Century 21
Accounting

10e General Journal

Claudia Bienias Gilbertson, CPA
Retired
North Hennepin Community College
Brooklyn Park, Minnesota

Mark W. Lehman, CPA, CFE
Associate Professor Emeritus
Richard C. Adkerson School of Accountancy
Mississippi State University
Starkville, Mississippi

Debra Harmon Gentene, NBCT
Business Teacher
Mason High School
Mason, Ohio

SOUTH-WESTERN
CENGAGE Learning·

Australia • Brazil • Japan • Korea • Mexico • Singapore • Spain • United Kingdom • United States

SOUTH-WESTERN
CENGAGE Learning®

**General Journal, Century 21 Accounting,
Tenth Edition**

**Claudia Bienias Gilbertson, CPA
Mark W. Lehman, CPA, CFE
Debra Harmon Gentene, NBCT**

Executive Vice President, Learning Operations and
Development: Sean Wakely

Senior Vice President, LRS/Acquisitions & Solutions
Planning: Jack W. Calhoun

Vice President/Editor-in-Chief: Karen Schmohe

Publisher: Mike Schenk

Editorial Assistant: Tristann Jones

Development Editor: Diane Bowdler

Senior Brand Manager: Robin LeFevre

Senior Market Development Manager: Mark Linton

Content Project Manager: Jana Lewis

Production Manager: Sharon Smith

Consulting Editors: Bill Lee, Bob First

Manager of Technology, Editorial: Matthew McKinney

Senior Website Project Manager: Ed Stubenrauch

Media Editor: Lysa Kosins

Manufacturing Planner: Kevin Kluck

Production Service: LEAP/Cenveo

Rights Acquisition Specialist Image/Text: Deanna Ettinger

Senior Art Directors: Tippy McIntosh/ Michelle Kunkler

Photo Researcher: Darren Wright

Internal Designer: Ke Design

Cover Designer: Ke Design

Cover Image: © Christopher Futcher/iStockphoto.com

For product information and technology assistance, contact us at
Cengage Learning Customer & Sales Support, 1-800-354-9706

For permission to use material from this text or product,
submit all requests online at **www.cengage.com/permissions**
Further permissions questions can be emailed to
permissionrequest@cengage.com

ISBN-13: 978-0-8400-6498-1
ISBN-10: 0-8400-6498-5

South-Western
5191 Natorp Boulevard
Mason, OH 45040
USA

Cengage Learning products are represented in Canada by
Nelson Education, Ltd.

For your course and learning solutions, visit **www.cengage.com/school**
Visit our company website at **www.cengage.com**

Microsoft Office Excel is a registered
trademark of Microsoft Corporation.

Intuit and QuickBooks are registered
trademarks of Intuit, Inc.

Sage Peachtree is a registered
trademark of Sage Software, Inc.

 The Career Clusters icons are being used with permission of
the States' Career Clusters Initiative, 2010,
www.careerclusters.org

**All illustrations, tables, and graphs are © Cengage Learning.

Intellectual Property
*All intellectual property on the Platform (except for User Generated
Content) is owned by NIKE or its licensors, which includes materials
protected by copyright, trademark, or patent laws. All trademarks, service
marks and trade names (e.g., the NIKE name and the Swoosh design) are
owned, registered and/or licensed by NIKE. All content on the Platform
(except for User Generated Content), including but not limited to text, software, scripts, code, designs, graphics, photos, sounds, music, videos, applications, interactive features and all other content ("Content") is a
collective work under the United States and other copyright laws and is the
proprietary property of NIKE; All rights reserved.*

The Nike Swoosh design is © Nike, Inc.

Printed in the United States of America
1 2 3 4 5 6 7 17 16 15 14 13

Contents

Part 2
Accounting
for a Merchandising Business Organized as a Corporation

Part 3
Accounting
for a Merchandising Business Organized as a Corporation—Adjustments and Valuation

Part 4
Additional
Accounting Procedures

Transform Your High School Accounting Course with Century 21 Accounting, from the leader in high school accounting education for 100+ years.

Input from educators, accounting professionals, content experts, and high school accounting students has shaped the 10th Edition of Century 21 Accounting. New critical-thinking activities, real-world applications, and enhanced online learning solutions—including Online Working Papers and Automated Accounting Online computerized accounting software—help you transform your accounting course.

▶ **Proven pedagogy** using a **renowned instructional design** supports teaching the mechanics of accounting and measuring learning outcomes in the 10th Edition.

▶ **Greater emphasis on conceptual understanding and financial statement analysis** encourages students to apply accounting concepts to real-world situations and develop higher-level thinking skills to make informed business decisions.

▶ **Critical thinking and technology use**, as defined by the Partnership for 21st Century Skills, have been expanded throughout with these new features to give students real-world practice and help them master valuable skills:

Forensic Accounting	*Think Like an Accountant*
Financial Literacy	*Why Accounting?*

▶ **Commercial technology** is integrated throughout the text to equip students to work with Microsoft Excel®, Peachtree®, QuickBooks®, and Automated Accounting Online. Students are given step-by-step instructions and the flexibility to use a variety of popular commercial software.

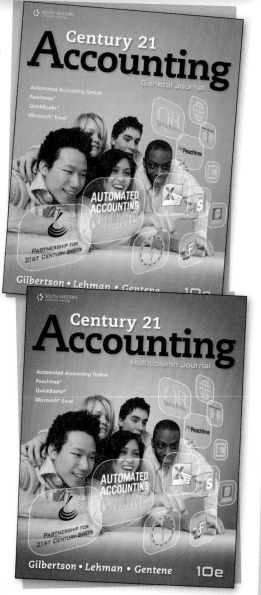

▶ **Unparalleled teaching tools and assessment resources**—in addition to exclusive CourseCare instructor training support—help ensure your success.

CourseCare

The Century 21 Accounting program provides students with a complete learning system designed to keep students on track and helps you measure outcomes.

The **organization** ensures clear student understanding. Students start with a service business organized as a proprietorship and merchandising businesses organized as corporations before concluding with special topics, partnerships, and the recording of international sales and electronic transactions.

The **step-by-step instructional approach** clearly reinforces text concepts, while the consistent use of T accounts increases student comprehension of journalizing transactions.

NEW! **Learning Objectives** connect the chapter coverage from beginning to end. Learning objectives are identified at point of introduction and in the end-of-chapter problems, making it easier for students to stay on track. By paying attention to the Learning Objectives, students can focus on what is important and you can better measure outcomes.

> " *The tagging of the Learning Objectives is such an easy and effective way for students to look back at a particular objective when they are working problems instead of having to flip through pages randomly until they find what they are looking for.* "
>
> Rosemary Hemsell,
> Grapevine High School,
> Grapevine, TX

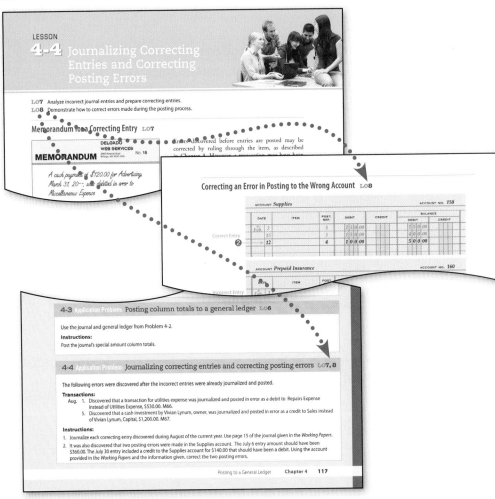

Measurable Outcomes

The **lesson structure** consists of three to five lessons per chapter and corresponding assessment activities. Each end-of-lesson section includes a **Work Together** problem and an **On Your Own** assignment. The Work Together problem allows you to demonstrate the new accounting concept to your class. Students can then check their understanding by completing the On Your Own assignment.

The **end-of-chapter material** includes short application problems to ensure students' understanding before they tackle the longer mastery and challenge problems.

> " *I like how the problems address objectives separately, then together in the Mastery problem, and at another level with the Challenge problem.* "
>
> Rosemary Hemsell,
> Grapevine High School,
> Grapevine, TX

End of Lesson Review

L04 Describe accounting procedures used in ordering merchandise.

L05 Discuss the purpose of a special journal.

L06 Journalize purchases of merchandise on account using a purchases journal.

Terms Review

inventory
merchandise inventory
perpetual inventory
periodic inventory
physical inventory
cost of merchandise
requisition
purchase order
special journal
purchase on account
purchases journal
special amount column
purchase invoice
terms of sale
due date

Audit your understanding

1. What is the difference between a periodic inventory system and a perpetual inventory system?
2. When the perpetual inventory system is used, in what account are purchases recorded? In what account are purchases recorded when the periodic inventory system is used?
3. Identify the four special journals typically used by a business.
4. How are special amount columns used in a journal?
5. Why are there two account titles in the amount column of the purchases journal?
6. What is the advantage of having special amount columns in a journal?
7. What information is contained on a purchase invoice?

Work together 9-2

Journalizing purchases using a purchases journal

The purchases journal for Golden Fabrics is given in the *Working Papers*. Your instructor will guide you through the following examples. Save your work to complete Work Together 9-3.

Using October of the current year, journalize these transactions on page 10 of the purchases journal. Purchase invoices are abbreviated as P.

Transactions:

Oct. 2. Purchased merchandise on account from Pacific Supply, $3,252.00. P162.
   7. Purchased merchandise on account from Coastal Company, $532.00. P163.
   11. Purchased merchandise on account from Yeatman Designs, $866.00. P164.

On your own 9-2

Journalizing purchases using a purchases journal

The purchases journal for Copperland Company is given in the *Working Papers*. Work this problem independently. Save your work to complete On Your Own 9-3.

Using November of the current year, journalize these transactions on page 11 of the purchases journal. Purchase invoices are abbreviated as P.

Transactions:

Nov. 5. Purchased merchandise on account from McKell Supply, Inc., $2,548.25. P244.
   10. Purchased merchandise on account from Tresler Corporation, $1,525.00. P245.
   17. Purchased merchandise on account from Lawes Imports, $2,643.50. P246.

©CANDICE CUSACK, ISTOCK

Transform Your Course

Problem Solving / Creativity

Greater emphasis on conceptual understanding and financial statement analysis has been incorporated into the 10th Edition, making it easier to balance coverage of accounting mechanics with how accounting information is used to make business decisions.

NEW! 21ST CENTURY SKILLS

included in the end-of-chapter material, provides activities that cultivate mastery of essential skills such as problem solving, communication, and technology use as defined by the Partnership for 21st Century Learning. Acquisition of the knowledge and skills taught in this feature will prepare students to compete in a workplace that demands creativity and innovation.

CRITICAL THINKING ACTIVITIES

are infused throughout the text to provide more opportunities for higher-level thinking and analysis, preparing students for college and career readiness.

CRITICAL THINKING

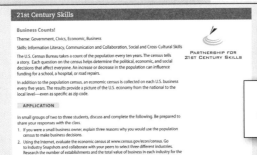

PARTNERSHIP FOR 21ST CENTURY SKILLS

NEW! THINK LIKE AN ACCOUNTANT

presents challenging problems that correspond to higher-level thinking skills based on the criteria established in Bloom's Taxonomy.

Excel templates are provided for students to use as an analysis tool to compare and contrast employer benefit plans and analyze how their decisions affect the company's bottom line.

with 21st Century Skills

Communication
Information Literacy

FINANCIAL LITERACY

guides students in the exploration of both business finance issues and critical personal finance topics through engaging activities that provide opportunities for students to apply valued skills such as problem solving, critical thinking, and technology use as defined by the Partnership for 21st Century Skills.

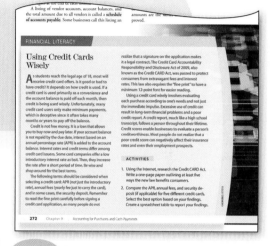

A listing of vendor accounts, account balances, and the total amount due to all vendors is called a **schedule of accounts payable**. Some businesses call this listing an ...amounts are the ... proved.

FINANCIAL LITERACY

Using Credit Cards Wisely

As students reach the legal age of 18, most will receive credit card offers. Is it good or bad to have credit? It depends on how credit is used. If a credit card is used primarily as a convenience and the account balance is paid off each month, then credit is being used wisely. Unfortunately, many credit card users only make minimum payments, which is deceptive since it often takes many months or years to pay off the balance.

Credit is not free money. It is a loan that allows you to buy now and pay later. If your account balance is not repaid by the due date, interest based on an annual percentage rate (APR) is added to the account balance. Interest rates and credit terms differ among credit card issuers. Some card companies offer a low introductory interest rate as bait. Then, they increase the rate after a short period of time. Be wise and shop around for the best terms.

The following terms should be considered when selecting a credit card: APR (not just the introductory rate), annual fees (yearly fee just to carry the card), and in some cases, the security deposit. Remember to read the fine print carefully before signing a credit card application, as many people do not

realize that a signature on the application makes it a legal contract. The Credit Card Accountability Responsibility and Disclosure Act of 2009, also known as the Credit CARD Act, was passed to protect consumers from extravagant fees and interest rates. This law also requires the "fine print" to have a minimum 12-point font for easier reading.

Using a credit card wisely involves evaluating each purchase according to one's needs and not just the immediate impulse. Excessive use of credit can result in long-term financial problems and a poor credit report. A credit report, much like a high school transcript, follows a person throughout their lifetime. Credit scores enable businesses to evaluate a person's creditworthiness. Most people do not realize that a poor credit score can negatively affect their insurance rates and even their employment prospects.

ACTIVITIES

1. Using the Internet, research the Credit CARD Act. Write a one-page paper outlining at least five ways the new law benefits consumers.

2. Compare the APR, annual fees, and security deposit (if applicable) for five different credit cards. Select the best option based on your findings. Create a spreadsheet table to report your findings.

272   Chapter 9   Accounting for Purchases and Cash Payments

GLOBAL AWARENESS

❶ Write the account title, Cash, after the word Account in the ...
❷ Write the account number, 110, after the words Account No. in the heading.

GLOBAL AWARENESS

International Weights and Measures

The primary system of measurement in the United States is the customary system. Among the units of measurement in the customary system are inches, feet, quarts, degrees Fahrenheit, and tablespoons. The United States is the only industrialized country that uses the customary system. Most of the rest of the world uses the International System of Units, which is also known as the metric system. Among the units of measurement in the metric system are centimeters, meters, liters, degrees Celsius, and grams. The metric system is based on a decimal system—like U.S. currency.

Many U.S. industries have converted to the metric system exclusively. Medicine and most pharmaceuticals use the metric system, as does the beverage industry. Other industries specify

measurements in both customary and metric systems, such as food products. In the United States, most measurements related to temperature are still given in degrees Fahrenheit. Companies that trade internationally may be forced to list weights and measures in both the customary and the metric system. These companies claim that this dual listing costs them millions of dollars each year. Even so, the United States continues to use the customary system.

CRITICAL THINKING

1. Look at five food packages. List the weights and measures indicated.

2. List arguments both for and against a proposal to convert all U.S. weights and measures to the metric system.

96   Chapter 4   Posting to a General Ledger

presents the role of accounting in a global environment and the cultural implications that occur as a result of the trans-migratory nature of the marketplace. It reflects current trends, concerns, and issues in global business, and cultural diversity in the workplace. Cultural topics will address both international and domestic issues.

ETHICS IN ACTION

responds to the increasing importance of ethics and personal character in accounting today. These ethical dilemmas assist students with decision-making and critical-thinking skills and challenge students' personal character development.

> *The use of Excel in this feature is an extremely important skill. Many of my high school students who come back to visit while they are in college have said they wish they would have used Excel more in class, because it is something they are doing a lot of in college business courses.*
>
> Kevin Willson, York Suburban School District, York, PA

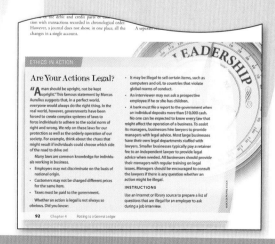

...in the debit and credit parts of... tion with transactions recorded in chronological order. However, a journal does not show, in one place, all the changes in a single account.   A separate ...

ETHICS IN ACTION

Are Your Actions Legal?

"A man should be upright, not be kept upright." This famous statement by Marcus Aurelius suggests that, in a perfect world, everyone would always do the right thing. In the real world, however, governments have been forced to create complex systems of laws to force individuals to adhere to the social norm of right and wrong. We rely on these laws for our protection as well as the orderly operation of our society. For example, think about the chaos that might result if individuals could choose which side of the road to drive on!

Many laws are common knowledge for individuals working in business.

• Employers may not discriminate on the basis of national origin.

• Customers may not be charged different prices for the same item.

• Taxes must be paid to the government.

Whether an action is legal is not always so obvious. Did you know:

• It may be illegal to sell certain items, such as computers and oil, to countries that violate global norms of conduct.

• An interviewer may not ask a prospective employee if he or she has children.

• A bank must file a report to the government when an individual deposits more than $10,000 cash.

No one can be expected to know every law that might affect the operation of a business. To assist its managers, businesses hire lawyers to provide managers with legal advice. Most large businesses have their own legal departments staffed with lawyers. Smaller businesses typically pay a retainer fee to an independent lawyer to provide legal advice when needed. All businesses should provide their managers with regular training on legal issues. Managers should be encouraged to consult the lawyers if there is any question whether an action might be illegal.

INSTRUCTIONS

Use an Internet or library source to prepare a list of questions that are illegal for an employer to ask during a job interview.

92   Chapter 4   Posting to a General Ledger

Transform Your Course by **Bringing**

Forensic Accounting presents criminal investigations involving fraud, providing students the opportunity to apply what they're learning in class to a real-world scenario. Students will examine the fraud scenarios using Excel® to analyze the data and continue the investigation.

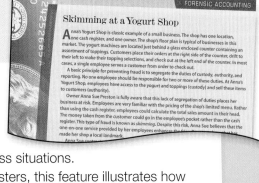

Why Accounting? provides examples of how accounting skills are applicable in a variety of business situations. Tied to the National Career Clusters, this feature illustrates how accounting knowledge transfers into the workplace and validates accounting's importance in the marketplace.

Careers in Accounting, designed to encourage students to think about their future in accounting, features a broad range of careers in the accounting field and promotes accounting as a profession through one-on-one interviews with various accounting professionals.

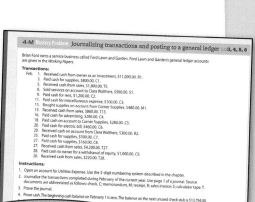

Accounting in the Real World: Fascinating chapter openers spotlight actual businesses that interest students, such as TOMs Shoes, iTunes, McDonald's, and Google, with intriguing questions that connect chapter topics to what's driving business decisions in today's organizations.

Commercial technology, integrated into the end of each chapter, equips students to work with **Microsoft Excel®, Peachtree®, QuickBooks®,** and **Automated Accounting Online** with step-by-step instructions and the flexibility to use multiple versions of software.

Accounting Practices to Life

Bring Accounting Practices to Life with *Relevant Simulations*

Manual and automated simulations for each cycle give your students hands-on, real-world experience in accounting practice. Automated simulations are completed using Automated Accounting Online, powered by CengageNOW.

First Year

Simulation 1: Red Carpet Events
Students encounter accounting principles and practical applications as they experience the challenges of operating an event-planning service business organized as a proprietorship. Students complete the simulation after Chapter 8. *Completion time 4-8 hours.*

Simulation 2: Authentic Threads
Students bring fashion trends into the world of accounting while they practice accounting applications in this dynamic merchandising business organized as a corporation. Students complete the simulation after Chapter 17. *Completion time 10-17 hours.*

Simulation 3: Digital Diversions
Students go digital in this engaging simulation with the latest retail software, cell phones, video cameras, music, and more in this merchandising business organized as a corporation. Students complete the simulation after Chapter 22. *Completion time 10-15 hours.*

Advanced

Simulation 1: Sounds, Inc.
From rock and pop to hip-hop and jazz, students listen up as this simulation demonstrates how accounting principles perform within a departmentalized merchandising business organized as a corporation. Students complete the simulation after Chapter 4. *Completion time 10-20 hours.*

Simulation 2: First Class Image Wear, Inc.
Style rules as students bring designer labels and fashion trends into the world of accounting within this merchandising business organized as a corporation. Students complete the simulation after Chapter 13. *Completion time 10-20 hours.*

Simulation 3: Progressive Badge Company
Accounting principles are reinforced as this engaging simulation features a manufacturing business, Progressive Badge Company, organized as a corporation that manufactures badges for specialty retailing. Students complete the simulation after Chapter 20. *Completion time 15-25 hours.*

Online Working Papers

The market's first **Online Working Papers**, *powered by Aplia*, feature automatic grading for instructors and immediate feedback for students. C21 Accounting Online Working Papers mirror the print working papers and tests including online journals, ledgers, worksheets, financial statements, and other forms students use to complete their textbook problems and tests.

- ▶ Mirror the C21 Accounting Print Working Papers
- ▶ Immediate Feedback for Students
- ▶ Automatically Graded Assignments for Instructors
- ▶ Chapter tests included

Students who stay engaged with material put more effort into the course. Century 21 Online Working Papers give **students instant feedback**, making sure they are learning from each question while gaining a better understanding of accounting basics.

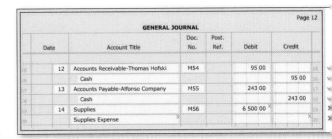

NEW TO ONLINE WORKING PAPERS FOR 10E

- ▶ Enhanced student feedback will provide students with additional instruction beyond right and wrong answers
- ▶ Algorithmic problems will provide students with additional opportunities to practice
- ▶ Device independent, the new online working papers will work on PCs, MACs, iPads, and other devices

The Online Working Papers **automatically grade assignments**, relieving instructors of the burden of grading homework by hand. As students complete the assignments, the instructor receives a complete assessment of their work and comprehension levels, while their grades are instantly recorded in the instructor's online grade book.

The Online Working Papers keep instructors informed about student participation, progress, and performance through real-time graphical reports. Instructors can easily download, save, manipulate, print, and import student grades into their current grading program.

What Users are Saying!

- ▶ **73%** say that **student performance has improved** in their class since using the Online Working Papers!
- ▶ **82%** report that their students are **more engaged** in the Accounting course.
- ▶ **75%** say their ability to **monitor student progress** has improved.
- ▶ **57%** say that after using Online Working Papers, their students are **more likely to enroll in further study in accounting** and/or other business education courses.

Visit **www.cengage.com/school/accounting** for a demo!

Accounting Digital Solutions

NEW! **Automated Accounting Online** is the next generation of the Automated Accounting software program that has successfully introduced students to computerized accounting for many years. Automated Accounting Online provides the functionality of commercial software incorporated with educational features that make teaching and learning computerized accounting easy. The completely redesigned interface is even more realistic and similar to what users see in commercial software programs such as Peachtree® and QuickBooks®.

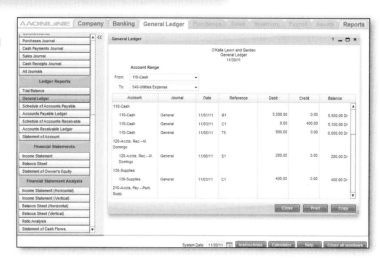

Automated Accounting Online:

▶ Is integrated into every chapter of Century 21 Accounting
▶ Provides immediate feedback for students
▶ Allows automatic grading for instructors
▶ Is compatible with PCs and MACs
▶ Is available anywhere with Internet connection

For a demo, visit **www.cengage.com/school/accounting**

Student Companion Website extends the learning experience well beyond the book with instructional games, study tools, chapter outlines, math worksheets, and data files.
www.c21accounting.com

Getting ready to start your class? Need help getting started?

Available exclusively from Cengage Learning, **CourseCare** is a revolutionary program designed to provide you with an unparalleled user experience with your Cengage Learning Digital Solution.

▶ 24/7 on-demand training resources
▶ Regularly scheduled professional training
▶ Dedicated Digital Solutions Coordinator

Please contact the CourseCare team at schoolscoursecare@cengage.com.

To learn more about the live and recorded training sessions available, please visit www.cengage.com/school/coursecare.

Transform Your Teaching Experience with **tools to make your job easier**

Automatic grading with Online Working Papers and Automated Accounting Online, designed to minimize your time grading, while maximizing your impact within the classroom. Immediate feedback for students and automatic grading for you will save you time and give you an instant sense of each student's comprehension. Grades are automatically entered in an instructor's online gradebook.

Wraparound Teacher's Edition features reduced student pages with comprehensive instructor support, including:

▶ An updated instructional design framework

▶ Common Core call outs

▶ Essential questions

▶ Tips for differentiated instruction

▶ Teaching ideas to increase student engagement

▶ An overview of each accounting part

▶ Resource Integration Guide

▶ Check figures

Written by high school accounting teachers, for high school accounting teachers.

Instructor's Resource Kit includes comprehensive teaching resources all in one place, including:

▶ Working Paper and Recycling Problem solutions (textbook problems)

▶ Chapter and Part Tests and solutions

▶ Simulation keys

Instructor's Resource CD places all key instructor resources at your fingertips in this all-in-one convenient tool that includes:

▶ Lesson plans and PowerPoint® presentations

▶ Chapter and Part Tests

▶ Solutions to Working Papers, Tests, Audit tests, Peachtree®, QuickBooks®, Simulations

▶ Crossword puzzles and solutions

▶ Competitive event prep for BPA and FBLA

▶ Correlation to the NBEA standards

▶ Transparency masters (Solutions, Ruling, Full Color Illustrations)

▶ Interactive spreadsheets

▶ Block scheduling correlation with Century 21 Accounting

Instructor Companion Site offers password-protected teacher resources including solutions, lesson plans, PowerPoint Presentations, and simulation keys.

Assessment Resources

▶ **ExamView® computerized test bank** allows you to easily create custom tests within minutes. Simply edit, add, delete, or rearrange questions with this easy-to-use software.

▶ **Chapter and Part Test Masters**
Two separate test masters for every chapter and part include problems and objective questions.

▶ **Teacher's Edition Chapter and Part Tests**
Provide solutions for convenient grading.

Reviewers

Cindy Anderson
Business and Computer Teacher
Wyndmere Public School
Wyndmere, North Dakota

Carolyn Holt Balis
Business Educator
Parma City School District
Parma, Ohio

Doris Curry
Business Teacher
Alief Kerr High School
Houston, Texas

Dan Doseck
Business Instructor
Alexander High School
Albany, Ohio

Fahryka P. Elliott
Business Education Teacher
Henrico High School
Henrico, Virginia

Kathryn L. Focht CPA
Educator
Wilson High School
West Lawn, Pennsylvania

Kathleen O'Connor Ford
Business Teacher
Rochester Adams High School
Rochester Hills, Michigan

Mike Hackman
Business and Accounting Teacher
Columbus North High School
Columbus, Indiana

Kathleen Harenza
Business Education Teacher
Mukwonago High chool
Mukwonago, Wisconsin

Rosemary Hemsell
CTE Teacher
Grapevine High School
Grapevine, Texas

Dana R. Hurda
Business and Accounting Instructor
Evansville High School
Evansville, Wisconsin

Joseph Kramer
Business and Information Technology
  Teacher
Seton-La Salle Catholic High School
Pittsburgh, Pennsylvania

Alvin R. Kroon
Teacher
Kamiak High School
Mukilteo, Washington

Cheryl L. Linthicum CPA, PhD
Accounting Professor
University of Texas
San Antonio, Texas

Claire Martin
Business Educator
Sully Buttes High School
Onida, South Dakota

Jane Melroy
Business Teacher
Skyline High School
Pratt, Kansas

James P. O'Connell
Business and Technology Teacher
Bishop Canevin High School
Pittsburgh, Pennsylvania

Rose Pettit
Business Education Teacher
Hopkins High School
Minnetonka, Minnesota

Matthew H. Pohlman
Business Instructor
CAL Community School District
Latimer, Iowa

Sherilyn Reynolds
Business Teacher
Sam Rayburn High School
Pasadena, Texas

Martha Scarberry
Vice Principal
B. Michael Caudill Middle School
Richmond, Kentucky

Lisa Slattery
Accounting Teacher
Spring Woods High School
Houston, Texas

Alice Smith
Business Teacher
Lafayette Central Catholic Jr./Sr. High
  School
Lafayette, Indiana

Jeynelle M. Strickland
Teacher and Chairperson
Savannah Christian Preparatory
  School
Savannah, Georgia

Eileen Wascisin
Business Teacher
Lynden High School
Lynden, Washington

Kevin W. Willson
Business Education Department
  Chairperson
York Suburban School District
York, Pennsylvania

Part

1 Accounting
for a Service Business
Organized as a
Proprietorship

©OLGALIS, ISTOCK

THE BUSINESS—
DELGADO WEB SERVICES

Delgado Web Services is the business used in the chapters in Part 1 to illustrate the accounting concepts and procedures for a service business organized as a proprietorship. Delgado Web Services is owned by Michael Delgado. Mr. Delgado designs, maintains, and hosts websites for small businesses.

Chart of Accounts
DELGADO WEB SERVICES

GENERAL LEDGER

Balance Sheet Accounts

(100) ASSETS
110 Cash
120 Petty Cash
130 Accounts Receivable—Main Street Services
140 Accounts Receivable—Valley Landscaping
150 Supplies
160 Prepaid Insurance

(200) LIABILITIES
210 Accounts Payable—Canyon Office Supplies
220 Accounts Payable—Mountain Graphic Arts

(300) OWNER'S EQUITY
310 Michael Delgado, Capital
320 Michael Delgado, Drawing
330 Income Summary

Income Statement Accounts

(400) REVENUE
410 Sales

(500) EXPENSES
510 Advertising Expense
520 Cash Short and Over
530 Communications Expense
540 Equipment Rental Expense
550 Insurance Expense
560 Miscellaneous Expense
570 Supplies Expense

The chart of accounts for Delgado Web Services is illustrated here for easy reference as you study the accounting cycle for a proprietorship in this textbook.

Chapter 1

Starting a Proprietorship: Changes That Affect the Accounting Equation

LEARNING OBJECTIVES

After studying Chapter 1, in addition to defining key terms, you will be able to:

LO1 Describe the different users of accounting information.

LO2 Prepare a net worth statement and explain its purpose.

LO3 Classify accounts as assets, liabilities, or owner's equity and demonstrate their relationship in the accounting equation.

LO4 Analyze the effects of transactions on the accounting equation.

LO5 Distinguish between cash and on account transactions.

LO6 Compare and contrast the types of transactions that increase and decrease owner's equity.

LO7 Explain the difference between expenses and liabilities.

©DANIEL KOUREY, ISTOCK/©JIM PRUITT, ISTOCK

THEBOOK/ISTOCKPHOTO.COM

Accounting In The Real World
TOMS Shoes

Have you ever thought about owning your own business? Someone who owns, operates, and takes the risk of a business venture is called an **entrepreneur**. America was built on the hard work of entrepreneurs as many men and women pursued their dream of business ownership by developing new ideas and turning them into business opportunities.

The goal of a business entrepreneur is to seek economic benefit. In recent years, a new type of entrepreneur has emerged. These new entrepreneurs are driven by the same innovation and productivity, yet they seek social value rather than profits. These entrepreneurs are also agents of change. They direct their entrepreneurial energy toward seeking solutions for society's problems.

Blake Mycoskie is one of today's leading social entrepreneurs. Blake sold his driver's education business to fund a social entrepreneurial idea. While visiting Argentina, Blake noticed the number of children who had no shoes. Being shoeless limited the children's ability to attend school. Even worse, being shoeless increased the risk of developing a disabling foot disease called *podoconiosis*. So Blake Mycoskie started a business called TOMS Shoes. The company name comes from the word "tomorrow" because Mycoskie wants to create a better future for impoverished children. Mycoskie's mission statement is: *"I'm going to start a shoe company. For every pair of shoes that we sell, I will give a pair to someone who needs them."*

Within a short period, TOMS Shoes has given hundreds of thousands of shoes to children in the United States, Argentina, Ethiopia, and South Africa.

CRITICAL THINKING

1. How is social entrepreneurship different from nonprofit organizations?
2. Identify a problem in your local community and create a solution for it by identifying a social entrepreneurship.

Key Terms

- accounting
- accounting system
- financial statements
- net worth statement
- asset
- liability
- personal net worth
- equity
- ethics
- business ethics
- service business
- proprietorship
- business plan
- GAAP
- equities
- owner's equity
- accounting equation
- transaction
- account
- account title
- account balance
- capital account
- creditor
- revenue
- sale on account
- expense
- withdrawals

LESSON
1-1 Accounting in Action

LO1 Describe the different users of accounting information.
LO2 Prepare a net worth statement and explain its purpose.

The Role of Accounting LO1

Every day, numerous business activities take place. For example, you may stop at a convenience store on the way to school to buy juice or school supplies. Have you ever wondered how many bottles of juice are sold each day? Or how much the store owner pays for rent or utilities? Or how much the store's employees are paid? Or how much the store owes to suppliers? Or would this business be a good investment?

Perhaps you have thought about starting a business by forming a local band. Do you know how to price your tickets to make a profit? Do you know the cost of renting a venue? Do you know how many tickets you will need to sell to make a profit?

All of these questions involve numbers. However, numbers alone cannot be used to make all business decisions. For instance, knowing how many bottles of orange juice were sold is important, but the data do not tell whether the store is making a profit. Data must be recorded and reported in accounting reports. Then, the information can be provided to business owners, managers, investors, and others to make business decisions and measure performance.

What Is Accounting?

Whether you are going to invest in a business, work for a multimillion-dollar company, or start your own business, you will always use financial information. Accounting provides financial information to users for making decisions. The information is communicated to everyone who needs it to make good business decisions. Therefore, accounting is often referred to as *the language of business*. Just like any language, it has its own terminology and rules that must be learned and practiced. Understanding this language is essential for using data to communicate effectively, making good financial decisions, and successfully operating a business. Inaccurate accounting records can make a business fail. A failure to understand accounting information can result in poor business decisions both personally and professionally.

Accounting is the process of planning, recording, analyzing, and interpreting financial information. The accounting process includes recording financial activities, but accounting is not the same as bookkeeping or recordkeeping. Bookkeeping is only the recording part of the accounting process. Accounting goes much further than just keeping records. Accounting involves analyzing and interpreting a business's operations to determine its financial well-being and plan its future success.

An **accounting system** is a planned process designed to compile financial data and summarize the results in accounting records and reports. Financial reports that summarize the financial condition and operations of a business are called **financial statements**. Business owners and managers use financial statements to make business decisions.

For many years, all accounting information was recorded using paper and ink. In today's business world, accounting software programs are widely used to record and process financial data. However, accounting software only processes data. Skill and knowledge in accounting are essential in order to effectively use the technology and correctly interpret results.

Accounting in Personal Life LO2

Accounting can be used to make personal financial decisions as well as business decisions. When buying a car, one of the first steps in the loan application is to complete a personal financial data sheet. A formal report that shows what an individual owns, what an individual owes, and the difference between the two is called a **net worth statement**. A net worth statement allows the person extending the loan to see the financial position of a borrower on a specific date and make a lending decision.

In order to calculate net worth, items that are owned must be identified and assigned a realistic value. Anything of value that is owned is called an **asset**. Examples of assets are cars, bikes, real estate, cash (including bank accounts), and jewelry. Amounts that are owed to others must be identified and assigned values. An amount owed is called a **liability**. Examples of liabilities include amounts owed to friends or relatives, car loans, and credit card bills. Net worth is the total estimated value of everything owned (assets) less the total of everything owed (liabilities). The difference between personal assets and personal liabilities is called **personal net worth**. Net worth shows the financial value of the owner after paying all liabilities. A larger number reflects a higher net worth. In business, net worth is also called *equity*. **Equity** is the difference between assets and liabilities.

$$\underset{\textbf{①}}{\begin{array}{c}\textbf{Total Assets}\\\textbf{(owned)}\end{array}} - \underset{\textbf{②}}{\begin{array}{c}\textbf{Total Liabilities}\\\textbf{(owed)}\end{array}} = \underset{\textbf{③}}{\begin{array}{c}\textbf{Net Worth (also}\\\textbf{known as Equity)}\end{array}}$$

PERSONAL NET WORTH STATEMENT

A personal net worth statement shows the assets, liabilities, and net worth of an individual. The personal net worth statement below shows a positive net worth. This means that Saida Khelchy owns more than she owes, something a lender looks upon favorably. A negative amount for net worth would reflect more debt than assets, something a lender would not favor.

	Saida Khelchy	
	Net Worth Statement	
	September 27, 20--	
	Assets	
① Total Assets	Savings Account	2,000.00
	Class Ring	250.00
	Total Assets	2,250.00
	Liabilities	
② Total Liabilities	Owed to Parents	50.00
	Ace Electronics	125.00
	Total Liabilities	175.00
③ Net Worth	Net Worth	2,075.00

Assets − Liabilities = Net Worth

Note: When statements are prepared on ruled accounting forms, it is standard practice to place double rules under the last amount on the statement to indicate that the amount is a total. Dollar signs are not used on these forms.

Accounting Scandals Rock the Financial World

Entering the 21st century, Enron, WorldCom, and Arthur Andersen were three of the most celebrated names in corporate America. But the actions of a few individuals forced financial mammoths Enron and WorldCom into bankruptcy. Arthur Andersen, once one of the prestigious "Big 5" accounting firms, was forced out of business. These accounting scandals caused hundreds of thousands of employees to lose their jobs. Millions of individuals lost billions of dollars in investment and retirement accounts. These scandals rocked the public's confidence in the accounting profession and the stock markets. Congress reacted by passing the Sarbanes-Oxley Act of 2002, requiring greater oversight of publicly traded companies.

INSTRUCTIONS

Search the Internet to obtain an article that describes an accounting scandal such as the Enron, WorldCom, Adelphia, HealthSouth, or Parmalat scandals. Write a one-paragraph summary that describes what happened and the individuals involved.

©LUCA DI FILIPPO, ISTOCK

Ethics in Business

A business and its owner have contacts with customers, suppliers, employees, government representatives, and many others. A successful business maintains a good relationship with all of these contacts. One way to maintain a good relationship with these contacts is to conduct all business in an ethical way. The principles of right and wrong that guide an individual in making decisions are called **ethics**. The use of ethics in making business decisions is called **business ethics**.

Making ethical business decisions is a skill that can be learned. Each chapter of this textbook contains a feature on business ethics. In Part 1, you will explore a model that guides evaluation of business decisions. In Part 2, you will apply that model to make ethical business decisions. The features in Part 3 will expand your knowledge of business ethics and encourage you to continue learning about business ethics long after you have completed this accounting course.

SHELLYGAMI-PHOTOAR/SHUTTERSTOCK.COM

End of Lesson Review

LO1 Describe the different users of accounting information.

LO2 Prepare a net worth statement and explain its purpose.

Terms Review

accounting

accounting system

financial statements

net worth statement

asset

liability

personal net worth

equity

ethics

business ethics

Audit your understanding

1. What is accounting?

2. Why is accounting called the language of business?

3. Describe a scenario in which you, as a nonaccountant, might use accounting.

Work together 1-1

Megan Finder, a recent college graduate, is applying for her first credit card. The creditor has asked for a personal net worth statement. Megan has $800.00 in her checking account and owns a scooter worth $2,000.00. She owes Jaycee Auto $920.00 and River College $125.00. Complete a net worth statement for Megan Finder. Use the current date.

On your own 1-1

Anthony Clement is applying for a car loan. The lending institution requires a personal net worth statement. Anthony currently has $1,085.00 in cash, and his camera is worth $635.00. He also owes Kelley Electronics $83.00, and Vista Travel $305.00. Complete a net worth statement for Anthony Clement. Use the current date.

©CANDICE CUSACK, ISTOCK

LESSON

1-2 How Business Activities Change the Accounting Equation

LO3 Classify accounts as assets, liabilities, or owner's equity and demonstrate their relationship in the accounting equation.

LO4 Analyze the effects of transactions on the accounting equation.

LO5 Distinguish between cash and on account transactions.

The Business—Delgado Web Services

Michael Delgado has designed his own personal website as well as websites for some friends. The father of one of his friends runs a plumbing business. He asked Michael if he could design a website for the plumbing business. After the website went live, the plumber's business increased by 25% in the first six months. Michael realized that he might be able to make a career from designing websites.

A business that performs an activity for a fee is called a **service business**. Examples of service businesses might include landscapers, salons, babysitters, or providers of medical services. Since Michael is the only owner of his business, the business is a proprietorship. A **proprietorship** is a business owned by one person. The owner is

legally responsible for all debts, taxes, and losses; therefore, the unlimited liability is a disadvantage. However, the owner receives all profits. The life of the business ends when the owner is no longer willing or able to continue the business. A proprietorship is sometimes referred to as a *sole proprietorship*.

Michael researches how to start a business. He learns that a common practice is to first write a business plan. A **business plan** is a formal written document that describes the nature of a business and how it will operate. The section of the business plan that describes the operation of the business is shown on this page. The financial part of the business plan will be developed as you study the chapters in Part 1.

DELGADO WEB SERVICES

Business Plan

Description: Delgado Web Services will be a sole proprietorship owned by Michael Delgado. The business has no employees. The business will design, maintain, and host websites for local businesses that want an Internet presence. A key function of the service is advising customers on the kinds of information that can be included on the website and ways to increase business.

Fees: Fees will vary depending on the size and amount of detail on each website, as well as the consulting time spent with the customer.

Suppliers: Artwork and photographic services will be purchased from Mountain Graphic Artists. Equipment will be rented for a monthly fee with a service agreement. The agreement will keep the computer, server, and software up to date.

Marketing: The business has business cards and a promotional brochure. Local businesses that could benefit from having an Internet presence have been identified. The marketing plan includes testimonials about existing websites the owner has already designed.

Watch Your Money Grow—The Rule of 72

One of the best ways to make money is to let money make more money. An amount paid for the use of money for a period of time is called **interest**. Money deposited in certain kinds of bank accounts increases when the bank pays interest on the deposit. Bank deposits are further increased with compound interest. **Compound interest** is interest paid on an original amount deposited in a bank plus any interest that has been paid. In other words, the original money deposited earns interest, and then the interest earns additional interest.

The "Rule of 72" is a simple way to see the power of compound interest. This formula calculates how long it will take an original investment to double its value at a given interest rate when left alone in an interest-bearing account.

When 72 is divided by the interest rate, the answer is the number of years it will take to double the money. This formula assumes that no additional deposits are made. The Rule of 72 illustrates the advantage of saving early. For example, if $500 is deposited in a bank account that earns 6% interest, it will take 12 years to double the $500. The calculation is $72 \div 6 = 12$ years.

ACTIVITIES

1. Rachel dreams of starting her own business. She will need a $6,000 investment to start; however, she has saved only $3,000. The bank pays a 4% interest rate that is compounded annually. How many years will it take for Rachel's money to double?

2. Rachel would like to open her business in two years. What percent interest would Rachel need to receive to double her money in two years?

3. Apply the Rule of 72 to debt. If Rachel's credit card charges 18% interest, and she makes no payments, how long will it take for Rachel's debt to double?

©NOREBBO, ISTOCK

Accounting Standards and Rules

The standards and rules that accountants follow while recording and reporting financial activities are commonly referred to as *generally accepted accounting principles* or **GAAP**. Pronounced as "gap," GAAP helps ensure that all companies follow the same set of guidelines and practices when reporting financial data. Following GAAP principles and concepts ensures consistent reporting.

An example of a GAAP concept is Unit of Measurement, in which business activities are stated in numbers that have common values—that is, using a common unit of measurement. In the United States, business activities are recorded in dollars. Using the unit of measurement concept, the financial reports of businesses can be clearly stated and understood in numbers that have comparable values. [CONCEPT: Unit of Measurement] Delgado Web Services will record all business activities using dollars as the unit of measurement.

Accounting concepts are described throughout this textbook. When an application of a concept first occurs, it is explained. When additional applications

occur, a concept reference, such as [CONCEPT: Business Entity], is used to indicate an application of a specific accounting concept. A brief description of each accounting concept used in this text is also provided on the Century 21 Accounting website at www.C21accounting.com.

Since Delgado Web Services is a new business, Michael must design the accounting system that will be used to keep the accounting records. Michael must be careful to keep these accounting records separate from his own personal financial records. For example, Michael owns a car for personal use. However, the financial records for Delgado Web Services must not include information about Michael's car or other personal belongings. The accounting concept Business Entity is applied when a business's financial information is recorded and reported separately from the owner's personal financial information. [CONCEPT: Business Entity]

Delgado Web Services will be used throughout Part 1 to illustrate the accounting concepts and procedures for a service business organized as a proprietorship.

Careers In Accounting

So You Want to Be an Accountant

STEPHEN COBURN/SHUTTERSTOCK.COM

Many high school students consider a career in accounting. However, not many understand the variety of positions that are available in the field of accounting or the differences in the duties performed. The range of positions also comes with a range of educational and experience requirements and a corresponding range of compensation.

Many of the accounting-related job titles in a company can be arranged in a hierarchy based on educational requirements and average salary. A typical hierarchy is given below.

The higher the position on the chart, the higher the level of education and experience required for the position and the higher the level of compensation. For example, at the top of the chart, a CEO (Chief Executive Officer) and a CFO (Chief Financial Officer) would typically earn higher salaries than positions further down on the chart in the same company.

There are many accounting fields that are not related to any one company. These include auditor, forensic accountant, government accountant, and accountants in education. Each of these areas has its own education and experience requirements.

Salary Range: Salaries in the broad field of accounting range from $35,000 to over $100,000.

Qualifications: Educational requirements range from a high school accounting course to a four-year degree and higher. Special certifications can be acquired, which usually increase the salary received.

Occupational Outlook: The projected growth in accounting positions varies, but many areas of accounting are expected to grow by up to 19% by 2020.

Source: O*Net Online (http://www.onetonline.org).

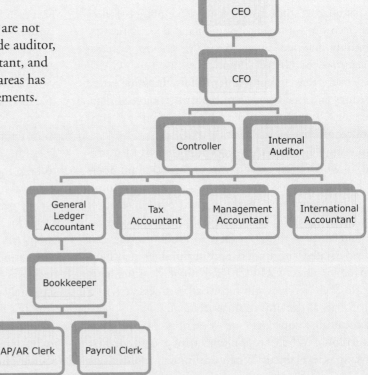

©MILENNY, ISTOCK

The Accounting Equation LO3

	Assets	=	Liabilities	+	Owner's Equity
	Left side amount		**Right side amounts**		
	$0	=	$0	+	$0

Delgado Web Services will own items such as cash and supplies that will be used to conduct daily operations. Anything of value that is owned is known as an asset. Assets have value because they can be used either to acquire other assets or to operate a business. For example, Delgado Web Services will use cash to buy supplies for the business. Delgado Web Services will then use the asset bought, supplies, to operate the web design service business.

Financial rights to the assets of a business are called **equities**. A business has two types of equities. (1) Equity of those to whom money is owed. For example, Delgado Web Services may buy some supplies and agree to pay for the supplies at a later date. The business from which supplies are bought will have a right to some of Delgado Web Services' assets until the business pays for the supplies. An amount owed by a business is known

as a liability. (2) Equity of the owner. Michael Delgado owns Delgado Web Services and invests in the assets of the business. Therefore, he has the right to decide how the assets will be used. The amount remaining after the value of all liabilities is subtracted from the value of all assets is called **owner's equity**.

The relationship among assets, liabilities, and owner's equity can be written as an equation. The equation showing the relationship among assets, liabilities, and owner's equity is called the **accounting equation**. The accounting equation is most often stated as:

Assets = Liabilities + Owner's Equity

The accounting equation must always be in balance. The total of the amounts on the left side must always equal the total of the amounts on the right side.

THINK LIKE AN ACCOUNTANT

Budgeting the Business Plan

Neil Logan came to your office with the idea of starting a web hosting service. Having previously worked in a similar company located in another state, he believes there is a need for a local web hosting business in your city. He believes this business would enable him to quit his $50,000-a-year job and "be his own boss."

After providing you with expense estimates, Neil stated, "I believe I can effectively service 20 clients. Each site would require about 75 hours a year to design, including periodic upgrades. This service would be billed to clients at $40 per hour. Then I would also receive a $30 monthly hosting fee."

OPEN THE SPREADSHEET TLA_CH01
Provide Neil with answers to the following questions:

1. Based on Neil's estimates, would you suggest he quit his job to start the business?

2. Determine to the nearest dollar what hourly billing rate he would need to charge to replace his current salary.

3. What if the market will not support a higher billing rate? Can Neil achieve his goal by obtaining more customers?

4. Can you think of a change in the worksheet that could make your analysis easier?

Receiving Cash LO4

	Assets	=	Liabilities	+	Owner's Equity
	Cash	=			Michael Delgado, Capital
Beginning Balances	$0		$0		$0
Received cash from owner as an investment	+2,000		0		+2,000
New Balances	$2,000		$0		$2,000

Any time a business spends money, receives money, or owes money, it engages in a business activity. Whenever a business activity takes place, amounts in the accounting equation change. Accountants call any business activity that changes assets, liabilities, or owner's equity a **transaction**. For example, paying cash for supplies is a transaction. After each transaction, the accounting equation must always remain in balance.

RECEIVED CASH INVESTMENT FROM OWNER

In the accounting equation above, the Beginning Balances line shows zero balances for assets, liabilities, and owner's equity. The values are zero because the business has not yet been started. To establish his new business, Michael invests $2,000.00 of personal money in his company. Delgado Web Services will only be concerned about the effect of this transaction on Delgado Web Services' accounting records, not on Michael's personal records. [CONCEPT: Business Entity]

> **Transaction 1.** January 2. Received cash from owner as an investment, $2,000.00.

In the accounting equation shown above, the asset Cash is increased by $2,000.00, the amount of cash received by the business. A record that summarizes all the transactions pertaining to a single item in the accounting equation is called an **account**. The name

given to an account is called an **account title**. Therefore, Cash is the account that summarizes all of the assets that are cash. Cash can include a bank checking account, savings accounts, and actual cash on hand that belongs to the business.

In the accounting equation above, the asset, Cash, is increased by $2,000.00. This increase is on the left side of the equation. The difference between the increases and decreases in an account is called the **account balance**. Before the owner's investment, the account balance of Cash was zero. After the owner's investment, the account balance of Cash is $2,000.00.

An account used to summarize the owner's equity in a business is called a **capital account**. The capital account is an owner's equity account. In the accounting equation shown above, the owner's equity account, Michael Delgado, Capital, is increased by $2,000.00. This increase is on the right side of the accounting equation. Before the owner's investment, the account balance of Michael Delgado, Capital was zero. After the owner's investment, the account balance of Michael Delgado, Capital is $2,000.00.

As a result of receiving cash, the accounting equation has changed. However, both sides changed by the same amount. The $2,000.00 increase on the left side of the equation equals the $2,000.00 increase on the right side of the equation. Therefore, the accounting equation is still in balance.

The left side of the accounting equation (assets) must always equal the right side (liabilities plus owner's equity).

Paying Cash

	Assets			=	Liabilities	+	Owner's Equity
	Cash	+ Supplies	+ Prepaid Insurance =				Michael Delgado, Capital
Balances	$2,000				$0		$2,000
Paid cash for supplies	−165	+165					
New Balances	$1,835	$165			$0		$2,000
Paid cash for insurance	−900		+900				
New Balances	$935	$165	$900		$0		$2,000

PAID CASH FOR SUPPLIES

Delgado Web Services needs supplies to operate the business. Michael Delgado uses some of the business's cash to buy supplies.

Transaction 2. January 2. Paid cash for supplies, $165.00.

In this transaction, two asset accounts are changed. One asset, Cash, has been exchanged for another asset, Supplies. Supplies are considered an asset because they are of value until they are used. The asset account, Cash, is decreased by $165.00, the amount of cash paid out. This decrease is on the left side of the accounting equation. The asset account, Supplies, is increased by $165.00, the amount of supplies bought. This increase is also on the left side of the accounting equation.

For this transaction, two asset accounts are changed. The two changes are both on the left side of the equation. When changes are made on only one side of the equation, the equation must still be in balance. Therefore, if one account is increased, another account on the same side of the equation must be decreased. After this transaction, the new account balance of Cash is $1,835.00. The new account balance of Supplies is $165.00. The sum of the amounts on the left side is $2,000.00 (Cash $1,835.00 + Supplies $165.00). The amount on the right side remains at $2,000.00. Therefore, the accounting equation is still in balance.

PAID CASH FOR INSURANCE

Delgado Web Services has business insurance that protects the business from losses due to accidents that might destroy the leased equipment or business

Transaction 3. January 3. Paid cash for insurance, $900.00.

records and contracts. Whenever a business buys insurance, the coverage is paid for in advance. Insurance premiums are an asset because they have value until they expire. Delgado Web Services pays a $900.00 insurance premium for insurance protection.

This payment gives Delgado Web Services insurance coverage for the length of the policy. Because insurance premiums are paid in advance, they are referred to as *prepaid*. The premiums (payments) are recorded in an asset account titled Prepaid Insurance.

This transaction is very much like the previous one in that two assets are changed. One asset, Cash, has been exchanged for another asset, Prepaid Insurance. The asset account, Cash, is decreased by $900.00, the amount of cash paid out. The asset account, Prepaid Insurance, is increased by $900.00, the amount of insurance bought.

After this transaction, the new account balance of Cash is $935.00. The new account balance of Prepaid Insurance is $900.00. The sum of the amounts on the left side is $2,000.00 (Cash, $935.00 + Supplies, $165.00 + Prepaid Insurance, $900.00). The amount on the right side remains at $2,000.00. Therefore, the accounting equation is still in balance.

	Assets			= Liabilities	+ Owner's Equity
	Cash +	Supplies +	Prepaid Insurance =	Accts. Pay.— Canyon Office Supplies +	Michael Delgado, Capital
Balances	$935	$165	$900	$0	$2,000
Bought supplies on account		+220		+220	
New Balances	$935	$385	$900	$220	$2,000
Paid cash on account	−100			−100	
New Balances	$835	$385	$900	$120	$2,000

BOUGHT SUPPLIES ON ACCOUNT

Delgado Web Services needs to buy additional supplies. The supplies are obtained from Canyon Office Supplies. Rather than paying with cash, Delgado Web Services arranges to buy with credit and pay at the end of the month. It is a common practice to buy items and pay for them at a future date, which is referred to as *buying on account*. Buying on account is an arrangement made between two businesses that allows a business to buy now and pay later. Buying on account is not the same as buying with a major credit card.

> **Transaction 4.** January 5. Bought supplies on account from Canyon Office Supplies, $220.00.

In this transaction, one asset and one liability are changed. The asset account, Supplies, is increased by $220.00, the amount of supplies bought. A person or business to whom a liability is owed is called a **creditor**. Delgado Web Services now owes Canyon Office Supplies $220.00. This means that Canyon Office Supplies has a claim against Delgado Web Services' assets until the debt is paid. Therefore, Canyon Office Supplies could legally force Delgado Web Services to pay with some of its assets. The word "payable" refers to a liability that promises a future payment. The liability account titled Accounts Payable—Canyon Office Supplies is increased by $220.00, the amount owed for the supplies.

After this transaction, the new account balance of Supplies is $385.00. The new account balance of Accounts Payable—Canyon Office Supplies is $220.00. The sum of the amounts on the left side is $2,220.00 (Cash, $935.00 + Supplies, $385.00 + Prepaid Insurance, $900.00). The sum of the amounts on the right side is also $2,220.00 (Accounts Payable— Canyon Office Supplies, $220.00 + Michael Delgado, Capital, $2.000.00). Therefore, the accounting equation is still in balance.

PAID CASH ON ACCOUNT

Canyon Office Supplies has allowed Delgado Web Services to buy on account. However, since it is a new business, Canyon Office Supplies has requested that Delgado Web Services send a check for $100.00 immediately. Delgado Web Services will pay the remaining portion of this liability at a later date.

> **Transaction 5.** January 9. Paid cash on account to Canyon Office Supplies, $100.00.

In this transaction, one asset and one liability are changed. The asset account, Cash, is decreased by $100.00, the amount of cash paid out. After this payment, Delgado Web Services owes less money to Canyon Office Supplies. Therefore, the liability account, Accounts Payable—Canyon Office Supplies, is decreased by $100.00, the amount paid on account.

After this transaction, the new account balance of Cash is $835.00. The new account balance of Accounts Payable—Canyon Office Supplies is $120.00. The sum of the amounts on the left side of the accounting equation is $2,120.00 (Cash, $835.00 + Supplies, $385.00 + Prepaid Insurance, $900.00). The sum of the amounts on the right side of the accounting equation is also $2,120.00 (Accounts Payable—Canyon Office Supplies, $120.00 + Michael Delgado, Capital, $2,000.00). Therefore, the accounting equation is still in balance.

End of Lesson Review

LO3 Classify accounts as assets, liabilities, or owner's equity and demonstrate their relationship in the accounting equation.

LO4 Analyze the effects of transactions on the accounting equation.

LO5 Distinguish between cash and on account transactions.

Terms Review

service business
proprietorship
business plan
GAAP
equities
owner's equity
accounting equation
transaction
account
account title
account balance
capital account
creditor

Audit your understanding

1. Give two examples of service businesses in your area.
2. What must be done if a transaction increases the left side of the equation?
3. How can a transaction affect only one side of the equation?
4. What does the term *on account* mean?

Work together 1-2

Determining how transactions change an accounting equation

Write the answers to the following problem in the *Working Papers*. Your instructor will guide you through the following example.

Trans. No.	Assets	=	Liabilities	+	Owner's Equity
1					

For each transaction, place a plus sign (+) in the appropriate column if the account classification asset, liability, or owner's equity is increased. Place a minus sign (–) in the appropriate column if the account classification is decreased.

Transactions:

1. Bought supplies on account.
2. Received cash from owner as an investment.
3. Paid cash for insurance.
4. Paid cash on account.

On your own 1-2

Determining how transactions change an accounting equation

Write the answers to the following problem in the *Working Papers*. Work this problem independently.

Place a plus sign (+) in the appropriate column if the classification is increased. Place a minus sign (–) in the appropriate column if the classification is decreased.

Trans. No.	Assets	=	Liabilities	+	Owner's Equity
1					

Transactions:

1. Received cash from owner as an investment.
2. Bought supplies on account.
3. Paid cash for supplies.
4. Paid cash for insurance.
5. Paid cash on account.

©CANDICE CUSACK, ISTOCK

1-3 How Transactions Change Owner's Equity in an Accounting Equation

LO6 Compare and contrast the types of transactions that increase and decrease owner's equity.

LO7 Explain the difference between expenses and liabilities.

Transactions Affecting Owner's Equity LO6

	Assets				=	Liabilities +	Owner's Equity
	Cash +	Accts. Rec.—Main Street Services +	Supplies +	Prepaid Insurance =		Accts. Pay.—Canyon Office Supplies +	Michael Delgado, Capital
Balances	$835	$0	$385	$900		$120	$2,000
Received cash from sales	+1,100						+1,100 (revenue)
New Balances	$1,935	$0	$385	$900		$120	$3,100
Sold services on account		+500					+500 (revenue)
New Balances	$1,935	$500	$385	$900		$120	$3,600

Total of left side:
$1,935 + $500 + $385 + $900 = $3,720

Total of right side:
$120 + $3,600 = $3,720

RECEIVED CASH FROM SALES

An increase in equity resulting from the sale of goods or services is called **revenue**. When cash is received from a sale, the total amount of both assets and owner's equity is increased.

> **Transaction 6.** January 10. Received cash from sales, $1,100.00.

SOLD SERVICES ON ACCOUNT

Just as Canyon Office Supplies allowed Delgado Web Services to buy on account, Delgado Web Services will allow its customers, Main Street Services and Valley Landscaping, to buy services and pay later. A sale for which payment will be received at a later date is called a **sale on account**. Regardless of when payment is made, the revenue should be recorded at the time of the sale. The accounting principle Realization of Revenue is applied when revenue is recorded at the time goods or services are sold. [CONCEPT: Realization of Revenue]

When Delgado Web Services receives cash for services performed, the asset account, Cash, is increased by the amount of cash received, $1,100.00. This increase is on the left side of the equation. The owner's equity account, Michael Delgado, Capital, is also increased by $1,100.00. This increase is on the right side of the equation. After this transaction is recorded, the equation is still in balance.

> **Transaction 7.** January 12. Sold services on account to Main Street Services, $500.00.

When Delgado Web Services sells services on account, it expects to receive payment in the future. Therefore, the asset account titled Accounts Receivable—Main Street Services, is increased by $500.00, the amount that will be received. This increase is on the left side of the equation. The owner's equity account, Michael Delgado, Capital, is also increased by $500.00 on the right side of the equation. The equation is still in balance.

Expense Transactions LO7

		Assets			=	Liabilities	+	Owner's Equity
	Cash +	Accts. Rec.— Main Street Services +	Supplies +	Prepaid Insurance	=	Accts. Pay.— Canyon Office Supplies	+	Michael Delgado, Capital
Balances	$1,935	$500	$385	$900		$120		$3,600
Paid cash for communications bill	−80							−80 (expense)
New Balances	$1,855	$500	$385	$900		$120		$3,520

Total of left side:
$1,855 + $500 + $385 + $900 = $3,640

Total of right side:
$120 + $3,520 = $3,640

Paid cash for equipment rental	−400							−400 (expense)
New Balances	$1,455	$500	$385	$900		$120		$3,120

Total of left side:
$1,455 + $500 + $385 + $900 = $3,240

Total of right side:
$120 + $3,120 = $3,240

PAID CASH FOR EXPENSES

Transaction 8. January 12. Paid cash for communications bill for cellphone and Internet service, $80.00.

Unlike a liability, which is an amount that is owed, the cost of goods or services used to operate a business is called an **expense**. Telephone and Internet service, rent, advertising, and utilities are common expense transactions. When cash is paid for expenses, the business has less cash. Therefore, the asset account **Cash** is decreased. Expenses decrease owner's equity. Therefore, the owner's equity account **Michael Delgado, Capital** is also decreased by the same amount.

The asset account, **Cash**, is decreased by $80.00, the amount of cash paid out. This decrease is on the left side of the equation. The owner's equity account **Michael Delgado, Capital** is also decreased by $80.00. This decrease is on the right side of the equation. After this transaction is recorded, the equation is still in balance.

All expense transactions affect the accounting equation in the same way as Transaction 8.

Transaction 9. January 13. Paid cash for equipment rental, $400.00.

This expense transaction is also shown in the accounting equation. The asset account **Cash** is decreased by $400.00. The owner's equity account **Michael Delgado, Capital** is also decreased by $400.00. After the transaction is recorded, the accounting equation is still in balance.

Sometimes people confuse expenses with liabilities. Remember, an expense is a cost as a result of doing business. A liability is debt owed by the business.

Other Cash Transactions

	Assets				= Liabilities +	Owner's Equity
	Cash +	Accts. Rec.—Main Street Services +	Supplies +	Prepaid Insurance =	Accts. Pay.—Canyon Office Supplies +	Michael Delgado, Capital
Balances	$1,455	$500	$385	$900	$120	$3,120
Received cash on account	+200	−200				
New Balances	$1,655	$300	$385	$900	$120	$3,120
Paid cash to owner for personal use	−350					−350 (withdrawal)
New Balances	$1,305	$300	$385	$900	$120	$2,770

Total of left side:
$1,305 + $300 + $385 + $900 = $2,890

Total of right side:
$120 + $2,770 = $2,890

RECEIVED CASH ON ACCOUNT

Transaction 10. January 16. Received cash on account from Main Street Services, $200.00.

When a business receives cash from a customer for a prior sale on account, the transaction increases the cash account balance and decreases the accounts receivable balance. The asset, Cash, increases because cash is received. The asset Accounts Receivable—Main Street Services decreases because the amount is no longer owed.

The asset account Cash is increased by $200.00. This increase is on the left side of the equation. The asset account Accounts Receivable—Main Street Services is decreased by $200.00. This decrease is also on the left side of the equation. After this transaction is recorded, the equation is still in balance.

PAID CASH TO OWNER FOR PERSONAL USE

Assets taken from the business for the owner's personal use are called **withdrawals**. A withdrawal decreases owner's equity. An owner may withdraw any kind of asset, but usually an owner withdraws cash. Therefore, the account balance of Cash decreases.

Transaction 11. January 16. Michael Delgado withdrew equity in the form of cash, $350.00.

The asset account Cash is decreased by $350.00. This decrease is on the left side of the accounting equation. The owner's equity account, Michael Delgado, Capital, is also decreased by $350.00. This decrease is on the right side of the equation. After this transaction is recorded, the equation is still in balance.

A decrease in owner's equity because of a withdrawal is not a result of the normal operations of a business. Therefore, a withdrawal is not considered an expense.

Summary of Changes in Owner's Equity

After recording the beginning investment used to start Delgado Web Services, the total owner's equity was $2,000.00, the investment by the owner, Michael Delgado. Since that initial investment, five additional transactions that changed owner's equity have been recorded in the accounting equation.

These transactions increased owner's equity by $770.00, from $2,000.00 to $2,770.00. Transaction 10, cash received on account, is not listed because it affects two accounts that are both on the left side of the accounting equation and had no impact on owner's equity. Owner's equity was not affected because the increase in owner's equity was recognized when the sale was made, not when payment was received.

Transaction Number	Kind of Transaction	Change in Owner's Equity
6	Revenue (cash)	+1,100.00
7	Revenue (on account)	+500.00
8	Expense (communications)	−80.00
9	Expense (equipment rental)	−400.00
11	Withdrawal of equity	−350.00
Net change in owner's equity		+770.00

Olympics—The Cost of Getting There

Accounting is often called the *language of business*. The knowledge of accounting is useful in many non-accounting positions. This Why Accounting feature will show you how accounting information is used in a variety of settings. It will focus on the 16 career clusters identified by the States' Career Clusters Initiative, 2010.

During the 2010 Winter Olympics in Vancouver, British Columbia, one of the major logistic challenges was planning how to move people. Crowds of 1.2 million spectators, 6,800 athletes, and over 10,000 media representatives were expected. All these people had to be moved around the city and Olympic venues. The locations of the events were separated by 75 miles, north to south. While all those people were moving between locations, the restaurants, stores, gas stations, and hotels providing goods and services

to the visitors also had to be restocked with supplies.

Transportation, Distribution & Logistics

To help reduce the amount of traffic, cars were prohibited on many roads. Spectators, athletes, and media personnel boarded shuttle buses to many of the events. Planners had to make many estimates. (1) The number of people who would use these services. (2) The number of buses needed. (3) The times the buses were needed. (4) The cost of these services. The price charged for these services was based on the estimated costs of providing these services. Estimating costs and determining the price to charge to cover those costs are part of the accounting function.

CRITICAL THINKING

1. What other costs would be included in the cost of the Olympics?
2. What other logistics would have to be planned for the Olympics?

End of Lesson Review

LO6 Compare and contrast the types of transactions that increase and decrease owner's equity.

LO7 Explain the difference between expenses and liabilities.

Terms Review

revenue

sale on account

expense

withdrawals

Audit your understanding

1. How is owner's equity affected when cash is received from sales?

2. How is owner's equity affected when services are sold on account?

3. How is owner's equity affected when cash is paid for expenses?

Work together 1-3

Determining how transactions change an accounting equation

Write the answers to the following problem in the *Working Papers*. Your instructor will guide you through the following example.

Place a plus sign (+) in the appropriate column if the account is increased. Place a minus sign (−) in the appropriate column if the account is decreased.

Trans. No.	Assets				=	Liabilities	+	Owner's Equity
	Cash +	Accts. Rec.— Harmon Co. +	Supplies +	Prepaid Insurance =		Accts. Pay.— Corona Supplies +		Nathaniel Conrad, Capital
1								

Transactions:

1. Received cash from sales.

2. Sold services on account to Harmon Co.

3. Paid cash for cell phone bill.

4. Received cash on account from Harmon Co.

5. Owner withdrew equity in the form of cash.

On your own 1-3

Determining how transactions change an accounting equation

Trans. No.	Assets				=	Liabilities	+	Owner's Equity
	Cash +	Accts. Rec.— Bethany Center +	Supplies +	Prepaid Insurance =		Accts. Pay.— McGrew Supplies +		Bryan Arnett, Capital
1								

Write the answers to the following problem in the *Working Papers*. Work this problem independently.

Place a plus sign (+) in the appropriate column if the account is increased. Place a minus sign (−) in the appropriate column if the account is decreased.

Transactions:

1. Sold services on account to Bethany Center.

2. Received cash from sales.

3. Received cash on account from Bethany Center.

4. Owner withdrew equity in the form of cash.

5. Paid cash for rent.

A Look at Accounting Software

Setting Up a New Company in the Company Setup Window

In a manual accounting system, the process of setting up a new company is done by writing or printing the proper headings on preprinted journal paper and ledger sheets. In a computerized accounting system, certain information about the business needs to be entered before the business starts up. With that information, the system will know how to properly account for the data that get keyed in from day to day.

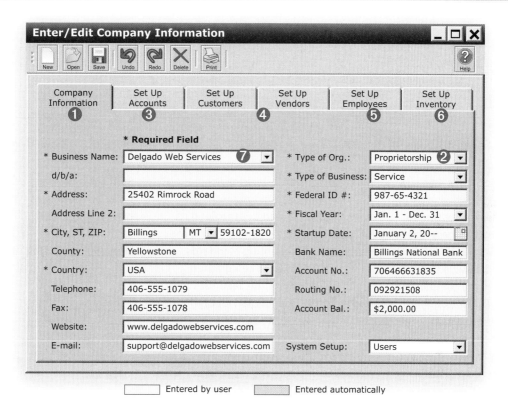

Entered by user   Entered automatically

1. Fields on the Company Information window provide the data the system needs for setting up forms and reports.

2. The type of business is selected here. Delgado Web Services is a proprietorship. Other business types you will learn about in this text are corporations and partnerships.

3. General accounts are set up here. You will learn more about accounts in Chapter 4.

4. Delgado Web Services is a very small business with no employees and only a few vendors and customers. All of its accounts would be set up here. Larger businesses have different types of accounts for customers and vendors.

5. If Michael Delgado decides to hire employees as his business grows, he will need to set up employee accounts to record the wages he pays them.

6. Delgado Web Services is a service business. That means it sells only services, not merchandise. Later in this text, you will learn about businesses that sell merchandise. These businesses need accounts to manage inventory.

7. Most accounting software systems enable more than one company's data to be managed. The company the user wants to work with is selected here. A new company can be started by clicking on New in the menu bar.

Chapter Summary

Accounting is a language used to communicate financial information so that individuals can make informed personal and business decisions. Financial information is communicated by using a planned accounting system to record, analyze, and interpret financial information.

In this chapter, you have learned that the accounting equation is stated as: Assets = Liabilities + Owner's Equity.

This equation must remain in balance at all times. This means that the left side of the equation (assets) must always equal the right side of the equation (liabilities + owner's equity). As transactions occur, they are analyzed to demonstrate their effect on the accounting equation while keeping it balanced.

EXPLORE ACCOUNTING

What Is GAAP?

GAAP, or Generally Accepted Accounting Principles, defines the standards and rules that accountants follow when reporting financial activities in the United States. Important business decisions are based on these financial data. GAAP principles provide consistency in reporting so companies can be compared. For example, Brad is evaluating whether to invest in Hewlett-Packard or Dell Inc. He compares financial information from both companies. Since both companies follow GAAP, Brad is assured that the financial data being evaluated are generated consistently. Therefore, he can make a better business decision.

Many different organizations have contributed to the rules over the years; however, since 1973, the Financial Accounting Standards Board (FASB) has been granted the authority by the Securities and Exchange Commission (SEC) to determine GAAP. GAAP has been the uniformity standard for U.S. companies. However, as many as 100 other countries follow another set of accounting rules and standards called *International Financial Reporting Standards (IFRS)*. IFRS are set by the International Accounting Standards Board (IASB). The SEC has recognized that global business opportunities and international competition present the need for a single set of accounting standards.

INSTRUCTIONS

Describe other situations in which consistency in standards helps to make informed comparisons and decisions.

©MAKHNACH_M_ISTOCK

PHOTOGRAPHER'S CHOICE/GETTY IMAGES

Apply Your Understanding

1-1 Application Problem: Preparing a net worth statement LO2

Lauren Juliana has been saving and would now like to purchase a boat. She does not have enough to pay cash, so she has contacted a lending institution about purchasing on credit. The lending institution has asked her to begin the loan process by completing a net worth statement.

Cash	$14,692
Owe Knapp College	10,981
Owe Ashley's Boutique	1,682
Owe Buzz Electronics	787
Jewelry	2,575

Instructions:

Use the form in your *Working Papers* to prepare a net worth statement for Lauren Juliana. Use today's date.

1-2 Application Problem: Completing the accounting equation LO4

Instructions:

For each line, fill in the missing amount to complete the accounting equation. Use the form in your *Working Papers* to complete the problem.

Assets	=	Liabilities	+	Owner's Equity
15,650		11,475		?
11,000		?		6,000
?		2,000		3,300
12,000		?		7,000
125,000		69,000		?
?		1,875		15,750
35,000		13,000		?
6,000		?		2,500
?		139,000		4,650
17,000		2,800		?
42,000		?		17,000
8,750		2,980		?
?		47,000		24,000
67,000		?		32,000
73,000		41,000		?
?		93,000		7,700
49,325		?		10,020
?		21,250		2,800

1-3 Application Problem: Determining how transactions change an accounting equation LO4, 5

Bethany Hartman is starting Hartman's Lawn Service, a small service business. Hartman's uses the accounts shown in the following equation. Use the form in your *Working Papers* to complete this problem.

Trans. No.	Assets			=	Liabilities		+	Owner's Equity
	Cash +	Supplies +	Prepaid Insurance =		Accts. Pay.— Knapp Co.	+	Accts. Pay.— Hickman Mowing +	Bethany Hartman, Capital
Beg. Bal. 1	0 +5,000	0	0		0		0	0 +5,000
New Bal. 2	5,000	0	0		0		0	5,000

Instructions:

For each transaction, complete the following. Transaction 1 is given as an example.

a. Analyze the transaction to determine which accounts in the accounting equation are affected.

b. Write the amount in the appropriate columns using a plus sign (+) if the account increases or a minus sign (–) if the account decreases.

c. Calculate a new balance for each transaction in the accounting equation.

d. Before going on to the next transaction, determine that the accounting equation is still in balance.

Transactions:

1. Received cash from owner as an investment, $5,000.00.
2. Paid cash for insurance, $1,800.00.
3. Bought supplies on account from Hickman Mowing, $700.00.
4. Bought supplies on account from Knapp Co., $200.00.
5. Paid cash on account to Hickman Mowing, $300.00.
6. Paid cash for supplies, $100.00.
7. Paid cash on account to Knapp Co., $100.00.
8. Received cash from owner as an investment, $1,000.00.

1-4 Application Problem: Determining how revenue, expense, and withdrawal transactions change an accounting equation LO4, 5, 6

Shannon O'Bryan operates a service business called Edgecliff Photography. Edgecliff Photography uses the accounts shown in the following accounting equation. Use the form in your *Working Papers* to complete this problem.

Trans. No.	Assets				=	Liabilities	+	Owner's Equity
	Cash +	Accts. Rec.— Eden Wedding Planners +	Supplies +	Prepaid Insurance =		Accts. Pay.— Shutter Supplies +		Shannon O'Bryan, Capital
Beg. Bal. 1	725 −400	0	200	300		200		1,025 −400 (expense)
New Bal. 2	325	0	200	300		200		625

Instructions:

For each transaction, complete the following. Transaction 1 is given as an example.

a. Analyze the transaction to determine which accounts in the accounting equation are affected.

b. Write the amount in the appropriate columns using a plus sign (+) if the account increases or a minus sign (–) if the account decreases.

c. For transactions that change owner's equity, write in parentheses a description of the transaction to the right of the amount.

d. Calculate a new balance for each transaction in the accounting equation.

e. Before going on to the next transaction, determine that the accounting equation is still in balance.

Transactions:

1. Paid cash for rent, $400.00.
2. Owner withdrew equity in the form of cash, $150.00.
3. Received cash from sales, $900.00.
4. Paid cash for camera repairs, $100.00.
5. Sold services on account to Eden Wedding Planners, $400.00.
6. Received cash from sales, $650.00.
7. Paid cash for charitable contributions, $35.00.
8. Received cash on account from Eden Wedding Planners, $300.00.

1-M Mastery Problem: Determining how transactions change an accounting equation LO4, 5, 6

Peter Gentry operates a service business called Doggywood Pet Suites. Doggywood Pet Suites uses the accounts shown in the following accounting equation. Use the form in your *Working Papers* to complete this problem.

Trans. No.	Assets				=	Liabilities	+	Owner's Equity
	Cash	+	Accts. Rec.— Dr. Shephard	+ Supplies +	Prepaid Insurance =	Accts. Pay.— Paws & Claws Co.	+	Peter Gentry, Capital
Beg. Bal.	2,500		0	200	100	1,300		1,500
1	−500							−500 (expense)
New Bal.	**2,000**		**0**	**200**	**100**	**1,300**		**1,000**
2								

Instructions:

For each transaction, complete the following. Transaction 1 is given as an example.

a. Analyze the transaction to determine which accounts in the accounting equation are affected.

b. Write the amount in the appropriate columns, using a plus sign (+) if the account increases or a minus sign (−) if the account decreases.

c. For transactions that change owner's equity, write in parentheses a description of the transaction to the right of the amount.

d. Calculate the new balance for each account in the accounting equation.

e. Before going on to the next transaction, determine that the accounting equation is still in balance.

Transactions:

1. Paid cash for rent, $500.00.
2. Received cash from owner as an investment, $700.00.
3. Paid cash for telephone bill, $75.00.
4. Received cash from sales, $1,050.00.
5. Bought supplies on account from Paws & Claws Co., $275.00.
6. Sold services on account to Dr. Shephard, $285.00.
7. Paid cash for advertising, $450.00.
8. Paid cash for supplies, $185.00.

9. Received cash on account from Dr. Shephard, $150.00.
10. Paid cash on account to Paws & Claws Co., $200.00.
11. Paid cash for one month of insurance, $100.00.
12. Received cash from sales, $475.00.
13. Owner withdrew equity in the form of cash, $800.00.

1-C Challenge Problem: Determining how transactions change an accounting equation LO4, 5, 6

Linda Liu owns a tutoring service called Homework Helper. On October 30, Homework Helper's accounting equation indicated the following account balances. Use the form in your *Working Papers* to complete this problem.

Trans. No.	Assets				=	Liabilities	+	Owner's Equity
	Cash +	Accts. Rec.— 4Kids Daycare +	Supplies +	Prepaid Insurance =		Accts. Pay.— Ashley Tech Services +		Linda Liu, Capital
Beg. Bal. 1	7,542	1,265	1,100	600		3,145		7,362

Instructions:

1. For each transaction, complete the following:
   a. Analyze the transaction to determine which accounts in the accounting equation are affected.
   b. Write the amount in the appropriate columns, using a plus sign (+) if the account increases or a minus sign (−) if the account decreases.
   c. For transactions that change owner's equity, write in parentheses a description of the transaction to the right of the amount.
   d. Calculate the new balance for each account in the accounting equation.
   e. Before going on to the next transaction, determine that the accounting equation is still in balance.
2. Answer the following questions.
   a. Why can the owner of a business withdraw assets from that business for personal use?
   b. Why would the owner withdraw assets other than cash?

Transactions:

1. Took $300.00 of supplies for personal use.
2. Had computer repaired at Ashley Tech Services and agreed to pay Ashley Tech Services at a later date, $225.00.
3. Linda Liu sold her personal book collection for $750.00 cash.
4. Paid Ashley Tech Services, $125.00.

21st Century Skills

Creativity and Innovation: Seize the Opportunity

Theme: Financial, Economic, Business, and Entrepreneurial Literacy

Skills: Critical Thinking and Problem Solving, Creativity and Innovation

PARTNERSHIP FOR
21ST CENTURY SKILLS

An entrepreneur is someone who creates a business. While an entrepreneur requires capital, determination, and risk-taking abilities, the entrepreneur must possess the vision to be a problem solver. When a problem is solved, a business opportunity is created. Famous inventor and entrepreneur Thomas Edison once said, "I find out what the world needs, then I proceed to invent it."

Corn flakes, Silly Putty, Play Dough, Frisbees, and potato chips all happened by accident. An entrepreneur had the vision to see that the new product would fill a consumer need or want. Other examples of entrepreneurs turning a discovery into an opportunity are disposable diapers, coffee makers, ice cream cones, and safety pins. Services such as delivery services and personal fitness can also be a business opportunity. An entrepreneur must have the vision and determination to discover these business opportunities. Sometimes just walking through a store to look for products that need improvement can lead to a new business. Other times, having a conversation with someone complaining about a need can also lead to a new product or idea for a service business.

APPLICATION

1. List five problems that you would like to solve that would help either at home, in your community, or at school.
2. From this list, describe a business opportunity (product or service) for each problem.

Analyzing Nike's financial statements

Selected published financial information for Nike, Inc., is reproduced in Appendix B. Look at pages B-5 through B-9, where you will find Nike's financial statements. To the left of the column headings on each page, you will see the phrase "In millions." This means that all dollar amounts are rounded to the nearest million. Therefore, an amount such as $174 actually means $174,000,000. Another way to think of this is that you can calculate the actual amount by multiplying the rounded amount by 1,000,000 ($174 × 1,000,000 = $174,000,000).

Not all companies round the amounts in their financial statements to the nearest million dollars. Many companies round to the nearest thousand dollars.

INSTRUCTIONS

1. List the actual amounts of Cash and equivalents and Accounts receivable, net for Nike for May 31, 2011.
2. The financial statements for Chipotle Mexican Grill, Inc., include the phrase "all numbers in thousands." In June 2010, the income statement included Total Revenue, $466,841, and Gross Profit, $178,357. List the actual amounts of Total Revenue and Gross Profit.

Chapter 2

Analyzing Transactions into Debit and Credit Parts

LEARNING OBJECTIVES

After studying Chapter 2, in addition to defining key terms, you will be able to:

LO1 Show the relationship between the accounting equation and a T account.

LO2 Identify the debit and credit side, the increase and decrease side, and the balance side of various accounts.

LO3 Restate and apply the two rules that are associated with the increase side of an account.

LO4 Restate and apply the four questions necessary to analyze transactions for starting a business into debit and credit parts.

LO5 Analyze transactions for operating a business into debit and credit parts.

Accounting In The Real World
Great Clips

When you need a new hair style or a new hair color, you may think of Great Clips. But, does Great Clips come to mind when you think of NASCAR racing? You might be surprised to learn that Great Clips is one of the longest-running sponsors of the NASCAR Nationwide Series.

Great Clips is a franchising operation. It was started near the University of Minnesota in 1982, by Ray Barton. Mr. Barton felt that the haircutting industry was changing and would soon be led by national franchise brands. With that in mind, Mr. Barton set out to grow the business. Currently, Great Clips is the largest no-appointment hair salon brand in North America, with over 2,700 salons. The Great Clips website states that its "hair salons are conveniently located in high-visibility strip malls and offer quality haircuts and perms for men, women, and children at competitive prices."

What does all of this have to do with NASCAR? Great Clips is a primary sponsor of NASCAR and has its own car in the Nationwide Series. The Great Clips car won its first victory in 2003.

As a service business similar to Delgado Web Services, each Great Clips salon keeps track of its own revenues and expenses. It must establish a list of accounts for recording its daily business transactions.

CRITICAL THINKING

1. If you owned a Great Clips franchise, why might you support Great Clips' sponsorship of NASCAR racing?

2. What asset and liability accounts might a Great Clips salon use to record its transactions?

3. List at least two transactions that a Great Clips salon might record.

Key Terms

- T account
- debit
- credit

- normal balance
- chart of accounts

- accounts payable
- accounts receivable

LESSON
2-1 Using T Accounts

LO1 Show the relationship between the accounting equation and a T account.
LO2 Identify the debit and credit side, the increase and decrease side, and the balance side of various accounts.
LO3 Restate and apply the two rules that are associated with the increase side of an account.

Analyzing the Accounting Equation LO1

In Chapter 1, the effects of transactions were recorded in an accounting equation. This procedure is not practical in an actual accounting system. Because of the number of accounts used by most businesses, recording transactions in the accounting equation would be cumbersome. Therefore, a separate record is commonly used for each account. The accounting equation can be represented as a T, as shown below.

Assets	=	Liabilities	+	Owner's Equity
Left side			Right side	

The values of all things owned (assets) are on the left side of the accounting equation. The values of all equities or claims against the assets (liabilities and owner's equity) are on the right side of the accounting equation. The total of amounts on the left side of the accounting equation must always equal the total of amounts on the right side. Therefore, the total of all assets on the left side of the accounting equation must always equal the total of all liabilities and owner's equity on the right side.

ETHICS IN ACTION

Ethics Versus Morality

Ethics and morality—these words are often used to refer to an individual's ability to "do what is right." These synonymous English words were derived from different languages. "Ethics" is derived from Greek, and "morality" is derived from Latin. Over time, our society has given a slightly different meaning to each word.

Over 100 years ago, C. C. Everett wrote, "Ethics is the science of morality." Morality is the standard of conduct that is acceptable in a society. Ethics is an organized method that relies on our morality to make moral decisions. Science students learn the scientific method—a model that guides how a proper experiment should be conducted. In the same manner, many ethical models have been proposed to guide individuals in applying their morality to business decisions.

The following ethical model will be used in this textbook:
1. Recognize you are facing an ethical dilemma.
2. Identify the action taken or the proposed action.
3. Analyze the action.
   a. Is the action illegal?
   b. Does the action violate company or professional standards?
   c. Who is affected, and how, by the action?
4. Determine if the action is ethical.

INSTRUCTIONS
Prepare a short report that contrasts the ethical model with the scientific method. How are the models similar? How are they different?

Accounts LO2

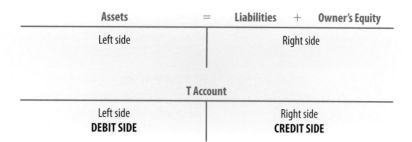

A record summarizing all the information affecting a single item in the accounting equation is known as an *account*. Transactions change the balances of accounts in the accounting equation. Accounting transactions must be analyzed to determine how account balances are changed. An accounting device used to analyze transactions is called a **T account**.

There are special names for amounts recorded on the left and right sides of an account. An amount recorded on the left side of an account is called a **debit**. An amount recorded on the right side of an account is called a **credit**. The words *debit* and *credit* come from the Latin and Italian words *debere* and *credere*. Common abbreviations are *dr.* for debit and *cr.* for credit. It is important to understand that in an accounting system, the words *debit* and *credit* do not have the same meaning as in everyday life. In an accounting system, the terms mean only the left side or right side of an account. Debit means an amount recorded on the left side of an account. Credit means an amount recorded on the right side of an account.

Increases, Decreases, and Balances in Accounts LO3

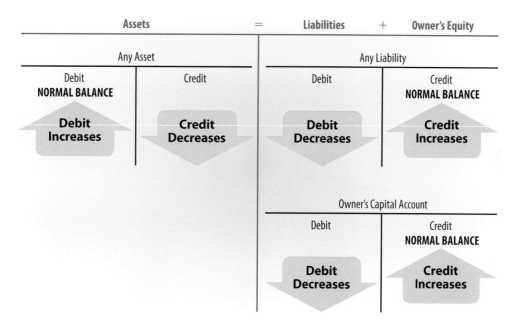

The sides of a T account are used to show increases and decreases in account balances. The increase side of each kind of account can be associated with the accounting equation using two rules:

1. Assets are on the left side of the accounting equation. Therefore, assets increase on the left, or debit, side of the account.
2. Liabilities and the owner's capital account are on the right side of the accounting equation. Therefore, liabilities and the owner's capital account increase on the right, or credit, side of the account.

The side of the account that is increased is called the **normal balance** of the account. Assets have normal debit balances because they increase on the debit side. Liabilities and the owner's capital account have normal credit balances because they increase on the credit side.

Accounts decrease on the side opposite their increase side. Therefore, assets decrease on the right, or credit, side of the account. Liabilities and the owner's capital account decrease on the left, or debit, side of the account.

Planning for College and Beyond

John Melby wants to be sure that he has enough money to send his newborn son to college. His college of choice is estimated to cost $100,000 for a four-year education, including tuition, books, room, and board. John wants to know whether a $5,000 annual contribution to a college fund will grow to $100,000 when his son enters college at the age of 18. The money would be invested in an account that is not subject to income taxes as long as the money will be used to pay educational expenses.

OPEN THE SPREADSHEET TLA_CH02

Answer the Following Questions about the College Fund Investment:

1. If John can earn a 6% annual return on the fund's investments, will he reach his $100,000 goal?

2. What amount would he need to contribute each year to reach his goal?

3. What annual contribution would be required if his son elects to enroll in a major that requires five years of coursework?

Planning for his son's college makes John realize that he needs to begin planning for his retirement. John is currently 25 years old and wants to have $1,000,000 in his retirement fund when he reaches age 65.

Answer the Following Questions about John's Retirement Fund Investment:

4. If John can earn a 6% annual return on the fund's investments, how much will he have to contribute each year to reach his goal?

5. What if John waits until his son begins college to start investing in his retirement fund (age 43)? How much would John have to contribute each year to reach his goal?

End of Lesson Review

LO1 Show the relationship between the accounting equation and a T account.

LO2 Identify the debit and credit side, the increase and decrease side, and the balance side of various accounts.

LO3 Restate and apply the two rules that are associated with the increase side of an account.

Terms Review

T account

debit

credit

normal balance

Audit your understanding

1. Draw the accounting equation on a T account.

2. What are the two accounting rules that explain increases of account balances?

Work together 2-1

Determining the increase and decrease and the normal balance sides for accounts

Write the answers to the following problems in the *Working Papers*. Your instructor will guide you through the following examples.

Cash
Accounts Receivable—Sullivan Company
Supplies
Prepaid Insurance

Accounts Payable—Sawyer Supplies
Accounts Payable—Oceanside Supplies
Parker Vogel, Capital

For each account, complete the following:

1. Prepare a T account.

2. Label the debit and credit side.

3. Draw an up arrow (↑) on the increase side.

4. Draw a down arrow (↓) on the decrease side.

5. Label the normal balance side.

On your own 2-1

Determining the increase and decrease and the normal balance sides for accounts

Write the answers to the following problems in the *Working Papers*. Work this problem independently.

Cash
Accounts Receivable—White Company
Accounts Receivable—Jagerstrom Inc.
Supplies

Prepaid Insurance
Accounts Payable—West End Hardware
Shelley Feinstein, Capital

For each account, complete the following:

1. Prepare a T account.

2. Label the debit and credit side.

3. Draw an up arrow (↑) on the increase side.

4. Draw a down arrow (↓) on the decrease side.

5. Label the normal balance side.

©CANDICE CUSACK, ISTOCK

LO4 Restate and apply the four questions necessary to analyze transactions for starting a business into debit and credit parts.

Received Cash from Owner as an Investment LO4

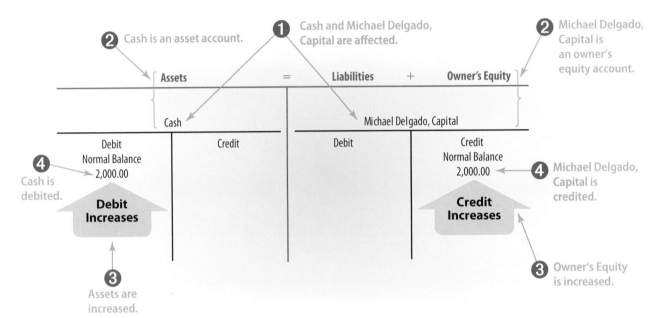

2 Cash is an asset account.

1 Cash and Michael Delgado, Capital are affected.

2 Michael Delgado, Capital is an owner's equity account.

Assets   =   Liabilities   +   Owner's Equity

Cash   Michael Delgado, Capital

Debit	Credit	Debit	Credit
Normal Balance			Normal Balance
2,000.00			2,000.00

4 Cash is debited.

Debit Increases

3 Assets are increased.

4 Michael Delgado, Capital is credited.

Credit Increases

3 Owner's Equity is increased.

January 2. Received cash from owner as an investment, $2,000.00.

The effect of this transaction is shown in the illustration. Before a transaction is recorded in the records of a business, the information is analyzed to determine which accounts are changed and how. Each transaction changes the balances of at least two accounts. A list of accounts used by a business is called a **chart of accounts**. The chart of accounts for Delgado Web Services is on page 3.

When accounts are analyzed, debits must equal credits for each transaction. In addition, after a transaction is recorded, total debits must equal total credits.

The same four questions are used every time a transaction is analyzed into its debit and credit parts.

Questions for Analyzing a Transaction into Its Debit and Credit Parts

1 **Which accounts are affected?**
Cash and *Michael Delgado, Capital*.

2 **How is each account classified?**
Cash is an asset account. *Michael Delgado, Capital* is an owner's equity account.

3 **How is each classification changed?**
Assets increase. Owner's equity increases.

4 **How is each amount entered in the accounts?**
Assets increase on the debit side. Therefore, debit the asset account, *Cash*. Owner's equity accounts increase on the credit side. Therefore, credit the owner's equity account, *Michael Delgado, Capital*.

Paid Cash for Supplies

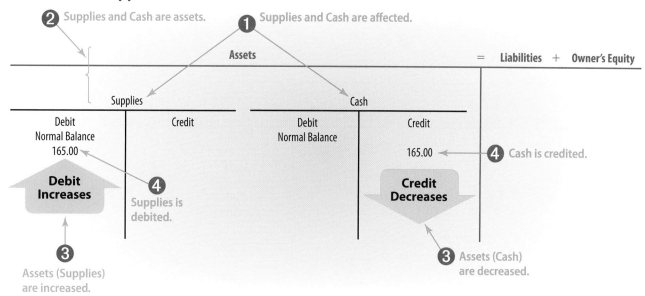

❷ Supplies and Cash are assets.

❶ Supplies and Cash are affected.

Assets = **Liabilities** + **Owner's Equity**

Supplies

Debit Normal Balance 165.00	Credit

Debit Increases

❹ Supplies is debited.

❸ Assets (Supplies) are increased.

Cash

Debit Normal Balance	Credit 165.00

❹ Cash is credited.

Credit Decreases

❸ Assets (Cash) are decreased.

January 2. Paid cash for supplies, $165.00.

The effect of this transaction on the accounting equation is shown in the illustration. In this transaction, two asset accounts are changed. One asset, cash, has been exchanged for another asset, supplies. The asset account, Cash, decreases by $165.00, the amount of cash paid out. This decrease is on the left side of the accounting equation. The asset account, Supplies, increases by $165.00, the amount of supplies bought. This increase is also on the left side of the accounting equation.

The two changes are both on the left side of the accounting equation. When changes are made on only one side of the accounting equation, the equation must still be in balance. Therefore, if one account is increased, another account on the same side of the equation must be decreased.

Transactions must always be carefully analyzed. A transaction may affect accounts from both sides of the accounting equation. Or, a transaction may affect accounts that are on the same side of the accounting equation, as is true in this example. A common error is to assume that every transaction must affect accounts on both sides of the accounting equation.

Do not attach any meaning to debit/ credit other than left side/right side. Don't think of them as "good" or "bad." Debit simply means left and credit simply means right.

↘ Questions for Analyzing a Transaction into Its Debit and Credit Parts

❶ Which accounts are affected?
Supplies and *Cash*

❷ How is each account classified?
Supplies is an asset account. *Cash* is an asset account.

❸ How is each classification changed?
One asset (*Supplies*) increases and another asset (*Cash*) decreases.

❹ How is each amount entered in the accounts?
Assets increase on the debit side. Therefore, debit the asset account, *Supplies*. Assets decrease on the credit side. Therefore, credit the asset account, *Cash*.

SZEFEI/ISTOCKPHOTO.COM

Paid Cash for Insurance

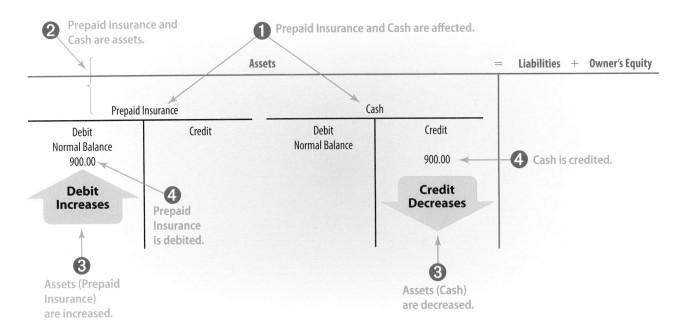

① Prepaid Insurance and Cash are affected.

② Prepaid Insurance and Cash are assets.

Assets				= **Liabilities** + **Owner's Equity**	

Prepaid Insurance

Debit Normal Balance 900.00	Credit
Debit Increases	**④** Prepaid Insurance is debited.

③ Assets (Prepaid Insurance) are increased.

Cash

Debit Normal Balance	Credit 900.00
	Credit Decreases

④ Cash is credited.

③ Assets (Cash) are decreased.

January 3. Paid cash for insurance, $900.00.

Paying cash for insurance is very similar to paying cash for supplies. One asset is increased and one asset is decreased.

The effect of this transaction on the accounting equation is shown in the illustration. In this transaction, two assets are changed. One asset, cash, has been exchanged for another asset, prepaid insurance. The asset account, Cash, decreases by $900.00, the amount of cash paid out. This decrease is on the left side of the accounting equation. The asset account, Prepaid Insurance, increases by $900.00, the amount of insurance bought. This increase is also on the left side of the accounting equation.

Questions for Analyzing a Transaction into Its Debit and Credit Parts

① Which accounts are affected?
Prepaid Insurance and *Cash*

② How is each account classified?
Prepaid Insurance is an asset account. *Cash* is an asset account.

③ How is each classification changed?
One asset (*Prepaid Insurance*) increases and another asset (*Cash*) decreases.

④ How is each amount entered in the accounts?
Assets increase on the debit side. Therefore, debit the asset account, *Prepaid Insurance*. Assets decrease on the credit side. Therefore, credit the asset account, *Cash*.

GLOBAL AWARENESS

The Global Business Day

When doing business internationally, time zone differences and cultural factors affect the business day. For example, in Spain, the normal business day is from 9 A.M. to 8 P.M. But many businesses traditionally close from 2 P.M. to 5 P.M. for a long lunch or *siesta*. In 2006, the Spanish government implemented new working hours for all government employees. Only one hour is allowed for lunch, and workers go home at 6 P.M. These new hours better align the Spanish business day with the rest of Central Europe.

CRITICAL THINKING

If your company has offices around the world, what methods could you use to facilitate working together on a team project?

Bought Supplies on Account

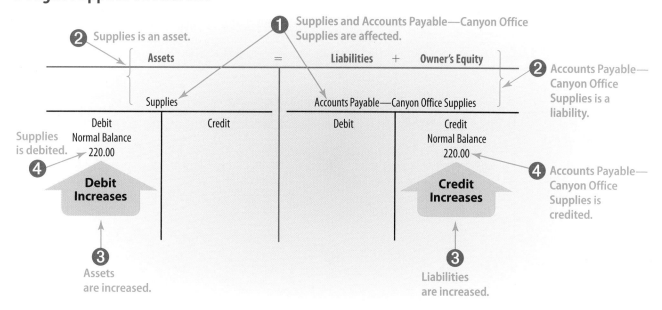

① Supplies and Accounts Payable—Canyon Office Supplies are affected.

② Supplies is an asset.

② Accounts Payable—Canyon Office Supplies is a liability.

| Assets | = | Liabilities | + | Owner's Equity |

Supplies

| Debit Normal Balance 220.00 | Credit |

Supplies is debited.

④

Debit Increases

③ Assets are increased.

Accounts Payable—Canyon Office Supplies

| Debit | Credit Normal Balance 220.00 |

④ Accounts Payable—Canyon Office Supplies is credited.

Credit Increases

③ Liabilities are increased.

January 5. Bought supplies on account from Canyon Office Supplies, $220.00.

The effect of this transaction on the accounting equation is shown in the illustration. In this transaction, one asset and one liability are changed. The asset account, Supplies, increases by $220.00, the amount of supplies bought. This increase is on the left side of the accounting equation. Amounts to be paid in the future for goods or services already acquired are called **accounts payable**. Canyon Office Supplies will have a claim against some of Delgado Web Services' assets until Delgado Web Services pays for the supplies bought. Therefore, Accounts Payable—Canyon Office Supplies is a liability account. The liability account, Accounts Payable—Canyon Office Supplies, increases by $220.00, the amount owed for the supplies. This increase is on the right side of the accounting equation.

⊗ Questions for Analyzing a Transaction into Its Debit and Credit Parts

① Which accounts are affected?
Supplies and *Accounts Payable—Canyon Office Supplies*

② How is each account classified?
Supplies is an asset account. *Accounts Payable—Canyon Office Supplies* is a liability account.

③ How is each classification changed?
Assets increase. Liabilities increase.

④ How is each amount entered in the accounts?
Assets increase on the debit side. Therefore, debit the asset account, Supplies. Liabilities increase on the credit side. Therefore, credit the liability, *Accounts Payable—Canyon Office Supplies.*

Paid Cash on Account

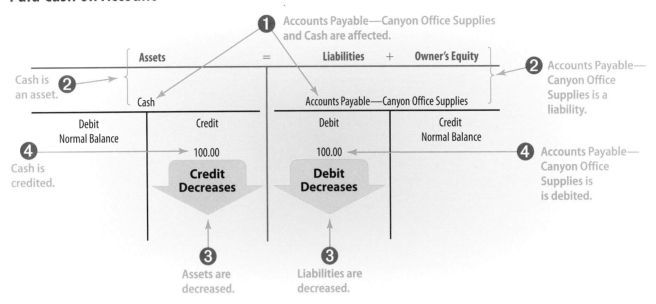

January 9. Paid cash on account to Canyon Office Supplies, $100.00.

The effect of this transaction on the accounting equation is shown in the illustration. In this transaction, one asset and one liability are changed. The asset account, Cash, is decreased by $100.00, the amount of cash paid out. This decrease is on the left side of the accounting equation. After this payment, Delgado Web Services owes less money to Canyon Office Supplies. Therefore, the liability account, Accounts Payable—Canyon Office Supplies, is decreased by $100.00, the amount paid on account. This decrease is on the right side of the accounting equation.

Questions for Analyzing a Transaction into Its Debit and Credit Parts

1. Which accounts are affected?
   Accounts Payable—Canyon Office Supplies and *Cash*

2. How is each account classified?
   Accounts Payable—Canyon Office Supplies is a liability account. *Cash* is an asset account.

3. How is each classification changed?
   Liabilities decrease. Assets decrease.

4. How is each amount entered in the accounts?
   Liabilities decrease on the debit side. Therefore, debit the liability account, *Accounts Payable—Canyon Office Supplies*. Assets decrease on the credit side. Therefore, credit the asset account, *Cash*.

remember

When you decrease an account balance, record the decrease on the side opposite the normal balance side of the account. The side opposite the normal balance side can be on the left or the right, depending on the type of account.

Record High Box Office Receipts + Accounting = Net Loss?

When you hear that a movie has broken all records for box office receipts, do you automatically assume that everyone connected with the movie received a share of the profits? That may not be the case. The answer depends on how those profits are calculated.

It is well known that some movies that have broken records for box office receipts have never shown a profit. How could this happen? For any company, revenues minus expenses equal net income. How those revenues and expenses are calculated has a dramatic effect on the calculation of net income.

There are three controversial costs involved in the making of a movie. (1) The cost of producing the movie. (2) The cost of distributing the movie. (3) The cost of advertising. Each of these costs includes the concept of overhead. Overhead costs are the costs of running the business. Overhead may include the cost of the administrative offices, electricity, heat, and payroll. Calculating the overhead costs of a movie usually involves estimating what percentage of the total cost should be applied to the specific movie. The higher the overhead estimate, the lower the net profit.

Actors are more often refusing to accept a percentage of net profits as part of their compensation. Instead, they negotiate for a flat fee in place of a percentage of net profits.

The next time you watch a movie, read through the credits at the end of the movie. In the listing of the crew, you will see the names of the accountants or controller for the movie. Then ask yourself if you think the movie will ever report a net profit.

CRITICAL THINKING

1. List three costs that would be included in the cost of advertising.
2. Use the Internet to search for the accountants for a recent movie. List the title of the movie and the name(s) of the accountants/controller.

LO4 Restate and apply the four questions necessary to analyze transactions for starting a business into debit and credit parts.

Terms Review

chart of accounts

accounts payable

Audit your understanding

1. State the four questions used to analyze a transaction.

2. What two accounts are affected when a business buys supplies on account?

Work together 2-2

Analyzing transactions into debit and credit parts

T accounts are given in the *Working Papers*. Your instructor will guide you through the following examples. Jensen Cleaning Service uses the following accounts. Some of the accounts will be explained in Lesson 2-3.

Cash	John Jensen, Capital
Accts. Rec.—Johannes Erickson	John Jensen, Drawing
Supplies	Sales
Prepaid Insurance	Rent Expense
Accts. Pay.—Supply Depot	Utilities Expense

Transactions:

Mar. 1. Received cash from owner as an investment, $4,000.00.

3. Paid cash for supplies, $95.00.

4. Bought supplies on account from Supply Depot, $120.00.

6. Paid cash for insurance, $250.00.

9. Paid cash on account to Supply Depot, $80.00.

1. Prepare two T accounts for each transaction. On each T account, write the account title of one of the accounts affected by the transaction.

2. Write the debit or credit amount in each T account to show the transaction's effect.

On your own 2-2

Analyzing transactions into debit and credit parts

T accounts are given in the *Working Papers*. Work this problem independently. Plumbing Solutions uses the following accounts. Some of the accounts will be explained in Lesson 2-3.

Cash	Brian Helfrey, Capital
Accts. Rec.—Theo Moses	Brian Helfrey, Drawing
Supplies	Sales
Prepaid Insurance	Advertising Expense
Accts. Pay.—Plumbing World	Rent Expense

Transactions:

June 2. Received cash from owner as an investment, $3,500.00.

4. Paid cash for insurance, $105.00.

5. Paid cash for supplies, $60.00.

8. Bought supplies on account from Plumbing World, $800.00.

9. Paid cash on account to Plumbing World, $500.00.

1. Prepare two T accounts for each transaction. On each T account, write the account title of one of the accounts affected by the transaction.

2. Write the debit or credit amount in each T account to show the transaction's effect.

2-3 Analyzing How Transactions Affect Owner's Equity Accounts

LO5 Analyze transactions for operating a business into debit and credit parts.

Received Cash from Sales LO5

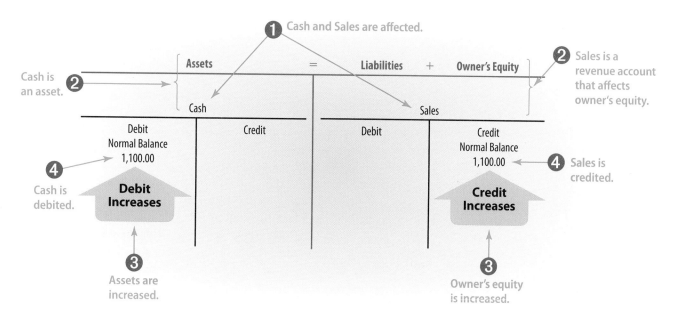

① Cash and Sales are affected.

Cash is an asset. ②

② Sales is a revenue account that affects owner's equity.

| Assets | = | Liabilities | + | Owner's Equity |

Cash

| Debit
Normal Balance
1,100.00 | Credit |

④ Cash is debited.

Debit Increases

③ Assets are increased.

Sales

| Debit | Credit
Normal Balance
1,100.00 |

④ Sales is credited.

Credit Increases

③ Owner's equity is increased.

January 10. Received cash from sales, $1,100.00.

Revenue increases owner's equity. The increases from revenue could be recorded directly in the owner's capital account. However, to avoid a capital account with a large number of entries and to summarize revenue information separately from the other records, Delgado Web Services uses a separate revenue account titled Sales.

The owner's capital account has a normal credit balance. Therefore, increases in the owner's capital account are shown as credits. Because revenue increases owner's equity, increases in revenue are also recorded as credits. Therefore, a revenue account has a normal credit balance.

⊗ Questions for Analyzing a Transaction into Its Debit and Credit Parts

❶ Which accounts are affected?
Cash and *Sales*

❷ How is each account classified?
Cash is an asset account. *Sales* is a revenue account that affects owner's equity.

❸ How is each classification changed?
Assets increase. Owner's equity increases.

❹ How is each amount entered in the accounts?
Assets increase on the debit side. Therefore, debit the asset account, *Cash*. Owner's equity accounts increase on the credit side. Revenue increases owner's equity. Therefore, credit the revenue account, *Sales*.

Sold Services on Account

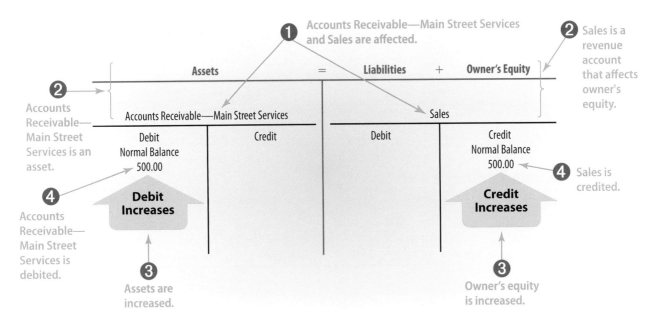

January 12. Sold services on account to Main Street Services, $500.00.

The analysis for selling services on account is similar to that for selling services for cash. The only difference is that cash is not received at the time of the transaction. Therefore, the **Cash** account is not affected by the transaction. Amounts to be received in the future due to the sale of goods or services are called **accounts receivable**. This transaction increases an accounts receivable account. The same four questions are used to analyze this transaction into its debit and credit parts.

Questions for Analyzing a Transaction into Its Debit and Credit Parts

1 **Which accounts are affected?**
Accounts Receivable—Main Street Services and *Sales*

2 **How is each account classified?**
Accounts Receivable—Main Street Services is an asset account. *Sales* is a revenue account that affects owner's equity.

3 **How is each classification changed?**
Assets increase. Owner's equity increases.

4 **How is each amount entered in the accounts?**
Assets increase on the debit side. Therefore, debit the asset account, *Accounts Receivable—Main Street Services*. Owner's equity accounts increase on the credit side. Revenue increases owner's equity. Therefore, credit the revenue account, *Sales*.

remember

Owner's equity is recorded on the right side of the accounting equation. The right side of a T account is the credit side. Therefore, owner's equity has a normal credit balance.

Paid Cash for an Expense

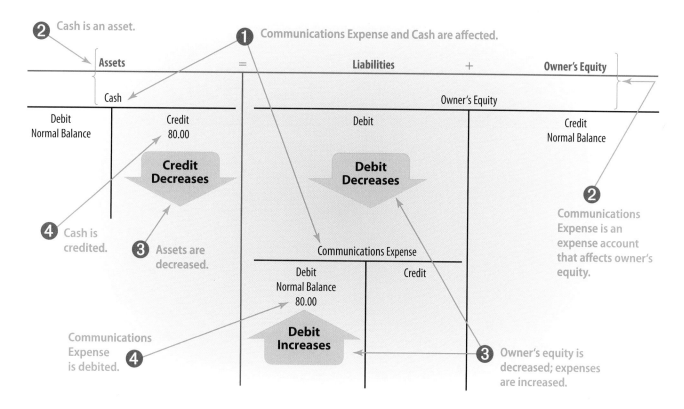

January 12. Paid cash for communications bill for cell phone and Internet service, $80.00.

Expenses decrease owner's equity. The decreases from expenses could be recorded directly in the owner's capital account. However, to avoid a capital account with a large number of entries and to summarize expense information separately from the other records, Delgado Web Services uses separate expense accounts.

The titles of Delgado Web Services' expense accounts are shown on its chart of accounts. The expense account, Communications Expense, is used for all payments for cell phone charges.

The owner's capital account has a normal credit balance. Decreases in the owner's capital account are shown as debits. Therefore, an expense account has a normal debit balance. Because expenses decrease owner's equity, increases in expenses are recorded as debits.

All expense transactions are recorded in a similar manner.

Questions for Analyzing a Transaction into Its Debit and Credit Parts

❶ Which accounts are affected?
Communications Expense and *Cash*

❷ How is each account classified?
Communications Expense is an expense account that affects owner's equity. *Cash* is an asset account.

❸ How is each classification changed?
Owner's equity decreases from an increase in expenses. Assets decrease.

❹ How is each amount entered in the accounts?
Owner's equity accounts decrease on the debit side. An increase in expenses decreases owner's equity. Expense accounts have normal debit balances. Therefore, debit the expense account, *Communications Expense*. Assets decrease on the credit side. Therefore, credit the asset account, *Cash*.

Received Cash on Account

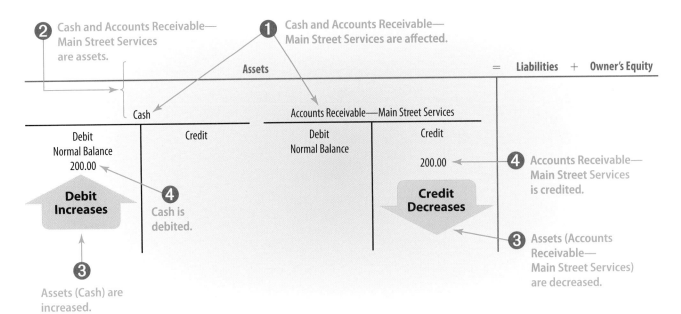

January 16. Received cash on account from Main Street Services, $200.00.

The effect of this transaction on the accounting equation is shown in the illustration. In this transaction, two asset accounts are changed. One asset, cash, has been exchanged for another asset, accounts receivable. The asset account, Cash, increases by $200.00, the amount of cash received. This increase is on the left side of the accounting equation. After this receipt of cash, Main Street Services owes less money to Delgado Web Services. The asset account, Accounts Receivable— Main Street Services decreases by $200.00, the amount of cash received on account. This decrease is also on the left side of the accounting equation.

Questions for Analyzing a Transaction into Its Debit and Credit Parts

❶ **Which accounts are affected?**
Cash and *Accounts Receivable—Main Street Services*

❷ **How is each account classified?**
Cash is an asset account. *Accounts Receivable—Main Street Services* is an asset account.

❸ **How is each classification changed?**
One asset (*Cash*) increases and another asset (*Accounts Receivable—Main Street Services*) decreases.

❹ **How is each amount entered in the accounts?**
Assets increase on the debit side. Therefore, debit the asset account, *Cash*. Assets decrease on the credit side. Therefore, credit the asset account, *Accounts Receivable—Main Street Services*.

Paid Cash to Owner for Personal Use

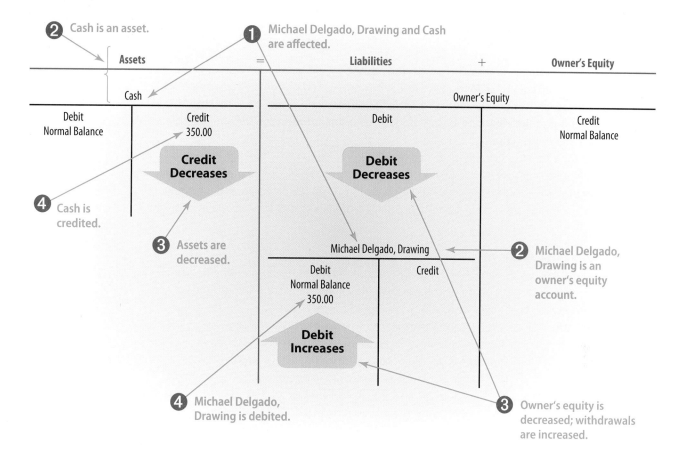

② Cash is an asset.

① Michael Delgado, Drawing and Cash are affected.

| Assets | = | Liabilities | + | Owner's Equity |

Cash

| Debit Normal Balance | Credit 350.00 |

Credit Decreases

④ Cash is credited.

③ Assets are decreased.

Owner's Equity

| Debit | | Credit Normal Balance |

Debit Decreases

Michael Delgado, Drawing

② Michael Delgado, Drawing is an owner's equity account.

| Debit Normal Balance 350.00 | Credit |

Debit Increases

④ Michael Delgado, Drawing is debited.

③ Owner's equity is decreased; withdrawals are increased.

January 16. Michael Delgado withdrew equity in the form of cash, $350.00.

Withdrawals decrease owner's equity. Withdrawals could be recorded directly in the owner's capital account. However, to avoid a capital account with a large number of entries and to summarize withdrawal information separately from the other records, Delgado Web Services uses a separate withdrawing account titled Michael Delgado, Drawing.

When drawing T accounts to analyze transactions, stack the accounts instead of writing them horizontally. Stacking the accounts will make it easier to recognize debits and credits.

⊘ Questions for Analyzing a Transaction into Its Debit and Credit Parts

① Which accounts are affected?
Michael Delgado, Drawing and *Cash*

② How is each account classified?
Michael Delgado, Drawing is an owner's equity account. *Cash* is an asset account.

③ How is each classification changed?
Owner's equity decreases from an increase in withdrawals. Assets decrease.

④ How is each amount entered in the accounts?
Owner's equity accounts decrease on the debit side. An increase in withdrawals decreases owner's equity. Withdrawal accounts have normal debit balances. Therefore, debit the owner's equity account, *Michael Delgado, Drawing*. Assets decrease on the credit side. Therefore, credit the asset account, *Cash*.

Pyramid Schemes

In 1912, Ivar Kreuger began his quest to take control of the European match market. He borrowed money and sold stock in the company to buy out his competitors. After World War I, he loaned money to war-torn countries that dropped trade restrictions that had prevented his company from entering their markets. He also bribed government officials to become the sole provider of matches in that country.

The stock of the company was widely owned and provided investors with a high return on their investments. Everyone wanted to own a piece of his company. Kreuger's fame and fortune landed him on the cover of *Time* magazine. He was welcome at the White House and enjoyed a lavish lifestyle including a Park Avenue penthouse in New York City furnished with paintings by Rembrandt.

THE PYRAMID COLLAPSES

Unknown to the public and undetected by accountants, Kreuger was running a fraud known as a *pyramid scheme*. Investors being paid a return on their investment from the earnings of the business are, in fact, being paid with money contributed by new investors. The scheme is destined to collapse when the new investors are no longer willing to invest.

The stock market crash of 1929 and the Great Depression left few banks and individuals with any money to invest in Kreuger's company. As rumors of his financial troubles grew, the value of the company's stock tumbled. Unable to continue the pyramid scheme, Kreuger committed suicide in 1932.

In response to public outcry, Congress passed the Securities Act of 1933 that established the Securities and Exchange Commission and increased the amount and quality of information companies must provide to investors.

HISTORY REPEATS ITSELF

Public outcry over the financial disasters of the early twenty-first century—Enron and WorldCom in particular—led Congress to pass the Sarbanes-Oxley Act in the hope that these disasters would never be repeated.

These Forensic Accounting features highlight famous frauds and how Congress and the accounting profession have reacted by reforming laws governing financial reporting information. You will also learn about typical occupational frauds involving employees stealing from their employers. An accountant who combines accounting and investigating skills to uncover fraudulent business activity, or to prevent such activity, is called a **forensic accountant**.

ACTIVITY

Peter Webb began his pool maintenance business in May. He visits each of his clients once a month for a three-hour cleaning procedure. Wanting to expand his business, he has provided a potential investor with financial information indicating that he is earning revenue of nearly $6,000 per month.

INSTRUCTIONS

Open the spreadsheet FA_CH02 and complete the steps on the Instructions tab.

Source: Called to Account, Paul M Clikeman, Routledge (New York), 2009.

End of Lesson Review

LO5 Analyze transactions for operating a business into debit and credit parts.

Term Review

accounts receivable

Audit your understanding

1. What two accounts are affected when a business pays cash for a cell phone bill?
2. What two accounts are affected when a business sells services on account?
3. What two accounts are affected when a business receives cash on account?
4. Is the drawing account increased on the debit side or credit side?
5. Are revenue accounts increased on the debit side or credit side?

Work together 2-3

Analyzing revenue, expense, and withdrawal transactions into debit and credit parts

T accounts are given in the *Working Papers*. Your instructor will guide you through the following examples. Use the chart of accounts for Jensen Cleaning Service in Work Together 2-2.

Transactions:

Mar. 11. Sold services on account to Johannes Erickson, $125.00.

13. Received cash from sales, $260.00.

14. Paid cash for telephone bill, $54.00.

16. Received cash on account from Johannes Erickson, $125.00.

19. Paid cash to owner for a withdrawal of equity, $200.00.

1. Prepare two T accounts for each transaction. On each T account, write the account title of one of the accounts affected by the transaction.

2. Write the debit or credit amount in each T account to show the transaction's effect.

On your own 2-3

Analyzing revenue, expense, and withdrawal transactions into debit and credit parts

T accounts are given in the *Working Papers*. Work this problem independently. Use the chart of accounts for Plumbing Solutions in On Your Own 2-2.

Transactions:

June 12. Paid cash for rent, $800.00.

14. Received cash from sales, $68.00.

15. Sold services on account to Theo Moses, $130.00.

18. Paid cash to owner for a withdrawal of equity, $280.00.

19. Received cash on account from Theo Moses, $130.00.

1. Prepare two T accounts for each transaction. On each T account, write the account title of one of the accounts affected by the transaction.

2. Write the debit or credit amount in each T account to show the transaction's effect.

©CANDICE CUSACK, ISTOCK

A Look at Accounting Software

Analyzing Transactions with Accounting Software Systems

You learned in this chapter that accountants use T accounts to analyze transactions. After doing accounting for a period of time, these analyses are done mentally without the help of T accounts. Occasionally, however, even experienced accountants will encounter complicated transactions and use T accounts to help them sort things out.

In a computerized system, with routine transactions, the system knows how to "analyze" the transaction. For example, when cash is received, the accountant tells the system where the money is coming from. The system knows how to correctly apply both debits and credits to the proper accounts. But even with computerized accounting systems, accountants still use T accounts to analyze more complicated transactions.

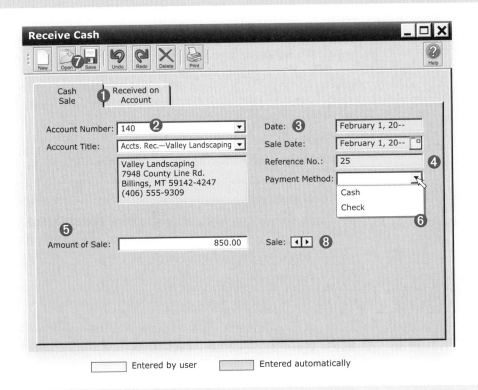

Entered by user   Entered automatically

❶ In a manual system, the accountant analyzes each transaction and decides which account to debit and which account to credit. In a computerized system, when cash is received, the user tells the system whether it is for a cash sale or for a payment on account. For the cash sale above, the system knows to debit **Cash** and credit **Sales**.

❷ The user can select the customer from drop menus either by account number or title. The system automatically displays the customer address and contact information. If this were cash received on account, the system would then know to debit **Cash** and to credit **Accts. Rec.—Valley Landscaping**.

❸ The system automatically displays the current date. The first field is the system date. That is the date the transaction is entered. It cannot be changed. However, if the sale date was earlier (for example, over a weekend), Sale Date can be changed.

❹ The system automatically assigns the next sequential number to the sale.

❺ The user enters the sale amount.

❻ A drop menu lets the user choose how the cash was received.

❼ The user clicks on Save to store the transaction.

❽ Navigation buttons allow the user to move forward or backward to review sales that have been entered.

Chapter Summary

This chapter introduced the concept of debits and credits. It is important to remember that sometimes a debit increases an account balance and sometimes a debit decreases an account balance. The rules for debits and credits can be tied to the accounting equation. Assets are on the left side of the accounting equation; therefore, assets increase on the left, or debit side, of the account. Liabilities and the owner's capital account are on the right side of the accounting equation; therefore, liabilities and the owner's capital account increase on the right, or credit, side of the account. T accounts can be used to help determine which accounts are debited and credited for each transaction. Four questions are used to analyze transactions into their debit and credit parts: (1) Which accounts are affected? (2) How is each account classified? (3) How is each classification changed? (4) How is each amount entered in the accounts?

Owner Withdrawals vs. Salary Expense

EXPLORE ACCOUNTING

When the owner of a business withdraws cash for personal use, that withdrawal decreases owner's equity. However, it is not considered an expense of the business. On the other hand, when wages or salaries are paid to employees, those wages or salaries are considered an expense of the business. These are called **Wages Expense** or **Salary Expense**.

The income of a business is calculated by subtracting total expenses from total revenue. Since employee wages and salaries are an expense of the business, they reduce the net income of the company. Since owner withdrawals are not considered an expense of the business, they do not reduce the net income of the company.

A business owned by one person is called a proprietorship. The Internal Revenue Service does not require the proprietorship, itself, to pay taxes. However, the owner of the proprietorship must include the net income of the proprietorship in his or her own taxable income.

The income of a proprietorship is affected by employee wages and salaries. Therefore, the income tax paid by the owner is affected by the amount of wages or salaries expense. The more wages or salaries expense the company has, the lower the net income will be. The lower the net income of a business, the lower the amount of income tax that will be paid on the net income. Because the income of a proprietorship is not affected by owner withdrawals, the income tax paid by the owner is not affected by how much cash the owner withdraws from the business.

If Bergum Consulting Company has revenues of $35,000.00 and expenses of $17,000.00, its income is $18,000.00 ($35,000.00 – $17,000.00). Bergum Consulting Company will have income of $18,000.00 whether the owner withdraws $300.00 or $3,000.00 from the business during that period.

INSTRUCTIONS

1. Amar Gupta owns St. Croix Photography. He is considering withdrawing $4,000.00 from St. Croix Photography for his personal use. What effect would this withdrawal have on the income tax Mr. Gupta must pay this year?

2. Mr. Gupta is also considering giving his employees a raise that would increase total salaries by $35,000.00 per year. What effect would this raise have on Mr. Gupta's income tax?

©MAKHNACH_M, ISTOCK

Apply Your Understanding

2-1 Application Problem: Determining the increase, decrease, and normal balance side for accounts LO2, 3

Write the answers for the following problem in the *Working Papers*.

Cash
Accounts Receivable—Tyler Choi
Accounts Receivable—Nolan Esby
Supplies

Prepaid Insurance
Accounts Payable—Green Solutions
Georganne Hayner, Capital

1	2	3	4	5	6	7	8
Account	Account Classification	Increase Side		Decrease Side		Account's Normal Balance	
		Debit	Credit	Debit	Credit	Debit	Credit
Cash	Asset	↑			↓	✔	

Instructions:

Do the following for each account. The Cash account is given as an example.

1. Write the account title in Column 1.
2. Write the account classification in Column 2.
3. Place an up arrow (↑) in either Column 3 or 4 to indicate the increase side of the account.
4. Place a down arrow (↓) in either Column 5 or 6 to indicate the decrease side of the account.
5. Place a check mark in either Column 7 or 8 to indicate the normal balance of the account.

2-2 Application Problem: Analyzing transactions into debit and credit parts LO4

Helfrey Marketing Services uses the following accounts.

Cash
Supplies
Prepaid Insurance
Accounts Receivable—Neco Valenza
Accounts Payable—All Star Company

Sawyer Helfrey, Capital
Sawyer Helfrey, Drawing
Sales
Advertising Expense
Rent Expense

Transactions:

June 1. Received cash from owner as an investment, $10,000.00.
      2. Paid cash for insurance, $4,000.00.
      4. Bought supplies on account from All Star Company, $6,000.00.
      5. Paid cash for supplies, $1,000.00.
      8. Paid cash on account to All Star Company, $4,000.00.

Instructions:

1. Prepare two T accounts for each transaction. On each T account, write the account title of one of the accounts affected by the transaction. Use the forms in your *Working Papers*.
2. Write the debit or credit amount in each T account to show how the transaction affected that account. T accounts for the first transaction are given as an example.

June 1.	Cash	
10,000.00		

	Sawyer Helfrey, Capital	
		10,000.00

2-3 Application Problem: Analyzing revenue, expense, and withdrawal transactions into debit and credit parts LO5

Use the chart of accounts for Helfrey Marketing Services given in Problem 2-2.

Transactions:

June 11. Received cash from sales, $22,000.00.
12. Paid cash for advertising, $1,500.00.
14. Sold services on account to Neco Valenza, $17,000.00.
18. Paid cash to owner for personal use, $5,000.00.
19. Received cash on account from Neco Valenza, $10,000.00.

Instructions:

1. Prepare two T accounts for each transaction. On each T account, write the account title of one of the accounts affected by the transaction. Use the forms in your *Working Papers*.

2. Write the debit or credit amount in each T account to show how the transaction affected that account.

2-M Mastery Problem: Analyzing transactions into debit and credit parts LO 4, 5

Gardens Plus uses the following accounts.

Cash	Simon Dirks, Drawing
Accounts Receivable—Lee Chen	Sales
Accounts Receivable—Ginger McCure	Advertising Expense
Supplies	Miscellaneous Expense
Prepaid Insurance	Rent Expense
Accounts Payable—West End Supplies	Repair Expense
Accounts Payable—Bellville Supplies	Utilities Expense
Simon Dirks, Capital	

Instructions:

1. Prepare a T account for each account. Use the forms in your *Working Papers*.

2. Analyze each transaction into its debit and credit parts. Write the debit and credit amounts in the proper T accounts to show how each transaction changes account balances. Write the date of the transactions before each amount.

May 1. Received cash from owner as an investment, $3,700.00.
2. Paid cash for rent, $600.00.
4. Paid cash for supplies, $400.00.
4. Received cash from sales, $950.00.
5. Paid cash for insurance, $375.00.
8. Sold services on account to Lee Chen, $800.00.
9. Bought supplies on account from Bellville Supplies, $300.00.
10. Paid cash for repairs, $85.00.
11. Received cash from owner as an investment, $2,900.00.

May 11. Received cash from sales, $1,000.00.
   12. Bought supplies on account from West End Supplies, $230.00.
   13. Received cash on account from Lee Chen, $650.00.
   15. Paid cash for miscellaneous expense, $35.00.
   16. Paid cash on account to Bellville Supplies, $60.00.
   22. Paid cash for electric bill (utilities expense), $65.00.
   23. Paid cash for advertising, $105.00.
   25. Sold services on account to Ginger McCure, $550.00.
   26. Paid cash to owner for personal use, $500.00.
   30. Received cash on account from Ginger McCure, $300.00.

2-C Challenge Problem: Analyzing transactions recorded in T accounts LO 4, 5

The following T accounts show the current financial situation for Sunshine Cleaners. Write the answers for the following problem in the *Working Papers*.

Cash

(1)	3,000.00	(2)	50.00
(5)	350.00	(3)	35.00
(8)	200.00	(6)	40.00
(9)	450.00	(7)	450.00
		(10)	300.00
		(11)	275.00
		(12)	250.00

Sales

(5)	350.00
(8)	200.00
(9)	450.00
(13)	115.00

Accounts Receivable—Ellie Morgan

(13)	115.00

Advertising Expense

(6)	40.00

Supplies

(4)	550.00
(10)	300.00

Miscellaneous Expense

(3)	35.00

Accounts Payable—Tri State Supplies

(11)	275.00	(4)	550.00

Rent Expense

(7)	450.00

Kelsey Guerrero, Capital

	(1)	3,000.00

Utilities Expense

(2)	50.00

Kelsey Guerrero, Drawing

(12)	250.00

1	2	3	4	5	6
Trans. No.	Accounts Affected	Account Classification	Entered in Account as a Debit	Entered in Account as a Credit	Description of Transaction
1	Cash	Asset	✔		Received cash from owner as an investment
	Kelsey Guerrero, Capital	Owner's Equity		✔	

Instructions:

1. Analyze each numbered transaction in the T accounts. Write the titles of accounts affected in Column 2. For each account, write the classification of the account in Column 3.

2. For each account, place a check mark in either Column 4 or 5 to indicate if the account is affected by a debit or a credit.

3. For each transaction, write a brief statement in column 6 describing the transaction. Information for Transaction 1 is given as an example.

21st Century Skills

Franchise—The Startup Alternative

Theme: Financial, Economic, Business, and Entrepreneurial Literacy

Skills: ICT Literacy, Critical Thinking and Problem Solving, Information Literacy

PARTNERSHIP FOR
21ST CENTURY SKILLS

Entrepreneurs may wish to explore an alternative to starting a business from scratch. Franchising is a popular alternative. A **franchise** is a right granted to an individual or business to sell the products or services of another, larger business within a defined geographical area. Franchises reduce some risk and often provide training for the franchisor. While others have already paved the way, there is no guarantee of success with a franchise. In addition, since rules are set by the franchisor, many entrepreneurs feel stifled in their ability to be creative.

Before considering the purchase of a franchise, the requirements of each company should be researched. Each company sets its own conditions for ownership of a franchise. An example of a condition is the franchise fee. This is the amount of money initially paid to use the franchise name. Another example is the yearly fee for the use of the name, called a royalty fee.

APPLICATION

1. Use the Internet to investigate five companies currently offering franchises and obtain their franchise and royalty fees. Search individual company websites or sites like www.entrepreneur.com/franzone to obtain the information. Organize your information in a spreadsheet.

2. Imagine that you have the funds to start a new business. Explain whether you would prefer to start a new business from scratch or purchase a franchise. Include the reasons for your preference.

Auditing for errors

The bookkeeper for The Wellness Center used T accounts to analyze three transactions as follows:

Transaction 1:

Abu Owusu, Drawing		Cash	
450.00			450.00

Transaction 2:

Accounts Receivable—Maria Chu		Sales	
450.00			450.00

Transaction 3:

Supplies		Accounts Payable—Northstar Supplies	
	150.00		150.00

Review the three sets of T accounts and answer the following questions.

1. Which T account analysis is incorrect? How did you determine it was incorrect?
2. What information would you need to determine the correct T account analysis for this transaction?

Analyzing Nike's financial statements

The Consolidated Balance Sheets in Appendix B on page B-6 list the assets, liabilities, and shareholders' equity for Nike for 2010 and 2011. Shareholders' equity for a corporation is similar to the capital for a proprietorship because it shows the value of the company to the owners.

INSTRUCTIONS

Find the total assets, total liabilities, and total equity for Nike for 2011 and 2010. Put your answer in the form of an accounting equation. You will have to add the total current liabilities, long-term debt, deferred income taxes and other liabilities, commitments and contingencies, and redeemable preferred stock to find the total liabilities.

Chapter 3 Journalizing Transactions

LEARNING OBJECTIVES

After studying Chapter 3, in addition to defining key terms, you will be able to:

LO1 Define what a journal is and explain why it is used to record transactions.

LO2 Compare and contrast different types of source documents.

LO3 Identify the four parts of a journal entry.

LO4 Analyze and record cash transactions using source documents.

LO5 Analyze and record transactions for buying and paying on account.

LO6 Analyze and record transactions that affect owner's equity.

LO7 Analyze and record sales and receipt of cash on account.

LO8 Demonstrate when to end and how to start a new journal page.

LO9 Identify and correct errors using standard accounting practices.

©DANIEL KOUREY, ISTOCK/©JIM PRUITT, ISTOCK

BLEND IMAGES/JUPITER IMAGES

Accounting In The Real World
iTunes

Is digital music catching on? To answer this question, all you have to do is look at the statistics. According to its website, iTunes offers more than 11 million songs for sale and has sold over 10 billion downloads.

Why is an online music store like iTunes so successful? There are many reasons. iTunes not only sells downloads, but it also provides a free player which can be used to manage many tasks.

iTunes' customers can take their music with them, wherever they go. They don't have to drive to the mall or wait for a CD in the mail. Songs can be downloaded at any time—24 hours a day, 7 days a week. Customers can preview a song before they buy it, which increases their satisfaction rate.

Since its customers don't have to drive to a store and don't physically purchase an item, iTunes is also friendly to the environment. Less driving helps the environment. In addition, no CDs means no packaging, CDs, or CD cases in the trash.

What if an iTunes customer doesn't like the order of songs on an album? iTunes lets one organize songs in any order. iTunes also allows listeners to enjoy tunes on many portable devices. Clients can download movies and college lectures as well as music.

CRITICAL THINKING

1. When iTunes sells a song or movie, it must record the transaction in accounts. Which accounts might iTunes use when it sells a song for cash?

2. What accounts might iTunes use when it has shipping costs on account?

Key Terms
- journal
- journalizing
- entry
- double-entry accounting
- source document
- check
- invoice
- sales invoice
- receipt
- memorandum

LESSON

3-1 Recording Transactions and the General Journal

LO1 Define what a journal is and explain why it is used to record transactions.

LO2 Compare and contrast different types of source documents.

LO3 Identify the four parts of a journal entry.

Journals and Journalizing LO1

In Chapter 2, transactions were analyzed into debit and credit parts using the accounting equation and T accounts. Transactions could be recorded this way in a business. However, as the number of accounts increases, the accounting equation would become very wide and difficult to use. A form for recording transactions in chronological order is called a **journal**. Most companies choose to use a journal to record transactions. Besides being more manageable, a journal also provides a more permanent record of the transactions of a business. Recording transactions in a journal is called **journalizing**.

There are several kinds of journals. Each business uses the kind of journal that best fits the needs of that business. The nature of a business and the number of transactions to be recorded determine the kind of journal to be used.

The word journal comes from the Latin *diurnalis*, meaning *daily*. Most businesses conduct transactions every day. To keep records up to date, businesses usually record transactions in their journals every day.

ETHICS IN ACTION

Recognizing Ethical Dilemmas and Actions

How often have you said something you later regretted? Chances are you spoke before you thought about how your words might affect others. Had you taken the time to think how your words would hurt someone else, you might have said something different or simply kept quiet.

The first step of the ethical model is to recognize that you are facing an ethical dilemma. Few business decisions will require you to act immediately. Take whatever time is required to determine whether your actions could harm someone else. If you have any doubts that your action will violate your morals, stop to evaluate the decision, using the ethical model.

The second step of the ethical model is to identify the action taken or the proposed action. Write down every possible action you think of, even if the idea might seem outrageous at first. Seek the advice of others who may have had similar dilemmas. Or ask someone you admire for his or her ethical behavior. Many companies assign a mentor to new employees to encourage them to seek advice.

INSTRUCTIONS

In private, write down the names of at least five individuals from whom you would feel comfortable seeking advice on ethical dilemmas.

A General Journal

GENERAL JOURNAL   PAGE

	DATE	ACCOUNT TITLE	DOC. NO.	POST. REF.	DEBIT	CREDIT	
1							1
2							2
3							3
4							4

USING A JOURNAL

Delgado Web Services uses a general journal. The general journal has two amount columns in which all kinds of entries can be recorded. The columns in Delgado Web Services' general journal are Date, Account Title, Doc. No., Post. Ref., Debit, and Credit. The use of each column is described later in this chapter.

ACCURACY

Information recorded in a journal includes the debit and credit parts of each transaction recorded in one place. The information can be verified by comparing the data in the journal with the transaction data.

CHRONOLOGICAL RECORD

Transactions are recorded in a journal in order by date. All information about a transaction is recorded in one place. This makes the information for a specific transaction easy to locate.

DOUBLE-ENTRY ACCOUNTING

Information for each transaction recorded in a journal is called an **entry**. The recording of debit and credit parts of a transaction is called **double-entry accounting**. In double-entry accounting, each transaction affects at least two accounts. Both the debit and the credit parts are recorded, reflecting the dual effect of each transaction. Double-entry accounting assures that debits equal credits.

Source Documents LO2

A business paper from which information is obtained for a journal entry is called a **source document**. Different types of source documents are used for different kinds of transactions. Each transaction is described by a source document that proves that the transaction did occur. For example, Delgado Web Services prepares a check stub for each cash payment made. The check stub describes information about the cash payment for which the check is prepared. The accounting concept

Objective Evidence is applied when a source document is prepared for each transaction. [CONCEPT: Objective Evidence]

A transaction should be journalized only if it actually occurs. The amounts recorded must be accurate and true. Nearly all transactions result in the preparation of a source document. Delgado Web Services uses five source documents: checks, sales invoices, receipts, memorandums, and calculator tapes.

CHECKS

NO. 1 $ *165.00*	
Date *January 2* 20 ==	
To *Eastside Supplies*	
For *Supplies*	
BALANCE BROUGHT FORWARD	0 | 00
AMOUNT DEPOSITED 1|2|-- Date	2,000 | 00
SUBTOTAL	2,000 | 00
OTHER:	
SUBTOTAL	2,000 | 00
AMOUNT THIS CHECK	165 | 00
BALANCE CARRIED FORWARD	1,835 | 00

DELGADO WEB SERVICES
25402 Rimrock Road
Billings, MT 59102-1820

NO. 1   93-2150/929

January 2   20 --

PAY TO THE ORDER OF *Eastside Supplies* $ *165.00*

One hundred sixty-five and no/100 ————————— DOLLARS

Billings National Bank
Billings, MT

FOR *Supplies*   *Michael Delgado*

⑈092921508⑈ 706466631⑉ 1

A business form ordering a bank to pay cash from a bank account is called a **check**. The source document for cash payments is a check. Delgado Web Services makes all cash payments by check. The checks are prenumbered to help account for all checks. Delgado Web Services' record of information on a check is the check stub prepared at the same time as the check.

Procedures for preparing checks and check stubs are described in Chapter 5.

SALES INVOICES

DELGADO WEB SERVICES
25402 Rimrock Road
Billings, MT 59102-1820

Sold to: Main Street Variety
3900 Grand Avenue
Billings, MT 59102

No. 1
Date 1/12/--
Terms 30 days

Description	Amount
Web Site Design	$500.00
Total	$500.00

When services are sold on account, the seller prepares a form showing information about the sale. A form describing the goods or services sold, the quantity, the price, and the terms of sale is called an **invoice**. Terms of sale could include the due date of the invoice and any penalties for late payment. An invoice used as a source document for recording a sale on account is called a **sales invoice**. A sales invoice is also referred to as a *sales ticket* or a *sales slip*.

A sales invoice is prepared in duplicate. The original is given to the customer. The copy is used as the source document for the sale on account transaction. [CONCEPT: Objective Evidence] Sales invoices are prenumbered in sequence to help account for all sales invoices.

fyi

Source documents can be critically important in tracking down errors. Businesses file their source documents so they can be referred to if it is necessary to verify information entered into their journals.

Other Source Documents

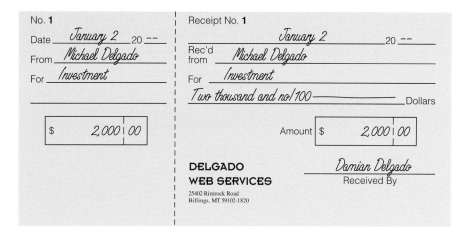

RECEIPTS

A business form giving written acknowledgement for cash received is called a **receipt**. When cash is received from sources other than sales, Delgado Web Services prepares a receipt. The receipts are prenumbered to help account for all of the receipts. A receipt is the source document for cash received from transactions other than sales. [CONCEPT: Objective Evidence]

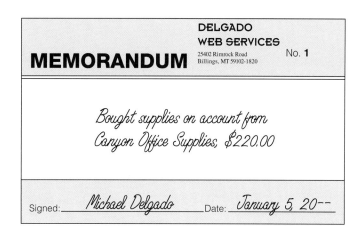

MEMORANDUMS

A form on which a brief message is written to describe a transaction is called a **memorandum**. A memorandum is used when there is no other source document for a transaction. A memorandum is also used when an additional explanation is needed about a transaction. [CONCEPT: Objective Evidence] Delgado Web Services' memorandums are prenumbered to help account for all memorandums. A brief note is written on the memorandum to describe the transaction.

CALCULATOR TAPES

Delgado Web Services collects cash at the time services are rendered to customers. At the end of each day, Delgado Web Services uses a printing electronic calculator to total the amount of cash received from sales for that day. By totaling all the individual sales, a single source document is produced for the total sales of the day. Thus, time and space are saved by recording only one entry for all of a day's sales. The calculator tape is the source document for daily sales. [CONCEPT: Objective Evidence] A calculator tape used as a source document is shown here.

Delgado Web Services dates and numbers each calculator tape. For example, in the illustration, the number *T10* indicates that the tape is for the tenth day of the month.

```
                      0·00 *
Jan 10, 20--     330·00 +
                 450·00 +
  T10            330·00 +
               1,100·00 *
```

Preparing Journal Entries

A company's journal is sometimes referred to as a "book of original entry." This means that the journal entry is the first place a business transaction becomes a permanent part of a company's accounting system.

Because the journal is a permanent record, accountants usually record journal entries in ink rather than pencil. When an entry in an amount column is an even dollar amount, "00" should be added to the cents column. If the column were left blank instead, there might be a question about whether an amount was omitted.

Received Cash from Owner as an Investment LO3

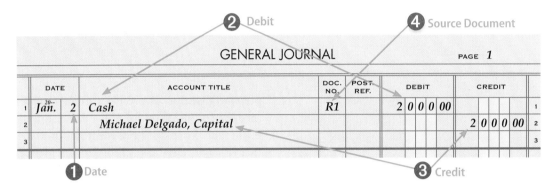

A journal entry consists of four parts: (1) date, (2) debit, (3) credit, and (4) source document. Before a transaction is recorded in a journal, the transaction is analyzed into its debit and credit parts.

> January 2. Received cash from owner as an investment, $2,000.00. Receipt No. 1.

The source document for this transaction is Receipt No. 1. [CONCEPT: Objective Evidence] The analysis of this transaction is shown in the T accounts.

The asset account, Cash, increases by a debit, $2,000.00. The owner's capital account, Michael Delgado, Capital, increases by a credit, $2,000.00.

Debits must equal credits for each entry in a journal. After the entry is journalized, the equality of debits and credits is verified. For this entry, the total debits, $2,000.00, equal the total credits, $2,000.00. The use of the Post. Ref. column is described in Chapter 4.

⬎ Journalizing Cash Received from Owner as an Investment

❶ Date. Write the date, 20-- Jan. 2, in the Date column. This entry is the first one on this journal page. Therefore, write both the year and the month for this entry. Do not write either the year or the month again on the same page.

❷ Debit. Write the title of the account debited, Cash, in the Account Title column. Write the debit amount, $2,000.00, in the Debit column.

❸ Credit. On the next line, indented about one centimeter, write the title of the account credited, Michael Delgado, Capital, in the Account Title column. This account title is indented to indicate that this account is credited. Write the credit amount, $2,000.00, in the Credit column.

❹ Source document. On the first line of the entry, write the source document number, R1, in the Doc. No. column. The source document number, R1, indicates that this is Receipt No. 1. (The source document number is a cross reference from the journal to the source document. Receipt No. 1 is filed in case more details about this transaction are needed.)

Dollars and cents signs and decimal points are not used when writing amounts on ruled accounting paper. Sometimes a color tint or a heavy vertical rule is used on printed accounting paper to separate the dollars and cents columns.

Paid Cash for Supplies

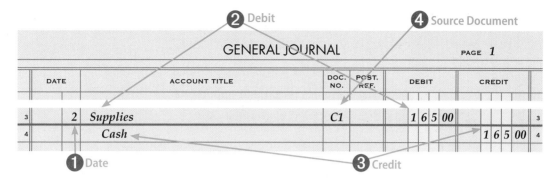

② Debit **④ Source Document**

GENERAL JOURNAL   PAGE 1

	DATE	ACCOUNT TITLE	DOC. NO.	POST. REF.	DEBIT	CREDIT	
3	2	Supplies	C1		1 6 5 00		3
4		Cash				1 6 5 00	4

① Date   **③ Credit**

January 2. Paid cash for supplies, $165.00. Check No. 1.

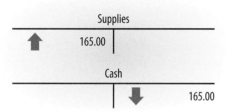

Supplies

165.00

Cash

165.00

The source document for this transaction is Check No. 1. [CONCEPT: Objective Evidence] The analysis of this transaction is shown in the T accounts.

The asset account **Supplies** increases by a debit, $165.00. The asset account **Cash** decreases by a credit, $165.00.

⊙ Journalizing Cash Paid for Supplies

① **Date.** Write the date, 2, in the Date column. This is not the first entry on the journal page. Therefore, do not write the year and month for this entry.

② **Debit.** Write the title of the account debited, Supplies, in the Account Title column. Write the debit amount, $165.00, in the Debit column.

③ **Credit.** On the next line, indented about one centimeter, write the title of the account credited, Cash, in the Account Title column. Write the credit amount, $165.00, in the Credit column.

④ **Source document.** On the first line of this entry, write the source document number, C1, in the Doc. No. column. The source document number, C1, indicates that this is Check No. 1.

For this entry, the total debits, $165.00, equal the total credits, $165.00.

remember If you misspell words in your written communications, people may mistrust the quality of your accounting skills. Note that in the word receipt, the "e" comes before the "i" and there is a silent "p" before the "t" at the end of the word.

End of Lesson Review

LO1 Define what a journal is and explain why it is used to record transactions.

LO2 Compare and contrast different types of source documents.

LO3 Identify the four parts of a journal entry.

Terms Review

journal

journalizing

entry

double-entry accounting

source document

check

invoice

sales invoice

receipt

memorandum

Audit your understanding

1. In what order are transactions recorded in a journal?

2. Why are source documents important?

3. List the four parts of a journal entry.

Work together 3-1

Journalizing entries in a general journal

A journal is given in the *Working Papers*. Your instructor will guide you through the following example.

Norma Dirks owns Dirks Copy Center, which uses the following accounts.

Cash	Norma Dirks, Capital
Accts. Rec.—K. Spah	Norma Dirks, Drawing
Supplies	Sales
Prepaid Insurance	Rent Expense
Accts. Pay.—Supply Mart	Utilities Expense

Transactions:

Apr. 1. Received cash from owner as an investment, $2,800.00. R1.

2. Paid cash for supplies, $415.00. C1.

Journalize each transaction completed during April of the current year. Use page 1 of the journal. Source documents are abbreviated as follows: check, C; receipt, R. Save your work to complete Work Together 3-2.

On your own 3-1

Journalizing entries in a general journal

A journal is given in the *Working Papers*. Work this problem independently.

Michelle Sullivan owns Sullivan's Service Center, which uses the following accounts.

Cash	Michelle Sullivan, Drawing
Accts. Rec.—G. Stratton	Sales
Supplies	Advertising Expense
Prepaid Insurance	Miscellaneous Expense
Accts. Pay.—Bayside Supplies	Rent Expense
Michelle Sullivan, Capital	

Transactions:

June 2. Received cash from owner as an investment, $3,200.00. R1.

3. Paid cash for supplies, $600.00. C1.

Journalize each transaction completed during June of the current year. Use page 1 of the journal. Source documents are abbreviated as follows: check, C; receipt, R. Save your work to complete On Your Own 3-2.

3-2 Transactions Affecting Prepaid Insurance and Supplies

LO4 Analyze and record cash transactions using source documents.

LO5 Analyze and record transactions for buying and paying on account.

Paid Cash for Insurance LO4

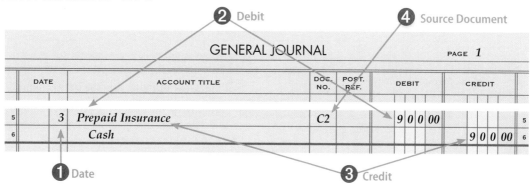

January 3. Paid cash for insurance, $900.00. Check No. 2.

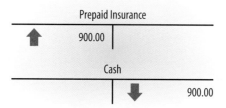

The source document for this transaction is Check No. 2. [CONCEPT: Objective Evidence] The analysis of this transaction is shown in the T accounts.

The asset account, Prepaid Insurance, increases by a debit, $900.00. The asset account, Cash, decreases by a credit, $900.00.

⬇ Journalizing Cash Paid for Insurance

① **Date.** Write the date, 3, in the Date column.

② **Debit.** Write the title of the account debited, Prepaid Insurance, in the Account Title column. Write the debit amount, $900.00, in the Debit column.

③ **Credit.** On the next line, indented about one centimeter, write the title of the account credited, Cash, in the Account Title column. Write the credit amount, $900.00, in the Credit column.

④ **Source document.** On the first line of this entry, write the source document number, C2, in the Doc. No. column.

For this entry, the total debits, $900.00, equal the total credits, $900.00.

remember All amounts written in the General Debit or General Credit columns must have an account title written in the Account Title column.

Bought Supplies on Account LO5

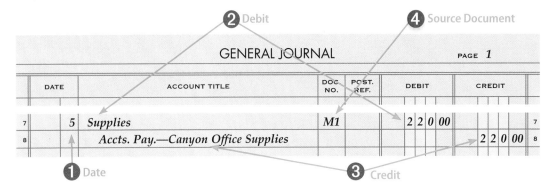

January 5. Bought supplies on account from Canyon Office Supplies, $220.00. Memorandum No. 1.

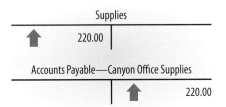

Delgado Web Services ordered these supplies by telephone. Delgado Web Services wishes to record this transaction immediately. Therefore, a memorandum is prepared that shows supplies bought on account.

The source document for this transaction is Memorandum No. 1. [CONCEPT: Objective Evidence] The analysis of this transaction is shown in the T accounts.

The asset account, Supplies, increases by a debit, $220.00. The liability account, Accounts Payable—Canyon Office Supplies, increases by a credit, $220.00.

Journalizing Supplies Bought on Account

1. **Date.** Write the date, 5, in the Date column.

2. **Debit.** Write the title of the account debited, Supplies, in the Account Title column. Write the debit amount, $220.00, in the Debit column.

3. **Credit.** On the next line, indented about one centimeter, write the abbreviated title of the account credited, Accts. Pay.—Canyon Office Supplies, in the Account Title column. Write the credit amount, $220.00, in the Credit column.

4. **Source document.** On the first line of this entry, write the source document number, M1, in the Doc. No. column.
   For this entry, the total debits, $220.00, equal the total credits, $220.00.

In the illustration, the account title is abbreviated. Account titles are usually written in full in journal entries; however, when the space is limited for a long account title, the title may be abbreviated. The abbreviation should clearly indicate the correct account title. The account title shown could also be abbreviated as "A/P—Canyon Office Supplies".

Paid Cash on Account

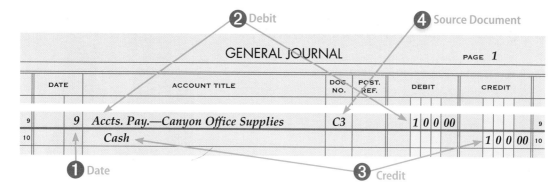

GENERAL JOURNAL PAGE **1**

❷ Debit ❹ Source Document

DATE	ACCOUNT TITLE	DOC. NO.	POST. REF.	DEBIT	CREDIT	
9	Accts. Pay.—Canyon Office Supplies	C3		1 0 0 00		9
	Cash				1 0 0 00	10

❶ Date ❸ Credit

January 9. Paid cash on account to Canyon Office Supplies, $100.00. Check No. 3.

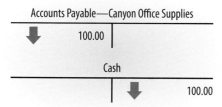

Accounts Payable—Canyon Office Supplies
| 100.00 | |

Cash
| | 100.00 |

The source document for this transaction is Check No. 3. [CONCEPT: Objective Evidence] The analysis of this transaction is shown in the T accounts.

The liability account, **Accounts Payable—Canyon Office Supplies**, decreases by a debit, $100.00. The asset account, **Cash**, decreases by a credit, $100.00.

Journalizing Cash Paid on Account

❶ **Date.** Write the date, 9, in the Date column.

❷ **Debit.** Write the abbreviated title of the account debited, Accts. Pay.—Canyon Office Supplies, in the Account Title column. Write the debit amount, $100.00, in the Debit column.

❸ **Credit.** On the next line, indented about one centimeter, write the title of the account credited, Cash, in the Account Title column. Write the credit amount, $100.00, in the Credit column.

❹ **Source document.** On the first line of this entry, write the source document number, C3, in the Doc. No. column.

For this entry, the total debits, $100.00, equal the total credits, $100.00.

The Small Business Administration (SBA) has programs that offer free management and accounting advice to small business owners. Visit its website at www.sba.gov.

Careers In Accounting

Diane Foley
FORENSIC ACCOUNTANT

Do you enjoy solving a puzzle? Maybe you like watching crime scene investigation television shows. Do you like accounting? Diane Foley enjoys all of these activities and she is a forensic accountant.

The word "forensic" means something that pertains to or is connected with a court of law. The work of a forensic accountant must be performed so that the findings can be used as evidence in court. Court work can include civil cases, such as divorces or disputes between landlords and tenant. Court work investigated by a forensic accountant may also include criminal cases, such as insurance fraud or breach of contract.

The work that Diane Foley performs as a forensic accountant involves investigative accounting. As a forensic accountant, she may investigate a case of employee fraud. Her job is to determine if a crime was committed. If a crime was committed, she must discover how it was done. For example, in the case of corporate theft, she must determine not only what was stolen from the company, but also how. She might also investigate a divorce proceeding to determine if one party is hiding assets.

Salary Range: Salary ranges from $30,000 to $50,000 but increases with experience. Earnings of six digits are possible for very successful forensic accountants.

Qualifications: To be successful, a forensic accountant must first have a thorough knowledge and complete understanding of accounting. However, being a good accountant does not necessarily make a good forensic accountant. A forensic accountant must possess additional skills. A recent study published by the Forensic and Valuation Services Section of the AICPA identified the following list of essential traits and characteristics. A forensic accountant should be analytical, detail-oriented, ethical, responsive, insightful, inquisitive, intuitive, persistent, and skeptical. Communication and presentation skills are also very important. The ability to communicate financial information clearly and at an understandable level is needed. An understanding of computer systems is necessary for success in this career field. Minimum education required for forensic accounting is a four-year accounting degree. Most forensic accountants are also Certified Public Accountants (CPAs). Work experience in the field of accounting is also desirable.

Occupational Outlook: Forensic accounting positions are currently in high demand. This trend is expected to continue. There is demand for more control in the financial sector. An increase in white-collar crimes also calls for more forensic accountants.

Sources: ForensicAccounting.com, forensic-accounting-information.com, fvs.aicpa.org, Monster.com, and AllBusinessSchools.com. *Characteristics and Skills of the Forensic Accountant* (published by AICPA/FVS Section). Survey completed Summer 2009.

ACTIVITY

Search the Internet for a school offering a certification in forensic accounting. Write a one-paragraph report about the requirements for the program.

End of Lesson Review

LO4 Analyze and record cash transactions using source documents.

LO5 Analyze and record transactions for buying and paying on account.

Audit your understanding

1. When cash is paid for insurance, which account is listed on the first line of the entry?

2. When supplies are bought on account, which account is listed on the first line of the entry?

3. When supplies are bought on account, which account is listed on the second line of the entry?

4. When cash is paid on account, which account is listed on the second line of the entry?

Work together 3-2

Journalizing entries in a general journal

Use the journal that you started for Work Together 3-1. Your instructor will guide you through the following example.

Norma Dirks owns Dirks Copy Center, which uses the following accounts.

Cash	Norma Dirks, Drawing
Accts. Rec.—K. Spah	Sales
Supplies	Miscellaneous Expense
Prepaid Insurance	Rent Expense
Accts. Pay.—Supply Mart	Utilities Expense
Norma Dirks, Capital	

Transactions:

Apr. 5. Bought supplies on account from Supply Mart, $600.00. M1.

7. Paid cash for insurance, $500.00. C2.

9. Paid cash on account to Supply Mart, $300.00. C3.

Journalize the transactions continuing on the next blank line of page 1 of the journal. Source documents are abbreviated as follows: check, C; memorandum, M. Save your work to complete Work Together 3-3.

On your own 3-2

Journalizing entries in a general journal

Use the chart of accounts below and the journal that you started for On Your Own 3-1. Work this problem independently.

Michelle Sullivan owns Sullivan's Service Center, which uses the following accounts.

Cash	Michelle Sullivan, Drawing
Accts. Rec.—G. Stratton	Sales
Supplies	Advertising Expense
Prepaid Insurance	Miscellaneous Expense
Accts. Pay.—Bayside Supplies	Rent Expense
Michelle Sullivan, Capital	

Transactions:

June 5. Paid cash for insurance, $300.00. C2.

9. Bought supplies on account from Bayside Supplies, $700.00. M1.

10. Paid cash on account to Bayside Supplies, $400.00. C3.

Journalize the transactions continuing on the next blank line of page 1 of the journal. Save your work to complete On Your Own 3-3.

LESSON
3-3 Transactions Affecting Owner's Equity and Asset Accounts

LO6 Analyze and record transactions that affect owner's equity.

LO7 Analyze and record sales and receipts of cash on account.

Received Cash from Sales LO6

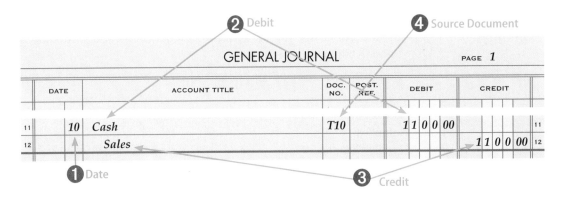

January 10. Received cash from sales, $1,100.00. Calculator Tape No. 10.

The source document for this transaction is Calculator Tape No. 10. [CONCEPT: Objective Evidence] The analysis of this transaction is shown in the T accounts.

The asset account, Cash, is increased by a debit, $1,100.00. The revenue account, Sales, is increased by a credit, $1,100.00.

The reason that Sales increases by a credit is discussed in the previous chapter. The owner's capital account increases on the credit side and has a normal credit balance. Because revenue increases owner's equity, increases in revenue are recorded as credits. A revenue account, therefore, has a normal credit balance.

Journalizing Cash Received from Sales

❶ **Date.** Write the date, 10, in the Date column.

❷ **Debit.** Write the title of the account debited, Cash, in the Account Title column. Write the debit amount, $1,100.00, in the Debit column.

❸ **Credit.** On the next line, indented about one centimeter, write the title of the account credited, Sales, in the Account Title column. Write the credit amount, $1,100.00, in the Credit column.

❹ **Source document.** On the first line of this entry, write the source document number, T10, in the Doc. No. column.

For this entry, the total debits, $1,100.00, equal the total credits, $1,100.00.

Sold Services on Account LO7

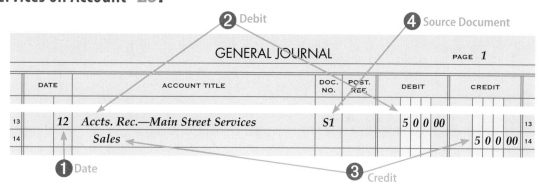

GENERAL JOURNAL

PAGE 1

	DATE	ACCOUNT TITLE	DOC. NO.	POST. REF.	DEBIT	CREDIT	
13	12	Accts. Rec.—Main Street Services	S1		5 0 0 00		13
14		Sales				5 0 0 00	14

① Date ② Debit ③ Credit ④ Source Document

January 12. Sold services on account to Main Street Services, $500.00. Sales Invoice No. 1.

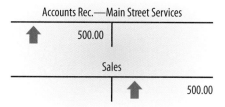

Accounts Rec.—Main Street Services

500.00

Sales

500.00

The source document for this transaction is Sales Invoice No. 1. [CONCEPT: Objective Evidence] The analysis of this transaction is shown in the T accounts.

The asset account, **Accounts Receivable—Main Street Services**, increases by a debit, $500.00. The revenue account, **Sales**, increases by a credit, $500.00.

Journalizing Services Sold on Account

① **Date.** Write the date, 12, in the Date column.

② **Debit.** Write the abbreviated name of the account debited, Accts. Rec.—Main Street Services, in the Account Title column. Write the debit amount, $500.00, in the Debit column.

③ **Credit.** On the next line, indented about one centimeter, write the title of the account credited, Sales, in the Account Title column. Write the credit amount, $500.00, in the Credit column.

④ **Source document.** Write the source document number, S1, in the Doc. No. column.

For this entry, the total debits, $500.00, equal the total credits, $500.00.

Accounting is not just for accountants. For example, a performing artist earns revenue from providing a service. Financial decisions must be made such as the cost of doing a performance, the percentage of revenue paid to a manager, travel expenses, and the cost of rehearsal space.

STOCKLITE/SHUTTERSTOCK.COM

Paid Cash for an Expense

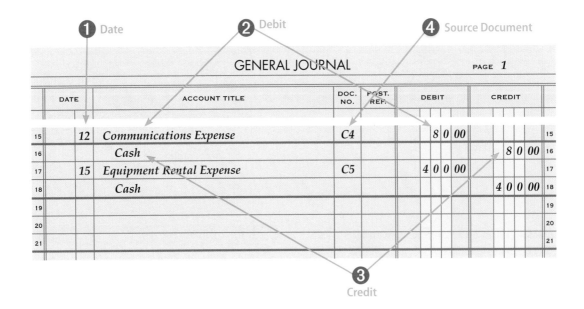

① Date　　**②** Debit　　**④** Source Document

GENERAL JOURNAL　　　　PAGE **1**

	DATE	ACCOUNT TITLE	DOC. NO.	POST. REF.	DEBIT	CREDIT	
15	12	*Communications Expense*	C4		8 0 00		15
16		*Cash*				8 0 00	16
17	15	*Equipment Rental Expense*	C5		4 0 0 00		17
18		*Cash*				4 0 0 00	18
19							19
20							20
21							21

③ Credit

January 12. Paid cash for communications bill, including cell phone and Internet service, $80.00. Check No. 4.

January 15. Paid cash for equipment rental, $400.00. Check No. 5.

Communications Expense

80.00

Cash

80.00

The source document for the first transaction is Check No. 4. [CONCEPT: Objective Evidence] The analysis of this transaction is shown in the T accounts.

The expense account, Communications Expense, increases by a debit, $80.00. The asset account, Cash, decreases by a credit, $80.00.

The reason that Communications Expense is increased by a debit is discussed in the previous chapter. The owner's capital account decreases on the debit side. Therefore, the owner's capital account has a normal credit balance.

Because expenses decrease owner's equity, increases in expenses are recorded as debits. An expense account, therefore, has a normal debit balance.

Whenever cash is paid for an expense, the journal entry is similar to the entry discussed above. Therefore, the journal entry to record paying cash for equipment rental is also illustrated.

❯ Journalizing Cash Paid for an Expense

① **Date.** Write the date, 12, in the Date column.

② **Debit.** Write the title of the account debited, Communications Expense, in the Account Title column. Write the debit amount, $80.00, in the Debit column.

③ **Credit.** On the next line, indented about one centimeter, write the title of the account credited, Cash, in the Account Title column. Write the credit amount, $80.00, in the Credit column.

④ **Source document.** Write the source document number, C4, in the Doc. No. column.

For this entry, the total debits, $80.00, equal the total credits, $80.00.

Drawing T accounts for analyzing transactions can make planning the journal entry easier.

Received Cash on Account

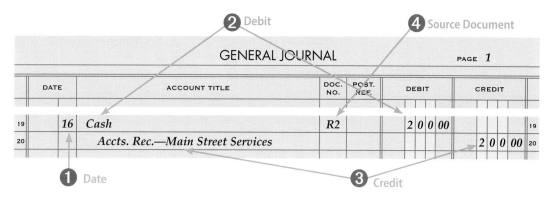

GENERAL JOURNAL   PAGE 1

2 Debit   4 Source Document

DATE	ACCOUNT TITLE	DOC. NO.	POST. REF.	DEBIT	CREDIT
16	Cash	R2		2 0 0 00	
	Accts. Rec.—Main Street Services				2 0 0 00

1 Date   3 Credit

January 16. Received cash on account from Main Street Services, $200.00. Receipt No. 2.

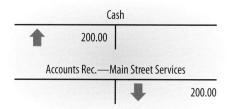

Cash

200.00

Accounts Rec.—Main Street Services

200.00

The source document for this transaction is Receipt No. 2. [CONCEPT: Objective Evidence] The analysis of this transaction is shown in the T accounts.

The asset account **Cash** increases by a debit, $200.00. The asset account **Accounts Receivable—Main Street Services** decreases by a credit, $200.00.

Journalizing Cash Received on Account

1. **Date.** Write the date, 16, in the Date column.

2. **Debit.** Write the title of the account debited, Cash, in the Account Title column. Write the debit amount, $200.00, in the Debit column.

3. **Credit.** On the next line, indented about one centimeter, write the abbreviated title of the account credited, Accts. Rec.—Main Street Services, in the Account Title column. Write the credit amount, $200.00, in the Credit column.

4. **Source document.** Write the source document number, R2, in the Doc. No. column.

   For this entry, the total debits, $200.00, equal the total credits, $200.00.

remember

Increases in expenses and in withdrawals decrease owner's equity. Decreases in owner's equity are recorded as debits. Therefore, increases in expenses and in withdrawals are recorded as debits.

Paid Cash to Owner as Withdrawal of Equity

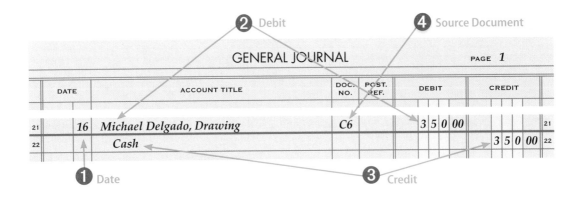

January 16. Paid cash to owner for a withdrawal of equity, $350.00. Check No. 6.

The source document for this transaction is Check No. 6. [CONCEPT: Objective Evidence] The analysis of this transaction is shown in the T accounts.

The reason that **Michael Delgado, Drawing** increased by a debit is discussed in the previous chapter. Decreases in the owner's capital account are shown as debits. Because withdrawals decrease owner's equity, increases in withdrawals are recorded as debits. A withdrawal account, therefore, has a normal debit balance.

Journalizing Cash Paid to Owner as Withdrawal of Equity

1 **Date.** Write the date, 16, in the Date column.

2 **Debit.** Write the title of the account debited, Michael Delgado, Drawing, in the Account Title column. Write the debit amount, $350.00, in the Debit column.

3 **Credit.** On the next line, indented about one centimeter, write the title of the account credited, Cash, in the Account Title column. Write the credit amount, $350.00, in the Credit column.

4 **Source document.** Write the source document number, C6, in the Doc. No. column.

For this entry, the total debits, $350.00, equal the total credits, $350.00.

Successful small business owners typically have the following characteristics. They have the confidence to make decisions. They keep trying during hard times for the business. They are willing to take risks. They have the creativity to surpass the competition. And they have an inner need to achieve.

End of Lesson Review

LO6 Analyze and record transactions that affect owner's equity.

LO7 Analyze and record sales and receipt of cash on account.

Audit your understanding

1. When cash is received from sales, which account is listed on the first line of the entry?

2. When cash is received from sales, which account is listed on the second line of the entry?

3. When services are sold on account, which account is listed on the second line of the entry?

4. When cash is paid for any reason, what abbreviation is used for the source document?

5. When cash is received on account, what abbreviation is used for the source document?

Work together 3-3

Journalizing transactions that affect owner's equity in a general journal

Use the chart of accounts and journal from Work Together 3-2. Your instructor will guide you through the following example.

Transactions:

Apr. 12. Paid cash for rent, $650.00. C4.

13. Received cash from sales, $2,500.00. T13.

14. Sold services on account to K. Spah, $480.00. S1.

19. Paid cash for electric bill, $220.00. C5.

20. Received cash on account from K. Spah, $255.00. R2.

21. Paid cash to owner as a withdrawal of equity, $1,500.00. C6.

Journalize the transactions continuing on the next blank line of page 1 of the journal. Source documents are abbreviated as follows: check, C; receipt, R; sales invoice, S; calculator tape, T. Save your work to complete Work Together 3-4.

On your own 3-3

Journalizing transactions that affect owner's equity in a general journal

Use the chart of accounts and journal from On Your Own 3-2. Work this problem independently.

Transactions:

June 11. Paid cash for rent, $750.00. C4.

12. Sold services on account to G. Stratton, $800.00. S1.

16. Received cash from sales, $4,300.00. T16.

17. Paid cash for postage (Miscellaneous Expense), $37.00. C5.

19. Received cash on account from G. Stratton, $500.00. R2.

20. Paid cash to owner as a withdrawal of equity, $1,200.00. C6.

Journalize the transactions continuing on the next blank line of page 1 of the journal. Source documents are abbreviated as follows: check, C; receipt, R; sales invoice, S; calculator tape, T. Save your work to complete On Your Own 3-4.

©CANDICE CUSACK, ISTOCK

3-4 Starting a New Journal Page

LO8 Demonstrate when to end and how to start a new journal page.

LO9 Identify and correct errors using standard accounting practices.

A Completed Journal Page LO8

GENERAL JOURNAL — PAGE 1

	DATE		ACCOUNT TITLE	DOC. NO.	POST. REF.	DEBIT	CREDIT	
1	Jan. 20--	2	Cash	R1		2 0 0 0 00		1
2			Michael Delgado, Capital				2 0 0 0 00	2
3		2	Supplies	C1		1 6 5 00		3
4			Cash				1 6 5 00	4
5		3	Prepaid Insurance	C2		9 0 0 00		5
6			Cash				9 0 0 00	6
33		22	Equipment Rental Expense	C9		5 1 0 00		33
34			Cash				5 1 0 00	34

A general journal page is complete when there is insufficient space to record any more entries. A partial view of Delgado Web Services' completed page 1 of the general journal is shown.

Delgado Web Services has one blank line remaining at the bottom of page 1. However, each journal entry requires at least two lines. If a journal entry is split between two different pages, the equality of debits and credits for the entry is not as easily verified. Also, to a person examining a single page, a split entry will appear incorrect. Therefore, a journal entry should not be split and journalized on two different pages. If there is only one blank line remaining on a journal page, a new page is started.

Starting a New General Journal Page

GENERAL JOURNAL — PAGE 2

	DATE	ACCOUNT TITLE	DOC. NO.	POST. REF.	DEBIT	CREDIT	
1							1
2							2
3							3
4							4
5							5

After one page of a general journal is filled, a new journal page is started. A new page is started by writing the page number in the space provided in the journal heading.

Playing It Safe with Renter's Insurance

Unexpected financial losses can affect your financial future. One way to manage this risk is to buy insurance.

Renter's insurance is a necessity when renting a home or business location. The building owner may have insurance, but that will protect only the building. The renter's personal belongings are not protected. A renter should carefully evaluate personal belongings to determine the amount of insurance coverage needed.

Renter's insurance should also provide liability protection for lawsuits or medical payments from injuries on your premises. You should also be sure the policy covers living expenses in case you have to relocate while damages are being repaired. In the case of a business, some renter's insurance provides compensation for the interruption in business due to the accident or emergency.

The amount reimbursed after a loss depends on the type of coverage. An actual cash value policy pays the price that the item's value is today regardless of the purchase price. For example, a five-year-old camera would be covered for the value after five years of use. It would not be covered for the original purchase price. A replacement cost policy pays the amount that it would cost to replace the item today. Most insurance policies have a deductible. A deductible is the amount that the insured pays out of pocket before the insurance coverage begins.

ACTIVITIES

Amy Tanner purchased renter's insurance with the following coverage: $100,000 liability for lawsuits and medical; $20,000 replacement cost for personal property, $500 deductible. One night, Amy left a candle burning that ended up causing a fire and destroying all of her personal belongings. The original cost of the belongings was $32,000.

1. How much did the insurance company pay for this claim?

2. How much did Amy pay to replace the personal property?

3. Explain the impact if Amy would have had an actual cash value policy instead of a replacement cost policy.

Correcting Errors In Journal Entries LO9

GENERAL JOURNAL   PAGE 14

	DATE	ACCOUNT TITLE	DOC. NO.	POST. REF.	DEBIT	CREDIT	
9	27	~~Advertising Expense~~	~~C10~~		~~5 5 00~~		9
10		~~Cash~~				~~5 5 00~~	10
11	27	Miscellaneous Expense	C10		5 5 00		11
12		Cash				5 5 00	12
13	28	Supplies	C11		~~3 0 0 00~~ 3 0 0 00		13
14		Cash				~~3 0 0 00~~ 3 0 0 00	14
15	29	Cash	T29		4 3 0 0 00		15
16		Sales				~~4 3 0 0 00~~ 4 3 0 0 00	16
17	31	Miscellaneous Expense	C12		3 5 00		17
18		Postage Expense			2 3 00		18
19		Cash				5 8 00	19

Delgado Web Services follows standard accounting practices for error corrections. Errors are corrected in a way that does not cause doubts about what the correct information is.

1. Sometimes an entire entry is incorrect and is discovered before the next entry is journalized. Draw neat lines through all parts of the incorrect entry. Journalize the entry correctly on the next blank line as shown on lines 9 through 12.
2. If an error is recorded, cancel the error by neatly drawing a line through the incorrect item. Write the correct item immediately above the canceled item as shown on lines 13 and 14.
3. Sometimes several correct entries are recorded after an incorrect entry is made. The next blank lines are several entries later. Draw neat lines through all incorrect parts of the entry. Record the correct items on the same lines as the incorrect items, directly above the canceled parts as shown on line 16. Always use a straight-edge or ruler to draw a precise, neat rule.

THINK LIKE AN ACCOUNTANT

Is Online Advertising Effective?

Your company, Nelson Sports, sells its products on an eCommerce site. To attract customers, Nelson Sports advertises on several Internet search and social networking sites. Each site bills Nelson Sports based on thousands of impressions. An impression is the number of times the advertisement appears on a web page. Nelson Sports pays an average of $20 per thousand impressions.

The chief operating officer (COO) has expressed her concern over the cost of Internet advertising. She has noticed that the monthly advertising expense has increased over 100% in just two years. At the same time, the click-through rate (the percent of viewers who click on the advertisement) has been declining. The COO is questioning whether this form of advertising results in an adequate number of potential customers visiting the eCommerce site.

The worksheet contains a table that includes the monthly advertising expense and the monthly click-through rate.

OPEN THE SPREADSHEET TLA_CH03

Using the two charts on the spreadsheet, prepare a response to the COO by answering the following questions:

1. Are more potential customers viewing the advertisements?
2. Is the increasing money spent on advertising resulting in more potential customers accessing the company's eCommerce site?
3. Should the company continue to pay for online advertising? What other information would you need?

RFID Tags and Public Safety

A radio frequency identification (RFID) tag can be used to track lost animals, products, or people. The tag transmits a radio frequency that can be detected several feet away. The message sent by the tag is specific to that tag. The message is received by an antenna which then interprets the radio signal.

RFID tags have major implications for public safety. The cost of searching for a lost child can be high. Salaries paid to rescue personnel are one cost. In addition, those rescue personnel are not available for other community service. The cost of an RFID tag is getting lower and lower. A tag may be as little as ten cents. But there is also the cost of putting a child through the implantation process.

The RFID tag is a good example of when the "numbers" are only a small part in the decision-making process. If the decision to implant an RFID tag into a child were only a matter of the monetary cost, many parents would agree that the cost of the tag is well worth the safety of the child. Most public safety departments would encourage the use of the RFID tag in order to reduce the cost of searching for a missing child. However, other items must also be considered. Implantation cost is one factor. The discomfort to the child is another factor. The chance that an RFID tag could be used improperly to track the movement of a child is also a factor.

CRITICAL THINKING

1. Use the Internet to research the use and cost of RFID tags to track inmates in prison. Write a short summary of your findings.
2. How could the use of RFID tags reduce costs for a company in tracking its products?

LO8 Demonstrate when to end and how to start a new journal page.

LO9 Identify and correct errors using standard accounting practices.

Audit your understanding

1. When is a general journal page complete?

2. If an entire entry is incorrect and is discovered before the next entry is journalized, how should the incorrect entry be corrected?

3. If several correct entries are recorded after an incorrect entry is made, how should the incorrect entry be corrected?

Work together 3-4

Journalizing transactions and starting a new journal page

Use the general journal from Work Together 3-3. Your instructor will guide you through the following examples.

Transactions:

Apr. 22. Paid cash for water bill (Utilities Expense), $180.00. C7.

23. Sold services on account to K. Spah, $345.00. S2.

26. Received cash from sales, $980.00. T26.

27. Paid cash to owner as a withdrawal of equity, $420.00. C8.

27. Paid cash for supplies, $66.00. C9.

28. Paid cash for postage (Miscellaneous Expense), $35.00. C10.

29. Received cash on account from K. Spah, $200.00. R3.

30. Received cash from sales, $745.00. T30.

1. Journalize the transactions for April 22 through 27. Source documents are abbreviated as follows: check, C; receipt, R; sales invoice, S; calculator tape, T.

2. Use page 2 of the journal to journalize the remaining transactions for April.

On your own 3-4

Journalizing transactions and starting a new journal page

Use the general journal from On Your Own 3-3. Work this problem independently.

Transactions:

June 23. Sold services on account to G. Stratton, $515.00. S2.

24. Paid cash for advertising, $165.00. C7.

25. Received cash from sales, $1,100.00. T25.

26. Paid cash for delivery charges (Miscellaneous Expense), $18.00. C8.

26. Received cash on account from G. Stratton, $635.00. R3.

27. Paid cash for postage (Miscellaneous Expense), $44.00. C9.

28. Paid cash for supplies, $210.00. C10.

30. Received cash from sales, $300.00. T30.

1. Journalize the transactions for June 23 through 26. Source documents are abbreviated as follows: check, C; receipt, R; sales invoice, S; calculator tape, T.

2. Use page 2 of the journal to journalize the remaining transactions for June.

A Look at Accounting Software
Making Journal Entries

In a computerized accounting system, the Make Journal Entries window serves the same function as the general journal you used in this chapter. But in a computerized accounting system, often-used transactions have special input windows like the Receive Cash window from the previous chapter. Those special input windows allow the user to make just one entry. Then the system automatically takes care of the rest of the transaction. That makes entry faster and reduces errors.

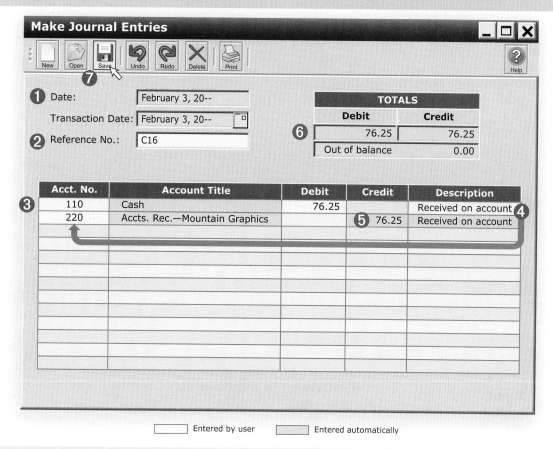

Entered by user   Entered automatically

❶ The current date is entered by the system. The system also enters the current date as the transaction date. However, if the transaction occurred on an earlier date, the user would enter the correct transaction date.

❷ The user enters a reference number.

❸ The window shows the entry for payment of cash on account to Mountain Graphics for $76.25. The debit part of the transaction is customarily entered first. To begin the entry, the account number or account title is keyed in. Systems use different methods to speed entry. Some use drop menus; some use autocomplete. Whichever field the user chooses to enter, the other field would be completed automatically.

❹ The typical method of entry is for the user to tab across the row, verifying or entering the correct information in each column. When the information in the entry row is all correct, the user presses Enter and the cursor moves to the beginning of the next row.

❺ To speed entry, and to reduce errors, the system may automatically enter data for the credit entry based on the data the user keyed for the debit. When the user enters the title or account number to begin the next row, the system would enter the credit amount ($76.25 for this transaction) and the description. Both could be overwritten if they were different from the first row.

❻ As the user makes each entry, the system updates the total debits and credits allowing the user to see at a glance if the transaction is in balance. Any out-of-balance condition is displayed to assist in correcting the error.

❼ The user clicks Save to end the transaction. If the user tries to save a transaction that is not in balance, the system will prompt the user to correct the out-of-balance condition.

Chapter Summary

This chapter introduces the basic input of the accounting system—the journal entry. The journal entry is the way business transactions are first recorded into the accounting system of any company. In this chapter, Delgado Web Services used the general journal to record its transactions. Other types of journals can be used. But the outcome is always the same: business transactions are entered into the accounting system. In a manual system, this is done by analyzing each transaction into its debit and credit parts and then manually recording it in a journal. In Chapter 4, you will learn how the journal is used to enter parts of each transaction into the accounts so that each account is up to date.

EXPLORE ACCOUNTING

Prenumbered Documents

Source documents are an important part of the accounting process. They provide information about business transactions. The use of prenumbered source documents also provides additional control. A prenumbered document is one that has the form number printed on it. The most common prenumbered document in everyday life is the personal check.

Businesses use several prenumbered documents. Examples include business checks, sales invoices, receipts, and memorandums.

Prenumbered documents provide a simple way to ensure that all documents are recorded. For example, when a business records the checks written during a period of time, all check numbers should be accounted for in numeric order. The person recording the checks must watch to see that no numbers are skipped.

Many computerized systems automatically generate numbered forms, using the next available number for that type of form. For example, if the last sales invoice was numbered 2108, the next sales invoice that is generated will be numbered 2109.

A business can also control operations by using batch totals. When many (sometimes hundreds of) documents are being recorded, the total amount can be used to help ensure that all documents are recorded. For example, the total of all sales invoices is calculated before the invoices are recorded. Once all invoices are recorded, another total is calculated from the journal entries. If the two totals are equal, it is assumed that all invoices have been recorded. If the totals do not equal, it may indicate that a document was skipped.

INSTRUCTIONS

With your instructor's permission, contact a local business and ask what prenumbered documents are used there. Determine how the business uses the documents to ensure that all documents are recorded properly.

Apply Your Understanding

INSTRUCTIONS: Download problem instructions for Excel, QuickBooks, and Peachtree from the textbook companion website at www.C21accounting.com.

3-1 Application Problem: Journalizing transactions in a general journal LO3, 4

D & M Company uses the following accounts.

Cash
Accounts Receivable—Scott Company
Accounts Payable—Supply Mart
Supplies
Prepaid Insurance
Dennis Marier, Capital
Dennis Marier, Drawing
Sales
Miscellaneous Expense
Rent Expense
Utilities Expense

Transactions:

Mar. 1. Received cash from owner as an investment, $5,000.00. R1.
4. Paid cash for supplies, $1,500.00. C1.

Instructions:

1. Journalize the transactions completed during March of the current year. Use page 1 of the journal given in the *Working Papers*. Source documents are abbreviated as follows: check, C; receipt, R.
2. Save your work to complete Problem 3-2.

3-2 Application Problem: Journalizing buying insurance, buying on account, and paying on account in a general journal LO3, 4, 5

Use the chart of accounts and journal from Problem 3-1.

Transactions:

Mar. 6. Paid cash for insurance, $300.00. C2.
7. Bought supplies on account from Supply Mart, $1,000.00. M1.
8. Paid cash on account to Supply Mart, $500.00. C3.
12. Paid cash on account to Supply Mart, $500.00. C4.

Instructions:

1. Journalize these transactions. Source documents are abbreviated as follows: check, C; memorandum, M.
2. Save your work to complete Problem 3-3.

3-3 Application Problem: Journalizing transactions that affect owner's equity and receiving cash on account in a general journal LO 3, 4, 5, 6, 7

Use the chart of accounts given in Problem 3-1 and the journal from Problem 3-2.

Transactions:

Mar. 12. Paid cash for rent, $400.00. C5.
13. Received cash from sales, $250.00. T13.
14. Sold services on account to Scott Company, $225.00. S1.
15. Paid cash to owner as withdrawal of equity, $1,400.00. C6.
18. Received cash from sales, $130.00. T18.
19. Paid cash for postage (Miscellaneous Expense), $32.00. C7.
21. Received cash on account from Scott Company, $125.00. R2.
22. Received cash from sales, $350.00. T22.
22. Paid cash for heating bill, $165.00. C8.

Instructions:

1. Journalize these transactions. Source documents are abbreviated as follows: check, C; memorandum, M; receipt, R; sales invoice, S; calculator tape, T.
2. Save your work to complete Problem 3-4.1.

3-4.1 Application Problem: Starting a new journal page LO 3, 4, 5, 6, 7, 8

Use the chart of accounts given in Problem 3-1 and the journal from Problem 3-3.

Transactions:

Mar. 26. Received cash on account from Scott Company, $100.00. R3.
26. Paid cash for a delivery (Miscellaneous Expense), $15.00. C9.
27. Sold services on account to Scott Company, $400.00. S2.
27. Paid cash for supplies, $22.00. C10.
28. Paid cash for rent, $100.00. C11.
29. Paid cash for postage (Miscellaneous Expense), $44.00. C15.
31. Received cash from sales, $685.00. T31.
31. Paid cash to owner as withdrawal of equity, $400.00. C13.

Instructions:

1. Journalize the first transaction for March 26. Source documents are abbreviated as follows: check, C; receipt, R; sales invoice, S; calculator tape, T.
2. Use page 2 of the journal to journalize the transactions for the rest of March.

3-4.2 Application Problem: Journalizing transactions LO3, 4, 5, 6, 7

Mundt Services uses the following accounts.

Cash
Accounts Receivable—J. Lepowsky
Supplies
Prepaid Insurance
Accounts Payable—Southern Supplies
Mikaela Mundt, Capital
Mikaela Mundt, Drawing
Sales
Advertising Expense
Utilities Expense

Transactions:

Aug. 1. Mikaela Mundt invested $2,000.00 of her own money in the business. Receipt No. 1.
3. Used business cash to purchase supplies costing $216.00. Wrote Check No. 1.
4. Wrote Check No. 2 for insurance, $245.00.
5. Purchased supplies for $68.00 over the phone from Southern Supplies, promising to send the check next week. Memo No. 1.
11. Sent Check No. 3 to Southern Supplies, $68.00.
12. Sent a check for the electricity bill, $180.00. Check No. 4.
15. Wrote an $800.00 check to Ms. Mundt as a withdrawal of equity for personal use. Used Check No. 5.
16. Sold services for $412.00 to J. Lepowsky, who agreed to pay for them within ten days. Sales Invoice No. 1.
17. Recorded cash sales of $1,179.00. Calculator tape dated March 17. T17.
18. Paid $132.00 for advertising. Wrote Check No. 6.
25. Received $412.00 from J. Lepowsky for the services performed last week. Wrote Receipt No. 2.

Instructions:

Journalize the transactions completed during August of the current year. Use page 1 of the journal given in the *Working Papers*. Remember to record appropriate source document numbers.

3-M Mastery Problem: Journalizing transactions and starting a new journal page
LO3, 4, 5, 6, 7, 8

Sadie's Car Wash uses the following accounts.

Cash
Supplies
Prepaid Insurance
Accounts Receivable—Zachary's Limos
Accounts Payable—OK Supplies
Accounts Payable—Archer Supplies
Sadie Berkowitz, Capital
Sadie Berkowitz, Drawing
Sales
Advertising Expense
Miscellaneous Expense
Rent Expense
Utilities Expense
Repairs Expense

Transactions:

May 1. Received cash from owner as an investment, $8,000.00. R1.
2. Paid cash for supplies, $150.00. C1.
3. Paid cash for rent, $450.00. C2.
4. Bought supplies on account from Archer Supplies, $850.00. M1.
5. Paid cash for electric bill, $123.00. C3.
8. Paid cash on account to Archer Supplies, $500.00. C4.
8. Received cash from sales, $490.00. T8.
8. Sold services on account to Zachary's Limos, $225.00. S1.
9. Paid cash for insurance, $600.00. C5.
10. Paid cash for repairs, $194.00. C6.
10. Received cash from sales, $238.00. T10.
11. Paid cash for miscellaneous expense, $20.00. C7.
11. Received cash from sales, $315.00. T11.
12. Received cash from sales, $450.00. T12.
15. Paid cash to owner as a withdrawal of equity for personal use, $2,000.00. C8.
15. Received cash from sales, $425.00. T15.
16. Paid cash for supplies, $550.00. C9.
17. Received cash on account from Zachary's Limos, $115.00. R2.
17. Bought supplies on account from OK Supplies, $300.00. M2.
17. Received cash from sales, $250.00. T17.
19. Received cash from sales, $325.00. T19.
22. Bought supplies on account from OK Supplies, $30.00. M3.
22. Received cash from sales, $305.00. T22.
23. Sold services on account to Zachary's Limos, $291.00. S2.
24. Paid cash for advertising, $75.00. C10.
24. Received cash from sales, $150.00. T24.
25. Received cash from sales, $385.00. T25.
26. Paid cash for supplies, $45.00. C11.
26. Received cash from sales, $150.00. T26.
29. Received cash on account from Zachary's Limos, $175.00. R3.
31. Paid cash to owner as withdrawal of equity, $2,250.00. C12.
31. Received cash from sales, $250.00. T31.

Instructions:

1. The journal for Sadie's Car Wash is given in the *Working Papers*. Use page 1 of the journal to journalize the transactions for May 1 through May 15. Source documents are abbreviated as follows: check, C; memorandum, M; receipt, R; sales invoice, S; calculator tape, T.
2. Use page 2 of the journal to journalize the transactions for the remainder of May.

Peachtree

1. Journalize transactions in the general journal.
2. From the menu bar, select Reports & Forms; General Ledger.
3. Make the selections to print the general journal.

 QuickBooks

1. Journalize transactions in the journal.
2. From the menu bar, select Reports; Accountant & Taxes.
3. Make the selections to print the journal.

1. Journalize transactions in the general journal.
2. From the Office button menu, select Print.
3. Print the worksheet.

AAONLINE

1. Go to www.cengage.com/login
2. Click on **AA Online** to access.
3. Go to the online assignment and follow the instructions.

3-S Source Documents Problem: Journalizing transactions from source documents
LO2, 3, 4, 5, 6, 7

White's Repair Service uses the following accounts.

Cash
Accounts Receivable—J. Puckett
Supplies
Prepaid Insurance
Accounts Payable—Atlas Supplies
Henry White, Capital
Henry White, Drawing
Sales
Miscellaneous Expense
Rent Expense
Utilities Expense

Source documents related to the transactions for White's Repair Service for June are provided in the *Working Papers*.

Instructions:

The journal for White's Repair Service is given in the *Working Papers*. Use page 1 of the journal to journalize the transactions for June. Source documents are abbreviated as follows: check, C; memorandum, M; receipt, R; sales invoice, S; calculator tape, T.

3-C Challenge Problem: Journalizing transactions using a variation of the general journal LO3, 4, 5, 6, 7

Malnick's Tailors uses the following accounts.

Cash
Accounts Receivable—Unique Uniforms
Supplies
Prepaid Insurance
Accounts Payable—Master Supplies
Misha Malnick, Capital
Misha Malnick, Drawing
Sales
Rent Expense
Utilities Expense

Transactions:

Sept. 1. Received cash from owner as an investment, $8,000.00. R1.
2. Paid cash for insurance, $2,500.00. C1.
3. Bought supplies on account from Master Supplies, $2,000.00. M1.
4. Paid cash for supplies, $1,500.00. C2.
8. Paid cash on account to Master Supplies, $2,000.00. C3.
9. Paid cash for rent, $1,000.00. C4.
12. Received cash from sales, $1,800.00. T12.
15. Sold services on account to Unique Uniforms, $400.00. S1.
16. Paid cash for telephone bill, $120.00. C5.
22. Received cash on account from Unique Uniforms, $400.00. R2.
25. Paid cash to owner as withdrawal of equity, $1,000.00. C6.

Instructions:

The journal for Malnick's Tailors is given in the *Working Papers*. Malnick's Tailors uses a journal with a column arrangement slightly different from the journal used in this chapter, as shown below.

			GENERAL JOURNAL				PAGE		
DEBIT	DATE		ACCOUNT TITLE	DOC. NO.	POST. REF.	CREDIT			
1									1
2									2
3									3
4									4
5									5

Use page 1 of the journal to journalize the transactions. Source documents are abbreviated as follows: check, C; memorandum, M; receipt, R; sales invoice, S; calculator tape, T.

 Peachtree

1. Journalize transactions in the general journal.
2. From the menu bar, select Reports & Forms; General Ledger.
3. Make the selections to print the general journal.

 Quick Books

1. Journalize transactions in the journal.
2. From the menu bar, select Reports; Accountant & Taxes.
3. Make the selections to print the journal.

1. Journalize transactions in the general journal.
2. From the Office button menu, select Print.
3. Print the worksheet.

AAONLINE

1. Go to www.cengage.com/login
2. Click on **AA Online** to access.
3. Go to the online assignment and follow the instructions.

21st Century Skills

Business Counts!

Theme: Government, Civics, Economic, Business

Skills: Information Literacy, Communication and Collaboration, Social and Cross-Cultural Skills, ICT Literacy

PARTNERSHIP FOR
21ST CENTURY SKILLS

The U.S. Census Bureau takes a count of the population every ten years. The census tells a story. Each question on the census helps determine the political, economic, and social decisions that affect everyone. An increase or decrease in the population can influence funding for a school, a hospital, or road repairs.

In addition to the population census, an economic census is collected on each U.S. business every five years. The results provide a picture of the U.S. economy from the national to the local level—even as specific as zip code.

 **APPLICATION**

In small groups of two to three students, discuss and complete the following. Be prepared to share your responses with the class.

1. If you were a small business owner, explain three reasons why you would use the population census to make business decisions.

2. Using the Internet, evaluate the economic census at www.census.gov/econ/census. Go to Industry Snapshots and collaborate with your peers to select three different industries. Research the number of establishments and the total value of business in each industry for the last two census periods. Prepare a bar graph to report your findings to the class. This can be graphed in Excel or drawn on a poster.

Analyzing Nike's financial statements

To calculate what percentage one amount is of another amount, you divide the smaller amount by the total that contains the smaller amount. Using Nike as an example, Cash for 2010 = $3,079,000,000. Total assets for 2010 = $14,419,000,000. To calculate what percentage cash is of total assets, use the following formula: Cash, $3,079,000,000 ÷ total assets, $14,419,000,000. The answer is 0.21354, or 21.35%.

INSTRUCTIONS

1. Use the information on page B-6 in Appendix B. Find the amount of accounts receivables and total assets for Nike for 2010 and 2011. Calculate what percentage accounts receivable are of total assets for 2011 and 2010.

2. Did the percentage increase or decrease over this period of time?

3. If this percentage would increase rapidly, what could be happening?

Chapter 4

Posting to a General Ledger

LEARNING OBJECTIVES

After studying Chapter 4, in addition to defining key terms, you will be able to:

LO1 Construct a chart of accounts for a service business organized as a proprietorship.

LO2 Demonstrate correct principles for numbering accounts.

LO3 Apply file maintenance principles to update a chart of accounts.

LO4 Complete the steps necessary to open general ledger accounts.

LO5 Post amounts from a general journal.

LO6 Demonstrate how to prove cash.

LO7 Analyze incorrect journal entries and prepare correcting entries.

LO8 Demonstrate how to correct errors made during the posting process.

©DANIEL KOUREY, ISTOCK/©JIM PRUITT, ISTOCK

STOCKBYTE/JUPITER IMAGES

Accounting In The Real World
Netflix

In 1998, Netflix announced that it was the "world's first Internet store to offer DVD rentals." A customer could order a DVD online and receive it in the mail. The customer would return the DVD in a postage-paid envelope provided by Netflix. In 2007, Netflix expanded to include streaming content over the Internet.

Virtually all of Netflix's revenue is derived from monthly subscription fees. GAAP requires that Netflix track all of these fees and report them as revenue on its financial statements. Besides tracking accounting transactions as required by GAAP, Netflix (and other companies) may choose to gather and analyze other financial information.

As part of its annual report, Netflix reports revenue per paying subscriber and the average number of subscribers per year. These data for the years 2007 through 2009 are as follows:

	2007	2008	2009
Average number of subscribers	6,718,000	8,268,000	10,464,000
Average revenue per subscriber	$14.95	$13.75	$13.30

As you can see, the average number of subscribers has increased each year since 2007. Also, the average revenue per subscriber has declined as lower-priced plans grow as a percentage of sales.

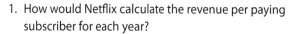

CRITICAL THINKING

1. How would Netflix calculate the revenue per paying subscriber for each year?

2. Who are some of Netflix's competitors?

Key Terms

- ledger
- general ledger
- account number
- file maintenance
- opening an account
- posting
- proving cash
- correcting entry

LESSON

4-1 Using Accounts and Preparing and Maintaining a Chart of Accounts

LO1 Construct a chart of accounts for a service business organized as a proprietorship.

LO2 Demonstrate correct principles for numbering accounts.

LO3 Apply file maintenance principles to update a chart of accounts.

LO4 Complete the steps necessary to open general ledger accounts.

Account Form

Delgado Web Services records transactions in a general journal, as described in Chapter 3. A journal is a permanent record of the debit and credit parts of each transaction with transactions recorded in chronological order. However, a journal does not show, in one place, all the changes in a single account.

If only a journal is used, a business must search through all journal pages to find items affecting a single account balance. For this reason, a form is used to summarize in one place all the changes to a single account. A separate form is used for each account.

Are Your Actions Legal?

"**A** man should be upright, not be kept upright." This famous statement by Marcus Aurelius suggests that, in a perfect world, everyone would always do the right thing. In the real world, however, governments have been forced to create complex systems of laws to force individuals to adhere to the social norm of right and wrong. We rely on these laws for our protection as well as the orderly operation of our society. For example, think about the chaos that might result if individuals could choose which side of the road to drive on!

Many laws are common knowledge for individuals working in business.

- Employers may not discriminate on the basis of national origin.
- Customers may not be charged different prices for the same item.
- Taxes must be paid to the government.

Whether an action is legal is not always so obvious. Did you know:

- It may be illegal to sell certain items, such as computers and oil, to countries that violate global norms of conduct.
- An interviewer may not ask a prospective employee if he or she has children.
- A bank must file a report to the government when an individual deposits more than $10,000 cash.

No one can be expected to know every law that might affect the operation of a business. To assist its managers, businesses hire lawyers to provide managers with legal advice. Most large businesses have their own legal departments staffed with lawyers. Smaller businesses typically pay a retainer fee to an independent lawyer to provide legal advice when needed. All businesses should provide their managers with regular training on legal issues. Managers should be encouraged to consult the lawyers if there is any question whether an action might be illegal.

INSTRUCTIONS

Use an Internet or library source to prepare a list of questions that are illegal for an employer to ask during a job interview.

Relationship of a T Account to an Account Form

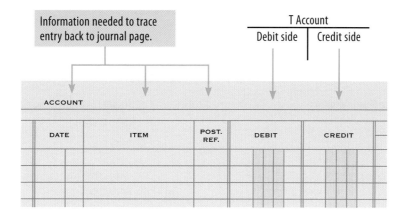

An account form is based on and includes the debit and credit sides of a T account. In addition to debit and credit columns, space is provided in the account form for recording the transaction date and journal page number. This information can be used to trace a specific entry back to where a transaction is recorded in a journal.

The major disadvantage of the account form illustrated above is that no current, up-to-date account balance is shown. If this form is used, an up-to-date balance must be calculated each time the account is examined. When an account has a large number of entries, it can be difficult and time-consuming to calculate the balance each time an entry is made. Therefore, a more commonly used account form has two additional columns, for the Debit and Credit Balances, as shown below.

Because the form has columns for the debit and credit balance, it is often referred to as the *balance-ruled account form.*

The account balance is calculated and recorded as each entry is recorded in the account. Recording information in an account is described later in this chapter. The T account is a useful device for analyzing transactions into debit and credit parts. However, the balance-ruled account form is more useful than the T account as a permanent record of changes to account balances. Delgado Web Services uses the balance-ruled account form.

Chart of Accounts LO1

Delgado Web Services
25402 Rimrock Road
Billings, MT 59102-1820

CHART OF ACCOUNTS

Balance Sheet Accounts	Income Statement Accounts
(100) ASSETS	**(400) REVENUE**
110 Cash	410 Sales
120 Petty Cash	
130 Accounts Receivable—Main Street Services	**(500) EXPENSES**
140 Accounts Receivable—Valley Landscaping	510 Advertising Expense
150 Supplies	520 Cash Short and Over
160 Prepaid Insurance	530 Communications Expense
	540 Equipment Rental Expense
(200) LIABILITIES	550 Insurance Expense
210 Accounts Payable—Canyon Office Supplies	560 Miscellaneous Expense
220 Accounts Payable—Mountain Graphic Arts	570 Supplies Expense
(300) OWNER'S EQUITY	
310 Michael Delgado, Capital	
320 Michael Delgado, Drawing	
330 Income Summary	

A group of accounts is called a **ledger**. A ledger that contains all accounts needed to prepare financial statements is called a **general ledger**. The name given to an account is known as an *account title*. The number assigned to an account is called an **account number**.

PREPARING A CHART OF ACCOUNTS

A list of account titles and numbers showing the location of each account in a ledger is known as a *chart of accounts*. Delgado Web Services' chart of accounts is shown above. For ease of use while studying the chapters in Part 1, Delgado Web Services' chart of accounts is also shown on page 3.

Accounts in a general ledger are arranged in the same order as they appear on financial statements. Delgado Web Services' chart of accounts shows five general ledger divisions: (1) Assets, (2) Liabilities, (3) Owner's Equity, (4) Revenue, and (5) Expenses.

Account Numbers LO2

1   5   0   **Supplies**

General ledger division   Location with general ledger division

Delgado Web Services assigns a 3-digit account number to each account. For example, Supplies is assigned the number 150, as shown.

The first digit of each account number shows the general ledger division in which the account is located. For example, the asset division accounts are numbered in the 100s. Therefore, the number for the asset account, Supplies, begins with a 1.

The second two digits indicate the location of each account within a general ledger division. The 50 in the account number for Supplies indicates that the account is located between account number 140 and account number 160.

Assigning Account Numbers LO3

Delgado Web Services initially assigns account numbers by 10s so that new accounts can be added easily. Nine numbers are unused between each account on Delgado Web Services' chart of accounts. For example, numbers 111 to 119 are unused between accounts numbered 110 and 120. New numbers can be assigned between existing account numbers without renumbering all existing accounts. The procedure for arranging accounts in a general ledger, assigning account numbers, and keeping records current is called **file maintenance**.

Unused account numbers are assigned to new accounts. Delgado Web Services records payments for postage in Miscellaneous Expense. If Mr. Delgado found that the amount paid each month for postage had become a major expense, he might decide to use a separate account. The account might be titled Postage Expense. Delgado Web Services arranges expense accounts in alphabetic order in its general ledger. Therefore, the new account would be inserted between Miscellaneous Expense and Supplies Expense.

560	Miscellaneous Expense	(Existing account)
	Postage Expense	*(New Account)*
570	Supplies Expense	(Existing account)

The number selected for the new account should leave some unused numbers on each side for other accounts that might need to be added. The middle, unused account number between existing numbers 560 and 570 is 565. Therefore, 565 is assigned as the account number for the new account.

560	Miscellaneous Expense	(Existing account)
565	*Postage Expense*	*(New Account)*
570	Supplies Expense	(Existing account)

Sometimes an account is no longer needed. For example, Delgado Web Services might buy its own equipment. Then it would no longer need the Equipment Rental Expense account. However, even though the account might never be used again, it is generally not removed from the chart of accounts. Companies often need to review past performance and if an account has been removed, there may be no way to recover the information that account contained.

When a new account is added at the end of a ledger division, the next number in a sequence of 10s is used. For example, suppose Delgado Web Services needs to add another expense account, Water Expense. The expense accounts are arranged in alphabetic order. Therefore, the new account would be added at the end of the expense section of the chart of accounts. The last used expense account number is 570, as shown on the chart of accounts. The next number in the sequence of 10s is 580, which is assigned as the number of the new account.

560	Miscellaneous Expense	(Existing account)
570	Supplies Expense	(Existing account)
580	*Water Expense*	*(New Account)*

Delgado Web Services has relatively few accounts in its general ledger and does not anticipate adding many new accounts in the future. Therefore, a 3-digit account number adequately provides for the few account numbers that might be added. However, as the number of general ledger accounts increases, a business may change to four or more digits.

Charts of accounts with more than three digits are described in later chapters.

STOCKLITE/SHUTTERSTOCK.COM

Opening an Account in a General Ledger LO4

Account Title ❶

Account Number ❷

ACCOUNT *Cash*   ACCOUNT NO. *110*

DATE	ITEM	POST. REF.	DEBIT	CREDIT	BALANCE	
					DEBIT	CREDIT

Writing an account title and number on the heading of an account is called **opening an account**. A general ledger account is opened for each account listed on a chart of accounts. Accounts are opened and arranged in a general ledger in the same order as on the chart of accounts.

Cash, account number 110, is the first account on Delgado Web Services' chart of accounts. The Cash account is opened using the steps shown below. The same procedure is used to open all accounts listed on Delgado Web Services' chart of accounts.

↘ Opening an Account in a General Ledger

❶ Write the account title, Cash, after the word *Account* in the heading.

❷ Write the account number, 110, after the words *Account No.* in the heading.

GLOBAL AWARENESS

International Weights and Measures

The primary system of measurement in the United States is the customary system. Among the units of measurement in the customary system are inches, feet, quarts, degrees Fahrenheit, and tablespoons. The United States is the only industrialized country that uses the customary system. Most of the rest of the world uses the International System of Units, which is also known as the metric system. Among the units of measurement in the metric system are centimeters, meters, liters, degrees Celsius, and grams. The metric system is based on a decimal system—like U.S. currency.

Many U.S. industries have converted to the metric system exclusively. Medicine and most pharmaceuticals use the metric system, as does the beverage industry. Other industries specify measurements in both customary and metric systems, such as food products. In the United States, most measurements related to temperature are still given in degrees Fahrenheit. Companies that trade internationally may be forced to list weights and measures in both the customary and the metric system. These companies claim that this dual listing costs them millions of dollars each year. Even so, the United States continues to use the customary system.

CRITICAL THINKING

1. Look at five food packages. List the weights and measures indicated.

2. List arguments both for and against a proposal to convert all U.S. weights and measures to the metric system.

End of Lesson Review

LO1 Construct a chart of accounts for a service business organized as a proprietorship.

LO2 Demonstrate correct principles for numbering accounts.

LO3 Apply file maintenance principles to update a chart of accounts.

LO4 Complete the steps necessary to open general ledger accounts.

Terms Review

ledger

general ledger

account number

file maintenance

opening an account

Audit your understanding

1. Describe the two parts of an account number.
2. List the two steps for opening an account.

Work together 4-1

Preparing a chart of accounts and opening an account

Forms are given in the *Working Papers*. Your instructor will guide you through the following examples.

Isabelle Seville owns a service business called Seville Company, which uses these accounts.

Accts. Pay.—Supply Mart   Cash
Accts. Rec.—L. North   Sales
Accts. Pay.—Anoka Supplies   Supplies
Accts. Rec.—Greg Varez   Supplies Expense
Miscellaneous Expense   Automobile Expense
Insurance Expense   Isabelle Seville, Capital
Prepaid Insurance   Rent Expense
Isabelle Seville, Drawing

1. Prepare a chart of accounts. Arrange any accounts receivable, accounts payable, or expense accounts in alphabetical order. Use 3-digit account numbers and number the accounts within a division by 10s.
2. Two new accounts, Postage Expense and Utilities Expense, are to be added to the chart of accounts prepared in Instruction 1. Assign account numbers to the two new accounts.
3. Using the account form in the *Working Papers*, open Cash.

On your own 4-1

Preparing a chart of accounts and opening an account

Forms are given in the *Working Papers*. Work this problem independently.

Parker Ross owns a service business called Ross Hair Care, which uses these accounts.

Accts. Pay.—Pine Supplies   Parker Ross, Capital
Accts. Rec.—G. Sieler   Cash
Prepaid Insurance   Sales
Parker Ross, Drawing   Supplies
Supplies Expense   Delivery Expense
Insurance Expense   Accts. Pay.—Ely Company
Telephone Expense   Accts. Rec.—T. Ryan

1. Prepare a chart of accounts. Arrange any accounts receivable, accounts payable, or expense accounts in alphabetical order. Use 3-digit account numbers and number the accounts within a division by 10s.
2. Two new accounts, Gasoline Expense and Water Expense, are to be added to the chart of accounts prepared in Instruction 1. Assign account numbers to the two new accounts.
3. Using the account form in the *Working Papers*, open Delivery Expense.

©CANDICE CUSACK, ISTOCK

4-2 Posting from a General Journal to a General Ledger and Proving Cash

LO5 Post amounts from a general journal.

LO6 Demonstrate how to prove cash.

Posting an Amount from the Debit Column of a General Journal **LO5**

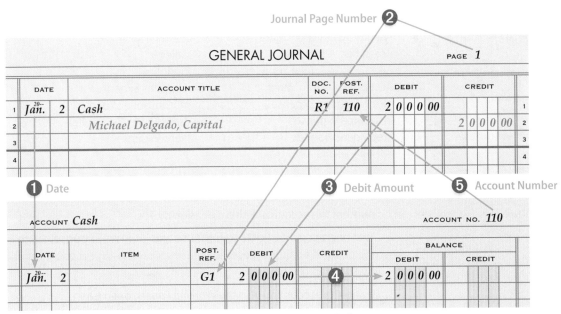

Account Balance

Transferring information from a journal entry to a ledger account is called **posting**. Posting sorts journal entries so that all debits and credits affecting each account are brought together. For example, all changes to Cash are brought together in the Cash account.

Each amount in the Debit and Credit columns of a general journal is posted to the account written in the Account Title column.

The numbers in the Post. Ref. columns of the general ledger account and the general journal serve three purposes: (1) An entry in an account can be traced to its source in a journal. (2) An entry in a journal can be traced to where it was posted in an account. (3) If posting is interrupted, the accounting personnel can easily see which entries in the general journal still need to be posted. A blank in the Post. Ref. column of the journal indicates that posting for that line still needs to be completed. Therefore, the posting reference is always recorded in the journal as the last step in the posting procedure.

Posting an Amount from the Debit Column of a General Journal

❶ Write the date, 20--, Jan. 2, in the Date column of the account, Cash.

❷ Write the journal page number, G1, in the Post. Ref. column of the account. The letter *G* is an abbreviation for the general journal. *Post. Ref.* is an abbreviation for Posting Reference.

❸ Write the debit amount, $2,000.00, in the Debit amount column of the account.

❹ Write the new account balance, $2,000.00, in the Balance Debit column. Because this entry is the first in the Cash account, the previous balance is zero.

	Previous Balance	+	Debit Column Amount	=	New Debit Balance
	$0.00		$2,000.00		$2,000.00

❺ Return to the journal and write the account number, 110, in the Post. Ref. column of the journal.

Posting an Amount from the Credit Column of a General Journal

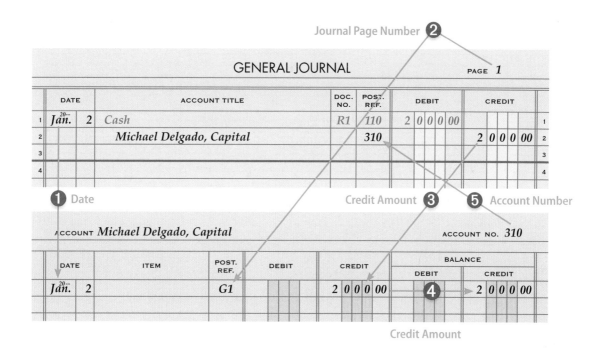

Journal Page Number ②

GENERAL JOURNAL

PAGE 1

	DATE		ACCOUNT TITLE	DOC. NO.	POST. REF.	DEBIT	CREDIT	
1	20-- Jan.	2	Cash	R1	110	2 0 0 0 00		1
2			Michael Delgado, Capital		310		2 0 0 0 00	2
3								3
4								4

① Date

Credit Amount ③   ⑤ Account Number

ACCOUNT Michael Delgado, Capital   ACCOUNT NO. 310

	DATE		ITEM	POST. REF.	DEBIT	CREDIT	BALANCE	
							DEBIT	CREDIT
	20-- Jan.	2		G1		2 0 0 0 00	④	2 0 0 0 00

Credit Amount

As stated previously, each amount in the Debit and Credit columns of a general journal is posted to the account written in the Account Title column. The five steps used to post an amount from the Credit column are described below.

remember Each amount in the Debit and Credit columns of a general journal is posted to the account written in the Account Title column.

Posting an Amount from the Credit Column of a General Journal

① Write the date, 20--, Jan. 2, in the Date column of the account, Michael Delgado, Capital.

② Write the journal page number, G1, in the Post. Ref. column of the account.

③ Write the credit amount, $2,000.00, in the Credit amount column of the account.

④ Write the new account balance, $2,000.00, in the Balance Credit column. Because this entry is the first in the capital account, the previous balance is zero. The new account balance is calculated as shown.

Previous Balance	+	Credit Column Amount	=	New Credit Balance
$0.00		$2,000.00		$2,000.00

⑤ Return to the journal and write the account number, 310, in the Post. Ref. column of the journal.

Posting a Debit Amount to an Account with a Balance

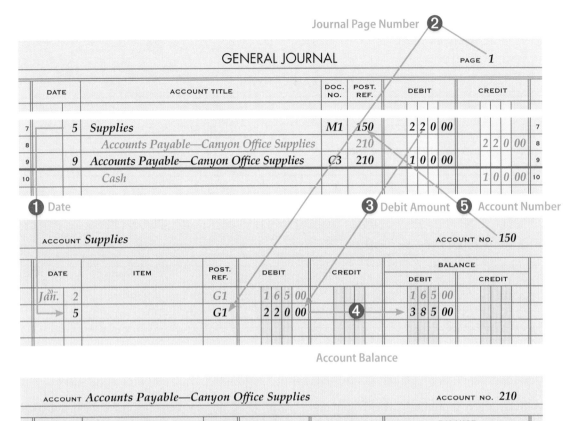

Journal Page Number ②

GENERAL JOURNAL PAGE 1

	DATE	ACCOUNT TITLE	DOC. NO.	POST. REF.	DEBIT	CREDIT	
7	5	*Supplies*	M1	150	2 2 0 00		7
8		*Accounts Payable—Canyon Office Supplies*		210		2 2 0 00	8
9	9	**Accounts Payable—Canyon Office Supplies**	C3	210	1 0 0 00		9
10		*Cash*				1 0 0 00	10

① Date   ③ Debit Amount   ⑤ Account Number

ACCOUNT *Supplies*   ACCOUNT NO. 150

DATE	ITEM	POST. REF.	DEBIT	CREDIT	BALANCE DEBIT	BALANCE CREDIT
Jan. 2		G1	1 6 5 00		1 6 5 00	
5		G1	2 2 0 00	④	3 8 5 00	

Account Balance

ACCOUNT *Accounts Payable—Canyon Office Supplies*   ACCOUNT NO. 210

DATE	ITEM	POST. REF.	DEBIT	CREDIT	BALANCE DEBIT	BALANCE CREDIT
Jan. 5		G1		2 2 0 00		2 2 0 00
① 9		② G1	③ 1 0 0 00	④		1 2 0 00

Only the first set of five steps is shown in the illustration. The second set of five steps is similar to the first set of steps and is described on the next page.

 remember

Two zeros are written in the cents column when an amount is in even dollars, such as $500.00. If the cents column is left blank, doubts may arise later about the correct amount.

➲ Posting a Debit Amount to an Account with a Balance

① Write the date, 5, in the Date column of the account, Supplies. The month and the year are written only once on a page of a ledger account unless the month or year changes.

② Write the journal page number, G1, in the Post. Ref. column of the account.

③ Write the debit amount, $220.00, in the Debit amount column.

④ Write the new account balance, $385.00, in the Balance Debit column. When both the previous balance and a newly posted amount are debits, the new balance is a debit.

Previous Balance	+	Debit Column Amount	=	New Debit Balance
$165.00		$220.00		$385.00

⑤ Return to the journal and write the account number, 150, in the Post. Ref. column of the journal.

① Write the date, **9**, in the Date column of the account, Accounts Payable—Canyon Office Supplies.

② Write the journal page number, **G1**, in the Post. Ref. column of the account.

③ Write the debit amount, **$100.00**, in the Debit amount column of the account.

④ Write the new account balance, **$120.00**, in the Balance Credit column. Whenever the credits in an account exceed the debits, the balance is a credit. Whenever the debits in an account exceed the credits, the balance is a debit.

Previous Balance	–	Debit Column Amount	=	New Credit Balance
$220.00		$100.00		$120.00

⑤ Return to the journal and write the account number, **210**, in the Post. Ref. column of the journal.

THINK LIKE AN ACCOUNTANT

Controlling Operating Expenses

Velcor Industries has over 70 expense accounts in its chart of accounts. Each month, the computerized accounting system generates a list of the accounts which includes the year-to-date account balance and the annual amount budgeted for the year.

The managers of the business want to receive a monthly report showing how effectively the business is controlling its expenses. For example, if the company expected to spend $12,000 on insurance for the entire year, it should only have spent $5,000 through May.

OPEN THE SPREADSHEET TLA_CH04

1. Follow the directions on the Instructions tab.

2. Prepare an analysis that highlights the five expense accounts that, as of May 31, are most over budget, as measured by the percent of the budgeted amount.

Journal Page with Posting Completed

	DATE		ACCOUNT TITLE	DOC. NO.	POST. REF.	DEBIT	CREDIT	
						GENERAL JOURNAL	PAGE 1	
1	Jan.	2	Cash	R1	110	2 0 0 0 00		1
2			Michael Delgado, Capital		310		2 0 0 0 00	2
3		2	Supplies	C1	150	1 6 5 00		3
4			Cash		110		1 6 5 00	4
5		3	Prepaid Insurance	C2	160	9 0 0 00		5
6			Cash		110		9 0 0 00	6
7		5	Supplies	M1	150	2 2 0 00		7
8			Accounts Payable—Canyon Office Supplies		210		2 2 0 00	8
9		9	Accounts Payable—Canyon Office Supplies	C3	210	1 0 0 00		9
10			Cash		110		1 0 0 00	10
11		10	Cash	T10	110	1 1 0 0 00		11
12			Sales		410		1 1 0 0 00	12
13		12	Accounts Receivable—Main Street Services	S1	130	5 0 0 00		13
14			Sales		410		5 0 0 00	14
15		12	Communications Expense	C4	530	8 0 00		15
16			Cash		110		8 0 00	16
17		15	Equipment Rental Expense	C5	540	4 0 0 00		17
18			Cash		110		4 0 0 00	18
19		16	Cash	R2	110	2 0 0 00		19
20			Accounts Receivable—Main Street Services		130		2 0 0 00	20
21		16	Michael Delgado, Drawing	C6	320	3 5 0 00		21
22			Cash		110		3 5 0 00	22
23		16	Accounts Receivable—Valley Landscaping	S2	140	4 0 0 00		23
24			Sales		410		4 0 0 00	24
25		17	Advertising Expense	C7	510	3 8 3 00		25
26			Cash		110		3 8 3 00	26
27		18	Cash	T18	110	5 3 5 00		27
28			Sales		410		5 3 5 00	28
29		19	Petty Cash	C8	120	1 0 0 00		29
30			Cash		110		1 0 0 00	30
31		19	Supplies	M2	150	1 0 5 00		31
32			Accounts Payable—Mountain Graphic Arts		220		1 0 5 00	32
33		22	Equipment Rental Expense	C9	540	5 1 0 00		33
34			Cash		110		5 1 0 00	34
35								35
36								36

Page 1 of Delgado Web Services' January general journal, after all posting has been completed, is shown above. Notice that the Post. Ref. column is completely filled in with account numbers.

remember

Posting will go smoothly if you consistently follow the five steps of posting. The last step in posting is to put the account number in the Post. Ref. column of the general journal.

General Ledger with Posting Completed

Delgado Web Services' general ledger, after all posting from the January journal is completed, is shown here and on the next several pages.

The use of the accounts Income Summary, Insurance Expense, and Supplies Expense is described in Chapter 6.

DATE	ITEM	POST. REF.	DEBIT	CREDIT	BALANCE DEBIT	BALANCE CREDIT
Jan. 2		G1	2 000 00		2 000 00	
2		G1		1 65 00	1 835 00	
3		G1		9 00 00	9 35 00	
9		G1		1 00 00	8 35 00	
10		G1	1 1 00 00		1 935 00	
12		G1		8 0 00	1 855 00	
15		G1		4 00 00	1 455 00	
16		G1	2 00 00		1 655 00	
16		G1		3 50 00	1 305 00	
17		G1		3 83 00	9 22 00	
18		G1	5 35 00		1 457 00	
19		G1		1 00 00	1 357 00	
22		G1		5 10 00	8 47 00	
24		G2	1 3 20 00		2 167 00	
28		G2		1 30 00	2 037 00	
29		G2	1 2 80 00		3 317 00	
31		G2		2 5 00	3 292 00	
31		G2		3 5 00	3 257 00	
31		G2		8 00 00	2 457 00	
31		G2	6 85 00		3 142 00	
31		G2		5 45 00	2 597 00	

ACCOUNT Cash — ACCOUNT NO. 110

DATE	ITEM	POST. REF.	DEBIT	CREDIT	BALANCE DEBIT	BALANCE CREDIT
Jan. 19		G1	1 00 00		1 00 00	

ACCOUNT Petty Cash — ACCOUNT NO. 120

A General Ledger after Posting Has Been Completed (continued)

ACCOUNT: Accounts Receivable—Main Street Services   ACCOUNT NO. 130

DATE	ITEM	POST. REF.	DEBIT	CREDIT	BALANCE DEBIT	BALANCE CREDIT
Jan. 20-- 12		G1	5 0 0 00		5 0 0 00	
16		G1		2 0 0 00	3 0 0 00	

ACCOUNT: Accounts Receivable—Valley Landscaping   ACCOUNT NO. 140

DATE	ITEM	POST. REF.	DEBIT	CREDIT	BALANCE DEBIT	BALANCE CREDIT
Jan. 20-- 16		G1	4 0 0 00		4 0 0 00	

ACCOUNT: Supplies   ACCOUNT NO. 150

DATE	ITEM	POST. REF.	DEBIT	CREDIT	BALANCE DEBIT	BALANCE CREDIT
Jan. 20-- 2		G1	1 6 5 00		1 6 5 00	
5		G1	2 2 0 00		3 8 5 00	
19		G1	1 0 5 00		4 9 0 00	
28		G2	1 3 0 00		6 2 0 00	

ACCOUNT: Prepaid Insurance   ACCOUNT NO. 160

DATE	ITEM	POST. REF.	DEBIT	CREDIT	BALANCE DEBIT	BALANCE CREDIT
Jan. 20-- 3		G1	9 0 0 00		9 0 0 00	

ACCOUNT: Accounts Payable—Canyon Office Supplies   ACCOUNT NO. 210

DATE	ITEM	POST. REF.	DEBIT	CREDIT	BALANCE DEBIT	BALANCE CREDIT
Jan. 20-- 5		G1		2 2 0 00		2 2 0 00
9		G1	1 0 0 00			1 2 0 00

ACCOUNT: Accounts Payable—Mountain Graphic Arts   ACCOUNT NO. 220

DATE	ITEM	POST. REF.	DEBIT	CREDIT	BALANCE DEBIT	BALANCE CREDIT
Jan. 20-- 19		G1		1 0 5 00		1 0 5 00

A General Ledger after Posting Has Been Completed (continued)

ACCOUNT Michael Delgado, Capital — ACCOUNT NO. 310

DATE	ITEM	POST. REF.	DEBIT	CREDIT	BALANCE DEBIT	BALANCE CREDIT
Jan. 2 (20--)		G1		2 000 00		2 000 00

ACCOUNT Michael Delgado, Drawing — ACCOUNT NO. 320

DATE	ITEM	POST. REF.	DEBIT	CREDIT	BALANCE DEBIT	BALANCE CREDIT
Jan. 16 (20--)		G1	3 5 0 00		3 5 0 00	
31		G2	8 0 0 00		1 1 5 0 00	

ACCOUNT Income Summary — ACCOUNT NO. 330

DATE	ITEM	POST. REF.	DEBIT	CREDIT	BALANCE DEBIT	BALANCE CREDIT

ACCOUNT Sales — ACCOUNT NO. 410

DATE	ITEM	POST. REF.	DEBIT	CREDIT	BALANCE DEBIT	BALANCE CREDIT
Jan. 10 (20--)		G1		1 1 0 0 00		1 1 0 0 00
12		G1		5 0 0 00		1 6 0 0 00
16		G1		4 0 0 00		2 0 0 0 00
18		G1		5 3 5 00		2 5 3 5 00
24		G2		1 3 2 0 00		3 8 5 5 00
29		G2		1 2 8 0 00		5 1 3 5 00
31		G2		6 8 5 00		5 8 2 0 00

ACCOUNT Advertising Expense — ACCOUNT NO. 510

DATE	ITEM	POST. REF.	DEBIT	CREDIT	BALANCE DEBIT	BALANCE CREDIT
Jan. 17 (20--)		G1	3 8 3 00		3 8 3 00	
31		G2	1 4 00		3 9 7 00	

A General Ledger after Posting Has Been Completed (continued)

ACCOUNT *Cash Short and Over*   ACCOUNT NO. **520**

DATE	ITEM	POST. REF.	DEBIT	CREDIT	BALANCE DEBIT	BALANCE CREDIT
Jan. 31		G2	1 00		1 00	

ACCOUNT *Communications Expense*   ACCOUNT NO. **530**

DATE	ITEM	POST. REF.	DEBIT	CREDIT	BALANCE DEBIT	BALANCE CREDIT
Jan. 12		G1	8 0 00		8 0 00	

ACCOUNT *Equipment Rental Expense*   ACCOUNT NO. **540**

DATE	ITEM	POST. REF.	DEBIT	CREDIT	BALANCE DEBIT	BALANCE CREDIT
Jan. 15		G1	4 0 0 00		4 0 0 00	
22		G1	5 1 0 00		9 1 0 00	
31		G2	5 4 5 00		1 4 5 5 00	

ACCOUNT *Insurance Expense*   ACCOUNT NO. **550**

DATE	ITEM	POST. REF.	DEBIT	CREDIT	BALANCE DEBIT	BALANCE CREDIT

ACCOUNT *Miscellaneous Expense*   ACCOUNT NO. **560**

DATE	ITEM	POST. REF.	DEBIT	CREDIT	BALANCE DEBIT	BALANCE CREDIT
Jan. 31		G2	2 5 00		2 5 00	
31		G2	2 0 00		4 5 00	

ACCOUNT *Supplies Expense*   ACCOUNT NO. **570**

DATE	ITEM	POST. REF.	DEBIT	CREDIT	BALANCE DEBIT	BALANCE CREDIT

A General Ledger after Posting Has Been Completed (concluded)

Proving Cash LO6

Check stub (left):

NO. **14** $ _____

Date _____ 20 ___

To _____

For _____

_____

BALANCE BROUGHT FORWARD	2,597	00
AMOUNT DEPOSITED _Date_		
SUBTOTAL		
AMOUNT THIS CHECK		
BALANCE CARRIED FORWARD		

Ledger account (right):

| ACCOUNT | Cash | | | | | ACCOUNT NO. | **110** |

DATE	ITEM	POST. REF.	DEBIT	CREDIT	BALANCE	
					DEBIT	CREDIT
31		G2		5 4 5 00	2 5 9 7 00	

Determining that the amount of cash agrees with the balance of the **Cash** account in the accounting records is called **proving cash**. Cash can be proved at any time Delgado Web Services wishes to verify the accuracy of the cash records. However, Delgado Web Services always proves cash at the end of a month. Delgado Web Services compares the cash balance as shown in the checkbook with the cash balance in the **Cash** account. If the two balances equal, cash is proved.

remember Whenever the debits in an account exceed the credits, the account balance is a debit. Whenever the credits in an account exceed the debits, the account balance is a credit.

WHY ACCOUNTING?

How Much Will You Pay for That Free Breakfast?

When you are looking for a hotel, what factors do you consider? Is location most important to you? Do you choose the lowest cost hotel? Are you willing to pay extra for an indoor pool? How do you feel about a hotel that accepts pets?

Hotels offer a wide variety of "extras" such as free breakfasts, on-site restaurants, workout facilities, etc. These extras are called *amenities*. Just as you consider which amenities are important to you and for which you are willing to pay more, so too, the hotel management must decide which amenities it wants to offer. This decision is usually based on how much

each amenity costs and which amenities the hotel's customers want.

A hotel that focuses on low cost may decide that the cost of a free breakfast would increase room rates so much that it would ultimately decrease business for the hotel. On the other hand, a hotel that focuses on service may be able to offer a wonderful free breakfast and raise room rates even more than the actual cost of the breakfast.

CRITICAL THINKING

1. What costs should hotel management consider when calculating the per-person cost of breakfast?
2. If the average cost of a breakfast is $8.00, why might a hotel only increase its room rates $6.00 once it offers a free breakfast?

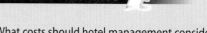

End of Lesson Review

LO5 Post amounts from a general journal.

LO6 Demonstrate how to prove cash.

Terms Review

posting

proving cash

Audit your understanding

1. List the five steps of posting from the general journal to the general ledger.

2. When both debit and credit amounts have been posted to an account, what determines whether the balance is a debit or a credit?

3. Which two amounts are compared when proving cash?

Work together 4-2

Posting to a general ledger

A completed journal and general ledger accounts are given in the *Working Papers*. Your instructor will guide you through the following example.

Omar Boje owns a service business that uses the following accounts.

Assets	**Owner's Equity**
110 Cash	310 Omar Boje, Capital
120 Accounts Receivable—Dan Carroll	320 Omar Boje, Drawing
130 Supplies	**Revenue**
140 Prepaid Insurance	410 Sales
Liabilities	**Expenses**
210 Accounts Payable—Ready Supply	510 Rent Expense

1. Post all the entries in the general journal.
2. Prove cash. The balance on the next available check stub is $1,720.00.

On your own 4-2

Posting to a general ledger

A completed journal and general ledger accounts are given in the *Working Papers*. Work this problem independently.

Helen Orr owns a service business which uses the following accounts.

Assets	**Owner's Equity**
110 Cash	310 Helen Orr, Capital
120 Accounts Receivable—K. Green	320 Helen Orr, Drawing
130 Supplies	**Revenue**
140 Prepaid Insurance	410 Sales
Liabilities	**Expenses**
210 Accounts Payable—Stein Company	510 Advertising Expense

1. Post all the entries in the general journal.
2. Prove cash. The balance on the next available check stub is $2,392.00.

LESSON
4-3 Journalizing Correcting Entries and Correcting Posting Errors

LO7 Analyze incorrect journal entries and prepare correcting entries.
LO8 Demonstrate how to correct errors made during the posting process.

Memorandum for a Correcting Entry LO7

DELGADO WEB SERVICES
MEMORANDUM No. 15
25402 Rimrock Road
Billings, MT 59102-1820

A cash payment of $120.00 for Advertising, March 31, 20--, was debited in error to Miscellaneous Expense

Signed: Michael Delgado   Date: April 17, 20--

Errors discovered before entries are posted may be corrected by ruling through the item, as described in Chapter 3. However, a transaction may have been improperly journalized and posted to the ledger. In such a case, the incorrect journal entry should be corrected with an additional journal entry, called a **correcting entry**.

If an accounting error is discovered, a memorandum is prepared as the source document describing the correction to be made.

Journal Entry to Record a Correcting Entry

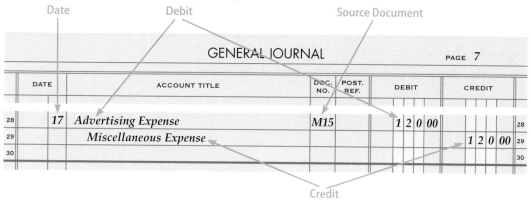

Date   Debit   Source Document

GENERAL JOURNAL   PAGE **7**

DATE	ACCOUNT TITLE	DOC. NO.	POST. REF.	DEBIT	CREDIT	
28	17 Advertising Expense	M15		1 2 0 00		28
29	Miscellaneous Expense				1 2 0 00	29
30						30

Credit

April 17. Discovered that a payment of cash for advertising in March was journalized and posted in error as a debit to Miscellaneous Expense instead of Advertising Expense, $120.00. Memorandum No. 15.

Advertising Expense
⬆ 120.00

Miscellaneous Expense
⬇ 120.00

To correct the error, an entry is made to add $120.00 to the Advertising Expense account. The entry must also deduct $120.00 from the Miscellaneous Expense account.

Because the Advertising Expense account has a normal debit balance, Advertising Expense is debited for $120.00 to show the increase in this expense account. The Miscellaneous Expense account also has a normal debit balance. Therefore, Miscellaneous Expense is credited for $120.00 to show the decrease in this expense account.

Correcting an Error in Posting to the Wrong Account LO8

ACCOUNT *Supplies*   **ACCOUNT NO.** *150*

DATE	ITEM	POST. REF.	DEBIT	CREDIT	BALANCE DEBIT	BALANCE CREDIT
Feb. 20-- 2		G3	2 5 0 00		2 5 0 00	
15		G3	1 5 0 00		4 0 0 00	
② → 12		G4	1 0 0 00		5 0 0 00	

Correct Entry **②**

ACCOUNT *Prepaid Insurance*   **ACCOUNT NO.** *160*

DATE	ITEM	POST. REF.	DEBIT	CREDIT	BALANCE DEBIT	BALANCE CREDIT
Feb. 20-- 3		G3	3 2 5 00		3 2 5 00	
① → ~~12~~		~~G4~~	~~1 0 0 00~~		~~4 2 5 00~~	

Incorrect Entry **①**

Sometimes, an error in posting is made but not discovered until additional postings have been made to the account. For example, assume that a debit to Supplies was incorrectly posted as a debit to Prepaid Insurance.

A line should be drawn through the incorrect posting in the Prepaid Insurance account. The correct posting should be made on the next available line in the correct account, Supplies.

Correcting an Error in Posting to the Wrong Account

① Draw a line through the entire incorrect entry.

② Record the posting in the correct account. Recalculate the account balance.

remember

Errors are corrected in a way that does not cause doubts about what the correct information is. If an error is recorded, cancel the error by neatly drawing a line through the incorrect item. Write the correct items immediately above the canceled item.

Correcting an Incorrect Amount and an Amount Posted to the Wrong Column

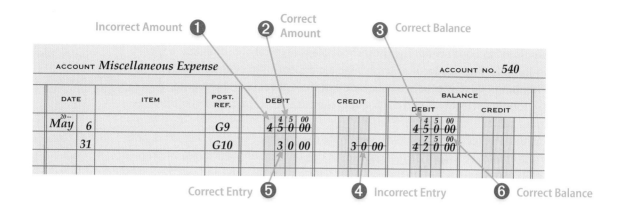

① Incorrect Amount   ② Correct Amount   ③ Correct Balance

DATE	ITEM	POST. REF.	DEBIT	CREDIT	BALANCE DEBIT	BALANCE CREDIT
May 6		G9	4 5 0 00		4 5 0 00	
31		G10	3 0 00	3 0 00	4 2 0 00	

(ACCOUNT Miscellaneous Expense — ACCOUNT NO. 540. DEBIT entry shows correction "45" over "450"; BALANCE DEBIT shows "75" over "420".)

⑤ Correct Entry   ④ Incorrect Entry   ⑥ Correct Balance

Other errors can be made when posting. An incorrect amount may be entered in the account. An amount may be entered in the wrong column. All corrections should be made in a way that leaves no question as to the correct amount.

⬎ Correcting an Incorrect Amount Posted in an Account

① Draw a line through the incorrect amount.

② Write the correct amount just above the correction in the same space.

③ Recalculate the account balance.

⬎ Correcting an Amount Posted to the Wrong Column

④ Draw a line through the incorrect item in the account.

⑤ Record the posting in the correct amount column.

⑥ Recalculate the account balance.

remember

General ledger accounts are part of the permanent records of a business and entries in the accounts are recorded in ink. Any corrections that need to be made should also be recorded in ink.

Skimming at a Yogurt Shop

Anna's Yogurt Shop is a classic example of a small business. The shop has one location, one cash register, and one owner. The shop's floor plan is typical of businesses in this market. The yogurt machines are located just behind a glass enclosed counter containing an assortment of toppings. Customers place their orders at the right side of the counter, drift to the left to make topping selections, and check out at the left end of the counter. In most cases, a single employee serves a customer from order to check out.

A basic principle for preventing fraud is to segregate the duties of custody, authority, and reporting. No one employee should be responsible for two or more of these duties. At Anna's Yogurt Shop, employees have access to the yogurt and toppings (custody) and sell these items to customers (authority).

Owner Anna Sue Preston is fully aware that this lack of segregation of duties places her business at risk. Employees are very familiar with the pricing of the shop's limited menu. Rather than using the cash register, employees could mentally calculate the total sales amount. The money taken from the customer could go in the employee's pocket rather than the cash register. This type of fraud is known as *skimming*. Despite this risk, Anna Sue believes that the one-on-one service provided by her employees enhances the friendly atmosphere that has made her shop a local landmark.

Anna Sue contracts with a local janitorial service to clean the store each morning. Unknown to shop employees, the janitorial service has also been instructed to measure the volume of product (yogurt and toppings). The daily difference in product volumes indicates how much product was actually sold. For example, selling ten small cones should use 60 ounces of yogurt and ten cones.

Anna Sue has asked you to perform an analysis to determine if any of her employees are skimming sales. She has provided you with data for the past four months. The data include the quantity sales of each menu item, the names of the two employees working that day, and the actual product usage as determined by the janitorial service. As a result of product spills and breakage, a 3.0% difference between the actual and expected volume of product used is considered acceptable.

INSTRUCTIONS

Open the spreadsheet FA_CH04. Click the Instructions tab. Follow the instructions and then provide Anna Sue with answers to the following questions:

1. Does an analysis of yogurt usage provide any evidence to suggest that an employee is involved in a skimming fraud?
2. Does an analysis of toppings, sugar cones, and waffle cones support the evidence identified in your analysis of yogurt usage?
3. Does this evidence prove that an employee is involved in a skimming fraud?
4. Suggest what action Anna Sue should take as a result of your analysis.

LO7 Analyze incorrect journal entries and prepare correcting entries.

LO8 Demonstrate how to correct errors made during the posting process.

Term Review

correcting entry

▶ ## Audit your understanding

1. What is a correcting entry?

2. When is a correcting entry necessary?

3. What are the three steps for correcting an incorrect amount posted to an account?

4. What are the three steps for correcting an amount posted to an incorrect column?

▶ ## Work together 4-3

Journalizing correcting entries and correcting posting errors

A journal and general ledger accounts are given in the *Working Papers*. Your instructor will guide you through the following example.

Transactions:

Dec. 1. Discovered that a transaction for supplies bought last month was journalized and posted in error as a debit to Prepaid Insurance instead of Supplies, $75.00. M15.

1. Discovered that a transaction for rent expense for last month was journalized and posted in error as a debit to Repair Expense instead of Rent Expense, $900.00. M16.

1. Journalize each correcting entry discovered during December of the current year. Use page 21 of the journal.

2. It was also discovered that two posting errors were made in the owner's drawing account. The Nov. 15 entry amount should have been $540.00. The Nov. 30 entry included a debit to the drawing account for $400.00 that was posted in error as a credit. Using the account provided in the *Working Papers* and the information given, correct the two posting errors.

▶ ## On your own 4-3

Journalizing correcting entries and correcting posting errors

A journal and general ledger accounts are given in the *Working Papers*. Work this problem independently.

Transactions:

July 1. Discovered that a transaction for supplies bought last month was journalized and posted in error as a debit to Prepaid Insurance instead of Supplies, $110.00. M23.

1. Discovered that a transaction for advertising expense for last month was journalized and posted in error as a debit to Miscellaneous Expense instead of Advertising Expense, $440.00. M24.

1. Journalize each correcting entry discovered during July of the current year. Use page 11 of the journal.

2. It was also discovered that two posting errors were made in the owner's capital account. The June 1 entry amount should have been $25,000.00. The June 15 entry included a credit to the capital account for $1,000.00 that was posted in error as a debit. Using the account provided in the *Working Papers* and the information given, correct the two posting errors.

©CANDICE CUSACK, ISTOCK

A Look at Accounting Software

Managing Accounts

In a manual system, the chart of accounts serves primarily as a reference document. All the accounts are written on paper forms, so it is easy to see what accounts are in use. Transactions are written in the lines of the account forms.

In a computerized accounting system, accounts are key-entered. Information about each account is stored in the computer's memory. When a transaction is keyed into the system, the user need only enter the number of each account. Related information, such as the account title and type, are retrieved from the computer's memory.

Note that the Income Summary account is missing. Computerized accounting systems do not need an Income Summary account. You will learn how that account is used in manual accounting systems in Chapter 8.

DELGADO WEB SERVICES
Chart of Accounts

Acct. No.	Account Title	Type ❶	Active? ❸
110	Cash	Asset	Yes
120	Petty Cash	Asset	Yes
130	Accounts Receivable—Main Street Services	Asset	Yes
140	Accounts Receivable—Valley Landscaping	Asset	Yes
150	Supplies	Asset	Yes
160	Prepaid Insurance	Asset	Yes
210	Accounts Payable—Canyon Office Supplies	Liability	Yes
220	Accounts Payable—Mountain Graphic Arts	Liability	Yes
310	Michael Delgado, Capital	Equity	Yes
320	Michael Delgado, Drawing	Equity	Yes
410	Sales	Revenue	Yes
510	Advertising Expense	Expense	Yes
510	Cash Short and Over	Expense	Yes
530	Communications Expense	Expense	Yes
540	Equipment Rental Expense	Expense	Yes
550	Insurance Expense	Expense	Yes
560	Miscellaneous Expense	Expense	Yes
570	Supplies Expense	Expense	Yes

(❷ brackets accounts 130 and 140)

❶ In a manual system, the chart of accounts would be a paper document like the one for Delgado Web Services on page 94. Each division has a heading, such as Assets. In a computerized system, the account type tells the system whether to add or subtract amounts debited or credited to each account.

❷ Computerized accounting systems allow users to set up different types of accounts and assign a range of numbers to each type. In this example, the range for Assets would probably be 100–199. The range for Liabilities would be 200–299, and so on.

❸ In a manual system, when an account is no longer needed it simply is not used anymore. In a computerized system, inactive accounts can clutter up reports with a lot of unnecessary lines showing zero amounts. If an account is marked "Inactive," it can no longer be used. When reports are run, the user can choose to include or exclude inactive accounts.

Chapter Summary

General ledger accounts are numbered using a numbering system specific to each company. The accounts used by a company and the numbers assigned to each account are recorded in a document called a chart of accounts. The journal is used to record all transactions in order by date. In addition to recording entries in the journal, amounts must be posted to general ledger accounts.

Posting transfers all information about an account into that account. Each amount in the Debit and Credit columns of a general journal is posted to the account written in the Account Title column. If errors are made in journal entries or in posting, corrections should be made following standard accounting principles. All corrections should clearly indicate the correct information.

Chart of Accounts

Each company designs its chart of accounts to meet its unique needs. Delgado Web Services, the company described in this section of the textbook, has a relatively simple chart of accounts, with a small number of accounts. Therefore, Delgado Web Services can use a 3-digit account number for each account. A company with more accounts may need to use a 4- or 5-digit account number for each account. The numbering system used by the company should ensure that each account can be assigned a unique number.

When setting up a chart of accounts, a company does not have to use a straight series of numbers. If a company has several departments, it may choose to use account numbers such as 12-150. The first two digits (12) can be used to designate a specific department. The last three digits (150) identify a unique account within that department. If this company has many departments or many accounts within each department, it may have to increase the number of digits in the account, such as 123-4567.

A large corporation made up of smaller companies may have one chart of accounts for the entire corporation. If the managers of the corporation also want to be able to separate out the accounts for each company, they may choose to set up the account numbers in an xx-yyy-zzzz format. The first two digits (xx) would be a unique number for each company, the second set of numbers (yyy) refers to a department number, and the third set of numbers (zzzz) is a unique account.

Another example would be a company that manufactures goods for its customers. Such a company may want to include the job order number in each account number, so that it can easily trace the cost of each job.

Many possible systems can be followed when assigning account numbers. A company should consider future growth when first setting up a system so that it can avoid having to renumber accounts at a later date.

INSTRUCTIONS

Develop a chart of accounts for an imaginary business. Write a detailed description of the company and a rationale for the account numbering system you have developed.

©MAKHNACH_M/ISTOCK

Apply Your Understanding

INSTRUCTIONS: Download problem instructions for Excel, QuickBooks, and Peachtree from the textbook companion website at www.C21accounting.com.

4-1 Application Problem: Preparing a chart of accounts and opening an account LO1, 2, 3, 4

Kajal Chauhan owns a service business called Deters Duplicating, which uses the following accounts.

Accounts Receivable—J. Chin
Accounts Receivable—A. Karn
Accounts Payable—River Company
Accounts Payable—Sharma Supply
Kajal Chauhan, Capital
Kajal Chauhan, Drawing
Prepaid Insurance
Advertising Expense

Postage Expense
Charitable Expense
Rent Expense
Insurance Expense
Supplies
Sales
Cash

Instructions:

1. Prepare a chart of accounts similar to the one described in this chapter. Arrange any accounts receivable, accounts payable, or expense accounts in alphabetical order. Use 3-digit account numbers and number the accounts within a division by 10s.

2. Two new accounts, Delivery Expense and Telephone Expense, are to be added to the chart of accounts prepared in Part 1. Assign account numbers to the two new accounts.

3. Using the forms in the *Working Papers*, open the Prepaid Insurance and the Postage Expense accounts.

4-2 Application Problem: Posting from a general journal to a general ledger and proving cash LO5, 6

A completed journal and general ledger accounts are given in the *Working Papers*.

Jing Suen owns a service business that uses the accounts given in the *Working Papers*.

Instructions:

1. Post all the entries in the general journal.

2. Prove cash. The balance on the next available check stub is $3,319.00.

4-3 Application Problem: Journalizing correcting entries and correcting posting errors LO7, 8

The following errors were discovered after the incorrect entries were already journalized and posted.

Transactions:

Aug. 1. Discovered that a transaction for utilities expense was journalized and posted in error as a debit to Repairs Expense instead of Utilities Expense, $530.00. M66.

5. Discovered that a cash investment by Vivian Lynum, owner, was journalized and posted in error as a credit to Sales instead of Vivian Lynum, Capital, $1,200.00. M67.

Instructions:

1. Journalize each correcting entry discovered during August of the current year. Use page 15 of the journal given in the *Working Papers*.

2. It was also discovered that two posting errors were made in the Supplies account. The July 6 entry amount should have been $360.00. The July 30 entry included a credit to the Supplies account for $140.00 that should have been a debit. Using the account provided in the *Working Papers* and the information given, correct the two posting errors.

4-M Mastery Problem: Journalizing transactions and posting to a general ledger LO3, 4, 5

Brian Ford owns a service business called Ford Lawn and Garden. Ford Lawn and Garden's general ledger accounts are given in the *Working Papers*.

Transactions:

Feb. 1. Received cash from owner as an investment, $11,000.00. R1.
  3. Paid cash for supplies, $800.00. C1.
  5. Received cash from sales, $1,800.00. T5.
  6. Sold services on account to Clara Walthers, $560.00. S1.
  9. Paid cash for rent, $1,200.00. C2.
  11. Paid cash for miscellaneous expense, $100.00. C3.
  13. Bought supplies on account from Corner Supplies, $480.00. M1.
  13. Received cash from sales, $860.00. T13.
  16. Paid cash for advertising, $286.00. C4.
  18. Paid cash on account to Corner Supplies, $280.00. C5.
  20. Paid cash for electric bill, $460.00. C6.
  20. Received cash on account from Clara Walthers, $300.00. R2.
  25. Paid cash for supplies, $300.00. C7.
  27. Paid cash for supplies, $160.00. C8.
  27. Received cash from sales, $4,200.00. T27.
  28. Paid cash to owner for personal use, $1,000.00. C9.
  28. Received cash from sales, $220.00. T28.

Instructions:

1. Open an account for Utilities Expense. Use the 3-digit numbering system described in the chapter.

2. Journalize the transactions completed during February of the current year. Use page 1 of a journal. Source documents are abbreviated as follows: check, C; memorandum, M; receipt, R; sales invoice, S; calculator tape, T.

3. Post from the general journal to the general ledger.

4. Prove cash. The balance on the next unused check stub is $13,794.00.

Peachtree

1. Journalize and post transactions to the general journal.
2. From the menu bar, select Reports & Forms; General Ledger.
3. Make the selections to print the general journal and general ledger.

Quick Books

1. Journalize and post transactions to the journal.
2. From the menu bar, select Reports; Accountant & Taxes.
3. Make the selections to print the journal and general ledger.

Excel

1. Journalize transactions in the general journal.
2. Post to the general ledger.
3. From the office button menu, select Print.
4. Print the worksheet.

AAONLINE

1. Go to www.cengage.com/login
2. Click on **AA Online** to access.
3. Go to the online assignment and follow the instructions.

4-S Source Documents Problem: Journalizing transactions and posting to a general ledger LO5, 6

Instructions:

1. The source documents and general journal for Darlene's Music Studio are given in the *Working Papers*. Use page 1 of the general journal to journalize the transactions for September.

2. Post from the journal to the general ledger.

3. Prove cash. The beginning cash balance on September 1 is zero. The balance on the next unused check stub is $3,120.00.

Peachtree

1. Journalize and post transactions to the general journal.
2. From the menu bar, select Reports & Forms; General Ledger.
3. Make the selections to print the general journal and general ledger.

Quick Books

1. Journalize and post transactions to the journal.
2. From the menu bar, select Reports; Accountant & Taxes.
3. Make the selections to print the journal and general ledger.

Excel

1. Journalize transactions to the general journal.
2. Post to general ledger.
3. From the office button menu, select Print.
4. Print the worksheet.

4-C Challenge Problem: Posting using a variation of the general journal LO5, 6

Lian Liu owns a service business that uses a general journal that is different from the journal used in this chapter. The May general journal and general ledger accounts (before posting) are given in the *Working Papers*.

Instructions:

1. Post from the general journal to the general ledger.
2. Prove cash. The balance on the next unused check stub is $8,525.00.

21st Century Skills

Creative Accounts

Theme: Financial, Economic, Business, and Entrepreneurial Literacy

Skills: Creativity and Innovation

PARTNERSHIP FOR
21ST CENTURY SKILLS

A chart of accounts is unique to each business. Accounts are created to fit the needs of the business. For example, the sources of revenue for a house-painting business might be simply sales. Revenue for a major-league baseball team might have several sales accounts. The team's revenue accounts might consist of ticket sales, concessions, parking, and souvenirs.

APPLICATION

Choose a fictitious character or person. You might use a character from a book or nursery rhyme or someone from history. Create account names that pertain to this character's business. Have fun, and put some creative thought into your accounts using the following guidelines.

a. Account numbers should have three digits.

b. Include five asset accounts, five liability accounts, one capital account, one drawing account, three revenue accounts, and five expense accounts.

Analyzing Nike's financial statements

When the financial statements of a company are inspected by the auditors, the auditors are investigating whether the company followed generally accepted accounting principles (GAAP) in preparing the financial statements. The auditors report their findings in a letter.

INSTRUCTIONS

Use the Report of Independent Registered Public Accounting Firm on page B-4 in Appendix B to answer the following questions.

1. To whom is the letter addressed?

2. What company performs an independent audit for Nike?

3. When was the letter dated?

Chapter 5 Cash Control Systems

LEARNING OBJECTIVES

After studying Chapter 5, in addition to defining key terms, you will be able to:

LO1 Record a deposit on a check stub.

LO2 Endorse checks using blank, special, and restrictive endorsements.

LO3 Prepare a check stub and a check.

LO4 Complete a bank statement reconciliation.

LO5 Record and journalize a bank service charge.

LO6 Complete recordkeeping for a dishonored check.

LO7 Journalize an electronic funds transfer.

LO8 Journalize a debit card transaction.

LO9 Establish a petty cash fund.

LO10 Prepare a petty cash report.

LO11 Replenish a petty cash fund.

©DANIEL KOUREY, ISTOCK/©JIM PRUITT, ISTOCK

EDYTA PAWLOWSKA/SHUTTERSTOCK.COM

Accounting In The Real World
Hard Rock

Anyone who has ever visited a Hard Rock Cafe knows it isn't just about the food. Although the food is known for being consistently high quality regardless of location, the food is only one part of the Hard Rock experience. Its website describes the company this way: "Hard Rock isn't just a name; it's a culture." The culture that is Hard Rock is summed up in its mission statement: "To spread the spirit of rock 'n' roll by creating authentic experiences that rock." Hard Rock's motto "Love All - Serve All" reflects its mission statement.

The spirit of rock 'n' roll has many aspects. Rock memorabilia is an important part of the spirit. Each of the 134 cafes in over 50 countries features rock memorabilia—over 70,000 pieces in total. It all started with a red Fender guitar, donated by its owner, Eric Clapton. The collection ranges from a lock of hair to a five-ton psychedelic bus and is still growing. If your dining experience is a pleasant one, you can take a piece of it home with you by shopping at the on-site store for articles that range from collector pins to one-of-a-kind guitars.

Hard Rock spreads the spirit of rock 'n' roll by supporting music in many ways. Annually, Hard Rock features the Artist of the Year on its website. The company sponsors concerts and performances around the world. Under its motto "All is One," Hard Rock supports music and music education, and partners with many music industry organizations and museums.

The spirit of rock 'n' roll is also about taking care of each other. Under Hard Rock's motto "Take Time to Be Kind," it supports many humanitarian causes around the globe. Under the motto "Save the Planet," Hard Rock supports environmental causes and groups.

One example of Hard Rock's donations to worldwide causes is its Signature Series. The series is a way for musicians and artists to support charities. Each artist donates a piece of original artwork. The artwork is reproduced on a limited-edition T-shirt which is sold by HR

worldwide. Proceeds from the sale of the shirts benefit the charity chosen by the artist. There are currently 27 shirts in the series, and over $11 million has been contributed to a wide variety of charities throughout the world.

If you can't make it to a Hard Rock Cafe, they may bring it to you with Hard Rock on Wheels. In honor of its 40th anniversary, Hard Rock is transforming a truck into a traveling museum that will contain some of the most historic memorabilia from their collection.

CRITICAL THINKING

1. At Hard Rock Cafe, customers use cash or credit cards to make purchases. What control problems may occur when employees accept cash for a sale?

2. What can Hard Rock do, in its own cafes, to help support its "Save the Planet" motto?

Source: www.hardrock.com.

Key Terms

- checking account
- deposit slip
- endorsement
- blank endorsement
- special endorsement
- restrictive endorsement
- postdated check
- voided check
- bank statement
- canceled check
- dishonored check
- non-sufficient funds check
- electronic funds transfer
- debit card
- petty cash
- petty cash slip
- cash short
- cash over

LO1 Record a deposit on a check stub.

LO2 Endorse checks using blank, special, and restrictive endorsements.

LO3 Prepare a check stub and a check.

How Businesses Use Cash

In accounting, money is usually referred to as cash. Most businesses make major cash payments by check. However, small cash payments for items such as postage and some supplies may be made from a cash fund kept at the place of business.

Because cash transactions occur more frequently than other types of transactions, more chances occur to make recording errors affecting cash. Cash can be transferred from one person to another without any question about ownership. Also, cash may be lost as it is moved from one place to another.

As a safety measure, Delgado Web Services keeps most of its cash in a bank. Because all cash receipts are placed in a bank, Delgado Web Services has written evidence to support its accounting records. Delgado Web Services can compare its record of checks written with the bank's record of checks paid. Greater control of Delgado Web Services' cash and greater accuracy of its cash records results from these procedures.

Business Codes of Conduct

A statement that guides the ethical behavior of a company and its employees is called a **code of conduct.** Merck & Co., Inc., a leading pharmaceutical company, makes its code of conduct available to its employees, consultants, and the public. The document, titled "Our Values and Standards, Edition II," begins by stating:

At Merck, our values and standards have always formed the basis of our success. They inspire trust and confidence on the part of the medical community, government officials, regulatory agencies, financial markets, our customers and patients, all whom are essential to our success.

The code of conduct contains sections that focus on Merck's relationship with customers, employees,

shareholders, suppliers, and communities/society. Each section contains specific guidance on Merck policies. Common questions and answers are provided to expand on these policies. Throughout the document, individuals are encouraged to seek the guidance of their supervisor, the Legal Department, and the Office of Ethics if they are unsure whether their actions comply with the code of conduct.

INSTRUCTIONS

Obtain access to Merck's code of conduct at www.merck.com. Can Merck employees do the following:

1. Give a physician a gift consisting of a medical textbook?

2. Use a cell phone to discuss new research methods with another Merck employee?

3. Accept a gift of two Super Bowl tickets from a customer?

©LUCA DI FILIPPO, ISTOCK

Depositing Cash

```
JAN 2 20-- D2000.00 HJS
```

Billings National Bank Billings, MT	Date _January 2,_ 20 _- -_		
	Currency		
	Coin		
For deposit to the account of	Checks		
DELGADO WEB SERVICES	22-1508	2,000	00
25402 Rimrock Road			
Billings, MT 59102-1820			
	TOTAL	2,000	00
⑈092921508⑈ 706466631835⑈	CUSTOMER RECEIPT		

A business form ordering a bank to pay cash from a bank account is known as a check. A bank account from which payments can be ordered by a depositor is called a **checking account**.

When a checking account is opened, the bank customer must provide a signature on a signature card for the bank records. If several persons are authorized to sign checks, each person's signature must be on the signature card.

A bank form which lists the checks, currency, and coins an account holder is adding to the bank account is called a **deposit slip**. A bank customer prepares a deposit slip each time cash or checks are deposited in a bank account. Deposit slips may differ slightly from one bank to another. Each bank designs its own deposit slips to fit the bank's recording machines. However, all deposit slips contain the same basic information.

Checks are listed on a deposit slip according to the bank routing number on each check. For example, the routing number 22-1508 identifies the bank on which the $2,000.00 check is written.

When a deposit is made, a bank gives the depositor a receipt. Many banks use a copy of the deposit slip with a printed or stamped verification as the receipt. The printed verification, *Jan 2, 20-- D2000.00 HJS*, is printed along the top left edge of the deposit slip. This printed verification means that a total of $2,000.00 was deposited on January 2. The initials *HJS* next to the amount are those of the bank employee who accepted the deposit.

Deposit Recorded on a Check Stub LO1

NO. **1**	$ _____		
Date: _____ 20__			
To: _____			
For: _____			
BALANCE BROUGHT FORWARD		0	00
AMOUNT DEPOSITED	1 2 -- Date	2,000	00
SUBTOTAL		2,000	00
OTHER:			
_____			
_____			
SUBTOTAL			
AMOUNT THIS CHECK			
BALANCE CARRIED FORWARD			

After the deposit is recorded on the check stub, a checkbook subtotal is calculated. The balance brought forward on Check Stub No. 1 is zero because the checking account has just been opened. The $2,000.00 deposit is the first transaction for this newly opened checking account. The previous balance, $0.00, plus the deposit, $2,000.00, equals the subtotal, $2,000.00.

Cash receipts are journalized at the time cash is received. Later, the cash receipts are deposited in the checking account. Therefore, no journal entry is needed for deposits because the cash receipts have already been journalized.

Blank Endorsement, Special Endorsement, and Restrictive Endorsement LO2

Ownership of a check can be transferred. The name of the first owner is stated on a check following the words *Pay to the order of.* Therefore, the person to whom payment is to be made must indicate that ownership of the check is being transferred. One person transfers ownership to another person by signing on the back of a check. A signature or stamp on the back of a check transferring ownership is called an **endorsement**. Federal regulations require that an endorsement be confined to a limited amount of space that is indicated on the back of a check.

An endorsement should be signed exactly as the person's name appears on the front of the check. For example, a check made payable to M. J. Delgado is endorsed on the back as *M. J. Delgado.* Immediately below that endorsement, Mr. Delgado would write his official signature, *Michael Delgado.*

Ownership of a check might be transferred several times, resulting in several endorsements. Each endorser guarantees payment of the check. If a bank does not receive payment from the person who signed the check, each endorser is individually liable for payment.

Three types of endorsements are commonly used, each having a specific use in transferring ownership.

BLANK ENDORSEMENT

An endorsement consisting only of the endorser's signature is called a **blank endorsement**. A blank endorsement indicates that the subsequent owner is whoever has the check.

If a check with a blank endorsement is lost or stolen, the check can be cashed by anyone who has possession of it. Ownership may be transferred without further endorsement. A blank endorsement should be used only when a person is at the bank ready to cash or deposit a check.

SPECIAL ENDORSEMENT

An endorsement indicating a new owner of a check is called a **special endorsement**. Special endorsements are sometimes known as *an endorsement in full.*

Special endorsements include the words *Pay to the order of* and the name of the new check owner. Only the person or business named in a special endorsement can cash, deposit, or further transfer ownership of the check. The original owner of the check also signs his or her name under the name of the new owner of the check.

Blank Endorsement

```
ENDORSE HERE
X        Michael Delgado



DO NOT WRITE, STAMP, OR SIGN BELOW THIS LINE
      RESERVED FOR FINANCIAL INSTITUTION USE
```

Special Endorsement

```
ENDORSE HERE
X        Pay to the order of
            Helen Goldsmith
            Michael Delgado

DO NOT WRITE, STAMP, OR SIGN BELOW THIS LINE
      RESERVED FOR FINANCIAL INSTITUTION USE
```

 Endorse all checks before presenting them to the bank for deposit.

Restrictive Endorsement

ENDORSE HERE
x   For deposit only to
the account of
DELGADO WEB SERVICES
Michael Delgado
DO NOT WRITE, STAMP, OR SIGN BELOW THIS LINE
RESERVED FOR FINANCIAL INSTITUTION USE

RESTRICTIVE ENDORSEMENT

An endorsement restricting further transfer of a check's ownership is called a **restrictive endorsement**. Depositing a check in a bank account is a common use of a restrictive endorsement. A restrictive endorsement limits use of the check to whatever purpose is stated in the endorsement.

Many businesses have a stamp prepared with a restrictive endorsement. When a check is received, it is immediately stamped with the restrictive endorsement. This prevents unauthorized persons from cashing the check if it is lost or stolen.

 If the amount of a check written in numbers is different than the amount written in words, the bank may refuse to process the check.

OTNAYDUR/SHUTTERSTOCK.COM

WHY ACCOUNTING?

The Cost of a College Course

Many students go on to a post-secondary school after high school. Students and their families try to save money to help pay for this post-secondary education. The cost of a college education varies with each college. What determines how much a college charges for each course it offers?

The first cost that may come to mind is the cost of the professor's salary. However, several other costs are involved. Many of these costs are not directly related to one specific course, but are general costs of running the college. One example is the college president's salary. The salaries of other employees, such as custodians,

registration personnel, and other administrators, must be included. Other costs must be incorporated into the calculation of the cost of tuition. Examples of additional costs are the cost of building upkeep, utilities, computers, desks, office space, student computer labs, and the library.

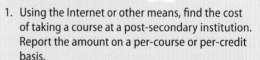

CRITICAL THINKING

1. Using the Internet or other means, find the cost of taking a course at a post-secondary institution. Report the amount on a per-course or per-credit basis.
2. What costs should the college consider when setting a price for board and room?

©ANEKCEN KOWEBHNKOB, ISTOCK

Completed Check Stub and Check LO3

① ②
NO. **1** $ *165.00*

② Date: *January 2,* 20--
③ To: *Eastside Supplies*

④ For: *Supplies*

BALANCE BROUGHT FORWARD	0	00
AMOUNT DEPOSITED `1 2 --` Date	2,000	00
SUBTOTAL	2,000	00
OTHER:		
⑤ SUBTOTAL	2,000	00
AMOUNT THIS CHECK	165	00
⑥ BALANCE CARRIED FORWARD	1,835	00

DELGADO WEB SERVICES
25402 Rimrock Road
Billings, MT 59102-1820

NO. **1**   93-2150 / 929

⑦ *January 2,* 20 --

PAY TO THE ORDER OF *Eastside Supplies*   **⑧** $ *165.00* **⑨**

One hundred sixty-five and ⁿᵒ/100 ————— DOLLARS **⑩**

Billings National Bank
Billings, MT

⑪ FOR *Supplies*   *Michael Delgado* **⑫**

⑆094292150⑆⑆ 7064666318354⑆ 001

Delgado Web Services uses printed checks with check stubs attached. Consecutive numbers are preprinted on Delgado Web Services' checks. Consecutive numbers on checks provide an easy way of identifying each check. Also, the numbers help keep track of all checks to ensure that none is lost or misplaced.

A check stub is a business's record of each check written for a cash payment transaction. [CONCEPT: Objective Evidence] To avoid forgetting to prepare a check stub, the check stub is prepared before the check is written.

After the check stub is completed, the check is written.

↘ Preparing Check Stubs and Checks

① Write the amount of the check, 165.00, in the space after the dollar sign at the top of the stub.

② Write the date of the check, January 2, 20--, on the Date line at the top of the stub.

③ Write to whom the check is to be paid, Eastside Supplies, on the To line at the top of the stub.

④ Record the purpose of the check, Supplies, on the For line.

⑤ Write the amount of the check, $165.00, in the amount column at the bottom of the stub on the line with the words "Amount This Check."

⑥ Calculate the new checking account balance, $1,835.00, and record the new balance in the amount column on the last line of the stub. The new balance is calculated as shown.

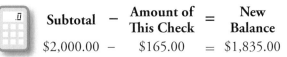

Subtotal	−	Amount of This Check	=	New Balance
$2,000.00	−	$165.00	=	$1,835.00

Preparing Checks

⑦ Write the date, January 2, 20--, in the space provided. The date should be the month, day, and year on which the check is issued. A check with a future date on it is called a **postdated check**. Most banks will not accept postdated checks because money cannot be withdrawn from a depositor's account until the date on the check.

⑧ Write to whom the check is to be paid, Eastside Supplies, following the words "Pay to the order of." If the person to whom a check is to be paid is a business, use the business's name rather than the owner's name. [CONCEPT: Business Entity] If the person to whom the check is to be paid is an individual, use that person's name.

⑨ Write the amount in figures, 165.00, following the dollar sign. Write the figures close to the printed dollar sign. This practice prevents anyone from writing another digit in front of the amount to change the amount of the check.

⑩ Write the amount in words, One hundred sixty-five and no/100, on the line with the word "Dollars." This written amount verifies the amount written in figures after the dollar sign. Begin the words at the extreme left. Draw a line through the unused space up to the word "Dollars." This line prevents anyone from writing in additional words to change the amount. If the amounts in words and in figures are not the same, a bank may pay only the amount in words. Often, when the amounts do not agree, a bank will refuse to pay the check.

11 Write the purpose of the check, Supplies, on the line labeled "For." (On some checks, this space is labeled "Memo.") Some checks do not have a line for writing the purpose of the check.

12 Sign the check. A check should not be signed until each item on the check and its stub has been verified for accuracy.

Recording a Voided Check

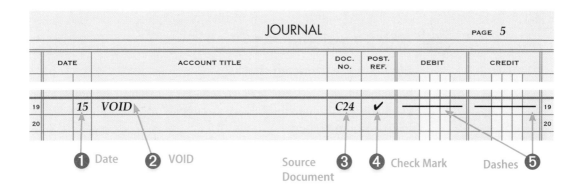

Banks usually refuse to accept altered checks. If any kind of error is made in preparing a check, a new check should be prepared. Because checks are prenumbered, all checks not used should be retained for the records. This practice helps account for all checks and assures that no checks have been lost or stolen.

A check that cannot be processed because the maker has made it invalid is called a **voided check**. The word *VOID* is written in large letters across both the check and its stub.

When Delgado Web Services records a check in its journal, the check number is placed in the journal's Doc. No. column. If a check number is missing from the Doc. No. column, there is a question whether all checks have been journalized. To ensure that all check numbers are listed in the journal, Delgado Web Services records voided checks in the journal.

FLASHON STUDIO/SHUTTERSTOCK.COM

Recording a Voided Check in the Journal

1 Record the date, 15, in the Date column.

2 Write the word, VOID, in the Account Title column.

3 Write the check number, C24, in the Doc. No. column.

4 Place a check mark in the Post. Ref. column.

5 Place a dash in both the Debit and Credit columns.

remember Always complete the check stub before writing the check. Otherwise you may forget to record the amount of the check on the check stub.

End of Lesson Review

LO1 Record a deposit on a check stub.

LO2 Endorse checks using blank, special, and restrictive endorsements.

LO3 Prepare a check stub and a check.

Terms Review

checking account

deposit slip

endorsement

blank endorsement

special endorsement

restrictive endorsement

postdated check

voided check

Audit your understanding

1. List the three types of endorsements.
2. List the steps for preparing a check stub.
3. List the steps for preparing a check.

Work together 5-1

Endorsing and writing checks

Write the answers to the following problems in the *Working Papers*. Your instructor will guide you through the following examples. You are authorized to sign checks for Grantsburg Accounting.

1. For each of these situations, prepare the appropriate endorsement.
    a. Write a blank endorsement.
    b. Write a special endorsement to transfer a check to Clara Kwon.
    c. Write a restrictive endorsement to deposit a check in the account of Grantsburg Accounting.
2. Record the balance brought forward on Check Stub No. 151, $2,145.88.
3. Record a deposit of $316.00 made on June 30 of the current year on Check Stub No. 151.
4. Prepare check stubs and write the following checks. Use June 30 of the current year as the date.
    a. Check No. 151 to A1 Computers for repairs, $148.00.
    b. Check No. 152 to Southwest Supply for supplies, $62.00.

On your own 5-1

Endorsing and writing checks

Write the answers to the following problems in the *Working Papers*. Work these problems independently. You are authorized to sign checks for Milltown Hair Care.

1. For each of these situations, prepare the appropriate endorsement.
    a. Write a special endorsement to transfer a check to Kevin Deters.
    b. Write a restrictive endorsement to deposit a check in the account of Milltown Hair Care.
2. Record the balance brought forward on Check Stub No. 317, $1,852.39.
3. Record a deposit of $135.79 made on March 31 of the current year on Check Stub No. 317.
4. Prepare check stubs and write the following checks. Use March 31 of the current year as the date.
    a. Check No. 317 to Uniform World for uniform rental, $195.00.
    b. Check No. 318 to Salon Supplies for supplies, $328.00.

©CANDICE CUSACK, ISTOCK

LESSON
5-2 Bank Reconciliation

LO4 Complete a bank statement reconciliation.

LO5 Record and journalize a bank service charge.

Bank Statement

Billings National Bank
Billings, MT

STATEMENT OF ACCOUNT FOR

DELGADO WEB SERVICES
25402 Rimrock Road
Billings, MT 59102-1820

ACCOUNT NUMBER
706466631835

STATEMENT DATE
January 30, 20--

BALANCE FROM PREVIOUS STATEMENT	NO. OF CHECKS	AMOUNT OF CHECKS	NO. OF DEPOSITS	AMOUNT OF DEPOSITS	SERVICE CHARGES	STATEMENT BALANCE
0.00	10	3,118.00	15	6,435.00	25.00	3,292.00

DATE	CHECK	AMOUNT	CHECK	AMOUNT	DEPOSIT	BALANCE
01/01/--						0.00
01/02/--					2,000.00	2,000.00
01/05/--	1	165.00				1,835.00
01/08/--	2	900.00				935.00
01/10/--					1,100.00	2,035.00
01/16/--					200.00	2,235.00
01/17/--					340.00	2,575.00
01/18/--	4	80.00	6	350.00	195.00	2,340.00
01/19/--	3	100.00			285.00	2,525.00
01/22/--	5	400.00	7	383.00	310.00	2,052.00
01/22/--					270.00	2,322.00
01/23/--	8	100.00			240.00	2,462.00
01/24/--					215.00	2,677.00
01/25/--					280.00	2,957.00
01/26/--					190.00	3,147.00
01/29/--	9	510.00			145.00	2,782.00
01/29/--					315.00	3,097.00
01/29/--					350.00	3,447.00
01/30/--	10	130.00				3,317.00
	SC	25.00				3,292.00
						3,292.00

PLEASE EXAMINE AT ONCE - IF NO ERRORS ARE REPORTED WITHIN 10 DAYS, THE ACCOUNT WILL BE CONSIDERED CORRECT. REFER ANY DISCREPANCY TO OUR ACCOUNTING DEPARTMENT IMMEDIATELY.

A report of deposits, withdrawals, and bank balances sent to a depositor by a bank is called a **bank statement**.

When a bank receives checks, the amount of each check is deducted from the depositor's account. A check which has been paid by the bank is called a **canceled check**. The bank stamps the checks to indicate that the checks are canceled and are not to be transferred further. Canceled checks may be returned to a depositor with a bank statement or may be kept on record by the bank. Account service charges are also listed on a bank statement.

Although banks seldom make mistakes, occasionally a check or deposit might be recorded in a wrong account. If errors are discovered, the bank should be notified at once. However, a bank's records and a depositor's records may differ for several reasons:

1. A service charge may not have been recorded in the depositor's business records.
2. Outstanding deposits may be recorded in the depositor's records but not on a bank statement.
3. Outstanding checks may be recorded in the depositor's records but not on a bank statement.
4. A depositor may have made math or recording errors.

Bank Reconciliation **Lesson 5-2** 129

Bank Statement Reconciliation LO4

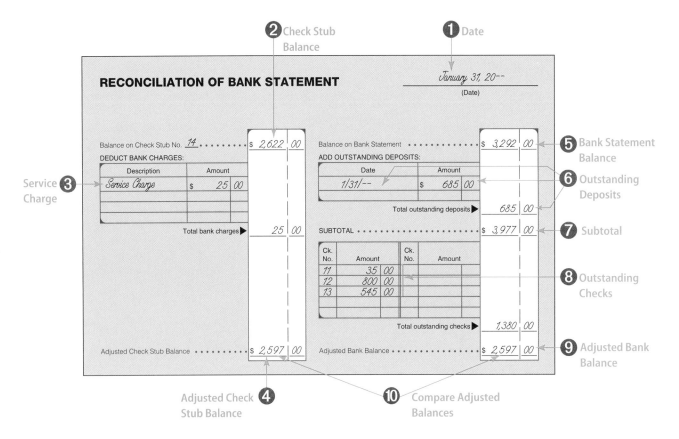

A bank statement is reconciled by verifying that information on a bank statement and a checkbook are in agreement. Reconciling immediately is an important aspect of cash control.

Delgado Web Services' canceled checks are kept on record at the bank. The bank statement is used to determine the canceled checks. For each canceled check listed on the bank statement, a check mark is placed on the corresponding check stub. A check stub with no check mark indicates an outstanding check. Outstanding checks are those checks issued by a depositor but not yet reported on a bank statement. Outstanding deposits are those deposits made at a bank but not yet shown on a bank statement.

Delgado Web Services receives a bank statement dated January 30 on January 31. Delgado Web Services uses a reconciliation form printed on the back of the bank statement.

↘ Reconciling a Bank Statement

1 Write the date on which the reconciliation is prepared, January 31, 20--.

2 In the left amount column, list the balance brought forward on Check Stub No. 14, the next unused check stub, $2,622.00.

3 In the space for bank charges, list any charges. The only such charge for Delgado Web Services is the bank service charge, $25.00. The bank service charge is labeled "SC" on the bank statement.

4 Write the adjusted check stub balance, $2,597.00, in the space provided at the bottom of the left amount column. The balance on the check stub, $2,622.00, minus the bank's service charge, $25.00, equals the adjusted check stub balance, $2,597.00.

5 Write the ending balance shown on the bank statement, $3,292.00, in the right amount column.

6. Write the date, 1/31/--, and the amount, $685.00, of any outstanding deposits in the space provided. Add the outstanding deposits. Write the total outstanding deposits, $685.00, in the right amount column.

7. Add the ending bank statement balance to the total outstanding deposits. Write the total, $3,977.00, in the space for the Subtotal.

8. List the outstanding checks, Nos. 11, 12, and 13, and their amounts, $35.00, $800.00, and $545.00, in the space provided. Add the amounts of the outstanding checks and write the total, $1,380.00, in the right amount column.

9. Calculate the adjusted bank balance, and write the amount, $2,597.00, in the space provided at the bottom of the right amount column. The subtotal, $3,977.00, minus the total outstanding checks, $1,380.00, equals the adjusted bank balance, $2,597.00.

10. Compare adjusted balances. The adjusted balances must be the same. The adjusted check stub balance is the same as the adjusted bank balance. Because the two amounts are the same, the bank statement is reconciled. The completed reconciliation form is filed for future reference. If the two adjusted balances are not the same, the error must be found and corrected before any more work is done.

FINANCIAL LITERACY

Shopping for a Checking Account

Opening a checking account is necessary when managing your money. A checking account is not only a safe and convenient method for controlling large sums of cash, but bills can be paid and canceled checks can serve as a record of spending.

However, not all checking accounts are the same, even within the same bank. You must shop around and compare features in order to find the checking account that best fits the needs of the business or individual. For example: Where is the nearest location? What is the minimum deposit to open an account? Does the bank offer online banking without a fee? Is there a monthly service fee? What is the cost of 200 checks? Is there a minimum balance required to avoid a fee? Is there unlimited check writing? Does the bank have interest-bearing accounts?

Fees should carefully be reviewed as well. Common fees include charges for ordering checks, automatic teller machine (ATM) withdrawals, monthly service fees, and a fee for insufficient funds should the amount on the check presented for payment exceed the available funds in the account.

ACTIVITIES

1. Compare and contrast the following two checking accounts. Based on your findings, which checking account would best fit the needs for a high school student who just started his or her first job? Explain your findings.

The Almighty Dollar Bank (ADB) Student Value Plus Checking Account requires $500 to open a checking account with no minimum balance requirement. There is a $5 monthly service charge but no ATM fees unless used at a bank other than ADB, in which case a $3 fee would be imposed by both ADB and the other bank. The first 200 checks are free. Subsequent check orders cost $17.95 for 200 checks. There is a $35 fee for insufficient funds. Online banking is offered free for the first three transactions each month.

The People Friendly Bank (PFB) Free Student Checking Account has no minimum initial balance but charges a $5 fee if the balance falls below $50. This account pays 1% annual interest on balances over $5,000 and has no monthly service charge. There is no charge for ATM withdrawals. Checks cost $12.95 per 200, and there is a $25 fee for insufficient funds. Online banking is free.

2. Explain why a business would open a checking account instead of a savings account to manage cash.

3. Compare/contrast the costs and features of checking accounts from three different banks. Summarize your findings in an Excel spreadsheet.

Recording a Bank Service Charge on a Check Stub LO5

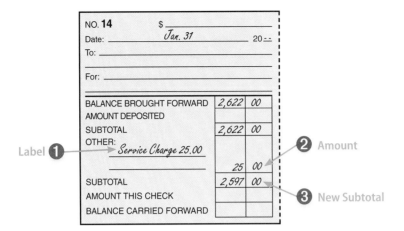

NO. **14**
$ _____
Date: _____ *Jan. 31* _____ 20 -_-_
To: _____
For: _____

BALANCE BROUGHT FORWARD	2,622	00
AMOUNT DEPOSITED		
SUBTOTAL	2,622	00
OTHER: *Service Charge 25.00*		
	25	00
SUBTOTAL	2,597	00
AMOUNT THIS CHECK		
BALANCE CARRIED FORWARD		

Label ❶

❷ Amount

❸ New Subtotal

The bank deducts the service charge from Delgado Web Services' checking account each month. Although Delgado Web Services did not write a check for the bank service charge, this cash payment must be recorded in Delgado Web Services' accounting records as a cash payment. Delgado Web Services makes a record of a bank service charge on a check stub.

↘ Recording a Bank Service Charge on a Check Stub

❶ Write Service Charge on the check stub under the heading "Other."

❷ Write the amount of the service charge, $25.00, in the amount column.

❸ Calculate and record the new subtotal, $2,597.00, on the Subtotal line. A new balance carried forward is not calculated until after Check No. 14 is written.

THINK LIKE AN ACCOUNTANT

Flowcharting the Bank Reconciliation Process

Your accounting clerks often struggle to understand the bank reconciliation process. To help them prepare the bank reconciliation, you have decided to create a flowchart summarizing the process. The objects available on an electronic spreadsheet can be used to create a flowchart.

A flowchart is a graphic representation of a process. Your flowchart uses two symbols. A rectangle represents a process, as briefly described by the text inside the symbol. The rounded rectangle denotes the start or end of a

process. An arrow between symbols represents the order in which processes are performed. Color coding the symbols can help the reader understand the process.

Complete the flowchart by replacing the question marks with text describing the appropriate process. Modify the color of symbols describing similar processes.

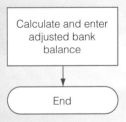

OPEN THE SPREADSHEET TLA_CH05
Follow the directions on the Instructions tab.

Journalizing a Bank Service Charge

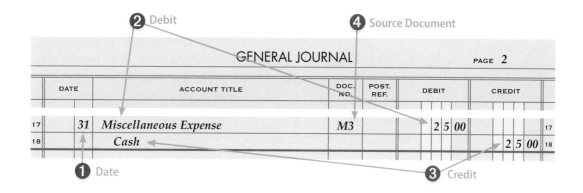

Because the bank service charge is a cash payment for which no check is written, Delgado Web Services prepares a memorandum as the source document. Delgado Web Services' bank service charges are relatively small and occur only once a month. Therefore, a separate ledger account for the expense is not used. Instead, Delgado Web Services records the bank service charge as a miscellaneous expense.

A memorandum is the source document for a bank service charge transaction. [CONCEPT: Objective Evidence] The analysis of this transaction is shown in the T accounts.

The expense account, Miscellaneous Expense, is debited for $25.00 to show the increase in owner's equity. The asset account, Cash, is credited for $25.00 to show the decrease in assets.

> January 31. Received bank statement showing January bank service charge, $25.00. Memorandum No. 3.

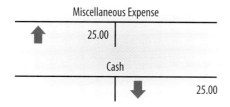

Journalizing a Bank Service Charge

1. **Date.** Write the date, 31, in the Date column.

2. **Debit.** Write the title of the account to be debited, Miscellaneous Expense, in the Account Title column. Record the amount debited, $25.00, in the Debit column.

3. **Credit.** On the next line, indented about one centimeter, write the title of the amount credited, Cash, in the Account Title column. Write the credit amount, $25.00, in the Credit column.

4. **Source document.** On the first line of the entry, write the source document number, M3, in the Doc. No. column.

The Federal Deposit Insurance Corporation (FDIC) protects depositors from banks that fail. Bank deposits are currently covered up to $250,000 per depositor.

End of Lesson Review

LO4 Complete a bank statement reconciliation.

LO5 Record and journalize a bank service charge.

Terms Review

bank statement

canceled check

Audit your understanding

1. List four reasons why a depositor's records and a bank's records may differ.
2. If a check mark is placed on the check stub of each canceled check, what does a check stub with no check mark indicate?

Work together 5-2

Reconciling a bank statement and recording a bank service charge

Forms are given in the *Working Papers*. Your instructor will guide you through the following examples.

On August 29 of the current year, Bright and White Laundry received a bank statement dated August 28. The following information is obtained from the bank statement and from the records of the business.

Bank statement balance	$2,712.00	Outstanding checks:	
Bank service charge	20.00	No. 306	$ 140.00
Outstanding deposit,		No. 308	70.00
August 28	300.00	Checkbook balance on	
		Check Stub No. 309	2,822.00

1. Prepare a bank statement reconciliation. Use August 29 of the current year as the date.
2. Record the service charge on Check Stub No. 309.
3. Record the service charge on journal page 16. Use Memorandum No. 77 as the source document.

On your own 5-2

Reconciling a bank statement and recording a bank service charge

Forms are given in the *Working Papers*. Work these problems independently.

On June 30 of the current year, Roettger Repair Co. received a bank statement dated June 29. The following information is obtained from the bank statement and from the records of the business.

Bank statement balance	$3,912.00	Outstanding checks:	
Bank service charge	25.00	No. 220	$ 140.00
Outstanding deposits:		No. 222	616.00
June 29	470.00	No. 223	160.00
June 30	660.00	Checkbook balance on	
		Check Stub No. 224	4,151.00

1. Prepare a bank statement reconciliation. Use June 30 of the current year as the date.
2. Record the service charge on Check Stub No. 224.
3. Record the service charge on journal page 12. Use Memorandum No. 75 as the source document.

©CANDICE CUSACK, ISTOCK

LESSON
5-3 Dishonored Checks and Electronic Banking

LO6 Complete recordkeeping for a dishonored check.

LO7 Journalize an electronic funds transfer.

LO8 Journalize a debit card transaction.

Recording a Dishonored Check on a Check Stub LO6

NO. **52**	$ _____			
Date: _____ 20__				
To: _____				
For: _____				
BALANCE BROUGHT FORWARD		2,112	00	
AMOUNT DEPOSITED				
SUBTOTAL Date		2,112	00	
OTHER:				
Dishonored Check				
		225	00	
SUBTOTAL		1,887	00	
AMOUNT THIS CHECK				
BALANCE CARRIED FORWARD				

① Label   ② Amount   ③ New Subtotal

A check that a bank refuses to pay is called a **dishonored check**. Banks dishonor a check for many reasons. A check dishonored by the bank because of insufficient funds in the account of the maker of the check is called a **non-sufficient funds check**. A non-sufficient funds check is also known as an *NSF check*. Banks may also dishonor a check for other reasons: (1) The check appears to be altered. (2) The signature of the person who signed the check does not match the one on the signature card at the bank. (3) The amounts written in figures and in words do not agree. (4) The check is post-dated. (5) The person who wrote the check has stopped payment on the check.

Issuing a check on an account with insufficient funds is illegal. Altering or forging a check is also illegal. An NSF check may affect the credit rating of the person or business that issued the check.

Sometimes money for an NSF check can be collected directly from the person or business that wrote the check. Often, however, the value of a dishonored check cannot be recovered and becomes an expense to the business.

Most banks charge a fee for handling NSF checks that have been previously accepted for deposit. This fee

is an expense of the business receiving such a check. Delgado Web Services' bank charges a $40.00 fee for handling NSF checks. Delgado Web Services attempts to collect the $40.00 fee in addition to the amount of the NSF check from the person or business that wrote the check.

When Delgado Web Services receives a check, it records the check as a debit to **Cash** and deposits the check in the bank. When a check is dishonored, the bank deducts the amount of the check plus the fee, $40.00, from Delgado Web Services' checking account. Therefore, Delgado Web Services records a dishonored check as a cash payment transaction.

↘ Recording a Dishonored Check on a Check Stub

① Write Dishonored Check under the heading "Other."

② Write the total of the dishonored check, $225.00, in the amount column. This is the amount of the dishonored check, $185.00, plus the service fee of $40.00.

③ Calculate and record the new subtotal, $1,887.00, on the Subtotal line. A new balance carried forward is not calculated until after Check No. 52 is written.

Journalizing a Dishonored Check

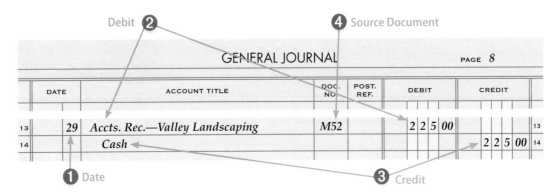

During January, Delgado Web Services received no checks that were subsequently dishonored. However, in August, Delgado Web Services did receive a check from Valley Landscaping that was eventually dishonored.

Delgado Web Services receives a notice of the dishonored check and the fee from the bank. Delgado Web Services attaches the notice to a memorandum, which is used as the source document. [CONCEPT: Objective Evidence] The analysis of this transaction is shown in the T accounts.

August 29. Received notice from the bank of a dishonored check from Valley Landscaping, $185.00, plus $40.00 fee; total, $225.00. Memorandum No. 52.

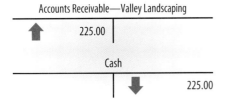

When a business is notified that a customer check is NSF, some companies will charge the customer for the bank fee plus an extra amount for the additional processing.

All checks received are deposited in Delgado Web Services' checking account. The entry for each cash receipts transaction includes a debit to **Cash**. If a check is subsequently returned as dishonored, the previous cash debit for the amount of the check must be offset by a cash credit. The asset account, **Cash**, is credited for $225.00 to show the decrease in assets.

When Delgado Web Services originally received the check from Valley Landscaping, **Accounts Receivable—Valley Landscaping** was credited to reduce the balance of the account. When Delgado Web Services finds out that the check was not accepted by the bank, the account, **Accounts Receivable—Valley Landscaping**, must be increased to show that this amount, plus the bank charge, is still owed to Delgado Web Services. The asset account, **Accounts Receivable—Valley Landscaping**, is debited for $225.00 to show the increase in assets.

Journalizing a Dishonored Check

1. **Date.** Write the date, 29, in the Date column.
2. **Debit.** Write the title of the account to be debited, Accounts Receivable—Valley Landscaping, in the Account Title column. Record the amount debited, $225.00, in the Debit column.
3. **Credit.** On the next line, indented about one centimeter, write the title of the account credited, Cash, in the Account Title column. Write the credit amount, $225.00, in the Credit column.
4. **Source document.** On the first line of this entry, write the source document number, M52, in the Doc. No. column.

Journalizing an Electronic Funds Transfer LO7

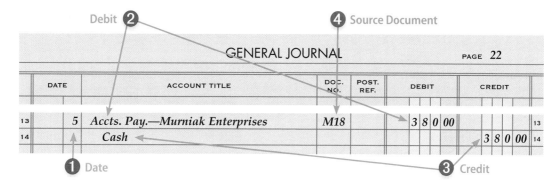

Debit ❷   **❹ Source Document**

	DATE	ACCOUNT TITLE	DOC. NO.	POST. REF.	DEBIT	CREDIT	
13	5	Accts. Pay.—Murniak Enterprises	M18		3 8 0 00		13
14		Cash				3 8 0 00	14

❶ Date   **❸ Credit**

A computerized cash payments system that transfers funds without the use of checks, currency, or other paper documents is called **electronic funds transfer.** Electronic funds transfer is also known as *EFT*. Many businesses use electronic funds transfer (EFT) to pay vendors. To use EFT, a business makes arrangements with its bank to process EFT transactions. Arrangements are also made with vendors to accept EFT payments on account. Then a transfer of funds from the business's account to the vendor's account can be completed via the Internet or a telephone call.

To control cash payments through EFT, the person responsible for requesting transfers should be given a password. The bank should not accept EFT requests from any person unable to provide an established password.

Delgado Web Services does not use electronic funds transfer. However, Bonita Beach Repair does use electronic funds transfer to make payments on account to vendors. The journal entry for making payments on account through EFT is the same as when a check is written. The only change is the source document used for the transaction. Bonita Beach Repair uses a memorandum as the source document for an EFT. A note is written on the memorandum to describe the transaction.

June 5. Paid cash on account to Murniak Enterprises, $380.00, using EFT. Memorandum No. 18.

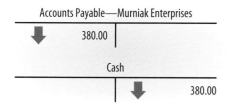

The source document for this transaction is Memorandum No. 18. [CONCEPT: Objective Evidence] The analysis of this transaction is shown in the T accounts.

The liability account, Accounts Payable—Murniak Enterprises, is decreased by a debit, $380.00. The asset account, Cash, is decreased by a credit, $380.00.

A cash payment made by EFT is recorded on the check stub as "Other." This procedure keeps the checkbook in balance during the time lag from when the EFT is made until receipt of the bank statement. The EFT payments are verified as part of the regular bank statement reconciliation process. EFT payments are identified in the Check column of the bank statement by the notation "EFT," rather than by a check number.

➥ Journalizing an Electronic Funds Transfer

❶ Date. Write the date, 5, in the Date column.

❷ Debit. Write the title of the account to be debited, Accounts Payable—Murniak Enterprises, in the Account Title column. Record the amount debited, $380.00, in the Debit column.

❸ Credit. On the next line, indented about 1 centimeter, write the title of the account credited, Cash, in the Account Title column. Write the credit amount, $380.00, in the Credit column.

❹ Source document. On the first line of this entry, write the source document number, M18, in the Doc. No. column.

Checking accounts and records should be maintained in such a way that all checks will be honored when presented to the bank.

Journalizing a Debit Card Transaction LO8

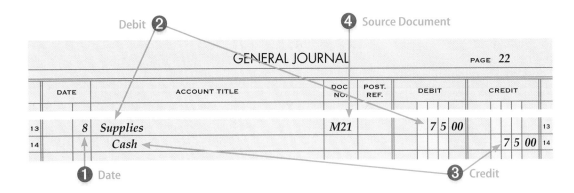

A bank card that automatically deducts the amount of a purchase from the checking account of the cardholder is called a **debit card.** There is one major difference between a debit card and a credit card. When a purchase is made with a debit card, the amount of the purchase is automatically deducted from the checking account of the cardholder. A debit card eliminates the need to write a check for the purchase. However, the effect is the same. The checking account balance is reduced by the amount of the purchase. A debit card also eliminates the need to carry a checkbook.

When using a debit card, it is important to remember to record all purchases to avoid errors in the checking account.

Bonita Beach Repair uses a debit card to make some purchases. Recording a cash payment made by a debit card is similar to recording a cash payment made by electronic funds transfer.

Bonita Beach Repair uses a memorandum as the source document for a debit card purchase. A note is written on the memorandum to describe the transaction.

June 8. Purchased supplies, $75.00, using debit card. Memorandum No. 21.

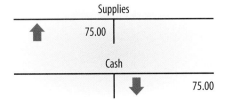

Journalizing a Debit Card Purchase

1 **Date.** Write the date, 8, in the Date column.

2 **Debit.** Write the title of the account to be debited, Supplies, in the Account Title column. Record the amount debited, $75.00, in the Debit column.

3 **Credit.** On the next line, indented about one centimeter, write the title of the account credited, Cash, in the Account Title column. Write the credit amount, $75.00, in the Credit column.

4 **Source document.** On the first line of this entry, write the source document number, M21, in the Doc. No. column.

The source document for this transaction is Memorandum No. 21. [CONCEPT: Objective Evidence] The analysis of this transaction is shown in the T accounts.

The asset account, Supplies, is increased by a debit, $75.00. The asset account, Cash, is decreased by a credit, $75.00.

A cash payment made with a debit card is recorded on the check stub as "Other." This procedure keeps the checkbook in balance during the time lag from when the debit card payment is made until receipt of the bank statement. The debit card payments are verified as part of the regular bank statement reconciliation process. Debit card payments are identified as a purchase on the bank statement, with the date, time, location, and amount of the debit card transaction stated.

Prepare a bank reconciliation every time you receive a statement of account from the bank.

Terms Review

dishonored check

non-sufficient funds check

electronic funds transfer

debit card

Audit your understanding

1. List six reasons why a bank may dishonor a check.

2. What account is credited when electronic funds transfer is used to pay cash on account?

3. What account is credited when a debit card is used to purchase supplies?

Work together 5-3

Recording dishonored checks, electronic funds transfers, and debit card purchases

Write the answers to this problem in the *Working Papers*. Your instructor will guide you through the following example.

Enter the following transactions on page 15 of a journal.

Transactions:

Aug. 18. Received notice from the bank of a dishonored check from Christine Iverson, $126.00, plus $25.00 fee; total, $151.00. Memorandum No. 312.

20. Paid cash on account to Schwartz Enterprises, $270.00, using EFT. Memorandum No. 313.

21. Purchased supplies, $62.00, using a debit card. Memorandum No. 314.

On your own 5-3

Recording dishonored checks, electronic funds transfers, and debit card purchases

Write the answers to this problem in the *Working Papers*. Work this problem independently.

Enter the following transactions on page 12 of a journal.

Transactions:

July 12. Received notice from the bank of a dishonored check from Tiffany Hooverman, $130.00, plus $30.00 fee; total, $160.00. Memorandum No. 78.

13. Paid cash on account to Alfredson Company, $486.00, using EFT. Memorandum No. 79.

14. Purchased supplies, $70.00, using a debit card. Memorandum No. 80.

5-4 Petty Cash

LO9 Establish a petty cash fund.
LO10 Prepare a petty cash report.
LO11 Replenish a petty cash fund.

Establishing a Petty Cash Fund LO9

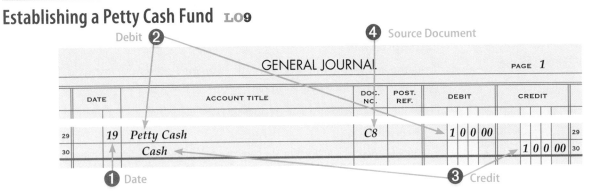

An amount of cash kept on hand and used for making small payments is called **petty cash**. A business usually has some small payments for which writing a check is not time or cost effective. Therefore, a business may maintain a separate cash fund for making small cash payments. The actual dollar amount considered to be a small payment differs from one business to another. Mr. Delgado has set $20.00 as the maximum amount to be paid at any one time from the petty cash fund.

The Petty Cash account is an asset with a normal debit balance. The balance of the Petty Cash increases on the debit side and decreases on the credit side.

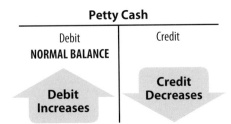

On January 19, Mr. Delgado decided that Delgado Web Services needed a petty cash fund of $100.00. This amount should provide for small cash payments during a month.

The source document for this transaction is Check No. 8. [CONCEPT: Objective Evidence] The analysis is shown in the T accounts. Petty Cash is debited for

January 19. Paid cash to establish a petty cash fund, $100.00. Check No. 8.

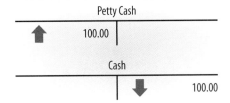

$100.00 to show the increase in this asset account balance. Cash is credited for $100.00 to show the decrease in this asset account balance.

Mr. Delgado cashed the check and placed the $100.00 in a locked petty cash box at his place of business. Only he is authorized to make payments from the petty cash fund.

↘ Establishing a Petty Cash Fund

❶ **Date.** Write the date, 19, in the Date column.

❷ **Debit.** Write the title of the account to be debited, Petty Cash, in the Account Title column. Record the amount debited, $100.00, in the Debit column.

❸ **Credit.** On the next line, indented about one centimeter, write the title of the account credited, Cash, in the Account Title column. Write the credit amount, $100.00, in the Credit column.

❹ **Source document.** Write the source document number, C8, in the Doc. No. column.

Making Payments from a Petty Cash Fund with a Petty Cash Slip

PETTY CASH SLIP	No. 1

Date: _January 19, 20- -_

Paid to: _Dispatch_

For: _Newspaper ad_ $ _14.00_

Account: _Advertising Expense_

Approved: _Michael Delgado_

Each time a small payment is made from the petty cash fund, Mr. Delgado prepares a form showing the purpose and amount of the payment. A form showing proof of a petty cash payment is called a **petty cash slip**.

A petty cash slip shows the following information: (1) petty cash slip number, (2) date of petty cash payment, (3) to whom paid, (4) reason for the payment, (5) amount paid, (6) account in which amount is to be recorded, and (7) signature of person approving the petty cash payment.

The petty cash slips are kept in the petty cash box until the fund is replenished. No entries are made in the journal for the individual petty cash payments.

Even though a petty cash fund usually contains only a small amount of cash, it is still important to have good controls over the system to guard against improper use of the cash in the fund.

PHOTODISC/GETTY IMAGES

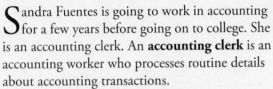

Careers In Accounting

Sandra Fuentes
ACCOUNTING CLERK

Sandra Fuentes is going to work in accounting for a few years before going on to college. She is an accounting clerk. An **accounting clerk** is an accounting worker who processes routine details about accounting transactions.

Accounting clerks usually work in one or more specific areas of an accounting department such as accounts payable, accounts receivable, or payroll. As an accounting clerk, Sandra performs calculations and verifies postings of transactions such as cash received or paid. She might also reconcile statements received from vendors or sent to customers. This could include contacting the customer or vendor to discuss payments and account balances. If she was a payroll clerk, she would probably verify hours worked, calculate wages paid, and calculate payroll deductions. Some accounting clerks verify computer-generated reports.

In Sandra's company, many of the people in higher-level accounting positions started out as accounting clerks. As an accounting clerk, Sandra will learn about the company and its products. When she does continue with her college education, she hopes it will help her to advance to other positions in the company. The company is supportive of this effort. It will reimburse one-half of the cost of tuition and books for any college accounting course she completes with a grade of B or better.

Sandra has also noticed that many accounting positions listed in the local newspaper require previous work experience in the field. Working as an accounting clerk is a good way for her to gain initial accounting work experience.

Salary Range: Salaries vary with job responsibilities but usually range from $27,000 to $33,000 annually.

Qualifications: Most accounting clerks are required to have a high school diploma or equivalent. It is helpful to have completed a high school accounting course. An accounting clerk must have a basic understanding of debits and credits and be attentive to detail. Since most accounting data are computerized, an accounting clerk needs good computer skills. Knowledge of spreadsheet software and/or accounting software is helpful. Good communication skills are necessary in order to communicate with customers and creditors. An accounting clerk also needs good math skills.

Occupational Outlook: The growth for accounting clerk positions is projected to be in the average range (between 7% and 13%) for the period from 2008 to 2018.

Source: online.onetcenter.org.

Petty Cash Report LO10

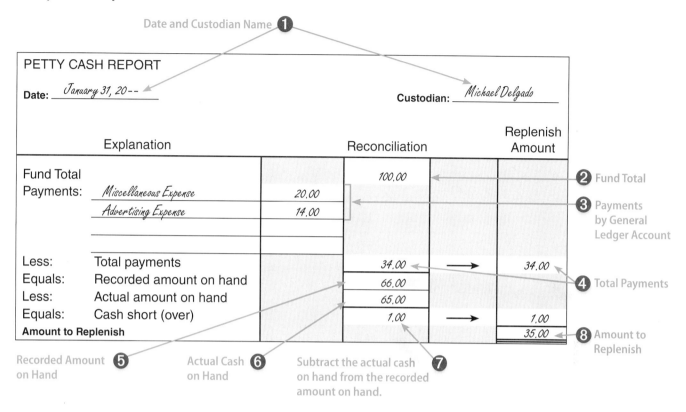

As petty cash is paid out, the amount in the petty cash box decreases. Eventually, the petty cash fund must be replenished and the petty cash payments recorded. Delgado Web Services replenishes its petty cash fund whenever the amount on hand is reduced to $25.00. Also, the petty cash fund is always replenished at the end of each month so that all of the expenses are recorded in the month they are incurred.

Before petty cash is replenished, a proof of the fund must be completed. The proof of the fund may be called a petty cash report. Delgado Web Services prepares a petty cash report on January 31, when the actual cash in the fund is $65.00.

Errors may be made when making payments from a petty cash fund. These errors cause a difference between actual cash on hand and the record of the amount of cash that should be on hand. A petty cash on hand amount that is less than the recorded amount is called **cash short**. A petty cash on hand amount that is more than the recorded amount is called **cash over**. The custodian prepares a petty cash report when the petty cash fund is to be replenished.

Preparing a Petty Cash Report

❶ Write the date, January 31, 20--, and custodian name, Michael Delgado, in the report heading.

❷ Write the fund total, $100.00, from the general ledger account.

❸ Summarize petty cash slips by totals for each general ledger account. Delgado Web Services' petty cash slips show $20.00 paid out for miscellaneous expense and $14.00 paid out for advertising expense.

❹ Calculate and write the total payments, $34.00, in the Reconciliation and Replenish Amount columns.

❺ Calculate and write the recorded amount on hand, $66.00 ($100.00 − $34.00).

❻ Write the actual amount of cash on hand, $65.00, in the Reconciliation column. This amount is determined by adding the coins and currency in the petty cash box.

❼ Subtract the actual amount on hand, $65.00, from the recorded amount on hand, $66.00, and write the amount short, $1.00, in the Reconciliation and Replenish Amount columns. The actual amount of petty cash on hand is $1.00 less than the recorded amount.

❽ Write the total of the amount to replenish, $35.00. The petty cash fund actually has $65.00 on hand. When replenishing the petty cash fund, the amount in the fund is brought back up to the original amount of the fund, $100.00 ($100.00 − $65.00 = $35.00).

Replenishing Petty Cash LO11

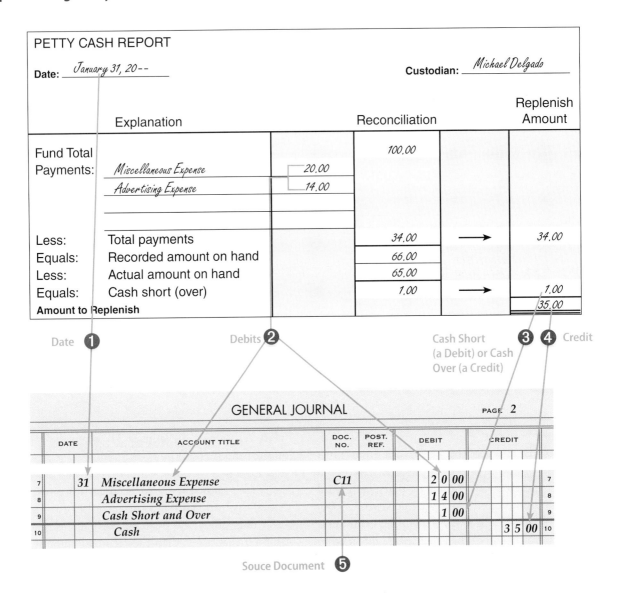

Once the petty cash report is complete, Delgado Web Services replenishes the petty cash fund.

> January 31. Paid cash to replenish the petty cash fund, $35.00: Miscellaneous Expense, $20.00; Advertising, $14.00, Cash Short and Over, $1.00. Check No. 11.

Petty cash short and petty cash over are recorded in an account titled Cash Short and Over. Cash Short and Over is debited when cash is short and credited when cash is over. Therefore, the balance of Cash Short and Over can be either a debit or credit. The balance is usually a debit because the petty cash fund is more likely to be short than over. A cash shortage adds to the cost of operating a business. Thus, the account is classified as an operating expense. Note that in Step 4,

the amount of petty cash short is recorded in the Debit column. If petty cash were over, the amount would be recorded in the Credit column.

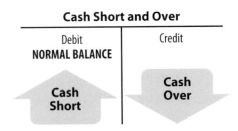

The source document for this transaction is Check No. 11. [CONCEPT: Objective Evidence] The analysis of this transaction is shown in the T accounts on the next page.

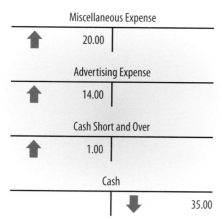

Miscellaneous Expense

20.00

Advertising Expense

14.00

Cash Short and Over

1.00

Cash

35.00

Unless the petty cash fund is permanently increased or decreased, the balance of the account is always the original amount of the fund. The check issued to replenish petty cash is a credit to Cash and does not affect the Petty Cash account. When the check is cashed, the money is placed in the petty cash box. The amount in the petty cash box changes, as shown below.

The total amount in the petty cash box, $100.00, is again the same as the balance of the Petty Cash account.

Amount in petty cash box before fund is replenished . . .	$ 65.00
Amount from check issued to replenish petty cash	+35.00
Amount in petty cash box after fund is replenished	$100.00

↘ Journalizing the Entry to Replenish Petty Cash

❶ Date. Write the date, 31, in the Date column.

❷ Debit Account Titles. Write the title of the first account debited, Miscellaneous Expense, in the Account Title column. Write the amount to be debited to Miscellaneous Expense, $20.00, in the Debit column on the same line as the account title. Write the title of the second account debited, Advertising Expense, on the next line in the Account Title column. Record the amount to be debited to Advertising Expense, $14.00, in the Debit column on the same line as the account title.

❸ Cash Short. Write the account title, Cash Short and Over, on the next line in the Account Title column. Record the amount of the shortage, $1.00, in the Debit column on the same line as the account title.

❹ Credit. On the next line, indented about one centimeter, write the title of the account credited Cash, in the Account Title column. Write the amount of the replenishment, $35.00, in the Credit column.

❺ Source Document. Write the source document number, C11, in the Doc. No. column.

End of Lesson Review

LO9 Establish a petty cash fund.

LO10 Prepare a petty cash report.

LO11 Replenish a petty cash fund.

Terms Review

petty cash

petty cash slip

cash short

cash over

Audit your understanding

1. Why do businesses use petty cash funds?

2. Why is Cash rather than Petty Cash credited when a petty cash fund is replenished?

Work together 5-4

Establishing and replenishing a petty cash fund

Write the answers to this problem in the *Working Papers*. Your instructor will guide you through the following example.

1. Prepare a petty cash report for November 30 of the current year using the following information: Amount in fund, $200.00. Petty cash slips supported payment of $24.00 for Postage Expense and $20.00 for Miscellaneous Expense. Actual amount of cash in the petty cash box is $154.00.

2. Journalize the following transactions related to petty cash completed during November of the current year. Use page 22 of a journal. The abbreviation for check is C.

   Transactions:

   Nov. 1. Paid cash to establish a petty cash fund, $200.00. C64.

   30. Paid cash to replenish the petty cash fund, $46.00. C86.

On your own 5-4

Establishing and replenishing a petty cash fund

Write the answers to this problem in the *Working Papers*. Work this problem independently.

1. Prepare a petty cash report for April 30 of the current year using the following information: Amount in fund, $250.00. Petty cash slips supported payment of $48.00 for Delivery Expense and $30.00 for Miscellaneous Expense. Actual amount of cash in the petty cash box is $171.00.

2. Journalize the following transactions related to petty cash completed during April. Use page 8 of a journal. The abbreviation for check is C.

   Transactions:

   Apr. 1. Paid cash to establish a petty cash fund, $250.00. C228.

   30. Paid cash to replenish the petty cash fund, $79.00. C253.

A Look at Accounting Software
Reconciling the Cash Account

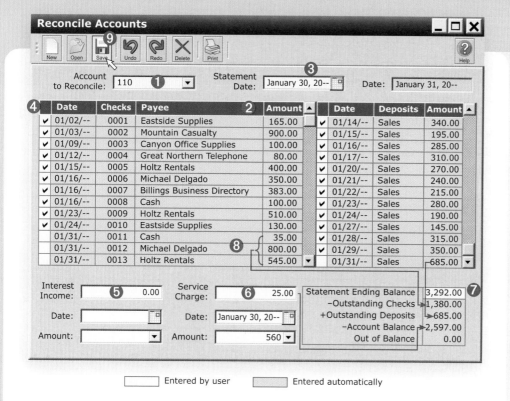

| Entered by user | Entered automatically |

In a manual accounting system, when a bank statement is reconciled, check marks may be placed on check stubs to indicate which checks and deposits have cleared the bank. A very similar procedure is followed with computerized accounting systems. Since there is no paper checkbook, the data from the Cash account is displayed in a window like the one above. The user clicks in fields provided by the system to indicate which items are cleared and which are not. Only a few other pieces of data from the statement are entered by the user, then the system displays an "in-balance" or "out-of-balance" amount. As in manual systems, the most important part of reconciling the cash account is to find and correct any errors.

1 The user selects the account to reconcile.

2 The system displays the checks that have been written and deposits that have been made. (Note that the Deposits scroll bar is at the bottom, indicating that other deposits have scrolled off the window at the top. Three deposits are not displayed.)

3 The user enters the statement date from the bank statement. The system displays the current date in the field to the right.

4 Checkboxes initially appear empty. The user clicks in the checkbox for each check or deposit that appears on the bank statement, indicating that the transaction has cleared the bank.

5 Delgado Web Services has a bank account that does not earn interest. If interest had been earned, the user would enter from the bank statement the amount of interest and the date it was paid. Then the user would select the account where the interest should be posted.

6 Most banks charge a monthly service fee. Delgado's bank charges $25.00 per month. That amount and the date it was drawn from the account by the bank are entered here. Then the user selects the account where the service charge is to be posted. Delgado posts these charges to Miscellaneous Expense, account number 560.

7 The user enters the ending balance from the bank statement.

8 The system sums all outstanding checks (those without check marks) and displays the total below the statement balance. The same is done for outstanding deposits on the next line. [$3,292.00 − $1,380.00 + $685.00 = $2,597.00] The system deducts the $25.00 service charge from the Cash account balance and displays the new balance, $2,597.00 on the next line. When the system subtracts that amount, the Out of Balance amount is zero. If the bank statement differed in any way from data in the system, this line would not be zero, and it would be necessary to find and correct the error(s).

9 The user clicks Save to post all account entries and to record the checks and deposits that have been cleared. A reconciliation report can be printed by clicking Print.

Chapter Summary

Cash is deposited often in order to safeguard this important asset. A deposit slip is prepared and the amount of the deposit is added to the cash balance on the next unused check stub. Any checks being deposited must be endorsed. When writing a check, the check stub is completed first. The check is prepared making sure that all figures and words are clear and accurate. Voided checks are recorded in the journal so that all check numbers are listed in the journal. A bank reconciliation is prepared on a regular basis. The bank service charge must be recorded on the next unused check stub and in the journal. Dishonored checks are also recorded on both the check stub and in the journal. Electronic funds transfers and debit card transactions are recorded on a check stub as "Other." A journal entry is made for both transactions. A petty cash fund is used to make small cash payments. A petty cash slip is prepared each time cash is paid out of the petty cash fund. The fund is replenished when the cash in the fund goes below a certain amount and at the end of each period. A petty cash report is prepared when the fund is replenished.

EXPLORE ACCOUNTING

Cash Controls

Cash transactions occur more frequently than other types of transactions. Because cash is easily transferred from one person to another, a business must try to safeguard its cash to protect it and other assets from errors.

An unintentional error occurs when someone mistakenly records an incorrect amount or forgets to record a transaction. An intentional error occurs when someone intentionally records an incorrect amount or does not record a transaction in order to cover up fraud or theft. Good cash control procedures should guard against both types of errors.

One common method of controlling cash is to insist that all cash payments over a certain amount be paid by check. In addition, checks should be prenumbered so that it is easy to account for each check. The Doc. No. column of a journal can be used to ensure that all checks issued are recorded in the journal. Other cash controls are to have one person responsible for authorizing all checks and to require a source document in support of each cash payment.

One of the best ways to safeguard assets is to separate duties so that one employee does not have total control of an entire set of processes. For example, one employee could receive and record the receipt of cash on account; a second employee could make and record deposits; and a third employee could reconcile the bank statement. By separating the duties, it is less likely that errors will be made. Separating the duties also makes it more difficult to defraud the company.

A company that does not have enough employees to institute the separation of duties concept may hire a certified public accountant (CPA) to perform some of these duties on a regular basis.

INSTRUCTIONS

Talk to a businessperson to determine what kinds of controls are in place in his or her business to safeguard cash. Schools, hospitals, charitable organizations, and government offices as well as retail, wholesale, and service businesses should have established controls that are being followed. Summarize and present your findings to your class.

Apply Your Understanding

INSTRUCTIONS: Download problem instructions for Excel, QuickBooks, and Peachtree from the textbook companion website at www.C21accounting.com.

5-1 Application Problem: Endorsing and writing checks LO1, 2, 3

You are authorized to sign checks for Wash N' Dry. Forms are given in the *Working Papers*.

Instructions:

1. For each of the following situations, prepare the appropriate endorsement.
   a. Write a blank endorsement.
   b. Write a special endorsement to transfer a check to Kim Lumas.
   c. Write a restrictive endorsement to deposit a check in the account of Wash N' Dry.
2. Record the balance brought forward on Check Stub No. 410, $4,125.15.
3. Record a deposit of $1,976.60 made on August 31 of the current year on Check Stub No. 410.
4. Prepare check stubs and write the following checks. Use August 31 of the current year as the date.
   a. Check No. 410 to Central Supplies for supplies, $649.50.
   b. Check No. 411 to *Evening Tribune* for advertising, $297.00.
   c. Check No. 412 to Barbaye Sam for rent, $600.00.

5-2 Application Problem: Reconciling a bank statement and recording a bank service charge LO4, 5

1. Use the required formulas to complete the account reconciliation.
2. Make the selections to print the worksheet.

AAONLINE

1. Go to www.cengage.com/login
2. Click on **AA Online** to access.
3. Go to the online assignment and follow the instructions.

Forms are given in the *Working Papers*. On April 30 of the current year, Clean Carpets received a bank statement dated April 29. The following information is obtained from the bank statement and from the records of the business.

Bank statement balance	$1,812.00
Bank service charge	25.00
Outstanding deposit, April 29	805.10
Outstanding checks:	
No. 475	325.95
No. 476	200.00
Checkbook balance on Check Stub No. 477	2,116.15

Instructions:

1. Prepare a bank statement reconciliation. Use April 30 of the current year as the date.
2. Record the service charge on Check Stub No. 477.
3. Record the service charge on journal page 8. Use Memorandum No. 36 as the source document.

5-3 Application Problem: Recording dishonored checks, electronic funds transfers, and debit card purchases LO6, 7, 8

Instructions:

Enter the following transactions on page 3 of the journal given in the *Working Papers*.

Transactions:

Feb. 25. Received notice from the bank of a dishonored check from Roland Ewing, $275.00, plus $30.00 fee; total, $305.00. Memorandum No. 414.
  26. Paid cash on account to Drew Geist, $310.00, using EFT. Memorandum No. 415.
  27. Purchased supplies, $67.00, using a debit card. Memorandum No. 416.

5-4 Application Problem: Establishing and replenishing a petty cash fund LO9, 10, 11

Instructions:

1. Prepare a petty cash report for June 30 of the current year using the following information: Amount in fund, $300.00. Petty cash slips supported payment of $155.00 for Postage Expense and $75.00 for Miscellaneous Expense. Actual amount of cash in the petty cash box is $66.00.

2. Journalize the following transactions related to petty cash completed during June of the current year. Use page 11 of a journal. The abbreviation for check is C.

Transactions:

June 3. Paid cash to establish a petty cash fund, $300.00. C44.
  30. Paid cash to replenish the petty cash fund, $234.00. C70.

5-M Mastery Problem: Reconciling a bank statement; journalizing a bank service charge, a dishonored check, and petty cash transactions LO4, 5, 6, 9, 10, 11

Lauryn Iverson owns a business called Fresh Flowers. Selected general ledger accounts are given below.

110 Cash	140 Prepaid Insurance	535 Repair Expense
115 Petty Cash	320 Lauryn Iverson, Drawing	540 Supplies Expense
120 Accts. Rec.—Aki Suzuki	520 Miscellaneous Expense	550 Utilities Expense
130 Supplies	530 Rent Expense	

Instructions:

1. Journalize the following transactions completed during March of the current year. Use page 25 of the journal given in the *Working Papers*. Source documents are abbreviated as follows: check, C; memorandum, M; calculator tape, T.

Transactions:

Mar. 21. Paid cash to establish a petty cash fund, $300.00. C220.
  24. Paid cash for repairs, $180.00. C221.
  26. Paid cash for supplies, $75.00. C222.
  27. Received notice from the bank of a dishonored check from Aki Suzuki, $215.00, plus $35.00 fee; total, $250.00. M44.
  28. Paid cash for miscellaneous expense, $60.00. C223.
  31. Paid cash to owner for a withdrawal of equity, $500.00. C224.
  31. Received cash from sales, $700.00. T31.

2. Prepare a petty cash report for March 31 of the current year using the following information: Petty cash slips supported payment of $97.00 for Supplies and $185.00 for Miscellaneous Expense. Actual amount of cash in the petty cash box is $15.00.

3. Continue using the journal and journalize the following transaction:
   Mar. 31. Paid cash to replenish the petty cash fund, $285.00. C225.

4. On March 31 of the current year, Fresh Flowers received a bank statement dated March 30. Prepare a bank statement reconciliation. Use March 31 of the current year as the date. The following information is obtained from the March 30 bank statement and from the records of the business.

Bank statement balance	$3,658.00
Bank service charge	30.00
Outstanding deposit, March 31	700.00
Outstanding checks, Nos. 224 and 225	
Checkbook balance on Check Stub No. 226	3,603.00

5. Continue using the journal and journalize the following transaction:

Transaction:
   Mar. 31. Received bank statement showing March bank service charge, $30.00. M45.

Peachtree

1. Journalize and post transactions to the general journal.
2. From the menu bar, select Tasks; Account Reconciliation to reconcile the bank statement.
3. Make the selections to print the general journal and the account reconciliation.

QB Quick Books

1. Journalize and post transactions to the journal.
2. From the menu bar, select Banking; Reconcile to complete the account reconciliation.
3. Make the selections to print the journal and the account reconciliation.

AAONLiNE

1. Go to www.cengage.com/login
2. Click on **AA Online** to access.
3. Go to the online assignment and follow the instructions.

5-C Challenge Problem: Reconciling a bank statement and recording a bank service charge and a dishonored check LO4, 5, 6

Use the bank statement, canceled checks, and check stubs for Pool Clean given in the *Working Papers*.

Instructions:

1. Compare the canceled checks with the check stubs. For each canceled check, place a check mark next to the appropriate check stub number. For each deposit shown on the bank statement, place a check mark next to the deposit amount on the appropriate check stub.

2. Prepare a bank statement reconciliation. Use July 29 of the current year as the date.

3. Record the following transactions on page 14 of a journal. The abbreviation for memorandum is M.

Transactions:
   Aug. 1. Received bank statement showing July bank service charge, $10.00. M114.
        1. Received notice from the bank of a dishonored check from Daric Cohen, $320.00, plus $30.00 fee; total, $350.00. M115.

4. Record the bank service charge and dishonored check on Check Stub No. 265.

Peachtree

1. Journalize and post transactions to the general journal.
2. From the menu bar, select Tasks; Account Reconciliation to reconcile the bank statement.
3. Make the selections to print the general journal and the account reconciliation.

QB Quick Books

1. Journalize and post transactions to the journal.
2. From the menu bar, select Banking; Reconcile to reconcile the bank statement.
3. Make the selections to print the journal and the account reconciliation.

X

1. Use the required formulas to complete the account reconciliation.
2. Make the selections to print the worksheet.

Veteran Police Officer Sentenced in Embezzlement Case

Theme: Financial, Economic, Business, and Entrepreneurial Literacy

Skills: Information Literacy, ICT Literacy, Social and Cross-Cultural Skills, Critical Thinking and Problem Solving

PARTNERSHIP FOR
21ST CENTURY SKILLS

Just pick up a daily newspaper and read headlines such as *"Nonprofit Executive Charged with Embezzlement," "Veteran Police Officer Sentenced in Embezzlement Case," "Restitution Ordered for Fast Food Embezzlement,"* and *"Doctor Accused of Embezzling More than 250K in Funds."* Most businesses will not experience an armed robbery, yet many will suffer from embezzlement.

Embezzlers come from all income levels and backgrounds. It is difficult to predict who will be dishonest. Most who embezzle will admit they had no intention of stealing from the company. Embezzlement usually begins with a plan to repay or an attempt to rationalize what they felt was owed to them. Unfortunately, this way of thinking costs businesses over $400 billion per year in lost assets such as cash, inventory, and supplies. Most embezzlement could be prevented with strict internal controls. Internal controls provide methods designed to detect and prevent theft, fraud, and errors.

APPLICATION

1. Interview managers at two local retail establishments to determine five of their internal controls. Compare and contrast the internal controls used for each of these businesses. Create a two-column table to compare the controls from each of the businesses. Be sure to list your source.

2. Conduct an Internet search for *fidelity bond*. Explain what a fidelity bond is. Compose a paragraph explaining the correlation between fidelity bonds, embezzlement, and internal controls.

3. Based on your personal experiences, create a list of five internal controls that you would create for your own fast-food business that hires high school age students.

Analyzing Nike's financial statements

On a financial statement, the term *Cash and equivalents* or *Cash and cash equivalents* includes more than just cash on hand. Checking accounts, savings accounts, and even some very short-term investments are also included in this total. Nike's financial statement in Appendix B on page B-6 shows the total Cash and equivalents for Nike for each year.

Published financial statements include notes that explain some of the titles and amounts used in the statements. Note 1 for Nike's financial statements begins on page B-10.

INSTRUCTIONS

1. List the amount of Nike's cash and cash equivalents for 2011 and 2010.
2. Look at Note 1 and list what Nike considers to be *cash and equivalents*.

Reinforcement Activity 1—Part A

An Accounting Cycle for a Proprietorship: Journalizing and Posting Transactions

   QB Quick Books   AAONLINE

Reinforcement activities strengthen the learning of accounting concepts and procedures. Reinforcement Activity 1 is a single problem divided into two parts. Part A includes learning from Chapters 1 through 5. Part B includes learning from Chapters 6 through 8. An accounting cycle is completed in Parts A and B for a single business—Peak Performance.

Peak Performance

In August of the current year, Jasmine Quinn starts a service business called Peak Performance. The business provides performance coaching services. Ms. Quinn helps individuals set and achieve goals, increase efficiency, identify talents, and improve skills. The business rents the facilities in which it operates, pays the utilities, and is responsible for maintenance. Peak Performance charges clients for each coaching session. Most of Peak Performance's sales are for cash. However, two private colleges hire Peak Performance to work with graduating seniors. These schools have an account with Peak Performance.

Chart of Accounts

Peak Performance uses the following chart of accounts.

Chart of Accounts

Balance Sheet Accounts

(100) ASSETS
110 Cash
120 Petty Cash
130 Accounts Receivable—Skiffton University
140 Accounts Receivable—Valley College
150 Supplies
160 Prepaid Insurance

(200) LIABILITIES
210 Accounts Payable—Dakota Supplies
220 Accounts Payable—Seaside Supplies

(300) OWNER'S EQUITY
310 Jasmine Quinn, Capital
320 Jasmine Quinn, Drawing
330 Income Summary

Income Statement Accounts

(400) REVENUE
410 Sales

(500) EXPENSES
510 Advertising Expense
520 Cash Short and Over
530 Insurance Expense
540 Miscellaneous Expense
550 Rent Expense
560 Repair Expense
570 Supplies Expense
580 Utilities Expense

An Accounting Cycle for a Proprietorship: Journalizing and Posting Transactions

Recording Transactions

INSTRUCTIONS

1. Journalize the following transactions completed during August of the current year. Use page 1 of the journal given in the *Working Papers*. Source documents are abbreviated as follows: check stub, C; memorandum, M; receipt, R; sales invoice, S; calculator tape, T.

Aug. 1. Received cash from owner as an investment, $18,000.00. R1.
   1. Paid cash for rent, $3,600.00. C1.
   2. Paid cash for electric bill, $210.00. C2.
   4. Paid cash for supplies, $900.00. C3.
   4. Paid cash for insurance, $2,400.00. C4.
   7. Bought supplies on account from Dakota Supplies, $1,000.00. M1.
   11. Paid cash to establish a petty cash fund, $200.00. C5.
   12. Received cash from sales, $950.00. T12.
   13. Paid cash for repairs, $500.00. C6.
   13. Paid cash for miscellaneous expense, $80.00. C7.
   13. Sold services on account to Valley College, $450.00. S1.
   14. Paid cash for advertising, $600.00. C8.
   15. Paid cash to owner for personal use, $500.00. C9.
   15. Paid cash on account to Dakota Supplies, $600.00. C10.
   15. Sold services on account to Skiffton University, $850.00. S2.
   18. Paid cash for miscellaneous expense, $190.00. C11.
   18. Received cash on account from Valley College, $250.00. R2.

2. Post from the general journal to the general ledger.

3. Use page 2 of the general journal. Journalize the following transactions.

Aug. 19. Received cash from sales, $2,040.00. T19.
   20. Paid cash for repairs, $320.00. C12.
   20. Bought supplies on account from Seaside Supplies, $240.00. M2.
   21. Paid cash for water bill, $530.00. C13.
   25. Paid cash for supplies, $85.00. C14.
   25. Received cash from sales, $2,240.00. T25.
   26. Paid cash for miscellaneous expense, $35.00. C15.
   26. Received cash on account from Skiffton University, $500.00. R3.
   28. Paid cash for telephone bill, $220.00. C16.
   28. Received cash from sales, $600.00. T28.

4. Peak Performance received a bank statement dated August 27. The following information is obtained from the bank statement and from the records of the business. Prepare a bank statement reconciliation. Use August 29 as the date.

Bank statement balance	$13,325.00
Bank service charge	25.00
Outstanding deposit, August 28	600.00
Outstanding checks:	
No. 14	85.00
No. 15	35.00
No. 16	220.00
Checkbook balance on Check Stub No. 17	$13,610.00

5. Continue using page 2 of the general journal, and journalize the following transactions.

Aug. 29. Received bank statement showing August bank service charge, $25.00. M3.
   29. Paid cash for supplies, $40.00. C17.

Aug. 31. Paid cash to replenish the petty cash fund, $130.00: miscellaneous expense, $70.00; repairs, $58.00; cash short, $2.00. C18.

31. Paid cash to owner as a withdrawal of equity, $1,200.00. C19.

31. Received cash from sales, $3,190.00. T31.

6. Post from the general journal to the general ledger.

7. Prove cash. The beginning cash balance on August 1 is zero. The balance on the next unused check stub is $15,405.00.

The general ledger prepared in Reinforcement Activity 1—Part A is needed to complete Reinforcement Activity 1—Part B.

Chapter 6

Work Sheet and Adjusting Entries for a Service Business

LEARNING OBJECTIVES

After studying Chapter 6, in addition to defining key terms, you will be able to:

LO1 Prepare the heading of a work sheet.

LO2 Prepare the trial balance section of a work sheet.

LO3 Analyze and explain the adjustments for supplies and prepaid insurance.

LO4 Complete the Adjustments columns of a work sheet.

LO5 Prepare the Balance Sheet and Income Statement columns of a work sheet.

LO6 Total and rule the work sheet.

LO7 Apply the steps for finding errors on a work sheet.

LO8 Journalize and post the adjusting entries for supplies and prepaid insurance.

©DANIEL KOUREY, ISTOCK/©JIM PRUITT, ISTOCK

PHOTOROLLER/SHUTTERSTOCK.COM

Accounting In The Real World

AICPA

An accountant who has passed the uniform certified public accounting exam and met licensing requirements for a state is called a **certified public accountant (CPA)**. Each state sets its own licensing requirements, but most states require a combination of work experience and education. Once certified and licensed, a CPA must complete continuing education requirements in order to maintain a CPA license. Again, each state sets its own rules for continuing education units.

The American Institute of Certified Public Accountants is the world's largest association representing the accounting profession, with nearly 370,000 members in 128 countries. Its mission is to provide members with the resources, information, and leadership that enable them to provide valuable services in the highest professional manner to benefit the public as well as employers and clients. In fulfilling its mission, the AICPA works with state CPA societies and national and international organizations, and gives priority to those areas where public reliance on accountants' CPA skills is most significant.

CPAs who work for public accounting firms provide many services to their clients, such as auditing financial statements, forensic accounting (sometimes called *fraud auditing*), consulting services, information technology services, evaluating operating performance, international accounting, and tax and financial planning services.

CPAs who are employed by corporations and other businesses often work in finance and accounting departments as financial analysts. They may also have the opportunity to rise up the ranks to positions such as controller, chief financial officer (CFO), and even chief executive officer (CEO). Others work in the areas of international finance, treasury, or internal auditing.

To find out more about CPA career opportunities, salary information, and the accounting profession, visit www.StartHereGoPlaces.com or www.aicpa.org. You may also e-mail the AICPA at educat@aicpa.org. In addition, each state has a CPA society or association that can provide more information. You can contact a state CPA society or association through the "Research/External Links" section of the AICPA website.

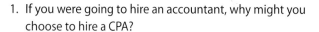

CRITICAL THINKING

1. If you were going to hire an accountant, why might you choose to hire a CPA?

2. If you were a CPA, why might you choose to join a professional association like the AICPA?

Source: www.aicpa.org.

Key Terms

- fiscal period
- fiscal year
- work sheet
- trial balance
- prepaid expense
- accrual basis of accounting
- cash basis of accounting
- adjustments
- balance sheet
- income statement
- net income
- net loss
- adjusting entries

6-1 Creating a Work Sheet

LO1 Prepare the heading of a work sheet.
LO2 Prepare the trial balance section of a work sheet.

Consistent Reporting

General ledger accounts contain information needed by managers and owners. Before the information can be used, however, it must be analyzed, summarized, and reported in a meaningful way. The accounting concept *Consistent Reporting* is applied when the same accounting procedures are followed in the same way in each accounting period. [CONCEPT: Consistent Reporting] For example, in one year, a delivery business might report the number of deliveries made. The next year, the same business reports the amount of revenue received for the deliveries made. The information for the two years cannot be compared because the business has not been consistent in reporting information about deliveries.

> A summary of preparing a work sheet is shown on the Work Sheet Overlay within this chapter.

ETHICS IN ACTION

Professional Codes of Conduct

Most professional organizations have a code of professional conduct to guide the actions of their members. One of the best-known codes of professional conduct is that of the American Institute of Certified Public Accountants (AICPA). A national organization of over 370,000 certified public accountants, the AICPA seeks to help its members provide professional services that benefit their employees, clients, and society. An important component of this mission is the AICPA Code of Professional Conduct.

The Code contains Rules of Conduct that its members must follow in their performance of professional services. The Rules address the topics of independence, integrity, objectivity, client relations, and colleague relations. Some Rules have Interpretations that provide further insight into the Rules. The Code is also supported by Ethics Rulings, a series of questions and answers that the AICPA elects to share with its members.

AICPA members who fail to adhere to the Code can be disciplined or expelled from the membership. Losing membership in the AICPA can result in serious consequences for a certified public accountant working in the profession.

INSTRUCTIONS

Access the AICPA's Code of Professional Conduct at www.aicpa.org. On the Membership tab, select Requirements. Citing the section number supporting each answer, determine whether a member of the AICPA may ethically do the following:

1. Accept an invitation to participate (free of charge) in a client's annual golf outing. (*Hint:* Search Section 100: Independence, Integrity and Objectivity.)

2. Charge a fee based on the net income reported on the audited income statement. (*Hint:* Search Section 300: Responsibilities to Clients.)

3. Advertise professional services in television commercials. (*Hint:* Search Section 500: Other Responsibilities and Practices.)

Fiscal Periods

The length of time for which a business summarizes its financial information and reports its financial performance is called a **fiscal period**. A fiscal period is also known as an *accounting period*. The accounting concept *Accounting Period Cycle* is applied when changes in financial information are reported for a specific period of time in the form of financial statements. [CONCEPT: Accounting Period Cycle] Each business chooses a fiscal period length that meets its needs. Because federal and state tax reports are based on one year, businesses must report their financial performance for a full year. A fiscal period consisting of twelve consecutive months is called a **fiscal year**. Because Delgado Web Services is a new business, Mr. Delgado wishes to have financial information reported frequently to help him make decisions. For

this reason, Delgado Web Services uses a one-month fiscal period.

A fiscal period can begin on any date. However, most businesses begin their fiscal periods on the first day of a month. Delgado Web Services started business on January 1. Therefore, Delgado Web Services' monthly fiscal period is for the period from January 1 through January 31, inclusive. Businesses often choose a one-year fiscal period that ends during a period of low business activity. In this way, the end-of-year accounting work comes at a time when other business activities are the lightest.

Financial information may be analyzed, summarized, and reported on any date a business needs the information. However, financial information is always summarized and reported at the end of a fiscal period.

Work Sheet

A columnar accounting form used to summarize the general ledger information needed to prepare financial statements is called a **work sheet.**

Accountants use a work sheet for four reasons: (1) to summarize general ledger account balances to prove that debits equal credits; (2) to plan needed changes to general ledger accounts to bring account balances up to date; (3) to separate general ledger account balances

according to the financial statements to be prepared; and (4) to calculate the amount of net income or net loss for a fiscal period.

Journals and ledgers are permanent records of a business and are usually prepared in ink or printed by a computer. However, a work sheet is a planning tool and is not considered a permanent accounting record. Therefore, a work sheet is prepared in pencil.

Preparing the Heading of a Work Sheet LO1

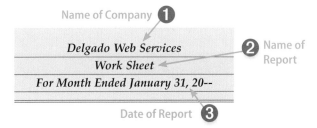

Name of Company ①

Delgado Web Services
Work Sheet
For Month Ended January 31, 20--

② Name of Report

Date of Report ③

The heading on a work sheet consists of three lines and contains the name of the business, the name of the report, and the date of the report.

The date on Delgado Web Services' work sheet indicates that the work sheet covers the 31 days from January 1 through and including January 31. If a work sheet were for a calendar year fiscal period, it might have a date stated as *For Year Ended December 31, 20--*.

Preparing a Trial Balance on a Work Sheet LO2

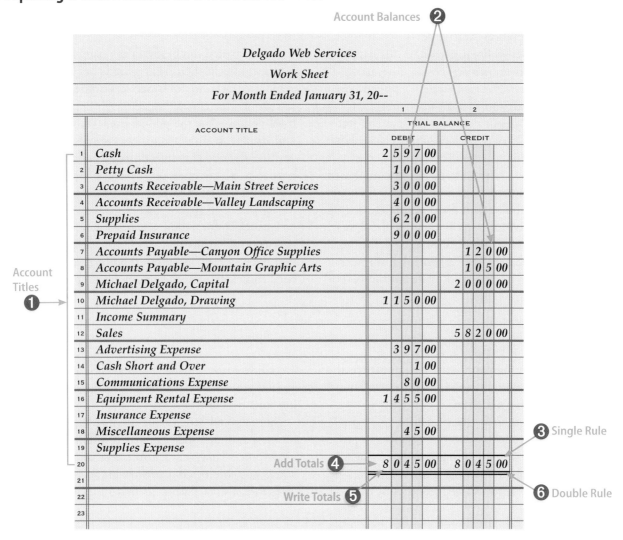

Account Balances ❷

Delgado Web Services

Work Sheet

For Month Ended January 31, 20--

	ACCOUNT TITLE	TRIAL BALANCE DEBIT	TRIAL BALANCE CREDIT
1	Cash	2 5 9 7 00	
2	Petty Cash	1 0 0 00	
3	Accounts Receivable—Main Street Services	3 0 0 00	
4	Accounts Receivable—Valley Landscaping	4 0 0 00	
5	Supplies	6 2 0 00	
6	Prepaid Insurance	9 0 0 00	
7	Accounts Payable—Canyon Office Supplies		1 2 0 00
8	Accounts Payable—Mountain Graphic Arts		1 0 5 00
9	Michael Delgado, Capital		2 0 0 0 00
10	Michael Delgado, Drawing	1 1 5 0 00	
11	Income Summary		
12	Sales		5 8 2 0 00
13	Advertising Expense	3 9 7 00	
14	Cash Short and Over	1 00	
15	Communications Expense	8 0 00	
16	Equipment Rental Expense	1 4 5 5 00	
17	Insurance Expense		
18	Miscellaneous Expense	4 5 00	
19	Supplies Expense		
20	Add Totals ❹	8 0 4 5 00	8 0 4 5 00
21			
22	Write Totals ❺		
23			

Account Titles ❶

❸ Single Rule
❻ Double Rule

The total of all debit account balances must equal the total of all credit account balances. A proof of the equality of debits and credits in a general ledger is called a **trial balance.**

Information for the trial balance is taken from the general ledger. General ledger account titles are listed on a trial balance in the same order as they are listed on the chart of accounts. All the account titles are listed, even if some accounts do not have balances.

↘ Preparing a Trial Balance on a Work Sheet

❶ Write the general ledger account titles in the work sheet's Account Title column.

❷ Write the general ledger debit account balances in the Trial Balance Debit column. Write the general ledger credit account balances in the Trial Balance Credit column. If an account does not have a balance, the space in the Trial Balance columns is left blank.

❸ Rule a single line across the two Trial Balance columns below the last line on which an account title is written. This single line shows that each column is to be added.

❹ Add both the Trial Balance Debit and Credit columns. If the two column totals are the same, then debits equal credits in the general ledger accounts. If the two column totals are not the same, recheck the Trial Balance columns to find the error. Other parts of a work sheet are not completed until the Trial Balance columns are proved. Suggestions for locating errors are described later in this chapter.

❺ Write each column's total below the single line.

❻ Rule double lines across both Trial Balance columns. The double lines mean that the Trial Balance column totals have been verified as correct.

ZZZZ Best

At the age of 16, Barry Minkow started a carpet cleaning business. Barry's goal was typical for a young man having just earned his driver's license—he wanted to earn enough money to purchase a car. By the age of 21, he was driving a Ferrari and living in a mansion. The listing of his company, ZZZZ Best, on the NASDAQ stock exchange made him a rich man. His success story earned him an invitation on the Oprah Winfrey Show where he explained his secret as "think big, be big." He expanded his business beyond carpet cleaning to include the restoration of buildings damaged by fire or floods.

THE FRAUD STORY

Unknown to his accountants, lawyers, and investors, the building restoration part of the business was complete fiction. The carpet cleaning business had never made a profit. The only way to obtain the money needed to support his lifestyle was to borrow the money from banks. But banks only lend money to profitable businesses. To create profit, Minkow created source documents that appeared to support the contracts and transactions of a building restoration business.

When accountants demanded to see one of his restoration projects, Minkow bribed a building guard to give him weekend access to an office building. He hung ZZZZ Best banners in the lobby and paid the guard to pretend that he knew Minkow and ZZZZ Best personnel. Fueled by the restoration business, ZZZZ Best grew into a $280 million business.

When the fraud was finally revealed, the assets of ZZZZ Best were sold for a mere $50,000. Minkow and members of his inner circle were charged with over 50 criminal counts, including securities fraud, tax evasion, and bank fraud. Minkow was sentenced to 25 years of prison and served just over seven years.

ACTIVITY

Amy Heath is a home stager, decorating homes to prepare them for sale. Her schedule does not include time to handle the accounting tasks of the business. So, she hired Barnes Bookkeeping to maintain her accounting records and write checks for her business. Each month, Amy reviews the bank reconciliation and financial statements prepared by Barnes Bookkeeping.

Despite her success, Amy does not seem to be earning the amount of money she expected. She has no reason to suspect that anything is wrong, especially since her friend Mary Kate Sanders is handling her account for Barnes Bookkeeping. Still, she has asked you to compare her bank records with a list of checks obtained from Barnes Bookkeeping.

INSTRUCTIONS

Open the spreadsheet FA_CH06. Follow the steps on the Instructions tab. After analyzing the data provided, answer the following questions:

1. Are there any differences in check amounts per the bank and the accounting records?

2. Do you believe any differences are the result of clerical errors? Support your answer.

3. What evidence would you want to examine next?

End of Lesson Review

LO1 Prepare the heading of a work sheet.

LO2 Prepare the trial balance section of a work sheet.

Terms Review

fiscal period

fiscal year

work sheet

trial balance

Audit your understanding

1. What is written on the three-line heading on a work sheet?

2. What general ledger accounts are listed in the Trial Balance columns of a work sheet?

Work together 6-1

Recording the trial balance on a work sheet

Use the work sheet given in the *Working Papers*. Your instructor will guide you through the following example.

On April 30 of the current year, Fix It Now has the following general ledger accounts and balances. The business uses a monthly fiscal period.

Account Titles	Account Balances	
	Debit	Credit
Cash	$4,900.00	
Petty Cash	75.00	
Accounts Receivable—B. Widell	1,387.00	
Supplies	228.00	
Prepaid Insurance	375.00	
Accounts Payable—Southside Supplies		$ 267.00
Connor Whitney, Capital		7,443.00
Connor Whitney, Drawing	1,700.00	
Income Summary		
Sales		2,160.00
Advertising Expense	460.00	
Cash Short and Over	6.00	
Insurance Expense		
Miscellaneous Expense	189.00	
Supplies Expense		
Utilities Expense	550.00	

Prepare the heading and trial balance on a work sheet. Total and rule the Trial Balance columns. Save your work to complete Work Together 6-2.

On your own 6-1

Recording the trial balance on a work sheet

Use the work sheet given in the *Working Papers*. Work this problem independently. On December 31 of the current year, Repair World has the following general ledger accounts and balances. The business uses a monthly fiscal period.

Account Titles	Account Balances	
	Debit	Credit
Cash	$13,600.00	
Petty Cash	150.00	
Accounts Receivable—Stephen Coates	2,996.00	
Supplies	476.00	
Prepaid Insurance	650.00	
Accounts Payable—Jill Stratton		$ 596.00
Isiah Clausen, Capital		14,886.00
Isiah Clausen, Drawing	3,400.00	
Income Summary		
Sales		8,280.00
Advertising Expense	910.00	
Cash Short and Over	2.00	
Insurance Expense		
Miscellaneous Expense	378.00	
Supplies Expense		
Utilities Expense	1,200.00	

Prepare the heading and trial balance on a work sheet. Total and rule the Trial Balance columns. Save your work to complete On Your Own 6-2.

©CANDICE CUSACK, ISTOCK

6-2 Planning Adjusting Entries on a Work Sheet

LO3 Analyze and explain the adjustments for supplies and prepaid insurance.

LO4 Complete the Adjustments columns of a work sheet.

Planning Adjustments on a Work Sheet LO3

Delgado Web Services buys supplies in quantity in January. Some of the supplies are used in January, but some supplies are not used until February or March. Cash paid for an expense in one fiscal period that is not used until a later period is called a **prepaid expense**. For example, only the value of the supplies used in January should be reported as expenses in January. The expense should be reported in the same fiscal period that it is used to produce revenue. The accounting concept *Matching Expenses with Revenue* is applied when revenue from business activities and expenses associated with earning that revenue are recorded in the same accounting period. In this way, January revenue and the supplies expense associated with earning the January revenue are recorded in the same accounting period. [CONCEPT: Matching Expenses with Revenue] Reporting income when it is earned and expenses when they are incurred is called the **accrual basis of accounting**. Generally accepted accounting principles (GAAP) require the use of the accrual basis of accounting.

Reporting income when the cash is received and expenses when the cash is paid is called the **cash basis of accounting**. Broadly speaking, GAAP requires the use of the accrual basis of accounting and does not allow the use of the cash basis of accounting. However, if the difference in results between the two methods is not large enough to affect decision making, a business could use the cash basis of accounting. The accounting concept *Materiality* is applied when the amount of an error or omission in the accounting records is not large enough to affect business decisions. [CONCEPT: Materiality] Materiality is affected by the size of the business. A $2,000,000 amount would be material to many businesses but could be immaterial to a large corporation.

The major difference between the accrual basis and the cash basis of accounting is in timing. For example, when the accrual basis is used, revenue from sales will be included in the financial statements even if the cash has not yet been collected. Expenses for the period will

be included in the financial statements even if the cash has not yet been paid. When the cash basis is used, revenue from sales will not be included in the financial statements until the cash has been collected. Expenses will not be included in the financial statements until the cash has been paid. Over time, the revenues and expenses reported will be the same. The differences are only caused by timing.

In order to give accurate information on financial statements, some general ledger accounts must be brought up to date at the end of a fiscal period. For example, Delgado Web Services debits an asset account, **Supplies**, each time supplies are bought. Supplies on hand are items of value owned by a business until the supplies are used. The value of supplies that are used becomes an expense to the business. However, recording an expense each time an individual supply, such as a pencil, is used would be impractical. Therefore, on January 31, the balance of the asset account, **Supplies**, is the value of all supplies bought rather than the value of only the supplies that have not yet been used. The amount of supplies that have been used must be deducted from the asset account, **Supplies**, and recorded in the expense account, **Supplies Expense**.

Likewise, the amount of insurance premium used during the fiscal period is also an expense of the business. When the insurance premium for a year of insurance coverage is paid, the entire amount is debited to an asset account, **Prepaid Insurance**. Recording each day's amount of insurance premium used during January is impractical. Therefore, at the end of a fiscal period, the amount of the insurance premium used must be deducted from the asset account, **Prepaid Insurance**, and recorded in the expense account, **Insurance Expense**.

Changes recorded on a work sheet to update general ledger accounts at the end of a fiscal period are called **adjustments**. The assets of a business, such as supplies and prepaid insurance, are used to earn revenue. The portions of the assets consumed in order to earn revenue become expenses of the business. The portions consumed are no longer assets but are now expenses. Therefore, adjustments must be made to both the asset and expense accounts for supplies and insurance. After the adjustments are made, the expenses incurred to earn revenue are reported in the same fiscal period as the revenue is earned and reported. [CONCEPT: Matching Expenses with Revenue]

A work sheet is used to plan adjustments. Changes are not made in general ledger accounts until adjustments are journalized and posted. The accuracy of the planning for adjustments is checked on a work sheet before adjustments are actually journalized.

Procedures for journalizing Delgado Web Services' adjustments are described later in this chapter.

Supplies Adjustment on a Work Sheet

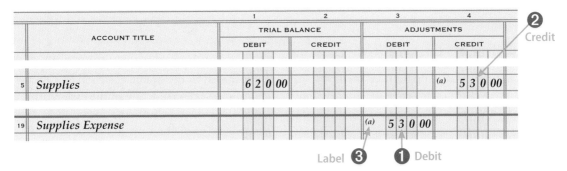

On January 31, before adjustments, the balance of Supplies is $620.00, and the balance of Supplies Expense is zero, as shown in the T accounts.

On January 31, Mr. Delgado counted the supplies on hand and found that the value of supplies still unused on that date was $90.00. The value of the supplies used is calculated as follows:

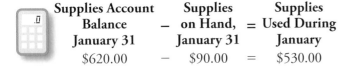

Supplies Account Balance January 31	−	Supplies on Hand, January 31	=	Supplies Used During January
$620.00	−	$90.00	=	$530.00

Four questions are asked in analyzing the adjustment for the asset account, Supplies.

1. **What is the balance of the account to be adjusted?** *$620.00*
2. **What should the balance be for this account?** *$90.00*
3. **What must be done to correct the account balance?** *Decrease $530.00*
4. **What adjustment is made?**
   Debit Supplies Expense, *$530.00*
   Credit Supplies, *$530.00*

The expense account, Supplies Expense, is increased by a debit, $530.00, the value of supplies used. The balance of Supplies Expense, $530.00, is the value of supplies used during the fiscal period from January 1 to January 31. [CONCEPT: Matching Expenses with Revenue]

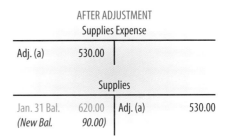

The asset account, Supplies, is decreased by a credit, $530.00, the value of supplies used. The debit balance, $620.00, less the credit adjustment, $530.00, equals the new balance, $90.00. The new balance of Supplies is the same as the value of supplies on hand on January 31.

↘ Recording the Supplies Adjustment on a Work Sheet

❶ Write the debit amount, $530.00, in the work sheet's Adjustments Debit column on the line with the account title Supplies Expense.

❷ Write the credit amount, $530.00, in the Adjustments Credit column on the line with the account title Supplies.

❸ Label the two parts of this adjustment with a small letter *a* in parentheses, (a). The letter *a* identifies the debit and credit amounts as part of the same adjustment.

Prepaid Insurance Adjustment on a Work Sheet

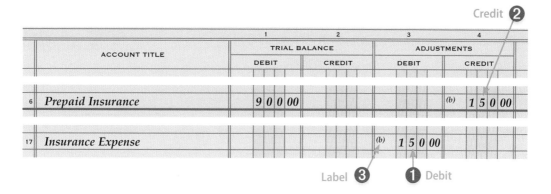

Credit ❷

	ACCOUNT TITLE	TRIAL BALANCE		ADJUSTMENTS	
		DEBIT	CREDIT	DEBIT	CREDIT
6	*Prepaid Insurance*	9 0 0 00			(b) 1 5 0 00
17	*Insurance Expense*			(b) 1 5 0 00	

Label ❸   ❶ Debit

On January 31, before adjustments, the balance of Prepaid Insurance is $900.00, and the balance of Insurance Expense is zero.

BEFORE ADJUSTMENT

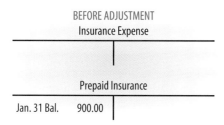

Insurance Expense

Prepaid Insurance

Jan. 31 Bal.   900.00

On January 31, Mr. Delgado checked the insurance records and found that the value of insurance premium remaining was $750.00. The value of the insurance premium used during the fiscal period is calculated as follows:

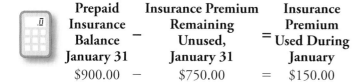

Prepaid Insurance Balance January 31	−	Insurance Premium Remaining Unused, January 31	=	Insurance Premium Used During January
$900.00	−	$750.00	=	$150.00

Four questions are asked in analyzing the adjustment for the asset account, Prepaid Insurance.

1. **What is the balance of the account to be adjusted?** *$900.00*
2. **What should the balance be for this account?** *$750.00*
3. **What must be done to correct the account balance?** *Decrease $150.00*
4. **What adjustment is made?**
   Debit Insurance Expense, *$150.00*
   Credit Prepaid Insurance, *$150.00*

The expense account, Insurance Expense, is increased by a debit, $150.00, the value of insurance premium used. The balance of Insurance Expense, $150.00, is the value of insurance premium used from January 1 to January 31. [CONCEPT: Matching Expenses with Revenue]

AFTER ADJUSTMENT

Insurance Expense

Adj. (b)   150.00

Prepaid Insurance

| Jan. 31 Bal. | 900.00 | Adj. (b) | 150.00 |
| (New Bal. | 750.00) | | |

The asset account, Prepaid Insurance, is decreased by a credit, $150.00, the value of insurance premium used. The debit balance, $900.00, less the credit adjustment, $150.00, equals the new balance, $750.00. The new balance of Prepaid Insurance is the same as the amount of insurance premium unused on January 31.

⬇ Recording the Prepaid Insurance Adjustment on a Work Sheet

❶ Write the debit amount, $150.00, in the work sheet's Adjustments Debit column on the line with the account title Insurance Expense.

❷ Write the credit amount, $150.00, in the Adjustments Credit column on the line with the account title Prepaid Insurance.

❸ Label the two parts of this adjustment with a small letter b in parentheses, (b). The letter b identifies the debit and credit amounts as part of the same adjustment.

Proving the Adjustments Columns of a Work Sheet LO4

		1	2	3	4
		TRIAL BALANCE		ADJUSTMENTS	
	ACCOUNT TITLE	DEBIT	CREDIT	DEBIT	CREDIT

Delgado Web Services
Work Sheet
For Month Ended January 31, 20--

	Account Title	Trial Balance Debit	Trial Balance Credit	Adjustments Debit	Adjustments Credit
5	Supplies	6 2 0 00			(a) 5 3 0 00
6	Prepaid Insurance	9 0 0 00			(b) 1 5 0 00
17	Insurance Expense			(b) 1 5 0 00	
18	Miscellaneous Expense	4 5 00			
19	Supplies Expense			(a) 5 3 0 00	
20		8 0 4 5 00	8 0 4 5 00	6 8 0 00	6 8 0 00

1 Single Rule
2 Totals

Double Rule **3**

After all adjustments are recorded in a work sheet's Adjustments columns, the equality of debits and credits for the two columns is proved by totaling and ruling the two columns.

Proving the Adjustments Columns of a Work Sheet

1 Rule a single line across the two Adjustments columns on the same line as the single line for the Trial Balance columns.

2 Add both the Adjustments Debit and Credit columns. If the two column totals are the same, then debits equal credits for these two columns, and the work sheet's Adjustments columns are in balance. Write each column's total below the single line. If the two Adjustments column totals are not the same, the Adjustments columns are rechecked and errors corrected before the work sheet is completed.

3 Rule double lines across both Adjustments columns. The double lines mean that the totals have been verified as correct.

Use a ruler when extending amounts on a work sheet to keep track of the line you are on.

Global Currencies

As global trade increases, U.S. businesses become more involved in transactions with foreign businesses. These transactions can be stated in terms of U.S. dollars or in the currency of the other country. If the transaction involves foreign currency, a U.S. business must convert the foreign currency into U.S. dollars before the transaction can be recorded. [CONCEPT: Unit of Measurement]

The value of foreign currency may change daily. In the United States, the exchange rate is the value of foreign currency in relation to the U.S. dollar. Banks, online services, and many daily newspapers list current exchange rates.

The exchange rate is stated in terms of one unit of foreign currency. Using China as an example, assume that one Chinese yuan is worth 0.15077 (or about 15 U.S. cents). This rate would be used when exchanging Chinese yuan for U.S. dollars.

A conversion formula can be used to find out how many foreign currency units can be purchased with one U.S. dollar. The formula is:

$$1 \text{ dollar} \div \text{Exchange Rate} = \text{Foreign Currency per U.S. dollar}$$

$$1 \text{ dollar} \div 0.15077 = 6.63262 \text{ yuan per U.S. dollar}$$

To convert an amount in Chinese yuan to U.S. dollars, divide the amount of yuan by the number of yuan per dollar as shown.

$$350 \text{ Chinese yuan} \div 6.63262 = \$52.77$$

CRITICAL THINKING

1. Current exchange rates change constantly. Do an Internet search and report the current exchange rate for the Chinese yuan.

2. If the exchange rate for one Mexican peso is 0.08142, what U.S. dollar amount would be recorded for a receipt of 5,000 Mexican pesos?

3. If the exchange rate for one European euro is 0.73320, what amount would be recorded in U.S. dollars for a receipt of 200 euros?

British Pound
US Dollar
Euro
Japanese Ye
Chinese Yu

End of Lesson Review

LO3 Analyze and explain the adjustments for supplies and prepaid insurance.

LO4 Complete the Adjustments columns of a work sheet.

Terms Review

prepaid expense

accrual basis of accounting

cash basis of accounting

adjustments

Audit your understanding

1. Explain how the concept of Matching Expenses with Revenue relates to adjustments.

2. List the four questions asked in analyzing an adjustment on a work sheet.

Work together 6-2

Planning adjustments on a work sheet

Use the work sheet from Work Together 6-1. Your instructor will guide you through the following examples.

1. Analyze the following adjustment information into debit and credit parts. Record the adjustments on the work sheet.

   Adjustment Information, April 30
   Supplies on hand $ 75.00
   Value of prepaid insurance   250.00

2. Total and rule the Adjustments columns. Save your work sheet to complete Work Together 6-3.

On your own 6-2

Planning adjustments on a work sheet

Use the work sheet from On Your Own 6-1. Work this problem independently.

1. Analyze the following adjustment information into debit and credit parts. Record the adjustments on the work sheet.

   Adjustment Information, December 31
   Supplies on hand $240.00
   Value of prepaid insurance   520.00

2. Total and rule the Adjustments columns. Save your work sheet to complete On Your Own 6-3.

©CANDICE CUSACK, ISTOCK

LESSON 6-3 Completing the Work Sheet and Finding Errors on a Work Sheet

LO5 Prepare the Balance Sheet and Income Statement columns of a work sheet.

LO6 Total and rule the work sheet.

LO7 Apply the steps for finding errors on a work sheet.

Extending Balance Sheet Account Balances on a Work Sheet LO5

1 Debit Balances without Adjustments

Delgado Web Services
Work Sheet
For Month Ended January 31, 20--

	ACCOUNT TITLE	TRIAL BALANCE		ADJUSTMENTS		INCOME STATEMENT		BALANCE SHEET		
		1 DEBIT	2 CREDIT	3 DEBIT	4 CREDIT	5 DEBIT	6 CREDIT	7 DEBIT	8 CREDIT	
1	Cash	2 5 9 7 00						2 5 9 7 00		1
2	Petty Cash	1 0 0 00						1 0 0 00		2
3	Accts. Rec.—Main Street Services	3 0 0 00						3 0 0 00		3
4	Accts. Rec.—Valley Landscaping	4 0 0 00						4 0 0 00		4
5	Supplies	6 2 0 00			(a) 5 3 0 00			9 0 00		5
6	Prepaid Insurance	9 0 0 00			(b) 1 5 0 00			7 5 0 00		6
7	Accts. Pay.—Canyon Office Supplies		1 2 0 00						1 2 0 00	7
8	Accts. Pay.—Mountain Graphic Arts		1 0 5 00						1 0 5 00	8
9	Michael Delgado, Capital		2 0 0 0 00						2 0 0 0 00	9
10	Michael Delgado, Drawing	1 1 5 0 00						1 1 5 0 00		10

2 Debit Balances with Adjustments   **3** Credit Balances without Adjustments

At the end of each fiscal period, Delgado Web Services prepares two financial statements from information on a work sheet. [CONCEPT: Accounting Period Cycle] The up-to-date account balances on a work sheet are extended to columns for the two financial statements.

A financial statement that reports the value of a business' assets, liabilities, and owner's equity on a specific date is called a **balance sheet.** The balance sheet accounts are the asset, liability, and owner's equity accounts. Up-to-date balance sheet account balances are extended to the Balance Sheet Debit and Credit columns of the work sheet.

↻ Extending Balance Sheet Account Balances on a Work Sheet

1 Extend the balance of Cash, $2,597.00, to the Balance Sheet Debit column. The balance of Cash in the Trial Balance Debit column is up to date because no adjustment affects this account. Extend to the Balance Sheet Debit column the balances of all accounts with debit balances that are not affected by adjustments.

2 Calculate the up-to-date adjusted balance of Supplies. The balance of Supplies in the Trial Balance Debit column is not up to date because it is affected by an adjustment. The debit balance, $620.00, minus the credit adjustment, $530.00, equals the up-to-date adjusted balance, $90.00. Extend the up-to-date balance, $90.00, to the Balance Sheet Debit column. Using the same procedure, calculate and extend the up-to-date adjusted balance of the other asset account affected by an adjustment, Prepaid Insurance.

3 Extend the up-to-date balance of Accounts Payable—Canyon Office Supplies, $120.00, to the Balance Sheet Credit column. The balance of Accounts Payable—Canyon Office Supplies in the Trial Balance Credit column is up to date because no adjustment affects this account. Extend to the Balance Sheet Credit column the balances of all accounts with credit balances that are not affected by adjustments.

Extending Income Statement Account Balances on a Work Sheet

Expense Balances without Adjustments **2**   **1** Sales Balance

Delgado Web Services
Work Sheet
For Month Ended January 31, 20--

		1	2	3	4	5	6	7	8	
	ACCOUNT TITLE	TRIAL BALANCE		ADJUSTMENTS		INCOME STATEMENT		BALANCE SHEET		
		DEBIT	CREDIT	DEBIT	CREDIT	DEBIT	CREDIT	DEBIT	CREDIT	
11	Income Summary									11
12	Sales		5 820 00				5 820 00			12
13	Advertising Expense	397 00				397 00				13
14	Cash Short and Over	1 00				1 00				14
15	Communications Expense	80 00				80 00				15
16	Equipment Rental Expense	1 455 00				1 455 00				16
17	Insurance Expense			(b) 150 00		150 00				17
18	Miscellaneous Expense	45 00				45 00				18
19	Supplies Expense			(a) 530 00		530 00				19
20		8 045 00	8 045 00	680 00	680 00					20
21										21
22										22
23										23

Expense Balances with Adjustments **3**

A financial statement showing the revenue and expenses for a fiscal period is called an **income statement.** Delgado Web Services' income statement accounts are the revenue and expense accounts. Up-to-date income statement account balances are extended to the Income Statement Debit and Credit columns of the work sheet.

A work sheet is prepared in manual accounting to adjust the accounts and sort amounts needed to prepare financial statements. However, in automated accounting, adjustments are prepared from the trial balance, and the software automatically generates the financial statements with no need for a work sheet.

> ### Extending Income Statement Account Balances on a Work Sheet
>
> **1** Extend the balance of Sales, $5,820.00, to the Income Statement Credit column. The balance of Sales in the Trial Balance Credit column is up to date because no adjustment affects this account.
>
> **2** Extend the balance of Advertising Expense, $397.00, to the Income Statement Debit column. The balance of Advertising Expense is up to date because no adjustment affects this account. Extend the balances of all expense accounts not affected by adjustments to the Income Statement Debit column.
>
> **3** Calculate the up-to-date adjusted balance of Insurance Expense. The balance of Insurance Expense in the Trial Balance Debit column is zero. This zero balance is not up to date because this account is affected by an adjustment. The debit balance, $0.00, plus the debit adjustment, $150.00, equals the adjusted balance, $150.00. Extend the up-to-date adjusted debit balance, $150.00, to the Income Statement Debit column. Using the same procedure, calculate and extend the up-to-date adjusted balance of each expense account affected by an adjustment.

Recording Net Income and Totaling and Ruling a Work Sheet L06

Delgado Web Services

Work Sheet

For Month Ended January 31, 20--

		ACCOUNT TITLE	1 TRIAL BALANCE DEBIT	2 TRIAL BALANCE CREDIT	3 ADJUSTMENTS DEBIT	4 ADJUSTMENTS CREDIT	5 INCOME STATEMENT DEBIT	6 INCOME STATEMENT CREDIT	7 BALANCE SHEET DEBIT	8 BALANCE SHEET CREDIT	
1		Cash	2 5 9 7 00						2 5 9 7 00		1
2		Petty Cash	1 0 0 00						1 0 0 00		2
3		Accts. Rec.—Main Street Services	3 0 0 00						3 0 0 00		3
4		Accts. Rec.—Valley Landscaping	4 0 0 00						4 0 0 00		4
5		Supplies	6 2 0 00			(a) 5 3 0 00			9 0 00		5
6		Prepaid Insurance	9 0 0 00			(b) 1 5 0 00			7 5 0 00		6
7		Accts. Pay.—Canyon Office Supplies		1 2 0 00						1 2 0 00	7
8		Accts. Pay.—Mountain Graphic Arts		1 0 5 00						1 0 5 00	8
9		Michael Delgado, Capital		2 0 0 0 00						2 0 0 0 00	9
10		Michael Delgado, Drawing	1 1 5 0 00						1 1 5 0 00		10
11		Income Summary									11
12		Sales		5 8 2 0 00				5 8 2 0 00			12
13		Advertising Expense	3 9 7 00				3 9 7 00				13
14		Cash Short and Over	1 00				1 00				14
15		Communications Expense	8 0 00				8 0 00				15
16		Equipment Rental Expense	1 4 5 5 00				1 4 5 5 00				16
17		Insurance Expense			(b) 1 5 0 00		1 5 0 00				17
18		Miscellaneous Expense	4 5 00				4 5 00				18
19		Supplies Expense			(a) 5 3 0 00		5 3 0 00				19
20			8 0 4 5 00	8 0 4 5 00	6 8 0 00	6 8 0 00	2 6 5 8 00	5 8 2 0 00	5 3 8 7 00	2 2 2 5 00	20
21		Net Income					3 1 6 2 00			3 1 6 2 00	21
22							5 8 2 0 00	5 8 2 0 00	5 3 8 7 00	5 3 8 7 00	22

❶ Single Rule ❸ Net Income ❻ Totals ❼ Double Rule ❹ Extend Net Income ❺ Single Rule ❷ Totals

The difference between total revenue and total expenses when total revenue is greater is called **net income.** Net income is sometimes also referred to as profit. Before the work sheet is complete, net income must be calculated and the work sheet must be totaled and ruled. A summary of preparing a work sheet is shown on the Work Sheet Overlay.

🔧 Calculating and Recording Net Income on a Work Sheet; Totaling and Ruling a Work Sheet

❶ Rule a single line across the four Income Statement and Balance Sheet columns.

❷ Add both the Income Statement and Balance Sheet columns. Write the totals below the single line.

❸ Calculate the net income. The Income Statement Credit column total, $5,820.00, minus the Income Statement Debit column total, $2,658.00, equals net income, $3,162.00. Write the amount of net income, $3,162.00, below the Income Statement Debit column total. Write the words Net Income on the same line in the Account Title column.

❹ Extend the amount of net income, $3,162.00, to the Balance Sheet Credit column. Since the owner's equity account, Michael Delgado, Capital, increases by a credit, extend the net income amount to the Balance Sheet Credit column.

❺ Rule a single line across the four Income Statement and Balance Sheet columns just below the net income amounts.

❻ Add the subtotal and net income amount for each column to get proving totals for the Income Statement and Balance Sheet columns. Write the totals below the single line. Check the equality for each pair of columns.

❼ Rule double lines across the Income Statement and Balance Sheet columns.

Calculating and Recording a Net Loss on a Work Sheet

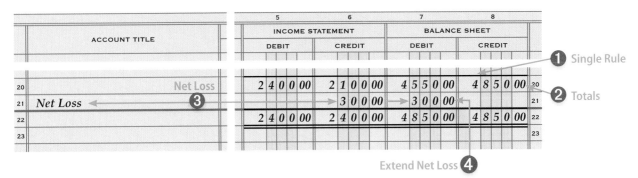

Delgado Web Services' completed work sheet shows a net income. However, a business might have a net loss to report. The difference between total revenue and total expenses when total expenses are greater is called a **net loss.**

Calculating and Recording a Net Loss on a Work Sheet

① Rule a single line across the four Income Statement and Balance Sheet columns.

② Add both the Income Statement and Balance Sheet columns. Write the totals below the single line.

③ Calculate the net loss. The Income Statement Debit column total, $2,400.00, minus the Income Statement Credit column total, $2,100.00, equals net loss, $300.00. The Income Statement Debit column total (expenses) is greater than the Income Statement Credit column total (revenue). Therefore, because expenses exceed revenue, there is a net loss. Write the amount of net loss, $300.00, below the Income Statement Credit column total. Write the words Net Loss on the same line in the Account Title column.

④ Extend the amount of net loss, $300.00, to the Balance Sheet Debit column on the same line as the words Net Loss. The owner's equity account, Michael Delgado, Capital, is decreased by a debit. Therefore, a net loss is extended to the Balance Sheet Debit column.

Marketing Management

Have you ever muted the sound on your television during an advertisement? Maybe you record and view your favorite show after it has been broadcast and skip the commercials completely. Have you ever thought about how much the advertiser is paying for that commercial spot?

Television commercials are only one small part of marketing. Marketing includes many activities from the original design of a product through selling and distribution. Marketing management is involved with making decisions as to how a firm's marketing resources will be used. In order to make wise decisions, marketing managers need to have a good understanding of how the sales of different products affect the profit of the company. Some products cost the

company very little to produce and sell. Other products have high costs associated with them. The accounting department works with marketing management to determine and communicate these costs.

CRITICAL THINKING

1. In this chapter, you learned that the Matching Expenses with Revenue concept requires that an expense should be reported in the same fiscal period that it is used to produce revenue. What might this mean for a company that pays for a television commercial?

2. What might a marketing manager consider when deciding on which channel and at what time to run a commercial?

Finding and Correcting Errors on the Work Sheet LO7

Several different kinds of errors may be made when preparing a work sheet.

1. There may be errors in the accounting records.
2. There may be errors in calculations.
3. An amount may be entered in the wrong column.

CORRECTING ACCOUNTING ERRORS ON THE WORK SHEET

Some errors in accounting records are not discovered until a work sheet is prepared. For example, a debit to Supplies may not have been posted from a journal to the general ledger Supplies account. The omission may not be discovered until the work sheet's trial balance does not balance. Also, information may be transferred incorrectly from general ledger accounts to the work sheet's trial balance. Additional errors may be made, such as recording adjustment information incorrectly or adding columns incorrectly. In addition, errors may be made in extending amounts to the Income Statement and Balance Sheet columns.

Any errors found on a work sheet should be corrected before any further work is completed. If an incorrect amount is found on a work sheet, erase the error and replace it with the correct amount. If an amount is written in an incorrect column, erase the amount and record it in the correct column.

CHECKING FOR TYPICAL CALCULATION ERRORS

When two column totals are not in balance, subtract the smaller total from the larger total to find the difference. Check the difference between the two amounts against the following guides.

1. **The difference is 1, such as $0.01, $0.10, $1.00, or $10.00.** For example, if the totals of the two columns are Debit, $14,657.00, and Credit, $14,658.00, the difference between the two columns is $1.00. The error is most likely in addition. Add the columns again.

2. **The difference can be divided evenly by 2.** For example, the difference between two column totals is $48.00, which can be divided by 2 with no remainder. Look for a $24.00 amount in the Trial Balance columns of the work sheet. If the amount is found, check to make sure it has been recorded in the correct Debit or Credit column. A $24.00 debit amount recorded in a Credit column results in a difference between column totals of $48.00. If the error is not found on the work sheet, check the general ledger accounts and journal entries. An entry for $24.00 may have been recorded in an incorrect column in the journal or in an account.

3. **The difference can be divided evenly by 9.** For example, the difference between two columns is $45.00, which can be divided by 9 with no remainder. When the difference can be divided equally by 9, look for transposed numbers such as 54 written as 45 or 19 written as 91. Also, check for a "slide." A slide occurs when numbers are moved to the right or left in an amount column. For example, $12.00 is recorded as $120.00 or $350.00 is recorded as $35.00.

4. **The difference is an omitted amount.** Look for an amount equal to the difference. If the difference is $50.00, look for an account balance of $50.00 that has not been extended. Look for any $50.00 amount on the work sheet and determine if it has been handled correctly. Look in the accounts and journals for a $50.00 amount, and check if that amount has been handled correctly. Failure to record a $50.00 account balance will make a work sheet's column totals differ by $50.00.

remember

The ending balance of the asset account, Supplies, should represent the amount of supplies remaining on hand at the end of the fiscal period. The amount of supplies used during the period should be recorded in the expense account, Supplies Expense.

CHECKING FOR ERRORS IN THE WORK SHEET

Check for Errors in the Trial Balance Columns

1. Have all general ledger account balances been copied in the Trial Balance column correctly?
2. Have all general ledger account balances been recorded in the correct Trial Balance column?

Check for Errors in the Adjustments Columns

1. Do the debits equal the credits for each adjustment? Use the small letters that label each part of an adjustment to help check accuracy and equality of debits and credits.
2. Is the amount for each adjustment correct?

Check for Errors in the Income Statement and Balance Sheet Columns

1. Has each amount been copied correctly when extended to the Income Statement or Balance Sheet column?
2. Has each account balance been extended to the correct Income Statement or Balance Sheet column?
3. Has the net income or net loss been calculated correctly?
4. Has the net income or net loss been recorded in the correct Income Statement or Balance Sheet column?

For all three of these cases, correct any errors found and add the columns again.

PREVENTING ERRORS

The best way to prevent errors is to work carefully. Check the work at each step in an accounting procedure. Most errors occur in doing arithmetic, especially in adding columns. When possible, use a calculator. When an error is discovered, do no more work until the cause of the error is found and corrections are made.

THINK LIKE AN ACCOUNTANT

Evaluating a New Sales Item

Tommy Dawson owns and operates Tigers' Den, a sports-oriented diner located near the campus of his alma mater, Central Georgia College. Tommy relies on his former classmate, Andre Miller, CPA, to assist him in evaluating the performance of his business.

Each month, Andre creates a series of charts to show Tommy how the business is performing. One of those charts reports the sales of what Tommy jokingly refers to as his "cash cow" items. Although nearly every customer orders an entrée, many do not order appetizers, side salads, beverages, and desserts. Tommy knows that getting customers to purchase these "cash cow" items can have a dramatic impact on earnings.

Tommy recently introduced a line of nonfood items with the Tigers' Den logo. "Getting people to pay us to advertise for us—I like it!" bragged Tommy. Similar to many national restaurant chains, Tommy created an area near the front entrance to display T-shirts, mugs, visors, and other items for sale.

During June, sales were as follows: appetizers, $4,093; desserts, $3,625; beverages, $3,743; side salads, $1,164; and logo items, $4,163.

OPEN THE SPREADSHEET TLA_CH06

The worksheet contains a schedule and chart reporting sales for January through May. Add the sales for June and answer the following questions:

1. What is the impact on sales of adding the merchandise?
2. Are there any categories that declined in sales from May to June?
3. Suggest reasons for the changes in sales between May and June.

©DAN BACHMAN, ISTOCK

End of Lesson Review

LO5 Prepare the Income Statement and Balance Sheet columns of a work sheet.

LO6 Total and rule the work sheet.

LO7 Apply the steps for finding errors on a work sheet.

Terms Review

balance sheet

income statement

net income

net loss

Audit your understanding

1. In which Balance Sheet column is net income recorded on the work sheet?

2. In which Balance Sheet column is net loss recorded on the work sheet?

3. What is the first step in checking for arithmetic errors when two column totals are not in balance?

4. What is one way to check for an error caused by transposed numbers?

5. What term is used to describe an error that occurs when numbers are moved to the right or left in an amount column?

Work together 6-3

Completing a work sheet

Use the work sheet from Work Together 6-2. Your instructor will guide you through the following examples.

1. Extend the up-to-date balances to the Balance Sheet and Income Statement columns.

2. Rule a single line across the Income Statement and Balance Sheet columns. Total each column. Calculate and record the net income or net loss. Label the amount in the Account Title column.

3. Total and rule the Income Statement and Balance Sheet columns. Save your work sheet to complete Work Together 6-4.

On your own 6-3

Completing a work sheet

Use the work sheet from On Your Own 6-2. Work this problem independently.

1. Extend the up-to-date balances to the Balance Sheet or Income Statement columns.

2. Rule a single line across the Income Statement and Balance Sheet columns. Total each column. Calculate and record the net income or net loss. Label the amount in the Account Title column.

3. Total and rule the Income Statement and Balance Sheet columns. Save your work sheet to complete On Your Own 6-4.

6-4 Journalizing and Posting Adjusting Entries

LO8 Journalize and post the adjusting entries for supplies and prepaid insurance.

Adjusting Entry for Supplies LO8

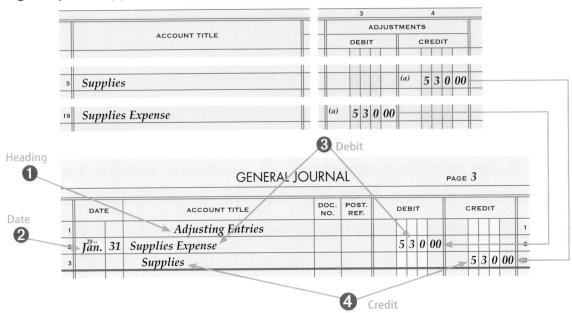

Delgado Web Services' adjustments are analyzed and planned on a work sheet. However, these adjustments must be journalized so they can be posted to the general ledger accounts. Journal entries recorded to update general ledger accounts at the end of a fiscal period are called **adjusting entries**. Adjusting entries are recorded on the next journal page following the page on which the last daily transactions for the month are recorded.

The information needed to journalize the adjusting entry for **Supplies** is obtained from lines 5 and 19 of the work sheet, as shown in the illustration. The entry must be recorded in a journal and posted to the general ledger accounts affected by the entry.

The effect of posting the adjusting entry for **Supplies** to the general ledger accounts is shown in the T accounts.

Supplies Expense has an up-to-date balance of $530.00, which is the value of the supplies used during the fiscal period. [CONCEPT: Matching Expenses with Revenue] **Supplies** has a new balance of $90.00, which is the cost of the supplies on hand at the end of the fiscal period.

Adjusting Entry for Supplies

❶ Write the heading, Adjusting Entries, in the middle of the Account Title column of the journal. Because no source document is prepared for adjusting entries, the entries are identified with a heading in the journal. The heading is written only once for all adjusting entries.

❷ Write the date, 20--, Jan. 31, in the Date column.

❸ Write the title of the account debited, Supplies Expense, in the Account Title column. Record the debit amount, $530.00, in the General Debit column on the same line as the account title.

❹ Write the title of the account credited, Supplies, on the next line in the Account Title column. Record the credit amount, $530.00, in the General Credit column on the same line as the account title.

Preparing a Work Sheet

1. Write the heading.
2. Record the trial balance.
   - Write the general ledger account titles in the Account Title column.
   - Write the account balances in either the Trial Balance Debit or Credit column.
   - Rule a single line across the Trial Balance columns.
   - Add the Trial Balance columns and compare the totals.
   - Rule double lines across both Trial Balance columns.
3. Record the supplies adjustment.
   - Write the debit amount in the Adjustments Debit column on the line with the account title **Supplies Expense.**
   - Write the credit amount in the Adjustments Credit column on the line with the account title **Supplies.**
   - Label this adjustment (a).
4. Record the prepaid insurance adjustment.
   - Write the debit amount in the Adjustments Debit column on the line with the account title **Insurance Expense.**
   - Write the credit amount in the Adjustments Credit column on the line with the account title **Prepaid Insurance.**
   - Label this adjustment (b).
5. Prove the Adjustments columns.
   - Rule a single line across the Adjustments columns.
   - Add the Adjustments columns and compare the totals to ensure that they are equal.
   - Write the proving totals below the single line.
   - Rule double lines across both Adjustments columns.
6. Extend all balance sheet account balances.
   - Extend the up-to-date asset account balances to the Balance Sheet Debit column.
   - Extend the up-to-date liability account balances to the Balance Sheet Credit column.
   - Extend the owner's capital and drawing account balances to the Balance Sheet columns.
7. Extend all income statement account balances.
   - Extend the up-to-date revenue account balance to the Income Statement Credit column.
   - Extend the up-to-date expense account balances to the Income Statement Debit column.
8. Calculate and record the net income (or net loss).
   - Rule a single line across the Income Statement and Balance Sheet columns.
   - Add the columns and write the totals below the single line.
   - Calculate the net income or net loss amount.
   - Write the amount of net income (or net loss) below the smaller of the two Income Statement column totals. Write the words *Net Income* or *Net Loss* in the Account Title column.
   - Extend the amount of net income (or net loss) to the Balance Sheet columns. Write the amount under the smaller of the two column totals. Write the amount on the same line as the words *Net Income* (or *Net Loss*).
9. Total and rule the Income Statement and Balance Sheet columns.
   - Rule a single line across the Income Statement and Balance Sheet columns immediately below the net income (or net loss) amounts.
   - Add the net income (or net loss) to the previous column totals. Compare the column totals to ensure that totals for each pair of columns are in balance.
   - Write the proving totals for each column below the single line.
   - Rule double lines across the Income Statement and Balance Sheet columns immediately below the proving totals.

Preparing a Work Sheet

Delgado Web Services
Work Sheet
For Month Ended January 31, 20--

	ACCOUNT TITLE	TRIAL BALANCE DEBIT	TRIAL BALANCE CREDIT	ADJUSTMENTS DEBIT	ADJUSTMENTS CREDIT	INCOME STATEMENT DEBIT	INCOME STATEMENT CREDIT	BALANCE SHEET DEBIT	BALANCE SHEET CREDIT	
1	Cash	2 5 9 7 00								1
2	Petty Cash	1 0 0 00								2
3	Accts. Rec.—Main Street Services	3 0 0 00								3
4	Accts. Rec.—Valley Landscaping	4 0 0 00								4
5	Supplies	6 2 0 00								5
6	Prepaid Insurance	9 0 0 00								6
7	Accts. Pay.—Canyon Office Supplies		1 2 0 00							7
8	Accts. Pay.—Mountain Graphic Arts		1 0 5 00							8
9	Michael Delgado, Capital		2 0 0 0 00							9
10	Michael Delgado, Drawing	1 1 5 0 00								10
11	Income Summary									11
12	Sales		5 8 2 0 00							12
13	Advertising Expense	3 9 7 00								13
14	Cash Short and Over	1 00								14
15	Communications Expense	8 0 00								15
16	Equipment Rental Expense	1 4 5 5 00								16
17	Insurance Expense									17
18	Miscellaneous Expense	4 5 00								18
19	Supplies Expense									19
20		8 0 4 5 00	8 0 4 5 00							20
21										21
22										22
23										23

C

Delgado Web Services

Work Sheet

For Month Ended January 31, 20--

	ACCOUNT TITLE	TRIAL BALANCE DEBIT	TRIAL BALANCE CREDIT	ADJUSTMENTS DEBIT	ADJUSTMENTS CREDIT	INCOME STATEMENT DEBIT	INCOME STATEMENT CREDIT	BALANCE SHEET DEBIT	BALANCE SHEET CREDIT
1	Cash	2 5 9 7 00							
2	Petty Cash	1 0 0 00							
3	Accts. Rec.—Main Street Services	3 0 0 00							
4	Accts. Rec.—Valley Landscaping	4 0 0 00							
5	Supplies	6 2 0 00			(b) 1 5 0 00				
6	Prepaid Insurance	9 0 0 00			(a) 5 3 0 00				
7	Accts. Pay.—Canyon Office Supplies		1 2 0 00						
8	Accts. Pay.—Mountain Graphic Arts		1 0 5 00						
9	Michael Delgado, Capital		2 0 0 0 00						
10	Michael Delgado, Drawing	1 1 5 0 00							
11	Income Summary								
12	Sales		5 8 2 0 00						
13	Advertising Expense	3 9 7 00							
14	Cash Short and Over	1 00							
15	Communications Expense	8 0 00							
16	Equipment Rental Expense	1 4 5 5 00							
17	Insurance Expense			(a) 5 3 0 00					
18	Miscellaneous Expense	4 5 00							
19	Supplies Expense			(b) 1 5 0 00					
20		8 0 4 5 00	8 0 4 5 00	6 8 0 00	6 8 0 00				
21									
22									
23									

D

Delgado Web Services

Work Sheet

For Month Ended January 31, 20--

	Account Title	Trial Balance Debit	Trial Balance Credit	Adjustments Debit	Adjustments Credit	Income Statement Debit	Income Statement Credit	Balance Sheet Debit	Balance Sheet Credit	
1	Cash	2 5 9 7 00						2 5 9 7 00		1
2	Petty Cash	1 0 0 00						1 0 0 00		2
3	Accts. Rec.—Main Street Services	3 0 0 00						3 0 0 00		3
4	Accts. Rec.—Valley Landscaping	4 0 0 00						4 0 0 00		4
5	Supplies	6 2 0 00			(a) 5 3 0 00			9 0 00		5
6	Prepaid Insurance	9 0 0 00			(b) 1 5 0 00			7 5 0 00		6
7	Accts. Pay.—Canyon Office Supplies		1 2 0 00						1 2 0 00	7
8	Accts. Pay.—Mountain Graphic Arts		1 0 5 00						1 0 5 00	8
9	Michael Delgado, Capital		2 0 0 0 00						2 0 0 0 00	9
10	Michael Delgado, Drawing	1 1 5 0 00						1 1 5 0 00		10
11	Income Summary									11
12	Sales		5 8 2 0 00							12
13	Advertising Expense	3 9 7 00								13
14	Cash Short and Over	1 00								14
15	Communications Expense	8 0 00								15
16	Equipment Rental Expense	1 4 5 5 00								16
17	Insurance Expense			(b) 1 5 0 00						17
18	Miscellaneous Expense	4 5 00								18
19	Supplies Expense			(a) 5 3 0 00						19
20		8 0 4 5 00	8 0 4 5 00	6 8 0 00	6 8 0 00					20
21										21
22										22
23										23

E

Delgado Web Services

Work Sheet

For Month Ended January 31, 20--

	TRIAL BALANCE		ADJUSTMENTS		INCOME STATEMENT		BALANCE SHEET	
ACCOUNT TITLE	DEBIT	CREDIT	DEBIT	CREDIT	DEBIT	CREDIT	DEBIT	CREDIT
1 Cash	2597 00						2597 00	
2 Petty Cash	100 00						100 00	
3 Accts. Rec.—Main Street Services	300 00						300 00	
4 Accts. Rec.—Valley Landscaping	400 00						400 00	
5 Supplies	620 00			(a) 530 00			90 00	
6 Prepaid Insurance	900 00			(b) 150 00			750 00	
7 Accts. Pay.—Canyon Office Supplies		120 00						120 00
8 Accts. Pay.—Mountain Graphic Arts		105 00						105 00
9 Michael Delgado, Capital		2000 00						2000 00
10 Michael Delgado, Drawing	1150 00						1150 00	
11 Income Summary								
12 Sales		5820 00				5820 00		
13 Advertising Expense	397 00				397 00			
14 Cash Short and Over	1 00				1 00			
15 Communications Expense	80 00				80 00			
16 Equipment Rental Expense	1455 00				1455 00			
17 Insurance Expense			(b) 150 00		150 00			
18 Miscellaneous Expense	45 00				45 00			
19 Supplies Expense			(a) 530 00		530 00			
20	8045 00	8045 00	680 00	680 00				
21								
22								
23								

F

Delgado Web Services
Work Sheet
For Month Ended January 31, 20---

	ACCOUNT TITLE	TRIAL BALANCE DEBIT	TRIAL BALANCE CREDIT	ADJUSTMENTS DEBIT	ADJUSTMENTS CREDIT	INCOME STATEMENT DEBIT	INCOME STATEMENT CREDIT	BALANCE SHEET DEBIT	BALANCE SHEET CREDIT	
1	Cash	2 5 9 7 00						2 5 9 7 00		1
2	Petty Cash	1 0 0 00						1 0 0 00		2
3	Accts. Rec.—Main Street Services	3 0 0 00						3 0 0 00		3
4	Accts. Rec.—Valley Landscaping	4 0 0 00						4 0 0 00		4
5	Supplies	6 2 0 00			(a) 5 3 0 00			9 0 00		5
6	Prepaid Insurance	9 0 0 00			(b) 1 5 0 00			7 5 0 00		6
7	Accts. Pay.—Canyon Office Supplies		1 2 0 00						1 2 0 00	7
8	Accts. Pay.—Mountain Graphic Arts		1 0 5 00						1 0 5 00	8
9	Michael Delgado, Capital		2 0 0 0 00						2 0 0 0 00	9
10	Michael Delgado, Drawing	1 1 5 0 00						1 1 5 0 00		10
11	Income Summary									11
12	Sales		5 8 2 0 00				5 8 2 0 00			12
13	Advertising Expense	3 9 7 00				3 9 7 00				13
14	Cash Short and Over	1 00				1 00				14
15	Communications Expense	8 0 00				8 0 00				15
16	Equipment Rental Expense	1 4 5 5 00				1 4 5 5 00				16
17	Insurance Expense			(b) 1 5 0 00		1 5 0 00				17
18	Miscellaneous Expense	4 5 00				4 5 00				18
19	Supplies Expense			(a) 5 3 0 00		5 3 0 00				19
20		8 0 4 5 00	8 0 4 5 00	6 8 0 00	6 8 0 00	2 6 5 8 00	5 8 2 0 00	5 3 8 7 00	2 2 2 5 00	20
21	Net Income					3 1 6 2 00			3 1 6 2 00	21
22						5 8 2 0 00	5 8 2 0 00	5 3 8 7 00	5 3 8 7 00	22
23										23

G

Adjusting Entry for Prepaid Insurance

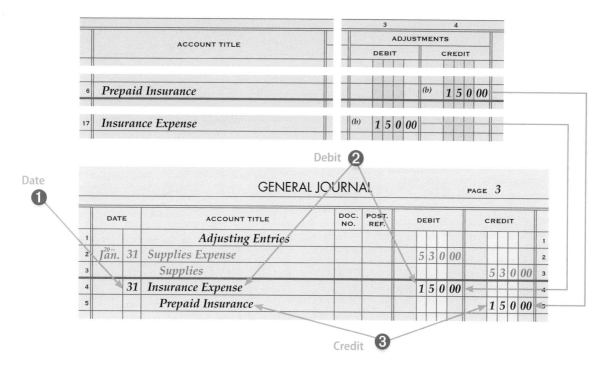

	ACCOUNT TITLE		ADJUSTMENTS	
			DEBIT	CREDIT
6	*Prepaid Insurance*			(b) 1 5 0 00
17	*Insurance Expense*		(b) 1 5 0 00	

GENERAL JOURNAL PAGE 3

	DATE	ACCOUNT TITLE	DOC. NO.	POST. REF.	DEBIT	CREDIT	
1		*Adjusting Entries*					1
2	20-- Jan. 31	Supplies Expense			5 3 0 00		2
3		Supplies				5 3 0 00	3
4	31	*Insurance Expense*			1 5 0 00		4
5		*Prepaid Insurance*				1 5 0 00	5

Date ①   Debit ②   Credit ③

The information needed to journalize the adjusting entry for **Prepaid Insurance** is obtained from lines 6 and 17 of the work sheet. The entry must be recorded in a journal and posted to the general ledger accounts affected by the entry.

The effect of posting the adjusting entry for **Prepaid Insurance** to the general ledger accounts is shown in the T accounts.

Insurance Expense

Adj. (b)	150.00	

Prepaid Insurance

Jan. 31 Bal.	900.00	Adj. (b)	150.00
(New Bal.	750.00)		

Adjusting Entry for Prepaid Insurance

① Write the date, **31**, in the Date column.

② Write the title of the account debited, **Insurance Expense**, in the Account Title column. Record the debit amount, **$150.00**, in the General Debit column on the same line as the account title.

③ Write the title of the account credited, **Prepaid Insurance**, on the next line in the Account Title column. Record the credit amount, **$150.00**, in the General Credit column on the same line as the account title.

remember

Adjusting entries are journalized on the next journal page following the page on which the last transaction of the month is recorded.

Partial Ledger Accounts after Posting Adjusting Entries

ACCOUNT *Supplies* **ACCOUNT NO.** *150*

DATE	ITEM	POST. REF.	DEBIT	CREDIT	BALANCE DEBIT	BALANCE CREDIT
Jan. 2		G1	1 6 5 00		1 6 5 00	
5		G1	2 2 0 00		3 8 5 00	
19		G1	1 0 5 00		4 9 0 00	
28		G2	1 3 0 00		6 2 0 00	
31		G3		5 3 0 00	9 0 00	

ACCOUNT *Prepaid Insurance* **ACCOUNT NO.** *160*

DATE	ITEM	POST. REF.	DEBIT	CREDIT	BALANCE DEBIT	BALANCE CREDIT
Jan. 3		G1	9 0 0 00		9 0 0 00	
31		G3		1 5 0 00	7 5 0 00	

ACCOUNT *Insurance Expense* **ACCOUNT NO.** *550*

DATE	ITEM	POST. REF.	DEBIT	CREDIT	BALANCE DEBIT	BALANCE CREDIT
Jan. 31		G3	1 5 0 00		1 5 0 00	

ACCOUNT *Supplies Expense* **ACCOUNT NO.** *570*

DATE	ITEM	POST. REF.	DEBIT	CREDIT	BALANCE DEBIT	BALANCE CREDIT
Jan. 31		G3	5 3 0 00		5 3 0 00	

Delgado Web Services' partial general ledger, after the adjusting entries are posted, is shown above.

remember

Planning and entering adjustments on a work sheet does not actually change any account balances. Adjusting entries must be journalized and posted in order to bring the general ledger accounts up to date.

End of Lesson Review

LO8 Journalize and post the adjusting entries for supplies and prepaid insurance.

Term Review

adjusting entries

Audit your understanding

1. Why are adjusting entries journalized?

2. Where is the information obtained to journalize adjusting entries?

3. What accounts are increased from zero balances after adjusting entries for supplies and prepaid insurance are journalized and posted?

Work together 6-4

Journalizing and posting adjusting entries

Use the work sheet from Work Together 6-3. A journal and general ledger accounts are given in the *Working Papers*. The general ledger accounts do not show all details for the fiscal period. The balance shown in each account is the account's balance before adjusting entries are posted. Your instructor will guide you through the following example.

Use page 8 of a journal. Journalize and post the adjusting entries.

On your own 6-4

Journalizing and posting adjusting entries

Use the work sheet from On Your Own 6-3. A journal and general ledger accounts are given in the *Working Papers*. The general ledger accounts do not show all details for the fiscal period. The balance shown in each account is the account's balance before adjusting entries are posted.

Use page 24 of a journal. Journalize and post the adjusting entries.

A Look at Accounting Software
Making Adjustments

You learned in this chapter that adjustments are made to the general ledger at the end of a fiscal period. The process of making adjustments is not much different in a computerized accounting system than it is in a manual accounting system. An accountant still needs to review the general ledger accounts to determine which accounts need to be adjusted and by how much.

You learned to use a work sheet to calculate adjustments and to extend account balances to the financial statement columns. When a computerized accounting system is being used, the accountant would print out a trial balance report and use that to find the accounts that need adjusted. Then, the accountant would access the Make Journal Entries window and enter the adjustments. After the adjustments are posted, the accountant would print out a new trial balance. A trial balance produced after adjustments are posted is called an **adjusted trial balance**. Finally, the adjusted trial balance is used to produce the financial statements.

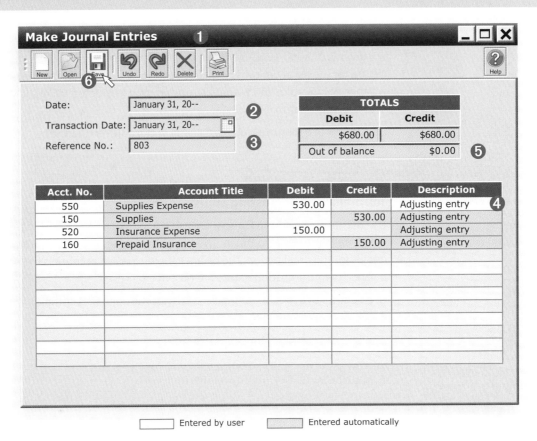

Entered by user   Entered automatically

❶ From the Reports window, the user prints out a trial balance.

❷ The user opens the Make Journal Entries window to enter adjustments. The system displays the current date. The transaction date is initially displayed the same, but it can be changed.

❸ The system enters a sequential reference number for the transaction.

❹ The user enters the first account number, 550, and the system automatically enters the account title. The user enters the debit amount and the description. For the credit entry, the system enters the same amount as the debit. It could be changed if necessary. The description will remain the same until changed by the user.

❺ The total of the debit and credit are entered by the system with each new entry. They should balance when all debits and credits are entered. The system will display an out of balance amount if debits and credits are not equal.

❻ Clicking Save posts the transaction. The system will not post if there is an out of balance condition.

❼ From the Reports window, again, the user prints out a new trial balance. This is an adjusted trial balance.

Delgado Web Services

① TRIAL BALANCE

As of January 31, 20--

Account	Debit	Credit
Cash	2,597.00	
Petty Cash	100.00	
Accounts Receivable—Main Street Services	300.00	
Accounts Receivable—Valley Landscaping	400.00	
Supplies	620.00	
Prepaid Insurance	900.00	
Accounts Payable—Canyon Office Supplies		120.00
Accounts Payable—Mountain Graphic Arts		105.00
Michael Delgado, Capital		2,000.00
Michael Delgado, Drawing	1,150.00	
Income Summary		
Sales		5,820.00
Advertising Expense	397.00	
Cash Short and Over	1.00	
Communications Expense	80.00	
Equipment Rental Expense	1,455.00	
Insurance Expense		
Miscellaneous Expense	45.00	
Supplies Expense		
Totals	8,045.00	8,045.00

Delgado Web Services

⑦ TRIAL BALANCE

As of January 31, 20--

Account	Debit	Credit
Cash	2,597.00	
Petty Cash	100.00	
Accounts Receivable—Main Street Services	300.00	
Accounts Receivable—Valley Landscaping	400.00	
Supplies	90.00	
Prepaid Insurance	750.00	
Accounts Payable—Canyon Office Supplies		120.00
Accounts Payable—Mountain Graphic Arts		105.00
Michael Delgado, Capital		2,000.00
Michael Delgado, Drawing	1,150.00	
Income Summary		
Sales		5,820.00
Advertising Expense	397.00	
Cash Short and Over	1.00	
Communications Expense	80.00	
Equipment Rental Expense	1,455.00	
Insurance Expense	150.00	
Miscellaneous Expense	45.00	
Supplies Expense	530.00	
Totals	8,045.00	8,045.00

Chapter Summary

Before accounting information can be used, it must be analyzed, summarized, and reported. The work sheet is a planning tool used to summarize general ledger information, analyze adjustments, and prepare financial statements. The work sheet is not considered a part of the permanent accounting records. The first step in completing a work sheet is to prepare a trial balance. The second step is to plan and enter the adjustments that must be made to bring all account balances up to date. Next, the new balances are extended to either the

Balance Sheet or Income Statement columns of the work sheet. The Income Statement and Balance Sheet columns are totaled, and net income or net loss is calculated. The last step is to calculate the final totals and rule the work sheet. Any errors revealed on the work sheet must be investigated and corrected. The work sheet is used to aid in journalizing the adjusting entries. Once the adjusting entries are posted, the general ledger accounts are up to date.

EXPLORE ACCOUNTING

Fiscal Periods

A fiscal period is the length of time for which a business summarizes and reports financial information. Many companies are required to prepare reports of their operations each year. These annual reports show the results of a company's operations for the year in the form of financial statements. These companies choose a year for the fiscal period. In such a case, a company will prepare financial statements every year.

A fiscal year can be any consecutive 12-month period. The Internal Revenue Service (IRS) requires many companies to report taxable income for the fiscal year January 1 through December 31. A fiscal year beginning January 1 can also be called a *calendar year*. Because they use a calendar year for reporting taxable income, many companies choose

to use the calendar year for issuing financial statements also.

However, there is no requirement to begin a fiscal year on January 1. Companies often choose a fiscal year that ends during a period of low business activity. Twelve consecutive months which end when business activities have reached the lowest point in their annual cycle are often referred to as a natural business year.

A survey of 500 businesses shows the number of companies that chose a fiscal year ending at the end of a specific month.

Fiscal Year-End	No. of Companies
January	27
February	8
March	17

Fiscal Year-End	No. of Companies
April	9
May	15
June	33
July	8
August	13
September	31
October	14
November	9
December	316

INSTRUCTIONS

Assume you work for a company that makes snowboards. You must determine what fiscal year should be used. Make a written recommendation to the owner. Explain why your recommendation is preferable.

Source: Accounting Trends and Techniques, 2006, published by the American Institute of Certified Public Accountants.

Apply Your Understanding

INSTRUCTIONS: Download problem files and instructions for Excel, QuickBooks, and Peachtree from the textbook companion website at www.C21accounting.com.

6-1 Application Problem: Recording the trial balance on a work sheet LO1, 2

1. Key the account balances in the trial balance section of the worksheet.
2. Use the required formulas to calculate the totals of the Trial Balance columns.
3. Key the adjusting entries in the Adjustments columns.
4. Create the appropriate formulas to extend amounts to the income statement and balance sheet.

Use the work sheet given in the *Working Papers*. On June 30 of the current year, Rosemount Copy Center has the following general ledger accounts and balances. The business uses a monthly fiscal period.

Account Titles	Account Balances	
	Debit	**Credit**
Cash	$8,715.00	
Petty Cash	75.00	
Accounts Receivable—Raymond O'Neil	642.00	
Supplies	518.00	
Prepaid Insurance	675.00	
Accounts Payable—Western Supply		$ 268.00
Akbar Sharma, Capital		9,695.00
Akbar Sharma, Drawing	375.00	
Income Summary		
Sales		1,704.00
Advertising Expense	255.00	
Cash Short and Over	2.00	
Insurance Expense		
Miscellaneous Expense	138.00	
Supplies Expense		
Utilities Expense	272.00	

Instructions:

Prepare the heading and trial balance on a work sheet. Total and rule the Trial Balance columns. Save your work to complete Problem 6-2.

6-2 Application Problem: Planning adjustments on a work sheet LO3, 4

Use the work sheet from Problem 6-1.

Instructions:

1. Analyze the following adjustment information into debit and credit parts. Record the adjustments on the work sheet.

    Adjustment Information, June 30
    Supplies on hand $188.00
    Value of prepaid insurance   540.00

2. Total and rule the Adjustments columns.
3. Save your work to complete Problem 6-3.

6-3 Application Problem: Completing a work sheet LO5, 6

Use the work sheet from Problem 6-2.

Instructions:

1. Extend the up-to-date balances to the Balance Sheet or Income Statement columns.
2. Rule a single line across the Income Statement and Balance Sheet columns. Total each column. Calculate and record the net income or net loss. Label the amount in the Account Title column.
3. Total and rule the Income Statement and Balance Sheet columns. Save your work to complete Problem 6-4.

6-4 Application Problem: Journalizing and posting adjusting entries LO8

AAONLiNE

1. Go to www.cengage.com/login
2. Click on **AA Online** to access.
3. Go to the online assignment and follow the instructions.

Use the work sheet from Problem 6-3. A journal and general ledger accounts are given in the *Working Papers*. The general ledger accounts do not show all details for the fiscal period. The balance shown in each account is the account's balance before adjusting entries are posted.

Instructions:

Use page 12 of a journal. Journalize and post the adjusting entries.

6-M Mastery Problem: Completing a work sheet; journalizing and posting adjusting entries LO1, 2, 3, 4, 5, 6, 8

Peachtree

1. Journalize and post adjusting entries to the general journal.
2. Make the selections to print the income statement and the balance sheet.
3. Make the selections to print the general journal and the adjusted trial balance.

1. Journalize and post adjusting entries to the journal.
2. Make the selections to print the balance sheet and the profit and loss statement.
3. Make the selections to print the journal and the adjusted trial balance.

1. Key the account balances in the trial balance section of the worksheet.
2. Use the required formulas to calculate the totals of the Trial Balance columns.
3. Key the adjusting entries in the Adjustments columns.
4. Create the appropriate formulas to extend amounts to the income statement and balance sheet.

On April 30 of the current year, Naples Electric Repair has the following general ledger accounts and balances. The business uses a monthly fiscal period. A work sheet is given in the *Working Papers*.

Account Titles	Account Balances	
	Debit	**Credit**
Cash	$5,658.00	
Petty Cash	300.00	
Accounts Receivable—Barbara Bye	3,022.00	
Supplies	1,710.00	
Prepaid Insurance	2,200.00	
Accounts Payable—Seaside Supplies		$1,000.00
Kaelynn Guerero, Capital		9,004.00
Kaelynn Guerero, Drawing	880.00	
Income Summary		
Sales		6,800.00
Advertising Expense	900.00	
Cash Short and Over	4.00	
Insurance Expense		
Miscellaneous Expense	380.00	
Rent Expense	750.00	
Supplies Expense		
Utilities Expense	1,000.00	

Instructions:

1. Prepare the heading and trial balance on a work sheet. Total and rule the Trial Balance columns.

2. Analyze the following adjustment information into debit and credit parts. Record the adjustments on the work sheet.

   Adjustment Information, April 30
   Supplies inventory $ 440.00
   Value of prepaid insurance   1,800.00

3. Total and rule the Adjustments columns.

1. Go to www.cengage.com/login
2. Click on **AA Online** to access.
3. Go to the online assignment and follow the instructions.

4. Extend the up-to-date balances to the Balance Sheet or Income Statement columns.

5. Rule a single line across the Income Statement and Balance Sheet columns. Total each column. Calculate and record the net income or net loss. Label the amount in the Account Title column.

6. Total and rule the Income Statement and Balance Sheet columns.

7. A journal and general ledger accounts are given in the *Working Papers*. The general ledger accounts do not show all details for the fiscal period. The balance shown in each account is the account's balance before adjusting entries are posted. Use page 8 of a journal. Journalize and post the adjusting entries.

6-C Challenge Problem: Completing a work sheet LO1, 2, 3, 4, 5, 6

ProSource Company had a small fire in its office. The fire destroyed some of the accounting records. On November 30 of the current year, the end of a monthly fiscal period, the following information was constructed from the remaining records and other sources. A work sheet is given in the *Working Papers*.

Remains of the general ledger:

Account Titles	Account Balances
Accounts Receivable—C. Grumpa	$1,650.00
Supplies	1,400.00
Donna Beggin, Drawing	600.00
Sales	7,600.00
Advertising Expense	400.00
Rent Expense	1,200.00
Utilities Expense	780.00
Information from the business's checkbook:	
Cash balance on last unused check stub	$6,238.00
Total payments for miscellaneous expense	100.00
Total payments for insurance	800.00
Information obtained through inquiries to other businesses:	
Owed to Century Supplies	$3,000.00
Value of prepaid insurance, November 30	500.00
Information obtained by counting supplies on hand after the fire:	
Supplies on hand	$400.00

Instructions:

1. From the information given, prepare a heading and reconstruct a trial balance on a work sheet. The owner's capital account balance is the difference between the total of all debit account balances minus the total of all credit account balances.

2. Complete the work sheet.

21st Century Skills

Insurance Expense

PARTNERSHIP FOR
21ST CENTURY SKILLS

Theme: Financial, Economic, Business, and Entrepreneurial Literacy

Skills: Workplace Competency, Information Literacy, Critical Thinking and Problem Solving

Adjustments for prepaid insurance are made by most companies. Insurance, or risk management, is crucial for owners to protect the business against unexpected loss or damage. In addition to the familiar property, liability, and automobile insurance, many other types of insurance coverage are available for a business.

One example is business interruption insurance. This insurance provides funds to make up for income that is lost due to something that disturbs the normal business operations. For example, a printing press that is struck by lightning might interrupt revenue until it can be repaired.

Another example is professional liability insurance that provides protection against being sued for professional negligence. Malpractice insurance, carried by physicians and other health professionals, is probably the most common professional liability insurance. Professional liability insurance is also used by architects, accountants, teachers, counselors, and other professionals. The rate for professional liability insurance varies by state and by specialty. Malpractice insurance for doctors may cost upwards of $100,000 per year!

APPLICATION

1. Use the Internet to find the malpractice insurance rates in your state, two nearby states, and two distant states. Prepare a chart showing how rates in your state compare to the others. What do you think could explain the variances?

2. With a partner, brainstorm at least five different business interruptions that might cause a business to suffer a loss of income.

Auditing for errors

The trial balance for Ogren Company is given below.

Account Titles	Account Balances	
	Debit	Credit
Cash		$2,196.00
Petty Cash	$ 150.00	
Accounts Receivable—Halstad Co.		1,475.00
Supplies		163.00
Accounts Payable—Eglund Inc.	625.00	
Wendy Mackerman, Capital		3,250.00
Wendy Mackerman, Drawing		300.00
Income Summary		
Sales	1,250.00	
Advertising Expense		716.00
Supplies Expense		
Rent Expense	125.00	
Totals	$2,150.00	$8,100.00

The Debit column does not equal the Credit column. The new bookkeeper knows that the amounts are correct but is not sure if the amounts are in the correct columns.

REVIEW AND ANSWER

1. Using what you know about the normal balance side of each account, find which amount(s) are in the wrong column.
2. On a separate piece of paper, copy the balances, putting them in the correct columns.
3. Total the columns to prove that debits now equal credits.

Analyzing Nike's financial statements

The length of time for which a business summarizes and reports financial information is known as a *fiscal period*. Annual statements use a fiscal period equal to one year. However, the fiscal year does not necessarily begin on January 1 and end on December 31 (a calendar year). A company's fiscal year can begin on any date. Most companies choose a fiscal year that ends during a period of low business activity, often after a period of high activity, when inventories are low. Look at Nike's financial statements in Appendix B beginning on page B-5.

INSTRUCTIONS

1. When does Nike's fiscal year end?
2. Why do you think Nike's management feels that this is a good time for a fiscal year-end?

Chapter 7

Financial Statements for a Proprietorship

LEARNING OBJECTIVES

After studying Chapter 7, in addition to defining key terms, you will be able to:

LO1 Prepare an income statement for a service business.

LO2 Calculate and analyze financial ratios using income statement amounts.

LO3 Prepare a balance sheet for a service business organized as a proprietorship.

Accounting In The Real World

American Eagle Outfitters

I f you have visited a shopping mall, you have probably seen at least one of the stores belonging to the American Eagle Outfitters (AEO) family. AEO markets its merchandise through three stores: American Eagle Outfitters, Aerie, and 77Kids. AEO "offers high-quality, on-trend clothing, accessories and personal care products at affordable prices." AEO brand targets 15- to 25-year-olds and has over 900 stores in the United States and Canada.

The AEO website states, "Since our first store opened in 1977, AEO has focused on innovation." One way AEO is trying to maintain its focus on innovation is by hiring young, creative new employees. The company is taking its motto (Live Your Life) one step further with a motto of "Live Your Life, Love Your Job" for employees and potential employees. In a campaign to attract new employees, AEO uses three methods: internships, full-time training programs, and campus visits.

College juniors can complete a paid summer internship at AEO's corporate office. The internship even includes furnished housing for students from outside the Pittsburgh area. Interns choose either a merchandising or planning and allocation program. The merchandising internship partners the intern with an AEO employee. The intern spends ten weeks learning how products are designed and produced. The planning and allocation internship focuses more on financial leadership on product and assortment choices. In this program, the intern spends time helping create sales goals for products and works with inventory distribution.

The full-time training program is designed for college graduates. The new employee is guided through a training program, based on a particular career path.

The three training program choices are merchandising, design, and planning and allocation leadership development. Within each training program, the new employee is guided and mentored to achieve the development and training required to succeed in the career area.

AEO visits college campuses throughout the year to introduce and recruit students to the internship and full-time training programs.

CRITICAL THINKING

1. What account titles might you find on a balance sheet for AEO?

2. Why would AEO be willing to participate in internship and training programs?

Source: www.ae.com.

Key Terms

- financial accounting
- managerial accounting
- financial ratio
- ratio analysis
- vertical analysis
- return on sales (ROS)

LESSON

7-1 Preparing an Income Statement

LO1 Prepare an income statement for a service business.
LO2 Calculate and analyze financial ratios using income statement amounts.

Reporting Financial Information

The financial information needed by managers and owners to make good business decisions can be found in the general ledger accounts. However, the information in the general ledger is very detailed. Therefore, to make this general ledger information more usable, the information is summarized, organized, and reported. The area of accounting that focuses on reporting information to external users is called **financial accounting**. Examples of external users include bankers, creditors, customers, government agencies, and stockholders. The area of accounting that focuses on reporting information to internal users is called **managerial accounting**. Examples of internal users include company managers and officers.

All financial information must be reported if good business decisions are to be made. A financial statement with incomplete information is similar to a book with missing pages. The complete story is not told. If a business has both rent and utilities expenses but reports only the rent expense, managers will have incomplete information on which to base decisions. The accounting

concept *Full Disclosure* is applied when financial statements contain all information necessary to understand a business's financial condition. Full Disclosure is also known as *Adequate Disclosure*. [CONCEPT: Full Disclosure]

Delgado Web Services prepares two financial statements: an income statement and a balance sheet. It always prepares these financial statements at the end of each monthly fiscal period. [CONCEPT: Accounting Period Cycle]

When a business is started, it is expected that the business will continue to operate indefinitely. For example, Michael Delgado assumes that he will own and operate Delgado Web Services for many years. When he retires, he expects to sell Delgado Web Services to someone else, who will continue its operation. The accounting concept *Going Concern* is applied when financial statements are prepared with the expectation that a business will remain in operation indefinitely. [CONCEPT: Going Concern]

COMSTOCK/GETTY IMAGES

Identifying Stakeholders

A majority of states have seat belt laws. The laws are unpopular with individuals who believe in freedom of choice. Most people recognize that wearing a seat belt provides the passenger with extra protection in a crash. Why not allow a passenger to accept the extra risk of driving without a seat belt?

A well-known ethical model, the **utilitarian theory**, states that an ethical action provides the greatest balance of good over harm. Any persons or groups affected by an action are called **stakeholders**. The impact of the action on the various stakeholders should be analyzed. Major stakeholders include owners, employees, customers, local communities, and society. Not every type of stakeholder will apply in each situation. However, the list of stakeholders provides a useful guide. It helps individuals see how their actions affect others.

Examine the table below. It analyzes the impact on stakeholders involved in a motorist's decision to drive without a seat belt.

Impact on Stakeholders of a Motorist's Decision to Drive Without a Seat Belt

Stakeholders	Negative Impact	Positive Impact
Motorist	• May incur serious injuries or death. • Insurance rates are likely to increase.	• Enjoys the perceived freedom of driving without the confinement of a seat belt.
Drivers of other vehicles	• May suffer mental anguish if a motorist incurs serious injuries. • Insurance rates for all drivers are likely to increase.	
Relatives of motorist	• Personal lives and careers may be negatively affected if an accident disables a motorist.	
Emergency personnel	• Risks to emergency personnel are greater because they may be more aggressive when responding to serious accidents.	
Insurance companies	• Higher medical bills resulting from more serious injuries may be only partially offset by higher insurance premiums.	
State government	• May be subject to lawsuits by individuals who believe the state was negligent in not passing seat belt laws. • More serious accidents require more emergency personnel and equipment, thus spending limited financial resources.	
Society	• Government programs may pay for medical bills and disability payments not provided by the motorist's insurance.	

This analysis demonstrates how a personal decision—not wearing a seat belt—can affect many people. Individuals must make their own conclusions. State legislators who voted for seat belt laws believed that benefits to the motorist failed to offset the negative impact on so many stakeholders. Individuals who oppose seat belt laws believe the benefits to the individual offset the negative impact on all other stakeholders.

INSTRUCTIONS

Most colleges and universities have minimum academic standards for admission. Create a table that analyzes the positive and negative impact of admission standards. Then answer the question: Are admission standards ethical?

©LUCA DI FILIPPO, ISTOCK

Preparing an Income Statement from Information on a Work Sheet LO1

	ACCOUNT TITLE	INCOME STATEMENT DEBIT	INCOME STATEMENT CREDIT	BALANCE SHEET DEBIT	BALANCE SHEET CREDIT	
		5	6	7	8	
12	Sales		5 8 2 0 00			12
13	Advertising Expense	3 9 7 00				13
14	Cash Short and Over	1 00				14
15	Communications Expense	8 0 00				15
16	Equipment Rental Expense	1 4 5 5 00				16
17	Insurance Expense	1 5 0 00				17
18	Miscellaneous Expense	4 5 00				18
19	Supplies Expense	5 3 0 00				19
20		2 6 5 8 00	5 8 2 0 00			20
21	Net Income	3 1 6 2 00				21
22		5 8 2 0 00	5 8 2 0 00			22
23						23

An income statement reports financial information over a specific period of time, indicating the financial progress of a business in earning a net income or a net loss. Expenses are the amounts a business pays to operate and earn revenue. The revenue earned and the expenses incurred to earn that revenue are reported in the same fiscal period. [CONCEPT: Matching Expenses with Revenue]

Information needed to prepare Delgado Web Services' income statement is obtained from two places on the work sheet. Account titles are obtained from the work sheet's Account Title column. Account balances are obtained from the work sheet's Income Statement columns. The income statement for a service business has four sections: (1) heading, (2) Revenue, (3) Expenses, and (4) Net Income or Net Loss.

Heading of an Income Statement

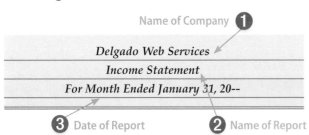

Name of Company ①

Delgado Web Services
Income Statement
For Month Ended January 31, 20--

③ Date of Report   ② Name of Report

Preparing the Heading of an Income Statement

① Center the name of the company, Delgado Web Services, on the first line.

② Center the name of the report, Income Statement, on the second line.

③ Center the date of the report, For Month Ended January 31, 20--, on the third line.

The income statement's date shows that this income statement reports information for the one-month period from January 1 through January 31.

remember

The work sheet is prepared as a planning tool to assist in preparing financial statements. It is an optional report.

A Budget Is a Road Map to Your Financial Future

A **budget** is a financial road map used by individuals and companies as a guide for spending and saving. Following a budget helps to avoid spending more than is earned. Businesses and individuals must periodically evaluate their financial condition and adjust their budgets to ensure the achievement of financial goals. The first step in creating a budget is to determine the amount of income you can expect. Then, expenses must be estimated. Fixed expenses are financial obligations that remain the same every period, such as rent, transportation, insurance, and loan payments. A strategy of setting aside at least 10% of after-tax income for saving and investing is called **pay yourself first.**

Variable expenses are those that change in value from month to month. These are more easily controlled than fixed expenses. Examples include utilities, groceries, recreation, and clothing.

A positive balance after total expenses are subtracted from total income is called a **surplus.** A surplus can be saved for future needs. A negative balance after total expenses are subtracted from total income is called a **deficit.** A deficit indicates that planned expenses must be reduced.

ACTIVITIES

Bethany has been working full time for one year and frequently finds herself short of cash. Her total income is $39,000, and her income after taxes is $2,500 per month. She has the following expenses:

- Car payment, $400/month
- Auto insurance, $3,000/year
- Gas, $50/week
- Groceries, $150/week
- Clothing, $50/week

- Entertainment, $25/week
- Utilities, (monthly average) $150/month
- Rent, $700/month
- Cell phone, $30/per month

1. Based on "pay yourself first," calculate the amount that Bethany should budget for savings.

2. List and total Bethany's fixed expenses. Be sure to include the amount for savings.

3. List and total the amount of variable expenses.

4. Calculate Bethany's current monthly surplus or deficit.

5. If there is a deficit, recommend what steps Bethany should take to avoid a deficit.

Revenue, Expenses, and Net Income Sections of an Income Statement

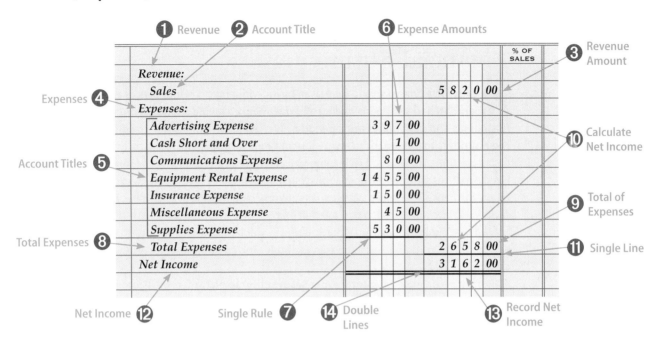

Preparing the Revenue, Expenses, and Net Income Sections of an Income Statement

1 Write the name of the first section, Revenue:, at the extreme left of the wide column on the first line.

2 Write the title of the revenue account, Sales, on the next line, indented about one centimeter.

3 Record the balance of the account, $5,820.00, on the same line in the second amount column.

4 Write the name of the second section, Expenses:, on the next line at the extreme left of the wide column.

5 Write the title of each expense account in the wide column, indented about one centimeter.

6 Record the balance of each expense account in the first amount column on the same line as the account title.

7 Rule a single line across the first amount column under the last expense account balance to indicate addition.

8 Write the words Total Expenses on the next blank line in the wide column, indented about one centimeter.

9 Record the amount of total expenses, $2,658.00, on the same line in the second amount column.

10 Calculate and verify the amount of net income.

a. Calculate net income from information on the income statement, as shown.

$$\underset{\textbf{Revenue}}{\textbf{Total}} - \underset{\textbf{Expenses}}{\textbf{Total}} = \underset{\textbf{Income}}{\textbf{Net}}$$

$$\$5,820.00 \ - \ \$2,658.00 \ = \ \$3,162.00$$

b. Compare the amount of net income, $3,162.00, with the net income on the work sheet. If the two amounts are not the same, an error has been made.

11 Rule a single line across the second amount column just below the amount of total expenses.

12 Write the words Net Income on the next line at the extreme left of the wide column.

13 On the same line, record the amount of net income, $3,162.00, in the second amount column.

14 Rule double lines across both amount columns below the amount of net income to show that the amount has been verified as correct.

Analyzing an Income Statement LO2

Vertical analysis percentages

Delgado Web Services Income Statement For Month Ended January 31, 20--												% OF SALES
Revenue:												
Sales							5	8	2	0	00	100.0
Expenses:												
Advertising Expense			3	9	7	00						
Cash Short and Over					1	00						
Communications Expense				8	0	00						
Equipment Rental Expense		1	4	5	5	00						
Insurance Expense			1	5	0	00						
Miscellaneous Expense				4	5	00						
Supplies Expense			5	3	0	00						
Total Expenses							2	6	5	8	00	45.7
Net Income							3	1	6	2	00	54.3

In order to be more useful, the income statement can contain additional information and calculations. For a service business, the revenue reported on an income statement is often compared to two items: (1) total expenses and (2) net income. To make decisions about future operations, a manager analyzes relationships between these two income statement components and the total sales. A comparison between two components of financial information is called a **financial ratio**. The calculation and interpretation of a financial ratio is called **ratio analysis**. On an income statement, financial ratios are calculated by dividing the amount of each component by the total amount of sales. Delgado Web Services calculates a ratio for total expenses and net income. The relationship between each component and total sales is shown in a separate column on the income statement at the right of the amount columns. Reporting an amount on a financial statement as a percentage of another item on the same financial statement is called **vertical analysis**.

remember

If expenses are more than revenue, the result is a net loss.

ACCEPTABLE FINANCIAL RATIOS

For a ratio to be useful, Mr. Delgado needs to know what ratios are acceptable for businesses similar to Delgado Web Services. Various industry organizations publish average ratios for similar businesses. In the future, Mr. Delgado could also compare Delgado Web Services' ratios from one fiscal period with the ratios of previous fiscal periods.

TOTAL EXPENSES RATIO

The total expenses ratio, based on information from the January income statement, is calculated as shown. For businesses similar to Delgado Web Services, an acceptable total expenses ratio is not more than 48.0%. Therefore, Delgado Web Services' percentage, 45.7%, is less than 48.0% and is acceptable.

Total Expenses	÷	Total Sales	=	Total Expenses Ratio
$2,658.00	÷	$5,820.00	=	45.7%

NET INCOME RATIO

The net income ratio, based on information from the January income statement, is calculated as shown. For businesses similar to Delgado Web Services, an acceptable net income ratio is not less than 52.0%. Therefore, Delgado Web Services' ratio, 54.3%, is greater than 52.0% and is acceptable. The ratio of net income to total sales is called **return on sales (ROS)**. Return on sales is a common financial ratio used to determine how much profit is being produced per dollar of sales. Delgado Web Services is producing 54.3 cents per dollar of sales.

Net Income	÷	Total Sales	=	Net Income Ratio
$3,162.00	÷	$5,820.00	=	54.3%

THINK LIKE AN ACCOUNTANT

Evaluating Manager Performance

Glade Media has three managers who are authorized to approve cash payments for operating expenses. Dan Smith is responsible for advertising and sales. John Nash is responsible for the upkeep of company offices. Karen Stevens is in charge of office operations. Cash payments recorded to each expense account are the responsibility of the manager in charge of the account.

Each year, the president, the three managers, and the accountant meet to estimate the expenses for the next fiscal year. Those estimates form the next year's budget. Before the meeting, the accountant prints a report of expense accounts from the accounting system. The report shows the actual and budgeted amounts for each account as well as the manager responsible. The information helps to evaluate each manager's performance. It also provides a basis to set the next fiscal year's budget.

OPEN THE SPREADSHEET TLA_CH07
Assume you are the accountant for Harris Company. Use the expense account report to prepare the additional reports listed and to answer the following questions.

1. Prepare a report of the budgeted and actual expenses for each account, grouped by manager.

2. Prepare a report of the actual and budgeted expenses for each manager.

3. Prepare a report that shows the expense accounts just for managers whose total actual expenses are over budget.

4. Can you think of a case where an actual account balance over budget might not indicate poor management performance? How does your answer affect the usefulness of this analysis?

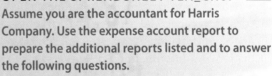

©DAN BACHMAN, ISTOCK

Income Statement with Two Sources of Revenue and a Net Loss

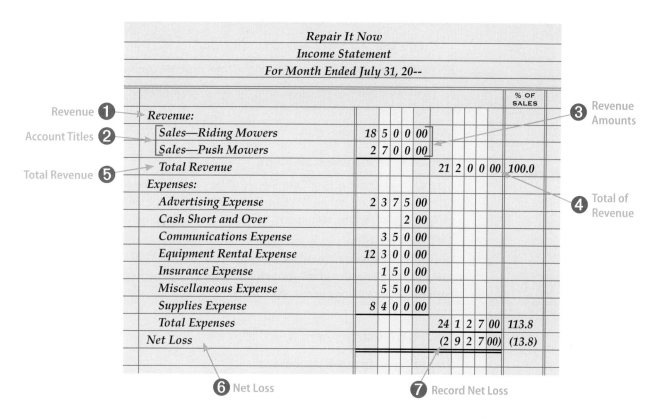

Repair It Now
Income Statement
For Month Ended July 31, 20--

				% OF SALES
Revenue:				
Sales—Riding Mowers	18 5 0 0 00			
Sales—Push Mowers	2 7 0 0 00			
Total Revenue		21 2 0 0 00	100.0	
Expenses:				
Advertising Expense	2 3 7 5 00			
Cash Short and Over	2 00			
Communications Expense	3 5 0 00			
Equipment Rental Expense	12 3 0 0 00			
Insurance Expense	1 5 0 00			
Miscellaneous Expense	5 5 0 00			
Supplies Expense	8 4 0 0 00			
Total Expenses		24 1 2 7 00	113.8	
Net Loss		(2 9 2 7 00)	(13.8)	

Labels on diagram:
- Revenue ❶
- Account Titles ❷
- Total Revenue ❺
- ❸ Revenue Amounts
- ❹ Total of Revenue
- ❻ Net Loss
- ❼ Record Net Loss

Delgado Web Services receives revenue from only one source, the sale of services for maintaining and hosting websites for small businesses. Repair It Now receives revenue from two sources, the sale of services to repair riding mowers and the sale of services to repair push mowers. The business's owner wants to know how much revenue is earned from each source. Therefore, the business uses two revenue accounts: Sales—Riding Mowers and Sales—Push Mowers.

When an income statement is prepared for Repair It Now, both revenue accounts are listed. The Revenue section for Repair It Now differs from the income statement prepared by Delgado Web Services.

If total expenses exceed total revenue, a net loss is reported on an income statement. Repair It Now reported a net loss on its July income statement.

Return on sales (ROS) is widely used by analysts in the investment field to evaluate a company.

Preparing the Revenue Section of an Income Statement with Two Sources of Revenue

❶ Write the section heading, Revenue:, at the left of the wide column.

❷ Write the titles of both revenue accounts in the wide column, indented about one centimeter.

❸ Record the balance of each account in the first amount column on the same line as the account title.

❹ Total the two revenue account balances. Write the total amount on the next line in the second amount column.

❺ Write the words Total Revenue in the wide column, indented about one centimeter on the same line as the total revenue amount.

Preparing the Net Loss Section of an Income Statement

❻ Write the words Net Loss at the extreme left of the wide column.

❼ Subtract the total expenses from the revenue to calculate the net loss. Record the amount of net loss in the second amount column in parentheses. An amount written in parentheses on a financial statement indicates a negative amount.

End of Lesson Review

LO1 Prepare an income statement for a service business.

LO2 Calculate and analyze financial ratios using income statement amounts.

Terms Review

financial accounting

managerial accounting

financial ratio

ratio analysis

vertical analysis

return on sales (ROS)

Audit your understanding

1. List the four sections of an income statement.

2. What is the formula for calculating the total expenses ratio?

3. What is the formula for calculating the net income ratio?

Work together 7-1

Preparing an income statement

A partial work sheet of Hair Care Salon for the month ended May 31 of the current year is given in the *Working Papers*. Also given is a blank form for completing an income statement. Your instructor will guide you through the following example.

Prepare an income statement for the month ended May 31 of the current year. Calculate and record the ratios for total expenses and net income. Round percentage calculations to the nearest 0.1%.

On your own 7-1

Preparing an income statement

A partial work sheet of Plumbing Solutions for the month ended February 28 of the current year is given in the *Working Papers*. Also given is a blank form for completing an income statement. Work this problem independently.

Prepare an income statement for the month ended February 28 of the current year. Calculate and record the ratios for total expenses and net income. Round percentage calculations to the nearest 0.1%.

198   Chapter 7   Financial Statements for a Proprietorship

LO3 Prepare a balance sheet for a service business organized as a proprietorship.

Preparing a Balance Sheet from Information on a Work Sheet LO3

	ACCOUNT TITLE	BALANCE SHEET					
		7		8			
		DEBIT		CREDIT			
1	Cash	2 5 9 7 00					1
2	Petty Cash	1 0 0 00					2
3	Accounts Receivable—Main Street Services	3 0 0 00					3
4	Accounts Receivable—Valley Landscaping	4 0 0 00					4
5	Supplies	9 0 00					5
6	Prepaid Insurance	7 5 0 00					6
7	Accounts Payable—Canyon Office Supplies			1 2 0 00			7
8	Accounts Payable—Mountain Graphic Arts			1 0 5 00			8
9	Michael Delgado, Capital			2 0 0 0 00			9
10	Michael Delgado, Drawing	1 1 5 0 00					10
20		5 3 8 7 00		2 2 2 5 00			20
21	Net Income			3 1 6 2 00			21
22		5 3 8 7 00		5 3 8 7 00			22
23							23

A balance sheet reports financial information on a specific date, indicating the financial condition of a business. The financial condition of a business refers to its financial strength. If a business has adequate available assets and few liabilities, that business is financially strong. If a business's financial condition is not strong, adverse changes in the economy might cause the business to fail.

Information about assets, liabilities, and owner's equity might be obtained from the general ledger accounts or from a work sheet. However, the information is easier to use if reported in an organized manner such as on a balance sheet.

Information needed to prepare Delgado Web Services' balance sheet is obtained from two places on the work sheet. Account titles are obtained from the work sheet's Account Title column. Account balances are obtained from the work sheet's Balance Sheet columns.

A balance sheet has four sections: (1) Heading, (2) Assets, (3) Liabilities, and (4) Owner's Equity.

Heading of a Balance Sheet

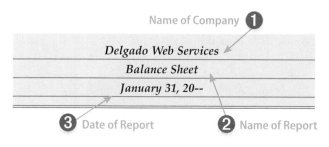

Name of Company ❶

Delgado Web Services
Balance Sheet
January 31, 20--

❸ Date of Report   ❷ Name of Report

❯ Preparing the Heading of a Balance Sheet

❶ Center the name of the company, Delgado Web Services, on the first line.

❷ Center the name of the report, Balance Sheet, on the second line.

❸ Center the date of the report, January 31, 20--, on the third line.

Pharmacists and Dentists in the Accounting Classroom

College accounting courses attract a diverse group of students. It is not surprising to find college accounting classes that include pharmacists and dentists. These professionals have already completed both a four-year and a graduate degree and are not planning on achieving a degree in accounting.

Many dentists and pharmacists own their own practice, which means they are also small business owners. Unfortunately, not all dental or pharmacy schools include an accounting course or other business courses in the required curriculum. Most of these small business owners hire accountants to do the accounting for their practice.

Dentists and pharmacists who do not want to hire an accountant can find help in the many accounting software packages designed specifically for dental practices and pharmacies. Either way, many report that they must still have at least an understanding of accounting so that they can interpret their financial statements.

CRITICAL THINKING

Using the Internet, find the name of one dental practice or pharmacy management company. List some of the costs that a dentist would have to consider when determining the cost of a dental filling.

Assets and Liabilities Sections of a Balance Sheet

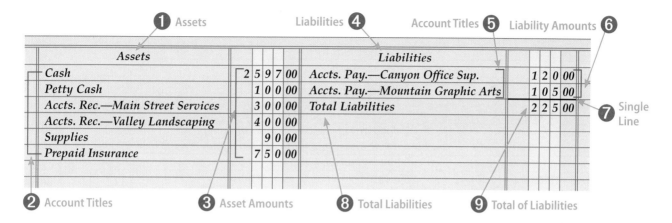

① Assets				**Liabilities ④**	**Account Titles ⑤**		**Liability Amounts ⑥**		
Assets				*Liabilities*					
Cash	2	5	9	7	00	Accts. Pay.—Canyon Office Sup.	1	2	0	00
Petty Cash		1	0	0	00	Accts. Pay.—Mountain Graphic Arts	1	0	5	00
Accts. Rec.—Main Street Services		3	0	0	00	Total Liabilities		2	2	5	00
Accts. Rec.—Valley Landscaping		4	0	0	00					
Supplies			9	0	00					
Prepaid Insurance		7	5	0	00					

② Account Titles   **③ Asset Amounts**   **⑧ Total Liabilities**   **⑨ Total of Liabilities**   **⑦ Single Line**

A balance sheet reports information about the elements of the accounting equation.

Assets = Liabilities + Owner's Equity

The assets are on the LEFT side of the accounting equation and on the LEFT side of Delgado Web Services' balance sheet.

Two kinds of equities are reported on a balance sheet: (1) liabilities and (2) owner's equity. Liabilities and owner's equity are on the RIGHT side of the accounting equation and on the RIGHT side of Delgado Web Services' balance sheet.

The information needed to prepare the Assets section is obtained from the work sheet's Account Title column and the Balance Sheet Debit column. The information needed to prepare the Liabilities section is obtained from the work sheet's Account Title column and the Balance Sheet Credit column.

↘ Preparing the Assets and Liabilities Sections of a Balance Sheet

① Write the title of the first section, Assets, in the middle of the left wide column.

② Write the titles of all asset accounts under the heading.

③ Record the balance of each asset account in the left amount column on the same line as the account title.

④ Write the title of the next section, Liabilities, in the middle of the right wide column.

⑤ Write the titles of all liability accounts under the heading.

⑥ Record the balance of each liability account in the right amount column on the same line as the account title.

⑦ Rule a single line across the right amount column under the last amount, to indicate addition.

⑧ Write the words Total Liabilities in the right wide column on the next blank line.

⑨ Record the total of all liabilities, $225.00, in the right amount column.

remember

The balance sheet proves the accounting equation (A = L + OE).

Owner's Equity Section of a Balance Sheet

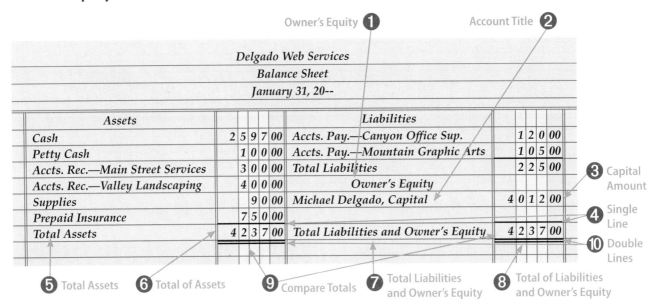

Only the amount of current capital is reported on Delgado Web Services' balance sheet. The amounts needed to calculate the current capital are found in the work sheet's Balance Sheet columns. The amount of current capital is calculated as shown.

Capital Account Balance	+	Net Income	−	Drawing Account Balance	=	Current Capital
$2,000.00	+	$3,162.00	−	$1,150.00	=	$4,012.00

When a business has a net loss, current capital is calculated as shown. The current capital is reported on the balance sheet in the same way as when the business has a net income.

Capital Account Balance	−	Net Loss	−	Drawing Account Balance	=	Current Capital
$6,000.00	−	$850.00	−	$500.00	=	$4,650.00

↘ Preparing the Owner's Equity Section of a Balance Sheet

1. Write the title of the section, Owner's Equity, in the middle of the right wide column on the next line below "Total Liabilities."

2. Write the title of the owner's capital account, Michael Delgado, Capital, on the next line.

3. Record the current amount of owner's equity, $4,012.00, in the right amount column.

4. Rule a single line under the last amount in the longer left amount column. Rule a single line in the right amount column on the same line.

5. Write the words Total Assets on the next line, in the left wide column.

6. Record the amount of total assets, $4,237.00, in the left amount column.

7. Write the words Total Liabilities and Owner's Equity in the right wide column on the same line as "Total Assets."

8. Record the amount of total liabilities and owner's equity, $4,237.00, in the right amount column.

9. Compare the totals of the two amount columns. The totals are the same, so the balance sheet is in balance.

10. Rule double lines across both the left and right amount columns just below the column totals to show that the totals have been verified as correct.

Owner's Equity Reported in Detail on a Balance Sheet

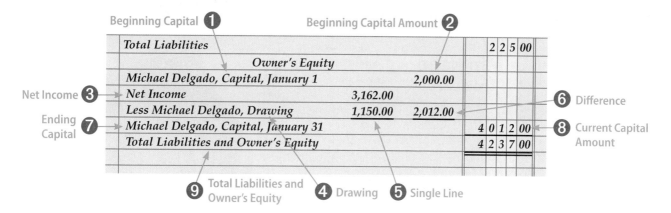

Total Liabilities			2 2 5 00
	Owner's Equity		
Michael Delgado, Capital, January 1		2,000.00	
Net Income	3,162.00		
Less Michael Delgado, Drawing	1,150.00	2,012.00	
Michael Delgado, Capital, January 31			4 0 1 2 00
Total Liabilities and Owner's Equity			4 2 3 7 00

- **①** Beginning Capital
- **②** Beginning Capital Amount
- **③** Net Income
- **⑦** Ending Capital
- **⑥** Difference
- **⑧** Current Capital Amount
- **⑨** Total Liabilities and Owner's Equity
- **④** Drawing
- **⑤** Single Line

Delgado Web Services' balance sheet reports the current capital on January 31 but does not show how this amount was calculated. Delgado Web Services is a small business with relatively few changes in owner's equity to report. Therefore, Michael Delgado decided that the business does not need to report all the details in the Owner's Equity section. However, some businesses prefer to report the details about how owner's equity is calculated.

If Delgado Web Services were to report details about owner's equity, the Owner's Equity section of the balance sheet would be prepared as shown in the illustration.

Preparing the Owner's Equity Section Reported in Detail on a Balance Sheet

① Write the words Michael Delgado, Capital, January 1 on the first line under the words "Owner's Equity."

② Record the owner's capital account balance on January 1, $2,000.00, in the wide column.

③ Write the words Net Income on the next line. Record the net income, $3,162.00, in the wide column to the left of the capital account balance.

④ Write the words Less Michael Delgado, Drawing on the next line. Record the balance of the drawing account, $1,150.00, in the wide column.

⑤ Rule a single line under the amount.

⑥ Subtract the balance of the drawing account from the net income. Record the difference, $2,012.00, in the wide column to the right of the drawing account balance.

⑦ Write the words Michael Delgado, Capital, January 31 on the next line.

⑧ Add the January 1 capital amount, $2,000.00, and the difference between the net income and the drawing account, $2,012.00. Record the sum, $4,012.00, in the right amount column.

⑨ Write the words Total Liabilities and Owner's Equity on the next line. Record the amount of total liabilities and owner's equity, $4,237.00, in the right amount column.

remember Capital is not copied from the work sheet to the balance sheet. Capital is calculated using beginning capital, plus net income or minus net loss, minus drawing.

Careers In Accounting

Min Kahn
BOOKKEEPER

Min Kahn is a bookkeeper in a midsize electronics company. As the title implies, she keeps the "books," that is, the financial records, for the company. Min supervises three accounting clerks. She verifies their work and performs other accounting tasks. These include journal entries, bank reconciliations, bank deposits and cash reports, as well as accounts receivable and accounts payable reports. Bookkeepers are often in charge of invoicing and managing the petty cash fund. Min is also in charge of the accounting software program used by the company. At the end of each fiscal period, she prepares the adjusting entries and does a trial balance. This is where the position of bookkeeper usually ends. However, in some small companies, the bookkeeper prepares the financial statements.

Min gives the trial balance to the accountant, who prepares the financial statements. The accountant also prepares other reports for managers to use in decision making.

Salary Range: Salaries vary with job responsibilities, but usually range from $31,000 to $40,000 annually. Bookkeepers who supervise other employees tend to earn higher salaries.

Qualifications: The qualifications for bookkeeper vary greatly with company size. A bookkeeper is sometimes an entry-level position. However, accounting clerks are often promoted to the job of bookkeeper.

A two-year accounting degree is helpful but not always required. A bookkeeper must have a sound understanding of the accounting cycle as well as basic knowledge of GAAP. When the position requires supervising accounting clerks, the bookkeeper must be able to direct, evaluate, and motivate those employees. Time management and project management skills are also important. Computer skills and an understanding of accounting software programs are essential. A bookkeeper must have good oral and written communications skills.

Occupational Outlook: The growth for bookkeeping positions is projected to be in the average range (between 7% and 13%) for the period from 2008 to 2018.

ACTIVITY
Research job openings for a bookkeeper in your area. Record the educational requirements and the salary range for five positions. Summarize your findings in a written report.

Sources: online.onetcenter.org; 2010 Accounting & Finance Salary Guide published by Robert Half.

End of Lesson Review

LO3 Prepare a balance sheet for a service business organized as a proprietorship.

▶ ## Audit your understanding

1. List the four sections on a balance sheet.
2. What is the formula for calculating current capital?

▶ ## Work together 7-2

Preparing a balance sheet

A partial work sheet of All Pro Painters for the month ended April 30 of the current year is given in the *Working Papers*. Also given is a blank form for completing a balance sheet. Your instructor will guide you through the following example.

Prepare a balance sheet for April 30 of the current year.

▶ ## On your own 7-2

Preparing a balance sheet

A partial work sheet of A-1 Computer Repair for the month ended October 31 of the current year is given in the *Working Papers*. Also given is a blank form for completing a balance sheet. Work this problem independently.

Prepare a balance sheet for October 31 of the current year.

©CANDICE CUSACK, ISTOCK

A Look at Accounting Software
Viewing Financial Statements in the Reports Window

One tremendous advantage of computerized accounting systems is their ability to produce accurate reports very quickly. If an error is discovered in the data, a correction can be made and a new report created in just minutes.

Most accounting systems come with dozens, or even hundreds, of available report forms. Many systems allow users to modify existing reports or to create new ones. Some systems have elaborate report formatting tools, while some offer very few. Some accounting systems offer interactive reports, while others display only plain text. An interactive report allows the user to click on numbers in the report to see the transactions that produced the numbers.

All managers need regular financial statements to guide their decision making and to report their progress to owners and creditors. So financial statements are among the most widely used reports. Usually, the user can select from several different formats for each statement. For example, one alternative income statement shows the current month and a range of previous months selected by the user.

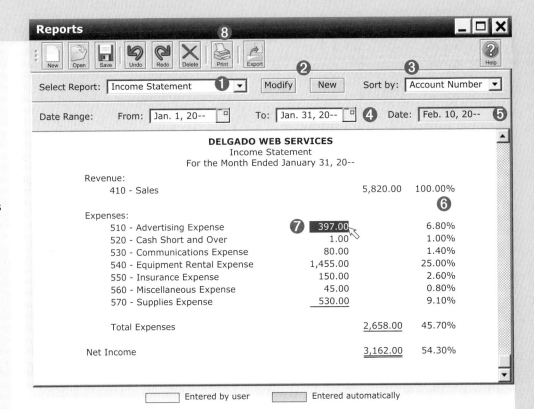

1. The user selects the income statement from the drop-down list.

2. To change the report, the user would click **Modify**. Tools available in the software would allow the user to add, edit, or delete fields and labels; change fonts; insert charts; etc. Clicking on **New** would allow the user to create an entirely new report.

3. Most reports can be sorted in a variety of ways. For example, this report could be sorted by account title or account number. Since Delgado Web Services' accounts are numbered in alphabetical order, it would not make a difference. The default selection is numerical.

4. The user selects the date range for the report. This option allows the user to prepare an income statement covering a single month, several months, or the year to date.

5. The current date cannot be changed by the user. If this statement is printed, the time and date will be printed in the footer. Time and date stamps are important in comparing like reports printed at different times.

6. On page 195 of this chapter, the income statement shows vertical analysis percentages only for Total Expenses and Net Income, with Sales being 100.0%. This income statement shows a complete vertical analysis, which allows management to compare all items on the income statement from one period to another. Vertical analysis gives management a better understanding of how different types of expenses and net income change over the course of the year in relation to sales.

7. This report is interactive. When the user positions the cursor over an active field, the field displays a frame. Clicking inside the frame opens a small window showing the data or the calculation that created the number. For example, clicking on the 397.00 advertising expense would show all the advertising transactions posted during the period.

8. If a printed statement is desired, the user would click **Print**.

Chapter Summary

Two financial statements prepared at the end of each fiscal period are the income statement and the balance sheet. Both financial statements are prepared using information found on the work sheet. The income statement summarizes the revenue, expenses, and net income or net loss of the company for a period of time. An income statement may show the total expense ratio and the net income ratio, which are used to evaluate the financial performance of the company.

The balance sheet lists the assets, liabilities, and owner's equity of the company on a specific date. The balance sheet proves that assets *equal* liabilities *plus* owner's equity. When preparing the balance sheet, the new capital account balance must be calculated. The balance sheet is used to evaluate the financial strength of the company.

Comparative and Interim Financial Statements

EXPLORE ACCOUNTING

A corporation that trades its stock on a U.S. stock exchange must submit an annual report to the Securities and Exchange Commission (SEC). The SEC has specific requirements as to what must be included in the financial statements.

One requirement is that the financial statements included in the annual report must show amounts for more than one year. The balance sheet must show ending balances for the current year and the previous year. The income statement and statement of stockholders' equity must show amounts for the current year and the two previous years. Financial statements providing information for multiple fiscal periods are called **comparative financial statements.**

These statements make it possible for a user to compare performance from year to year. For example, the net income for the current year can be compared to the net income for the two previous years. In this way, the user can determine if there is a positive or negative trend occurring in net income. On the balance sheet, the ending cash balance for the current year can be compared to the ending cash balance from the previous year to determine if the amount of cash on hand is increasing or decreasing.

Businesses that are required to submit an annual report to the SEC must also submit a quarterly report. This report is not as detailed as the annual report, but it must include the financial statements for the quarter. Financial statements providing information for a time period shorter than the fiscal year are called **interim**

financial statements. Users of financial information are able to evaluate the progress of the firm every three months rather than waiting an entire year. The importance of interim financial statements can be verified by the fact that the results reported in these statements are often summarized and reported in financial news sources, such as *The Wall Street Journal* and CNBC.

INSTRUCTIONS

Contact a corporation near you. Ask if the business prepares interim financial statements and, if it does, find out how often these statements are prepared.

©MAKHNACH_M_ISTOCK

Apply Your Understanding

INSTRUCTIONS: Download problem instructions for Excel, QuickBooks, and Peachtree from the textbook companion website at www.C21accounting.com.

7-1 Application Problem: Preparing an income statement LO1, 2

AAONLINE

1. Go to www.cengage.com/login
2. Click on **AA Online** to access.
3. Go to the online assignment and follow the instructions.

A form is given in the *Working Papers*. The following information is obtained from the work sheet of Lincoln Lawn Service for the month ended January 31 of the current year.

	ACCOUNT TITLE	INCOME STATEMENT		BALANCE SHEET		
		DEBIT	CREDIT	DEBIT	CREDIT	
12	Sales		4 1 1 3 00			12
13	Advertising Expense	2 5 0 00				13
14	Cash Short and Over	2 00				14
15	Insurance Expense	4 7 5 00				15
16	Miscellaneous Expense	5 8 00				16
17	Supplies Expense	3 1 9 00				17
18	Utilities Expense	1 6 3 00				18
19		1 2 6 7 00	4 1 1 3 00	6 2 8 7 00	3 4 4 1 00	19
20	Net Income	2 8 4 6 00			2 8 4 6 00	20
21		4 1 1 3 00	4 1 1 3 00	6 2 8 7 00	6 2 8 7 00	21

Instructions:

1. Prepare an income statement for the month ended January 31 of the current year.
2. Calculate and record the ratios for total expenses and net income. Round percentage calculations to the nearest 0.1%.

7-2 Application Problem: Preparing a balance sheet LO3

AAONLINE

1. Go to www.cengage.com/login
2. Click on **AA Online** to access.
3. Go to the online assignment and follow the instructions.

A form is given in the *Working Papers*. The following information is obtained from the work sheet of Lee's Home Repair for the month ended January 31 of the current year.

	ACCOUNT TITLE	BALANCE SHEET		
		DEBIT	CREDIT	
1	Cash	1 9 0 0 00		1
2	Petty Cash	2 0 0 00		2
3	Accounts Receivable—J. Greenstein	1 7 5 00		3
4	Supplies	1 6 0 00		4
5	Prepaid Insurance	2 4 0 00		5
6	Accounts Payable—Superior Supplies		4 0 0 00	6
7	Accounts Payable—Media Plus		3 0 0 00	7
8	Timothy Lee, Capital		2 1 2 8 00	8
9	Timothy Lee, Drawing	9 5 0 00		9
10	Income Summary			10
20		3 6 2 5 00	2 8 2 8 00	20
21	Net Income		7 9 7 00	21
22		3 6 2 5 00	3 6 2 5 00	22
23				23

Instructions:

Prepare a balance sheet for January 31 of the current year.

Forms are given in the *Working Papers*. The following information is obtained from the work sheet of Eiler Copy Service for the month ended September 30 of the current year.

	ACCOUNT TITLE	INCOME STATEMENT		BALANCE SHEET		
		5 DEBIT	6 CREDIT	7 DEBIT	8 CREDIT	
1	Cash			3 4 8 0 00		1
2	Petty Cash			7 5 00		2
3	Accounts Receivable—S. Romano			9 8 00		3
4	Supplies			3 9 0 00		4
5	Prepaid Insurance			4 0 0 00		5
6	Accounts Payable—Supplies Plus				3 0 6 00	6
7	Cheryl Eiler, Capital				4 6 6 8 00	7
8	Cheryl Eiler, Drawing			3 0 0 00		8
9	Income Summary					9
10	Sales		1 6 3 5 00			10
11	Advertising Expense	2 2 5 00				11
12	Cash Short and Over	1 00				12
13	Insurance Expense	7 8 00				13
14	Miscellaneous Expense	4 2 00				14
15	Supplies Expense	7 0 0 00				15
16	Utilities Expense	8 2 0 00				16
17		1 8 6 6 00	1 6 3 5 00	4 7 4 3 00	4 9 7 4 00	17
18	Net Loss	(2 3 1 00)			(2 3 1 00)	18
19		1 6 3 5 00	1 6 3 5 00	4 7 4 3 00	4 7 4 3 00	19
20						20

Instructions:

1. Prepare an income statement for the month ended September 30 of the current year.

2. Calculate and record the ratios for total expenses and net loss. Place the percentage for net loss in parentheses to show that it is for a net loss. Round percentage calculations to the nearest 0.1%.

3. Prepare a balance sheet for September 30 of the current year.

Peachtree

1. From the menu bar, select Reports & Forms; Financial Statements.
2. Make the selections to print the income statement and balance sheet.

QB
Quick Books

1. From the menu bar, select Reports; Company & Financial.
2. Make the selections to print the profit and loss statement and balance sheet.

X

1. Complete the income statement and balance sheet spreadsheets.
2. Make the selections to print.

Forms are given in the *Working Papers*. The information below is obtained from the work sheet of Scow Art School for the month ended October 31 of the current year.

	ACCOUNT TITLE		INCOME STATEMENT		BALANCE SHEET		
			5 DEBIT	**6** CREDIT	**7** DEBIT	**8** CREDIT	
1	Cash				2 0 6 0 00		1
2	Accounts Receivable—J. Holben				1 9 0 00		2
3	Supplies				8 2 5 00		3
4	Prepaid Insurance				1 1 0 0 00		4
5	Accounts Payable—Tampa Supply					5 4 5 00	5
6	Accounts Payable—Supply Depot					9 3 0 00	6
7	Greg Scow, Capital					4 5 2 7 00	7
8	Greg Scow, Drawing				1 0 0 0 00		8
9	Income Summary						9
10	Sales—Lessons			2 1 0 0 00			10
11	Sales—Group Classes			3 6 0 0 00			11
12	Advertising Expense		6 8 5 00				12
13	Insurance Expense		1 5 0 00				13
14	Miscellaneous Expense		4 2 00				14
15	Rent Expense		2 5 0 0 00				15
16	Supplies Expense		3 1 5 0 00				16
17			6 5 2 7 00	5 7 0 0 00	5 1 7 5 00	6 0 0 2 00	17
18	Net Loss		(8 2 7 00)			(8 2 7 00)	18
19			5 7 0 0 00	5 7 0 0 00	5 1 7 5 00	5 1 7 5 00	19
20							20

Instructions:

1. Prepare an income statement for the month ended October 31 of the current year.

2. Calculate and record the ratios for total expenses and net loss. Place the percentage for net loss in parentheses to show that it is for a net loss. Round percentage calculations to the nearest 0.1%.

3. Prepare a balance sheet for October 31 of the current year.

Peachtree

1. From the menu bar, select Reports & Forms; Financial Statements.
2. Make the selections to print the income statement and balance sheet.

 Quick Books

1. From the menu bar, select Reports; Company & Financial.
2. Make the selections to print the profit and loss statement and balance sheet.

21st Century Skills

Comparing Financial Statements

Theme: Financial, Economic, Business, and Entrepreneurial Literacy

Skills: ICT Literacy, Critical Thinking and Problem Solving

PARTNERSHIP FOR
21ST CENTURY SKILLS

Select three companies within the same industry. Go to the home page for each company. Search each site for its most current financial statements. This information is typically found under one of the following headings: About Us, Investor Relations, or History. Then, locate the income statement to obtain the following information. An income statement is also called a profit and loss statement (or a P&L).

APPLICATION

1. List the total revenue, total expenses, and net income or net loss for each company.
2. For each company, calculate and record the ratios for total expenses and net income by dividing each item by the amount of total sales. Round percentage calculations to the nearest 0.1%.
3. Compare these ratios for net income for each company. Which company has the best ratio?
4. Assume you are an accountant. What recommendation(s) would you suggest for the company to increase its net income by 20% for the next fiscal period?

Analyzing Nike's financial statements

Nike's financial reports include a Consolidated Statement of Income, which is shown in Appendix B on page B-5. This statement reports revenue, expenses, and operating income similar to an income statement for a proprietorship. Nike's statement of income is more complex than the income statement described in this chapter. Besides reporting net income, it also reports other items that will be covered later in this course. The first line of the statement is Revenues. As part of GAAP, Nike must report when that revenue is recognized, or counted as revenue. The first note to the financial statement, titled Summary of Significant Accounting Policies, covers items such as revenue recognition.

INSTRUCTIONS

1. Look through Note 1 on page B-10 for a paragraph titled Recognition of Revenues. When are revenues from wholesale sales recognized?
2. When are retail store revenues recognized?

Chapter 8

Recording Closing Entries and Preparing a Post-Closing Trial Balance for a Service Business

LEARNING OBJECTIVES

After studying Chapter 8, in addition to defining key terms, you will be able to:

LO1 Journalize and post closing entries for a service business organized as a proprietorship.

LO2 Prepare a post-closing trial balance.

©DANIEL KOUREY, ISTOCK/©JIM PRUITT, ISTOCK

FANCY/JUPITER IMAGES

Accounting In The Real World

Ben & Jerry's

What is your favorite flavor of ice cream? If your answer is Cherry Garcia, Magic Brownie, or Chunky Monkey, you are already acquainted with Ben & Jerry's ice cream. Ben & Jerry's is known for its unusual ice cream flavors and its even more unusual names for those flavors. This ice cream maker began in an old gas station. It is has now become a socially and environmentally responsible company while still earning a profit for its stockholders.

One example of Ben & Jerry's social responsibility involves the brownies used in many of its ice cream flavors such as Magic Brownie. All the brownie chunks in this flavor come from Greyston Bakery, which started as a small bakery in Yonkers, New York. Greyston Bakery has an "open hiring" policy, which focuses on employing the chronically unemployed. Its reason for existing is to "provide jobs to homeless people, ex-convicts, teenage moms, and other people in difficult circumstances."

Another example is Ben & Jerry's commitment to pay its employees no less than a livable wage. A livable wage is defined as the starting wage for a single person that will sustain a reasonable quality of life. It is to include expenditures for housing, utilities, out-of-pocket health care, transportation, food, recreation, savings, taxes, and miscellaneous expenses. Each year, the company recalculates the livable wage to make sure it keeps up with the actual cost of living. Since 2008, Ben & Jerry's livable wage has been almost double the national minimum wage.

CRITICAL THINKING

1. List at least two reasons why Ben & Jerry's pays more than the current minimum wage to its employees.

2. Go to www.benjerry.com and find two additional examples that demonstrate the company's social or environmental responsibility.

3. Name three expense accounts that might be found on an income statement for Ben & Jerry's.

Sources: www.benjerry.com; www.greystonbakery.com.

Key Terms

- permanent accounts
- temporary accounts
- closing entries
- post-closing trial balance
- accounting cycle

8-1 Recording Closing Entries

LO1 Journalize and post closing entries for a service business organized as a proprietorship

Need for Permanent and Temporary Accounts

Delgado Web Services prepares a work sheet at the end of each fiscal period. The work sheet is used to journalize adjusting entries (Chapter 6) and to prepare financial statements (Chapter 7). [CONCEPT: Accounting Period Cycle] The work sheet is also used to complete other end-of-period work.

Accounts used to accumulate information from one fiscal period to the next are called **permanent accounts**. Permanent accounts are also referred to as *real accounts*. Permanent accounts include the asset and liability accounts and the owner's capital account. The ending account balances of permanent accounts for one fiscal period are the beginning account balances for the next fiscal period.

Accounts used to accumulate information until it is transferred to the owner's capital account are called **temporary accounts**. Temporary accounts are also referred to as *nominal accounts*. Temporary accounts include the revenue, expense, and owner's drawing accounts plus the Income Summary account. Temporary accounts show changes in the owner's capital for a single fiscal period. Therefore, at the end of a fiscal period, the balances of temporary accounts are summarized and transferred to the owner's capital account. The temporary accounts begin a new fiscal period with zero balances.

Need for Closing Temporary Accounts

Journal entries used to prepare temporary accounts for a new fiscal period are called **closing entries**. The temporary account balances must be reduced to zero at the end of each fiscal period. This procedure prepares the temporary accounts for recording information about the next fiscal period. Otherwise, the amounts for the next fiscal period would be added to amounts for previous fiscal periods. [CONCEPT: Matching Expenses with Revenue] The net income for the next fiscal period

would be difficult to calculate because amounts from several fiscal periods remain in the accounts. Therefore, the temporary accounts must start each new fiscal period with zero balances.

To close a temporary account, an amount equal to its balance is recorded in the account on the side opposite to its balance. For example, if an account has a credit balance of $3,565.00, a debit of $3,565.00 is recorded to close the account.

Can I Say This on My Résumé?

Kendra Wheeler applied for an accounting assistant position with Hampton Group. She slightly exaggerated her work experience on her résumé. She felt uncomfortable with this decision, but she was desperate to get a job.

Based on the résumé, Kendra was hired. After one year, she received above-average ratings during her annual review. Then, her boss met Kendra's former supervisor and learned the truth.

INSTRUCTIONS

Was Kendra's action unethical? Let's apply the ethical model to this situation.

1. *Recognize you are facing an ethical dilemma.* Kendra should have realized that her uncomfortable feelings were a sign that her actions might not be ethical.

2. *Identify the action taken or the proposed action.* Kendra could have stated her qualifications honestly. However, she elected to exaggerate her work experience.

3. *Analyze the action.*

   a. *Is the action illegal?* Possibly. Overstating qualifications is generally not illegal, but the employer could terminate her employment. However, overstating qualifications when applying for a government position may be illegal.

   b. *Does the action violate company or professional standards?* No. Kendra was neither an employee of the company nor a member of any profession at the time she was hired.

   c. *Who is affected, and how, by the action?*

Stakeholders	Negative Impact	Positive Impact
Kendra	• When the truth is discovered, she may be terminated. If retained, she may not be promoted.	• Obtained employment.
Other applicants	• More highly qualified applicants lost an employment opportunity.	
Hampton Group	• The company lost the opportunity of receiving the services of a more qualified employee. • If Kendra is terminated, the company must train another employee. • If Kendra is retained, managers may hesitate to give her responsibilities necessary for the efficient operation of the company.	

4. *Determine if the action is ethical.* Kendra's action was not ethical. Exaggerating her résumé provided her with a short-term benefit. However, this benefit does not outweigh the negative impact on other applicants and the Hampton Group. In fact, Kendra's action could possibly cause her more harm in the long run.

Need for the Income Summary Account

Whenever a temporary account is closed, the closing entry must have equal debits and credits. If an account is debited for $3,000.00 to close the account, some other account must be credited for the same amount. A temporary account titled Income Summary is used to summarize the closing entries for the revenue and expense accounts.

The Income Summary account is unique because it does not have a normal balance side. The balance of this account is determined by the amounts posted to the account at the end of a fiscal period. When revenue is greater than total expenses, resulting in a net income, the Income Summary account has a credit balance, as shown in the T account.

Income Summary	
Debit	Credit
Total expenses	Revenue (greater than expenses)
	(Credit balance is the net income.)

When total expenses are greater than revenue, resulting in a net loss, the Income Summary account has a debit balance, as shown in the T account.

Income Summary	
Debit	Credit
Total expenses (greater than revenue)	Revenue
(Debit balance is the net loss.)	

Thus, whether the balance of the Income Summary account is a credit or a debit depends upon whether the business earns a net income or incurs a net loss. Because Income Summary is a temporary account, the account is also closed at the end of a fiscal period when the net income or net loss is recorded.

Delgado Web Services records four closing entries:

(1) An entry to close income statement accounts with credit balances.

(2) An entry to close income statement accounts with debit balances,

(3) An entry to record net income or net loss and close Income Summary, and

(4) An entry to close the owner's drawing account.

Information needed to record the four closing entries is found in the Income Statement and Balance Sheet columns of the work sheet.

Closing Entry for an Income Statement Account with a Credit Balance LO1

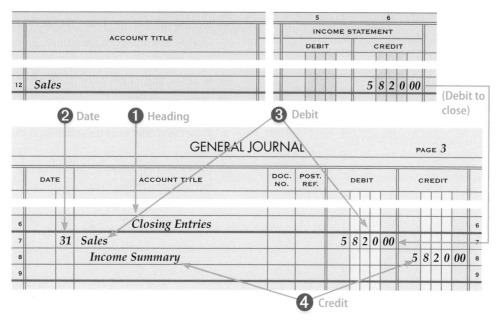

② Date **①** Heading **③** Debit (Debit to close)

④ Credit

Delgado Web Services has one income statement account with a credit balance, **Sales**. This credit balance must be reduced to zero to prepare the account for the next fiscal period. To reduce the balance to zero, **Sales** is debited for the amount of the balance. Because debits must equal credits for each journal entry, some other account must be credited. The account used for the credit part of this closing entry is **Income Summary**.

The effect of this closing entry on the general ledger accounts is shown in the T accounts on the next page.

Global Quality Standards

The quality of products is a major concern for industry, especially when those products are traded among nations. In order for some products to be used in other nations, they must be standardized. A standard is a technical specification for a product. The company providing the product must be able to consistently produce a quality product that meets certain standards. According to the organizations that help establish these standards, the "product" can be a physical product, a service, or software.

International quality standards have changed over time. They focus on inspecting and measuring the final product to see that it matches defined specifications. They also emphasize process management. Process management includes monitoring all processes and activities involved in the development or production of the product, with the goal of continuous improvement in the efficiency of the operation.

Quality standards have been established for many fields, including information processing and communications, textiles, packaging, energy production, shipbuilding, and banking and financial services.

More recently, a series of standards is being developed to address environmental issues for organizations involved in international trade.

CRITICAL THINKING

1. How would your company benefit from global quality standards if it were buying the same product from different vendors in different countries?

2. Could meeting international quality standards give a company a competitive advantage?

Sales

Closing	5,820.00	Bal.	5,820.00	
		(New Bal.	0.00)	

Income Summary

		Closing (revenue)	5,820.00

The balance of Sales is now zero, and the account is ready for the next fiscal period. The credit balance of Sales is transferred to Income Summary.

Most small businesses use the calendar year as their fiscal year because it matches the way in which the owners have to file their personal income tax returns.

❥ Closing Entry for an Income Statement Account with a Credit Balance

❶ Write the heading, Closing Entries, in the middle of the Account Title column of the journal. For Delgado Web Services, this heading is placed in the journal on the first blank line after the last adjusting entry.

❷ Write the date, 31, on the next line in the Date column.

❸ Write the title of the account debited, Sales, in the Account Title column. Record the debit amount, $5,820.00, in the Debit column on the same line as the account title.

❹ On the next line, indented one centimeter, write the title of the account credited, Income Summary, in the Account Title column. Record the credit amount, $5,820.00, in the Credit column on the same line as the account title.

THINK LIKE AN ACCOUNTANT

Analyzing Financial Statements

Lenny Bethune has come to your accounting office seeking your advice. He has operated a heating and air conditioning repair service for several years. Despite a steady increase in revenues, his net income continues to decline.

As you examine a schedule containing his income statement information for the past four years, Lenny explains some of his business decisions. "I used to rent part of an old building in the industrial park. Two years ago, I decided to get serious. I moved my office to a new retail center located on the main drag. I thought that would give me some visibility. People would see my office on a daily basis. They would remember my name when their systems failed. So I figured I wouldn't need to spend as much on advertising."

His income statement information reflects his story. His rent expense jumped in the next year. The new office also caused his insurance and utility expenses to rise.

"After a year," Lenny continued, "I wasn't seeing the increase in service calls that I had hoped. So I started to do more advertising again, in the local newspaper and on the radio. I just don't know what to do next." Lenny has asked you to evaluate his financial information and provide him with some recommendations.

OPEN THE SPREADSHEET TLA_CH08
Click on the Instructions tab. The file contains a structure for writing the memorandum. The memorandum should contain a chart that shows the change in Lenny's expenses and income for the past four years. Consider the following questions in preparing the memo.

1. How do potential customers select a service company when their heat or air conditioning has failed?

2. Does advertising appear to have increased revenue?

3. Did the move to a new office have a positive impact on revenue?

4. What could Lenny do to better understand the increase in Miscellaneous Expense?

©DAN BACHMAN, ISTOCK

Closing Entry for Income Statement Accounts with Debit Balances

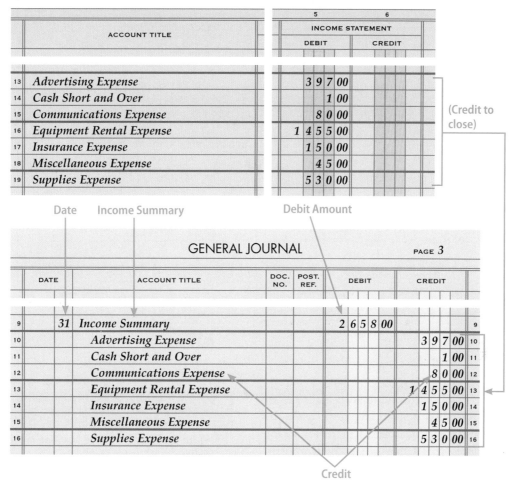

	ACCOUNT TITLE		INCOME STATEMENT	
			5 DEBIT	6 CREDIT
13	*Advertising Expense*		3 9 7 00	
14	*Cash Short and Over*		1 00	
15	*Communications Expense*		8 0 00	
16	*Equipment Rental Expense*		1 4 5 5 00	
17	*Insurance Expense*		1 5 0 00	
18	*Miscellaneous Expense*		4 5 00	
19	*Supplies Expense*		5 3 0 00	

(Credit to close)

Date Income Summary Debit Amount

GENERAL JOURNAL
PAGE 3

	DATE	ACCOUNT TITLE	DOC. NO.	POST. REF.	DEBIT	CREDIT	
9	31	*Income Summary*			2 6 5 8 00		9
10		*Advertising Expense*				3 9 7 00	10
11		*Cash Short and Over*				1 00	11
12		*Communications Expense*				8 0 00	12
13		*Equipment Rental Expense*				1 4 5 5 00	13
14		*Insurance Expense*				1 5 0 00	14
15		*Miscellaneous Expense*				4 5 00	15
16		*Supplies Expense*				5 3 0 00	16

Credit

Delgado Web Services has seven income statement accounts with debit balances. The seven expense accounts have normal debit balances at the end of a fiscal period. The balances of the expense accounts must be reduced to zero to prepare the accounts for the next fiscal period. Each expense account is credited for an amount equal to its balance. Income Summary is debited for the total of all the expense account balances. The amount debited to Income Summary is not entered in the amount column until all expenses have been journalized and the total amount calculated.

The effect of this closing entry on the general ledger accounts is shown in the T accounts. The balance of each expense account is returned to zero, and the accounts are ready for the next fiscal period. The balance of Income Summary is the net income for the fiscal period, $3,162.00.

Income Summary			
Closing (expenses)	2,658.00	Closing (revenue)	5,820.00
		(New Bal.	3,162.00)

Equipment Rental Expense			
Bal.	1,455.00	Closing	1,455.00
(New Bal.	0.00)		

Advertising Expense			
Bal.	397.00	Closing	397.00
(New Bal.	0.00)		

Insurance Expense			
Bal.	150.00	Closing	150.00
(New Bal.	0.00)		

Cash Short and Over			
Bal.	1.00	Closing	1.00
(New Bal.	0.00)		

Miscellaneous Expense			
Bal.	45.00	Closing	45.00
(New Bal.	0.00)		

Communications Expense			
Bal.	80.00	Closing	80.00
(New Bal.	0.00)		

Supplies Expense			
Bal.	530.00	Closing	530.00
(New Bal.	0.00)		

Closing Entry to Record Net Income or Loss and Close the Income Summary Account

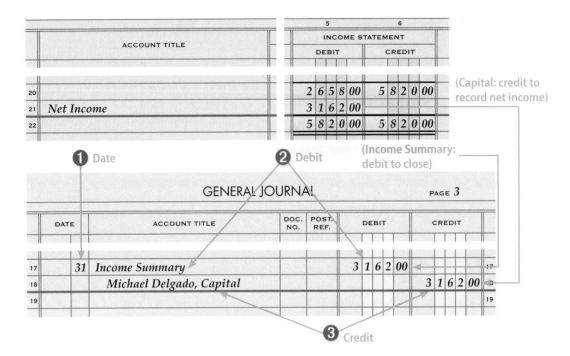

Delgado Web Services' net income appears on line 21 of the work sheet. The amount of net income increases the owner's capital and, therefore, must be credited to the owner's capital account. The balance of the temporary account, Income Summary, must be reduced to zero to prepare the account for the next fiscal period.

The effect of this closing entry on the general ledger accounts is shown in the T accounts. The debit to the Income Summary account, $3,162.00, reduces the account balance to zero and prepares the account for the next fiscal period. The credit, $3,162.00, increases the balance of the owner's capital account, Michael Delgado, Capital.

Income Summary

Closing (expenses)	2,658.00	Closing (revenue)	5,820.00
Closing	3,162.00	(New Bal.	0.00)

Michael Delgado, Capital

	Bal.	2,000.00
	Closing (net inc.)	3,162.00
	(New Bal.	5,162.00)

If a business incurs a net loss, the closing entry is a debit to the owner's capital account and a credit to the Income Summary account.

Closing Entry to Record Net Income or Loss and Close the Income Summary Account

❶ Write the date, 31, on the next line in the Date column.

❷ Write the title of the account debited, Income Summary, in the Account Title column. Record the debit amount, $3,162.00, in the Debit column on the same line as the account title.

❸ On the next line, indented one centimeter, write the title of the account credited, Michael Delgado, Capital, in the Account Title column. Record the credit amount, $3,162.00, in the Credit column on the same line as the account title.

Amounts for closing entries are taken from the Income Statement and Balance Sheet columns of the work sheet.

Closing Entry for the Owner's Drawing Account

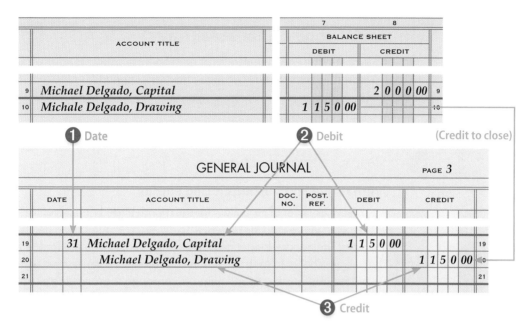

Withdrawals are assets that the owner takes out of a business and which decrease the amount of the owner's equity. The drawing account is a temporary account that accumulates information separately for each fiscal period. Therefore, the drawing account balance must be reduced to zero at the end of one fiscal period to prepare the account for the next fiscal period.

The drawing account is neither a revenue nor an expense account. Therefore, the drawing account is not closed through Income Summary. The drawing account balance is closed directly to the owner's capital account.

The effect of the entry to close the drawing account is shown in the T accounts.

The drawing account has a zero balance and is ready for the next fiscal period. The capital account's new balance, $4,012.00, is verified by comparing the balance to the amount of capital shown on the balance sheet prepared at the end of the fiscal period. The capital account balance shown on Delgado Web Services' balance sheet in Chapter 7 is $4,012.00. The two amounts are the same, and the capital account balance is verified.

Michael Delgado, Capital

Closing (drawing)	1,150.00	Bal.	2,000.00
		Net Income	3,162.00
		(New Bal.	*4,012.00)*

Michael Delgado, Drawing

Bal.	1,150.00	Closing	1,150.00
(New Bal.	*0.00)*		

◆ Closing Entry for the Owner's Drawing Account

❶ Write the date, 31, in the Date column.

❷ Write the title of the account debited, Michael Delgado, Capital, in the Account Title column. Record the debit amount, $1,150.00, in the Debit column on the same line as the account title.

❸ On the next line, indented one centimeter, write the title of the account credited, Michael Delgado, Drawing, in the Account Title column. Record the credit amount, $1,150.00, in the Credit column on the same line as the account title.

remember Delgado Web Services makes four closing entries: (1) close income statement accounts with credit balances. (2) Close income statement accounts with debit balances. (3) Record net income or loss in the owner's capital account and close Income Summary. (4) Close the owner's drawing account.

End of Lesson Review

LO1 Journalize and post closing entries for a service business organized as a proprietorship.

Terms Review

permanent accounts

temporary accounts

closing entries

Audit your understanding

1. What do the ending balances of permanent accounts for one fiscal period represent at the beginning of the next fiscal period?
2. What do the balances of temporary accounts show?
3. List the four closing entries.

Work together 8-1

Journalizing and posting closing entries

A partial work sheet of Fix It Now for the month ended April 30 of the current year is given in the *Working Papers*. Also given are a journal and general ledger accounts. The general ledger accounts do not show all details for the fiscal period. The balance shown in each account is the account's balance after adjusting entries are posted. Your instructor will guide you through the following example.

Continue on page 8. Journalize and post the closing entries. Save your work to complete Work Together 8-2.

On your own 8-1

Journalizing and posting closing entries

A partial work sheet of Repair World for the month ended December 31 of the current year is given in the *Working Papers*. Also given are a journal and general ledger accounts. The general ledger accounts do not show all details for the fiscal period. The balance shown in each account is the account's balance after adjusting entries are posted. Work this problem independently.

Continue on page 24. Journalize and post the closing entries. Save your work to complete On Your Own 8-2.

©CANDICE CUSACK, ISTOCK

LO2 Prepare a post-closing trial balance.

General Ledger Accounts after Closing Entries Are Posted

Delgado Web Services' general ledger, after the closing entries are posted, is shown here and on the next several pages. When an account has a zero balance, lines are drawn in both the Balance Debit and Balance Credit columns. The lines assure a reader that a balance has not been omitted.

ACCOUNT **Cash**   ACCOUNT NO. **110**

DATE		ITEM	POST. REF.	DEBIT	CREDIT	BALANCE DEBIT	BALANCE CREDIT
Jan.	2		G1	2 000 00		2 000 00	
	2		G1		1 65 00	1 835 00	
	3		G1		9 00 00	9 35 00	
	9		G1		1 00 00	8 35 00	
	10		G1	1 1 00 00		1 935 00	
	12		G1		80 00	1 855 00	
	15		G1		4 00 00	1 455 00	
	16		G1	2 00 00		1 655 00	
	16		G1		3 50 00	1 305 00	
	17		G1		3 83 00	9 22 00	
	18		G1	5 35 00		1 457 00	
	19		G1		1 00 00	1 357 00	
	22		G1		5 10 00	8 47 00	
	24		G2	1 3 20 00		2 167 00	
	28		G2		1 30 00	2 037 00	
	29		G2	1 2 80 00		3 317 00	
	31		G2		35 00	3 282 00	
	31		G2		8 00 00	2 482 00	
	31		G2	6 85 00		3 167 00	
	31		G2		5 45 00	2 622 00	
	31		G2		25 00	2 597 00	

ACCOUNT **Petty Cash**   ACCOUNT NO. **120**

DATE		ITEM	POST. REF.	DEBIT	CREDIT	BALANCE DEBIT	BALANCE CREDIT
Jan.	19		G1	1 00 00		1 00 00	

ACCOUNT **Accounts Receivable—Main Street Services**   ACCOUNT NO. **130**

DATE		ITEM	POST. REF.	DEBIT	CREDIT	BALANCE DEBIT	BALANCE CREDIT
Jan.	12		G1	5 00 00		5 00 00	
	16		G1		2 00 00	3 00 00	

A General Ledger after Closing Entries Are Posted (continued)

ACCOUNT Accounts Receivable—Valley Landscaping ACCOUNT NO. 140

DATE		ITEM	POST. REF.	DEBIT	CREDIT	BALANCE DEBIT	BALANCE CREDIT
Jan.	16		G1	4 0 0 00		4 0 0 00	

ACCOUNT Supplies ACCOUNT NO. 150

DATE		ITEM	POST. REF.	DEBIT	CREDIT	BALANCE DEBIT	BALANCE CREDIT
Jan.	2		G1	1 6 5 00		1 6 5 00	
	5		G1	2 2 0 00		3 8 5 00	
	19		G1	1 0 5 00		4 9 0 00	
	28		G2	1 3 0 00		6 2 0 00	
	31		G3		5 3 0 00	9 0 00	

ACCOUNT Prepaid Insurance ACCOUNT NO. 160

DATE		ITEM	POST. REF.	DEBIT	CREDIT	BALANCE DEBIT	BALANCE CREDIT
Jan.	1		G1	9 0 0 00		9 0 0 00	
	31		G3		1 5 0 00	7 5 0 00	

ACCOUNT Accounts Payable—Canyon Office Supplies ACCOUNT NO. 210

DATE		ITEM	POST. REF.	DEBIT	CREDIT	BALANCE DEBIT	BALANCE CREDIT
Jan.	5		G1		2 2 0 00		2 2 0 00
	9		G1	1 0 0 00			1 2 0 00

ACCOUNT Accounts Payable—Mountain Graphic Arts ACCOUNT NO. 220

DATE		ITEM	POST. REF.	DEBIT	CREDIT	BALANCE DEBIT	BALANCE CREDIT
Jan.	19		G1		1 0 5 00		1 0 5 00

ACCOUNT Michael Delgado, Capital ACCOUNT NO. 310

DATE		ITEM	POST. REF.	DEBIT	CREDIT	BALANCE DEBIT	BALANCE CREDIT
Jan.	2		G1		2 0 0 0 00		2 0 0 0 00
	31		G3		3 1 6 2 00		5 1 6 2 00
	31		G3	1 1 5 0 00			4 0 1 2 00

ACCOUNT Michael Delgado, Drawing ACCOUNT NO. 320

DATE		ITEM	POST. REF.	DEBIT	CREDIT	BALANCE DEBIT	BALANCE CREDIT
Jan.	16		G1	3 5 0 00		3 5 0 00	
	31		G2	8 0 0 00		1 1 5 0 00	
	31		G3		1 1 5 0 00	—	

ACCOUNT Income Summary ACCOUNT NO. 330

DATE		ITEM	POST. REF.	DEBIT	CREDIT	BALANCE DEBIT	BALANCE CREDIT
Jan.	31		G3		5 8 2 0 00		5 8 2 0 00
	31		G3	2 6 5 8 00			3 1 6 2 00
	31		G3	3 1 6 2 00		—	

A General Ledger after Closing Entries Are Posted (continued)

ACCOUNT Sales   ACCOUNT NO. 410

DATE		ITEM	POST. REF.	DEBIT	CREDIT	BALANCE DEBIT	BALANCE CREDIT
Jan.	10		G1		1 1 0 0 00		1 1 0 0 00
	12		G1		5 0 0 00		1 6 0 0 00
	16		G1		4 0 0 00		2 0 0 0 00
	18		G1		5 3 5 00		2 5 3 5 00
	24		G2		1 3 2 0 00		3 8 5 5 00
	29		G2		1 2 8 0 00		5 1 3 5 00
	31		G2		6 8 5 00		5 8 2 0 00
	31		G3	5 8 2 0 00			

ACCOUNT Advertising Expense   ACCOUNT NO. 510

DATE		ITEM	POST. REF.	DEBIT	CREDIT	BALANCE DEBIT	BALANCE CREDIT
Jan.	17		G1	3 8 3 00		3 8 3 00	
	31		G2	1 4 00		3 9 7 00	
	31		G3		3 9 7 00		

ACCOUNT Cash Short and Over   ACCOUNT NO. 520

DATE		ITEM	POST. REF.	DEBIT	CREDIT	BALANCE DEBIT	BALANCE CREDIT
Jan.	31		G2	1 00		1 00	
	31		G3		1 00		

ACCOUNT Communications Expense   ACCOUNT NO. 530

DATE		ITEM	POST. REF.	DEBIT	CREDIT	BALANCE DEBIT	BALANCE CREDIT
Jan.	12		G1	8 0 00		8 0 00	
	31		G3		8 0 00		

ACCOUNT Equipment Rental Expense   ACCOUNT NO. 540

DATE		ITEM	POST. REF.	DEBIT	CREDIT	BALANCE DEBIT	BALANCE CREDIT
Jan.	15		G1	4 0 0 00		4 0 0 00	
	22		G1	5 1 0 00		9 1 0 00	
	31		G2	5 4 5 00		1 4 5 5 00	
	31		G3		1 4 5 5 00		

ACCOUNT Insurance Expense   ACCOUNT NO. 550

DATE		ITEM	POST. REF.	DEBIT	CREDIT	BALANCE DEBIT	BALANCE CREDIT
Jan.	31		G3	1 5 0 00		1 5 0 00	
	31		G3		1 5 0 00		

A General Ledger after Closing Entries Are Posted (continued)

ACCOUNT *Miscellaneous Expense*   **ACCOUNT NO.** *560*

DATE		ITEM	POST. REF.	DEBIT	CREDIT	BALANCE DEBIT	BALANCE CREDIT
Jan. 20--	31		G2	2 0 00		2 0 00	
	31		G2	2 5 00		4 5 00	
	31		G3		4 5 00	—	—

ACCOUNT *Supplies Expense*   **ACCOUNT NO.** *570*

DATE		ITEM	POST. REF.	DEBIT	CREDIT	BALANCE DEBIT	BALANCE CREDIT
Jan. 20--	31		G3	5 3 0 00		5 3 0 00	
	31		G3		5 3 0 00	—	—

A General Ledger after Closing Entries Are Posted (concluded)

Group Homes

A group home is usually a private residence that has been converted to house a group of unrelated persons. It provides a caring and safe home for people who could not otherwise live on their own. In most cases, the people living at the group home share a trait such as being developmentally disabled. The group home supervisors, sometimes called "parents," are trained caregivers who provide assistance to the residents as needed. A group home allows the residents to live in a home setting and learn how to help manage a budget or do household tasks.

Group homes are often licensed by the state. Therefore, besides providing direct care and assistance to the group home residents, the group home parents must keep accurate records required by the state. This could include what and how much food each resident consumes and the medicines given to each resident. Group parents may also have to keep track of personal spending money for each resident and a budget for the household.

Group homes are often owned by private companies. A person moving from the position of group home parent to a higher-level position within the company will most likely need to have more experience in recordkeeping, budgeting, and accounting.

CRITICAL THINKING

1. Using the Internet, find the name of one group home in your area. List the name, location, and type of home it is.
2. Besides good recordkeeping skills, what other skills would a group parent need to possess?

Post-Closing Trial Balance LO2

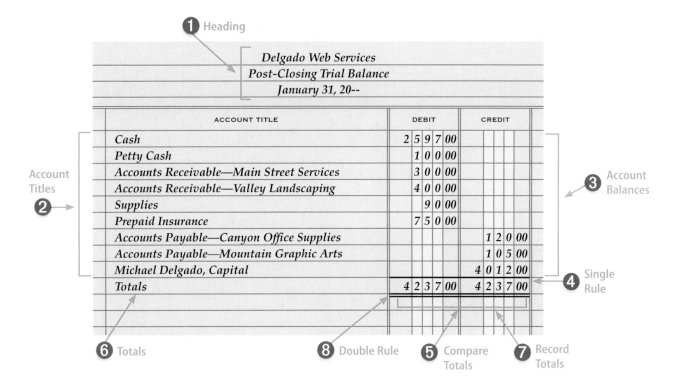

① Heading

Delgado Web Services
Post-Closing Trial Balance
January 31, 20--

ACCOUNT TITLE	DEBIT	CREDIT
Cash	2 5 9 7 00	
Petty Cash	1 0 0 00	
Accounts Receivable—Main Street Services	3 0 0 00	
Accounts Receivable—Valley Landscaping	4 0 0 00	
Supplies	9 0 00	
Prepaid Insurance	7 5 0 00	
Accounts Payable—Canyon Office Supplies		1 2 0 00
Accounts Payable—Mountain Graphic Arts		1 0 5 00
Michael Delgado, Capital		4 0 1 2 00
Totals	4 2 3 7 00	4 2 3 7 00

② Account Titles

③ Account Balances

④ Single Rule

⑥ Totals **⑧** Double Rule **⑤** Compare Totals **⑦** Record Totals

After the closing entries are posted, Delgado Web Services verifies that debits equal credits in the general ledger accounts by preparing a trial balance. A trial balance prepared after the closing entries are posted is called a **post-closing trial balance**.

Only general ledger accounts with balances are included on a post-closing trial balance. The permanent accounts (assets, liabilities, and owner's capital) have balances and do appear on a post-closing trial balance. Because the temporary accounts (Income Summary, revenue, expense, and drawing) are closed and have zero balances, they do not appear on a post-closing trial balance.

The total of all debits must equal the total of all credits in a general ledger. The totals of both columns on Delgado Web Services' post-closing trial balance are the same, $4,237.00. Delgado Web Services' post-closing trial balance shows that the general ledger account balances are in balance and ready for the new fiscal period.

Preparing a Post-Closing Trial Balance

① Write the heading on three lines.

② Write the titles of all general ledger accounts with balances in the Account Title column.

③ On the same line with each account title, write each account's balance in either the Debit or Credit column.

④ Rule a single line across both amount columns below the last amount, and add each amount column.

⑤ Compare the two column totals. The two column totals must be the same. If the two column totals are not the same, the errors must be found and corrected before any more work is completed.

⑥ Write the word Totals on the line below the last account title.

⑦ Write the column totals, $4,237.00, below the single line.

⑧ Rule double lines across both amount columns to show that the totals have been verified as correct.

Accounting Cycle for a Service Business

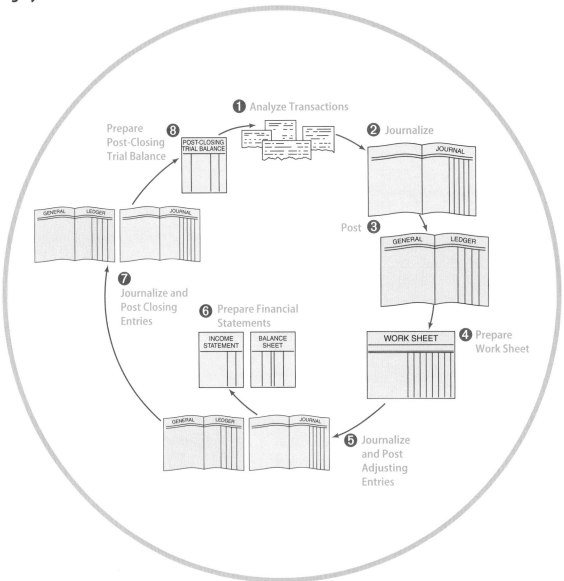

Chapters 1 through 8 describe Delgado Web Services' accounting activities for a one-month fiscal period. The series of accounting activities included in recording financial information for a fiscal period is called an **accounting cycle**. [CONCEPT: Accounting Period Cycle]

For the next fiscal period, the cycle begins again at Step 1.

The word *post* means *after*. The Post-Closing Trial Balance is prepared *after* closing entries.

Steps in an Accounting Cycle

1. Check source documents for accuracy and analyze transactions into debit and credit parts.
2. Record transactions from information on source documents in a journal.
3. Post journal entries to the general ledger.
4. Prepare a work sheet, including a trial balance, from the general ledger.
5. Journalize adjusting entries and post them to the general ledger.
6. Prepare financial statements from the work sheet.
7. Journalize and post closing entries.
8. Prepare a post-closing trial balance of the general ledger.

HealthSouth Inflates Earnings

Financial analysts use a variety of information sources and data analysis models to predict corporate earnings. Financial media sources survey financial analysts to get consensus estimates. The resulting "street expectations" for revenue and earnings are reported in the financial news.

The pressure to meet street expectations can cause honest people to do things they ordinarily would not do. Such was the case at HealthSouth. HealthSouth was a provider of outpatient rehabilitation services. At its peak, HealthSouth was the largest company based in Alabama.

But in 1995, fueled by HealthSouth's success, competitors entered the market, and the federal government tightened its Medicare reimbursement policies. These events had a negative impact on HealthSouth's revenue and earnings. For the first time in over 40 quarters, HealthSouth was going to miss street expectations. A scheme was hatched to falsify revenues to achieve street expectations.

By the end of the next quarter, the company had again missed street expectations. The company again falsified its revenues. The fraud continued for over seven years. Managing the fraud became increasingly complex, requiring 120,000 fraudulent journal entries each quarter. The fraud was finally revealed in 2003 when the chief financial officer, Wesley Smith, alerted government officials.

Fraudsters use many methods to inflate sales, but each method leaves behind a trail of evidence in the accounting system. Forensic accountants can search computer data for signs, or red flags, of each method used to inflate sales.

ACTIVITY

Kelly Boatman dreamed of selling her restaurant supply business and retiring. However, sales began to decline, and the business started to lose money. How could she sell the company if it was losing money? Desperate to return the business to profitability, Kelly began a scheme to record false sales. She created imaginary customers and entered sales invoices to those customers. After each quarter's actual sales were known, she would determine how many false sales to record. Kelly usually waited until her employees left for the day to enter the transactions.

Relying on her new and improved financial statements, Ambro Corporation is considering buying Kelly's business. However, before making a firm offer, the company wants you to perform some basic analysis of the financial data.

1. Identify the number of invoices having different transaction and posting dates.
2. Identify the number of invoices entered after normal working hours (11:00 A.M. to 6:00 P.M.).
3. Identify the number of invoices that require further investigation.

INSTRUCTIONS

Open the spreadsheet FA_CH08 and complete the steps on the Instructions tab.

End of Lesson Review

LO2 Prepare a post-closing trial balance.

Terms Review

post-closing trial balance

accounting cycle

Audit your understanding

1. Why are lines drawn in both the Balance Debit and Balance Credit columns when an account has a zero balance?
2. Which accounts go on the post-closing trial balance?
3. Why are temporary accounts omitted from a post-closing trial balance?
4. What are the steps in the accounting cycle?

Work together 8-2

Preparing a post-closing trial balance

Use the general ledger accounts from Work Together 8-1. Your instructor will guide you through the following example. A form to complete a post-closing trial balance is given in the *Working Papers*.

Prepare a post-closing trial balance for Fix It Now on April 30 of the current year.

On your own 8-2

Preparing a post-closing trial balance

Use the general ledger accounts from On Your Own 8-1. Work this problem independently. A form to complete a post-closing trial balance is given in the *Working Papers*.

Prepare a post-closing trial balance for Repair World on December 31 of the current year.

©CANDICE CUSACK, ISTOCK

A Look at Accounting Software

Exporting Report Data to Excel

Computerized accounting systems can display or print many different kinds of reports. Accountants, however, need to do more with reports than look at them.

Virtually all accounting systems can export report data in a variety of formats. One common format is "comma separated values." CSV files, which have a .csv file extension, are usable in database programs.

Most accountants, however, prefer to use spreadsheet software like Excel to analyze report data. The computational and charting features of Excel enable accountants to better understand what the report data say about the business's performance.

In Chapters 16 and 17, you will learn about the types of analysis performed by accountants, managers, and investors.

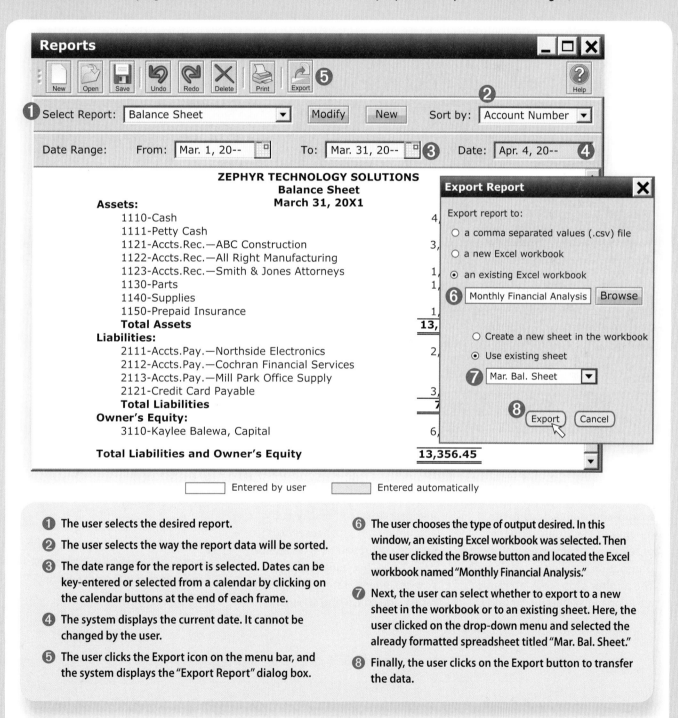

| | Entered by user | | Entered automatically |

1. The user selects the desired report.

2. The user selects the way the report data will be sorted.

3. The date range for the report is selected. Dates can be key-entered or selected from a calendar by clicking on the calendar buttons at the end of each frame.

4. The system displays the current date. It cannot be changed by the user.

5. The user clicks the Export icon on the menu bar, and the system displays the "Export Report" dialog box.

6. The user chooses the type of output desired. In this window, an existing Excel workbook was selected. Then the user clicked the Browse button and located the Excel workbook named "Monthly Financial Analysis."

7. Next, the user can select whether to export to a new sheet in the workbook or to an existing sheet. Here, the user clicked on the drop-down menu and selected the already formatted spreadsheet titled "Mar. Bal. Sheet."

8. Finally, the user clicks on the Export button to transfer the data.

Chapter Summary

After the financial statements are prepared at the end of an accounting period, the temporary accounts are closed. There are four closing entries. First, revenue accounts are closed and the balances are transferred to the Income Summary account. The second closing entry is to close expense accounts and transfer the balances to the Income Summary account. The third closing entry closes the Income Summary account and transfers the net income (or net loss) to the capital account. The last closing entry closes the drawing account and transfers the balance to the capital account. After closing, the equality of the general ledger is proven by preparing a post-closing trial balance. The steps in the accounting cycle are completed each accounting period.

EXPLORE ACCOUNTING

Audits and Public Accounting Firms

An examination of financial records, accounts, and supporting documents to check their accuracy is called an **audit**. An audit is performed periodically so that users of financial statements can trust the accuracy of the reports. The accountant who conducts the audit is called an **auditor**.

When performing an audit for a client, the auditor looks closely at the client's financial statements and the way the client records transactions. The auditor traces transactions from the ledger accounts back to the journal entries and source documents. A paper or electronic path that provides a documented history of a transaction is called an **audit trail**. The auditor's job is to determine if the financial statements fairly present the financial position of the client. The auditor issues an opinion, which is a statement as to whether the financial statements follow standard accounting rules (GAAP). (GAAP stands for *Generally Accepted Accounting Principles*.) This "opinion" is used by bankers deciding to lend money to the company. It is also used by investors when making investment decisions.

An accounting business that helps other businesses with accounting issues is called a **public accounting firm**. An audit is only one of many services provided by public accounting firms. Other services include tax preparation, tax advice, payroll services, bookkeeping services, financial statement preparation, and consulting services.

These other services often make up a higher percentage of business for the accounting firm than performing audits.

Many accounting firms report that they are getting more requests for consulting services than for other services they can provide. In many cases, consulting is also the area that produces the largest profit margin for the public accounting firm. Therefore, some firms are actively advertising their ability to provide management consulting services for clients.

INSTRUCTIONS

Contact a public accounting firm in your area. Research what services the firm provides and which service area (if any) is growing. Present your findings to your class.

Apply Your Understanding

INSTRUCTIONS: Download problem instructions for Excel, QuickBooks, and Peachtree from the textbook companion website at www.C21accounting.com.

8-1 Application Problem: Journalizing and posting closing entries LO1

A journal and general ledger accounts for Rosemount Copy Center are given in the *Working Papers*. A partial work sheet for the month ended June 30 of the current year is shown below.

	ACCOUNT TITLE	INCOME STATEMENT		BALANCE SHEET		
		5 DEBIT	**6** CREDIT	**7** DEBIT	**8** CREDIT	
1	Cash			8 7 1 5 00		1
2	Petty Cash			7 5 00		2
3	Accounts Receivable—Raymond O'Neil			6 4 2 00		3
4	Supplies			1 8 8 00		4
5	Prepaid Insurance			5 4 0 00		5
6	Accounts Payable—Western Supplies				2 6 8 00	6
7	Akbar Sharma, Capital				9 6 9 5 00	7
8	Akbar Sharma, Drawing			3 7 5 00		8
9	Income Summary					9
10	Sales		1 7 0 4 00			10
11	Advertising Expense	2 5 5 00				11
12	Cash Short and Over	2 00				12
13	Insurance Expense	1 3 5 00				13
14	Miscellaneous Expense	1 3 8 00				14
15	Supplies Expense	3 3 0 00				15
16	Utilities Expense	2 7 2 00				16
17		1 1 3 2 00	1 7 0 4 00	10 5 3 5 00	9 9 6 3 00	17
18	Net Income	5 7 2 00			5 7 2 00	18
19		1 7 0 4 00	1 7 0 4 00	10 5 3 5 00	10 5 3 5 00	19
20						20
21						21
22						22
23						23

Instructions:

Continue on page 12 of the journal. Journalize and post the closing entries. Save your work to complete Problem 8-2.

8-2 Application Problem: Preparing a post-closing trial balance LO2

Use the general ledger accounts for Rosemount Copy Center from Problem 8-1. A form to complete a post-closing trial balance is given in the *Working Papers*.

Instructions:

Prepare a post-closing trial balance for Rosemount Copy Center on June 30 of the current year.

8-M Mastery Problem: Journalizing and posting closing entries with a net loss; preparing a post-closing trial balance LO1, 2

Rausch Company's partial work sheet for the month ended May 31 of the current year is given below. The general ledger accounts are given in the *Working Papers*. The general ledger accounts do not show all details for the fiscal period. The balance shown in each account is the account's balance before closing entries are posted.

	ACCOUNT TITLE	INCOME STATEMENT DEBIT	INCOME STATEMENT CREDIT	BALANCE SHEET DEBIT	BALANCE SHEET CREDIT	
1	Cash			3 4 7 5 00		1
2	Petty Cash			2 0 0 00		2
3	Accounts Receivable—M. Monesrud			3 7 5 00		3
4	Supplies			3 9 0 00		4
5	Prepaid Insurance			4 0 0 00		5
6	Accounts Payable—Lexington Supply				3 0 0 00	6
7	Rhonda Rausch, Capital				5 0 1 2 00	7
8	Rhonda Rausch, Drawing			3 0 0 00		8
9	Income Summary					9
10	Sales		1 7 9 0 00			10
11	Advertising Expense	2 2 5 00				11
12	Cash Short and Over	2 00				12
13	Insurance Expense	1 7 5 00				13
14	Miscellaneous Expense	4 0 00				14
15	Supplies Expense	7 0 0 00				15
16	Utilities Expense	8 2 0 00				16
17		1 9 6 2 00	1 7 9 0 00	5 1 4 0 00	5 3 1 2 00	17
18	Net Loss		1 7 2 00	1 7 2 00		18
19		1 9 6 2 00	1 9 6 2 00	5 3 1 2 00	5 3 1 2 00	19
20						20
21						21
22						22
23						23

Instructions:

1. Continue on page 10 of the journal. Journalize and post the closing entries.

2. Prepare a post-closing trial balance.

Peachtree

1. Journalize and post adjusting and closing entries to the general journal.
2. From the menu bar, select Reports & Forms; General Ledger.
3. Make the selections to print the general journal and post-closing trial balance.

QuickBooks

1. Journalize and post adjusting and closing entries to the journal.
2. From the menu bar, select Reports; Accountant and Taxes.
3. Make the selections to print the journal and post-closing trial balance.

X

1. Key the account balances to complete the post-closing trial balance.
2. Use the required formulas to calculate the totals of the Trial Balance columns.
3. Prepare a chart of accounts that only includes asset accounts.
4. Make the selections to print the spreadsheet.

AAONLINE

1. Go to www.cengage.com/login
2. Click on **AA Online** to access.
3. Go to the online assignment and follow the instructions.

Yanta's Yard Care's partial work sheet for the month ended June 30 of the current year is given below. The general ledger accounts are given in the *Working Papers*. The general ledger accounts do not show all details for the fiscal period. The balance shown in each account is the account's balance before closing entries are posted.

	ACCOUNT TITLE	INCOME STATEMENT		BALANCE SHEET		
		DEBIT	CREDIT	DEBIT	CREDIT	
1	Cash			3 7 9 6 00		1
2	Accounts Receivable—V. Mathaney			1 9 0 00		2
3	Supplies			1 3 0 0 00		3
4	Prepaid Insurance			2 4 0 0 00		4
5	Accounts Payable—Eveleth Repair				1 1 6 00	5
6	Accounts Payable—Fremont Supplies				2 2 0 00	6
7	Accounts Payable—Olmstad Company				4 3 0 00	7
8	Jon Yanta, Capital				8 0 0 0 00	8
9	Jon Yanta, Drawing			2 0 0 00		9
10	Income Summary					10
11	Sales—Lawn Care		9 8 0 0 00			11
12	Sales—Shrub Care		5 0 0 0 00			12
13	Advertising Expense	7 8 0 00				13
14	Insurance Expense	8 0 0 00				14
15	Miscellaneous Expense	1 1 0 0 00				15
16	Rent Expense	6 6 0 0 00				16
17	Supplies Expense	6 4 0 0 00				17
18		15 6 8 0 00	14 8 0 0 00	7 8 8 6 00	8 7 6 6 00	18
19	Net Loss		8 8 0 00	8 8 0 00		19
20		15 6 8 0 00	15 6 8 0 00	8 7 6 6 00	8 7 6 6 00	20
21						21
22						22
23						23

Instructions:

1. Continue on page 12 of the journal. Journalize and post the closing entries.

2. Prepare a post-closing trial balance.

3. Jon Yanta, owner of Yanta's Yard Care, is disappointed that his business incurred a net loss for June of the current year. Mr. Yanta would have preferred not to have to reduce his capital by $880.00. He knows that you are studying accounting, so Mr. Yanta asks you to analyze his work sheet for June. Based on your analysis of the work sheet, what would you suggest might have caused the net loss for Yanta's Yard Care? What steps would you suggest so that Mr. Yanta can avoid a net loss in future months?

Peachtree

1. Journalize and post adjusting and closing entries to the general journal.
2. From the menu bar, select Reports & Forms; General Ledger.
3. Make the selections to print the general journal and post-closing trial balance.

QB Quick Books

1. Journalize and post adjusting and closing entries to the journal.
2. From the menu bar, select Reports; Accountant and Taxes.
3. Make the selections to print the journal and post-closing trial balance.

AAONLINE

1. Go to www.cengage.com/login
2. Click on **AA Online** to access.
3. Go to the online assignment and follow the instructions.

21st Century Skills

Advertising—Just Do It!

Theme: Financial, Economic, Business, and Entrepreneurial Literacy; Health Literacy

Skills: ICT Literacy, Creativity and Innovation, Critical Thinking and Problem Solving

PARTNERSHIP FOR
21st CENTURY SKILLS

At the end of an accounting period, a business owner usually reflects on the expenses incurred. One of the most costly expenses is advertising expense. What is advertising? What is the difference between advertising and marketing? Who utilizes advertising?

Advertising is just a part of marketing; however, advertising is often more expensive than marketing. Marketing is the process of trying to understand the customer and what influences customer behavior. Advertising promotes the company and its products or services in various media. The media may include the method the company will use to reach the customer. Advertising includes television, radio, billboards, Internet websites or promotions, magazines, and newspapers. Almost all businesses pay for advertising to persuade customers to purchase products or services. Advertising for nonprofit organizations is sometimes in the form of public service announcements. Almost all businesses need to spend money on advertising. Businesses with poor sales may especially need to buy advertising to increase sales. Advertising might just be what a company needs to "jump start" its business.

APPLICATION

1. Use the Internet to research nutritional guidelines for teens. Select an advertising medium of your choice to create a public service announcement advertising the nutritional guidelines.
2. Compare and contrast the costs of advertising for three different types of advertising.
3. With a partner, brainstorm three nontraditional forms of advertising that a business on a budget might want to utilize.
4. Create an income statement for a nonprofit organization that educates young people on nutrition. Explain how an income statement for a nonprofit will look different from an income statement for a for-profit business.

Auditing for errors

The closing entries for Clausen Enterprises are given below.

REVIEW AND ANSWER

Assuming all account balances are correct, review the entries. List any errors you find.

Date	Account Title	Doc. No.	Post. Ref.	General Debit	General Credit
20-- July 31	Sales			16,000	
	Income Summary				16,000
31	Insurance Expense			450	
	Rent Expense			1,250	
	Supplies Expense			600	
	Utilities Expense			1,700	
	Income Summary				4,000
31	Income Summary			20,000	
	Jennifer Clausen, Capital				20,000
31	Jennifer Clausen, Drawing			4,500	
	Jennifer Clausen, Capital				4,500

Analyzing Nike's financial statements

Refer to Nike's Consolidated Statements of Income in Appendix B on page B-5. To calculate what percentage an item increased or decreased from one year to another, calculate the difference between the two amounts and divide this difference by the amount for the earlier year. For example, Nike's percentage of increase in revenue from 2009 to 2010 would be calculated as follows: ($19,014,000,000 − $19,176,000,000) ÷ $19,176,000,000 = 0.8% decrease.

INSTRUCTIONS

1. What is Nike's revenue (sales) for each of the three years? Is this a favorable or an unfavorable trend?

2. Calculate the percentage of increase in revenue from 2010 to 2011.

Reinforcement Activity 1—Part B

An Accounting Cycle for a Proprietorship: End-of-Fiscal-Period Work

  Peachtree QuickBooks AAONLiNE

The general ledger prepared in Reinforcement Activity 1—Part A is needed to complete Reinforcement Activity 1—Part B. Reinforcement Activity 1—Part B includes end-of-fiscal-period activities studied in Chapters 6 through 8.

Work Sheet

INSTRUCTIONS

8. Prepare a trial balance on the work sheet given in the *Working Papers*. Use a one-month fiscal period ended August 31 of the current year.

9. Analyze the following adjustment information into debit and credit parts. Record the adjustments on the work sheet.

Adjustment Information, August 31	
Supplies on hand	$ 845.00
Value of prepaid insurance	2,200.00

10. Total and rule the Adjustments columns.

11. Extend the up-to-date account balances to the Balance Sheet and Income Statement columns.

12. Complete the work sheet.

Adjusting Entries

INSTRUCTIONS

13. Use page 3 of the general journal. Journalize and post the adjusting entries.

Financial Statements

INSTRUCTIONS

14. Prepare an income statement. Figure and record the component percentages for sales, total expenses, and net income. Round percentage calculations to the nearest 0.1%.

15. Prepare a balance sheet.

Closing Entries

INSTRUCTIONS

16. Continue using page 3 of the general journal. Journalize and post the closing entries.

Post-Closing Trial Balance

INSTRUCTIONS

17. Prepare a post-closing trial balance.

This simulation covers the transactions completed by Red Carpet Events, an event planning service business organized as a proprietorship. Morgan Hartley, the owner, began the event planning business on June 1 of the current year. Morgan provides party planning services for a wide variety of events including parties, banquets, and weddings.

The activities included in the accounting cycle for Red Carpet Events are listed below. The company uses a general journal and a general ledger similar to those described for Delgado Web Services in Part 1.

This simulation is available in manual and in automated versions, for use with Automated Accounting Online software.

The following activities are included in this simulation:

1 Journalizing transactions in a general journal.

2 Preparing a bank statement reconciliation and recording a bank service charge.

3 Proving cash.

4 Posting from a general journal to a general ledger.

5 Preparing a trial balance on a work sheet.

6 Recording adjustments on a work sheet.

7 Completing a work sheet.

8 Preparing financial statements (income statement and balance sheet).

9 Journalizing and posting adjusting entries.

10 Journalizing and posting closing entries.

11 Preparing a post-closing trial balance.

12 Completing the Think Like an Accountant Financial Analysis activities.

Part
2 Accounting
for a Merchandising Business Organized as a Corporation

©OLGALIS, ISTOCK

THE BUSINESS—
THREEGREEN PRODUCTS, INC.

ThreeGreen Products, Inc., the business described in Part 2, is a retail merchandising business organized as a corporation. It rents store space in a shopping center. ThreeGreen purchases and sells a wide variety of environmentally friendly products, from light bulbs to cleaning supplies. Purchases are made directly from businesses that manufacture the items.

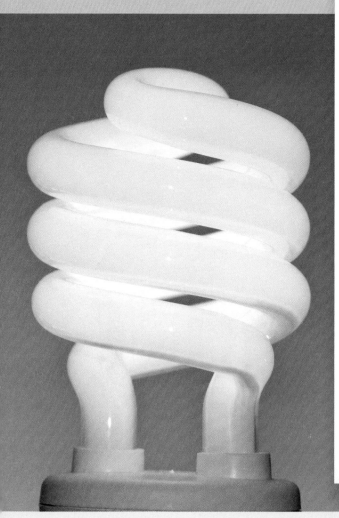

Chart of Accounts
THREEGREEN PRODUCTS, INC.

GENERAL LEDGER

Balance Sheet Accounts

(1000) ASSETS
1100 Current Assets
1110 Cash
1120 Petty Cash
1130 Accounts Receivable
1135 Allowance for Uncollectible Accounts
1140 Merchandise Inventory
1145 Supplies—Office
1150 Supplies—Store
1160 Prepaid Insurance
1170 Notes Receivable
1175 Interest Receivable
1200 Plant Assets
1205 Office Equipment
1210 Accumulated Depreciation—Office Equipment
1215 Store Equipment
1220 Accumulated Depreciation—Store Equipment

(2000) LIABILITIES
2100 Current Liabilities
2110 Accounts Payable
2120 Sales Tax Payable
2130 Employee Income Tax Payable
2135 Social Security Tax Payable
2140 Medicare Tax Payable
2145 Medical Insurance Payable
2150 Retirement Benefits Payable
2160 Unemployment Tax Payable—Federal
2165 Unemployment Tax Payable—State
2170 Federal Income Tax Payable
2180 Dividends Payable

(3000) STOCKHOLDERS' EQUITY
3110 Capital Stock
3120 Paid-in Capital in Excess of Par
3130 Retained Earnings
3140 Dividends
3150 Income Summary

Income Statement Accounts

(4000) OPERATING REVENUE
4110 Sales
4120 Sales Discount
4130 Sales Returns and Allowances

(5000) COST OF GOODS SOLD
5110 Purchases
5120 Purchases Discount
5130 Purchases Returns and Allowances

(6000) OPERATING EXPENSES
6105 Advertising Expense
6110 Cash Short and Over
6115 Credit Card Fee Expense
6120 Depreciation Expense—Office Equipment
6125 Depreciation Expense—Store Equipment
6130 Insurance Expense
6135 Miscellaneous Expense
6140 Payroll Taxes Expense
6145 Rent Expense
6150 Salary Expense
6155 Supplies Expense—Office
6160 Supplies Expense—Store
6165 Uncollectible Accounts Expense
6170 Utilities Expense
6200 Income Tax Expense
6205 Federal Income Tax Expense

(7000) OTHER REVENUE
7110 Interest Income

SUBSIDIARY LEDGERS
Accounts Receivable Ledger
110 Belk & Jensen
120 Edmonds Hospital
130 Lake Automotive
140 Palmer Dentistry
150 Skinner College
160 Wells Apartments

Accounts Payable Ledger
210 Bearden Chemicals
220 Estes Supply
230 Galle Electric
240 Mobley Tools
250 S&R Imports
260 Wynn Lighting

The chart of accounts for ThreeGreen Products, Inc., is illustrated here for ready reference as you study Part 2 of this textbook.

Chapter 9

Accounting for Purchases and Cash Payments

LEARNING OBJECTIVES

After studying Chapter 9, in addition to defining key terms, you will be able to:

LO1 Distinguish among service, retail merchandising, and wholesale merchandising businesses.

LO2 Identify differences between a sole proprietorship and a corporation.

LO3 Explain the relationship between a subsidiary ledger and a controlling account.

LO4 Describe accounting procedures used in ordering merchandise.

LO5 Discuss the purpose of a special journal.

LO6 Journalize purchases of merchandise on account using a purchases journal.

LO7 Post merchandise purchases to an accounts payable ledger and a general ledger.

LO8 Record cash payments using a cash payments journal.

LO9 Record replenishment of a petty cash fund.

LO10 Post cash payments to an accounts payable ledger and a general ledger.

©DANIEL KOUREY, ISTOCK/©JIM PRUITT, ISTOCK

BLEND IMAGES/JUPITER IMAGES

Accounting In The Real World

Yum! Brands, Inc.

Ask someone if they have eaten at a Yum! restaurant. Chances are they will look a bit confused. Although Yum! may not be a household word yet, its collection of brands—including Pizza Hut, Taco Bell, and KFC—is very well known.

Yum! Brands, Inc., has more than 35,000 restaurants in over 110 countries. It is committed to providing customers with safe and nutritious meals. To make that happen, Yum! takes responsibility for its supply chain.

Yum! is not satisfied with simply seeking out quality ingredients. The company is actively involved in the production processes of its supplier partners. Yum! monitors suppliers using its Supplier Tracking and Recognition (STAR) system. STAR is an audit system that measures each supplier's food safety and security practices. Pest control and sanitation are two examples. The system ensures that the supply chain provides Yum! with raw materials that meet or exceed government requirements.

Yum! also monitors its suppliers to ensure that humane procedures are used for the care of animals. Its KFC Animal Welfare Advisory Council guides research in the development of improved practices for raising and processing animals to all of Yum!'s businesses.

CRITICAL THINKING

1. How can Yum!'s involvement in its supplier partners' production processes reduce the cost of raw materials?

2. Can you think of additional businesses, other than restaurants, that could benefit from getting involved with suppliers in their supply chain?

Source: www.yum.com.

Key Terms

- merchandise
- merchandising business
- retail merchandising business
- wholesale merchandising business
- corporation
- capital
- share of stock
- stockholder
- capital stock

- articles of incorporation
- charter
- vendor
- subsidiary ledger
- accounts payable ledger
- controlling account
- inventory
- merchandise inventory
- perpetual inventory
- periodic inventory
- physical inventory

- cost of merchandise
- requisition
- purchase order
- special journal
- purchase on account
- purchases journal
- special amount column
- purchase invoice
- terms of sale
- due date
- cash payments journal

- list price
- trade discount
- net price
- cash discount
- general amount column
- discount period
- purchases discount
- contra account
- credit limit
- schedule of accounts payable

LESSON
9-1 Subsidiary Ledgers and Controlling Accounts

LO1 Distinguish among service, retail merchandising, and wholesale merchandising businesses.
LO2 Identify differences between a sole proprietorship and a corporation.
LO3 Explain the relationship between a subsidiary ledger and a controlling account.

Merchandising Businesses LO1

Delgado Web Services, the business in Part 1, is a service business; it sells services for a fee. Another type of business purchases goods to sell. Goods that a business purchases to sell are called **merchandise**. A business that purchases and resells goods is called a **merchandising business**. A merchandising business that sells to those who use or consume the goods is called a **retail merchandising business**. A **wholesale merchandising business** buys and resells merchandise primarily to other merchandising businesses. Some wholesale businesses also sell to individual consumers.

Service and merchandising businesses use many of the same accounts. However, merchandising businesses have additional accounts on their balance sheets and income statements to account for the purchase and sale of merchandise.

Forming a Corporation LO2

Many businesses need amounts of capital that cannot be easily acquired as a proprietorship. These businesses choose to organize as corporations. A **corporation** is an organization with the legal rights of a person which many persons or other corporations may own. For example, a corporation can own property, incur liabilities, and enter into contracts in its own name.

The assets or other financial resources available to a business are called **capital**. One way that a corporation obtains capital to operate or grow its business is by selling units of ownership in the company. Each unit of ownership in a corporation is called a **share of stock**. The owner of one or more shares of stock is called a **stockholder**. The total shares of ownership in a corporation are called **capital stock**. Another way corporations raise capital is by borrowing money.

A corporation is formed by applying to a state government. The **articles of incorporation**, a legal document that identifies basic characteristics of a corporation, is a part of the application submitted to a state to become a corporation. The articles of incorporation typically include the name and address of the business, its purpose for operating, any limitations on its activities, and rules for dissolving the corporation. The articles of incorporation also describe how the business is to be governed and how capital may be acquired. A state approves the formation of a corporation by issuing a **charter**, the legal right for a business to conduct operations as a corporation.

The main difference between the accounting records of proprietorships and corporations is in the capital accounts. Proprietorships have a single capital and drawing account for the owner. A corporation has separate capital accounts for the stock issued and for the earnings kept in the business. This will be explained in more detail in later chapters. As in proprietorships, information in a corporation's accounting system is kept separate from the personal records of its owners. [CONCEPT: Business Entity] Periodic financial statements must be sent to the stockholders of the corporation to report the financial activities of the business.

At What Price, Safety?

Willcutt Industries assembles a safety system for passenger cars. This system substantially reduces severe injuries to drivers involved in accidents. Willcutt recently took steps to increase its profits. The company cut costs and increased production. It began using some less-expensive parts, which reduced production costs by $50.00 per unit. The new parts increase the system's estimated failure rate from 12 to 15 failures per 10,000 accidents. Still, Willcutt continues to exceed the government's safety standard of 20 failures per 10,000 accidents. The company also reduced the unit price by $40.00. The lower price has allowed the component to be installed on other car models, resulting in significant unit sales growth.

INSTRUCTIONS

Access the *Ford Motor Company Standards of Corporate Conduct*. Use this code along with the ethical model to determine whether this action by Willcutt Industries is ethical.

©LUCA DI FILIPPO, ISTOCK

THE BUSINESS—THREEGREEN PRODUCTS, INC.

Individuals occasionally see a need for a new product or service, or they believe they can improve a process. But it takes more than a great idea to start a successful business—it requires a passion for the idea. Many of today's most well-known businesses were started by individuals who were passionate about their ideas. Thomas Edison's passion to invent a light bulb started General Electric. As a struggling actor, Danny Thomas made a spiritual promise that would be fulfilled in the building of St. Jude Children's Research Hospital.

Mary Prisock has always had a passion for saving the environment. She has spent hours surfing the Internet to purchase products for her home that are safe for the environment. She grew frustrated with having to purchase from dozens of online retailers. Eventually, she decided to open ThreeGreen Products, Inc., a store that provides local residents with a wide variety of products that are friendly to the environment. The name "ThreeGreen" was inspired by the three green arrows in the universal recycling symbol.

Mary developed a business plan to operate the store from a location in a new shopping center. However, she did not have the capital to launch the business. With the help of a small group of investors, though, Mary was able to form a corporation and open her business. Each investor received a number of shares of stock based on the amount invested.

Unlike a proprietorship, a corporation exists independent of its owners. Mary expects ThreeGreen Products, Inc., to continue beyond her lifetime and plans to give her shares of stock to her children. [CONCEPT: Going Concern]

ROMAN SOTOLA/SHUTTERSTOCK.COM

Subsidiary Ledgers and Controlling Accounts LO3

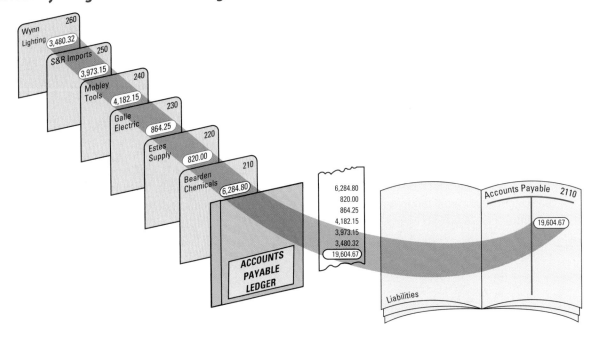

A business can have several types of ledgers. The general ledger is a collection of accounts used to assemble similar transactions, such as those that affect **Cash**. General ledger accounts are used to prepare financial statements.

A business from which merchandise, supplies, or other assets are purchased is called a **vendor**. Merchandising businesses often purchase merchandise on account from many vendors, so they have many vendor accounts. A business needs to know the amount owed to each vendor to ensure it pays its bills on time. Delgado Web Services, the business in Part 1, used general ledger accounts to assemble the transactions with, and maintain the amount owed to, each vendor. This method is not practical for a business having a large number of vendors. This is why most businesses maintain a separate ledger with separate accounts for each vendor. A ledger that is summarized in a single general ledger account is called a **subsidiary ledger**. Accountants often refer to a subsidiary ledger as a *subledger*. The subsidiary ledger containing vendor accounts is called an **accounts payable ledger**.

ThreeGreen has six vendor accounts in its accounts payable ledger. The total amount owed to these vendors equals the balance in a single general ledger account

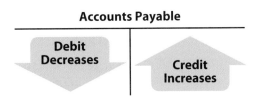

titled **Accounts Payable**. An account in a general ledger that summarizes all accounts in a subsidiary ledger is called a **controlling account**. Accounts Payable, a liability account, is increased by a credit and decreased by a debit, as shown in the T account. Therefore, it has a normal credit balance.

Although any numbering scheme can be used, ThreeGreen uses three-digit numbers for its accounts payable ledger. The first digit identifies the division in which the controlling account appears in the general ledger. The next two digits are unique to the vendor. Accounts in the subsidiary ledgers can be located by either number or name. For example, the vendor number for Bearden Chemicals is 210. The first digit, *2*, shows that **Accounts Payable** is a liability. The second and third digits, *10*, are the unique number assigned to Bearden Chemicals.

Subsidiary Ledger Form

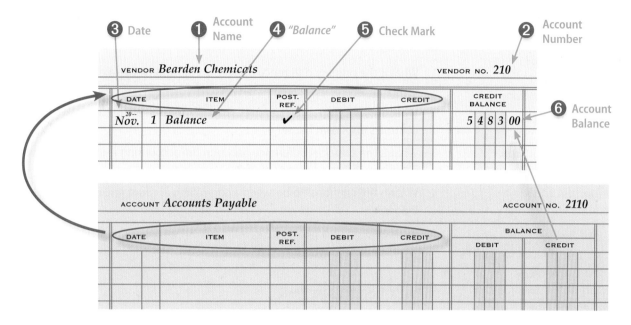

Accounts payable ledger forms are similar to general ledger forms. The accounts payable ledger form contains the same columns as the general ledger except that it lacks a Debit Balance column. **Accounts Payable** has a normal credit balance, so the accounts payable ledger form does not require a Debit Balance column. On November 1, ThreeGreen prepared a new page for Bearden Chemicals in the accounts payable ledger because the existing page was full. On that day, the account balance was $5,483.00.

⬇ Starting a New Page in a Subsidiary Ledger

1. Write the account name, Bearden Chemicals.
2. Write the account number, 210.
3. Write the date, 20--, Nov. 1, in the Date column.
4. Write the word Balance in the Item column.
5. Place a check mark in the Post. Ref. column to show that the amount has been carried forward from a previous page rather than posted from a journal.
6. Write the balance, $5,483.00, in the Credit Balance column.

A business can include letters in its subsidiary account numbers. Letters can have meaning that is useful to company employees. For example, the IL in account IL5234 would indicate that the customer is from Illinois. The S in account 6345S could indicate the customer's rank as a "silver" member in a customer rewards program.

End of Lesson Review

Terms Review

merchandise

merchandising business

retail merchandising business

wholesale merchandising business

corporation

capital

share of stock

stockholder

capital stock

articles of incorporation

charter

vendor

subsidiary ledger

accounts payable ledger

controlling account

Audit your understanding

1. What is the primary difference between retail and wholesale merchandising businesses?

2. What allows a corporation to own property, incur liabilities, and enter into contracts in its own name?

3. What is the principal difference between the accounting records of proprietorships and corporations?

4. What is the relationship between a controlling account and a subsidiary ledger?

5. What column on a general ledger form is not on an accounts payable ledger form?

Work together 9-1

Starting an accounts payable ledger form

Accounts payable ledger forms are given in the *Working Papers*. Your instructor will guide you through the following examples.

1. Start a new page for an accounts payable ledger account for Warren River Supply. The account number is 240, and the balance on October 1 of the current year is $1,489.50.

2. Start a new page for an accounts payable ledger account for Zodiac Industries. The account number is 250, and the balance for October 1 of the current year is $2,491.80.

On your own 9-1

Starting an accounts payable ledger form

Accounts payable ledger forms are given in the *Working Papers*. Work this problem independently.

1. Start a new page for an accounts payable ledger account for Tilson Corporation. The account number is 240, and the balance on November 1 of the current year is $948.25.

2. Start a new page for an accounts payable ledger account for Value Distributors. The account number is 250, and the balance on November 1 of the current year is $3,231.60.

LESSON 9-2 Accounting for Merchandise Purchases

LO4 Describe accounting procedures used in ordering merchandise.

LO5 Discuss the purpose of a special journal.

LO6 Journalize purchases of merchandise on account using a purchases journal.

Measuring Inventory LO4

A list of assets, usually containing the value of individual items, is called an **inventory**. There are different kinds of inventories. For example, a company might have an inventory of office or store supplies, equipment, or goods for sale. The goods a business has on hand for sale to customers is called **merchandise inventory**. Its value is recorded in a general ledger account titled Merchandise Inventory, an asset account. Two principal methods are used to determine the value of inventory.

PERPETUAL INVENTORY METHOD

An inventory determined by keeping a continuous record of increases, decreases, and the balance on hand of each item of merchandise is called a **perpetual inventory**. When a perpetual inventory system is used, purchases of merchandise are accounted for directly to the Merchandise Inventory account. Businesses that use the perpetual inventory method usually have computerized accounting systems to efficiently maintain the detailed records that are required. Those records would include a record of the units purchased and sold as well as the current quantity on hand. When the bar code on merchandise is scanned, the system instantly records the sale price and updates the merchandise inventory records. The perpetual inventory method provides a business with better information for controlling the cost of the merchandise it sells.

PERIODIC INVENTORY METHOD

A merchandise inventory evaluated at the end of a fiscal period is called a **periodic inventory**. When a periodic inventory is conducted by counting, weighing, or measuring items of merchandise on hand, it is called a **physical inventory**. A merchandising business may conduct a periodic inventory once at the end of the fiscal year, every quarter, or every month. It depends on the volume of its sales. The periodic inventory method is easier to maintain than the perpetual method. That's because the periodic method does not require records of the quantity and cost of individual goods. Merchandising businesses with manual accounting systems usually use the periodic inventory method.

WAVEBREAKMEDIA LTD/SHUTTERSTOCK.COM

fyi

How would a company count the number of golf balls in its inventory? A fork lift carries each bin to be weighed on an industrial scale. The weight of an empty bin is subtracted to determine the weight of the golf balls in the bin. The weight of ten golf balls is measured using a small scale with precision accuracy. Then a simple calculation can determine the number of balls in each bin.

Cost of Goods Sold

The amount a business pays for goods it purchases to sell is called **cost of merchandise**. ThreeGreen has chosen to use a periodic inventory system. When a periodic inventory system is used, the cost of merchandise is recorded to the Purchases account. Purchases is increased by a debit and decreased by a credit, so it has a normal debit balance.

No other items bought, such as store supplies, are recorded in the Purchases account. These items are recorded in other accounts, such as Supplies—Store. Merchandise and other items bought are recorded and reported at the purchase price. [CONCEPT: Historical Cost]

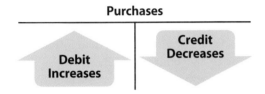

Purchases

Debit Increases | Credit Decreases

The income statement of a merchandising business places Purchases in a section titled Cost of Goods Sold, separate from other expenses. Accounts in the Cost of Goods Sold section include all the costs necessary to make an item of merchandise available for sale. That includes the purchase price and any related costs or discounts. For example, freight charges paid to ship items to the merchandising business are a cost of making the item available for sale. So they would be recorded in Purchases. In contrast, the freight charge paid to ship an item to a customer would be accounted for as an expense. It would be recorded in an account such as Freight Expense.

The cost of merchandise sold should appear on the income statement only when the goods are sold. [CONCEPT: Matching Expenses with Revenue] For a business using the perpetual inventory method, the cost of merchandise is recorded in the Merchandise Inventory account until the goods are sold. When goods are sold, the cost of that merchandise is removed from Merchandise Inventory and recorded to accounts in the Cost of Goods Sold section.

For a business using the periodic inventory method, the cost of merchandise purchased is recorded directly to the Cost of Goods Sold accounts. These accounts and merchandise inventory balances are used to calculate the cost of goods sold reported on the income statement. Regardless of which inventory method is used, the cost of goods sold reported on the income statement will be the same.

WHY ACCOUNTING?

Cost of Construction

Constructing a new building involves many companies working together, each with a specific function such as structural steel, concrete, wiring, carpentry, plumbing, drywall, and carpeting. The activity of all of these construction companies and their workers must be coordinated. For example, drywall cannot be installed until the electrical and plumbing work is finished. If drywall installers are hired too early, they will not be able to work efficiently, which will unnecessarily increase the cost of the building.

The person or company that manages a construction project is called a *general contractor*. The general contractor usually hires the other companies, called *subcontractors*, and coordinates all activity on the project.

Construction projects generally begin with a bidding phase where subcontractors who want to work on the project submit bids, or estimates, for the work they would do. At most construction companies, assigning costs to tasks and determining the cost of a job is the responsibility of the estimator. It is essential that the estimator's bid accurately covers the costs involved. If the bid is too high, the general contractor may reject it and hire another subcontractor to do the work. If the bid is too low, the subcontractor may lose money on the project.

CRITICAL THINKING

1. The website, www.stateuniversity.com, lists the minimum educational requirements for a professional cost estimator as a "high school education with courses in mathematics and accounting." Explain how an accounting course would be helpful to the estimator.

2. Name one problem that may result from a delay in the completion of the electrical work on a building project.

PURCHASE ORDER

Three△Green Products, Inc.

255 Chestnut Street
Harrisburg, PA 17101

PO Number: **153**
Date: 10/28/--

Purchase From:
Wynn Lighting
1532 Industrial Parkway
Birmingham, AL 35217

Ship To:
ThreeGreen Products, Inc.
255 Chestnut Street
Harrisburg, PA 17101

Qty	Stock #	Description	Unit Price	Total
200	B-50	50 watt compact fluorescent lamp	$3.05	**$610.00**
150	B-100	100 watt compact fluorescent lamp	$3.15	**$472.50**
			Total	**$1,082.50**

Ordering Merchandise

The process of ordering merchandise begins when an authorized employee submits a purchase request. A form requesting the purchase of merchandise is called a **requisition**. The requisition includes a description of the merchandise to be ordered, the quantity to be purchased, and the required delivery date. Requisitions generally require management approval. After a requisition is approved, it is submitted to another employee who is responsible for placing an order with whichever supplier provides the best combination of quality and price.

A form requesting that a vendor sell merchandise to a business is called a **purchase order**. The purchase order lists the number, description, quantity, and unit price of each item ordered. The vendor uses the purchase order to (1) approve the sale and (2) process the order. No transaction occurs until the customer receives the goods from the vendor. Thus, no journal entry is recorded when a purchase order is prepared.

For many small businesses, Internet commerce sites provide an alternative method for ordering merchandise. Rather than sending a purchase order to a vendor, the customer simply orders the merchandise online. This offers several advantages. First, delivery of the merchandise is faster. Second, the vendor does not have to enter the purchase order information into its computerized accounting system. For this reason, some vendors offer customers a discount off the purchase price for placing their orders online.

Using Special Journals LO5

The accounting procedures taught in Part 1 provide an effective system for a small business with a limited number of transactions. However, a business having many daily transactions could not efficiently operate using a single journal. To increase efficiency, separate journals were developed to record transactions impacting similar accounts. A journal used to record only one kind of transaction is called a **special journal**. Businesses typically use five journals:

1. Purchases journal—for all purchases of merchandise on account
2. Cash payments journal—for all cash payments
3. Sales journal—for all sales of merchandise on account
4. Cash receipts journal—for all cash receipts
5. General journal—for all other transactions

This chapter teaches the accounting for purchases and cash payments. Chapter 10 will cover the recording of sales and cash receipts. All other transactions recorded in the general journal will be described in Chapter 11.

Purchases Journal LO6

		PURCHASES JOURNAL			PAGE	
	DATE	ACCOUNT CREDITED	PURCH. NO.	POST. REF.	PURCHASES DR. ACCTS. PAY. CR	
1						1
2						2

A transaction in which the items purchased are to be paid for later is called a **purchase on account**. A business can purchase merchandise or buy services and supplies on account.

A **purchases journal** is a special journal used to record only purchases of merchandise on account. Each purchase of merchandise on account transaction is recorded on one line of the purchases journal. The amount column has two account titles in its heading: Purchases Debit and Accounts Payable Credit. A journal amount column headed with an account title is called a **special amount column**. Special amount columns are used for frequently occurring transactions. All transactions for purchasing merchandise on account involve a debit to Purchases and a credit to Accounts Payable. Therefore, the special amount column in the purchases journal includes those accounts in the heading.

Using special amount columns eliminates writing general ledger account titles in the Account Credited column. Recording entries in a journal with special amount columns saves time and helps to reduce mistakes.

Purchase Invoice

When a vendor sells merchandise to a buyer, the vendor prepares an invoice showing what has been sold. An invoice used as a source document for recording a purchase on account transaction is called a **purchase invoice**. [CONCEPT: Objective Evidence] A purchase invoice lists the quantity, the description, and the price of each item and shows the total amount of the purchase. It provides the information needed for recording a purchase on account.

When the invoice is received, an employee verifies the accuracy of the invoice. A stamp may be used to provide a place to enter his or her initials, the date the invoice is received, and the purchase invoice number assigned. The date entered in the stamp should not be confused with the vendor's date on the invoice, *11/4*. ThreeGreen assigns numbers in sequence to easily identify all purchase invoices. The number recorded on the invoice, *525*, is the number assigned by ThreeGreen to this purchase invoice. This number should not be confused with the invoice number, *15648*, assigned by the vendor. Each vendor uses a different numbering system. Therefore, vendor invoice numbers would not be recorded in sequence. That would make it impossible to detect a missing purchase invoice.

An agreement between a buyer and a seller about payment for merchandise is called the **terms of sale**. The terms of sale on this invoice are net 30 days, usually abbreviated n/30. These terms mean that the net amount of the invoice is due within 30 days from the vendor's invoice date. The invoice is dated November 4. Therefore, payment must be received by the vendor by December 4. The date by which an invoice must be paid is called the **due date**. A business that pays an invoice after the due date is usually required to pay a late fee. Some businesses file purchase invoices by the date the check should be written to ensure that the vendor receives the payment by the due date.

 All purchases of merchandise on account are recorded in the purchases journal. If a purchase is made for cash, the transaction is NOT recorded in the purchases journal.

Wynn Lighting
1532 Industrial Parkway
Birmingham, AL 35217

Protecting Our Environment

Ship To:

ThreeGreen Products, Inc.
255 Chestnut Street
Harrisburg, PA 17101

Invoice

REC'D ACL
DATE 11/6
DOC 525

Invoice #: 15648
Date: 11/4/--

Packed by	Shipping Method	Ship Date	Delivery Date	Terms	Payment Due
JBL	UPS	11/2/--	11/6/--	n/30	12/4/--

Qty	Item #	Description	Unit Price	Total
200	B-50	50 watt compact fluorescent lamp	$ 3.05	$ 610.00 ✓
150	B-100	100 watt compact fluorescent lamp	$ 3.15	$ 472.50 ✓
			Total	$ 1,082.50 ✓

Thank you for your business!

⬇ Receiving a Purchase Invoice

❶ Record the initials of the employee processing the invoice, ACL, date received, 11/6/--, and ThreeGreen's purchase invoice number, 525, in the stamp.

❷ Place a check mark by each of the amounts in the Total column to show that the items have been received and that amounts have been checked and are correct.

❸ Review the vendor's terms and the payment due date.

Purchasing Merchandise on Account

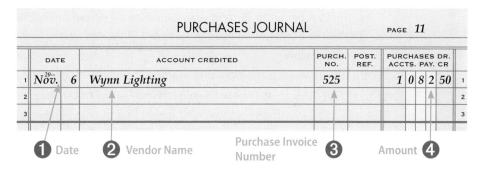

	DATE	ACCOUNT CREDITED	PURCH. NO.	POST. REF.	PURCHASES DR. ACCTS. PAY. CR	
1	Nov. 6	Wynn Lighting	525		1 0 8 2 50	1
2						2
3						3

PURCHASES JOURNAL   PAGE 11

❶ Date   **❷** Vendor Name   Purchase Invoice Number   **❸**   Amount **❹**

November 6. Purchased merchandise on account from Wynn Lighting, $1,082.50. Purchase Invoice No. 525.

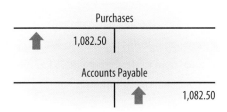

Purchases
1,082.50 ⬆

Accounts Payable
⬆ 1,082.50

A purchase on account transaction increases the amount owed to a vendor. This transaction increases the Purchases balance and increases the Accounts Payable balance. Because Purchases is increased by a debit, it is debited for

$1,082.50. Therefore, Accounts Payable is credited for $1,082.50 to show the increase in this liability account.

⬇ Journalizing a Purchase of Merchandise on Account

❶ Write the date, 20--, Nov. 6, in the Date column.

❷ Write the vendor account title, Wynn Lighting, in the Account Credited column.

❸ Write the purchase invoice number, 525, in the Purch. No. column.

❹ Write the amount of the invoice, $1,082.50, in the special amount column. This single amount is both a debit to Purchases and a credit to Accounts Payable. Therefore, it is not necessary to write the title of either general ledger account.

End of Lesson Review

Terms Review

inventory

merchandise inventory

perpetual inventory

periodic inventory

physical inventory

cost of merchandise

requisition

purchase order

special journal

purchase on account

purchases journal

special amount column

purchase invoice

terms of sale

due date

Audit your understanding

1. What is the difference between a periodic inventory system and a perpetual inventory system?

2. When the perpetual inventory system is used, in what account are purchases recorded? In what account are purchases recorded when the periodic inventory system is used?

3. Identify the four special journals typically used by a business.

4. How are special amount columns used in a journal?

5. Why are there two account titles in the amount column of the purchases journal?

6. What is the advantage of having special amount columns in a journal?

7. What information is contained on a purchase invoice?

Work together 9-2

Journalizing purchases using a purchases journal

The purchases journal for Golden Fabrics is given in the *Working Papers*. Your instructor will guide you through the following examples. Save your work to complete Work Together 9-3.

Using October of the current year, journalize these transactions on page 10 of the purchases journal. Purchase invoices are abbreviated as P.

Transactions:

Oct. 2. Purchased merchandise on account from Pacific Supply, $3,252.00. P162.

7. Purchased merchandise on account from Coastal Company, $532.00. P163.

11. Purchased merchandise on account from Yeatman Designs, $866.00. P164.

On your own 9-2

Journalizing purchases using a purchases journal

The purchases journal for Copperland Company is given in the *Working Papers*. Work this problem independently. Save your work to complete On Your Own 9-3.

Using November of the current year, journalize these transactions on page 11 of the purchases journal. Purchase invoices are abbreviated as P.

Transactions:

Nov. 5. Purchased merchandise on account from McKell Supply, Inc., $2,548.25. P244.

10. Purchased merchandise on account from Tresler Corporation, $1,525.00. P245.

17. Purchased merchandise on account from Lawes Imports, $2,643.50. P246.

©CANDICE CUSACK, ISTOCK

9-3 Posting from a Purchases Journal

LO7 Post merchandise purchases to an accounts payable ledger and a general ledger.

Posting from a Purchases Journal to an Accounts Payable Ledger **LO7**

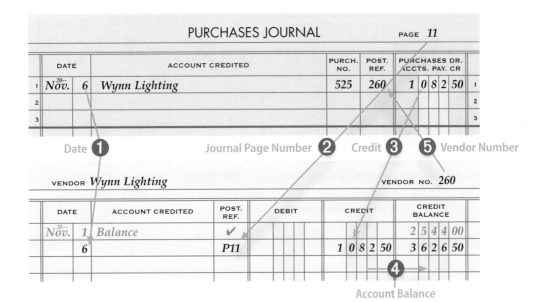

	PURCHASES JOURNAL		PAGE 11		
DATE	ACCOUNT CREDITED	PURCH. NO.	POST. REF.	PURCHASES DR. ACCTS. PAY. CR	
¹ Nov.²⁰⁻⁻ 6	*Wynn Lighting*	525	260	1 0 8 2 50	1
2					2
3					3

Date **1**   Journal Page Number **2**   Credit **3**   **5** Vendor Number

VENDOR *Wynn Lighting*   VENDOR NO. 260

DATE	ACCOUNT CREDITED	POST. REF.	DEBIT	CREDIT	CREDIT BALANCE
Nov.²⁰⁻⁻ 1	*Balance*	✔			2 5 4 4 00
6		P11		1 0 8 2 50	3 6 2 6 50

4

Account Balance

Each entry in the purchases journal affects the account of the vendor named in the Account Credited column. The amount on each line of a purchases journal is posted as a credit to a vendor account in the accounts payable ledger. Posting frequently helps ensure that vendor accounts are paid on time. ThreeGreen must maintain a reputation for paying its accounts on time if it wishes to continue purchasing goods and services on account.

When several journals are used, an abbreviation is used to show from which journal the posting is made. *P* is the abbreviation used for the purchases journal. The abbreviation *P11* means page 11 of the purchases journal. This additional information is necessary to provide a clear audit trail. Thus, an employee working with Wynn Lighting's account can trace the transaction back to the correct journal and page number.

> **Posting from a Purchases Journal to an Accounts Payable Ledger**
>
> **1** Write the date, 20--, Nov. 6, in the Date column of the vendor account.
>
> **2** Write the journal page number, P11, in the Post. Ref. column of the account to provide an audit trail back to the journal where the transaction was recorded.
>
> **3** Write the credit amount, $1,082.50, in the Credit column of the vendor account, Wynn Lighting.
>
> **4** Add the amount in the Credit column to the previous balance in the Credit Balance column. (Wynn Lighting has a previous balance of $2,544.00; therefore, $2,544.00 + $1,082.50 = $3,626.50.) Write the new account balance, $3,626.50, in the Credit Balance column.
>
> **5** Write the vendor number, 260, in the Post. Ref. column of the journal to provide an audit trail to the account where the transaction was posted.

Totaling and Ruling a Purchases Journal

	DATE		ACCOUNT CREDITED	PURCH. NO.	POST. REF.	PURCHASES DR. ACCTS. PAY. CR	
1	Nov.²⁰⁻⁻	6	Wynn Lighting	525		1 0 8 2 50	1
2		8	Galle Electric	526		6 4 0 00	2
3		13	Bearden Chemicals	527		6 2 8 4 80	3
4		15	Mobley Tools	528		4 1 8 2 15	4
5		21	Wynn Lighting	529		3 4 8 0 32	5
6		22	Galle Electric	530		1 0 8 0 00	6
7		27	S&R Imports	531		3 9 7 3 15	7
8		29	Galle Electric	532		8 6 4 25	8
9		30	Total			21 5 8 7 17	9

PURCHASES JOURNAL   PAGE **11**

Date **2**   **3** "Total"   Single **1** Line   Total **4** Column   Double **6** Lines   **5** Total Amount

ThreeGreen rules its purchases journal whenever a journal page is filled, and always at the end of each month. Calculating the total does more than report the total value of inventory purchased on account during a period of time. Using a purchases journal, ThreeGreen can post all the purchases on a journal page to the general ledger using a single journal entry. In this way, special journals significantly reduce the time required to post transactions.

Totaling and Ruling a Purchases Journal

1 Rule a single line across the amount column under the last entry.

2 Write the date, 30, in the Date column.

3 Write the word Total in the Account Credited column.

4 Add the amount column. Verify the total by re-adding the column in reverse order.

5 Write the total, $21,587.17, directly below the single line in the amount column.

6 Rule double lines across the amount column directly below the total amount to show that the total has been verified as correct.

Employees who specialize in purchasing merchandise might consider earning certification by the Institute for Supply Management. A Certified Professional in Supply Management understands the challenges involved in purchasing merchandise and recognizes opportunities to help the business maximize its profits.

Posting the Total of a Purchases Journal to a General Ledger

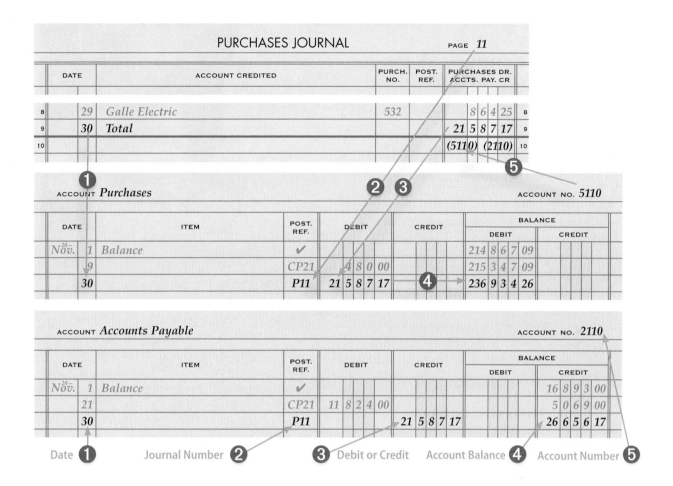

The total amount of the purchases journal is posted to two general ledger accounts, Purchases and Accounts Payable.

The debit to Purchases increases the balance of the account. The credit to Accounts Payable increases the balance of the account. The transactions with the posting reference CP21 will be discussed later in the chapter.

Posting the Total of a Purchases Journal to the General Ledger Accounts

1. Write the date, 30, in the Date columns of the accounts.

2. Write the purchases journal page number, P11, in the Post. Ref. columns of the accounts. The abbreviation P11 means page 11 of the purchases journal.

3. For each account, write the purchases journal column total, $21,587.17, in the Debit or Credit column.

4. For each account, calculate and write the new account balance in the Balance Debit or Credit column.

5. Return to the purchases journal and write the Purchases general ledger account number, (5110), and the Accounts Payable general ledger account number, (2110), in parentheses below the column total.

Careers In Accounting

Courtney Bloom
MANAGEMENT ACCOUNTANT

YURI_ARCURS/ISTOCKPHOTO.COM

A manager is a person who controls an area of a business by planning and directing courses of action. Making good business decisions requires accurate and timely information. The area of accounting that focuses on reporting information to internal users is called *managerial accounting*.

As a management accountant, Courtney Bloom supports the management of her company by gathering, summarizing, and reporting financial data. Those reports are needed for informed decision making. Managers need financial data for planning, controlling, measuring, and providing feedback.

Courtney's role as a management accountant is different from a financial accountant in several ways. The management accountant is usually looking ahead to predict some future costs or outcomes. The financial accountant is usually summarizing and reporting past results. The management accountant is not bound by rules and standards as the financial accountant is by the rules of GAAP. The management accountant creates reports to meet the needs of the company's managers. The financial accountant creates financial statements for external users. Those would include lenders, investors, and business partners.

In her role as management accountant, Courtney produces a wide range of reports to help managers make decisions. One example is a listing of all the costs involved in making a product. This helps managers when setting the price of the product. Another example is a cash budget. A cash budget helps managers to plan ahead for times when it may be necessary to borrow cash or when excess cash can be invested. A third example is reporting all the expenses associated with employees so that management can develop a sound compensation policy.

Salary Range: Varies greatly according to region and job requirements, but averages between $35,000 and $45,000.

Qualifications: The management accountant is an integral player on the management team. He or she needs to have a thorough knowledge of management accounting. It is just as important to understand what managers do, what information managers need, and how the company operates. The management accountant must also possess the written and oral communication skills to present complex financial information so that managers not trained in accounting can understand it and use it.

Most management accountants have a four-year degree, with an emphasis in accounting. Those who want higher credentials can obtain the Certified Management Accountant (CMA) designation.

Occupational Outlook: Overall, the accounting field has a better than average outlook for the period from 2008 to 2018, with a greater than 20% growth in the field. The specific occupation of management accountant is expected to see comparable growth.

Sources: ima.org; online.onetcenter.org; mysalary.com.

ACTIVITY

Go to a job search website such as monster.com and find a job opening for a management accountant. Write a paragraph about the position, including educational requirements and salary range.

©MILENNY, ISTOCK

End of Lesson Review

LO7 Post merchandise purchases to an accounts payable ledger and a general ledger.

Audit your understanding

1. Why should a business frequently post from the purchases journal to the accounts payable ledger?

2. Why is it important to record a posting reference in the accounts payable ledger?

3. Why is the vendor number written in the Post. Ref. column of the purchases journal?

Work together 9-3

Posting a purchases journal

Selected accounts payable and general ledger accounts for Golden Fabrics are given in the *Working Papers*. Use the purchases journal from Work Together 9-2. Your instructor will guide you through the following examples. Save your work to complete Work Together 9-5.

1. Post the transactions from the purchases journal to the accounts payable ledger.

2. Total and rule the purchases journal.

3. Post the purchases journal to the general ledger.

On your own 9-3

Posting a purchases journal

Selected accounts payable and general ledger accounts for Copperland Company are given in the *Working Papers*. Use the purchases journal from On Your Own 9-2. Work this problem independently. Save your work to complete On Your Own 9-5.

1. Post the transactions from the purchases journal to the accounts payable ledger.

2. Total and rule the purchases journal.

3. Post the purchases journal to the general ledger.

©CANDICE CUSACK, ISTOCK

LESSON
9-4 Accounting for Cash Payments

LO8 Record cash payments using a cash payments journal.
LO9 Record replenishment of a petty cash fund.

Cash Payments Journal LO8

	DATE	ACCOUNT TITLE	CK. NO.	POST. REF.	GENERAL		ACCOUNTS PAYABLE DEBIT	PURCHASES DISCOUNT CREDIT	CASH CREDIT	
					DEBIT	CREDIT				
1										1
2										2
3										3

A **cash payments journal** is a special journal used to record only cash payment transactions. Only those columns needed to record cash payment transactions are included in ThreeGreen's cash payments journal. A cash payments journal may be set up to accommodate a business's frequent cash payment transactions. Since all cash payment transactions affect **Cash**, and all cash payments are credits, a special amount column is provided for Cash Credit. In addition, ThreeGreen has many cash payment transactions affecting the **Accounts Payable** account. Therefore, a special amount column is provided in the cash payments journal for Accounts Payable Debit.

TRADE DISCOUNT

Most manufacturers and wholesalers print catalogs and maintain Internet sites that describe their products. Generally, the prices listed are the manufacturers' suggested retail prices. The retail price listed in a catalog or on an Internet site is called a **list price**. When a merchandising business purchases a number of products from a manufacturer, the price frequently is quoted as "list price less trade discount." A **trade discount** is a reduction in the list price granted to a merchandising business. Trade discounts are also used to quote different prices for different quantities purchased without changing catalog or list prices. The price after the trade discount has been deducted from the list price is referred to as the **net price**. For example, an item with a list price of $500.00 and a 40% trade discount would be purchased for a net price of $300.00 ($500.00 less trade discount of $200.00, 40% of $500.00 equals $200.00).

When a trade discount is granted, the seller's invoice shows the net price. Only the invoice amount is used in a journal entry. [CONCEPT: Historical Cost] No journal entry is made to show the amount of a trade discount.

CASH DISCOUNT

When a company purchases goods, the purchase invoice shows the amount the company is expected to pay. To encourage early payment, a vendor may allow a deduction from the invoice amount. A **cash discount** is a deduction that a vendor allows on an invoice amount to encourage prompt payment. Cash discounts taken when purchasing goods are recorded to **Purchases Discount**. Taking cash discounts reduces the company's cost of merchandise. ThreeGreen uses a cash payments journal with a Purchases Discount Credit column because it often takes cash discounts.

A journal amount column that is not headed with an account title is called a **general amount column**. ThreeGreen's cash payments journal has General Debit and General Credit columns for cash payment transactions that do not occur often. Monthly rent is one example.

All cash payments made by ThreeGreen are recorded in a cash payments journal. The source document for most cash payments is the check issued. A few payments, such as bank service charges, are made as direct withdrawals from the company's bank account. For payments not using a check, the source document is a memorandum. Most of ThreeGreen's cash payments are paid by check to vendors.

Cash Payment of an Expense

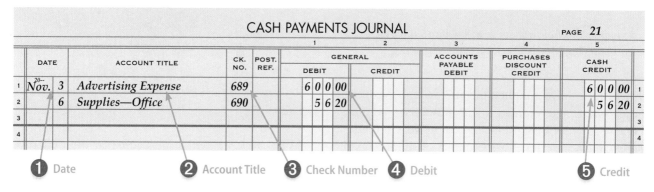

CASH PAYMENTS JOURNAL

PAGE 21

	DATE	ACCOUNT TITLE	CK. NO.	POST. REF.	GENERAL DEBIT	GENERAL CREDIT	ACCOUNTS PAYABLE DEBIT	PURCHASES DISCOUNT CREDIT	CASH CREDIT	
1	Nov. 3	Advertising Expense	689		6 0 0 00				6 0 0 00	1
2	6	Supplies—Office	690		5 6 20				5 6 20	2
3										3
4										4

1 Date **2** Account Title **3** Check Number **4** Debit **5** Credit

---

November 3. Wrote a check to Kelser Promotions for advertising, $600.00. Check No. 689.

ThreeGreen usually pays for an expense at the time the transaction occurs. This cash payment increases the Advertising Expense balance and decreases the balance in Cash. Advertising Expense has a normal debit balance and is increased by this $600.00 debit. Cash

```
         Advertising Expense
   ↑      600.00
              Cash
              ↓       600.00
```

also has a normal debit balance and is decreased by this $600.00 credit.

Journalizing a Cash Payment of an Expense

1 Write the date, 20--, Nov. 3, in the Date column.

2 Write the account title, Advertising Expense, in the Account Title column.

3 Write the check number, 689, in the Ck. No. column.

4 Write the debit amount to Advertising Expense, $600.00, in the General Debit column.

5 Write the credit amount, $600.00, in the Cash Credit column.

THINK LIKE AN ACCOUNTANT

Evaluating Alternative Purchase Offers

In difficult economic times, vendors may offer incentives for their customers to purchase merchandise. These offers often take the form of a choice, such as "$3,000.00 discount or 0% financing" for the purchase of a car. Which of those offers provides your business the best benefit?

Your company purchases merchandise from Keller Wholesale. Keller provides you a catalog with suggested retail prices and offers a standard 45% trade discount. Periodically, Keller offers its customers an extra percentage trade discount or free shipping.

The current offer reads "Take an additional 10% off your discounted price or receive free shipping." You understand Keller's offer to be 10% off the discounted amount, not a 55% (45% + 10%) trade discount.

OPEN THE SPREADSHEET TLA_CH09

Using the worksheet, make a decision on whether to accept the extra percentage trade discount or free shipping on the following purchases:

1. Speaker wire with a list price of $4,560.00 plus $185.00 shipping. Keller regularly offers a 45% trade discount on wire.

2. Surveillance cameras with a list price of $9,250.00 plus $490.00 shipping. Keller's regular trade discount on electronic equipment is 58%.

3. Entertainment centers with a list price of $12,870.00 plus $1,650.00 shipping. Keller offers a 46% trade discount on furniture.

©DAN BACHMAN, ISTOCK

Buying Supplies for Cash

> **November 6. Wrote a check to Wells Office Supply for store supplies, $56.20. Check No. 690.**

ThreeGreen buys supplies for use in the business. Supplies are not recorded in the Purchases account because supplies are not intended for resale. Computer paper and printer toner are examples of supplies used in a business.

Buying supplies increases the Supplies—Office account balance and decreases the Cash account balance. Although Supplies—Office is an asset account, the steps for journalizing buying supplies for cash are similar to journalizing the payment of cash for an expense.

Note: This transaction is illustrated at the top of the previous page.

Any check written is journalized in the cash payments journal. The amount of the check is always entered in the Cash Credit column. Unless a special column is provided for the debit portion of the transaction, the account description is entered in the Account Title column. The related amount is then recorded in the General Debit column.

Cash Payments for Purchases

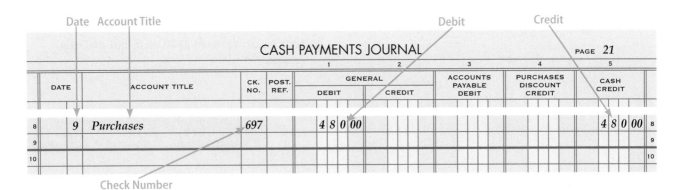

Businesses usually purchase merchandise on account. However, vendors may choose not to extend credit to all of their customers. Businesses not offered credit must pay the vendor before the merchandise is shipped or delivered.

> **November 9. Purchased merchandise from Polar Refrigeration for cash, $480.00. Check No. 697.**

ThreeGreen writes a check for ten energy efficient dorm refrigerators with an invoice amount of $480.00. Because the transaction involves a cash payment, it is recorded in the cash payments journal. Only purchases on account are recorded in the purchases journal.

Only cash payment transactions are recorded in the cash payments journal.

Cash Payments on Account with Purchases Discounts

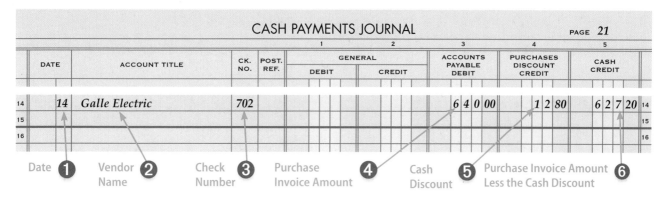

A cash discount is stated as a percentage deducted from the invoice amount. For example, *2/10, n/30* is a common term of sale, which is read *two ten, net thirty. Two ten* means that 2% of the invoice amount may be deducted if the invoice is paid within ten days of the invoice date. The period of time during which a customer may take a cash discount is called the **discount period**. *Net thirty* means that the total invoice amount must be paid within 30 days.

Purchases Discount

Debit Decreases	Credit Increases

When a company that has purchased merchandise on account takes a cash discount, it is called a **purchases discount**. Purchases discounts are recorded in a general ledger account titled Purchases Discount. An account that reduces a related account on a financial statement is called a **contra account**. Purchases Discount is a contra account to Purchases and is included in the Cost of Goods Sold section of the general ledger. On an income statement, the balance of Purchases Discount is deducted from the balance of Purchases.

Since contra accounts are deductions from their related accounts, contra account normal balances are opposite the normal balances of their related accounts. The normal balance for Purchases is a debit. Therefore, the normal balance for Purchases Discount, a contra account to Purchases, is a credit. Unlike trade discounts, cash discounts are recorded because they decrease the invoice amount due.

November 14. Paid cash on account to Galle Electric, $627.20, covering Purchase Invoice No. 489 for $640.00, less 2% discount, $12.80. Check No. 702.

STEP 1

Purchase Invoice Amount	×	Discount Rate	=	Cash Discount
$640.00	×	2%	=	$12.80

STEP 2

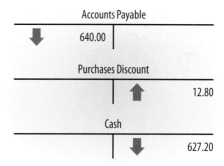

Purchase Invoice Amount	−	Cash Discount	=	Invoice Amount
$640.00	−	$12.80	=	$627.20

Accounts Payable

640.00

Purchases Discount

12.80

Cash

627.20

Journalizing a Cash Payment on Account with Purchases Discount

1. Write the date, 14, in the Date column.
2. Write the account title of the vendor, Galle Electric, in the Account Title column.
3. Write the check number, 702, in the Ck. No. column.
4. Write the debit amount to Accounts Payable, $640.00, in the Accounts Payable Debit column.
5. Write the credit amount, $12.80, in the Purchases Discount Credit column.
6. Write the credit amount, $627.20, in the Cash Credit column.

Cash Payments on Account without Purchases Discounts

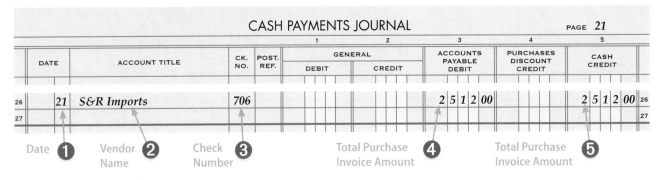

				1	2	3	4	5
				GENERAL		ACCOUNTS PAYABLE DEBIT	PURCHASES DISCOUNT CREDIT	CASH CREDIT
DATE	ACCOUNT TITLE	CK. NO.	POST. REF.	DEBIT	CREDIT			
26	21	S&R Imports	706				2 5 1 2 00		2 5 1 2 00	26
27									27

Date ➊ Vendor Name ➋ Check Number ➌ Total Purchase Invoice Amount ➍ Total Purchase Invoice Amount ➎

Many vendors do not offer cash discounts. Sometimes a business does not have the cash available to take advantage of a cash discount. In both cases, the full purchase invoice amount is paid.

ThreeGreen purchased merchandise on account from S&R Imports on October 24. S&R Imports' credit terms are n/30. Therefore, ThreeGreen will pay the full amount of the purchase invoice, $2,512.00, within 30 days of the invoice date, October 24.

November 21. Wrote a check to S&R Imports to pay on account, $2,512.00, covering Purchase Invoice No. 468. Check No. 706.

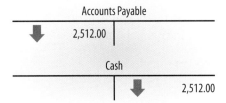

Accounts Payable

2,512.00

Cash

2,512.00

▶ Journalizing a Cash Payment on Account without Purchases Discount

➊ Write the date, 21, in the Date column.

➋ Write the vendor account title, S&R Imports, in the Account Title column.

➌ Write the check number, 706, in the Ck. No. column.

➍ Write the debit amount to Accounts Payable, $2,512.00, in the Accounts Payable Debit column.

➎ Write the credit amount, $2,512.00, in the Cash Credit column.

fyi

The employee responsible for signing a check should have no other purchasing functions. The vendor name and amount on the check should be compared to the requisition, purchase order, and purchase invoice. This review is an important control to prevent the business from paying for unauthorized merchandise.

Replenishing a Petty Cash Fund LO9

```
PETTY CASH REPORT

Date: November 22, 20--                                    Custodian: Jon Butler
```

Explanation		Reconciliation		Replenish Amount
Fund Total		250.00		
Payments: *Advertising*	124.00			
Supplies—Store	62.18			
Miscellaneous	28.95			
Less: Total payments		215.13	→	215.13
Equals: Recorded amount on hand		34.87		
Less: Actual amount on hand		35.18		
Equals: Cash short (over)		(0.31)	→	(0.31)
Amount to Replenish				214.82

Date — Check Number — Amounts — Cash Short is a Debit, Cash Over is a Credit — Total Cash Payment

CASH PAYMENTS JOURNAL   PAGE 22

					1		2		3	4	5	
	DATE	ACCOUNT TITLE	CK. NO.	POST. REF.	GENERAL DEBIT		CREDIT		ACCOUNTS PAYABLE DEBIT	PURCHASES DISCOUNT CREDIT	CASH CREDIT	
1	20-- Nov. 22	*Advertising Expense*	707		1 2 4 00						2 1 4 82	1
2		*Supplies—Store*			6 2 18							2
3		*Miscellaneous Expense*			2 8 95							3
4		*Cash Short and Over*					0 31					4
5												5

Account Titles

Accounting for petty cash was introduced in Chapter 5. In that chapter, it was shown that the petty cash report is used to determine the amount of cash needed to replenish the petty cash fund. If total petty cash payments do not balance with petty cash on hand, the fund is either short or over. Petty cash short and petty cash over are recorded in an account titled Cash Short and Over. The account is a temporary account. At the end of the fiscal year, Cash Short and Over is closed to Income Summary.

The balance of Cash Short and Over can be either a debit or credit. In Chapter 5, the petty cash fund of Delgado Web Services was $1.00 short. In November, ThreeGreen's petty cash fund is over $0.31. Note that

in Step 5, the amount of petty cash over is recorded in the General Credit column. If petty cash were short, the amount would be recorded in the General Debit column.

> **November 22.** Paid cash to replenish the petty cash fund, $214.82: advertising, $124.00; store supplies, $62.18; miscellaneous, $28.95; cash over, $0.31. Check No. 707.

The petty cash fund is replenished for the amount paid out, $215.13, less cash over, $0.31. This total amount, $214.82, restores the fund's cash balance to its original amount, $250.00 ($215.13 − $0.31 + $35.18 cash on hand).

LO8 Record cash payments using a cash payments journal.

LO9 Record replenishment of a petty cash fund.

Terms Review

cash payments journal

list price

trade discount

net price

cash discount

general amount column

discount period

purchases discount

contra account

Audit your understanding

1. What is the net price of an item with a $1,200.00 list price having a 60% trade discount?

2. Why would a vendor offer a cash discount to a customer?

3. What is recorded in the general amount columns of the cash payments journal?

4. What is meant by terms of sale 2/10, n/30?

5. When journalizing a cash payment to replenish petty cash, what is entered in the Account Title column of the cash payments journal?

6. How is cash short recorded in the account, Cash Short and Over?

Work together 9-4

Journalizing cash payments using a cash payments journal

The cash payments journal for Golden Fabrics and the petty cash report are given in the *Working Papers*. Your instructor will guide you through the following example. Save your work to complete Work Together 9-5.

Using October of the current year, journalize these transactions on page 10 of a cash payments journal. The checks used as source documents are abbreviated as C.

Transactions:

Oct. 2. Wrote a check to Bilton Communications for telephone bill, $124.00. C521.

3. Wrote a check on account to Grey Manufacturing, Inc., covering Purchase Invoice No. 532 for $1,640.00, less 2% cash discount. C522.

9. Wrote a check to LPF Manufacturing for merchandise with a list price of $1,575.00. C523.

12. Wrote a check to Village Supply for office supplies, $64.00. C524.

16. Wrote a check on account to Westland Supply covering Purchase Invoice No. 516 for $426.00. No cash discount was offered. C525.

31. Record the replenishment of the petty cash fund on October 31. C526.

On your own 9-4

Journalizing cash payments using a cash payments journal

The cash payments journal for Copperland Company and the petty cash report are given in the *Working Papers*. Work this problem independently. Save your work to complete On Your Own 9-5.

Using November of the current year, journalize these transactions on page 11 of the cash payments journal. The checks used as source documents are abbreviated as C.

Transactions:

Nov. 3. Wrote a check on account to Gillis Glass Co. covering Purchase Invoice No. 765 for $2,120.00, less 2% cash discount. C832.

7. Wrote a check to Anders Office Supply for office supplies, $164.00. C833.

8. Wrote a check to Taylor Energy for the electric bill, $324.00. C834.

14. Wrote a check to Metal Magic for merchandise with a list price of $1,560.00. C835.

18. Paid cash on account to Sheng Industries covering Purchase Invoice No. 724 for $1,816.00. No cash discount was offered. C836.

30. Record the replenishment of the petty cash fund on November 30. C837.

9-5 Posting from a Cash Payments Journal

LO10 Post cash payments to an accounts payable ledger and a general ledger.

Posting from a Cash Payments Journal to an Accounts Payable Ledger LO10

Journal Page Number ②

CASH PAYMENTS JOURNAL PAGE 21

				1	2	3	4	5
DATE	ACCOUNT TITLE	CK. NO.	POST. REF.	GENERAL DEBIT	GENERAL CREDIT	ACCOUNTS PAYABLE DEBIT	PURCHASES DISCOUNT CREDIT	CASH CREDIT
14	Bearden Chemicals	698	210			5 4 8 3 00		5 4 8 3 00

Date ① Vendor Number ⑤ Debit ③

VENDOR *Bearden Chemicals*   VENDOR NO. 210

DATE	ITEM	POST. REF.	DEBIT	CREDIT	CREDIT BALANCE
Nov. 1	Balance	✔			5 4 8 3 00
13		P11		6 2 8 4 80	11 7 6 7 80
14		CP21	5 4 8 3 00		6 2 8 4 80

④ Account Balance

Each entry in the Accounts Payable Debit column of a cash payments journal affects a vendor account. Individual amounts in the Accounts Payable Debit column are posted frequently to the proper vendor accounts in the accounts payable ledger. Frequent posting ensures that each vendor's account is up to date.

A business needs to monitor its outstanding accounts payable balances to ensure that it can continue to purchase goods and services on account. Many vendors establish limits on the outstanding balances of their customers. A **credit limit** is the maximum outstanding balance allowed to a customer by a vendor. Bearden Chemicals has established a $12,000.00 credit limit for ThreeGreen. To continue purchasing merchandise from Bearden Chemicals, ThreeGreen must ensure that it does not exceed its credit limit. Any disruption in the purchase of merchandise can lead to lost sales and dissatisfied customers. Keeping a fully stocked inventory is critical for the success of a merchandising business.

➤ Posting from a Cash Payments Journal to an Accounts Payable Ledger

① Write the date, 14, in the Date column of the vendor account.

② Write the journal page number, CP21, in the Post. Ref. column of the account. The abbreviation CP21 means page 21 of the cash payments journal.

③ Write the debit amount, $5,483.00, in the Debit column of the vendor account.

④ Subtract the amount in the Debit column from the previous balance in the Credit Balance column ($11,767.80 − $5,483.00 = $6,284.80). Write the new balance, $6,284.80, in the Credit Balance column.

⑤ Write the vendor number, 210, in the Post. Ref. column of the cash payments journal.

Posting from the General Amount Columns of a Cash Payments Journal to a General Ledger

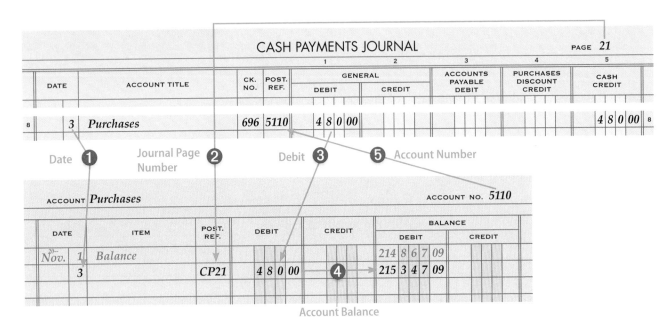

Date ❶   Journal Page Number ❷   Debit ❸   ❺ Account Number

Account Balance

Entries in a cash payments journal are recorded in either the general amount columns or the special amount columns. Each amount in the General columns of a cash payments journal is posted individually to the general ledger account written in the Account Title column.

Writing the account number in a special journal provides an audit trail. An employee working with the journal can trace the transaction to the account where it was posted.

> ↘ **Posting from the General Amount Columns of a Cash Payments Journal to a General Ledger**
>
> ❶ Write the date, 9, in the Date column of the account.
>
> ❷ Write the journal page number, CP21, in the Post. Ref. column of the account. The abbreviation CP21 means page 21 of the cash payments journal.
>
> ❸ Write the debit amount, $480.00, in the account's Debit column. (A credit amount would be written in the Credit column.)
>
> ❹ Add the amount in the Debit column to the previous balance in the Balance Debit column ($480.00 + $214,867.09 = $215,347.09). Write the new account balance, $215,347.09, in the Balance Debit column of the account.
>
> ❺ Write the general ledger account number, 5110, in the Post. Ref. column of the cash payments journal.

Totaling, Proving, and Ruling a Cash Payments Journal

	DATE	ACCOUNT TITLE	CK. NO.	POST. REF.	GENERAL DEBIT	GENERAL CREDIT	ACCOUNTS PAYABLE DEBIT	PURCHASES DISCOUNT CREDIT	CASH CREDIT	
					1	2	3	4	5	
20	28	Galle Electric	719	230	1 0 8 0 00		1 0 8 0 00	2 1 60	1 0 5 8 40	20
21	30	Wynn Lighting	720	260			1 0 8 2 50		1 0 8 2 50	21
22	30	Rent Expense	721	6145	7 0 0 00				7 0 0 00	22
23	30	Totals			7 1 5 4 58	1 9 1 5 20	7 0 5 1 50	2 1 60	12 2 6 9 28	23

CASH PAYMENTS JOURNAL — PAGE 22

2 Date **3** "Totals" **1** Single Line **4** Column Totals **5** Double Line

Column Title	Debit Column Totals	Credit Column Totals
General Debit	$ 7,154.58	
General Credit		$ 1,915.20
Accounts Payable Debit	7,051.50	
Purchases Discount Credit		21.60
Cash Credit		12,269.28
Totals	$14,206.08	$14,206.08

A journal is proved and ruled whenever a journal page is filled and always at the end of a month. The total for each column is written in the next available line. These totals are used to prove that the debits equal the credits.

The two totals, $14,206.08, are equal. Equality of debits and credits in ThreeGreen's cash payments journal for November is proved. If the total debits do not equal the total credits, the errors must be found and corrected before any more work is completed. Common errors include entering amounts incorrectly and entering a correct amount in the wrong column. Sometimes amounts are entered in the wrong journal.

Ruling a Cash Payments Journal

1 Rule a single line across all amount columns directly below the last entry to indicate that all the columns are to be added.

2 On the next line, write the date, 30, in the Date column.

3 Write the word Totals in the Account Title column.

4 Write each column total below the single line.

5 Rule double lines across all amount columns to show that the totals have been verified as correct.

Posting from the Special Amount Columns of a Cash Payments Journal to a General Ledger

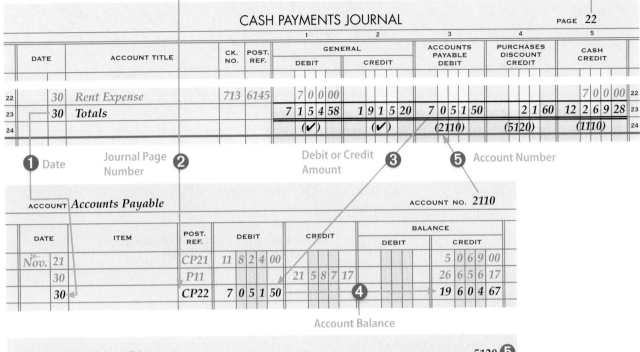

The total of each special amount column is posted to the account named in the column's heading whenever a page is filled and always at the end of the month. The totals of the General amount columns are not posted. Each amount in these columns was posted individually to a general ledger account. To indicate that these totals are not posted, a check mark is placed in parentheses below each column total.

Posting the Total of a Cash Payments Journal to the General Ledger Accounts

1. Write the date, 30, in the Date column of the accounts.
2. Write the cash payments journal page number, CP22, in the Post. Ref. column of the accounts. The abbreviation CP22 means page 22 of the cash payments journal.
3. For each account, write the cash payments journal column total in the Debit or Credit column.
4. For each account, calculate and write the new account balance in the Balance Debit or Balance Credit column.
5. Return to the cash payments journal and write the general ledger account number in parentheses below the column total.

Completed Accounts Payable Ledger

VENDOR *Bearden Chemicals* **VENDOR NO.** *210*

DATE		ITEM	POST. REF.	DEBIT	CREDIT	CREDIT BALANCE
Nov.	1	Balance	✔			5 4 8 3 00
	13		P11		6 2 8 4 80	11 7 6 7 80
	14		CP21	5 4 8 3 00		6 2 8 4 80

VENDOR *Estes Supply* **VENDOR NO.** *220*

DATE		ITEM	POST. REF.	DEBIT	CREDIT	CREDIT BALANCE
Nov.	1	Balance	✔			3 1 6 5 00
	25		CP22	2 3 4 5 00		8 2 0 00

VENDOR *Galle Electric* **VENDOR NO.** *230*

DATE		ITEM	POST. REF.	DEBIT	CREDIT	CREDIT BALANCE
Nov.	8		P11		6 4 0 00	6 4 0 00
	14		CP21	6 4 0 00		——
	22		P11		1 0 8 0 00	1 0 8 0 00
	28		CP22	1 0 8 0 00		——
	29		P11		8 6 4 25	8 6 4 25

VENDOR *Mobley Tools* **VENDOR NO.** *240*

DATE		ITEM	POST. REF.	DEBIT	CREDIT	CREDIT BALANCE
Nov.	1	Balance	✔			3 1 8 9 00
	15		P11		4 1 8 2 15	7 3 7 1 15
	19		CP21	3 1 8 9 00		4 1 8 2 15

VENDOR *S&R Imports* **VENDOR NO.** *250*

DATE		ITEM	POST. REF.	DEBIT	CREDIT	CREDIT BALANCE
Nov.	1	Balance	✔			2 5 1 2 00
	21		CP21	2 5 1 2 00		——
	27		P11		3 9 7 3 15	3 9 7 3 15

VENDOR *Wynn Lighting* **VENDOR NO.** *260*

DATE		ITEM	POST. REF.	DEBIT	CREDIT	CREDIT BALANCE
Nov.	1	Balance	✔			2 5 4 4 00
	6		P11		1 0 8 2 50	3 6 2 6 50
	21		P11		3 4 8 0 32	7 1 0 6 82
	23		CP22	2 5 4 4 00		4 5 6 2 82
	30		CP22	1 0 8 2 50		3 4 8 0 32

ThreeGreen's accounts payable ledger has been posted for the month of November.

Proving the Accounts Payable Ledger

ThreeGreen Products, Inc.						
Schedule of Accounts Payable						
November 30, 20--						
Bearden Chemicals	6	2	8	4	80
Estes Supply		8	2	0	00
Galle Electric		8	6	4	25
Mobley Tools	4	1	8	2	15
S&R Imports	3	9	7	3	15
Wynn Lighting	3	4	8	0	32
Total Accounts Payable	19	6	0	4	67

A controlling account balance in a general ledger must equal the sum of all account balances in a subsidiary ledger. Like most businesses, ThreeGreen proves subsidiary ledgers at the end of each month.

A listing of vendor accounts, account balances, and the total amount due to all vendors is called a **schedule of accounts payable**. Some businesses call this listing an *accounts payable trial balance*. A schedule of accounts payable is prepared after all entries in all journals are posted. The balance of Accounts Payable in the general ledger is $19,604.67. The total of the schedule of accounts payable is $19,604.67. Because the two amounts are the same, the accounts payable ledger is proved.

Using Credit Cards Wisely

As students reach the legal age of 18, most will receive credit card offers. Is it good or bad to have credit? It depends on how credit is used. If a credit card is used primarily as a convenience and the account balance is paid off each month, then credit is being used wisely. Unfortunately, many credit card users only make minimum payments, which is deceptive since it often takes many months or years to pay off the balance.

Credit is not free money. It is a loan that allows you to buy now and pay later. If your account balance is not repaid by the due date, interest based on an annual percentage rate (APR) is added to the account balance. Interest rates and credit terms differ among credit card issuers. Some card companies offer a low introductory interest rate as bait. Then, they increase the rate after a short period of time. Be wise and shop around for the best terms.

The following terms should be considered when selecting a credit card: APR (not just the introductory rate), annual fees (yearly fee just to carry the card), and in some cases, the security deposit. Remember to read the fine print carefully before signing a credit card application, as many people do not realize that a signature on the application makes it a legal contract. The Credit Card Accountability Responsibility and Disclosure Act of 2009, also known as the Credit CARD Act, was passed to protect consumers from extravagant fees and interest rates. This law also requires the "fine print" to have a minimum 12-point font for easier reading.

Using a credit card wisely involves evaluating each purchase according to one's needs and not just the immediate impulse. Excessive use of credit can result in long-term financial problems and a poor credit report. A credit report, much like a high school transcript, follows a person throughout their lifetime. Credit scores enable businesses to evaluate a person's creditworthiness. Most people do not realize that a poor credit score can negatively affect their insurance rates and even their employment prospects.

ACTIVITIES

1. Using the Internet, research the Credit CARD Act. Write a one-page paper outlining at least five ways the new law benefits consumers.

2. Compare the APR, annual fees, and security deposit (if applicable) for five different credit cards. Select the best option based on your findings. Create a spreadsheet table to report your findings.

©NOREBBO, ISTOCK

End of Lesson Review

LO10 Post cash payments to an accounts payable ledger and a general ledger.

Terms Review

credit limit

schedule of accounts payable

Audit your understanding

1. In which column of the cash payments journal are the amounts that are posted individually to the accounts payable ledger?
2. List the five steps for ruling a cash payments journal at the end of the month.
3. What is the relationship between a controlling account and a subsidiary ledger?

Work together 9-5

Posting a cash payments journal

A blank schedule of accounts payable is given in the *Working Papers*. Use Golden Fabrics' cash payments journal from Work Together 9-4 and the accounts payable and general ledgers from Work Together 9-3. Your instructor will guide you through the following examples.

1. Post the transactions from the cash payments journal to the accounts payable ledger.
2. Total, prove, and rule the cash payments journal.
3. Post the cash payments journal to the general ledger.
4. Prepare a schedule of accounts payable.

On your own 9-5

Posting a cash payments journal

A blank schedule of accounts payable is given in the *Working Papers*. Use Copperland Company's cash payments journal from On Your Own 9-4 and the accounts payable and general ledgers from On Your Own 9-3. Work this problem independently.

1. Post the transactions from the cash payments journal to the accounts payable ledger.
2. Total, prove, and rule the cash payments journal.
3. Post the cash payments journal to the general ledger.
4. Prepare a schedule of accounts payable.

A Look at Accounting Software

Like special journals in a manual accounting system, the windows of a computerized accounting system are designed to capture similar transactions affecting commonly used accounts. In this chapter, Mary Prisock had to decide which special journal to use for each transaction. In a computerized accounting system, rather than selecting the appropriate special journal, the user must select the appropriate window to enter a transaction.

Vendor invoices entered in the Receive Inventory window capture the same information as a purchases journal. The window also allows for the display or entry of other information related to the vendor and the parts purchased. Cash payments entered in the Write Checks window capture the same information as a cash payments journal plus some additional information.

Entering a Purchase Invoice in the Receive Inventory Window

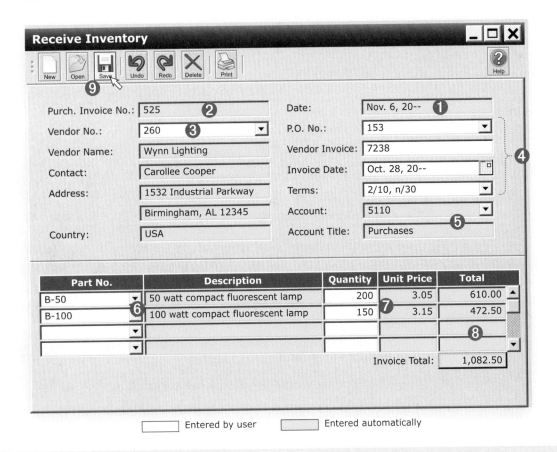

① The current date is entered by the system.

② The system automatically enters the next available purchase invoice number.

③ The source document for an entry in this window is the vendor invoice. The vendor can be selected either by number (as above) or by name. Information about the vendor is displayed automatically.

④ The purchase order number, as well as vendor invoice number, date, and terms, are keyed or selected using list boxes or calendars.

⑤ The system displays the default **Purchases** account number. It can be changed if needed.

⑥ A part number is selected from the list box field. The part description is automatically retrieved from the inventory file. Part descriptions would be protected, preventing the user from making unauthorized changes to the data. New items would have to be added to the inventory file before they could be entered in this window.

⑦ The user enters the quantity. The unit price is entered by the system from the company's inventory file. The price can be overwritten if it has changed.

⑧ The system calculates line and invoice totals.

⑨ Clicking **Save** posts the transaction to Accounts Payable, Purchases, and the vendor's accounts payable account. Inventory quantities are also updated.

Processing Cash Payments in the Write Checks Window

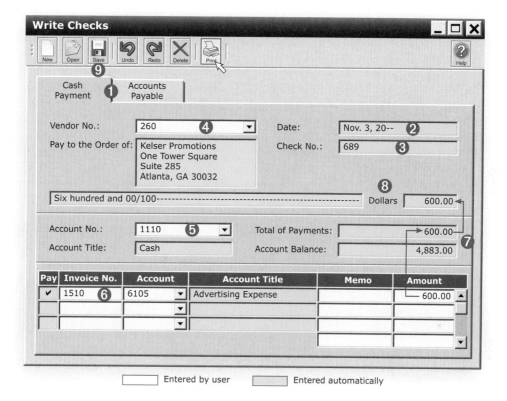

Entered by user   Entered automatically

① The user would click the **Cash Payment** tab to write a check for an immediate expense. If the **Accounts Payable** tab were selected, invoices previously approved for payment in the accounts payable window would appear in the rows at the bottom of this window. The user would deselect any **Pay** boxes for checks that were not to be written at this time. Payment information for any row selected would appear in the top section of the window.

② The current date is entered by the system.

③ The system enters the next available check number.

④ The vendor is selected from the Vendor No. list box. Information about the vendor is automatically retrieved.

⑤ The system displays the default cash account, but if the company maintains different cash accounts, a different account could be selected.

⑥ The user keys the invoice number and selects the account number. The account title and the check mark in the **Pay** box are automatically displayed. A description of the payment can be keyed in the memo box. The user keys the check amount.

⑦ The total of all checks to be written and the remaining balance of the Cash account are displayed.

⑧ The system displays text and numeric versions of the check amount.

⑨ Clicking **Save** posts the transaction and updates Cash, Accounts Payable (if applicable), the selected expense accounts, and the vendor's accounts payable account. The user clicks **Print** to print the checks. Checks cannot be printed until the window is saved.

Chapter Summary

A merchandising business purchases goods to sell to its customers. Many merchandising businesses organize as corporations in order to have access to the capital needed for purchasing goods. A corporation raises capital by selling its capital stock to investors or by borrowing.

A merchandising business may purchase merchandise on account from many vendors. The business must maintain an accounting system that ensures these bills are paid on time. Businesses using the periodic inventory method record merchandise purchases to the **Purchases** account. Each purchase on account is efficiently recorded in the special amount column of the purchases journal. The transaction is immediately posted in the vendor's accounts payable ledger account to update the amount owed to the vendor. The totals of the special columns of a completed purchases journal are posted to the general ledger.

All cash payments are recorded in the cash payments journal. The journal contains a special amount column to efficiently record the many cash payments made for purchases on account. To encourage early payment, some vendors offer a cash discount that allows the customer to pay less than the full amount of the purchase invoice. **Purchases Discount**, a contra account to **Purchases**, is used to account for cash discounts. The cash payments journal includes a special amount column, Purchases Discount Credit, to record cash discounts.

Cash payments for other purchases and expenses are also recorded in the cash payments journal. Small expenses, paid using a petty cash fund, are recorded in the cash payments journal when a check is written to reimburse the fund. The totals of the special columns of a completed cash payments journal are posted to the general ledger. A business can ensure the accuracy of its accounts payable ledger by preparing a schedule of accounts payable. The total of the schedule should equal the updated balance of **Accounts Payable**, the controlling account for the accounts payable ledger.

EXPLORE ACCOUNTING

One Size Does Not Fit All

What do cars and computerized accounting systems have in common?

Henry Ford revolutionized automobile production by applying mass production techniques and limiting personal choice. He said buyers of Ford's Model T could select "any colour, so long as it is black."* Imagine for a moment that, as part of a national directive to make cars more affordable, a team of experts is charged with revolutionizing today's automobile industry. Inspired by the success of the Model T, the team sets out to design a single car that everyone would be required to drive. No

longer would consumers be allowed to select from a sport coupe, four-door sedan, pickup truck, convertible, minivan, etc. Everyone would drive the same car (and it would be black!). Imagine what that car might look like! Would many people want to drive it? The answer is likely to be a resounding "NO!"

Similar questions could be asked about the design of a computerized accounting system. Can one system meet the accounting and financial reporting needs of every organization? Can one system be used by ExxonMobil, Walmart, and Apple? Can that same system be used by a local clothing store and your

school district? The answer to each of these questions would also be a resounding "NO!"

For this reason, a business can select from a large number of computerized accounting systems. These systems offer a wide variety of features targeted to businesses of every type and size. QuickBooks and Peachtree, for example, are two of many systems developed for small businesses. In contrast, Oracle and SAP are two of several systems capable of handling the demands of today's largest international corporations.

Just as a driver selects a car based on his or her transportation needs,

*Source: ge.com.

a business selects a system based on its business needs. Common questions might include:

1. How many users can use the system at the same time?
2. What type of computer equipment is required?
3. Does the system contain suggested charts of accounts for various types of businesses?
4. Does the system track amounts owed to vendors?
5. Does the system support Internet access by vendors? Customers?
6. Can the system alert managers to the need to order merchandise?
7. Can master file data be exported to an electronic spreadsheet?
8. Can the system automatically back up data files to a remote location?

INSTRUCTIONS

Use the Internet to research the special features of a computerized accounting system. Identify at least eight special features offered by the system. Suggest at least two local businesses that you believe could, and at least two that could not, use this system. Support your answers.

Apply Your Understanding

INSTRUCTIONS: Download problem instructions for Excel, QuickBooks, and Peachtree from the textbook companion website at www.C21accounting.com.

9-1 Application Problem: Starting an accounts payable ledger form LO3

Accounts payable ledger forms are given in the *Working Papers*.

Instructions:

1. Start a new page for an accounts payable ledger account for Newton Industries. The account number is 240, and the balance on September 1 of the current year is $2,489.90.
2. Start a new page for an accounts payable ledger account for Reston Corporation. The account number is 250, and the balance for September 1 of the current year is $3,047.40.

9-2 Application Problem: Journalizing purchases using a purchases journal LO6

1. Journalize and post transactions on account to the purchases journal.
2. Print the purchases journal and accounts payable ledger.

AAONLiNE

1. Go to www.cengage.com/login
2. Click on **AA Online** to access.
3. Go to the online assignment and follow the instructions.

The purchases journal for Electronic Source is given in the *Working Papers*.

Instructions:

Use page 9 of the purchases journal to journalize the following transactions completed during September of the current year. The purchase invoices used as source documents are abbreviated as P. Save the purchases journal to complete Problem 9-3.

Transactions:

Sept. 2. Purchased merchandise on account from Henson Audio, $980.00. P354.
5. Purchased merchandise on account from Peterson Electronics, $2,450.00. P355.
13. Purchased merchandise on account from Atlanta Systems, $2,845.00. P356.
19. Purchased merchandise on account from Lester Corporation, $680.00. P357.
22. Purchased merchandise on account from Masonville Music, $4,890.00. P358.

9-3 Application Problem: Posting a purchases journal LO7

Select accounts payable and general ledger accounts for Electronic Source are given in the *Working Papers*. Use the purchases journal from Problem 9-2. Save your work to complete Problem 9-5.

Instructions:

1. Post the transactions on the purchases journal to the accounts payable ledger.
2. Total and rule the purchases journal.
3. Post the purchases journal to the general ledger.

9-4 Application Problem: Journalizing cash payments using a cash payments journal LO8

1. Journalize and post transactions on account to the cash payments journal.
2. Complete the petty cash report by classifying each expense to compute the actual cash on hand.
3. Print the cash payments journal and petty cash report.

AAONLiNE

1. Go to www.cengage.com/login
2. Click on **AA Online** to access.
3. Go to the online assignment and follow the instructions.

The cash payments journal and a petty cash report for Electronic Source are given in the *Working Papers*.

Instructions:

Use page 9 of a cash payments journal to journalize the following transactions completed during September of the current year. Source documents are abbreviated as follows: check, C; purchase invoice, P. Save your work to complete Problem 9-5.

Transactions:

Sept. 2. Paid cash for advertising, $125.00. C388.
5. Paid cash on account to Henson Audio, $2,489.00, covering P346, less 2% discount. C389.
8. Paid cash for heating bill, $240.00. C390.
10. Paid cash on account to Peterson Electronics, $3,484.00, covering P349, less 2% discount. C391.
12. Paid cash for office supplies, $43.00. C392.
15. Paid cash to KLP Mfg. for merchandise with a list price of $2,136.00. C393.
16. Purchased merchandise for cash from O'Brian Industries, $349.00. C394.
18. Paid cash on account to Atlanta Systems, $1,925.00, covering P348. No cash discount was offered. C395.
21. Purchased merchandise for cash from Evansville Sound Company, $300.00. C396.
23. Paid cash on account to Masonville Music, $659.00. No cash discount was offered. C397.
30. Record the replenishment of the petty cash fund on September 30. C398.

9-5 Application Problem: Posting a cash payments journal LO10

A blank schedule of accounts payable is given in the *Working Papers*. Use Electronic Source's cash payments journal from Problem 9-4 and the accounts payable and general ledgers from Problem 9-3.

Instructions:

1. Post the transactions from the cash payments journal to the accounts payable ledger.
2. Total, prove, and rule the cash payments journal.
3. Post the cash payments journal to the general ledger.
4. Prepare a schedule of accounts payable.

9-M Mastery Problem: Journalizing purchases, cash payments, and other transactions LO6, 7, 8, 10

Denmar Automotive sells car parts and accessories.

Instructions:

1. Using the journals given in the *Working Papers*, journalize the following transactions completed during July of the current year. Use page 7 of a purchases journal and page 7 of a cash payments journal. Post the following transactions when journalized: (1) transactions impacting Accounts Payable to the accounts payable subsidiary ledger, and (2) cash payments, entered in a general amount column of the cash payments journal, to the general ledger. Source documents are abbreviated as follows: check, C; purchase invoice, P.

Transactions:

July 2. Purchased merchandise on account from Rackley Industries, $2,950.00. P184.
  3. Paid cash on account to Helms Supply, $1,280.00, covering P166, less 2% discount. C318.
  6. Purchased merchandise on account from Kelsay Parts, $3,560.00. P185.
  7. Paid cash to WCKF Radio for advertising, $800.00. C319.
  8. Paid cash on account to Kelsay Parts, $3,940.00, covering P167, less 2% discount. C320.
  10. Paid cash to Southern Bell for telephone bill, $221.00. C321.
  12. Paid cash on account to Rackley Industries, $2,119.00, covering P162. No cash discount was offered. C322.
  12. Purchased merchandise on account from Helms Supply, $1,450.00. P186.
  13. Paid cash to Edmondson Supply for store supplies, $315.00. C323.
  14. Paid cash to Deanes Electronics for merchandise, $1,392.00. C324.
  15. Paid cash on account to Kelsay Parts, $3,560.00, covering P174, less 2% discount. C325.
  15. Purchased merchandise on account from Delmar, Inc., $2,480.00. P187.
  18. Purchased merchandise for cash from Columbus Industries, $615.00. C326.
  20. Paid cash on account to Delmar, Inc., $2,290.00, covering P159. No cash discount was offered. C327.
  23. Paid cash to Regional Electric for the electric bill, $920.00. C328.
  28. Paid cash to Williams Stores for store supplies, $121.00. C329.
  29. Purchased merchandise on account from Rackley Industries, $985.00. P188.
  31. Replenished the $200.00 petty cash fund. Receipts were submitted for the following: office supplies, $45.60; store supplies, $67.30; and miscellaneous, $23.89. A cash count shows $61.98 in the petty cash box. C330.

2. Total and rule the purchases journal.

3. Post the purchases journal to the general ledger.

4. Total, prove, and rule the cash payments journal.

5. Post the special columns of the cash payments journal to the general ledger.

6. Prepare a schedule of accounts payable as of July 31.

Peachtree

1. Journalize and post to the purchase journal and cash disbursements journal.
2. From the menu bar, select Reports and Forms; Accounts Payable.
3. Make the selections to print the purchase journal and the cash disbursements journal.

QuickBooks

1. Journalize and post purchases on account in the Enter Bills window.
2. Journalize and post payments to vendors in the Pay Bills window.
3. From the menu bar, select Reports; Vendors & Payables, Vendor Balance Detail.
4. In the Dates drop-down box, select All and make the selections to print.

9-S Source Documents Problem: Journalizing purchases, cash payments, and other transactions from source documents LO6, 8

Messler Sailing sells sailboats, parts, and accessories. Source documents related to the purchases and cash payments of Messler Sailing for October are provided in the *Working Papers*.

Instructions:

1. Using journals given in the *Working Papers*, journalize the transactions for October of the current year. Use page 10 of a purchases journal and page 15 of a cash payments journal. Source documents are abbreviated as follows: check, C; purchase invoice, P.

2. Total and rule the purchases journal.

3. Total the amount columns of cash payments journal page 15. Prove the equality of debits and credits and rule the cash payments journal.

9-C Challenge Problem: Journalizing purchases and cash payments LO6, 8

SoundStage Music is a merchandising company that specializes in instrument and music sales to professional musicians and schools. The company was organized in October and began purchasing inventory in November in anticipation of its grand opening on November 20.

The company was able to negotiate accounts with five vendors. Three of those vendors, Abraham Instruments, Pacific Guitar, and Southern Music Supply, offer 2/10, n/30 credit terms. The remaining vendors have n/30 credit terms.

The accounts payable ledger in the *Working Papers* shows SoundStage Music's November purchases on account. In an effort to conserve cash, the company did not take advantage of any cash discounts. These unpaid invoices will, therefore, be paid by the 30-day due date.

With the company now open for business, the company has the money available to pay all of its accounts on time. The company allows three days for the mail to deliver a check to a vendor. For example, an invoice dated November 28 due in ten days, December 8, would be written and mailed on December 5.

During December, the company made the following merchandise purchases:

Transactions:

	Vendor	Purchase Invoice	Amount
Dec. 2	Brassworks	9	$2,950.00
6	Pratt Publishing	10	3,560.00
9	Southern Music Supply	11	1,450.00
12	Abraham Instruments	12	2,480.00
14	Pratt Publishing	13	1,495.00
19	Pacific Guitar	14	4,310.00
22	Abraham Instruments	15	4,805.00
28	Pacific Guitar	16	1,648.00

Instructions:

1. Using the purchases and cash payments journals and accounts payable ledger forms given in the *Working Papers*, journalize the purchases and cash payments made during December. Post the transactions to the accounts payable ledger when the transactions are recorded in the journals. Record a check in the cash payments journal on the appropriate due date of an unpaid purchase invoice.

   Hint: Beginning with December 1, examine the unpaid purchase invoices and the table of purchases for any transactions that should be journalized. For example, the November 24 purchase from Pacific Guitar is due on December 4 (to take advantage of the cash discount). Thus, a payment must be made on December 1. This transaction has been journalized and posted as an example. No purchases were made on December 1. Continue this process for every day in December.

2. Prepare a schedule of accounts payable as of December 31.

 Peachtree

1. Journalize and post to the purchase journal and cash disbursements journal.
2. From the menu bar, select Reports & Forms; Accounts Payable.
3. Make the selections to print the purchase journal and the cash disbursements journal.

 Quick Books

1. Journalize and post purchases on account in the Enter Bills window.
2. Journalize and post payments to vendors in the Pay Bills window.
3. From the menu bar, select Reports; Vendors & Payables, Vendor Balance Detail.
4. In the Dates drop-down box, select All and make the selections to print.

21st Century Skills

Where in the World?

Theme: World, Global Awareness

Skills: ICT Literacy, Information Literacy

PARTNERSHIP FOR
21ST CENTURY SKILLS

In today's global economy, many foreign vendors and manufacturers supply merchandise sold in the United States. When dealing with foreign suppliers, business owners must be aware of the risks associated with conducting business outside the United States. Legal uncertainties as well as political and economic instability can result in long delays in receiving the merchandise, and quality standards are not always consistent or acceptable to U.S. customers. In many countries, business practices lag behind those in developed nations.

Whenever a foreign supplier is being sought, a business owner must be vigilant in selecting a supplier that is trustworthy. In addition to seeking acceptable warranties, prices, and minimum order quantities, a business owner should visit the supplier to observe firsthand its production, labor, and business practices.

APPLICATION

1. Many clothing items are imported from other countries. Make a list of ten articles among your clothing and shoes. Check the label on each item, and create a table indicating the item and the country in which it was made.

2. Your table undoubtedly lists mostly foreign countries. Were any items made in the United States? What cost factors, do you suppose, have driven clothing manufacturing overseas?

Analyzing Nike's financial statements

The Nike "swoosh" and the "Just Do It" slogan are part of today's culture. Its creative ad campaigns have made Nike one of the world's most recognizable brands. Nike gains public attention by signing famous athletes to endorse its products. The company also promotes its brand by sponsoring athletic and charity events.

INSTRUCTIONS

1. Using page B-10 in Appendix B, refer to the Demand creation expense section of Note 1 to identify the total advertising and promotion expenses for the three years ended May 31, 2011.

2. When does Nike expense the production costs of its advertisements?

Chapter 10

Accounting for Sales and Cash Receipts

LEARNING OBJECTIVES

After studying Chapter 10, in addition to understanding key terms, you will be able to:

LO1 Explain the relationship between the accounts receivable ledger and its controlling account.

LO2 Record sales on account using a sales journal.

LO3 Post sales on account to an accounts receivable ledger and a general ledger.

LO4 Record cash and credit card sales using a cash receipts journal.

LO5 Journalize cash receipts on account using a cash receipts journal.

LO6 Post cash receipts to an accounts receivable ledger and a general ledger.

LO7 Prepare a schedule of accounts receivable.

©DANIEL KOUREY, ISTOCK/©JIM PRUITT, ISTOCK

BLEND IMAGES/JUPITER IMAGES

Accounting In The Real World

Best Buy

With over 1,000 stores in the United States, Best Buy has established itself as a leader in retail electronics. The company has achieved consistent sales growth by responding to innovations in consumer electronics. By acquiring related technology businesses, such as Geek Squad and Napster, Best Buy has expanded its products and services to reach new markets.

Recognizing the opportunities in the international market, Best Buy expanded into Canada in 2002, followed by China in 2007 and Europe in 2009. In each case, Best Buy bought existing electronics stores to gain an immediate presence in those countries and, in doing so, gained valuable knowledge about local consumers. Where other businesses had failed in their attempts to expand internationally, Best Buy knew to avoid an "if it works here, it can work there" approach to international expansion. Rather than rebranding each store, Best Buy strategically kept the names of the stores it acquired, using the market strength of each as a foundation while expanding product offerings with Best Buy-branded products.

Thus, Canadian consumers purchase Best Buy merchandise at Future Shop, while Chinese consumers shop at Jiangsu Five Star. Best Buy's consolidated income statement includes the total sales from each of its brands: Best Buy, Audiovisions, The Carphone Warehouse, Future Shop, Geek Squad, Jiangsu Five Star, Magnolia Audio Video, Napster, Pacific Sales, The Phone House, and Speakeasy.

Any corporation that buys another business faces many challenges. One challenge involves the accounting system. Will the purchased business be allowed to retain its own accounting system? Or will the corporation require the purchased business to adopt its accounting system?

CRITICAL THINKING

1. Discuss Best Buy's strategy of maintaining local brands. What impact do you think this strategy would have on employees of an acquired business?

2. What accounting problems might exist in combining the accounting systems of two businesses?

Key Terms

- selling price
- markup
- accounts receivable ledger
- sales tax
- sales journal
- cash sale
- point-of-sale (POS) terminal
- terminal summary
- batch report
- batching out
- cash receipts journal
- sales discount
- schedule of accounts receivable

10-1 Accounting for Sales on Account

LO1 Explain the relationship between the accounts receivable ledger and its controlling account.

LO2 Record sales on account using a sales journal.

Subsidiary Ledgers and Controlling Accounts LO1

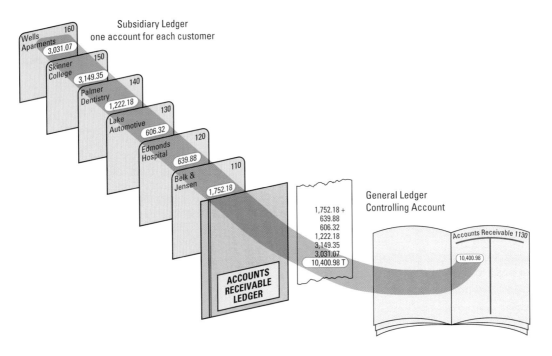

Subsidiary Ledger
one account for each customer

Wells Aparments 160
3,031.07

Skinner College 150
3,149.35

Palmer Dentistry 140
1,222.18

Lake Automotive 130
606.32

Edmonds Hospital 120
639.88

Belk & Jensen 110
1,752.18

ACCOUNTS RECEIVABLE LEDGER

1,752.18 +
639.88
606.32
1,222.18
3,149.35
3,031.07
10,400.98 T

General Ledger
Controlling Account

Accounts Receivable 1130
10,400.98

A merchandising business gets its revenue from the sale of merchandise. The amount a business receives from the sale of an item of merchandise is called the **selling price**. For a business to survive and grow, it must earn a profit. The amount a business adds to the cost of merchandise to establish the selling price is called **markup**. (Cost of merchandise + Markup = Selling price.) The share of total revenue that results from the markup is what covers all the expenses of the business and returns a profit to the owners.

A sale of merchandise may be (1) on account or (2) for cash. Regardless of when payment is received, the revenue should be recorded when a sale is made, not on the date cash is received. [CONCEPT: Realization of Revenue] For example, on June 15, ThreeGreen sold merchandise on account to a customer. The customer paid ThreeGreen

for the merchandise on July 9. ThreeGreen records the revenue on June 15, the date of the sale.

Delgado Web Services, the business in Part 1, used general ledger accounts to record transactions with each charge customer. This method is not practical for a business having a large number of customers. Like most businesses, ThreeGreen maintains a subsidiary ledger for its receivables. An **accounts receivable ledger** is a subsidiary ledger containing all accounts for charge customers. The total amount owed by these customers equals the balance in the controlling account, **Accounts Receivable**. An accurate accounts receivable ledger provides a business with the information necessary to ensure the collection of money owed the business while maintaining good relations with its charge customers.

Accounts Receivable, an asset account, is increased by a debit and decreased by a credit, so it has a normal debit balance.

Accounts Receivable

Debit Increases	Credit Decreases

Although any numbering scheme can be used, ThreeGreen uses three-digit numbers for its accounts receivable ledger. The first digit identifies the division of the chart of accounts where the controlling account appears. The second two digits are unique to the customer. For example, the customer number for Skinner College is 150. The first digit, *1*, shows that the controlling account, **Accounts Receivable,** is an asset. The second and third digits, *50*, are the unique number assigned to Skinner College. Accounts in the subsidiary ledgers can be located by either number or name.

ETHICS IN ACTION

Sharing the News

The plant manager was somber as he announced the news to his three department managers. "Corporate headquarters has just informed me that this plant is going to be closed." Pausing to let the managers absorb the bad news, he continued, "The four of us have been offered positions in the new plant overseas. We have 30 days to quietly get this plant ready to close. The employees will learn about it when they report to work on closing day. Corporate has authorized us to give them two weeks' severance pay and free enrollment in a trade school. Have their checks ready on that day."

Phillip Walters, human resources manager, left the meeting and went straight to the phone to call his wife. "Corporate just informed us they're closing the plant. They're going to make the announcement in a month. I'll be able to keep my job if we're willing to move overseas."

INSTRUCTIONS

Access the *Code of Business Conduct* of The Dow Chemical Company at http://www.dow.com/company/aboutdow/code_conduct/ethics_conduct.htm. Using this information and the ethical model, determine whether Phillip acted ethically by informing his wife of the impending plant closing.

Subsidiary Ledger Form

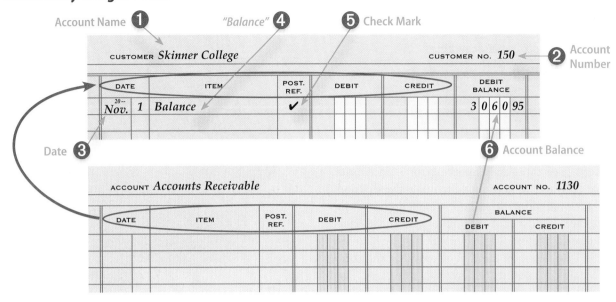

The accounts receivable ledger form is based on the general ledger form and contains the same columns, except the Credit Balance amount column. Because Accounts Receivable has a normal debit balance, the accounts receivable ledger form does not require a Credit Balance column. On November 1, ThreeGreen prepared a new page for Skinner College in the accounts receivable ledger, showing the account balance was $3,060.95.

> **Starting a New Page in a Subsidiary Ledger**
>
> ① Write the account name, Skinner College.
> ② Write the account number, 150.
> ③ Write the date, 20--, Nov. 1, in the Date column.
> ④ Write the word Balance in the Item column.
> ⑤ Place a check mark in the Post. Ref. column to show that the amount has been carried forward from a previous page rather than posted from a journal.
> ⑥ Write the balance, $3,060.95, in the Debit Balance column.

Sales Tax LO2

ThreeGreen sells merchandise to a variety of customers, including individuals, businesses, schools, and churches. ThreeGreen uses the special journals described in this chapter to record transactions related to sales.

Laws of most states and some cities require that a tax be collected from customers for each sale made. A tax on a sale of merchandise or services is called a **sales tax**. Sales tax rates are usually stated as a percentage of sales. Regardless of the tax rates used, accounting procedures are the same.

Businesses must file reports with the proper government agency and pay the amount of sales tax collected. Every business collecting a sales tax needs accurate records of the amount of (1) total sales and (2) total sales tax collected. The amount of sales tax collected is a business liability until paid to the government agency. Therefore, the sales tax amount is recorded in a separate liability account titled Sales Tax Payable. Sales

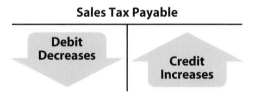

Tax Payable is increased by a credit and decreased by a debit, so it has a normal credit balance.

A state can choose to exempt from sales taxes some types of merchandise or sales to certain types of customers. For example, a sale of merchandise to a business that expects to resell the merchandise to its customers is normally exempt from sales tax. Only the final consumer of a product is normally required to pay sales tax. Some other common exemptions are:

1. Sales of necessities such as food, medicines, and clothing
2. Sales to nonprofit organizations such as schools, churches, and government agencies

Sales Journal

	DATE	ACCOUNT DEBITED	SALE NO.	POST. REF.	ACCOUNTS RECEIVABLE DEBIT	SALES CREDIT	SALES TAX PAYABLE CREDIT	
					1	2	3	
1								1
2								2
3								3

A **sales journal** is a special journal used to record only sales of merchandise on account. ThreeGreen uses a sales journal to record all sales of merchandise on account transactions.

The special amount columns in this sales journal are Accounts Receivable Debit, Sales Credit, and Sales Tax Payable Credit. With these special amount columns, each sale on account transaction can be recorded on one line of the sales journal.

Sales Invoice

When merchandise is sold on account, the seller prepares an invoice to document the sale. An invoice is a form that describes the goods or services sold, the quantity and the price, and the terms of the sale. [CONCEPT: Objective Evidence] The invoice used as a source document for recording a sale on account is often referred to as a sales invoice, a *sales ticket,* or a *sales slip.* While the seller considers an invoice for a sale on account to be a sales invoice, the same invoice is considered by the customer to be a purchase invoice.

Mary Prisock uses a template in an electronic spreadsheet to prepare ThreeGreen's sales invoices. She prints two copies of each sales invoice. The original copy is given to the customer. The second copy is used as the source document for the sale on account transaction. Sales invoices are numbered in sequence. Number 498 is the number of the sales invoice issued to Wells Apartments.

ThreeGreen operates in a state with a 6% sales tax rate. The total amount of the sale of merchandise in the invoice above is calculated as shown on page 288.

Sale on Account

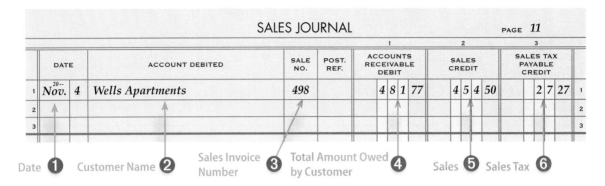

ThreeGreen sells on account only to businesses that have previously applied and been approved to purchase on account. Other customers must either pay cash or use a credit or debit card.

> November 4. Sold merchandise on account to Wells Apartments, $454.50, plus sales tax, $27.27; total, $481.77. Sales Invoice No. 498.

Price of Goods	×	Sales Tax Rate	=	Sales Tax
$454.50	×	6%	=	$27.27

Price of Goods	+	Sales Tax	=	Total Amount
$454.50	+	$27.27	=	$481.77

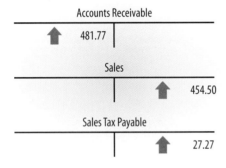

A sale on account transaction increases the amount to be collected later from a customer. Payment for this sale will be received at a later date. However, the sale is recorded at the time the sale is made because the sale has taken place and payment is due to ThreeGreen. [CONCEPT: Realization of Revenue]

Accounts Receivable is increased with a debit, so it is debited for the total amount of the sale plus sales tax, $481.77, to show the increase in this asset account. Sales increases with a credit; therefore, Sales is credited for the price of the goods, $454.50, to show the increase in this revenue account. Sales Tax Payable also increases with a credit, so a credit to Sales Tax Payable for the amount of sales tax, $27.27, increases this liability account.

The debit and credit amounts are recorded in special amount columns. So, writing the titles of the general ledger accounts in the Account Debited column is not necessary. However, the name of the customer is written in the Account Debited column to show who owes the amount.

Some states exempt schools and other nonprofit organizations from paying sales tax. A sale to a tax-exempt organization would be recorded using the same amount in the Sales Credit and Accounts Receivable Debit columns. No amount would be entered in the Sales Tax Payable Credit column.

Journalizing a Sale on Account

1. Write the date, 20--, Nov. 4, in the Date column.

2. Write the account name, Wells Apartments, in the Account Debited column.

3. Write the sales invoice number, 498, in the Sale No. column.

4. Write the total amount owed by the customer, $481.77, in the Accounts Receivable Debit column.

5. Write the sales amount, $454.50, in the Sales Credit column.

6. Write the sales tax amount, $27.27, in the Sales Tax Payable Credit column.

End of Lesson Review

LO1 Explain the relationship between the accounts receivable ledger and its controlling account.

LO2 Record sales on account using a sales journal.

Terms Review

selling price

markup

accounts receivable ledger

sales tax

sales journal

Audit your understanding

1. How are selling price and markup related?

2. What is the relationship between the accounts receivable ledger and its controlling account?

3. What column on a general ledger form is not on an accounts receivable ledger form?

4. What is the title of the general ledger account used to summarize the total amount due from all charge customers?

5. How are sales tax rates usually stated?

6. Why is sales tax collected considered a liability?

Work together 10-1

Accounting for sales on account

The sales journal and accounts receivable ledger forms for Classic Appliances are given in the *Working Papers*. Your instructor will guide you through the following examples. Save your work to complete Work Together 10-2.

1. Start a new page for an accounts receivable ledger account for Venice Café. The account number is 120, and the balance on September 1 of the current year is $390.34.

2. Using the current year, journalize the following transactions on page 9 of the sales journal. Classic Appliances operates in a state with a 6% sales tax. The sales invoice source document is abbreviated as S.

   Transactions:

   Sept. 2. Sold merchandise on account to Lenny Stanford, $1,600.00, plus sales tax. S221.

   6. Sold merchandise on account to Washington City Schools, $680.00. Washington City Schools is exempt from sales taxes. S222.

   7. Sold merchandise on account to Venice Café, $2,560.00, plus sales tax. S223.

   15. Sold merchandise on account to Washington City Schools, $1,849.00. S224.

On your own 10-1

Accounting for sales on account

The sales journal and accounts receivable ledger forms for Johnston Supplies are given in the *Working Papers*. Work this problem independently. Save your work to complete On Your Own 10-2.

1. Start a new page for an accounts receivable ledger account for Kelly Diller. The account number is 110, and the balance on June 1 of the current year is $185.00.

2. Using the current year, journalize the following transactions on page 6 of the sales journal. Johnston Supplies operates in a state with a 6% sales tax. The sales invoice source document is abbreviated as S.

   Transactions:

   June 2. Sold merchandise on account to Kelly Diller, $750.00, plus sales tax. S340.

   9. Sold merchandise on account to FJT Plumbing, $265.00, plus sales tax. S341.

   14. Sold merchandise on account to Roberts College, $692.00. Roberts College is exempt from sales taxes. S342.

   16. Sold merchandise on account to FJT Plumbing, $3,480.00, plus sales tax. S343.

LESSON
10-2 Posting from a Sales Journal

LO3 Post sales on account to an accounts receivable ledger and a general ledger.

Posting from a Sales Journal to an Accounts Receivable Ledger LO3

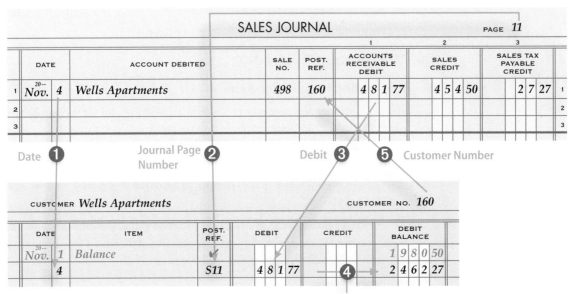

The only significant difference between the accounts payable and accounts receivable ledger forms is the column head above the balance column. The accounts payable ledger form has a Credit Balance column, while the accounts receivable ledger form shown above has a Debit Balance column. Because the ledger forms are similar, the process of posting transactions to the ledger forms is also similar.

A business should post sales transactions frequently to the accounts receivable ledger so that each customer account will show an up-to-date balance.

> **Posting from a Sales Journal to an Accounts Receivable Ledger**
>
> ❶ Write the date, 4, in the Date column of the account.
>
> ❷ Write the sales journal page number, S11, in the Post. Ref. column of the account. S is the abbreviation used for the sales journal.
>
> ❸ Write the debit amount, $481.77, in the Debit column of the customer account.
>
> ❹ Add the amount in the Debit column to the previous balance in the Debit Balance column ($1,980.50 + $481.77 = $2,462.27). Write the new account balance, $2,462.27, in the Debit Balance column.
>
> ❺ Write the customer number, 160, in the Post. Ref. column of the sales journal.

Totaling, Proving, and Ruling a Sales Journal

	DATE		ACCOUNT DEBITED	SALE NO.	POST. REF.	ACCOUNTS RECEIVABLE DEBIT (1)	SALES CREDIT (2)	SALES TAX PAYABLE CREDIT (3)	
1	20-- Nov.	4	Wells Apartments	498		4 8 1 77	4 5 4 50	2 7 27	1
2		5	Skinner College	499		1 9 0 8 00	1 9 0 8 00		2
3		9	Lake Automotive	500		6 0 6 32	5 7 2 00	3 4 32	3
4		11	Palmer Dentistry	501		7 6 8 50	7 2 5 00	4 3 50	4
5		16	Belk & Jensen	502		1 7 5 2 18	1 6 5 3 00	9 9 18	5
6		19	Wells Apartments	503		2 5 4 9 30	2 4 0 5 00	1 4 4 30	6
7		24	Edmonds Hospital	504		1 6 7 48	1 5 8 00	9 48	7
8		24	Skinner College	505		3 3 4 00	3 3 4 00		8
9		29	Palmer Dentistry	506		4 5 3 68	4 2 8 00	2 5 68	9
10		30	*Totals*			9 0 2 1 23	8 6 3 7 50	3 8 3 73	10
11									11
12									12
13									13
14									14
15									15

SALES JOURNAL   PAGE *11*

Date ❷   "Totals" ❸   Single Rule ❶   Column Totals ❹   Double Rule ❺

At the end of each month, ThreeGreen totals, proves, and rules its sales journal. The proof for ThreeGreen's sales journal is calculated below.

The two totals, $9,021.23, are equal. Equality of debits and credits in ThreeGreen's sales journal for November is proved.

Totaling and Ruling a Sales Journal

❶ Rule a single line across all amount columns directly below the last entry to indicate that all the columns are to be added.

❷ On the next line, write the date, 30, in the Date column.

❸ Write the word Totals in the Account Debited column.

❹ Write each column total below the single rule.

❺ Rule double lines across all amount columns to show that the totals have been verified as correct.

Column Title	Debit Totals	Credit Totals
Accounts Receivable Debit......................	$9,021.23	
Sales Credit...		$8,637.50
Sales Tax Payable Credit........................		383.73
Totals	$9,021.23	$9,021.23

Posting Totals of a Sales Journal to a General Ledger

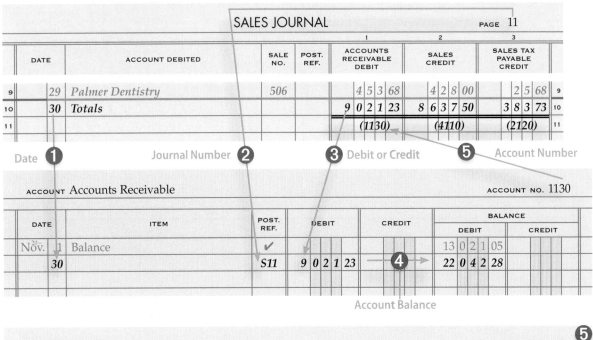

Posting Special Amount Columns of a Sales Journal

① Write the date, 30, in the Date column of the accounts.

② Write the sales journal page number, S11, in the Post. Ref. column of the accounts.

③ For each special amount column and account, write the column total in the Debit or Credit column of the related account.

④ For each account, calculate and write the new account balance in the Balance Debit or Credit column.

⑤ In the sales journal, write the general ledger account number in parentheses below each special amount column total.

End of Lesson Review

LO3 Post sales on account to an accounts receivable ledger and a general ledger.

Audit your understanding

1. Which accounts are impacted, and how, by the posting of the special columns of a sales journal?

2. List the five steps for posting transactions to accounts receivable ledger forms.

Work together 10-2

Posting from a sales journal

Use the sales journal and accounts receivable ledger forms for Work Together 10-1. Selected general ledger accounts for Classic Appliances are given in the *Working Papers*. Your instructor will guide you through the following examples. Save your work to complete Work Together 10-4.

1. Post the transactions from the sales journal to the accounts receivable ledger.

2. Total, prove, and rule the sales journal.

3. Post the sales journal to the general ledger.

On your own 10-2

Posting from a sales journal

Use the sales journal and accounts receivable ledger forms for On Your Own 10-1. Selected general ledger accounts for Johnston Supplies are given in the *Working Papers*. Work this problem independently. Save your work to complete On Your Own 10-4.

1. Post the transactions from the sales journal to the accounts receivable ledger.

2. Total, prove, and rule the sales journal.

3. Post the sales journal to the general ledger.

©CANDICE CUSACK, ISTOCK

LESSON
10-3 Accounting for Cash and Credit Card Sales

LO4 Record cash and credit card sales using a cash receipts journal.

LO5 Journalize cash receipts on account using a cash receipts journal.

Processing Sales Transactions LO4

A sale in which the customer pays for the total amount of the sale at the time of the transaction is called a **cash sale**. ThreeGreen accepts cash, credit cards, and debit cards. Credit card and debit card sales are treated as cash sales because the business receives its cash in a very short time. A specialized computer used to collect, store, and report all the information about a sales transaction is called a **point-of-sale (POS) terminal**. Before any sale

VEF/SHUTTERSTOCK.COM

7 805386 774629

The UPC symbol on merchandise is scanned to enter data into a point-of-sale (POS) terminal.

is entered, the number, description, price, and quantity on hand of each item of merchandise are stored in the POS terminal. When processing a sale, the sales clerk uses a scanning device to scan the Universal Product Code (UPC) symbol on the item.

The POS terminal matches the number represented by the UPC symbol with the merchandise number to obtain the description and price of the merchandise. When all the merchandise has been scanned, the sales clerk enters the customer's method of payment. For a cash sale, the sales clerk enters the amount of cash given by the customer, and the POS terminal computes the amount of change. For credit and debit card sales, the customer swipes the card in the card scanner and identifies whether the card is a credit or debit card. The POS system produces a receipt that contains detailed information about the sale.

Periodically, ThreeGreen instructs the POS terminal to print a report of all sales. The report that summarizes the cash and credit card sales of a point-of-sale terminal is called a **terminal summary**. A terminal summary is also known as a *Z tape*. ThreeGreen uses the terminal summary as the source document for recording sales in its journals. [CONCEPT: Objective Evidence] At any time, the POS system can produce a variety of reports to help management make decisions. For example:

1. A report of sales by sales clerk would assist management to analyze a sales clerk's efficiency.
2. A report of sales by time of day would assist management in scheduling sales clerks to match busy periods.
3. A report of the average sale amount would enable management to track customer buying habits.

TERMINAL SUMMARY		
ThreeGreen Products, Inc.		
Code:		35
Date:		11/4/--
Time:		19:34
VISA	033	
Sales		689.40
Sales Tax		41.36
Total		730.76
MasterCard	029	
Sales		784.60
Sales Tax		47.08
Total		831.68
Debit Cards	063	
Sales		2,184.50
Sales Tax		131.07
Total		2,315.57
Cash	162	
Sales		2,621.50
Sales Tax		157.29
Total		2,778.79
Totals		
Sales		6,280.00
Sales Tax		376.80
Total		6,656.80

294 Chapter 10 Accounting for Sales and Cash Receipts

Processing Credit Cards

Using a credit card will produce a different outcome for a consumer than using a debit card, but merchandising businesses account for them as if they were the same. Therefore, in this chapter, the term *credit card* will include both debit and credit cards.

Sales information for credit card sales is stored in the POS terminals. Periodically, ThreeGreen instructs the terminal to produce a summary and print a report of credit card sales. A report of credit card sales produced by a point-of-sale terminal is called a **batch report**. A batch report can be detailed, showing every credit card sale. Or, the batch report can be a summary, showing only the number and total of sales by credit card type. The process of preparing a batch report from a point-of-sale terminal is called **batching out**.

There are several methods for a business to process credit card sales. ThreeGreen has contracted with an independent company, CreditCorp, to process its credit card sales. When ThreeGreen batches out, the POS terminal transmits a summary batch report to CreditCorp. CreditCorp combines the batch reports for all of its customers and submits the information to a credit card association, such as VISA or MasterCard. The association collects the funds from the banks that issued the cards and transfers the funds to CreditCorp. For example, suppose a customer having a VISA card issued by Capital National Bank buys $500.00 of merchandise from ThreeGreen. When ThreeGreen batches out, a message goes to CreditCorp with the credit card number and amount of the sale. When VISA receives the information, it collects $500.00 from Capital National and transfers $500.00 to CreditCorp, who then deposits the funds to ThreeGreen's bank account. The cash is typically deposited in ThreeGreen's account within two to three business days.

EDULEITE/ISTOCKPHOTO.COM

BATCH REPORT		
MERCHANT:	02984893	155
TERMINAL:		934844
DATE:	11/4/--	19:35
BATCH:		37
VISA		
COUNT		033
SALES		743.01
RETURNS		12.25
NET		730.76
MASTERCARD		
COUNT		029
SALES		869.83
RETURNS		38.15
NET		831.68
DEBIT CARDS		
COUNT		063
SALES		2,320.87
RETURNS		5.30
NET		2,315.57
TOTALS		
COUNT		125
SALES		3,933.71
RETURNS		55.70
NET		3,878.01
CONTROL NUMBER: 0934849534		

POS terminals are often used to support a perpetual inventory system by maintaining an up-to-date quantity of all merchandise on hand.

Cash Receipts Journal

<table>
<tr><td colspan="16" align="center">CASH RECEIPTS JOURNAL</td><td>PAGE</td></tr>
<tr><td></td><td></td><td></td><td></td><td>1</td><td>2</td><td>3</td><td>4</td><td>5</td><td>6</td><td>7</td></tr>
<tr><td rowspan="2">DATE</td><td rowspan="2">ACCOUNT TITLE</td><td rowspan="2">DOC. NO.</td><td rowspan="2">POST. REF.</td><td colspan="2" align="center">GENERAL</td><td>ACCOUNTS RECEIVABLE CREDIT</td><td>SALES CREDIT</td><td>SALES TAX PAYABLE CREDIT</td><td>SALES DISCOUNT DEBIT</td><td>CASH DEBIT</td></tr>
<tr><td>DEBIT</td><td>CREDIT</td></tr>
<tr><td>1</td><td></td><td></td><td></td><td></td><td></td><td></td><td></td><td></td><td></td><td></td><td>1</td></tr>
<tr><td>2</td><td></td><td></td><td></td><td></td><td></td><td></td><td></td><td></td><td></td><td></td><td>2</td></tr>
<tr><td>3</td><td></td><td></td><td></td><td></td><td></td><td></td><td></td><td></td><td></td><td></td><td>3</td></tr>
</table>

ThreeGreen has many transactions involving the receipt of cash, so it uses a special journal for recording cash transactions. A **cash receipts journal** is a special journal used to record only cash receipt transactions.

Only those columns needed to record cash receipt transactions are included in ThreeGreen's cash receipts journal. Since all cash receipt transactions affect Cash, a special column is provided for this general ledger account. In addition, ThreeGreen has many cash receipt transactions affecting Accounts Receivable, Sales, and Sales Tax Payable. Therefore, special columns are provided in ThreeGreen's cash receipts journal for these general ledger accounts.

To encourage early payment, ThreeGreen allows some customers who purchase merchandise on account to take a deduction from the invoice amount. A cash discount on a sale taken by the customer is called a **sales discount**. When a sales discount is taken, the customer pays less than the invoice amount previously recorded in Accounts Receivable. Sales discounts reduce the amount of cash ThreeGreen receives on sales on account. Because customers often take these discounts, ThreeGreen's cash receipts journal has a special column titled Sales Discount Debit. Cash receipts that do not occur often are recorded in the General columns.

Cash and Credit Card Sales

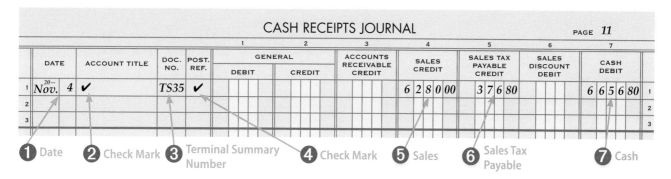

| | | | DATE | ACCOUNT TITLE | DOC. NO. | POST. REF. | GENERAL DEBIT | GENERAL CREDIT | ACCOUNTS RECEIVABLE CREDIT | SALES CREDIT | SALES TAX PAYABLE CREDIT | SALES DISCOUNT DEBIT | CASH DEBIT | |

CASH RECEIPTS JOURNAL — PAGE 11

DATE	ACCOUNT TITLE	DOC. NO.	POST. REF.	GENERAL DEBIT	GENERAL CREDIT	ACCOUNTS RECEIVABLE CREDIT	SALES CREDIT	SALES TAX PAYABLE CREDIT	SALES DISCOUNT DEBIT	CASH DEBIT
Nov. 4	✔	TS35	✔				6 2 8 0 00	3 7 6 80		6 6 5 6 80

① Date ② Check Mark ③ Terminal Summary Number ④ Check Mark ⑤ Sales ⑥ Sales Tax Payable ⑦ Cash

At the end of each week, ThreeGreen batches out and prints a terminal summary, which is assigned a sequential number by the POS terminal. The terminal summary serves as the source document for weekly cash and credit card sales transactions. The total of the terminal summary is recorded as a single cash sale transaction. ThreeGreen also batches out and prints a terminal summary at the end of each month so the company can analyze its monthly sales.

> **November 4. Recorded cash and credit card sales, $6,280.00, plus sales tax, $376.80; total, $6,656.80. Terminal Summary 35.**

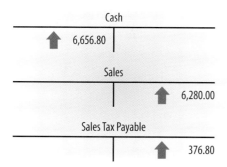

Cash
▲ 6,656.80

Sales
▲ 6,280.00

Sales Tax Payable
▲ 376.80

Management is responsible for determining how often the business should batch out, deposit cash, and record sales in the sales journal. Most businesses perform these tasks at the end of every business day. (The weekly processing demonstrated in this textbook was selected to simplify the textbook illustrations and problems.)

The cash from sales, $2,778.79, as shown on the terminal summary, is deposited directly in the bank. The cash from credit card sales is received two or three days later when CreditCorp transfers $3,878.01 to ThreeGreen's account at American Bank. The two deposits equal the total sales reported on the terminal summary.

Cash Sales	+	Credit Card Sales	=	Total Sales
$2,778.79	+	$3,878.01	=	$6,656.80

Because **Cash** is increased by a debit, **Cash** is debited for the total sales and sales tax, $6,656.80, to show the increase in this asset account. The **Sales** account is increased by a credit, so **Sales** is credited for the total price of all goods sold, $6,280.00, to show the increase in this revenue account. The **Sales Tax Payable** account is also increased by a credit. Therefore, **Sales Tax Payable** is credited for the total sales tax, $376.80, to show the increase in this liability account.

Journalizing Cash and Credit Card Sales

① Write the date, 20--, Nov. 4, in the Date column.

② Place a check mark in the Account Title column to show that no account title needs to be written. The debit and credit amounts will be recorded in special amount columns.

③ Write the terminal summary document number, TS35, in the Doc. No. column.

④ Place a check mark in the Post. Ref. column to show that amounts on this line are not to be posted individually.

⑤ Write the sales amount, $6,280.00, in the Sales Credit column.

⑥ Write the sales tax amount, $376.80, in the Sales Tax Payable Credit column.

⑦ Write the cash amount, $6,656.80, in the Cash Debit column.

Cash Receipts on Account LO5

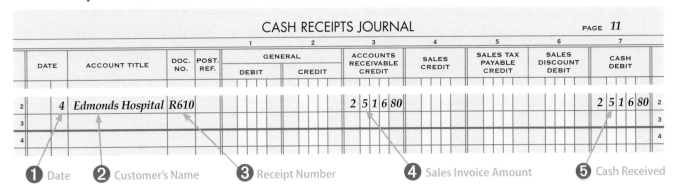

CASH RECEIPTS JOURNAL

PAGE 11

	DATE	ACCOUNT TITLE	DOC. NO.	POST. REF.	GENERAL DEBIT	GENERAL CREDIT	ACCOUNTS RECEIVABLE CREDIT	SALES CREDIT	SALES TAX PAYABLE CREDIT	SALES DISCOUNT DEBIT	CASH DEBIT	
2	4	Edmonds Hospital	R610				2 5 1 6 80				2 5 1 6 80	2
3												3
4												4

① Date **②** Customer's Name **③** Receipt Number **④** Sales Invoice Amount **⑤** Cash Received

ThreeGreen prepares a receipt whenever cash is received on account from a customer. The receipts are prenumbered so that all receipts can be accounted for. Receipts are prepared in duplicate. The original receipt is given to the customer. The copy of the receipt is used as the source document for the cash receipt on account transaction. [CONCEPT: Objective Evidence]

A transaction in which cash is received on account will increase the balance in Cash and decrease the future amount to be collected from the customer, so the balance in Accounts Receivable decreases. Cash is debited for the amount of cash received, $2,516.80, to show the increase in this asset account, and Accounts Receivable is credited for $2,516.80 to show the decrease in this asset account.

> **November 4. Received cash on account from Edmonds Hospital, $2,516.80, covering S448. Receipt No. 610.**

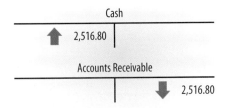

Cash
⬆ 2,516.80

Accounts Receivable
⬇ 2,516.80

⤷ Journalizing Cash Receipts on Account

① Write the date, 4, in the Date column.

② Write only the account name, Edmonds Hospital, in the Account Title column. The debit and credit amounts are entered in special amount columns. Therefore, the titles of the two general ledger accounts do not need to be written in the Account Title column.

③ Write the receipt number, R610, in the Doc. No. column.

④ Write the credit amount, $2,516.80, in the Accounts Receivable Credit column.

⑤ Write the debit amount, $2,516.80, in the Cash Debit column.

Merchants are charged a fee every time a customer pays with a credit card. The fee can be a combination of a percent of the transaction and a charge per transaction. The fee is negotiated between the merchant and the business contracted to process the transactions. For example, a company having a 2% plus $0.20 per transaction fee would pay a $2.20 fee on a $100.00 sale. For this reason, some merchants offer discounts to customers who pay cash.

Calculating Cash Receipts on Account with Sales Discount

ThreeGreen offers credit terms of 2/10, n/30 to selected customers. When a customer pays the amount owed within ten days, ThreeGreen records a 2% sales discount. If the discount is not taken, the net amount is due in 30 days.

On October 27, ThreeGreen sold merchandise on account to Palmer Dentistry for $1,450.00. On November 5, ThreeGreen received payment for this sale on account within the discount period. Because it made the payment within the discount period, Palmer Dentistry was entitled to deduct 2% from the $1,450.00 it owed.

	Sales Invoice Amount	×	Sales Discount Rate	=	Sales Discount
	$1,450.00	×	2%	=	$29.00

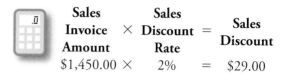

International Financial Reporting Standards

In the United States, accounting rules and principles are called generally accepted accounting principles, or GAAP. All publicly held U.S. companies must follow these rules when preparing financial statements.

Historically, each country had its own set of rules and regulations, which had to be followed when preparing financial statements in that country. In earlier times, when most companies only operated in their own countries, this was not a problem. However, as international trade increased, an effort was made to develop a set of international accounting rules.

The International Accounting Standards Board (IASB) is responsible for the development and publication of International Financial Reporting Standards (IFRS, pronounced ī-fers). Beginning in 1973, acceptance of international accounting standards was very slow. Only a few countries were willing to follow them.

Recently, the momentum has increased. Today, more than 110 countries allow businesses to use international accounting standards. The United States is slowly moving toward acceptance of IFRS. Currently, foreign private companies are allowed to prepare and issue financial statements in the United States following IFRS. In February 2010, the Securities and Exchange Commission (SEC) issued a release which stated, "... we continue to encourage the convergence of U.S. GAAP and IFRS and expect that the differences will become fewer and narrower over time...."

Someday, there may be one set of international accounting standards with which all countries will comply.

CRITICAL THINKING

1. What problems do you think the IASB might encounter when attempting to develop one set of international accounting standards?
2. The AICPA hosts an IFRS Resources site at www .ifrs.com. Go to that website and research the progress of one new standard. Write a report summarizing your findings.

Source: Securities and Exchange Commission Release Nos. 33-9109; 34-61578 Commission Statement in Support of Convergence and Global Accounting Standards, dated February 24, 2010.

©FONTMONSTER, ISTOCK

Journalizing Cash Receipts on Account with Sales Discounts

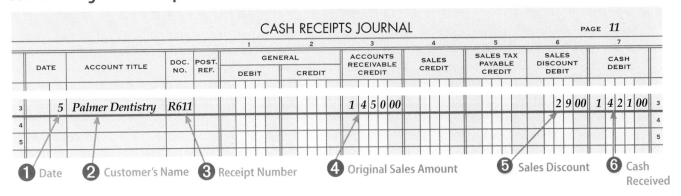

CASH RECEIPTS JOURNAL   PAGE 11

						1 GENERAL DEBIT	2 GENERAL CREDIT	3 ACCOUNTS RECEIVABLE CREDIT	4 SALES CREDIT	5 SALES TAX PAYABLE CREDIT	6 SALES DISCOUNT DEBIT	7 CASH DEBIT	
	DATE	ACCOUNT TITLE	DOC. NO.	POST. REF.									
3	5	*Palmer Dentistry*	R611					1 4 5 0 00			2 9 00	1 4 2 1 00	3
4													4
5													5

① Date ② Customer's Name ③ Receipt Number ④ Original Sales Amount ⑤ Sales Discount ⑥ Cash Received

Sales discounts are recorded in a general ledger account titled **Sales Discount**. Since sales discounts decrease sales, **Sales Discount** is a contra account to **Sales** and has a normal debit balance.

Sales Discount

| Debit Increases | Credit Decreases |

A business could debit **Sales** for the amount of the sales discount. However, better information is provided to management if these amounts are debited to **Sales Discount**. It enables business managers to determine the cost effectiveness of encouraging early payments.

> November 5. Received cash on account from Palmer Dentistry, $1,421.00, covering Sales Invoice No. 462 for $1,450.00, less 2% discount, $29.00. Receipt No. 611.

If a customer does not pay the amount owed within the discount period, the full invoice amount is due. If Palmer Dentistry had not taken advantage of the discount, the journal entry would be a debit to **Cash**, $1,450.00, and a credit to **Accounts Receivable**, $1,450.00.

↘ Journalizing Cash Receipts on Account with Sales Discounts

① Write the date, **5**, in the Date column.

② Write the customer's name, **Palmer Dentistry**, in the Account Title column.

③ Write the receipt number, **R611**, in the Doc. No. column.

④ Write the original invoice amount, **$1,450.00**, in the Accounts Receivable Credit column.

⑤ Write the amount of sales discount, **$29.00**, in the Sales Discount Debit column.

⑥ Write the amount of cash received, **$1,421.00**, in the Cash Debit column.

Cash
↑ 1,421.00

Accounts Receivable
↓ 1,450.00

Sales Discount
↑ 29.00

STOCKBYTE/GETTY IMAGES

End of Lesson Review

LO4 Record cash and credit card sales using a cash receipts journal.

LO5 Journalize cash receipts on account using a cash receipts journal.

Terms Review

cash sale

point-of-sale (POS) terminal

terminal summary

batch report

batching out

cash receipts journal

sales discount

Audit your understanding

1. How does a POS terminal determine the price of an item?
2. What are the two types of batch reports?
3. What is meant by 2/10, n/30 credit terms?

Work together 10-3

Accounting for cash and credit card sales

The cash receipts journal for Classic Appliances is given in the *Working Papers*. Your instructor will guide you through the following examples. Save your work to complete Work Together 10-4.

Using the current year, journalize the following transactions on page 9 of the cash receipts journal. Source documents are abbreviated as follows: receipt, R; terminal summary, TS.

Transactions:

Sept. 3. Received cash on account from Lenny Stafford covering S216, $2,189.36, less 2% discount. R264.

6. Recorded cash and credit card sales, $5,326.30, plus sales tax, $298.15; total, $5,624.45. TS38.

8. Received cash on account from Venice Café covering S218 for $390.34, less 2% discount. R265.

20. Recorded cash and credit card sales, $5,624.45, plus sales tax, $320.59; total, $5,945.04. TS39.

28. Received cash on account from Washington City Schools covering S199 for $1,509.45. R266.

On your own 10-3

Accounting for cash and credit card sales

The cash receipts journal for Johnston Supplies is given in the *Working Papers*. Work this problem independently. Save your work to complete On Your Own 10-4.

Using the current year, journalize the following transactions on page 6 of the cash receipts journal. Source documents are abbreviated as follows: receipt, R; terminal summary, TS.

Transactions:

June 3. Received cash on account from Kelly Diller, covering S330 for $185.00, less 2% discount. R408.

5. Recorded cash and credit card sales, $2,583.00, plus sales tax, $154.98; total, $2,737.98. TS23.

7. Received cash on account from FJT Plumbing, covering S332 for $2,989.20, less 2% discount. R409.

12. Received cash on account from Roberts College, $381.60, covering S319. R410.

18. Recorded cash and credit card sales, $3,825.30, plus sales tax, $229.52; total, $4,054.82. TS24.

Accounting for Cash and Credit Card Sales   **Lesson 10-3**   **301**

LESSON
10-4 Posting from a Cash Receipts Journal

LO6 Post cash receipts to an accounts receivable ledger and a general ledger.

LO7 Prepare a schedule of accounts receivable.

Posting from a Cash Receipts Journal to an Accounts Receivable Ledger **LO6**

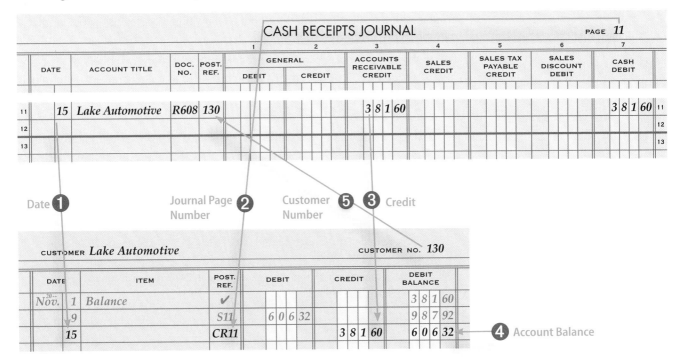

Each entry in the Accounts Receivable Credit column of the cash receipts journal is posted to the accounts receivable ledger account of the customer shown in the Account Title column. The updated accounts receivable ledger form provides a history of activity with the customer. If a customer questions a charge on an invoice or whether a payment was credited to its account, the posting references on the accounts receivable ledger form enable the company to locate the sales invoices and receipts supporting each transaction.

> **Posting from a Cash Receipts Journal to an Accounts Receivable Ledger**
>
> ① Write the date, 15, in the Date column of the account.
>
> ② Write the cash receipts journal page number, CR11, in the Post. Ref. column of the account. *CR* is the abbreviation for the cash receipts journal.
>
> ③ Write the credit amount, $381.60, in the Credit column of the customer account.
>
> ④ Subtract the amount in the Credit column from the previous balance in the Debit Balance column ($987.92 − $381.60 = $606.32). Write the new balance, $606.32, in the Debit Balance column.
>
> ⑤ Write the customer number, 130, in the Post. Ref. column of the cash receipts journal.

Totaling, Proving, and Ruling a Cash Receipts Journal

					GENERAL		ACCOUNTS RECEIVABLE CREDIT	SALES CREDIT	SALES TAX PAYABLE CREDIT	SALES DISCOUNT DEBIT	CASH DEBIT	
	DATE	ACCOUNT TITLE	DOC. NO.	POST. REF.	DEBIT	CREDIT						
25	30 ✔		TS40 ✔					3 1 8 4 00	1 9 1 04		3 3 7 5 04	25
26	30	Totals					11 6 4 1 30	43 1 1 9 33	2 3 8 1 46	7 2 25	57 0 6 9 84	26
27												27

CASH RECEIPTS JOURNAL PAGE **11**

The procedures for totaling, proving, and ruling a cash receipts journal are the same as the procedures described for ThreeGreen's sales journal. At the end of each month, equality of debits and credits is proved for a cash receipts journal. The proof for ThreeGreen's cash receipts journal for November is calculated as shown below. The two totals, $57,142.09, are equal. Equality of debits and credits is proved.

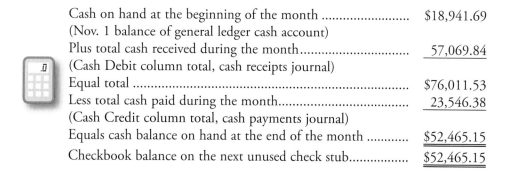

Column Title	Debit Totals	Credit Totals
General Debit	———	
General Credit		———
Accounts Receivable Credit		$11,641.30
Sales Credit		43,119.33
Sales Tax Payable Credit		2,381.46
Sales Discount Debit	$ 72.25	
Cash Debit	57,069.84	
Totals	$57,142.09	$57,142.09

Proving Cash at the End of a Month

After the cash receipts journal is proved at the end of each month, cash is proved. ThreeGreen's cash proof at the end of November is calculated as shown. The balance on the next unused check stub is $52,465.15. Since the balance on the next unused check stub is the same as the cash proof, cash is proved.

Cash on hand at the beginning of the month	$18,941.69
(Nov. 1 balance of general ledger cash account)	
Plus total cash received during the month.............................	57,069.84
(Cash Debit column total, cash receipts journal)	
Equal total	$76,011.53
Less total cash paid during the month....................................	23,546.38
(Cash Credit column total, cash payments journal)	
Equals cash balance on hand at the end of the month	$52,465.15
Checkbook balance on the next unused check stub.................	$52,465.15

Posting Special Amount Column Totals of a Cash Receipts Journal to a General Ledger

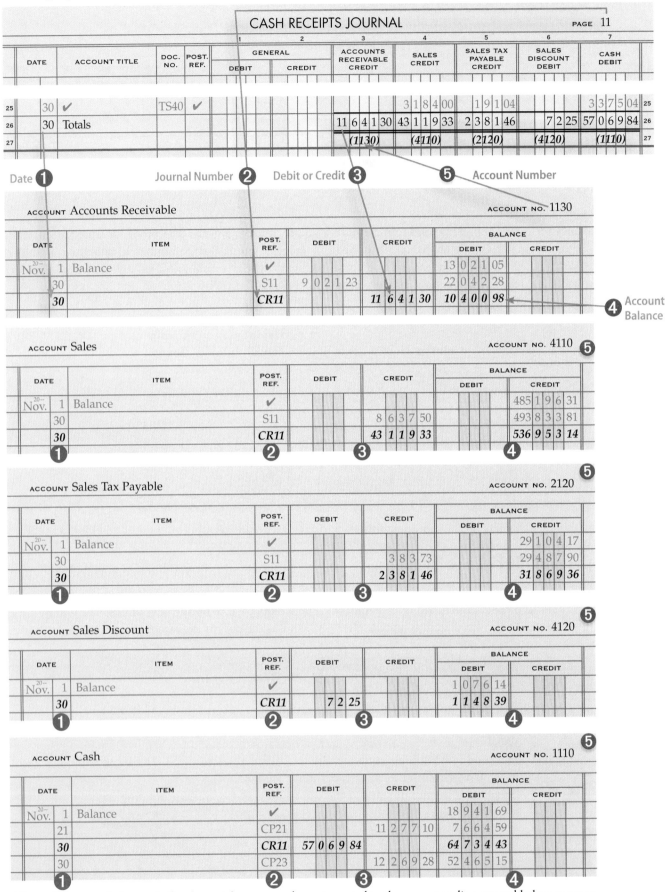

After cash is proved, the total of each special amount column is posted to the corresponding general ledger account.

Analyzing Home Sales

Donovan Homes builds homes in select communities across the nation. The company is organized into geographic regions under the control of regional managers. Each regional manager is responsible for maximizing sales within that region.

Customers can select from over 25 house plans and contract for upgrades such as extra garage space, granite counter tops, and hardwood floors. The calculation of the sales price for a home begins with the base price for the selected model. The base price is multiplied by an adjustment ratio that reflects differences in building costs among the regions. For example, a $256,000 base price home built in the Atlantic region is multiplied by an adjustment factor of 1.67, resulting in an adjusted base price of $427,520. Any upgrades are added to the adjusted base price to calculate the total sales price.

The national sales manager is preparing for a sales meeting and wants an analysis of home sales for the past year.

OPEN THE SPREADSHEET TLA_CH10
Answer the following questions:

1. What were the most and least popular models? Identify the total sales for these two models in millions of dollars, e.g., $7.8 million.

2. Last year, Donovan Homes implemented a special upgrades promotion for the Newport model. How successful was that promotion in the Northeast region, as measured by the average upgrades?

3. The architect of the Coastal, Islands, and Tidewater models will be attending the sales meeting. Donovan Homes may suggest that the architect modify the plans for any model that is not selling well. How many of each of these models were sold?

©DAN BACHMAN, ISTOCK

↘ Posting Special Amount Column Totals of a Cash Receipts Journal

1 Write the date, 30, in the Date column of each account.

2 Write the cash receipts journal page number, CR11, in the Post. Ref. column of each account. The abbreviation *CR11* means page 11 of the cash receipts journal.

3 For each special amount column and account, write the special amount column total in the Debit or Credit column of the account.

4 For each account, calculate and write the new account balance in the Balance Debit or Credit column.

5 Return to the cash receipts journal and write the general ledger account number in parentheses below each special amount column total.

PHOTOALTO AGENCY RF COLLECTIONS/GETTY IMAGES

Occupational Fraud: Theft at Pirate's Treasure Miniature Golf

Craig Carpenter thought he had designed an effective system of internal controls for his new business, Pirate's Treasure Miniature Golf. Then, one day, some green golf balls appeared in the collection containers at the 18th hole. Pirate's Treasure uses blue golf balls.

The 18th hole is a key internal control for most miniature golf courses. Each attendant begins the day with an established number of balls provided by another employee or the owner. The last hole is designed to limit the player to a single shot, capturing the ball regardless of the accuracy of the putt. If the player sinks the putt in a single shot—a hole-in-one—the ball drops into a separate container and a bell rings notifying the attendant to issue a "Free Play" certificate.

Each morning, Craig arrives at the course well before it opens. He counts the number of balls in both containers at the 18th hole. Then he compares the number of balls in the hole-in-one container to the number of pre-numbered "Free Play" certificates issued the previous day. He also reconciles the total number of balls in both containers to the revenue recorded in the point-of-sale terminal.

Since Craig opened Pirate's Treasure, there has never been a problem reconciling the number of "Free Play" certificates. In contrast, the total number of golf balls is frequently a few short of the number indicated by the cash register. Craig knows why. He has witnessed some energetic customers accidently hit their shots over the fence, across the parking lot, and down the street.

But the green golf balls trouble him. Especially so, considering that revenue at the course did not increase as expected during the summer months. Unsure what he should do, he downloaded his sales data from the point-of-sale terminal and asked you to "take a look."

Performing a forensic investigation requires a full understanding of the business. Your first step is to spend an evening playing several rounds at Pirate's Treasure. As you are playing, you pay particular attention to the color of balls being used and make a note of anything unusual.

Nothing appears out of the ordinary until later in the evening when you notice a group of individuals playing with green golf balls. As they finish the 17th hole, the group walks right past the 18th hole. They return their golf balls to the attendant and talk a while before leaving the course.

Based on this information, you believe an employee may be providing selected customers with his own green golf balls. In exchange for not playing the 18th hole, he may be allowing them to play at a discounted price with the proceeds going into his own pocket. Using a different color golf ball would enable him to keep track of his fraudulent activity. Unfortunately for the employee, it appears that some of those individuals decided to play the 18th hole with their green golf balls.

INSTRUCTIONS

Open the spreadsheet FA_CH10 and use the sales data in the workbook to answer the following questions:

1. Do the hourly sales for any employee differ significantly from the hourly sales trends of other employees?

2. Does the sales trend for any employee support your suspicions of fraud?

3. What would you suggest as the next step in your forensic investigation?

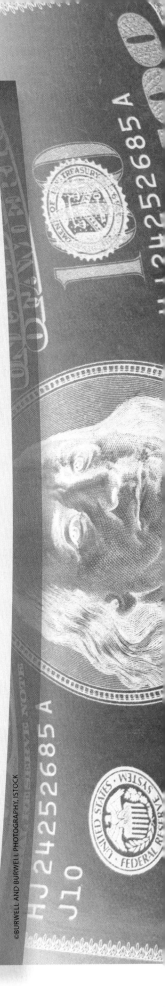

Completed Accounts Receivable Ledger

CUSTOMER Belk & Jensen   **CUSTOMER NO.** 110

DATE		ITEM	POST. REF.	DEBIT	CREDIT	DEBIT BALANCE
Nov. 20--	1	Balance	✔			3 1 5 8 80
	6		CR11		2 1 6 2 40	9 9 6 40
	16		S11	1 7 5 2 18		2 7 4 8 58
	29		CR11		9 9 6 40	1 7 5 2 18

CUSTOMER Edmonds Hospital   **CUSTOMER NO.** 120

DATE		ITEM	POST. REF.	DEBIT	CREDIT	DEBIT BALANCE
Nov. 20--	1	Balance	✔			2 9 8 9 20
	4		CR11		2 5 1 6 80	4 7 2 40
	24		S11	1 6 7 48		6 3 9 88

CUSTOMER Lake Automotive   **CUSTOMER NO.** 130

DATE		ITEM	POST. REF.	DEBIT	CREDIT	DEBIT BALANCE
Nov. 20--	1	Balance	✔			3 8 1 60
	9		S11	6 0 6 32		9 8 7 92
	15		CR11		3 8 1 60	6 0 6 32

CUSTOMER Palmer Dentistry   **CUSTOMER NO.** 140

DATE		ITEM	POST. REF.	DEBIT	CREDIT	DEBIT BALANCE
Nov. 20--	1	Balance	✔			1 4 5 0 00
	5		CR11		1 4 5 0 00	
	11		S11	7 6 8 50		7 6 8 50
	29		S11	4 5 3 68		1 2 2 2 18

CUSTOMER Skinner College   **CUSTOMER NO.** 150

DATE		ITEM	POST. REF.	DEBIT	CREDIT	DEBIT BALANCE
Nov. 20--	1	Balance	✔			3 0 6 0 95
	4		CR11		4 8 2 60	2 5 7 8 35
	5		S11	1 9 0 8 00		4 4 8 6 35
	24		S11	3 3 4 00		4 8 2 0 35
	28		CR11		1 6 7 1 00	3 1 4 9 35

CUSTOMER Wells Apartments   **CUSTOMER NO.** 160

DATE		ITEM	POST. REF.	DEBIT	CREDIT	DEBIT BALANCE
Nov. 20--	1	Balance	✔			1 9 8 0 50
	4		S11	4 8 1 77		2 4 6 2 27
	12		CR11		1 9 8 0 50	4 8 1 77
	19		S11	2 5 4 9 30		3 0 3 1 07

ThreeGreen's accounts receivable ledger has been posted for the month of November.

Proving the Accounts Receivable Ledger LO7

ThreeGreen Products, Inc.						
Schedule of Accounts Receivable						
November 30, 20--						
Belk & Jensen	1	7	5	2	18	
Edmonds Hospital		6	3	9	88	
Lake Automotive		6	0	6	32	
Palmer Dentistry	1	2	2	2	18	
Skinner College	3	1	4	9	35	
Wells Apartments	3	0	3	1	07	
Total Accounts Receivable	10	4	0	0	98	

A listing of customer accounts, account balances, and total amount due from all customers is called a **schedule of accounts receivable**. Some businesses call the listing the *accounts receivable trial balance*. A schedule of accounts receivable is prepared after all entries in a journal are posted. The balance of Accounts Receivable in the general ledger is $10,400.98. The total of the schedule of accounts receivable is $10,400.98. Because the two amounts are the same, the accounts receivable ledger is proved.

LO6 Post cash receipts to an accounts receivable ledger and a general ledger.

LO7 Prepare a schedule of accounts receivable.

Term Review

schedule of accounts receivable

Audit your understanding

1. From which column of the cash receipts journal are amounts posted individually to the accounts receivable ledger?

2. What is another name for the schedule of accounts receivable?

Work together 10-4

Posting from a cash receipts journal

Use the cash receipts journal for Work Together 10-3 and the accounts receivable and general ledger forms from Work Together 10-2. A blank form for a schedule of accounts receivable is given in the *Working Papers*. Your instructor will guide you through the following examples.

1. Post the transactions on the cash receipts journal to the accounts receivable ledger.

2. Total and prove the cash receipts journal.

3. Prove cash. On September 30, the balance on the next unused check stub was $17,608.96.

4. Rule the cash receipts journal.

5. Post the cash receipts journal to the general ledger.

6. Prepare a schedule of accounts receivable.

On your own 10-4

Posting from a cash receipts journal

Use the cash receipts journal for On Your Own 10-3 and the accounts receivable and general ledger forms from On Your Own 10-2. A blank form for a schedule of accounts receivable is given in the *Working Papers*. Work this problem independently.

1. Post the transactions on the cash receipts journal to the accounts receivable ledger.

2. Total and prove the cash receipts journal.

3. Prove cash. On June 30, the balance on the next unused check stub was $11,953.98.

4. Rule the cash receipts journal.

5. Post the cash receipts journal to the general ledger.

6. Prepare a schedule of accounts receivable.

A Look at Accounting Software

In a manual accounting system, accounting for a sales transaction requires entry in a sales journal and posting to both general and subsidiary ledgers. At each step, errors can occur. Accounting for cash receipts can be even more complicated and leads to many errors in the real world. A computerized accounting system simplifies both the journalizing and posting of these transactions.

You can see from the windows illustrated here how few entries users need to make to record the transactions. Since most calculations and all postings are directed by the system, the opportunity for error is greatly minimized and much time is saved. When sales reports are needed, they can be produced in seconds and customized easily. With a manual system, these reports can require hours. Requested changes in report formats can take equally as much time.

Creating a New Sales Invoice

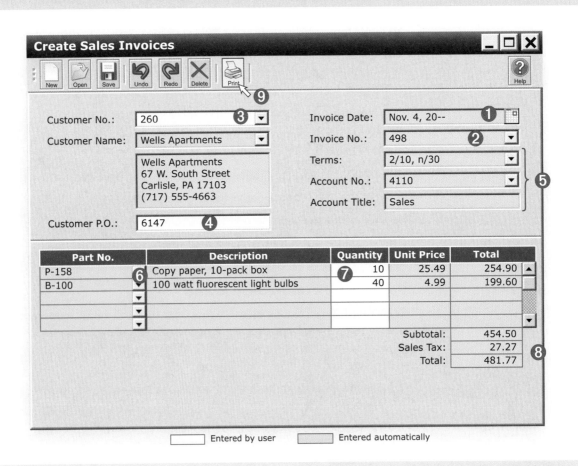

Entered by user   Entered automatically

❶ The current date is entered by the system. It can be changed if the sale occurred on an earlier date.

❷ The system automatically enters the next available sales invoice number.

❸ The customer can be entered either by number (as above) or by name. Information about the customer is displayed automatically.

❹ The source document for an entry in this window is the customer purchase order. The user enters the purchase order number here.

❺ The system displays the company's standard terms as well as the general ledger account number and title. The terms or the account number can be changed if appropriate.

❻ Part numbers are selected from list boxes. Part descriptions are automatically retrieved from the inventory file.

❼ The user enters the quantity. The unit price is entered by the system from the inventory file. The price can be overwritten if it has changed or if the customer has been offered a lower price.

⑧ The system calculates line and invoice totals. Sales tax is computed and added automatically, but can be deleted if the customer is exempt from sales tax.

⑨ Clicking Save posts the transaction to **Sales**, **Accounts Receivable**, **Sales Tax Payable**, and the customer's account. Inventory quantities are also updated. The user clicks **Print** to print the invoice. Print cannot be selected until the window is saved. Multiple copies will probably be printed. Usually, two or more copies go to the customer and one is retained in the company files.

Receiving a Cash Payment on Account

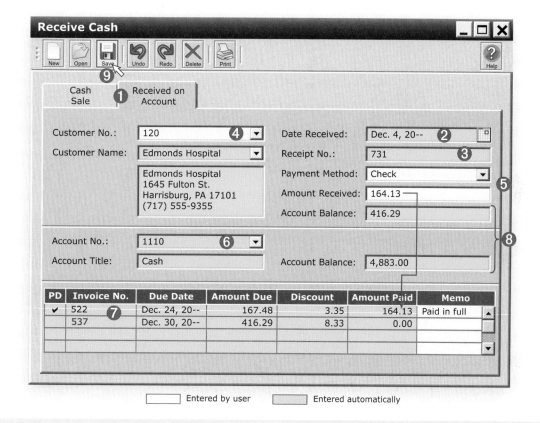

Entered by user   Entered automatically

① The user may choose to enter a cash sale or an amount received on account. In the window above, the user is receiving cash on account from Edmonds Hospital. Cash sales would be entered in this window, not in the Create Sales Invoices window. Receipt from a cash sale was illustrated in Chapter 2.

② The system enters the date.

③ The system enters the next available cash receipt number.

④ The user enters the customer by number or name, and the system displays the customer information.

⑤ The user selects the customer's method of payment and the amount received. Payment options would be cash, check, credit card, or debit card.

⑥ The system enters the default cash account. However, if the company maintains more than one cash account, a different account could be selected.

⑦ All unpaid invoices issued to Edmonds Hospital would be listed in these rows. Data from the accounts receivable file would populate the invoice numbers, due dates, amounts due, and discounts, if earned. The amount paid is entered automatically from the Amount Received field. The user may enter a memo notation.

⑧ The system displays the new customer account balance and new cash account balance.

⑨ The user clicks **Save** to post the transaction to **Cash**, **Accounts Receivable**, **Sales Discount**, and the customer's account.

Chapter Summary

A merchandising business must maintain an accounting system that provides its managers with the information necessary to ensure the collection of money owed by its charge customers. Each sale on account, including any sales taxes owed, is efficiently recorded on a single line of a sales journal. The transaction is immediately posted to the customer's accounts receivable ledger account to update the amount owed by the customer. The totals of the special columns of a completed sales journal are posted to the general ledger.

Each state determines its sales tax rate and how sales taxes are applied. State sales tax laws may exempt the collection of sales tax on sales to nonprofit organizations such as schools and churches. A state can also exempt from sales taxes the sales of selected merchandise, such as food, medicine, and clothing.

A business receives cash from cash sales and collections of its sales on account. Cash sales for a period of time are summarized and recorded on a single line of the cash receipts journal. Cash sales include sales to customers who paid with a credit or debit card.

When a charge customer pays on account, the transaction is recorded individually in the cash receipts journal and posted to the accounts receivable ledger, reducing the amount owed by the customer. To encourage early payment, a business may allow its charge customers to take a cash discount. When a customer takes a cash discount, the merchandising business regards it as a discount on sales, and a journal entry is made in the cash receipts journal to Sales Discount and Accounts Receivable. Sales Discount is a contra account to Sales.

The totals of the special columns of a completed cash receipts journal are posted to the general ledger. A business can ensure the accuracy of its accounts receivable ledger by preparing a schedule of accounts receivable. The total of the schedule should equal the updated balance of Accounts Receivable, the controlling account for the accounts receivable ledger.

EXPLORE ACCOUNTING

Journalizing Sales Discounts

Most retail sales are made to individuals who pay with cash or a credit card. Individual customers are expected to pay the full amount of the invoice at the time of the sale. In contrast, most sales to other businesses are made on account. A sale on account to a business customer usually includes an offer of a cash discount. Cash discount terms such as 2/10, n/30, as discussed in Chapter 9, encourage early payment. Remember, when a cash discount is taken by a customer, it is recorded as a sales discount.

Sales on account that involve both sales taxes and cash discounts present an interesting accounting problem. Assume Country Crafters purchases $100.00 of merchandise, plus $6.00 sales tax, for a total sale of $106.00, with 2/10, n/30 payment

terms. Nine days later, Country Crafters pays $103.88 in full payment of the invoice. How should the cash receipt be journalized?

Because the payment is received within the discount period, the sales amount is reduced by the amount of the discount, $2.12. The amount of sales tax may also be reduced because the amount of the sale is reduced. Thus, the following journal entry may be recorded:

Cash	103.88	
Sales Tax Payable	0.12	
Sales Discount	2.00	
Accounts Receivable		106.00

The net sales amount is $98.00—the original $100.00 sales less a 2% discount of $2.00. The net sales tax payable is $5.88—the original $6.00 sales tax less a 2% discount of $0.12.

The end result is that a $98.00 sale was made on which $5.88 sales tax ($98.00 × 6%) was collected.

It is essential for accountants to be familiar with the sales tax laws in states where their companies do business. Each state regulates how sales taxes should be paid. In some states, state regulations may require that sales taxes be paid only on actual sales realized—$5.88 for this transaction. In some states, sales taxes must be paid on the original invoice amount of a sale—$6.00 for this transaction. In these states, a sales discount would not result in a reduction in the sales tax liability. The following journal entry would be recorded:

Cash	103.88	
Sales Discount	2.12	
Accounts Receivable		106.00

Some states may allow a business to pay a percent of its original or gross sales rather than the amount of sales tax collected, assuming the amounts will be nearly identical. The business may elect not to recognize any impact on the amount of sales tax due to the relatively small dollar amount involved.

INSTRUCTIONS

Research the sales tax laws of your state. Contact a local business or use the Internet to determine how state law instructs a business to calculate its sales tax liability. Does the law explain how sales discounts impact the amount of sales tax owed?

Apply Your Understanding

INSTRUCTIONS: Download problem instructions for Excel, QuickBooks, and Peachtree from the textbook companion website at www.C21accounting.com.

10-1 Application Problem: Journalizing sales on account LO2

1. Journalize and post transactions on account to the sales journal.
2. Print the sales journal and accounts receivable ledger.

AAONLiNE

1. Go to www.cengage.com/login
2. Click on **AA Online** to access.
3. Go to the online assignment and follow the instructions.

Health Fashions is a clothing store specializing in uniforms for medical providers.

Instructions:

Journalize the following transactions completed during November of the current year on page 11 of the sales journal given in the *Working Papers*. The sales tax rate is 6%. The sales invoice source document is abbreviated as S. Save your work to complete Problem 10-2.

Transactions:

Nov. 2. Sold merchandise on account to Paulson Medical Clinic, $2,049.00, plus sales tax. S589.
4. Sold merchandise on account to Central Medical Clinic, $694.00, plus sales tax. S590.
7. Sold merchandise on account to Mason College, $1,648.00. Mason College is exempt from paying sales tax. S591.
9. Sold merchandise on account to Trannon Emergency Center, $828.00, plus sales tax. S592.
19. Sold merchandise on account to Fairview Hospital, $1,948.00, plus sales tax. S593.
25. Sold merchandise on account to Central Medical Clinic, $3,482.00, plus sales tax. S594.

10-2 Application Problem: Posting from a sales journal LO3

The accounts receivable ledger forms and selected general ledger accounts for Health Fashions are given in the *Working Papers*. Use the sales journal from Problem 10-1. Save your work to complete Problem 10-4.

Instructions:

1. Post the transactions on the sales journal to the accounts receivable ledger.
2. Total, prove, and rule the sales journal.
3. Post the sales journal to the general ledger.

10-3 Application Problem: Journalizing cash receipts LO4, 5

The cash receipts journal for Health Fashions is given in the *Working Papers*.

Instructions:

Journalize the following transactions completed during November of the current year on page 11 of the cash receipts journal. Source documents are abbreviated as follows: receipt, R; sales invoice, S; terminal summary, TS. Save the cash receipts journal to complete Problem 10-4.

Transactions:

Nov. 6. Received cash on account from Paulson Medical Clinic covering S587 for $1,547.15, less 2% discount. R568.
7. Recorded cash and credit card sales, $3,480.00, plus sales tax, $208.80; total, $3,688.80. TS41.
8. Received cash on account from Mason College covering S588 for $679.19, less 2% discount. R569.
14. Recorded cash and credit card sales, $2,940.00, plus sales tax, $176.40; total, $3,116.40. TS42.
16. Received cash on account from Trannon Emergency Center, $2,184.14, covering S585. R570.
21. Recorded cash and credit card sales, $2,875.00, plus sales tax, $172.50; total, $3,047.50. TS43.
28. Received cash on account from Central Medical Clinic, $1,648.96, covering S584. R571.

10-4 Application Problem: Posting from a cash receipts journal LO6, 7

AAONLiNE

1. Go to www.cengage.com/login
2. Click on **AA Online** to access.
3. Go to the online assignment and follow the instructions.

Use Health Fashions' cash receipts journal from Problem 10-3 and the accounts receivable and general ledgers from Problem 10-2.

Instructions:

1. Post the transactions from the cash receipts journal to the accounts receivable ledger.
2. Total and prove the cash receipts journal.
3. Prove cash. On November 30, the balance on the next unused check stub was $17,882.35.
4. Rule the cash receipts journal.
5. Post the cash receipts journal to the general ledger.
6. Prepare a schedule of accounts receivable.

10-M Mastery Problem: Journalizing sales and cash receipts transactions LO2, 3, 4, 5, 6, 7

University Designs sells custom imprinted products.

The sales journal, cash receipts journal, account receivable ledger forms, and selected general ledger accounts are given in the *Working Papers*.

Instructions:

1. Journalize the transactions on page 315 completed during the remainder of March in the appropriate journal. Use page 3 for the sales journal and page 3 for the cash receipts journal. Post any transaction impacting Accounts Receivable to the accounts receivable subsidiary ledger when the transaction is journalized. The sales tax rate is 7%. Source documents are abbreviated as follows: receipt, R; sales invoice, S; terminal summary, TS.

Transactions:

Mar. 3. Sold merchandise on account to Trailor Stores, $3,248.00, plus sales tax. S321.

4. Received cash on account from Jenkins & Sanders LLP, covering S312 for $945.00. R348.

5. Recorded cash and credit card sales, $1,485.00, plus sales tax, $92.14; total, $1,577.14. TS6.

9. Received cash on account from Luxury Suites, $4,219.00, covering S320, less a 2% discount. R349.

10. Sold merchandise on account to Southwestern University, $1,435.00. Southwestern University is exempt from sales tax. S322.

12. Received cash on account from Daniel Smith Promotions, $1,471.00 covering S345. R350.

16. Recorded cash and credit card sales, $1,020.50, plus sales tax, $64.59; total, $1,085.09. TS7.

2. Total, prove, and rule the sales journal.

3. Post the sales journal to the general ledger.

4. Total and prove the cash receipts journal.

5. Prove cash. On March 31, the balance on the next unused check stub was $11,582.54.

6. Rule the cash receipts journal.

7. Post the cash receipts journal to the general ledger.

8. Prepare a schedule of accounts receivable.

1. Journalize and post transactions on account to the sales journal and cash receipts journal.
2. On the Customers worksheet, sort the customer information.
3. Print the worksheets.

Peachtree

1. Journalize and post to the sales journal and cash receipts journal.
2. From the menu bar, select Reports & Forms; Accounts Receivable.
3. Print the sales journal and cash receipts journal.

QB Quick Books

1. Journalize and post sales on account in the Create Invoices window.
2. Journalize and post cash receipts in the Receive Payments window.
3. From the menu bar, select Reports; Customers and Receivables, Customer Balance Detail.
4. In the Dates drop-down box, select All and make the selections to print.

AAONLiNE

1. Go to www.cengage.com/login
2. Click on **AA Online** to access.
3. Go to the online assignment and follow the instructions.

10-S Source Documents Problem: Journalizing sales and cash receipts transactions; proving and ruling journals LO2, 3, 4, 5, 6

Golfer's Paradise sells golf and other recreational equipment. Source documents related to the sales and cash receipts are provided in the *Working Papers*.

Sales journal page 11 and cash receipts journal page 13 for Golfer's Paradise are given in the *Working Papers*.

Instructions:

1. Journalize the transactions shown in the source documents in the appropriate journal. The sales tax rate is 7.5%.

2. Total, prove, and rule the sales journal.

3. Total, prove, and rule the cash receipts journal.

AAONLiNE

1. Go to www.cengage.com/login
2. Click on **AA Online** to access.
3. Go to the online assignment and follow the instructions.

Innovative Technology is a merchandising company that specializes in selling computer and network equipment to small businesses. To encourage prompt payment, the company offers 2/10, n/30 credit terms. Unfortunately, many of its customers claim the sales discount despite sending their payments after the ten-day discount period. Because Innovative Technology has been giving its customers the discount regardless of when payment is received, customers have been increasingly taking advantage of the discount policy.

Innovative Technology's president has directed the accounting department to track these unearned sales discounts. To accomplish this task, an additional column labeled "Unearned Sales Discount Debit" has been added to the cash receipts journal.

Instructions:

1. Using the sales and cash receipts journals and accounts receivable ledger forms given in the *Working Papers*, journalize the sales and cash receipts made during December. Use page 12 for the sales journal and page 12 for the cash receipts journal. The sales tax rate is 6%. Post the transactions to the accounts receivable ledger when the transactions are recorded in the journals.

Hint: Innovative Technology records the sales invoice number in the Item column of the accounts receivable ledger forms. When a customer pays an invoice, determine whether any claimed discount is earned (received within ten days of the sale) or unearned (received after ten days). Record the sales discount in the appropriate column.

Transactions:

Dec.
2. Sold merchandise on account to Andersen & Smith LLP, $3,248.00, plus sales tax. S898.
3. Received a check for $2,947.77 from Jenson College in full payment of S894. R948.
4. Sold merchandise on account to Olsen Manufacturing, $627.19, plus sales tax. S899.
6. Received a check for $1,554.96 cash from Andersen & Smith LLP in full payment of S893. R949.
7. Received a $3,000.00 check from Randle Distribution Centers in partial payment of S895. R950.
8. Received a check for $958.51 from Olsen Manufacturing in full payment of S892 and S897. R951.
9. Received a check for $4,900.00 from Northern Regional Airlines with a note stating "partial payment of $5,000.00 against our account." R952.
14. Sold merchandise on account to Jenson College, $1,436.00. Jenson College is not subject to sales tax. S900.
15. Sold merchandise on account to Randle Distribution Centers, $2,498.00, plus sales tax. S901.
16. Received a $3,374.02 check from Andersen & Smith LLP in full payment of S898. R953.
23. Received a check for $1,135.25 from Randle Distribution Centers with the note "for the outstanding amount due on our November 28 purchase." R954.
24. Sold merchandise on account to Northern Regional Airlines, $1,249.19, plus sales tax. S902.

2. Total, prove, and rule the journals.

3. Prepare an email message to the company president describing the amount of unearned sales discounts.

Peachtree

1. Journalize and post to the sales journal and cash receipts journal.
2. From the menu bar, select Reports & Forms; Accounts Receivable.
3. Make the selections to print the sales journal and cash receipts journal.

QuickBooks

1. Journalize and post sales on account in the Create Invoices window.
2. Journalize and post cash receipts in the Receive Payments window.
3. From the menu bar, select Reports; Customers and Receivables, Customer Balance Detail.
4. In the Dates drop-down box, select All and make the selections to print.

AAONLINE

1. Go to www.cengage.com/login
2. Click on **AA Online** to access.
3. Go to the online assignment and follow the instructions.

21st Century Skills

Engineering Meets Business

PARTNERSHIP FOR
21ST CENTURY SKILLS

Theme: Science, Business Literacy

Skills: Critical Thinking and Problem Solving, ICT Literacy

Collaboration between engineering and other departments within a business is vital. An engineer's design work would likely be flawed without the support of others. In addition to design work, engineers are often required to write business plans, conduct market research, and figure out how best to build their designs. To do that successfully and at low cost, engineers must work hand in hand with other professionals such as accountants, marketers, and sales representatives.

A resource often used by engineers to find a manufacturer for a new product, or parts for its assembly, is the Thomas Register. This online directory lists manufacturers for all types of products. So, when an engineer needs a source for a part, the Thomas Register is often the first place to look. Sometimes a manufacturer only sells through a distributor. Distributors can also be found in the Thomas Register.

APPLICATION

1. You have designed the following products and you need to find a manufacturer or distributor for parts to build each product. Log on to ThomasRegister.com to find suppliers. Complete the table below.

New Product	Part Needed	Supplier Needed	Supplier Found
Security camera	Lens	Manufacturer	
Computer	Hard drive	Manufacturer	
Lamp	Socket	Distributor	
Coffee pot	Rubber handle	Distributor	
Luggage	Wheels	Manufacturer	

2. Contact a local distributor. Ask what advantages they provide versus buying direct from a manufacturer.

Analyzing Nike's financial statements

What do Kentucky Fried Chicken, Pizza Hut, and Taco Bell have in common? Each of these well-known companies is owned by Yum! Brands, Inc. A company that is owned by another company is known as a subsidiary. When Yum! Brands prepares its financial statements, it includes financial information from each subsidiary. These financial statements are referred to as consolidated financial statements.

INSTRUCTIONS

1. Use the Description of Business section of Note 1 on page B-10 in Appendix B to identify Nike's subsidiaries.
2. What do these subsidiaries have in common with Nike?

Chapter 11

Accounting for Transactions Using a General Journal

LEARNING OBJECTIVES

After studying Chapter 11, in addition to defining key terms, you will be able to:

LO1 Explain the purpose of a general journal.

LO2 Account for purchases returns and allowances.

LO3 Post a general journal to the accounts payable ledger and general ledger.

LO4 Account for sales returns and allowances.

LO5 Post a general journal to the accounts receivable ledger and general ledger.

LO6 Record a correcting entry to the accounts receivable ledger.

LO7 Explain the relationship between retained earnings and dividends.

LO8 Account for the declaration and payment of dividends.

©DANIEL KOUREY, ISTOCK/©JIM PRUITT, ISTOCK

NYUL/ISTOCKPHOTO.COM

Accounting In The Real World

LG Electronics

"Life's good!" LG's familiar logo has become a common sight in electronics and appliance stores. From cell phones to televisions to refrigerators, LG Electronics is a leader in today's consumer electronics market.

LG Electronics was founded in 1958 as GoldStar. Initially, it focused on supplying the Korean market with radios, televisions, and appliances. The company took a big step in 1982 when it became an international company by building a television manufacturing plant in Huntsville, Alabama. LG became a global leader in consumer electronics by acquiring U.S.-based Zenith Electronics in 1995.

In recent years, LG has fueled its growth through strategic partnerships with other companies that manufacture similar technologies. For example, LG and General Electric share patents on kitchenware and refrigerators. Schneider Electric and LG are partners in producing camera lenses for mobile phones. LG launched a smartphone that uses Microsoft's Windows Mobile 6.0, offering access to documents in Word, Excel, and PowerPoint. Through a partnership with Dolby Laboratories, LG expects to be the first handset maker to build Dolby Mobile technology into its cell phones.

CRITICAL THINKING

Suppose LG and Dolby are planning a joint venture to produce a media player. Dolby's contribution will be a part costing it $8 to produce. LG expects to add another $32 of costs and sell the product to retailers for $70.

1. How should the $30-per-unit profit be divided between LG and Dolby?

2. LG and Dolby together expect to spend $40 to produce the player. What other types of expenses do you think each company will incur to sell the product to retailers? Does this change your answer to part (1)?

Source: www.lg.com.

Background: ©CYBERTRONE, SHUTTERSTOCK; Real World: IMAGE CHINA VIA AP IMAGES

Key Terms

- general journal
- purchases return
- purchases allowance
- debit memorandum
- sales return
- sales allowance
- credit memorandum
- retained earnings
- dividends
- board of directors
- declaring a dividend

LESSON 11-1 Accounting for Purchases Transactions Using a General Journal

LO1 Explain the purpose of a general journal.
LO2 Account for purchases returns and allowances.
LO3 Post a general journal to the accounts payable ledger and general ledger.

General Journal LO1

A journal with two amount columns in which all kinds of entries can be recorded is called a **general journal**. Not every transaction can be recorded in a special journal. For example, when ThreeGreen buys store supplies on account, the transaction results in a debit to Supplies—Store and a credit to Accounts Payable.

The transaction is not a cash payment, so it cannot be recorded in the cash payments journal. Nor is the transaction a purchase of merchandise on account, so it cannot be recorded in the purchases journal. Transactions that cannot be recorded in a special journal are recorded in a general journal.

Memorandum for Buying Supplies on Account

ThreeGreen receives an invoice from a vendor when it buys store supplies on account. A pre-numbered memorandum is attached to the invoice noting that it is for store supplies and not for purchases. This is done to ensure that the invoice gets paid and recorded correctly.

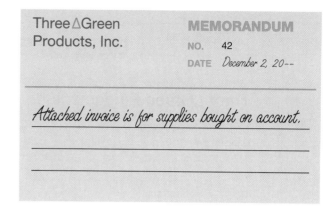

Three△Green Products, Inc.

MEMORANDUM

NO. 42

DATE *December 2, 20--*

Attached invoice is for supplies bought on account.

BUYING SUPPLIES ON ACCOUNT

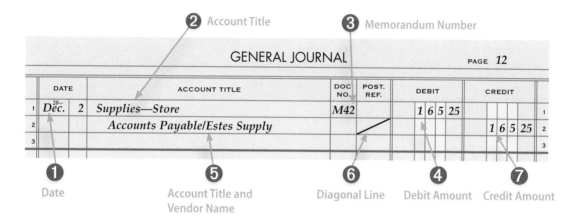

2 Account Title **3** Memorandum Number

GENERAL JOURNAL   PAGE 12

	DATE		ACCOUNT TITLE	DOC. NO.	POST. REF.	DEBIT	CREDIT	
1	Dec.	2	Supplies—Store	M42		1 6 5 25		1
2			Accounts Payable/Estes Supply				1 6 5 25	2
3								3

1 Date **5** Account Title and Vendor Name **6** Diagonal Line **4** Debit Amount **7** Credit Amount

---

December 2. Bought store supplies on account from Estes Supply, $165.25. Memorandum No. 42.

Supplies—Store

165.25 |

Accounts Payable

| 165.25

When store supplies are bought on account, both the value of store supplies on hand and the amount owed to vendors increase. Therefore, the journal entry for this transaction is a $165.25 debit to Supplies—Store and a $165.25 credit to Accounts Payable.

The equality of debits and credits is checked after each general journal entry is recorded. For this entry, the debit is $165.25 and the credit is $165.25. The debits equal the credits.

A general journal entry posted to a controlling account, such as Accounts Payable, will also be posted to a subsidiary ledger account. This process maintains the equality of the controlling account balance with the sum of the subsidiary ledger account balances.

Journalizing Buying Supplies on Account

1 Write the date, 20--, Dec. 2, in the Date column.

2 Write the account title, Supplies—Store, in the Account Title column.

3 Write the memorandum number, M42, in the Doc. No. column.

4 Write the debit amount to Supplies—Store, $165.25, in the Debit column on the same line as the account title.

5 On the next line indented about one centimeter, write Accounts Payable/Estes Supply, in the Account Title column. Place a diagonal line between the two account titles.

6 Place a diagonal line in the Post. Ref. column on the same line to show that the single credit amount is posted to the general ledger account, Accounts Payable, and the accounts payable ledger account, Estes Supply.

7 Write the credit amount for Accounts Payable and Estes Supply, $165.25, in the Credit column on the same line as the two account titles.

DEBIT MEMORANDUM

Three△Green Products, Inc.

1501 Commerce Street
Carlisle, PA 17013
717-555-4868

Date: December 8, 20--
Debit Memorandum #: 38
Vendor ID: 240

To:

Mobley Tools
2533 Interstate Drive
Crossville, TN 38558

Quantity	Item #	Description	Unit Price	Line Total
2	T-253	18 watt power tool batteries	$21.95	$43.90
			Subtotal	$43.90
			Sales Tax	
			Total	**$43.90**

Customers generally do not want to keep merchandise that is inferior in quality, different from what they ordered, or damaged when received. If that happens, the customer may be allowed to return part or all of the merchandise purchased. Credit allowed for the purchase price of returned merchandise, resulting in a decrease in the customer's account payable to the vendor, is called a **purchases return**.

When merchandise is damaged but still usable, or is of a different quality than that ordered, the vendor may let the customer keep the merchandise at a reduced price. Credit allowed for part of the purchase price of merchandise that is not returned, resulting in a decrease in the customer's account payable to the vendor, is called a **purchases allowance**.

A purchases return or allowance should be confirmed in writing. A form prepared by the customer showing the price deduction taken by the customer for a return or an allowance is called a **debit memorandum**. The form is called a debit memorandum because the customer records the amount as a debit to the vendor's account. The result is a decrease in the amount owed.

A customer may use the debit memorandum as the source document for journalizing a purchases return or allowance. Or, the customer may wait for written confirmation from the vendor and use that confirmation as the source document.

ThreeGreen issues a debit memorandum for each purchases return or allowance. These debit memorandums are used as source documents for purchases returns and allowances transactions. [CONCEPT: Objective Evidence] Using debit memorandums makes it possible for these transactions to be recorded immediately without waiting for written confirmation from the vendors. The original of each debit memorandum is sent to the vendor and ThreeGreen files a copy in its records.

A business could credit Purchases for the amount of a purchases return or allowance. However, better information is provided if these amounts are credited to a separate account titled Purchases Returns and Allowances. This allows the business to track the amount of purchases returns and allowances in a fiscal period and makes it possible to evaluate the efficiency of its purchasing activities.

Journalizing Purchases Returns and Allowances

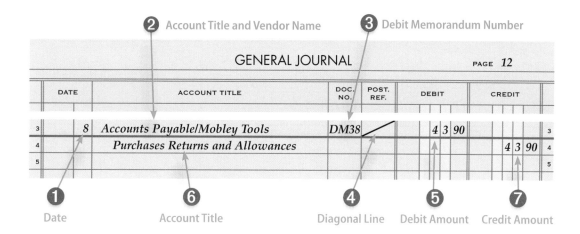

Account Title and Vendor Name ② ③ Debit Memorandum Number

GENERAL JOURNAL   PAGE 12

	DATE	ACCOUNT TITLE	DOC. NO.	POST. REF.	DEBIT	CREDIT	
3	8	Accounts Payable/Mobley Tools	DM38	/	4 3 90		3
4		Purchases Returns and Allowances				4 3 90	4
5							5

① Date   ⑥ Account Title   ④ Diagonal Line   ⑤ Debit Amount   ⑦ Credit Amount

Purchases Returns and Allowances

Debit Decreases	Credit Increases

Merchandise returns and purchase allowances decrease the total value of merchandise purchased. **Purchases Returns and Allowances** is a contra account to Purchases. Thus, the normal account balance of Purchases Returns and Allowances is a credit, the opposite of the normal debit balance of Purchases. Both Purchases and Purchases Returns and Allowances are listed in the Cost of Goods Sold division of ThreeGreen's chart of accounts.

December 8. Returned merchandise to Mobley Tools, $43.90, covering Purchase Invoice No. 528. Debit Memorandum No. 38.

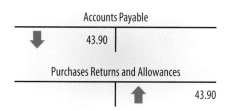

Accounts Payable

↓ 43.90

Purchases Returns and Allowances

↑ 43.90

Journalizing Purchases Returns and Allowances

① Write the date, 8, in the Date column.

② Write the account title and vendor name, Accounts Payable/Mobley Tools, in the Account Title column. A diagonal line is placed between the two accounts.

③ Write the debit memorandum number, DM38, in the Doc. No. column.

④ Place a diagonal line in the Post. Ref. column to show that the single debit amount is posted to the general ledger account, Accounts Payable, and the accounts payable ledger account, Mobley Tools.

⑤ Write the amount, $43.90, in the Debit column of the first line.

⑥ On the next line indented about one centimeter, write Purchases Returns and Allowances in the Account Title column.

⑦ Write the amount, $43.90, in the Credit column of the second line.

Posting from a General Journal to an Accounts Payable Ledger LO3

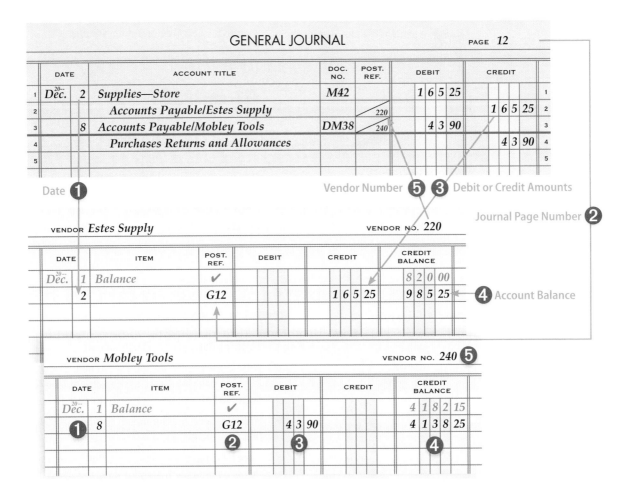

An entry in the general journal that affects **Accounts Payable**, a general ledger account, also affects a vendor's account in the accounts payable ledger.

The diagonal line in the Post. Ref. column allows the posting references of both the general ledger and subsidiary ledger accounts to be recorded.

Posting from a General Journal to an Accounts Payable Ledger

Posting a Credit Entry

1 Write the date, 2, in the Date column of the vendor account.

2 Write the general journal page number, G12, in the Post. Ref. column of the account. G12 signifies page 12 of the general journal.

3 Write the amount, $165.25, in the Credit column of the vendor account.

4 Add the amount in the Credit column to the previous balance in the Credit Balance column ($820.00 + $165.25 = $985.25). Write the new balance, $985.25, in the Credit Balance column.

5 Write the vendor number, 220, to the right of the diagonal line in the Post. Ref. column of the general journal.

Posting a Debit Entry

1 Write the date, 8, in the Date column of the vendor account.

2 Write the general journal page number, G12, in the Post. Ref. column of the account.

3 Write the amount, $43.90, in the Debit column of the vendor account.

4 Subtract the amount in the Debit column from the previous balance in the Credit Balance column ($4,182.15 − $43.90 = $4,138.25). Write the new balance, $4,138.25, in the Credit Balance column.

5 Write the vendor number, 240, to the right of the diagonal line in the Post. Ref. column of the general journal.

Posting from a General Journal to a General Ledger

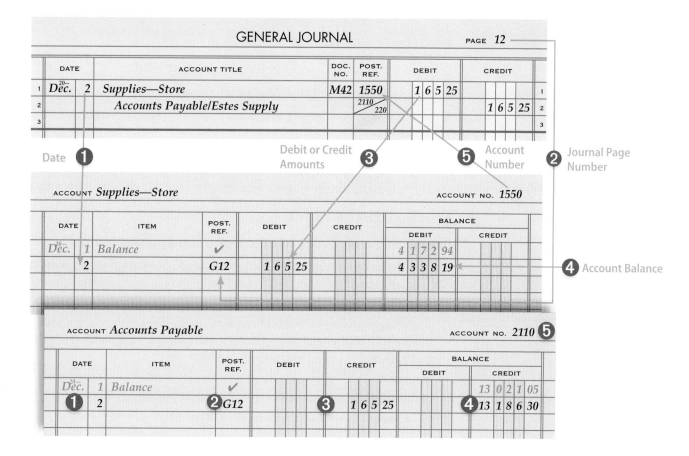

Transactions recorded in the general journal can affect both general ledger and subsidiary ledger accounts. Buying supplies on account, for example, results in a debit to the general ledger account, Supplies—Store. The transaction also results in credits to the general ledger account, Accounts Payable, and the accounts payable ledger account, Estes Supply.

In a computerized accounting system, transactions are posted immediately after they are entered. In a manual accounting system, general journal transactions may be posted immediately, at the end of each day, or less frequently. How often posting is done depends on the number and types of transactions. Since daily posting is most commonly practiced, this text will show daily posting.

At the end of each day, each line of the entry can be posted in sequence to the general ledger and any subsidiary ledger. Or, amounts can be posted first to the subsidiary ledgers, then to the general ledger. The first method makes it less likely that a transaction will be overlooked in the posting process. The second method is more efficient because it uses only one ledger at a time. Whichever method is chosen, it should be applied consistently. Using a consistent method to post general journal entries helps to ensure that all amounts are posted. Always review a completed general journal page to be sure that all postings have been made.

Posting a General Journal to a General Ledger

① Write the date, 2, in the Date column of the account.

② Write the general journal page number, G12, in the Post. Ref. column of the account.

③ Write each amount in the Debit or Credit column of the general ledger account in the Account Title column.

④ For each account, calculate and write the new account balance in the Balance Debit or Credit column.

⑤ Write the general ledger account number in the Post. Ref. column of each line of the journal entry. For the debit to Supplies—Store, write 1550 in the Post. Ref. column. For the credit to Accounts Payable, write 2110 to the left of the diagonal line in the Post. Ref. column of the general journal. The vendor account number, 220, to the right of the diagonal line, indicates the accounts payable ledger account where the transaction was posted.

LO1 Explain the purpose of a general journal.

LO2 Account for purchases returns and allowances.

LO3 Post a general journal to the accounts payable ledger and general ledger.

Terms Review

general journal

purchases return

purchases allowance

debit memorandum

Audit your understanding

1. When is a transaction recorded in a general journal?

2. When is the equality of debits and credits proved for a general journal?

3. What is a primary difference between a purchases return and a purchases allowance?

4. If purchases returns and allowances decrease the value of Purchases, why are returns and allowances credited to a separate account?

Work together 11-1

Journalizing and posting transactions using a general journal

A general journal and selected accounts payable and general ledger accounts for Evans Equipment are given in the *Working Papers*. Your instructor will guide you through the following examples.

1. Journalize the following transactions during December of the current year. Use page 12 of a general journal. Source documents are abbreviated as follows: memorandum, M; debit memorandum, DM.

   Transactions:

   Dec. 5. Bought office supplies on account from Milam Corp., $532.00. M57.

   　　　7. Returned merchandise to Griffin, Inc., $248.00. DM32.

2. Post each general journal entry to the accounts payable and general ledgers.

On your own 11-1

Journalizing and posting transactions using a general journal

A general journal and selected accounts payable and general ledger accounts for Steil Florist are given in the *Working Papers*. Work this problem independently.

1. Journalize the following transactions during December of the current year and January of the next year. Use page 12 of a general journal. Source documents are abbreviated as follows: memorandum, M; debit memorandum, DM.

   Transactions:

   Dec. 15. Returned merchandise to Olen, Inc., $255.00. DM33.

   　　　22. Bought store supplies on account from Gould Depot, $251.00. M58.

   　　　23. Returned merchandise to Branker Supply, $69.00. DM34.

   　　　28. Bought office supplies on account from Plette Corp., $198.00. M59.

2. Post each general journal entry to the accounts payable and general ledgers.

11-2 Recording Sales Transactions Using a General Journal

LO4 Account for sales returns and allowances.

LO5 Post a general journal to the accounts receivable ledger and general ledger.

LO6 Record a correcting entry to the accounts receivable ledger.

Credit Memorandum for Sales Returns and Allowances LO4

CREDIT MEMORANDUM

Three△Green Products, Inc.

1501 Commerce Street
Carlisle, PA 17013
717-555-4868

Date: November 16, 20--
Credit Memorandum#: 14
Vendor ID: 130

To:
Lake Automotive
152 S. Queen Street
Shippensburg, PA 17257

Quantity	Item #	Description	Unit Price	Totals
3	T-253	18 watt power tool batteries	$21.95	$65.85
			Subtotal	$65.85
			Sales Tax	3.95
			Total	**$69.80**

Most merchandising businesses expect to have some merchandise returned. A customer may receive the wrong item or get damaged goods. A customer may return merchandise for a credit on account or a cash refund. Credit allowed to a customer for the sales price of returned merchandise, resulting in a decrease in the accounts receivable of the merchandising business, is called a **sales return**.

Credit may be granted to a customer without requiring the return of merchandise. Credit may also be given because of a shortage in a shipment. Credit allowed to a customer for part of the sales price of merchandise that is not returned, resulting in a decrease in the accounts receivable of the merchandising business, is called a **sales allowance**.

A vendor usually informs a customer in writing when a sales return or a sales allowance is granted. A form prepared by the vendor showing the amount deducted for returns and allowances is called a **credit memorandum**. The form is called a credit memorandum because the vendor credits the customer's account, reducing the amount owed to the vendor. The original of a credit memorandum is given to the customer. The copy is used as the source document

for recording the sales returns and allowances transaction. [CONCEPT: Objective Evidence]

Sales returns and sales allowances decrease the amount of a business's sales. **Sales Returns and Allowances** is a contra account to the revenue account **Sales**. The normal account balance of **Sales Returns and Allowances** is a debit, the opposite of the normal credit balance of **Sales**. Both **Sales** and **Sales Returns and Allowances** are listed in the Revenue division of ThreeGreen's chart of accounts.

Sales Returns and Allowances

Debit Increases	Credit Decreases

A business could debit the **Sales** account for the amount of a return or allowance. However, better information is provided if these amounts are debited to **Sales Returns and Allowances**. This contra account enables management to quickly learn if the percent of sales returns and allowances to sales is greater than expected.

Journalizing Sales Returns and Allowances

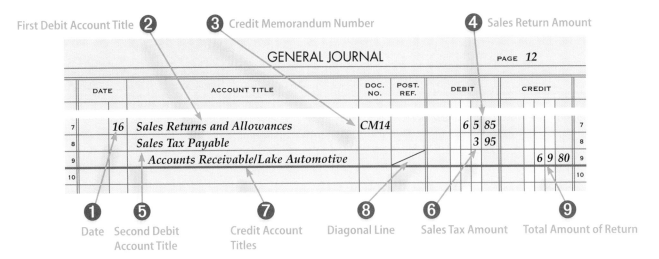

First Debit Account Title ❷   ❸ Credit Memorandum Number   ❹ Sales Return Amount

GENERAL JOURNAL   PAGE 12

DATE	ACCOUNT TITLE	DOC. NO.	POST. REF.	DEBIT	CREDIT	
7	16	Sales Returns and Allowances	CM14		6 5 85		7
8		Sales Tax Payable			3 95		8
9		Accounts Receivable/Lake Automotive				6 9 80	9
10							10

❶ Date   ❺ Second Debit Account Title   ❼ Credit Account Titles   ❽ Diagonal Line   ❻ Sales Tax Amount   ❾ Total Amount of Return

On November 9, ThreeGreen sold merchandise on account to Lake Automotive for $606.32 including tax. Later, on December 16, Lake Automotive returned merchandise it purchased for $65.85. The sales return reduces the amount owed by Lake Automotive by $69.80 ($65.85 sales plus $3.95 sales tax).

Because the transaction is not a cash receipt, it cannot be recorded in the cash receipts journal. Since the transaction is not a sale on account, it cannot be recorded in the sales journal. Transactions that cannot be recorded in a special journal are recorded in the general journal.

December 16. Granted credit to Lake Automotive for merchandise returned, $65.85, plus sales tax, $3.95, from S500; total, $69.80. Credit Memorandum No. 14.

Journalizing Sales Returns and Allowances

❶ Write the date, 16, in the Date column.

❷ Write Sales Returns and Allowances in the Account Title column.

❸ Write CM and the credit memorandum number, 14, in the Doc. No. column.

❹ Write the amount of the sales return, $65.85, in the Debit column.

❺ Write Sales Tax Payable on the next line in the Account Title column.

❻ Write the sales tax amount, $3.95, in the Debit column.

❼ On the next line, in the Account Title column, indented about one centimeter, write the general ledger and accounts payable ledger accounts to be credited, Accounts Receivable/Lake Automotive.

❽ Draw a diagonal line in the Post. Ref. column.

❾ Write the total accounts receivable amount, $69.80, in the Credit column.

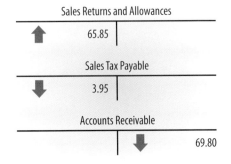

Posting from a General Journal to an Accounts Receivable Ledger LO5

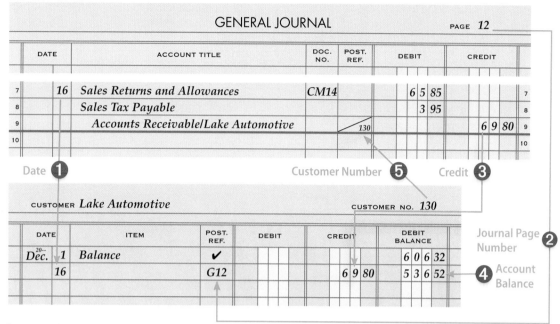

Entries in the general journal may affect account balances in both general ledger and subsidiary ledger accounts.

The posting of the transaction to the general ledger follows the same steps presented earlier in the chapter.

Posting from a General Journal to an Accounts Receivable Ledger

1. Write the date, 16, in the Date column of the customer account.

2. Write the general journal page number, G12, in the Post. Ref. column of the account. G12 signifies page 12 of the general journal.

3. Write the amount, $69.80, in the Credit column of the customer account.

4. Subtract the amount in the Credit column from the previous balance in the Debit Balance column ($606.32 − $69.80 = $536.52). Write the new balance, $536.52, in the Debit Balance column.

5. Write the customer number, 130, to the right of the diagonal line in the Post. Ref. column of the general journal.

THINK LIKE AN ACCOUNTANT

Sales Returns Are Expensive

Not only does a sales return eliminate the financial benefit of a sale, but the time and effort involved in receiving and restocking returned items are also expensive. Over the past year, the level of sales returns at Midwest Equipment Supply has risen. The company's management has hired your accounting firm to address the problem, and you've been given the assignment.

Your first step for correcting the problem is to talk to customers having a high level of sales returns. You will attempt to discover the most common reason for their sales returns. Is the customer unhappy with the quality of the items?

Were the wrong goods shipped? Was an incorrect quantity of goods shipped? Once you understand the problem, you can begin to develop the solution.

Your client's computer system contains a report that summarizes its sales and sales returns for each customer over a period of time. To determine which customers to call, you need to calculate a return rate for each customer. Those customers having the highest return rate should be contacted.

OPEN THE SPREADSHEET TLA_CH11
Follow the steps on the Instructions worksheet. The Analysis worksheet contains the most recent summary report of sales and sales returns. Prepare a report of the five customers having the highest return rates. Why might you also interview customers having the lowest return rates?

Correcting Errors in Subsidiary Ledger Accounts LO6

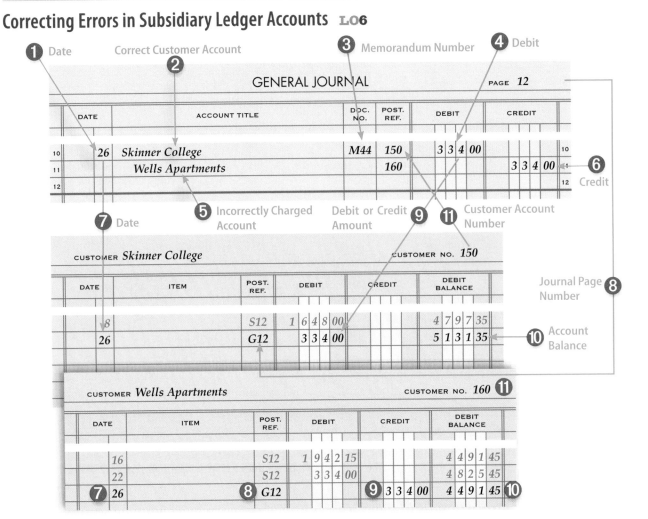

Errors may be made in recording amounts in subsidiary ledgers that do not affect the general ledger controlling account. For example, a sale on account may be recorded to the wrong customer in the sales journal.

> **December 26.** Found that a sale on account to Skinner College was incorrectly charged to the account of Wells Apartments, $334.00. Memorandum No. 44.

The correcting entry recorded in the general journal involves only subsidiary ledger accounts. Skinner College's account is debited for $334.00 to record the charge sale in the correct account. Wells Apartments' account is credited for $334.00 to cancel the incorrect entry.

The steps for posting a journal entry to correct customer accounts are the same as posting other transactions to subsidiary ledgers with one exception. A diagonal line is not needed in the Post. Ref. column to separate the references to the general ledger and subsidiary ledger account. Only a reference to the subsidiary ledger account is entered in the Post. Ref. column of the general journal because the correcting transaction does not affect a general ledger account.

Journalizing and Posting Correcting Entries Affecting Customer Accounts

1. Write the date, 26, in the Date column of a general journal.
2. Write the name of the correct customer, Skinner College, in the Account Title column.
3. Write the memorandum number, M44, in the Doc. No. column.
4. Write the amount, $334.00, in the Debit column.
5. Indent and write the name of the incorrectly charged customer, Wells Apartments.
6. Write the amount, $334.00, in the Credit column.
7. Write the date, 26, in the Date column of each customer account.
8. Write the general journal page number, G12, in the Post. Ref. column of each customer account.
9. Write the amount, $334.00, in the appropriate Debit or Credit column of each customer account.
10. For each account, calculate and write the new account balance in the Debit Balance column.
11. Write the appropriate customer numbers in the Post. Ref. column of the general journal.

LO4 Account for sales returns and allowances.

LO5 Post a general journal to the accounts receivable ledger and general ledger.

LO6 Record a correcting entry to the accounts receivable ledger.

Terms Review

sales return

sales allowance

credit memorandum

Audit your understanding

1. What is the difference between a sales return and a sales allowance?
2. What is the source document for journalizing sales returns and allowances?
3. Why are sales returns and allowances not debited to the Sales account?
4. Which general ledger accounts are affected, and how, by a sales returns and allowances transaction?

Work together 11-2

Accounting for sales returns and allowances using a general journal

A general journal and selected accounts receivable and general ledger accounts for Cline Interiors are given in the *Working Papers*. Your instructor will guide you through the following examples.

1. Using the current year, journalize the following transactions on page 6 of a general journal. Source documents are abbreviated as follows: credit memorandum, CM; sales invoice, S.

   Transactions:

   June 4. Granted credit to Keller Associates for merchandise returned, $245.00, plus sales tax, $14.70, from S645; total, $259.70. CM28.

   9. Learned that a sale on account to Ashston & Lindsay LLP was incorrectly charged to the account of Abraham Corporation, $623.00. Memorandum No. 61.

   12. Granted credit to Lambert Schools for damaged merchandise, $206.00 (no sales tax), from S633. CM29.

   26. Found that a sale on account to Keller Associates was incorrectly charged to the account of Karson Properties, $598.00. Memorandum No. 62.

2. Post each general journal entry to the accounts receivable and general ledgers.

On your own 11-2

Accounting for sales returns and allowances using a general journal

The general journal and accounts receivable ledger for Food Warehouse are given in the *Working Papers*. Work this problem independently.

1. Using the current year, journalize the following transactions on page 7 of a general journal. Source documents are abbreviated as follows: credit memorandum, CM; sales invoice, S.

   Transactions:

   July 5. Granted credit to City Food Bank for damaged merchandise, $245.00 (no sales tax), from S764. CM36.

   8. Found that a sale on account to Learning Playhouse was incorrectly charged to the account of RPL Corporation, $846.00. Memorandum No. 92.

   19. Granted credit to Paulson Café for merchandise returned, $158.50, plus sales tax, $9.51, from S758; total, $168.01. CM37.

   23. Learned that a sale on account to City Food Bank was incorrectly charged to the account of Bettsworth Hospital, $489.00. Memorandum No. 93.

2. Post each general journal entry to the accounts receivable and general ledgers.

LO7 Explain the relationship between retained earnings and dividends.

LO8 Account for the declaration and payment of dividends.

Stockholders' Equity Accounts Used by a Corporation LO7

(3000)	STOCKHOLDERS' EQUITY
3110	Capital Stock
3120	Paid-In Capital in Excess of Par
3130	Retained Earnings
3140	Dividends
3150	Income Summary

Dividends

Debit
Increases

Credit
Decreases

The owners' equity accounts for a corporation are listed under a major chart of accounts division titled Stockholders' Equity.

Most corporations have many stockholders. It is not practical to have a separate owner's equity account for each stockholder. Instead, a single owners' equity account titled **Capital Stock** is used for the investment of all owners.

Net income increases a corporation's total stockholders' equity. Some income may be retained by a corporation for business expansion. An amount earned by a corporation and not yet distributed to stockholders is called **retained**

earnings. Retained Earnings is the stockholders' equity account used to record a corporation's earnings.

Some of a corporation's income may be given to stockholders as a return on their investments. Earnings distributed to stockholders are called **dividends**. A corporation's dividend account is a temporary account similar to a proprietorship's drawing account. Each time a dividend is declared, the stockholders' equity account, Dividends, is debited. At the end of each fiscal period, the balance in Dividends is closed to Retained Earnings.

FINANCIAL LITERACY

Charitable Contributions

Americans should be proud of their charitable giving. The average American family donates $2,000 per year. Small businesses donate as much as 6% of their profits. Both families and businesses give more than in any other country. Charitable giving is a vital contribution to society.

Picking a charity that will use contributions wisely requires some effort. In an effort to pressure donors, many charities create a false sense of urgency. It is never wise to give money under pressure. That can result in a poor choice of charities and adversely impact one's budget.

The first step in selecting a charity is to identify an issue that holds personal significance. Then, become familiar with the charities that support your cause. Study the charity's finances and see how they spend their donations. At least 75% should go directly to the cause. Be cautious of organizations

that spend heavily on administrative expenses, program development, or education (usually advertising). CharityWatch.org, the Better Business Bureau, and Charityguide.org are examples of watchdog organizations. They monitor and report how effectively charities spend their money.

ACTIVITIES

1. Assume you are the owner of a small business that sells children's toys.
   a. Using the Internet (search *children's charities*), find three charities pertaining to children that you might support. Explain why you chose these charities.
   b. Using Excel, create a chart for each charity displaying its use of funds as a percent of expenses.
2. Explain how a small business that is not making a profit can still donate to charity.
3. List at least three ways businesses benefit from their charitable contributions.

© NOREBBO, ISTOCK

Declaring a Dividend LO8

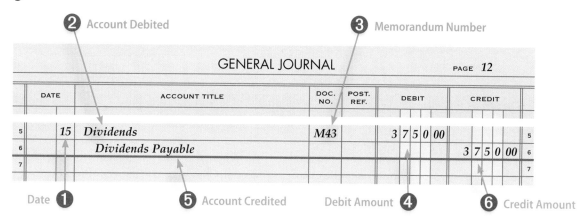

2 Account Debited   **3** Memorandum Number

GENERAL JOURNAL   PAGE 12

DATE	ACCOUNT TITLE	DOC. NO.	POST. REF.	DEBIT	CREDIT	
5	15	Dividends	M43		3 7 5 0 00		5
6		Dividends Payable				3 7 5 0 00	6
7							7

Date **1**   **5** Account Credited   Debit Amount **4**   **6** Credit Amount

A group of persons elected by the stockholders to govern a corporation is called the **board of directors**. Dividends can be distributed to stockholders only by formal action of a corporation's board of directors. (CONCEPT: Business Entity) Action by a board of directors to distribute corporate earnings to stockholders is called **declaring a dividend**. Dividends are normally declared on one date and paid on a later date.

Not all corporations declare dividends. A corporation's board of directors must consider how the dividend impacts the corporation and the desire of stockholders to receive a dividend. However, when a dividend is declared, the corporation is obligated to pay it. The dividend is a liability that must be recorded in the corporation's accounts. A dividend cannot exceed the balance of the Retained Earnings account.

ThreeGreen's board of directors declares a dividend every three months so that stockholders can share the corporation's earnings throughout the year. ThreeGreen declares dividends each March 15, June 15, September 15, and December 15. The dividends are then paid on the 15th of the month following the declaration.

> December 15. ThreeGreen's board of directors declared a quarterly dividend of $0.05 per share; capital stock issued is 75,000 shares; total dividend, $3,750.00. Date of payment is January 15. Memorandum No. 43.

Number of Shares Outstanding	×	Quarterly Dividend per Share	=	Total Quarterly Dividend
75,000	×	$0.05	=	$3,750.00

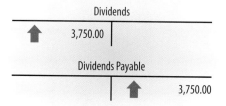

```
           Dividends
   3,750.00 |

        Dividends Payable
                |  3,750.00
```

The stockholders' equity account, **Dividends**, increases by a debit and has a normal debit balance. Therefore, **Dividends** is debited for $3,750.00. **Dividends Payable** is credited for $3,750.00 to show the increase in this liability account.

The journal entry is posted to general ledger accounts using the same procedures illustrated earlier in this chapter.

▶ Journalizing a Declared Dividend

1 Write the date, 15, in the Date column.

2 Write the title of the account debited, Dividends, in the Account Title column.

3 Write the memorandum number, M43, in the Doc. No. column.

4 Write the debit amount, $3,750.00, in the Debit column.

5 Write the title of the account credited, Dividends Payable, on the next line of the Account Title column, indented about one centimeter.

6 Write the credit amount, $3,750.00, in the Credit column.

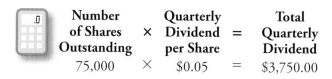

remember   Dividends is a temporary account that is closed to Retained Earnings at the end of the fiscal period.

Paying Declared Dividends

					GENERAL		ACCOUNTS PAYABLE DEBIT	PURCHASES DISCOUNT CREDIT	CASH CREDIT	
	DATE	ACCOUNT TITLE	CK. NO.	POST. REF.	DEBIT	CREDIT				
10	15	*Dividends Payable*	742		3 7 5 0 00				3 7 5 0 00	10
11	①		②	③		④			⑤	11

CASH PAYMENTS JOURNAL   PAGE 1

ThreeGreen issues one check for the amount of the total dividend to be paid. Most corporations make the check payable to an agent, such as a bank. The agent then handles the details of sending dividend checks to individual stockholders.

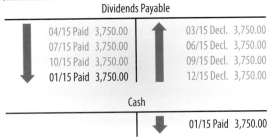

Dividends Payable

04/15 Paid 3,750.00	03/15 Decl. 3,750.00
07/15 Paid 3,750.00	06/15 Decl. 3,750.00
10/15 Paid 3,750.00	09/15 Decl. 3,750.00
01/15 Paid 3,750.00	12/15 Decl. 3,750.00

Cash

	01/15 Paid 3,750.00

January 15. Paid cash for quarterly dividend declared December 15, $3,750.00. Check No. 742.

When this entry is posted, the Dividends Payable account has a zero balance. Procedures for posting a cash payments journal were presented in Chapter 9.

Journalizing the Payment of a Dividend

① Write the date, 15, in the Date column.

② Write the account title, Dividends Payable, in the Account Title column.

③ Write the check number, 742, in the Ck. No. column.

④ Write the debit amount to Dividends Payable, $3,750.00, in the General Debit column.

⑤ Write the credit amount, $3,750.00, in the Cash Credit column.

WHY ACCOUNTING?

Cost of Surgery

For a patient needing surgery, many questions will arise: How will the surgery be done? Who will perform the surgery? What will be the recovery time? What precautions will be taken to prevent infection? How much will it cost? What if the surgery isn't successful? The answer to the first question will affect the answers to all of the other questions.

In the past, surgery required an incision large enough to allow the surgeon's hands and instruments to access the affected area. Today, there are many new approaches to surgery which permit less invasive procedures. Some of these are laparoscopy, robotics, microwaves, radiofrequency ablation, cryoablation (freezing), cold plasma, and lasers.

Alternative surgical procedures will very likely decrease the pain from an operation, decrease the length of any hospital stay, reduce the chance of infection, and improve the likelihood of a successful outcome. However, advanced surgical procedures will likely limit the number of surgeons who can

perform the operation and increase the expense of each surgery.

Science, Technology, Engineering & Mathematics

The revenue earned on each surgery must cover many expenses related to developing and using the alternative surgical method. These would include:

1. Research and development
2. Patent and other legal activities
3. FDA approval
4. Quality control
5. Production
6. Training
7. Marketing and selling

CRITICAL THINKING

1. Search the Internet for an article about an alternative form of surgery. For example, you could visit the website of the FDA (www.fda.gov). Write a one-paragraph summary about the procedure you researched.

2. List three expenses that may have been affected by the alternative form of surgery you chose in part (1). Explain why.

Careers In Accounting

Jose Soto
ACCOUNTANT/GENERAL LEDGER ACCOUNTANT

STARUSH/ISTOCKPHOTO.COM

The job title "accountant" is used for many positions in the broad field of accounting. It is often the job title for general ledger accountants. However, the position of general ledger accountant is quite specific with tasks and responsibilities that are very different from other accounting positions.

Jose Soto is a general ledger accountant. He is responsible for a variety of tasks related to the general ledger. Some of these tasks are:

1. Accurately record all transactions
2. Make appropriate adjusting and closing entries
3. Reconcile accounts
4. Manage the computerized accounting system
5. Compare budgeted to actual costs
6. Prepare financial statements
7. Prepare other schedules and reports required by management
8. Prepare tax returns

The size of the company usually determines the specific duties of the general ledger accountant. In the large company where Jose works, he has responsibility for certain areas of the accounting process and supervises the accounting clerks. In small companies, the general ledger accountant would be responsible for a wider range of tasks.

Salary Range: Salaries vary with job responsibilities. An entry-level general ledger accountant usually earns between $34,000 and $45,000 annually, plus bonuses and/or profit sharing.

Qualifications: The general ledger accountant must have a complete understanding of accounting and accounting systems. Since most of accounting is automated, the general ledger accountant must be able to work with computer systems. Good communication skills are required. The ability to work well with subordinates and others at all levels is essential. Other required skills include:

1. The ability to work alone
2. The discipline to plan and complete projects
3. The knowledge to apply GAAP to specific situations
4. The analytical skills to interpret data and solve problems

Most general ledger accountants have a four-year accounting degree, although some do not. Many have the Certified Public Accountant (CPA) certification.

Occupational Outlook: The growth in the number of general ledger accounting positions is expected to be much faster than average (20% or more by 2018).

Sources: payscale.com; online.onetcenter.org; accountingcoach.com.

ACTIVITY
Search a newspaper or job search site on the Internet for job openings in your area for general ledger accountants. Select five postings and write a summary of the education requirements, salary range, and job descriptions for all five postings.

© MILENNY, ISTOCK

Terms Review

retained earnings

dividends

board of directors

declaring a dividend

Audit your understanding

1. Under what major chart of accounts division are the owners' equity accounts for a corporation normally listed?

2. Why is only one account maintained for the investment of all owners of a corporation?

3. Which account does a corporation use to record earnings not yet distributed to stockholders?

4. How and when do net income and dividends impact permanent stockholders' equity accounts?

5. What action is required before a corporation can distribute income to its stockholders?

Work together 11-3

Journalizing the declaration and payment of dividends

Journals for LPF Corporation are given in the *Working Papers*. Your instructor will guide you through the following examples.

Journalize the following transactions during December of the current year and January of the next year. Use page 12 of a general journal and page 15 of a cash payments journal. Source documents are abbreviated as follows: check, C; memorandum, M.

Transactions:

Dec. 15. The board of directors declared a dividend of $2.00 per share; capital stock issued is 6,000 shares. M112.

Jan. 15. Paid cash for dividend declared December 15. C556.

On your own 11-3

Journalizing the declaration and payment of dividends

Journals for Badge Crafts are given in the *Working Papers*. Work this problem independently.

Journalize the following transactions during December of the current year and January of the next year. Use page 12 of a general journal and page 14 of a cash payments journal. Source documents are abbreviated as follows: check, C; memorandum, M.

Transactions:

Dec. 15. The board of directors declared a dividend of $3.00 per share; capital stock issued is 7,000 shares. M98.

Jan. 15. Paid cash for dividend declared December 15. C632.

A Look at Accounting Software

In a manual accounting system, paper journals and ledgers make it easy to view transactions that have been entered and posted. Posting references make it easy to track journal entries in the ledgers. An auditor can quickly follow all the transactions that lead to the financial results at the end of a fiscal period.

In a computerized accounting system, tracking transactions can be much more difficult. Multiple windows need to be opened to see all effects of the many transactions. Navigating through so many windows can be awkward.

All computerized accounting systems allow the user to print a variety of transaction reports. Paper records can make tracking transactions and finding errors easier. If desired, a report of each transaction can be printed out as soon as it has been posted, as in Figure 1, below. All transactions within a given date range and within a specified range of account numbers can be printed out. Or, users could choose to print a report of all the transactions in any single general ledger or subsidiary ledger account for a given date range, as in Figure 2, below.

Reviewing Transactions That Have Been Entered and Posted

Figure 1

THREE△GREEN PRODUCTS, INC.
GL Transaction Detail
Dec. 2, 20--

② ③ ①

Account	Type	Date	Refer.	Memo	Debit	Credit	Balance
1550 - Supplies—Store							
	General	12/2/--	M42	Purchased supplies on account from Estes Supply	165.25		4,338.19 Dr
2110 - Accounts Payable						④	
	General	12/2/--	M42	Purchased supplies on account from Estes Supply		165.25	13,186.30 Cr

Figure 2

THREE△GREEN PRODUCTS, INC.
Account Detail
220 - Estes Supply
Nov. 1, 20-- to Dec. 31, 20--

⑥ ⑤ ⑦

Date	Type	Refer.	Memo	Tran. No.	Amount	Balance
11/1/--			Balance			3,165.00 Cr
11/25/--	General	CP22	1110 - Cash	394	−2,345.00	820.00 Cr
12/2/--	General	M42	1550 - Supplies—Store	461	165.25	985.25 Cr

① Figure 1 shows a general ledger detail report of the transaction on December 2, 20--, shown on page 324 in this chapter. It was printed right after the transaction was posted.

② Note that the transactions are listed by account. Only general ledger accounts are shown on this report. If there had been other GL accounts affected, **Sales Tax Payable**, for example, they would appear in order by account number in this listing.

③ The Type column, under the account title, displays the type of journal window the transaction was entered in.

④ As with manual accounting systems, computerized systems post accounts payable and accounts receivable transactions to both general ledger and subsidiary ledger accounts. Note how the Transaction Detail report (Fig. 1) corresponds to the Account Detail for Estes Supply (Fig. 2).

⑤ For this Account Detail report, the user selected the months of November and December of the current year. Any range could have been selected, from a single day to multiple years.

⑥ This report lists postings in date order.

⑦ Account detail reports usually include just two amount columns—one showing the amount posted as a positive or negative number and the other showing the running account balance. The normal account balance, whether debit or credit, is always positive. So, on this report, since Estes Supply would have a normal credit balance, debits are shown as negative numbers.

Chapter Summary

A general journal is used to record transactions that cannot be recorded in a special journal. Examples illustrated in this chapter include:

1. The purchase of supplies on account
2. Purchases returns and allowances
3. Sales returns and allowances
4. The declaration of a dividend

Since no cash is involved, none of these transactions can be recorded in a cash payments or cash receipts journal. The transactions do not involve the purchase or sale of merchandise on account so they would not be recorded in a purchases or sales journal.

Customers may be allowed to return merchandise to a vendor. Examples are merchandise that is inferior in quality, different from what was ordered, or damaged when received. A purchases return occurs when a customer returns merchandise to a vendor. A purchases allowance occurs when a vendor allows a customer to keep the merchandise at a reduced price. Both transactions increase **Purchases Returns and Allowances**, a contra account to **Purchases**, and reduce **Accounts Payable**. The customer prepares a debit memorandum to document the transaction.

Vendors record the merchandise returned by a customer as a sales return. A sales allowance occurs when a customer is allowed to keep the merchandise at a reduced price. Both transactions increase **Sales Returns and Allowances**, a contra account to **Sales**, and reduce **Accounts Receivable**. The vendor prepares a credit memorandum to document the transaction and sends a copy to the customer.

A dividend is a distribution of a corporation's earnings to its stockholders. When the board of directors declares a dividend, the **Dividends Payable** account is increased to reflect the corporation's obligation to pay the dividend.

EXPLORE ACCOUNTING

Categories of Internal Control

It's a fact of life—people make mistakes. It's not a matter of if, but how often. For this reason, accounting procedures must be set up to minimize the problems caused by these mistakes. One type of error is the posting of a transaction from a journal to both the general ledger and a subsidiary ledger. For example, ThreeGreen might fail to record a sale to a customer's account. As a result, ThreeGreen may never collect that account receivable. To avoid errors and the losses they cause, businesses should establish effective controls. Processes and procedures employed within a business to ensure that its operations are conducted ethically, accurately, and reliably are called **internal controls**.

Internal controls are of three types: (1) preventive, (2) detective, and (3) corrective. A preventive control attempts to prevent an employee from making the error. Establishing and following consistent procedures for posting transactions is a preventive control. A detective control actively looks for errors. Preparing a trial balance is a detective control. A corrective control restores the business to normal after an error has occurred. Insurance on employees who handle cash is a corrective control meant to protect the business from any fraudulent activity by those employees.

Businesses with enough employees should split duties among several of them to reduce the chances of error. This segregation of duties enables one employee to check the work of another. For example, one employee should post transactions to the general ledger while another employee should post transactions to the subsidiary ledger.

INSTRUCTIONS

1. Determine whether the following control procedures are preventive, detective, or corrective:

   a. A computerized accounting system requires the debits and credits of a journal entry to be equal.

   b. A manager recounts the cash in an employee's cash drawer before the cash total is written on a deposit slip.

   c. An accountant uses a computer program to search the accounting records for credit entries to expense accounts.

   d. A company replaces a hand-prepared sales invoice system with a point-of-sale system.

   e. Customers at a fast-food restaurant receive a free meal if they inform the manager that they did not receive a sales receipt.

2. Discuss whether a policeman scanning a highway with radar is a preventive or detective control of the speed limit.

Apply Your Understanding

INSTRUCTIONS: Download problem instructions for Excel, QuickBooks, and Peachtree from the textbook companion website at www.C21accounting.com.

11-1 Application Problem: Journalizing and posting purchases transactions using a general journal LO2, 3

1. Journalize and post vendor transactions to the general journal and accounts payable ledger.
2. Print the worksheets.

A general journal and selected accounts payable and general ledger accounts for Holiday Ceramics are given in the *Working Papers*.

Instructions:

1. Journalize the following transactions during December of the current year. Use page 12 of a general journal. Source documents are abbreviated as follows: memorandum, M; debit memorandum, DM.

Transactions:

Dec. 2. Bought store supplies on account from Daniels Supply, $153.00. M85.
6. Returned merchandise to Mason Molds, $107.00. DM23.
7. Returned merchandise to Harris Paints, $129.00. DM24.
9. Bought office supplies on account from Office Zone, $292.00. M86.

2. Post each general journal entry to the accounts payable and general ledgers.

11-2 Application Problem: Accounting for sales returns and allowances using a general journal LO4, 5, 6

1. Journalize and post sales transactions to the general journal and accounts receivable ledger.
2. Print the worksheets.

A general journal and selected accounts receivable and general ledger accounts for Quality Furniture Center are given in the *Working Papers*.

Instructions:

1. Using the current year, journalize the following transactions on page 9 of a general journal. Source documents are abbreviated as follows: credit memorandum, CM; sales invoice, S.

Transactions:

Sept. 3. Found that a sale on account to John Auburn was incorrectly charged to the account of Mary Best, $1,562.00. Memorandum No. 160.
5. Granted credit to Anna Jackson for merchandise returned, $657.00, plus sales tax, $39.42, from S884; total, $696.42. CM88.
14. Granted credit to Metsville Schools for damaged merchandise, $398.00 (no sales tax), from S879. CM89.
19. Found that a sale on account to Burns & Associates was incorrectly charged to the account of Cassidy Corporation, $993.00. Memorandum No. 161.

2. Post each general journal entry to the accounts receivable and general ledgers.

11-3 Application Problem: Journalizing the declaration and payment of dividends LO8

Journals for Meridian Industries are given in the *Working Papers*.

Instructions:
Journalize the following transactions during December of the current year and January of the next year.
Use page 12 of a general journal and page 16 of a cash payments journal. Source documents are abbreviated as follows: check, C; memorandum, M.

Transactions:

Dec. 15. The board of directors declared a dividend of $0.24 per share; capital stock issued is 120,000 shares. M260.
Jan. 15. Paid cash for dividend declared December 15. C954.

11-M.1 Mastery Problem: Journalizing and posting transactions using a general journal and a cash payments journal LO2, 3, 4, 5, 6, 8

Journals and selected accounts payable, accounts receivable, and general ledger accounts for Williams Market are given in the *Working Papers*.

Instructions:

1. Journalize the following transactions during December of the current year. Use page 12 of a general journal. Journalize the January transaction on page 16 of a cash payments journal. Source documents are abbreviated as follows: memorandum, M; debit memorandum, DM; credit memorandum, CM; sales invoice, S.

Transactions:

Dec. 2. Granted credit to JD's Café for damaged merchandise, $49.00, plus sales tax, $3.92, from S678; total, $52.92. CM68.
     3. Bought store supplies on account from Kelsar Supply, $231.00. M335.
     6. Learned that a sale on account to Rib Shack was incorrectly charged to the account of Restaurant Deville, $754.00. M336.
    12. Returned merchandise to Great Lakes Produce, $256.00. DM93.
    15. The board of directors declared a dividend of $0.34 per share; capital stock issued is 8,600 shares. M337.
    23. Granted credit to Connie's Bakery for merchandise returned, $189.00, plus sales tax, $15.12, from S680; total, $204.12. CM69.
    28. Returned merchandise to Century Foods, $358.00. DM94.
Jan. 15. Paid cash for dividend declared December 15. C881.

2. Post each general journal entry to the appropriate subsidiary ledger and the general ledger.

3. Post the Jan. 15 transaction in the General Debit column of the cash payments journal.

Peachtree

1. Journalize and post sales returns in the Credit Memos window.
2. Journalize and post purchase returns in the Vendor Credit Memos window.
3. Print the sales journal, cash receipts journal and purchase journal.
4. Print the vendor ledgers and the customer ledgers.

QuickBooks

1. Journalize and post sales returns in the Create Credit Memos/Refunds window.
2. Journalize and post purchase returns in the Enter Bills window.
3. From the menu bar, select Reports; Accountant & Taxes, Journal.
4. Make the selections to print the December 1-31, 2011 journal.

AAONLINE

1. Go to www.cengage.com/login
2. Click on **AA Online** to access.
3. Go to the online assignment and follow the instructions.

11-M.2 Mastery Problem (Review of Chapters 9, 10, and 11): Journalizing and posting transactions

Journals and selected accounts payable, accounts receivable, and general ledger accounts for Innovative Solutions are given in the *Working Papers*.

Instructions:

1. Journalize the following transactions during December of the current year. Use page 12 of a general journal, page 12 of a sales journal, page 12 of a purchases journal, page 12 of a cash receipts journal, and page 15 of a cash payments journal. The company offers sales terms of 2/10, n/30. The sales tax rate is 6%. Post the following transactions when journalized: (a) transactions impacting the accounts receivable or accounts payable subsidiary ledgers, (b) transactions recorded in the general journal, and (c) cash payments entered in a general amount column of the cash payments journal. Source documents are abbreviated as follows: check, C; memorandum, M; purchase invoice, P; receipt, R; sales invoice, S; terminal summary, TS; debit memorandum, DM; credit memorandum, CM.

Transactions:

Dec. 1. Sold merchandise on account to Larry Simpson, $4,780.00, plus sales tax. S395.
    2. Paid cash to Perkins Properties for rent, $800.00. C518.
    3. The board of directors declared a dividend of $0.20 per share; capital stock issued is 20,000 shares. M68.
    4. Received cash on account from Coastal County Schools, $814.80, less 2% sales discount. R289.
    5. Paid cash to Ulman Paper for office supplies, $169.00. C519.
    6. Paid cash on account to Jing Corporation for $2,618.00, less 2% discount. C520.
    7. Purchased merchandise on account from Wilson Metals, $9,000.00, less a 60% trade discount. P315.
    8. Bought office supplies on account from Barger Office Supply, $148.00. M69.

Dec. 9. Paid cash to Dave's Signs for miscellaneous expense, $42.00. C521.
    10. Sold merchandise on account to LaDonna Atkins, $2,410.00, plus sales tax. S396.
    12. Paid cash to Daniel Promotions for advertising, $590.00. C522.
    13. Paid cash to City Utilities for electric bill, $347.50. C523.
    14. Purchased merchandise on account from Quitman Manufacturing, $4,818.00. P316.
    15. Sold merchandise on account to Coastal County Schools, $3,448.00. Coastal County Schools is exempt from sales tax. S397.
    16. Granted credit to Larry Simpson for merchandise returned, $229.00, plus sales tax, $13.74; total, $242.74. CM21.
    17. Recorded cash and credit card sales, $6,148.90, plus sales tax, $332.04; total, $6,480.94. TS49.
    18. Returned merchandise to Jing Corporation, $540.00. DM8.
    22. Received cash on account from Joseph Greggs, $2,219.15. R290.
    28. Paid cash for dividend declared December 3. C524.
    30. Paid cash to replenish the petty cash fund: advertising expense, $49.00; miscellaneous, $25.00; cash short, $2.00. C525.

2. Prove and rule the sales journal. Post the totals of the special columns to the general ledger.

3. Total and rule the purchases journal. Post the total to the general ledger.

4. Prove the equality of debits and credits for the cash receipts journal. Post the totals of the special columns to the general ledger.

5. Prove and rule the cash payments journal. Post the totals of the special columns to the general ledger.

6. Prove cash. The balance on the next unused check stub is $22,267.95.

7. Prepare a schedule of accounts receivable and a schedule of accounts payable.

AAONLiNE

1. Go to www.cengage.com/login
2. Click on **AA Online** to access.
3. Go to the online assignment and follow the instructions.

11-C Challenge Problem: Journalizing business transactions LO2, 6

The general journal for Discount Warehouse is given in the *Working Papers*.

Instructions:

Using the current year, journalize the following transactions on page 10 of a general journal. Source documents are abbreviated as follows: memorandum, M; debit memorandum, DM; credit memorandum, CM.

Transactions:
Oct. 2. Returned office supplies purchased on account from Best Office Supply, $122.00. DM46.
    6. Learned that a purchase of merchandise on account from Harris Industries was incorrectly charged to the account of Hall Corporation, $5,463.00. M249.
    12. Opened a box of store supplies from Display Warehouse, only to discover that the items were defective. Display Warehouse asked that the goods, costing $425.00, be destroyed. DM47.
    17. Found that the transaction to record the declaration of dividends was recorded as an $8,000.00 debit to Dividends Payable and a credit to Dividends. M250.
    21. Received a call from Columbus College stating it did not receive credit for $25.20 of sales tax on CM89 for $420.00. Columbus College, a for-profit business, is not exempt from sales tax. CM92.
    24. Credit memorandum 88 for $327.00 was incorrectly recorded as a credit to the account of Aaron Company. The memorandum should have been recorded as a credit to the account of Ashton Corporation. M251.

Peachtree

1. Journalize and post sales returns in the Credit Memos window.
2. Journalize and post purchase returns in the Vendor Credit Memos window.
3. Print the sales journal, cash receipts journal and purchase journal.
4. Print the vendor ledgers and the customer ledgers.

1. Journalize and post sales returns in the Create Credit Memos/Refunds window.
2. Journalize and post purchase returns in the Enter Bills window.
3. From the menu bar, select Reports; Accountant & Taxes, Journal.
4. Make the selections to print the October 1-31, 2011 journal.

Balancing Returns

PARTNERSHIP FOR
21ST CENTURY SKILLS

Theme: Financial, Economic, Business, and Entrepreneurial Literacy

Skills: Creativity and Innovation, Problem Solving and Critical Thinking, Information Literacy

It's the wrong size. It's a duplicate gift. It's an ugly color. Merchandise is returned for many reasons. Billions of dollars worth of goods are returned to retailers each year. Many returns are for legitimate reasons. However, thieves may produce fake receipts. They may switch price tags. Thieves may steal merchandise and then return it for a cash refund. Fraudulent sales returns cost retailers an estimated $10 billion per year.

To reduce the number of fraudulent sales returns, businesses try to create returns policies that encourage customer loyalty and discourage dishonesty.

APPLICATION

1. Using the Internet, compare and contrast the returns policies for five retailers.
2. Why do you think some retailers include a restocking fee for items such as electronics?
3. Assume you are a small business owner. Write your own returns policy. Be sure to include policies that involve lack of sales receipts, returns of electronics, and time limitations.

Auditing for errors

LaDonna Smith has just completed posting sales and cash receipts transactions to the general and subsidiary ledgers. According to the company's internal control procedures, you are assigned the task of checking her work.

REVIEW AND ANSWER

Three accounts receivable ledger accounts are shown below and to the right. Assume that the posting references and the amounts are correct. From your knowledge of transactions that impact the accounts receivable ledger, determine if any of the amounts are recorded in the wrong column. List any incorrect amounts and calculate new ending balances for the accounts.

CUSTOMER Jenni Beckman   CUSTOMER NO. 110

DATE		ITEM	POST. REF.	DEBIT	CREDIT	DEBIT BALANCE
July 1	Balance	✔			8 9 5 25
16		S7	8 4 9 30		1 7 4 4 55
25		CR7	3 6 2 42		2 1 0 6 97
28		G7		4 8 0 60	1 6 2 6 37

CUSTOMER Andrew Estes   CUSTOMER NO. 120

DATE		ITEM	POST. REF.	DEBIT	CREDIT	DEBIT BALANCE
July 1	Balance	✔			1 6 4 9 17
24		S7		4 8 0 60	1 1 6 8 57
28		G7	4 8 0 60		1 6 4 9 17

CUSTOMER Blake Gentry												CUSTOMER NO. 130					

DATE		ITEM	POST. REF.	DEBIT	CREDIT	DEBIT BALANCE
July²⁰⁻⁻	1	Balance	✔			3 1 9 4 44
	5		CR7	9 5 8 95		4 1 5 3 39
	22		S7		3 2 2 9 46	9 2 3 93

Analyzing Nike's financial statements

Graphics are an effective way to communicate financial information. A stacked column chart is especially useful to present income statement data. The chart can show trends in sales, expenses, and net income for multiple fiscal years.

INSTRUCTIONS

1. Prepare an electronic spreadsheet containing information from Nike's Consolidated Statements of Income on page B-5 in Appendix B. (Use a sheet of paper if spreadsheet software is not available.) Enter the following headings in the first column:

   Row 2: Cost of sales

   Row 3: Total expenses

   Row 4: Income taxes

   Row 5: Net income

2. Across the first row, beginning in the second column, enter the years 2011 to 2009.

3. Enter the data from the Consolidated Statements of Income. For total expenses, add the six amounts from Total selling and administrative expense through Other (Income), net.

4. Prepare a stacked column chart of the data.

5. What does the top of each column represent?

Chapter 12 | Preparing Payroll Records

LEARNING OBJECTIVES

After studying Chapter 12, in addition to defining key terms, you will be able to:

LO1 Explain how employees are paid.

LO2 Calculate hourly employee earnings.

LO3 Demonstrate the process for determining federal income tax withholdings.

LO4 Demonstrate the process for calculating social security and Medicare taxes.

LO5 Explain the benefit of funding medical and retirement plans with pretax contributions.

LO6 Prepare a payroll register.

LO7 Prepare employee earnings records.

LO8 Justify the use of a payroll checking account.

LO9 Prepare employee payroll checks.

©DANIEL KOUREY, ISTOCK/©JIM PRUITT, ISTOCK

STEPHEN COBURN/SHUTTERSTOCK.COM

Accounting In The Real World
The Walt Disney Company

Every child dreams of going to Disneyland®. Whether you are 4 or 40, your first visit to Disneyland is a magical moment. From riding an attraction, to watching a show, to having your picture taken in the arms of a famous Disney character, the Disney experience is certain to spark your imagination.

Could you be a cast member for Disney? No, you don't have to be a dancer, actor, or singer, although Disney needs people with these skills. All you need is a passion to share the magic of Disney. The variety of talents required to operate Disneyland is truly amazing.

- Do you like animals? Stable attendants help guests interact with the animals, operate horse-drawn vehicles, and care for animals at the guest kennels.
- Do you enjoy photography? Photo-imaging cast members take guest portraits framed by famous Disney landmarks and join families for the day to capture their Disney experience.
- Are costumes your thing? Costume and cosmetology cast members help entertainers with costumes, wigs, and makeup.

These are just of a few of the many positions required to deliver the Disney experience. Are you ready to explore joining the team? The Disneyland CareerStart Program allows high school seniors and recent graduates to work as cast members. The program enables cast members to attend seminars featuring Disney executives and enroll in hospitality management courses offered for college credit.

CRITICAL THINKING

1. Select one of the cast member positions available with the Disneyland CareerStart Program. What expense accounts, other than payroll, might Disney need to account for activities related to this position? For example, attractions cast members wear costumes provided by Disney. Therefore, Disney would require costumes and laundry expense accounts.

2. Suppose a cast member begins her day by attending a two-hour seminar featuring a Disney sales manager. Leaving the off-site training facility, she travels 45 minutes to the park and spends an hour in makeup. Waiting an hour for a storm to pass, she finally dances alongside a float and entertains guests during the 30-minute parade. After spending 15 minutes to remove makeup, she returns to the training facility. There, she spends three hours training a new cast member to perform her character.

   a. Summarize the cast member's hours by activity.
   b. How would this information be useful to a manager?

Source: http://disney.go.com/disneycareers/careerstart/index.html.

Key Terms

- wage
- salary
- commission
- total earnings
- pay period
- payroll
- payroll clerk
- time clock

- payroll taxes
- withholding allowance
- payroll deduction
- social security tax
- Medicare tax
- accumulated earnings
- tax base
- qualified retirement plan

- 401(k)
- individual retirement account (IRA)
- Roth individual retirement account (Roth IRA)
- payroll register
- net pay

- employee earnings record
- voucher check
- direct deposit

LESSON
12-1 Calculating Employee Earnings

LO1 Explain how employees are paid.

LO2 Calculate hourly employee earnings.

Paying Employees LO1

The amount paid to an employee for every hour worked is called a **wage**. Under the federal wage and hour laws, hourly employees must be paid for every hour they are on the job. The wage and hour laws allow employers to exempt owners and managers from this hourly payment rule. Those employees are often paid a fixed amount regardless of the number of hours worked. A fixed annual sum of money divided among equal pay periods is called a **salary**. To encourage higher sales, many companies pay their sales employees based on the sales they achieve. A **commission** is a method of paying an employee based on the amount of sales the employee generates. Commissions are normally calculated as a percent of an employee's sales. The total amount paid by a business for an employee's work, earned by a wage, salary, or commission, is called **total earnings**. Total earnings are sometimes referred to as *gross pay*, *gross wages*, or *gross earnings*.

ThreeGreen employs several people to work in the business. These employees record the time they work for ThreeGreen each day. Periodically, ThreeGreen pays its employees for the number of hours each employee has worked. A **pay period** is the number of days or weeks of work covered by an employee's paycheck. A business may decide to pay its employees every week (weekly), every two weeks (biweekly), twice a month (semimonthly), or once a month (monthly). ThreeGreen uses a semi-monthly pay period. Employees are paid on the 15th and last day of each month.

The total amount earned by all employees for a pay period is called a **payroll**. But the total payroll is not the amount actually paid to employees. The payroll amount paid to employees is reduced by state and federal taxes and other deductions such as health insurance. Special payroll records support the recording of payroll transactions in a journal. The business also uses these records to inform employees of their annual earnings and to prepare payroll reports for federal, state, and local governments. The accounting staff position that compiles and computes payroll data and then prepares, journalizes, and posts payroll transactions is called a **payroll clerk**.

ETHICS IN ACTION

Is It Discrimination or Poor Judgment?

Your group at CyberMarket has an opening for a research analyst. You are on the team to pick candidates to be interviewed. Your company has a code of conduct that bars discrimination on the basis of "race, color, religion, national origin, gender, sexual orientation, age, disability, or veteran status." In a recent meeting, team members gave the following reasons for wanting to drop two candidates.

Candidate A: "She's 52 years old. I wasn't even born when she graduated from college. How can she possibly know anything about our business?"

Candidate B: "The ad said two to five years of experience. But we really need someone with more than two years of experience."

INSTRUCTIONS

Use the ethical model to help evaluate hiring decisions based on each of the statements above. Use online sources, as appropriate, to determine whether any actions are illegal.

©LUCA DI FILIPPO, ISTOCK

Calculating Employee Hours Worked

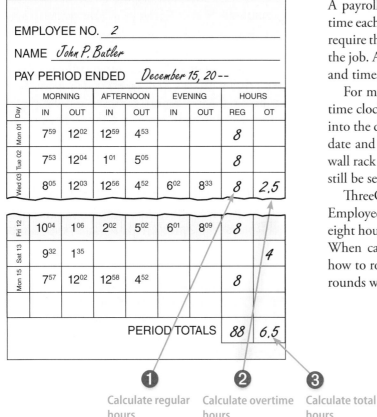

EMPLOYEE NO. _2_							
NAME _John P. Butler_							
PAY PERIOD ENDED _December 15, 20--_							

Day	MORNING		AFTERNOON		EVENING		HOURS	
	IN	OUT	IN	OUT	IN	OUT	REG	OT
Mon 01	7⁵⁹	12⁰²	12⁵⁹	4⁵³			8	
Tue 02	7⁵³	12⁰⁴	1⁰¹	5⁰⁵			8	
Wed 03	8⁰⁵	12⁰³	12⁵⁶	4⁵²	6⁰²	8³³	8	2.5
Fri 12	10⁰⁴	1⁰⁶	2⁰²	5⁰²	6⁰¹	8⁰⁹	8	
Sat 13	9³²	1³⁵						4
Mon 15	7⁵⁷	12⁰²	12⁵⁸	4⁵²			8	
PERIOD TOTALS							88	6.5

❶ Calculate regular hours

❷ Calculate overtime hours

❸ Calculate total hours

A payroll system must keep an accurate record of the time each hourly employee has worked. Most businesses require their employees to make a record of their time on the job. A **time clock** is a device used to record the dates and times of every employee's arrivals and departures.

For more than a century, the most common type of time clock required each employee to insert a time card into the device. The time clock stamped or punched the date and time on the next available line of the card. A wall rack full of time cards was a common sight and can still be seen in many businesses today.

ThreeGreen uses a traditional time card system. Employees earn overtime pay for working more than eight hours in any day or more than 40 hours in a week. When calculating hours worked, a business can elect how to round arrival and departure times. ThreeGreen rounds work hours to the nearest quarter hour.

Calculating Employee Hours Worked

❶ Calculate the number of regular hours for each day. Enter the amounts in the Hours/Reg column. The hours worked on December 3, the third line of the time card, are calculated using the arrival and departure times imprinted on the time card.

	Departure Time	−	Arrival Time	=	Hours Worked
Morning:					
Time card	12:03		8:05		
Nearest quarter hour	12:00	−	8:00	=	4
Afternoon:					
Time card	4:52		12:56		
Nearest quarter hour	5:00	−	1:00	=	4
Total regular hours worked on December 3					8

The hours worked in the morning, afternoon, and evening are calculated separately. The morning departure time of 12:03 is rounded to the nearest quarter hour, 12:00. The 8:00 arrival time (rounded from 8:05), subtracted from the 12:00 departure time, equals four hours. Record the total regular hours worked, 8, on the time card in the Hours/Reg column.

❷ Calculate the number of overtime hours for each day. Overtime hours for December 3 are calculated using the same procedure as for regular hours. Record Mr. Butler's overtime hours worked, 2.5, in the Hours/OT column.

	Departure Time	−	Arrival Time	=	Hours Worked
Time card	8:33		6:02		
Nearest quarter hour	8:30	−	6:00	=	2.5

❸ Add Mr. Butler's hours worked in the Hours/Reg and Hours/OT columns and enter the totals, 88 regular hours and 6.5 overtime hours, in the spaces provided at the bottom of the time card.

Time Clock Systems

Hour Summary

Payroll Period: 12/1/20-- to 12/15/20--
Employee No.: 2
Employee Name: John P. Butler

Date	Day	Regular	Overtime	Other	Total
12/1/20--	Mon	8.0			8.0
12/2/20--	Tue	8.0			8.0
12/3/20--	Wed	8.0	2.5		10.5
12/4/20--	Thu	8.0			8.0
12/5/20--	Fri	8.0			8.0
12/8/20--	Mon	8.0			8.0
12/9/20--	Tue	8.0			8.0
12/10/20--	Wed	8.0			8.0
12/11/20--	Thu	8.0			8.0
12/12/20--	Fri	8.0			8.0
12/13/20--	Sat		4.0		4.0
12/15/20--	Mon	8.0			8.0
Totals		88.0	6.5	—	94.5

Employee No.: 4
Employee Name: Cary B. Wells

Date	Day	Regular	Overtime	Other	Total
12/2/20--	Tue	4.0			4.0
12/3/20--	Wed	8.0			8.0
12/4/20--	Thu	8.0	2.5		10.5
12/5/20--	Fri	6.0			6.0

Computer technology offers new methods for recording employee time. Employees can swipe a name badge, key in a PIN, or press a finger on a biometric pad to record their arrival or departure. Today's time clocks feed data directly into a company's computer system. At the end of every pay period, the system can print a report showing the daily regular and overtime hours worked by each employee. The report to the left shows how Mr. Butler's hours for the pay period ending December 15 would be reported. The data could also be used to prepare other reports. For example, one report could show the exact times employees arrived and departed. Another report could show a list of employees who arrived late for work.

Larger companies can afford more expensive systems to record employee arrival and departure times. A popular system requires employees to scan a personal identification card through a card scanner. At the end of the pay period, the system prints a report similar to the time card.

GLOBAL AWARENESS

European Union

The European Union (EU) is an association of 27 European countries. It was formed to enhance political, economic, and social cooperation. The EU ensures the free movement of people, goods, services, and capital within and between the 27 countries. This means that no passport is required to move from one EU country to another. It also means that goods can move between the EU countries without additional taxes or tariffs. This is known as the "single market."

The single market is possible because there is one set of laws which apply in all member states. These laws are created by several organizations. The major law-making organization is the Council of the European Union.

The standard unit of money for the EU is the euro. Currently, however, only 17 EU countries use the euro. In those countries, it is no longer necessary to worry about exchange rates or calculating the true price of a product.

The EU hopes to grow by adding even more countries to the union.

CRITICAL THINKING

1. Name the 10 EU countries that do not use the euro as their monetary unit.

2. Use the Internet to research the EU and International Financial Reporting Standards (IFRS). (IFRS were discussed in the Global Awareness feature in Chapter 10.) Summarize the EU's use or nonuse of IFRS.

Calculating Hourly Employee Total Earnings LO2

Hourly employee earnings are calculated using time card data. Hourly wage rates are obtained from personnel records.

The Fair Labor Standards Act, often referred to as the federal wage and hour laws, set the minimum wage and rules for the payment of overtime. The law requires most businesses involved in interstate commerce to pay employees at least 1½ times their normal hourly rate for hours worked in excess of 40 hours per week. ThreeGreen complies with the Fair Labor Standards Act. But the company goes even further and pays its employees overtime when they work more than eight hours in a day.

Mr. Butler earned $1,466.25 for his work during the pay period ending December 15. However, taxes and other deductions are taken out of total earnings to determine the actual amount ThreeGreen will pay Mr. Butler.

Calculate regular earnings ❶

Regular Hours	×	Regular Rate	=	Regular Earnings
88	×	$15.00	=	$1,320.00

Calculate the overtime rate ❷

Regular Rate	×	1½	=	Overtime Rate
$15.00	×	1½	=	$22.50

Calculate overtime earnings ❸

Overtime Hours	×	Overtime Rate	=	Overtime Earnings
6.5	×	$22.50	=	$146.25

Calculate total earnings ❹

Regular Earnings	+	Overtime Earnings	=	Total Earnings
$1,320.00	+	$146.25	=	$1,466.25

Calculating an Hourly Employee's Total Earnings

❶ Multiply the regular hours, 88, by the regular rate, $15.00, to calculate regular earnings, $1,320.00.

❷ Multiply the regular rate, $15.00, by 1½ to calculate the overtime rate, $22.50.

❸ Multiply the overtime hours, 6.5, by the overtime rate, $22.50, to calculate the overtime earnings, $146.25.

❹ Add the regular earnings, $1,320.00, and the overtime earnings, $146.25, to calculate the total earnings, $1,466.25.

WHY ACCOUNTING?

Cost of Legislation

The U.S. Senate and the House of Representatives, which constitute the Congress of the United States, are responsible for writing the laws that govern the nation. Those laws generally have a cost. Many Americans may not realize how Congress determines the cost of legislation it is debating.

The Congressional Budget Office (CBO) is a government agency whose mandate is "to provide Congress with objective, nonpartisan, and timely analyses to aid in economic and budgetary decisions...." Congress established the CBO in 1974. The Speaker of the House of Representatives and the president pro tempore of the Senate act jointly to appoint the CBO's director. The director serves a four-year term, but can be reappointed for an unlimited number of terms. Currently, about 250 people are employed by the CBO to provide the reports required by law and requested by Congress.

The CBO has a very important role in the legislative process. Clearly, Congress must have accurate estimates for the cost of proposed legislation if it is to make well-informed decisions.

Government & Public Administration

CRITICAL THINKING

Visit the Congressional Budget Office website (www.cbo.gov). Find the estimated cost for one piece of proposed or recently passed legislation. Write a one-paragraph report summarizing the legislation and stating the estimated cost.

End of Lesson Review

Terms Review

Audit your understanding

1. What is a payroll?
2. Identify three methods used by modern time clock systems to record employee arrival and departure times.
3. Describe the overtime rules of the Fair Labor Standards Act.
4. How does ThreeGreen calculate overtime earnings?

Work together 12-1

Calculating hourly employee total earnings

The October 15 time card for Alice R. Webster and time card data for other employees are provided in the *Working Papers*. Your instructor will guide you through the following example. Round hours to the nearest quarter hour.

1. Calculate the regular, overtime, and total hours worked by Ms. Webster. Any hours over eight hours per day or 40 hours per week are considered overtime. Each work week begins on Monday. Record the total hours on the time card.

2. Enter the regular and overtime hours for Ms. Webster in the schedule. For each employee, calculate the amount of regular, overtime, and total earnings. Overtime hours are paid at 1½ times the regular rate. Round dollar amounts to the nearest cent.

On your own 12-1

Calculating hourly employee total earnings

The June 30 time card for Mary Carol Prestwood and time card data for other employees are provided in the *Working Papers*. Work this problem independently. Round hours to the nearest quarter hour.

1. Calculate the regular, overtime, and total hours worked by Ms. Prestwood. Any hours over eight hours per day or 40 hours per week are considered overtime. Each work week begins on Monday. Record the total hours on the time card.

2. Enter the regular and overtime hours for Ms. Prestwood in the schedule. For each employee, calculate the amount of regular, overtime, and total earnings. Overtime hours are paid at 1½ times the regular rate. Round dollar amounts to the nearest cent.

LESSON
12-2 Determining Payroll Tax Withholding

LO3 Demonstrate the process for determining federal income tax withholdings.

LO4 Demonstrate the process for calculating social security and Medicare taxes.

LO5 Explain the benefit of funding medical and retirement plans with pretax contributions.

Payroll Taxes LO3

Federal income tax is withheld from employee earnings in all 50 states. Employers in many states also are required to withhold state, city, or county income taxes from employee earnings. The amounts withheld ensure that the employee has paid an amount about equal to the employee's annual tax liability. Income taxes withheld must be sent periodically to the respective government agencies.

Taxes based on the payroll of a business are called **payroll taxes**. All payroll taxes are based on employee earnings. Therefore, accurate and detailed payroll records must be maintained. Errors in payroll records could cause incorrect payroll tax payments. Government agencies may assess penalties for failure to pay correct payroll taxes when they are due. Payroll taxes withheld represent liabilities for the employer until payments are made to the respective government tax agencies.

THINK LIKE AN ACCOUNTANT

Evaluating Employee Performance

Gerald Murphy is the sole accountant at Jenkins Vacations. The business rents and manages vacation rental property. Owners of homes at popular vacation destinations hire Jenkins Vacations to rent their properties. These "members" receive 60% of all rental fees.

In addition to managing the accounting system, Gerald is responsible for ensuring that the company meets its income goals. A major factor in achieving that goal is the quality of the service provided to customers.

The company employs 24 sales agents in its call center. Agents work with customers to arrange rentals from its inventory of properties. After each call is completed, the customer is asked to complete a survey to rate the quality of the service received. Customers rate the consultants on a scale of 1 (poor) to 5 (excellent).

Each week, the computer system provides Gerald with the ratings for each consultant. Gerald examines these ratings to identify consultants who are not meeting the company's quality standards. Gerald works with the consultants who are underperforming to improve the quality of their service.

OPEN THE SPREADSHEET TLA_CH12
Follow the steps on the Instructions tab. The worksheets on the Analysis and Week 15 Data tabs contain the ratings for two weeks. Using the worksheets, identify sales agents who meet the following criteria:

1. For week 14, identify the agents whose:
   a. weekly change is in the top quarter of all agents.
   b. average score is in the bottom quarter of all agents.

2. Answer the same questions for week 15.

3. What recommendations would you make regarding those consultants who consistently have poor performance?

©DAN BACHMAN, ISTOCK

Employee's Withholding Allowance Certificate

③ Marital Status

① Name and Address

② Social Security Number

④ Withholding Allowances

⑤ Signature and Date

A deduction from total earnings for each person legally supported by a taxpayer, including the employee, is called a **withholding allowance**. The information used to determine how much income tax to withhold is found on Form W-4, Employee's Withholding Allowance Certificate. Employers are required to have a current Form W-4 on file for every employee. The amount of income tax withheld is based on an employee's marital status and number of allowances. A married employee will have less income tax withheld than a single employee with the same earnings. The larger the number of allowances claimed, the smaller the amount of income tax withheld.

Most employees are required to have federal income taxes withheld from their wages. An exemption from withholding is available for certain low-income and part-time employees. The employee must meet the requirements listed in item 7 of the Form W-4. However, individuals cannot claim exemption from withholding if (1) their income exceeds $950.00 and includes more than $300.00 of unearned income such as interest and dividends and (2) another person can claim them as a dependent on their tax return. These requirements are subject to change.

Any amount withheld from an employee's gross earnings is called a **payroll deduction**. Federal income tax is just one of many amounts that are withheld.

Other taxes described in this chapter are withheld from all employees. Some employees elect to have retirement plan contributions, health care premiums, and charitable contributions withheld.

⬎ Preparing an Employee's Withholding Allowance Certificate

❶ Write the employee's name and address.

❷ Write the employee's social security number.

❸ Check the appropriate marital status block. Mr. Butler checked the married box for item 3.

❹ Write the total number of withholding allowances claimed. Mr. Butler claimed four withholding allowances, one each for himself, his wife, and their two children.

❺ The employee must sign and date the form.

Each employee must have a social security number. Current law ensures that most infants who are at least one year old by the end of a tax year will have a social security number. Therefore, most employees will have received their social security number as a child. Employees without social security numbers can apply for a number at the nearest social security office.

Employee's Income Tax Withholding—Single Persons

SINGLE Persons—**SEMIMONTHLY** Payroll Period
(For Wages Paid Through December 20--)

And the wages are—		And the number of withholding allowances claimed is—										
At least	But less than	0	1	2	3	4	5	6	7	8	9	10
		The amount of income tax to be withheld is—										
$0	$260	$0	$0	$0	$0	$0	$0	$0	$0	$0	$0	$0
260	270	1	0	0	0	0	0	0	0	0	0	0
270	280	2	0	0	0	0	0	0	0	0	0	0
280	290	3	0	0	0	0	0	0	0	0	0	0
290	300	4	0	0	0	0	0	0	0	0	0	0
900	920	90	67	44	21	5	0	0	0	0	0	0
920	940	93	70	47	24	7	0	0	0	0	0	0
940	960	96	73	50	27	9	0	0	0	0	0	0
960	980	99	76	53	30	11	0	0	0	0	0	0
980	1000	102	79	56	33	13	0	0	0	0	0	0
1000	1020	105	82	59	36	15	0	0	0	0	0	0
1020	1040	108	85	62	39	17	2	0	0	0	0	0
1040	1060	111	88	65	42	19	4	0	0	0	0	0
1060	1080	114	91	68	45	22	6	0	0	0	0	0
1080	1100	117	94	71	48	25	8	0	0	0	0	0
1100	1120	120	97	74	51	28	10	0	0	0	0	0
1120	1140	123	100	77	54	31	12	0	0	0	0	0
1140	1160	126	103	80	57	34	14	0	0	0	0	0
1160	1180	129	106	83	60	37	16	1	0	0	0	0
1180	1200	132	109	86	63	40	18	3	0	0	0	0
1200	1220	135	112	89	66	43	21	5	0	0	0	0
1220	1240	138	115	92	69	46	24	7	0	0	0	0
1240	1260	141	118	95	72	49	27	9	0	0	0	0
1260	1280	144	121	98	75	52	30	11	0	0	0	0
1280	1300	147	124	101	78	55	33	13	0	0	0	0
1300	1320	150	127	104	81	58	36	15	0	0	0	0
1320	1340	153	130	107	84	61	39	17	1	0	0	0
1340	1360	156	133	110	87	64	42	19	3	0	0	0
1360	1380	159	136	113	90	67	45	22	5	0	0	0
1380	1400	162	139	116	93	70	48	25	7	0	0	0
1400	1420	165	142	119	96	73	51	28	9	0	0	0
1420	1440	168	145	122	99	76	54	31	11	0	0	0
1440	1460	171	148	125	102	79	57	34	13	0	0	0
1460	1480	174	151	128	105	82	60	37	15	0	0	0
1480	1500	177	154	131	108	85	63	40	17	2	0	0
1500	1520	180	157	134	111	88	66	43	20	4	0	0
1520	1540	185	160	137	114	91	69	46	23	6	0	0
1540	1560	190	163	140	117	94	72	49	26	8	0	0
1560	1580	195	166	143	120	97	75	52	29	10	0	0
1580	1600	200	169	146	123	100	78	55	32	12	0	0
1600	1620	205	172	149	126	103	81	58	35	14	0	0
1620	1640	210	175	152	129	106	84	61	38	16	1	0
1640	1660	215	178	155	132	109	87	64	41	18	3	0
1660	1680	220	182	158	135	112	90	67	44	21	5	0
1680	1700	225	187	161	138	115	93	70	47	24	7	0

Federal income tax laws are written and passed by Congress. The Internal Revenue Service (IRS), an agency of the U.S. Department of the Treasury, administers the tax laws. The amount of federal income tax to withhold from each employee's total earnings is found in withholding tables. These withholding tables are revised each year and are available from the IRS in Publication 15 (Circular E), Employer's Tax Guide. The withholding tables shown in this chapter are those available when this textbook was prepared.

There are tables for various payroll periods—monthly, semimonthly, biweekly, weekly, and daily. Single persons are taxed at different levels of income than married persons. Single persons and married persons tables are available for each pay period. ThreeGreen's pay period is semimonthly, so ThreeGreen uses the semimonthly withholding tables.

The federal income tax withholding tables on pages 353–354 contain a column for 0 dependents. How can an employee have 0 dependents if the employee is a dependent? Some employees claim fewer dependents than they are allowed—even as low as zero—to increase the amount of tax withheld. An employee who has other taxable income, such as interest and dividends, can use payroll withholding to pay the additional income taxes owed on this income. As a result, the employee avoids having a large income tax payment when the tax return is filed.

Employee's Income Tax Withholding—Married Persons

Select the appropriate table ❶

MARRIED Persons—SEMIMONTHLY Payroll Period
(For Wages Paid Through December 20--)

And the wages are—		And the number of withholding allowances claimed is—										
At least	But less than	0	1	2	3	4	5	6	7	8	9	10
		The amount of income tax to be withheld is—										
1060	1080	52	35	19	4	0	0	0	0	0	0	0
1080	1100	55	37	21	6	0	0	0	0	0	0	0
1100	1120	58	39	23	8	0	0	0	0	0	0	0
1120	1140	61	41	25	10	0	0	0	0	0	0	0
1140	1160	64	43	27	12	0	0	0	0	0	0	0
1160	1180	67	45	29	14	0	0	0	0	0	0	0
1180	1200	70	47	31	16	1	0	0	0	0	0	0
1200	1220	73	50	33	18	3	0	0	0	0	0	0
1220	1240	76	53	35	20	5	0	0	0	0	0	0
1240	1260	79	56	37	22	7	0	0	0	0	0	0
1260	1280	82	59	39	24	9	0	0	0	0	0	0
1280	1300	85	62	41	26	11	0	0	0	0	0	0
1300	1320	88	65	43	28	13	0	0	0	0	0	0
1320	1340	91	68	46	30	15	0	0	0	0	0	0
1340	1360	94	71	49	32	17	2	0	0	0	0	0
1360	1380	97	74	52	34	19	4	0	0	0	0	0
1380	1400	100	77	55	36	21	6	0	0	0	0	0
1400	1420	103	80	58	38	23	8	0	0	0	0	0
1420	1440	106	83	61	40	25	10	0	0	0	0	0
1440	1460	109	86	64	42	27	12	0	0	0	0	0
1460	1480	112	89	67	44	29	14	0	0	0	0	0
1480	1500	115	92	70	47	31	16	0	0	0	0	0
1500	1520	118	95	73	50	33	18	2	0	0	0	0
1520	1540	121	98	76	53	35	20	4	0	0	0	0
1540	1560	124	101	79	56	37	22	6	0	0	0	0
1560	1580	127	104	82	59	39	24	8	0	0	0	0
1580	1600	130	107	85	62	41	26	10	0	0	0	0
1600	1620	133	110	88	65	43	28	12	0	0	0	0
1620	1640	136	113	91	68	45	30	14	0	0	0	0
1640	1660	139	116	94	71	48	32	16	1	0	0	0
1660	1680	142	119	97	74	51	34	18	3	0	0	0
1680	1700	145	122	100	77	54	36	20	5	0	0	0
1700	1720	148	125	103	80	57	38	22	7	0	0	0
1720	1740	151	128	106	83	60	40	24	9	0	0	0
1740	1760	154	131	109	86	63	42	26	11	0	0	0
1760	1780	157	134	112	89	66	44	28	13	0	0	0
1780	1800	160	137	115	92	69	46	30	15	0	0	0
1800	1820	163	140	118	95	72	49	32	17	2	0	0
1820	1840	166	143	121	98	75	52	34	19	4	0	0
1840	1860	169	146	124	101	78	55	36	21	6	0	0
1860	1880	172	149	127	104	81	58	38	23	8	0	0
1880	1900	175	152	130	107	84	61	40	25	10	0	0
1900	1920	178	155	133	110	87	64	42	27	12	0	0
1920	1940	181	158	136	113	90	67	44	29	14	0	0
1940	1960	184	161	139	116	93	70	47	31	16	1	0
1960	1980	187	164	142	119	96	73	50	33	18	3	0
1980	2000	190	167	145	122	99	76	53	35	20	5	0
2000	2020	193	170	148	125	102	79	56	37	22	7	0
2020	2040	196	173	151	128	105	82	59	39	24	9	0
2040	2060	199	176	154	131	108	85	62	41	26	11	0
2060	2080	202	179	157	134	111	88	65	43	28	13	0
2080	2100	205	182	160	137	114	91	68	45	30	15	0
2100	2120	208	185	163	140	117	94	71	48	32	17	2
2120	2140	211	188	166	143	120	97	74	51	34	19	4
2140	2160	214	191	169	146	123	100	77	54	36	21	6
2160	2180	217	194	172	149	126	103	80	57	38	23	8
2180	2200	220	197	175	152	129	106	83	60	40	25	10
2200	2220	223	200	178	155	132	109	86	63	42	27	12
2220	2240	226	203	181	158	135	112	89	66	44	29	14
2240	2260	229	206	184	161	138	115	92	69	47	31	16

❷ Locate employee's total earnings ❸ Intersection of earnings and withholding allowance

---

↘ Determining an Employee's Income Tax Withholding

❶ Select the correct table. Married Persons—Semimonthly Payroll Period is used to determine income tax withholding for John P. Butler.

❷ Locate the employee's total earnings between the appropriate lines of the At Least and But Less Than columns. Mr. Butler's total earnings for the pay period ended December 15, 20--, were $1,466.25. Locate the line At Least $1,460.00 But Less Than $1,480.00.

❸ Follow the selected wages line across to the column headed by the employee's number of withholding allowances. The amount listed at the intersection of the wages line and number of withholding allowances column is the amount of income tax to withhold. Mr. Butler's federal income tax withholding, with total earnings of $1,466.25 and four withholding allowances, is $29.00 for the semimonthly pay period ended December 15, 20--.

Employee Social Security and Medicare Tax LO4

The Federal Insurance Contributions Act (FICA) established a federal program for old-age, survivors, disability, and hospital insurance. A federal tax paid for old-age, survivors, and disability insurance is called **social security tax**. A federal tax paid for hospital insurance is called **Medicare tax**. Each of these taxes is accounted for and reported separately.

Social security and Medicare taxes are paid by both employees and employers. Employers are required to withhold and deposit the employees' taxes and pay a matching amount of these taxes. Thus, if an employer withholds $85.00 from an employee's earnings, the business must also pay taxes of $85.00, for a total of $170.00. A self-employed individual must pay both the employee and employer tax.

Social security tax is calculated on employee earnings up to a maximum paid in a calendar year. The total gross earnings year to date for an employee is called **accumulated earnings**. The maximum amount of earnings on which a tax is calculated is called a **tax base**. When the amount of accumulated earnings equals the tax base, no additional taxes must be paid. Congress sets the tax base and the tax rates for the social security tax. An act of Congress can change the tax base and tax rate at any time. The social security tax rate and base used in this text are 6.2% of earnings up to a maximum of $106,800.00 in each calendar year.

Between January 1 and December 15, Mr. Butler's earnings are less than the social security tax base. Therefore, Mr. Butler's social security tax deduction for the semimonthly pay period ended December 15, 20--, is calculated as shown.

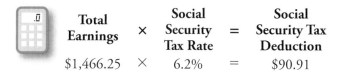

	Total Earnings	×	Social Security Tax Rate	=	Social Security Tax Deduction
	$1,466.25	×	6.2%	=	$90.91

The Medicare tax does not have a tax base. Therefore, Medicare tax is calculated on total employee earnings. The Medicare tax rate used in this text is 1.45% of total employee earnings. Mr. Butler's Medicare tax deduction for the semimonthly pay period ended December 15, 20--, is calculated as shown.

	Total Earnings	×	Medicare Tax Rate	=	Medicare Tax Deduction
	$1,466.25	×	1.45%	=	$21.26

fyi Accounting procedures are the same regardless of changes in the tax base and tax rate. The social security tax rate of 6.2% and the tax base of $106,800.00 are assumed for all payroll calculations in this textbook.

Voluntary Deductions from Earnings LO5

The U.S. Congress uses tax law to motivate individuals to save for retirement. Tax laws also encourage employers to sponsor retirement savings plans for their employees. A retirement savings plan approved by the Internal Revenue Service that provides individuals with a tax benefit is called a **qualified retirement plan**. Contributions to a qualified retirement plan are deposited in an investment account with a bank or other financial institution. Individuals can select from a range of investment options based upon the level of risk they wish to accept. Three popular qualified retirement plans are summarized below.

A **401(k)** is a qualified retirement plan sponsored by an employer. Employee contributions to a 401(k) are not taxable. These contributions are deducted from the employee's earnings subject to federal income taxes, thereby reducing the amount of taxes withheld. For this reason, contributions made to a 401(k) are referred to as pretax contributions.

Some businesses, as a fringe benefit, match their employees' 401(k) plan contributions. If an employer offers its employees a one-to-one match, it would contribute another $2,000.00 to the account of an employee who contributed $2,000.00. Thus, a total of $4,000.00 would be contributed to the plan.

Contributions to a 401(k) and the investment income are generally not taxable to the employee until they are withdrawn. Thus, the federal income tax is deferred, or postponed, from the year the funds were deposited until the year the funds are withdrawn.

An **individual retirement account (IRA)** is a qualified retirement plan that provides most individuals with a deferred federal income tax benefit. Individuals can make contributions directly into their IRA accounts. Individuals can also direct their employers to withhold contributions from their earnings. IRA contributions made through payroll withholdings do not reduce earnings subject to federal income taxes. Individuals who qualify receive a tax benefit when filing their annual tax returns. Federal income taxes on qualified contributions and investment income are deferred until the funds are withdrawn.

A **Roth individual retirement account (Roth IRA)** is a qualified retirement plan that allows tax-free withdrawals from the account. Contributions to a Roth IRA are not deducted from total earnings and do not provide a current tax benefit. However, the contributions and investment income in a Roth IRA are not subject to federal income taxes when withdrawn. As they can do with an IRA, individuals can contribute to their Roth IRA accounts through direct deposits or payroll withholdings.

As a fringe benefit, businesses often provide employees with access to group health insurance plans. Employees are usually required to pay a portion of their health insurance premiums, especially for coverage of family members. A business may elect to have its health insurance plan approved by the IRS. Approved health insurance plans enable employees to pay their portion of the insurance premiums with pretax contributions. These contributions reduce the amount of wages subject to social security, Medicare, and federal income taxes.

The benefit of pretax contributions can be significant. Assuming a federal income tax rate of 30%, the following example shows the impact of paying medical insurance premiums and retirement plan contributions with pretax dollars. Larry and Sandra have equal incomes, but only Larry's employer sponsors pretax medical and 401(k) plans. Sandra's employer does not sponsor a pretax medical plan, but she makes contributions to a Roth IRA.

	Larry	**Sandra**
Total earnings	$3,000.00	$3,000.00
Medical insurance premiums	(150.00)	
401(k) contribution	(250.00)	
Earnings subject to federal income taxes	$2,600.00	$3,000.00
Federal income taxes (30%)	780.00	900.00
Net earnings after federal income taxes	$1,820.00	$2,100.00
Medical insurance premiums		(150.00)
Roth IRA		(250.00)
Cash available	$1,820.00	$1,700.00

By deducting his contributions from his total earnings subject to federal income taxes, Larry saved $120.00 ($1,820.00 − $1,700.00). Both employees' $250.00 retirement contributions will earn investment income free of tax until the funds are withdrawn. However, only Larry will have to pay income tax on withdrawals from his account.

ThreeGreen has elected to encourage its employees to make contributions to a Roth IRA. The business is considering whether to sponsor a pretax medical insurance plan.

 Tax laws limit the annual amount a taxpayer can contribute to each type of qualified retirement plan.

End of Lesson Review

LO3 Demonstrate the process for determining federal income tax withholdings.

LO4 Demonstrate the process for calculating social security and Medicare taxes.

LO5 Explain the benefit of funding medical and retirement plans with pretax contributions.

Terms Review

payroll taxes

withholding allowance

payroll deduction

social security tax

Medicare tax

accumulated earnings

tax base

qualified retirement plan

401(k)

individual retirement account (IRA)

Roth individual retirement account (Roth IRA)

Audit your understanding

1. Where does an employer get the information used to determine the amount of federal income tax to withhold from employees' earnings?

2. Employee federal income tax withholdings are based on what two factors?

3. Does the employer or employee pay social security tax and Medicare tax?

4. What is the difference in the tax impact of contributions between a 401(k), an IRA, and a Roth IRA?

5. Are the withdrawals from a 401(k), an IRA, and a Roth IRA subject to income taxes?

Work together 12-2

Determining payroll tax withholding

Information taken from a semimonthly payroll is given in the *Working Papers*. Your instructor will guide you through the following examples.

1. Determine the federal income tax that must be withheld for each employee. Use the tax withholding tables in this lesson.

2. Calculate the amount of social security tax and Medicare tax that must be withheld for each employee. Use a social security tax rate of 6.2% and a Medicare tax rate of 1.45%. None of the employees has accumulated earnings greater than the tax base. Round dollar amounts to the nearest cent.

On your own 12-2

Determining payroll tax withholding

Information taken from a semimonthly payroll is given in the *Working Papers*. Work this problem independently.

1. Determine the federal income tax that must be withheld for each employee. Use the tax withholding tables in this lesson.

2. Calculate the amount of social security tax and Medicare tax that must be withheld for each employee. Use a social security tax rate of 6.2% and a Medicare tax rate of 1.45%. None of the employees has accumulated earnings greater than the tax base. Round dollar amounts to the nearest cent.

12-3 Preparing Payroll Records

LO6 Prepare a payroll register.
LO7 Prepare employee earnings records.

Payroll Register LO6

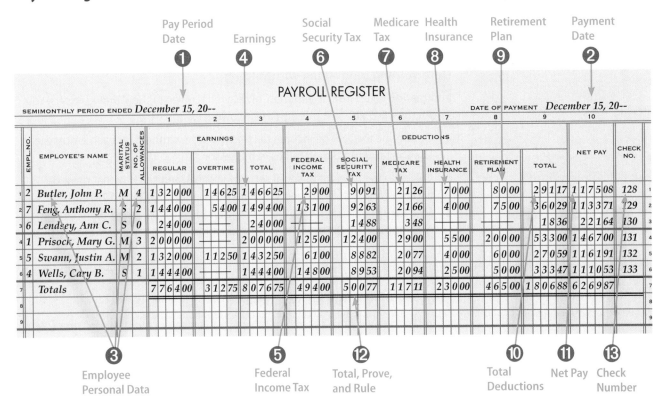

A **payroll register** summarizes the earnings, deductions, and net pay of all employees for one pay period. ThreeGreen prepares a separate payroll register for each semimonthly payroll.

Most states and some local governments have an income tax system. The methods of calculating state and local income taxes are significantly different from federal tax calculations. A business must understand the tax laws of every state and locality in which it operates and where its employees reside. For these reasons, state and local income taxes are ignored in this textbook.

⚙ Preparing a Payroll Register

❶ Write the last date of the semimonthly payroll period, December 15, 20--, at the top of the payroll register.

❷ Write the date of payment, December 15, 20--, also at the top of the payroll register.

❸ For each employee, enter employee number, name, marital status, and number of allowances. This information is taken from personnel records. Entries for John P. Butler are on line 1 of the register.

❹ Enter regular earnings, overtime earnings, and total earnings for each employee in columns 1, 2, and 3 of the payroll register. This information is taken from each employee's time card.

⑤ Enter in column 4 the federal income tax withheld from each employee. Mr. Butler's federal tax withholding is $29.00.

⑥ Enter in column 5 of the payroll register the social security tax withheld from each employee. Mr. Butler's social security tax deduction, $90.91, is recorded in column 5 of the payroll register. Mr. Butler's total earnings for the year have not exceeded the social security tax base. Thus, his total earnings for the pay period are taxed.

⑦ Enter in column 6 the Medicare tax withheld from each employee. Mr. Butler's Medicare tax deduction is $21.26.

⑧ Enter in column 7 the health insurance premium deductions. Full-time ThreeGreen employees participate in a group health insurance plan. Mr. Butler's semimonthly health insurance premium is $70.00. Premiums are set by the insurance company and are usually based on the employee marital status and the number of individuals covered.

⑨ Enter in column 8 the employee's contribution to a retirement plan. Mr. Butler has instructed ThreeGreen to withhold $80.00 per pay period for his Roth IRA.

⑩ After all deductions are entered in the payroll register, add all the deduction amounts for each employee and enter the totals in column 9. Mr. Butler's total deductions, $291.17, are calculated as shown.

	Federal Income Tax	+	Social Security Tax	+	Medicare Tax	+	Health Insurance	+	Retirement Plan	=	Total Deductions
	$29.00	+	$90.91	+	$21.26	+	$70.00	+	$80.00	=	$291.17

⑪ Determine the net pay for each employee. The total earnings paid to an employee after payroll taxes and other deductions is called **net pay**. Subtract the total deductions, column 9, from total earnings, column 3, to determine net pay. Enter net pay in column 10. Mr. Butler's net pay, $1,175.08, is calculated as shown.

	Total Earnings	−	Total Deductions	=	Net Pay
	$1,466.25	−	$291.17	=	$1,175.08

⑫ Total, prove, and rule the payroll register. Total each amount column. Subtract the Total Deductions column from the Total Earnings column. The result should equal the total of the Net Pay column. If the totals do not agree, the errors must be found and corrected. Proving the accuracy of ThreeGreen's payroll register for the pay period ended December 15, 20--, is shown.

	Total Earnings	−	Total Deductions	=	Net Pay
	$8,076.75	−	$1,806.88	=	$6,269.87

The net pay, $6,269.87, is the same as the total of the Net Pay column. The payroll register is proved. After the payroll register is proved, rule double lines below all amount column totals to show the totals have been verified as correct.

⑬ Payroll checks are written after a manager approves the payroll. Write the payroll check numbers in the Check No. column.

Employee Earnings Records LO7

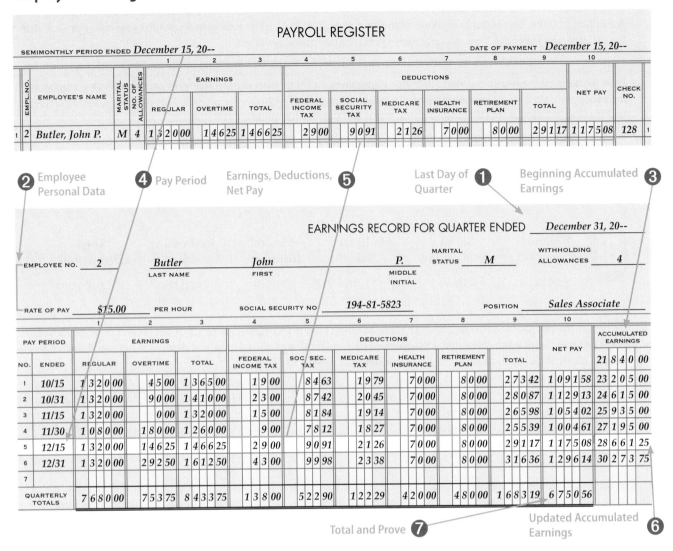

A business must send the IRS quarterly and annual reports of employee earnings and tax withholdings. Maintaining a record of each employee's payroll activity for a quarter is useful in preparing these reports. For example, that record is useful for identifying when individual employees exceed a tax base. A business form used to record details of an employee's earnings and deductions is called an **employee earnings record**. The employee's earnings and deductions for each pay period are recorded on one line of the employee earnings record. A new earnings record is prepared for each employee each quarter. John Butler's earnings record for the fourth quarter is shown.

The steps for completing the employee earnings record are on the next page.

The 401(k) name relates to a section of the Internal Revenue Code. The 401(k) is just one of several methods available that enable employees to deduct their contributions from total earnings. A 403(b) plan, for example, allows pretax contributions for government employees and employees of tax-exempt organizations such as schools and churches. Amounts withdrawn from these plans are generally taxable when the funds are withdrawn.

➲ Preparing an Employee Earnings Record

① Enter the last day of the yearly quarter, December 31, 20--, at the top of the earnings record.

② Enter the employee's number, name, marital status, withholding allowances, hourly rate, social security number, and position in the space provided. This information is taken from the employee's personnel records.

③ Enter the fiscal year's accumulated earnings for the beginning of the current quarter. This information is taken from the ending accumulated earnings for the previous quarter. Mr. Butler's accumulated earnings for the first three quarters ended September 30 are $21,840.00. The Accumulated Earnings column of the employee earnings record shows the total earnings from the beginning of the fiscal year.

④ Enter the ending date of the pay period being recorded, 12/15.

⑤ Enter the earnings, deductions, and net pay in the columns of the employee earnings record. This information is taken from the current pay period's payroll register.

⑥ Add the current pay period's total earnings to the previous period's accumulated earnings. Mr. Butler's accumulated earnings as of December 15 are calculated as shown.

Accumulated Earnings as of December 1	+	Total Earnings for Pay Period Ended December 15	=	Accumulated Earnings as of December 15
$27,195.00	+	$1,466.25	=	$28,661.25

The amounts in the Accumulated Earnings column supply an up-to-date reference for an employee's year-to-date earnings. When employee earnings reach the tax base, certain payroll taxes cease. For example, social security taxes are not owed beyond the first $106,800.00 of earnings.

⑦ At the end of each quarter, total and prove the earnings record for each employee. Calculate quarterly totals for each amount column. Subtract the Total Deductions column from the Total Earnings column. The result should equal the total of the Net Pay column. If the totals do not agree, the errors must be found and corrected. Proving the accuracy of Mr. Butler's fourth quarterly totals is shown below.

Total Earnings	−	Total Deductions	=	Net Pay
$8,433.75	−	$1,683.19	=	$6,750.56

The net pay, $6,750.56, is compared to the total of the Net Pay column. The earnings record is proved because these amounts are equal. These totals are needed to prepare required government reports.

↗↗↗
remember

Total earnings, not net pay, is added to the previous accumulated earnings amount on the earnings record. Total earnings is the amount compared to the tax base to determine whether social security taxes should be withheld.

Occupational Fraud: Detecting Shell Companies

Ruth Holder was patiently waiting her turn at a stop light. Watching the traffic cross in front of her, she saw something that surprised her. Alice Scott, an accounts payable clerk at her company, zoomed by in an expensive sports car. "How can someone earning $35,000 a year afford a $100,000 sports car?" she thought.

When Ruth returned to the office, she went straight to the office of Jack Torres, internal auditor. As she explained what she saw, Ruth was relieved that Jack understood her concern. "Anyone who is part of the purchasing function has, under certain circumstances, the ability to have checks processed to a shell company," he said. Sensing that Ruth did not understand, Jack continued. "A shell company is a fictitious company created by an employee. The employee submits invoices for the payment of goods or services that were not ordered or received. Alice may have found a weakness in our controls. Or, she may be working with someone else in purchasing to avoid our controls."

Soon after Ruth left his office, Jack entered your office and shut the door. Handing you a folder containing some papers and instructions, he began, "I have reason to suspect that checks may be getting processed to one or more shell companies. There are many tests that can detect a shell company," he said. "Let's begin with the most basic test. The folder includes a list of employees who are involved with our purchasing function. Search our accounts payable data to determine if any of our vendors' names contain the last name of one of these employees. Having checks written to a shell company containing an employee's name makes it easier for that employee to cash the checks."

Jack continued. "If an employee is involved in a shell company, chances are that the purchases will be for a service-related expense, not for such things as inventory or equipment. Other employees would discover those things were missing. Due to the sensitive nature of this investigation, report your findings directly to me. Do not make contact with any personnel in purchasing until we complete this initial phase of our investigation. After you get the results of this test, let's discuss our next step. Let me know if you have any questions."

INSTRUCTIONS

Open the spreadsheet FA_CH12. Use the data in the workbook to identify any evidence of a shell company.

End of Lesson Review

LO6 Prepare a payroll register.

LO7 Prepare employee earnings records.

Terms Review

payroll register

net pay

employee earnings record

Audit your understanding

1. What does the payroll register summarize?

2. How is net pay calculated?

3. Why do companies complete employee earnings records?

Work together 12-3

Preparing payroll records

A payroll register for Judy's Fashions is provided in the *Working Papers*. Your instructor will guide you through the following examples.

1. Complete the payroll register for the semimonthly pay period ended July 15, 20--. Use the federal income tax withholding tables in Lesson 12-2. Use tax rates of 6.2% for social security tax and 1.45% for Medicare tax. Round dollar amounts to the nearest cent. Neither employee has reached the tax base. Withhold $60.00 for health insurance and $15.00 for a Roth IRA for each employee. The voluntary deductions are not eligible to be deducted from total earnings to calculate payroll taxes.

2. Total all the amount columns of the payroll register. Prove the payroll register.

3. Enter the July 15 payroll information on Mr. Johnson's quarterly earnings record. Mr. Johnson is employee number 2; rate of pay is $15.00 per hour; social security number is 954-15-1568; position is sales manager. Accumulated earnings at the end of the second quarter are $17,218.00. Save your work to complete Work Together 12-4.

On your own 12-3

Preparing payroll records

A payroll register for Russell Company is provided in the *Working Papers*. Work this problem independently.

1. Complete the payroll register for the semimonthly pay period ended July 15, 20--. Use the federal income tax withholding tables in Lesson 12-2. Use tax rates of 6.2% for social security tax and 1.45% for Medicare tax. Round dollar amounts to the nearest cent. Withhold $75.00 for health insurance and $30.00 for a Roth IRA for each employee. The voluntary deductions are not eligible to be deducted from total earnings to calculate payroll taxes.

2. Total all the amount columns of the payroll register. Prove the payroll register.

3. Enter the July 15 payroll information on Mr. Patterson's quarterly earnings record. Mr. Patterson's employee number is 3; rate of pay is $18.25 per hour; social security number is 941-74-4818; position is production scheduler. Accumulated earnings at the end of the second quarter are $19,150.00. Save your work to complete On Your Own 12-4.

12-4 Preparing Payroll Checks

LO8 Justify the use of a payroll checking account.

LO9 Prepare employee payroll checks.

Payroll Bank Account LO8

THREEGREEN PRODUCTS, INC.		DATE 12/15/20--		No. 312
PAYEE	First American Bank			
ACCOUNT	**TITLE**		**DESCRIPTION**	**AMOUNT**
			December 15, 20-- payroll	$6,269.87 ①

Prepare the check stub

THREEGREEN PRODUCTS, INC.
1501 Commerce Street
Carlisle, PA 17013

FIRST AMERICAN BANK
109 Delaware Street
Harrisburg, PA 17101

No. 312

GENERAL ACCOUNT

DATE 12/15/20--

AMOUNT $ 6,269.87 ②

Prepare the check

Six thousand two hundred sixty-nine and 87/100 _____ Dollars

FOR CLASSROOM USE ONLY

PAY TO THE
ORDER OF

First American Bank
Payroll Account 006863274
109 Delaware Street
Harrisburg, PA 17101

Mary G. Prisock

⑈61003114⑈ 006⑈8632⑈072⑈ 0312

⟩ Preparing a Check for Total Net Pay

① **Prepare the check stub.** The payee is First American Bank, the location of ThreeGreen's payroll checking account. The date is 12/15/20-- and the description is the December 15, 20-- payroll. The amount, $6,269.87, is the total of the Net Pay column of the payroll register.

② **Prepare the check from the information on the check stub.** Include the address of the payee. The check is signed by Mary G. Prisock.

ThreeGreen pays its employees with checks written on a separate payroll checking account. A check for the total net pay is written on ThreeGreen's general checking account. That check is deposited in the payroll checking account.

A separate payroll checking account helps to protect and control payroll payments. The exact amount needed to pay the payroll is deposited in the payroll checking account. If amounts on checks are altered or unauthorized payroll checks are prepared, the amount in the payroll account would be insufficient to cover all the checks. The bank and

ThreeGreen would be alerted quickly to an unauthorized payroll check. Also, since payroll checks are drawn on the separate account, any balance in this account will correspond to the sum of outstanding payroll checks.

ThreeGreen uses a different style of check than Delgado Web Services in Part 1. A **voucher check** has a detachable check stub, or voucher, that contains detailed information about the cash payment. Most computerized accounting systems are designed to print voucher checks. The voucher, usually referred to as the check stub, contains spaces to enter the date, payee, description, and amount. When paying expenses, the general ledger account number and title would be entered. The address of the payee on the check is in a position that allows it to appear in the window of a mailing envelope. Voucher checks are prepared in duplicate. The original check with the voucher attached is mailed to the vendor and the copy is filed.

Employee's Payroll Check LO9

① Record earnings information from the time card and payroll register

③ Record current deductions from the payroll register

④ Add current deductions to YTD deductions from the prior check stub

John P. Butler

December 15, 20--

Type	Hours	Rate	Gross Pay	Deductions	Current	YTD
				Federal Income Tax	29.00	580.00
Regular	80.00	15.00	1,320.00	Social Security Tax	90.91	1,777.00
Overtime	6.50	22.50	146.25	Medicare Tax	21.26	415.59
				Health Insurance	70.00	1,330.00
				Retirement	80.00	1,520.00
Current Total Earnings			1,466.25	Totals	291.17	5,622.59
YTD Total Earnings			28,661.25	Net Pay	1,175.08	23,038.66

PAYROLL ACCOUNT	66-311 / 610

December 15, 20--

THREEGREEN PRODUCTS, INC.

No. 67

Pay to the order of John P. Butler $ 1,175.08

One thousand one hundred seventy-five and 08/100   Dollars

FOR CLASSROOM USE ONLY

FIRST AMERICAN BANK
Harrisburg, PA 17101

Mary G. Prisock

⑇610031140 006863274 067⑇

② Record YTD total earnings from the employee earnings record

⑥ Prepare the employee's payroll check in the amount of net pay

⑤ Enter column totals and net pay

Preparing an Employee's Payroll Check

① Enter earnings information from the payroll register and the employee's time card. The total current earnings, $1,466.25, should match the total earnings on the payroll register.

② Enter the YTD Total Earnings, $28,661.25, from the employee earnings record.

③ Enter the employee's current deductions from the payroll register and record the total, $291.17.

④ Add each current deduction amount to the YTD amount reported on the employee's prior check stub and record the total, $5,622.59. For example, John Butler's November 30 check stub reported year-to-date federal income taxes of $551.00. The YTD federal income tax deduction is $580.00 ($551.00 + $29.00).

⑤ Total the Current and YTD deductions columns. Calculate and enter the amounts for Current and YTD net pay ($1,466.25 – $291.17 = $1,175.08; $28,661.25 – $5,622.59 = $23,038.66).

⑥ Prepare each employee's payroll check payable for the amount of net pay. John P. Butler's net pay is $1,175.08.

The time card and payroll register are the primary sources of information to prepare a payroll check. Year-to-date information is calculated using information from the employee earnings record and the prior payroll. The payroll checks have vouchers, detachable stubs, for recording earnings and deductions. Employees keep their paycheck stubs as a record of deductions and cash received.

Electronic Funds Transfer

John P. Butler   *December 15, 20--*

Type	Hours	Rate	Gross Pay	Deductions	Current	YTD
				Federal Income Tax	29.00	580.00
Regular	80.00	15.00	1,320.00	Social Security Tax	90.91	1,777.00
Overtime	6.50	22.50	146.25	Medicare Tax	21.26	415.59
				Health Insurance	70.00	1,330.00
				Retirement	80.00	1,520.00
Current Total Earnings			1,466.25	Totals	291.17	5,622.59
YTD Total Earnings			28,661.25	Net Pay	1,175.08	23,038.66

Direct Deposit Distribution
Checking XXXXXXXX74   1,175.08

THREEGREEN PRODUCTS, INC.   December 15, 20--

Advice Number: 00000123456

Pay to the order of   John P. Butler $ 1,175.08

One thousand one hundred seventy-five and 08/100   **Dollars**

THIS IS NOT A CHECK
FOR CLASSROOM USE ONLY

NON-NEGOTIABLE

**Direct Deposit
Confirmation Only
Not a Valid Check**

A computerized cash payments system that transfers funds without the use of checks, currency, or other paper documents is called electronic funds transfer (EFT). The payment of an employee's net pay using electronic funds transfer is called **direct deposit**. A business that pays its employees using direct deposit transmits payroll information to its bank. The bank electronically deducts the total amount of employees' net pay from the business's payroll checking account. Each employee's net pay is deposited in his or her bank account.

The payroll must still be calculated, but payroll checks are not written and do not have to be distributed. Each employee receives a printed or electronic statement of earnings and deductions resembling a payroll check. The voucher portion at the top includes a reference to the employee's checking account number and the amount deposited. The bottom portion contains several notations clearly indicating that the document is not a negotiable check. Bank information, such as the bank routing number and account number, are not displayed.

remember

Using a separate checking account for payroll checks provides internal control and helps to prevent fraud.

Personal Federal Income Taxes

Individuals are required to prepare an annual tax return, Form 1040, to report the amount of income tax owed to the government. Payroll withholding tables attempt to estimate the amount of income tax an individual will be required to pay based on earnings. However, income tax is also due on other sources of income, such as interest and dividends. The sum of all sources of income reported on Form 1040 is labeled **total income**.

When preparing their tax returns, individuals are allowed to subtract from their total income certain *adjustments*, such as retirement plan contributions, tuition, and moving expenses. The amount of total income minus adjustments, reported on Form 1040, is called **adjusted gross income**.

Tax laws allow taxpayers to deduct certain expenses from adjusted gross income. Individuals can elect to *itemize* deductions by listing these expenses on Schedule A. Or, they can elect to take a *standard* deduction using a fixed amount based on their filing status—married or single. Next, individuals can deduct from adjusted gross income the amount of their *exemptions* (computed as a standard amount per person multiplied by the number of individuals supported by the taxpayer). The value that results after subtracting deductions and exemptions from adjusted gross income is the amount used to calculate income tax. The amount of total income minus adjustments, deductions, and exemptions that is used to calculate income tax is called **taxable income**.

ACTIVITIES

1. Visit the IRS website at www.irs.gov and research Form 1040 Schedule A. List and explain five deductions that taxpayers can itemize in calculating their income tax.

2. Even after the income tax is calculated, tax law allows several reductions in the amount of income tax owed. What are these reductions called? List and explain two of these reductions.

 Employees are responsible for contacting their employer when the number of their dependents changes. A new W-4 form should be completed and a copy of the form sent to the Internal Revenue Service.

End of Lesson Review

LO8 Justify the use of a payroll checking account.

LO9 Prepare employee payroll checks.

Terms Review

voucher check

direct deposit

Audit your understanding

1. Why does ThreeGreen have a separate checking account for payroll checks?

2. What is the source of the information that is recorded on each employee's payroll check voucher?

3. How do payroll procedures differ for employees who request direct deposit of their pay?

Work together 12-4

Preparing payroll checks

Use the payroll register from Work Together 12-3. The *Working Papers* contain (1) one blank general account check, (2) two blank payroll account checks, and (3) prior pay period pay stubs for each employee. Your instructor will guide you through the following examples.

1. Prepare Judy's Fashions' general account check for the pay period ended July 15, 20--. The payment date is July 15. Prepare the check to the order of First Community Bank. The payroll account number is 148-164-118. Sign your name as the manager of Judy's Fashions.

2. Complete the payroll checks for the pay period ended July 15, 20--. The payment date is July 15. Sign your name as the manager of Judy's Fashions. Record the two payroll check numbers in the payroll register.

On your own 12-4

Preparing payroll checks

Use the payroll register from On Your Own 12-3. The *Working Papers* contain (1) one blank general account check, (2) two blank payroll account checks, and (3) prior pay period pay stubs for each employee. Work this problem independently.

1. Prepare Russell Company's general account check for the pay period ended July 15, 20--. The payment date is July 15. Prepare the check to the order of First American Bank. The payroll account number is 748-476-7. Sign your name as the manager of Russell Company.

2. Complete the payroll checks for the pay period ended July 15, 20--. The payment date is July 15. Sign your name as the manager of Russell Company. Record the two payroll check numbers in the payroll register.

A Look at Accounting Software

Processing Payroll in the Enter Payroll Window

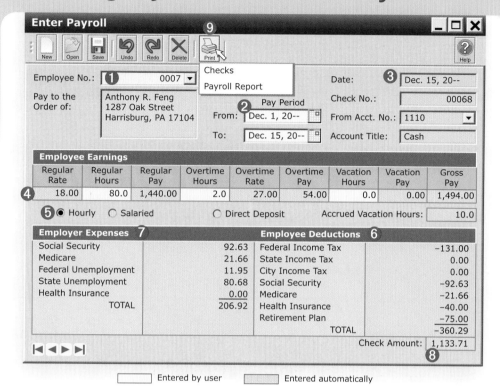

Entered by user	Entered automatically

In the manual payroll system used by ThreeGreen, the business maintains paper copies of employee earnings records and computes its payroll using a paper payroll register. Employee time cards are the source documents for the payroll register. Other companies might use technology such as spreadsheet software and electronic time clock systems.

In a computerized accounting system, most of the fields in the Enter Payroll window are populated by the system from data contained in individual employee payroll records. The user simply selects an employee and enters the number of hours worked. As an alternative, the hours worked could be entered off of a report printed from an electronic time clock system. More advanced time clock systems can transfer an electronic file containing the hours worked directly into the computerized accounting system. As a result, no manual entry of employee hours would be required. However, management would review and verify the hours worked before printing paychecks.

1 After the user selects this employee's number, his name and address are retrieved by the system from his individual payroll record. The arrow keys, lower left, are used to navigate from one employee to another.

2 The user selects beginning and ending dates for the pay period. These dates only need to be selected when entering the first employee for each pay period. The dates remain the same until changed.

3 The system sets the current date, the next check number, and the Cash account. The Cash account can be changed if it is different.

4 On the Employee Earnings line, the user can only enter the hours. Pay rates as well as exemptions and marital status are retrieved by the system from each employee's payroll record. For a salaried employee, the Regular Rate would be their semimonthly salary. No hours would be entered for a salaried employee.

5 This row is for information only. If any items were incorrect, they would have to be updated in the individual employee payroll record. If the employee had taken vacation during the pay period, those hours would be entered under Vacation Hours and the Accrued Vacation Hours field would show the new balance.

6 Tax rates are downloaded into the system from the IRS website. The system uses those rates to compute the withholding amounts. Deductions for health insurance and retirement are retrieved from each employee's payroll record.

7 Employer payroll expenses are also computed by the system. These expenses and the related liabilities will be posted to the various employer general ledger accounts.

8 The system computes the employee's net pay and enters it in the Check Amount field.

9 The user clicks Save after entering each employee's payroll information. A new, blank screen automatically appears, allowing the user to enter the hours for the next employee. When all payroll entries are complete, the user clicks Print and selects Checks from the drop-down menu to print all paychecks. A payroll report similar to a payroll register may also be printed.

Chapter Summary

A business uses a time card system to collect information on the number of hours worked by each hourly employee. Most employers are required to pay employees overtime pay for hours worked over 40 hours per week. The overtime pay rate is typically 1½ times the regular pay rate. The total of regular and overtime pay is called total earnings and is also known as gross pay.

Employers are required to withhold federal income taxes, social security taxes, and Medicare taxes from the employees' total earnings. Employees may be able to have medical insurance, retirement contributions, and other items deducted from their total earnings. Payroll taxes and voluntary deductions are deducted from total earnings to determine net pay, the amount actually paid to the employees. Tax laws enable employees to deduct some voluntary deductions, such as health insurance and retirement contributions, before the calculation of federal income taxes.

A payroll register is used to summarize earnings, deductions, and net pay of all employees. A payroll register is prepared for each pay period. The payroll register is used to update an employee earnings record, a form useful in submitting quarterly and annual payroll tax reports to government agencies.

A check for the total net pay of all employees is written to a special payroll account. Payroll checks for each employee are written on the payroll account using the information in the payroll register.

EXPLORE ACCOUNTING   Progressive Income Taxes

The tax tables used in this chapter provide an easy method of determining federal income tax withholdings. The tables are based on (1) an annual $3,650.00 per person withholding allowance and (2) tax rates that change in relation to the employee's total earnings. A progressive tax increases the tax rate as the taxpayer's taxable earnings increase.

The annual tax rates for a married person (effective when this book was written) are shown below. Note that a taxpayer does not begin paying income taxes until his or her wages exceed $13,750.00 (after deducting withholding allowances). To use a tax rate table, locate the employee's total earnings between the appropriate lines of the Over and But not over columns. Each line of a tax table is referred to as a tax bracket and is often identified by the tax rate. Thus, a taxpayer earning $100,000.00 is said to be "in the 27% tax bracket." The bracket tax rate is also referred to as a *marginal tax rate*.

For the December 15 payroll, Mary Prisock earned $2,000.00. If Ms. Prisock earned that salary for the whole year, she would earn an annual salary of $48,000.00. After deducting $3,650.00 for each of her three withholding allowances, she would have $37,050.00 of earnings subject to income taxes. That would place her "in the 15% tax bracket." So, she would pay $1,075.00 plus 15% of the excess earnings over $24,500.00, as shown on the next page.

(b) MARRIED person—

If the amount of wages (after subtracting withholding allowances) is:

The amount of income tax to withhold is:

Not over $13,750 . . . . $0

Over—	But not over—		of excess over—
$13,750	—$24,500	. . . 10%	—$13,750
$24,500	—$75,750	. . . $1,075.00 plus 15%	—$24,500
$75,750	—$94,050	. . . $8,762.50 plus 25%	—$75,750
$94,050	—$124,050	. . . $13,337.50 plus 27%	—$94,050
$124,050	—$145,050	. . . $21,437.50 plus 25%	—$124,050
$145,050	—$217,000	. . . $26,687.50 plus 28%	—$145,050
$217,000	—$381,400	. . . $46,833.50 plus 33%	—$217,000
$381,400	. . . .	$101,085.50 plus 35%	—$381,400

Annual gross wages	$48,000.00
Less: Withholding allowances ($3,650.00 × 3)	10,950.00
Equals: Wages subject to federal income tax	$37,050.00
15% bracket minimum tax	$ 1,075.00
Plus: Additional tax ($37,050.00 – $24,500.00) × 15%	1,882.50
Equals: Annual federal income tax	$ 2,957.50

The annual income tax of $2,957.50 is divided by 24 to determine the $123.00 amount to be withheld from each semimonthly pay period. ($2,957.50 ÷ 24 periods = $123.23, rounded to $123.00). Using the tax tables in this chapter, taxes of $125.00 would be withheld ($2,000.00 earnings with 3 withholding allowances). Both methods produce nearly identical amounts. The IRS will accept either method.

A common misconception of a progressive income tax is that a taxpayer pays the bracket percentage on all earnings. The effective tax rate, the actual income tax divided by total earnings, is a measure of the amount of tax actually paid. Ms. Prisock's effective tax rate is only 6.16% ($2,957.50 ÷ $48,000.00). However, she will pay 15% of every additional dollar earned until she earns the minimum of the next tax bracket.

INSTRUCTIONS

Obtain a current version of Publication 15 (Circular E), Employer's Tax Guide. Locate the tax rate table for married persons for annual payroll periods.

1. How have the amounts and rates in the tax brackets changed from the table shown above?
2. What political and economic forces can explain the differences, especially in the tax rates, for the higher income tax brackets?
3. What was the highest marginal tax rate for married taxpayers in 1970?

Apply Your Understanding

INSTRUCTIONS: Download problem instructions for Excel, QuickBooks, and Peachtree from the textbook companion website at www.C21accounting.com.

12-1 Application Problem: Calculating total earnings LO1, 2

The December 15 time card for Marcus T. Groves and time card information for other employees are provided in the *Working Papers*.

Instructions:

1. Calculate the regular, overtime, and total hours worked by Mr. Groves. Any hours over eight hours per day or 40 hours per week are considered overtime. Each work week begins on Monday. Record the hours on the time card.
2. Enter the regular and overtime hours for Mr. Groves in the schedule. For each employee, calculate the amount of regular, overtime, and total earnings. Overtime hours are paid at 1½ times the regular rate.

12-2 Application Problem: Determining payroll tax withholding LO3, 4

Information taken from the semimonthly payroll register is given in the *Working Papers*.

Instructions:

1. Determine the federal income tax that must be withheld for each of the eight employees. Use the tax withholding tables in Lesson 12-2.
2. Calculate the amount of social security tax and Medicare tax that must be withheld for each employee using 6.2% and 1.45% tax rates, respectively. None of the eight employees has accumulated earnings greater than the tax base.

12-3 Application Problem: Preparing payroll records LO6, 7

1. Record the regular and overtime earnings for each employee on the payroll register.
2. Print the payroll register.

The information for Warne Company's semimonthly pay period, September 16–30 of the current year, and the earnings record for Mary A. Terrell are given in the *Working Papers*.

Instructions:

1. Complete a payroll register. Use the tax withholding tables in Lesson 12-2 to find the federal income tax withholding for each employee. Calculate withholdings for social security and Medicare taxes using 6.2% and 1.45% tax rates, respectively. None of the employees has accumulated earnings greater than the social security tax base. Each employee's health insurance and retirement plan deductions have been entered in the payroll register. The voluntary deductions are not eligible to be deducted from total earnings to calculate payroll taxes.
2. Record the information for Ms. Terrell from the September 30 payroll register in the earnings record.
3. Record the quarterly totals on Ms. Terrell's earnings record.

12-4 Application Problem: Preparing payroll checks LO9

1. Journalize and post payroll-related transactions in the Payments window.
2. Print the cash disbursements journal.

1. Journalize and post payroll-related transactions in the Write Checks window.
2. From the menu bar, select Reports; Banking, Check Detail.
3. In the Dates drop-down box, select All and make the selections to print.

Castle Electronics' net payroll for the semimonthly pay period ended May 15, 20--, is $7,498.80. Payroll checks are prepared on May 15, 20--. Blank checks and the prior period paycheck stubs are provided in the *Working Papers*.

Instructions:

1. Prepare a general account check for the total amount of the net pay. Make the check payable to The Peoples Bank, Payroll Account 518-481-148, and sign your name as manager of Castle Electronics.
2. Prepare payroll checks for two employees of Castle Electronics. Payroll information for the two employees is as follows. Sign your name as a manager of Castle Electronics.

   a. Mitchell R. Haynes
      Check No. 658

Regular earnings	$1,280.00
Overtime earnings	60.00
Deductions:	
Federal income tax	$71.00
Social security tax	83.08
Medicare tax	19.43
Health insurance	50.00
Retirement	25.00

   b. Sharon V. Bricken
      Check No. 659

Regular earnings	$1,160.00
Overtime earnings	36.98
Deductions:	
Federal income tax	$86.00
Social security tax	74.21
Medicare tax	17.36
Health insurance	65.00
Retirement	40.00

12-M Mastery Problem: Preparing a semimonthly payroll LO3, 4, 6, 9

Prior pay period paycheck stubs and selected payroll data for Malone Company are provided in a payroll register in the *Working Papers.*

Instructions:

1. Prepare a payroll register. Use the tax withholding tables in Lesson 12-2 to find the federal income tax withholding for each employee. Calculate withholdings for social security and Medicare taxes using 6.2% and 1.45% tax rates, respectively. None of the employees has accumulated earnings greater than the social security tax base. The voluntary deductions are not eligible to be deducted from total earnings to calculate payroll taxes.

2. Prepare a check for the total amount of the net pay. Make the check payable to First American Bank, Payroll Account 345-59-721, and sign your name as the manager of Malone Company.

3. Prepare payroll checks for Henry W. Davis, Check No. 452, and Juan S. Garcia, Check No. 453. Sign your name as the manager of Malone Company. Record the two payroll check numbers in the payroll register.

 Peachtree

1. Journalize and post payroll-related transactions in the Payments window.
2. Print the cash disbursements journal.

 Quick Books

1. Journalize and post payroll-related transactions in the Write Checks window.
2. From the menu bar, select Reports; Banking, Check Detail.
3. In the Dates drop-down box, select All and make the selections to print.

AAONLINE

1. Go to www.cengage.com/login
2. Click on **AA Online** to access.
3. Go to the online assignment and follow the instructions.

12-S Source Documents Problem: Preparing a semimonthly payroll LO2, 3, 4, 6, 7, 9

Jenkins Cabinets uses a computerized time card system. Payroll forms and selected payroll data are provided in a payroll register in the *Working Papers.*

Instructions:

1. Prepare the payroll register. Use the tax withholding tables in Lesson 12-2 to find the federal income tax withholding for each employee. Calculate withholdings for social security and Medicare taxes using 6.2% and 1.45% tax rates, respectively. None of the employees has accumulated earnings greater than the social security tax base. The voluntary deductions are not eligible to be deducted from total earnings to calculate payroll taxes.

2. Update each employee's earnings record.

3. Prepare a check for the total amount of the net pay. Make the check payable to First National Savings Bank, Payroll Account 481-154-488. Sign your name as the manager of Jenkins Cabinets.

4. Prepare payroll checks for each employee. Sign your name as the manager of Jenkins Cabinets.

AAONLINE

1. Go to www.cengage.com/login
2. Click on **AA Online** to access.
3. Go to the online assignment and follow the instructions.

12-C Challenge Problem: Preparing a semimonthly payroll with pretax medical and retirement plans LO3, 4, 6

Assume Malone Company (Problem 12-M) offers its employees pretax medical and 401(k) plans. Earnings and voluntary deduction information are provided on the payroll register in the *Working Papers*.

Instructions:

1. Prepare a payroll register. Health insurance premiums and retirement plan contributions are eligible to be deducted from total earnings to calculate federal income taxes. Only health insurance premiums are eligible to be deducted from total earnings to calculate social security and Medicare taxes. Use the income tax withholding tables in Lesson 12-2 to find the income tax withholding for each employee. Calculate withholdings for social security and Medicare taxes using 6.2% and 1.45% tax rates, respectively. None of the employees has accumulated earnings greater than the social security tax base.

2. Prepare a schedule that calculates the difference in each employee's net pay.

1. Record the regular and overtime earnings for each employee on the payroll register.
2. Print the payroll register.

21st Century Skills

What's Your Story? Preparing a Resume

Theme: Financial, Economic, Business, and Entrepreneurial Literacy

Skills: Creativity and Innovation, Information Literacy

PARTNERSHIP FOR
21ST CENTURY SKILLS

A resume is the first thing an employer sees when reviewing a candidate for a job. Therefore, having an exceptional resume improves your chances of getting a job interview. However, creating a resume with little or no work experience can be challenging. Hiring managers may receive hundreds of resumes. You can make yours stand out and get the interview by following some simple guidelines.

A resume provides a statement of your education, experience, and qualifications. It should highlight your strengths and accomplishments. Jobs in accounting require attention to detail as well as problem-solving, mathematical, communication, computer, and people skills. Therefore, your resume for an accounting job should include classes you have taken that required analytical skills and cite examples of situations where you have worked as a team player. Most accounting jobs involve the use of accounting software, so be sure to include your experience with computers and software.

A bulleted list summarizing your qualifications is a great way to begin your resume. Many employers use technology to screen applicants by placing resumes in a keyword searchable database. Searching a database of resumes helps the employer determine which applicants align with the skills they want in an employee. Don't forget to use key terms to improve the likelihood that your resume will be found in a database search. A resume is an advertisement of who you are. Tell your story!

APPLICATION

1. Using the library or Internet, research sample resumes. Then, prepare a resume that you could send to a prospective employer. Remember to emphasize skills and qualifications necessary to the position.

2. Phil Knight, founder of Nike and famous author, John Grisham, were both accountants. Using the Internet, research one of the above or another famous accountant. Imagine that this person has decided to re-enter the accounting profession. Create a resume outlining his or her skills and qualifications.

Analyzing Nike's financial statements

Each annual report contains a section that tells how the financial statements were prepared. Accounting and management policies that were followed are described in detail. The report provides assurance that amounts on the financial statements can be relied upon to make business decisions.

INSTRUCTIONS

Use Management's Annual Report on Internal Control Over Financial Reporting on page B-4 in Appendix B to answer the following questions.

1. Who is responsible for preparing Nike's financial statements?
2. What is the system of internal control designed to do?
3. Can internal controls prevent or detect all misstatements?

Chapter 13

Accounting for Payroll and Payroll Taxes

LEARNING OBJECTIVES

After studying Chapter 13, in addition to defining key terms, you will be able to:

LO1 Analyze a payroll transaction.

LO2 Journalize a payroll including employee payroll taxes.

LO3 Calculate and record employer payroll taxes.

LO4 Prepare selected payroll tax reports.

LO5 Pay and record withholding and payroll taxes.

©DANIEL KOUREY, ISTOCK/©JIM PRUITT, ISTOCK

DMITRIY SHIRONOSOV/SHUTTERSTOCK.COM

Accounting In The Real World

Google

To stay competitive, technology companies must continually reinvent themselves. They must introduce a steady stream of new products along with applications for those products. Since its inception in 1996, Google has revolutionized how people surf the Internet. In its rise to dominance, Google acquired over 50 businesses, capturing a multitude of products and the creative talents that developed them. Its most notable acquisitions are YouTube and DoubleClick.

To retain a creative workforce, companies must provide a supportive work environment that encourages and rewards creativity. Google has the financial strength to offer many innovative benefits designed to make its employees' lives healthier, less complicated, and more fun. Beyond comprehensive health and retirement benefits, employees earn up to 25 vacation days per year. They can attend financial planning classes and receive reimbursement for furthering their college education.

Google is family friendly. New mothers receive up to 18 weeks of paid maternity leave. Fathers also receive up to seven weeks of parental leave. New parents are reimbursed up to $500 for take-out meals during the first three months the new baby is home. Google also provides financial assistance to pay legal and other fees for the adoption of a child.

Employees at Google's Mountain View, California, headquarters can ride to work in a shuttle that serves the San Francisco area. Once at work, employees can:

- Eat a free lunch or dinner cooked by gourmet chefs.

- Visit a doctor or receive a massage.

- Have their laundry dry cleaned or a bicycle repaired.

- Exercise in the gym or on the volleyball court.

CRITICAL THINKING

1. Google has offices all over the world. Identify three services you would suggest any company offer that would uniquely serve employees living in your city or state.

2. In what accounts should Google record the expense of these employee benefits?

Source: www.google.com.

Key Terms

- salary expense
- federal unemployment tax
- state unemployment tax
- deposit
- lookback period

LESSON
13-1 Recording a Payroll

LO1 Analyze a payroll transaction.

LO2 Journalize a payroll including employee payroll taxes.

Different Forms of Payroll Information

Payroll information for each pay period is recorded in a payroll register. Each pay period, payroll information is also recorded on employees' earnings records. Separate payroll accounts for each employee are not kept in the general ledger. Instead, accounts that summarize total earnings and deductions for all employees are kept in the general ledger. The total of gross earnings for all employees earning hourly wages, salaries, and commissions is called **salary expense**.

The payroll register and employee earnings records provide all the payroll information needed to prepare payroll and payroll tax reports. Journal entries are made to record the payment of the payroll and employer payroll taxes. In addition, various quarterly and annual payroll tax reports are required to report the payment of payroll taxes.

ETHICS IN ACTION

Age Discrimination?

Marist Industries maintains its own exercise facility for employees and their families. To show its commitment to employee health, the company hired Thom Dyer, an Olympic hopeful in weight lifting, as the facility manager. The company gave Thom a $20,000 budget to upgrade the exercise equipment. He used all the money to buy free weights, the equipment of choice for serious weightlifters.

To make room for the new weights, Thom removed several stationary bikes. Mary Ester, a 55-year-old manager, complained to Thom that he was "pushing out" the older employees.

She told him that free weights would only be used by "younger" employees. In response, Thom explained his belief that weight training was the most effective exercise for people of all ages. Not satisfied with his answer, Mary filed an employment discrimination complaint against Thom.

INSTRUCTIONS

Determine whether Thom acted ethically when he modified the mix of exercise equipment. Use the *Employee Handbook for the Emerson Business Ethics Program* as a guide. To access the handbook, enter its title in your Internet browser's search engine.

©LUCA DI FILIPPO, ISTOCK

Analyzing Payment of Payroll LO1

PAYROLL REGISTER

SEMIMONTHLY PERIOD ENDED December 15, 20--   DATE OF PAYMENT December 15, 20--

	EMPL. NO.	EMPLOYEE'S NAME	MARITAL STATUS	NO. OF ALLOWANCES	EARNINGS			DEDUCTIONS						NET PAY	CHECK NO.
					REGULAR	OVERTIME	TOTAL	FEDERAL INCOME TAX	SOCIAL SECURITY TAX	MEDICARE TAX	HEALTH INSURANCE	RETIREMENT PLAN	TOTAL		
1	2	Butler, John P.	M	4	1 3 2 0 00	1 4 6 25	1 4 6 6 25	2 9 00	9 0 91	2 1 26	7 0 00	8 0 00	2 9 1 17	1 1 7 5 08	128
2	7	Feng, Anthony R.	S	2	1 4 4 0 00	5 4 00	1 4 9 4 00	1 3 1 00	9 2 63	2 1 66	4 0 00	7 5 00	3 6 0 29	1 1 3 3 71	129
3	6	Lendsey, Ann C.	S	0	2 4 0 00	—	2 4 0 00	—	1 4 88	3 48	—	—	1 8 36	2 2 1 64	130
4	1	Prisock, Mary G.	M	3	2 0 0 0 00	—	2 0 0 0 00	1 2 5 00	1 2 4 00	2 9 00	5 5 00	2 0 0 00	5 3 3 00	1 4 6 7 00	131
5	5	Swann, Justin A.	M	2	1 3 2 0 00	1 1 2 50	1 4 3 2 50	6 1 00	8 8 82	2 0 77	4 0 00	6 0 00	2 7 0 59	1 1 6 1 91	132
6	4	Wells, Cary B.	S	1	1 4 4 4 00	—	1 4 4 4 00	1 4 8 00	8 9 53	2 0 94	2 5 00	5 0 00	3 3 3 47	1 1 1 0 53	133
7		Totals			7 7 6 4 00	3 1 2 75	8 0 7 6 75	4 9 4 00	5 0 0 77	1 1 7 11	2 3 0 00	4 6 5 00	1 8 0 6 88	6 2 6 9 87	

Similar to a special journal, the column totals of a payroll register provide the debit and credit amounts needed to journalize a payroll. Data from the payroll register for ThreeGreen's semimonthly pay period ended December 15 are summarized in the T accounts below.

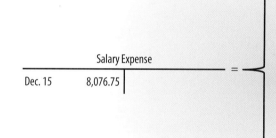

The sum of the Total Earnings column, $8,076.75, is the salary expense for the period. **Salary Expense** is debited for this amount. The total of each Deductions column (except for the Total column) is credited to a liability account. For example, federal income taxes of $494.00 were withheld from the employees' gross wages. The amount withheld is a liability of the business until the taxes are sent to the federal government. Therefore, **Employee Income Tax Payable** is credited for $494.00 to record this liability. Each of the other Deductions column totals is credited to a related liability account.

The Net Pay column total, $6,269.87, is the net amount paid to employees. So, **Cash** is credited for $6,269.87. A check for the total net pay amount, $6,269.87, is drawn on ThreeGreen's general checking account and is deposited in a separate payroll checking account. Individual payroll checks are then written on the payroll checking account.

remember Total Earnings is the debit amount for Salary Expense. Net Pay is the credit amount for cash.

fyi The totals of the Earnings Regular, Earnings Overtime, and Deductions Total columns are not used to journalize the payroll.

Journalizing Payment of a Payroll LO2

Date ❶ ❷ Account Debited ❸ Check Number

	DATE	ACCOUNT TITLE	CK. NO.	POST. REF.	GENERAL		ACCOUNTS PAYABLE DEBIT	PURCHASES DISCOUNT CREDIT	CASH CREDIT	
					DEBIT	CREDIT				
11	15	Salary Expense	732		8 0 7 6 75				6 2 6 9 87	11
12		Employee Income Tax Payable				4 9 4 00				12
13		Social Security Tax Payable				5 0 0 77				13
14		Medicare Tax Payable				1 1 7 11				14
15		Health Insurance Premiums Payable				2 3 0 00				15
16		Retirement Contributions Payable				4 6 5 00				16
17										17

CASH PAYMENTS JOURNAL   PAGE 12

Accounts Credited ❻   Total Earnings ❹   Payroll Deductions ❼   Amount Paid to Employees ❺

ThreeGreen journalized the company's payroll for the semimonthly period ended December 15, 20--.

> December 15. Paid cash for semimonthly payroll, $6,269.87 (total payroll, $8,076.75, less deductions: employee income tax, $494.00; social security tax, $500.77; Medicare tax, $117.11; health insurance premiums, $230.00; retirement contributions, $465.00). Check No. 732.

Amounts recorded in the General columns of a cash payments journal are posted individually to general ledger accounts. The credit to **Cash**, $6,269.87, is not posted separately to the **Cash** account. The amount is included in the journal's Cash Credit column total that is posted at the end of the month. The same procedures are followed to post this journal entry to the appropriate accounts as were described in Chapter 9.

↘ Journalizing Payment of a Payroll

❶ Write the date, 15, in the Date column.

❷ Write the title of the account debited, Salary Expense, in the Account Title column.

❸ Write the check number, 732, in the Ck. No. column.

❹ Write the total earnings for the pay period to Salary Expense, $8,076.75, in the General Debit column.

❺ On the same line, write the total amount paid to employees, $6,269.87, in the Cash Credit column.

❻ On the next five lines, write the titles of the accounts relating to each payroll deduction: Employee Income Tax Payable, Social Security Tax Payable, Medicare Tax Payable, Health Insurance Premiums Payable, and Retirement Contributions Payable in the Account Title column.

❼ On the same five lines, write the payroll deduction amounts for the corresponding liability accounts, $494.00, $500.77, $117.11, $230.00, and $465.00 in the General Credit column.

End of Lesson Review

LO1 Analyze a payroll transaction.

LO2 Journalize a payroll including employee payroll taxes.

Term Review

salary expense

Audit your understanding

1. What account title is used to journalize the Total Earnings column of the payroll register?
2. What account title is used to journalize the Federal Income Tax column of the payroll register?
3. What account title is used to journalize the Social Security Tax column of the payroll register?
4. What account title is used to journalize the Medicare Tax column of the payroll register?

Work together 13-1

Recording a payroll

Lakeland Company's payroll register has the following totals for the semimonthly pay period, May 1–15, of the current year. T accounts and a cash payments journal page are provided in the *Working Papers*. Your instructor will guide you through the following examples.

Total Earnings	Federal Income Tax Withheld	Social Security Tax Withheld	Medicare Withheld
$13,800.00	$925.00	$855.60	$200.10

1. Use the T accounts provided to analyze Lakeland's May 1–15 payroll.
2. Journalize the payment of Lakeland's May 1–15 payroll on page 6 of the cash payments journal. The payroll was paid by Check No. 564 on May 15 of the current year.

On your own 13-1

Recording a payroll

Houston Company's payroll register has the following totals for the semimonthly pay period, June 16–30, of the current year. T accounts and a cash payments journal page are provided in the *Working Papers*. Work this problem independently.

Total Earnings	Federal Income Tax Withheld	Social Security Tax Withheld	Medicare Withheld
$15,640.00	$1,015.00	$969.68	$226.78

1. Use the T accounts provided to analyze Houston's June 16–30 payroll.
2. Journalize the payment of Houston's June 16–30 payroll on page 8 of a cash payments journal. The payroll was paid by Check No. 776 on June 30 of the current year.

©CANDICE CUSACK, ISTOCK

13-2 Recording Employer Payroll Taxes

LO3 Calculate and record employer payroll taxes.

Employer Payroll Taxes

Employers must pay to the government the taxes withheld from employee earnings. ThreeGreen has withheld federal income tax, social security tax, and Medicare tax from employee wages and salaries. The amounts withheld are liabilities to the business until they are actually paid to the government.

In addition, employers must pay several of their own payroll taxes. Employer payroll taxes are business expenses and are recorded in the **Payroll Tax Expense** account.

Most employers must pay four separate payroll taxes. These taxes are (1) social security tax, (2) Medicare tax, (3) federal unemployment tax, and (4) state unemployment tax.

EMPLOYER SOCIAL SECURITY AND MEDICARE TAXES

Social security and Medicare taxes are the only payroll taxes paid by both employees and employers. ThreeGreen withheld $500.77 in social security tax and $117.11 in Medicare tax from employee wages for the pay period ended December 15. The business owes the same amount of social security and Medicare taxes as the amount withheld from employees. ThreeGreen's social security and Medicare taxes for the pay period ended December 15 are also $500.77 and $117.11, respectively.

Congress sets the social security and Medicare tax rates for employees and employers. Congress often changes the tax rates and tax base. The social security tax rate used in this text is 6.2% of earnings up to the tax base—a maximum of $106,800.00 each calendar

year. Medicare does not have a tax base. Therefore, Medicare tax is calculated on total employee earnings. The Medicare tax rate used in this text is 1.45% of total employee earnings.

FEDERAL UNEMPLOYMENT TAX

The Federal Unemployment Tax Act (FUTA) created a national program to provide cash payments to employees who lose their jobs through no fault of their own. Federal unemployment insurance laws require that employers pay taxes to fund unemployment benefits. These taxes are used to pay workers' benefits for limited periods of unemployment and to administer the unemployment benefit program. A federal tax paid by employers to administer the unemployment program is called **federal unemployment tax**, commonly referred to as *FUTA*. The tax rate and tax base for FUTA taxes are referred to as the *FUTA tax rate* and *FUTA tax base*.

STATE UNEMPLOYMENT TAX

Unemployment benefits are paid by state unemployment programs. A state tax paid by employers that is used to pay benefits to unemployed workers is called **state unemployment tax**, commonly referred to as *SUTA*. The Social Security Act specifies certain standards for unemployment benefit laws. Therefore, state unemployment laws differ very little. However, each employer must know the requirements of the state in which it operates. The tax rate for SUTA taxes is referred to as the *SUTA tax rate*. The SUTA tax uses the FUTA tax base.

Social security tax and Medicare tax are the only payroll taxes paid by both the employer and employee. A business pays the same amount of social security tax and Medicare tax as the amount withheld from employees.

Employers must pay four taxes on employee earnings—social security tax, Medicare tax, FUTA tax, and SUTA tax.

Calculating Unemployment Taxes LO3

THREE△GREEN PRODUCTS, INC. Calculation of FUTA Earnings for December 15, 20-- Pay Period				
1	2	3	4	5
Employee	Prior Accumulated Earnings	Earnings to Equal FUTA Tax Base	Earnings for Current Pay Period	FUTA Earnings
Butler, John P.	$27,195.00	$ 0.00	$1,466.25	$ 0.00
Feng, Anthony R.	5,260.00	1,740.00	1,494.00	1,494.00
Lendsey, Ann C.	1,648.00	5,352.00	240.00	240.00
Prisock, Mary G.	44,000.00	0.00	2,000.00	0.00
Swann, Justin A.	16,089.00	0.00	1,432.50	0.00
Wells, Cary B.	6,490.00	510.00	1,444.00	510.00
				$2,244.00

1 Enter prior accumulated earnings

2 Enter the difference between the FUTA tax base and prior accumulated earnings

3 Enter earnings for the current pay period

4 Enter the FUTA earnings

The FUTA tax rate is 6.2% of the FUTA tax base; currently, the first $7,000.00 earned by each employee. Earnings subject to unemployment taxes are referred to as *FUTA earnings*.

Employers can generally deduct from federal unemployment payments the amounts they pay to state unemployment programs. But the deduction cannot be more than 5.4% of FUTA earnings. The effective FUTA tax rate in most states is, therefore, 0.8% on the first $7,000.00 earned by each employee (federal, 6.2% − deductible for state, 5.4% = 0.8%).

The amount of FUTA earnings for ThreeGreen's pay period ended December 15, 20--, is shown in the illustration.

↘ Calculating FUTA Earnings

1 From each employee's earnings record, enter total earnings prior to the current pay period. John P. Butler's prior earnings as of November 30, $27,195.00, are recorded in the first column.

2 Enter the amount of earnings needed for each employee to reach the $7,000.00 FUTA tax base. Subtract the prior total earnings, column 2, from $7,000.00. Enter zero if the amount is less than zero. Mr. Butler's amount ($7,000.00 − $27,195.00) is negative; therefore, $0.00 is entered in column 3.

3 Enter the current pay period earnings in column 4. Mr. Butler's earnings for the December 15 pay period are $1,466.25.

4 Enter in column 5 the lesser of the amounts in columns 3 and 4, then total column 5.

- If the earnings for the current pay period (column 4) are less than or equal to the earnings needed to reach the FUTA tax base, then all current earnings are FUTA earnings. Enter the current earnings amount in column 5. Anthony R. Feng and Ann C. Lendsey have earnings that match this test.

- If the earnings for the current pay period are greater than the amount in column 3, then FUTA earnings are the amount in column 3. For Cary B. Wells, the earnings for the current pay period, $1,444.00, are greater than the $510.00 of earnings needed to reach the $7,000.00 FUTA tax base. Therefore, $510.00 is entered for Mr. Wells' FUTA earnings.

- Total the FUTA Earnings column. This total amount, $2,244.00, is used to calculate the unemployment taxes.

Earnings are subject to FUTA taxes until an employee's accumulated earnings reach the FUTA tax base.

Journalizing Employer Payroll Taxes

Account Debited ❷   Memorandum Number ❸   ❹ Amount Debited

GENERAL JOURNAL   PAGE 12

	DATE	ACCOUNT TITLE	DOC. NO.	POST. REF.	DEBIT	CREDIT	
7	15	Payroll Taxes Expense	M44		7 5 7 01		7
8		Social Security Tax Payable				5 0 0 77	8
9		Medicare Tax Payable				1 1 7 11	9
10		Unemployment Tax Payable—Federal				1 7 95	10
11		Unemployment Tax Payable—State				1 2 1 18	11

Employer payroll taxes are paid to the government at later dates than when they are journalized. However, the liabilities are incurred when salaries are paid. Therefore, the transaction to record employer payroll taxes expense is journalized on the same date the payroll is journalized. The salary expense and the employer payroll taxes expense are both recorded in the same accounting period.

> **December 15. Recorded employer payroll taxes expense, $757.01, for the semimonthly pay period ended December 15. Taxes owed are: social security tax, $500.77; Medicare tax, $117.11; federal unemployment tax, $17.95; state unemployment tax, $121.18. Memorandum No. 44.**

Payroll Taxes Expense is debited for $757.01 to show the increase in the balance of this expense account. Four liability accounts are credited to show the increase in payroll tax liabilities. Amounts recorded in the general journal are posted individually to general ledger accounts. The same procedures are followed to post this journal entry to the appropriate accounts as were described in Chapter 12.

The December 15 transactions in **Social Security Tax Payable** and **Medicare Tax Payable**, shown in the T accounts in gray, are the amounts withheld from employees' wages. These amounts were posted from the payment of the payroll in the cash payments journal.

Payroll Taxes Expense	
Dec. 15 757.01	

Social Security Tax Payable	
	Dec. 15 500.77
	500.77

Medicare Tax Payable	
	Dec. 15 117.11
	117.11

Unemployment Tax Payable—Federal	
	Dec. 15 17.95

Unemployment Tax Payable—State	
	Dec. 15 121.18

Journalizing Employer Payroll Taxes

❶ Write the date, 15, in the Date column.

❷ Write the title of the expense account debited, Payroll Taxes Expense, in the Account Title column.

❸ Write the memorandum number, M44, in the Doc. No. column.

❹ Write the debit amount, $757.01, in the Debit column.

❺ Write the titles of the liability accounts credited, Social Security Tax Payable, Medicare Tax Payable, Unemployment Tax Payable—Federal, and Unemployment Tax Payable—State, on the next four lines of the Account Title column, indented about one centimeter.

❻ Write the credit amounts, $500.77, $117.11, $17.95, and $121.18, respectively, in the Credit column.

	FUTA Earnings	×	Tax Rate	=	Tax
FUTA	$2,244.00	×	0.8%	=	$ 17.95
SUTA	2,244.00	×	5.4%	=	121.18

Careers In Accounting

Tuan Nguyen
CONTROLLER

TAN KIAN KHOON/SHUTTERSTOCK.COM

Do you want to be in charge of an entire accounting department? Do you like managing people? Do you like having authority and making decisions? If so, you may want to consider the top position. The chief accountant in an organization, having responsibility for both financial and managerial accounting activities, is called a **controller** or sometimes a *comptroller*.

Depending on the size and type of company, the controller is the highest or second highest accounting position. Tuan Nguyen is the controller for Asian Pacific Imports. He is in charge of the entire range of accounting functions for his company. Recently, Tuan was involved in setting up and managing a new automated accounting system. It is his responsibility to:

1. Manage the company's accounting system.
2. Produce annual and interim financial statements.
3. Work with external auditors.
4. Establish internal control policies.
5. Interact with other managers to understand the kind of data they need to make decisions.
6. Explain accounting rules to non-accounting personnel.
7. Manage accounting department employees.
8. Develop new reports for internal use.
9. Supervise the preparation of tax returns and reports.

Salary Range: $100,000 to more than $250,000.

Qualifications: The position of controller requires a thorough understanding of GAAP and automated accounting systems. Excellent oral and written communication skills and effective presentation skills are essential. Like all managers, this person must be able to direct, motivate, and evaluate employees and respect confidentiality. Excellent math skills are needed to be able to analyze financial statements and understand tax rules and reporting deadlines. Most companies require ten or more years of experience in the field. A four-year college degree is required with a masters degree preferred. A Certified Public Accountant (CPA) certification is usually required.

Occupational Outlook: The growth for controller positions is expected to be average (between 7% and 13%) for the period from 2008 to 2018.

ACTIVITY

Contact two companies in your community or region and ask if you can interview the controller. Some questions you might ask are: What was his/her education and experience when he/she was hired as controller? To what position in the company does he/she report? What are some of his/her biggest challenges? What does he/she enjoy most about the job? Write a summary of your findings.

Sources: www.onetcenter.org, www.salary.com/Controller-salary.html.

©MILENNY, ISTOCK

End of Lesson Review

LO3 Calculate and record employer payroll taxes.

Terms Review

federal unemployment tax

state unemployment tax

Audit your understanding

1. What is the tax rate ThreeGreen must pay on employees for each of the following taxes: social security, Medicare, federal unemployment, and state unemployment?

2. What is the amount of each employee's earnings that is subject to federal and state unemployment taxes at ThreeGreen?

Work together 13-2

Recording employer payroll taxes

Payroll information taken from employee earnings records is given below. A form and general journal page are provided in the *Working Papers*. Your instructor will guide you through the following examples.

Employee Name	Accumulated Earnings, April 30	Total Earnings for May 1–15 Pay Period
Ellis, Nick C.	$6,100.00	$ 762.50
Jennings, Evan P.	7,980.00	1,040.00
Powers, Virginia A.	4,380.00	527.00
Wolfe, Kerry T.	6,850.00	849.50

1. Calculate the FUTA taxes. Unemployment taxes are owed on the first $7,000.00 of earnings for each employee.

2. Calculate the amount of employer payroll taxes owed for the May 1–15 pay period. Use the employer payroll tax rates shown in this chapter.

3. Journalize the employer's payroll taxes for the May 1–15 pay period on May 15 of the current year. Use general journal page 10 and Memorandum No. 46.

On your own 13-2

Recording employer payroll taxes

Payroll information taken from employee earnings records is given below. A form and general journal page are provided in the *Working Papers*. Work this problem independently.

Employee Name	Accumulated Earnings, May 31	Total Earnings for June 1–15 Pay Period
Holt, Stephanie L.	$6,380.00	$653.00
Klein, Jacob S.	3,840.00	521.00
Singh, Irene M.	7,290.00	736.50
Tate, Joyce B.	6,270.00	614.00

1. Calculate the FUTA taxes. Unemployment taxes are owed on the first $7,000.00 of earnings for each employee.

2. Calculate the amount of employer payroll taxes owed for the June 1–15 pay period. Use the employer payroll tax rates shown in this chapter.

3. Journalize the employer's payroll taxes for the June 1–15 pay period on June 15 of the current year. Use general journal page 12 and Memorandum No. 97.

LESSON
13-3 Reporting Withholding and Payroll Taxes

LO4 Prepare selected payroll tax reports.

Employer Annual Report to Employees of Taxes Withheld LO4

22222	**a** Employee's social security number 194-81-5823	OMB No. 1545-0008		
b Employer identification number (EIN) 31-0429632			**1** Wages, tips, other compensation 30,273.75	**2** Federal income tax withheld 620.00
c Employer's name, address, and ZIP code ThreeGreen Products, Inc. 1501 Commerce Street Carlisle, PA 17013			**3** Social security wages 30,273.75	**4** Social security tax withheld 1,876.97
			5 Medicare wages and tips 30,273.75	**6** Medicare tax withheld 438.97
			7 Social security tips	**8** Allocated tips
d Control number			**9**	**10** Dependent care benefits
e Employee's first name and initial Last name Suff. John P. Butler		**11** Nonqualified plans		**12a**
		13 Statutory employee ☐ Retirement plan ☐ Third-party sick pay ☐		**12b**
1014 Bosler Ave. Carlisle, PA 17013		**14** Other		**12c**
				12d
f Employee's address and ZIP code				
15 State Employer's state ID number	**16** State wages, tips, etc.	**17** State income tax	**18** Local wages, tips, etc.	**19** Local income tax **20** Locality name

Form **W-2** Wage and Tax Statement   **20 - -**   Department of the Treasury—Internal Revenue Service

Copy 1—For State, City, or Local Tax Department

An employer who withholds taxes from employee earnings must furnish each employee with an annual report of these withholdings. The report shows total year's earnings and the amounts withheld for taxes for an employee. These amounts are obtained from the employee earnings records. The report is prepared on the Internal Revenue Service Form W-2, Wage and Tax Statement.

Employers must furnish Form W-2 to each employee by January 31 of the next year. If requested by the employee, Form W-2 must be furnished within 30 days of the last date of employment.

Four copies (A to D) of Form W-2 are prepared. The employer sends Copy A to the Social Security Administration and keeps Copy D for the business's records. Copies B and C are given to the employee. The employee attaches Copy B to a personal federal income tax return and keeps Copy C for a personal record. Businesses in states with state income tax must prepare an additional copy to be attached to the employee's state tax return.

Some federal tax forms can be printed from copies available on the Internet. Other tax forms, such as the W-2 and W-3, are designed to be machine readable and must be obtained directly from the Internal Revenue Service.

Employer's Quarterly Federal Tax Return

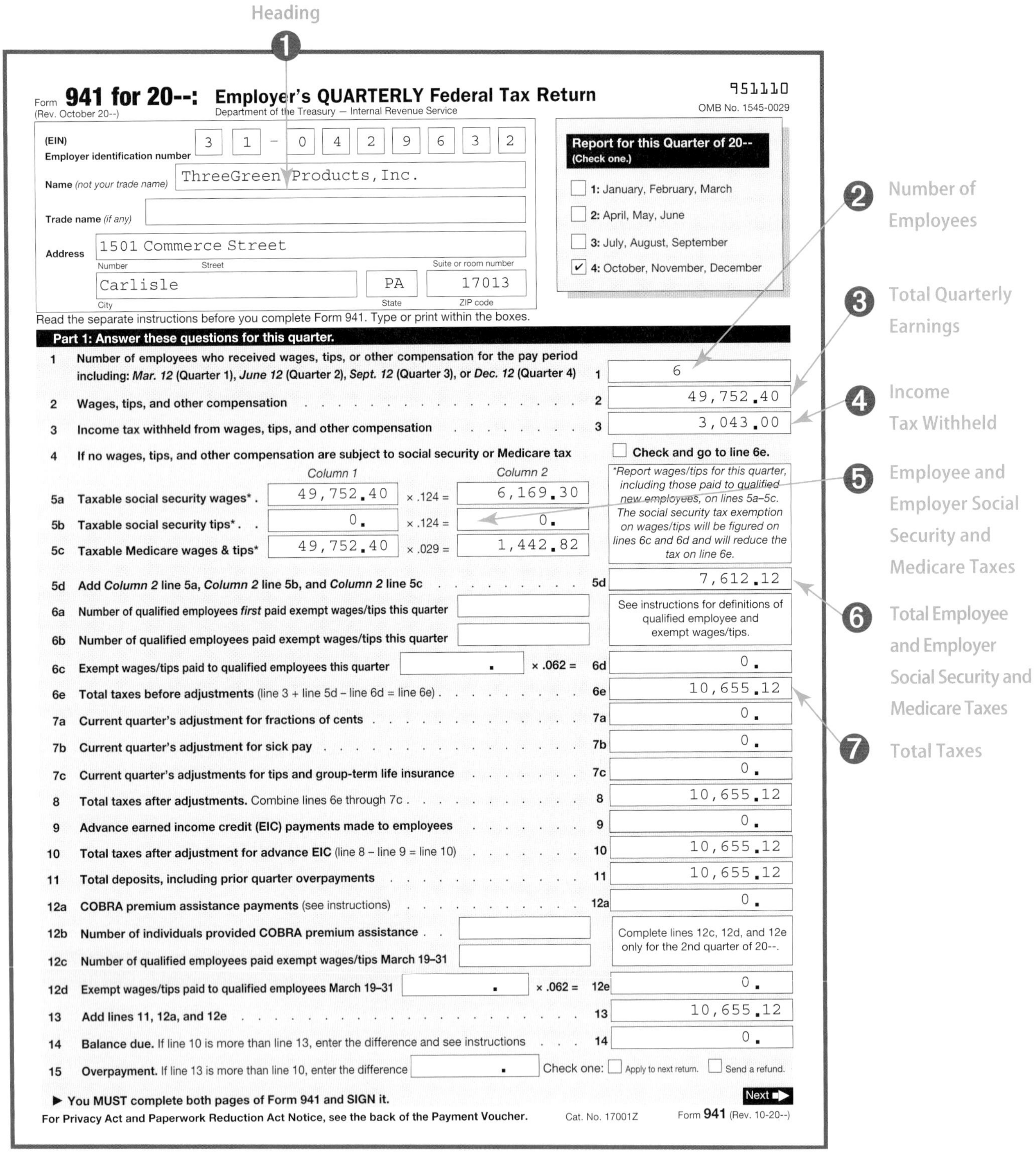

Heading

①

② Number of Employees

③ Total Quarterly Earnings

④ Income Tax Withheld

⑤ Employee and Employer Social Security and Medicare Taxes

⑥ Total Employee and Employer Social Security and Medicare Taxes

⑦ Total Taxes

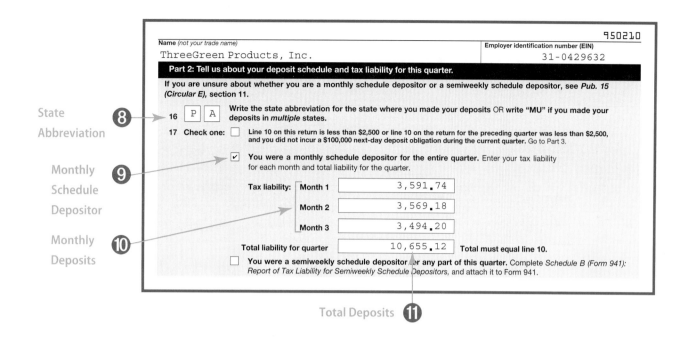

State Abbreviation ⑧

Monthly Schedule Depositor ⑨

Monthly Deposits ⑩

Total Deposits ⑪

Preparing Employer's Quarterly Federal Tax Return

Each employer is required by law to periodically report to the government the payroll taxes withheld from employee salaries, and to report the employer payroll taxes due. Some reports are submitted quarterly and others, annually.

Each employer must file Form 941, Employer's Quarterly Federal Tax Return, showing the federal income tax, social security tax, and Medicare taxes owed to the government. The form must be filed before the last day of the month following the end of a calendar quarter. ThreeGreen's Form 941 for the quarter ended December 31 is shown on the previous page. The information needed to prepare Form 941 is obtained from employee earnings records.

Preparing an Employer's Quarterly Federal Tax Return

① Enter the company name, address, employer identification number, and the date the quarter ended in the heading section of Form 941.

② Enter the number of employees, 6, on line 1.

③ Enter total quarterly earnings, $49,752.40, on lines 2, 5a, and 5c. This amount is the sum of the fourth quarter total earnings of all employees.

④ Enter the income tax withheld, $3,043.00, on line 3. This amount is the total of the fourth quarter federal income tax withheld from all employees.

⑤ Calculate and enter the quarterly employee and employer social security taxes, $6,169.30, and Medicare taxes, $1,442.82, in column 2 on lines 5a and 5c, respectively. The 12.4% tax rate is the sum of the employee 6.2% and the employer 6.2% social security tax rates. The 2.9% tax rate is the sum of the employee 1.45% and the employer 1.45% Medicare tax rates.

⑥ Enter the total social security and Medicare taxes, $7,612.12 ($6,169.30 + $1,442.82), on line 5d.

⑦ Enter the total payroll taxes, $10,655.12 ($3,043.00 + $7,612.12), on line 6e. Since ThreeGreen has no adjustments to its taxes, the total is also entered on lines 8 and 10.

⑧ Enter the two-letter state abbreviation, PA, on line 16.

⑨ ThreeGreen deposits tax withholdings every month. Check the box next to the statement "You were a monthly schedule depositor for the entire quarter."

⑩ Enter the monthly deposits, $3,591.74 + $3,569.18 + $3,494.20, in the boxes provided in line 17.

⑪ Enter the sum of the monthly totals, $10,655.12 ($3,591.74 + $3,569.18 + $3,494.20), on lines 11 and 13 and in the box under the monthly deposits.

Employer Annual Reporting of Payroll Taxes

33333	a Control number	For Official Use Only ▶ OMB No. 1545-0008

| b Kind of Payer (Check one) | 941 [X] CT-1 | Military [ ] Hshld. emp. [ ] | 943 [ ] Medicare govt. emp. [ ] | 944 [ ] | Kind of Employer (Check one) | None apply [ ] State/local non-501c [X] | 501c non-govt. [ ] State/local 501c [ ] | Federal govt. [ ] | Third-party sick pay (Check if applicable) [ ] |

c Total number of Forms W-2 6	d Establishment number

1 Wages, tips, other compensation 168,365.60	2 Federal income tax withheld 12,048.00
e Employer identification number (EIN) 31-0429632	3 Social security wages 168,365.60	4 Social security tax withheld 12,298.67
f Employer's name ThreeGreen Products, Inc. 1501 Commerce Street Carlisle, PA 17013	5 Medicare wages and tips 168,365.60	6 Medicare tax withheld 2,876.30
	7 Social security tips	8 Allocated tips
	9	10 Dependent care benefits
g Employer's address and ZIP code	11 Nonqualified plans	12a Deferred compensation
h Other EIN used this year	13 For third-party sick pay use only	12b
15 State Employer's state ID number	14 Income tax withheld by payer of third-party sick pay	
16 State wages, tips, etc.	17 State income tax	18 Local wages, tips, etc.	19 Local income tax
Contact person Mary G. Prisock	Telephone number (717) 555-8490	For Official Use Only
Email address mprisock@threegreen.com	Fax number	

Under penalties of perjury, I declare that I have examined this return and accompanying documents, and, to the best of my knowledge and belief, they are true, correct, and complete.

Signature ▶ *Mary G. Prisock*   Title ▶ *President*   Date ▶ 2/26/--

Form **W-3** Transmittal of Wage and Tax Statements   20- -   Department of the Treasury Internal Revenue Service

Send this entire page with the entire Copy A page of Form(s) W-2 to the Social Security Administration.
Do not send any payment (cash, checks, money orders, etc.) with Forms W-2 and W-3.

Form W-3, Transmittal of Wage and Tax Statements, is sent to the Social Security Administration by February 28 each year. Form W-3 reports the prior year's earnings and payroll taxes withheld for all employees. Attached to Form W-3 is Copy A of each employee's Form W-2. Employers with more than 250 employees must send the information to the Internal Revenue Service in computer files rather than the actual Forms W-2 and W-3.

At the end of a calendar year, employers must also report to the federal and state governments a summary of all earnings paid to employees during the 12 months.

WHY ACCOUNTING?

Hybrid Crops

If you are connected with agriculture, the terms "high yield" and "disease resistant" sound like money in your pocket. Yield is the amount of product the farmer can produce per acre. The higher the yield, the more product the farmer has available to sell. A plant that is resistant to disease will also increase the yield. However, high-yield and disease-resistant crops may actually decrease the net revenue to the farmer.

One way to increase both yield and disease resistance is to alter the seeds used for planting. Hybrid seeds and plants are those in which cross-pollination has been artificially structured to encourage different outcomes such as high yield and/or disease resistance.

Agriculture, Food & Natural Resources

CRITICAL THINKING

1. Search the Internet to find crops other than corn for which hybrid seeds are used. List three such crops.

2. If genetically modified corn increases worldwide production by 10%, what effect could this have on the price per bushel of corn?

End of Lesson Review

LO4 Prepare selected payroll tax reports.

Audit your understanding

1. When must employers furnish a W-2 statement to their employees?
2. What taxes are included in the quarterly federal tax return filed by the employer?

Work together 13-3

Reporting withholding and payroll taxes

A Form 941, Employer's Quarterly Federal Tax Return, is given in the *Working Papers*. Your instructor will guide you through the following example. The following data are for Concept Designs.

Date Paid	Total Earnings	Federal Income Tax Withheld	Employee Social Security Tax Withheld	Employee Medicare Tax Withheld
Jan. 31	$11,640.00	$698.00	$721.68	$168.78
Feb. 28	11,900.00	718.00	737.80	172.55
Mar. 31	12,100.00	728.00	750.20	175.45

   a. Company address: 12043 Washington Street, Naperville, Illinois 60540-4158

   b. Employer identification number: 70-8418625

   c. Number of employees: 8

Prepare a Form 941 for Concept Designs for the first quarter of the current year.

On your own 13-3

Reporting withholding and payroll taxes

A Form 941, Employer's Quarterly Federal Tax Return, is given in the *Working Papers*. Work this problem independently. The following data are for Concept Designs. The company address, employer identification number, and number of employees are the same as in Work Together 13-3.

Date Paid	Total Earnings	Federal Income Tax Withheld	Employee Social Security Tax Withheld	Employee Medicare Tax Withheld
Apr. 30	$11,820.00	$712.00	$732.84	$171.39
May 31	12,280.00	738.00	761.36	178.06
Jun. 30	11,920.00	724.00	739.04	172.84

Prepare a Form 941 for Concept Designs for the second quarter of the current year.

LESSON
13-4 Paying Withholding and Payroll Taxes

LO5 Pay and record withholding and payroll taxes.

Paying the Liability for Employee Income Tax, Social Security Tax, and Medicare Tax LO5

Employers must pay to the federal, state, and local governments all payroll taxes withheld from employee earnings as well as the employer payroll taxes. The payment of payroll taxes to the government is referred to as a **deposit**. Two amounts determine how often deposits are made to the federal government: (1) the amount of payroll taxes collected during the current deposit period and (2) the amount of payroll taxes owed during a prior 12-month period. The 12-month period that ends on June 30 of the prior year that is used to determine how frequently a business must deposit payroll taxes is called the **lookback period**. The Internal Revenue Service provides businesses with the following flowchart to assist them in determining when to make tax deposits.

When to Deposit Form 941 Employment Taxes

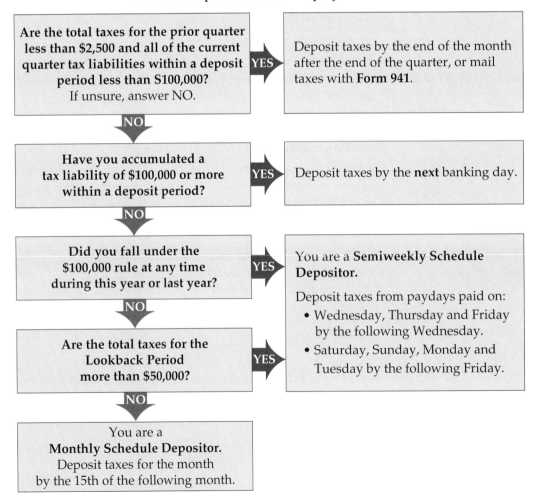

Are the total taxes for the prior quarter less than $2,500 and all of the current quarter tax liabilities within a deposit period less than $100,000? If unsure, answer NO. — **YES** → Deposit taxes by the end of the month after the end of the quarter, or mail taxes with **Form 941**.

NO ↓

Have you accumulated a tax liability of $100,000 or more within a deposit period? — **YES** → Deposit taxes by the **next** banking day.

NO ↓

Did you fall under the $100,000 rule at any time during this year or last year? — **YES** → You are a **Semiweekly Schedule Depositor.**

Deposit taxes from paydays paid on:
- Wednesday, Thursday and Friday by the following Wednesday.
- Saturday, Sunday, Monday and Tuesday by the following Friday.

NO ↓

Are the total taxes for the Lookback Period more than $50,000? — **YES** →

NO ↓

You are a **Monthly Schedule Depositor.** Deposit taxes for the month by the 15th of the following month.

Making Federal Tax Deposits

New employers are monthly schedule depositors for the first calendar year of business. After a lookback period is established, the business must evaluate whether a change in its deposit period is required.

ThreeGreen is classified as a monthly depositor. So, every month the payroll taxes must be paid by the 15th day of the following month. The payment includes all the federal income, social security, and Medicare taxes that ThreeGreen withheld from employee salaries. ThreeGreen must also pay the employer share of the social security and Medicare taxes.

Federal tax deposits must be paid using electronic fund transfer. Businesses are encouraged to make deposits using the Electronic Federal Tax Payment System (EFTPS). Either by computer or telephone, the business can have the deposit transferred directly from its bank account to the government.

A business may choose to have a tax professional, financial institution, or other third party deposit its taxes electronically. ThreeGreen prepares a check to its bank for the amount for December, $3,494.20. The bank uses its electronic fund transfer system to deposit the taxes for ThreeGreen.

Tax rules change periodically. Always check the most current tax information before calculating any tax amount and the tax deposit requirements.

 remember Employee payroll taxes are paid by employees through payroll withholdings. Employers must pay their own payroll taxes.

FINANCIAL LITERACY

Wage Garnishment

Employers are required by law to withhold deductions from employees' wages. Examples include federal income tax, social security and Medicare taxes, and, in some cases, state and local income taxes. Employers may also withhold deductions that an employee has agreed to for such things as insurance, savings, meals, union dues, uniforms, and charitable contributions.

Many employers and employees may encounter another legal deduction from an employee's paycheck. **Wage garnishment** is a process that requires an employer to withhold a portion of an employee's paycheck to pay a court-ordered debt settlement. Common settlements include child support and damages awarded to an individual or a business. Generally, the employer sends the garnisheed amount to the court. The court then pays the employee's creditor. All states permit wage garnishment, but limitations and types of wage garnishment vary by state.

Someone considering a loan or credit purchase that they can't afford should think twice. Garnishment may add to financial hardship. Even worse, it will result in one's employer learning that he or she is not very responsible about money.

ACTIVITIES

1. Explain the purpose of wage garnishment.

2. Explain why wage garnishment is not a voluntary deduction.

3. Research the types of wage garnishments that are permissible in your state. Compare your findings to the garnishment laws of two other states of your choice.

©NOREBBO, ISTOCK

Journalizing Payment of Liability for Employee Income Tax, Social Security Tax, and Medicare Tax

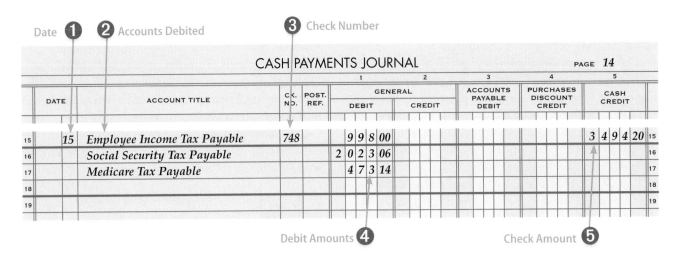

Date ❶ ❷ Accounts Debited ❸ Check Number

CASH PAYMENTS JOURNAL   PAGE *14*

DATE	ACCOUNT TITLE	CK. NO.	POST. REF.	GENERAL DEBIT	GENERAL CREDIT	ACCOUNTS PAYABLE DEBIT	PURCHASES DISCOUNT CREDIT	CASH CREDIT	
15	Employee Income Tax Payable	748		9 9 8 00				3 4 9 4 20	15
	Social Security Tax Payable			2 0 2 3 06					16
	Medicare Tax Payable			4 7 3 14					17
									18
									19

Debit Amounts ❹   Check Amount ❺

January 15. Paid cash for liability for employee income tax, $998.00; social security tax, $2,023.06; and Medicare tax, $473.14; total, $3,494.20. Check No. 748.

The January 15 balance of each liability account is a result of payroll transactions recorded in December. The transactions in **Employee Income Tax Payable** are the amounts withheld on the December 15 and December 31 payrolls. There are two transactions recorded in **Social Security Tax Payable** and **Medicare Tax Payable** for each payroll. The first transaction is the amount withheld from the December 15 payroll recorded on a cash payments journal. The second December 15 transaction represents the employer's share of payroll taxes recorded on a general journal. The two December 31 transactions represent the employee and employer payroll taxes for the December 31 payroll.

The debit to each liability account reduces the balance to zero. The balance of Cash is decreased by a credit for the total payment, $3,494.20.

Employee Income Tax Payable

		Dec. 15	494.00
		Dec. 31	504.00
Jan. 15	998.00	Jan. 15 Bal.	998.00

Social Security Tax Payable

		Dec. 15	500.76
		Dec. 15	500.76
		Dec. 31	510.77
		Dec. 31	510.77
Jan. 15	2,023.06	Jan. 15 Bal.	2,023.06

Medicare Tax Payable

		Dec. 15	117.11
		Dec. 15	117.11
		Dec. 31	119.46
		Dec. 31	119.46
Jan. 15	473.14	Jan. 15 Bal.	473.14

Cash

Jan. 15	3,494.20		

⤵ Journalizing a Payment of Liability for Employee Income Tax, Social Security Tax, and Medicare Tax

❶ Write the date, 15, in the Date column.

❷ Write the titles of the three accounts debited, Employee Income Tax Payable, Social Security Tax Payable, and Medicare Tax Payable, in the Account Title column.

❸ Write the check number, 748, in the Ck. No. column.

❹ Write the three debit amounts, $998.00, $2,023.06, and $473.14, in the General Debit column.

❺ Write the amount of the credit to Cash, $3,494.20, in the Cash Credit column.

Paying the Liability for Federal Unemployment Tax

FUTA taxes are paid by the end of the month following each quarter if the liability amount is more than $500.00. However, all unemployment tax liabilities outstanding at the end of a calendar year must be paid. FUTA tax is paid to the federal government using electronic funds transfer or the Electronic Federal Tax Payment System. The deposit for FUTA tax is similar to the deposit required for income tax, social security tax, and Medicare tax.

The total of FUTA taxes paid during a calendar year is reported on Form 940. ThreeGreen's FUTA tax liability for the entire year is $297.02. Therefore, ThreeGreen was not required to make any quarterly tax deposits.

The Internal Revenue Service encourages all businesses to deposit federal payroll taxes using the Electronic Federal Tax Payment System.

THINK LIKE AN ACCOUNTANT

Accountant Billing Rates

Public accounting firms earn revenue by selling the services of staff accountants to clients. Each accountant's time is charged to the client at an hourly billing rate. Billing rates are based on the accountant's annual salary, employer payroll taxes, employee benefits, office expenses, and profit.

Morse and Poole, CPAs, is preparing for its annual recruiting drive for new staff accountants. As the firm's recruiting director, Barbara Edmonds evaluates and recommends competitive employment offers for the partners to consider. She believes the firm must offer today's college graduates more than a good salary. Some job candidates want wellness benefits to pay for preventive health care, including fitness center fees. Other individuals want paid time off to serve their community.

To prepare for the annual partners' meeting, Ms. Edmonds has decided to "run the numbers" on three alternative employment offers:

1. Individuals who value preventive health care would be offered a $50,000 annual salary. Those employees would also receive a $2,500 wellness benefit.

2. Individuals who want extra time to serve the community would be offered a $48,000 salary. Those employees would receive 15 days of paid time off for community service.

3. Individuals who value preventive health care and community service would be offered a $46,000 salary. They would also receive a $2,500 wellness benefit and ten days off for community service.

This year, in addition to the above compensation, the firm will offer first-year staff three weeks of paid vacation, five days of sick leave, and free health insurance.

Staff accountants are expected to bill 80% of their available hours. To pay for office expenses and earn a profit, the firm charges an hourly billing rate of about 220% of each accountant's hourly payroll expense.

OPEN THE SPREADSHEET TLA_CH13

Follow the steps on the Instructions tab. The worksheet on the Analysis tab contains payroll expense and billing rates for the prior year. Complete the analysis to determine the billing rate that would result from each offer. Answer these questions:

1. How could the offers be changed to make the billing rates similar?

2. The firm will use the same billing rate for all first-year staff, regardless of the offer selected by individual accountants. What would you recommend for a new billing rate?

3. Can you think of a fourth alternative the firm should consider? What salary and benefits would be included?

Journalizing Payment of Liability for Federal Unemployment Tax

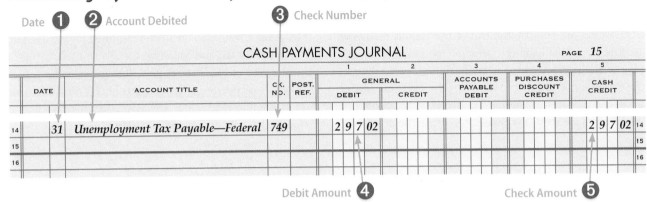

Date ❶ ❷ Account Debited ❸ Check Number

CASH PAYMENTS JOURNAL PAGE 15

					GENERAL		ACCOUNTS PAYABLE DEBIT	PURCHASES DISCOUNT CREDIT	CASH CREDIT	
	DATE	ACCOUNT TITLE	CK. NO.	POST. REF.	DEBIT	CREDIT				
14	31	Unemployment Tax Payable—Federal	749		2 9 7 02				2 9 7 02	14
15										15
16										16

Debit Amount ❹   Check Amount ❺

January 31. Paid cash for federal unemployment (FUTA) tax liability for quarter ended December 31, $297.02. Check No. 749.

For each payroll period, a credit entry was recorded to Unemployment Tax Payable—Federal. The T account shows the entries for the December pay periods. The account balance on December 31, $297.02, is the total FUTA tax liability for the year. The balance of the liability account is reduced to zero by this transaction.

Unemployment Tax Payable—Federal

Jan. 31	297.02	Nov. 30 Bal.	290.84
		Dec. 15	3.89
		Dec. 31	2.29
		Dec. 31 Bal.	297.02

Cash

| | | Jan. 31 | 297.02 |

↘ Journalizing a Payment of Liability for Federal Unemployment Tax

❶ Write the date, 31, in the Date column.
❷ Write the title of the account debited, Unemployment Tax Payable—Federal, in the Account Title column.
❸ Write the check number, 749, in the Ck. No. column.
❹ Write the debit amount, $297.02, in the General Debit column.
❺ Write the amount of the credit to Cash, $297.02, in the Cash Credit column.

Journalizing Payment of Liability for State Unemployment Tax

CASH PAYMENTS JOURNAL PAGE 15

					GENERAL		ACCOUNTS PAYABLE DEBIT	PURCHASES DISCOUNT CREDIT	CASH CREDIT	
	DATE	ACCOUNT TITLE	CK. NO.	POST. REF.	DEBIT	CREDIT				
15	31	Unemployment Tax Payable—State	750		1 4 7 42				1 4 7 42	15
16	❶	❷	❸		❹				❺	16

January 31. Paid cash for state unemployment (SUTA) tax liability for quarter ended December 31, $147.42. Check No. 750.

The T account shows the entries to Unemployment Tax Payable—State for the two December pay periods. The balance of the liability account is reduced to zero by this transaction.

State requirements for reporting and paying SUTA taxes vary. Employers are generally required to pay the SUTA tax during the month following each calendar quarter. The steps for recording the transactions are the same as for FUTA tax.

Unemployment Tax Payable—State

Jan. 31	147.42	Nov. 30 Bal.	105.74
		Dec. 15	26.24
		Dec. 31	15.44
		Dec. 31 Bal.	147.42

Cash

| | | Jan. 31 | 147.42 |

End of Lesson Review

LO5 Pay and record withholding and payroll taxes.

Terms Review

deposit

lookback period

Audit your understanding

1. For a monthly schedule depositor, when are payroll taxes paid to the federal government?

2. By what method are businesses encouraged to deposit federal payroll taxes?

Work together 13-4

Paying withholding and payroll taxes

A cash payments journal page is given in the *Working Papers*. Your instructor will guide you through the following examples. The following payroll data are for Tessler Electric for the monthly pay period ended March 31 of the current year.

Date Paid	Federal Income Tax Withheld	Employee Social Security Tax Withheld	Employee Medicare Tax Withheld
Mar. 31	$1,320.00	$1,331.76	$311.46

Credit balances on March 31 for the unemployment tax accounts are as follows: Unemployment Tax Payable—Federal, $515.52; Unemployment Tax Payable—State, $1,159.92.

1. Prepare a journal entry for payment of the withheld taxes. Tessler Electric is a monthly schedule depositor. Journalize Check No. 495 on cash payments journal page 14 using the date the taxes are due to the federal government.

2. Prepare journal entries for payment of the FUTA and SUTA tax liabilities. Assume both checks were prepared on the due date for the federal tax deposit. Check Nos. 522 and 523.

On your own 13-4

Paying withholding and payroll taxes

A cash payments journal page is given in the *Working Papers*. Work this problem independently. The following payroll data are for Sunburst Stores for the monthly pay period ended June 30 of the current year.

Date Paid	Federal Income Tax Withheld	Employee Social Security Tax Withheld	Employee Medicare Tax Withheld
June 30	$1,035.00	$1,021.76	$238.96

Credit balances on June 30 for the unemployment tax accounts are as follows: Unemployment Tax Payable—Federal, $532.83; Unemployment Tax Payable—State, $533.95.

1. Prepare a journal entry for payment of the withheld taxes. Sunburst Stores is a monthly schedule depositor. Journalize Check No. 878 on cash payments journal page 19 using the date the taxes are due to the federal government.

2. Prepare journal entries for payment of the FUTA and SUTA tax liabilities. Assume both checks were prepared on the due date for the federal tax deposit. Check Nos. 903 and 904.

A Look at Accounting Software

Using the Payroll Report to Check Payroll Entries

Accounting for payroll is one of the most complicated functions for accountants. As you have learned in the past two chapters, salaries, wages, and commissions need to be calculated. Vacation and sick leave need to be monitored. Employee benefits need to be taken into account. Then deductions need to be calculated. In addition to federal and state income taxes, tax deductions may also be required for local taxing authorities. These may include cities, counties, and school districts. Some taxes have limiting tax bases; others do not. In all payroll calculations, there is no room for error. Payroll information needs to be kept highly confidential.

Finally, employer taxes and taxes withheld from employees need to be reported to taxing authorities, each with its own regulations, rate schedules, deadlines, and forms. Is it any wonder that payroll accounting was one of the first business activities to be computerized and among the first to be contracted out? Today, many small businesses contract with other businesses that specialize in payroll accounting to process their payroll.

THREE△GREEN PRODUCTS, INC.
Payroll Report
December 1, 20-- to December 15, 20--

	Hours	Butler, John P.	Hours	Feng, Anthony R.	Hours	Wells, Cary B.	Total
Salary		0.00		0.00		0.00	0.00
Regular Wages	88.00	1,320.00	80.00	1,440.00	76.00	1,444.00	7,764.00
Overtime Wages	6.50	146.25	2.00	54.00	0.00	0.00	312.75
Vacation	0.00	0.00	0.00	0.00	0.00	0.00	0.00
Total Earnings		**1,466.25**		**1,494.00**		**1,444.00**	**8,076.75**
Federal Income Tax		−29.00		−131.00		−148.00	−494.00
State Income Tax		0.00		0.00		0.00	0.00
City Income Tax		0.00		0.00		0.00	0.00
Social Security		−90.91		−92.63		−89.53	−500.77
Medicare		−21.26		−21.66		−20.94	−117.11
Total Taxes		**−141.17**		**−245.29**		**−258.47**	**−1,111.88**
Health Insurance		−70.00		−40.00		−25.00	−230.00
Retirement		−80.00		−75.00		−50.00	−465.00
Total Deductions		**−291.17**		**−360.29**		**−333.47**	**−1,806.88**
Net Pay		**1,175.08**		**1,133.71**		**1,110.53**	**6,269.87**
Employer Expenses							
FUTA		0.00		11.95		4.08	17.95
SUTA		0.00		80.68		27.54	121.18
Social Security		90.91		92.63		89.53	500.77
Medicare		21.26		21.66		20.94	117.11
Employer Total		**112.17**		**206.92**		**142.09**	**757.01**

❶ This payroll report is an example of what would have printed out after all the entries for the payroll period had been made in the Enter Payroll window, shown in the Using Accounting Software illustration in Chapter 12.

❷ The header row lists the names of all employees.

❸ Similar to the payroll register shown on page 379, except for its vertical structure, the report shows the earnings, taxes, deductions, and net pay for each employee. Most accounting software reports can be customized by the user. On this report, for example, employee hours have been added and taxes have been subtotaled.

❹ Unlike the payroll register, this report also shows the employer expense for each employee.

❺ Totals for each row are shown in the last column on the right.

Chapter Summary

Employee payroll taxes are withheld from employees' earnings. Each tax creates a liability when payment of the payroll is recorded in the cash payments journal. These taxes are a liability until paid to the federal and state governments.

Employer payroll taxes are an expense of the business. **Payroll Taxes Expense** is debited, and various liability accounts are credited by a journal entry recorded in the general journal. These taxes are also a liability of the business until paid to the federal and state governments.

The following table identifies who pays each payroll tax and how the tax is calculated. Only social security and Medicare taxes are paid by both employees and employers.

A business must understand the laws that govern how and when payroll tax liabilities are paid. Employee income, social security, and Medicare taxes are paid to the government by making a tax deposit using an electronic funds transfer or using the Electronic Federal Tax Payment System. Monthly schedule depositors must make the deposit by the 15th day of the subsequent month.

Each quarter, the business submits Form 941, Employer's Quarterly Federal Tax Return, before the last day of the next month. The form reports employee earnings and tax deposits for the quarter.

FUTA taxes are paid by the end of the month following each quarter if the liability amount is more than $500.00. Tax payments to state governments are usually paid each month. The reporting and deposit requirements vary by state.

Tax	Employee Payroll Taxes	Employer Payroll Taxes
Federal Income (Employee)	Different rates based on employee's earnings, withholding allowances, and marital status	—
Social Security	6.2% of earnings up to $106,800.00	6.2% of each employee's earnings up to $106,800.00
Medicare	1.45% of earnings	1.45% of earnings
Federal Unemployment (FUTA)	—	0.8% of each employee's earnings up to $7,000.00
State Unemployment (SUTA)	—	5.4% of each employee's earnings up to $7,000.00

Income for Financial Reporting versus Income for Tax Reporting

Financial statements should provide important information that is accurate, reliable, comparable, and consistent. For over 100 years, the accounting profession has been the leader in developing a standard set of accounting principles and concepts. These guidelines are known as Generally Accepted Accounting Principles (GAAP). Businesses whose stock is traded on stock exchanges must use GAAP. Most privately owned businesses also use GAAP in preparing their financial statements and determining their net income.

The Internal Revenue Service (IRS) is responsible for collecting money to operate the federal government. Federal income taxes are calculated as a percentage of business or individual income. The Internal Revenue Code, written and passed by Congress, provides the rules that govern the reporting of taxable revenue and expenses.

The objectives of the accounting profession and business community, however, are not necessarily the same as those of the federal government and the IRS. The accounting profession and business community want financial statements to be accurate, reliable, comparable, and consistent. The concepts cited throughout the textbook, such as *Business Entity, Adequate Disclosure, Going Concern,* and *Historical Cost,* are the basic principles on which more specific GAAP rules have been developed.

Congress has two primary objectives when writing tax law. The most obvious objective is to generate funds to operate the government. A more subtle objective is to modify the behavior of businesses and taxpayers. For example, during an economic recession Congress often provides small businesses with tax incentives to hire new workers.

Tax law often differs from GAAP. For example, a GAAP concept, *Matching Expenses with Revenue,* requires that the cost of business equipment be expensed over the usable life of the equipment. However, to encourage businesses to replace equipment more rapidly, the Internal Revenue Code may permit the cost of equipment to be expensed more rapidly. So, in a certain year, the expense for allocating the cost of equipment would be greater for tax purposes than for financial reporting purposes. Most businesses follow GAAP in preparing their financial statements but must follow the Internal Revenue Code in preparing their tax returns. As a result, net income on financial statements generally differs from the income reported on tax returns.

INSTRUCTIONS

Examine at least two company annual reports. Study the financial statements and the notes connected with those statements. Is there any information indicating a difference between net income reported on the financial statements and the income reported for tax purposes? What are they, if any?

©MAKHNACH_M_ISTOCK

Apply Your Understanding

INSTRUCTIONS: Download problem instructions for Excel, QuickBooks, and Peachtree from the textbook companion website at www.C21accounting.com.

13-1 Application Problem: Recording a payroll LO2

James Company's payroll register has the following totals for two semimonthly pay periods, August 1–15 and August 16–31 of the current year.

| Period | Total Earnings | Deductions | | | | | Net Pay |
		Federal Income Tax	Social Security Tax	Medicare Tax	Health Insurance	Retirement Contributions	
August 1-15	$7,280.00	$492.00	$451.36	$105.56	$390.00	$450.00	$5,391.08
August 16-31	$7,490.00	$518.00	$464.38	$108.61	$390.00	$450.00	$5,559.01

Instructions:

Journalize payment of the two payrolls on page 10 of the cash payments journal given in the *Working Papers*. The first payroll was paid by Check No. 692 on August 15 of the current year. The second payroll was paid by Check No. 708 on August 31 of the current year.

AAONLiNE
1. Go to www.cengage.com/login
2. Click on **AA Online** to access.
3. Go to the online assignment and follow the instructions.

13-2 Application Problem: Recording employer payroll taxes LO3

Use Malone's selected payroll information for the two semimonthly pay periods, April 1–15 and April 16–30 of the current year. Forms and a general journal are given in the *Working Papers*.

Employee Name	Accumulated Earnings, March 31	Total Earnings for April 1–15 Pay Period	Total Earnings for April 16–30 Pay Period
Campos, Regina P.	$4,980.00	$ 830.00	$ 850.00
Duran, Erica A.	5,490.00	915.00	895.00
Glover, Brandon T.	7,080.00	1,180.00	1,180.00
Norton, Authur S.	5,340.00	890.00	795.00
Rivas, Pearl S.	6,900.00	1,150.00	1,060.00

Employer payroll tax rates are as follows: social security, 6.2%; Medicare, 1.45%; FUTA, 0.8%; SUTA, 5.4%. Unemployment taxes are owed on the first $7,000.00 of earnings for each employee.

Instructions:

1. Calculate the amount of FUTA earnings for the April 1–15 pay period.
2. Calculate the employer payroll tax amounts for the April 1–15 pay period.

3. Journalize the employer payroll taxes on page 5 of a general journal. Use the date of April 15 of the current year. The source document is Memorandum No. 87.

4. Calculate the employer payroll taxes for the April 16–30 pay period. Calculate April 15 accumulated earnings by adding total earnings for the April 1–15 pay period to the March 31 accumulated earnings.

5. Journalize the employer payroll taxes on page 5 of a general journal. Use the date of April 30 of the current year. The source document is Memorandum No. 95.

13-3 Application Problem: Reporting withholding and payroll taxes LO4

The following payroll data are for Lance Clothiers for the second quarter of the current year.

Date Paid	Total Earnings	Federal Income Tax Withheld	Employee Social Security Tax Withheld	Employee Medicare Tax Withheld
Apr. 30	$ 9,525.00	$580.00	$590.55	$138.11
May 31	9,996.00	625.00	619.75	144.94
Jun. 30	10,439.00	646.00	647.22	151.37

Additional data:

a. Company address: 154 N. Morgan Street, Tampa, FL 33601-2500

b. Employer identification number: 70-7154845

c. Number of employees: 5

d. Federal tax payments have been made on May 15, June 15, and July 15.

Instructions:

Prepare the Form 941, Employer's Quarterly Federal Tax Return, given in the *Working Papers*.

13-4 Application Problem: Paying withholding and payroll taxes LO5

Peachtree

1. Journalize and post payroll transactions to the cash disbursements journal.
2. Print the cash disbursements journal and the general ledger trial balance.

1. Journalize and post payroll transactions in the Write Checks window.
2. Print the check detail and the trial balance.

1. Enter Excel formulas to solve for unemployment taxable earnings.
2. Print the worksheet.

AAONLINE

1. Go to www.cengage.com/login
2. Click on **AA Online** to access.
3. Go to the online assignment and follow the instructions.

The following payroll data are for Webster Company for the first quarter of the current year.

Period	Total Earnings	Federal Income Tax Withheld
March	$21,640.00	$1,395.00
First Quarter	63,180.00	—

In addition, total earnings are subject to 6.2% employee and 6.2% employer social security tax, plus 1.45% employee and 1.45% employer Medicare tax. The FUTA tax rate is 0.8%, and the state SUTA tax rate is 5.4% of total earnings. No total earnings have exceeded the tax base for calculating unemployment taxes.

Instructions:

1. Calculate the appropriate liability amount of social security and Medicare taxes for March. Journalize the payment of the withheld taxes on page 6 of the cash payments journal given in the *Working Papers*. The taxes were paid by Check No. 789 on April 15 of the current year.

2. Calculate the appropriate FUTA tax liability for the first quarter. Journalize payment of this liability in the cash payments journal. The tax was paid by Check No. 822 on April 30 of the current year.

3. Calculate the appropriate SUTA tax liability for the first quarter. Journalize payment of this liability in the cash payments journal. The tax was paid by Check No. 823 on April 30 of the current year.

Keller Systems, Inc., completed payroll transactions during the period January 1 to February 15 of the current year. Payroll tax rates are as follows: social security, 6.2%; Medicare, 1.45%; FUTA, 0.8%; SUTA, 5.4%. No total earnings have exceeded the tax base for calculating unemployment taxes. Keller Systems is a monthly schedule depositor for payroll taxes.

Instructions:

1. Journalize the following transactions on page 14 of the cash payments journal and page 13 of the general journal given in the *Working Papers*. Source documents are abbreviated as follows: check, C, and memorandum, M.

Transactions:

Jan. 15. Paid cash for December's payroll tax liability. Withheld taxes from December payrolls: employee income tax, $790.00; social security tax, $778.72; and Medicare tax, $182.12. C621.

15. Paid cash for semimonthly payroll. Total earnings, $6,420.00; withholdings: employee income tax, $410.00; health insurance premiums, $360.00 (calculate the social security and Medicare deductions). C622.

15. Recorded employer payroll taxes expense for the January 15 payroll. M64.

15. Paid cash for employees' health insurance premiums, $720.00. C623.

31. Paid cash for semimonthly payroll. Gross wages, $6,810.00; withholdings: employee income tax, $445.00; health insurance premiums, $360.00. C661.

31. Recorded employer payroll taxes expense for the January 31 payroll. M65.

31. Paid cash for FUTA tax liability for quarter ended December 31, $43.20. C662.

31. Paid cash for SUTA tax liability for quarter ended December 31, $291.60. C663.

Feb. 15. Paid cash for the January liability for employee income tax, social security tax, and Medicare tax, C687.

15. Paid cash for semimonthly payroll. Gross wages, $6,280.00; withholdings: employee income tax, $398.00; health insurance premiums, $360.00. C688.

15. Recorded employer payroll taxes expense. M66.

2. Prove and rule the cash payments journal.

🍑 Peachtree

1. Journalize and post payroll transactions to the cash disbursements journal.
2. Journalize and post payroll transactions to the general journal.
3. Print the cash disbursements journal, general journal, and general ledger trial balance.

Quick Books

1. Journalize and post payroll transactions in the Write Checks window.
2. Journalize and post payroll transactions to the journal.
3. Print the check detail, journal, and the trial balance.

X〕

1. Enter Excel formulas to complete the payroll register.
2. Print the worksheet.

Heath Company is searching for a new chief executive officer. The company believes it will be able to hire a qualified individual for a $95,000.00 annual salary. The company pays $150.00 of each employee's $400.00 monthly insurance premium.

Instructions:

1. Determine the total annual salary and payroll tax expense for the employee, assuming the company does not have an IRS-approved health care plan.

2. What would be the total annual salary and payroll tax expense for the employee, assuming the company receives IRS approval for its health care plan? Remember, contributions to an approved health care plan reduce the amount of wages subject to social security, Medicare, and federal income taxes.

3. Does the company have an incentive to seek IRS approval for its health care plan?

Adding Up the Benefits

Theme: Financial, Economic, Business, and Entrepreneurial Literacy

Skills: Creativity and Innovation, Critical Thinking and Problem Solving, Communication and Collaboration, ICT Literacy

Today's generation of workers, known as Gen Y, changes jobs more often than previous generations. In the past, it was not uncommon for an employee to stay with a company for an entire career spanning 30 or more years.

High employee turnover is costly. It can influence a company's financial health. In order to reduce employee turnover, companies have become more employee friendly. Benefits such as sick leave, paid vacation, and health insurance are becoming more flexible. Free day care, wardrobe assistance, eight-week sabbaticals, and on-site dog parks are just a few examples of the generous benefits companies are offering to lure and keep employees.

For the 13th year, software company SAS was named one of *Fortune Magazine*'s 100 Best Companies To Work For. While some companies have reduced benefits, SAS has chosen to be different. Founder and CEO Jim Goodnight looks for benefits that might increase productivity or foster creativity. Offering on-site health care and free M&Ms has proven to be a winner. At a company where employees are encouraged to balance their work and personal life, SAS has one of industry's lowest turnover rates, and it has been extremely profitable.

APPLICATION

1. With a partner, brainstorm at least ten benefits that you feel would make you a more loyal and productive employee.
2. Using the Internet or personal interviews, research the benefits offered by two companies in your community or nearest city. Draw a Venn diagram on a poster to compare/contrast your findings.
3. If you had the option of receiving 20% additional salary or an eight-week paid sabbatical, which would you choose, and why? Explain your answer in one to two paragraphs.

Auditing for errors

In April, the liability for FUTA and SUTA taxes for Riverside Corporation is recorded at about the same amount as for previous months. Philip Jenkins suggests that it usually begins to decrease in April. You have been asked to investigate the payroll data to discover whether there is a problem.

REVIEW AND ANSWER

1. Why would the liability for unemployment tax begin to decline in April?
2. If there is an error in the unemployment liability amounts, what is the likely cause?
3. Examine the information below and on a separate sheet of paper write the correct amounts for the unemployment tax liabilities.

Accumulated Earnings, January–March	April Total Earnings	FUTA Tax	SUTA Tax
$3,680.00	$1,270.00	$10.16	$ 68.58
6,250.00	2,160.00	17.28	116.64
5,370.00	1,620.00	12.96	87.48
6,730.00	2,080.00	16.64	112.32
4,980.00	1,680.00	13.44	90.72

Analyzing Nike's financial statements

The list of personalities that endorse Nike products is dominated by famous athletes, many of whom are destined for their respective sport's hall of fame. Nike typically signs these stars to multiyear endorsement contracts that include signing bonuses—prepayments made at the signing of the contract.

INSTRUCTIONS

Use the Demand Creation Expense section in Note 1 of Nike's financial statements in Appendix B, page B-10, to answer the following questions.

1. How does Nike expense endorsement payments?
2. How are signing bonuses accounted for?

Reinforcement Activity 2—Part A

An Accounting Cycle for a Corporation: Journalizing and Posting Transactions

Reinforcement Activity 2 reinforces learning from Part 2, Chapters 9 through 17. Activities cover a complete accounting cycle for a merchandising business organized as a corporation. Reinforcement Activity 2 is a single problem divided into two parts. Part A includes learning from Chapters 9 through 13. Part B includes learning from Chapters 14 through 17.

The accounting work of a single merchandising business for the last month of a yearly fiscal period is used in this reinforcement activity. The records kept and reports prepared, however, illustrate the application of accounting concepts for all merchandising businesses.

Gulf Uniform Supply, Inc. (GUS)

Gulf Uniform Supply, Inc. (GUS), a merchandising business, is organized as a corporation. The business sells a complete line of uniforms for a variety of businesses and organizations, including schools, medical offices, and retail stores. GUS is located in an open-area shopping center and is open for business Monday through Saturday. A monthly rent is paid for its store space in the shopping center. GUS accepts credit sales for approved customers and credit cards from individual customers.

Chart of Accounts

GUS uses the chart of accounts shown on the next page.

Journals and Ledgers

The journals and ledgers used by GUS are listed below. Models of the journals and ledgers are shown in the textbook chapters indicated.

Journal and Ledgers	Chapter
Purchases journal	9
Cash payments journal	9
Accounts payable ledger	9 and 11
Sales journal	10
Cash receipts journal	10
Accounts receivable ledger	10 and 11
General journal	11

Chart of Accounts
General Ledger

Balance Sheet Accounts

(1000) ASSETS
<u>1100   Current Assets</u>
1110   Cash
1120   Petty Cash
1130   Accounts Receivable
1135   Allowance for Uncollectible Accounts
1140   Merchandise Inventory
1145   Supplies—Office
1150   Supplies—Store
1160   Prepaid Insurance
1170   Notes Receivable
1175   Interest Receivable
<u>1200   Plant Assets</u>
1205   Office Equipment
1210   Accumulated Depreciation—Office Equipment
1215   Store Equipment
1220   Accumulated Depreciation—Store Equipment

(2000) LIABILITIES
2110   Accounts Payable
2120   Sales Tax Payable
2130   Employee Income Tax Payable
2135   Social Security Tax Payable
2140   Medicare Tax Payable
2145   Health Insurance Premiums Payable
2150   Retirement Benefits Payable
2160   Unemployment Tax Payable—Federal
2165   Unemployment Tax Payable—State
2170   Federal Income Tax Payable
2180   Dividends Payable

(3000) OWNER'S EQUITY
3110   Capital Stock
3120   Retained Earnings
3130   Dividends
3140   Income Summary

Income Statement Accounts

(4000) OPERATING REVENUE
4110   Sales
4120   Sales Discount
4130   Sales Returns and Allowances

(5000) COST OF MERCHANDISE
5110   Purchases
5120   Purchases Discount
5130   Purchases Returns and Allowances

(6000) OPERATING EXPENSES
6105   Advertising Expense
6110   Cash Short and Over
6115   Credit Card Fee Expense
6120   Depreciation Expense—Office Equipment
6125   Depreciation Expense—Store Equipment
6130   Insurance Expense
6135   Miscellaneous Expense
6140   Payroll Taxes Expense
6145   Rent Expense
6150   Salary Expense
6155   Supplies Expense—Office
6160   Supplies Expense—Store
6165   Uncollectible Accounts Expense
6170   Utilities Expense

(6200) INCOME TAX EXPENSE
6205   Federal Income Tax Expense

(7000) OTHER REVENUE
7110   Interest Income

Subsidiary Ledgers

Accounts Receivable Ledger
110   Batesville Manufacturing
120   Chandler City Schools
130   Hubbard Medical Clinic
140   Musheer Orthopedics
150   Pacific Stores
160   Western Theaters

Accounts Payable Ledger
210   Alpha Supply
220   Distinctive Garments
230   Klein Industries
240   Medical Clothiers
250   Singh Imports
260   Trevino Company

An Accounting Cycle for a Corporation: Journalizing and Posting Transactions

Recording Transactions

The December 1 account balances for the general and subsidiary ledgers are given in the *Working Papers*.

> **INSTRUCTIONS**

1. Journalize the following transactions completed during December of the current year. GUS offers sales terms of 2/10, n/30. The sales tax rate is 6%. Post the following transactions when journalized: (1) transactions impacting the accounts receivable or accounts payable subsidiary ledgers, (2) transactions recorded in the general journal, and (3) cash payments entered in a general amount column of the cash payments journal. Source documents are abbreviated as follows: check, C; memorandum, M; purchase invoice, P; receipt, R; sales invoice, S; terminal summary, TS; debit memorandum, DM; credit memorandum, CM.

Dec. 1. Paid cash to Riverside Properties for rent, $1,600.00. C456.

2. Paid cash to City Office Source for office supplies, $216.00. C457.

2. The board of directors declared a dividend of $0.50 per share; capital stock issued is 6,000 shares. M56.

3. Received cash on account from Chandler City Schools, covering S392 for $814.80, less 2% sales discount. R402.

3. Sold merchandise on account to Pacific Stores, $4,795.00, plus sales tax. S395.

4. Paid cash to Downtown Hardware for miscellaneous expense, $85.00. C458.

6. Recorded cash and credit card sales, $5,845.00, plus sales tax, $315.63; total, $6,160.63. TS45.

7. Bought $225.00 of office supplies and $312.00 of store supplies from Alpha Supply on account, $537.00. M57.

8. Paid cash on account to Singh Imports, covering P243 for $1,589.00, less 2% discount. C459.

8. Sold merchandise on account to Batesville Manufacturing, $1,208.00, plus sales tax. S396.

8. Purchased merchandise on account from Trevino Company, $4,000.00, less a 40% trade discount. P245.

10. Paid cash to Cantrell Energy for electric bill, $482.50. C460.

10. Purchased merchandise on account from Singh Imports, $3,925.00. P246.

11. Received a $3,000.00 check from Pacific Stores. The check pays $3,061.22 of the Dec. 3 sale on account, S395, less 2% discount. R403.

11. Paid cash on account to Klein Industries, $2,618.00, covering P240. C461.

13. Paid cash to City Office Source for store supplies, $235.00. C462.

13. Recorded cash and credit card sales, $7,125.00, plus sales tax, $384.75; total, $7,509.75. TS46.

13. Purchased merchandise on account from Klein Industries, $4,958.00. P247.

14. Sold merchandise on account to Chandler City Schools, $5,580.00. Chandler City Schools is exempt from sales tax. S397.

14. Paid cash to Innovative Communications for advertising, $325.00. C463.

14. Returned $410.00 of merchandise to Klein Industries from P247. DM14.

14. Received cash on account from Musheer Orthopedics, $831.50, covering S385. R404.

15. Paid cash on account to Alpha Supply, $942.00, covering P241. C464.

15. Paid cash for liability for employee income tax, $471.00, social security tax, $899.00, and Medicare tax, $210.25; total, $1,580.25. C465.

15. Paid cash for semimonthly payroll, $2,670.10 (total payroll, $3,528.00, less deductions: employee income tax, $228.00; social security tax, $218.74; Medicare tax, $51.16; health insurance premiums, $240.00; retirement benefits, $120.00). C466.

15. Recorded employer payroll taxes, $309.89, for the semimonthly pay period ended December 15. Taxes owed are: social security tax, $218.74; Medicare tax, $51.16; federal unemployment tax, $5.16; and state unemployment tax, $34.83. M58.

Dec. 16. Discovered that a sale on account to Musheer Orthopedic for $627.50 was incorrectly charged to the account of Hubbard Medical Clinic. M59.

18. Sold merchandise on account to Pacific Stores, $3,640.00, plus sales tax. S398.

20. Recorded cash and credit card sales, $6,890.00, plus sales tax, $367.93; total, $7,257.93. TS47.

22. Received cash on account from Hubbard Medical Clinic, covering S390 for $1,057.50. R405.

23. Paid cash on account to Medical Clothiers, $548.00, covering P239. C467.

24. Granted credit to Pacific Stores for merchandise returned, $128.00, plus sales tax, $7.68, from S395; total, $135.68. CM25.

27. Recorded cash and credit card sales, $6,295.00, plus sales tax, $347.48; total, $6,642.48. TS48.

28. Gulf Uniform Supply's bank charges a fee for handling the collection of credit card sales deposited during the month. The credit card fee is deducted from its bank account. The amount is then shown on the bank statement. The credit card fee is recorded in the cash payments journal as a reduction in cash. Recorded credit card fee expense, $442.00. M60. (Debit Credit Card Fee Expense; credit Cash.)

29. Paid cash for dividend declared December 2. C468.

29. Purchased merchandise on account from Distinctive Garments, $3,528.00. P248.

2. Prove and total page 23 of the cash payments journal. Post the totals of the special columns to the general ledger.

3. Journalize the following transactions, applying the same posting procedures used above.

Dec. 31. Paid cash to replenish the petty cash fund, $90.30: office supplies, $42.50; store supplies, $16.40; advertising, $25.00; miscellaneous, $5.40; cash short, $1.00. C469.

31. Paid cash for semimonthly payroll, $2,745.07 (total payroll, $3,620.00, less deductions: employee income tax, $238.00; social security tax, $224.44; Medicare tax, $52.49; health insurance premiums, $240.00; retirement benefits, $120.00). C470.

31. Recorded employer payroll taxes, $318.78, for the semimonthly pay period ended December 31. Taxes owed are: social security tax, $224.44: Medicare tax, $52.49; federal unemployment tax, $5.40; and state unemployment tax, $36.45. M61.

31. Recorded cash and credit card sales, $3,920.00, plus sales tax, $216.38; total, $4,136.38. TS49.

4. Prove and rule the sales journal. Post the totals of the special columns.

5. Total and rule the purchases journal. Post the total.

6. Prove the equality of debits and credits for the cash receipts journal and the cash payments journals.

7. Prove cash. The balance on the next unused check stub is $49,743.48.

8. Rule the cash receipts journal. Post the totals of the special columns.

9. Rule the cash payments journals. Post the totals of the special columns of page 24 of the cash payments journal.

10. Prepare a schedule of accounts receivable and a schedule of accounts payable. Prove the accuracy of the subsidiary ledgers by comparing the schedule totals with the balances of the controlling accounts in the general ledger. If the totals are not the same, find and correct the errors.

The ledgers used in Reinforcement Activity 2—Part A are needed to complete Reinforcement Activity 2—Part B.

Chapter 14

Accounting for Uncollectible Accounts Receivable

©DANIEL KOUREY, ISTOCK/©JIM PRUITT, ISTOCK

BANANASTOCK/JUPITER IMAGES

Accounting In The Real World
Delta Air Lines

Imagine you are booking a flight on Delta.com. You identify the date and destination of your flight. Then you select your seats. Next is your personal information. To pay for your ticket, can you click the "Sales on Account" button? No! Individual travelers booking flights on Delta must pay for their tickets when making reservations. So why does Delta have over $1.3 billion in accounts receivable?

In its annual report, Delta reports that its accounts receivable includes amounts due from credit card companies. Delta also sells aircraft maintenance and cargo transportation services on account to selected customers. Delta's accounts receivables also include amounts other companies and airlines owe Delta for frequent-flyer program transactions.

Any business that sells on account faces the risk that some customers will not pay their accounts. Some of Delta's aircraft maintenance and cargo transportation customers, even other airlines, may go out of business before paying their accounts. Delta refers to these amounts as uncollectible accounts. For many businesses, the expense of their uncollectible accounts can significantly reduce net income.

Fortunately for Delta, it considers the amount of these uncollected accounts to be "immaterial." An immaterial amount is too small to be reported individually on its income statement. According to generally accepted accounting principles (GAAP), Delta is required to report an estimate of uncollectible accounts on its balance sheet. The airline estimates that $47 million of its $1.3 billion accounts receivable may never be collected. Forty seven million is a lot of money. However, the amount is "immaterial" when compared to Delta's $43.5 billion in total assets.

CRITICAL THINKING

1. What percent of Delta's total assets is the estimate of its uncollectible accounts?

2. Do you believe the GAAP requirement that Delta report its estimate of uncollectible accounts provides useful information for the reader of its financial statements?

Source: www.delta.com (2009 Annual Report).

Background: ©MC_PP, SHUTTERSTOCK; Real World: COURTESY OF DELTA AIR LINES

Key Terms

- uncollectible accounts
- allowance method
- book value
- book value of accounts receivable
- net realizable value

- percent of sales method
- percent of accounts receivable method
- aging of accounts receivable
- writing off an account

- direct write-off method
- promissory note
- note payable
- note receivable
- maker of a note
- payee

- principal
- interest rate
- maturity date
- time of a note
- maturity value
- interest income
- dishonored note

14-1 Uncollectible Accounts Receivable

LO1 Explain the purpose of the allowance method for recording losses from uncollectible accounts.

LO2 Estimate uncollectible accounts expense using an aging of accounts receivable.

LO3 Record the adjusting entry for the allowance for uncollectible accounts.

Allowance Method of Recording Losses from Uncollectible Accounts LO1

ThreeGreen uses terms of 2/10, n/30 when selling to customers on account. The company expects customers to pay in full within 30 days. ThreeGreen begins sending customers periodic reminders when their accounts are more than 30 days past due. More serious actions may be taken if a customer account is not paid within 90 days. ThreeGreen may stop selling on account to a customer until payment is received. ThreeGreen is aware that a small percentage of its customers will never pay their account in full.

With each sale on account, a business takes the risk that the customer will never pay the amount owed. This risk is an expense of doing business. The expense must be recorded in the same accounting period that the revenue is earned. Accurate financial reporting requires that expenses be recorded in the fiscal period in which the expenses contribute to earning revenue. [CONCEPT: Matching Expenses with Revenue]

Accounts receivable that cannot be collected are called **uncollectible accounts**. The expense is recorded in Uncollectible Accounts Expense. Some businesses refer to uncollectible accounts as *bad debts* and use the account title Bad Debt Expense.

A business cannot know the amount of money it will fail to collect from uncollectible accounts. Generally accepted accounting principles (GAAP) require a business to record an estimate of its uncollectible accounts. Estimating uncollectible accounts expense at the end of a fiscal period records the expense of uncollectible accounts in the same period as the related revenue.

The adjusting entry to record estimated uncollectible accounts affects two general ledger accounts. The amount is debited to Uncollectible Accounts Expense and credited to an account titled Allowance for Uncollectible Accounts. Allowance for Uncollectible Accounts is a contra account to its related asset account, Accounts Receivable.

Crediting the estimated value of uncollectible accounts to a contra account is called the **allowance method** of recording losses from uncollectible accounts. The difference between an asset's account balance and its related contra account balance is called **book value**. The difference between the balance of Accounts Receivable and its contra account, Allowance for Uncollectible Accounts, is called the **book value of accounts receivable**. The book value of accounts receivable, reported on the balance sheet, represents an estimate of the total

amount of accounts receivable the business expects to collect in the future. The amount of accounts receivable a business expects to collect is called the **net realizable value**.

A contra account is usually assigned the next number of the account number sequence after its related account in the chart of accounts. ThreeGreen's Accounts Receivable account is numbered 1130. The contra account, Allowance for Uncollectible Accounts, is numbered 1135.

Methods of Estimating Uncollectible Accounts Receivable LO2

Two methods are commonly used to estimate uncollectible accounts receivable:

1. The **percent of sales method** assumes that a percent of credit sales will become uncollectible. For example, a business might estimate that 0.5% of its sales on account will become uncollectible. A business with credit sales of $700,000.00 would estimate that $3,500.00 will not be collectible ($700,000.00 × 0.5% = $3,500.00).
2. The **percent of accounts receivable method** uses an analysis of accounts receivable to estimate the amount that will be uncollectible.

Percents are usually based on past experience. A business that has experienced a 1.0% rate of uncollectible accounts can reasonably expect that 1.0% of future accounts receivable will become uncollectible. However, the business may have valid reasons to change its estimate. For example, an economic downturn could cause more customers than before to be unable to pay their accounts. Or, the business might tighten its credit policy so only customers with good credit scores are allowed to buy on account.

When conditions change, should the business raise its estimate of uncollectible accounts to 1.5% or 2.0%? Should the estimate be reduced to 0.5%? There is no correct answer. Historically, accountants have used conservative estimates when preparing financial statements. Using 2.0% rather than 1.5% would be a more conservative approach. The higher percentage increases the estimate of uncollectible accounts, which decreases net income.

A business must not, however, change its estimate to achieve some other goal, such as reducing net income to avoid income taxes. The book value of accounts receivable in the financial accounts must be a reasonable and unbiased estimate of the money a business expects to collect in the future. The accounting concept *Neutrality* is applied when the process of making accounting estimates is free from bias. [CONCEPT: Neutrality]

A business may use either the percent of sales or the percent of accounts receivable method to estimate its uncollectible accounts. Regardless of the method used, the business must ensure that it reports a reasonable and unbiased estimate of future uncollectible accounts. ThreeGreen uses the percent of accounts receivable method.

ETHICS IN ACTION

A Farewell Performance

Janice opened an envelope stamped "Secret and Confidential" and began to cry as she read the letter. For six years, she had enjoyed sailing the Caribbean working as a dancer for the nightly shows on the *Merriment*, a cruise ship of the Vibrance Cruise Line. Janice knew the ship was scheduled for renovation in four months. The company even found her a temporary spot in a Las Vegas show while the ship was in dry dock. But she never expected the news contained in the letter.

"The cruise industry is experiencing radical changes. The size and services offered by the new mega ships have made the *Merriment* obsolete. Renovation of the ship is no longer a financially viable option. Vibrance has no choice but to decommission the *Merriment* at the end of this season. As a result, we regret that your contract will not be renewed."

Sitting in her cabin, she pulled out her notebook computer and logged on to her favorite social networking site. Janice felt the need to share her unknown future with her family and friends. Her post read: "I'm in tears. Just learned this is my last season on the *Merriment*. ☹ The ship is being scrapped."

INSTRUCTIONS

Determine whether Janice acted ethically when she posted the message on her social networking site. Use the Code of Business Conduct and Ethics of Carnival Corporation as a guide. Go to www.Carnival.com, find "About Carnival," select "Investor Relations," then "Corporate Governance."

©LUCA DI FILIPPO, ISTOCK

Estimating Uncollectible Accounts Expense

			Days Account Balance Past Due			
Customer	**Account Balance**	**Current**	**1–30**	**31–60**	**61–90**	**Over 90**
Belk & Jensen	$ 3,247.36	$ 1,495.18	$1,752.18			
Edmonds Hospital	639.88		167.48	$195.36	$277.04	
Lake Automotive	3,757.82	3,151.50	606.32			
Mason City Schools	2,489.64	2,489.64				
Skinner College	2,578.35					$2,578.35
Triangle Health	3,154.48	3,154.48				
Wells Apartments	4,514.28	1,483.21	3,031.07			
	$20,381.81	$11,774.01	$5,557.05	$195.36	$277.04	$2,578.35
Percent		1.0%	4.0%	12.0%	30.0%	80.0%

Accounts Receivable as of December 31, 20--

The first step in using the percent of accounts receivable method is to total accounts by "age" groups. Analyzing accounts receivable according to when they are due is called the **aging of accounts receivable**. Most businesses group accounts in 30-day periods, such as 31–60 days past due.

ThreeGreen uses past cash receipts data to estimate the percent of each age group that will become uncollectible in the future. For example, the company estimates that 4.0% of its accounts 1–30 days overdue will become uncollectible.

Age Group	Amount	Percent	Uncollectible	
Current	$11,774.01	1.0%	$ 117.74	
1–30	5,557.05	4.0%	222.28	
31–60	195.36	12.0%	23.44	❶ Compute an estimate of each age group
61–90	277.04	30.0%	83.11	
Over 90	2,578.35	80.0%	2,062.68	
	$20,381.81		$2,509.25	❷ Compute the total estimate
Current Balance of Allowance for Uncollectible Accounts			125.15	
Estimated Addition to Allowance for Uncollectible Accounts			$2,384.10	❸ Compute the addition to the allowance account

The percent for each age group is used to calculate the total estimate of uncollectible accounts. Of the total accounts receivable on December 31, $20,381.81, the company estimates that $2,509.25 will become uncollectible.

ThreeGreen's general ledger shows that Allowance for Uncollectible Accounts has a $125.15 credit balance. This balance is what remains of estimates made in prior fiscal periods. To bring the balance up to the new estimate, the current balance must be increased by a $2,384.10 credit. Allowance for Uncollectible Accounts is increased by $2,384.10 to equal the new balance of $2,509.25.

Estimating Uncollectible Accounts Expense

❶ Compute the estimate for each age group. Multiply the amount of each age group by the estimated uncollectible percent.

❷ Compute the total of the uncollectible estimates, $2,509.25.

❸ Subtract the current balance, $125.15, from the total estimate, $2,509.25, to determine the addition to the allowance account, $2,384.10. (If the allowance account has a debit balance, add the current balance to the total estimate.)

Adjusting Entry for Allowance for Uncollectible Accounts LO3

Write "Adjusting Entries" **1**

GENERAL JOURNAL
PAGE **13**

	DATE		ACCOUNT TITLE	DOC. NO.	POST. REF.	DEBIT	CREDIT	
1			*Adjusting Entries*					1
2	Dec.	31	Uncollectible Accounts Expense			2 3 8 4 10		2
3			Allowance for Uncollectible Accounts				2 3 8 4 10	3
4								4

Date **2** **3** Account Title **5** Account Title Debit Amount **4** **6** Credit Amount

At the end of a fiscal period, some general ledger accounts need to be brought up to date before financial statements are prepared. In Part 1, Delgado Web Services recorded adjusting entries to bring Supplies and Prepaid Insurance up to date.

ThreeGreen has estimated that $2,509.25 of its accounts receivable will become uncollectible. ThreeGreen needs to record an adjusting entry to bring its Allowance for Uncollectible Accounts balance to a $2,509.25 credit. (Other adjusting entries will be presented in the next chapter.)

The general ledger balance of Allowance for Uncollectible Accounts is a $125.15 credit. This balance is the unused allowance estimate from the prior fiscal period. That is, it was not needed to cover any uncollectible accounts.

When the allowance account has a previous credit balance, the amount of the adjusting entry, $2,384.10, is added to the previous balance. The new account balance, $2,509.25, is the estimated amount of uncollectible accounts.

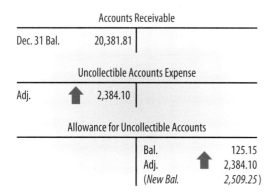

Four questions are asked to analyze the adjustments for the allowance for uncollectible accounts.

1. What is the balance of the account being adjusted?
Allowance for Uncollectible Accounts, $125.15

2. What should the balance be for this account?
Allowance for Uncollectible Accounts, $2,509.25

3. What must be done to correct the account balance?
Increase $2,384.10 ($2,509.25 − $125.15)

4. What adjusting entry is made?
Debit Uncollectible Accounts Expense, $2,384.10
Credit Allowance for Uncollectible Accounts, $2,384.10

This new balance of the allowance account, subtracted from Accounts Receivable, $20,381.81, is the book value of accounts receivable. ThreeGreen estimates that it will collect $17,872.56 from its outstanding accounts receivable.

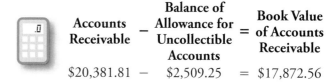

Accounts Receivable	−	Balance of Allowance for Uncollectible Accounts	=	Book Value of Accounts Receivable
$20,381.81	−	$2,509.25	=	$17,872.56

> **Journalizing an Adjusting Entry for the Allowance for Uncollectible Accounts**

1 Write the heading, Adjusting Entries, in the middle of the general journal's Account Title column. This heading explains all of the adjusting entries that will follow. Indicating a source document is unnecessary. The first adjusting entry is recorded on the first two lines under the heading.

2 Write the date, Dec. 31, in the Date column.

3 Write the account title, Uncollectible Accounts Expense, in the Account Title column.

4 Write the amount, $2,384.10, in the Debit column.

5 On the next line indented about one centimeter, write Allowance for Uncollectible Accounts in the Account Title column.

6 Write the amount, $2,384.10, in the Credit column of the second line.

McKesson & Robbins

McKesson Corporation is one of the world's largest health care companies with over $100 billion in annual revenues. McKesson distributes medicines and installs technology solutions. The company has experienced both good and bad times since its founding in 1833. One of the worst chapters in its history began in 1926 when the company, then known as McKesson & Robbins, was sold to Frank Coster.

Frank Coster was actually Phillip Musica. As a young man, Musica had twice been convicted and jailed for illegal business activities. Beginning in 1919, Musica, using his new name, founded two drug companies. The companies produced legitimate alcohol-based health and drug products. However, Coster's best customers were bootleggers. During prohibition, these bootleggers distilled the alcohol out of his products. Coster used his new wealth to purchase control of McKesson & Robbins.

With the help of his brothers, Coster began a fraud to skim profits from McKesson & Robbins. The brothers set up a division in Canada to make international sales. They created false documents to show the purchase and sale of merchandise. In 1937, the Canadian division reported having $10 million of inventory and $9 million in accounts receivable. The division made up a large portion of McKesson & Robbins' $87 million in assets. In reality, it owned little more than the typewriters used to prepare the false documents.

Beginning in 1932, the Securities and Exchange Commission began requiring publicly traded companies to have annual audits. McKesson & Robbins' stock was traded on the New York Stock Exchange. So why didn't its auditors detect the fraud? In that day, auditors conducted audits in their offices. Corporations brought their accounting records and source documents to the auditors. The fraud was discovered in 1938 by the company's treasurer. He began to question certain transactions and discovered forged documents.

This fraud led the accounting profession to change how audits are conducted. New rules were set up to improve the quality of audits. Auditors now must physically observe inventory. They must confirm accounts receivable with customers. Auditors now perform audits at their clients' offices.

ACTIVITY

Jesse Dawkins, the treasurer of Naper Distribution, has become suspicious of his credit manager. He overheard the credit manager instruct an accounts receivable clerk to write off an account. What surprised him was the customer's name, Jenkins Construction. Jesse remembered seeing a transaction to write off the same customer account several months ago. "Why would we be selling to that account again?" he wondered.

Jesse has asked you to analyze sales and transactions to write off accounts receivable. Provide him with answers to the following questions:

1. How many customers have had transactions written off?
2. Has the company sold merchandise to any customer after the customer's account has been written off?
3. Which customer accounts would you examine first? Explain.

INSTRUCTIONS

Open the spreadsheet FA_CH14 and complete the steps on the Instructions tab.

Sources: http://academic.cengage.com/resource_uploads/downloads/0324312148_70201.pdf; http://www.mckesson.com; *Called to Account,* Paul M. Clikeman, Routledge (New York), 2009

End of Lesson Review

LO1 Explain the purpose of the allowance method for recording losses from uncollectible accounts.

LO2 Estimate uncollectible accounts expense using an aging of accounts receivable.

LO3 Record the adjusting entry for the allowance for uncollectible accounts.

Terms Review

uncollectible accounts

allowance method

book value

book value of accounts receivable

net realizable value

percent of sales method

percent of accounts receivable method

aging of accounts receivable

Audit your understanding

1. What general ledger accounts are used to account for uncollectible accounts receivable?

2. Explain why an adjustment for uncollectible accounts is an application of the *Matching Expenses with Revenue* concept.

3. What are the two methods used to estimate uncollectible accounts receivable?

4. How is Accounts Receivable affected by the estimate of uncollectible accounts?

Work together 14-1

Journalizing the adjusting entry for Allowance for Uncollectible Accounts

The aging of accounts receivable for Brett Company as of December 31 of the current year and estimated percentages of uncollectible accounts by age group are presented in the *Working Papers*. Use page 13 of a general journal, also given in the *Working Papers*. Your instructor will guide you through the following examples.

1. Calculate the estimate of uncollectible accounts expense. The balance of Allowance for Uncollectible Accounts on December 31, before the adjusting entry is recorded, is a $236.89 credit.

2. Journalize the adjusting entry for Allowance for Uncollectible Accounts.

On your own 14-1

Journalizing the adjusting entry for Allowance for Uncollectible Accounts

The aging of accounts receivable for PCZ Corporation as of December 31 of the current year and estimated percentages of uncollectible accounts by age group are presented in the *Working Papers*. Use page 13 of a general journal, also given in the *Working Papers*. Work this problem independently.

1. Calculate the estimate of uncollectible accounts expense. The balance of Allowance for Uncollectible Accounts on December 31, before the adjusting entry is recorded, is a $1,841.63 credit.

2. Journalize the adjusting entry for Allowance for Uncollectible Accounts.

©CANDICE CUSACK, ISTOCK

14-2 Writing Off and Collecting Uncollectible Accounts Receivable

LO4 Write off an uncollectible account receivable.

LO5 Account for the collection of an account receivable that was written off.

Journalizing the Writing Off of an Uncollectible Account Receivable **LO4**

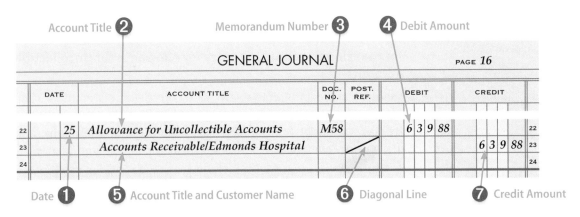

When a customer account is determined to be uncollectible, a journal entry is made to cancel the uncollectible account. This entry cancels the uncollectible amount from Accounts Receivable in the general ledger as well as the customer account in the accounts receivable ledger. Canceling the balance of a customer account because the customer does not pay is called **writing off an account**. A customer should not be told that its account has been written off. A business should continue its efforts to collect the account.

After months of unsuccessful collection efforts, ThreeGreen decides that Edmonds Hospital is unable to pay its account.

> **January 25. Wrote off Edmonds Hospital's past due account as uncollectible, $639.88. Memorandum No. 58.**

Because the account has been determined to be uncollectible, the $639.88 is now an actual uncollectible amount. The amount of the uncollectible account is deducted from the allowance account.

Accounts Receivable is credited to reduce the balance due from customers. **Edmonds Hospital** is also credited to cancel the debit balance of the account. Edmonds Hospital's account is written off. **Allowance for Uncollectible Accounts** is debited to reduce the estimate of future uncollectible accounts.

GENERAL LEDGER

Allowance for Uncollectible Accounts

| Jan. 25 | ⬇ 639.88 | Bal. | 2,509.25 |
| | | (New Bal. | 1,869.37) |

Accounts Receivable

| Bal. | 21,843.15 | Jan. 25 | ⬇ 639.88 |
| (New Bal. | 21,203.27) | | |

ACCOUNTS RECEIVABLE LEDGER

Edmonds Hospital

| Bal. | 639.88 | Jan. 25 | ⬇ 639.88 |
| (New Bal. | 0.00) | | |

The book value of accounts receivable is the same before and after writing off an uncollectible account. This is true because the same amount is deducted from both Accounts Receivable and Allowance for Uncollectible Accounts.

Journalizing the Writing Off of an Uncollectible Account Receivable

1. Write the date, 25, in the Date column.

2. Write the account title, Allowance for Uncollectible Accounts, in the Account Title column.

3. Write the memorandum number, M58, in the Doc. No. column.

④ Write the amount, $639.88, in the Debit column on the same line as the account title.

⑤ On the next line indented about one centimeter, write Accounts Receivable/Edmonds Hospital in the Account Title column. A diagonal line is placed between the two accounts.

⑥ Place a diagonal line in the Post. Ref. column to show that the single credit amount is posted to the general ledger account, Accounts Receivable, and the accounts receivable ledger account, Edmonds Hospital.

⑦ Write the amount, $639.88, in the Credit column of the second line.

The allowance method does not recognize an expense when an account is written off. Some businesses use a different method of writing off uncollectible accounts. Recording uncollectible accounts expense only when an amount is actually known to be uncollectible is called the **direct write-off method**. Although this method is easier to apply, it does not match the expense to the revenue that is earned in the same period. As a result, the direct write-off method does not comply with GAAP.

GLOBAL AWARENESS

Doing Business in Russia

Until December 1991, Russia was part of the Union of Soviet Socialist Republics (USSR). The USSR was also called the Soviet Union. The Soviet Union was run by a centralized government in a planned economy. In a planned economy, the central government controls all resources and makes all decisions about their use. Enterprises are told what to produce in order to meet national objectives.

In December 1991, the USSR was dissolved. The former USSR became 15 independent countries. Russia, the largest of the countries, is approximately 6.5 million square miles. It covers nine time zones. The country has over 140 million consumers. Many foreign companies would like to enter a new market of that size.

But there are also many limiting factors foreign companies must consider. The transition away from central control has not been complete. The government still controls many industries. In industries not totally controlled by government, many new laws interfere with business matters. Most business is transacted in Russian. Therefore, interpreters must be hired. Most imports are subject to high tariffs and severe quotas.

In the United States, businesses follow generally accepted accounting principles (GAAP) to ensure fair and accurate financial reporting. Russian accounting rules are called Russian Accounting Standards (RAS). RAS are designed to support tax authorities. Therefore, they follow Russian tax laws.

CRITICAL THINKING

1. Use the Internet to research Russia and International Financial Reporting Standards (IFRS). (IFRS were discussed in the Global Awareness feature in Chapter 10.)

2. List one area in which RAS differ from IFRS.

Posting an Entry to Write Off an Uncollectible Account Receivable

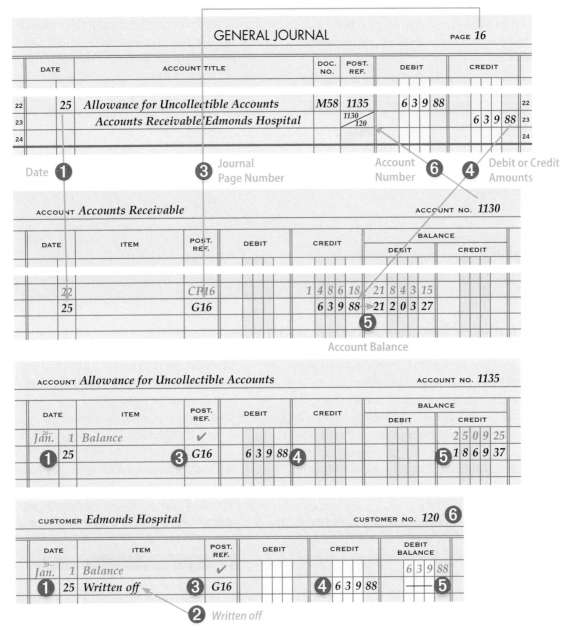

The journal entry to write off an uncollectible account affects the two general ledger accounts and the customer account. The words *Written off* are written in the Item column of the customer account to show the full credit history for the customer.

⊗ Posting an Entry to Write Off an Uncollectible Account Receivable

1️⃣ Write the date, 25, in the Date column of the account.

2️⃣ Write the words Written off in the Item column of the customer account.

3️⃣ Write the general journal page number, G16, in the Post. Ref. column of the account.

4️⃣ Write each amount in the Debit or Credit column of the general ledger account.

5️⃣ For each account, calculate and write the new account balance in the Balance column.

6️⃣ Write the general ledger account number in the Post. Ref. column of each line of the journal entry. For the credit to Accounts Receivable, write 1130 to the left of the diagonal line. Write the customer account number, 120, to the right of the diagonal line.

Reopening an Account Previously Written Off LO5

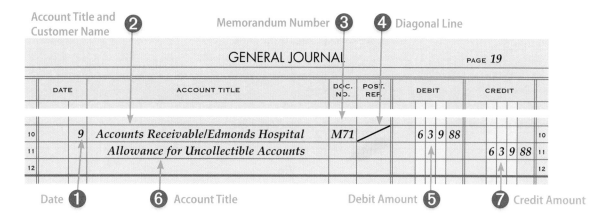

A business writes off a specific account receivable after determining it probably will not be collected. Sometimes, after an account has been written off, the customer pays the delinquent account.

> March 9. Received cash in full payment of Edmonds Hospital's account, previously written off as uncollectible, $639.88. Memorandum No. 71 and Receipt No. 695.

GENERAL LEDGER
Accounts Receivable

Bal.	21,843.15	Jan. 25	639.88
Mar. 9	639.88		
(New Bal.	21,843.15)		

Allowance for Uncollectible Accounts

Jan. 25	639.88	Bal.	2,509.25
		Mar. 9	639.88
		(New Bal.	2,509.25)

ACCOUNTS RECEIVABLE LEDGER
Edmonds Hospital

Bal.	639.88	Jan. 25	639.88
Mar. 9	639.88		
(New Bal.	639.88)		

Several accounts must be changed to show that Edmonds Hospital paid its account. The accounts also should be changed to show a complete credit history of Edmonds Hospital with ThreeGreen.

Two journal entries are recorded for the collection of a written-off account receivable. (1) A general journal entry reopens the customer account. (2) An entry in the cash receipts journal records the cash received on account.

To show an accurate credit history, Edmonds Hospital is reopened. Accounts Receivable is debited for $639.88 to replace the amount previously written off in the general ledger account. Allowance for Uncollectible Accounts is credited for $639.88 to replace the amount that was removed when Edmonds Hospital's account was written off. Also, Edmonds Hospital's account in the accounts receivable ledger is debited for $639.88. This entry to reopen the account is the exact reverse of the entry to write off Edmonds Hospital's account.

Reopening an Account Previously Written Off

1. Write the date, 9, in the Date column.

2. Write the account title, Accounts Receivable/Edmonds Hospital, in the Account Title column. A diagonal line is placed between the two accounts.

3. Write the memorandum number, M71, in the Doc. No. column.

4. Place a diagonal line in the Post. Ref. column to show that the single credit amount is posted to the general ledger account, Accounts Receivable, and the accounts receivable ledger account, Edmonds Hospital.

5. Write the amount, $639.88, in the Debit column on the same line as the account title.

6. On the next line indented about one centimeter, write Allowance for Uncollectible Accounts in the Account Title column.

7. Write the amount, $639.88, in the Credit column of the second line.

Recording Cash Received for an Account Previously Written Off

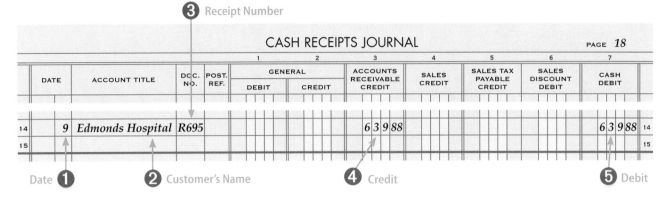

❸ Receipt Number

CASH RECEIPTS JOURNAL   PAGE **18**

					GENERAL		ACCOUNTS RECEIVABLE CREDIT	SALES CREDIT	SALES TAX PAYABLE CREDIT	SALES DISCOUNT DEBIT	CASH DEBIT	
					1	2	3	4	5	6	7	
	DATE	ACCOUNT TITLE	DOC. NO.	POST. REF.	DEBIT	CREDIT						
14	9	Edmonds Hospital	R695				6 3 9 88				6 3 9 88	14
15												15

Date **❶**   **❷** Customer's Name   **❹** Credit   **❺** Debit

After the entry to reopen Edmonds Hospital's account is recorded, an entry is made to record the cash received on Edmonds Hospital's account.

GENERAL LEDGER

Cash

Mar. 9	⬆	639.88	

Accounts Receivable

Bal.	21,843.15	Jan. 25		639.88
Mar. 9	639.88	Mar. 9	⬇	639.88
(New Bal.	21,203.27)			

ACCOUNTS RECEIVABLE LEDGER

Edmonds Hospital

Bal.	639.88	Jan. 25		639.88
Mar. 9	639.88	Mar. 9	⬇	639.88
(New Bal.	0.00)			

March 9. Received cash in full payment of Edmonds Hospital's account, previously written off as uncollectible, $639.88. Memorandum No. 71 and Receipt No. 695.

> **↘ Recording Cash Received for an Account Previously Written Off**
>
> **❶** Write the date, **9**, in the Date column.
>
> **❷** Write only the customer's name, **Edmonds Hospital**, in the Account Title column. The debit and credit amounts are entered in special amount columns. Therefore, the titles of the two general ledger accounts do not need to be written in the Account Title column.
>
> **❸** Write the receipt number, **R695**, in the Doc. No. column.
>
> **❹** Write the credit amount, **$639.88**, in the Accounts Receivable Credit column.
>
> **❺** Write the debit amount, **$639.88**, in the Cash Debit column.

Yield Management

Assume you are going on a vacation. You paid $250 for a plane ticket. Now you are sitting on the plane waiting for takeoff. While talking to your seatmates, you learn that Maja paid $160 for her ticket. John paid $300 for his. You are glad you didn't have to pay $300. However, you also feel it is unfair that Maja only paid $160. What caused the difference in price?

It could be a concept called *yield management*, also referred to as *revenue management*. The goal of yield management is to maximize revenue by understanding and influencing consumer behavior. A company may charge different customers different prices for the same goods or services. Yield management is done by higher-level managers. It requires data from several areas of a business and executive decision making.

Yield management is often limited to goods and services which are considered perishable—meaning there is a limited time to sell the product or service. An airline ticket is considered perishable because once the plane takes off, all empty seats have no value.

CRITICAL THINKING

1. Name an additional industry that could implement yield management.
2. Why would someone responsible for yield management benefit from accounting?

©ANEKCEN KOWEBHKOB, ISTOCK

Posting Entries for Collecting a Written-Off Account Receivable

GENERAL JOURNAL
PAGE 19

	DATE	ACCOUNT TITLE	DOC. NO.	POST. REF.	DEBIT	CREDIT	
10	9	Accounts Receivable/Edmonds Hospital	M71	1130 / 120	6 3 9 88		10
11		Allowance for Uncollectible Accounts		1135		6 3 9 88	11
12							12

① Post general journal entry to general ledger

ACCOUNT Accounts Receivable — ACCOUNT NO. 1130

DATE	ITEM	POST. REF.	DEBIT	CREDIT	BALANCE DEBIT	BALANCE CREDIT
Jan. 1	Balance	✔			21 8 4 3 15	
25		G16		6 3 9 88	21 2 0 3 27	
Mar. 9		G19	6 3 9 88		21 8 4 3 15	

①

ACCOUNT Allowance for Uncollectible Accounts — ACCOUNT NO. 1135

DATE	ITEM	POST. REF.	DEBIT	CREDIT	BALANCE DEBIT	BALANCE CREDIT
Jan. 1	Balance	✔				2 5 0 9 25
25		G16	6 3 9 88			1 8 6 9 37
Mar. 9		G19		6 3 9 88		2 5 0 9 25

② Post general journal entry to customer account

CUSTOMER Edmonds Hospital — CUSTOMER NO. 120

DATE	ITEM	POST. REF.	DEBIT	CREDIT	DEBIT BALANCE
Jan. 1	Balance	✔			6 3 9 88
25	Written off	G16		6 3 9 88	—
Mar. 9	Reopen account	G19	6 3 9 88		6 3 9 88
9		CR18		6 3 9 88	—

③ Write "Reopen account" in customer account   **④** Post cash receipts journal entry to customer account

CASH RECEIPTS JOURNAL
PAGE 18

	DATE	ACCOUNT TITLE	DOC. NO.	POST. REF.	1 GENERAL DEBIT	2 GENERAL CREDIT	3 ACCOUNTS RECEIVABLE CREDIT	4 SALES CREDIT	5 SALES TAX PAYABLE CREDIT	6 SALES DISCOUNT DEBIT	7 CASH DEBIT	
14	9	Edmonds Hospital	R695	120			6 3 9 88				6 3 9 88	14
15												15

⌑ Posting Entries for Collecting a Written-Off Account Receivable

① Post the general journal entry to the general ledger.

② Post the debit portion of the general journal entry to the customer account.

③ Write the words Reopen account in the Item column of the customer account.

④ Post the cash receipts journal entry to the customer account.

End of Lesson Review

Terms Review

writing off an account

direct write-off method

Audit your understanding

1. Why is Allowance for Uncollectible Accounts debited when a customer account is written off?

2. Does the book value of accounts receivable differ before and after writing off an account? Explain.

3. Why is a customer account reopened when the account is paid after being previously written off?

Work together 14-2

Recording entries related to uncollectible accounts receivable

Page 15 of a general journal, page 24 of a cash receipts journal, and selected ledger accounts for Olsen Company are given in the *Working Papers*. Your instructor will guide you through the following examples.

1. Journalize the following transactions completed during November and December of the current year. Post the transactions to the accounts receivable ledger when the transactions are recorded in the journals.

   Transactions:

   Nov. 4. Wrote off Mellon Corp.'s past-due account as uncollectible, $494.00. M145.

   15. Wrote off Horne Co.'s past-due account as uncollectible, $1,548.00. M147.

   Dec. 8. Received cash in full payment of Mellon Corp.'s account, previously written off as uncollectible, $494.00. M158 and R341.

   14. Wrote off Fischer Industries' past-due account as uncollectible, $1,360.00. M161.

   16. Received cash in full payment of Horne Co.'s account, previously written off as uncollectible, $1,548.00. M169 and R349.

2. Post general journal entries to the general ledger.

On your own 14-2

Recording entries related to uncollectible accounts receivable

Page 10 of a general journal, page 22 of a cash receipts journal, and selected ledger accounts for Hillside Company are given in the *Working Papers*. Work this problem independently.

1. Journalize the following transactions completed during October and November of the current year. Post the transactions to the accounts receivable ledger when the transactions are recorded in the journals.

   Transactions:

   Oct. 5. Wrote off Janice Harrell's past-due account as uncollectible, $527.00. M145.

   26. Wrote off Daniel Pruitt's past-due account as uncollectible, $249.00. M147.

   Nov. 12. Received cash in full payment of Tom Sloan's account, previously written off as uncollectible, $750.00. M151 and R213.

   16. Wrote off Nancy Brown's past-due account as uncollectible, $428.00. M158.

   23. Received cash in full payment of Janice Harrell's account, previously written off as uncollectible, $527.00. M161 and R225.

2. Post general journal entries to the general ledger.

LESSON

14-3 Promissory Notes

LO6 Record the acceptance of a note receivable.

LO7 Account for the collection of a note receivable.

LO8 Account for a dishonored note receivable.

Understanding Promissory Notes

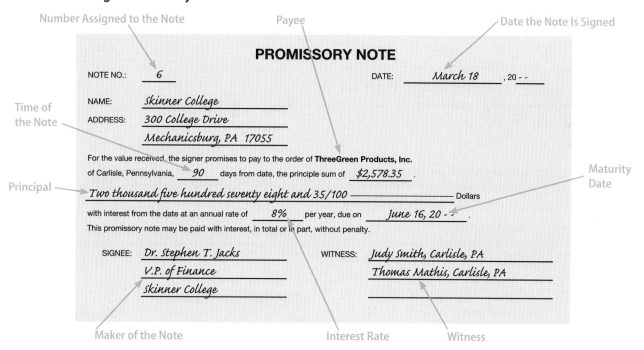

Number Assigned to the Note

Payee

Date the Note Is Signed

Time of the Note

Principal

Maturity Date

Maker of the Note

Interest Rate

Witness

PROMISSORY NOTE

NOTE NO.: _6_ DATE: _March 18_ , 20 - -

NAME: _Skinner College_

ADDRESS: _300 College Drive_
Mechanicsburg, PA 17055

For the value received, the signer promises to pay to the order of **ThreeGreen Products, Inc.**
of Carlisle, Pennsylvania, _90_ days from date, the principle sum of _$2,578.35_ .

Two thousand five hundred seventy eight and 35/100 _____ Dollars

with interest from the date at an annual rate of _8%_ per year, due on _June 16, 20 - -_ .
This promissory note may be paid with interest, in total or in part, without penalty.

SIGNEE: _Dr. Stephen T. Jacks_ WITNESS: _Judy Smith, Carlisle, PA_
V.P. of Finance _Thomas Mathis, Carlisle, PA_
Skinner College

Cash is the primary medium of exchange for business transactions. [CONCEPT: Unit of Measurement] Cash is used to purchase merchandise and to pay salaries and other expenses. In turn, businesses receive cash when they sell their products or services and collect payment. The cash received can be used to purchase more merchandise and continue to pay salaries and other expenses.

Sometimes, the receipt of cash from sales does not occur at the same time and in amounts sufficient to pay for needed purchases and expenses. When this occurs, a business must make arrangements with its vendors to delay payments or to borrow additional cash. Generally, when a bank or business lends money to another business, a loan agreement is made in writing.

A written and signed promise to pay a sum of money at a specified time is called a **promissory note**. A person or business to whom a liability is owed is called a *creditor*. A promissory note signed by a business and given to a creditor is entered in the businesses books as a **note**

payable. A promissory note that a business accepts from a customer is entered in the business's books as a **note receivable**. Notes payable and notes receivable are frequently referred to simply as *notes*.

The person or business that signs a note, and thus promises to make payment, is called the **maker of a note**. The person or business to whom the amount of a note is payable is called the **payee**. The original amount of a note, sometimes referred to as the *face amount*, is called the **principal**. The percent of the principal that is due for the use of the funds secured by a note is called the **interest rate**. The date on which the principal of a note is due to be repaid is called the **maturity date**. The length of time from the signing date to the maturity date, usually expressed as the number of days, may be referred to as the **time of a note**, or *term*. To be legally enforceable, the signing of a promissory note must be witnessed by a person who is not a party to the agreement. The witness must also sign the note.

Accepting a Note Receivable from a Customer LO6

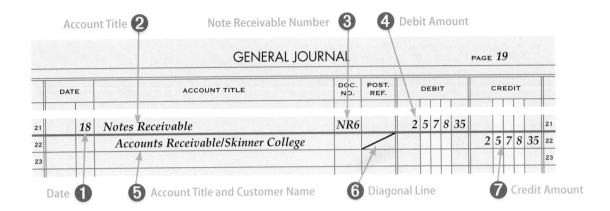

On occasion, a customer may be unable to pay an amount owed to a business by the due date and might request additional time. The business should require the customer to sign a promissory note. A note does not pay the amount the customer owes. However, the form of the asset is changed from an account receivable to a note receivable. Notes provide an advantage over oral promises and accounts receivable or payable. The note is a written confirmation of the amount owed that provides the business with legal evidence of the debt should it be necessary to go to court to collect.

When a customer signs a note, the principal amount is debited to an asset account titled **Notes Receivable**. Like **Accounts Receivable**, **Notes Receivable** is an asset with a normal debit balance. One asset, an account receivable, is replaced by another asset, a note receivable.

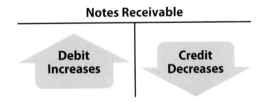

Notes Receivable

| Debit Increases | Credit Decreases |

March 18. Accepted a 90-day, 8% note from Skinner College for an extension of time on its account, $2,578.35. Note Receivable No. 6.

The transaction is posted to the general ledger and accounts receivable ledger accounts using the same posting procedure illustrated on page 423. The words *Accepted note* are written in the Item column of the customer account to show the full credit history for the customer.

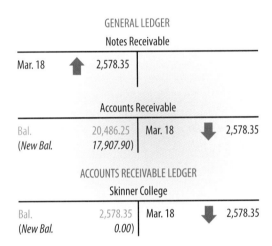

GENERAL LEDGER

Notes Receivable

| Mar. 18 | 2,578.35 | |

Accounts Receivable

| Bal. | 20,486.25 | Mar. 18 | 2,578.35 |
| (New Bal. | 17,907.90) | | |

ACCOUNTS RECEIVABLE LEDGER

Skinner College

| Bal. | 2,578.35 | Mar. 18 | 2,578.35 |
| (New Bal. | 0.00) | | |

➘ Journalizing Accepting a Note for an Extension of Time on an Account Receivable

① Write the date, 18, in the Date column.

② Write the account title, Notes Receivable, in the Account Title column.

③ Write the note number, NR6, in the Doc. No. column.

④ Write the amount, $2,578.35, in the Debit column on the same line as the account title.

⑤ On the next line indented about one centimeter, write Accounts Receivable/Skinner College in the Account Title column. A diagonal line is placed between the two accounts.

⑥ Place a diagonal in the Post. Ref. column to show that the single credit amount is posted to the general ledger account, Accounts Receivable, and the accounts receivable ledger account, Skinner College.

⑦ Write the amount, $2,578.35, in the Credit column of the second line.

Interest on Promissory Notes LO7

An amount paid for the use of money for a period of time is called *interest*. Banks and other lending institutions charge interest on money loaned to their customers. The interest rate is stated as a percentage of the principal. Interest at 8% means that eight cents will be paid for the use of each dollar borrowed for a full year. Thus, the interest on a $1,000.00, 8% note would be $80.00 ($1,000.00 × 8%).

The time of a note issued for less than one year is typically stated as a number of days, such as 30 days, 60 days, or 90 days. The time used in calculating interest is often stated as a fraction of 360 days. The interest on Skinner College's $2,578.35, 8% note for 90 days is $51.27.

	Principal	×	Annual Interest Rate	×	Time as Fraction of a Year	=	Interest for Fraction of Year
	$2,578.35	×	8%	×	90/360	=	$51.57

The amount that is due on the maturity date of a note is called the **maturity value**. Skinner College's 90-day note with a principal of $2,578.35 and interest rate of 8% will have a maturity value of $2,629.92.

	Principal	+	Interest	=	Maturity Value
	$2,578.35	+	$51.57	=	$2,629.92

Maturity Date of Promissory Notes

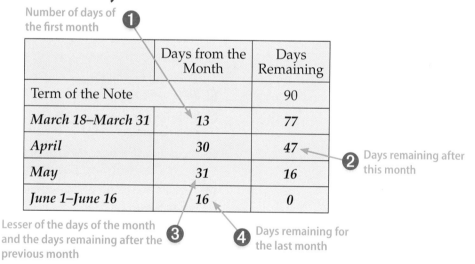

	Days from the Month	Days Remaining
Term of the Note		90
March 18–March 31	13	77
April	30	47
May	31	16
June 1–June 16	16	0

① Number of days of the first month

② Days remaining after this month

③ Lesser of the days of the month and the days remaining after the previous month

④ Days remaining for the last month

Calculating the Maturity Date of a Note

① Calculate the number of days remaining in March, 13, by subtracting the date of the note, 18, from the number of days in March, 31.

② For each month, calculate the days remaining by subtracting Days from the Month from the Days Remaining in the previous month. For example, the days from April, 30, are subtracted from the days remaining after March, 77, to calculate the days remaining after April, 47.

③ For each month, enter the lesser of the number of days in the month or the number of days remaining after the previous month. For example, the number of days from May, 31, is the lesser of the days in May, 31, and the days remaining after April, 47.

④ When the number of days in the month is greater than the days remaining after the previous month, enter the days remaining. Because 16 is less than the number of days in June, add only 16 days in June.

Collecting Principal and Interest on a Note Receivable

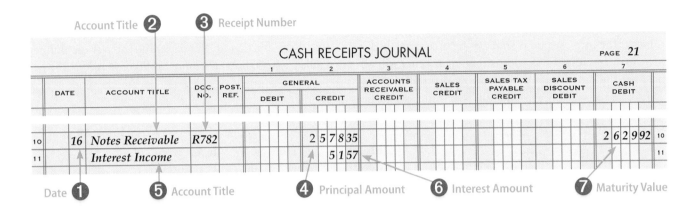

When a note receivable reaches its maturity date, the maker of the note is expected to pay the maturity value to the payee. The interest earned on money loaned is called **interest income**. The interest earned on a note receivable is credited to a revenue account titled Interest Income.

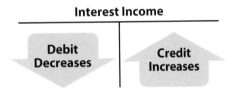

Interest income is investment revenue rather than revenue from normal operations. Therefore, Interest Income is listed in the chart of accounts under a classification titled *Other Revenue*.

June 16. Received cash for the maturity value of Note Receivable No. 6, a 90-day, 8% note: principal, $2,578.35, plus interest, $51.57; total, $2,629.92. Receipt No. 782.

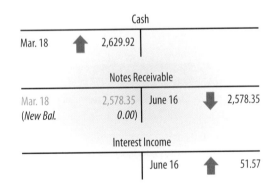

Interest income is calculated using the same method as that used for notes payable. The principal is multiplied by the interest rate and the fraction of the year ($2,578.35 × 8% × 90/360) to calculate interest income, $51.57.

After the entry is recorded, the original of Note Receivable No. 6 is marked *Paid*. The original is given to the maker of the note and a copy is kept by ThreeGreen.

⤵ Journalizing Cash Received for Maturity Value of a Note Receivable

❶ Write the date, 16, in the Date column of the cash receipts journal.

❷ Write the account title, Notes Receivable, in the Account Title column.

❸ Write the receipt number, R782, in the Doc. No. column.

❹ Write the principal amount, $2,578.35, in the General Credit column.

❺ On the next line, write the account title, Interest Income, in the Account Title column.

❻ Calculate and write the interest amount, $51.57, in the General Credit column.

❼ Write the maturity value, $2,629.92, in the Cash Debit column on the first line of the entry.

Sometimes partial payments on a note are made each month. This arrangement is common when an individual buys a car and signs a note for the amount owed. Each monthly payment includes part of the principal and part of the interest to be paid.

Recording a Dishonored Note Receivable LO8

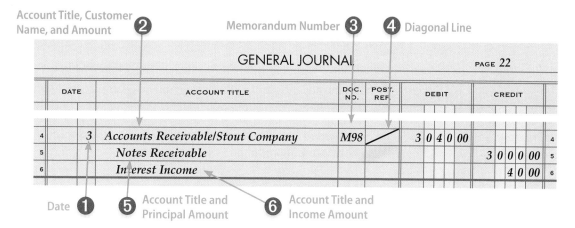

A note that is not paid when due is called a **dishonored note**. The balance of the Notes Receivable account should show only the total amount of notes that probably will be collected. The amount of a dishonored note receivable should be removed from Notes Receivable.

The amount of the note plus interest income earned on the note is still owed by the customer. Therefore, the total amount owed should be debited to Accounts Receivable in the general ledger. The amount owed should also be debited to the customer account in the accounts receivable ledger. This information may be important if the customer requests credit in the future or if collection is achieved later.

June 3. Stout Company dishonored Note Receivable No. 4, a 60-day, 8% note, maturity value due today: principal, $3,000.00; interest, $40.00; total, $3,040.00. Memorandum No. 98.

The interest income on the note has been earned as of the maturity date even though the note has not been paid. Stout Company owes the principal amount of the note plus the interest earned. Therefore, the maturity value, $3,040.00, is debited to Accounts Receivable and to Stout Company in the accounts receivable ledger. One asset, a note receivable, is replaced by another asset, an account receivable.

ThreeGreen does not write off Stout Company's account when the note is dishonored. The company continues to try to collect the account. Later, ThreeGreen may decide that the account cannot be collected. At that time, the balance of the account will be written off as an uncollectible account.

The transaction is posted to the general ledger and accounts receivable ledger accounts using the same posting procedure illustrated in the previous lesson. The words *Dishonored note* are written in the Item column of the customer account to show the full credit history for the customer.

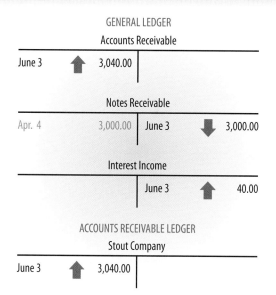

Journalizing a Dishonored Note Receivable

❶ Write the date, 3, in the Date column of the general journal.

❷ Record a debit to Accounts Receivable/Stout Company for the total maturity value of the note, $3,040.00.

❸ Write the memorandum number, M98, in the Doc. No. column.

❹ Place a diagonal line in the Post. Ref. column to show that the single debit amount is posted to the general ledger account, Accounts Receivable, and the accounts receivable ledger account, Stout Company.

❺ Record a credit to Notes Receivable for the amount of principal of the note, $3,000.00.

❻ Record a credit to Interest Income for the amount of the interest earned on the note, $40.00.

End of Lesson Review

Terms Review

promissory note

note payable

note receivable

maker of a note

payee

principal

interest rate

maturity date

time of a note

maturity value

interest income

dishonored note

Audit your understanding

1. What conditions might cause a business to delay payment to a vendor?

2. What is the advantage of a promissory note over an account receivable?

3. What does an interest rate of 10% mean?

4. What is written in a customer's account when (1) a note is accepted and (2) a note is dishonored?

Work together 14-3

Recording notes receivable

The journals and selected ledger accounts for PLD, Inc. are provided in the *Working Papers*. Your instructor will guide you through the following examples.

1. For each of the following notes, calculate (a) the maturity date of the note, (b) the interest on the note, and (c) the maturity value of the note. Use the form provided in the *Working Papers*.

Note	Date	Principal	Interest Rate	Time
NR3	June 5	$20,000.00	8%	90 days
NR4	June 12	$10,000.00	6%	120 days

2. Journalize the following transactions completed during July of the current year. Use page 7 of a general journal and page 8 of a cash receipts journal. Source documents are abbreviated as follows: note receivable, NR; receipt, R; memorandum, M.

Transactions:

July 5. Accepted a 90-day, 8% note from Gary Kinney for an extension of time on his account, $1,800.00. NR5.

12. Received cash from Mary James for the maturity value of NR1, a 60-day, 9% note for $500.00. R113.

26. Dennis Craft dishonored NR2, a 90-day, 9% note, for $400.00. M25.

3. Post transactions in the general journal to the general ledger and the accounts receivable ledger when each transaction is journalized. Also post any entries in the General columns of the cash receipts journal to the general ledger accounts as transactions are journalized.

On your own 14-3

Recording notes receivable

The journals and selected ledger accounts for Lance Supply are provided in the *Working Papers*. Work this problem independently.

1. For each of the following notes, calculate (a) the maturity date of the note, (b) the interest on the note, and (c) the maturity value of the note. Use the form provided in the *Working Papers*.

Note	Date	Principal	Interest Rate	Time
NR12	March 22	$8,000.00	6%	120 days
NR13	April 7	$6,000.00	7%	90 days

©CANDICE CUSACK, ISTOCK

On your own 14-3 (Continued)

2. Journalize the following transactions completed during May of the current year. Use page 15 of a general journal and page 20 of a cash receipts journal. Source documents are abbreviated as follows: note receivable, NR; receipt, R; memorandum, M.

Transactions:

May 8. Accepted a 120-day, 8% note from Marshall Sykes for an extension of time on his account, $3,200.00. NR14.

16. Received cash from Jenni Downey for the maturity value of NR7, a 90-day, 8% note for $6,000.00. R243.

21. Roger Hamm dishonored NR6, a 120-day, 6% note, for $2,800.00. M46.

3. Post transactions in the general journal to the general ledger and the accounts receivable ledger when each transaction is journalized. Also post any entries in the General columns of the cash receipts journal to the general ledger accounts as transactions are journalized.

THINK LIKE AN ACCOUNTANT

Revising Aging Percentages

Most of Steele Company's sales are on account. The company works hard to ensure it receives payment for credit sales. Each month, the accounting manager prints an aging of accounts receivable report. The manager uses the monthly report to monitor the company's success in collecting its unpaid accounts receivable.

At the end of the fiscal year, the aging schedule is used to calculate the adjustment to the allowance for uncollectible accounts. For years, the company has used the same percentages to estimate the uncollectible amount from each age group. These percentages are as follows:

Current	2%
1–30 Days	5%
31–60 Days	10%
61–90 Days	30%
91–120 Days	50%
121–150 Days	85%
Over 150 Days	95%

No one in the company knows when or how these percentages were determined. Amy Drake, the new controller, is not satisfied to use percentages that no one is able to justify. Thus, she has asked you to analyze past collection history to propose a new set of percentages. To assist you with your analysis, she has provided you with a list of all unpaid invoices as of December 31 of the prior year. The list includes the amount of each invoice paid to date.

OPEN THE SPREADSHEET TLA_CH14

Follow the steps on the Instructions tab. Use the data in the workbook to analyze cash collections from the list of unpaid invoices. Use the analysis to answer the following questions:

1. What percentages would you recommend be used to determine the allowance for uncollectible accounts?
2. Prepare a memo that describes how your recommended percentages differ from those used in prior years.

A Look at Accounting Software

Using an Accounts Receivable Aging Report

In this chapter, you learned that an aging of accounts receivable is used to determine the allowance for uncollectible accounts. However, accountants use accounts receivable aging for other tasks as well. The aging report is a useful tool in managing the collection of past-due accounts.

Imagine that ThreeGreen's accountant is making calls to collect old amounts due. She has decided to call Edmonds Hospital about its $277.04 outstanding balance. The accounts payable clerk at Edmonds Hospital asks what

invoices ThreeGreen is calling about and what purchase orders the merchandise was ordered on. That information is just a couple of clicks away.

This follow-up process would likely be used to determine if and when an account should be written off. For example, the Skinner College account for $2,578.35 is now more than 90 days old. If mailed requests and follow-up phone calls have failed to result in payment, the accountant may decide that it is time to write off that account as uncollectible.

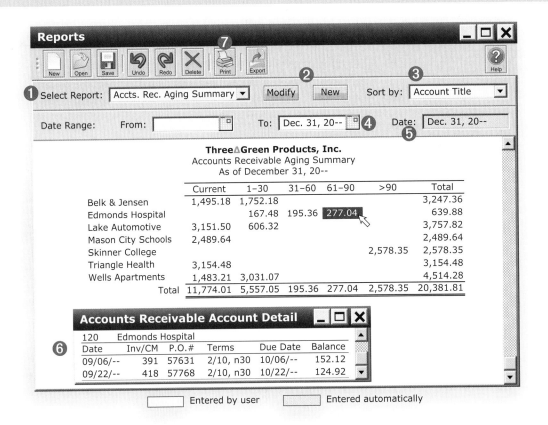

	Current	1–30	31–60	61–90	>90	Total
Belk & Jensen	1,495.18	1,752.18				3,247.36
Edmonds Hospital		167.48	195.36	277.04		639.88
Lake Automotive	3,151.50	606.32				3,757.82
Mason City Schools	2,489.64					2,489.64
Skinner College					2,578.35	2,578.35
Triangle Health	3,154.48					3,154.48
Wells Apartments	1,483.21	3,031.07				4,514.28
Total	11,774.01	5,557.05	195.36	277.04	2,578.35	20,381.81

Accounts Receivable Account Detail

120   Edmonds Hospital

Date	Inv/CM	P.O. #	Terms	Due Date	Balance
09/06/--	391	57631	2/10, n30	10/06/--	152.12
09/22/--	418	57768	2/10, n30	10/22/--	124.92

☐ Entered by user   ☐ Entered automatically

1. The user selects the desired report from the drop-down list. The user could choose a detailed aging report, which would show every open invoice sorted by customer.

2. To change the report, the user would click **Modify**. Clicking on **New** would allow the user to create an entirely new report.

3. Most reports can be sorted in a variety of ways. For example, this report might be sorted by highest to lowest account totals. When trying to collect past due accounts, that would allow the user to focus on the largest outstanding amounts.

4. The user selects the date range. The **From** date is left blank for this report to show all open amounts from previous dates.

5. The current date cannot be changed by the user.

6. In this interactive report, the user has clicked on the 277.04 past due amount from Edmonds Hospital. The system has opened a small window showing the billings that make up that amount.

7. If a printed report is desired, the user would click **Print**.

Chapter Summary

The allowance method of recording losses from uncollectible accounts is an application of the *Matching Expenses with Revenue* concept. This method records the expense of uncollectible accounts in the same period as the related revenue. Estimates of uncollectible accounts are recorded to Allowance for Uncollectible Accounts, a contra asset account to Accounts Receivable. The expense of uncollectible accounts is recorded in Uncollectible Accounts Expense.

The percent of accounts receivable method assumes that a percent of the Accounts Receivable account balance may become uncollectible. Percentages are multiplied by the total of receivables in each age group in an aging of accounts receivable. The total of these calculations equals an estimate of the accounts that may never be collected. The amount needed to increase the balance of Allowance for Uncollectible Accounts to the estimate of uncollectible accounts is recorded as an expense.

An account receivable is written off when the account is determined to be uncollectible. Writing off an account reduces Accounts Receivable, Allowance for Uncollectible Accounts, and the customer's account. However, writing off an account does not change the book value of accounts receivable or impact expenses.

Occasionally, after an account has been written off, the customer pays the delinquent account. A journal entry is recorded to reopen the account. This procedure provides a complete credit history in the customer's account.

A customer who is unable to pay an account on the due date may request additional time. The business may require the customer to sign a promissory note. A promissory note is often referred to as a *note receivable* or *note*. An account receivable is replaced by a note receivable. The note requires the creditor to pay the note principal plus interest on the maturity date. The interest earned on a note receivable is recorded in Interest Income. If the creditor fails to pay the note on the due date, the amount due is recorded as an account receivable.

Accounting Estimates Use Interesting Assumptions

Accountants use many accounting estimates to adjust the historical cost of certain transactions to better reflect the company's financial condition.

One of the most interesting accounting estimates concerns an expense known as **postretirement benefits other than pensions.** Some companies offer their employees free health care and other services during their retirement. For many years, companies expensed these benefits when the services were provided and paid for in cash. Accounting rules now require that these benefits be recognized as an expense over the employee's years of work. Free health care during retirement is part of the total payment that a company provides an employee in exchange for the employee's services.

For example, TGX Industries has promised free health care to its retired employees, their spouses, and their family members under 21 years of age. Manuel Saenz is expected to work for TGX Industries for 30 years. Health care costs for Manuel, his wife, and any future children during his retirement are currently estimated to be $60,000. Rather than expense the $60,000 when the bills are paid during Manuel's retirement, the accounting rule requires that the $60,000 be expensed over Manuel's 30 years of service. Therefore, $2,000 will be expensed each year.

To estimate the projected benefit, assumptions must be made regarding the following items: (1) annual growth rate in health care costs, (2) life expectancy, (3) retirement age, (4) number of children, and (5) interest costs. Management's assumptions can dramatically affect accounting estimates. Companies that prepare public financial statements have independent auditors examine the assumptions used to compute accounting estimates to ensure that these assumptions are reasonable.

INSTRUCTIONS

Research the annual growth rate of health care costs. What is the likelihood that this growth rate will continue at its current level? Identify factors that might cause further increases or decreases in the growth rate.

©MAKHNACH_M_ISTOCK

Apply Your Understanding

INSTRUCTIONS: Download problem instructions for Excel, QuickBooks, and Peachtree from the textbook companion website at www.C21accounting.com.

14-1 Application Problem: Journalizing the adjusting entry for Allowance for Uncollectible Accounts LO 2, 3

The aging of accounts receivable for SMG Corporation as of December 31 of the current year and estimated percent of uncollectible accounts by age group are presented in the *Working Papers*. Use page 13 of a general journal, also given in the *Working Papers*.

Instructions:

1. Calculate the estimate of uncollectible accounts expense. The balance of Allowance for Uncollectible Accounts on December 31, before the adjusting entry is recorded, is a $548.97 credit.

2. Journalize the adjusting entry for uncollectible accounts expense.

14-2 Application Problem: Recording entries related to uncollectible accounts receivable LO 4, 5

Page 6 of a general journal, page 11 of a cash receipts journal, and selected ledger accounts for Rosario Equipment are given in the *Working Papers*.

Instructions:

1. Journalize the following transactions completed during May and June of the current year. Post the transactions to the accounts receivable ledger when the transactions are recorded in the journals.

Transactions:

May 6. Wrote off Suarez Consulting's past-due account as uncollectible, $1,648.11. M89.
14. Wrote off Durham Supply's past-due account as uncollectible, $948.50. M92.
23. Received cash in full payment of Foley Corp.'s account, previously written off as uncollectible, $1,109.80. M98 and R334.
June 7. Wrote off Pennington Co.'s past-due account as uncollectible, $488.93. M104.
29. Received cash in full payment of Suarez Consulting's account, previously written off as uncollectible, $1,648.11. M109 and R356.

2. Post general journal entries to the general ledger.

Peachtree

1. Journalize and post transactions related to allowance for uncollectible accounts to the cash receipts journal.
2. Journalize and post accounts receivable transactions previously written off as uncollectible to the sales journal and cash receipts journal.
3. Print the general ledger trial balance, sales journal, and cash receipts journal.

QuickBooks

1. Journalize and post transactions related to allowance for uncollectible accounts to the journal.
2. Journalize and post accounts receivable transactions previously written off in the Create Invoices – Accounts Receivable window and the Receive Payments window.
3. Print the journal, trial balance, and customer balance detail report.

Excel

1. Calculate financial ratios that help evaluate accounts receivable and trends related to uncollectible accounts.
2. Create and key formulas to complete the worksheet.
3. Print the worksheet.

AAONLINE

1. Go to www.cengage.com/login
2. Click on **AA Online** to access.
3. Go to the online assignment and follow the instructions.

14-3 Application Problem: Recording notes receivable LO6, 7, 8

The journals and selected ledger accounts for Hillside Co. are provided in the *Working Papers*.

Instructions:

1. For each of the following notes, calculate (a) the maturity date of the note, (b) the interest on the note, and (c) the maturity value of the note. Use the form provided in the *Working Papers*.

Note	Date	Principal	Interest Rate	Time
NR8	April 16	$25,000.00	8%	90 days
NR9	May 3	$ 8,000.00	9%	180 days

2. Journalize the following transactions completed during June of the current year. Use page 16 of a general journal and page 23 of a cash receipts journal. Source documents are abbreviated as follows: note receivable, NR; receipt, R; memorandum, M.

Transactions:

June 3. Accepted a 120-day, 8% note from Daniel Burris for an extension of time on his account, $6,800.00. NR10.
　　12. Received cash from Dan Slaughter for the maturity value of NR6, a 90-day, 8% note for $2,000.00. R204.
　　18. Maggie Singer dishonored NR6, a 90-day, 8% note for $3,800.00. M240.

3. Post transactions in the general journal to the general ledger and the accounts receivable ledger when each transaction is journalized. Also post any entries in the General columns of the cash receipts journal to the general ledger accounts as transactions are journalized.

14-M Mastery Problem: Recording entries for uncollectible accounts LO4, 5, 6, 7, 8

A general journal, a cash receipts journal, and selected accounts receivable and general ledger accounts for Sing Industries are given in the *Working Papers*. The following transactions relating to uncollectible accounts receivable occurred during December of the current year.

Instructions:

1. Journalize the following transactions. Use page 12 of a general journal and page 22 of a cash receipts journal. Post transactions in the general journal to the general ledger and the accounts receivable ledger when the transaction is journalized. Post any transaction in the cash receipts journal impacting Accounts Receivable to the accounts receivable ledger when the transaction is journalized.

Transactions:

Dec. 3. Wrote off Patel Corporation's past-due account as uncollectible, $498.25. M243.
　　4. Received cash from Industrial Fittings for the maturity value of NR5, a 90-day, 8% note for $5,000.00. R889.
　　6. Received cash in full payment of Banda Company's account, previously written off as uncollectible, $1,548.25. M244 and R890.
　　10. Broyles Industries dishonored NR6, a 90-day, 8% note, for $4,800.00. M245.
　　14. Wrote off Murrell, Inc.'s past-due account as uncollectible, $1,645.00. M246.
　　18. Accepted a 120-day, 8% note from Maples Corporation for an extension of time on its account, $4,500.00. NR10.
　　21. Received cash from Cochran Metals for the maturity value of NR7, a 120-day, 9% note for $4,000.00. R891.

2. Prove the cash receipts journal. Post the total of the Accounts Receivable Credit column to the general ledger account.

3. Journalize the December 31 adjusting entry for estimated uncollectible accounts expense for the year. Use page 13 of the general journal. Use the aging of accounts receivable given in the *Working Papers* to calculate the adjustment. Post the adjusting entry to the general ledger accounts.

Peachtree

1. Journalize and post transactions related to allowance for uncollectible accounts to the cash receipts journal.
2. Journalize and post accounts receivable transactions previously written off as uncollectible to the sales journal and cash receipts journal.
3. Print the general ledger trial balance, sales journal, and cash receipts journal.

Quick Books

1. Journalize and post transactions related to allowance for uncollectible accounts to the journal.
2. Journalize and post accounts receivable transactions previously written off in the Create Invoices – Accounts Receivable window and the Receive Payments window.
3. Print the journal, trial balance, and customer balance detail report.

X

1. Calculate financial ratios that help evaluate accounts receivable and trends related to uncollectible accounts.
2. Create and key formulas to complete the worksheet.
3. Print the worksheet.

AAONLINE

1. Go to www.cengage.com/login
2. Click on **AA Online** to access.
3. Go to the online assignment and follow the instructions.

Wood Company makes a monthly adjustment for its allowance for uncollectible accounts. The November 30 aging of accounts receivable follows:

	Wood Company Aging of Accounts Receivable 11/30/20--			
Age Group	**Amount**	**Percent**	**Uncollectible**
Current	$ 65,489.02	2.0%	$ 1,309.78
1–30	28,184.25	4.0%	1,127.37
31–60	13,484.81	8.0%	1,078.78
61–90	7,491.06	30.0%	2,247.32
Over 90	13,495.15	80.0%	10,796.12
	$128,144.29		$16,559.37
Current Balance of Allowance for Uncollectible Accounts			(1,548.02)
Estimated Addition to Allowance for Uncollectible Accounts			$18,107.39

The aging of accounts receivable as of December 31 is given in the *Working Papers*.

Instructions:

1. Apply the percentages used in the prior month to calculate the amount to be added to the allowance account in December.

2. Use the aging of accounts receivable to estimate the December adjustment to the allowance for uncollectible accounts. The current balance in Allowance for Uncollectible Accounts is a $6,481.18 debit.

3. Do you believe that the percentages used by Wood Company are a correct application of the concept, *Matching Revenue and Expenses*? Explain your answer.

21st Century Skills

Promises, Promises

Theme: Financial, Economic, Business, and Entrepreneurial Literacy; Global Awareness

Skills: Critical Thinking and Problem Solving, Information Literacy, ICT Literacy

PARTNERSHIP FOR
21ST CENTURY SKILLS

Technological advances have made it easier than ever for businesses to operate in foreign markets. Exports can increase sales and imported goods can make a business more competitive. However, before deciding to do business outside the United States, there are many things to consider. One of these is the risk of extending credit and being unable to collect.

Foreign customers, no different from domestic customers, will want an open line of credit. Extending credit privileges is always risky but can be financially rewarding for a business. Any customer can suffer from bad management, market conditions, economic uncertainty, and changes in government regulations. However, with foreign customers, there are added risks: civil unrest, war, unstable currency, different laws and accounting standards, and the basic difficulties of doing business over great distances. Collecting accounts receivable can be much more difficult.

How do you protect yourself against a foreign customer who cannot, or will not, honor its promise to pay? Where do you turn if a foreign customer is unable to pay? The Export-Import Bank of the United States (Ex-Im Bank) helps businesses by limiting their risk. The Ex-Im Bank assumes credit risks by providing credit insurance and loan guarantees for U.S. businesses.

APPLICATION

1. Go to www.exim.gov. Research the Export-Import Bank of the United States. Create a poster (by hand) or a flyer (using a computer) "advertising" the mission of the Ex-Im Bank and why it would be advantageous for a small business owner to use the services of Ex-Im Bank.

2. As you will learn while researching the Ex-Im Bank, it charges a fee for its services. Why do you think a fee is necessary? Explain.

3. Go to www.census.gov/foreign-trade/statistics/highlights/top/index.html. Select the most current "Year-to-Date" option and answer the following questions.

   a. What are the top five countries to which the United States exports?

   b. Based on current political and economic conditions, what risks could be incurred in extending credit to customers in these countries?

Analyzing Nike's financial statements

Nike markets its products to retail merchandising businesses, through its company-owned retail stores and Internet site, and to independent distributors and licensees. Individual customers must pay cash or use a credit card to purchase Nike merchandise. Business customers can purchase merchandise on account. Each time Nike sells to a business on account, it accepts the risk that the business may be unable to pay its account. Nike uses the allowance method of recording losses from uncollectible accounts.

INSTRUCTIONS

Use the Allowance for Uncollectible Accounts Receivable section of Note 1 on page B-10 to answer the following questions:

1. What factors does Nike take into account when estimating the amount of its allowance for uncollectible accounts receivable?

2. What was the balance of the allowance for uncollectible accounts receivable on May 31, 2011 and 2010?

Chapter 15

Preparing Adjusting Entries and a Trial Balance

LEARNING OBJECTIVES

After studying Chapter 15, in addition to defining key terms, you will be able to:

LO1 Prepare an unadjusted trial balance.

LO2 Adjust supplies and prepaid insurance.

LO3 Adjust merchandise inventory.

LO4 Adjust interest receivable.

LO5 Calculate depreciation expense using the straight-line method.

LO6 Adjust accumulated depreciation.

LO7 Post adjusting entries.

LO8 Adjust federal income tax payable.

LO9 Prepare an adjusted trial balance.

Accounting In The Real World
Gap Inc.

Gap operates five brands: Gap, Banana Republic, Old Navy, Piperlime, and Athleta. Gap's retail website, www.gap.com, is focused on the consumer. Most people who visit Gap online are buying apparel, shoes, and accessories. Its Web pages display colorful pictures of garments and special promotions. Gap maintains a second website, www.gapinc.com, that focuses on the company's operations. Click on the "Investors" tab of that website and you will get a completely different perspective of the company. That tab links investors to a wealth of information about the company and its financial performance.

Like most retailers, Gap is constantly opening new stores and closing stores to maximize its profitability. The number of stores in any month has a significant impact on total sales. The number of days in a month impacts the days the company can generate sales. Thus, analyzing the month-to-month changes in total sales is not an accurate measure of a company's performance.

To provide investors with better information, retailers announce their sales using a ratio known as *comparable store sales*. This ratio is also referred to as *same store sales*. Gap investors can download an Excel file containing ten years of monthly changes in comparable store sales.

Comparable store sales is calculated by dividing the current month's total sales by the number of stores. Only sales for stores open at least one year are included in the calculation. The change in comparable store sales is calculated by dividing the current month's comparable store sales by the same monthly amount for the previous year. Established companies consider small positive percentage increases to be a sign of success. New retailers often experience double-digit changes in the early years of their existence.

Comparable store sales is just one of many interesting facts available on the Investors page. Gap's "Real Estate"

section provides store designs for developers. The "Stock Information" link reports current and historical stock market information. Investors can look up Gap's stock price for any day since 1990. The "Governance" section reports facts concerning the management of the company, such as the number of individuals on the company's board of directors.

CRITICAL THINKING

1. In March of the current year, PRG Fashions' 368 stores generated total sales of $126 million. In the previous year, those stores earned total sales of $123 million. Describe the company's financial performance based on comparable store sales.

2. What other factors could cause month-to-month comparable stores sales (e.g., August to July) to be an unreliable measure of financial performance?

Source: www.gapinc.com.

Key Terms

- unadjusted trial balance
- beginning inventory
- ending inventory
- accrued revenue
- accrued interest income
- current assets

- plant assets
- depreciation
- depreciation expense
- salvage value
- useful life
- straight-line method of depreciation

- accumulated depreciation
- book value of a plant asset
- adjusted trial balance
- tax bracket
- marginal tax rate

LESSON

15-1 Planning Adjusting Entries

LO1 Prepare an unadjusted trial balance.
LO2 Adjust supplies and prepaid insurance.

Adjusting Account Balances

Management decisions about future business operations are often based on financial information. This information shows whether the business is making a profit or incurring a loss. Profit or loss information helps a business plan for future changes. Financial information is also needed to prepare required tax reports.

Businesses may choose any 12-month period, or fiscal year, for reporting their financial performance. In choosing its fiscal year, a business will take into account the way its business activity flows throughout the calendar year. ThreeGreen uses a fiscal year that begins on January 1 and ends on December 31. Therefore, ThreeGreen summarizes its financial information on December 31 of each year.

Some general ledger accounts need to be brought up to date before financial statements are prepared.

Adjusting entries are used to bring a general ledger account up to date. In Chapter 6, Delgado Web Services entered adjusting entries for supplies and prepaid insurance.

ThreeGreen also makes adjusting entries to supplies and prepaid insurance. However, ThreeGreen adjusts these accounts as well: (1) **Merchandise Inventory**, (2) **Accumulated Depreciation**, (3) **Interest Receivable**, and (4) **Federal Income Tax Payable**. The adjusting entry for **Merchandise Inventory** is unique to a merchandising business. The other adjusting entries could also be made by a service business. The adjusting entry for **Federal Income Tax Payable** is unique to corporations. This adjusting entry is not made for a proprietorship because taxes are paid by the owner, not the business.

ETHICS IN ACTION

To Tell or Not to Tell, That Is the Question

Kelly Franklin was waiting to board a ski lift when she saw Leslie Best climbing into a limousine. Kelly and Leslie both work as clerks in the production office for DLT Industries. "No way can she afford to be driven around in a limo," thought Kelly. "Her husband has been out of work for years." Kelly also recalled that the company has been experiencing inventory losses. An internal investigation failed to identify any reason for the shortages. "Has Leslie been stealing inventory?" she wondered.

DLT requires employees to file a report if they believe someone has violated the law or a company policy. But feeling that she has little more than her suspicions, Kelly elects not to make a report to the company's ethics hotline.

INSTRUCTIONS

Go to www.generalmills.com, find "Responsibility" and select "Ethics and integrity," then "Code of conduct." Determine whether Kelly acted ethically by deciding not to report her suspicions. Use *A Champion's Code of Conduct* from General Mills as a guide. If Kelly came to you for advice, what would you tell her?

©LUCA DI FILIPPO, ISTOCK

Preparing an Unadjusted Trial Balance LO1

① Write account titles
② Enter account balances

ThreeGreen Products, Inc.
Unadjusted Trial Balance
December 31, 20--

ACCOUNT TITLE	DEBIT	CREDIT
Cash	54 1 9 4 34	
Petty Cash	2 5 0 00	
Accounts Receivable	20 3 8 1 81	
Allowance for Uncollectible Accounts		1 2 5 15
Merchandise Inventory	108 4 8 6 44	
Supplies—Office	4 5 4 8 17	
Supplies—Store	5 0 4 9 61	
Prepaid Insurance	11 0 0 0 00	
Notes Receivable	6 2 0 0 00	
Interest Receivable		
Salary Expense	184 2 3 4 95	
Supplies Expense—Office		
Supplies Expense—Store		
Uncollectible Accounts Expense		
Utilities Expense	4 9 6 5 42	
Federal Income Tax Expense	20 0 0 0 00	
Interest Income		4 6 4 00
Totals	818 9 1 0 27	818 9 1 0 27

Total, prove, and rule column totals ③

The first step in preparing adjusting entries is to prepare a trial balance. A trial balance prepared before adjusting entries are posted is called an **unadjusted trial balance**. A trial balance provides a proof that the debits and credits in the general ledger are equal. A trial balance also provides a complete list of accounts that may need to be brought up to date.

In Part 1, Delgado Web Services used a work sheet to plan its adjustments. The work sheet contained a trial balance and columns to enter adjustments. Rather than using a work sheet, ThreeGreen uses an unadjusted trial balance and records adjustments directly to a general journal.

> **◉ Preparing an Unadjusted Trial Balance**
>
> ❶ Write the title of each general ledger account in the Account Title column. Write the accounts in the same order they appear in the general ledger. All accounts are listed regardless of whether or not there is a balance. Listing all accounts reduces the possibility of overlooking an account that needs to be brought up to date.
>
> ❷ Write the balance of each account in the appropriate Debit or Credit column. The amounts are taken from the general ledger accounts.
>
> ❸ Total, prove, and rule the Debit and Credit columns.

Recording Adjusting Entries for Supplies LO2

ThreeGreen Products, Inc.																			
Unadjusted Trial Balance																			
December 31, 20--																			

ACCOUNT TITLE	DEBIT	CREDIT
Merchandise Inventory	108 4 8 6 44	
Supplies—Office	4 5 4 8 17	
Supplies—Store	5 0 4 9 61	
Prepaid Insurance	11 0 0 0 00	

① Debit Supplies Expense—Office   **③** Debit Supplies Expense—Store

GENERAL JOURNAL   PAGE 15

	DATE	ACCOUNT TITLE	DOC. NO.	POST. REF.	DEBIT	CREDIT	
6	31	Supplies Expense—Office			3 9 3 8 17		6
7		Supplies—Office				3 9 3 8 17	7
8	31	Supplies Expense—Store			4 5 8 4 61		8
9		Supplies—Store				4 5 8 4 61	9

② Credit Supplies—Office   **④** Credit Supplies—Store

The balance of Supplies—Office in the unadjusted trial balance is $4,548.17. The amount is the cost of office supplies on hand at the beginning of the year plus the office supplies purchased during the year. The account balance needs to be adjusted to reflect the office supplies on hand on December 31. The office supplies on hand are counted and determined to be $610.00. The difference is the value of office supplies used during the year, which is an expense.

The balance of Supplies—Store in the unadjusted trial balance is $5,049.61. The amount is the cost of store supplies on hand at the beginning of the year plus the store supplies purchased during the year. The account balance needs to be adjusted to reflect the store supplies on hand on December 31. The store supplies on hand are counted and determined to be $465.00. The difference is the value of store supplies used during the year, which is an expense.

Four questions are asked to analyze the adjustments for supplies.

1. **What are the balances of the accounts being adjusted?**
   Supplies—Office, $4,548.17
   Supplies—Store, $5,049.61
2. **What should the balances be for these accounts?**
   Supplies—Office, $610.00
   Supplies—Store, $465.00

3. **What must be done to correct the account balances?**
   Decrease Supplies—Office, $3,938.17 ($4,548.17 – $610.00)
   Decrease Supplies—Store, $4,584.61 ($5,049.61 – $465.00)
4. **What adjusting entries are made?**
   Debit Supplies Expense—Office, $3,938.17
   Credit Supplies—Office, $3,938.17
   Debit Supplies Expense—Store, $4,584.61
   Credit Supplies—Store, $4,584.61

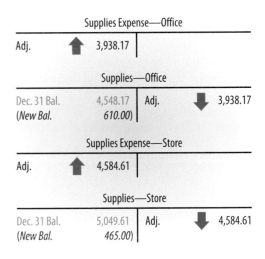

The adjusting entries for supplies are shown in the T accounts. The December 31 balances are the amounts reported in the unadjusted trial balance. The new balances are the amount of supplies on hand on December 31.

⟱ Journalizing the Adjusting Entries for Supplies

① Record a debit, $3,938.17, to Supplies Expense—Office in the general journal.

② Record a credit, $3,938.17, to Supplies—Office in the general journal.

③ Record a debit, $4,584.61, to Supplies Expense—Store in the general journal.

④ Record a credit, $4,584.61, to Supplies—Store in the general journal.

remember Whether you prefer to think of adjusting an asset account, such as Supplies, or an expense account, such as Supplies Expense, the adjusting journal entry is identical.

Many types of transactions are journalized in a general journal. These transactions can affect both the general ledger and subsidiary accounts. For example, the purchase of supplies on account affects two general ledger accounts and the vendor's accounts payable account. These transactions should be posted often to ensure management makes decisions using up-to-date information.

Adjusting entries are different from typical journal entries. The process of planning adjusting entries does not require the same need for management to have up-to-date information. It takes time for a business to obtain all the information necessary to plan adjusting entries. Determining the value of ending inventory can take several days. Therefore, adjusting entries only need to be posted after all adjusting entries are journalized.

Debt Collection—Know Your Rights

Consumers sometimes become financially overextended. A sudden illness or loss of a job may leave a person unable to pay for the goods or services they've purchased. As a result, banks and businesses find that they have uncollectible accounts.

When consumers don't pay their debts, creditors often hire debt collectors to recover the money. Debt collectors, however, are limited by law in the methods they may use to collect a debt. They may not attempt to collect the debt from anyone other than the signer(s) of the note. For example, they may not go after a parent of the debtor unless the parent cosigned the note.

Consumers should be aware of the protections offered by the Fair Debt Collections Practices Act (FDCPA), which is enforced by the Federal Trade Commission. The FDCPA prohibits debt collectors from

contacting debtors before 8 A.M. and after 9 P.M. unless given permission. Debt collectors may not call debtors at work without a request that they do so. They may not contact anyone else regarding a debtor's account except to obtain contact information. Most importantly, harassing behaviors, threats, obscenities, and profane language are prohibited.

ACTIVITIES

1. Assume you are a debtor receiving calls from a debt collector. What would be a reasonable way to try to work through the problem and avoid damaging your credit score any further?

2. Assume you cosigned on a student loan for a friend. You are now receiving calls from a debt collector because your friend is unable to pay. Is the debt collector wrong in contacting you in his effort to collect your friend's debt? Explain.

Source: www.ftc.gov/bcp/edu/pubs/consumer/credit/cre18.shtm.

©NOREBBO, ISTOCK

Recording an Adjusting Entry for Prepaid Insurance

ThreeGreen Products, Inc.			
Unadjusted Trial Balance			
December 31, 20--			
ACCOUNT TITLE		DEBIT	CREDIT
Supplies—Store		5 0 4 9 61	
Prepaid Insurance		11 0 0 0 00	
Notes Receivable		6 2 0 0 00	

① Debit Insurance Expense

GENERAL JOURNAL PAGE 15

	DATE	ACCOUNT TITLE	DOC. NO.	POST. REF.	DEBIT	CREDIT	
10	31	Insurance Expense			8 2 0 0 00		10
11		Prepaid Insurance				8 2 0 0 00	11

② Credit Prepaid Insurance

Insurance premiums are debited to **Prepaid Insurance** when paid. The January 1 balance in the account was $2,600.00. During the year, ThreeGreen paid $8,400.00 of insurance premiums. Thus, the balance in the unadjusted trial balance is $11,000.00.

ThreeGreen determined that the value of prepaid insurance on December 31 is $2,800.00. Therefore, the amount of insurance used during the year is $8,200.00 ($11,000.00 − $2,800.00). This difference is the expense for insurance premiums during the year. **Prepaid Insurance** is credited and **Insurance Expense** is debited at the end of the fiscal period for the value of premiums used.

Four questions are asked to analyze the adjustment for prepaid insurance.

1. **What is the balance of the account being adjusted?**
   Prepaid Insurance, $11,000.00
2. **What should the balance be for this account?**
   Prepaid Insurance, $2,800.00
3. **What must be done to correct the account balance?**
   Decrease $8,200.00 ($11,000.00 − $2,800.00)
4. **What adjustment is made?**
   Debit Insurance Expense, $8,200.00
   Credit Prepaid Insurance, $8,200.00

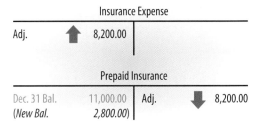

The adjusting entry for **Prepaid Insurance** is shown in the T accounts. The December 31 balance is the amount reported in the unadjusted trial balance. The new balance is the amount of insurance premiums to be used in the next fiscal period.

⌘ Journalizing the Adjusting Entry for Prepaid Insurance

① Record a debit, $8,200.00, to Insurance Expense in the general journal.

② Record a credit, $8,200.00, to Prepaid Insurance in the general journal.

LO1 Prepare an unadjusted trial balance.

LO2 Adjust supplies and prepaid insurance.

Term Review

unadjusted trial balance

Audit your understanding

1. What adjusting entry is unique to a corporation?
2. What four questions are used to analyze the adjustment of an account?
3. Which accounts are used for the adjustment to office supplies?
4. Which accounts are used for the adjustment to prepaid insurance?

Work together 15-1

Journalizing the adjusting entries for supplies and prepaid insurance

Page 15 of a general journal and a partially completed unadjusted trial balance are given in the *Working Papers*. Selected general ledger accounts for Southside Electric are provided on pages 429–431 of the *Working Papers*. Prepare the adjusting entries for supplies and prepaid insurance. Your instructor will guide you through the following examples. Save your work to complete Work Together 15-2.

1. Enter the following accounts on the unadjusted trial balance. Obtain the account balances from the general ledger accounts.

> Allowance for Uncollectible Accounts
> Supplies—Store
> Accumulated Depreciation—Office Equipment
> Insurance Expense

2. Total, prove, and rule the unadjusted trial balance.
3. Journalize the adjusting entries for supplies and prepaid insurance. The adjusting entry for the allowance for uncollectible accounts has been recorded on the general journal. The December 31 value of supplies and prepaid insurance are determined to be:

Office supplies	$ 548.00
Store supplies	640.00
Prepaid insurance	1,600.00

On your own 15-1

Journalizing the adjusting entries for supplies and prepaid insurance

Page 18 of a general journal and a partially completed unadjusted trial balance are given in the *Working Papers*. Selected general ledger accounts for Idaho Adventures are provided on pages 439–441 of the *Working Papers*. Prepare the adjusting entries for supplies and prepaid insurance. Work these problems independently. Save your work to complete to complete On Your Own 15-2.

1. Enter the following accounts on the unadjusted trial balance. Obtain the account balances from the general ledger accounts.

> Allowance for Uncollectible Accounts
> Supplies—Office
> Accumulated Depreciation—Store Equipment
> Interest Income

2. Total, prove, and rule the unadjusted trial balance.
3. Journalize the adjusting entries for supplies and prepaid insurance. The adjusting entry for the allowance for uncollectible accounts has been recorded on the general journal. The December 31 value of supplies and prepaid insurance are determined to be:

Office supplies	$ 684.00
Store supplies	775.00
Prepaid insurance	2,400.00

©CANDICE CUSACK, ISTOCK

LESSON

15-2 Adjusting Merchandise Inventory and Interest Receivable

LO3 Adjust merchandise inventory.
LO4 Adjust interest receivable.

Recording an Adjusting Entry for Merchandise Inventory LO3

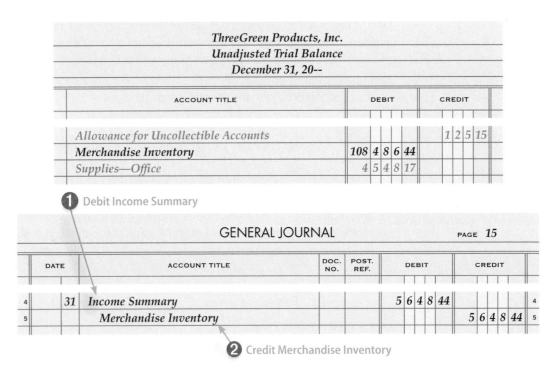

ThreeGreen Products, Inc.
Unadjusted Trial Balance
December 31, 20--

ACCOUNT TITLE	DEBIT	CREDIT
Allowance for Uncollectible Accounts		1 2 5 15
Merchandise Inventory	108 4 8 6 44	
Supplies—Office	4 5 4 8 17	

① Debit Income Summary

GENERAL JOURNAL PAGE 15

	DATE	ACCOUNT TITLE	DOC. NO.	POST. REF.	DEBIT	CREDIT	
4	31	*Income Summary*			5 6 4 8 44		4
5		*Merchandise Inventory*				5 6 4 8 44	5

② Credit Merchandise Inventory

ThreeGreen uses the periodic inventory method. During a fiscal period, all purchases of merchandise are recorded in **Purchases**. No changes in the amount of inventory resulting from purchases and sales are recorded in **Merchandise Inventory**. As a result, the balance of **Merchandise Inventory** on December 31, $108,486.44, has not changed from its January 1 balance.

The amount of inventory on hand at the beginning of a fiscal period is called **beginning inventory**. During the period, merchandise is purchased and merchandise is sold. To determine how much merchandise remains in inventory at the end of the period, a physical inventory is conducted. The actual count of merchandise at the end of a fiscal period is called **ending inventory**. A physical inventory is always conducted at the end of the fiscal year. Some businesses conduct physical inventories

more frequently. The balance of the **Merchandise Inventory** account at the end of the fiscal year must equal the actual ending inventory balance.

ThreeGreen's year-end physical inventory revealed that the merchandise on hand was purchased at a cost of $102,838.00. Therefore, **Merchandise Inventory** must be adjusted to equal the current cost of merchandise on hand.

Most accounts needing adjustment at the end of a fiscal period have a related expense account. Expense accounts are temporary accounts. For example, when **Prepaid Insurance** is adjusted, **Insurance Expense** is the related expense account. **Merchandise Inventory**, however, does not have a related expense account. Therefore, **Income Summary**, also a temporary account, is used to adjust **Merchandise Inventory** at the end of the fiscal year.

Four questions are asked to analyze the adjustment for merchandise inventory.

1. What is the balance of the account being adjusted?
Merchandise Inventory, $108,486.44

2. What should the balance be for this account?
Merchandise Inventory, $102,838.00

3. What must be done to correct the account balance?
Decrease $5,648.44

4. What adjustment is made?
Debit Income Summary, $5,648.44
Credit Merchandise Inventory, $5,648.44

Merchandise Inventory			
Dec. 31 Bal.	108,486.44	Adj.	5,648.44
(New Bal.	102,838.00)		

Income Summary	
Adj.	5,648.44

The adjusting entry for merchandise inventory is shown in the T accounts. The December 31 balance is the amount reported in the unadjusted trial balance. The beginning debit balance of Merchandise Inventory, $108,486.44, minus the adjustment credit amount, $5,648.44, equals the ending debit balance,

$102,838.00. Income Summary is a unique account in that it does not have a normal balance. Thus, the debit to Income Summary is not marked in the T account as increasing or decreasing the account.

In this example, ThreeGreen's ending inventory was lower than its beginning inventory. If the amount of merchandise on hand were greater than the January 1 balance of Merchandise Inventory, opposite entries would be made—debit Merchandise Inventory and credit Income Summary. Thus, if ThreeGreen's December 31 actual count had been $112,700.00, the adjusting entry would increase Merchandise Inventory by $4,213.56.

Journalizing the Adjusting Entry for Merchandise Inventory

1 Record a debit, **$5,648.44**, to Income Summary in the general journal.

2 Record a credit, **$5,648.44**, to Merchandise Inventory in the general journal.

remember When an account that requires adjusting does not have a related expense account, the temporary account Income Summary is used.

Accounting for Accrued Revenue LO4

Generally accepted accounting principles (GAAP) require that revenue be recorded in the accounting period in which the revenue is earned. [CONCEPT: Realization of Revenue] For a sale on account, revenue is earned on the day the goods are delivered to the customer. The sale increases the revenue account, Sales, and increases an asset account, Accounts Receivable.

Unlike sales on account, some revenues are earned over time. For example, a $10,000.00, 9% note receivable earns $2.50 of interest income every day the note is outstanding ($10,000.00 × 0.09 × 1/360). Making a journal entry for each day's interest income and the related receivable is impractical. However, the amount of interest earned must be recorded when financial statements are prepared.

Revenue earned in one fiscal period but not received until a later fiscal period is called **accrued revenue**. A company must identify the period of time for which accrued revenue should be recorded. The number of days is used to calculate the amount of the adjusting entry. The adjusting entry for accrued revenue increases a revenue account (a credit) and increases a receivable account (a debit). The income statement will then report all revenue earned for the period even though some of the revenue has not yet been received. The balance sheet will report all the assets, including the related receivable. [CONCEPT: Adequate Disclosure]

BLAJ BABRIEL/SHUTTERSTOCK.COM

Journalizing the Adjusting Entry for Interest Receivable

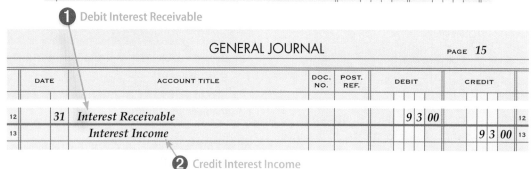

ThreeGreen Products, Inc.
Unadjusted Trial Balance
December 31, 20--

ACCOUNT TITLE	DEBIT	CREDIT
Prepaid Insurance	11 0 0 0 00	
Notes Receivable	6 2 0 0 00	
Interest Receivable		
Office Equipment	24 8 9 5 18	

1 Debit Interest Receivable

GENERAL JOURNAL   PAGE 15

DATE		ACCOUNT TITLE	DOC. NO.	POST. REF.	DEBIT	CREDIT	
12	31	Interest Receivable			9 3 00		12
13		Interest Income				9 3 00	13

2 Credit Interest Income

Interest Receivable

Debit Increases	Credit Decreases

Interest Income

Debit Decreases	Credit Increases

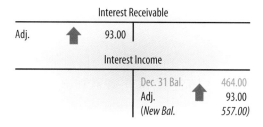

Interest Receivable

Adj.   93.00

Interest Income

Dec. 31 Bal.   464.00
Adj.   93.00
(New Bal.   557.00)

At the end of each fiscal period, ThreeGreen examines the notes receivable on hand. The amount of interest income earned but not yet collected is calculated. The interest owed to the business is an asset and is recorded in Interest Receivable. The interest earned must be recorded as revenue on the income statement. Interest earned but not yet received is called **accrued interest income**. Interest earned on notes receivable is recorded in Interest Income.

On December 31, ThreeGreen has one note receivable on hand, a 90-day, 9%, $6,200.00 note dated November 1. The time period from November 1 to December 31 is 60 days. Therefore, the interest earned on the note is calculated for 60/360 of a year.

Principal	×	Interest Rate	×	Time as Fraction of a Year	=	Accrued Interest Income
$6,200.00	×	9%	×	60/360	=	$93.00

Four questions are asked to analyze the adjustment for interest receivable.

1. **What is the balance of the account being adjusted?**
   Interest Receivable, zero
2. **What should the balance be for this account?**
   Interest Receivable, $93.00
3. **What must be done to correct the account balance?**
   Increase $93.00
4. **What adjustment is made?**
   Debit Interest Receivable, $93.00
   Credit Interest Income, $93.00

The adjusting entry is shown in the T accounts. The December 31 balance in Interest Income, $464.00, is the interest earned on notes that matured during the fiscal year. Interest Receivable is debited for $93.00 to record the accrued interest income. The interest earned is credited to Interest Income. Interest income is reported on the income statement.

Journalizing the Adjusting Entry for Interest Receivable

1 Record a debit, $93.00, to Interest Receivable in the general journal.

2 Record a credit, $93.00, to Interest Income in the general journal.

End of Lesson Review

LO3 Adjust merchandise inventory.

LO4 Adjust interest receivable.

Terms Review

beginning inventory

ending inventory

accrued revenue

accrued interest income

Audit your understanding

1. How is the amount of merchandise inventory on hand at the end of the fiscal year determined?

2. What adjusting entry is recorded when the ending merchandise inventory is greater than the beginning value?

3. How often is revenue earned on an outstanding note receivable?

4. What types of accounts are increased by recording an adjusting entry for accrued revenue?

Work together 15-2

Journalizing the adjusting entries for merchandise inventory and interest receivable

Use the general journal and unadjusted trial balance from Work Together 15-1. Your instructor will guide you through the following example. Save your work to complete Work Together 15-3.

1. From a physical count of merchandise inventory, the December 31 balance is determined to be $96,471.25. Journalize the adjusting entry for merchandise inventory.

2. A single note receivable is outstanding on December 31. The 90-day, 8% note was signed on November 22. Journalize the adjusting entry for interest receivable.

On your own 15-2

Journalizing the adjusting entries for merchandise inventory and interest receivable

Use the general journal and unadjusted trial balance from On Your Own 15-1. Your instructor will guide you through the following example. Save your work to complete On Your Own 15-3.

1. From a physical count of merchandise inventory, the December 31 balance is determined to be $158,420.00. Journalize the adjusting entry for merchandise inventory.

2. A single note receivable is outstanding on December 31. The 120-day, 9% note was signed on October 18. Journalize the adjusting entry for interest receivable.

15-3 Adjusting Accumulated Depreciation

LO5 Calculate depreciation expense using the straight-line method.

LO6 Adjust accumulated depreciation.

Categories of Assets

Most businesses use several broad categories of assets in their operations. Cash and other assets expected to be exchanged for cash or consumed within a year are called **current assets**. Physical assets that will be used for a number of years in the operation of a business are called **plant assets**. Some of ThreeGreen's plant assets are computers, cash registers, and sales display cases.

Businesses may have three major types of plant assets—equipment, buildings, and land. ThreeGreen records its equipment in two different equipment accounts—**Office Equipment** and **Store Equipment**. ThreeGreen rents the building and the land where the business is located. Therefore, the company does not need plant asset accounts for buildings and land.

Depreciating Plant Assets

A business buys plant assets to use in earning revenue. For example, ThreeGreen bought a new lighted display case to draw attention to its products. The display case will be useful for only a limited period of time. After several years, most display cases become worn from use and no longer offer an attractive display. A loss in the usefulness of a plant asset as a result of wear or obsolescence is called **depreciation**.

To match revenue with the expenses used to earn the revenue, the cost of a plant asset must be expensed over the asset's useful life. A portion of a plant asset's cost is transferred to an expense account in each fiscal period that the asset is used to earn revenue. [CONCEPT: Matching Expenses with Revenue] The portion of a plant asset's cost that is transferred to an expense account in each fiscal period during that asset's useful life is called **depreciation expense**.

Three factors are considered in calculating the annual amount of depreciation expense for a plant asset.

Original Cost. The original cost of a plant asset includes all costs paid to make the asset usable to a business. These costs include the price of the asset plus delivery and any necessary installation costs.

Salvage Value. A business removes a plant asset from use when the asset is no longer usable. The asset may be sold to another business or sold for scrap. An estimate of the amount that will be received for an asset at the time of its disposal is called its **salvage value**. Salvage value may also be referred to as *residual value* or *scrap value*. Since salvage value cannot be known when the asset is bought, it must be estimated. The amount an owner expects to receive when a plant asset is removed from use is its estimated salvage value.

Useful Life. The period of time over which an asset contributes to the earnings of a business is called its **useful life**. When a plant asset is bought, the exact length of useful life cannot be known. Therefore, the number of years of useful life must be estimated. The total amount of depreciation expense is distributed over the estimated useful life of a plant asset.

Two factors affect the useful life of a plant asset: (1) physical depreciation and (2) functional depreciation. Physical depreciation is caused by wear and deterioration from aging and weathering. Functional depreciation occurs when a plant asset becomes inadequate or obsolete. An asset is inadequate when it can no longer perform at an acceptable level of efficiency. A new asset of the same design and capability might replace it. An asset is obsolete when a more modern asset, perhaps using new technology, can operate more efficiently or produce better service.

Calculating Depreciation Expense and Book Value LO5

STRAIGHT-LINE DEPRECIATION

Recording an equal amount of depreciation expense for a plant asset in each year of its useful life is called the **straight-line method of depreciation**.

On January 2, 20X1, ThreeGreen bought a lighted display case for $2,500.00. The display case has an estimated salvage value of $500.00 and an estimated useful life of five years. Using the straight-line method of depreciation, the annual depreciation expense is $400.00. The depreciation expense is the same for each year in which the asset is used.

	Original Cost	−	Estimated Salvage Value	=	Estimated Total Depreciation Expense
	$2,500.00	−	$500.00	=	$2,000.00

	Estimated Total Depreciation Expense	÷	Years of Estimated Useful Life	=	Annual Depreciation Expense
	$2,000.00	÷	5	=	$400.00

ACCUMULATED DEPRECIATION

The total amount of depreciation expense that has been recorded since the purchase of a plant asset is called **accumulated depreciation**. The amount accumulates each year of the plant asset's useful life. The depreciation expense for the current year is added to the prior year's accumulated depreciation to update accumulated depreciation.

	20X2 Accumulated Depreciation	+	20X3 Depreciation Expense	=	20X3 Accumulated Depreciation
	$800.00	+	$400.00	=	$1,200.00

BOOK VALUE

The original cost of a plant asset minus accumulated depreciation is called the **book value of a plant asset**.

The book value is calculated by subtracting the accumulated depreciation from the original cost of the asset.

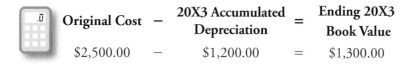

	Original Cost	−	20X3 Accumulated Depreciation	=	Ending 20X3 Book Value
	$2,500.00	−	$1,200.00	=	$1,300.00

Procedures for recording the accumulated depreciation and book value of individual assets are presented in Chapter 19.

Journalizing the Adjusting Entry for Accumulated Depreciation LO6

ThreeGreen Products, Inc.
Unadjusted Trial Balance
December 31, 20--

ACCOUNT TITLE	DEBIT	CREDIT
Office Equipment	24 8 9 5 18	
Accumulated Depreciation—Office Equipment		6 1 8 9 00
Store Equipment	59 1 4 8 11	
Accumulated Depreciation—Store Equipment		8 4 9 5 00

GENERAL JOURNAL PAGE 15

	DATE	ACCOUNT TITLE	DOC. NO.	POST. REF.	DEBIT	CREDIT	
14	31	Depreciation Expense—Office Equip.			7 4 8 5 00		14
15		Accumulated Depreciation—Office Equip.				7 4 8 5 00	15
16	31	Depreciation Expense—Store Equip.			9 8 3 0 00		16
17		Accum. Depreciation—Store Equip.				9 8 3 0 00	17

① Debit Depreciation Expense—Office Equipment and credit Accumulated Depreciation—Office Equipment

② Debit Depreciation Expense—Store Equipment and credit Accumulated Depreciation—Store Equipment

Accumulated Depreciation

Debit Decreases	Credit Increases

At the end of the fiscal year, ThreeGreen needs to bring the balance of each accumulated depreciation account up to date. To do that, it calculates the depreciation expense for each plant asset. Then, the depreciation amounts for each class of plant assets, such as office equipment, are totaled. After making the calculations, ThreeGreen determined that the total depreciation expense for its office equipment is $7,485.00.

The balance of Accumulated Depreciation—Office Equipment on December 31 is $6,189.00. Thus, the balance of that account needs to be increased by $7,485.00, the amount of the current year's depreciation. The new balance of Accumulated Depreciation—Office Equipment is $13,674.00 ($6,189.00 + $7,485.00).

It is important to retain original cost information for plant assets. If depreciation expense for office equipment were credited directly to the asset account, Office Equipment, that account would no longer show the total amount of the cost of office equipment. The account would be reduced by the amount of the depreciation. Instead, depreciation is recorded to the contra account, Accumulated Depreciation—Office Equipment.

Each plant asset account, except for Land, has a contra account. Land is not depreciated because it rarely loses its value or usefulness. Therefore, Land does not have a contra account.

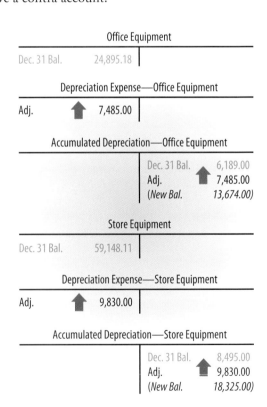

Four questions are asked to analyze the adjustments for accumulated depreciation.

1. **What is the balance of the account being adjusted?**
   Accumulated Depreciation—Office Equipment, $6,189.00

2. **What should the balance be for this account?**
   Accumulated Depreciation—Office Equipment, $13,674.00

3. **What must be done to correct the account balance?**
   Increase $7,485.00

4. **What adjustment is made?**
   Debit Depreciation Expense—Office Equipment, $7,485.00
   Credit Accumulated Depreciation—Office Equipment, $7,485.00

A similar analysis is performed to identify the adjusting journal entry for **Accumulated Depreciation—Store Equipment**. The adjusting entries for both plant assets are shown in the T accounts.

At any time, the book value of plant assets can be calculated by subtracting accumulated depreciation from its related plant asset account. The book value of office equipment is $11,221.18 ($24,895.18 − $13,674.00).

Journalizing the Adjusting Entries for Accumulated Depreciation

1 Record a debit, $7,485.00, to Depreciation Expense—Office Equipment and a credit to Accumulated Depreciation—Office Equipment.

2 Record a debit, $9,830.00, to Depreciation Expense—Store Equipment and a credit to Accumulated Depreciation—Store Equipment.

Project Manager: Implementing a New Software Program

Imagine you are in charge of implementing a new software program for use throughout a company. You have several responsibilities to perform:

- Make sure the computers can run the new software.
- Load the software on all the company's computers.
- Check to make sure the program runs correctly.
- Conduct initial and follow-up training for all employees on how to use the program.
- Plan the timelines for all of these tasks.

You must make sure that all of these tasks are completed on schedule. You also have a budget for the project that must be followed. As the project manager, you must work closely with other departments to plan the budget and the project schedule. You must consider the costs of time, money, and other resources the project will require.

The information technology (IT) department of a company faces a challenge. Although it provides a very important service to the company, it does not generate revenue for the company. Because of this, every cost must be carefully measured and understood so that it can be justified when presenting a proposed project budget for approval.

CRITICAL THINKING

1. You are a project manager proposing a budget to implement a new word processing program throughout the company. The company management wants to cut the training portion of the budget in half. What arguments might you present to encourage management to keep the full training budget?

2. The IT department is also in charge of computer security. In most companies, each employee has access only to certain parts of the computer system. Why?

End of Lesson Review

LO5 Calculate depreciation expense using the straight-line method.

LO6 Adjust accumulated depreciation.

Terms Review

current assets

plant assets

depreciation

depreciation expense

salvage value

useful life

straight-line method of depreciation

accumulated depreciation

book value of a plant asset

Audit your understanding

1. What are two categories of assets?

2. What three factors are used to calculate a plant asset's annual depreciation expense?

3. What plant asset account does not have a contra account for accumulated depreciation?

4. How does an adjusting entry for accumulated depreciation affect the related plant asset account?

Work together 15-3

Journalizing the adjusting entries for accumulated depreciation

Use the general journal and unadjusted trial balance from Work Together 15-2 and the schedule provided in the *Working Papers*. Your instructor will guide you through the following example. Save your work to complete Work Together 15-4.

1. Calculate depreciation expense for a color printer costing $950.00. The printer has an estimated salvage value of $150.00 and a useful life of five years.

2. Calculate the book value of the color printer at the end of its second year of service.

3. On December 31, Southside Electric determined its total depreciation expense. Total depreciation expense is $2,150.00 for office equipment and $7,440.00 for store equipment. Journalize the adjusting entries for accumulated depreciation.

On your own 15-3

Journalizing the adjusting entries for accumulated depreciation

Use the general journal and unadjusted trial balance from On Your Own 15-2 and the schedule provided in the *Working Papers*. Work this problem independently. Save your work to complete On Your Own 15-4.

1. Calculate depreciation expense for a security system costing $3,750.00. The system has an estimated salvage value of $500.00 and a useful life of eight years.

2. Calculate the book value of the security system at the end of its second year of service.

3. On December 31, Idaho Adventures determined its total depreciation expense. Total depreciation is $4,890.00 for office equipment and $6,950.00 for store equipment. Journalize the adjusting entries for accumulated depreciation.

©CANDICE CUSACK, ISTOCK

15-4 Calculating Federal Income Tax

LO7 Post adjusting entries.
LO8 Adjust federal income tax payable.
LO9 Prepare an adjusted trial balance.

Adjusting Entries LO7

			GENERAL JOURNAL						PAGE 15		
	DATE		ACCOUNT TITLE	DOC. NO.	POST. REF.	DEBIT			CREDIT		
1			*Adjusting Entries*								1
2	Dec.	31	Uncollectible Accounts Expense			2 3 8 4 10					2
3			Allowance for Uncollectible Accounts						2 3 8 4 10		3
4		31	Income Summary			5 6 4 8 44					4
5			Merchandise Inventory						5 6 4 8 44		5
6		31	Supplies Expense—Office			3 9 3 8 17					6
7			Supplies—Office						3 9 3 8 17		7
8		31	Supplies Expense—Store			4 5 8 4 61					8
9			Supplies—Store						4 5 8 4 61		9
10		31	Insurance Expense			8 2 0 0 00					10
11			Prepaid Insurance						8 2 0 0 00		11
12		31	Interest Receivable			9 3 00					12
13			Interest Income						9 3 00		13
14		31	Depreciation Expense—Office Equip.			7 4 8 5 00					14
15			Accum. Depreciation—Office Equip.						7 4 8 5 00		15
16		31	Depreciation Expense—Store Equip.			9 8 3 0 00					16
17			Accum. Depreciation—Store Equip.						9 8 3 0 00		17
18											18

The unadjusted trial balance acts as a check list to ensure that the business brings every account up to date. The accountant can start by examining each asset account to determine if the account needs adjustment. This process continues through the liability and owners' equity accounts.

Adjusting entries are made in the order that the accounts appear on the trial balance. **Allowance for Uncollectible Accounts** is the first account that needs to be adjusted. **Merchandise Inventory** is adjusted next, then **Supplies—Office**, and so forth. The process does not end once every asset, liability, and owners' equity account is examined. ThreeGreen's accountant would also review the revenue and expense accounts.

This process ensures that every account on the trial balance is up to date.

An accountant can perform this process in reverse order by first examining revenue and expense accounts. Then, the asset, liability, and owners' equity accounts would be reviewed. The adjusting entries would be the same but would be journalized in a different order.

Two accounts are not adjusted at this time: **Federal Income Tax Payable** and **Federal Income Tax Expense**. These accounts will be adjusted after all other adjusting entries are posted and the net income before federal income tax is determined.

The adjusting entries are posted to the general ledger to bring the account balances up to date.

Posting Adjusting Entries

GENERAL JOURNAL

PAGE 15

	DATE		ACCOUNT TITLE	DOC. NO.	POST. REF.	DEBIT	CREDIT	
1			*Adjusting Entries*					1
2	*20--* *Dec.*	31	*Uncollectible Accounts Expense*		6165	2 3 8 4 10		2
3			*Allowance for Uncollectible Accounts*		1135		2 3 8 4 10	3
4		31	*Income Summary*		3150	5 6 4 8 44		4
5			*Merchandise Inventory*		1140		5 6 4 8 44	5
6		31	*Supplies Expense—Office*		6155	3 9 3 8 17		6
7			*Supplies—Office*		1145		3 9 3 8 17	7
8		31	*Supplies Expense—Store*		6160	4 5 8 4 61		8
9			*Supplies—Store*		1150		4 5 8 4 61	9

Enter general ledger account numbers in general journal ③

Post the debit ❶   ❷ Post the credit

ACCOUNT *Allowance for Uncollectible Accounts*   ACCOUNT NO. 1135

DATE		ITEM	POST. REF.	DEBIT	CREDIT	BALANCE DEBIT	BALANCE CREDIT
20-- *Dec.*	31	*Balance*	✔				1 2 5 15
	31		G15		2 3 8 4 10		2 5 0 9 25

ACCOUNT *Uncollectible Accounts Expense*   ACCOUNT NO. 6165 ③

DATE		ITEM	POST. REF.	DEBIT	CREDIT	BALANCE DEBIT	BALANCE CREDIT
20-- *Dec.*	31		G15	2 3 8 4 10		2 3 8 4 10	

🔾 Posting Adjusting Entries

❶ Post the debit portion of the adjusting entry to the general ledger account.

❷ Post the credit portion of the adjusting journal entry to the general ledger account.

❸ Write the account numbers of the accounts in the Post. Ref. column of the general journal.

THINK LIKE AN ACCOUNTANT

Calculating Quarterly Income Tax Payments

Marcus Bass was shocked when he met his tax accountant to sign his annual federal tax return. Not only did his company owe an extra $23,000.00 in taxes, but he also had to pay $2,000.00 in penalties. "I paid my quarterly tax estimates on time. Why do I owe a penalty?" he asked.

"The government expects you to pay reasonable estimates each quarter," explained Latisha Hilton, his tax accountant. "You made quarterly tax payments on time, but your employees assumed the company would owe only $70,000.00 in federal income taxes. The good news is your net income was much higher than you expected. The bad news is you failed to increase the quarterly tax payments. The penalty is for underpaying the estimates."

Marcus asked Latisha if she would help his employees calculate the amount of the quarterly tax payments. "Let me propose another plan," she said. "I'll create a spreadsheet to help your employees do this on their own.

OPEN THE SPREADSHEET TLA_CH15

Complete the work sheet to create a schedule for calculating quarterly tax payments. The company paid $26,000.00 for its first quarterly tax payment. The company currently expects to earn a net income before federal income tax of $320,000.00 this year.

1. Calculate the estimated tax payment for the second quarter.

2. The company's sales continue to increase. At the end of the third quarter, the company now expects an annual net income before federal income tax of $350,000.00. Calculate the estimated tax payment for the third quarter.

©DAN BACHMAN, ISTOCK

Calculating Income Before Federal Income Taxes LO8

ThreeGreen Products, Inc.
Adjusted Trial Balance
December 31, 20--

❶ Enter account titles

❷ Enter account balances except Federal Income Tax Expense

ACCOUNT TITLE	DEBIT	CREDIT
Cash	54 1 9 4 34	
Petty Cash	2 5 0 00	
Accounts Receivable	20 3 8 1 81	
Income Summary	5 6 4 8 44	
Sales		632 3 7 1 75
Sales Discount	1 6 4 8 19	
Sales Returns and Allowances	3 9 4 1 57	
Purchases	254 8 5 1 26	
Purchases Discount		9 2 2 14
Purchases Returns and Allowances		1 4 9 5 01
Advertising Expense	4 6 8 0 00	
Credit Card Fee Expense	6 8 4 2 20	
Depreciation Expense—Office Equipment	7 4 8 5 00	
Depreciation Expense—Store Equipment	9 8 3 0 00	
Insurance Expense	8 2 0 0 00	
Miscellaneous Expense	3 4 9 5 04	
Payroll Taxes Expense	16 6 9 7 98	
Rent Expense	8 4 0 0 00	
Salary Expense	184 2 3 4 95	
Supplies Expense—Office	3 9 3 8 17	
Supplies Expense—Store	4 5 8 4 61	
Uncollectible Accounts Expense	2 3 8 4 10	
Utilities Expense	4 9 6 5 42	
Federal Income Tax Expense		
Interest Income		5 5 7 00

❸ Total income statement credit accounts

❹ Total income statement debit accounts

Total of income statement credit accounts . . . . $ 635,345.90 ❸

Less total of income statement debit accounts
excluding federal income tax . . . . −531,826.93 ❹

Equals net income before federal income tax . . . . . . $ 103,518.97 ❺ Subtract debit total from credit total

After the adjusting entries are posted, an updated trial balance can be prepared. A trial balance prepared after adjusting entries are posted is called an **adjusted trial balance**. The adjusted trial balance is prepared in two steps. First, all account balances, except for Federal Income Tax Expense, are entered on the trial balance. This information is used to plan the adjustment for federal income tax expense. Then, after the adjustment is posted, the account balances for Federal Income Tax Expense and Federal Income Tax Payable are entered.

⊌ Calculating Net Income Before Federal Income Tax

❶ Enter the account titles of all general ledger accounts.

❷ Enter the account balances of all accounts except Federal Income Tax Expense.

❸ Calculate the total account balances of income statement credit accounts. Include the account balance of Income Summary if the account has a credit balance.

❹ Calculate the total account balances of income statement debit accounts, excluding the balance of Federal Income Tax Expense. Include the account balance of Income Summary if the account has a debit balance.

❺ Subtract the total of debits from the total of credits to calculate net income before federal income taxes.

Calculating Federal Income Tax

Corporations anticipating annual federal income taxes of $500.00 or more are required to pay estimated taxes each quarter. Estimated income tax is paid in quarterly installments in April, June, September, and December. The actual federal income tax owed is calculated at the end of a fiscal year. A corporation must file an annual tax return reporting the actual income tax owed. Any additional tax owed that was not paid in quarterly installments must be paid when the final return is filed.

Early in the current year, ThreeGreen estimated it would owe $20,000.00 in federal income taxes for the year. Thus, ThreeGreen paid quarterly installments of $5,000.00. Each tax payment is recorded as a debit to Federal Income Tax Expense and a credit to Cash. Now that the actual amount of net income before income taxes is known, the actual amount of federal income tax is calculated.

Tax Rate Schedule			
If taxable income (line 30, Form 1120, or line 26, Form 1120-A) is:			
Over—	But not over—	Tax is:	Of the amount over—
$0	50,000	15%	-0-
50,000	75,000	$7,500 + 25%	$50,000
75,000	100,000	13,750 + 34%	75,000
100,000	335,000	22,250 + 39%	100,000
335,000	10,000,000	113,900 + 34%	335,000
10,000,000	15,000,000	3,400,000 + 35%	10,000,000
15,000,000	18,333,333	5,150,000 + 38%	15,000,000
18,333,333	—	35%	-0-

The amount of federal income tax a corporation must pay is calculated using a tax rate table issued by the Internal Revenue Service. Tax rates for corporations can be changed by an act of Congress. The tax rates in effect when this text was written are used to calculate federal income taxes.

Different tax rates are applied to different levels of net income. Each tax rate and taxable income amount on one line of a tax table is called a **tax bracket**. The tax rate associated with a tax bracket is called a **marginal tax rate**.

The first step in calculating federal income tax is to find the correct tax bracket. ThreeGreen's net income before federal income tax is $103,518.97. That places ThreeGreen in the Over 100,000 But not over 335,000 tax bracket (highlighted in the tax table). ThreeGreen's income tax will be $22,250.00, plus 39% of income above $100,000.00.

	Net Income before Federal Income Taxes	−	Of the Amount Over	=	Net Income Subject to Marginal Tax Rate	×	Marginal Tax Rate	=	Marginal Income Tax
	$103,518.97	−	$100,000.00	=	$3,518.97	×	39%	=	$1,372.40

The second step is to calculate the amount of net income subject to the marginal tax rate. This amount, $3,518.97, is multiplied by the marginal tax rate, 39%, to calculate the marginal income tax, $1,372.40.

The minimum amount of tax owed by a business in the 100,000 to 335,000 tax bracket is $22,250.00.

This amount is provided in the third column of the tax table. The bracket minimum income tax, $22,250.00, is added to the marginal income tax, $1,372.40, to calculate the total income tax owed for the fiscal year, $23,622.40.

	Bracket Minimum Income Tax	+	Marginal Income Tax	=	Federal Income Tax
	$22,250.00	+	$1,372.40	=	$23,622.40

Journalizing the Adjusting Entry for Federal Income Tax Payable

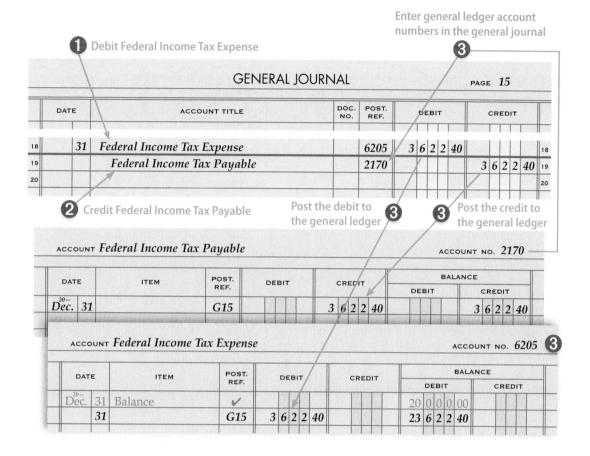

Enter general ledger account numbers in the general journal ③

① Debit Federal Income Tax Expense

② Credit Federal Income Tax Payable

Post the debit to the general ledger ③

Post the credit to the general ledger ③

ThreeGreen made four quarterly tax payments of $5,000.00. The total payments of $20,000.00 are less than the income tax owed of $23,622.40. ThreeGreen must adjust the balance of Federal Income Tax Payable to recognize the additional $3,622.40 of taxes owed. ThreeGreen will pay this amount when it files its tax return with the Internal Revenue Service.

Four questions are asked to analyze the adjustment for federal income tax payable.

1. What is the balance of the account being adjusted?
Federal Income Tax Payable, zero

2. What should the balance be for this account?
Federal Income Tax Payable, $3,622.40

3. What must be done to correct the account balance?
Increase $3,622.40

4. What adjustment is made?
Debit Federal Income Tax Expense, $3,622.40
Credit Federal Income Tax Payable, $3 622.40

The adjusting entry is shown in the T accounts. The new balance of Federal Income Tax Expense, $23,622.40, is the total amount of taxes owed to the federal government. The adjusted balance of Federal

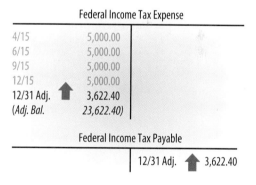

Income Tax Payable, $3,622.40, is the remaining amount of taxes to be paid.

⊙ Journalizing the Adjusting Entry for Federal Income Tax Payable

① Record a debit, **$3,622.40**, to **Federal Income Tax Expense** in the general journal.

② Record a credit, **$3,622.40**, to **Federal Income Tax Payable** in the general journal.

③ Post the adjusting entry to the general ledger.

Completing an Adjusted Trial Balance LO9

<table>
<tr><td colspan="3" align="center">ThreeGreen Products, Inc.
Adjusted Trial Balance
December 31, 20--</td></tr>
<tr><th>ACCOUNT TITLE</th><th>DEBIT</th><th>CREDIT</th></tr>
<tr><td>Cash</td><td>54 1 9 4 34</td><td></td></tr>
<tr><td>Petty Cash</td><td>2 5 0 00</td><td></td></tr>
<tr><td colspan="3"></td></tr>
<tr><td>Unemployment Tax Payable—State</td><td></td><td>1 4 7 42</td></tr>
<tr><td>Federal Income Tax Payable</td><td></td><td>3 6 2 2 40</td></tr>
<tr><td>Dividends Payable</td><td></td><td>3 7 5 0 00</td></tr>
<tr><td>Capital Stock</td><td></td><td>75 0 0 0 00</td></tr>
<tr><td>Retained Earnings</td><td></td><td>65 2 1 8 84</td></tr>
<tr><td>Dividends</td><td>15 0 0 0 00</td><td></td></tr>
<tr><td>Income Summary</td><td>5 6 4 8 44</td><td></td></tr>
<tr><td>Sales</td><td></td><td>632 3 7 1 75</td></tr>
<tr><td>Sales Discount</td><td>1 6 4 8 19</td><td></td></tr>
<tr><td>Sales Returns and Allowances</td><td>3 9 4 1 57</td><td></td></tr>
<tr><td>Purchases</td><td>254 8 5 1 26</td><td></td></tr>
<tr><td>Purchases Discount</td><td></td><td>9 2 2 14</td></tr>
<tr><td>Purchases Returns and Allowances</td><td></td><td>1 4 9 5 01</td></tr>
<tr><td>Advertising Expense</td><td>4 6 8 0 00</td><td></td></tr>
<tr><td>Credit Card Fee Expense</td><td>6 8 4 2 20</td><td></td></tr>
<tr><td>Depreciation Expense—Office Equipment</td><td>7 4 8 5 00</td><td></td></tr>
<tr><td>Depreciation Expense—Store Equipment</td><td>9 8 3 0 00</td><td></td></tr>
<tr><td>Insurance Expense</td><td>8 2 0 0 00</td><td></td></tr>
<tr><td>Miscellaneous Expense</td><td>3 4 9 5 04</td><td></td></tr>
<tr><td>Payroll Taxes Expense</td><td>16 6 9 7 98</td><td></td></tr>
<tr><td>Rent Expense</td><td>8 4 0 0 00</td><td></td></tr>
<tr><td>Salary Expense</td><td>184 2 3 4 95</td><td></td></tr>
<tr><td>Supplies Expense—Office</td><td>3 9 3 8 17</td><td></td></tr>
<tr><td>Supplies Expense—Store</td><td>4 5 8 4 61</td><td></td></tr>
<tr><td>Uncollectible Accounts Expense</td><td>2 3 8 4 10</td><td></td></tr>
<tr><td>Utilities Expense</td><td>4 9 6 5 42</td><td></td></tr>
<tr><td>Federal Income Tax Expense</td><td>23 6 2 2 40</td><td></td></tr>
<tr><td>Interest Income</td><td></td><td>5 5 7 00</td></tr>
<tr><td>Totals</td><td>842 3 2 4 77</td><td>842 3 2 4 77</td></tr>
</table>

Enter balance for Federal Income Tax Payable ❶

Update balance for Federal Income Tax Expense ❷

Total, prove, and rule the trial balance ❸

The adjusted trial balance can be completed after the federal income tax expense adjustment is posted. The account balances for Federal Income Tax Payable and Federal Income Tax Expense are entered in the adjusted trial balance.

Completing an Adjusted Trial Balance

❶ Enter the adjusted balance of Federal Income Tax Payable, $3,622.40.

❷ Replace the unadjusted balance of Federal Income Tax Expense, $20,000.00, with the adjusted balance, $23,622.40.

❸ Total, prove, and rule the adjusted trial balance.

Careers In Accounting

Kalika Patel
CHIEF FINANCIAL OFFICER

YURI_ARCURS/ISTOCKPHOTO.COM

Kalika Patel is vice president and chief financial officer (CFO) of her company. The CFO is the top financial position in an organization. Generally, only large companies employ CFOs. Where no CFO position exists, the controller is likely the chief accounting officer. As a member of the executive management team, Kalika helps run the entire company. She takes the lead in formulating decisions that relate to finance and accounting. Kalika reports directly to the chief executive officer (CEO).

As CFO, Kalika is ultimately responsible for her company's financial statements. However, she leaves their preparation to her accounting department. She devotes her efforts, instead, to the things executives are concerned about: planning, directing, and controlling the business. Her specific duties would include:

1. Reviewing reports submitted to the Securities and Exchange Commission (SEC)
2. Overseeing company investments
3. Managing cash flow
4. Negotiating the acquisition of capital assets, including other companies
5. Planning for taxes
6. Negotiating contracts
7. Arranging capital financing

Many CFOs also supervise investor relations and invest pension plan funds. As CFO, Kalika interprets operating results for both the company management and the board of directors.

Salary Range: Approximately $160,000, although this varies greatly with the size of the company and can be as high as several hundred thousand dollars.

Qualifications: A CFO must be able to relate to the needs of senior executives in order to ensure that financial reports support their needs. This requires strong interpersonal and problem-solving skills as well as creativity. The CFO must be able to use sound judgment to make good decisions. He/she must possess integrity and dependability. Most companies require ten or more years of accounting experience in progressively responsible roles. A four-year college degree is required with a master's degree, and/or a Certified Public Accountant (CPA) certification is highly desirable.

Occupational Outlook: The growth for chief financial officer positions is expected to remain the same (–2% to +2%) for the period from 2008 to 2018.

ACTIVITY

Use the Internet to access the home page of a corporation that interests you. Find the name of the chief financial officer for that company. Search for additional information about that person's education and past work experience.

©MILENNY, ISTOCK

End of Lesson Review

LO7 Post adjusting entries.

LO8 Adjust federal income tax payable.

LO9 Prepare an adjusted trial balance.

Terms Review

adjusted trial balance

tax bracket

marginal tax rate

Audit your understanding

1. How does the trial balance serve as a check list for preparing adjusting entries?

2. In what order can the adjusting entries be journalized?

3. Which accounts are totaled to determine net income before federal income taxes?

4. What is the bracket minimum tax and marginal tax rate of the 25% tax bracket?

Work together 15-4

Preparing the adjusting entry for federal income tax and an adjusted trial balance

Use the general journal and general ledger accounts from Work Together 15-3. An incomplete adjusted trial balance is given in the *Working Papers*. Your instructor will guide you through the following example.

1. Post the adjusting entries in the general ledger.

2. Record all account balances, except for Federal Income Tax Expense, on an adjusted trial balance.

3. Using the tax table shown in this chapter, calculate the federal income tax owed for the fiscal year.

4. Journalize and post the adjusting entry for federal income tax payable.

5. Complete the adjusted trial balance.

6. Total, prove, and rule the adjusted trial balance.

On your own 15-4

Preparing the adjusting entry for federal income tax and an adjusted trial balance

Use the general journal and general ledger accounts from On Your Own 15-3. An incomplete adjusted trial balance is given in the *Working Papers*. Work this problem independently.

1. Post the adjusting entries in the general ledger.

2. Record all account balances, except for Federal Income Tax Expense, on an adjusted trial balance.

3. Using the tax table shown in this chapter, calculate the federal income tax owed for the fiscal year.

4. Journalize and post the adjusting entry for federal income tax payable.

5. Complete the adjusted trial balance.

6. Total, prove, and rule the adjusted trial balance.

A Look at Accounting Software
Setting up Recurring Entries

In computerized accounting systems, transactions that are set up for automated entry are called **recurring entries**. These are sometimes referred to as *recurring transactions*. Any transaction that is repeated frequently can be set up as a recurring entry. One example is fulfillment of a standing purchase order, where a fixed selection of merchandise is shipped to the same customer every month. Likewise, recurring entries can be used to enter purchases of merchandise that occur every month.

In this chapter, ThreeGreen made adjusting entries at the end of its fiscal year. Businesses using computerized accounting systems can easily prepare monthly financial statements. These businesses, however, must prepare and post monthly adjusting entries. Since these are the same, or nearly the same, every month, using a recurring entry saves time and ensures that all adjustments are recorded every month.

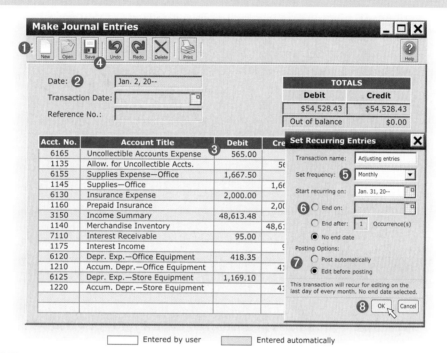

Entered by user ☐   Entered automatically ☐

❶ Clicking **New** on the menu bar opens a pick list. The user selects *Create Recurring Entry*.

❷ The system sets the current date. It cannot be changed. Note that no transaction date is selected.

❸ Recurring entries can be set up individually or in a single transaction as shown in the window. In this case, the user has entered all adjusting entries as a single transaction.

❹ When the transaction is complete, the user clicks **Save**. The system opens the **Set Recurring Entries** dialog box.

❺ The user enters a name for the transaction and selects the frequency from the pick list. Choices would be *Weekly*, *Monthly*, *Quarterly*, and *None*.

❻ The date of the first occurrence is entered. If the recurring entry is expected to be in effect for only a limited number of periods, such as rent on a short-term lease, either an "End on" date or a specific number of periods could be entered. The recurring entry for adjustments would not have an end date.

❼ In this window, the user has selected the option of editing the entry before posting. The amount of each adjusting entry may be different from month to month. The user might elect to have other recurring entries posted automatically. Whenever a recurring entry is posted automatically, the system displays a message confirming the entry.

Note: The user also has the option of setting up an entry as a template. Templates are useful for entries that recur frequently but irregularly. To make an entry a template, the user would select *None* in the **Set frequency** field, leave the start date blank, and not set any options.

❽ The system displays a summary of the options selected, and the user clicks **OK** to record the recurring entry.

On January 31, and at the end of every month to follow, the system will alert the user that the entry is ready for editing. It will be retrieved from memory with the transaction date and reference number assigned by the system. The user will enter the correct adjustments and click **Save** to post the entry.

Chapter Summary

At the end of a fiscal year, some general ledger accounts must be brought up to date before financial statements are prepared. The first step in recording adjusting entries is to prepare an unadjusted trial balance.

Four questions must be answered to analyze an adjustment.

1. What are the balances of the accounts being adjusted?
2. What should the balances be for these accounts?
3. What must be done to correct the account balances?
4. What adjusting entries are made?

Most asset and liability accounts have a related revenue or expense account. For example, the adjusting entry for prepaid insurance includes a debit to **Insurance Expense**. **Merchandise Inventory** does not have a related income statement account. Therefore, the adjusting entry for merchandise inventory includes an entry to the temporary account, **Income Summary**.

Accrued revenue is recorded when revenue has been earned but not collected. Interest income is one example of accrued revenue. The adjusting entry consists of a debit to **Interest Receivable** and a credit to **Interest Income**.

Current assets include cash and other assets expected to be consumed within a year. Plant assets include physical assets that will be used for many years. Over time, plant assets depreciate. That is, their usefulness and value are reduced due to wear or obsolescence. Depreciation expense recognizes a portion of each plant asset's cost every fiscal year. The amount of depreciation expense recorded each year is based on the asset's original cost, useful life, and salvage value. The adjusting entry includes a credit to **Accumulated Depreciation**, a contra account to the related plant asset account, and a debit to **Depreciation Expense**.

An adjusted trial balance is prepared after adjusting entries are posted. Total debits and credits of all income statement accounts, excluding **Federal Income Tax Expense**, are computed. The excess of the credit total over the debit total equals the net income before federal income taxes. The federal income tax owed is based on the minimum tax and marginal tax rate of the appropriate tax bracket. After the adjusting entry for federal income tax is posted, the federal income tax adjustment is entered in the adjusted trial balance.

EXPLORE ACCOUNTING

Accounting Systems Design

The role filled by accountants in preparing financial statements and filing tax returns for businesses is well understood. In addition, many accountants fill another important role. They design the accounting systems used to prepare the various financial reports needed for successful business operations.

An accounting system should be designed to meet the needs of the business it serves. Several factors to consider are:

1. Size of the company
2. Number of business locations
3. Geographic area of operations (local, statewide, national, or international)
4. Number of employees
5. Type of organization (service, merchandising, or manufacturing)

Also to be considered are the intended uses of the information:

1. Required financial reports (income statement, balance sheet, and cash flow statement)
2. Income tax reporting
3. Management decision making
4. Management controls
5. Product pricing

An accounting system is built around a chart of accounts, which provides the organizational structure for the data that will be collected and the information that will be reported.

A small business owned and operated by one person may not need detailed information. However, as a business grows in size and complexity, more detailed information is required. Large international businesses need very complex accounting systems with thousands of accounts. As businesses grow, accountants constantly look for ways to provide better information. Thus, accountants play a key role in business.

INSTRUCTIONS

Sunshine Gifts has decided to start manufacturing its own unique ceramic products. The company has ordered a set of custom molds, materials, and equipment. Two new employees have been hired to do the manufacturing. What additional accounts will need to be added to the company's chart of accounts to enable it to manage its new business activities?

Apply Your Understanding

INSTRUCTIONS: Download problem instructions for Excel, QuickBooks, and Peachtree from the textbook companion website at www.C21accounting.com.

15-1 Application Problem: Preparing adjusting entries for supplies and prepaid insurance LO1, 2

Page 20 of a general journal and a partially completed unadjusted trial balance are given in the *Working Papers*. Selected general ledger accounts for New England Arts are provided on pages 449–451 of the *Working Papers*. Prepare the adjusting entries for supplies and prepaid insurance. Save your work to complete Problem 15-2.

Instructions:

1. Enter the following accounts on the unadjusted trial balance. Obtain the account balances from the general ledger accounts.

   Merchandise Inventory
   Accumulated Depreciation—Office Equipment
   Depreciation Expense—Office Equipment
   Uncollectible Accounts Expense

2. Total, prove, and rule the unadjusted trial balance.

3. Journalize the adjusting entries for supplies and prepaid insurance. The adjusting entry for the allowance for uncollectible accounts has been recorded in the general journal. The December 31 value of supplies and prepaid insurance are determined to be:

Office supplies	$ 950.00
Store supplies	1,550.00
Prepaid insurance	2,000.00

15-2 Application Problem: Journalizing the adjusting entries for merchandise inventory and interest receivable LO3, 4

Use the general journal and unadjusted trial balance from Problem 15-1. Save your work to complete Problem 15-3.

Instructions:

1. From a physical count of merchandise inventory, the December 31 balance is determined to be $83,205.00. Journalize the adjusting entry for merchandise inventory.

2. A single note receivable is outstanding on December 31. The 120-day, 9% note was signed on November 28. Journalize the adjusting entry for interest receivable.

15-3 Application Problem: Journalizing the adjusting entries for accumulated depreciation LO5, 6

Use the general journal and unadjusted trial balance from Problem 15-2. Save your work to complete Problem 15-4.

Instructions:

1. Calculate depreciation expense for a display case costing $4,700.00; estimated salvage value, $500.00, useful life, three years.

2. Calculate the book value of the display case at the end of its second year of service.

3. On December 31, New England Arts determined the total depreciation expense: office equipment, $4,150.00; store equipment, $6,440.00. Journalize the adjusting entries for accumulated depreciation.

15-4 Application Problem: Preparing the adjusting entry for federal income tax and an adjusted trial balance LO7, 8, 9

Use the general journal and general ledger accounts used in Problem 15-3. An incomplete adjusted trial balance is given in the *Working Papers*.

Instructions:
1. Post the adjusting entries to the general ledger.
2. Record all account balances, except for Federal Income Tax Expense, on an adjusted trial balance.
3. Using the tax table shown on page 458 of this chapter, calculate the federal income tax owed for the fiscal year.
4. Journalize and post the adjusting entry for federal income tax payable.
5. Complete the adjusted trial balance.
6. Total, prove, and rule the adjusted trial balance.

 Peachtree

1. Journalize and post adjusting entries to the general journal.
2. Make the selections to print the income statement and the balance sheet.
3. Make the selections to print the general journal and the adjusted trial balance.

 Quick Books

1. Journalize and post adjusting entries to the journal.
2. Make the selections to print the balance sheet and the profit and loss statement.
3. Make the selections to print the journal and the adjusted trial balance.

1. Use the required formulas to calculate the totals of the Trial Balance columns.
2. Key the adjusting entries in the Adjustments columns.
3. Create the appropriate formulas to extend amounts to the Adjusted Trial Balance columns.

15-M Mastery Problem: Journalizing adjusting entries and preparing an adjusted trial balance LO2, 3, 4, 6, 7, 8, 9

Page 16 of a general journal, a partially completed adjusted trial balance, and selected general ledger accounts for Winterland Rentals are given in the *Working Papers*.

Instructions:
1. Use the following information collected on December 31 to prepare the adjusting entries.

a.	Estimate of uncollectible accounts receivable	$ 1,200.00
b.	Merchandise inventory	55,830.00
c.	Office supplies inventory	1,090.00
d.	Store supplies inventory	870.00
e.	Value of prepaid insurance	3,000.00
f.	Note receivable, 90-day, 6% note, dated November 21	
g.	Estimate of office equipment depreciation	3,600.00
h.	Estimate of store equipment depreciation	12,950.00

2. Post the adjusting entries in the general ledger.
3. Record all account balances, except for Federal Income Tax Expense, on an adjusted trial balance.
4. Using the tax table shown in this chapter, calculate the federal income tax owed for the fiscal year.
5. Journalize and post the adjusting entry for federal income tax payable.
6. Complete the adjusted trial balance.
7. Total, prove, and rule the adjusted trial balance.

 Peachtree

1. Journalize and post adjusting entries to the general journal.
2. Make the selections to print the income statement and the balance sheet.
3. Make the selections to print the general journal and the adjusted trial balance.

Quick Books

1. Journalize and post adjusting entries to the journal.
2. Make the selections to print the balance sheet and the profit and loss statement.
3. Make the selections to print the journal and the adjusted trial balance.

1. Use the required formulas to calculate the totals of the Trial Balance columns.
2. Key the adjusting entries in the Adjustments columns.
3. Create the appropriate formulas to extend amounts to the Adjusted Trial Balance columns.

AAONLINE

1. Go to www.cengage.com/login
2. Click on **AA Online** to access.
3. Go to the online assignment and follow the instructions.

15-C Challenge Problem: Journalizing adjusting entries LO2, 8

Use page 16 of the general journal given in the *Working Papers* to journalize the following adjusting entries for Renovation Central.

Instructions:

1. A large account previously written off in a prior year was unexpectedly collected in the current year. As a result, the current credit balance of Allowance for Uncollectible Accounts is $17,460.00. The December 31 estimate of uncollectible accounts is only $15,450.00.

2. While counting the merchandise inventory on December 31, the company discovered $3,500.00 of store supplies that had been incorrectly recorded as purchases. The unadjusted balance of Supplies—Store is $4,500.00. With the addition of the newly discovered supplies, the actual value of store supplies on December 31 is $4,800.00.

3. The company has fallen short of its expected net income for the current year. As a result, the actual amount of federal income tax owed is $12,980.00. The company had made quarterly federal income tax payments of $4,000.00.

21st Century Skills

Don't Lose a Chunk!

Theme: Financial, Economic, Business, and Entrepreneurial Literacy

Skills: Creativity and Innovation, Critical Thinking and Problem Solving, Communication and Collaboration, ICT Literacy

PARTNERSHIP FOR
21ST CENTURY SKILLS

There are many items that lose their value over time. One you can probably relate to easily is an automobile. While owning a car can be expensive, with costs for fuel, maintenance, repair, insurance, and interest on the loan, the largest cost is depreciation. Did you realize that as soon as you drive your new car off the dealer's lot, it is worth less money than you just paid for it?

Some vehicles depreciate faster than others. There are factors that should be considered when buying a new car in order to minimize your monetary loss. Look for one with wide appeal, not one that only satisfies your own preferences. To maximize resale value, follow these guidelines:

- *Color:* Stay away from trendy, flashy colors. Cars with common, neutral exterior colors such as black, white, or silver are more likely to be popular in the long run.
- *Supply and Demand:* Buy a car that's a little harder to find, and you won't have as much competition at resale time.
- *Safety:* Everyone appreciates safety features such as tire pressure warnings, pedestrian friendly bumpers, and rollover air bags.
- *Comfort:* Options such as automatic climate control, auxiliary jack for MP3s, and navigation systems enhance the value of a vehicle.
- *Reliability:* Some brands and models have track records for experiencing few maintenance problems, which could reduce the overall cost of owning a vehicle.
- *Fuel Efficiency:* Some cars get better gas mileage. This not only helps with resale but also with overall vehicle costs.

Once you own the vehicle, there are factors you should consider to reduce depreciation. Maintenance records showing regularly scheduled services, low mileage, and cleanliness can help you get the highest price at resale.

APPLICATION

1. a. Shop for a car. Using the Internet, research the retail price for a new car—make and model of your choice. Be sure to indicate the options that you choose for the vehicle such as power seats, CD changer, etc.

    b. Go to Kelley Blue Book at www.kbb.com. Research the value of the same make and model that is three years old with 36,000 miles, and five years old with 60,000 miles. Then, make the same comparison changing the mileage to 60,000 for the three-year-old model and 100,000 for the five-year-old model. Explain your findings.

2. Using the above instructions, research three other vehicles. Create a table or spreadsheet to display your findings.

3. Assume that you are a car salesman and your sales commission is based on selling the cars that will depreciate the fastest. Create an advertisement (written or video) highlighting the features of this car. Be sure to include factors in your advertisement that will increase depreciation. (Example: Color—bright lemon yellow.)

Auditing for errors

The following information was used to prepare the adjusting entries shown in the general journal:

a. Uncollectible accounts are estimated to be $4,345.00. The balance of the allowance account before adjustment was a $652.00 debit.

b. Merchandise inventory on hand, $194,831.25, is $5,518.00 less than the amount of inventory from the prior year.

c. Office supplies inventory used during the year, $3,210.00.

d. A single note receivable is outstanding on December 31. The 90-day, 8% note was signed on November 27.

e. Office equipment has a seven-year useful life and a $3,500 salvage value.

f. After the adjusting entries were posted, the corporation's net income before federal income taxes was $342,500.00. The company has made four quarterly income tax deposits of $25,000.00.

GENERAL JOURNAL   PAGE 22

	DATE		ACCOUNT TITLE	DOC. NO.	POST. REF.	DEBIT	CREDIT	
1			*Adjusting Entries*					1
2	Dec.	31	Uncollectible Accounts Expense			3 6 9 3 00		2
3			Allowance for Uncollectible Accounts				3 6 9 3 00	3
4		31	Merchandise Inventory			5 5 1 8 00		4
5			Income Summary				5 5 1 8 00	5
6		31	Supplies Expense—Office			3 2 1 0 00		6
7			Supplies—Office				3 2 1 0 00	7
8		31	Interest Receivable			2 1 0 00		8
9			Interest Income				2 1 0 00	9
10		31	Depreciation Expense—Office Equip.			5 7 3 0 00		10
11			Accum. Depreciation—Office Equip.				5 7 3 0 00	11
12		31	Federal Income Tax Expense			16 4 5 0 00		12
13			Federal Income Tax Payable				16 4 5 0 00	13

Selected accounts from the adjusted trial balance are shown.

ACCOUNT TITLE	DEBIT	CREDIT
Accounts Receivable	49 8 4 2 25	
Allowance for Uncollectible Accounts		3 0 4 1 00
Merchandise Inventory	205 8 6 7 25	
Supplies—Office	5 8 7 00	
Notes Receivable	10 5 0 0 00	
Interest Receivable		2 1 0 00
Office Equipment	40 1 1 0 00	
Accumulated Depreciation—Office Equipment		12 4 8 0 00
Federal Income Tax Payable		16 4 5 0 00
Income Summary		5 5 1 8 00

REVIEW AND ANSWER

Audit the adjusting entries to determine if the balances in the adjusted trial balance are correct. Prepare a list that describes any errors you discover and how they should be corrected.

Analyzing Nike's financial statements

Accounting terms are not always used consistently. *Gross profit* and *gross margin* are both used to describe the amount of revenue remaining after the cost of merchandise has been deducted. Nike's gross margin has gone up over the past three fiscal periods, a favorable trend. But sales have gone up as well. That makes it difficult to tell how well Nike has controlled its cost of merchandise sold.

The ratio of gross margin to revenue may be referred to as *gross margin, gross margin percent,* or *gross profit rate.* This ratio provides management and investors with a better measure of how well the company has controlled its merchandise costs.

INSTRUCTIONS

1. Use Nike's Selected Financial Data on page B-3 in Appendix B to identify the gross margin percent for 2007–2011. Round gross margin percents to one decimal place.

2. Is the trend in the gross profit rate favorable or unfavorable?

3. Show how amounts on Nike's Consolidated Statements of Income, on page B-5, were used to calculate the gross profit rate for 2011.

Chapter 16 Financial Statements and Closing Entries for a Corporation

LEARNING OBJECTIVES

After studying Chapter 16, in addition to defining key terms, you will be able to:

LO1 Prepare an income statement for a merchandising business organized as a corporation.

LO2 Prepare a statement of stockholders' equity.

LO3 Prepare a balance sheet for a business organized as a corporation.

LO4 Prepare closing entries.

LO5 Prepare a post-closing trial balance.

©DANIEL KOUREY, ISTOCK/©JIM PRUITT, ISTOCK

BLEND IMAGES/JUPITER IMAGES

Accounting In The Real World

Boeing

Since 1916, The Boeing Company has been a leader in the aerospace industry. The company's first aircraft was its Model C, a two-man seaplane with a cruising speed of merely 65 miles per hour and a range of 200 miles. Today, Boeing is best known for its 7X7 line of commercial aircraft. The Boeing 737, introduced in 1964, continues to be the dominant aircraft flown by commercial passenger airlines. The latest model carries up to 215 passengers with a cruising speed of 500 miles per hour and a range of 3,200 miles.

Boeing is also a leading defense and space contractor. Boeing manufactures a diverse line of military products, including manned and unmanned combat aircraft, surveillance aircraft, missile defense systems, and satellites. The company is also winding down operations as a contractor for the space shuttle and international space station projects.

Are you short of the $85 million needed to buy a 737? Boeing can also arrange for a commercial airline to finance its aircraft purchases.

So, is Boeing an aircraft, space exploration, or financial company? The income statement Boeing prepares in accordance with GAAP provides no answer to that question. Like other large corporations, Boeing's income statement reports a single amount of product sales.

Fortunately, the Securities and Exchange Commission (SEC) requires publicly traded corporations to report more detailed financial information. The document filed with the SEC is known as Form 10-K. Boeing's 10-K contains detailed sales information for each of its products. A table shows that Boeing sells more 737s than all other commercial models combined. A reader can also learn the percent of total company revenue generated from each group of products.

CRITICAL THINKING

1. Identify a company that has extended its product line beyond its original market. Find its 10-K report on its website. How are its sales reported?

2. How else could Boeing report its net sales to provide readers with more detailed information?

Source: www.boeing.com.

Key Terms

- operating revenue
- net sales
- cost of merchandise sold
- gross profit

- operating expenses
- income from operations
- statement of stockholders' equity
- par value

- current liabilities
- long-term liabilities
- supporting schedule

LESSON
16-1 Preparing an Income Statement

LO1 Prepare an income statement for a merchandising business organized as a corporation.

Uses of Financial Statements

Financial statements provide the primary source of information needed by owners and managers to make decisions on the future activity of a business. All financial information must be reported in order to make sound business decisions. The financial statements should provide information about a business's current financial condition, changes from its previously reported financial condition, and the progress of its operations. [CONCEPT: Adequate Disclosure]

Comparing the financial condition and progress for more than one fiscal period helps owners and managers make sound business decisions. Therefore, financial information must be reported the same way from one fiscal period to the next. [CONCEPT: Consistent Reporting]

ThreeGreen prepares three financial statements to report financial progress and condition. A corporation prepares an income statement and a balance sheet similar to those used by a proprietorship. A corporation also prepares a statement of stockholders' equity.

ETHICS IN ACTION

Don't Bite the Hand That Feeds You

Many grocery and department stores package their damaged, returned, and overstocked nonperishable items for sale to salvage stores. The items are packed into large crates and sold by the crate at a substantial discount over retail price. The salvage stores do not even know what items are in the crates until the crates are delivered and opened.

Source: www.thekrogerco.com/documents/EthicsPolicy.pdf

Patti Dexter has worked in the floral department of Harvest Grocery Store for several years. In her spare time, she has been helping her parents open a salvage store within one mile of Harvest Grocery Store. Patti intends to keep her current job and help her parents only on crate delivery day.

INSTRUCTIONS

Determine whether it is ethical for Patti to work for both Harvest Grocery Store and her parents' salvage store. Use *The Kroger Co. Policy on Business Ethics* as a guide.

©LUCA DI FILIPPO, ISTOCK

Preparing an Income Statement from a Trial Balance LO1

<table>
<tr><td colspan="3">ThreeGreen Products, Inc.
Adjusted Trial Balance
December 31, 20--</td></tr>
<tr><th>ACCOUNT TITLE</th><th>DEBIT</th><th>CREDIT</th></tr>
<tr><td>Merchandise Inventory</td><td>102 8 3 8 00</td><td></td></tr>
<tr><td>Income Summary</td><td>5 6 4 8 44</td><td></td></tr>
<tr><td>Sales</td><td></td><td>632 3 7 1 75</td></tr>
<tr><td>Sales Discount</td><td>1 6 4 8 19</td><td></td></tr>
<tr><td>Sales Returns and Allowances</td><td>3 9 4 1 57</td><td></td></tr>
<tr><td>Purchases</td><td>254 8 5 1 26</td><td></td></tr>
<tr><td>Purchases Discount</td><td></td><td>9 2 2 14</td></tr>
<tr><td>Purchases Returns and Allowances</td><td></td><td>1 4 9 5 01</td></tr>
<tr><td>Advertising Expense</td><td>4 6 8 0 00</td><td></td></tr>
<tr><td>Credit Card Fee Expense</td><td>6 8 4 2 20</td><td></td></tr>
<tr><td>Depreciation Expense—Office Equipment</td><td>7 4 8 5 00</td><td></td></tr>
<tr><td>Depreciation Expense—Store Equipment</td><td>9 8 3 0 00</td><td></td></tr>
<tr><td>Insurance Expense</td><td>8 2 0 0 00</td><td></td></tr>
<tr><td>Miscellaneous Expense</td><td>3 4 9 5 04</td><td></td></tr>
<tr><td>Payroll Taxes Expense</td><td>16 6 9 7 98</td><td></td></tr>
<tr><td>Rent Expense</td><td>8 4 0 0 00</td><td></td></tr>
<tr><td>Salary Expense</td><td>184 2 3 4 95</td><td></td></tr>
<tr><td>Supplies Expense—Office</td><td>3 9 3 8 17</td><td></td></tr>
<tr><td>Supplies Expense—Store</td><td>4 5 8 4 61</td><td></td></tr>
<tr><td>Uncollectible Accounts Expense</td><td>2 3 8 4 10</td><td></td></tr>
<tr><td>Utilities Expense</td><td>4 9 6 5 42</td><td></td></tr>
<tr><td>Federal Income Tax Expense</td><td>23 6 2 2 40</td><td></td></tr>
<tr><td>Interest Income</td><td></td><td>5 5 7 00</td></tr>
<tr><td>Totals</td><td>842 3 2 4 77</td><td>842 3 2 4 77</td></tr>
</table>

The income statement of a merchandising business has four main sections: (1) Operating Revenue, (2) Cost of Merchandise Sold, (3) Operating Expenses, and (4) Other Revenue. Information from an adjusted trial balance is used to prepare the income statement. Amounts in all revenue and expense accounts and **Merchandise Inventory** are reported on an income statement.

ThreeGreen's income statement, illustrated on the next page, is one of many different styles used by various businesses. This four-column style was chosen because it clearly shows the calculations that are made. This income statement differs from Delgado Web Services' income statement shown in Chapter 7. First, ThreeGreen has more accounts to report on its income statement. Second, the Operating Revenue section is more detailed than the Revenue section on Delgado's income statement. Also, ThreeGreen's income statement includes sections for Cost of Merchandise Sold and Other Revenue.

ThreeGreen Products, Inc.

Income Statement

For Year Ended December 31, 20--

					% OF NET SALES
Operating Revenue:					
Sales			632 3 7 1 75		
Less: Sales Discount		1 6 4 8 19			
Sales Returns and Allowances		3 9 4 1 57	5 5 8 9 76		
Net Sales				626 7 8 1 99	100.0
Cost of Merchandise Sold:					
Merchandise Inventory, Jan. 1, 20--			108 4 8 6 44		
Purchases		254 8 5 1 26			
Less: Purchases Discount	9 2 2 14				
Purchases Returns and Allowances	1 4 9 5 01	2 4 1 7 15			
Net Purchases			252 4 3 4 11		
Total Cost of Mdse. Avail. for Sale			360 9 2 0 55		
Less Mdse. Inventory, Dec. 31, 20--			102 8 3 8 00		
Cost of Merchandise Sold				258 0 8 2 55	41.2
Gross Profit				368 6 9 9 44	58.8
Operating Expenses:					
Advertising Expense			4 6 8 0 00		
Credit Card Fee Expense			6 8 4 2 20		
Depreciation Expense—Office Equipment			7 4 8 5 00		
Depreciation Expense—Store Equipment			9 8 3 0 00		
Insurance Expense			8 2 0 0 00		
Miscellaneous Expense			3 4 9 5 04		
Payroll Taxes Expense			16 6 9 7 98		
Rent Expense			8 4 0 0 00		
Salary Expense			184 2 3 4 95		
Supplies Expense—Office			3 9 3 8 17		
Supplies Expense—Store			4 5 8 4 61		
Uncollectible Accounts Expense			2 3 8 4 10		
Utilities Expense			4 9 6 5 42		
Total Operating Expenses				265 7 3 7 47	42.4
Income from Operations				102 9 6 1 97	16.4
Other Revenue:					
Interest Income				5 5 7 00	0.1
Net Income before Federal Income Tax				103 5 1 8 97	16.5
Less Federal Income Tax Expense				23 6 2 2 40	3.8
Net Income after Federal Income Tax				79 8 9 6 57	12.7

 Net income after federal income tax is typically referred to as net income.

 Due to rounding, vertical analysis percents may not total 100.0%.

Operating Revenue Section of an Income Statement for a Merchandising Business

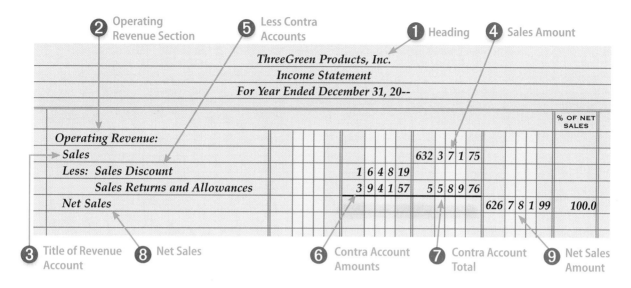

② Operating Revenue Section **⑤ Less Contra Accounts** **① Heading** **④ Sales Amount**

ThreeGreen Products, Inc.
Income Statement
For Year Ended December 31, 20--

					% OF NET SALES
Operating Revenue:					
Sales			632 3 7 1 75		
Less: Sales Discount	1 6 4 8 19				
Sales Returns and Allowances	3 9 4 1 57	5 5 8 9 76			
Net Sales				626 7 8 1 99	100.0

③ Title of Revenue Account **⑧ Net Sales** **⑥ Contra Account Amounts** **⑦ Contra Account Total** **⑨ Net Sales Amount**

ThreeGreen's normal business activity is the sale of ecologically friendly products. The revenue earned by a business from its normal business operations is called **operating revenue**. The Operating Revenue section of the income statement lists the Sales account and its contra accounts, Sales Discount and Sales Returns and Allowances. The amount of sales, less sales discounts and sales returns and allowances, is called **net sales**.

> ## ⓢ Preparing the Operating Revenue Section of an Income Statement
>
> **①** Write the income statement heading on three lines.
>
> **②** Write the name of this section, Operating Revenue:, at the extreme left of the wide column on the first line.
>
> **③** Write the title of the revenue account, Sales, on the next line, indented about one centimeter.
>
> **④** Write the amount of sales, $632,371.75, in the third amount column.
>
> **⑤** Write Less: on the next line, indented about one centimeter, followed by Sales Discount and Sales Returns and Allowances on the line after that.
>
> **⑥** Write the amount of the sales discounts, $1,648.19, and sales returns and allowances, $3,941.57, in the second amount column.
>
> **⑦** Add sales discounts, $1,648.19, and sales returns and allowances, $3,941.57, and write the amount, $5,589.76, in the third amount column.
>
> **⑧** Write Net Sales on the next line, indented about one centimeter.
>
> **⑨** Subtract the total of the contra accounts, $5,589.76, from sales, $632,371.75, to calculate net sales, $626,781.99. Write that amount in the fourth amount column.

Cost of Merchandise Sold Section of an Income Statement for a Merchandising Business

① Cost of Merchandise Sold Section **②** Beginning Inventory   **⑧** Vertical Analysis Percentages

ThreeGreen Products, Inc.							
Income Statement							
For Year Ended December 31, 20--							

				% OF NET SALES
Operating Revenue:				
Sales			632 3 7 1 75	
Less: Sales Discount	1 6 4 8 19			
Sales Returns and Allowances	3 9 4 1 57	5 5 8 9 76		
Net Sales			626 7 8 1 99	100.0
Cost of Merchandise Sold:				
Merchandise Inventory, Jan. 1, 20--		108 4 8 6 44		
Purchases		254 8 5 1 26		
Less: Purchases Discount	9 2 2 14			
Purchases Returns and Allowances	1 4 9 5 01	2 4 1 7 15		
Net Purchases		252 4 3 4 11		
Total Cost of Mdse. Avail. for Sale		360 9 2 0 55		
Less Mdse. Inventory, Dec. 31, 20--		102 8 3 8 00		
Cost of Merchandise Sold			258 0 8 2 55	41.2
Gross Profit			368 6 9 9 44	58.8

③ Purchases Section   **⑤** Ending Inventory   **⑦** Gross Profit   **⑥** Cost of Merchandise Sold   **④** Total Cost of Merchandise Available for Sale

The original price of all merchandise sold during a fiscal period is called the **cost of merchandise sold**. [CONCEPT: Historical Cost] Cost of merchandise sold is also known as *cost of goods sold* or *cost of sales*. The operating revenue remaining after cost of merchandise sold has been deducted is called **gross profit**. Gross profit is often referred to as *gross profit on sales*. Management uses gross profit as a measure for how effectively the business is performing in its primary functions of buying and selling merchandise. Calculating a ratio between gross profit and net sales enables management to compare its performance to prior fiscal periods.

Most calculated amounts reported on a financial statement have a related description. Net sales and net purchases are two examples. However, the totals of the sales contra accounts, $5,589.76, and the purchases contra accounts, $2,417.15, are not described. Instead, the reader of the financial statement is expected to understand the amount by its physical position on the statement. Each amount is immediately to the right of an amount column ruled with a single line.

The single ruled line shown in the illustration below indicates that the column is being totaled. The amount adjacent to the column is the sum of that column.

ThreeGreen Products, Inc.					
Income Statement					
For Year Ended December 31, 20--					

				% OF NET SALES
Operating Revenue:				
Sales			632 3 7 1 75	
Less: Sales Discount	1 6 4 8 19			
Sales Returns and Allowances	3 9 4 1 57	5 5 8 9 76		
Net Sales			626 7 8 1 99	100.0

Total of adjacent column

Preparing the Cost of Merchandise Sold Section of an Income Statement

1 Write the name of this section, Cost of Merchandise Sold:, at the extreme left of the wide column.

2 Write the beginning inventory.

    a. Indent about one centimeter on the next line and write Merchandise Inventory, Jan. 1, 20--.

    b. Write the beginning merchandise inventory balance, $108,486.44, in the third amount column. The amount of beginning inventory is the January 1 balance of the Merchandise Inventory general ledger account.

3 Prepare the Purchases subsection.

    a. Indent about one centimeter on the next line and write Purchases. Enter the purchases amount, $254,851.26, in the second amount column.

    b. Write Less: on the next line, indented about one centimeter, followed by Purchases Discount and Purchases Returns and Allowances aligned below it. It is permissible to abbreviate long titles when necessary.

    c. Write the amount of the purchases discounts, $922.14, and purchases returns and allowances, $1,495.01, in the first amount column.

    d. Add purchases discounts, $922.14, and purchases returns and allowances, $1,495.01, and write the amount, $2,417.15, in the second amount column.

    e. Write Net Purchases on the next line, indented about one centimeter.

    f. Subtract the total of the contra accounts, $2,417.15, from Purchases, $254,851.26, to calculate net purchases, $252,434.11. Write that amount in the third amount column.

4 Calculate the total cost of merchandise available for sale.

    a. Indent about one centimeter on the next line, and write Total Cost of Merchandise Available for Sale.

    b. Add the beginning merchandise inventory, $108,486.44, and net purchases, $252,434.11, to calculate the total cost of merchandise available for sale, $360,920.55. Write that amount in the third amount column.

5 Write the amount of the ending inventory found in the adjusted trial balance.

    a. Indent about one centimeter on the next line, and write Less Merchandise Inventory, Dec. 31, 20--.

    b. Write the ending merchandise inventory, $102,838.00, found in the adjusted trial balance, in the third amount column.

6 Calculate the cost of merchandise sold.

    a. Indent about one centimeter on the next line, and write Cost of Merchandise Sold.

    b. Subtract the ending merchandise inventory, $102,838.00, from the total cost of merchandise available for sale, $360,920.55, to calculate the cost of merchandise sold, $258,082.55. Write that amount in the fourth amount column.

7 Calculate the gross profit.

    a. Write Gross Profit on the next line at the extreme left of the wide column.

    b. Write the gross profit, $368,699.44, in the fourth amount column. (Total operating revenue, $626,781.99, less cost of merchandise sold, $258,082.55, equals gross profit, $368,699.44.)

8 Prepare a vertical analysis.

    a. Divide each amount in the fourth amount column by the amount of net sales. Round each percentage to the nearest 0.1%.

    b. Write the percentage in the % of Net Sales column.

Other titles for an income statement include a statement of earnings, profit and loss statement, statement of operations, and statement of income.

Completing an Income Statement for a Merchandising Business

1 Operating Expenses Section

8 Vertical Analysis Percentages

ThreeGreen Products, Inc.
Income Statement
For Year Ended December 31, 20--

Gross Profit		368 6 9 9 44	58.8
Operating Expenses:			
Advertising Expense	4 6 8 0 00		
Credit Card Fee Expense	6 8 4 2 20		
Depreciation Expense—Office Equipment	7 4 8 5 00		
Depreciation Expense—Store Equipment	9 8 3 0 00		
Insurance Expense	8 2 0 0 00		
Miscellaneous Expense	3 4 9 5 04		
Payroll Taxes Expense	16 6 9 7 98		
Rent Expense	8 4 0 0 00		
Salary Expense	184 2 3 4 95		
Supplies Expense—Office	3 9 3 8 17		
Supplies Expense—Store	4 5 8 4 61		
Uncollectible Accounts Expense	2 3 8 4 10		
Utilities Expense	4 9 6 5 42		
Total Operating Expenses		265 7 3 7 47	42.4
Income from Operations		102 9 6 1 97	16.4
Other Revenue:			
Interest Income		5 5 7 00	0.1
Net Income before Federal Income Tax		103 5 1 8 97	16.5
Less Federal Income Tax Expense		23 6 2 2 40	3.8
Net Income after Federal Income Tax		79 8 9 6 57	12.7

3 Other Revenue Section

6 Net Income after Federal Income Tax

5 Less Federal Income Tax Expense

4 Net Income before Federal Income Tax

2 Income from Operations

7 Double Lines

The expenses incurred by a business in its normal operations are called **operating expenses**. The operating revenue remaining after the cost of merchandise sold and operating expenses have been deducted is called **income from operations**. Income from operations is also referred to as *operating income*.

Businesses often earn income unrelated to their normal business operations. One example is interest earned on invested or loaned funds. On the income statement, Interest Income is presented after Income from Operations in a section labeled Other Revenue.

❯ Completing an Income Statement

1 **Prepare the Operating Expenses section.**

   a. Write the name of this section, Operating Expenses:, at the extreme left of the wide column.

   b. On the next line, indented about one centimeter, list the expense account titles, one per line, in the order in which they appear on the trial balance.

   c. Write the amount of each expense account balance in the third amount column.

   d. Indent about one centimeter, and write Total Operating Expenses on the next line in the wide column below the last expense account title.

   e. Total the individual expense amounts and write the total, $265,737.47, in the fourth amount column on the total line.

2 Calculate the income from operations.

    a. Write Income from Operations on the next line at the extreme left of the wide column.

    b. Write the amount, $102,961.97, in the fourth amount column. (Gross profit, $368,699.44, less total operating expenses, $265,737.47, equals income from operations, $102,961.97.)

3 Prepare the Other Revenue section.

    a. Write the name of this section, Other Revenue:, at the extreme left of the wide column.

    b. Indent about one centimeter, and write Interest Income on the next line in the wide column. Write the amount, $557.00, on the same line in the fourth amount column.

4 Calculate the net income before federal income tax.

    a. Write Net Income before Federal Income Tax on the next line at the extreme left of the wide column.

    b. Write the amount, $103,518.97, in the fourth amount column. (Income from operations, $102,961.97, plus other revenue, $557.00, equals net income before federal income tax, $103,518.97.)

5 Write Less Federal Income Tax Expense on the next line at the extreme left of the wide column. Write the amount, $23,622.40, on the same line in the fourth amount column.

6 Calculate net income after federal income tax.

    a. Write Net Income after Federal Income Tax on the next line at the extreme left of the wide column.

    b. Write the amount, $79,896.57, in the fourth amount column. (Net income before federal income tax, $103,518.97, less federal income tax expense, $23,622.40, equals net income after federal income tax, $79,896.57.)

7 Rule double lines across the four amount columns to show that the income statement is complete.

8 Prepare a vertical analysis.

    a. Divide each amount in the fourth amount column by the amount of net sales. Round each percentage to the nearest 0.1%.

    b. Write the percentage in the % of Net Sales column.

THINK LIKE AN ACCOUNTANT

Managing a Stock Portfolio

Lakeland Marina operates six marinas on Lake Martin. Located in a northern climate, the company earns more than 70% of its annual revenues during three summer months. The money earned during these months is needed to operate the marinas during the cold winter months when sales plummet.

Daniel Ellis, CPA, is the chief financial officer of the company. He is responsible for investing excess cash until it is needed to pay operating expenses during the winter months. The company's board of directors has a policy that restricts how Daniel can invest the cash. Daniel is limited to buying the stock of companies listed in the S&P 500. The S&P 500 is a collection of large American companies. He constantly monitors the market prices of stocks in the portfolio to evaluate his investment decisions.

The company maintains investment accounts with five local financial advisors. Each financial advisor is affiliated with a national investment firm. Daniel likes having access to the variety of investment research that each advisor's firm offers. Spreading the investments around is also good business. Each of the financial advisors has a boat docked at one of the marinas.

Unfortunately, using five financial advisors means that Daniel receives five investment reports. He needs one place where he can monitor the value of the entire stock portfolio.

OPEN THE SPREADSHEET TLA_CH16

Complete the worksheet to determine the current value of the investments. Answer the following questions:

1. Identify the stocks having the highest positive percentage change, as denoted by the green arrow in the % Change column.

2. Which stock has the highest total value?

3. What ratio using two items of information from the schedule could provide Daniel with useful information about the performance of each stock?

The Demise of Arthur Andersen

For nearly a century, the name Arthur Andersen stood for quality accounting services. Arthur Andersen's clients included many of the world's best-known companies: FedEx, Merck, Sara Lee, Walgreens, and Delta Air Lines. One of the "Big Five" accounting firms, Arthur Andersen employed over 85,000 employees worldwide. The number of staff and clients attending classes at its suburban Chicago training center made the firm the largest corporate user of O'Hare Airport.

In a stunning turn of events in 2002, the Big Five became the "Big Four." In 2001, energy company Enron announced that its financial statements were inflated by a massive accounting fraud. Of course, Enron's stockholders wanted to know why its auditor, Arthur Andersen, failed to detect the fraud. The investigations and lawsuits that followed delved into the actions of both Enron executives and Arthur Andersen employees.

Arthur Andersen was no stranger to lawsuits. Investors often sue auditors when a corporation fails or announces an accounting fraud. But the Enron failure was different. Investigators learned that Arthur Andersen employees had shredded documents related to the firm's Enron audit. Arthur Andersen was convicted of obstruction of justice. Due to the conviction, the firm was banned from auditing any financial statements submitted to the Securities and Exchange Commission. The loss of its publicly traded corporate clients effectively killed the firm.

At the time, the Enron bankruptcy was the largest in U.S. history. Enron would only hold that dubious honor for a month. Telecommunications giant WorldCom, another Arthur Andersen client, filed for bankruptcy in July 2002.

Enron and WorldCom share a common story. Each company was heralded for its innovative, dynamic business model. Each company's financial statements reported increasing earnings. In reality, those financial statements were hiding the fact that earnings were declining. Each accounting fraud was a failed attempt by executives to protect their reputations and maintain inflated stock prices. In each case, Arthur Andersen failed to detect the frauds.

ACTIVITY
Cress Valley Electronics, with one store located in Nashville, has submitted its financial statements to your bank. Its owner, Donald Morris, is seeking a loan to expand his business.

INSTRUCTIONS
Open the spreadsheet FA_CH16 and complete the steps on the Instructions tab.

End of Lesson Review

LO1 Prepare an income statement for a merchandising business organized as a corporation.

Terms Review

operating revenue

net sales

cost of merchandise sold

gross profit

operating expenses

income from operations

Audit your understanding

1. What is the major difference between the income statements for merchandising businesses and service businesses?

2. How is the cost of merchandise sold calculated?

3. Why is interest income presented in a section other than Operating Revenue?

Work together 16-1

Preparing an income statement for a merchandising business

The adjusted trial balance for Superior Corporation for the year ended December 31 of the current year is given in the *Working Papers*. The beginning merchandise inventory amount is $86,789.15. Your instructor will guide you through the following examples.

1. Prepare an income statement.

2. Prepare a vertical analysis of each amount in the fourth amount column. Round calculations to the nearest 0.1%. Save your work to complete Work Together 16-2.

On your own 16-1

Preparing an income statement for a merchandising business

Eastern Imports' adjusted trial balance for the year ended December 31 of the current year is given in the *Working Papers*. The beginning merchandise inventory amount is $128,110.24. Work this problem independently.

1. Prepare an income statement.

2. Prepare a vertical analysis of each amount in the fourth amount column. Round calculations to the nearest 0.1%. Save your work to complete On Your Own 16-2.

Preparing an Income Statement **Lesson 16-1** **481**

16-2 Preparing a Statement of Stockholders' Equity

LO2 Prepare a statement of stockholders' equity.

Stockholders' Equity Information LO2

ThreeGreen Products, Inc. Income Statement For Year Ended December 31, 20--		
Net Income before Federal Income Tax		103 5 1 8 97
Less Federal Income Tax Expense		23 6 2 2 40
Net Income after Federal Income Tax		79 8 9 6 57

ACCOUNT *Capital Stock* **ACCOUNT NO.** *3110*

DATE	ITEM	POST. REF.	DEBIT	CREDIT	BALANCE DEBIT	BALANCE CREDIT
20-- Jan. 1	Balance	✔				70 0 0 0 00
May 14		CR5		5 0 0 0 00		75 0 0 0 00

ThreeGreen Products, Inc. Adjusted Trial Balance December 31, 20--		
ACCOUNT TITLE	DEBIT	CREDIT
Capital Stock		75 0 0 0 00
Retained Earnings		65 2 1 8 84
Dividends	15 0 0 0 00	

A financial statement that shows changes in a corporation's ownership for a fiscal period is called a **statement of stockholders' equity**. The information to prepare a statement of stockholders' equity is obtained from several sources. The current year's income statement summarizes the change in retained earnings from the operation of the business. The general ledger provides the beginning balance and activity in the **Capital Stock** account. The current year's adjusted trial balance provides the current balances of other capital accounts.

Capital Stock Section of the Statement of Stockholders' Equity

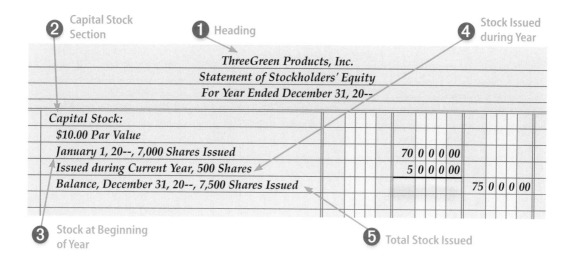

② Capital Stock Section   **①** Heading   **④** Stock Issued during Year

ThreeGreen Products, Inc.
Statement of Stockholders' Equity
For Year Ended December 31, 20--

Capital Stock:
$10.00 Par Value
January 1, 20--, 7,000 Shares Issued   70 0 0 0 00
Issued during Current Year, 500 Shares   5 0 0 0 00
Balance, December 31, 20--, 7,500 Shares Issued   75 0 0 0 00

③ Stock at Beginning of Year   **⑤** Total Stock Issued

A statement of stockholders' equity contains two major sections: (1) Capital Stock and (2) Retained Earnings. The amount of capital stock issued as of the beginning of the year is the beginning balance of the **Capital Stock** general ledger account. Any additional stock transactions during the fiscal year are recorded in the same account. Thus, the amounts in the Capital Stock section of the statement of stockholders' equity are obtained from **Capital Stock**.

Each share of stock issued by a corporation has a monetary value. A value assigned to a share of stock and printed on the stock certificate is called **par value**. When issuing shares of stock, a corporation can assign any par value allowed by laws in the state in which it incorporates.

◈ Preparing the Capital Stock Section of a Statement of Stockholders' Equity

① Write the heading: company name, ThreeGreen Products, Inc.; statement name, Statement of Stockholders' Equity; and fiscal period, For Year Ended December 31, 20--.

② Write the heading, Capital Stock:. On the next line, write the par value of the stock, $10.00 Par Value, indented about one centimeter.

③ On the next line, write January 1, 20--, the number of shares, 7,000, and Shares Issued. In the second amount column enter $70,000.00, the dollar amount of stock issued as of the beginning of the year.

④ On the next line, write Issued during Current Year, 500 Shares, the number of shares issued. In the second amount column, write the dollar amount of stock issued during the year, $5,000.00.

⑤ On the next line, write Balance, December 31, 20--, 7,500 Shares Issued, the current amount of shares outstanding. Calculate the total dollar amount of stock issued as of the end of the year by adding the dollar amount of beginning stock, $70,000.00, and the dollar amount of shares issued during the year, $5,000.00. Write the total amount, $75,000.00, in the third amount column.

Retained Earnings Section of the Statement of Stockholders' Equity

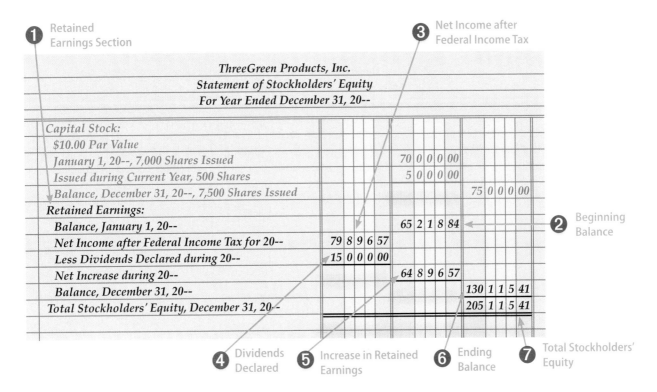

1 Retained Earnings Section

3 Net Income after Federal Income Tax

ThreeGreen Products, Inc.
Statement of Stockholders' Equity
For Year Ended December 31, 20--

Capital Stock:			
$10.00 Par Value			
January 1, 20--, 7,000 Shares Issued		70 0 0 0 00	
Issued during Current Year, 500 Shares		5 0 0 0 00	
Balance, December 31, 20--, 7,500 Shares Issued			75 0 0 0 00
Retained Earnings:			
Balance, January 1, 20--		65 2 1 8 84	
Net Income after Federal Income Tax for 20--	79 8 9 6 57		
Less Dividends Declared during 20--	15 0 0 0 00		
Net Increase during 20--		64 8 9 6 57	
Balance, December 31, 20--			130 1 1 5 41
Total Stockholders' Equity, December 31, 20--			205 1 1 5 41

2 Beginning Balance

4 Dividends Declared

5 Increase in Retained Earnings

6 Ending Balance

7 Total Stockholders' Equity

Net income increases a corporation's total capital. Some income may be retained by a corporation for business expansion. Some income may be distributed as dividends to provide stockholders with a return on their investments. During the year, ThreeGreen's board of directors declared $15,000.00 in dividends.

The Retained Earnings section of the Statement of Stockholders' Equity is prepared using amounts on the adjusted trial balance and the income statement. The beginning balance of **Retained Earnings** and the amount of dividends declared are obtained from the adjusted trial balance. The net income after federal income taxes is obtained from the income statement.

It is not uncommon for a business to have a net loss during its early years of existence. The losses would result in a debit balance in Retained Earnings. This amount would be reported as an accumulated deficit on the statement of retained earnings.

> **Preparing the Retained Earnings Section of a Statement of Stockholders' Equity**

1 Write the heading, Retained Earnings:.

2 Write the beginning balance of Retained Earnings, $65,218.84, from the adjusted trial balance, indented about one centimeter.

3 Write the net income after federal income tax, $79,896.57, from the income statement.

4 Write the amount of dividends, $15,000.00, from the adjusted trial balance.

5 Subtract dividends, $15,000.00, from net income after federal income tax, $79,896.57, to calculate the increase in retained earnings, $64,896.57. Write that amount in the second amount column.

6 Add the beginning balance of retained earnings, $65,218.84, and the increase in retained earnings, $64,896.57, to calculate the ending balance of retained earnings, $130,115.41. Write that amount in the third amount column.

7 Add the ending amounts of capital stock, $75,000.00, and retained earnings, $130,115.41, to calculate the total amount of stockholders' equity, $205,115.41. Write that amount in the third amount column.

End of Lesson Review

LO2 Prepare a statement of stockholders' equity.

Terms Review

statement of stockholders' equity

par value

Audit your understanding

1. What financial information does a statement of stockholders' equity report?

2. What are the two major sections of a statement of stockholders' equity?

3. Where is the information found to prepare the Capital Stock section of a statement of stockholders' equity?

4. Where is the beginning balance of retained earnings found?

5. When issuing shares of stock, what par value can a corporation assign to each share?

6. Where is net income after federal income taxes found?

Work together 16-2

Preparing a statement of stockholders' equity

Use the trial balance and income statement for Superior Corporation from Work Together 16-1. A form for the statement of stockholders' equity is given in the *Working Papers*. Your instructor will guide you through the following example.

Prepare a statement of stockholders' equity for the current year. As of January 1, Superior Corporation had issued 8,000 shares of capital stock with a par value of $10.00 per share. During the fiscal year, the corporation issued 250 additional shares of capital stock. Save your work to complete Work Together 16-3.

On your own 16-2

Preparing a statement of stockholders' equity

Use the trial balance and income statement for Eastern Imports from On Your Own 16-1. A form for the statement of stockholders' equity is given in the *Working Papers*. Work this problem independently.

Prepare a statement of stockholders' equity for the current year. As of January 1, Eastern Imports had issued 124,000 shares of capital stock with a par value of $1.00 per share. During the fiscal year, the corporation issued 12,000 additional shares of stock. Save your work to complete On Your Own 16-3.

LESSON

16-3 Preparing a Balance Sheet

LO3 Prepare a balance sheet for a business organized as a corporation.

Balance Sheet Information on a Trial Balance LO3

ThreeGreen Products, Inc. Adjusted Trial Balance December 31, 20--		
ACCOUNT TITLE	DEBIT	CREDIT
Cash	54 1 9 4 34	
Petty Cash	2 5 0 0 00	
Accounts Receivable	20 3 8 1 81	
Allowance for Uncollectible Accounts		2 5 0 9 25
Merchandise Inventory	102 8 3 8 00	
Supplies—Office	6 1 0 00	
Supplies—Store	4 6 5 00	
Prepaid Insurance	2 8 0 0 00	
Notes Receivable	6 2 0 0 00	
Interest Receivable	9 3 00	
Office Equipment	24 8 9 5 18	
Accumulated Depreciation—Office Equipment		13 6 7 4 00
Store Equipment	59 1 4 8 11	
Accumulated Depreciation—Store Equipment		18 3 2 5 00
Accounts Payable		16 4 8 9 10
Sales Tax Payable		3 5 7 4 64
Employee Income Tax Payable		9 5 0 00
Social Security Tax Payable		2 0 2 3 06
Medicare Tax Payable		4 7 3 14
Health Insurance Premiums Payable		4 6 0 00
Retirement Benefits Payable		4 6 5 00
Unemployment Tax Payable—Federal		2 9 7 02
Unemployment Tax Payable—State		1 4 7 42
Federal Income Tax Payable		3 6 2 2 40
Dividends Payable		3 7 5 0 00

A corporation's balance sheet reports assets, liabilities, and stockholders' equity on a specific date. [CONCEPT: Accounting Period Cycle] Some management decisions can best be made after owners have analyzed the balance sheet. For example, balance sheet information would help management to decide whether the corporation should incur additional liabilities to acquire additional plant assets.

The information used to prepare a balance sheet is obtained from two sources: (1) the trial balance and (2) the statement of stockholders' equity.

Current Assets Section of a Balance Sheet

Current Assets Section ②   ① Heading   Book Value of Accounts Receivable ③

ThreeGreen Products, Inc.								
Balance Sheet								
December 31, 20--								
Assets								
Current Assets:								
Cash				54 1 9 4 34				
Petty Cash				2 5 0 00				
Accounts Receivable	20 3 8 1 81							
Less Allowance for Uncollectible Accounts	2 5 0 9 25		17 8 7 2 56					
Merchandise Inventory			102 8 3 8 00					
Supplies—Office			6 1 0 00					
Supplies—Store			4 6 5 00					
Prepaid Insurance			2 8 0 0 00					
Notes Receivable			6 2 0 0 00					
Interest Receivable			9 3 00					
Total Current Assets					185 3 2 2 90			

④ Remaining Current Asset Accounts   ⑤ Total Current Assets

ThreeGreen classifies its assets as current assets and plant assets. A business owning both current and plant assets usually lists them under separate headings on a balance sheet. Some of ThreeGreen's asset accounts have related contra accounts that reduce the related account on the balance sheet. The difference between an asset's account balance and its related contra account balance is known as book value. An asset's book value is reported on a balance sheet by listing three amounts: (1) the balance of the asset account, (2) the balance of the asset's contra account, and (3) the book value.

↻ Preparing the Current Assets Section of a Balance Sheet

① Write the balance sheet heading on three lines.

② Begin preparing the Assets section of the balance sheet. Use information from the adjusted trial balance.

   a. Write the section title, Assets, on the first line in the middle of the wide column.

   b. Write the section title, Current Assets:, on the next line at the extreme left of the wide column.

   c. Beginning on the next line, indented about one centimeter, write Cash and Petty Cash in the order in which they appear on the adjusted trial balance.

   d. Write the balance of each asset account in the second column.

③ Calculate the book value of accounts receivable.

   a. Write Accounts Receivable on the next line, indented about one centimeter.

   b. Write the total amount of accounts receivable, $20,381.81, in the first amount column.

   c. Write Less Allowance for Uncollectible Accounts on the next line, indented about two centimeters.

   d. Write the amount of the allowance for uncollectible accounts, $2,509.25, in the first amount column.

   e. Subtract the allowance for uncollectible accounts, $2,509.25, from the total amount of accounts receivable, $20,381.81, to calculate the book value of accounts receivable, $17,872.56. Write that amount in the second amount column on the same line.

④ Write the remaining current asset account titles and amounts.

⑤ Calculate total current assets.

   a. Write Total Current Assets on the next line, indented about one centimeter.

   b. Add the amounts in the second amount column and write the total, $185,322.90, in the third amount column.

Plant Assets Section of a Balance Sheet

② Book Value of Office Equipment

ThreeGreen Products, Inc.
Balance Sheet
December 31, 20--

Total Current Assets			185 3 2 2 90
Plant Assets:			
Office Equipment	24 8 9 5 18		
Less Accumulated Depreciation—Office Equipment	13 6 7 4 00	11 2 2 1 18	
Store Equipment	59 1 4 8 11		
Less Accumulated Depreciation—Store Equipment	18 3 2 5 00	40 8 2 3 11	
Total Plant Assets			52 0 4 4 29
Total Assets			237 3 6 7 19

① Plant Assets Section

③ Book Value of Store Equipment   **④ Total Plant Assets**   **⑤ Total Assets**

⊗ Preparing the Plant Assets Section of a Balance Sheet

① Write the heading, Plant Assets:, on the next line at the extreme left of the wide column.

② Calculate the book value of office equipment using information from the adjusted trial balance.

a. Write Office Equipment on the next line, indented about one centimeter.

b. Write the total amount of office equipment, $24,895.18, in the first amount column.

c. Write Less Accumulated Depreciation—Office Equipment on the next line, indented about two centimeters.

d. Write the amount of the accumulated depreciation—office equipment, $13,674.00, in the first amount column.

e. Subtract the accumulated depreciation—office equipment, $13,674.00, from the total amount of office equipment, $24,895.18, to calculate the book value of office equipment, $11,221.18. Write that amount in the second amount column on the same line.

③ Use the same procedure to calculate the book value of store equipment.

④ Calculate total plant assets.

a. Write Total Plant Assets on the next line, indented about one centimeter.

b. Add the amounts in the second amount column and write the total, $52,044.29, in the third amount column.

⑤ Calculate total assets.

a. Write Total Assets on the next line at the extreme left of the wide column.

b. Add the totals of current assets, $185,322.90, and plant assets, $52,044.29, and write the amount, $237,367.19, on the same line in the third amount column.

Liabilities Section of a Balance Sheet

ThreeGreen Products, Inc.																		
Balance Sheet																		
December 31, 20--																		

Total Assets											237	3	6	7	19
Liabilities															
Current Liabilities:															
Accounts Payable				16	4	8	9	10							
Sales Tax Payable				3	5	7	4	64							
Employee Income Tax Payable—Federal					9	5	0	00							
Social Security Tax Payable				2	0	2	3	06							
Medicare Tax Payable					4	7	3	14							
Health Insurance Premiums Payable					4	6	0	00							
Retirement Benefits Payable					4	6	5	00							
Unemployment Tax Payable—Federal					2	9	7	02							
Unemployment Tax Payable—State					1	4	7	42							
Federal Income Tax Payable				3	6	2	2	40							
Dividends Payable				3	7	5	0	00							
Total Liabilities									32	2	5	1	78		

① Liabilities Section

② Account Title and Amount of Each Current Liability

③ Total Liabilities

Liabilities are classified according to the length of time until they are due. Liabilities due within a short time, usually within a year, are called **current liabilities**. Liabilities owed for more than a year are called **long-term liabilities**. One example of a long-term liability would be a mortgage loan. On December 31 of the current year, ThreeGreen does not have any long-term liabilities.

To prepare the Liabilities section of the balance sheet, use information from the adjusted trial balance.

A company having both current liabilities and long-term liabilities would include headings and totals for each category. The process is similar to preparing the Assets section of a balance sheet.

Preparing the Liabilities Section of a Balance Sheet

① Write the section title, Liabilities, on the next line in the middle of the wide column.

② Write the title, Current Liabilities:, on the next line at the extreme left of the wide column.

   a. Beginning on the next line, indented about one centimeter, write the liability account titles in the order in which they appear on the adjusted trial balance.

   b. Write the balance of each liability account in the second amount column.

③ Calculate total liabilities.

   a. Write Total Liabilities on the next line below the last liability account title at the extreme left of the wide column.

   b. Write the amount of the total liabilities, $32,251.78, on the same line in the third amount column.

Stockholders' Equity Section of a Balance Sheet

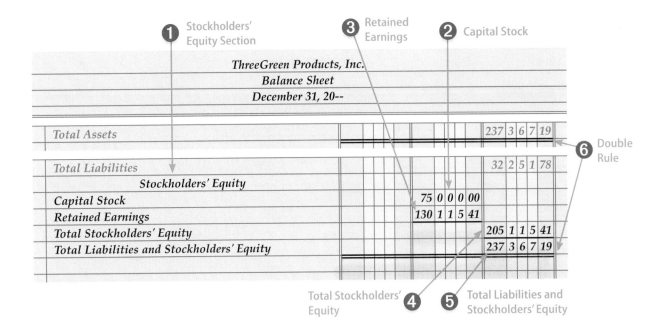

A major difference between the balance sheets of a corporation and a proprietorship is the Owners' Equity section. The Owners' Equity section of ThreeGreen's balance sheet is labeled Stockholders' Equity. Some corporations use the same label, Owners' Equity, as proprietorships. Either label is acceptable.

The Stockholders' Equity section contains the total amounts of capital stock and retained earnings. These amounts are calculated and reported on the statement of stockholders' equity.

ThreeGreen's completed balance sheet is shown on the following page.

Preparing the Stockholders' Equity Section of a Balance Sheet

1 Write the heading, Stockholders' Equity, on the next line, centered in the wide column.

2 Write Capital Stock on the next line. Write the amount of capital stock, $75,000.00, calculated on the statement of stockholders' equity, in the second amount column.

3 Write Retained Earnings on the next line. Write the amount of retained earnings, $130,115.41, calculated on the statement of stockholders' equity, in the second amount column.

4 Add the amount of capital stock, $75,000.00, and retained earnings, $130,115.41, to calculate the total of stockholders' equity, $205,115.41. Enter that amount in the third amount column.

5 Add the amount of total liabilities, $32,251.78, and total stockholders' equity, $205,115.41, to calculate the total of liabilities and stockholders' equity, $237,367.19. Enter that amount in the third amount column. Verify the accuracy by comparing the total amount of assets and the total amount of liabilities and stockholders' equity. These two amounts must be the same.

6 Draw double rules across the three columns at the end of the Assets section and the Stockholders' Equity section to show that assets equal liabilities plus owners' equity.

Completed Balance Sheet

ThreeGreen Products, Inc.
Balance Sheet
December 31, 20--

Assets					
Current Assets:					
Cash			54 1 9 4 34		
Petty Cash			2 5 0 00		
Accounts Receivable	20 3 8 1 81				
Less Allowance for Uncollectible Accounts	2 5 0 9 25		17 8 7 2 56		
Merchandise Inventory			102 8 3 8 00		
Supplies—Office			6 1 0 00		
Supplies—Store			4 6 5 00		
Prepaid Insurance			2 8 0 0 00		
Notes Receivable			6 2 0 0 00		
Interest Receivable			9 3 00		
Total Current Assets				185 3 2 2 90	
Plant Assets:					
Office Equipment	24 8 9 5 18				
Less Accumulated Depreciation—Office Equipment	13 6 7 4 00		11 2 2 1 18		
Store Equipment	59 1 4 8 11				
Less Accumulated Depreciation—Store Equipment	18 3 2 5 00		40 8 2 3 11		
Total Plant Assets				52 0 4 4 29	
Total Assets				237 3 6 7 19	
Liabilities					
Current Liabilities:					
Accounts Payable			16 4 8 9 10		
Sales Tax Payable			3 5 7 4 64		
Employee Income Tax Payable			9 5 0 00		
Social Security Tax Payable			2 0 2 3 06		
Medicare Tax Payable			4 7 3 14		
Health Insurance Premiums Payable			4 6 0 00		
Retirement Benefits Payable			4 6 5 00		
Unemployment Tax Payable—Federal			2 9 7 02		
Unemployment Tax Payable—State			1 4 7 42		
Federal Income Tax Payable			3 6 2 2 40		
Dividends Payable			3 7 5 0 00		
Total Liabilities				32 2 5 1 78	
Stockholders' Equity					
Capital Stock			75 0 0 0 00		
Retained Earnings			130 1 1 5 41		
Total Stockholders' Equity				205 1 1 5 41	
Total Liabilities and Stockholders' Equity				237 3 6 7 19	

Total assets must equal the total of liabilities and stockholders' equity. If these totals are not equal, identify the errors before preparing adjusting and closing entries.

Supporting Schedules for a Balance Sheet

A report prepared to give details about an item on a principal financial statement is called a **supporting schedule**. A supporting schedule is sometimes referred to as a *supplementary report* or an *exhibit*.

ThreeGreen prepares two supporting schedules to accompany the balance sheet. The supporting schedules are a schedule of accounts payable and a schedule of accounts receivable. A balance sheet shows only the accounts payable total amount. The account balance for each vendor is not shown. When detailed information is needed, a supporting schedule of accounts payable is prepared, showing the balance for each vendor. A balance sheet also shows only the accounts receivable total amount. When information about the account balance for each customer is needed, a supporting schedule of accounts receivable is prepared. ThreeGreen's supporting schedules on December 31 are similar to the supporting schedules for November 30 shown in Chapters 9 and 10.

IMAGERYMAJESTIC/SHUTTERSTOCK.COM

End of Lesson Review

LO3 Prepare a balance sheet for a business organized as a corporation.

Terms Review

current liabilities

long-term liabilities

supporting schedule

Audit your understanding

1. How does ThreeGreen classify its assets?

2. What three items are listed on the balance sheet for an account having a related contra asset account?

3. What is an example of a long-term liability?

4. Where are the amounts obtained for the Stockholders' Equity section of the balance sheet?

5. What are two supporting schedules that might accompany a balance sheet?

Work together 16-3

Preparing a balance sheet for a corporation

Use Superior Corporation's trial balance and statement of stockholders' equity from Work Together 16-2. A form for the balance sheet is given in the *Working Papers*. Your instructor will guide you through the following example.

Prepare a balance sheet for the current year. Save your work to complete Work Together 16-4.

On your own 16-3

Preparing a balance sheet for a corporation

Use Eastern Imports' trial balance and statement of stockholders' equity from On Your Own 16-2. A form for the balance sheet is given in the *Working Papers*. Work this problem independently.

Prepare a balance sheet for the current year. Save your work to complete On Your Own 16-4.

16-4 Recording Closing Entries for Income Statement Accounts

LO4 Prepare closing entries.

Closing Entries LO4

Closing entries for a corporation are made from information in the adjusted trial balance. Closing entries for revenue and expense accounts are similar to those for proprietorships. A corporation's closing entries to close net income and temporary equity accounts are also similar to those for a proprietorship. However, these closing entries affect different accounts. A corporation records four closing entries:

1. A closing entry for income statement accounts with credit balances (revenue and contra-cost accounts).

2. A closing entry for income statement accounts with debit balances (cost, contra revenue, and expense accounts).

3. A closing entry to record net income or net loss in the **Retained Earnings** account and close the **Income Summary** account.

4. A closing entry for the **Dividends** account.

The Income Summary Account

At the end of a fiscal period, the temporary accounts are closed to prepare the general ledger for the next fiscal period. [CONCEPT: Matching Expenses with Revenue] To close a temporary account, an amount equal to its balance is recorded on the side opposite the balance. Amounts needed for the closing entries are obtained from the adjusted trial balance and from the statement of stockholders' equity. Closing entries are recorded in the general journal.

Chapter 8 discusses the difference between permanent accounts and temporary accounts. Permanent accounts, also referred to as *real accounts*, include the asset and liability accounts as well as the owners' capital accounts. The ending account balances of permanent accounts for one fiscal period are the beginning account balances for the next fiscal period. Temporary accounts, also referred to as *nominal accounts*, include the revenue, cost, expense, and dividend accounts.

Another temporary account is used to summarize the closing entries for revenue, cost, and expenses. The account is titled **Income Summary** because it is used to summarize information about net income. **Income Summary** is used only at the end of a fiscal period to help prepare other accounts for a new fiscal period.

The **Income Summary** account is unique because it does not have a normal balance side. The balance of this account is determined by the amounts posted to the account at the end of a fiscal period. When revenue is greater than total expenses, resulting in a net income, the **Income Summary** account has a credit balance, as shown in the T account.

Income Summary	
Debit	Credit
Expenses	Revenue (greater than expenses)
	(Credit balance is the net income.)

remember A corporation is not required to pay a dividend to its shareholders. Thus, some corporations only prepare three closing entries.

Closing Entry for Accounts with Credit Balances

ThreeGreen Products, Inc.
Adjusted Trial Balance
December 31, 20--

ACCOUNT TITLE	DEBIT	CREDIT
Sales		632 371 75
Sales Discount	1 648 19	
Sales Returns and Allowances	3 941 57	
Purchases	254 851 26	
Purchases Discount		9 2 2 14
Purchases Returns and Allowances		1 495 01
Interest Income		5 5 7 00
Totals	842 324 77	842 324 77

❸ ❷ Date ❶ Heading   Debit to Close ❸

GENERAL JOURNAL   PAGE 16

	DATE	ACCOUNT TITLE	DOC. NO.	POST. REF.	DEBIT	CREDIT	
1		*Closing Entries*					1
2	Dec. 31	Sales			632 371 75		2
3		Purchases Discount			9 2 2 14		3
4		Purchases Returns and Allowances			1 495 01		4
5		Interest Income			5 5 7 00		5
6		Income Summary				635 345 90	6
7							7

❹ Credit to Income Summary

ThreeGreen's adjusted trial balance has four income statement accounts with credit balances. One account, Sales, is a revenue account. Two accounts, Purchases Discount and Purchases Returns and Allowances, are contra cost accounts. The fourth account is an Other Revenue account. Each account has a normal credit balance that must be reduced to zero to prepare the account for the next fiscal period. [CONCEPT: Matching Expenses with Revenue]

To reduce each balance to zero, each account is debited for the amount of the balance. The impact of the closing entry on Sales is shown in the T account.

Income Summary is credited for $635,345.90, the total of the four debits in this closing entry.

Sales			
Closing	632,371.75	Bal.	632,371.75
		(New Bal.	0.00)

Income Summary			
Adj. (mdse. inv.)	5,648.44	Closing	635,345.90
		(credit accounts)	

The balance in Income Summary will be adjusted by other closing entries.

Closing Income Statement Accounts with Credit Balances

❶ Write the heading, Closing Entries, in the middle of the general journal's Account Title column on a new page. This heading explains all of the closing entries that follow. Therefore, indicating a source document is unnecessary. The first closing entry is recorded on the first four lines below the heading.

❷ Write the date, Dec. 31, 20--, in the Date column.

❸ Write the account title of each revenue and contra cost account in the Account Title column. Write the balance of each revenue and contra cost account in the Debit column.

❹ Write the title of the account credited, Income Summary, in the Account Title column, indented about one centimeter. Write the amount, $635,345.90, in the Credit column.

Closing Entry for Income Statement Accounts with Debit Balances

	Debit	Credit
Income Summary	5 6 4 8 44	
Sales		632 3 7 1 75
Sales Discount	1 6 4 8 19	
Sales Returns and Allowances	3 9 4 1 57	
Purchases	254 8 5 1 26	
Purchases Discount		9 2 2 14
Purchases Returns and Allowances		1 4 9 5 01
Advertising Expense	4 6 8 0 00	
Credit Card Fee Expense	6 8 4 2 20	
Utilities Expense	4 9 6 5 42	
Federal Income Tax Expense	23 6 2 2 40	

③ Date ⟶ **①** **②** Income Summary **④** Debit to Income Summary **③** Credit to Close

GENERAL JOURNAL

PAGE **16**

	DATE	ACCOUNT TITLE	DOC. NO.	POST. REF.	DEBIT	CREDIT	
7	31	Income Summary			549 8 0 0 89		7
8		Sales Discount				1 6 4 8 19	8
9		Sales Returns and Allowances				3 9 4 1 57	9
10		Purchases				254 8 5 1 26	10
11		Advertising Expense				4 6 8 0 00	11
12		Credit Card Fee Expense				6 8 4 2 20	12
13		Depreciation Expense—Office Equipment				7 4 8 5 00	13
14		Depreciation Expense—Store Equipment				9 8 3 0 00	14
15		Insurance Expense				8 2 0 0 00	15
16		Miscellaneous Expense				3 4 9 5 04	16
17		Payroll Taxes Expense				16 6 9 7 98	17
18		Rent Expense				8 4 0 0 00	18
19		Salary Expense				184 2 3 4 95	19
20		Supplies Expense—Office				3 9 3 8 17	20
21		Supplies Expense—Store				4 5 8 4 61	21
22		Uncollectible Accounts Expense				2 3 8 4 10	22
23		Utilities Expense				4 9 6 5 42	23
24		Federal Income Tax Expense				23 6 2 2 40	24

ThreeGreen's adjusted trial balance has many income statement accounts with debit balances—contra revenue accounts, Purchases, and the expense accounts. These debit balances must be reduced to zero to prepare the accounts for the next fiscal period. [CONCEPT: Matching Expenses with Revenue] To reduce the balances to zero, the accounts are credited for the amount of their balances. Income Summary is debited for the total amount.

Closing Income Statement Accounts with Debit Balances

① Write the date, 31, in the Date column.

② Write the title of the account debited, Income Summary, in the Account Title column. The debit to Income Summary is not entered in the amount column until all contra revenue, cost, and expense balances have been journalized and the total amount calculated.

③ Write the account title of each contra revenue, cost, and expense account in the Account Title column, each indented about one centimeter. Write the balance of each account in the Credit column.

④ Add the credit amounts for this entry. Write the total of the credited accounts, $549,800.89, in the Debit column on the same line as the account title Income Summary.

Summary of Closing Entry for Income Statement Accounts with Debit Balances

The second closing entry reduces the balance of the contra revenue, Purchases, and expense accounts to a zero balance. The effect of the closing entry on Purchases is shown in the T account.

Purchases			
Bal.	254,851.26	Closing	254,851.26
(New Bal.	0.00)		

After recording this closing entry, Income Summary has three amounts:

1. A debit of $5,648.44, the amount of the merchandise inventory adjustment.
2. A credit of $635,345.90, the amount of the entry to close the revenue and contra cost accounts.

3. A debit of $549,800.89, the amount of the entry to close the contra revenue, cost, and expense accounts.

Income Summary			
Adj. (mdse. inv.)	5,648.44	Closing (credit	
Closing (debit		accounts)	635,345.90
accounts)	549,800.89	(New Bal.	79,896.57)

The credit balance of Income Summary, $79,896.57, is equal to the net income after federal income tax amount shown on the income statement. However, Income Summary is not closed as part of this closing entry. Instead, the account is closed with the third closing entry when net income is recorded.

Closing Entry to Record Net Income

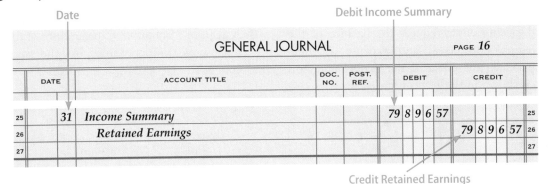

After closing entries for the income statement accounts are posted, Income Summary has a credit balance of $79,896.57. This credit balance equals the net income reported on the statement of stockholders' equity and income statement.

A corporation's net income should be recorded in the Retained Earnings account at the end of the fiscal year. After the closing entry is posted, Income Summary has a zero balance.

The new balance in Retained Earnings, $145,115.41, does not yet equal the amount reported on the statement of stockholders' equity. A fourth closing entry is required to adjust Retained Earnings to the correct amount.

Income Summary

Adj. (mdse. inv.)	5,648.44	Closing (credit	
Closing (debit		accounts)	635,345.90
accounts)	549,800.89		
Closing (Retained			
Earnings)	79,896.57	(New Bal.	0.00)

Retained Earnings

	Bal.	65,218.84
	Closing (Income	
	Summary)	79,896.57
	(New Bal.	145,115.41)

Closing Entry for Dividends

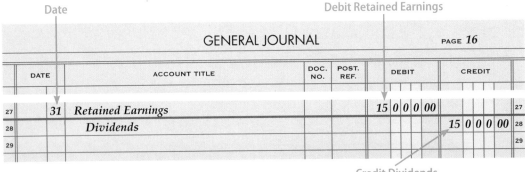

Because dividends decrease the earnings retained by a corporation, the Dividends account is closed to Retained Earnings. After the closing entry is posted, Dividends has a zero balance. The amount of the Dividends account, $15,000.00, has reduced the balance of Retained Earnings. The new balance in Retained Earnings, $130,115.41, now equals the amount reported on the statement of stockholders' equity. Therefore, the Retained Earnings account is up to date.

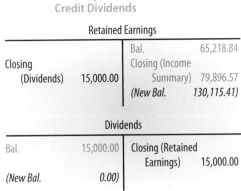

Retained Earnings

		Bal.	65,218.84
Closing		Closing (Income	
(Dividends)	15,000.00	Summary)	79,896.57
		(New Bal.	130,115.41)

Dividends

Bal.	15,000.00	Closing (Retained	
		Earnings)	15,000.00
(New Bal.	0.00)		

Completed Closing Entries for a Corporation Recorded in a Journal

GENERAL JOURNAL

	DATE		ACCOUNT TITLE	DOC. NO.	POST. REF.	DEBIT	CREDIT	
1			*Closing Entries*					1
2	Dec. 20--	31	Sales			632 3 7 1 75		2
3			Purchases Discount			9 2 2 14		3
4			Purchases Returns and Allowances			1 4 9 5 01		4
5			Interest Income			5 5 7 00		5
6			Income Summary				635 3 4 5 90	6
7		31	Income Summary			549 8 0 0 89		7
8			Sales Discount				1 6 4 8 19	8
9			Sales Returns and Allowances				3 9 4 1 57	9
10			Purchases				254 8 5 1 26	10
11			Advertising Expense				4 6 8 0 00	11
12			Credit Card Fee Expense				6 8 4 2 20	12
13			Depreciation Expense—Office Equipment				7 4 8 5 00	13
14			Depreciation Expense—Store Equipment				9 8 3 0 00	14
15			Insurance Expense				8 2 0 0 00	15
16			Miscellaneous Expense				3 4 9 5 04	16
17			Payroll Taxes Expense				16 6 9 7 98	17
18			Rent Expense				8 4 0 0 00	18
19			Salary Expense				184 2 3 4 95	19
20			Supplies Expense—Office				3 9 3 8 17	20
21			Supplies Expense—Store				4 5 8 4 61	21
22			Uncollectible Accounts Expense				2 3 8 4 10	22
23			Utilities Expense				4 9 6 5 42	23
24			Federal Income Tax Expense				23 6 2 2 40	24
25		31	Income Summary			79 8 9 6 57		25
26			Retained Earnings				79 8 9 6 57	26
27		31	Retained Earnings			15 0 0 0 00		27
28			Dividends				15 0 0 0 00	28
29								29

After all closing entries have been recorded, ThreeGreen's general journal appears as shown above. The next step is to post these closing entries to the general ledger.

It is not uncommon for a business to have hundreds, even thousands, of accounts. Preparing a closing entry by entering each account balance would be a monumental task subject to human error. Computerized accounting systems provide a single command that prepares and posts the entries.

Major Changes in China's Accounting Standards

When the People's Republic of China (PRC) was formed in 1949, all the businesses in China came under state ownership. This meant that companies were owned and controlled by the government. All accounting standards were determined by the government. The accounting system and financial statements focused on accounting for state-owned assets. There was no measure of profit or loss and no accounting for the debts of an organization.

Since 1979, new laws have been passed that allow foreign investors to invest in Chinese businesses. As a result of demands by these foreign investors, Chinese accounting standards began to change. The standards moved Chinese accounting away from just measuring and recording assets to a focus on profit and loss.

These new standards paved the way for a major change to occur in Chinese accounting standards in 2006. The Ministry of Finance announced new rules called Accounting Standards for Business Enterprises (or ASBEs). With only a few exceptions, the ASBEs follow the International Financial Reporting Standards (IFRS).

This move to ASBEs has resulted in great savings for Chinese corporations. At one point in time, a Chinese company that sold shares of stock in the United States had to prepare three sets of financial statements—one following the original standards established by the PRC, one following IFRS, and one following U.S. GAAP. Since 2008, the U.S. Securities and Exchange Commission (SEC) has allowed foreign companies selling shares of stock in the United States to submit financial statements prepared following IFRS. Today, Chinese businesses selling shares of stock in the United States only have to prepare one set of financial statements, using the new ASBEs.

CRITICAL THINKING

1. Use the Internet to research China's ASBEs and IFRS. (IFRS were discussed in the Global Awareness feature in Chapter 10.)
2. List one area in which the ASBEs differ from IFRS.

Sources: www.chinaorbit.com and www.law.upenn.edu.

©FONTMONSTER, ISTOCK

TESTING/SHUTTERSTOCK.COM

LO4 Prepare closing entries.

Audit your understanding

1. Where is the information obtained to journalize closing entries for revenue, cost, and expenses?
2. What is the name of the temporary account used to summarize the closing entries for revenue, cost, and expenses?

Work together 16-4

Journalizing closing entries

Use Superior Corporation's trial balance and financial statements from Work Together 16-3. A general journal is given in the *Working Papers*. Your instructor will guide you through the following example.

Record the following closing entries on page 19 of the general journal.

a. Close the income statement accounts with credit balances.
b. Close the income statement accounts with debit balances.
c. Close the Income Summary account.
d. Close the Dividends account.

On your own 16-4

Journalizing closing entries

Use Eastern Imports' trial balance and financial statements from On Your Own 16-3. A general journal is given in the *Working Papers*. Work this problem independently.

Record the following closing entries on page 25 of the general journal.

a. Close the income statement accounts with credit balances.
b. Close the income statement accounts with debit balances.
c. Close the Income Summary account.
d. Close the Dividends account.

©CANDICE CUSACK, ISTOCK

LO5 Prepare a post-closing trial balance.

General Ledger After Closing Entries Are Posted

ACCOUNT Merchandise Inventory   **ACCOUNT NO.** 1140

DATE	ITEM	POST. REF.	DEBIT	CREDIT	BALANCE DEBIT	BALANCE CREDIT
Dec. 20-- 31	Balance	✔			108 486 44	
31		G15		5 648 44	102 838 00	

ACCOUNT Retained Earnings   **ACCOUNT NO.** 3130

DATE	ITEM	POST. REF.	DEBIT	CREDIT	BALANCE DEBIT	BALANCE CREDIT
Dec. 20-- 1	Balance	✔				65 218 84
31		G16		79 896 57		145 115 41
31		G16	15 000 00			130 115 41

ACCOUNT Dividends   **ACCOUNT NO.** 3140

DATE	ITEM	POST. REF.	DEBIT	CREDIT	BALANCE DEBIT	BALANCE CREDIT
Dec. 20-- 31	Balance	✔			15 000 00	
31		G16		15 000 00		

ACCOUNT Income Summary   **ACCOUNT NO.** 3150

DATE	ITEM	POST. REF.	DEBIT	CREDIT	BALANCE DEBIT	BALANCE CREDIT
Dec. 20-- 31		G15	5 648 44		5 648 44	
31		G16		635 345 90		629 697 46
31		G16	549 800 89			79 896 57
31		G16	79 896 57			

ACCOUNT Sales   **ACCOUNT NO.** 4110

DATE	ITEM	POST. REF.	DEBIT	CREDIT	BALANCE DEBIT	BALANCE CREDIT
Dec. 20-- 31	Balance	✔				632 371 75
31		G16	632 371 75			

Closing entries do not change asset and liability accounts such as **Merchandise Inventory**. Revenue, cost, and expense accounts, such as **Sales**, have zero balances.

Three closing entries affect **Income Summary**: the $635,345.90 credit closes the credit accounts; the $549,800.89 debit closes expense accounts; the $79,896.57 debit, ThreeGreen's net income after federal income tax, is closed to **Retained Earnings** leaving **Income Summary** with a zero balance. The $15,000.00 balance in **Dividends** is also closed to **Retained Earnings** leaving **Dividends** with a zero balance. The ledger is now ready for the next fiscal period.

Post-Closing Trial Balance LO5

① Heading

ThreeGreen Products, Inc.
Post-Closing Trial Balance
December 31, 20--

② Accounts with Balances

③ Account Balances

ACCOUNT TITLE	DEBIT	CREDIT
Cash	54 1 9 4 34	
Petty Cash	2 5 0 00	
Accounts Receivable	20 3 8 1 81	
Allowance for Uncollectible Accounts		2 5 0 9 25
Merchandise Inventory	102 8 3 8 00	
Supplies—Office	6 1 0 00	
Supplies—Store	4 6 5 00	
Prepaid Insurance	2 8 0 0 00	
Notes Receivable	6 2 0 0 00	
Interest Receivable	9 3 00	
Office Equipment	24 8 9 5 18	
Accumulated Depreciation—Office Equipment		13 6 7 4 00
Store Equipment	59 1 4 8 11	
Accumulated Depreciation—Store Equipment		18 3 2 5 00
Accounts Payable		16 4 8 9 10
Sales Tax Payable		3 5 7 4 64
Employee Income Tax Payable—Federal		9 5 0 00
Social Security Tax Payable		2 0 2 3 06
Medicare Tax Payable		4 7 3 14
Health Insurance Premiums Payable		4 6 0 00
Retirement Benefits Payable		4 6 5 00
Unemployment Tax Payable—Federal		2 9 7 02
Unemployment Tax Payable—State		1 4 7 42
Federal Income Tax Payable		3 6 2 2 40
Dividends Payable		3 7 5 0 00
Capital Stock		75 0 0 0 00
Retained Earnings		130 1 1 5 41
Totals	271 8 7 5 44	271 8 7 5 44

④ Totals **⑤ Column Totals** **⑥ Double Rule**

A post-closing trial balance is prepared to prove the equality of debits and credits in the general ledger. Account balances on the post-closing trial balance agree with the balances on the balance sheet shown on page 491.

Recording adjusting and closing entries can be a time-consuming process for large, multinational companies. After financial statements are prepared, an audit still must still be performed. More adjustments may result from the audit. For this reason, the SEC allows publicly-held companies up to three months to submit their financial statements.

❯ Preparing a Post-Closing Trial Balance

① Write the post-closing trial balance heading on three lines.

② List all general ledger accounts that have balances in the Account Title column.

③ Write the balance of each asset account in the Debit column. Write the balance of each contra asset, liability, and capital account in the Credit column.

④ Write the word Totals on the next line below the last account title.

⑤ Total the columns and write the totals, $271,875.44, on the Totals line.

⑥ Verify that the column totals equal. Rule double lines below both column totals.

Accounting Cycle for a Merchandising Business Organized as a Corporation

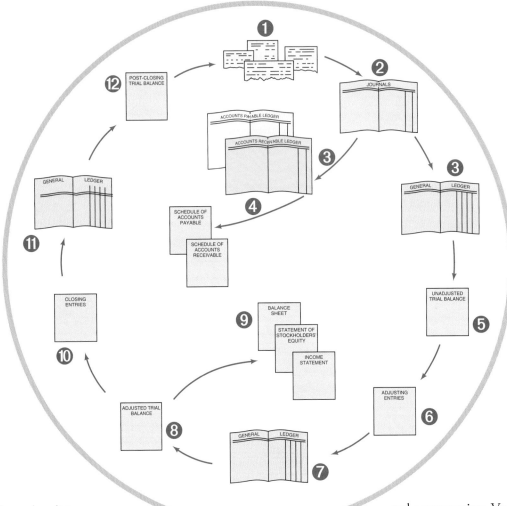

Service and merchandising businesses use a similar accounting cycle. The accounting cycles are also similar for a proprietorship and a corporation. Variations occur when subsidiary ledgers are used. Variations also occur in preparing financial statements.

↘ Using the Accounting Cycle for a Merchandising Business

1. Source documents are checked for accuracy, and transactions are analyzed into debit and credit parts.
2. Transactions, from information on source documents, are recorded in journals.
3. Journal entries are posted to the accounts payable ledger, the accounts receivable ledger, and the general ledger.
4. Schedules of accounts payable and accounts receivable are prepared from the subsidiary ledgers.
5. An unadjusted trial balance is prepared from the general ledger.
6. Adjusting entries are journalized.
7. Adjusting entries are posted to the general ledger.
8. An adjusted trial balance is prepared from the general ledger.
9. Financial statements are prepared from the adjusted trial balance.
10. Closing entries are journalized.
11. Closing entries are posted to the general ledger.
12. A post-closing trial balance is prepared from the general ledger.

End of Lesson Review

LO5 Prepare a post-closing trial balance.

Audit your understanding

1. Which accounts and balances are listed on a post-closing trial balance? In what order are they listed?

2. What is the purpose of preparing a post-closing trial balance?

3. What two steps in the accounting cycle occur after adjusting entries are posted to the general ledger?

Work together 16-5

Preparing a post-closing trial balance

Plumbing Central's December 31 account balances for the current year are shown below. The balances include the adjusting and closing entries. Your instructor will guide you through the following example.

Account	Balance
Cash	$ 12,810.20
Petty Cash	350.00
Accounts Receivable	18,398.80
Allowance for Uncollectible Accounts	1,200.00
Merchandise Inventory	140,980.00
Supplies—Store	2,268.00
Prepaid Insurance	1,980.00
Accounts Payable	11,676.50
Sales Tax Payable	1,584.00
Capital Stock	50,000.00
Retained Earnings	112,326.50

Prepare a post-closing trial balance on the form provided in the *Working Papers*.

On your own 16-5

Preparing a post-closing trial balance

Foreign Auto Supply's December 31 account balances for the current year are shown below. The balances include the adjusting and closing entries. Work this problem independently.

Account	Balance
Cash	$ 13,485.00
Merchandise Inventory	121,152.00
Supplies—Office	741.00
Notes Receivable	3,560.00
Equipment	35,487.00
Accumulated Depreciation—Equipment	12,450.00
Accounts Payable	23,154.00
Sales Tax Payable	1,548.00
Federal Income Tax Payable	2,489.00
Dividends Payable	5,000.00
Capital Stock	75,000.00
Retained Earnings	54,784.00

Prepare a post-closing trial balance on the form provided in the *Working Papers*.

A Look at Accounting Software

Using the System Manager to Navigate a Computerized Accounting System

Computerized accounting systems are typically composed of from five to several dozen modules. The modules are individual applications that perform unique functions. Modules tend to mirror the specific functions performed in an accounting department: general ledger, accounts receivable, accounts payable, payroll, etc. These individual applications are linked together by another module—a controlling program often called the system manager. The system manager acts as a portal to each of the modules and provides utilities that are shared by each of them. For example, banking functions need to be accessed by both Accounts Payable and Accounts Receivable modules, and banking transactions affect General Ledger accounts. So the banking utility works best as part of the system manager.

Likewise, reports are used in virtually all modules, so the Reports utility usually resides within the system manager as well.

Most small-business accounting systems contain the six modules illustrated below, although there are variations. One software consultant counted over 90 different modules available for computerized accounting systems. The larger and more complex a business is, the more modules it is likely to need. Many accounting systems allow businesses to add modules as they grow. These added modules, or applications, are also accessed by the user through the system manager. A few examples of these additional modules would be Human Resource Management, Customer Service, Web Business Tools, and Point-of-Sale.

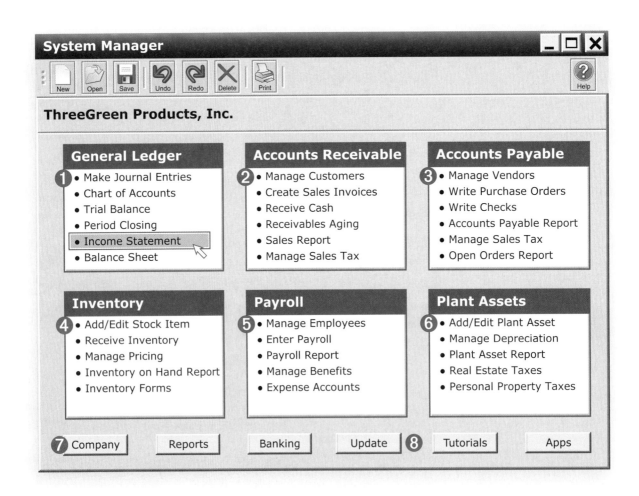

① The General Ledger module contains all general ledger accounts. Accounts are created, edited, or deactivated by selecting Chart of Accounts.

- A trial balance can be viewed or printed at any time.

- Some common reports are made available to the user directly from the modules. They may be listed under the module heading, as illustrated above. The user has selected the income statement. The reports listed here could also be accessed from the module's main menu. A larger number of reports, especially custom reports, are accessed by clicking on the Reports button. Examples might include an income statement with a vertical analysis and a statement of stockholders' equity.

② The Accounts Receivable module is primarily designed to manage a business's customer accounts. Cash receipts are linked to the banking utility and the general ledger accounts.

- Some computerized accounting systems provide separate modules for sales orders. Some, like the one illustrated here, include basic sales entry functions in the Accounts Receivable module.

- Businesses that sell in several states and municipalities will encounter sales tax rates that vary from state to state, from county to county, and from city to city. The wider a business's operating area, the more likely it is to need a sales tax management utility. It can be included in a module, as it is here, or it can be a module on its own.

③ The Accounts Payable module is primarily designed to manage a business's vendor accounts. The cash payments function is linked to the banking utility and the general ledger accounts.

- Purchase orders can be a part of the Accounts Payable module, as shown here, or a separate module.

- Managing sales tax as part of the purchasing process is less complex than it is for sales. These taxes are paid to vendors. However, some purchases may be tax-exempt. States generally require businesses to file reports of their tax-exempt purchases. This utility helps to manage that obligation.

④ Recall that computerized accounting systems use perpetual inventory systems (Chapter 9, Lesson 9-2). The Inventory module is designed to track the receipt and sale of inventory items and to maintain a record of the cost of each item. When a sale is recorded in the Accounts Receivable module, items sold are automatically deducted from the inventory on hand. The cost of the items is automatically recorded in the Cost of Merchandise Sold account. You will learn more about inventory in Chapter 20.

⑤ The Payroll module is designed to manage a business's employee records and to enable the business to accurately and efficiently compensate its employees. Many small businesses contract with payroll service providers to handle their payroll. In that case, this module would not be in active use.

⑥ Plant assets, commonly called *fixed assets*, are managed through the Plant Assets module. Depreciation and property taxes are managed in this module as well. You will learn more about plant assets in Chapter 19.

⑦ Some large business organizations operate multiple companies. Most computerized accounting systems allow businesses to handle the accounting for more than one business. When there is more than one company, the company for which transactions are to be entered is selected by clicking on the Company button.

⑧ As with most application software, the publisher of the application periodically releases updates. The Update button accesses those releases. The Tutorials button allows the user to learn how to use the features of the system. The software publisher usually provides these tutorials as part of the software.

Chapter Summary

Financial statements are prepared using information from three sources: (1) end-of-fiscal-period account balances from the adjusted trial balance, (2) selected beginning account balances from general ledger accounts, and (3) amounts calculated on another financial statement.

The income statement of a merchandising business has four main sections: (1) Operating Revenue, (2) Cost of Merchandise Sold, (3) Operating Expenses, and (4) Other Revenue. The Operating Revenue section uses sales less its contra accounts to calculate net sales. The Cost of Merchandise Sold section uses the amounts of merchandise inventory, purchases, and purchases contra accounts to calculate the cost of merchandise sold. The cost of merchandise sold is subtracted from net sales to calculate the gross profit. The total of all operating expense accounts, subtracted from gross profit, equals income from operations. The Other Revenue section contains any revenue account not directly related to the normal operating activities of the business. Federal income tax expense is then deducted to yield net income after federal income tax.

The statement of stockholders' equity reports the changes in equity accounts. The statement contains two sections: (1) Capital Stock and (2) Retained Earnings. Each section begins with the beginning balance and reports changes during the fiscal period.

The balance sheet reports the asset and liability accounts on the adjusted trial balance. Assets are classified as current assets and plant assets. The book value of any account having a contra asset account is presented. Stockholders' equity amounts are obtained from the statement of stockholders' equity.

Temporary accounts are closed after financial statements are prepared. Four entries are recorded: (1) income statement accounts with credit balances, (2) income statement accounts with debit balances, (3) net income to retained earnings, and (4) dividends to retained earnings. After the closing entries are posted, a post-closing trial balance is prepared. The post-closing trial balance is prepared to ensure that the general ledger is prepared for the next fiscal period.

EXPLORE ACCOUNTING

Alternative Fiscal Years

Many small companies use a fiscal year that is the same as the calendar year, January 1 to December 31. However, there may be several reasons why a different fiscal period would be beneficial. If the calendar year-end comes in the middle of a high sales period, a fiscal year ending at this time can be more difficult. All employees are extremely busy with sales and shipping. Because of this activity, accurately identifying sales, inventory, and accounts receivable is more difficult. If the calendar year-end comes just before the high sales period begins, an analysis of the company's financial condition will not be as favorable. The company may have borrowed money to buy a high level of inventory, so the company has higher debt and high inventory levels. Therefore, some companies choose to use a natural business year as the fiscal year, as discussed in Chapter 6.

Baker's Dozen, Inc., is a corporation that makes and sells decorative cakes, cookies, and candies. Approximately 90% of its sales are made between November 1 and February 15 because of the three holidays of Thanksgiving, Christmas, and Valentine's Day. The company spends six months—May to November—preparing for its heavy sales period. The company has selected April 1 to March 31 as its fiscal year. By March 31, inventory is low, most accounts receivable have been collected, and the company has not yet replaced inventory to begin preparing for the next season. Thus, this is an ideal time to end the fiscal year. Inventory is easier to count, the level of accounts receivable is lower, and more employees are available to help with the closing activities.

INSTRUCTIONS

What other types of companies may find it beneficial to use a fiscal year different from the calendar year? What would be the ideal fiscal period for these companies? You may wish to find a local business that has a fiscal period different from the calendar year. If so, determine the reasons for selecting the fiscal period it now uses.

Apply Your Understanding

INSTRUCTIONS: Download problem instructions for Excel, QuickBooks, and Peachtree from the textbook companion website at www.C21accounting.com.

16-1 Application Problem: Preparing an income statement for a merchandising business LO1

A form for completing this problem and an adjusted trial balance for Top-Light Corporation for the year ended December 31 of the current year are given in the *Working Papers*. The beginning balance of Merchandise Inventory is $90,260.72. Save your work to complete Problem 16-2.

Instructions:

1. Prepare an income statement.

2. Prepare a vertical analysis of each amount in the fourth amount column. Round percentage calculations to the nearest 0.1%.

16-2 Application Problem: Preparing a statement of stockholders' equity LO2

A form for completing this problem is given in the *Working Papers*. Use the income statement and trial balance from Problem 16-1. Save your work to complete Problem 16-3.

Instructions:

Prepare a statement of stockholders' equity for Top-Light Corporation for the fiscal year ended on December 31 of the current year. Use the following additional information.

Capital stock outstanding on January 1	2,000 shares
Capital stock issued during the year	300 shares
Capital stock par value	$25.00
Retained earnings, January 1	$50,403.31

16-3 Application Problem: Preparing a balance sheet for a corporation LO3

A form for completing this problem is given in the *Working Papers*. Use the trial balance and financial statements from Problem 16-2. Save your work to complete Problem 16-4.

Instructions:

Prepare a balance sheet for the current year.

16-4 Application Problem: Journalizing closing entries LO4

Use Top-Light Corporation's trial balance and financial statements from Problems 16-1 and 16-2. A general journal is given in the *Working Papers*.

Instructions:

Record the following closing entries on page 21 of the general journal.

a. Close the income statement accounts with credit balances.

b. Close the income statement accounts with debit balances.

c. Close the Income Summary account.

d. Close the Dividends account.

Peachtree

1. Journalize and post closing entries to the general journal.
2. Make the selections to print the balance sheet and income statement.
3. Make the selections to print the general journal and the post-closing trial balance.

QuickBooks

1. Journalize and post adjusting entries to the journal.
2. Make the selections to print the balance sheet and the profit and loss statement.
3. Make the selections to print the journal and the post-closing trial balance.

Excel

1. Key the account balances in the trial balance section of the worksheet.
2. Use the required formulas to calculate the totals of the Trial Balance columns.
3. Key the closing entries in the Adjustments columns.
4. Create the appropriate formulas to extend amounts to the income statement and balance sheet.

AAONLiNE

1. Go to www.cengage.com/login
2. Click on **AA Online** to access.
3. Go to the online assignment and follow the instructions.

16-5 Application Problem: Preparing a post-closing trial balance LO5

AAONLiNE

1. Go to www.cengage.com/login
2. Click on **AA Online** to access.
3. Go to the online assignment and follow the instructions.

MidSouth Electric's balance sheet accounts with December 31 balances for the current year, after adjusting and closing entries have been posted, are shown below.

Account	Balance	Account	Balance
Cash	$ 23,524.22	Interest Receivable	$ 32.45
Petty Cash	250.00	Accounts Payable	11,676.50
Accounts Receivable	23,643.44	Sales Tax Payable	1,584.00
Allowance for Uncollectible Accounts	3,980.00	Federal Income Tax Payable	3,790.00
Merchandise Inventory	156,262.33	Dividends Payable	4,000.00
Supplies	352.00	Capital Stock	72,000.00
Notes Receivable	6,490.00	Retained Earnings	113,523.94

Instructions:

Prepare a post-closing trial balance on the form provided in the *Working Papers*.

16-M Mastery Problem: Preparing financial statements and closing entries LO1, 2, 3, 4

The adjusted trial balance for Paulson Corporation for the year ended December 31 of the current year and forms for completing this problem are given in the *Working Papers*. The beginning balance of Merchandise Inventory is $112,825.90.

Instructions:

1. Prepare an income statement.

2. Prepare a vertical analysis of each amount in the fourth amount column. Round percentage calculations to the nearest 0.1%.

3. Prepare a statement of stockholders' equity. The company had 4,500 shares of $10.00 par value stock outstanding on January 1. The company issued an additional 500 shares during the year.

4. Prepare a balance sheet for the current year.

5. Journalize the closing entries on page 19 of the general journal.

 Peachtree

1. Journalize and post closing entries to the general journal.
2. Make the selections to print the balance sheet and income statement.
3. Make the selections to print the general journal and the post-closing trial balance.

 Quick Books

1. Journalize and post adjusting entries to the journal.
2. Make the selections to print the balance sheet and the profit and loss statement.
3. Make the selections to print the journal and the post-closing trial balance.

X

1. Key the account balances in the trial balance section of the worksheet.
2. Use the required formulas to calculate the totals of the Trial Balance columns.
3. Key the closing entries in the Adjustments columns.
4. Create the appropriate formulas to extend amounts to the income statement and balance sheet.

16-C Challenge Problem: Preparing an income statement LO1

Selected sections of the adjusted trial balance for KLT Corporation are presented in the *Working Papers*. The corporation's chart of accounts contains several sales accounts. KLT Corporation also has an account for interest expense. A form for completing this problem is also given in the *Working Papers*. The beginning balance of Merchandise Inventory is $66,964.96.

Instructions:

1. Prepare the income statement for KLT Corporation.

2. Prepare a vertical analysis of the income statement.

PARTNERSHIP FOR
21ST CENTURY SKILLS

Should You Buy Stock?

Theme: Financial, Economic, Business, and Entrepreneurial Literacy

Skills: Creativity and Innovation, Critical Thinking and Problem Solving, Communication and Collaboration, ICT Literacy

A share of stock is a unit of ownership in a corporation. Stock may be purchased by individuals, investment companies, pension funds, institutions, banks, and other companies. Publicly traded stocks are bought and sold on stock exchanges throughout the world. Ownership of a corporation's stock entitles the owner to distributions of earnings if dividends are declared. Many investors, however, buy stock with the expectation that it will increase in value and the stock can be sold for a profit.

Stock ownership entitles the owner to vote at stockholders' meetings proportional to the number of shares owned. Important issues regarding the corporation may be decided at these meetings including the election of the members of the board of directors. Sometimes an individual or group of stockholders will attempt to gain a majority of a company's stock in order to elect their choice of directors and thus take control of the company.

Investors might determine which stocks they will purchase based on political or social issues. For example, an investor might buy stocks only of companies that have environmental policies. Another investor might buy stocks only of companies that have family-friendly policies allowing for a balance in work and family life for their employees.

APPLICATION

1. Assume that as a stockholder you are responsible for selecting the membership of the board of directors for a new social network company. Identify 9–11 individuals (by name or title) whom you would like to serve on the board of directors. Explain why each individual would be a valuable contributor.

2. Compose a letter to one of these individuals asking them to serve on the board of directors for your company. Using persuasion, explain why their involvement would be beneficial to everyone.

3. Many investors are unsure of the right time to buy or sell stock. Using websites like www .finance.yahoo.com, research *dollar cost averaging*, a common investment strategy. Write a financial advice column explaining to new investors the meaning of this concept and how it can be implemented.

Analyzing Nike's financial statements

Nike has two classes of common stock—Class A and Class B. The majority of Class A stock is owned by Philip H. Knight, cofounder and chairman of the board of directors. This class of stock has different voting rights than Class B stock. For example, the Class A stockholders can elect three-fourths of the members of the board of directors. This right allows the Class A stockholders to have more control over the individuals who govern the corporation. Class B shares are publicly traded under the symbol NKE. Quarterly dividends are paid to both classes of stock.

Class A stockholders also have the right to convert their shares, one for one, into Class B shares. This right allows Class A stockholders to sell their shares on the stock market.

INSTRUCTIONS

Use the Consolidated Statements of Shareholders' Equity on pages B-8 and B-9 of Appendix B to answer the following questions.

1. How many shares of Class A and Class B shares are outstanding as of May 31, 2011?

2. How many Class A shares were converted into Class B shares in fiscal year 2011?

3. What change in the dollar amounts of the stockholders' equity accounts results from Class A stock being issued to employees?

Chapter 17

Financial Statement Analysis

LEARNING OBJECTIVES

After studying Chapter 17, in addition to defining key terms, you will be able to:

LO1 Analyze an income statement using vertical analysis.

LO2 Perform vertical analysis of a balance sheet.

LO3 Analyze a balance sheet using vertical analysis.

LO4 Perform horizontal analysis on an income statement.

LO5 Perform horizontal analysis on a balance sheet.

LO6 Calculate earnings per share.

LO7 Calculate and interpret market ratios.

LO8 Calculate and interpret liquidity ratios.

©DANIEL KOUREY, ISTOCK/©JIM PRUITT, ISTOCK

GOLDENKB/ISTOCKPHOTO.COM

Accounting In The Real World
E*TRADE

The Internet revolutionized how individual investors buy and sell stock. Before the Internet, an investor could only trade stock using a stock broker. Through their investment firms, stock brokers had access to financial information not available elsewhere. As a result, most investors relied on their stock brokers for investment advice. When an investor made a decision on an investment, the stock broker would make the purchase on the stock exchange.

Today's investors can manage their own investments using an online investing site. For over 20 years, E*TRADE has been a leader in online investing. E*TRADE customers have 24/7 access to financial information and the tools to place stock trades. An E*TRADE customer can enter the stock symbol of a corporation and gain instant access to a wealth of information, including:

- recent news articles about the corporation,
- projected earnings,
- research reports, and
- charts of the stock prices for one day to over 30 years.

A link on E*TRADE's website opens to a wide range of financial ratios for the selected company. A section for AT&T Inc. (stock symbol, T) is shown.

The financial community has assigned names to the most commonly used vertical analysis ratios. For example, profit margin is the name given to the vertical analysis ratio for net income after federal income taxes. E*TRADE uses two methods to help investors compare AT&T's profit margin to other companies in the same industry. The illustration at the top of the next column indicates, from low to high, how the company's ratios compare to those of other companies. AT&T's profit margin, 17.28%, is in the upper range of other communications services companies.

Below the ratios, E*TRADE provides an explanation of the ratios. This statement helps E*TRADE's customers make more informed investment decisions.

PROFITABILITY (TTM)		
Gross Margin	54.66%	
Operating Margin	18.13%	
EBITDA Margin	33.92%	
Profit Margin	17.28%	

T's **Gross Margin** is comparable to other companies in the Communications Services industry, which means it has relatively the same amount of cash to spend on business operations as its peers. As indicated by the **Operating Margin**, T controls its costs and expenses better than 79% of its peers.

CRITICAL THINKING

1. Access etrade.com and enter a stock symbol to obtain a current stock quote for a company. Use the available links to view its financial ratios. Identify the four ratios shown in the illustration above.

2. With this information, compare the company's performance to other companies in its industry group.

Source: www.etrade.com.

Key Terms

- profitability ratio
- benchmark
- comparative financial statements
- trend analysis
- profit margin

- gross margin
- operating margin
- operating expense ratio
- solvency ratio
- debt ratio
- horizontal analysis

- earnings per share
- market ratio
- dividend yield
- price-earnings ratio
- liquidity ratio
- working capital

- current ratio
- quick assets
- quick ratio

LESSON
17-1 Vertical Analysis of an Income Statement

LO1 Analyze an income statement using vertical analysis.

Vertical Analysis Ratios LO1

Vertical analysis ratios measure the relationship between one financial statement item and another item on the same financial statement. On the income statement, vertical analysis ratios focus on the ability of a business to earn a profit. A ratio that measures the ability of a business to generate income is called a **profitability ratio**. Vertical analysis ratios on an income statement are examples of profitability ratios.

Managers use vertical analysis ratios to help make business decisions. For vertical analysis to be an effective tool, a business must set a target, or standard, for each ratio. A standard used to compare financial performance is called a **benchmark**.

Benchmark ratios can be determined using many factors. These include:

1. **Actual ratios from prior fiscal periods**. Current fiscal period ratios tend to be similar to prior-period ratios.

2. **Industry standards published by industry organizations**. A business can be expected to have ratios similar to other businesses in the same industry.

3. **Business plans**. Managers often make decisions that change how they conduct business. For example, managers may decide to advertise more with the goal of increasing sales. As a result, advertising expense as a percent of sales is likely to change.

4. **Unexpected events**. Unexpected events may require a business to revise its benchmark ratios. For example, a hard freeze in Florida can result in higher food prices.

Based on these factors, ThreeGreen sets a benchmark for each vertical analysis ratio. A benchmark ratio can be stated as a single value or a range of values. ThreeGreen expects that its gross profit should be between 59.5% and 60.5% of net sales. If a ratio falls outside the target range, ThreeGreen should look for what caused the unfavorable results.

ETHICS IN ACTION

An Unethical Invitation?

John Gatlin's e-commerce site has grown from a one-person operation to a company that employs over 100 people. When he needs more computer equipment, John heads to Nance Office Supply to talk with Blake Nash, its computer expert. Blake makes sure that John buys the right equipment, but he never tries to sell him more than he needs. For this reason, John will only buy his computer equipment from Blake.

John enjoys following his college football team by traveling to games in his motor home. At the last minute, John's parents said they couldn't make the trip to the upcoming game. John has invited Blake and his wife to join him and his family. John already purchased the game tickets and the food for the tailgate party. "I've already paid for everything," insisted John, when Blake offered to pay for his share of the trip. Blake asked John if he could call back and give him a decision in a few hours. Before he accepts John's invitation, Blake has asked for your advice.

INSTRUCTIONS

Determine whether it would be ethical for Blake to accept John's invitation. Use Staples' *Code of Ethics* at www.staples.com/sbd/cre/marketing/staples_soul /documents/staples-code-of-ethics_english.pdf as a guide.

©LUCA DI FILIPPO, ISTOCK

Analyzing Trends with Vertical Analysis

ThreeGreen Products, Inc.
Comparative Income Statement
For Years Ended December 31, 20-- and 20--

	CURRENT YEAR		PRIOR YEAR	
	AMOUNT	PERCENT	AMOUNT	PERCENT
Net Sales	626 7 8 1 99	100.0	548 9 1 5 25	100.0
Cost of Merchandise Sold	258 0 8 2 55	41.2	214 8 9 5 25	39.1
Gross Profit	368 6 9 9 44	58.8	334 0 2 0 00	60.9
Operating Expenses:				
Advertising Expense	4 6 8 0 00	0.7	4 5 0 0 00	0.8
Credit Card Fee Expense	6 8 4 2 20	1.1	5 4 8 1 29	1.0
Depreciation Expense—Office Equipment	7 4 8 5 00	1.2	7 2 1 8 00	1.3
Depreciation Expense—Store Equipment	9 8 3 0 00	1.6	9 2 4 0 00	1.7
Insurance Expense	8 2 0 0 00	1.3	7 8 0 0 00	1.4
Miscellaneous Expense	3 4 9 5 04	0.6	5 4 1 8 78	1.0
Payroll Taxes Expense	16 6 9 7 98	2.7	14 8 8 1 67	2.7
Rent Expense	8 4 0 0 00	1.3	8 4 0 0 00	1.5
Salary Expense	184 2 3 4 95	29.4	164 1 9 4 91	29.9
Supplies Expense—Office	3 9 3 8 17	0.6	3 4 8 1 19	0.6
Supplies Expense—Store	4 5 8 4 61	0.7	5 0 1 9 92	0.9
Uncollectible Accounts Expense	2 3 8 4 10	0.4	2 1 4 9 92	0.4
Utilities Expense	4 9 6 5 42	0.8	3 1 9 4 99	0.6
Total Operating Expenses	265 7 3 7 47	42.4	240 9 8 0 67	43.9
Income from Operations	102 9 6 1 97	16.4	93 0 3 9 33	16.9
Other Revenue	5 5 7 00	0.1	2 4 9 00	0.0
Net Income before Federal Income Tax	103 5 1 8 97	16.5	93 2 8 8 33	17.0
Less Federal Income Tax Expense	23 6 2 2 40	3.8	19 9 6 8 03	3.6
Net Income after Federal Income Tax	79 8 9 6 57	12.7	73 3 2 0 30	13.4

Financial statements that provide information for multiple fiscal periods are called **comparative financial statements**. The format of ThreeGreen's comparative income statement differs from the income statement shown in Chapter 16. Each fiscal year's amounts are listed in a single column. Three amounts, Net Sales, Cost of Merchandise Sold, and Other Revenue, are listed without their underlying accounts. The vertical analysis ratios are presented next to each year's income statement amounts.

An analysis of changes over time is called **trend analysis**. Comparing financial statement ratios over two or more periods is useful for identifying and correcting unfavorable trends. Management should analyze the trends indicated by changes in vertical analysis ratios. The first vertical analysis ratio a manager would likely analyze would be for net income after federal income taxes. This ratio reveals how successfully the business has performed in generating income.

Net income after federal income tax as a percent of net sales is called **profit margin**. ThreeGreen's profit margin has decreased from 13.4% to 12.7% of net sales. ThreeGreen would like its net income after federal income tax to be a larger part of each sales dollar. Thus, these ratios show an unfavorable trend. However, to determine how to correct this unfavorable trend, management will need to analyze each item on the income statement. For example, utilities expense has increased from 0.6% to 0.8% of net sales. This unfavorable trend alerts management to evaluate its energy policies and investigate payments posted to this account.

A corporation having a net loss before federal income taxes can file for a tax refund from the federal government. To qualify for this benefit, the corporation must have paid at least an equal amount of federal income taxes in the previous three years. The tax refund is calculated using the same tax schedule that ThreeGreen used to calculate its federal income tax expense.

Using Vertical Analysis to Analyze Gross Profit

	ThreeGreen Products, Inc. Comparative Income Statement For Years Ended December 31, 20-- and 20--				
	CURRENT YEAR		PRIOR YEAR	
	AMOUNT	PERCENT	AMOUNT	PERCENT
Net Sales	626 781 99	100.0	548 915 25	100.0
Cost of Merchandise Sold	258 082 55	41.2	214 895 25	39.1
Gross Profit	368 699 44	58.8	334 020 00	60.9

For most retail businesses, the cost of merchandise is the largest cost of doing business. Controlling the cost of merchandise is necessary to maximize gross profit. Gross profit must be large enough to cover total operating expenses and produce the desired amount of net income.

The vertical analysis ratios for the cost of merchandise sold and gross profit are similar. Both ratios focus on the relationship between sales and the cost of merchandise sold. Any increase in the cost of merchandise sold reduces gross profit. Therefore, a manager can focus on either ratio in an effort to maximize the gross profit.

Managers often focus on the cost of merchandise sold ratio. Jenn Quitman, the manager of Main Street Café, constantly monitors her "food cost." For a café, the food cost is the cost of merchandise sold. Jenn expects her food cost to be between 36.0% and 38.0%. If her food cost exceeds 38.0%, she immediately investigates what has caused it to go up.

Most managers and investors watch the vertical analysis ratio for gross profit. The ratio is so widely used that it has been given an alternative name. Gross profit as a percent of net sales is called **gross margin**. This ratio is also referred to as *gross profit margin*. Online investing sites and company annual reports report gross margins.

ThreeGreen's benchmark gross margin is between 59.5% and 60.5%. ThreeGreen's gross margin has decreased from 60.9% to 58.8% of net sales—an unfavorable trend. The ratio for the current year is lower than the benchmark—also an unfavorable result. Therefore, ThreeGreen's managers need to investigate why this ratio has decreased below the target range.

CORRECTING AN UNFAVORABLE GROSS MARGIN

Two actions can enable a business to achieve its gross margin benchmark:

(1) Increase unit sales prices. The amount a business adds to the cost of merchandise to establish the selling price is called markup. The markup of an item purchased for $4.00 and sold for $10.00 is $6.00. To increase sales revenue, a business may consider increasing its markups. A business must be cautious when increasing its markups. If a markup is too large, a decrease in sales revenue could occur. The higher sales price may exceed what customers are willing to pay. Or, customers may elect to purchase from competing businesses having lower prices.

(2) Decrease the unit cost of merchandise. Decreasing the unit cost of merchandise will increase the gross margin. To decrease its cost of merchandise, a business should review purchasing practices. For example, the business could purchase items in larger quantities or from other vendors that offer a lower cost.

Management may need to take both actions to achieve its gross margin benchmark.

MANAGING AN UNFAVORABLE GROSS MARGIN

A business must work to maintain or reduce its cost of merchandise. However, gradual increases in the cost of merchandise are unavoidable. Any increase in merchandise costs reduces the gross margin, leaving less gross profit to cover operating expenses. To maintain its target gross margin when the cost of merchandise rises, a business must increase its unit sales prices. Before deciding to increase prices, a business must try to determine the impact that higher prices will have on its sales. Often, it's possible for a business to absorb a lower gross profit by reducing operating expenses.

Unfavorable ratios serve as a warning that management action is necessary. Vertical analysis ratios are an example of how accounting information can help management planning and decision making. Effective managers rely on the information provided from accounting records.

Using Vertical Analysis to Analyze Operating Expenses

ThreeGreen Products, Inc.
Comparative Income Statement
For Years Ended December 31, 20-- and 20--

	CURRENT YEAR		PRIOR YEAR	
	AMOUNT	PERCENT	AMOUNT	PERCENT
Utilities Expense	4 9 6 5 42	0.8	3 1 9 4 99	0.6
Total Operating Expenses	265 7 3 7 47	42.4	240 9 8 0 67	43.9
Income from Operations	102 9 6 1 97	16.4	93 0 3 9 33	16.9

The vertical analysis ratio for income from operations, like the gross margin, has an alternate name. Income from operations as a percent of net sales is called the **operating margin**. This ratio is also referred to as the *rate of return on sales*. Investors are interested in the operating margin. This ratio gives the best indication of how effectively a business is earning a profit from its normal business operations. ThreeGreen's normal business operations involve the sale of ecologically friendly merchandise. Its operating margin for the current year, 16.4%, means that ThreeGreen nets 16.4 cents of every dollar of sales before taxes.

Investors can compare the operating margin to other businesses in the same industry to assist them in making investment decisions. However, managers who want to control operating expenses will be more interested in another ratio. Total operating expenses as a percent of net sales is called the **operating expense ratio**. Unlike the operating margin, the operating expense ratio does not include the effect of merchandise costs.

ThreeGreen's benchmark total operating expense ratio is between 40.0% and 42.0%. Its actual operating expense ratio has declined from 43.9% to 42.4% of net sales—a favorable trend. The current year's ratio is still higher than the target range—an unfavorable result. Therefore, ThreeGreen's managers need to continue their efforts to decrease operating expenses.

CORRECTING AN UNFAVORABLE OPERATING EXPENSE RATIO

An operating expense ratio that is higher than expected only alerts management that there may be a problem. The ratio does not reveal specific problems nor suggest any solutions. Management must investigate individual expense accounts until the reason for the unfavorable ratio is identified.

ThreeGreen should begin by analyzing its largest operating expense, wages and salaries. Salary expense is 29.4%

of net sales. In the prior year, salary expense was 29.9% of sales. The decrease in the ratio suggests that ThreeGreen has been effective in managing its salary expense.

ThreeGreen should evaluate each expense. Several courses of action are possible.

(1) Reduce operating expenses. Having identified which operating expenses are higher than expected, management can take action to reduce them. The actions required are often unique to the business and different for each expense account. For example:

- Supplies Expense. Employees can be trained to use supplies more efficiently. Management can also try to obtain lower prices from vendors.
- Insurance Expense. Management can try to lower its insurance expense by comparing premiums from other insurance companies. The business can also elect to reduce the amount of coverage.
- Credit Card Fee Expense. Management can offer customers incentives to pay with cash rather than using a credit card.

(2) Modify the benchmark. Management may be unable to reduce an expense. ThreeGreen's utilities expense has increased from 0.6% to 0.8% of net sales. The local utility company raised its rates during the current year. ThreeGreen changed its thermostat settings to conserve energy. Still, it was unable to offset the rate increases. ThreeGreen may have to accept that its utility expenses will be higher in future fiscal periods.

(3) Increase net sales. Management can offset an increase in operating expenses by increasing net sales. The business can increase its unit sales prices if customers are willing to pay higher prices. The business can also take actions to increase the number of items sold.

It is natural for management to focus on expenses that exceed the target range. However, it may be as important for managers to focus on expenses that fall short of the target range. Spending too little may have a negative impact on the business. Examples:

- A store cuts back on the number of sales clerks to reduce the expense of their wages. The action forces customers to stand in long lines to check out. Eventually, customers avoid shopping at the store.

- A café reduces its advertising, but loses sales to other restaurants that do more advertising.
- To reduce its depreciation expense, a business does not replace its old computer systems. As a result, its employees are less productive. The business might also be unable to take advantage of business opportunities on the Internet.

Rollover and Protect Your Investment

Most companies today offer their employees a 401(k) retirement plan. Since you are likely to change jobs more than 10 times between the ages of 18 and 44, what happens to your employer-sponsored 401(k) when you leave an employer? What are your options? You can do one of the following:

1. Leave your 401(k) with your former employer. Although your account will remain active, be aware that many companies impose fees to maintain 401(k) accounts for former employees.
2. Move your 401(k) funds to a different qualified retirement plan. The movement of funds from one qualified retirement plan to another is called a **rollover**. For example, funds may be withdrawn from your 401(k) plan with a former employer and deposited to another 401(k) offered by your new employer. Or the funds can be rolled over to an individual retirement account (IRA) at a bank or other financial institution, which can give you more flexibility in managing the invested funds. Funds withdrawn from a qualified retirement plan must be rolled over to another qualified plan within 60 days or the IRS will impose taxes and penalties on the amount withdrawn. Rollovers are important to saving for your retirement because they allow your retirement savings to keep growing tax-free.
3. Take a lump-sum distribution. Some employers will require 401(k) accounts with small

balances ($5,000 or less) to be closed. If the funds are taken in cash (not rolled over), the IRS will require the payment of taxes and penalties for early withdrawal. You will also be subject to additional state and local income taxes. Funds in a qualified retirement plan must be left in the plan until at least age 59½ to avoid penalties.

Understand your 401(k) rollover options and make smart choices about your investment future!

ACTIVITIES

Determine the best option for the following scenarios:

1. Nathan will soon leave his employer to return to graduate school. What is the best option for his current 401(k) of $15,000?

2. Ashley was just terminated from her employer of five years and has not found another job. What is the best option for her 401(k)?

3. Courtney just obtained a new job and will begin two weeks after her termination from her former job. Her new employer matches 401(k) employee contributions up to 5%. What is the best option for her 401(k)?

4. Nikki has an IRA with a local financial institution. She is considering cashing in her IRA of $18,000 because she needs the full amount for a down payment on a condo. What would you suggest? Why?

Source: Bureau of Labor Statistics.

©NOREBBO, ISTOCK

LO1 Analyze an income statement using vertical analysis.

Terms Review

profitability ratio

benchmark

comparative financial
 statements

trend analysis

profit margin

gross margin

operating margin

operating expense ratio

Audit your understanding

1. Identify four factors that management can use to determine benchmark financial ratios.

2. Why should a business be cautious about increasing the markup on merchandise purchased for sale?

3. What are two practices that can be used to reduce the cost of merchandise?

4. Should managers interested in reducing operating expenses focus more on the operating expense ratio or the operating margin?

5. What are three possible actions to correct an unfavorable operating expense ratio?

Work together 17-1

Analyzing an income statement

The comparative income statement for Tri-State Pipe and a form for completing this problem are given in the *Working Papers*. Your instructor will guide you through the following examples.

1. Complete the vertical analysis of the comparative income statement. Round percentage calculations to the nearest 0.1%.

2. Compare selected vertical analysis ratios to Tri-State Pipe's benchmark ratios. Identify whether each ratio indicates a favorable trend and is within management's target range.

On your own 17-1

Analyzing an income statement

The comparative income statement for PBH Corporation and a form for completing this problem are given in the *Working Papers*. Work this problem independently.

1. Complete the vertical analysis of the comparative income statement. Round percentage calculations to the nearest 0.1%.

2. Compare the vertical analysis ratios to PBH Corporation's benchmark ratios. Identify whether each ratio indicates a favorable trend and is within management's target range.

17-2 Vertical Analysis of a Balance Sheet

LO2 Perform vertical analysis of a balance sheet.

LO3 Analyze a balance sheet using vertical analysis.

Calculating Vertical Analysis Ratios on a Balance Sheet LO2

1 Asset Amounts Divided by Total Assets

2 Liability and Stockholders' Equity Amounts Divided by Total Assets

ThreeGreen Products, Inc.
Comparative Balance Sheet
December 31, 20-- and 20--

	CURRENT YEAR		PRIOR YEAR	
	AMOUNT	PERCENT	AMOUNT	PERCENT
ASSETS				
Current Assets:				
Cash	54 1 9 4 34	22.8	5 4 2 6 55	2.9
Petty Cash	2 5 0 00	0.1	2 5 0 00	0.1
Accounts Receivable (net)	17 8 7 2 56	7.5	12 1 9 4 00	6.6
Merchandise Inventory	102 8 3 8 00	43.3	108 4 8 6 44	58.4
Supplies—Office	6 1 0 00	0.3	5 0 9 00	0.3
Supplies—Store	4 6 5 00	0.2	2 8 9 00	0.2
Prepaid Insurance	2 8 0 0 00	1.2	1 2 0 0 00	0.6
Notes Receivable	6 2 0 0 00	2.6	2 2 0 0 00	1.2
Interest Receivable	9 3 00	0.0	1 8 00	0.0
Total Current Assets	185 3 2 2 90	78.1	130 5 7 2 99	70.3
Plant Assets:				
Office Equipment (net)	11 2 2 1 18	4.7	12 9 4 8 69	7.0
Store Equipment (net)	40 8 2 3 11	17.2	42 1 9 4 26	22.7
Total Plant Assets	52 0 4 4 29	21.9	55 1 4 2 95	29.7
Total Assets	237 3 6 7 19	100.0	185 7 1 5 94	100.0
LIABILITIES				
Current Liabilities:				
Accounts Payable	16 4 8 9 10	6.9	36 2 3 8 07	19.5
Sales Tax Payable	3 5 7 4 64	1.5	3 2 4 9 25	1.7
Employee Income Tax Payable	9 5 0 00	0.4	8 9 0 00	0.5
Social Security Tax Payable	2 0 2 3 06	0.9	1 9 0 1 68	1.0
Medicare Tax Payable	4 7 3 14	0.2	4 4 4 75	0.2
Health Insurance Premiums Payable	4 6 0 00	0.2	4 2 4 00	0.2
Retirement Benefits Payable	4 6 5 00	0.2	3 8 0 00	0.2
Unemployment Tax Payable—Federal	2 9 7 02	0.1	2 5 6 86	0.1
Unemployment Tax Payable—State	1 4 7 42	0.1	1 2 7 49	0.1
Federal Income Tax Payable	3 6 2 2 40	1.5	3 0 8 5 00	1.7
Dividends Payable	3 7 5 0 00	1.6	3 5 0 0 00	1.9
Total Liabilities	32 2 5 1 78	13.6	50 4 9 7 10	27.2
STOCKHOLDERS' EQUITY				
Capital Stock	75 0 0 0 00	31.6	70 0 0 0 00	37.7
Retained Earnings	130 1 1 5 41	54.8	65 2 1 8 84	35.1
Total Stockholders' Equity	205 1 1 5 41	86.4	135 2 1 8 84	72.8
Total Liabilities and Stockholders' Equity	237 3 6 7 19	100.0	185 7 1 5 94	100.0

Vertical analysis ratios measure the relationship between one financial statement item and another item on the same financial statement. On an income statement, each item is divided by net sales. On a balance sheet, each item is divided by the amount of Total Assets.

ThreeGreen's comparative balance sheet contains columns to report the vertical analysis ratios for each year.

⤵ Calculating Vertical Analysis Ratios

① Divide each asset amount by the amount of Total Assets. Round each percent to the nearest 0.1%. For the current year, dividing Total Current Assets, $185,322.90, by Total Assets, $237,367.19, results in 78.1%.

② Divide each liability and stockholders' equity amount by the amount of Total Assets. For the current year, dividing Total Current Liabilities, $32,251.78, by Total Assets, $237,367.19, results in 13.6%.

Forms of Business Organization

EXPLORE ACCOUNTING

When forming a new business, there are several types of organization to choose from. The factors that must be considered in deciding on a form of organization are state and federal requirements, capital needs, taxation, and owner liability. In Part 1 of this textbook, you learned about sole proprietorships. In Parts 2 and 3, the corporate form of business was illustrated. Part 4 will introduce partnerships.

The standard corporate form is the "C" Corporation, named for Subchapter C of the Internal Revenue Code. Below, three forms of business organization not used in this textbook are compared to the C Corporation.

Corporations that have more than 30 stockholders must organize as C Corporations. These must have a board of directors, conduct annual stockholders meetings, and publish financial reports with the SEC and other government agencies. Since all corporate income is taxed, and dividends (paid after federal income tax) are taxed again to the stockholders, corporate income distributions are taxed twice. However, there are two big advantages to this form of organization. One is limited liability for

the owners, which means they cannot be held individually responsible for the liabilities of the company. Their liability is limited to the amount of their investment. The second is the ability to issue stock to raise capital.

S Corporation. These companies are named for Subchapter S of the Internal Revenue Code. They are regular corporations, with fewer than 100 stockholders, that have elected to be taxed in the same way as proprietorships and partnerships. Like C Corporations, these companies must have boards of directors, conduct annual meetings, and file the same reports. Unlike C Corporations, all corporate earnings (and losses) pass through the corporation to the stockholders in proportion to their ownership to be reported on their individual tax returns. That eliminates "double taxation."

Limited Liability Company (LLC). Owners of limited liability companies are called *members*. In most states, LLCs can consist of one, two, or more members. Members enjoy the same limited liability as stockholders in a corporation. These entities are not required to maintain boards of directors, conduct annual meetings,

or file returns with the SEC. LLCs are not recognized by the IRS for tax purposes, so each must elect to be taxed as a proprietorship, partnership, or corporation.

Limited Liability Partnership (LLP). Many states that allow LLPs limit them to professional organizations—doctors, dentists, lawyers, CPAs, etc. At least two partners are necessary to form an LLP, and most states restrict the number of partners. As a rule, each partner must be registered as either a general or limited partner. Only limited partners enjoy limited liability. Some states require that at least one partner be registered as a general partner. The primary advantage of forming an LLP is that partners can manage their organization and allocate profits and losses among themselves according to their partnership agreement.

INSTRUCTIONS

You own a small, but growing, retail business organized as a proprietorship. You need to raise capital for expansion. Several family members and friends are eager to invest in your business. Which form of organization would be best for you? For your investors? Why?

©MAKHNACH_M, ISTOCK

Evaluating Vertical Analysis Asset Ratios LO3

<table>
<thead>
<tr>
<th colspan="5" style="text-align:center">ThreeGreen Products, Inc.
Comparative Balance Sheet
December 31, 20-- and 20--</th>
</tr>
<tr>
<th rowspan="2"></th>
<th colspan="2">CURRENT YEAR</th>
<th colspan="2">PRIOR YEAR</th>
</tr>
<tr>
<th>AMOUNT</th>
<th>PERCENT</th>
<th>AMOUNT</th>
<th>PERCENT</th>
</tr>
</thead>
<tbody>
<tr><td>ASSETS</td><td></td><td></td><td></td><td></td></tr>
<tr><td>Current Assets:</td><td></td><td></td><td></td><td></td></tr>
<tr><td>Cash</td><td>54 1 9 4 34</td><td>22.8</td><td>5 4 2 6 55</td><td>2.9</td></tr>
<tr><td>Petty Cash</td><td>2 5 0 00</td><td>0.1</td><td>2 5 0 00</td><td>0.1</td></tr>
<tr><td>Accounts Receivable (net)</td><td>17 8 7 2 56</td><td>7.5</td><td>12 1 9 4 00</td><td>6.6</td></tr>
<tr><td>Merchandise Inventory</td><td>102 8 3 8 00</td><td>43.3</td><td>108 4 8 6 44</td><td>58.4</td></tr>
<tr><td>Supplies—Office</td><td>6 1 0 00</td><td>0.3</td><td>5 0 9 00</td><td>0.3</td></tr>
<tr><td>Supplies—Store</td><td>4 6 5 00</td><td>0.2</td><td>2 8 9 00</td><td>0.2</td></tr>
<tr><td>Prepaid Insurance</td><td>2 8 0 0 00</td><td>1.2</td><td>1 2 0 0 00</td><td>0.6</td></tr>
<tr><td>Notes Receivable</td><td>6 2 0 0 00</td><td>2.6</td><td>2 2 0 0 00</td><td>1.2</td></tr>
<tr><td>Interest Receivable</td><td>9 3 00</td><td>0.0</td><td>1 8 00</td><td>0.0</td></tr>
<tr><td>Total Current Assets</td><td>185 3 2 2 90</td><td>78.1</td><td>130 5 7 2 99</td><td>70.3</td></tr>
<tr><td>Plant Assets:</td><td></td><td></td><td></td><td></td></tr>
<tr><td>Office Equipment (net)</td><td>11 2 2 1 18</td><td>4.7</td><td>12 9 4 8 69</td><td>7.0</td></tr>
<tr><td>Store Equipment (net)</td><td>40 8 2 3 11</td><td>17.2</td><td>42 1 9 4 26</td><td>22.7</td></tr>
<tr><td>Total Plant Assets</td><td>52 0 4 4 29</td><td>21.9</td><td>55 1 4 2 95</td><td>29.7</td></tr>
<tr><td>Total Assets</td><td>237 3 6 7 19</td><td>100.0</td><td>185 7 1 5 94</td><td>100.0</td></tr>
</tbody>
</table>

A business determines its benchmark vertical analysis ratios for its balance sheet in the same way it determined its income statement ratios. It uses (1) actual ratios from prior fiscal periods, (2) industry standards published by industry organizations, (3) business plans, and (4) unexpected events.

A business should never make a business decision for the sole purpose of meeting a benchmark ratio. However, if the benchmark ratios correctly reflect the company's financial goals, management should consider whether actions are necessary to bring a ratio within the target range.

A leading publication of industry standards presents vertical analysis ratios for only three asset items: net accounts receivable, merchandise inventory, and net plant assets. These items represent the majority of the total assets of a business. Therefore, ThreeGreen closely monitors its vertical analysis ratios for these items.

CORRECTING AN UNFAVORABLE VERTICAL ANALYSIS RATIO FOR ACCOUNTS RECEIVABLE

ThreeGreen has determined that the vertical analysis ratio for accounts receivable should be between 8.0% and 10.0% of total assets. A favorable trend moves the ratio toward 9.0%, the middle of the target range. A ratio below the favorable target range may indicate that ThreeGreen is restricting customers' ability to purchase on account. Credit sales can be an effective tool to increase the revenue of a business. A ratio above the target range may indicate that ThreeGreen is too freely extending credit to its customers. The company might not be able to collect accounts from less creditworthy customers.

ThreeGreen's ratio for accounts receivable has increased from 6.6% to 7.5%—a favorable trend. The current-year ratio, 7.5%, is still below the target range. That ratio should cause management to reevaluate how the company approves credit customers. Allowing more credit sales will likely increase both sales and uncollectible accounts. But, if managed carefully, sales should increase at a higher rate than uncollectible accounts.

CORRECTING AN UNFAVORABLE VERTICAL ANALYSIS RATIO FOR MERCHANDISE INVENTORY

ThreeGreen determines that its vertical analysis ratio for merchandise inventory should be between 42.0% and 45.0% of total assets. A business should strive to have the lowest possible amount of inventory, while ensuring that merchandise is always available when a customer places an order. A ratio below the target range may indicate that the business is not stocking an adequate supply of goods. Or, the business might not stock the right variety of merchandise. The business will lose sales if the right quantity and selection of merchandise are not available for sale. A ratio above the target range may indicate that the business is stocking more merchandise than it needs. Carrying more merchandise than needed can increase some operating expenses, such as rent, utilities, and insurance.

ThreeGreen's ratio for merchandise inventory ratio has declined from 58.4% to 43.3%. The prior-year ratio was higher than the target range. Thus, the decline in the ratio is a favorable trend. The current year's ratio, 43.3%, is within the target range. ThreeGreen prepared a list of its inventory items having the largest cost. Then it assessed whether the proper quantity of each item was available for sale. This information allowed ThreeGreen to reduce the quantities of many items.

CORRECTING AN UNFAVORABLE VERTICAL ANALYSIS RATIO FOR PLANT ASSET

ThreeGreen determines that its vertical analysis ratio for plant assets should be between 20.0% and 25.0% of total assets. A business must have plant assets to operate. A ratio below the target range may indicate that ThreeGreen has not invested enough in plant assets. Too few plant assets could force the business to operate inefficiently. A ratio above the target range may indicate that ThreeGreen owns more plant assets than necessary. Or it may have spent more than it should on the assets it owns.

ThreeGreen's ratio for plant assets, 21.9%, is within the target range. This ratio is difficult for a business to change over a short period of time. Therefore, the target ratio should be considered when acquiring plant assets in the future. Buying used plant assets can help to reduce the ratio. A company below its target range might consider buying additional or higher-quality plant assets.

Architecture for Humanity

Almost every person in the world has benefited from the work of an architect. The homes we live in and the schools we attend were designed by architects. Architects provide planning, design, and construction oversight services.

Architecture for Humanity (AH) is a nonprofit organization that provides services for those who cannot afford the services of an architect. AH provides a network of over 40,000 professionals who are ready to contribute their expertise to help others. AH also helps raise funds to cover the costs of construction. Once a structure is built, the city or a local organization must maintain it. So designing durability into structures is a major focus.

AH provides direct services to thousands of people each year. Perhaps its biggest contribution, though, is its Open Architecture Network. This is a website where hundreds of building plans and designs are shared and can be viewed or downloaded for free by anyone around the world.

CRITICAL THINKING

1. Go to the website for Architecture for Humanity (http://architectureforhumanity.org). Research one project (in process or completed). In a written report, list the name, a one-paragraph summary, and the location of the project.

2. Architecture for Humanity gives the following uses for contributions received: 88% spent on construction and design services, 9% spent on administrative costs, and 3% spent on fundraising. Why might AH's accountants collect and distribute this information?

Evaluating Vertical Analysis Liability Ratios

ThreeGreen Products, Inc.
Comparative Balance Sheet
December 31, 20-- and 20--

	CURRENT YEAR		PRIOR YEAR	
	AMOUNT	PERCENT	AMOUNT	PERCENT
LIABILITIES				
Current Liabilities:				
Accounts Payable	16 4 8 9 10	6.9	36 2 3 8 07	19.5
Sales Tax Payable	3 5 7 4 64	1.5	3 2 4 9 25	1.7
Employee Income Tax Payable	9 5 0 00	0.4	8 9 0 00	0.5
Social Security Tax Payable	2 0 2 3 06	0.9	1 9 0 1 68	1.0
Medicare Tax Payable	4 7 3 14	0.2	4 4 4 75	0.2
Health Insurance Premiums Payable	4 6 0 00	0.2	4 2 4 00	0.2
Retirement Benefits Payable	4 6 5 00	0.2	3 8 0 00	0.2
Unemployment Tax Payable—Federal	2 9 7 02	0.1	2 5 6 86	0.1
Unemployment Tax Payable—State	1 4 7 42	0.1	1 2 7 49	0.1
Federal Income Tax Payable	3 6 2 2 40	1.5	3 0 8 5 00	1.7
Dividends Payable	3 7 5 0 00	1.6	3 5 0 0 00	1.9
Total Liabilities	32 2 5 1 78	13.6	50 4 9 7 10	27.2
STOCKHOLDERS' EQUITY				
Capital Stock	75 0 0 0 00	31.6	70 0 0 0 00	37.7
Retained Earnings	130 1 1 5 41	54.8	65 2 1 8 84	35.1
Total Stockholders' Equity	205 1 1 5 41	86.4	135 2 1 8 84	72.8
Total Liabilities and Stockholders' Equity	237 3 6 7 19	100.0	185 7 1 5 94	100.0

A ratio that measures the ability of a business to pay its long-term liabilities is called a **solvency ratio**. The vertical analysis ratio for total liabilities is one type of solvency ratio. Similar to other ratios used by investors, the ratio for total liabilities has another name. Total liabilities divided by total assets is called the **debt ratio**. Although solvency ratios are generally considered long-term measures, the debt ratio can be used to rate the ability of a business to pay its current and long-term liabilities.

CORRECTING AN UNFAVORABLE DEBT RATIO

The ability to borrow money and delay the payment of expenses can benefit both individuals and businesses. Borrowing money enables individuals to purchase major items, such as houses and cars. Paying for daily expenses with a credit card can delay payment of these expenses.

Borrowing too much money, however, can be risky. It can be easy for individuals to buy houses or cars that they can't afford. Monthly loan and credit card payments can leave little money to pay for daily expenses. Individuals often abuse credit cards by making impulsive purchases of things they don't need or can't afford. Monthly debt payments, then, become overwhelming when someone becomes ill or loses a job.

Businesses face the same benefits and risks as individuals. A business can borrow money to purchase the equipment necessary to operate. Delaying payment for expenses and merchandise inventory purchases enables the business to use its cash for other transactions. However, a business can have too many liabilities. The business must be able to pay its liabilities on a timely basis. If sales decline during difficult financial times, the business may be unable to make its monthly payments.

ThreeGreen determines that total liabilities should be between 12.0% and 18.0% of total assets. ThreeGreen's debt ratio declined from 27.2% to 13.6%, a positive trend. The current-year debt ratio, 13.6%, is within the target range. Analyzing individual vertical analysis ratios provides more insight into the change in the debt ratio. ThreeGreen achieved its goal by reducing accounts payable from 19.5% to 6.9% of total assets.

A business having a debt ratio below its target range is able to increase its liabilities. For example, a business could borrow money to expand its store. The business could obtain a bank loan to pay for the expansion, purchase new store equipment, and increase its level of inventory.

A business having a debt ratio above the target range needs to restrict its purchases on account. The business may also be able to raise cash by selling more stock. Increasing assets will lower the debt ratio. Or the extra cash could be used to pay off some liabilities, which would also lower the debt ratio.

End of Lesson Review

LO2 Perform vertical analysis of a balance sheet.

LO3 Analyze a balance sheet using vertical analysis.

Terms Review

solvency ratio

debt ratio

Audit your understanding

1. Why do many retailers perform vertical analysis on the Accounts Receivable and Merchandise Inventory accounts?

2. What may cause a vertical analysis ratio for accounts receivable to be below the target range?

3. What may cause a vertical analysis ratio for merchandise inventory to be below the target range?

4. What should a company do if the vertical analysis ratio for merchandise inventory is above the target range?

5. Why is it risky for a business to have too many liabilities?

Work together 17-2

Analyzing a balance sheet

The comparative balance sheet for Tri-State Pipe and a form for completing this problem are given in the *Working Papers*. Your instructor will guide you through the following examples.

1. Complete the vertical analysis of the comparative balance sheet. Round percentage calculations to the nearest 0.1%.

2. Compare actual vertical analysis ratios to Tri-State Pipe's target ratios. Identify whether each ratio indicates a favorable trend and is within management's target range.

On your own 17-2

Analyzing a balance sheet

The comparative balance sheet for PBH Corporation and a form for completing this problem are given in the *Working Papers*. Work this problem independently.

1. Complete the vertical analysis of the comparative balance sheet. Round percentage calculations to the nearest 0.1%.

2. Compare actual vertical analysis ratios to PBH Corporation's target ratios. Identify whether each ratio indicates a favorable trend and is within management's target range.

17-3 Horizontal Analysis

LO4 Perform horizontal analysis on an income statement.
LO5 Perform horizontal analysis on a balance sheet.

Analyzing Trends with Horizontal Analysis

People often search for trends by comparing current information to prior-period information. These comparisons are used in all facets of life, including academic achievement, sports records, and business performance. For example, a high school increasing the average ACT score of its students from 22.9 to 24.1 would proudly claim a 5.2% increase in test scores—a favorable trend. In contrast, a 2.4% decrease in sales is an unfavorable trend that should cause concern for a corporation's board of directors.

A comparison of one item on a financial statement with the same item on a previous period's financial statement is called **horizontal analysis**. A horizontal analysis ratio is calculated by dividing the difference between the current- and prior-period amounts by the prior-period amount. The horizontal analysis ratio for a corporation's salary expense is calculated below.

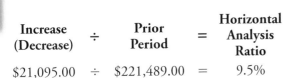

Current Period	−	Prior Period	=	Increase (Decrease)
$242,584.00	−	$221,489.00	=	$21,095.00

Increase (Decrease)	÷	Prior Period	=	Horizontal Analysis Ratio
$21,095.00	÷	$221,489.00	=	9.5%

Horizontal analysis ratios must be evaluated along with other information. For example, did the sales of the corporation also increase? Did management expect, or even plan, for wages and salaries to increase? Consider the following two cases:

Alton Company. Believing it would win a large government contract, Alton Company hired several new employees to support the planned increase in sales. Unfortunately, the government delayed awarding the contract until a month before the end of the fiscal year. Thus, salary expense increased by 9.5% while sales increased by just 2.0%.

Burke Company. Burke Company had expected the current year to be "business as usual." As expected, the company's sales increased a modest 2.0%. However, Burke did not foresee that several employees would leave the company and need to be replaced at significantly higher pay. As a result, the company's salary expense increased by 9.5%.

Each company's sales increased by 2.0% while salary expense increased by 9.5%. Yet the reason for the increase at each company tells a different story about management's performance. Horizontal analysis does not, by itself, provide any answers. An increase in sales is not necessarily favorable, while an increase in an operating expense is not always unfavorable. Horizontal analysis does motivate managers to investigate why changes have occurred. Management can then use what it learns to improve company performance.

Horizontal Analysis of an Income Statement LO4

Current Year Less Prior Year ❶

Difference Amount Divided by Prior Year ❷

ThreeGreen Products, Inc. Comparative Income Statement For Years Ended December 31, 20-- and 20--			INCREASE (DECREASE)	
	CURRENT YEAR	PRIOR YEAR	AMOUNT	PERCENT
Net Sales	626 7 8 1 99	548 9 1 5 25	77 8 6 6 74	14.2
Cost of Merchandise Sold	258 0 8 2 55	214 8 9 5 25	43 1 8 7 30	20.1
Gross Profit	368 6 9 9 44	334 0 2 0 00	34 6 7 9 44	10.4
Operating Expenses:				
Advertising Expense	4 6 8 0 00	4 5 0 0 00	1 8 0 00	4.0
Credit Card Fee Expense	6 8 4 2 20	5 4 8 1 29	1 3 6 0 91	24.8
Depreciation Expense—Office Equipment	7 4 8 5 00	7 2 1 8 00	2 6 7 00	3.7
Depreciation Expense—Store Equipment	9 8 3 0 00	9 2 4 0 00	5 9 0 00	6.4
Insurance Expense	8 2 0 0 00	7 8 0 0 00	4 0 0 00	5.1
Miscellaneous Expense	3 4 9 5 04	5 4 1 8 78	(1 9 2 3 74)	(35.5)
Payroll Taxes Expense	16 6 9 7 98	14 8 8 1 67	1 8 1 6 31	12.2
Rent Expense	8 4 0 0 00	8 4 0 0 00	—	0.0
Salary Expense	184 2 3 4 95	164 1 9 4 91	20 0 4 0 04	12.2
Supplies Expense—Office	3 9 3 8 17	3 4 8 1 19	4 5 6 98	13.1
Supplies Expense—Store	4 5 8 4 61	5 0 1 9 92	(4 3 5 31)	(8.7)
Uncollectible Accounts Expense	2 3 8 4 10	2 1 4 9 92	2 3 4 18	10.9
Utilities Expense	4 9 6 5 42	3 1 9 4 99	1 7 7 0 43	55.4
Total Operating Expenses	265 7 3 7 47	240 9 8 0 67	24 7 5 6 80	10.3
Income from Operations	102 9 6 1 97	93 0 3 9 33	9 9 2 2 64	10.7
Other Revenue	5 5 7 00	2 4 9 00	3 0 8 00	123.7
Net Income before Federal Income Tax	103 5 1 8 97	93 2 8 8 33	10 2 3 0 64	11.0
Less Federal Income Tax Expense	23 6 2 2 40	19 9 6 8 03	3 6 5 4 37	18.3
Net Income after Federal Income Tax	79 8 9 6 57	73 3 2 0 30	6 5 7 6 27	9.0

This comparative income statement differs slightly from the income statement used to prepare a vertical analysis. Each fiscal year's amounts are listed in a single column.

The dollar amount of the increase or decrease is entered in the third column. The horizontal analysis ratio is written in the fourth column.

❯ Calculating a Horizontal Analysis Ratio

❶ Calculate the difference by subtracting the prior-year amount from the current-year amount. The difference for net sales, $77,866.74, is calculated by subtracting prior-year net sales, $548,915.25, from current-year net sales, $626,781.99.

❷ Calculate the horizontal analysis ratio by dividing the difference by the prior-year amount. The horizontal analysis ratio for net sales, 14.2%, is calculated by dividing the difference, $77,866.74, by prior-year net sales, $548,915.25. The ratio is typically rounded to the nearest tenth of a percent.

Net income after federal income tax is typically referred to as *net income*.

Horizontal Analysis of a Balance Sheet LO5

	CURRENT YEAR	PRIOR YEAR	INCREASE (DECREASE) AMOUNT	PERCENT
ThreeGreen Products, Inc.				
Comparative Balance Sheet				
December 31, 20-- and 20--				
ASSETS				
Current Assets:				
Cash	54 1 9 4 34	5 4 2 6 55	48 7 6 7 79	898.7
Petty Cash	2 5 0 00	2 5 0 00	———	0.0
Accounts Receivable (net)	17 8 7 2 56	12 1 9 4 00	5 6 7 8 56	46.6
Merchandise Inventory	102 8 3 8 00	108 4 8 6 44	(5 6 4 8 44)	(5.2)
Supplies—Office	6 1 0 00	5 0 9 00	1 0 1 00	19.8
Supplies—Store	4 6 5 00	2 8 9 00	1 7 6 00	60.9
Prepaid Insurance	2 8 0 0 00	1 2 0 0 00	1 6 0 0 00	133.3
Notes Receivable	6 2 0 0 00	2 2 0 0 00	4 0 0 0 00	181.8
Interest Receivable	9 3 00	1 8 00	7 5 00	416.7
Total Current Assets	185 3 2 2 90	130 5 7 2 99	54 7 4 9 91	41.9
Plant Assets:				
Office Equipment (net)	11 2 2 1 18	12 9 4 8 69	(1 7 2 7 51)	(13.3)
Store Equipment (net)	40 8 2 3 11	42 1 9 4 26	(1 3 7 1 15)	(3.2)
Total Plant Assets	52 0 4 4 29	55 1 4 2 95	(3 0 9 8 66)	(5.6)
Total Assets	237 3 6 7 19	185 7 1 5 94	51 6 5 1 25	27.8
LIABILITIES				
Current Liabilities:				
Accounts Payable	16 4 8 9 10	36 2 3 8 07	(19 7 4 8 97)	(54.5)
Sales Tax Payable	3 5 7 4 64	3 2 4 9 25	3 2 5 39	10.0
Employee Income Tax Payable	9 5 0 00	8 9 0 00	6 0 00	6.7
Social Security Tax Payable	2 0 2 3 06	1 9 0 1 68	1 2 1 38	6.4
Medicare Tax Payable	4 7 3 14	4 4 4 75	2 8 39	6.4
Health Insurance Premiums Payable	4 6 0 00	4 2 4 00	3 6 00	8.5
Retirement Benefits Payable	4 6 5 00	3 8 0 00	8 5 00	22.4
Unemployment Tax Payable—Federal	2 9 7 02	2 5 6 86	4 0 16	15.6
Unemployment Tax Payable—State	1 4 7 42	1 2 7 49	1 9 93	15.6
Federal Income Tax Payable	3 6 2 2 40	3 0 8 5 00	5 3 7 40	17.4
Dividends Payable	3 7 5 0 00	3 5 0 0 00	2 5 0 00	7.1
Total Liabilities	32 2 5 1 78	50 4 9 7 10	(18 2 4 5 32)	(36.1)
STOCKHOLDERS' EQUITY				
Capital Stock	75 0 0 0 00	70 0 0 0 00	5 0 0 0 00	6.7
Retained Earnings	130 1 1 5 41	65 2 1 8 84	64 8 9 6 57	99.5
Total Stockholders' Equity	205 1 1 5 41	135 2 1 8 84	69 8 9 6 57	51.7
Total Liabilities and Stockholders' Equity	237 3 6 7 19	185 7 1 5 94	51 6 5 1 25	27.8

ThreeGreen performs a horizontal analysis on its comparative balance sheet. Accounts receivable and plant assets are presented at book value. The horizontal analysis ratios for a balance sheet are calculated using the same steps illustrated for the income statement.

The ratios show that total assets increased by 27.8% during the current year. The increase resulted from a 51.7% increase in stockholders' equity and a 36.1% decrease in liabilities. While these ratios appear to be favorable, only those who have day-to-day knowledge of the business can properly evaluate them. For example, ThreeGreen's 5.2% decrease in merchandise inventory might be seen as unfavorable by observers outside the company. However, because ThreeGreen took actions to reduce its inventory, its managers view this trend as favorable.

Managers use horizontal analysis ratios to help identify and explain significant trends. Publicly held corporations must file documents with the Securities and Exchange Commission that contain a section titled *Management's Discussion and Analysis of Financial Condition and Results of Operations*. Management often cites these ratios to explain the current year's results of operations.

Financial Analysis

For years, BJ's BBQ has expanded by opening new restaurants in major cities in Tennessee and Kentucky. The company performs a market study to identify a city lacking in the number of barbeque restaurants. The company tries to find a building previously occupied by another restaurant. The building is then renovated to reflect the casual, campfire style that has made BJ's BBQ a regional favorite.

Each month, the company performs a financial analysis of its financial statements. The analysis includes vertical analysis and other classic ratios. The company also calculates a set of ratios unique to restaurants. BJ's strives to increase each of these ratios over time.

Average ticket price: Dollar sales divided by the number of sales tickets. BJ's offers specials that encourage patrons to purchase additional items, such as beverages and desserts.
Sales per square foot: Dollar sales per day divided by square footage in the dining area. This ratio measures how effectively the company's dining area generates sales.
Table turns: The number of tickets per day divided by the number of tables. This ratio

indicates how effectively the restaurant is servicing customers. BJ's offers early dinner specials in an effort to attract customers and increase its table turns ratio. BJ's BBQ has a table turns ratio of 4.39, meaning that just over four groups of customers are served daily at each table.

In a surprise move, the chief executive officer has announced his plan to purchase Barbeque Hut, a chain of 16 restaurants in North Carolina and Virginia. Before the deal closes, however, he has asked you to analyze the financial statements of the company.

OPEN THE SPREADSHEET TLA_CH17
Follow the steps on the Instructions tab. The worksheet on the Analysis tab contains five-year information for Barbeque Hut. Calculate the three ratios described above. On the Charts tab, create charts to contrast the ratios for BJ's BBQ and Barbeque Hut. Use the charts to answer the following questions.

1. Is Barbeque Hut effective in increasing its ratios over the five-year period? Explain.

2. Based on the information provided, would you recommend that the company continue to pursue the purchase of Barbeque Hut?

End of Lesson Review

Term Review

horizontal analysis

Audit your understanding

1. How could a 2.0% decrease in supplies expense be an unfavorable trend?
2. How does a publicly held corporation use horizontal analysis when reporting to the Securities and Exchange Commission?

Work together 17-3

Analyzing financial statements using horizontal analysis

The comparative financial statements for Tri-State Pipe are given in the *Working Papers*. Your instructor will guide you through the following example.

Complete the horizontal analysis of the income statement. Round percentage calculations to the nearest 0.1%.

On your own 17-3

Analyzing financial statements using horizontal analysis

The comparative financial statements for Tri-State Pipe are given in the *Working Papers*. Work this problem independently.

Complete the horizontal analysis of the balance sheet. Round percentage calculations to the nearest 0.1%.

©CANDICE CUSACK, ISTOCK

LO6 Calculate earnings per share.
LO7 Calculate and interpret market ratios.
LO8 Calculate and interpret liquidity ratios.

Earnings per Share LO6

Net income after federal income tax divided by the number of outstanding shares of stock is called **earnings per share**. Earnings per share is often abbreviated as EPS. EPS is the most widely recognized measure of a corporation's financial performance. Corporations must include earnings per share on income statements submitted to the Securities and Exchange Commission.

There are no industry standards for earnings per share. Nor can a corporation's EPS be compared to the EPS of other corporations. Each corporation's EPS is a unique number because corporations can issue any number of shares. The earnings of each corporation are divided by a different number of shares. ThreeGreen's earnings per share would be different if it had issued more shares. ThreeGreen issued 7,500 shares of $10.00 par value stock, raising $75,000 of capital. If ThreeGreen had elected to issue 75,000 shares of $1.00 par value stock, it would still have raised $75,000 of capital. But the decision would have had a dramatic impact on EPS.

Net Income after Federal Income Tax	$79,896.57	$79,896.57
Number of Shares Outstanding	÷ 7,500	÷ 75,000
Earnings per Share	$ 10.65	$ 1.07

A corporation's earnings per share can only be compared to (1) the prior period's earnings per share and (2) projected earnings per share. Many corporations share estimates of their projected earnings per share with investors. A corporation strives to have its actual EPS increase from the prior year and to meet or exceed projections. Horizontal analysis can be used to calculate the change in EPS from prior years.

STOCKBYTE/GETTY IMAGES

Market Ratios LO7

Stock is traded on stock exchanges around the world. Investors use financial information and other information to place a value on a corporation's stock. A ratio that measures a corporation's financial performance in relation to the market value of its stock is called a **market ratio**. Investors rely on market ratios to make informed investment decisions.

DIVIDEND YIELD

The relationship between dividends per share and market price per share is called the **dividend yield**. Each corporation can decide the amount of dividends to pay to its stockholders. Corporations in some industries tend to have similar dividend yields. For example, most utility companies have high dividend yields—between 3% and 6%. Investors seeking a constant income will buy stock in companies with high dividend yields. For this reason, investors refer to stocks of these corporations as *income stocks*.

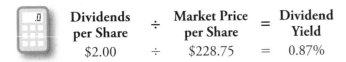

	Dividends per Share	÷	Market Price per Share	=	Dividend Yield
	$2.00	÷	$228.75	=	0.87%

In contrast, some corporations pay little, if any, dividends. These corporations have very small, or zero, dividend yields. These corporations prefer to retain their earnings to support their future growth. Investors refer to stocks of these corporations as *growth stocks*. Investors who buy a growth stock expect to benefit through an increase in the market value of the stock.

PRICE-EARNINGS RATIO

The relationship between the market value per share and earnings per share of a stock is called the **price-earnings ratio**. It is often referred to as the *P/E ratio*.

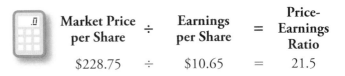

	Market Price per Share	÷	Earnings per Share	=	Price-Earnings Ratio
	$228.75	÷	$10.65	=	21.5

The P/E ratio is calculated as the market price per share divided by the earnings per share. The P/E ratio measures the price of the company's stock relative to its earnings. Income stocks typically have low P/E ratios. In contrast, growth stocks typically have high P/E ratios. Investors are willing to pay more for growth stocks that are expected to have dynamic earnings growth.

Online sources of financial information highlight the EPS and P/E ratios over several years. Investors analyze the trends in the P/E ratio to project a company's future earnings. Then, using historical P/E ratios, investors can predict future market prices of the corporation's stock.

Based on its dividend yield of 0.87% and its price-earnings ratio of 21.5, investors perceive ThreeGreen to be a growth stock.

©RTIMAGES/FOTOLIA.COM

Liquidity Ratios LO8

A ratio that measures the ability of a business to pay its current financial obligations is called a **liquidity ratio**. A business must have adequate financial resources to buy additional merchandise, pay employees, and pay for other operating expenses. The balance sheet is the primary source of data to calculate liquidity ratios.

Companies use liquidity ratios to analyze their financial strength. A company must understand its financial strength to plan for future periods and to ensure that adequate resources are available to operate the business. Creditors, vendors, and investors use liquidity ratios to help determine if a company is a good credit or investment risk. Before creditors will lend money to a business, or vendors will sell merchandise on account, they must believe that the company will later make good on its debt. A company that has been determined to be a poor credit risk is usually a bad investment as well.

WORKING CAPITAL

The amount of current assets less current liabilities is called **working capital**. The amount is stated in dollars. Working capital is a measure of the financial resources available for the daily operations of a business. ThreeGreen's working capital for the current year is calculated as shown below.

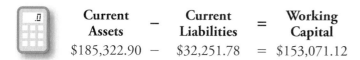

Current Assets	−	Current Liabilities	=	Working Capital
$185,322.90	−	$32,251.78	=	$153,071.12

Working capital should not be confused with cash. ThreeGreen does not have $153,071.12 in cash. The company does have $153,071.12 of assets that are available for use in daily operations of the business.

CURRENT RATIO

A business cannot compare itself to industry standards based on the value of its working capital. Nor is a horizontal analysis of working capital meaningful. A more useful measure is needed.

A ratio that measures the relationship of current assets to current liabilities is called the **current ratio**. The current ratio measures a company's ability to pay its current liabilities when due.

On December 31 of the current year, ThreeGreen calculated its current ratio at 5.75, as shown below. The current ratio may be stated as 5.75 to 1. ThreeGreen's current assets are 5.75 times its current liabilities. Based on previous experience, industry

guidelines, and the need to maintain sufficient merchandise inventory, ThreeGreen wants to maintain a current ratio between 4.0 and 6.0. ThreeGreen's current ratio of 5.75 is within the target range and a favorable indication of its financial strength.

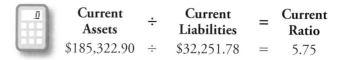

Current Assets	÷	Current Liabilities	=	Current Ratio
$185,322.90	÷	$32,251.78	=	5.75

QUICK RATIO

The current ratio assumes a business could sell its merchandise inventory quickly to pay its current liabilities. For many businesses, that may not be possible. Thus, some creditors prefer to use a more conservative measure of liquidity. Cash and other current assets that can be quickly converted into cash are called **quick assets**. Quick assets are also referred to as *liquid assets*. ThreeGreen's quick assets include cash, petty cash, and the book value of accounts receivable. A ratio that measures the relationship of quick assets to current liabilities is called the **quick ratio**.

On December 31 of the current year, ThreeGreen's quick ratio was 2.24. The quick ratio may be stated as 2.24 to 1. ThreeGreen's quick assets are 2.24 times its current liabilities. Most businesses strive to have a quick ratio of at least 1.00. ThreeGreen wants to maintain a quick ratio between 2.00 and 3.00, so 2.24 is within the target range and a favorable indication of its liquidity.

Cash	+	Accounts Receivable	=	Quick Assets
$54,444.34	+	$17,872.56	=	$72,316.90

Quick Assets	÷	Current Liabilities	=	Quick Ratio
$72,316.90	÷	$32,251.78	=	2.24

fyi

Liquidity ratios are used by managers, vendors, and creditors to help determine the ability of a business to meet its current debt obligations.

Careers In Accounting

Gerald Bozeman
INTERNAL AUDITOR

Gerald Bozeman is an internal auditor for a large financial services company. In Chapter 8 (page 232), an audit was described as an examination of financial records, accounts, and supporting documents to check their accuracy. An accountant who conducts an audit is known as an auditor. An internal auditor is an employee of a company who evaluates and monitors his or her company's internal control processes and procedures.

An internal auditor often reports to more than one person. On administrative and support issues, Mr. Bozeman reports to Ms. Gutzman, the chief executive officer (CEO). He also reports to the audit committee of the board of directors on issues of accountability.

In Chapter 11 (page 338), internal controls were defined as the processes and procedures employed within a business to ensure that its operations are conducted ethically, accurately, and reliably. Among Mr. Bozeman's major tasks is making sure that the internal control processes and procedures are being followed by company employees. He collects data and looks for deficient controls; duplicated effort; and noncompliance with laws, regulations, and company policies. Computers and calculators are the tools he relies on to perform these tasks.

Mr. Bozeman prepares both written and oral reports of his internal audits. These reports detail his findings and recommend corrective actions. His reports are presented to the audit committee. If the audit committee approves his recommendations, he will follow up to ensure that the recommendations are implemented.

Mr. Bozeman is a Certified Internal Auditor (CIA). This means that he has met the requirements of The Institute of Internal Auditors. These include education credits, work experience, and passing a certification exam.

Salary Range: Salaries vary depending on company size, job responsibilities, and experience. The average range is $43,000 to $95,000.

Qualifications: Minimum education for an internal auditor is a bachelor's degree in accounting. A master's degree is often preferred. Most employers also require past experience in the field of accounting. Many internal auditors have some education in law, forensics, finance, math, and economics.

Internal auditors interact with coworkers, other executives, and external professionals. They also prepare oral and written reports for senior management. So, it is necessary to have excellent communication skills as well as a cooperative attitude. To perform well in their positions, internal auditors must have good organizational, analytical, math, reasoning, and problem-solving skills. They must be able to plan and direct projects, deal with high-stress situations, prioritize tasks, and keep up to date with technology. An internal auditor must also be ethical, reliable, and responsible.

Occupational Outlook: The growth for auditor positions is projected to be faster than average (20% or higher for the period from 2008 to 2018).

ACTIVITIES

1. Go to the website for The Institute of Internal Auditors (www.theiia.org). Find the specific education and work experience required to become a Certified Internal Auditor.
2. On the same website, find the Code of Ethics for internal auditors. List the four principles that make up the code.

LO6 Calculate earnings per share.

LO7 Calculate and interpret market ratios.

LO8 Calculate and interpret liquidity ratios.

Terms Review

earnings per share

market ratio

dividend yield

price-earnings ratio

liquidity ratio

working capital

current ratio

quick assets

quick ratio

Audit your understanding

1. Why can one corporation's earnings per share not be compared to the EPS of other corporations?
2. What group is the primary user of market ratios?
3. Do income stocks typically have low or high dividend yields?
4. Do growth stocks typically have low or high price-earnings ratios?
5. What is the primary source of data to calculate liquidity ratios?
6. What does working capital measure?
7. Why is the current ratio a useful measure of financial strength?

Work together 17-4

Analyzing financial statements using financial ratios

Selected financial information for Eagle Corporation is presented below. A form for completing this problem is given in the *Working Papers*. Your instructor will guide you through the following example.

Net income after federal income taxes	$148,186.18
Number of shares outstanding	40,000
Dividends per share	$2.48
Market price	$37.90
Quick assets	$484,943.00
Current assets	$604,984.00
Current liabilities	$418,493.00

1. Calculate the (a) earnings per share, (b) dividend yield, and (c) price-earnings ratio. Round the dividend yield to the nearest 0.01%. Round the P/E ratio to the nearest 0.1.
2. Evaluate each ratio relative to prior-year ratios. Investors consider Eagle Corporation to be an income stock.
3. Calculate the (a) working capital and (b) current and quick ratios. Round ratios to the nearest 0.01.
4. Determine if the liquidity ratios are within management's target range.

On your own 17-4

Analyzing financial statements using financial ratios

Selected financial information for Mid-State Corporation is presented below. A form for completing this problem is given in the *Working Papers*. Work this problem independently.

Net income after federal income taxes	$6,118,089.54
Number of shares outstanding	8,500,000
Dividends per share	$0.06
Market price	$42.15
Quick assets	$2,814,974.00
Current assets	$4,657,856.00
Current liabilities	$3,253,053.00

1. Calculate the (a) earnings per share, (b) dividend yield, and (c) price-earnings ratio. Round the dividend yield to the nearest 0.01%. Round the P/E ratio to the nearest 0.1.
2. Evaluate each ratio relative to prior-year ratios. Investors consider Mid-State Corporation to be a growth stock.
3. Calculate the (a) working capital and (b) current and quick ratios. Round ratios to the nearest 0.01.
4. Determine if the liquidity ratios are within management's target range.

A Look at Accounting Software

Analyzing the Printout of a Five-Year Comparative Income Statement

In this chapter, you learned about comparative financial statements and trend analysis. The comparative income statement in the chapter compares the current year to the prior year. While that is a common and useful analysis, managers often need a longer-term view.

Some high-end accounting software systems come with preformatted reports similar to the one illustrated here. However, this report could be created in most accounting systems using the custom report tools supplied in the software. Five-year comparative statements like this one are especially useful to investors and creditors. They are also useful to management for making more accurate projections of future revenue, expenses, and net income.

Some financial analysts argue that a comparison of two sequential periods only indicates the direction of a change. They contend that it requires three or more periods to reveal a trend. Several trends can be seen in this five-year comparative statement. Can you identify some of them?

MUSIC MANIA, INC. ❶
5-Year Comparative Income Statement
Year-to-Date, December 31

❸	20X1 ❹	% of Sales	% Δ	20X2	% of Sales	% Δ
Revenue	1,589,741.18	100.0%	6.6%	1,727,571.74	100.0%	8.7%
Cost of Goods Sold	864,819.20	54.4%	11.2%	961,048.16	55.6%	11.1%
Gross Profit	724,921.98	45.6%	1.5%	766,523.58	44.4%	5.7%
Operating Expenses:						
Advertising Expense	15,696.38	1.0%	10.3%	17,209.51	1.0%	9.6%
Cash Short and Over	116.37	0.0%	6.3%	149.70	0.0%	28.6%
Credit Card Fee Expense	5,723.07	0.4%	11.0%	6,219.26	0.4%	8.7%
Depr. Exp.—Office Equip.	7,675.11	0.5%	13.0%	8,447.23	0.5%	10.1%
Depr. Exp.—Store Equip.	7,862.73	0.5%	–9.6%	10,232.56	0.6%	30.1%
Insurance Expense	17,421.29	1.1%	0.5%	17,614.67	1.0%	1.1%
Miscellaneous Expense	5,143.43	0.3%	0.9%	5,690.69	0.3%	10.6%
Payroll Taxes Expense	28,214.62	1.8%	2.3%	31,047.37	1.8%	10.0%
Professional Fees	9,866.98	0.6%	4.2%	10,369.21	0.6%	5.1%
Rent Expense	49,200.00	3.1%	0.0%	49,200.00	2.8%	0.0%
Salary Expense	311,419.62	19.6%	2.3%	342,686.15	19.8%	10.0%
Supplies Exp.—Office	3,462.52	0.2%	5.7%	4,107.93	0.2%	18.6%
Supplies Exp.—Store	15,602.75	1.0%	6.0%	17,028.84	1.0%	9.1%
Uncollectible Accts. Exp.	4,677.62	0.3%	16.3%	5,005.71	0.3%	7.0%
Utilities Expense	7,442.74	0.5%	4.0%	7,770.22	0.4%	4.4%
Total Operating Exp.	489,525.23	30.8%	2.5%	532,779.05	30.8%	8.8%
Income from Operations	235,396.75	14.8%	–0.6%	233,744.53	13.5%	–0.7%
Other Revenue	2,633.67	0.2%	5.8%	3,071.91	0.2%	16.6%
Net Income before FIT	238,030.42	15.0%	–0.5%	236,816.44	13.7%	–0.5%
Federal Income Tax Exp.	76,081.86	4.8%	–0.6%	75,608.41	4.4%	–0.6%
Net Income after FIT	161,948.56	10.2%	–0.4%	161,208.03	9.3%	–0.5%

① Music Mania, Inc., is a retail merchandising business that sells musical instruments and supplies.

② This report shows five years of income statements. For each year, it includes columns for a vertical analysis and the percent change from the prior year. Analysts commonly use the symbol Δ (delta) to represent an amount of change.

③ Computerized accounting systems generally put limits on the number of characters or numbers that can be entered in a particular type of field. For example, the account titles on this report are limited to 26 characters, including spaces and punctuation. The reason for limiting field lengths is clear when the fields are displayed in columns on a report such as this one.

④ When a report is being designed, numerical fields, shown here in dollars and cents, can be rounded to the nearest dollar or the nearest thousand dollars (000). The point is to show the amount of detail that will be meaningful to the reader and still be easy to read.

⑤ The designer of this report chose to use a shaded-bar style. For long reports, the bars aid the reader in following data across the page.

20X3	% of Sales	% Δ	20X4	% of Sales	% Δ	20X5	% of Sales	% Δ
1,901,538.21	100.0%	10.1%	1,963,528.36	100.0%	3.3%	1,943,304.02	100.0%	−1.0%
1,064,861.40	56.0%	10.8%	998,945.05	50.9%	−6.2%	994,194.34	51.2%	−0.5%
836,676.81	44.0%	9.2%	964,583.31	49.1%	15.3%	949,109.68	48.8%	−1.6%
14,869.02	0.8%	−13.6%	13,406.50	0.7%	−9.8%	13,026.29	0.7%	−2.8%
119.26	0.0%	−20.3%	127.66	0.0%	7.0%	419.54	0.0%	228.6%
6,845.54	0.4%	10.1%	7,068.70	0.4%	3.3%	6,995.89	0.4%	−1.0%
8,332.35	0.4%	−1.4%	7,385.80	0.4%	−11.4%	7,211.50	0.4%	−2.4%
11,515.72	0.6%	12.5%	11,128.79	0.6%	−3.4%	10,977.44	0.6%	−1.4%
20,322.04	1.1%	15.4%	20,330.17	1.0%	0.0%	20,431.82	1.1%	0.5%
5,613.30	0.3%	−1.4%	6,115.13	0.3%	8.9%	6,264.34	0.3%	2.4%
33,326.24	1.8%	7.3%	34,206.05	1.7%	2.6%	35,998.45	1.9%	5.2%
10,610.81	0.6%	2.3%	11,679.32	0.6%	10.1%	11,683.99	0.6%	0.0%
56,580.00	3.0%	15.0%	56,580.00	2.9%	0.0%	56,580.00	2.9%	0.0%
367,839.31	19.3%	7.3%	377,550.27	19.2%	2.6%	397,333.90	20.4%	5.2%
4,627.17	0.2%	12.6%	4,564.24	0.2%	−1.4%	4,567.43	0.2%	0.1%
18,707.88	1.0%	9.9%	20,137.16	1.0%	7.6%	18,816.16	1.0%	−6.6%
4,548.39	0.2%	−9.1%	4,941.37	0.3%	8.6%	5,368.30	0.3%	8.6%
8,800.55	0.5%	13.3%	9,011.76	0.5%	2.4%	10,012.07	0.5%	11.1%
572,657.58	30.1%	7.5%	584,232.92	29.8%	2.0%	605,687.12	31.2%	3.7%
264,019.23	13.9%	13.0%	380,350.39	19.4%	44.1%	343,422.56	17.7%	−9.7%
2,555.83	0.1%	−16.8%	2,359.03	0.1%	−7.7%	2,941.71	0.2%	24.7%
266,575.06	14.0%	12.6%	382,709.42	19.5%	43.6%	346,364.27	17.8%	−9.5%
87,214.27	4.6%	15.3%	130,121.20	6.6%	49.2%	118,332.07	6.1%	−9.1%
179,360.79	9.4%	11.3%	252,588.22	12.9%	40.8%	228,032.20	11.7%	−9.7%

Chapter Summary

Financial ratios allow managers to compare the financial performance of a business to established benchmarks. Management can determine benchmark ratios using many factors, including (1) actual ratios from prior fiscal periods, (2) industry standards published by industry organizations, (3) business plans, and (4) unexpected events. Organizations that publish industry standards analyze large numbers of financial statements to develop average financial ratios by industry.

Benchmark ratios are often stated in terms of a target range. When a ratio falls outside the target range, the business should investigate what factors or events resulted in the unfavorable results.

Vertical analysis ratios measure the relationship between one financial statement item and the total that includes that item. For an income statement, the total is net sales. For a balance sheet, total assets or the sum of total liabilities plus stockholder's equity are used. However, since those two totals are equal, total assets can be used to calculate all vertical analysis ratios on the balance sheet. Certain vertical analysis ratios have alternate names, including the gross margin, operating margin, profit margin, and debt ratio.

Horizontal analysis focuses on the percentage change in a financial statement amount between fiscal periods. A horizontal analysis ratio is calculated by dividing the difference of the current- and prior-period amounts by the prior-period amount.

Earnings per share (EPS) is likely the most widely recognized financial ratio. EPS is unique to each corporation. There are no industry benchmarks for EPS. However, managers and investors can use horizontal analysis to compare the current period's EPS to those of prior periods.

Financial ratios can be classified as profitability, solvency, market, and liquidity ratios. Each ratio measures a certain aspect of a corporation's operations. These ratios can be compared to benchmark ratios to measure the corporation's performance.

EXPLORE ACCOUNTING

Annual Reports—Financial Information and More

Corporations publish annual reports to communicate the results of operations to interested parties, such as stockholders, creditors, and government agencies. The typical annual report is a colorful, soft-cover brochure printed on glossy paper and 40 to 60 pages in length. Most companies encourage their stockholders to register for electronic delivery of the annual report. Other individuals can access the annual report on the corporation's website. The reports are grouped in two sections:

1. *Management's Analysis and Discussion.* This section provides management with an opportunity to promote the corporation. Through the use of pictures, graphs, and narrative, management can highlight the achievements of the past fiscal year and present its plans. Some corporations report on how the volunteer work of their employees is having a positive impact in their communities. They might include discussions of environmental and recycling programs to demonstrate efforts toward social responsibility.

   The ultimate objective of any corporation is to increase the market price of its stock, thereby raising stockholders' investment. By "putting its best foot forward" in this section, management can increase the demand for the corporation's products and stock, thus increasing the stock's price.

2. *Financial Statements.* This section contains several items in addition to the basic financial statements. Most of the additional items are required by GAAP or the Securities and Exchange Commission. As a result, these items are similar among corporations.

   a. *Notes to the Financial Statements.* The notes contain additional, detailed information about items presented on the financial statements. For example, the note related to long-term debt would include the projected loan repayments for the next five years.

   b. *Auditor's Report.* The report of the independent auditor states that a public accounting firm has tested the financial statements and found them accurate and free of misrepresentation. The auditor's report is not meant as an endorsement of the corporation's investment quality. It does, however, give the reader confidence to use the financial statements to make business or investment decisions.

   c. *Financial Analysis.* Summary financial information, such as total assets, net income, and common financial ratios, is presented for several years.

INSTRUCTIONS

Access an annual report using a library or the Internet. Prepare a detailed outline of its contents. Summarize the major topics in management's analysis and discussion. Did management do a good job of "putting its best foot forward"? Would you recommend that a friend purchase the corporation's stock? Support your answers.

Apply Your Understanding

INSTRUCTIONS: Download problem instructions for Excel, QuickBooks, and Peachtree from the textbook companion website at www.C21accounting.com.

17-1 Application Problem: Analyzing an income statement LO1

AAONLiNE
1. Go to www.cengage.com/login
2. Click on **AA Online** to access.
3. Go to the online assignment and follow the instructions.

1. Review the comparative income statement.
2. Complete the vertical analysis.
3. Print the worksheet.

The comparative income statement for TR's Quik Mart and a form for completing this problem are given in the *Working Papers*.

Instructions:

1. Complete the vertical analysis of the comparative income statement. Round the calculation of percents to the nearest 0.1%.

2. Compare selected vertical analysis ratios to TR's Quik Mart's benchmark ratios. Identify whether each ratio indicates a favorable trend and is within management's target range.

17-2 Application Problem: Analyzing a balance sheet LO2, 3

1. Review the comparative balance sheet.
2. Complete the Current Ratios section.
3. Complete the vertical analysis.
4. Print the worksheet.

The comparative balance sheet for TR's Quik Mart and a form for completing this problem are given in the *Working Papers*.

Instructions:

1. Complete the vertical analysis of the comparative balance sheet. Round the calculation of percents to the nearest 0.1%.

2. Compare selected vertical analysis ratios to TR's Quik Mart's target ratios. Identify whether each ratio indicates a favorable trend and is within management's target range.

17-3 Application Problem: Analyzing financial statements using horizontal analysis LO4, 5

1. Review the comparative financial statements.
2. Complete the horizontal analysis.
3. Print the worksheets.

The comparative financial statements for Vector Industries are given in the *Working Papers*. Round the calculation of percents to the nearest 0.1%.

Instructions:

1. Complete the horizontal analysis of the income statement.

2. Complete the horizontal analysis of the balance sheet.

17-4 Application Problem: Analyzing financial statements using financial ratios LO6, 7, 8

AAONLiNE
1. Go to www.cengage.com/login
2. Click on **AA Online** to access.
3. Go to the online assignment and follow the instructions.

Selected financial information for Lakeside Furniture is presented below. A form for completing this problem is given in the *Working Papers*.

Net income after federal income taxes	$7,948,184.15
Number of shares outstanding	2,500,000
Dividends per share	$2.40
Market price	$38.15
Quick assets	$2,618,419.19
Current assets	$3,418,461.04
Current liabilities	$2,491,894.11

Instructions:

1. Calculate the (a) earnings per share, (b) dividend yield, and (c) price-earnings ratio. Round the dividend yield to the nearest 0.01%. Round the price-earnings ratio to the nearest 0.1.

2. Evaluate each ratio relative to prior-year ratios. Investors consider Lakeside Furniture to be an income stock.

3. Calculate the (a) working capital and (b) current and quick ratios. Round ratios to the nearest 0.01.

4. Determine if these items are within management's target range.

17-M Mastery Problem: Analyzing financial statements LO1, 2, 3, 4, 5, 6, 7, 8

1. Review the comparative financial statements.
2. Complete the vertical analysis.
3. Complete the horizontal analysis.
4. Print the worksheets.

The income statement and balance sheet for Aqua Products, Inc., and forms for completing this problem are given in the *Working Papers*.

Instructions:

1. Prepare a vertical analysis of the income statement and balance sheet. Round percentage calculations to the nearest 0.1%.

2. Prepare a horizontal analysis of the comparative income statement and balance sheet. Round percentage calculations to the nearest 0.1%.

3. Compare the actual vertical analysis ratios to management's benchmark ratios. Identify whether each ratio is within management's target range.

4. Using the following information, calculate the following ratios for the current year: (a) earnings per share,
(b) dividend yield, and (c) price-earnings ratio. Round the dividend yield to the nearest 0.01%. Round the price-earnings ratio to the nearest 0.1. Evaluate each ratio relative to prior-year ratios.

Number of shares outstanding	10,000
Dividends per share	$0.80
Market price	$92.40

5. Calculate the (a) working capital and (b) current and quick ratios. Round ratios to the nearest 0.01. Determine if these ratios are within management's target range.

17-C Challenge Problem: Analyzing industry standards LO1, 3, 8

Selected financial ratios for the five industries below are represented in the table by the letters A through E. Match each industry, 1 through 5, to a set of ratios, A through E. A form for completing this problem is given in the *Working Papers*.

Ratio \ Industry	A	B	C	D	E
Profitability Ratios					
Gross Margin	36.8%	94.6%	9.0%	84.5%	100.0%
Profit Margin	3.6%	8.4%	1.0%	10.2%	8.7%
Vertical Analysis Ratios					
Account Receivable	10.7%	9.8%	10.5%	3.3%	55.8%
Merchandise Inventory	40.6%	0.4%	11.4%	1.0%	0.0%
Plant Assets	22.5%	26.1%	47.4%	35.8%	1.5%
Debt Ratio	47.8%	77.3%	65.7%	73.5%	88.5%
Liquidity Ratio					
Current Ratio	2.70	1.40	1.30	1.20	1.00
Quick Ratio	0.8	1.2	0.7	0.8	0.9

1. Accommodations (hotels and motels)
2. Commercial banking
3. Gasoline stations
4. Hardware stores
5. Offices of physicians

Source: Almanac of Business and Industrial Financial Ratios, 2011 Edition, Leo Troy, CCH, Chicago, Illinois.

21st Century Skills

Savings and Investing

Theme: Financial, Economic, Business, and Entrepreneurial Literacy

Skills: Critical Thinking and Problem Solving, Communication and Collaboration, ICT Literacy

PARTNERSHIP FOR
21ST CENTURY SKILLS

A common method of planning finances is the 70-20-10 rule. The guideline for spending (including debt payments) is 70%, the guideline for saving is 20%, and the guideline for investing is 10%. Therefore, when budgeting, you will begin to set money aside for savings. That will allow you to plan for opportunities and emergencies and reach long-term financial goals. Although many consider saving and investing to be the same thing, they really are quite different.

The purpose of saving is to store money in a safe place, such as a bank, where it earns interest. That gives you easy access to the cash for short-term needs. Examples include saving for a car or a computer and maintaining an emergency fund. Emergency funds are critical as they provide a safety net for unexpected repairs, medical expenses, or job loss. A guideline for an emergency fund is savings equal to six months of expenses.

There are a number of ways you can save money for short-term needs: savings accounts, money market accounts, and certificates of deposit (CDs). These methods of savings offer low risk, but the tradeoff is that they earn low interest. Interest is the percentage rate paid on money saved or invested. Most banks and savings and loans provide similar, competitive savings plans.

The purpose of investing is to build wealth for future needs—a commitment greater than five years. Common investments include stocks, bonds, mutual funds, real estate, IRAs, and 401(k)s. Depending on the type of investment, the risk is likely to be greater. The tradeoff is that the rate of return will be higher, and you will begin to build wealth while you are young. Unlike savings accounts, investments carry some risk of losing the entire amount invested. Due to the risk factor, most investors diversify by putting their money in multiple investments. Selecting the best investments to build wealth requires assessing the tradeoffs between risk and rate of return. A good investment plan provides more opportunity to grow your money over time.

APPLICATION

1. Research the methods of saving and investing. Create a model or diagram summarizing the types of savings and investment plans and their levels of risk. Which plan would be the best for an emergency fund? Explain your answer.
2. Based on your findings in part (1), do you think buying stock in a strong company would be a good short-term savings strategy?
3. Interview five adults about the methods they use to save and invest. Record your finding in a table or spreadsheet. Share your findings with the class and explain why you think they selected these methods based on their ages and family situations.

Auditing for errors

The Sarbanes-Oxley Act requires publicly traded corporations to document and test their accounting systems. The documentation for River Corporation contains the following section related to the analysis of comparative financial statements.

REVIEW AND ANSWER

Identify the errors in this section of the documentation.

FINANCIAL STATEMENT ANALYSIS

The accounting department will provide the board of directors with an analysis of monthly comparative financial statements. This report must be submitted by the tenth business day after the end of the month. The calculation method for each ratio to be included in the report follows.

1. Vertical analysis: Divide every item on the financial statements by sales.
2. Horizontal analysis: Divide the month-to-month change of each item on the financial statements by the current month's amount of the item.
3. Earnings per share: Divide income from operations by the number of shares.
4. Dividend yield: Divide the most recent dividend per share by the market price of the stock on the last day of the month.
5. Price-earnings ratio: Divide the market price of the stock on the last day of the month by the earnings per share.
6. Working capital: Divide current assets by current liabilities.

Analyzing Nike's financial statements

Nike's Selected Financial Data page provides investors with a summary of the most important amounts in the financial statements. The Year Ended May 31 section provides amounts from the Consolidated Statements of Income. The At May 31 section reports amounts from the Consolidated Balance Sheets.

The Financial Ratios section reports five financial ratios for each of the five years. Nike's management must believe that these financial ratios provide investors with the best and quickest way of assessing the performance and financial stability of the corporation.

INSTRUCTIONS

Use the Selected Financial Data on page B-3 of Appendix B to answer the following questions.
1. Identify the five financial ratios presented on the Selected Financial Data page.
2. What other financial ratios are presented in the Year Ended May 31 section?

Reinforcement Activity 2—Part B

An Accounting Cycle for a Corporation: End-of-Fiscal-Period Work

  **AA**ONLINE

The ledgers used in Reinforcement Activity 2—Part A are needed to complete Reinforcement Activity 2—Part B.

Reinforcement Activity 2—Part B includes those accounting activities needed to complete the accounting cycle of Gulf Uniform Supply, Inc. (GUS), and to evaluate a proposed corporate acquisition.

End-of-Fiscal-Period Work

INSTRUCTIONS

11. After preparing the schedule of accounts receivable, the company accepted an offer from Western Theaters to settle its account for $1,500.00. Enter the following transactions on a new general journal page. Post each transaction to the general ledger and the accounts receivable ledger.

   Dec. 31.   Accepted a $1,500.00, 120-day, 8% note from Western Theaters. NR7.

   31.   Wrote off the remaining balance of Western Theaters' account. M62.

12. Prepare a new schedule of accounts receivable.

13. Prepare an unadjusted trial balance.

14. Complete the aging of accounts receivable. Journalize the December 31 adjusting entry for estimated uncollectible accounts expense for the year.

15. Use the information below, collected on December 31, to journalize the adjusting entries.

a. Merchandise inventory	$53,148.00
b. Office supplies inventory	845.00
c. Store supplies inventory	995.00
e. Value of prepaid insurance	2,400.00
f. Note receivable—6%, 90-day, dated November 10, face amount	4,000.00
g. Estimate of office equipment depreciation	5,460.00
h. Estimate of store equipment depreciation	6,980.00

16. Post the adjusting entries in the general ledger.

17. Prepare an adjusted trial balance, including all account balances except Federal Income Tax Expense, and total the columns.

18. Using the tax table shown in Chapter 15, calculate the federal income tax owed for the fiscal year.

19. Journalize and post the adjusting entry for federal income tax payable.

20. Complete the adjusted trial balance.

21. Prepare an income statement for the current year. Prepare a vertical analysis of each amount in the fourth amount column. Round calculations to the nearest 0.1%.

22. Prepare a statement of stockholders' equity. The company had 5,500 shares of $10.00 par value stock outstanding on January 1. The company issued an additional 500 shares during the year.

23. Prepare a balance sheet for the current year.

24. Journalize and post the closing entries.

Proposed corporate acquisition: The board of directors of Health Fashions, Inc. (HFI), is seeking a buyer for the company. HFI sells uniforms to doctors' offices and hospitals. Thus, HFI and GUS operate similar businesses. Acquiring HFI would enable GUS to expand into a bordering state.

GUS obtained the comparative income statement and balance sheet from HFI. For the acquisition to work, GUS's management would want HFI's financial ratios to be in line with its own benchmarks. GUS considers HFI to be an income stock.

25. Prepare a vertical analysis of HFI's comparative income statement and balance sheet. Round calculations to the nearest 0.1%.

26. Prepare a horizontal analysis of HFI's comparative income statement and balance sheet. Round calculations to the nearest 0.1%.

27. Compare HFI's vertical analysis ratios to GUS's benchmark ratios. Determine whether each ratio shows a favorable trend and is within GUS's target range.

28. Using the following information, calculate the following ratios: (a) earnings per share, (b) dividend yield, and (c) price-earnings ratio. Round the dividend yield to the nearest 0.01%. Round the price-earnings ratio to the

nearest 0.1. Evaluate each ratio relative to prior-year ratios.

	Current Year	Prior Year
Number of shares outstanding	50,000	50,000
Dividends per share	$0.16	$0.14
Market price	$12.50	$11.50

29. Calculate (a) the working capital and (b) the current and quick ratios for the current year. Round ratios to the nearest 0.01. Determine if these ratios are within GUS's target range. Is HFI a good fit for GUS?

© Robbi/Shutterstock

AUTHENTIC THREADS

Featuring
"THINK LIKE AN ACCOUNTANT"
Critical Thinking Activities

Authentic Threads is a merchandising business organized as a corporation. The company specializes in selling a unique variety of trendy clothing, shoes, jewelry, and accessories for the teen and young adult market. This simulation includes the realistic transactions made both in store and on the company's website. In this simulation, you will do accounting work for Authentic Threads.

Source documents are provided for transactions that are recorded in special journals and a general journal, similar to the ones used by ThreeGreen Products, Inc., in Part 2.

This real-life business simulation is available in manual and automated versions. The automated version is used with Automated Accounting Online software.

The following activities are included in this simulation:

1 Recording transactions in special journals from source documents.

2 Posting items to be posted individually to a general ledger and subsidiary ledgers.

3 Recording a payroll in a payroll register. Updating the employee earnings records. Recording payroll journal entries.

4 Posting column totals to a general ledger.

5 Preparing schedules of accounts receivable and accounts payable from subsidiary ledgers.

6 Preparing a trial balance on a work sheet.

7 Planning adjustments and completing a work sheet.

8 Preparing financial statements.

9 Journalizing and posting adjusting entries.

10 Journalizing and posting closing entries.

11 Preparing a post-closing trial balance.

12 Completing the Think Like an Accountant Financial Analysis activities.

Part

3

Accounting

for a Merchandising Business Organized as a Corporation—Adjustments and Valuation

©OLGALIS, ISTOCK

SUN TREASURES, INC.

Sun Treasures, Inc., the business described in Part 3, is a retail merchandising business organized as a corporation. Sun Treasures purchases and sells a wide variety of souvenirs. It rents free-standing buildings near east Florida beaches.

The corporation was originally organized and owned by Nathan Morgan. Over time, he sold common stock to family members and gave stock to his children. Several years ago, the company sold common stock to the public. The Morgan family still owns over 50% of the outstanding shares. The Morgan family holds five of the seven positions on the corporation's board of directors.

The board has adopted a ten-year plan to expand its business to the Florida west coast. The strategy includes opening new retail stores and a distribution center in central Florida.

Chart of Accounts
SUN TREASURES, INC.

GENERAL LEDGER

Balance Sheet Accounts

(1000) ASSETS
1100   Current Assets
1110   Cash
1120   Petty Cash
1130   Accounts Receivable
1135   Allowance for Uncollectible Accounts
1140   Notes Receivable
1145   Interest Receivable
1150   Merchandise Inventory
1160   Supplies—Office
1170   Supplies—Store
1180   Prepaid Insurance
1200   Plant Assets
1210   Office Equipment
1215   Accumulated Depreciation—Office Equipment
1220   Store Equipment
1225   Accumulated Depreciation—Store Equipment

(2000) LIABILITIES
2100   Current Liabilities
2110   Accounts Payable
2120   Sales Tax Payable
2130   Notes Payable
2140   Interest Payable
2145   Line of Credit
2147   Unearned Rent Income
2150   Employee Income Tax Payable
2155   Social Security Tax Payable
2160   Medicare Tax Payable
2165   Medical Insurance Payable
2170   Retirement Benefits Payable
2175   Unemployment Tax Payable—State
2180   Unemployment Tax Payable—Federal
2185   Federal Income Tax Payable
2200   Long-term Liabilities
2210   Long-term Notes Payable
2220   Bonds Payable

(3000) STOCKHOLDERS' EQUITY
3110   Capital Stock—Common
3120   Paid-in Capital in Excess of Par—Common
3130   Capital Stock—Preferred
3210   Retained Earnings
3220   Dividends
3230   Income Summary

Income Statement Accounts

(4000) OPERATING REVENUE
4110   Sales
4120   Sales Discount
4130   Sales Returns and Allowances

(5000) COST OF GOODS SOLD
5110   Purchases
5120   Purchases Discount
5130   Purchases Returns and Allowances

(6000) OPERATING EXPENSES
6105   Advertising Expense
6110   Cash Short and Over
6115   Credit Card Fee Expense
6120   Depreciation Expense—Office Equipment
6125   Depreciation Expense—Store Equipment
6130   Insurance Expense
6135   Miscellaneous Expense
6140   Payroll Taxes Expense
6145   Rent Expense
6150   Salary Expense
6155   Supplies Expense—Office
6160   Supplies Expense—Store
6165   Uncollectible Accounts Expense
6170   Utilities Expense
6200   Income Tax Expense
6205   Federal Income Tax Expense

(7000) OTHER REVENUE
7105   Gain on Plant Assets
7107   Rent Income
7110   Interest Income

(8000) OTHER EXPENSES
8105   Interest Expense
8110   Loss on Plant Assets

The chart of accounts for Sun Treasures, Inc., is illustrated here for ready reference as you study Part 3 of this textbook.

Chapter 18

Acquiring Capital for Growth and Development

LEARNING OBJECTIVES

After studying Chapter 18, in addition to defining key terms, you will be able to:

LO1 Identify available sources of debt financing.

LO2 Journalize transactions related to short-term debt financing.

LO3 Identify the components of a loan application.

LO4 Journalize transactions related to long-term financing.

LO5 Journalize transactions related to equity financing.

LO6 Identify factors influencing financing decisions.

LO7 Analyze the impact of financial leverage.

©DANIEL KOUREY, ISTOCK/©JIM PRUITT, ISTOCK

EDHAR/SHUTTERSTOCK.COM

Accounting In The Real World
DreamWorks Animation SKG

He's crude, loud, and green. Yet the lovable ogre, Shrek, has taken his place among widely recognized animated characters. The creative minds at DreamWorks Animation SKG (DreamWorks) have entertained both young and old with over 20 animated feature films, including *Madagascar*, *Bee Movie*, and *Kung Fu Panda*.

DreamWorks was once a division of Old DreamWorks Studios. The studios were created in 1994 through a partnership of Steven Spielberg, Jeffrey Katzenberg, and David Geffen. In 2004, the animation division was spun off to form a new company, DreamWorks Animation SKG, with Katzenberg serving as its chief executive officer. The new corporation raised additional capital by issuing common stock on the New York Stock Exchange. Its Class A stock trades under the stock symbol DWA and has over 70 million shares outstanding. The stock now trades on the NASDAQ exchange.

A second class of common stock, Class B, is owned entirely by Katzenberg and Geffen. Class B stock has different voting rights than the Class A stock available to independent investors. Each share of Class A stock has a single vote. Each share of Class B stock has 15 votes. Class B stock represents 13% of DreamWorks' total stockholders' equity and 69% of its voting rights. As a result, Katzenberg and Geffen can control all issues brought to a vote by the stockholders.

DreamWorks' capital structure is not uncommon. Individuals who start a business often maintain control of the corporation after stock is sold to the public.

Potential investors should understand the capital structure of a corporation before investing in its common stock.

CRITICAL THINKING

1. As a potential investor, what are the pros and cons of investing in a corporation controlled by its founders?

2. Suppose the corporation you created intends to issue stock to the public. Why would you want to maintain control?

Source: DreamWorks Animation SKG, Form 10-K, 2010.

Key Terms

- revenue expenditure
- debt financing
- line of credit
- prime interest rate
- interest expense

- non-operating expenses
- capital expenditures
- collateral
- bond

- bond issue
- stated interest rate
- equity financing
- par value

- issue date
- preferred stock
- cost of capital
- financial leverage

LESSON

18-1 Short-Term Debt Financing

LO1 Identify available sources of debt financing.
LO2 Journalize transactions related to short-term debt financing.

Short-Term Debt Financing Options LO1

Every business needs cash to pay its operating expenses. Purchasing inventory and paying the payroll are examples of daily activities that require a business to earn revenue. The payment of an operating expense necessary to earn revenue is called a **revenue expenditure**. Over an extended period of time, a business must generate enough cash from sales to pay these expenses. However, from time to time, a business may find itself short of cash. When this happens, the business may need to borrow money for a short period of time.

Many business events and decisions make it necessary for a business to borrow money. For example, a garden center has its peak season in the spring. Extra cash may be required to purchase an adequate supply of merchandise to meet customer needs. Additional employees are usually hired to service a larger number of customers, so extra cash may be needed for higher payroll expenses.

A business might experience an emergency. For example, a storm can damage plant assets and destroy merchandise inventory. The business must quickly pay for repairs and restock its merchandise inventory to avoid lost sales.

Obtaining capital by borrowing money for a period of time is called **debt financing**. There are several ways for a business to borrow money from a bank or other financial institution. A bank loan agreement that provides immediate short-term access to cash is called a **line of credit**, or *credit line*. There are different kinds of credit lines. The loan agreement sets the maximum amount that can be borrowed and the repayment terms. It will also set the interest rate and the length of time the agreement will be in effect. The business can draw any amount it needs within the terms of the loan agreement.

The interest rate charged on a line of credit can change based on market interest rates. The interest rate charged to a bank's most creditworthy customers is called the **prime interest rate**. Interest rates are often based on the prime interest rate. For example, a line of credit may have an interest rate of 2% over the prime interest rate. This rate would be stated as *prime plus 2%*.

A business needing to borrow money might elect to sign a promissory note, which it would record as a note payable. The note would state the principal, interest rate, and repayment terms. Unlike a line of credit, a note is signed for a specific number of months and the interest rate is fixed for the term of the note.

ETHICS IN ACTION

The Newspaper Test

A code of conduct should provide employees with a guide for making an ethical decision. The ethical model presented in Chapter 2 provides employees with a structured method of evaluating all the implications of an action. Yet, even with these aids, employees can still find it difficult to make a decision.

Some companies provide their employees with a simple set of questions. One popular question is: "Would I be comfortable if my actions were reported in the newspaper?" If employees are uncomfortable with their actions becoming public knowledge, chances are their actions are unethical. At the very least, employees should know that, if they are in doubt about an ethical question, they should consult their company's ethics officer or legal department.

INSTRUCTIONS

Use the Internet to access the code of conduct for Lockheed Martin Corporation, Yahoo! Inc., and Royal Dutch Shell plc. Prepare a list of questions that could help you determine if an action is ethical.

©LUCA DI FILIPPO, ISTOCK

Drawing on a Line of Credit LO2

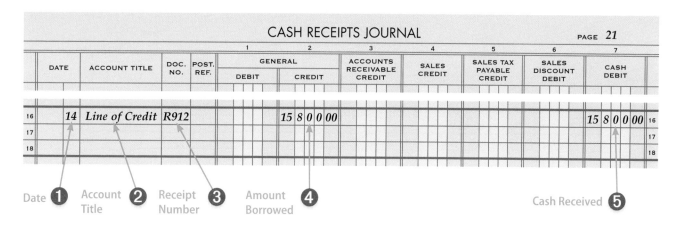

CASH RECEIPTS JOURNAL   PAGE **21**

	DATE	ACCOUNT TITLE	DOC. NO.	POST. REF.	GENERAL DEBIT	GENERAL CREDIT	ACCOUNTS RECEIVABLE CREDIT	SALES CREDIT	SALES TAX PAYABLE CREDIT	SALES DISCOUNT DEBIT	CASH DEBIT	
16	14	Line of Credit	R912			15 8 0 0 00					15 8 0 0 00	16
17												17
18												18

Date ❶   Account Title ❷   Receipt Number ❸   Amount Borrowed ❹   Cash Received ❺

Line of Credit

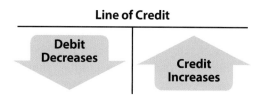

Debit Decreases | Credit Increases

Sun Treasures has arranged a line of credit with First National Bank that provides the company with immediate access to a maximum of $50,000.00. Sun Treasures can transfer money from its line of credit to its checking account using an Internet site or by calling a bank loan officer. Sun Treasures pays an annual interest rate of prime plus 2.5% on its daily outstanding balance. The line of credit requires Sun Treasures to pay monthly interest and at least 10% of its outstanding balance at the end of every month.

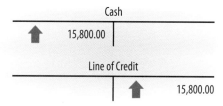

Cash

15,800.00

Line of Credit

15,800.00

Sun Treasures draws on its line of credit to prepare for its peak selling season. The company regularly maintains an inventory of about $150,000.00. However, prior to its peak selling season, the company increases its inventory to over $200,000.00. Sun Treasures plans to repay the borrowed funds as it collects cash from the sale of this extra inventory.

> November 14. Drew $15,800.00 on its line of credit. Receipt No. 912.

A receipt is prepared to document the amount of funds drawn on the credit line. [CONCEPT: Objective Evidence]

↘ Journalizing the Receipt of Cash from a Line of Credit

❶ Write the date, 14, in the Date column.

❷ Write the account name, Line of Credit, in the Account Title column.

❸ Write the cash receipt number, R912, in the Doc. No. column.

❹ Write the total amount borrowed, $15,800.00, in the General Credit column.

❺ Write the cash deposited, $15,800.00, in the Cash Debit column.

Note to Student:

The journals and ledgers illustrated in Parts 1 and 2 of this textbook included detailed steps for recording the date, source document, and other information about the transactions. Because you now know these standard steps, future illustrations will focus on the account titles and amounts of the transactions.

Signing a Promissory Note for an Extension of Time

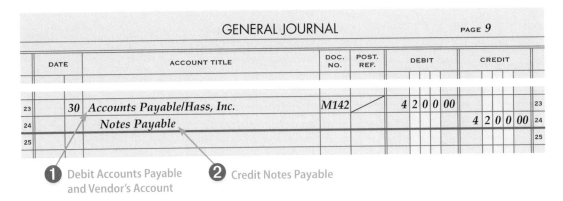

1 Debit Accounts Payable and Vendor's Account   **2** Credit Notes Payable

A business that is unable to pay its account when due might ask the vendor for an extension of time. The vendor may ask the business to sign a promissory note. The note does not pay the amount owed to the vendor. However, the form of the liability is changed from an account payable to a note payable. When this entry is posted, the balance of the Accounts Payable account for Hass, Inc., will be zero. One liability, Accounts Payable, is replaced by another liability, Notes Payable.

> September 30. Sun Treasures signed a 60-day, 12% note to Hass, Inc., for an extension of time on its account payable, $4,200.00. Memorandum No. 142.

The interest rate on promissory notes signed with a vendor may be rather high. A business should avoid signing a note for an extension of time. Instead, the business should consider borrowing funds against a line of credit or obtaining a loan from its bank.

GENERAL LEDGER

Accounts Payable

⬇ 4,200.00 |

Notes Payable

| ⬆ 4,200.00

ACCOUNTS PAYABLE LEDGER

Hass, Inc.

⬇ 4,200.00 | Bal.   4,200.00

> **↘ Journalizing Signing a Promissory Note for an Extension of Time**
>
> **1** Record a debit, $4,200.00, to Accounts Payable/Hass, Inc., in the general journal.
>
> **2** Record a credit, $4,200.00, to Notes Payable.

For transactions to Accounts Payable or Accounts Receivable, draw a diagonal in the Post. Ref. column. The line allows for the posting of the transaction to the general ledger and subsidiary ledger account.

Paying Principal and Interest on a Promissory Note

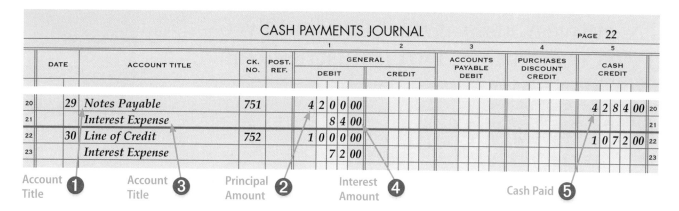

	DATE	ACCOUNT TITLE	CK. NO.	POST. REF.	GENERAL DEBIT	GENERAL CREDIT	ACCOUNTS PAYABLE DEBIT	PURCHASES DISCOUNT CREDIT	CASH CREDIT	
20	29	Notes Payable	751		4 2 0 0 00				4 2 8 4 00	20
21		Interest Expense				8 4 00				21
22	30	Line of Credit	752		1 0 0 0 00				1 0 7 2 00	22
23		Interest Expense				7 2 00				23

Account Title ❶ Account Title ❸ Principal Amount ❷ Interest Amount ❹ Cash Paid ❺

When a promissory note reaches its maturity date, the maker of the note pays the maturity value to the payee. Interest incurred on borrowed funds is called **interest expense**. The interest incurred on a note is debited to an expense account titled Interest Expense.

Interest Expense are listed in a section of the chart of accounts titled Other Expenses.

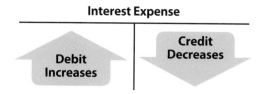

Interest Expense

Debit Increases | **Credit Decreases**

Expenses that are not related to a business's normal operations are called **non-operating expenses**. Interest expense is a financing expense rather than an operating expense. Non-operating expense accounts such as

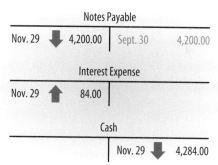

Sun Treasures paid the 60-day note it signed on September 30.

Principal	×	Annual Interest Rate	×	Time as Fraction of a Year	=	Interest for Fraction of Year
$4,200.00	×	12%	×	60/360	=	$84.00

November 29. Paid cash for the maturity value of the August 30 note: principal, $4,200.00, plus interest, $84.00; total, $4,284.00. Check No. 751.

Sun Treasures also makes monthly interest payments on its line of credit. On November 30, Sun Treasures paid $1,000.00 on its outstanding balance plus $72.00 of interest. This transaction is also recorded in the cash payments journal. The debit reduces the balance of Line of Credit and increases Interest Expense.

⬎ Journalizing the Payment of Principal and Interest on a Promissory Note

❶ Write the account name, Notes Payable, in the Account Title column.

❷ Write the note's principal amount, $4,200.00, in the General Debit column.

❸ Write the account title, Interest Expense, in the Account Title column on the next line.

❹ Write the interest expense amount, $84.00, in the General Debit column.

❺ Write the amount of cash paid, $4,284.00, in the Cash Credit column on the first line of the entry.

Executive Abuses at Adelphia and Tyco— Two Corporations, Two Industries, One Common Story

At its peak, Adelphia Communication Corporation was one of the largest cable television providers in the United States. Adelphia was founded in 1952 by John Rigas and headquartered in Pennsylvania. Adelphia's stock was traded on NASDAQ. In 2003, its revenues exceeded $3.6 billion.

Tyco International was a diversified business that specialized in security, fire protection, and flow control equipment. Tyco was founded in 1960 and headquartered in New York. Its stock traded on the New York Stock Exchange (NYSE). In 2007, its revenues exceeded $17 billion.

What could these corporations possibly have in common? Each chief executive officer was charged and convicted of using corporation funds to support a lavish personal lifestyle.

John Rigas and two of his sons were accused of spending $100 million of Adelphia funds on personal assets and expenses. For example, Rigas used $26 million to purchase land surrounding his estate to ensure that his view would not be obstructed. They spent $12.8 million to construct a golf course on land they controlled. They had sole use of several luxurious condominiums and private jets. At the age of 80, John Rigas was sentenced to 15 years in prison.

Dennis Kozlowski became the chief executive officer of Tyco in 1992. In 2002, it was learned that he illegally avoided $1 million of New York sales taxes on the purchase of paintings for his apartment. That accusation prompted an investigation which revealed that Kozlowski had used $600 million of Tyco funds on personal assets and expenses. Some of those purchases included a $30 million Fifth Avenue apartment, a $29 million vacation home, and a $5 million diamond ring. Tyco even paid for half of his wife's $2 million birthday party featuring entertainment by Jimmy Buffett. Kozlowski was sentenced to a minimum of eight years and four months in prison.

In each case, the abuse of corporate funds was the tip of the iceberg. Adelphia used fraudulent accounting entries to hide over $3 billion in loans to the Rigas family. Tyco used questionable methods in accounting for its acquisition of over 1,000 companies. Both Adelphia and Tyco were forced to restate some prior-year financial statements.

There the similarities end. Adelphia declared bankruptcy in 2002 and soon went out of business. Its assets were sold to Time Warner and Comcast. In contrast, Tyco survived its scandal and continues to be a profitable business.

ACTIVITY

PlyCorp Industries has hired you to search for any signs of fraudulent accounting entries. One of your standard tests is to search for entries contrary to the normal balance of income statement accounts.

INSTRUCTIONS

Open the spreadsheet FA_CH18 and complete the steps on the Instructions tab.

Sources: http://en.wikipedia.org; Cecil W. Jackson, *Business Fairy Tales* (Thomson, 2006); Jerry W. Markham and M. E. Sharpe, *A Financial History of Modern U.S. Corporate Scandals* (Armonk, New York and London, England, 2006).

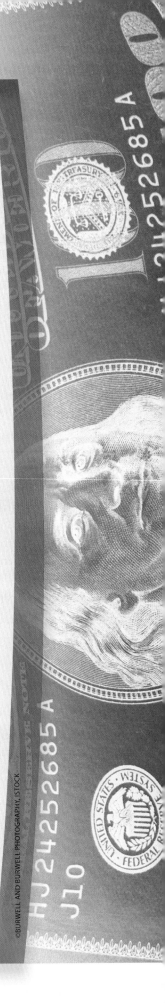

LO1 Identify available sources of debt financing.

LO2 Journalize transactions related to short-term debt financing.

Terms Review

revenue expenditure

debt financing

line of credit

prime interest rate

interest expense

non-operating expenses

Audit your understanding

1. What information is specified in the loan agreement for a line of credit?

2. On a line of credit, how would an interest rate of 3% over the prime rate be stated?

3. Is interest expense an operating or a non-operating expense?

4. Where is interest expense listed in a chart of accounts?

Work together 18-1

Journalizing entries for short-term debt

The journals for Klein, Inc., are given in the *Working Papers*. Your instructor will guide you through the following examples.

Using the current year, journalize the following transactions on page 5 of a cash receipts journal, page 8 of a cash payments journal, and page 4 of a general journal. Source documents are abbreviated as: check, C; receipt, R; memorandum, M.

Transactions:

Mar. 3. Drew $6,500.00 on its line of credit. R146.

26. Signed a 90-day, 10% note to MVT Supply for an extension of time on its account payable, $2,400.00. M92.

June 24. Paid cash for the maturity value of the March 26 note: principal, $2,400.00, plus interest. C362.

30. Paid cash for the monthly payment on its line of credit: principal, $1,500.00, plus interest, $64.20. C369.

On your own 18-1

Journalizing entries for short-term debt

The journals for Placid Stores are given in the *Working Papers*. Work this problem independently.

Using the current year, journalize the following transactions on page 7 of a cash receipts journal, page 10 of a cash payments journal, and page 5 of a general journal. Source documents are abbreviated as: check, C; receipt, R; memorandum, M.

Transactions:

Apr. 16. Drew $2,250.00 on its line of credit. R206.

May 28. Signed a 60-day, 12% note to Gates Supply for an extension of time on its account payable, $3,660.00. M85.

July 27. Paid cash for the maturity value of the May 28 note: principal, $3,660.00, plus interest. C421.

31. Paid cash for the monthly payment on its line of credit: principal, $800.00, plus interest, $24.10. C426.

18-2 Long-Term Debt Financing

LO3 Identify the components of a loan application.
LO4 Journalize transactions related to long-term financing.

Applying for a Business Loan LO3

As a business expands, it must purchase more equipment and other plant assets. The assets or other financial resources available to a business are called capital. Purchases of plant assets used in the operation of a business are called **capital expenditures**. These plant assets will be used for many years to support the operations of the business.

Corporations often require large amounts of capital to finance capital expenditures. A business can obtain this capital from both internal and external sources. The portion of net income not paid as a dividend is an internal source of capital. But internal capital may not be adequate. Thus, a corporation must acquire additional capital from external sources. These might include borrowing money or selling stock.

Banks are a convenient source of external capital. The first step in obtaining a loan is completing the bank's loan application. The application collects basic information about the business and its primary owners. Before approving the loan, the bank must be confident that the business is capable of repaying the funds. The business must convince the bank to approve the loan. Thus, the business should submit a business plan describing how the borrowed funds will be used and how they will be repaid.

THINK LIKE AN ACCOUNTANT

Authorizing a Dividend

At each November meeting, the board of directors of Natchez Finance Corporation reviews the company's financial performance. The information is used to determine the dividend per share for the next four quarters. For the past 24 years, the board has authorized an increase in the quarterly dividend.

Board members are aware that many stockholders are retirees who rely on the income provided by the quarterly dividend. However, the corporation cannot afford to pay out all of its earnings in dividends. The business must retain some of its earnings to finance future growth.

The board considers two financial ratios in making its decision:

Payout Ratio: The board attempts to pay out between 60%–70% of its earnings. The board believes stockholders deserve to receive a dividend of at least 60% of company earnings. However, the board needs to retain at least 30% of company earnings to finance future growth.

Dividend Yield: The board wants the financial markets to view the corporation's stock as an *income stock* that yields at least a 5.0% dividend.

During 20X4, Natchez Finance Corporation was negatively impacted by a severe economic downturn. To obtain the funds needed to operate, the corporation was forced to issue more stock than usual. Further complicating the situation was a decline in the market price of the common stock. Although the board believes the economy is recovering, it is seeking your recommendation on the amount of the dividend for the next year.

OPEN THE SPREADSHEET TLA_CH18

The worksheet contains the relevant data for 20X1–20X4. Analyze the data to suggest an amount for the new quarterly dividend. Answer the following questions:

1. How often has the corporation achieved the payout ratio target?
2. How often has the corporation achieved the dividend yield target?
3. What dividend per share do you recommend? Support your answer.

With each loan, the bank takes a risk that the borrower will not repay it. Banks only earn money if borrowers repay borrowed funds with interest. Banks will often require a business to pledge certain assets to secure a loan. Assets pledged to a creditor to guarantee repayment of a loan are called **collateral**. If the borrower is unable to repay the loan, the creditor can take the collateral and sell it to pay off the debt.

Sun Treasures has a goal of opening two new stores on the west Florida coast. It estimates it will need $400,000.00 to fund the expansion. Of this amount, $300,000.00 must come from external sources. A summary of the primary sections of Sun Treasures' business plan follows. Each section addresses common questions that will be asked by the bank's loan officers.

Section Title	Questions of Interest to Bank Officers	Summary of Sun Treasures' Business Plan
Use of funds	What portion of the funds will be used for revenue expenditures and capital expenditures?	Sun Treasures expects to use $150,000.00 for equipment at each location. Another $50,000.00 per store will be used to purchase inventory.
Business experience	What experience do the primary owners and managers have in the industry? Do the decision makers understand how to operate the business? Can they anticipate problems and react to ensure success?	Sun Treasures has been in this business for 15 years. The primary owner and chief operating officer have a combined 40 years of experience in the industry. The manager of the west coast stores has been in a management position with Sun Treasures for nine years.
Market demand	Is there a proven consumer demand for the product or service? What competition does the business face?	Sun Treasures contracted Delson Marketing to perform a market survey. The survey indicated that opportunities exist for souvenir stores in Venice and Fort Myers Beach.
Financial projections	When will the project become profitable? What assumptions is the business using to make its projections?	The new locations are expected to lose $50,000.00 over the first 18 months of operation. A loss is common while new stores develop a loyal customer base. This loss will be funded with profits from the existing stores. Based on a conservative 6% per year growth in sales, the new stores will be able to repay the loan in five years.
Collateral	What assets will be offered as collateral that could be claimed if the business is unable to pay the loan? How easy will it be to resell those assets?	All store equipment from the existing and new stores will be offered as collateral. This equipment will be purchased from vendors that also actively repurchase equipment.
Capital profile	What is the business risking in the project? Does the business have an adequate stake in the project to ensure management is motivated to succeed?	Sun Treasures plans to issue common and preferred stock to fund at least 10% of the project.

 Other financial institutions include insurance companies, investment firms, and mutual funds.

Signing a Long-Term Note Payable LO4

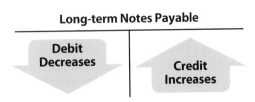

					GENERAL		ACCOUNTS RECEIVABLE CREDIT	SALES CREDIT	SALES TAX PAYABLE CREDIT	SALES DISCOUNT DEBIT	CASH DEBIT
	DATE	ACCOUNT TITLE	DOC. NO.	POST. REF.	DEBIT	CREDIT					
1	20-- Apr. 1	Long-term Notes Payable	R628			120 000 00					120 000 00

CASH RECEIPTS JOURNAL PAGE 7

Account Title **①**   Amount Borrowed **②**   Cash Received **③**

Long-term Notes Payable

Debit Decreases	Credit Increases

A note payable is signed as evidence of the debt when receiving a bank loan. Notes payable signed to fund revenue expenditures usually have terms of 12 months or less. However, long-term notes are common when the borrowed funds are used to purchase plant assets. That's because plant assets are useable as collateral for the notes that are issued to fund them. When a note payable is signed for a period greater than one year, it is usually recorded to an account titled Long-term Notes Payable.

In response to Sun Treasures' loan application, the bank agreed to provide only a portion of the funds needed to open the new stores. After Sun Treasures signs the note, the bank deposits the principal amount of the note in Sun Treasures' checking account.

April 1. Signed a 5-year, 8.0% note for $120,000.00. Receipt No. 628.

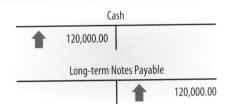

A receipt is prepared as evidence of the deposit of the principal amount in Sun Treasures' bank account. [CONCEPT: Objective Evidence] No entry is made for interest until a later date when interest is paid.

⊌ Journalizing the Signing of a Long-term Note Payable

① Write the account name, Long-term Notes Payable, in the Account Title column.

② Write the total amount borrowed, $120,000.00, in the General Credit column.

③ Write the cash received, $120,000.00, in the Cash Debit column.

Making a Monthly Payment on a Long-Term Note Payable

					GENERAL		ACCOUNTS PAYABLE DEBIT	PURCHASES DISCOUNT CREDIT	CASH CREDIT	
	DATE	ACCOUNT TITLE	CK. NO.	POST. REF.	DEBIT	CREDIT				
					1	2	3	4	5	
1	Aug. 1	Long-term Notes Payable	673		1 6 6 6 05				2 4 3 3 17	1
2		Interest Expense			7 6 7 12					2
3										3
4										4

CASH PAYMENTS JOURNAL   PAGE **15**

❶ Account Title   **❸** Account Title   **❷** Principal Amount   **❹** Interest Amount   Cash Paid **❺**

Amount Borrowed	$120,000.00
Term of Note (Months)	60
Annual Interest Rate	8%
Monthly Payment	$2,433.17

Payment Number	Payable 1st day of	Beginning Balance	Interest	Principal	Ending Balance
1	May	$120,000.00	$800.00	$1,633.17	$118,366.83
2	June	$118,366.83	$789.11	$1,644.06	$116,722.77
3	July	$116,722.77	$778.15	$1,655.02	$115,067.75
4	August	$115,067.75	$767.12	$1,666.05	$113,401.70
5	September	$113,401.70	$756.01	$1,677.16	$111,724.54
6	October	$111,724.54	$744.83	$1,688.34	$110,036.20
7	November	$110,036.20	$733.57	$1,699.60	$108,336.60
8	December	$108,336.60	$722.24	$1,710.93	$106,625.67

Sun Treasures' note agreement requires that it make a payment on the first of every month. Upon signing the note, the bank provided Sun Treasures with a schedule of monthly payments.

August 1. Paid cash for monthly loan payment, $1,666.05, interest, $767.12; total, $2,433.17. Check No. 673.

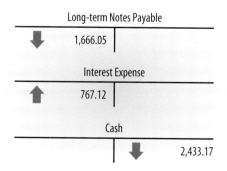

Sun Treasures is required to pay $2,433.17 each month. A portion of the payment is interest on the

outstanding balance of the loan. The remaining amount reduces the outstanding loan principal. The interest and principal portions of the August payment are highlighted in the payment schedule. The monthly payment will enable Sun Treasures to fully repay the loan by the end of the five years (60 months).

↘ Journalizing the Monthly Payment on a Long-term Note Payable

❶ Write the account name, Long-term Notes Payable, in the Account Title column.

❷ Write the principal portion of the August payment, $1,666.05, in the General Debit column.

❸ Write the account title, Interest Expense, in the Account Title column on the next line.

❹ Write the interest portion of the August payment, $767.12, in the General Debit column.

❺ Write the amount of cash paid, $2,433.17, in the Cash Credit column on the first line of the entry.

Issuing Bonds

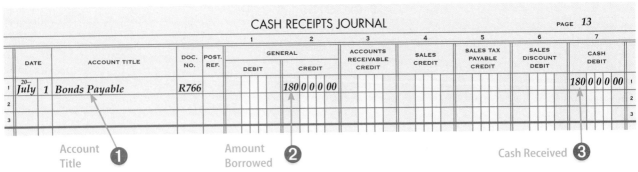

Large loans can be difficult to obtain from a single bank. An alternative to borrowing money from a bank is to borrow money from individual investors. A long-term promise to pay a specified amount on a specified date and to pay interest at stated intervals is called a **bond**. Like notes payable, bonds are written promises to pay. Bonds generally have extended terms such as 5, 10, or 20 years. Also, bonds payable tend to be issued for larger amounts than notes payable.

Bonds Payable

Debit Decreases	Credit Increases

All bonds representing the total amount of a loan are called a **bond issue**. A corporation usually sells an entire bond issue to a securities dealer who sells individual bonds to individual investors. The process of selling bonds is commonly referred to as *issuing bonds*.

Each bond states the face value, interest rate, and due date. The face value is the amount to be repaid at the end of the bond term. The interest rate used to calculate periodic interest payments on a bond is called the **stated interest rate**. The face value is multiplied by the stated interest rate to calculate periodic interest payments to investors. Many bonds pay interest semiannually.

July 1. Issued 20-year, 6.5%, $5,000.00 bonds, $180,000.00. Receipt No. 766.

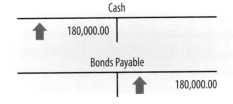

Journalizing the Issuance of Bonds Payable

1. Write the account name, Bonds Payable, in the Account Title column.
2. Write the bonds' total face value, $180,000.00, in the General Credit column.
3. Write the amount of cash received, $180,000.00, in the Cash Debit column.

Paying Interest on Bonds

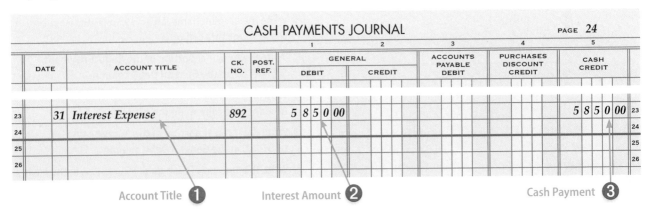

Similar to stock, bonds are securities that can be bought and sold. Sales between investors have no impact on the corporation. However, the corporation does need to maintain current records of who owns each bond in order to make proper interest payments. Corporations issue one check for the amount of interest to be paid, usually to an agent such as a bank. The agent then handles the details of sending interest checks to individual bondholders.

Sun Treasures' bonds require that interest be paid semiannually on June 30 and December 31. Interest on the bond is calculated as the face value multiplied by the stated interest rate.

	Face Value	×	Stated Interest Rate	×	Time as Fraction of a Year	=	Interest Payment
	$180,000.00	×	6.5%	×	180/360	=	$5,850.00

December 31. Paid cash for semiannual interest on bonds, $5,850.00. Check No. 892.

Interest Expense

↑ 5,850.00

Cash

↓ 5,850.00

Sun Treasures writes a single check to its agent who then writes individual checks to the bondholders. The investors who own the bonds on the payment date receive the interest payments. Thus, an investor who purchases a bond from another investor on December 29 would receive a check for $162.50 ($5,000.00 × 6.5% × 180/360 = $162.50 per bond).

Journalizing the Payment of Interest on Bonds Payable

① Write the account name, Interest Expense, in the Account Title column.

② Write the interest expense amount, $5,850.00, in the General Debit column.

③ Write the amount of cash paid, $5,850.00, in the Cash Credit column.

Costs Determine Pricing

Have you ever thought that the price you paid for a product was too high? Did you think about all the costs that went into making the product available to you? Manufacturers and retailers must charge enough to cover all their costs plus make a reasonable profit.

You can probably imagine most of the retailer's costs, but consider the manufacturer's costs. Calculating the manufacturing cost is not as easy as it may seem. Take a bicycle for example. Besides the actual materials used in the bike, there are many other costs that must be included such as:

- Machines used, as well as the parts and supplies required to maintain the machines.
- Labor, including factory supervisors.
- Utilities for the factory.
- Labor and supplies to keep the factory clean.
- Employee benefits, vacations, and training.

Manufacturing

The price charged for the bike must also include all the administrative costs of the company and produce a profit for the company's stockholders. It is the job of the company's accountants to make sure all of these costs are identified and measured accurately. If any costs are missed, the company will make less profit on each bicycle it sells. If enough costs are missed, the company might actually lose money on every bike it sells. The field of accounting that identifies and measures costs is called **cost accounting**.

CRITICAL THINKING

Select a product of your choice and make a list of all the costs that went into the making of the product. Be prepared to defend your list in class.

©ANEKEN KOWEBİNKOB, ISTOCK

End of Lesson Review

LO3 Identify the components of a loan application.

LO4 Journalize transactions related to long-term financing.

Terms Review

capital expenditures

collateral

bond

bond issue

stated interest rate

Audit your understanding

1. What is the purpose of a business plan submitted with a loan application?

2. What can happen to collateral if a borrower is unable to repay a bank loan?

3. Identify the primary sections of a business plan.

4. Investor A sells a bond to investor B just days before the interest payment is made. Which investor receives the interest payment?

5. What are two common differences between notes payable and bonds?

Work together 18-2

Journalizing entries for long-term debt

The journals and a loan payment schedule for Lambers Stores are given in the *Working Papers*. Your instructor will guide you through the following examples.

Using the current year, journalize the following transactions on page 6 of a cash receipts journal and page 12 of a cash payments journal. Refer to the loan payment schedule when journalizing the December 1 transaction. Source documents are abbreviated as: check, C; receipt, R.

Transactions:

June 1. Signed a five-year, 9.0% note, $25,000.00. R337.

July 1. Issued 20-year, 6%, $5,000.00 bonds, $200,000.00. R345.

Dec. 1. Paid cash for the December payment on the June 1 note payable, $518.96. C842.

31. Paid cash for the semiannual interest on bonds. C861.

On your own 18-2

Journalizing entries for long-term debt

The journals and a loan payment schedule for Belmar Co. are given in the *Working Papers*. Work this problem independently.

Using the current year, journalize the following transactions on page 8 of a cash receipts journal and page 15 of a cash payments journal. Refer to the loan payment schedule when journalizing the November 1 transaction. Source documents are abbreviated as: check, C; receipt, R.

Transactions:

July 1. Issued 20-year, 5.5%, $10,000.00 bonds, $300,000.00. R621.

1. Signed a four-year, 7.5% note, $32,000.00. R622.

Nov. 1. Paid cash for the November payment on the August 1 note payable, $773.72. C902.

Dec. 31. Paid cash for the semiannual interest on bonds. C928.

LO5 Journalize transactions related to equity financing.

Issuing Capital Stock LO5

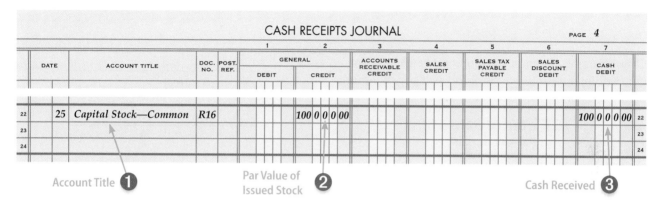

		CASH RECEIPTS JOURNAL						PAGE 4	
			1	2	3	4	5	6	7
DATE	ACCOUNT TITLE	DOC. NO.	POST. REF.	GENERAL DEBIT	GENERAL CREDIT	ACCOUNTS RECEIVABLE CREDIT	SALES CREDIT	SALES TAX PAYABLE CREDIT	SALES DISCOUNT DEBIT	CASH DEBIT

| | 25 | Capital Stock—Common | R16 | | 100 00 0 00 | | | | | 100 00 0 00 | |

Account Title ❶   Par Value of Issued Stock ❷   Cash Received ❸

A corporation may elect to raise capital by selling stock. Obtaining capital by issuing stock in a corporation is called **equity financing**. Selling stock increases the stockholders' equity in the business.

Capital Stock—Common

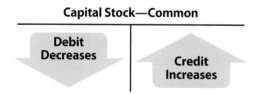

Debit Decreases

Credit Increases

An advantage of selling stock is that the capital becomes a part of a corporation's permanent capital. Permanent capital does not have to be returned to stockholders as long as the business continues to operate. Another advantage is that dividends do not have to be paid to stockholders unless the earnings are sufficient to warrant such payments. A disadvantage of selling more stock is that the ownership is spread over more shares and more owners.

Shares of stock are often assigned a value. A value assigned to a share of stock is called the **par value**. The par value has nothing to do with the market value of the stock. State laws use the par value to determine the minimum amount of equity that must be retained in the corporation.

Several years ago, Sun Treasures issued stock to raise the capital required to open its first store.

> February 25. Sold 10,000 shares of $10.00 par value common stock at par value, $100,000.00. Receipt No. 16.

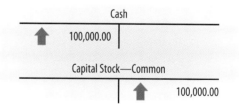

Cash

100,000.00 |

Capital Stock—Common

| 100,000.00

The date on which a business issues a note, bond, or stock is called the **issue date**. The issue date is required to determine the proper payments of interest or dividends.

Journalizing the Sale of Common Stock at Par Value

❶ Write the account name, Capital Stock—Common, in the Account Title column.

❷ Write the stocks' total par value, $100,000.00, in the General Credit column.

❸ Write the amount of cash received, $100,000.00, in the Cash Debit column.

Issuing Stock in Excess of Par Value

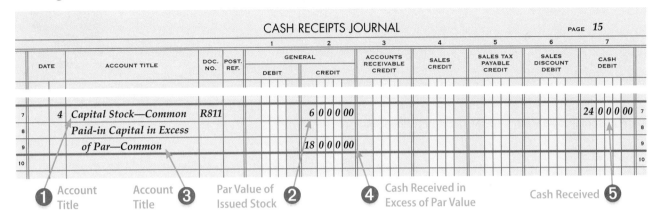

CASH RECEIPTS JOURNAL — PAGE 15

	DATE	ACCOUNT TITLE	DOC. NO.	POST. REF.	GENERAL DEBIT	GENERAL CREDIT	ACCOUNTS RECEIVABLE CREDIT	SALES CREDIT	SALES TAX PAYABLE CREDIT	SALES DISCOUNT DEBIT	CASH DEBIT	
7	4	Capital Stock—Common	R811			6 000 00					24 000 00	7
8		Paid-in Capital in Excess										8
9		of Par—Common				18 000 00						9
10												10

① Account Title ③ Account Title Par Value of Issued Stock ② ④ Cash Received in Excess of Par Value Cash Received ⑤

Over time, the common stock of a profitable corporation will increase in value. Investors will be willing to pay more than the par value of the stock.

Paid-in Capital in Excess of Par—Common

Debit Decreases	Credit Increases

The par value of the issued stock is recorded in Capital Stock—Common. Any additional amount received is recorded to Paid-in Capital in Excess of Par—Common. The account is an equity account and appears on the statement of stockholders' equity under common stock.

> August 4. Sold 600 shares of $10.00 par value common stock at $40.00 per share, $40,000.00. Receipt No. 811.

The amount credited to Capital Stock—Common is always the par value multiplied by the number of shares issued. The issue price of the stock does not have any impact on this amount. The balance of Capital Stock—Common is useful to satisfy information required by certain state laws and taxing authorities.

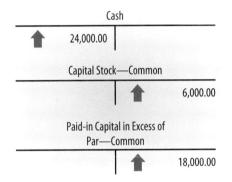

Cash
24,000.00

Capital Stock—Common
6,000.00

Paid-in Capital in Excess of Par—Common
18,000.00

Journalizing the Issuance of Stock in Excess of Par Value

① Write the account name, Capital Stock—Common, in the Account Title column.

② Write the total par value amount, $6,000.00, in the General Credit column.

③ Write the account title, Paid-in Capital in Excess of Par—Common, in the Account Title column on the next two lines.

④ Write the difference between the total par value and the cash received, $18,000.00, in the General Credit column.

⑤ Write the total cash received, $24,000.00, in the Cash Debit column.

	No. of Shares	×	Value per Share	=	Value
Total received	600	×	$40.00	=	$24,000.00
Par value	600	×	$10.00	=	6,000.00
Amount received in excess of par value					$18,000.00

Issuing Preferred Stock at Par Value

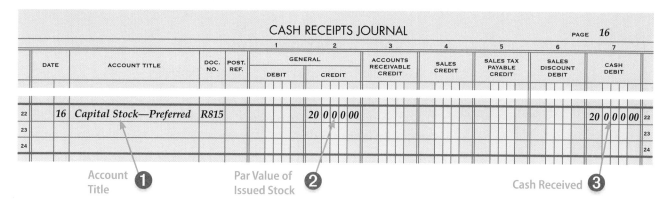

① Account Title
② Par Value of Issued Stock
③ Cash Received

Some investors are uncomfortable with the risks of owning common stock, especially if dividends have not been paid consistently. To attract these investors, some corporations offer a different class of stock in addition to their common shares. **Preferred stock** is a class of stock that gives preferred shareholders preference over common shareholders in dividends along with other rights. Preferred stock is typically described by referring to the stock's dividend rate and par value. Sun Treasures plans to issue 6%, $50.00 par value preferred stock.

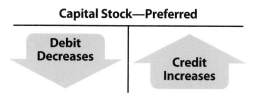

August 16. Issued 400 shares of 6%, $50.00 par value preferred stock at par value, $20,000.00. Receipt No. 815.

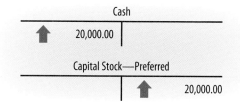

Corporations are not required to pay dividends on stock, whether common or preferred. However, when dividends are paid, all the dividends owed the preferred stockholders must be paid first. Preferred stock dividends are determined by the par value and the stated interest rate. Sun Treasures' annual preferred dividend is $3.00 (6% × $50.00) per share. Thus, Sun Treasures is expected to pay annual total dividends of $1,200.00 ($3.00 × 400 shares) to preferred stockholders. Any additional dividends declared are paid to common stockholders.

Preferred stockholders can have other preferences over common stockholders. Unpaid dividends may accumulate from one year to another. These dividends must be paid before common stockholders receive any dividends. If the corporation is dissolved, preferred stockholders receive cash for their stock before any cash is distributed to common stockholders. However, preferred stockholders do not have the same voting rights as common stockholders.

Journalizing the Sale of Preferred Stock at Par Value

① Write the account name, Capital Stock—Preferred, in the Account Title column.

② Write the total par value amount, $20,000.00, in the General Credit column.

③ Write the total cash received, $20,000.00, in the Cash Debit column.

End of Lesson Review

LO5 Journalize transactions related to equity financing.

Terms Review

equity financing

par value

issue date

preferred stock

Audit your understanding

1. Is a corporation required to issue dividends? Explain.

2. How is preferred stock typically described?

3. In what order is cash paid to preferred and common stockholders if a corporation is dissolved?

4. What is the most common reason that investors purchase preferred stock?

Work together 18-3

Journalizing the sale of common and preferred stock

A cash receipts journal for Center Fashion is given in the *Working Papers*. Your instructor will guide you through the following examples.

Using the current year, journalize the following transactions on page 6 of a cash receipts journal. Source documents are abbreviated as: receipt, R.

Transactions:

June 1. Sold 6,000 shares of $10.00 par value common stock at par value, $60,000.00. R258.

9. Sold 2,000 shares of $10.00 par value common stock at $10.50 per share, $21,000.00. R267.

22. Issued 500 shares of 5%, $60.00 par value preferred stock at par value, $30,000.00. R289.

30. Issued 500 shares of $10.00 par value common stock at $11.25 per share. R301.

On your own 18-3

Journalizing the sale of common and preferred stock

A cash receipts journal for Main Station is given in the *Working Papers*. Work this problem independently.

Using the current year, journalize the following transactions on page 8 of a cash receipts journal. Source documents are abbreviated as: receipt, R.

Transactions:

Aug. 3. Sold 40,000 shares of $1.00 par value common stock at par value, $40,000.00. R311.

14. Issued 2,000 shares of 6%, $50.00 par value preferred stock at par value, $100,000.00. R325.

21. Sold 8,000 shares of $1.00 par value common stock at $1.40 per share, $11,200.00. R330.

29. Issued 6,000 shares of $1.00 par value common stock at $1.60 per share. R338.

LESSON
18-4 Acquiring Additional Capital

LO6 Identify factors influencing financing decisions.

LO7 Analyze the impact of financial leverage.

Making Financing Decisions LO6

Most businesses need additional capital to finance a major expansion or the purchase of expensive plant assets such as buildings and machinery. How a business elects to obtain funds for expansion or development will impact its earnings. Each method has a different impact on earnings. Borrowing money increases interest expense. Issuing stock may result in dividend payments.

The ratio of interest and dividend payments to the proceeds from debt and capital financing is called the **cost of capital**. A business should only raise capital if the projected increase in earnings exceeds the cost of capital. A business that elects to raise capital has several options: a line of credit, notes payable, bonds, common stock, and preferred stock. Each option can have positive and negative effects on a business and its owners. The following factors should be considered in deciding how a business should raise capital.

Interest Rate. A business seeks to minimize its interest expense. The interest rate of a loan or bond is dependent on several factors. Short-term interest rates are usually less than long-term interest rates. Interest rates can change from events in the regional or global economy. Creditors demand higher interest rates if they loan money to a business with a less than perfect credit history.

Impact on Earnings. Interest on debt financing is an expense that reduces net income before federal income taxes. But interest payments also reduce federal income taxes. For a company with a marginal tax rate of 25%, a $1,000.00 interest payment reduces its federal income taxes by $250.00. Thus, the net cash outlay is only $750.00. In contrast, dividends are not an expense and do not reduce federal income taxes. The primary benefit of dividends is that the payments are made to the stockholders rather than creditors and bondholders.

Repayment Terms. A business must decide how quickly it wants to repay borrowed funds. Debt financing is often extended for a term similar to the useful life of the assets purchased. Funds used to purchase extra merchandise for a busy season should be repaid quickly. Funds used to purchase plant assets are often repaid over several years. Bonds usually provide the longest repayment terms. In contrast, equity financing is typically never repaid.

Ownership Control. The existing owners of a business maintain full control of a business when expansion is achieved with debt financing. If funding is obtained through equity financing, a proportional share in the control of the business goes with each new share of stock. This spreading of the control over the business is known as *dilution of control*.

Debt Ratio. A business may not have total control over which financing method it selects. Creditors may be unwilling to lend money to a business with a high debt ratio. Such a business is perceived to be a high credit risk. The business may have no choice but to issue additional stock. In contrast, lenders are more willing to lend money to a business with a low debt ratio. Creditors perceive such a business to be a low credit risk.

India—An Expanding Market

A company that wants to expand into a foreign market should consider India. With 1.16 billion people and 240 million households, India is the fourth largest economy in the world. It is also a nation with a young population. The average age of an Indian citizen is 25.3 (compared to 36.7 in the United States). India is known for its competitive education system and large pool of highly skilled workers.

Like any nation, India has unique political and cultural practices. It is very important to be aware of these practices in order to have a successful business relationship. India is a culturally diverse country. Four factors affect the difficulty of doing business there: regionalism, religion, language, and caste. The first three factors are closely related. India is made up of several states. These states (or regions) vary greatly in religious beliefs and language. For example, Hindi is the official language of India, but states within India have their own official languages—21 in all. English is considered an associate language and is used in most business dealings.

Historically, India's social structure involved a caste system—class distinctions based on the occupation and ethnicity of the family into which a person is born. Although this system has been officially dismantled, there are still many signs of it in Indian culture. Organizations have a hierarchy which is strictly followed. A simple task can take hours because a worker at the right level must complete it. This hierarchy determines each individual's role and status. Most decisions are made by the owner of a business rather than someone in a lower-level position.

Relationships are critical in business practices. Business decisions are not based solely on financial facts and figures. A person hoping to do business with an Indian firm must be patient and allow a relationship to develop. In negotiations, being forceful might be misinterpreted as a sign of disrespect.

Many foreign businesspeople find it extremely helpful to follow two strategies when beginning an expansion into India:

1. Work at a local level rather than marketing to the entire country.

2. Form a partnership with an Indian businessperson or company instead of operating individually. A local partner can provide priceless information on local customs and practices.

CRITICAL THINKING

Although a handshake is usually required when meeting someone in India, Namaste is also practiced. Use the Internet to research the word "Namaste" and the gesture that accompanies the greeting. In a written report, explain the meaning of the word and the gesture.

Sources: www.buyusa.gov/india; www.export.gov/india; Doing Business in India, Ernst & Young, India; and www.kwintessential.co.uk.

©FONTMONSTER, ISTOCK

Financial Leverage LO7

Suppose a business wants to purchase $50,000.00 of equipment. The equipment will enable the business to serve more customers and earn more income. The company only has $10,000.00 it can afford to invest in the equipment. Should the company borrow the $40,000.00 needed to complete the purchase? If so, how should the company raise the necessary cash?

The ability of a business to use borrowed funds to increase its earnings is called **financial leverage**. For financial leverage to be a benefit, the borrowed funds must be invested in the business and increase income by more than the interest paid. The following table presents three possible outcomes of borrowing $40,000.00 at 8.0%.

	Outcome			
	8.0%	10.0%	12.0%	6.0%
Operating income	$ 4,000.00	$ 5,000.00	$ 6,000.00	$ 3,000.00
Interest expense	3,200.00	3,200.00	3,200.00	3,200.00
Net income (loss) before federal income tax	$ 800.00	$ 1,800.00	$ 2,800.00	$ (200.00)
Federal income tax (25%)	200.00	450.00	700.00	(50.00)
Net income after federal income tax	$ 600.00	$ 1,350.00	$ 2,100.00	$ (150.00)
Investment	10,000.00	10,000.00	10,000.00	10,000.00
Return on investment	6.0%	13.5%	21.0%	–1.5%

In the first column, the business earns an annual operating income of $4,000.00, a return of 8.0% on its $50,000.00 purchase of equipment. After interest expense and federal income taxes, the business earns an additional $600.00. However, the business only invested $10,000.00 of internal capital. Thus, the business earns 6.0% ($600.00 ÷ $10,000.00) on its investment.

What if the company can earn $5,000.00 in operating income, a return of 10.0% on the $50,000.00 purchased equipment? The second column shows the power of financial leverage. The return on the company's investment jumps to 13.5%. The interest expense is unchanged. Thus, the $1,000.00 of additional operating income belongs to the business. Earning a 12.0% return on the purchased equipment, as shown in the third column, results in the business earning 21.0% on its investment.

It might appear that a business should always borrow money when it needs additional capital. That is not the case. Borrowing money can be risky. The fourth column shows how financial leverage can be harmful. What if an economic decline causes the company to earn only $3,000.00, or 6.0% on the purchased equipment? Interest must be paid regardless of the income earned with the borrowed funds. As a result, the business loses $150.00, a negative return of 1.5% on its investment.

A business can have too much debt. A business having a high level of debt is perceived to be a credit risk. Creditors and investors may be unwilling to loan money or invest in the business. A business having a high level of debt is said to be *highly leveraged* or possibly *over-leveraged*.

©ORANGE LINE MEDIA/FOTOLIA.COM

Selecting Financing Methods

A business needing to raise additional capital has many decisions to make. Does it use debt financing, equity financing, or a combination of both? What form of debt financing should be used? Should equity financing involve common or preferred stock? The best choice will be unique for each business.

A business wants to take advantage of financial leverage. At the same time, a business cannot risk having too much debt. It is very hard to determine the exact amount of capital that should be raised by debt versus equity financing.

Several years after opening its west coast stores, Sun Treasures is ready to expand again. Sun Treasures needs to raise $340,000.00 of capital to finance a third store and a distribution center. The company will need $250,000.00 to purchase equipment and $60,000.00 to purchase inventory. The remaining $30,000.00 will be required to pay expenses prior to opening.

The board of directors used the following schedule to guide its decision-making. Using current balances of the liability and equity accounts, the schedule enabled the board to examine the new balances after financing decisions were made.

	Current	Debt Financing	Equity Financing	New Balances
Financial statement balances				
Line of credit	$ 14,200.00	$ 18,000.00		$ 32,200.00
Notes payable	50,000.00	160,000.00		210,000.00
Bonds payable	100,000.00			100,000.00
Other liabilities	16,800.00			16,800.00
Total liabilities	$181,000.00			$359,000.00
Stockholders' equity	190,000.00		$162,000.00	352,000.00
Total liabilities and stockholders' equity	$371,000.00			$711,000.00
New capital financing		$178,000.00	$162,000.00	$340,000.00
Other information				
Debt ratio	48.8%			50.5%
Shares owned by majority owners	48,000		1,000	49,000
Total shares outstanding	90,000		3,500	93,500
Percent of shares owned by majority owners	53.3%			52.4%

The board decided to take the following actions to finance the expansion of the business:

1. Draw $18,000.00 on its $50,000.00 line of credit. This debt financing source has the lowest interest rate, 6.0%, of the three debt financing options. The new balance of $32,200.00 will preserve the board's target emergency balance of approximately $15,000.00.

2. Sign a $160,000.00, 7.5% note payable on the equipment. The interest rate on this debt is higher than the interest rate of the bonds. Sun Treasures projects that company earnings will enable the loan to be repaid within four to six years. The board elected to pay a slightly higher interest rate for a few years rather than be obligated to pay interest on additional 6.5% bonds for 20 years.

3. Sell 4,500 shares of common stock at the current market price of $36.00 per share. The stock will

generate the remaining $162,000.00 of financing needed to fund the expansion ($178,000.00 + $162,000.00 = $340,000.00).

The debt financing alone would raise the company's debt ratio to 65.4%. This ratio exceeds the board's maximum benchmark of 60.0%. Thus, equity financing is required to raise the additional funds and bring the debt ratio down.

The total number of shares outstanding will increase to 94,500 (90,000 + 4,500). To hold onto a majority of the outstanding shares, the founding family has elected to purchase 1,000 shares. The family will then own 52.4% of the outstanding shares. A family united in its decisions can guarantee its control over the corporation by owning a majority of the common stock.

After the equity financing, the debt ratio of 50.5% will be within the benchmark range of 40.0% and 60.0%.

LO6 Identify factors influencing financing decisions.

LO7 Analyze the impact of financial leverage.

Terms Review

cost of capital

financial leverage

Audit your understanding

1. Identify five options available to a business to raise capital.

2. Identify five factors that a business should consider in deciding how to raise capital.

3. What is necessary for financial leverage to increase earnings?

4. How might individuals describe a business having a high level of debt?

5. What might force a corporation to issue additional stock?

Work together 18-4

Analyzing the impact of financial leverage

A form is given in the *Working Papers*. Your instructor will guide you through the following example.

1. KMT Stores is considering a renovation of its store. The project will cost $100,000.00. The company can issue 7%, $5,000.00 bonds to finance 90% of the project. The remaining capital will come from internal sources. The renovation should enable the business to serve more customers. Complete the form to evaluate the effect of financial leverage on the proposed renovation. Evaluate the earnings potential of the project assuming that operating income will increase by 6%, 7%, or 8% of the project cost.

2. Under what conditions should KMT Stores renovate the store?

On your own 18-4

Analyzing the impact of financial leverage

A form is given in the *Working Papers*. Work this problem independently.

1. Daniel Electric is planning to open a distribution center. The center will cost $500,000.00. The company can finance 96% of the project with 8.2%, $10,000.00 bonds. The remaining capital will come from internal sources. Complete the form to evaluate the effect of financial leverage on the proposed center. Evaluate the earnings potential of the project assuming that operating income will increase by 7.6%, 7.8%, or 8.0% of the center cost.

2. Under what conditions should Daniel Electric open the distribution center?

©CANDICE CUSACK, ISTOCK

A Look at Accounting Software

Accounting for Credit Card Payments in the Banking Module

In this chapter, you learned several different ways that businesses can raise capital for growth and development. But notes payable, credit lines, bond issues, and stock issues don't provide the cash a business needs for its daily operations.

Just like consumers, businesses use credit cards to finance some of their day-to-day expenses.

Unlike the usual expenditures for inventory and supplies, credit card charges tend to be small and occur in large numbers. These are tedious to account for manually, but technology simplifies the process significantly.

Using the Internet, a business can link directly to its bank's accounting system. Credit card charges can be downloaded from the bank directly into the business's accounting system, where each charge can easily be posted to the proper account.

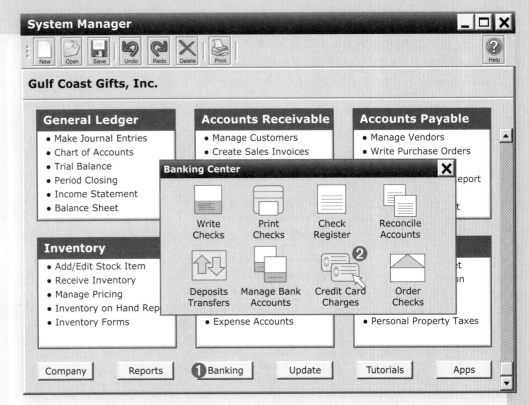

1. The user clicks on the Banking button to open the Banking Center navigation pane.

2. The user clicks on the Credit Card Charges icon to open the Credit Card Charges window.

3. From the drop-down list, the user selects a credit card account. Many businesses have more than one credit card account.

4. The user clicks on the Download button and the current charges are listed in the frame below. The Internet connection data were entered when the American Express—First American Bank account was set up. The system makes that connection and does the download automatically.

5. The current charges are displayed the same as they would appear on a credit card account statement. Gulf Coast Gifts, Inc., has provided three employees with cards on this account. The Card column identifies the employee who made each charge.

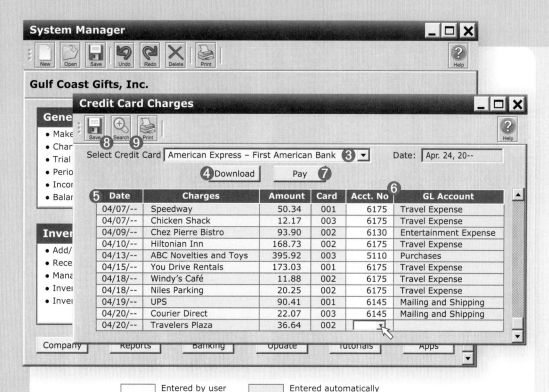

System Manager

New · Open · Save · Undo · Redo · Delete · Print · Help

Gulf Coast Gifts, Inc.

Gene...
- Make...
- Char...
- Trial...
- Perio...
- Incor...
- Balar...

Inver...
- Add/...
- Rece...
- Mana...
- Inver...
- Inver...

Credit Card Charges

Save ⑧ · Search ⑨ · Print · Help

Select Credit Card ⑤ American Express – First American Bank ③ ▼   Date: Apr. 24, 20--

④ Download   Pay ⑦

⑥

⑤ Date	Charges	Amount	Card	Acct. No	GL Account
04/07/--	Speedway	50.34	001	6175	Travel Expense
04/07/--	Chicken Shack	12.17	003	6175	Travel Expense
04/09/--	Chez Pierre Bistro	93.90	002	6130	Entertainment Expense
04/10/--	Hiltonian Inn	168.73	002	6175	Travel Expense
04/13/--	ABC Novelties and Toys	395.92	003	5110	Purchases
04/15/--	You Drive Rentals	173.03	001	6175	Travel Expense
04/18/--	Windy's Café	11.88	002	6175	Travel Expense
04/18/--	Niles Parking	20.25	002	6175	Travel Expense
04/19/--	UPS	90.41	001	6145	Mailing and Shipping
04/20/--	Courier Direct	22.07	003	6145	Mailing and Shipping
04/20/--	Travelers Plaza	36.64	002		

Company · Reports · Banking · Update · Tutorials · Apps

☐ Entered by user   ☐ Entered automatically

It is not uncommon for questions to arise later about specific charges. With paper records, it might be necessary to search through stacks of charge statements and charge slips to find them. In an automated system, a simple search can quickly locate any charge and make it easy to examine the details.

⑥ The Acct. No. and GL Account columns are empty until the user begins to assign account numbers to the charges. As account numbers are assigned, the system automatically displays the GL account titles.

⑦ At any time the user chooses, he or she can access the Credit Card Charges window, select a credit card account, and click the Pay button. That opens a new dialog box in which the user will designate the bank account the funds are to be paid from and the amount of the payment. The funds are automatically drawn from the business's checking account and paid on the credit card account. The system automatically credits the Cash account and debits the American Express—First American Bank account.

⑧ When the user has finished assigning the charges to the proper accounts, he or she clicks Save to post the charges. The next time charges are downloaded, only charges not posted will appear in the window.

⑨ Clicking on Search opens a search box allowing the user to quickly find and review any individual charge that has been posted. Clicking Print gives the user a choice of reports, including a report of the charges that have been posted.

Chapter Summary

At some point, every business needs to raise capital. A business might need extra cash to prepare for its prime selling season. An unexpected event, such as a storm, may cause a business to need extra cash for repairs. Businesses also need capital to fund expansion plans.

A business can raise capital through internal or external sources. The portion of net income not paid as a dividend is an internal source of capital. This source is rarely adequate to fund major expansion plans. In these cases, a business must raise capital from external sources. External sources include debt and equity financing.

Several types of debt financing are available. A line of credit is a flexible, short-term bank loan. A note payable is a bank loan for a stated amount, period, and interest rate. Notes can be signed for several months or several years. The term of the note determines whether the transaction is recorded to Notes Payable, a current liability, or Long-term Notes Payable, a long-term liability. Bonds are long-term promises to pay that are sold to investors. Bonds are often issued for 5, 10, and 20 years.

A business can raise equity financing by selling common or preferred stock. Common stockholders have voting rights and the right to the earnings of the business. A business can, but is not required to, pay dividends on its common stock. Preferred stockholders expect to earn a stated dividend rate along with other preferred rights. Preferred stockholders, though, do not have voting rights. Shares of both common and preferred stock are often assigned a par value. The par value has nothing to do with the market value of the stock. The amount of a stock sale above the par value is credited to an account titled Paid-in Capital in Excess of Par.

How a business raises needed capital is a complex decision. A business wants to reduce its obligation to pay interest to external sources. Each type of debt financing has different repayment terms. In contrast, equity financing does not have to be repaid. But equity financing may reduce the amount of control held by current stockholders by giving a share of the control to new stockholders.

The financial leverage of using debt financing can be a powerful tool to increase earnings. Whichever way a business elects to fund its operations, it must take care not to become over leveraged.

EXPLORE ACCOUNTING

Corporate Reporting with EDGAR

Public mistrust stemming from the 1929 stock market crash threatened the ability of corporations to obtain equity financing. In response, Congress created the Securities and Exchange Commission (SEC) in 1933 to restore public confidence in the financial markets. Corporations offering stock and bonds for sale to the public must register these securities with the SEC. Each quarter, corporations must submit financial reports containing their financial statements. The most common SEC reports include the Form 10-Q quarterly report and the Form 10-K annual report. Corporations also commonly file a Form 8-K to report significant events, such as a change in auditor, corporate mergers, and changes in the board of directors. Corporations have only four days after such an event to file Form 8-K.

The SEC has the authority to establish the accounting principles that must be used in preparing financial reports. However, the SEC has permitted the accounting profession to develop generally accepted accounting principles (GAAP). The SEC does require additional information not normally found in financial statements prepared in accordance with GAAP. For example, a corporation must describe its business and list the members of its board of directors.

Investors can obtain access to the SEC reports from many sources. Most corporations post these reports on their websites. Key search words such as *investor relations* or *corporate governance* are useful in searching for the reports. The SEC also posts reports to its Electronic Data Gathering, Analysis, and Retrieval (EDGAR) system at http://www.sec.gov/edgar.shtml. An investor can enter a company name or stock symbol to access the reports.

INSTRUCTIONS

Use EDGAR or a corporate website to access the latest Form 10-K for a corporation of your choice. Prepare a list of the topics discussed in the Item 2—Properties section of the report.

Source: www.sec.gov.

Apply Your Understanding

INSTRUCTIONS: Download problem instructions for Excel, QuickBooks, and Peachtree from the textbook companion website at www.C21accounting.com.

18-1 Application Problem: Journalizing entries for short-term debt LO2

The journals for Gift Shack are given in the *Working Papers*.

Instructions:

Using the current year, journalize the following transactions on page 9 of a cash receipts journal, page 14 of a cash payments journal, and page 8 of a general journal. Source documents are abbreviated as: check, C; receipt, R; memorandum, M.

Transactions:

Aug. 29. Signed a 90-day, 15% note to Mann Co. for an extension of time on its account payable, $2,950.00. M153.
Sept. 24. Drew $12,900.00 on its line of credit. R337.
Nov. 27. Paid cash for the maturity value of the August 29 note: principal, $2,950.00, plus interest. C669.
    30. Paid cash for the monthly payment on its line of credit: principal, $2,400.00, plus interest, $108.90. C674.

18-2 Application Problem: Journalizing entries for long-term debt LO4

AAONLINE

1. Go to www.cengage.com/login
2. Click on **AA Online** to access.
3. Go to the online assignment and follow the instructions.

The journals and a loan payment schedule for PAL Industries are given in the *Working Papers*.

Instructions:

Using the current year, journalize the following transactions on page 7 of a cash receipts journal and page14 of a cash payments journal. Refer to the loan payment schedule when journalizing the December 1 transaction. Source documents are abbreviated as: check, C; receipt, R.

Transactions:

Apr. 1. Signed a six-year, 7% note, $16,000.00. R552.
July 1. Issued 20-year, 5%, $5,000.00 bonds, $250,000.00. R606.
Dec. 1. Paid cash for the December payment on the April 1 note payable, $272.78. C968.
    31. Paid cash for the semiannual interest on bonds. C997.

18-3 Application Problem: Journalizing the sale of common and preferred stock LO5

Peachtree

1. Journalize and post transactions related to the sale of common and preferred stock to the general journal.
2. Print the general journal and the trial balance.

QB
Quick Books

1. Journalize and post transactions related to the sale of common and preferred stock to the journal.
2. Print the journal and the trial balance.

A cash receipts journal for Southern Supply is given in the *Working Papers*.

Instructions:

Using the current year, journalize the following transactions on page 9 of a cash receipts journal. Source documents are abbreviated as: receipt, R.

Transactions:

Sept. 2. Sold 350 shares of 7.5%, $100.00 par value preferred stock at par value. R525.
8. Issued 20,000 shares of $1.00 par value common stock at par value. R531.
10. Issued 4,000 shares of $1.00 par value common stock at $1.30 per share. R533.
21. Sold 250 shares of 7.5%, $100.00 par value preferred stock at par value. R543.
28. Sold 6,000 shares of $1.00 par value common stock at $1.40 per share. R549.

18-4 Application Problem: Analyzing the impact of financial leverage LO7

A form is given in the *Working Papers*.

Instructions:

1. UpTown Café wants to begin providing live music in its dining area. The plan will require the company to invest $30,000.00 in sound equipment. The vendor maintains that other restaurants have increased their annual operating income by 8.5% to 9.5% of the cost of the equipment. The vendor has offered to finance $28,000.00 of the purchase with a 9% note. The remaining capital will come from internal sources. Complete the form to evaluate the effect of financial leverage on the proposed center. Evaluate the earnings potential of the project assuming that operating income will increase by 8.5%, 9.0%, or 9.5% of the equipment cost.

2. Assume the company is successful in increasing its operating income by 9.5% of the sound equipment cost. Explain the impact of financial leverage on the return on UpTown Café's investment.

The journals for Teller Tires are given in the *Working Papers*.

Instructions:

Using the current year, journalize the following transactions on page 7 of a cash receipts journal, page 12 of a cash payments journal, and page 7 of a general journal. Refer to the loan payment schedule when journalizing the December 1 transaction. Source documents are abbreviated as: check, C; receipt, R; memorandum, M.

Transactions:

July	1.	Issued twenty-five 20-year, 6%, $10,000.00 bonds. R359.
	3.	Signed a 180-day, 12% note to PTS Corp. for an extension of time on its account payable, $3,200.00. M98.
	8.	Issued 8,000 shares of $25.00 par value common stock at par value. R362.
	12.	Sold 500 shares of 6.5%, $50.00 par value preferred stock at par value. R370.
	18.	Drew $24,800.00 on its line of credit. R376.
	23.	Issued 6,000 shares of $25.00 par value common stock at $28.00 per share. R385.
	31.	Signed a five-year, 8% note, $45,000.00. R392.
Dec.	1.	Paid cash for the December payment on the July 31 note payable, $912.44. C745.
	2.	Paid cash for the monthly payment on its line of credit: principal, $3,000.00, plus interest, $128.95. C746.
	30.	Paid cash for the maturity value of the July 3 note to PTS Corp., $3,200.00, plus interest. C762.
	31.	Paid cash for the semiannual interest on bonds. C763.

AAONLINE

1. Go to www.cengage.com/login
2. Click on **AA Online** to access.
3. Go to the online assignment and follow the instructions.

Peachtree

1. Journalize and post the July transactions to the general journal.
2. Journalize and post the December transactions in the Write Checks window.
3. Print the general journal, cash disbursements journal, and trial balance.

QuickBooks

1. Journalize and post the July transactions to the journal.
2. Journalize and post the December transactions in the Write Checks window.
3. Print the journal, check detail, and trial balance.

1. Journalize and post the July transactions to the journal.
2. Journalize and post the December transactions to the cash payments journal.
3. Print the general journal and cash payments journal.

18-C Challenge Problem: Selecting financing methods LO7

Windsong Corporation needs to obtain $500,000.00 of financing for a distribution center. Using the form provided in the *Working Papers*, develop a financing plan to fund the project.

Instructions:

1. Use the following information to determine an appropriate amount of debt and equity funding.

   a. Current liability and equity account balances are presented on the form.

   b. The project involves the opening of a distribution center. The funds will be used to purchase $380,000.00 of equipment and $70,000.00 of additional merchandise inventory. The remaining funds will cover pre-opening expenses.

   c. The company has a $25,000.00 line of credit with a 6.5% interest rate.

   d. A bank is willing to loan up to $250,000.00 at 8% for up to ten years.

   e. The company can issue up to $200,000.00 of 7%, 20-year $5,000.00 bonds.

   f. The Windsong family currently owns 8,000 of the 12,000 outstanding shares. The Windsong family wishes to keep control of a majority of the outstanding common stock.

   g. The company can sell up to 20,000 of its $10.00 par value common stock to independent investors for $15.00 per share.

   h. The board has a target debt ratio benchmark of 30% to 50%.

   i. Windsong projects that it will earn 12% on its investment in the project.

2. What number of shares of common stock should be purchased by the Windsong family to maintain voting control?

1. Use the worksheet to develop a financing plan to fund the distribution center project.
2. Select an appropriate mixture of debt versus equity financing.
3. Print the worksheet.

21st Century Skills

PARTNERSHIP FOR
21ST CENTURY SKILLS

Heavenly Deals

Theme: Financial, Economic, Business, and Entrepreneurial Literacy

Skills: Critical Thinking and Problem Solving, Communication and Collaboration

Many great business ideas never become reality because entrepreneurs are unable to raise the capital to get started. The types of financing that businesses normally use to raise capital are seldom available for high-risk ventures. Many of those ideas are simply left behind.

The business of raising capital is rarely considered a heavenly undertaking—unless an angel is providing the financing. The term *angel* originally came from Broadway in the 1900s. It described a wealthy individual who provided money for theatrical productions. Today, an *angel investor* is usually a successful businessperson who wants to invest in startup companies with the potential to produce huge returns on their investments. Angel investors seek startups that would be too risky for banks; and they often contribute expertise and experience in addition to capital.

Many angel investors choose to invest for reasons that go beyond a monetary return. They may choose to invest close to home in an effort to help their local community with technological or environmental advancements, or to help create jobs. It is difficult to account for the number of angel investors. Some studies indicate there may be over 12,000 of them. The angel investor might be a name you recognize, like Jeff Bezos, founder of Amazon. He was an angel investor for both Google and Twitter. Or, PayPal's cofounder, Peter Thiel, who helped Facebook get its start. There might be an angel investor in your own community willing to invest in your idea!

APPLICATION

1. You have created a more efficient solar panel, and you have identified potential customers who have said they would be willing to purchase a large number of panels. Unfortunately, you do not have the production capacity to manufacture the panels, which will cost $10,000,000.00. Compose a persuasive letter to a potential angel investor. Describe your business idea and state the amount of capital needed. Be sure to list at least three reasons why this would be a worthwhile investment.

2. Together with a classmate, brainstorm at least five characteristics of an angel investor who might be interested in investing in your Online Homework Tutoring business.

Analyzing Nike's financial statements

Investors use a ratio known as the *dividend yield* when making investment decisions. The dividend yield is calculated as follows: Dividend Yield = Dividend per Share ÷ Market Price per Share.

Companies with large dividend yields (greater than 3%) are typically considered to be *income stocks*, meaning that investors own the stock primarily to earn the dividend. In contrast, companies with no dividend or small dividend yields (less than 2%) are often referred to as *growth stocks*, meaning that investors are counting on the market value of the stock to increase over time.

INSTRUCTIONS

Use Nike's Selected Financial Data on page B-3 in Appendix B to answer the following questions.

1. For each year, calculate Nike's dividend yield using the high price of common stock. Calculate percents to one decimal place.

2. Would you classify Nike as an income or growth stock?

Chapter 19

Accounting for Plant Assets, Depreciation, and Intangible Assets

LEARNING OBJECTIVES

After studying Chapter 19, in addition to defining key terms, you will be able to:

LO1 Record the buying of a plant asset.

LO2 Analyze the cost of individual assets bought as a bundle.

LO3 Calculate and record the payment of property tax.

LO4 Calculate depreciation expense.

LO5 Calculate depreciation for a partial year.

LO6 Calculate accumulated depreciation and book value.

LO7 Prepare plant asset records.

LO8 Journalize annual depreciation expense.

LO9 Record the sale of a plant asset for book value.

LO10 Record the sale of a plant asset for more/less than book value.

LO11 Calculate depreciation using the double declining-balance method.

LO12 Record the buying of an intangible asset.

LO13 Calculate and record amortization expense.

Accounting In The Real World
Cinemark Holdings, Inc.

At a movie theater, the experience begins when you walk through the door and smell the popcorn. These days, it is about more than just the movie. How you feel about the experience is a combination of many items, including seating, theater size, audio system, and visual impact.

Cinemark Holdings, Inc., of Plano, Texas, is in the process of improving your experience. Cinemark's circuit is the third largest in the United States. It has 292 theaters and 3,816 screens in 39 states. Cinemark also has 139 theaters and 1,125 screens in 13 countries in Latin America. It is opening more screens and plans to continue doing so in the future. Cinemark features stadium seating in 86% of its first-run theaters.

Besides opening new theaters, Cinemark is making a huge investment in state-of-the-art equipment in many of its current theaters. It has developed a large-screen digital format which it calls XD Extreme Digital Cinema. XD theaters include wall-to-wall and ceiling-to-floor screens and wrap-around sound. Cinemark feels that all of these investments will add to the total experience of each customer.

Cinemark also offers Summer Movie Clubhouse Fun Film for Kids. Available at over 150 locations, this is a ten-week series of G- or PG-rated movies. The best part of this series is the price—$1 per person per show. A series punch card is available for $5 and is good for all ten movies. The Cinemark website states that "The Summer Movie Clubhouse offers an affordable way to beat the summer heat and enjoy some great family films. Our customers look forward to this successful program every year."

The large investment in equipment and special programming seem to be paying off. During a recent year, Cinemark ranked either 1 or 2 in box office revenues in 25 of its top 30 markets.

Cinemark estimates that its furniture and equipment will last for five to 15 years. In compliance with GAAP, Cinemark depreciates the costs of the furniture and equipment over their estimated useful lives. Thus, a portion of each item of furniture and equipment is recorded as an expense every period until only the salvage value remains.

CRITICAL THINKING

1. The digital projection equipment may last longer than Cinemark's estimated useful life. Why do you think Cinemark estimates a shorter useful life for its equipment?

2. What is the effect on the income statement of estimating a useful life of ten years rather than 15 years for projection equipment?

Key Terms

- return on investment
- real property
- personal property
- assessed value
- plant asset record
- gain
- gain on plant assets
- loss
- loss on plant assets
- accelerated depreciation
- declining-balance method of depreciation
- double declining-balance method of depreciation
- intangible asset
- amortization

LO1 Record the buying of a plant asset.

LO2 Analyze the cost of individual assets bought as a bundle.

LO3 Calculate and record the payment of property tax.

Plant Assets

Physical assets that will be used for a number of years in the operation of a business are known as *plant assets*. A business may have several types of plant assets, including equipment, buildings, and land. Businesses often subdivide plant assets into more focused categories and create an account for each category. For example, a company may divide its equipment into office, store, warehouse, and transportation equipment.

Sun Treasures, Inc., owns its equipment but rents the building and the land where the business is located. Therefore, Sun Treasures only has accounts for equipment. To provide more detailed financial information, Sun Treasures records its equipment in two different equipment accounts—**Office Equipment** and **Store Equipment**. [CONCEPT: Adequate Disclosure]

Sun Treasures is going to be investing in plant assets as it opens new stores. When a company buys a plant asset, it expects that the asset will help the company earn revenue. Since companies have limited resources

to invest in plant assets, managers must often decide between investment opportunities. Accounting data can be used to predict the efficiency of an investment. The ratio of the money earned on an investment relative to the amount of the investment is called **return on investment**, or *ROI*. The more efficient the investment, the higher its ROI. These predictions will help company managers decide which assets to buy.

Most plant assets are useful for only a limited period of time. Over time, most equipment wears out and can no longer perform its functions. Other equipment, such as computers, becomes technologically outdated. Regardless of the reason, the cost of a plant asset should be depreciated over its useful life. Each plant asset account should have a related accumulated depreciation account—a contra asset account—to accumulate the annual depreciation expense of the plant assets in the account.

ETHICS IN ACTION

Lifelong Learning

When you are ill, you expect your doctor to know the latest methods and medicines to restore your health. Businesses should expect nothing less from their accountants. Therefore, accountants must constantly improve their knowledge and skills to provide their clients, employees, and the public with the highest level of professional service.

The code of conduct for every major accounting organization includes some reference to lifelong learning. Most organizations require their members to continue their education

throughout their careers. For example, certified public accountants must complete a minimum number of continuing education hours every year. This education may be in the form of self-study courses, college courses, seminars, and conferences.

INSTRUCTIONS

Access the codes of conduct from the American Institute of Certified Public Accountants (AICPA), the Institute of Internal Auditors (IIA), the Institute of Management Accountants (IMA), and the Association of Certified Fraud Examiners (ACFE). Identify what each code states about lifelong learning.

©LUCA DI FILIPPO, ISTOCK

Recording the Buying of a Plant Asset LO1

						GENERAL		ACCOUNTS PAYABLE DEBIT	PURCHASES DISCOUNT CREDIT	CASH CREDIT	
	DATE	ACCOUNT TITLE	CK. NO.	POST. REF.		DEBIT	CREDIT				
						1	2	3	4	5	
8	3	*Store Equipment*	612			8 5 0 0 00				8 5 0 0 00	8
9											9
10											10

CASH PAYMENTS JOURNAL   PAGE 1

① Account Title   **②** Cost of the Plant Asset   **③** Cash Paid

Procedures for recording the buying of a plant asset are similar to procedures for recording the buying of current assets such as supplies. The amount paid for a plant asset is debited to a plant asset account with a title such as Store Equipment. Regardless of their actual value, plant assets are always recorded at their original cost. [CONCEPT: Historical Cost]

Store Equipment
⬆ 8,500.00

Cash
⬇ 8,500.00

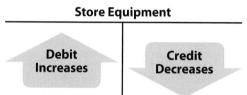

Store Equipment

Debit Increases	Credit Decreases

January 3, 20X1. Paid cash for a shelving unit, $8,500.00. Check No. 612.

↘ Journalizing the Buying of a Plant Asset

① Write the plant asset account, Store Equipment, in the Account Title column of the cash payments journal.

② Enter the cost of the plant asset, $8,500.00, in the General Debit column.

③ Enter the same amount, $8,500.00, in the Cash Credit column.

FINANCIAL LITERACY

Don't Be Caught "Upside Down"

As soon as a new car is driven off the lot, it depreciates approximately 20%. The same car will continue depreciating significantly for the next several years. If the car is wrecked, totaled, or stolen within those few years, the owner could be left *upside down*.

Upside down means the amount still owed on the automobile exceeds the amount the insurance company would pay if the vehicle were totaled or stolen. For example, someone pays $30,000 for a car and a year later it is totaled. The car owner still owes the lender $25,000. The insurance company values the vehicle at $22,000 due to depreciation. That leaves the owner upside down, owing the difference of $3,000 to the lender. Statistics show that as many as 40% of consumers would be left upside down in the event of theft or total loss in an accident.

If your automobile insurance does not offer full replacement cost, you might consider Guaranteed Auto Protection (GAP) insurance. GAP insurance covers the difference between the actual cash value and what you owe to the lender. Most automobile lease contracts require GAP insurance.

ACTIVITIES

1. Can you think of other products besides automobiles that might need to be covered with GAP insurance?

2. How do you think your decision to purchase GAP insurance might change for different makes and models of automobiles?

Recording the Buying of a Group of Assets LO2

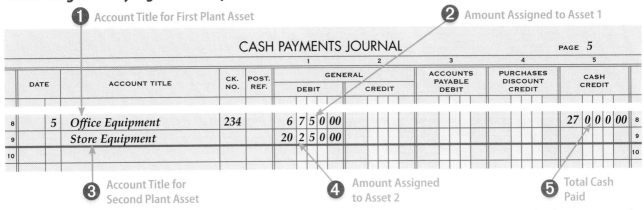

1 Account Title for First Plant Asset

2 Amount Assigned to Asset 1

3 Account Title for Second Plant Asset

4 Amount Assigned to Asset 2

5 Total Cash Paid

A company may buy several assets as a group with a single discounted price for all the assets. That often happens when a vendor offers a bundled price to encourage the sale of more items. Even though one price is paid for all the assets, each asset must be assigned (or allocated) a price. The cost allocated to each asset is debited to that plant asset account. [CONCEPT: Historical Cost] This allocation must be done so that each plant asset can be depreciated individually.

Dufore Company buys a copy machine (office equipment) and a display case (store equipment) for a total cost of $27,000.00. The copy machine has an estimated value of $7,500.00. The display case has an estimated value of $22,500.00.

The first step is to calculate the total estimated value of all the assets bought:

Estimated Value of Asset 1	+	Estimated Value of Asset 2	=	Total Estimated Value of All Assets Bought
$7,500.00	+	$22,500.00	=	$30,000.00

The cost assigned to the copy machine (Asset 1) is calculated as follows:

Estimated Value of Asset 1	÷	Total Estimated Value of All Assets Bought	=	Percentage of Total Estimated Value
$7,500.00	÷	$30,000.00	=	25%

Total Purchase Price	×	Percentage of Total Estimated Value	=	Cost Assigned to Asset 1
$27,000.00	×	25%	=	$6,750.00

The cost assigned to the display case (Asset 2) is calculated as follows:

Estimated Value of Asset 2	÷	Total Estimated Value of All Assets Bought	=	Percentage of Total Estimated Value
$22,500.00	÷	$30,000.00	=	75%

Total Purchase Price	×	Percentage of Total Estimated Value	=	Cost Assigned to Asset 1
$27,000.00	×	75%	=	$20,250.00

March 5, 20X1. Dufore Company bought a copy machine and a display case for $27,000.00. Check No. 234.

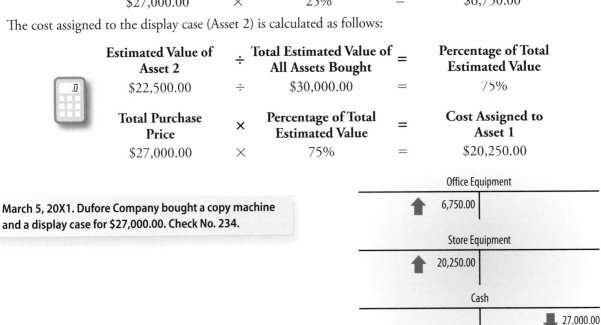

① Write the title of the first plant asset account, Office Equipment, in the Account Title column of the cash payments journal.

② Enter the cost assigned to the copy machine, $6,750.00, in the General Debit column.

③ Write the title of the second plant asset account, Store Equipment, in the Account Title column on the next line of the cash payments journal.

④ Enter the cost assigned to the display unit, $20,250.00, in the General Debit column on the same line.

⑤ Enter the total cash paid, $27,000.00, in the Cash Credit column.

Calculating and Paying Property Tax LO3

						GENERAL		ACCOUNTS PAYABLE DEBIT	PURCHASES DISCOUNT CREDIT	CASH CREDIT	
	DATE	ACCOUNT TITLE	CK. NO.	POST. REF.		DEBIT	CREDIT				
14	15	Property Tax Expense	551			1 0 4 0 00				1 0 4 0 00	14
15											15
16											16

CASH PAYMENTS JOURNAL — PAGE 3

① Account Title **②** Amount of Tax **③** Cash Paid

For tax purposes, state and federal governments define two kinds of property—real and personal. Land and anything attached to the land is called **real property**. Real property is sometimes referred to as *real estate*. All property not classified as real property is called **personal property**. For tax purposes, these definitions apply whether the property is owned by a business or an individual.

Most governmental units with taxing power impose taxes based on the value of real property. Real property taxes are assessed on buildings and land. Some governmental units also tax personal property such as cars, boats, trailers, and airplanes.

The value of an asset determined by tax authorities for the purpose of calculating taxes is called the **assessed value**. Assessed value is usually based on the judgment of officials referred to as *assessors*. Assessors are elected by citizens or are specially trained employees of a local (usually county) government.

A tax rate is used to calculate property tax. The tax rate is multiplied by an asset's assessed value, not the value recorded on a business's records.

Brighton Bikes, Inc., owns real property that has been assessed for a total of $80,000.00. The city tax rate is 1.3%.

The assessed value of an asset may not be the same as the value on the business's or individual's records. The assessed value is assigned to an asset for tax purposes only. Often, the assessed value is only a part of the true value of the asset.

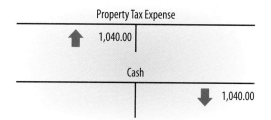

Property Tax Expense

⬆ 1,040.00

Cash

⬇ 1,040.00

Assessed Value	×	Tax Rate	=	Annual Property Tax
$80,000.00	×	1.3%	=	$1,040.00

February 15, 20X1. Brighton Bikes, Inc., paid cash for property tax, $1,040.00. Check No. 551.

Payment of property taxes is necessary for a firm to continue in business. Therefore, Brighton Bikes classifies property tax as an operating expense.

① Write the title of the account, Property Tax Expense, in the Account Title column of the cash payments journal.

② Enter the amount of the property tax, $1,040.00, in the General Debit column.

③ Enter the same amount, $1,040.00, in the Cash Credit column.

End of Lesson Review

LO1 Record the buying of a plant asset.

LO2 Analyze the cost of individual assets bought as a bundle.

LO3 Calculate and record the payment of property tax.

Terms Review

return on investment

real property

personal property

assessed value

Audit your understanding

1. Which accounts are affected, and how, when cash is paid for office equipment?

2. Why must a cost be allocated to each asset bought in a group?

3. What items are included in real property?

Work together 19-1

Journalizing buying plant assets and paying property tax

The cash payments journal for O'Donnel Copy Center is given in the *Working Papers*. Your instructor will guide you through the following examples.

Journalize the following transactions completed during the current year. Use page 1 of a cash payments journal. The abbreviation for a check is C.

Transactions:

Jan. 3. Paid cash for a copy machine for use in the store, $800.00. C241.

5. Paid cash for an office chair, $500.00. C244.

Feb. 26. Paid property taxes on real property with an assessed value of $200,000.00. The tax rate in the city where the property is located is 2.0% of assessed value. C268.

July 2. Paid cash for a filing cabinet (office equipment) and a paper cutter (store equipment), $600.00. The filing cabinet has an estimated value of $300.00, and the paper cutter has an estimated value of $450.00. C331.

On your own 19-1

Journalizing buying plant assets and paying property tax

The cash payments journal for Foreman Floor Center is given in the *Working Papers*. Work this problem independently.

Journalize the following transactions completed during the current year. Use page 3 of a cash payments journal. The abbreviation for a check is C.

Transactions:

Feb. 2. Paid cash for a computer for use in the office, $1,200.00. C335.

5. Paid cash for a carpet stretcher, $600.00. C340.

Mar. 24. Paid property taxes on real property with an assessed value of $84,000.00. The tax rate in the city where the property is located is 3.5% of assessed value. C371.

28. Paid cash for a desk (office equipment) and a display case (store equipment), $2,100.00. The desk has an estimated value of $600.00, and the display case has an estimated value of $1,800.00. C380.

LESSON

19-2 Calculating Depreciation Expense

LO4 Calculate depreciation expense.

LO5 Calculate depreciation for a partial year.

LO6 Calculate accumulated depreciation and book value.

Calculating Straight-Line Depreciation **LO4**

Original Cost	–	Estimated Salvage Value	=	Estimated Total Depreciation Expense	
$8,500.00	–	$500.00	=	$8,000.00	❶ Calculate Total Depreciation Expense

Estimated Total Depreciation Expense	÷	Years of Estimated Useful Life	=	Annual Depreciation Expense	
$8,000.00	÷	4	=	$2,000.00	❷ Calculate Annual Depreciation Expense

Plant assets are expected to be used in the business for many years. GAAP requires that the cost of a plant asset be expensed over the plant asset's useful life. [CONCEPT: Matching Expenses with Revenue] The annual expense is recorded in Depreciation Expense and the contra asset account Accumulated Depreciation.

Several methods for calculating depreciation expense are available. The easiest and most widely used method is known as the *straight-line method of depreciation*. This method requires the business to know the cost of the plant asset and to estimate two amounts:

1. The amount the business expects to receive when a plant asset is disposed of, known as the *estimated salvage value*. The salvage value of an asset can be zero if the company plans to discard it when it is no longer useful.
2. The number of years a plant asset is expected to contribute to the earnings of a business, known as the *estimated useful life*.

The straight-line method of depreciation charges an equal amount of depreciation expense in each full year in which the asset is used. Other methods of depreciation will be explained later in this chapter.

On January 3, 20X1, Sun Treasures bought a shelving unit for $8,500.00 with an estimated salvage value of $500.00 and an estimated useful life of four years.

⬇ Calculating Annual Depreciation Expense

❶ Subtract the asset's estimated salvage value from the asset's original cost. This difference is the estimated total depreciation expense for the asset's entire useful life.

❷ Divide the estimated total depreciation expense by the years of estimated useful life. The result is the annual depreciation expense.

The estimated useful life should be based on prior experience with similar assets and on available guidelines. Trade associations frequently publish guidelines for specialized plant assets. The Internal Revenue Service also publishes depreciation guidelines for plant assets.

Careers In Accounting

Casey Hepburn
AUDITOR

Casey Hepburn, CPA, is an auditor for a major public accounting firm. He works with a variety of clients ranging from small companies to huge multinational corporations. It is an auditor's responsibility to determine if a client's financial statements have been prepared and reported in compliance with generally accepted accounting principles (GAAP). If the client is a large firm, Mr. Hepburn will work with a team of accountants to perform the audit.

When auditing a company's accounts and transactions, the team cannot possibly look at all transactions to see if they are recorded correctly. Instead, the team uses a technique called *sampling*. In sampling, only selected transactions are verified. If those transactions were recorded according to GAAP, the team makes the assumption that all similar transactions have also been recorded correctly. In order to do a thorough job, the audit team must have access to all necessary company records. The audit team follows established standard procedures to ensure that their audits are done correctly.

As a requirement of the Sarbanes-Oxley Act of 2002, the audit team must also review the client's internal control system as it relates to financial reporting. The audit team must point out any weaknesses it finds in the internal control system.

At the conclusion of the audit, the auditor issues an *opinion*. The opinion is directed to the client's board of directors and shareholders. Without this opinion, the shareholders would have no assurance that the financial statements were prepared in compliance with GAAP.

As an auditor, Mr. Hepburn must be objective. This means that he must be independent of his client. An auditor must not have any personal stake in the client's financial position, whether good or bad. The audit team usually reports to an audit committee, which is a subcommittee of the board of directors. It is essential that the auditor have unrestricted access to the audit committee without needing permission from the board.

Salary Range: Salaries vary depending on company size, job responsibilities, and experience. The average entry-level salary is $44,000 to $55,000. The average salary for a senior audit manager is $96,000 to $141,500, plus bonuses.

Qualifications: Minimum education for an auditor is a bachelor's degree in accounting and a CPA certificate. A master's degree is often preferred. Most employers also require past experience in the field of accounting. Many auditors have some education in law, forensics, finance, math, and economics.

Effective communication skills are essential for an auditor. Auditors interact with the client's employees, managers, customers, vendors, bankers, and directors. They often must explain accounting standards and clarify expectations. The preparation of written reports is also required.

To perform well in their positions, auditors must be able to gather, organize, and process information; solve problems; understand the consequence of errors; and keep up to date with technology. They must be able to plan and direct projects, deal with high-stress situations, maintain confidentiality, and prioritize tasks. An auditor must also be ethical, reliable, and responsible.

Occupational Outlook: The growth for auditor positions is projected to be faster than average (20% or higher) for the period from 2008 to 2018.

Sources: www.investopedia.com, www.online.onetcenter.org, and www.roberthalffinance.com/SalaryCenter.

ACTIVITY

Look for a job opening in auditing. Write a paragraph about the position, including educational requirements and salary range.

Calculating Depreciation Expense for Part of a Year LO5

Annual Depreciation Expense	÷	Months in a Year	=	Monthly Depreciation Expense	
$900.00	÷	12	=	$75.00	← ❶ Calculate Monthly Depreciation Expense

Monthly Depreciation Expense	×	Number of Months Asset Is Used	=	Partial Year's Depreciation Expense	
$75.00	×	4	=	$300.00	← ❷ Calculate Partial Year's Depreciation Expense

A month is the smallest unit of time used to calculate depreciation. A plant asset may be placed in service at a date other than the first day of a fiscal period. In such cases, a business may elect to calculate depreciation expense to the nearest first of a month. A partial year's depreciation may also be recorded in the year the plant asset is sold or disposed of.

Sun Treasures bought an office computer on September 3, 20X1. The annual straight-line depreciation expense is $900.00. The depreciation expense is $300.00 for the remaining four months of the year in which Sun Treasures used the computer.

Calculating Partial Year's Depreciation Expense

❶ Divide the annual depreciation expense by 12, the number of months in a year. The result is the monthly depreciation expense.

❷ Multiply the monthly depreciation expense by the number of months the plant asset is used in a year. The result is the partial year's depreciation expense.

The three years' depreciation expense is illustrated below. In the first year, a partial year's depreciation is recorded: September 3, 20X1, to December 31, 20X1—four months. If the asset had been bought September 16 or later, only three months' depreciation would be

expensed because the date would be closer to October 1 than September 1. In the next two years, a full year's depreciation, $900.00, would be expensed each year. In 20X4, the original three-year useful life ends August 31, so eight months' depreciation would be recorded.

Office computer: $3,000.00
Estimated salvage value: $300.00
Useful life: 3 years
Annual depreciation ($3,000.00 − $300.00) ÷ 3 = $900.00 per year
Monthly depreciation: $900.00 ÷ 12 = $75 per month

20X1 Sept. 3	20X1 Dec. 31	20X2 Dec. 31	20X3 Dec. 31	20X4 Aug. 31
	4 months	1 year	1 year	8 months
	$75 × 4 = $300.00	$900.00	$900.00	$75 × 8 = $600.00

Calculating Accumulated Depreciation and Book Value LO6

Plant asset:	*Office Computer*	Original cost:		$3,000.00
Depreciation method:	*Straight-line*	Estimated salvage value:		$300.00
		Estimated useful life:		*3 years*
		Date bought:		*September 3, 20X1*

Year	Beginning Book Value	Annual Depreciation	Accumulated Depreciation	Ending Book Value
20X1	$3,000.00	$300.00	$ 300.00	$2,700.00
20X2	2,700.00	900.00	1,200.00	1,800.00
20X3	1,800.00	900.00	2,100.00	900.00
20X4	900.00	600.00	2,700.00	300.00

CALCULATING ACCUMULATED DEPRECIATION

Depreciation is not recorded as a reduction of the plant asset account. Instead, the depreciation expense for each year of a plant asset's useful life is recorded in an accumulated depreciation account. The accumulated depreciation for a plant asset in the current year is calculated by adding the depreciation expense for the current year to the prior year's accumulated depreciation.

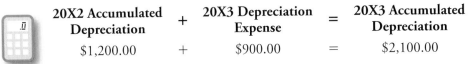

	20X2 Accumulated Depreciation	+	20X3 Depreciation Expense	=	20X3 Accumulated Depreciation
	$1,200.00	+	$900.00	=	$2,100.00

CALCULATING BOOK VALUE

The original cost of a plant asset minus accumulated depreciation is known as the *book value of a plant asset*. The book value is calculated by subtracting the accumulated depreciation from the original cost of the plant asset. The ending book value, at the end of the fiscal year, is the beginning book value for the next year. Plant assets may continue to be used after their estimated useful lives have ended; however, no additional depreciation is recorded.

The book value can also be calculated by subtracting the year's depreciation from that year's beginning book value. Either method of calculating a book value is acceptable because both methods calculate the same amount.

	Original Cost	−	Accumulated Depreciation	=	Ending Book Value
	$3,000.00	−	$2,700.00	=	$300.00

End of Lesson Review

LO4 Calculate depreciation expense.

LO5 Calculate depreciation for a partial year.

LO6 Calculate accumulated depreciation and book value.

Audit your understanding

1. Which accounting concept is being applied when depreciation expense is recorded for plant assets?

2. What three amounts are used to calculate a plant asset's annual depreciation expense using the straight-line method of depreciation?

Work together 19-2

Calculating depreciation

Forms are given in the *Working Papers.* Your instructor will guide you through the following example.

Brookdale Banners bought the following assets during 20X1. Brookdale uses the straight-line depreciation method. Calculate beginning book value, annual depreciation, accumulated depreciation, and ending book value for each asset for each year of estimated useful life. If the asset was not bought at the beginning of 20X1, calculate the depreciation expense for the part of 20X1 in which the company owned the asset. Save your work to complete Work Together 19-3.

Transactions:

Jan. 4. Bought a display case costing $4,040.00; estimated salvage value, $200.00; estimated useful life, 8 years.

Sept. 20. Bought a work station, $4,800.00; estimated salvage value, $0.00; estimated useful life, 5 years.

On your own 19-2

Calculating depreciation

Forms are given in the *Working Papers.* Work this problem independently.

Royal Repair Co. bought the following assets during 20X1. Royal uses the straight-line depreciation method. Calculate beginning book value, annual depreciation, accumulated depreciation, and ending book value for each asset for each year of estimated useful life. If the asset was not bought at the beginning of 20X1, calculate the depreciation expense for the part of 20X1 in which the company owned the asset. Save your work to complete On Your Own 19-3.

Transactions:

Jan. 5. Bought a stitching machine costing $2,500.00; estimated salvage value, $340.00; estimated useful life, 6 years.

June 13. Bought a notebook computer, $2,070.00; estimated salvage value, $150.00; estimated useful life, 4 years.

LESSON 19-3 *Journalizing Depreciation Expense*

LO7 Prepare plant asset records.

LO8 Journalize annual depreciation expense.

Preparing Plant Asset Records LO7

PLANT ASSET RECORD No. __62__   General Ledger Account No. __1120__

Description __Shelving Unit__   General Ledger Account __Store Equipment__   ❶

Date Bought __January 2, 20X1__   Serial Number _____   Original Cost __$8,500.00__

Estimated Useful Life __4 years__   Estimated Salvage Value __$500.00__   Depreciation Method __Straight-line__

Disposed of: Discarded _____   Sold _____   Traded _____   ❷

Date _____   Disposal Amount _____

Year	Annual Depreciation Expense	Accumulated Depreciation	Ending Book Value	
20X1	$2,000.00	$2,000.00	$6,500.00	
20X2	2,000.00	4,000.00	4,500.00	❸
20X3	2,000.00	6,000.00	2,500.00	
20X4	2,000.00	8,000.00	500.00	

Continue record on back of card

Accountants keep a separate record for each plant asset. An accounting form on which a business records information about each plant asset is called a **plant asset record**.

Plant asset records may vary in arrangement for different businesses, but most records contain similar information. Sun Treasures' plant asset record has three sections. Section 1 is prepared when a plant asset is bought. Section 2 provides space for recording the disposition of the plant asset. When the asset is disposed of, this information will be filled in. Section 3 provides space for recording annual depreciation expense and the changing book value of the asset each year it is used.

At the end of each fiscal period, Sun Treasures brings each plant asset record up to date by recording three amounts: (1) annual depreciation expense, (2) accumulated depreciation, and (3) ending book value.

The amount recorded in the Annual Depreciation Expense column is the amount calculated for each year. These amounts may be different if the asset is bought or sold at a time other than near the fiscal year beginning or end.

For any plant asset, accumulated depreciation for the first year is the annual depreciation expense for the first year. For each year thereafter, accumulated depreciation for any plant asset is the depreciation expense that has accumulated over all prior years added to that year's annual depreciation expense.

The ending book value for any given year is the original cost less that year's accumulated depreciation.

PHOTODISC/GETTY IMAGES

Preparing a Plant Asset Record

1. Write the information in Section 1 when the plant asset is bought.

2. Do not write in Section 2 until the asset is disposed of.

3. Each year the asset is owned, record the year's annual depreciation expense in Section 3. Calculate and record accumulated depreciation and ending book value.

THINK LIKE AN ACCOUNTANT

Applying International Accounting Standards

Accountants using GAAP commonly assign a useful life of 25 or 30 years to a building. The cost of a building includes everything needed to occupy a building, including its foundation, electrical wiring, plumbing, light fixtures, and carpet. All of these costs are combined and depreciated as one asset having one cost, one salvage value, and one useful life.

Does every part of the building depreciate over the same number of years? The answer is no. A foundation can last a lifetime, depending on how it is constructed. In contrast, carpet usually becomes worn or goes out of style as early as five to seven years.

International financial reporting standards (IFRS, pronounced i'fers) take a different approach to depreciating a building. IFRS require that a building be divided into its component parts. Each component is depreciated over its expected useful life. Thus, the foundation may be depreciated over 30 or more years. In contrast, the carpet may be depreciated over a shorter period, such as seven years.

Most of today's computerized accounting systems are designed to apply GAAP depreciation methods. A company having purchased a building would have recorded the entire cost as a single asset in its accounting system. Until accounting systems are modified to comply with IFRS rules, accountants must use other computer technologies to generate the required information.

OPEN THE SPREADSHEET TLA_CH19
Follow the steps on the Instructions tab.

Bryan Creek Stores has completed a project to divide the costs of its existing plant assets. Each plant asset is assigned a number in the format XXXX-YY. The XXXX is the plant asset number in its existing accounting system. The YY is a code for each component part, such as foundation and carpet. Use the worksheet to complete a table of plant asset information supporting amounts in IFRS financial statements.

Journalizing Annual Depreciation Expense LO8

Sun Treasures, Inc.		
Unadjusted Trial Balance		
December 31, 20--		
ACCOUNT TITLE	DEBIT	CREDIT
Office Equipment	325 6 4 8 16	
Accumulated Depreciation—Office Equipment		79 7 2 7 00

① Debit Depreciation Expense

GENERAL JOURNAL						PAGE 13
DATE	ACCOUNT TITLE	DOC. NO.	POST. REF.	DEBIT	CREDIT	
	Adjusting Entries					1
14 31	Depreciation Expense—Office Equipment			25 1 4 6 00		14
15	Accum. Depreciation—Office Equipment				25 1 4 6 00	15
16						16

② Credit Accumulated Depreciation

At the end of the fiscal year, Sun Treasures calculates the depreciation expense for each plant asset. The depreciation expense for each asset is recorded on its plant asset record. Next, the total depreciation expense is calculated for all plant assets recorded in the same plant asset account.

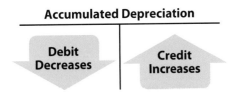

Accumulated Depreciation

Debit Decreases | Credit Increases

Sun Treasures determined that total depreciation expense for store equipment is $25,146.00. Using this information, an adjusting entry is then recorded in a general journal.

It is important to retain original cost information for plant assets. Rather than credit depreciation to a plant asset account, depreciation is recorded to the asset's accumulated depreciation contra account. At any time, the book value of a plant asset can be calculated by subtracting its accumulated depreciation from the plant asset account.

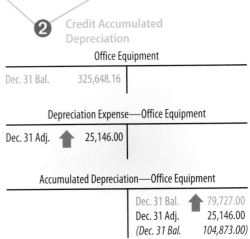

Office Equipment

Dec. 31 Bal.   325,648.16

Depreciation Expense—Office Equipment

Dec. 31 Adj.   ⬆ 25,146.00

Accumulated Depreciation—Office Equipment

Dec. 31 Bal.   ⬆ 79,727.00
Dec. 31 Adj.   25,146.00
(Dec. 31 Bal.   104,873.00)

⊗ Journalizing Annual Depreciation Expense

① Debit Depreciation Expense—Office Equipment for the amount of depreciation expense, $25,146.00.

② Credit Accum. Depreciation—Office Equipment for the same amount, $25,146.00.

End of Lesson Review

LO7 Prepare plant asset records.

LO8 Journalize annual depreciation expense.

Term Review

plant asset record

> ### Audit your understanding
>
> 1. How is accumulated depreciation recorded so as to retain the original cost information for plant assets?
> 2. How does an adjusting entry for depreciation expense change the balance of the asset account?

> ### Work together 19-3
>
> #### Journalizing depreciation
>
> Use the depreciation calculations from Work Together 19-2. Additional forms are given in the *Working Papers*. Your instructor will guide you through the following examples.
>
> 1. Complete each plant asset record for the years 20X1 through 20X3. Use the following additional information:

Description	General Ledger Account	Date Bought	Plant Asset No.	Serial No.
Display Case	1220—Store Equipment	Jan. 4	105	374-02
Work Station	1210—Office Equipment	Sept. 20	106	X56Y17

> 2. On December 31, 20X3, Brookdale Banners determined that total depreciation expense for office equipment for the year was $13,125.00. Record the adjusting entry on page 23 of a general journal. Save your work to complete Work Together 19-4.

> ### On your own 19-3
>
> #### Journalizing depreciation
>
> Use the depreciation calculations from On Your Own 19-2. Additional forms are given in the *Working Papers*. Work this problem independently.
>
> 1. Complete each plant asset record from the years 20X1 through 20X3. Use the following additional information:

Description	General Ledger Account	Date Bought	Plant Asset No.	Serial No.
Stitching Machine	1220—Store Equipment	Jan. 5	276	GH-422-J
Notebook Computer	1210—Office Equipment	June 13	277	81763273

> 2. On December 31, 20X3, Royal Repair Co. determined that total depreciation expense for store equipment for the year was $15,775.00. Record the adjusting entry on page 20 of a general journal. Save your work to complete On Your Own 19-4.

©CANDICE CUSACK, ISTOCK

LESSON

19-4 Disposing of Plant Assets

LO9 Record the sale of a plant asset for book value.

LO10 Record the sale of a plant asset for more/less than book value.

Selling a Plant Asset for Book Value LO9

					1	2	3	4	5	6	7	
					GENERAL		ACCOUNTS RECEIVABLE CREDIT	SALES CREDIT	SALES TAX PAYABLE CREDIT	SALES DISCOUNT DEBIT	CASH DEBIT	
	DATE	ACCOUNT TITLE	DOC. NO.	POST. REF.	DEBIT	CREDIT						
4	2	Accum. Depr.—Store Equip.	R543		8 0 0 0 00						5 0 0 00	4
5		Store Equipment				8 5 0 0 00						5

CASH RECEIPTS JOURNAL PAGE 1

① Remove the original cost of the plant asset and its related accumulated depreciation. Record the cash received.

② Complete Section 2 of the plant asset record.

Disposed of:	Discarded _____	Sold ✓	Traded _____
Date	*January 2, 20X5*	Disposal Amount	*$500.00*

When a plant asset is no longer useful to a business, the asset may be disposed of. The old plant asset may be sold, traded for a new asset, or discarded.

When a plant asset is disposed of, a journal entry is recorded that achieves the following:

1. Removes the original cost of the plant asset and its related accumulated depreciation.
2. Recognizes any cash or other asset received for the old plant asset.
3. Recognizes any gain or loss on the disposal.

Cash

⬆ 500.00

Accumulated Depreciation—Store Equipment

⬇ 8,000.00 | Bal. 8,000.00

Store Equipment

Bal. 8,500.00 | ⬇ 8,500.00

January 2, 20X5. Received cash from sale of shelving unit, $500.00: original cost, $8,500.00; total accumulated depreciation through December 31, 20X4, $8,000.00. Receipt No. 543.

Cash received		$500.00
Less: Book value of asset sold:		
Cost	$8,500.00	
Accumulated depreciation	8,000.00	500.00
Gain (loss) on sale of plant asset		$ 0.00

The amount of gain or loss, if any, is calculated by subtracting the book value from the cash received. The display case was sold for its book value. Therefore, no gain or loss exists.

⬎ Recording Sale of a Plant Asset for Book Value

① Record an entry in the cash receipts journal to remove the original cost, $8,500.00, from Store Equipment and $8,000.00 from Accum. Depr.—Store Equip. Record the cash received from the sale, $500.00, as a debit to Cash.

② Check the type of disposal, Sold, and write the date, January 2, 20X5, and disposal amount, $500.00, in Section 2 of the plant asset record.

Recording Depreciation Expense on Disposal of an Asset

GENERAL JOURNAL

PAGE 5

	DATE		ACCOUNT TITLE	DOC. NO.	POST. REF.	DEBIT	CREDIT	
1	20X5 May	1	Depreciation Expense—Store Equipment	M72		1 0 0 00		1
2			Accum. Depreciation—Store Equipment				1 0 0 00	2
3								3

❸ Update Section 3 of the plant asset record.

Debit Depreciation Expense account. **❶**

❷ Credit the Accumulated Depreciation account.

Year	Annual Depreciation Expense	Accumulated Depreciation	Ending Book Value
20X1	$300.00	$ 300.00	$1,700.00
20X2	300.00	600.00	1,400.00
20X3	300.00	900.00	1,100.00
20X4	300.00	1,200.00	800.00
20X5	100.00	1,300.00	700.00

Plant assets may be disposed of in different ways. They may be discarded, sold, or traded. A plant asset may be disposed of at any time during its useful life. When a plant asset that has not been fully depreciated is disposed of, its depreciation from the beginning of the current fiscal year to the date of disposal must be recorded.

On May 1, 20X5, Sun Treasures intends to sell a desk that was bought on January 10, 20X1, for $2,000.00. Annual depreciation expense for the desk is $300.00. Depreciation recorded through December 31, 20X4, is $1,200.00.

The method to calculate depreciation on disposal of a plant asset is the same as calculating depreciation for a partial year when an asset is bought during the fiscal year. The monthly depreciation expense is multiplied by the number of months the asset is used during the current fiscal year. Depreciation is calculated for each month prior to the month the plant asset is sold. Thus, Sun Treasures will depreciate the desk for four months, January through April.

> May 1, 20X5. Recorded a partial year's depreciation on a desk to be sold, $100.00. Memorandum No. 72.

The depreciation is also recorded on the plant asset record for the desk.

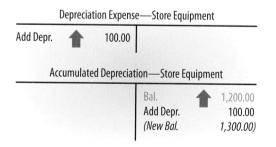

Depreciation Expense—Store Equipment

Add Depr. ⬆ 100.00

Accumulated Depreciation—Store Equipment

Bal. ⬆ 1,200.00
Add Depr. 100.00
(New Bal. 1,300.00)

❯ Recording a Partial Year's Depreciation on Disposal of a Plant Asset

❶ Record a debit, $100.00, to Depreciation Expense— Store Equipment in the general journal.

❷ Record a credit, $100.00, to Accum. Depreciation— Store Equipment in the general journal.

❸ Record the depreciation expense in Section 3 of the plant asset record for the desk. Calculate and record accumulated depreciation and ending book value.

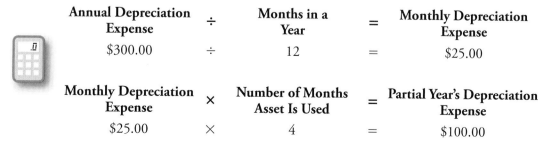

Annual Depreciation Expense	÷	Months in a Year	=	Monthly Depreciation Expense
$300.00	÷	12	=	$25.00

Monthly Depreciation Expense	×	Number of Months Asset Is Used	=	Partial Year's Depreciation Expense
$25.00	×	4	=	$100.00

Selling a Plant Asset for More Than Book Value LO10

					1	2	3	4	5	6	7	
					GENERAL		ACCOUNTS RECEIVABLE CREDIT	SALES CREDIT	SALES TAX PAYABLE CREDIT	SALES DISCOUNT DEBIT	CASH DEBIT	
	DATE	ACCOUNT TITLE	DOC. NO.	POST. REF.	DEBIT	CREDIT						
1	20X5 May 1	Accum. Depr.—Store Equip.	R582		1 3 0 0 00						8 5 0 00	1
2		Store Equipment				2 0 0 0 00						2
3		Gain on Plant Assets				1 5 0 00						3

CASH RECEIPTS JOURNAL   PAGE **19**

① Record an entry to remove the asset and its accumulated depreciation, record the gain, and record cash.

Complete Section 2 of the plant asset record. ②

Disposed of:	Discarded _____	Sold ✓	Traded _____	
Date	May 1, 20X5	Disposal Amount	$850.00	

An increase in equity resulting from the sale of goods or services is known as *revenue*. Revenue results from the normal operation of the business and appears at the top of the income statement under the heading Revenues. However, an increase in equity resulting from activity other than selling goods or services is called a **gain**. A gain is related to a supplemental activity, such as selling a plant asset. Gains are listed further down on the income statement, usually under the heading, Other Revenue.

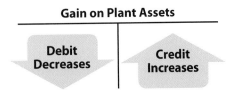

Gain on Plant Assets

Debit Decreases   Credit Increases

An increase in equity that results when a plant asset is sold for more than book value is called **gain on plant assets**. Sun Treasures is selling a desk for $850.00. After the partial year's depreciation is recorded, a journal entry is made to record the sale of the desk.

> **May 1, 20X5. Received cash from sale of desk, $850.00: original cost, $2,000.00; accumulated depreciation through May 1, 20X5, $1,300.00. Receipt No. 582.**

The gain or loss on the sale of a plant asset is the book value subtracted from cash received.

Cash received		$850.00
Less book value of asset sold:		
Cost	$2,000.00	
Accumulated depreciation	1,300.00	700.00
Gain (loss) on sale of plant asset		$150.00

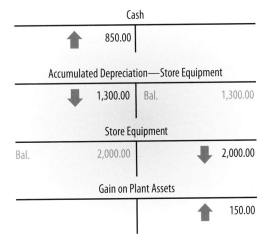

The gain realized on the disposal of a plant asset is credited to a revenue account titled Gain on Plant Assets.

A gain from the sale of plant assets is not operating revenue. Therefore, Gain on Plant Assets is listed in a classification titled Other Revenue in the chart of accounts.

↘ Recording Sale of a Plant Asset for More Than Book Value

① Record an entry in the cash receipts journal to remove the original cost, $2,000.00, from Store Equipment and $1,300.00 from Accum. Depr.—Store Equip. Record the gain on the sale, $150.00, as a credit to Gain on Plant Assets. Record the cash received from the sale, $850.00, as a debit to Cash.

② Check the type of disposal, Sold, and write the date, May 1, 20X5, and disposal amount, $850.00, in Section 2 of the plant asset record for the desk.

Selling a Plant Asset for Less Than Book Value

CASH RECEIPTS JOURNAL														PAGE 19		
					1		2		3	4	5	6	7			
	DATE	ACCOUNT TITLE	DOC. NO.	POST. REF.	GENERAL				ACCOUNTS RECEIVABLE CREDIT	SALES CREDIT	SALES TAX PAYABLE CREDIT	SALES DISCOUNT DEBIT	CASH DEBIT			
					DEBIT		CREDIT									
1	20X6 Oct. 6	Accum. Depr.—Office Equip.	R645		3 3 0 0 00								2 0 0 00			1
2		Loss on Plant Assets			3 0 0 00											2
3		Office Equipment					3 8 0 0 00									3

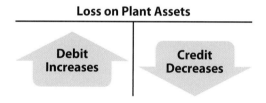

① Record an entry to remove the asset and its accumulated depreciation, record the loss, and record cash.

② Complete Section 2 of the plant asset record.

Disposed of: Discarded _____ Sold ✓ Traded _____

Date *October 6, 20X6* Disposal Amount *$200.00*

The cost of goods or services used to operate a business is known as an *expense*. Expenses result from the normal operation of the business and appear on the income statement under the heading, Operating Expenses. A decrease in equity resulting from activity other than selling goods or services is called a **loss**. A loss is related to a supplemental activity, such as selling a plant asset. Losses are listed further down on the income statement, usually under the heading, Other Expenses.

Loss on Plant Assets

Debit Increases	Credit Decreases

The decrease in equity that results when a plant asset is sold for less than book value is called **loss on plant assets**. Sun Treasures sold a computer after three years of use. After the partial year's depreciation is recorded, a journal entry is made to record the sale of the computer.

> October 6, 20X6. Received cash from sale of a computer, $200.00: original cost, $3,800.00; total accumulated depreciation through October 1, 20X6, $3,300.00. Receipt No. 645.

The gain or loss on the sale of a plant asset is the book value subtracted from cash received.

Cash received		$ 200.00
Less book value of asset sold:		
Cost	$3,800.00	
Accumulated depreciation	3,300.00	500.00
Gain (loss) on sale of plant asset		$(300.00)

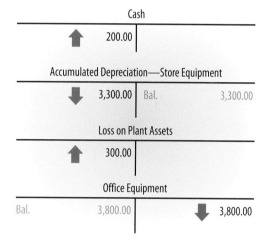

The loss realized on the disposal of a plant asset is debited to another expense account titled Loss on Plant Assets. A loss from the sale of plant assets is not an operating expense. Therefore, Loss on Plant Assets is listed in a classification titled Other Expenses in the chart of accounts.

Recording Sale of a Plant Asset for Less Than Book Value

① Record an entry in the cash receipts journal to remove the original cost, $3,800.00, from Office Equipment and $3,300.00 from Accum. Depr.—Office Equip. Record the loss on the sale, $300.00, as a debit to Loss on Plant Assets. Record the cash received from the sale, $200.00, as a debit to Cash.

② Check the type of disposal, Sold, and write the date, October 6, 20X6, and disposal amount, $200.00, in Section 2 of the plant asset record for the computer.

End of Lesson Review

LO9 Record the sale of a plant asset for book value.

LO10 Record the sale of a plant asset for more/less than book value.

Terms Review

gain

gain on plant assets

loss

loss on plant assets

Audit your understanding

1. What is recorded on plant asset records for plant assets that have been disposed of?

2. When an asset is disposed of after the beginning of the fiscal year, what entry may need to be recorded before an entry is made for the discarding of a plant asset?

3. What is the formula to calculate the gain or loss on the sale of a plant asset?

4. In which account classification is Loss on Plant Assets listed?

Work together 19-4

Recording the disposal of plant assets

Use the plant asset records from Work Together 19-3. Your instructor will guide you through the following examples.

1. For each of the following transactions completed in 20X4, journalize an entry for additional depreciation, if needed. Use page 15 of a general journal given in the *Working Papers*. Source documents are abbreviated as follows: memorandum, M; receipt, R.

   Transactions:

   Jan. 5. Received cash for sale of a display case, plant asset No. 105, $3,000.00. R217.

   Aug. 10. Received cash for sale of a work station, plant asset No. 106, $2,000.00. M61 and R281.

2. Use page 3 of a cash receipts journal to record the disposal of each plant asset.

3. Make appropriate notations in the plant asset records.

On your own 19-4

Recording the disposal of plant assets

Use the plant asset records from On Your Own 19-3. Work this problem independently.

1. For each of the following transactions completed in 20X4, journalize an entry for additional depreciation, if needed. Use page 10 of a general journal given in the *Working Papers*. Source documents are abbreviated as follows: memorandum, M; receipt, R.

   Transactions:

   Jan. 4. Received cash for sale of a stitching machine, plant asset No. 276, $1,300.00. R441.

   23. Received cash for sale of a notebook computer, plant asset No. 277, $850.00. M71 and R450.

2. Use page 2 of a cash receipts journal to record the disposal of each plant asset.

3. Make appropriate notations in the plant asset records.

LESSON

19-5 Declining-Balance Method of Depreciation

LO11 Calculate depreciation using the double declining-balance method.

Calculating Depreciation Using the Double Declining-Balance Method LO11

Plant Asset: Automobile
Depreciation Method: Double Declining-Balance

Original Cost: $30,000.00
Estimated Salvage Value: $2,500.00
Estimated Useful Life: 5 years

Year	Beginning Book Value	Declining-Balance Rate	Annual Depreciation	Ending Book Value
1	$30,000.00	40%	$12,000.00	$18,000.00
2	18,000.00	40%	7,200.00	10,800.00

4 Transfer the book value to the following year.

1 Calculate rate.

2 Determine the annual depreciation expense.

3 Determine the ending book value.

The straight-line method charges an equal amount of depreciation expense each year. However, many plant assets depreciate more in the early years of useful life than in later years. For example, a truck's value will decrease more in the first year than in later years. Therefore, charging more depreciation expense in the early years may be more accurate than charging the same amount each year. [CONCEPT: Matching Expenses with Revenue] Any method of depreciation that records greater depreciation expense in the early years and less depreciation expense in the later years is called **accelerated depreciation**. GAAP allows the use of either straight-line or accelerated depreciation.

A common accelerated depreciation method bases its calculations on the book value of the asset, which declines each period. The **declining-balance method of depreciation** is a type of accelerated depreciation that multiplies the book value of an asset by a constant depreciation rate to determine annual depreciation. The declining-balance depreciation rate is some multiple of the straight-line rate. Many businesses use a declining-balance rate that is two times the straight-line rate. A declining-balance rate that is two times the straight-line rate is called the **double declining-balance method of depreciation**.

Calculating Depreciation Using the Double Declining-Balance Method

1 Calculate the double declining-balance rate. An example of a plant asset with a five-year life is shown.

Estimated Depreciation Expense	÷	Years of Estimated Useful Life	=	Straight-Line Rate of Depreciation
100%	÷	5	=	20%

Straight-Line Rate of Depreciation	×	Multiply by Two	=	Double Declining-Balance Rate of Depreciation
20%	×	2	=	40%

2 Multiply the double declining-balance rate by the beginning book value to determine the annual depreciation expense for a given year ($30,000.00 × 40% = $12,000.00).

3 Subtract the annual depreciation expense from the beginning book value to determine the ending book value ($30,000.00 − $12,000.00 = $18,000.00).

4 Transfer the ending book value to the beginning book value for the following year. Calculating the depreciation expense in the last year of an asset's life is described on the next page.

Calculating Depreciation Expense in the Final Year

Plant Asset: Automobile
Depreciation Method: Double Declining-Balance

Original Cost: $30,000.00
Estimated Salvage Value: $2,500.00
Estimated Useful Life: 5 years

Year	Beginning Book Value	Declining-Balance Rate	Annual Depreciation	Ending Book Value
1	$30,000.00	40%	$12,000.00	$18,000.00
2	18,000.00	40%	7,200.00	10,800.00
3	10,800.00	40%	4,320.00	6,480.00
4	6,480.00	40%	2,592.00	3,888.00
5	3,888.00	—	1,388.00	2,500.00
Total Depreciation			$27,500.00	

1 Transfer the book value.

2 Determine the last year's depreciation.

3 Verify the ending book value.

Although the depreciation rate is the same each year, the annual depreciation expense declines from one year to the next. A plant asset is never depreciated below its estimated salvage value. Therefore, in the final year, only enough depreciation expense is recorded to reduce the book value of the plant asset to its salvage value.

Sometimes, the formula for the declining-balance method results in an ending book value that is greater than the estimated salvage value in the final year of a plant asset's useful life. In other words, the depreciation formula does not create enough depreciation to reduce the asset's book value down to its estimated salvage value.

When this situation occurs, the amount of depreciation recorded should be more than the amount calculated using the double declining-balance method. The amount of depreciation in the final year of an asset's life should be the amount needed to make the book value of the asset equal to the estimated salvage value of the asset.

Calculating the Last Year's Depreciation Expense

1 Transfer the ending book value from Year 4 to the beginning book value of Year 5.

2 Subtract the salvage value of the plant asset from the beginning book value to determine the depreciation expense for the final year of useful life ($3,888.00 − $2,500.00 = $1,388.00).

3 Verify that the ending book value is equal to the salvage value.

Accelerated Depreciation Methods

The double declining-balance method of depreciation is one method of accelerated depreciation. Other methods are also acceptable. All accelerated methods have one thing in common—more depreciation is charged in the first year than in the later years. GAAP allows each business to choose either straight-line or accelerated depreciation for financial reporting. But, once chosen, the business should use the same method from year to year. [CONCEPT: Consistent Reporting]

The U.S. Internal Revenue Service has published rules that must be applied when calculating the amount of depreciation expense that is used to compute a business's federal income tax obligation. Those rules are called the Modified Accelerated Cost Recovery System (MACRS). MACRS is an accelerated depreciation method. If a business chooses a different method of calculating depreciation for financial reporting, it must maintain two sets of financial records, one to support its financial reports and one to substantiate its federal income tax return. Some businesses choose to use MACRS for their financial reporting as well, allowing them to keep just one set of books. For more information about the differences between GAAP and IRS tax rules, see Explore Accounting on page 400.

Unlike the straight-line method, the declining-balance method does not use the estimated salvage value to calculate depreciation. The estimated salvage value is used only to limit the last year's depreciation expense.

Comparing Two Methods of Depreciation

Plant Asset:
Depreciation Method: Comparison of Two Methods

Original Cost: $6,000.00
Estimated Salvage Value: $500.00
Estimated Useful Life: 5 years

Year	Straight-Line Method			Double Declining-Balance Method		
	Beginning Book Value	Annual Depreciation	Ending Book Value	Beginning Book Value	Annual Depreciation	Ending Book Value
1	$6,000.00	$1,100.00	$4,900.00	$6,000.00	$2,400.00	$3,600.00
2	4,900.00	1,100.00	3,800.00	3,600.00	1,440.00	2,160.00
3	3,800.00	1,100.00	2,700.00	2,160.00	864.00	1,296.00
4	2,700.00	1,100.00	1,600.00	1,296.00	518.40	777.60
5	1,600.00	1,100.00	500.00	777.60	277.60	500.00
Total Depreciation	$5,500.00			$5,500.00		

Regardless of the depreciation method used, the total depreciation expense over the useful life of a plant asset is the same. The accounts used in the journal entries to record depreciation expense and the sale of plant assets are also the same.

Since both straight-line and accelerated depreciation methods are acceptable under GAAP, the company must decide which method to use. The straight-line method is easy to calculate. The same amount of depreciation expense is recorded for each year of estimated useful life.

An accelerated method is more complicated to use. A different depreciation expense amount must be calculated each year. One advantage of an accelerated method is that it records more depreciation expense in the earlier years. The result is lower income in the early years, which reduces the taxes paid on the income. However, this advantage is only true in the earlier years. In the later years of the asset, less depreciation will be recorded, which will increase net income and the taxes paid on the income.

Resource Allocation

Every company has a limited amount of resources (human, monetary, and material) to invest. Therefore, when a company invests in a plant asset, it wants to choose the investment that yields the biggest return. Finance is the branch of business that looks at investments and returns. Larger businesses have finance departments that analyze cost and payback information to decide between investment opportunities.

Resource allocation is planning which items or projects should be funded and what level of funding each should receive. *Funding* in this analysis refers to providing resources, whether human, monetary, or material. The plan would rank items or projects recommended for funding. Therefore, if fewer resources are available, items with the lowest rankings would be removed from the list. The plan would also include a ranking of items that are not recommended for funding. If more funds become available, the next highest-ranking item would be funded.

For example, a company may have the following five projects under consideration: buy a new cutting machine, buy an air purifier system, add a second shift of production, retool the factory to be more efficient, or buy robots to perform some tasks. The finance department recommends that the company resources be used to (1) buy an air purifier system and (2) buy a new cutting machine. The projects not recommended for funding are ranked as follows: (3) remodel the factory, (4) add a second shift of production, and (5) buy robots. If more resources become available, they should be used to remodel the factory. If fewer resources become available, the new cutting machine would not be funded.

CRITICAL THINKING

As a class, using the five projects listed above, brainstorm a list of factors that the resource allocation team may consider when choosing which projects to recommend for funding.

End of Lesson Review

LO11 Calculate depreciation using the double declining-balance method.

Terms Review

acelerated depreciation

declining-balance method of depreciation

double declining-balance method of depreciation

Audit your understanding

1. When calculating depreciation expense using the declining-balance method, what number stays constant each fiscal period?

2. What is the declining-balance method that uses twice the straight-line rate?

3. What change occurs in the annual depreciation expense calculated using the declining-balance method?

4. An asset is never depreciated below what amount?

Work together 19-5

Calculating depreciation using the double declining-balance depreciation method

Forms are given in the *Working Papers*. Your instructor will guide you through the following example.

Calculate beginning book value, annual depreciation, and ending book value for each of the following plant assets bought during the current year. Use the double declining-balance depreciation method. Round amounts to the nearest cent.

Date	Description	Original Cost	Estimated Salvage Value	Estimated Useful Life
Jan. 4	Painting Machine	$27,000.00	$1,000.00	4 years
Jan. 6	Office Computer	2,200.00	200.00	5 years
Jan. 7	Sander	800.00	80.00	8 years

On your own 19-5

Calculating depreciation using the double declining-balance depreciation method

Forms are given in the *Working Papers*. Work this problem independently.

Calculate beginning book value, annual depreciation, and ending book value for each of the following plant assets bought during the current year. Use the double declining-balance depreciation method. Round amounts to the nearest cent.

Date	Description	Original Cost	Estimated Salvage Value	Estimated Useful Life
Jan. 2	Skate Rack	$ 3,000.00	$ 200.00	5 years
Jan. 4	Delivery Truck	75,000.00	8,000.00	8 years
Jan. 6	Office Shredder	600.00	50.00	4 years

©CANDICE CUSACK, ISTOCK

19-6 Buying Intangible Assets and Calculating Amortization Expense

LO12 Record the buying of an intangible asset.
LO13 Calculate and record amortization expense.

Recording the Buying of an Intangible Asset LO12

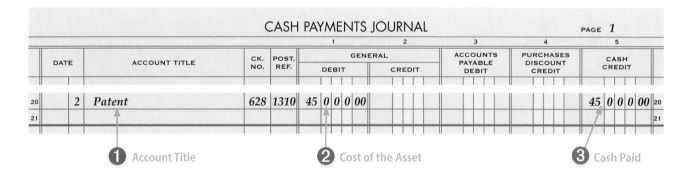

	DATE	ACCOUNT TITLE	CK. NO.	POST. REF.	GENERAL DEBIT	GENERAL CREDIT	ACCOUNTS PAYABLE DEBIT	PURCHASES DISCOUNT CREDIT	CASH CREDIT	
20	2	Patent	628	1310	45 0 0 0 00				45 0 0 0 00	20
21										21

CASH PAYMENTS JOURNAL   PAGE *1*

① Account Title   **②** Cost of the Asset   **③** Cash Paid

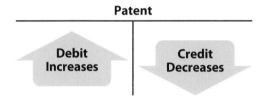

Patent

Debit Increases	Credit Decreases

An asset that does not have physical substance is called an **intangible asset**. Intangible assets include patents, copyrights, trademarks, and other similar items. The value of an intangible asset such as a patent comes from the rights it gives to the patent holder, not from the piece of paper that ensures those rights.

Some intangible assets have an easily determined legal life. For example, most patents are granted for 20 years. During those 20 years, no other company or individual can copy that product. However, after the patent expires, any individual or company can reproduce and sell that product.

Recording the buying of an intangible asset is very similar to buying any other asset. Sharp Company wishes to buy a patent from another company. The patent's legal remaining life is 14 years. However, Sharp

Company feels that the patent will only be useful for ten years. After that time, other new technology will exist that will reduce the patent's value to zero.

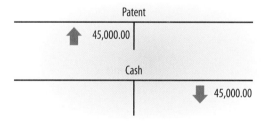

Patent	
45,000.00	

Cash	
	45,000.00

January 2, 20X1. Paid cash for a patent, $45,000.00. Check No. 628.

> **Journalizing the Buying of a Plant Asset**

① Write the intangible asset account, Patent, in the Account Title column of the cash payments journal.

② Enter the cost of the patent, $45,000.00, in the General Debit column.

③ Enter the same amount, $45,000.00, in the Cash Credit column.

Calculating and Recording Amortization Expense LO13

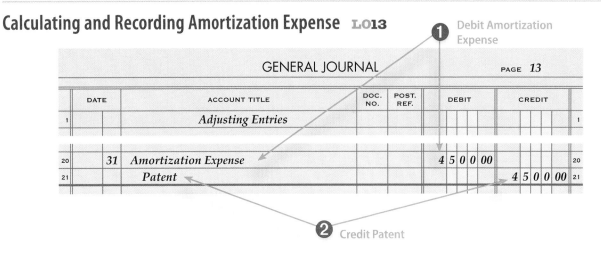

1 Debit Amortization Expense

2 Credit Patent

Amortization is the spreading of the cost of an intangible asset over its useful life. Amortization is similar to depreciation, which applies only to physical assets. Some intangible assets have a legal life, such as a patent. If an intangible asset has a useful or legal life that can be determined, the asset should be amortized. Amortization is based on an estimate of the useful, or legal, life of the intangible asset, whichever is less. Unlike the depreciation of a physical asset, there is no estimated salvage value of an intangible asset. Amortization is recorded as an adjusting entry each fiscal period until the value is zero.

The patent bought by Sharp Company will expire in 14 years. Therefore, the patent's legal life is 14 years.

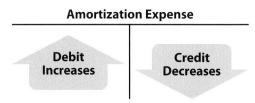

However, Sharp Company feels that new technology will mean that its patent will only have a useful life of ten years. Sharp Company must amortize the patent over no more than ten years. Amortization Expense will be debited for $4,500.00 to record one year of amortization. The asset account, Patent, is credited for $4,500.00.

Original Cost	−	Estimated Salvage Value	=	Estimated Total Amortization Expense
$45,000.00	−	$0.00	=	$45,000.00

Estimated Total Amortization Expense	÷	Years of Legal/ Useful Life	=	Annual Amortization Expense
$45,000.00	÷	10	=	$4,500.00

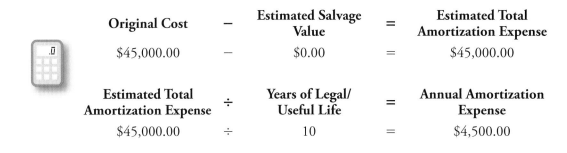

The balance in the Patent account represents the cost of the patent that has not yet been amortized.

Intangible assets appear on the balance sheet, usually as the last category of assets. The Amortization Expense account will appear on the income statement, as an operating expense.

Recording Amortization Expense

1 Debit Amortization Expense for the amount of amortization expense, $4,500.00.

2 Credit Patent for the same amount, $4,500.00.

LO12 Record the buying of an intangible asset.

LO13 Calculate and record amortization expense.

Terms Review

intangible asset

amortization

Audit your understanding

1. Which account is debited when recording amortization on a patent?

2. Which account is credited when recording amortization on a patent?

Work together 19-6

Journalizing buying intangible assets and calculating amortization expense

The cash payments journal for River Falls Publishing is given in the *Working Papers*. Your instructor will guide you through the following examples.

1. Journalize the following transactions completed during the current year. Use page 1 of a cash payments journal. The abbreviation for a check is C.

   Transactions:

   Jan. 4. Paid cash for a patent, $18,000.00. C532.

   6. Paid cash for a trademark, $30,000.00. C538.

2. Use the following data to record amortization expense for December 31, 20X1. Use page 1 of a general journal.

Asset	Estimated Useful Life	Estimated Legal Life	Estimated Salvage Value
Patent	9 years	12 years	$0.00
Trademark	14 years	10 years	$0.00

On your own 19-6

Journalizing buying intangible assets and calculating amortization expense

The cash payments journal for High Tech, Inc., is given in the *Working Papers*. Work this problem independently.

1. Journalize the following transactions completed during the current year. Use page 1 of a cash payments journal. The abbreviation for a check is C.

   Transactions:

   Jan. 4. Paid cash for a trademark, $35,000.00. C112.

   6. Paid cash for a patent, $98,000.00. C115.

2. Use the following data to record amortization expense for December 31, 20X1. Use page 1 of a general journal.

Asset	Estimated Useful Life	Estimated Legal Life	Estimated Salvage Value
Trademark	8 years	10 years	$0.00
Patent	9 years	7 years	$0.00

A Look at Accounting Software
Accounting for Plant Assets

Plant (fixed) asset management, which includes calculation of depreciation, is an important part of the accounting responsibility in a corporation. That is especially true for companies with big investments in furniture, fixtures, and equipment. To facilitate plant asset management, specialized programs (usually called *fixed asset management* software) are available. Some *off-the-shelf* accounting software programs include plant asset management utilities. Built-in utilities, however, usually have limited capability. Large corporations generally choose software uniquely designed for plant asset management.

Sun Treasures, Inc., as described in this chapter, uses a manual accounting system and manages its plant assets using plant asset record forms. The company uses straight-line depreciation. In reality, even a company the size of Sun Treasures would certainly use a computerized accounting system, including some type of plant asset utility. It's likely that accelerated depreciation would be

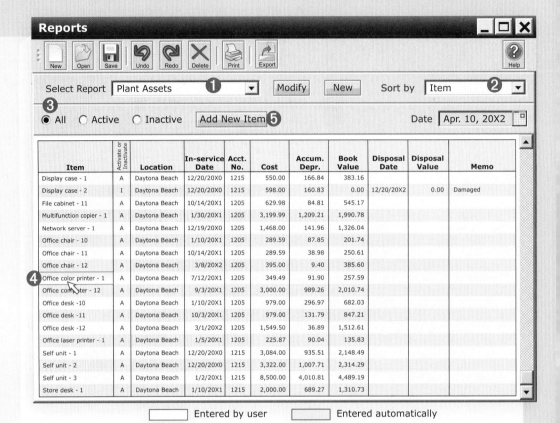

Reports

Select Report: Plant Assets ❶   Modify   New   Sort by: Item ❷

❸ ● All   ○ Active   ○ Inactive   Add New Item ❺   Date Apr. 10, 20X2

Item	Activate or Inactivate	Location	In-service Date	Acct. No.	Cost	Accum. Depr.	Book Value	Disposal Date	Disposal Value	Memo
Display case - 1	A	Daytona Beach	12/20/20X0	1215	550.00	166.84	383.16			
Display case - 2	I	Daytona Beach	12/20/20X0	1215	598.00	160.83	0.00	12/20/20X2	0.00	Damaged
File cabinet - 11	A	Daytona Beach	10/14/20X1	1205	629.98	84.81	545.17			
Multifunction copier - 1	A	Daytona Beach	1/30/20X1	1205	3,199.99	1,209.21	1,990.78			
Network server - 1	A	Daytona Beach	12/19/20X0	1205	1,468.00	141.96	1,326.04			
Office chair - 10	A	Daytona Beach	1/10/20X1	1205	289.59	87.85	201.74			
Office chair - 11	A	Daytona Beach	10/14/20X1	1205	289.59	38.98	250.61			
Office chair - 12	A	Daytona Beach	3/8/20X2	1205	395.00	9.40	385.60			
Office color printer - 1	A	Daytona Beach	7/12/20X1	1205	349.49	91.90	257.59			
Office computer - 12	A	Daytona Beach	9/3/20X1	1205	3,000.00	989.26	2,010.74			
Office desk -10	A	Daytona Beach	1/10/20X1	1205	979.00	296.97	682.03			
Office desk -11	A	Daytona Beach	10/3/20X1	1205	979.00	131.79	847.21			
Office desk -12	A	Daytona Beach	3/1/20X2	1205	1,549.50	36.89	1,512.61			
Office laser printer - 1	A	Daytona Beach	1/5/20X2	1205	225.87	90.04	135.83			
Self unit - 1	A	Daytona Beach	12/20/20X0	1215	3,084.00	935.51	2,148.49			
Self unit - 2	A	Daytona Beach	12/20/20X0	1215	3,322.00	1,007.71	2,314.29			
Self unit - 3	A	Daytona Beach	1/2/20X1	1215	8,500.00	4,010.81	4,489.19			
Store desk - 1	A	Daytona Beach	1/10/20X1	1215	2,000.00	689.27	1,310.73			

❹ (Office color printer - 1 selected for editing)

☐ Entered by user   ☐ Entered automatically

❶ To view the current list of plant assets, the user selects Plant Assets from the drop-down list in the Reports window.

❷ The user chooses the way the list is sorted by making a selection from the Sort by drop-down list.

❸ If the user wishes to see all the plant assets the company has ever owned, the All button would be clicked. Clicking on Active omits plant assets no longer owned or in use. Clicking Inactive lists only inactive items.

❹ To edit an item, the user double-clicks on the item name. Here, Office color printer - 1 has been selected for editing.

❺ If the user wants to add a new item, he or she would click on Add New Item on the Reports window or on New in the Add/Edit Plant Asset pop-up window. In either case, a blank pop-up window like the one shown here would allow the user to set up the new item.

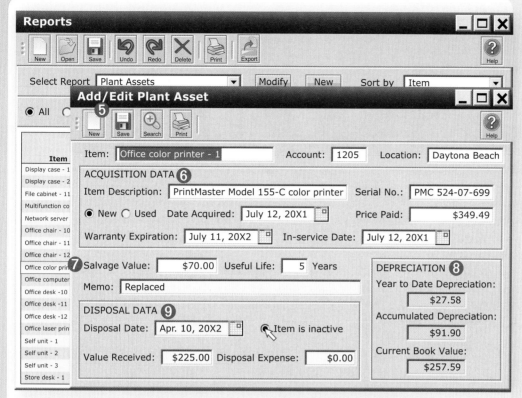

Add/Edit Plant Asset (⑤) window with toolbar (New, Save, Search, Print, Help)

Item: Office color printer - 1   Account: 1205   Location: Daytona Beach

ACQUISITION DATA ⑥

Item Description: PrintMaster Model 155-C color printer   Serial No.: PMC 524-07-699

◉ New ◯ Used   Date Acquired: July 12, 20X1   Price Paid: $349.49

Warranty Expiration: July 11, 20X2   In-service Date: July 12, 20X1

⑦ Salvage Value: $70.00   Useful Life: 5 Years

Memo: Replaced

DISPOSAL DATA ⑨

Disposal Date: Apr. 10, 20X2   ◉ Item is inactive

Value Received: $225.00   Disposal Expense: $0.00

DEPRECIATION ⑧

Year to Date Depreciation: $27.58

Accumulated Depreciation: $91.90

Current Book Value: $257.59

☐ Entered by user   ☐ Entered automatically

⑥ After naming the new item, assigning the general ledger account number, and entering its location, the user would enter the acquisition data. All dates are entered by clicking the calendar button and selecting the appropriate date. Some information, such as the price paid and in-service date, are used by the system to calculate depreciation. Other data, such as the serial number and warranty expiration, are helpful in managing the use of the item.

⑦ The user would enter estimates of the salvage value and useful life. The Memo field is used to note any information about the purchase, use, or disposal of the item that may be helpful at a later date. Clicking Save would add the new item to the list of plant assets.

⑧ The Depreciation section displays three system-calculated fields. It is for information only. No user entry is enabled.

⑨ The user has opened this window to record the disposal of the office color printer. After entering the disposal date, value received, and the disposal expense ($0.00 in this example), the user has keyed "Replaced" in the Memo field to note the reason for the item's disposal. Finally, the user clicks the button to set the item to inactive and then clicks Save to record the changes.

used as well because it allows businesses to reduce taxable income in the short term.

If Sun Treasures used a computerized accounting system, its plant asset list, when selected in the Reports window, might appear as it does here. The accountant has double-clicked on Office color printer - 1 to select it for editing. Much of the information in the Add/Edit Plant Asset pop-up window is the same as would be found on a plant asset record. Notice that this window does not show the method of depreciation nor the depreciation schedule.

To set, change, or view depreciation data, the user would go to the System Manager and open the Manage Depreciation window. For this example, double declining-balance is the default depreciation method applied to all new plant assets. To change an asset from double declining-balance to straight-line, the user would access the Manage Depreciation window and select the asset to be changed. The user could also view and print a depreciation schedule from the Manage Depreciation window.

Chapter Summary

Plant assets are assets that will be used in the operation of a business for a number of years. Plant assets are recorded at cost. The cost of a plant asset must be spread out over its useful life. This is recorded each year as depreciation expense. If a group of assets is bought for one price, the cost of each asset must be allocated so that each asset can be depreciated separately. When recording depreciation for a plant asset, the plant asset account is not credited. A separate accumulated depreciation account is used to record the total depreciation for that plant asset.

Plant assets are depreciated using one of a variety of methods. Straight-line depreciation spreads the cost of the asset equally over its useful life. Accelerated methods, such as the declining-balance method, charge more depreciation expense in the early years of the asset's life, with the amount of depreciation decreasing each year. Over the life of the asset, both methods record the same total amount of depreciation expense. During the life of the plant asset, its book value can be calculated by subtracting accumulated depreciation from the cost of the asset.

When a company sells a plant asset, it must determine if a gain or loss was incurred on the sale. The cash received for the asset is subtracted from the book value of the asset. If the cash received is more than the book value, the asset is sold for a gain. If the cash received is less than the book value, the asset is sold for a loss. The gain or loss is recorded at the time of the sale and is reported on the income statement under the heading, Other Revenues or Other Expenses.

Intangible assets are assets that have no physical substance, such as a patent. Intangible assets are amortized over the lesser of their legal or useful life. There is no estimated salvage value of an intangible asset and no accumulated amortization account. When an intangible asset is amortized, the asset's account is credited. Amortization expense decreases net income.

EXPLORE ACCOUNTING

Natural Resource Assets

©MAKHNACH_M_ISTOCK

Assets can be categorized into several subdivisions: current assets, plant assets, and intangible assets. An additional category of assets is natural resources. Natural resources include assets such as gold mines, timber forests, and oil wells.

When a natural resource is purchased, it is recorded at its historical cost plus any related expenses needed to make the natural resource useable. Assume that Coal Company bought a coal mine for $4,000,000. In addition, Coal Company estimates that it will spend $200,000 getting the land ready for mining to begin. The asset Coal Mine would be debited for the total, $4,200,000, as follows:

Coal Mine	4,200,000	
Cash		4,200,000

Natural resource assets are not depreciated or amortized. As coal is mined, a depletion expense will be recorded. Coal Company estimates that it will be able to mine 2,000,000 tons of coal from the mine and sell the land for $400,000 once all mining is finished. A depletion rate is calculated as follows:

Depletion Rate = (Cost of Asset – Salvage Value) ÷ Estimated Units to Be Mined

Depletion Rate = ($4,200,000 – $400,000) ÷ 2,000,000

Depletion Rate = $3,800,000 ÷ 2,000,000

Depletion Rate = $1.90 per ton

Coal Company mines 450,000 tons of coal in 20X1. The annual depletion expense would be calculated as:

Annual Depletion Expense = Depletion Rate × Tons Mined

Annual Depletion Expense = $1.90 × 450,000

Annual Depletion Expense = $855,000

The expense would be recorded as follows:

Depletion Expense	855,000	
Coal Mine		855,000

As with amortization, an accumulated depletion account is not used.

Rather, the asset account is decreased. The depletion expense will appear on the income statement under the heading Operating Expenses. The asset account, Coal Mine, is decreased by the entry and will appear on the balance sheet under the heading Natural Resources.

INSTRUCTIONS

1. List five types of natural resource assets. For each asset, suggest which unit of measure would be used to measure the depletion of the natural resource.

2. On January 2, 20X1, Big Coal Company bought a coal mine for $5,500,000. Big Coal expects to mine 2,750,000 tons of coal from the mine. By December 31, 20X1, Big Coal has extracted 356,000 tons of coal.

   Using T accounts, record the effect of the purchase of the mine and any depletion expense Big Coal Company should record for the year.

Apply Your Understanding

INSTRUCTIONS: Download problem instructions for Excel, QuickBooks, and Peachtree from the textbook companion website at www.C21accounting.com.

19-1 Application Problem: Journalizing buying plant assets and paying property tax LO1, 2, 3

The cash payments journal for White Cleaners is given in the *Working Papers*.

Instructions:

Journalize the following transactions completed during the current year. Use page 1 of a cash payments journal. The abbreviation for a check is C.

Transactions:

Jan. 4. Paid cash for office computer, $600.00. C226.

5. Paid cash for a pressing machine, $4,200.00. C230.

Feb. 24. Paid property taxes on real property with an assessed value of $360,000.00. The tax rate in the city where the property is located is 1.2% of assessed value. C278.

May 12. Paid cash for office desk (office equipment) and display rack (store equipment), $3,800.00. The office desk has an estimated value of $1,000.00, and the display rack has an estimated value of $3,000.00. C354.

19-2 Application Problem: Calculating straight-line depreciation LO4, 5, 6

AAONLINE

1. Go to www.cengage.com/login
2. Click on **AA Online** to access.
3. Go to the online assignment and follow the instructions.

1. Create and key formulas using the straight-line method to complete the depreciation table.
2. Print the worksheet.

Forms are given in the *Working Papers*.

Instructions:

Quick Mart bought the following assets during 20X1. Quick Mart uses the straight-line depreciation method. Calculate beginning book value, annual depreciation, accumulated depreciation, and ending book value for each asset for each year of estimated useful life. If the asset was not bought at the beginning of 20X1, calculate the depreciation expense for the part of 20X1 in which the company owned the asset. Save your work to complete Problem 19-3.1.

Transactions:

Jan. 4. Bought a freezer costing $15,000.00; estimated salvage value, $600.00; estimated useful life, 6 years; plant asset No. 561; serial number, 674-653B.

Mar. 30. Bought a conference table (office equipment), $3,000.00; estimated salvage value, $250.00; estimated useful life, 5 years; plant asset No. 562; serial number, FX27J482.

Aug. 2. Bought a microwave oven (store equipment), $2,200.00; estimated salvage value, $100.00; estimated useful life, 5 years; plant asset no. 563; serial number, 7-ST1-003.

19-3.1 Application Problem: Preparing plant asset records LO7

Instructions:

Quick Mart records plant assets in two accounts: Office Equipment, Account No. 1210, and Store Equipment, Account No. 1220. Using the transaction data and depreciation calculations from Problem 19-2, prepare a plant asset record for each plant asset. Plant asset records are given in the *Working Papers*. Record the depreciation and book values for 20X1–20X4. Save the plant asset records for use in Problem 19-4.

19-3.2 Application Problem: Journalizing annual depreciation expense LO8

Instructions:

On December 31, 20X4, Pierce, Inc., determined that total depreciation expense for office equipment for the year was $19,358.00 and total depreciation expense for store equipment was $38,954.00. Record the adjusting entries on page 23 of a general journal given in the *Working Papers*.

19-4 Application Problem: Recording the disposal of plant assets LO9, 10

During 20X5, Quick Mart had the following transactions involving the sale of plant assets. Use the plant asset records completed in Problem 19-3.1. Journals are given in the *Working Papers*.

Instructions:

1. For each plant asset disposed of in 20X5, journalize an entry for additional depreciation, if needed. Use page 3 of a general journal. Source documents are abbreviated as follows: check, C; memorandum, M; receipt, R.

2. Use page 3 of a cash receipts journal to record the disposal of each plant asset.

3. Make appropriate notations in the plant asset records.

Transactions:

Jan. 6. Received cash for sale of a conference table, plant asset No. 562, $1,200.00. R375.
Mar. 29. Received cash for sale of a microwave oven, plant asset No. 563, $660.00. M35 and R398.
July 8. Received cash for sale of a freezer, plant asset No. 561, $3,000.00. M78 and R421.

19-5 Application Problem: Calculating depreciation using the double declining-balance depreciation method LO11

Peachtree

1. Journalize and post depreciation related to the disposal of plant assets to the general journal.
2. Journalize and post cash received for the disposal of assets to the cash receipts journal.
3. Print the cash receipts journal, general journal, and trial balance.

Quick Books

1. Journalize and post transactions related to the disposal of plant assets to the journal.
2. Print the journal and trial balance.

Instructions:

Forms are given in the *Working Papers*. Calculate beginning book value, annual depreciation, and ending book value for each of the following plant assets bought during 20X1. Use the double declining-balance depreciation method. Round amounts to the nearest cent.

Date	Description	Original Cost	Estimated Salvage Value	Estimated Useful Life
Jan. 3	Forklift	$20,000.00	$2,500.00	8 years
Jan. 5	Cutting Machine	$40,000.00	$3,000.00	4 years
Jan. 8	Scale	$16,000.00	$1,000.00	5 years

19-6 Application Problem: Accounting for intangible assets LO12, 13

The cash payments journal for Tobie Industries is given in the *Working Papers*.

Instructions:

1. Journalize the following transactions completed during the current year. Use page 1 of a cash payments journal. The abbreviation for a check is C.

Transactions:

Jan. 5. Paid cash for a patent, $700,000. C315.
     6. Paid cash for a trademark, $85,000. C320.

2. Use the following data to record amortization expense for December 31, 20X1. Use page 1 of a general journal.

Asset	Estimated Useful Life	Estimated Legal Life	Estimated Salvage Value
Patent	10 years	13 years	$0.00
Trademark	10 years	5 years	$0.00

19-M Mastery Problem: Recording transactions for plant assets LO1, 2, 3, 4, 5, 6, 7, 8, 9, 10, 11

Hillside Resort records plant assets in two accounts: Furniture, Account No. 1205, and Equipment, Account No. 1215. Furniture is depreciated using the double declining-balance method. Equipment is depreciated using the straight-line method. Forms are given in the *Working Papers*.

Instructions:

1. Record the following transactions completed during 20X1 on page 1 of a cash payments journal.

Transactions:

Jan. 5. Bought an X-ray machine and a supply cabinet: cost, $30,000.00. C521. X-ray machine: estimated value, $22,000.00; estimated salvage value, $0.00; estimated useful life, 5 years; plant asset No. 715; serial number, ZYX487-6. Supply cabinet: estimated value, $11,000.00; estimated salvage value, $800.00; estimated useful life, 5 years; plant asset No. 716; serial number, 74-3554-L8.

Feb. 26. Paid property taxes on plant assets assessed at $600,000.00. The tax rate is 1.1%. C560.

Apr. 5. Bought a testing machine for the exam room: cost, $6,500.00; estimated salvage value, $500.00; estimated useful life, 6 years; plant asset No. 717; serial number, 7-H256. C602.

2. Complete Section 1 of a plant asset record for each new plant asset.

3. Use the forms provided in the *Working Papers* to calculate beginning book value, annual depreciation, accumulated depreciation, and ending book value for the life of each new plant asset.

4. Complete Section 3 of the plant asset records for 20X1–20X4.

5. Record the following transactions completed during 20X5. Use page 2 of a cash receipts journal and page 1 of a general journal.

Transactions:

Jan. 6. Received cash for sale of a supply cabinet, plant asset No. 716, $1,500.00. R321.

July 2. Received cash for sale of an X-ray machine, plant asset No. 715, $1,700.00. M112 and R382.

Dec. 31. Recorded the adjusting entry for depreciation. Total 20X5 depreciation expense of furniture was $29,500.00. Total 20X5 depreciation expense of equipment was $65,750.00.

6. Complete the plant asset records for each plant asset sold during 20X5.

7. Complete Section 3 of the plant asset record for the testing machine for 20X5.

AAONLINE

1. Go to www.cengage.com/login
2. Click on **AA Online** to access.
3. Go to the online assignment and follow the instructions.

Peachtree

1. Journalize and post transactions related to plant assets to the cash disbursements journal.
2. Journalize and post transactions related to plant assets to the cash receipts journal and general journal.
3. Print the cash disbursements journal, cash receipts journal, general journal, and trial balance.

QB Quick Books

1. Journalize and post transactions related to plant assets in the Write Checks window.
2. Journalize and post transactions related to plant assets to the journal.
3. Print the check detail, journal, and trial balance.

19-C Challenge Problem: Calculating a partial year's depreciation using the double declining-balance method LO4, 5, 6, 11

Quick Repair, Inc., uses the double declining-balance depreciation method for its equipment. Because many items are bought during the year, Quick Repair must calculate a partial year's depreciation in the first year. Quick Repair uses the same method to calculate a partial year's depreciation as was described for Sun Treasures on page 591. The annual depreciation expense is calculated then divided by 12 to get the monthly depreciation. The monthly depreciation is then multiplied by the number of months the plant asset was owned during the year. For subsequent years, the annual depreciation is calculated using the normal method—book value multiplied by the depreciation rate.

Instructions:

Forms are given in the *Working Papers*. Calculate beginning book value, annual depreciation, accumulated depreciation, and ending book value for the following assets bought in 20X1. Round to the nearest cent.

Transactions:
Apr. 2. Bought an extension ladder, $3,000.00; estimated salvage value, $200.00; estimated useful life, 5 years.
July 24. Bought a power sprayer, $4,800.00; estimated salvage value, $250.00; estimated useful life, 4 years.

1. Create and key formulas using the double declining-balance method to complete the depreciation tables.
2. Print the worksheet.

21st Century Skills

Green Advantage

Theme: Financial, Economic, Business, and Entrepreneurial Literacy

Skills: Creativity and Innovation, Critical Thinking and Problem Solving, Communication and Collaboration, ICT Literacy

PARTNERSHIP FOR 21ST CENTURY SKILLS

It is often said, "If something is worth copying, it is worth protecting." This philosophy is what drives a company or individual to protect an invention by having it patented. In the United States, a patent is an exclusive right issued by the U.S. Patent and Trademark Office (USPTO) that legally excludes others from making, using, or selling an invention or a new process within the United States.

By some estimates, 45% to 75% of the wealth of market-leading companies like Procter & Gamble and Sony is made up of intangible assets such as patents and trademarks. These companies are acutely aware of the role patents and trademarks play in maintaining a competitive edge and maximizing revenues.

The patent process can be complex, taking an average of 40 months for review and approval by the USPTO. In December 2009, the U.S. government expedited the application process to an average of 49 days for patents involving "green" technology, reducing the review and approval time by about a year. In addition to promoting U.S. competitiveness and creating "green" jobs, the goal was to also encourage innovations that benefit the environment.

Many companies recognize the advantages of using green technology. To them, conserving energy to protect the environment is just as motivating as saving money. Bank of America (BOA) is one example of an eco-friendly business. Its internal paper recycling program saves approximately 200,000 trees each year. BOA was also able to reduce paper use by 32% while generating a 24% increase in customers.

We all can do some simple things to reduce energy consumption. The World Watch Institute, a global environmental organization, is just one resource for information on the environment. Its purpose is to educate and inform individuals on how to create an environmentally sustainable society.

APPLICATION

1. Go to www.worldwatch.org or an eco-friendly website of your choice and create a list of ten ways that an individual or a company can "Go Green and Save Green." Inform others by displaying posters in your classroom or throughout the school.

2. Using the above list, create a "Top Ten Tweets" to inform others on how they can help the environment.

Sources: www.uspto.gov/news/pr/2009/09_33.jsp, www.wipo.int/sme/en/documents/valuing_patents.htm, and www.businesspundit.com/25-big-companies-that-are-going-green/.

Clausen, Inc., recently bought two new plant assets. David Hetland, accounting clerk, has prepared the following depreciation schedule for the assets.

Plant Asset: Refrigerator Case
Depreciation Method: Straight-line

Original Cost: $12,000.00
Estimated Salvage Value: $2,000.00
Estimated Useful Life: 5 years

Year	Beginning Book Value	Annual Depreciation	Accumulated Depreciation	Ending Book Value
20X1	$12,000.00	$2,400.00	$ 2,400.00	$9,600.00
20X2	9,600.00	2,400.00	4,800.00	7,200.00
20X3	7,200.00	2,400.00	7,200.00	4,800.00
20X4	4,800.00	2,400.00	9,600.00	2,400.00
20X5	2,400.00	2,400.00	12,000.00	0.00

Plant Asset: Freezer
Depreciation Method: Declining-balance

Original Cost: $16,000.00
Estimated Salvage Value: $2,000.00
Estimated Useful Life: 5 years

Year	Beginning Book Value	Annual Depreciation	Accumulated Depreciation	Ending Book Value
20X1	$16,000.00	$5,600.00	$ 5,600.00	$10,400.00
20X2	10,400.00	4,160.00	9,760.00	6,240.00
20X3	16,240.00	2,496.00	12,256.00	3,744.00
20X4	3,744.00	1,497.60	13,753.60	2,246.40
20X5	2,246.40	898.56	14,652.16	1,347.84

REVIEW AND ANSWER

Determine the accuracy of each depreciation schedule. Identify any corrections that David should make.

Merchandising businesses often rent buildings from companies that specialize in building management. Any modifications made to the building become the property of the building owner at the end of the lease. These fixed assets are known as *leasehold improvements*.

INSTRUCTIONS

1. Review Nike's annual report in Appendix B. Referring to Note 3 on page B-12, what was the amount of leasehold improvements for 2011 and 2010?

2. Referring to Note 1 on page B-10, what method of depreciation does Nike use to depreciate property, plant and equipment?

3. What range of years does Nike use for the estimated useful life of leasehold improvements?

Chapter 20

Accounting for Inventory

LEARNING OBJECTIVES

After studying Chapter 20, in addition to defining key terms, you will be able to:

LO1 Prepare a stock record.

LO2 Calculate the cost of merchandise inventory using the first-in, first-out (FIFO) inventory costing method.

LO3 Calculate the cost of merchandise inventory using the last-in, first-out (LIFO) inventory costing method.

LO4 Calculate the cost of merchandise inventory using the weighted-average inventory costing method.

LO5 Estimate the cost of merchandise inventory using the gross profit method of estimating inventory.

©DANIEL KOUREY, ISTOCK/©JIM PRUITT, ISTOCK

TETRA IMAGES/JUPITER IMAGES

Accounting In The Real World
OfficeMax

Background: ©MICHAL STRZELECKI, ISTOCK; Real World: © SG CITYSCAPES/ALAMY

For any retail company, inventory makes up a large percentage of its current assets. The larger the store, the more inventory it has on hand. Think of a typical OfficeMax store. It offers hundreds of different products. Each product must be sufficiently stocked so that it is available when the customer wants it. The OfficeMax mission is: We help our customers do their best work. In order to fulfill this mission, OfficeMax must maintain up-to-date inventory that is wanted by its customers.

However, too much inventory is not desirable. Excess inventory takes space, either on the shelves or in a warehouse. Excess inventory uses capital that could be used for other revenue-generating projects. Inventory that takes a long time to sell could become obsolete.

OfficeMax recently won an award for its inventory management. Its website states that "OfficeMax has used greater forecast accuracy to reduce inventory while improving customer service levels." The annual reports for OfficeMax support the claim of reduction in inventory level. In 2005, inventory was over $1.1 billion. In 2010, inventory had dropped to $846 million. Not only did actual levels of inventory decrease, but inventory as a percentage of total current assets also decreased. In 2005, inventory was 57% of total current assets. By 2010, inventory was only 42% of total current assets.

CRITICAL THINKING

1. The companies from which OfficeMax purchases its inventory are called vendors. These vendors may offer OfficeMax a high volume purchase rebate program. This means that the more OfficeMax buys of that product, the lower the cost will be per unit. What action would this encourage on the part of OfficeMax?

2. If OfficeMax takes advantage of these high volume purchase rebate programs and purchases some items in high volume, what is the risk for OfficeMax?

Source: officemax.com.

Key Terms

- inventory record
- stock record
- stock ledger
- first-in, first-out inventory costing method (FIFO)

- last-in, first-out inventory costing method (LIFO)
- weighted-average inventory costing method

- market value
- lower of cost or market inventory costing method (LCM)

- gross profit method of estimating inventory

LESSON
20-1 Determining the Quantity of Merchandise Inventory

LO1 Prepare a stock record.

Why Merchandise Inventory Is Important

Merchandise inventory on hand is typically the largest asset of a merchandising business. Successful businesses must have merchandise available for sale that customers want. A business therefore needs controls that help managers to maintain a merchandise inventory of sufficient quantity, variety, and price.

The cost of merchandise inventory is reported on both the balance sheet and the income statement. An accurate cost of merchandise inventory is required to correctly report current assets and retained earnings on the balance sheet. The accuracy of the inventory cost will also ensure that gross profit and net income are reported correctly on the income statement. [CONCEPT: Adequate Disclosure]

ETHICS IN ACTION

Hotlines

The accounting scandals of the early 21st century led the U.S. Congress to pass legislation designed to protect investors by improving the accuracy and reliability of financial reporting. The bill, known as the Sarbanes-Oxley Act of 2002 (SOX), contains a section that requires management to make a written statement about the effectiveness of its internal control system.

In an effective internal control system, employees and other stakeholders must be able to communicate possible ethics violations. A phone number called a *hotline* may be provided to allow an individual to provide confidential information about possible ethics violations. An effective ethics hotline must ensure an individual that:

1. Management takes hotline calls seriously.
2. The information provided will be maintained on an anonymous or confidential basis.
3. No retaliation or harassment will be tolerated.

INSTRUCTIONS

HealthSouth's compliance hotline is available to HealthSouth employees to report possible violations of its *Standards of Business Conduct*. Describe how the compliance hotline is designed to meet the three criteria presented above. You may also do a Google search for HealthSouth's *Standards of Business Conduct*.

© LUCA DI FILIPPO, ISTOCK

The Most Efficient Quantity of Inventory

To determine the most efficient quantity of inventory, a business makes frequent analysis of purchases, sales, and inventory records. Many businesses fail because too much or too little merchandise inventory is kept on hand. A business that stocks merchandise that does not satisfy the demand of its customers is also likely to fail.

A merchandise inventory that is larger than needed may decrease the net income of a business for several reasons.

1. Excess inventory requires a business to spend money for expensive store and warehouse space.
2. Excess inventory uses capital that could be invested in other assets to earn a profit for the business.
3. Excess inventory requires a business to spend money for expenses, such as taxes and insurance premiums, which increase with the cost of the merchandise inventory.
4. Excess inventory may become obsolete and unsalable.

Merchandise inventory that is smaller than needed may also decrease the net income of a business for several reasons.

1. Sales may be lost to competitors if items wanted by customers are not on hand.
2. Sales may be lost to competitors if there is an insufficient variety of merchandise to satisfy customers.
3. When a business frequently orders small quantities of an item, the price paid is often more per unit than when merchandise is ordered in large quantities.

Methods Used to Determine the Quantity of Merchandise Inventory

To control their inventory, businesses may take a physical count monthly, quarterly, semiannually, or annually. Usually, the volume of items on hand and the volume of sales determines how frequently a physical inventory is taken. However, the quantity of items in inventory at the end of a fiscal year must be determined in order to calculate the cost of merchandise sold.

As described in Chapter 9, two principal methods are used to determine the quantity of each item of merchandise on hand.

1. A merchandise inventory evaluated at the end of a fiscal period is known as a *periodic inventory*.
2. A merchandise inventory determined by keeping a continuous record of increases, decreases, and the balance on hand of each item of merchandise is known as a *perpetual inventory*. A perpetual inventory is also referred to as a *book inventory*.

Because controlling the quantity of merchandise inventory is so important to a business's success, many methods of keeping inventory records are used. Today, most companies use computers to keep track of the inventory on hand.

Keeping track of merchandise inventory also involves knowing the ideal quantity for each kind of merchandise in inventory. To ensure having the appropriate quantity, companies frequently establish an ideal minimum quantity and an ideal reorder quantity. When the minimum quantity is reached, new merchandise is ordered.

Minimum quantity levels must be established with consideration for how long it may take to receive new inventory. Otherwise, merchandise may not be available when a customer wants to buy it. Those who order new merchandise must also be aware of the ideal quantities to order to get the best prices and trade discounts.

A business usually determines the order in which products are sold, based on the type of inventory. A grocery store, for example, must sell its earliest purchases first. A hardware store, on the other hand, could sell its most recent purchases first. The inventory costing method used to calculate the cost of merchandise sold should not be determined by the order in which items are sold. A business should choose the inventory costing method that provides its managers with the best accounting information.

Inventory Record

❶ Stock Number and Description

❸ Unit Price and Total Cost

INVENTORY RECORD

DATE _December 31, 20--_ ITEM _Beach Totes_

1	2	3	4	5
STOCK NUMBER	DESCRIPTIONS	NO. OF UNITS ON HAND	UNIT PRICE	TOTAL COST
BB715-S	Beach Tote—Small	22	15.95	350.90
BB715-M	Beach Tote—Medium	14	4 @ 16.95	
			10 @ 18.95	257.30
BB715-L	Beach Tote—Large	10	19.50	195.00
	Total			2,941.25

❷ Actual Units on Hand

As described in Chapter 9, a periodic inventory conducted by counting, weighing, or measuring items of merchandise on hand is known as a physical inventory. Employees count each item of inventory and record the quantities on special forms. To ensure an accurate and complete count, a business will typically be closed during the physical inventory.

A business frequently establishes its fiscal year to end when inventory is at a minimum because it takes less time to count a smaller inventory. For example, a department store may take an inventory at the end of December. The amount of merchandise on hand is smaller because of holiday sales. Few purchases of additional merchandise are made in December after the holiday sales. All of these activities make the merchandise inventory smaller at the end of December.

A form used during a physical inventory to record information about each item of merchandise on hand is called an **inventory record**. The inventory record has space to record the stock number, description, number of units on hand, unit price, and total cost of each item. Columns 1–3 are completed when the business is taking a physical inventory. Columns 4–5 are completed after the physical inventory. The methods used to determine the unit prices are discussed later in this chapter.

❯ Preparing an Inventory Record

❶ Write the stock number and description before the physical inventory begins.

❷ Write the actual count in the No. of Units on Hand column.

❸ Write the unit price and calculate the total cost after the physical inventory is completed. These columns are usually completed by the accounting department.

Taking an inventory is an involved and expensive task. An efficient inventory count requires extensive management planning and employee training. Some businesses hire independent companies that specialize in taking inventories to assist in planning for and counting the inventory.

Stock Record LO1

STOCK RECORD						
Description *Beach Tote—Small*			Stock No. *BB715-S*			
Reorder *20*			Minimum *10*		Location *Rack 45*	
1	2	3	4	5	6	7
INCREASES			DECREASES			BALANCE
DATE	PURCHASE INVOICE NO.	QUANTITY	DATE	SALES INVOICE NO.	QUANTITY	QUANTITY
			Oct. 10		*2*	*9*
Nov. 2	*410*	*20*				*29*
			Nov. 12	*1531*	*2*	*27*
			Nov. 29	*1601*	*4*	*23*
			Dec. 6	*1647*	*1*	*22*

Purchase Information   Sales Information   New Balance on Hand

Some businesses keep inventory records that show continuously the quantity on hand for each kind of merchandise. A form used to show the kind of merchandise, quantity received, quantity sold, and balance on hand is called a **stock record**. A separate stock record is prepared for each kind of merchandise on hand. A file of stock records for all merchandise on hand is called a **stock ledger**.

A perpetual inventory system provides day-to-day information about the quantity of merchandise on hand. The minimum balance allowed before a reorder must be placed is also shown on each stock record. The minimum balance is the quantity that will typically last until the ordered merchandise can be received from the vendors. When the quantity falls below the minimum, additional merchandise is ordered in the quantity shown on the reorder line of the stock record. A stock record shows the quantity but usually not the cost of the merchandise.

Purchase information is recorded in the Increases columns when additional merchandise is received. Sales information is recorded in the Decreases columns when merchandise is sold. The new balance on hand is recorded after each purchase and sale.

When a perpetual inventory is kept, errors may be made in recording or calculating amounts. Also, some stock records may be incorrect because merchandise is taken from stock and not recorded on stock records. A business should at least take a physical inventory at the end of its fiscal year. The perpetual records are then corrected to reflect the actual quantity on hand as determined by the physical inventory.

Perpetual Inventory Using a Computer

UPC (Universal Product Code) symbol on merchandise is scanned to enter data into a point-of-sale (POS) terminal

Many merchandising businesses use a computer to keep perpetual inventory records. The point-of-sale terminals at the customer check-out counters are connected to the computer. The terminals read the Universal Product Codes (UPC) marked on products.

The stock ledger is stored in the computer. When a UPC is read at the terminal, the product description and the sales price are retrieved from the stock ledger and displayed on the terminal. The computer reduces the units on hand to reflect the item sold. The computer may also periodically check the quantities in the stock ledger and print a list of items that need to be reordered. Even with a computerized system, errors may occur. Therefore, companies that use a product's UPC code and a point-of-sale terminal should at least take a physical inventory at the end of the fiscal year.

Periodic Physical Inventory Counts

Classic Furniture counts its inventory at the end of each fiscal year. The physical inventory is an expensive and time-consuming undertaking. A special team of 40 temporary workers is employed. The physical inventory is actually performed on New Year's Day before any sales occur in the new year.

The company's inventory manager, Renee Schaeffer, is not satisfied with having only one physical count per year. She would like to have a monthly count to ensure she is making accurate buying decisions. But closing the store for a day, once a month, is not an option.

Instead, the inventory manager would like to perform daily counts of a few inventory items. Differences between the actual quantity on hand and the quantity stored in the accounting system could be investigated. Any loss of inventory could be entered in the accounting system to revise the recorded quantity of inventory.

OPEN THE SPREADSHEET TLA_CH20

The inventory manager has e-mailed the accounting manager asking for assistance in creating these daily lists. The worksheet contains a list of nearly 500 inventory items downloaded from the accounting system. Use the list to create two random lists of the inventory items.

1. Create a list of 5 inventory items.

2. Create a list consisting of 2% of the inventory items.

   Click on the Instructions tab and follow the instructions.

LO1 Prepare a stock record.

Terms Review

inventory record

stock record

stock ledger

Audit your understanding

1. Identify four reasons why a merchandise inventory that is larger than needed may decrease the net income of a business.

2. When are physical inventories normally taken?

3. How do inventory levels affect the period a business selects for its fiscal year? Why?

4. How is the accuracy of a perpetual inventory checked?

Work together 20-1

Preparing a stock record

A stock record for Green Gardens is given in the *Working Papers*. Your instructor will guide you through the following example.

Enter the following transactions on the stock record of Stock No. GL764-3, soaker hose. Source documents are abbreviated as follows: purchase invoice, P; sales invoice, S.

Transactions:

Oct. 3. Sold 3 of GL764-3 soaker hose. S835.

27. Purchased 40 of GL764-3 soaker hose. P1121.

29. Sold 5 of GL764-3, soaker hose. S886.

Dec. 4. Sold 3 of GL764-3, soaker hose. S912.

On your own 20-1

Preparing a stock record

A stock record for Plumbing World is given in the *Working Papers*. Work this problem independently.

Enter the following transactions on the stock record of Stock No. 7461XG, O-rings. Source documents are abbreviated as follows: purchase invoice, P; sales invoice, S.

Transactions:

Nov. 4. Sold 10 7461XG, O-rings. S237.

16. Sold 20 7461XG, O-rings. S286.

17. Sold 18 7461XG, O-rings. S312.

Dec. 9. Purchased 150 7461XG, O-rings. P323.

LESSON

20-2 Determining the Cost of Merchandise Inventory

LO2 Calculate the cost of merchandise inventory using the first-in, first-out (FIFO) inventory costing method.

LO3 Calculate the cost of merchandise inventory using the last-in, first-out (LIFO) inventory costing method.

LO4 Calculate the cost of merchandise inventory using the weighted-average inventory costing method.

First-In, First-Out Inventory Costing Method LO2

Units Needed to Equal the Total Units on Hand **3**

Unit Price Times **4** FIFO Units

Purchase Dates	Units Purchased	Unit Price	Total Cost	FIFO Units on Hand	FIFO Cost
January 1, beginning inventory	10	$20.80	$ 208.00		
February 16, purchases	6	21.60	129.60		
April 17, purchases	14	22.40	313.60		
September 5, purchases	12	23.40	280.80	10	$234.00
November 22, purchases	8	23.50	188.00	8	188.00
	50		$1,120.00	18	$422.00

Units from the Most Recent Purchase **2**

Total Units on Hand **1**

Total **5** FIFO Cost

After the quantities of merchandise on hand are counted, purchase invoices are used to find merchandise unit prices. The total costs are then calculated using the quantities and unit prices recorded on the inventory records. Most businesses use one of three inventory costing methods: (1) first-in, first-out, (2) last-in, first-out, or (3) weighted-average.

Sun Treasures, Inc., uses the most recent invoices for purchases to determine the unit price of an item in inventory. The earliest invoices for purchases, therefore, are used to determine the cost of merchandise sold. Using the price of merchandise purchased first to calculate the cost of merchandise sold first is called the **first-in, first-out inventory costing method (FIFO)**. The first-in, first-out method is frequently abbreviated as *FIFO*.

On December 31, a physical inventory of Extra Large Beach Totes, Model No. BB715-XL, showed 18 units on hand. Using the FIFO method, the 18 units would show a total cost of $422.00.

Costing Inventory Using the FIFO Method

1 Enter the total number of units on hand, 18.

2 From the most recent purchase, November 22, enter the number of units purchased, 8. In some cases, the number of units of the most recent purchase will be greater than or equal to the total number of units on hand. In such a case, enter the total number of units on hand and do not complete Step 3 below.

3 From the next most recent purchase, September 5, enter the number of units, 10, needed for the FIFO units to equal the total number on hand, 18. Continue with the next invoices as needed.

4 Multiply the unit price of each appropriate purchase by the FIFO units on hand to determine the FIFO cost.

5 Add the individual FIFO costs to determine the FIFO cost of the total number of units in ending inventory.

Last-In, First-Out Inventory Costing Method LO3

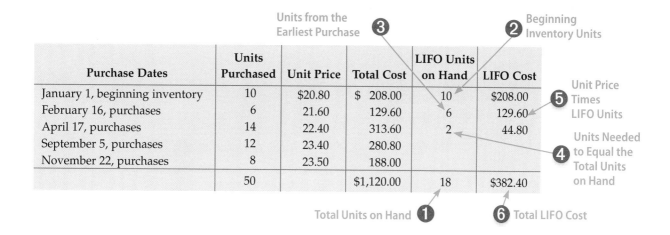

Units from the Earliest Purchase ③

Beginning ② Inventory Units

Purchase Dates	Units Purchased	Unit Price	Total Cost	LIFO Units on Hand	LIFO Cost
January 1, beginning inventory	10	$20.80	$ 208.00	10	$208.00
February 16, purchases	6	21.60	129.60	6	129.60
April 17, purchases	14	22.40	313.60	2	44.80
September 5, purchases	12	23.40	280.80		
November 22, purchases	8	23.50	188.00		
	50		$1,120.00	18	$382.40

⑤ Unit Price Times LIFO Units

④ Units Needed to Equal the Total Units on Hand

Total Units on Hand ①

⑥ Total LIFO Cost

Using the price of merchandise purchased last to calculate the cost of merchandise sold first is called the **last-in, first-out inventory costing method (LIFO)**. The last-in, first-out method is frequently abbreviated as *LIFO*. This method is based on the idea that the most recent costs of merchandise should be charged against current revenue. [CONCEPT: Matching Expenses with Revenue]

Using the LIFO method, each item on the inventory records is recorded at the earliest prices paid for the merchandise.

The earliest prices for the 18 beach totes would consist of the 10 units in the January 1 beginning inventory. The next earliest purchase, February 16, of 6 units is then used to cost 6 units in ending inventory. The remaining 2 units in ending inventory are costed using the next earliest purchase, April 17. On the inventory record, the 18 units would show a total cost of $382.40.

Costing Inventory Using the LIFO Method

① Enter the total number of units on hand, 18.

② Enter the number of units in beginning inventory, 10. In some cases, the number of units of beginning inventory will be greater than or equal to the total number of units on hand. In such a case, enter the total number of units on hand and do not complete Steps 3 and 4 below.

③ From the earliest purchase, February 16, enter the number of units purchased, 6.

④ From the next earliest purchase, April 17, enter the number of units, 2, needed for the LIFO units to equal the total number of units on hand, 18.

⑤ Multiply the unit price of the beginning inventory by the LIFO units on hand to determine the LIFO cost for beginning inventory. Repeat this process for each appropriate purchase.

⑥ Add the LIFO cost for the beginning inventory and each appropriate purchase to determine the LIFO cost of the total number of units in ending inventory.

remember

In the LIFO method, the latest purchases are assumed to be sold first (first-out). Therefore, ending inventory consists of the units purchased the earliest, and the earliest purchase invoice costs are used to value the ending inventory.

Weighted-Average Inventory Costing Method LO4

Purchases			Total
Date	Units	Unit Price	Cost
January 1, beginning inventory	10	$20.80	$ 208.00
February 16, purchases	6	21.60	129.60
April 17, purchases	14	22.40	313.60
September 5, purchases	12	23.40	280.80
November 22, purchases	8	23.50	188.00
	50		$1,120.00

1 Total Cost of Inventory Available

Total of Beginning Inventory and Purchases	÷	Total Units	=	Weighted-Average Price per Unit
$1,120.00	÷	50	=	$22.40

2 Weighted-Average Price per Unit

Units in Ending Inventory	×	Weighted-Average Price per Unit	=	Cost of Ending Inventory
18	×	$22.40	=	$403.20

3 Cost of Ending Inventory

Using the average cost of beginning inventory plus merchandise purchased during a fiscal period to calculate the cost of merchandise sold is called the **weighted-average inventory costing method**. The average unit price of the total inventory available is calculated. This average unit price is used to calculate both ending inventory and cost of merchandise sold. The average cost of merchandise is then charged against current revenue. [CONCEPT: Matching Expenses with Revenue]

Using the weighted-average method, the inventory is costed at the average price per unit of the beginning inventory plus the cost of all purchases during the fiscal year. On the inventory record, the 18 units would show a total cost of $403.20.

> **Costing Inventory Using the Weighted-Average Method**
>
> **1** Calculate the total cost of beginning inventory and each purchase, $1,120.00, by multiplying the units by each unit price.
>
> **2** Calculate the weighted-average price per unit, $22.40, by dividing the total cost, $1,120.00, by the total number of units available, 50.
>
> **3** Calculate the cost of ending inventory, $403.20, by multiplying the weighted-average price per unit, $22.40, by the units in ending inventory, 18.

Inventory Costing Method and Actual Flow of Inventory

The actual flow of inventory in a company does not have to match the inventory costing method a company chooses. For example, a grocery store will usually stock to the back so that the first goods purchased are the first goods sold. Therefore, the actual flow of the groceries is on a FIFO basis. A hardware store may decide to stock its new inventory in front of its older inventory. Therefore, the actual flow of the hardware is on a LIFO basis. A gas station, where all the gas is put into a large underground tank, sells its gas on a weighted-average basis. However, each of these three kinds of businesses can decide which inventory method (FIFO, LIFO, or weighted-average) it uses. The inventory method chosen by a company to determine the cost of merchandise sold does not have to match the actual flow of inventory for that company.

The Rise and Fall of WorldCom

Telecommunications giant WorldCom collapsed in 2003. What could have caused the failure of the nation's second largest long-distance service provider, boasting over $100 billion in assets?

The roots of WorldCom were planted during the historic breakup of AT&T in 1984. AT&T dominated the long-distance and local phone service market. To increase competition, the Federal Trade Commission (FTC) forced AT&T to divest itself of its local phone service companies. The seven new independent local phone companies were dubbed the "Baby Bells."

Long-distance phone service instantly became a commodity that could be bought and sold. WorldCom was one of several corporations created to take advantage of this new business opportunity. WorldCom bought a huge volume of long-distance service from AT&T and resold the minutes to small businesses.

From its humble beginnings, WorldCom embarked on a path of growth through acquisitions. WorldCom bought a variety of telecom businesses, most often paying for the acquisitions with WorldCom stock. Its most notable acquisition was its 1997 merger with MCI Communications. The $37 billion price tag was triple the size of WorldCom. The new MCI WorldCom then set its sights on Sprint Corporation, announcing in 1999 a staggering $129 billion merger. Fearing that a combined Sprint and MCI WorldCom would decrease competition, the government did not approve the merger.

But hidden behind by the smoke screen of its merger activity, WorldCom was experiencing decreasing sales and incurring losses. To hide the losses, WorldCom began recording fraudulent journal entries. The fraud involved the accounting for line costs, the fees paid to other telecom companies. The journal entries reduced line cost expenses and recorded the expenses as plant assets.

WorldCom's internal auditors were suspicious that a fraud was occurring. During their investigation, one auditor noted an unusual transaction to a plant asset account. It wasn't so much that the amount was large. After all, WorldCom was often involved in acquisitions in the billions of dollars. But it was the amount, exactly $500,000,000.00, that caught the internal auditor's attention. Why would the amount of an addition to plant assets be a rounded number? When all the investigations were complete, it was revealed that WorldCom had reported $3.8 billion of line costs as plant assets.

ACTIVITY

The board of directors of Royal Imports has launched an internal investigation. The board suspects an accounting fraud at its foreign operations. Begin the investigation by analyzing the corporation's journal entries for any signs of a fraud. At the direction of the manager of internal audit, complete the following steps.

INSTRUCTIONS

Open the spreadsheet FA_CH20 and complete the steps on the Instructions tab.

1. Prepare a list of transactions greater than $25,000.00 that end in 000.00.

2. Identify any transaction that appears unusual. Support your conclusion.

3. What would you suggest as the next step in your investigation?

Sources: Richard B. Lanza and Scott Gilbert, "A Risk-Based Approach to Journal Entry Testing," *Journal of Accountancy* (July 2007) and Cecil W. Jackson, *Business Fairy Tales* (Thomson, 2006).

Calculating the Cost of Merchandise Sold

The cost of ending inventory determined using any of the three inventory costing methods can be used to calculate the cost of merchandise sold. The cost of ending inventory is subtracted from the total cost of units available for sale. Although the formula is the same, under each inventory costing method the amount determined will be different. Sun Treasures uses the FIFO method. Therefore, the FIFO cost of $422.00 is subtracted from the total cost of merchandise available for sale, $1,120.00, to calculate the cost of merchandise sold of $698.00.

Cost of Merchandise Available for Sale	−	FIFO Cost of Ending Inventory	=	Cost of Merchandise Sold
$1,120.00	−	$422.00	=	$698.00

Comparison of Inventory Methods

	FIFO	LIFO	Weighted-Average
Cost of merchandise sold:			
Merchandise inventory, Jan. 1.............	$ 208.00	$ 208.00	$ 208.00
Net purchases	912.00	912.00	912.00
Merchandise available for sale	$1,120.00	$1,120.00	$1,120.00
Less ending inventory, Dec. 31...........	422.00	382.40	403.20
Cost of merchandise sold.............	$ 698.00	$ 737.60	$ 716.80
In a period of rising prices: Relative cost of ending inventory	highest	lowest	intermediate
Relative cost of merchandise sold	lowest	highest	intermediate

In a *period of rising prices*, the FIFO method gives the highest possible ending inventory cost and the lowest cost of merchandise sold. The LIFO method gives the lowest possible ending inventory cost and the highest cost of merchandise sold. The weighted-average method gives ending inventory cost and cost of merchandise sold between FIFO and LIFO. As the cost of merchandise sold increases, gross profit and net income decrease. Thus, net income is highest under the FIFO method, lowest under the LIFO method, and intermediate under the weighted-average method.

In a *period of declining prices*, the results for the FIFO and LIFO methods are reversed.

All three inventory costing methods are acceptable accounting practices. A business should select one method and use that same method continuously for each fiscal period. If a business changed inventory costing methods, part of the difference in gross profit and net income would be caused by the change in methods. To provide financial statements that can be analyzed and compared with statements of other fiscal periods, the same inventory costing method must be used for each fiscal period. [CONCEPT: Consistent Reporting]

Lower of Cost or Market Inventory Costing Method

The price that must be paid to replace an asset is called the **market value**. Using the lower of cost or market price to calculate the cost of ending merchandise inventory is called the **lower of cost or market inventory costing method (LCM)**. In this context, *cost* refers to the actual amount paid for the unit of inventory on hand. *Market* refers to the amount that must be paid to replace the unit of inventory. For example, assume that a permanent change in market conditions means that Sun Treasures may currently have to pay a vendor $22.50 to purchase the extra large beach tote.

Two amounts are needed to apply the lower of cost or market method:

1. The cost of the inventory using the FIFO, LIFO, or weighted-average method.
2. The current market value of the inventory.

These two amounts are then compared and the lower of the two is used to cost the inventory. For example, Sun Treasures uses the FIFO method of costing inventory. The FIFO cost and the current market value for 18 beach totes are shown below. The FIFO cost is $422.00, and the current market value is $405.00. Using the lower of cost or market method, the market value of the beach totes is lower than the FIFO cost. Therefore, the market value of $405.00 is used as the cost of the totes.

If Sun Treasures used the LIFO method, the LIFO cost would be $382.40. The LIFO cost of $382.40 is lower than the market value, so the LIFO cost would be used instead of the market value. If Sun Treasures used the weighted-average method, the weighted-average cost would be $403.20. The weighted-average cost of $403.20 is lower than the market value, so the weighted-average cost would be used instead of the market value.

The LCM method is designed to prevent inventory values from being overstated. This is especially important in industries where the cost of component parts tends to decrease rather than increase. Without the LCM method, these inventories would be stated at older, higher prices. The use of the LCM method ensures that the inventory value will not be reported at a value higher than current market value.

Lower of Cost or Market Inventory Costing Method			
Costing Method	Cost	Market Value (18 units × $22.50 current market price)	Lower of Cost or Market
FIFO	$422.00	$405.00	$405.00
LIFO	382.40	405.00	382.40
Weighted-average	403.20	405.00	403.20

Calculate the cost ↗   Calculate the market price ⌐

Determine the smaller number to use as the lower of cost or market ←

Inventory Management

The cost of inventory is usually a large portion of a retail, manufacturing, or wholesale company's current assets. The efficient management of inventory, therefore, can lead to major cost savings for many companies. Inventory management deals with the fine line between having too much inventory and running out of inventory. It is broad in nature, starting with identifying inventory requirements and covering each step until the inventory is received at the correct location. It requires trying to forecast demand, price levels, defective goods, available space, and handling costs.

Many of the decisions made by an inventory manager will have an effect on the financial statements of a company. Too much inventory will tie up capital that could be used for other projects. Inventory requires storage space and handlers, which decrease profit. Excess inventory may have to be sold at below cost prices, which further decreases profits.

Too little inventory also has an effect on financial statements. Lost sales will decrease net income.

Business Management & Administration

CRITICAL THINKING

1. Inventory management companies help their clients manage inventory. Search the Internet for an inventory management company and write a one-sentence summary of the services it provides.
2. Search the Internet for an inventory management software program. List the name of the software and write a one-sentence summary of its features.

Source: Inventory Management, published by the U.S. Small Business Administration.

LO2 Calculate the cost of merchandise inventory using the first-in, first-out (FIFO) inventory costing method.

LO3 Calculate the cost of merchandise inventory using the last-in, first-out (LIFO) inventory costing method.

LO4 Calculate the cost of merchandise inventory using the weighted-average inventory costing method.

Terms Review

first-in, first-out inventory costing method (FIFO)

last-in, first-out inventory costing method (LIFO)

weighted-average inventory costing method

market value

lower of cost or market inventory costing method (LCM)

Audit your understanding

1. On what idea is the FIFO method based?

2. When the LIFO method is used, at what price is each item in ending merchandise inventory recorded?

3. In a period of rising prices, which inventory costing method gives the lowest cost of merchandise sold?

4. Why should a business select one inventory costing method and use that same method continuously for each fiscal period?

Work together 20-2

Determining the cost of inventory using the FIFO, LIFO, and weighted-average inventory costing methods

Inventory costing information for Sunshine Spas is given in the *Working Papers.* Your instructor will guide you through the following example.

Calculate the cost of ending inventory using the FIFO, LIFO, and weighted-average methods. There are 15 units in ending inventory.

On your own 20-2

Determining the cost of inventory using the FIFO, LIFO, and weighted-average inventory costing methods

Inventory costing information for Electronics Plus is given in the *Working Papers.* Work this problem independently.

Calculate the cost of ending inventory using the FIFO, LIFO, and weighted-average methods. There are 26 units in ending inventory.

20-3 Estimating Inventory

LO5 Estimate the cost of merchandise inventory using the gross profit method of estimating inventory.

Gross Profit Method of Estimating Inventory LO5

STEP 1: Beginning inventory, January 1 .... $ 331,235.20
   Plus   net purchases for January 1 to January 31. .... +64,516.21
   Equals cost of merchandise available for sale .... $ 395,751.41

STEP 2: Net sales for January 1 to January 31 .... $ 122,367.00
   Times   previous year's gross profit percentage. .... ×   40.00%
   Equals estimated gross profit on operations .... $ 48,946.80

STEP 3: Net sales for January 1 to January 31 .... $ 122,367.00
   Less   estimated gross profit on operations .... −48,946.80
   Equals estimated cost of merchandise sold .... $ 73,420.20

STEP 4: Cost of merchandise available for sale .... $ 395,751.41
   Less   estimated cost of merchandise sold .... −73,420.20
   Equals estimated ending merchandise inventory............. $ 322,331.21

Restaurant Supply Co.
Income Statement
For Month Ended January 31, 20--

			% of Net Sales
Operating Revenue:			
Net Sales		$122,367.00	100.0
Cost of Merchandise Sold:			
Beginning Inventory, January 1	$331,235.20		
Net Purchases........................	64,516.21		
Merchandise Available for Sale	$395,751.41		
Less Est. Ending Inv., January 31.	322,331.21		
Cost of Merchandise Sold..............		73,420.20	60.0
Gross Profit on Operations..............		$ 48,946.80	40.0
Operating Expenses...................		43,807.39	35.8
Net Income		$ 5,139.41	4.2

Estimating inventory by using the previous year's percentage of gross profit on operations is called the **gross profit method of estimating inventory**. The gross profit method is often used to estimate the cost of the ending inventory reported on monthly financial statements. The gross profit method is a less expensive method of calculating inventory costs than taking a physical inventory or maintaining a perpetual inventory system.

Four values are needed to perform this four-step process. Actual net sales and net purchases amounts are obtained from the general ledger. The beginning inventory amount is obtained from the prior period's financial statements. The gross profit percentage is estimated by management based on the previous year's actual percentage, adjusted for any significant changes in economic conditions.

Estimating Inventory for Other Months

When the gross profit method of estimating inventory is used for months other than the first month of the fiscal year, the process is the same as that just illustrated. Net sales and purchases amounts are obtained from the general ledger. For the sales account, the previous month's ending balance is subtracted from the current month's ending balance to calculate the amount of sales for just the current month. The same process is used for the purchases account. The beginning inventory for the month is the same as the ending inventory from the previous month. Note that both the beginning and ending inventory amounts will be based on estimated amounts.

Accounting in Ancient Civilizations

Five thousand years before the appearance of double-entry accounting, Mesopotamian scribes were among the few people who could read and write. These scribes became the equivalent of today's accountants.

Public scribes would meet business partners at the gates of the city. The scribe would listen as the partners described their agreement. The scribe would then record the contract on moist clay tablets. The business partners would sign their names by pressing their seals into the clay. The tablets were then dried in the sun or a kiln. The development of accounting in Egypt was similar, except that the Egyptians used papyrus rather than clay tablets, allowing for more details to be recorded.

The major problem with these systems was the lack of a single unit of valuation to use in measuring the value of each transaction. This issue was solved when the Greeks introduced coined money about 600 BC. Although it took many years for the usage of coins to spread, this is often identified as a major event in the development of accounting records.

The Babylonians in Asia Minor used an early form of banking. They transferred funds with a system resembling our checking accounts, one of the first uses of business documents.

These early practices provided the foundation for today's financial system and recordkeeping methods.

CRITICAL THINKING

1. Estimate how many transactions might occur in a single day in a mid-sized bank.

2. List the number of different methods of payment that are accepted by a local department store.

Sources: www.accountancystudents.co.uk and John R. Alexander, *History of Accounting*, Association of Chartered Accountants in the United States.

©FONTMONSTER, ISTOCK

LO5 Estimate the cost of merchandise inventory using the gross profit method of estimating inventory.

Term Review

gross profit method of estimating inventory

▶ Audit your understanding

1. When neither a perpetual system is maintained nor a physical inventory is taken, how can an ending merchandise inventory be determined that is accurate enough for a monthly income statement?

2. What amounts are needed to estimate ending merchandise inventory?

3. What amount is used for beginning inventory for a month that is not the first month of a fiscal year?

▶ Work together 20-3

Estimating ending inventory using the gross profit method

A form for making estimated inventory calculations and a form for completing an income statement are given in the *Working Papers*. Your instructor will guide you through the following examples.

1. Use the following information obtained from the records and management of Goldsmith Company to estimate the cost of the ending inventory on June 30.

Estimated beginning inventory, June 1	$77,400.00
Actual net purchases for June	$23,900.00
Actual net sales for June	$122,500.00
Estimated gross profit percentage	45.0%
Actual operating expenses for June	$38,465.00

2. Prepare an income statement for the month ended June 30 of the current year.

▶ On your own 20-3

Estimating ending inventory using the gross profit method

A form for making estimated inventory calculations and a form for completing an income statement are given in the *Working Papers*. Work this problem independently.

1. Use the following information obtained from the records and management of Leah Enterprises to estimate the cost of the ending inventory on April 30.

Estimated beginning inventory, April 1	$49,000.00
Actual net purchases for April	$24,200.00
Actual net sales for April	$112,000.00
Estimated gross profit percentage	55.0%
Actual operating expenses for April	$35,840.00

2. Prepare an income statement for the month ended April 30 of the current year.

A Look at Accounting Software

Managing Inventory

The inventory management module of a computerized accounting system is very complex. It has links to accounts payable, accounts receivable, and the general ledger. It must receive data from, and pass data to, each of those modules. Computerized inventory systems today are so powerful they can track the sales of specific items to specific customers. That data can be used to send targeted sales offers to those customers. Inventory systems are also capable of issuing automatic reorders when stock levels drop to designated reorder quantities.

The illustration shows a new inventory stock item being entered. This window would also be used to edit information for an existing stock item. In that case, the user would double-click one of the stock items in the report to open the window. Then the user could, for example, change the preferred vendor, the location of the item, or the reorder quantity. By clicking the Inactive button, the user would prevent the item from being reordered.

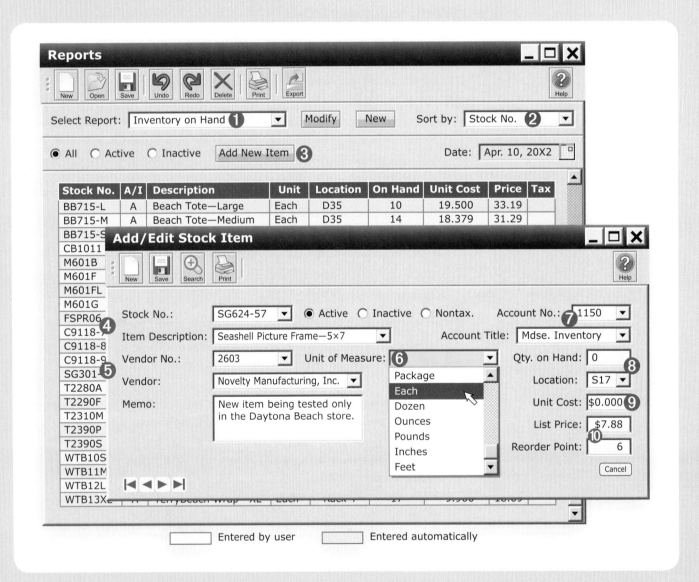

1. To view an inventory report, the user opens the Reports window and selects Inventory on Hand from the drop list.

2. The user has chosen to have this report sorted by stock number.

3. The user has clicked on the Add New Item button to open the Add/Edit Stock Item pop-up window.

4. The user enters the new stock number and description. The Active button is on by default. States determine which types of products are exempt from sales tax. When Nontax is selected, point-of-sale (POS) terminals will print the item on the customer receipt with an NT, and no sales tax will be charged for it.

5. The user may enter a preferred vendor (by vendor number or name). This can speed up order entry when creating a purchase order, although the vendor could be changed in the Write Purchase Orders window.

6. The user must select a unit of measure. Here, the user is selecting Each from the drop list.

7. The system automatically selects the Merchandise Inventory account—number 1150. In the manual system used by Sun Treasures, Inc., inventory is maintained using the periodic system. When a computer system is used, inventory is maintained using a perpetual system, so inventory purchases are debited to Merchandise Inventory rather than to Purchases.

8. The quantity on hand for this new item is zero because no orders have been entered yet. The system will update this number as new orders increase it and sales decrease it. The user would select the storage location for the item. That information helps salespeople know where to look for replacement items when stock is depleted on the sales floor. It also is helpful when counting the inventory.

9. The system computes an average unit cost of all the items currently in inventory. Sun Treasures uses LIFO, so as items are sold, the most recently purchased items will be deducted from inventory first. The system then computes a new average cost of the remaining items in inventory.

10. The user enters the list price. The POS terminals use this price to compute the value of each sale. Finally, the user enters a reorder quantity. If the accounting system is not programmed to do an automatic reorder, the purchasing department would reorder the item when the stock level dropped to this quantity.

Chapter Summary

The quantity of inventory on hand can be kept on a perpetual or periodic basis. The perpetual basis provides an up-to-date balance in the **Merchandise Inventory** account throughout the period. The periodic basis does not update inventory throughout the period. Both methods require that a physical inventory be taken at least once a year. Once the quantity of inventory is determined, a cost must be applied to each unit of inventory. This can be done using the FIFO, LIFO, or weighted-average methods. Each method results in different amounts for the cost of ending inventory and the cost of merchandise sold. In times of rising prices, the FIFO method will result in the highest net income amount. When the ending inventory cannot be counted, ending inventory can be estimated using the gross profit method.

EXPLORE ACCOUNTING

Activity-Based Costing

A company must accurately calculate the cost of a product in order to determine the selling price of that product. The materials and labor costs for most products are not difficult to determine. Other costs that must be measured include custodial services in the factory, machine maintenance costs, supervisory labor costs, and the cost of factory supplies. All expenses other than direct materials and direct labor that apply to making products are called **factory overhead.**

Several methods can be used to calculate factory overhead costs. A method commonly used is to relate factory overhead costs to the number of hours of labor that each product requires. Using this method, a product using one hour of labor per unit would be allocated four times more factory overhead costs than a product using 15 minutes of labor per unit. This method was more practical when production was labor intensive. Today, many automated manufacturing processes involve little, if any, direct labor. Therefore, a newer method of allocating factory overhead costs is one based on activities. Major activities in the manufacturing process are identified and factory overhead costs are allocated based on these activities. Allocating factory overhead based on the level of major activities is referred to as **activity-based costing (ABC).**

For example, the production of a pizza at a local pizza parlor involves two significant activities: assembling the ingredients and cooking the pizza. The first activity involves direct labor, but the second activity involves only cooking time in the oven. In contrast, the production of a sub sandwich involves three times as much direct labor as a pizza but no cooking in the oven. If factory overhead were applied based solely on direct labor, the sub sandwich would improperly receive three times as much overhead cost as the pizza.

Using ABC, the accountant recognizes that a significant amount of overhead costs of the pizza parlor results from the ovens: the cost of the ovens, heating the ovens, and cooling the kitchen from the heat that escapes from the ovens. These overhead costs should be allocated to those products that require cooking. Thus, factory overhead costs related to the ovens would be applied to pizza production based on cooking time.

ABC is also used by service businesses to determine the cost of providing various services. ABC results in more accurate estimates on the cost of producing individual products and services. Managers can use this information to assist them in making better decisions, such as the price of products and the profitability of different product lines.

INSTRUCTIONS

The challenge of implementing ABC is to match costs with related activities that are easy to measure. Identify the measurable activities in two different lawn maintenance services: mowing a lawn and cutting down a tree.

Apply Your Understanding

INSTRUCTIONS: Download problem instructions for Excel, QuickBooks, and Peachtree from the textbook companion website at www.C21accounting.com.

20-1 Application Problem: Preparing a stock record LO1

A stock record for Electronics World is given in the *Working Papers*.

Instructions:

Enter the following transactions on the stock record of a 42-inch flat-screen television, Stock No. 891DC-5. Source documents are abbreviated as follows: purchase invoice, P; sales invoice, S.

Transactions:

Feb.   4.   Sold 2 Model No. 891DC-5 televisions to Country Motel, n/30. S910.

      28.   Sold 1 Model No. 891DC-5 television to Janice Olson, 2/10, n/30. S984.

Mar. 10.   Received 10 units of Model No. 891DC-5 televisions from GLC Electronics, 2/10, n/30. P1012.

      24.   Sold 2 Model No. 891DC-5 televisions to Seaside Restaurant, n/30. S1062.

20-2 Application Problem: Determining the cost of inventory using the FIFO, LIFO, and weighted-average inventory costing methods LO2, 3, 4

Forms for costing inventory for Oakland Supply are given in the *Working Papers*. There are 192 units in ending inventory.

Purchase Date	Quantity	Unit Price
January 1, beginning inventory	100	$4.00
March 13, purchases	88	4.10
June 8, purchases	90	4.25
September 16, purchases	94	4.30
December 22, purchases	98	4.40

Instructions:

Calculate the cost of ending inventory using the FIFO, LIFO, and weighted-average methods.

 Peachtree

1. Journalize and post purchases of inventory on account in the Purchases/ Receive Inventory window.
2. Journalize and post sales of inventory on account in the Sales/Invoicing window.
3. Print the purchases journal, sales journal, inventory valuation report, and trial balance.

 QuickBooks

1. Journalize and post purchases of inventory on account in the Enter Bills window.
2. Journalize and post sales of inventory on account in the Create Invoices window.
3. Print the vendor balance detail, inventory valuation summary, and trial balance.

1. Key the inventory-related transactions on the stock record.
2. Use the inventory costing methods to calculate year-end inventory.
3. Print the worksheet.

AAONLINE

1. Go to www.cengage.com/login
2. Click on **AA Online** to access.
3. Go to the online assignment and follow the instructions.

20-3 Application Problem: Estimating ending inventory using the gross profit method LO5

Use the following information obtained from the records and management of Lee Industries. A form for making inventory calculations and a form for completing an income statement are given in the *Working Papers*.

Instructions:

1. Estimate the cost of the ending inventory on March 31.

Estimated beginning inventory, March 1	$49,350.00
Actual net purchases for March	$22,900.00
Actual net sales for March	$93,000.00
Estimated gross profit percentage	55.0%
Actual operating expenses for March	$40,176.00

2. Prepare an income statement for the month ended March 31 of the current year.

20-M Mastery Problem: Determining the cost of inventory using the FIFO, LIFO, and weighted-average inventory costing methods LO2, 3, 4

Computer Supply Company began the year with 16 units of its model 120-HP print cartridge in beginning inventory. Each unit sells for $39.95. The following transactions involving model 120-HP occurred during the year. Forms are given in the *Working Papers*. Source documents are abbreviated as follows: purchase invoice, P; sales invoice, S.

Transactions:

Jan.	6.	Purchased 40 units from Printers Plus for $10.24 per unit, 2/10, n/30. P361.
Apr.	5.	Sold 44 units to Glenville Hospital, n/30. S812.
	14.	Purchased 40 units from Printers Plus for $10.36 per unit, 2/10, n/30. P437.
July	5.	Sold 50 units to Hills Department Store, n/30. S971.
Aug.	3.	Purchased 40 units from Printers Plus for $10.46 per unit, 2/10, n/30. P512.
Dec.	2.	Sold 30 units to ABC Company, n/30. S1186.
	12.	Purchased 40 units from Printers Plus for $10.54 per unit, 2/10, n/30. P556.

Instructions:

1. Enter the transactions on the stock record and determine the number of units in ending inventory.

2. Calculate the cost of ending inventory using the FIFO, LIFO, and weighted-average methods.

3. Which of the inventory costing methods resulted in the lowest cost of merchandise sold? Merchandise available for sale is the total cost of beginning inventory plus all purchases during the year.

Peachtree

1. Journalize and post purchases of inventory on account in the Purchases/Receive Inventory window.
2. Journalize and post sales of inventory on account in the Sales/Invoicing window.
3. Print the purchases journal, sales journal, inventory valuation report, and trial balance.

QuickBooks

1. Journalize and post purchases of inventory on account in the Enter Bills window.
2. Journalize and post sales of inventory on account in the Create Invoices window.
3. Print the vendor balance detail, inventory valuation summary, and trial balance.

X

1. Key the inventory-related transactions on the stock record.
2. Use the inventory costing methods to calculate year-end inventory.
3. Print the worksheet.

AAONLINE

1. Go to www.cengage.com/login
2. Click on **AA Online** to access.
3. Go to the online assignment and follow the instructions.

20-C Challenge Problem: Determining the cost of merchandise inventory destroyed in a fire LO5

A fire completely destroyed the warehouse of Albertson Painting Company on the night of May 12 of the current year. The accounting records of the company and $945.00 of merchandise inventory were salvaged. The company does not maintain a perpetual inventory system. The insurance company therefore has requested an estimate of the merchandise inventory destroyed in the fire. Forms are given in the *Working Papers*. The following income statement is for the previous fiscal year.

Albertson Painting Company
Income Statement
For Year Ended April 30, 20--

Operating Revenue:		
Net Sales		$316,308.00
Cost of Merchandise Sold:		
Beginning Inventory, May 1 (Prior Year) .	$ 15,348.27	
Net Purchases.	156,282.02	
Merchandise Available for Sale	$171,630.29	
Less Est. Ending Inv., April 30.	17,271.99	
Cost of Merchandise Sold.		154,358.30
Gross Profit on Operations.		$161,949.70
Operating Expenses.		142,267.61
Net Income		$ 19,682.09

The following additional financial information is obtained from the current year's accounting records.

Net purchases, May 1 to May 12 $ 3,377.02
Net sales, May 1 to May 12   11,216.44
Operating expenses, May 1 to May 12   4,937.70

Instructions:

1. Calculate the prior year's gross profit on operations as a percentage of net sales. Round the percentage calculation to the nearest 0.1%.

2. Use the percentage calculated in part (1) and the current year's financial information to calculate an estimate of the total merchandise inventory as of May 12.

3. To calculate the cost of the inventory destroyed in the fire, subtract the cost of the merchandise inventory that was not destroyed from the estimate of the total merchandise inventory as of May 12.

4. Prepare an income statement for the period May 1 through May 12.

The insurance company maintains that it is liable for paying only the book value of the inventory destroyed by fire. Albertson Painting Company maintains that the insurance company should pay the replacement cost of the destroyed inventory.

5. What is meant by the book value and the replacement value of the inventory?

6. Albertson Painting Company uses the FIFO inventory costing method. How does using FIFO affect the difference between the book value and the replacement value of the destroyed inventory?

7. What should determine which value the insurance company uses?

21st Century Skills

Piggly Wiggly—Just In Time!

Theme: Financial, Economic, Business, and Entrepreneurial Literacy

Skills: Critical Thinking and Problem Solving, Communication and Collaboration

PARTNERSHIP FOR
21ST CENTURY SKILLS

For a small business, inventory is often the most important asset. If not managed properly, inventory costs can also become the greatest expense on the income statement keeping a business from being profitable. The cost of inventory consists of more than just the cost of the actual item and its shipping. One of the greatest costs associated with inventory is the cost of storing, or holding the merchandise, as well as having excessive inventory.

To keep inventory costs down, many companies have implemented an inventory strategy called just-in-time delivery (JIT). Toyota, now a leader in the automotive industry, developed JIT as part of its management strategy after its delegates observed the Piggly Wiggly grocery store while on a visit to the United States to view auto manufacturers. While not all that impressed with the Ford manufacturing processes, the delegates were fascinated with how the supermarket only reordered and restocked goods after customers had made purchases. The JIT strategy maintains that inventory is not reordered until stock is close to depletion. This saves warehouse space and costs.

While JIT may save costs, a business must not underestimate the risks involved. The products must arrive exactly when needed. Uncontrollable circumstances such as natural disasters, untimely weather, supplier misfortunes, and political risks can damage business credibility and reduce revenue. The best intentions to become more profitable can leave a company vulnerable. Management must carefully develop a risk management plan to implement if using the JIT strategy.

When planning an event to occur on a specific date, one must assess the risks involved so proactive measures can be taken to offset the risks, deliver the product, and make a profit.

Your business has been asked to design and provide t-shirts for a local benefit sponsored by your school. Individuals in your school will be participating in the event as well as some members from the local community. Your supplier needs five days to complete and deliver the order. The organizer of the event estimates that approximately 1,000 t-shirts will be needed. The shirts will cost you $5.00 each to purchase. The organizer will only pay for the number of shirts for those participating. You must make a profit.

1. Create a table with two columns. Label with the following: (1) Risks, (2) Measures.

2. Create a bulleted list with at least five risks associated with this order.

3. Create a bulleted list next to the risks, under the heading Measures, and explain measures you will take to offset the risks in order to make a profit. Present your risk assessment to the class.

Analyzing Nike's financial statements

The managers at Nike need to constantly monitor the amount of inventory available for sale. Having too little inventory can result in products running out of stock, which can cause the company to lose sales. Holding too much inventory increases the company's operating expenses. A financial ratio that evaluates the amount of inventory available for sale is known as the inventory turnover ratio. The ratio is calculated as follows:

$$\text{Inventory Turnover} = \frac{\text{Cost of Goods Sold}}{(\text{Beginning Inventory} + \text{Ending Inventory}) \div 2}$$

Dividing the sum of the beginning and ending inventory by 2 approximates the average inventory for the fiscal year. As one example, the inventory turnover for Domino's Pizza, Inc., based on its 2011 fiscal year financial statements (www.dominos.com), is calculated below.

$$\text{Inventory Turnover} = \frac{\$1,181,677,000}{(\$26,998,000 + \$30,702,000) \div 2} = 41.17$$

Dividing 365 by the turnover ratio yields a financial ratio known as *number of days' sales in inventory*. Domino's number of days' sales in inventory is 8.87 days. Thus, the average item remains in its inventory for approximately 9 days.

INSTRUCTIONS

1. Using the financial information in Appendix B of this text, calculate Nike's inventory turnover ratio and number of days' sales in inventory for 2011.

2. Why would the inventory turnover ratios for Nike and Domino's differ?

Reinforcement Activity 3—Part A

An Accounting Cycle for a Corporation: Journalizing and Posting Transactions

  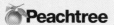   **AAONLiNE**

Reinforcement Activity 3 reinforces learning from Parts 2 and 3. Activities cover a complete accounting cycle for a merchandising business organized as a corporation. Reinforcement Activity 3 is a single problem divided into two parts. Part A includes learning from Part 2 and Chapters 18 through 20 of Part 3. Part B includes learning from Chapters 21 and 22.

The accounting work of a single merchandising business for the last month of a fiscal year is used in this reinforcement activity. The records kept and reports prepared, however, illustrate the application of accounting concepts for all merchandising businesses.

Restaurant Warehouse, Inc.

Restaurant Warehouse, Inc., a merchandising business, is organized as a corporation. The business sells a complete line of restaurant supplies, mostly to business customers. Restaurant Warehouse is located within an industrial park and is open for business Monday through Saturday. A monthly rent is paid for the building. Restaurant Warehouse subleases some of its warehouse space. Restaurant Warehouse sells to some businesses on account and accepts cash or credit cards from small business owners.

Chart of Accounts

Restaurant Warehouse uses the chart of accounts shown on the next page.

Journals and Ledgers

The journals, ledgers, and forms used by Restaurant Warehouse are listed below. Models of these items are shown in the textbook chapters indicated.

Journals and Ledgers	Chapter(s)
Purchases journal	9
Cash payments journal	9
Accounts payable ledger	9 and 11
Sales journal	10
Cash receipts journal	10
Accounts receivable ledger	10 and 11
General journal	11
General ledger	11
Plant asset record	19

Restaurant Warehouse, Inc., Chart of Accounts

General Ledger

Balance Sheet Accounts

(1000) ASSETS

1100   Current Assets
1105   Cash
1110   Petty Cash
1115   Accounts Receivable
1120   Allowance for Uncollectible Accounts
1125   Notes Receivable
1130   Interest Receivable
1135   Merchandise Inventory
1140   Supplies
1145   Prepaid Insurance
1200   Plant Assets
1205   Office Equipment
1210   Accumulated Depreciation—Office Equipment
1215   Warehouse Equipment
1220   Accumulated Depreciation—Warehouse Equipment

(2000) LIABILITIES

2100   Current Liabilities
2105   Accounts Payable
2110   Sales Tax Payable
2115   Notes Payable
2120   Interest Payable
2125   Unearned Rent Income
2130   Employee Income Tax Payable
2135   Social Security Tax Payable
2140   Medicare Tax Payable
2145   Medical Insurance Payable
2150   Unemployment Tax Payable—State
2155   Unemployment Tax Payable—Federal
2160   Federal Income Tax Payable
2165   Dividends Payable
2200   Long-Term Liabilities
2205   Bonds Payable

(3000) STOCKHOLDERS' EQUITY

3105   Capital Stock—Common
3110   Paid-in Capital in Excess of Par—Common
3115   Capital Stock—Preferred

3120   Paid-in Capital in Excess of Par—Preferred
3205   Retained Earnings
3210   Dividends
3215   Income Summary

Income Statement Accounts

(4000) OPERATING REVENUE

4105   Sales
4110   Sales Discount
4115   Sales Returns and Allowances

(5000) COST OF GOODS SOLD

5105   Purchases
5110   Purchases Discount
5115   Purchases Returns and Allowances

(6000) OPERATING EXPENSES

6105   Advertising Expense
6110   Cash Short and Over
6115   Credit Card Fee Expense
6120   Depreciation Expense—Office Equipment
6125   Depreciation Expense—Warehouse Equipment
6130   Insurance Expense
6135   Miscellaneous Expense
6140   Payroll Taxes Expense
6145   Rent Expense
6150   Repairs Expense
6155   Salary Expense
6160   Supplies Expense
6165   Uncollectible Accounts Expense
6170   Utilities Expense
6200   Income Tax Expense
6205   Federal Income Tax Expense

(7000) OTHER REVENUE

7105   Interest Income
7110   Rent Income
7115   Gain on Plant Assets

(8000) OTHER EXPENSES

8105   Interest Expense
8110   Loss on Plant Assets

Subsidiary Ledgers

Accounts Receivable Ledger

110   Bakery Depot
120   Ferndale Café
130   Hilltop Hospital
140   Huang Restaurant
150   Northside Catering
160   Rao Deli

Accounts Payable Ledger

210   Bok Supply Company
220   Dreyfus Company
230   Glommen Company
240   Hilton Supply
250   Sarr Corp.
260   Winona Manufacturing

Recording Transactions

The December 1, 20X4, account balances for the general and subsidiary ledgers are given in the *Working Papers*. Transactions from the period December 1 through December 23 have already been journalized and individual items have been posted.

INSTRUCTIONS

1. Journalize the following transactions completed during the last week in December of the current year. Restaurant Warehouse offers sales terms of 2/10, n/30. The sales tax rate is 6%. Post the following transactions when journalized: (1) transactions affecting the accounts receivable or accounts payable subsidiary ledgers, (2) transactions recorded in the general journal, and (3) amounts entered in a general amount column of the cash payments and cash receipts journals. Source documents are abbreviated as follows: check, C; memorandum, M; purchase invoice, P; receipt, R; sales invoice, S; terminal summary, TS; debit memorandum, DM; credit memorandum, CM; note payable, NP.

Dec. 26. Received cash for the maturity value of NR28, a 90-day, 12% note for $11,600.00. R454.

27. Recorded cash and credit card sales, $4,674.00, plus sales tax, $280.44; total, $4,954.44. TS40.

28. Sold merchandise on account to Huang Restaurant, $5,000.00, plus sales tax. S428.

28. Purchased merchandise on account from Dreyfus Company, $12,296.00. P190.

28. Signed a 90-day, 10% note, for $12,000.00 with Northstar National Bank. NP22 and R455.

28. Received cash for sale of a computer, plant asset No. 284, $300.00. M29 and R456. Update the plant asset record and record the sale.

28. Received cash in full payment of Bakery Depot's account, previously written off as uncollectible, $1,896.00. M30 and R457.

29. Paid $1,000.00 on the outstanding balance of the Sarr Corp. account. C343.

29. Issued 500 shares of $10.00 par value common stock at $50.00 per share. R458.

29. Issued 300 shares of 5%, $50.00 par value preferred stock at par value, $15,000.00. R459.

30. Rao Deli dishonored NR29, a 60-day, 12% note, for $6,000.00. M31.

Dec. 30. Recorded payment of credit card fee expense, $836.00. M32.

30. Purchased a work station for use in the office and a forklift for use in the warehouse in a lump-sum transaction, $30,000.00. The work station has an estimated value of $11,000, and the forklift has an estimated value of $22,000.00. C344. Open a plant asset record for each item. Work station: plant asset No. 452; serial number, M251; useful life, 4 years; estimated salvage value, $1,000.00. Forklift: plant asset No. 453; serial number, 124XYG; useful life, 5 years; estimated salvage value, $3,000.00.

31. Paid cash to replenish the petty cash fund, $169.92: supplies, $25.00; advertising, $100.00; miscellaneous, $44.74; cash short, $0.18. C345.

31. Paid cash for semimonthly payroll, $4,413.72 (total payroll, $5,520.00, less deductions: employee income tax, $304.00; social security tax, $342.24; Medicare tax, $80.04; medical insurance, $380.00). C346.

31. Recorded employer payroll taxes, $484.28, for the semimonthly pay period ended December 31. Taxes owed are: social security tax, $342.24; Medicare tax, $80.04; state unemployment tax, $54.00; and federal unemployment tax, $8.00. M33.

31. Recorded cash and credit card sales, $930.00, plus sales tax, $55.80; total, $985.80. TS41.

31. Paid semiannual interest on bonds payable, $1,200.00. C347.

2. Prove and rule the sales journal. Post the totals of the special columns.

3. Total and rule the purchases journal. Post the total.

4. Prove the equality of debits and credits for the cash receipts and cash payments journals.

5. Prove cash. The balance on the next unused check stub is $25,001.40.

6. Rule the cash receipts journal. Post the totals of the special columns.

7. Rule the cash payments journal. Post the totals of the special columns.

8. Prepare a schedule of accounts receivable and a schedule of accounts payable. Prove the accuracy of the subsidiary ledgers by comparing the schedule totals with the balances of the controlling accounts in the general ledger. If the totals are not the same, find and correct the errors.

The ledgers and plant asset records used in Reinforcement Activity 3—Part A are needed to complete Reinforcement Activity—3 Part B.

Chapter 21

Accounting for Accruals, Deferrals, and Reversing Entries

LEARNING OBJECTIVES

After studying Chapter 21, in addition to defining key terms, you will be able to:

LO1 Record the reversing entry for accrued revenue.

LO2 Record an entry to receive payment on a note receivable with accrued interest.

LO3 Calculate accrued interest expense.

LO4 Record the adjusting entry for an accrued expense.

LO5 Record the reversing entry for an accrued expense.

LO6 Record an entry to pay an installment on a note payable with accrued interest.

LO7 Record an entry to receive cash on deferred revenue.

LO8 Calculate the amount and record the entry for deferred revenue when earned.

LO9 Record an entry to pay cash on a deferred expense.

LO10 Calculate the amount and record the entry for a deferred expense when incurred.

©DANIEL KOUREY, ISTOCK/©JIM PRUITT, ISTOCK

PIERREDESVARRE/ISTOCKPHOTO.COM

Accounting In The Real World
USA Today

You've probably heard someone ask, "Did you read *USA Today* today?" *USA Today* is a national newspaper with an average daily circulation of over 1.8 million, not including online subscriptions. *USA Today* is published Monday through Friday. It is known for color-coding its four sections: News (blue), Money (green), Sports (red), and Life (purple).

USA Today has two major sources of revenue: advertising and subscriptions. Both kinds of revenue are collected in advance. *USA Today* collects fees for advertising before the advertisements appear. Customers pay subscriptions for paper delivery or online editions as much as a year in advance. Receiving these fees does not, however, mean that *USA Today* can record the amounts as current revenue.

In accordance with GAAP, advertising fees are recorded as revenue when the advertising is printed or placed on a website. In the same manner, subscription fees are recorded as revenue when purchased newspapers are delivered. When preparing financial statements, accountants at *USA Today* must analyze the money collected from advertising and subscriptions to determine what amount should be recorded as revenue.

CRITICAL THINKING

1. Suppose you purchase a $150 annual subscription to *USA Today* on November 1. How much should *USA Today* recognize as revenue on its December financial statements?

2. Would your answer to question 1 differ if the customer selected online delivery of *USA Today*?

Sources: www.gannett.com; www.wikipedia.com.

Key Terms

- accrual
- deferral
- reversing entry
- accrued expenses
- accrued interest expense
- deferred revenue
- deferred expenses

21-1 Accruals

LO1 Record the reversing entry for accrued revenue.

LO2 Record an entry to receive payment on a note receivable with accrued interest.

LO3 Calculate accrued interest expense.

LO4 Record the adjusting entry for an accrued expense.

LO5 Record the reversing entry for an accrued expense.

LO6 Record an entry to pay an installment on a note payable with accrued interest.

Accruals and Deferrals

Generally accepted accounting principles (GAAP) require that revenue and expenses be recorded in the accounting period in which revenue is earned and expenses are incurred. [CONCEPT: Matching Expenses with Revenue] However, some revenues, such as interest income, are earned each day but are recorded only when the interest is actually received. Likewise, some expenses may be incurred before they are actually paid. For example, a note payable incurs interest expense each day the note is outstanding, but the interest may not be paid until the note's maturity date. An entry recording revenue before the cash is received, or an expense before the cash is paid, is called an **accrual**. An accrual can be illustrated as follows:

Some revenues, such as rental income, are received before they are earned. Some expenses, such as rent expense, are paid before they are incurred. An entry recording the receipt of cash before the related revenue is earned, or payment of cash before the related expense is incurred, is called a **deferral**. A deferral can be illustrated as follows:

Deferral

Cash is recorded when received/paid.	→	Revenue/Expense is recorded in a future period.

Accrual

Revenue/Expense recorded at end of period.	→	Cash is received/paid in a future period.

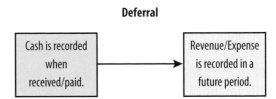

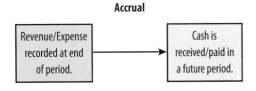

ETHICS IN ACTION

Guarding Intellectual Property

Is it ethical to use file-sharing software to download music from the Internet? Is it ethical to purchase a DVD that you know has been pirated? If you purchase software that allows for three installations, is it ethical to install the software on a friend's computer?

Anything, or any process, that is protected by patent, trademark, or copyright is called **intellectual property**. Music, videos, and computer software are examples of intellectual property. The individual or business that creates intellectual property retains the exclusive right to control the use of the property. The authorized use is

stated in the terms of service, often called the terms of use. When installing computer software, the consumer must agree to the terms of service to proceed with the installation. Violating the terms of service, including the sharing or purchasing of unauthorized copies, is illegal.

Businesses recognize the need to comply with the licensing agreements of computer software. Many companies address this issue in their code of conduct.

INSTRUCTIONS

Do an Internet search to access "Everyday Values," the code of conduct for Harley-Davidson, Inc. What guidance does Harley-Davidson provide its employees about copying software for both business and personal use?

Reversing Entry for Accrued Interest Income LO1

	DATE	ACCOUNT TITLE	DOC. NO.	POST. REF.	DEBIT	CREDIT	
		Adjusting Entries					1
4	31	*Interest Receivable*			1 7 5 00		4
5		*Interest Income*				1 7 5 00	5

GENERAL JOURNAL PAGE **13**

In Chapter 15, ThreeGreen Products, Inc., made an adjusting entry to record accrued interest income. Sun Treasures makes a similar entry for accrued interest income. On December 31, Sun Treasures has one note receivable on hand, a 90-day, 7%, $15,000.00 note dated November 1. Accrued interest on this note is $175.00. Interest Receivable is debited, and Interest Income is credited for this amount, as shown above.

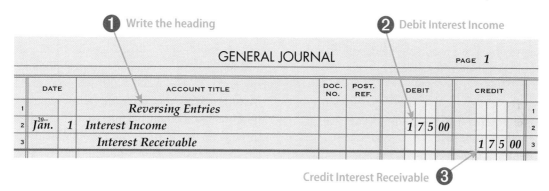

1 Write the heading   **2** Debit Interest Income

GENERAL JOURNAL PAGE **1**

	DATE	ACCOUNT TITLE	DOC. NO.	POST. REF.	DEBIT	CREDIT	
1		*Reversing Entries*					1
2	Jan. 1	*Interest Income*			1 7 5 00		2
3		*Interest Receivable*				1 7 5 00	3

Credit Interest Receivable **3**

On December 31, Interest Income is closed as part of the regular closing entry for income statement accounts with credit balances. Interest Income is debited for $2,512.80 to reduce the account balance to zero.

Interest Income

Dec. 31 Closing	2,512.80	Dec. 31 Unadj. Bal.	2,337.80
Jan. 1 Rev.	175.00	Dec. 31 Adj.	175.00
(New Bal.	175.00)		

Interest Receivable

Dec. 31 Adj.	175.00	Jan. 1 Rev.	175.00
(New Bal.	0.00)		

Adjusting entries for accrued revenues have an effect on transactions that will be recorded in the following fiscal period. On the maturity date of the outstanding 90-day note receivable, Sun Treasures will receive interest of $262.50.

However, an adjusting entry was made to record the amount of interest earned last year, $175.00. Thus, $175.00 of the $262.50 total interest income has already been recorded as revenue. The remaining $87.50 of the $262.50 total interest will be earned during the current fiscal period.

It is not convenient to determine how much, if any, of cash received from notes receivable relates to interest accrued during the prior fiscal period. To avoid this inconvenience, an entry is made at the beginning of the new fiscal period to reverse the adjusting entry. An entry made at the beginning of one fiscal period to reverse an adjusting entry made in the previous fiscal period is called a **reversing entry**.

The reversing entry is the opposite of the adjusting entry. The entry creates a debit balance of $175.00 in Interest Income. A debit balance is the opposite of the normal balance of Interest Income. When the full amount of interest is received, the $262.50 will be credited to Interest Income, resulting in an $87.50 credit balance ($262.50 credit − $175.00 debit), the amount of interest earned in the new year.

The reversing entry reduced the balance in Interest Receivable to zero. When the interest is received, no entry will be made to Interest Receivable. Instead, the total amount of interest received will be credited to Interest Income.

> **Reversing an Adjusting Entry for Accrued Interest Income**
>
> **1** Write the heading, Reversing Entries, in the middle of the general journal's Account Title column. This heading explains all the reversing entries that follow. There is no source document.
>
> **2** Record a debit, $175.00, to Interest Income.
>
> **3** Record a credit, $175.00, to Interest Receivable.

Collecting a Note Receivable with Accrued Interest LO2

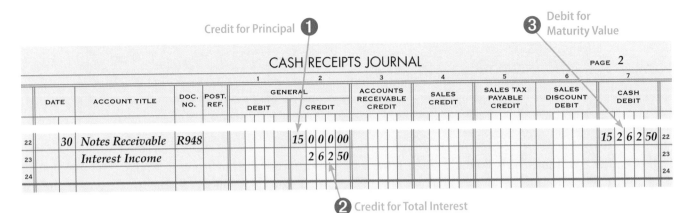

Credit for Principal ❶   ❸ Debit for Maturity Value

CASH RECEIPTS JOURNAL   PAGE 2

	DATE	ACCOUNT TITLE	DOC. NO.	POST. REF.	GENERAL DEBIT	GENERAL CREDIT	ACCOUNTS RECEIVABLE CREDIT	SALES CREDIT	SALES TAX PAYABLE CREDIT	SALES DISCOUNT DEBIT	CASH DEBIT	
22	30	Notes Receivable	R948			15 0 0 0 00					15 2 6 2 50	22
23		Interest Income				2 6 2 50						23
24												24

❷ Credit for Total Interest

On January 30, Sun Treasures received the maturity value of the only note receivable on hand on December 31, the end of the previous fiscal year.

> **January 30. Received cash for the maturity value of a 90-day, 7% note: principal, $15,000.00, plus interest, $262.50; total, $15,262.50. Receipt No. 948.**

Cash

Jan. 30 ⬆ 15,262.50	

Notes Receivable

Nov. 1 15,000.00	Jan. 30 ⬇ 15,000.00

Interest Income

Dec. 31 Closing 2,512.80	Dec. 31 Unadj. Bal. 2,337.80
Jan. 1 Rev. 175.00	Dec. 31 Adj. 175.00
	Jan. 30 ⬆ 262.50
	(New Bal. 87.50)

The total interest, $262.50, was earned during two fiscal periods—$175.00 during the previous fiscal period and $87.50 during the current fiscal period. The reversing entry created a $175.00 debit balance in Interest Income. After the $262.50 credit is posted, Interest Income has a credit balance of $87.50, the amount of interest earned during the current fiscal period. After the $15,000.00 credit is posted, Notes Receivable has a zero balance.

❯ Collecting a Note Receivable with Accrued Interest

❶ Record a credit to Notes Receivable in the General Credit column of the cash receipts journal for the principal of the note, $15,000.00.

❷ Record a credit to Interest Income in the General Credit column for the total interest, $262.50.

❸ Record a debit in the Cash Debit column for the maturity value of the note, $15,262.50.

Careers In Accounting

Jonathon Lopez
ACCOUNTING INSTRUCTOR

IMAGE SOURCE/JUPITER IMAGES

Jonathon Lopez is an accounting instructor at Forest Valley High School. Jonathon always wanted to be a high school teacher. He enjoyed taking accounting in high school and continued studying business in college.

As a secondary teacher, Mr. Lopez develops daily lesson plans and prepares materials for classroom activities. He presents accounting concepts via lectures, discussions, and demonstrations. He also guides students through activities and helps students as they independently complete problems and assignments. Mr. Lopez evaluates his students' growing knowledge of accounting and adjusts his teaching as necessary. Other tasks include grading assignments, administering and grading tests, assigning grades for reporting purposes, coordinating fund-raising activities, and serving as advisor to the Business Professionals of America Club.

Forest Valley School is publically supported, so Mr. Lopez is required by his local administration and by state and federal law to maintain accurate student records. He must plan his teaching so that students fulfill stated objectives for each course he teaches. In addition, he is responsible for establishing and enforcing rules for student behavior and maintaining a good learning environment.

The accounting classroom has an interactive white board and other up-to-date technology. To complete their accounting assignments, students use spreadsheet and accounting software as well as the Internet. Mr. Lopez has been trained on all the technology used in his classroom.

Mr. Lopez teaches both first-year and advanced accounting. He works with local two- and four-year colleges so that when his advanced students finish the course they are allowed to take a college-level test. If the student passes the test, he or she receives college credit for the course.

To keep himself up to date in the accounting field, Mr. Lopez attends conferences and seminars.

He can learn about new accounting rules, discover new resource materials for teaching, and interact with other teachers to exchange ideas.

All members of the Forest Valley High School faculty serve on a school-wide committee and chaperone various student activities. Mr. Lopez also meets with parents for conferences and communicates with parents via e-mail and phone.

Salary Range: The national median range for a secondary teacher in vocational education is $53,000. However, individual salaries vary greatly. Salaries are dependent on local school contracts, level of education completed, and years of teaching experience.

Qualifications: Most states require a four-year bachelor's degree in order to be certified to teach, but there are exceptions to this standard. In order to teach business courses, most degree programs require extensive coursework in the business area. In addition, most states require continuing education units in order to renew a state teaching license.

Occupational Outlook: The growth for secondary vocational educators is projected to be average (7 to 13% for the period from 2008 to 2018).

ACTIVITY

Use the Internet to research the qualifications required in your state to be a secondary teacher. Write a one-page report summarizing your findings.

Source: www.online.onetcenter.org.

©MILENNY, ISTOCK

Analyzing an Adjustment for Accrued Interest Expense LO3, 4

Sun Treasures, Inc. Unadjusted Trial Balance December 31, 20--		
ACCOUNT TITLE	DEBIT	CREDIT
Interest Payable		
Long-term Notes Payable		106 625 67
Interest Expense	17 636 26	

Debit Interest Expense ❶

GENERAL JOURNAL   PAGE 13

	DATE	ACCOUNT TITLE	DOC. NO.	POST. REF.	DEBIT	CREDIT	
1		*Adjusting Entries*					1
18	31	Interest Expense			710 84		18
19		Interest Payable				710 84	19

Credit Interest Payable ❷

Expenses incurred in one fiscal period, but not paid until a later fiscal period, are called **accrued expenses**. At the end of a fiscal period, an accrued expense is recorded by an adjusting entry. [CONCEPT: Matching Expenses with Revenue] The adjusting entry increases an expense account. The adjusting entry also increases a payable account.

Interest incurred but not yet paid is called **accrued interest expense**. On December 31, Sun Treasures has one long-term note payable outstanding. On April 1,

Sun Treasures signed a five-year, 8.0% note payable for $120,000. The terms of the note state that Sun Treasures must make a payment of $2,433.17 on the first of each month. The payment is first applied to the interest for the prior month. Any additional amount reduces the principal of the note. The balance of the note after the December 31 payment is $106,625.67. On December 31, Sun Treasures owes 30 days of accrued interest expense and must make an adjusting entry for this amount.

	Principal	×	Interest Rate	×	Time as Fraction of Year	=	Accrued Interest Expense
	$106,625.67	×	8%	×	30/360	=	$710.84

Before the adjusting entry is made, Interest Expense has a balance of $17,636.26, which represents the interest expense incurred throughout the year on all other debt. In the adjusting entry, Interest Expense is debited for $710.84 to show the increase in the

balance of this Other Expense account. The credit to Interest Payable creates a $710.84 account balance that represents the interest owed on December 31 that will be paid in the next fiscal period, on January 1, 20X2.

After posting, Interest Payable has a credit balance of $710.84 and will appear on the December 31 balance sheet as a current liability. This credit balance is the accrued interest expense incurred but not yet paid at the end of the year. The new balance of Interest Expense, $18,347.10, is the total amount of interest expense incurred during the fiscal period and will appear on the income statement for the year ended December 31 as an Other Expense.

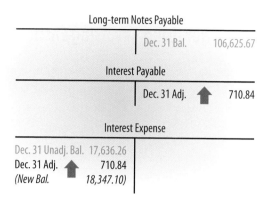

Long-term Notes Payable	
	Dec. 31 Bal. 106,625.67

Interest Payable	
	Dec. 31 Adj. ▲ 710.84

Interest Expense	
Dec. 31 Unadj. Bal. 17,636.26	
Dec. 31 Adj. ▲ 710.84	
(New Bal. 18,347.10)	

Recording an Adjusting Entry for Accrued Interest Expense

1. Record a debit, $710.84, to Interest Expense.
2. Record a credit, $710.84, to Interest Payable.

remember The Interest Payable account appears in the Current Liabilities section of the balance sheet. The Interest Expense account appears in the Other Expenses section of the income statement.

Reversing Entry for Accrued Interest Expense LO5

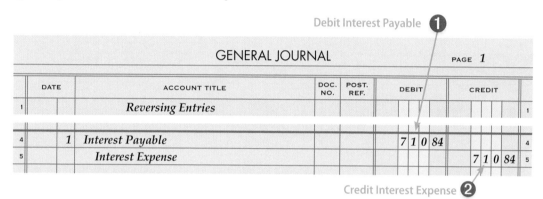

Debit Interest Payable ❶

	DATE	ACCOUNT TITLE	DOC. NO.	POST. REF.	DEBIT	CREDIT	
1		*Reversing Entries*					1
4	1	*Interest Payable*			7 1 0 84		4
5		*Interest Expense*				7 1 0 84	5

GENERAL JOURNAL — PAGE 1

Credit Interest Expense ❷

On December 31, Interest Expense is closed as part of the regular closing entries. Interest Expense is credited for $18,347.10 to reduce the account balance to zero. After the closing entry is posted, the Interest Expense account is closed.

Interest Expense	
Dec. 31 Unadj. Bal. 17,636.26	Dec. 31 Closing 18,347.10
Dec. 31 Adj. 710.84	Jan. 1 Rev. ▼ 710.84
	(New Bal. 710.84)

Interest Payable	
Jan. 1 Rev. ▼ 710.84	Dec. 31 Adj. 710.84
(New Bal. 0.00)	

Adjusting entries for accrued expenses have an effect on transactions to be recorded in the following fiscal period. For example, on January 1, Sun Treasures will pay the monthly payment which will decrease the principal balance and pay the interest of $710.84.

However, an adjusting entry was made to record the amount of accrued interest expense last year, $710.84. Thus, the total interest expense was incurred and recorded in the previous year.

Having to remember that the cash paid for interest is for accrued interest expense is an inconvenience. To avoid the inconvenience, a reversing entry is made at the beginning of the new fiscal period.

The reversing entry is the opposite of the adjusting entry. The entry creates a credit balance of $710.84 in Interest Expense. A credit balance is the opposite of the normal balance of the Interest Expense account. When the interest is paid, $710.84 will be debited to Interest Expense. The account will then have a zero balance.

The reversing entry to Interest Payable reduces that account to a zero balance. Thus, when the interest is paid, no debit entry will be required to recognize payment of the balance of Interest Payable. The total amount of interest paid will be debited to Interest Expense.

Reversing an Adjusting Entry for Accrued Interest Expense

1. Record a debit, $710.84, to Interest Payable in the general journal.
2. Record a credit, $710.84, to Interest Expense.

Effect of Not Using Reversing Entries

Reversing entries are not required in accounting. A company can choose to use reversing entries or not. If Sun Treasures did not use a reversing entry for accrued interest expense, there is a possibility that the interest could be reported twice. The $710.84 amount is recorded once as an adjusting entry to Interest Expense in the previous fiscal period. The amount could be recorded a second time as a debit to Interest Expense in the current fiscal period when the note is paid. The double charge will be avoided only if accounting personnel remember that the interest chargeable to the previous

fiscal period should be recorded as a debit to Interest Payable, not to Interest Expense. In large companies with hundreds of accounts, making sure that these double charges do not occur can be difficult.

Companies that choose to use reversing entries do not want to force their accountants to have to go back and check prior entries when notes are paid or received in the next period. Like other companies that use reversing entries, Sun Treasures records a reversing entry whenever an adjusting entry creates a balance in an asset or a liability account that initially had a zero balance.

Paying an Installment Note Payable with Accrued Interest LO6

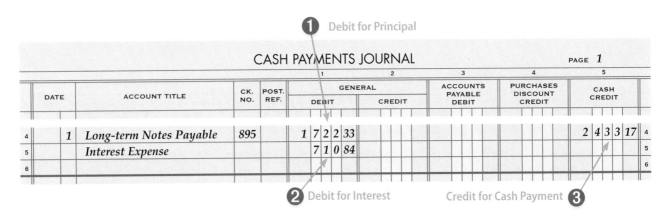

January 1. Paid cash for the monthly payment on the long-term note payable: principal, $1,722.33, plus interest, $710.84; total, $2,433.17. Check No. 895.

Sun Treasures is required to make monthly cash payments of $2,433.17. The difference between the total cash paid and the amount of interest expense is the amount by which the principal is reduced. The principal balance of the notes payable will be reduced $1,722.33 by the January 1 payment.

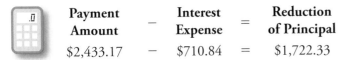

Payment Amount	−	Interest Expense	=	Reduction of Principal
$2,433.17	−	$710.84	=	$1,722.33

The total interest, $710.84, was incurred during the previous fiscal period. The reversing entry created a $710.84 credit balance in Interest Expense. After the $710.84 debit is recorded, Interest Expense has a zero balance.

Not all notes payable require a monthly payment, which covers interest expense for the month plus a

reduction in principal. Some notes payable are paid in full on the maturity date of the note. If the maturity date is in a different fiscal period than when the note was signed, an adjusting entry is required at the end of the fiscal period to record accrued interest expense. The accrued interest expense would cover the number of days between the issue date of the note and the end of the period. The reversing entry and the entry to show the payment of the maturity value would be the same as the note payable illustrated in this lesson.

> **Paying an Installment Note Payable with Accrued Interest**
>
> ❶ Record a debit to Long-term Notes Payable in the General Debit column for the reduction of principal, $1,722.33.
>
> ❷ Record a debit to Interest Expense in the General Debit column for the total interest, $710.84.
>
> ❸ Record a credit to Cash in the Cash Credit column for the monthly payment amount, $2,433.17.

Analyzing Accruals

The adjusting entries for accrued revenue and accrued expenses must be recorded at the end of a fiscal period in order for the financial statements to be accurate. Each accrual entry affects a balance sheet account and an income statement account. If an accrual entry is not recorded, both the balance sheet and the income statement will be incorrect.

Since accrual entries do not involve an outside business or customer, Sun Treasures must remember to record these entries. When determining its accrued revenue, Sun Treasures must include all forms of revenue earned but not yet received. This lesson illustrated accrued interest income. There are many other forms of accrued revenue. A utility company that bills its customers in January for utilities it supplied in December records an entry for estimated revenue earned in December even though the cash will not be received until January. Some rental agreements allow the renter to pay in the following month. The company renting the property must record rent earned in December even though the cash will not be received until January.

In a similar manner, when determining its accrued expenses, Sun Treasures must include all forms of expenses incurred but not yet paid. This lesson illustrated accrued interest expense. There are many other forms of accrued expenses. Payroll is an accrued expense for many companies. If a company pays its employees two weeks after the end of a payroll period, on December 31, that company will owe two weeks of wages. An accrued expense must be recorded. If a renter is allowed to pay December rent on January 15, the renter must record an accrued expense for the December rent incurred but not yet paid.

remember The adjusting entry for accrued interest income affects both the income statement and the balance sheet. The income statement will report all income for the period even though some of the income has not yet been received. The balance sheet will report all assets, including the accrued income receivable.

remember The adjusting entry for accrued interest expense affects both the income statement and the balance sheet. The income statement will report all expenses for the period even though some of the expenses have not yet been paid. The balance sheet will report all liabilities, including the accrued expenses payable. [CONCEPT: Adequate Disclosure]

WHY ACCOUNTING?

Government's Role in Regulating Accounting Practices

Government & Public Administration

Government, both federal and state, plays a very important role in the regulation of the field of accounting. From the establishment of GAAP to the criteria for becoming a CPA, federal and/or state laws must be followed. It is critical that lawmakers and policy setters have an understanding of accounting in order to make laws that enable the desired outcome.

Sometimes laws are a result of an event that had a tremendous impact on society. The Securities Act of 1933 was the first federal legislation to regulate the offer and sale of securities. The Securities Exchange Act of 1934 established the Securities and Exchange Commission. Both of these acts were enacted in response to the stock market crash of 1929. The Sarbanes-Oxley Act of 2002 (SOX) set new standards for boards of directors, company management, and public accounting firms. The law was enacted in direct response to a number of major accounting scandals. SOX addresses many issues including auditor independence, internal control, and financial disclosure. It is the intent of the government that these laws will prevent stock market crashes and accounting scandals in the future.

CRITICAL THINKING

Research either the Securities Act of 1933, the Securities Exchange Act of 1934, or the Sarbanes-Oxley Act of 2002 and do the following:

1. Formulate questions to analyze the event that led to the formation of the law.
2. Gather and list relevant sources of information to answer the questions.
3. Determine the reliability of the sources.
4. Present an oral or written report stating how the law serves to prevent the same event from happening in the future.

LO1 Record the reversing entry for accrued revenue.

LO2 Record an entry to receive payment on a note receivable with accrued interest.

LO3 Calculate accrued interest expense.

LO4 Record the adjusting entry for an accrued expense.

LO5 Record the reversing entry for an accrued expense.

LO6 Record an entry to pay an installment on a note payable with accrued interest.

Terms Review

accrual

deferral

reversing entry

accrued expenses

accrued interest expense

Audit your understanding

1. Which accounting concept is being applied when an adjusting entry is made at the end of the fiscal period to record accrued revenue?

2. Why does a business use reversing entries as part of its procedures for accounting for accrued interest expense?

Work together 21-1

Journalizing entries for accruals

Accounting forms and a partial unadjusted trial balance for Kufas Corporation are given in the *Working Papers*. After each journal entry, update the T accounts given in the *Working Papers*. Your instructor will guide you through the following examples.

On December 31, 20X1, Kufas Corporation has one note receivable outstanding, a 120-day, 6%, $10,000.00 note dated November 16, and one note payable outstanding, a 90-day, 6%, $12,000.00 note dated December 1.

1. Journalize the adjusting entries for accrued interest income and accrued interest expense on December 31. Use page 14 of a general journal.

2. Journalize the closing entries for interest income and interest expense using page 14 of a general journal.

3. Journalize the January 1, 20X2, reversing entries for accrued interest income and accrued interest expense on page 15 of a general journal.

4. Journalize the payment of cash for the maturity value of the note payable on March 1, 20X2. Check No. 478. Use page 25 of a cash payments journal.

5. Journalize the receipt of cash for the maturity value of the note receivable on March 16, 20X2. Receipt No. 278. Use page 16 of a cash receipts journal.

6. List the amount of interest income from this note receivable that will be shown on the income statements for 20X1 and 20X2.

7. List the amount of interest expense from this note payable that will be shown on the income statements for 20X1 and 20X2.

On your own 21-1

Journalizing entries for accruals

Accounting forms and a partial unadjusted trial balance for Craven, Inc., are given in the *Working Papers*. After each journal entry, update the T accounts given in the *Working Papers*. Work this problem independently.

On December 31, 20X1, Craven, Inc., has one note receivable outstanding, a 90-day, 10%, $12,000.00 note dated December 1, and one note payable outstanding, a 180-day, 5%, $20,000.00 note dated October 17.

1. Journalize the adjusting entries for accrued interest income and accrued interest expense on December 31. Use page 14 of a general journal.

2. Journalize the closing entries for interest income and interest expense using page 14 of a general journal.

©CANDICE CUSACK, ISTOCK

On your own 21-1 (Continued)

3. Journalize the January 1, 20X2, reversing entries for accrued interest income and accrued interest expense on page 15 of a general journal.

4. Journalize the receipt of cash for the maturity value of the note receivable on March 1, 20X2. Receipt No. 241. Use page 19 of a cash receipts journal.

5. Journalize the payment of cash for the maturity value of the note payable on April 15, Check No. 512. Use page 30 of a cash payments journal.

6. List the amount of interest income from this note receivable that will be shown on the income statements for 20X1 and 20X2.

7. List the amount of interest expense from this note payable that will be shown on the income statements for 20X1 and 20X2.

LESSON
21-2 Deferrals

LO7 Record an entry to receive cash on deferred revenue.

LO8 Calculate the amount and record the entry for deferred revenue when earned.

LO9 Record an entry to pay cash on a deferred expense.

LO10 Calculate the amount and record the entry for a deferred expense when incurred.

Recording Revenue Received in Advance LO7

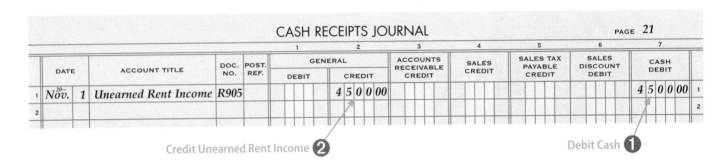

Credit Unearned Rent Income **2**   Debit Cash **1**

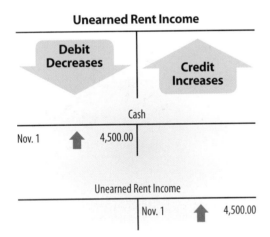

Unearned Rent Income

Debit Decreases

Credit Increases

Cash

Nov. 1 ↑ 4,500.00

Unearned Rent Income

Nov. 1 ↑ 4,500.00

Sun Treasures rents its store space. The lease allows Sun Treasures to sublease extra space. In November, Sun Treasures signs an agreement to sublease a portion of the store space to Cones N More, an ice cream business.

November 1. Received cash for three months' rent in advance, $4,500.00. Receipt No. 905.

Sun Treasures has received cash, but has not yet earned income. Cash received for goods or services which have not yet been provided is called **deferred revenue**. Deferred revenue is sometimes called *unearned revenue*. Deferred revenue is a liability until the services have been provided. Sun Treasures has incurred a liability to provide store space to Cones N More. Therefore, a liability account, Unearned Rent Income, is used to record the cash received in advance. Unearned Rent Income is a liability account with a normal credit balance. It is increased by a credit and decreased by a debit.

⊗ Recording Revenue Received in Advance

1 Record a debit to Cash in the Cash Debit column of the cash receipts journal for the cash received, $4,500.00.

2 Record a credit to Unearned Rent Income in the General Credit column for the total liability, $4,500.00.

Recording Adjusting Entry for Deferred Revenue Earned LO8

Debit Unearned Rent Income **1**

	DATE		ACCOUNT TITLE	DOC. NO.	POST. REF.	DEBIT	CREDIT	
1			*Adjusting Entries*					1
20	20	31	*Unearned Rent Income*			3 0 0 0 00		20
21			*Rent Income*				3 0 0 0 00	21

GENERAL JOURNAL   PAGE **13**

Credit Rent Income **2**

Sun Treasures will earn rent income each day that it allows Cones N More to use its store space. It is not practical to record this revenue every day. However, any rent income earned by the end of the fiscal period must be shown on the financial statements. Therefore, Sun Treasures makes an adjusting entry on December 31 to show how much rent income has been earned to date. Sun Treasures has earned two months' rent and must make an adjusting entry for this amount.

Total Rent Received	÷	Number of Months	=	Rent per Month
$4,500.00	÷	3	=	$1,500.00

Rent per Month	×	Months Earned	=	Amount of Adjustment
$1,500.00	×	2	=	$3,000.00

Sun Treasures will record this income in a separate income account, Rent Income. Rent Income increases with a credit and decreases with a debit. Unearned Rent Income is debited for $3,000.00 to reduce this liability account by the amount of rent income earned. Rent Income is credited for the same amount, $3,000.00.

After this entry is posted, Unearned Rent Income will have a balance of $1,500.00, which represents one month of rent that is still unearned. Because this entry does not establish a balance in a payable or receivable account, no reversing entry will be necessary.

> **Recording the Adjusting Entry for Deferred Revenue Earned**
>
> **1** Record a debit, $3,000.00, to Unearned Rent Income in the general journal.
>
> **2** Record a credit, $3,000.00, to Rent Income.

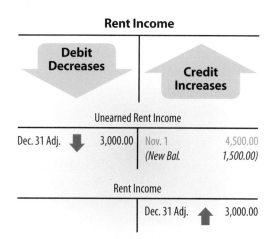

Rent Income

Debit Decreases	Credit Increases

Unearned Rent Income

| Dec. 31 Adj. | 3,000.00 | Nov. 1 | 4,500.00 |
| | | (New Bal. | 1,500.00) |

Rent Income

| | Dec. 31 Adj. | 3,000.00 |

remember

When cash is received before the related revenue has been earned, the revenue must be deferred until it is earned.

Recording an Expense Paid in Advance LO9

Debit Prepaid Rent ❶   Credit Cash ❷

CASH PAYMENTS JOURNAL

PAGE 1

	DATE	ACCOUNT TITLE	CK. NO.	POST. REF.	GENERAL DEBIT	GENERAL CREDIT	ACCOUNTS PAYABLE DEBIT	PURCHASES DISCOUNT CREDIT	CASH CREDIT	
1	Nov. 1	Prepaid Rent	231		4 5 0 0 00				4 5 0 0 00	1

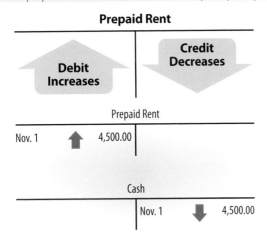

Prepaid Rent

Debit Increases | Credit Decreases

Prepaid Rent

Nov. 1 ⬆ 4,500.00

Cash

Nov. 1 ⬇ 4,500.00

When Cones N More paid $4,500.00 to Sun Treasures for three months' rent in advance, it was deferred revenue for Sun Treasures. This required Sun Treasures to record the amount initially as a liability and to defer calling it income until it was earned. Cones N More also records an entry for the transaction.

November 1. Paid cash for three months' rent in advance, $4,500.00. Check No. 231.

Cones N More will eventually record the rent as an expense. But the rent is not an expense at the time of payment because the expense will be incurred over the three-month period. Payments for goods or services which have not yet been received are called **deferred expenses**. Deferred expenses are often listed as *prepaid expenses* (see page 163). Deferred expenses are assets until the services have been received. Therefore, Cones N More records an asset, Prepaid Rent, at the time the rent is paid. Prepaid Rent is increased on the debit side and decreased on the credit side.

> ↘ **Recording an Expense Paid in Advance**

❶ Record a debit to Prepaid Rent in the General Debit column of the cash payments journal for the rent paid in advance, $4,500.00.

❷ Record a credit to Cash in the Cash Credit column for the cash paid, $4,500.00.

FINANCIAL LITERACY

What Is a Good Credit Risk?

When a creditor lends money, it wants to be sure it will get repaid. While each lender is unique, most use some variation of the five C's of credit to help determine the creditworthiness of the borrower before approving a loan.

1. Character—What is the borrower's general attitude about payment obligations? What is the educational background?

2. Capacity—What is the capacity to repay the loan? Checking previous payment history and comparing income against debt help assess the ability to repay.

3. Capital—What is the borrower's net worth—total assets minus total debt? Usually the greater the capital, the greater the ability to repay.

4. Collateral—What assets is the borrower willing to pledge as a guarantee of repayment?

5. Conditions—What are the current economic conditions? Is the borrower's source of income secure?

By determining creditworthiness, the lender reduces the likelihood of default on the debt and reduces the amount of its uncollectable accounts.

ACTIVITIES

1. Assume you are a small business owner. Create your own credit application including ten questions that would help you ensure creditworthiness.

2. If you had to pick the top three C's of credit, which three do you think are the best predictors of creditworthiness? Explain why.

Recording Adjusting Entry for Deferred Expenses Incurred LO10

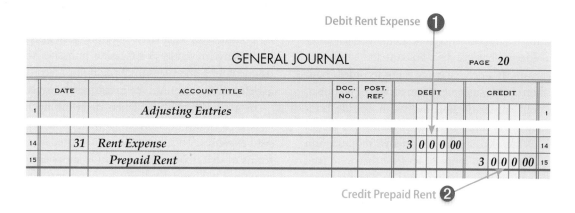

Debit Rent Expense ❶

GENERAL JOURNAL   PAGE 20

	DATE	ACCOUNT TITLE	DOC. NO.	POST. REF.	DEBIT	CREDIT	
1		*Adjusting Entries*					1
14	31	*Rent Expense*			3 0 0 0 00		14
15		*Prepaid Rent*				3 0 0 0 00	15

Credit Prepaid Rent ❷

Cones N More will incur rent expense each day it is allowed to use store space. It is not practical to record this expense every day. However, any rent expense incurred by the end of the fiscal period must be shown on the financial statements. Therefore, Cones N More makes an adjusting entry on December 31 to show how much rent expense has been incurred to date. Cones N More has *used* two months' rent and must make an adjusting entry for this amount.

Total Rent Paid	÷	Number of Months	=	Rent per Month
$4,500.00	÷	3	=	$1,500.00

Rent per Month	×	Months Incurred	=	Amount of Adjustment
$1,500.00	×	2	=	$3,000.00

Cones N More will record this adjustment in the expense account, Rent Expense. Rent Expense is debited for $3,000.00 to show the amount of this adjustment for November and December. Prepaid Rent is credited for $3,000.00 to reduce this asset by the amount of rent expense incurred.

After this entry is posted, Prepaid Rent will have a balance of $1,500.00, which represents one month of rent that is still prepaid. Because this entry does not establish a balance in a payable or receivable account, no reversing entry will be necessary.

> **Recording the Adjusting Entry for Deferred Expenses Incurred**
>
> ❶ Record a debit, $3,000.00, to Rent Expense in the general journal.
>
> ❷ Record a credit, $3,000.00, to Prepaid Rent.

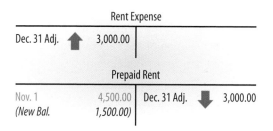

Rent Expense

Dec. 31 Adj. ↑	3,000.00	

Prepaid Rent

| Nov. 1 | 4,500.00 | Dec. 31 Adj. ↓ | 3,000.00 |
| (New Bal. | 1,500.00) | | |

remember When cash is paid in advance for a future expense, the expense is deferred until it is actually incurred.

Analyzing Deferrals

The adjusting entries for deferred revenue and deferred expenses must be recorded at the end of a fiscal period in order for the financial statements to be accurate. Each entry for a deferral affects a balance sheet account and an income statement account. If a deferral entry is not recorded, both the balance sheet and the income statement will be incorrect.

Since deferral entries do not involve an outside business or customer, the company must remember to record these entries. When determining its deferred revenue, Sun Treasures must include all forms of revenue that were paid for previously and have now been earned. While this lesson illustrated deferred rent revenue, there are many other kinds of deferred revenue. For example, a law firm that is retained by a business for legal services for one year, paid in advance, has deferred revenue. A magazine publisher who receives payment for a one-year subscription must record the receipt as deferred revenue until the magazines are issued.

In a similar manner, when determining its deferred expenses, Cones N More must include all forms of prepaid expenses. This lesson illustrated prepaid rent. Other forms of deferred expenses include supplies and prepaid insurance, which were discussed in Chapters 6 and 15.

THINK LIKE AN ACCOUNTANT

Estimating Product Costs

In the comedy classic *Father of the Bride*, actor Steve Martin's character, George Banks, has had enough. Faced with the reality of his daughter's extravagant wedding expenses, he escapes to the grocery store to buy hot dogs for dinner. Standing in front of the bread isle, he tears four buns from the package. The following interaction ensues.

> *Stock Boy*: What are you doing?
> *George Banks*: I'll tell you what I'm doing. I want to buy eight hot dogs and eight hot dog buns to go with them. But no one sells eight hot dog buns. They only sell twelve hot dog buns. So I end up paying for four buns I don't need. So I am removing the superfluous buns.
> *Stock Boy*: But I'm sorry sir, you're going to have to pay for all twelve buns. They're not marked individually.
> *George Banks*: Yeah. And you want to know why? Because some big-shot over at the wiener company got together with some big-shot over at the bun company and decided to rip off the American public.

George Banks' dilemma is not that uncommon in business. Merchandise is often packaged in a quantity that results in unneeded extras. When those extras go unused, their cost has to be considered when making business decisions.

Dave's Dogs is a local institution and favorite with local college students. Alumni returning for football games dream of devouring one of Dave's special hot dogs. So Dave rents concession booths at football games. But Dave faces some of the same problems as George Banks. Hot dogs come in packages of 100. Hot dog buns are packaged by the dozen.

Based on the weather, the opponent, and the success of the team, Dave estimates how many hot dogs he will sell. But Dave has asked you to help determine a better way of determining the quantity of merchandise he needs to order as well as the number of employees he must hire.

OPEN THE SPREADSHEET TLA_CH21

The worksheet contains an incomplete schedule containing relevant assumptions. Comments provide detailed explanation of each assumption. Use the data to answer following questions:

1. Determine Dave's operating income if he estimates game attendance at 28,000, 30,000, and 32,000, assuming he sells every hot dog.

2. What is the cost per hot dog if Dave estimates game attendance at 38,000, 40,000, and 42,000?

3. Provide Dave with an explanation of why the cost per hot dog changes. Support your answer.

©DAN BACHMAN, ISTOCK

LO7 Record an entry to receive cash on deferred revenue.

LO8 Calculate the amount and record the entry for deferred revenue when earned.

LO9 Record an entry to pay cash on a deferred expense.

LO10 Calculate the amount and record the entry for a deferred expense when incurred.

Terms Review

deferred revenue

deferred expenses

Audit your understanding

1. When a business receives cash for services that will be performed in the future, what type of account is credited?

2. The adjusting entry for deferred expenses that have now been incurred includes a debit to what type of account?

Work together 21-2

Journalizing entries for deferrals

The appropriate accounting forms are given in the *Working Papers*. After each journal entry, update the T accounts given in the *Working Papers*. Your instructor will guide you through the following examples.

1. Journalize the following transactions for Boje Law Firm.

    Sept. 1. Signed a contract to provide legal services to Johnson Corporation for six months. Received cash in advance, $12,000.00. R345.

    Dec. 31. Journalized the adjusting entry for legal services performed for Johnson Corporation.

2. Journalize the following transactions for Johnson Corporation.

    Sept. 1. Signed a contract to receive legal services from Boje Law Firm for six months. Paid cash in advance, $12,000.00. C672.

    Dec. 31. Journalized the adjusting entry for expense incurred for legal services provided by Boje Law Firm.

3. What is the balance in the Prepaid Legal Fees account? What does it represent?

On your own 21-2

Journalizing entries for deferrals

The appropriate accounting forms are given in the *Working Papers*. After each journal entry, update the T accounts given in the *Working Papers*. Work this problem independently.

1. Journalize the following transactions for Smythe Manufacturing.

    Nov. 1. Signed a contract to lease excess warehouse space to Fredrickson Company for six months. Received cash in advance, $9,000.00. R487.

    Dec. 31. Journalized the adjusting entry for rent earned.

2. Journalize the following transactions for Fredrickson Company.

    Nov. 1. Signed a contract to lease a warehouse from Smythe Manufacturing for six months. Paid cash in advance, $9,000.00. C212.

    Dec. 31. Journalized the adjusting entry for rent expense.

3. What is the balance in the Prepaid Rent account? What does it represent?

©CANDICE CUSACK, ISTOCK

A Look at Accounting Software

Maintaining Vendor Information and Setting up a Loan

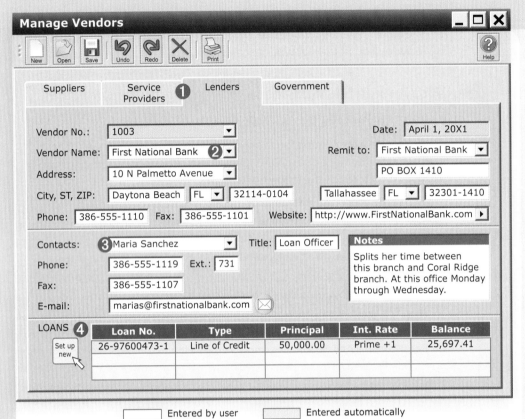

Manage Vendors

| | New | Open | Save | Undo | Redo | Delete | Print | Help |

Tabs: Suppliers | Service Providers ❶ | Lenders | Government

Vendor No.: 1003
Vendor Name: ❷ First National Bank
Address: 10 N Palmetto Avenue
City, ST, ZIP: Daytona Beach FL 32114-0104
Phone: 386-555-1110   Fax: 386-555-1101   Website: http://www.FirstNationalBank.com

Date: April 1, 20X1
Remit to: First National Bank
PO BOX 1410
Tallahassee FL 32301-1410

Contacts: ❸ Maria Sanchez   Title: Loan Officer
Phone: 386-555-1119   Ext.: 731
Fax: 386-555-1107
E-mail: marias@firstnationalbank.com

Notes
Splits her time between this branch and Coral Ridge branch. At this office Monday through Wednesday.

LOANS ❹   Set up new

Loan No.	Type	Principal	Int. Rate	Balance
26-97600473-1	Line of Credit	50,000.00	Prime +1	25,697.41

☐ Entered by user   ☐ Entered automatically

❶ Different types of vendors require different kinds of information. The user has selected the Lenders tab in the Manage Vendors window. The top two sections of the tab are similar for all vendor types; however, the bottom section is unique to lenders.

❷ The user has selected First National Bank from the Vendor Name drop-down menu. The system enters the vendor number automatically. The vendor could also have been selected by number. When a new vendor is added, the system enters the same information in the Remit to cells by default. However, if the vendor has a different address for receiving payments, the information can be changed as it has been for First National Bank.

❸ Multiple contacts, each with their own contact information, can be entered for each vendor. Contacts are selected from the drop-down menu. Clicking the button at the end of the e-mail address opens a new message to the contact in the user's e-mail program.

❹ Loans owed to this vendor are listed in this section. Currently, Sun Treasures has a $50,000.00 line of credit with First National Bank. As of April 1, there is a $25,697.41 balance drawn on the line of credit. Sun Treasures has just signed a new loan with the bank and is now setting it up in the accounting system.

In a manual accounting system, customer and vendor information might be kept in a file cabinet. Since many individuals in the business might need access to that information, it is often duplicated and kept in several different offices. Computerized accounting systems make it easy to provide customer and vendor information to everyone in the organization who has access to the accounting system.

To protect the integrity of the data in a computerized accounting system, users are assigned limited rights to access it. For example, sales reps might be given the right to view customer and vendor information but have no authority to enter or change it. An accounting clerk in the payroll department can be given the authority to enter or edit payroll data, but not purchasing or sales data. The controller would likely have full access to the system.

This feature focuses on maintaining vendor information. Businesses rely on different kinds of vendors. Suppliers provide the merchandise and supplies that merchandising businesses need to operate. Service providers include advertisers, insurance companies, utilities, maintenance personnel, financial services, data services, etc. Lenders are a type of service provider, but the need to track individual loans and their repayment requirements makes lenders unique. There are several types of vendors that fall into the general category of government. These are taxing authorities, as well as licensing and regulatory agencies, at federal, state, and local levels.

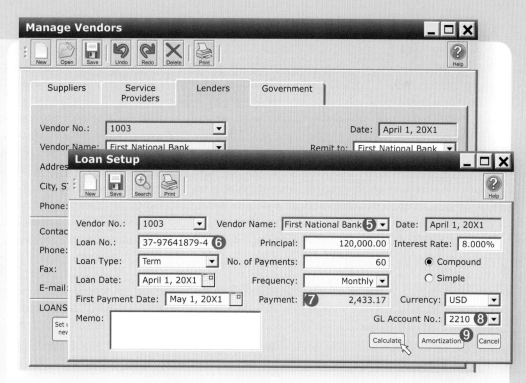

⑤ Because the user launched the Loan Setup pop-up window from the First National Bank vendor tab, the system automatically fills in the vendor name and number. If Loan Setup had been launched from the Banking module, the user would then select the lender from the drop-down menu.

⑥ The user completes all the other fields in the pop-up window except for the amount of the payment. This loan is a $120,000.00, five-year, 8% compound interest term loan requiring monthly payments beginning on May 1. USD is the international banking symbol for the U.S. dollar.

⑦ After entering the loan information, the user clicks the Calculate button. The system computes and enters the payment amount, $2,433.17. This amount would be confirmed with the loan document. If the amount were different, the user could overwrite the amount to match the loan document.

⑧ The user must enter a general ledger account number before the system will complete the loan setup.

⑨ If the user wants an amortization schedule for this loan, clicking the Amortization button will open the schedule, which can then be printed, saved, and even e-mailed, if desired. A recurring transaction could be set up to partially or fully automate the monthly payment on the loan. Monthly payments can be made either through the Write Checks window or by electronic funds transfer from the Banking module.

Chapter Summary

Accrued revenue must be recorded as an adjusting entry at the end of a fiscal period. The adjusting entry increases a receivable account and a revenue account. The adjusting entry for accrued interest income can be reversed by a reversing entry. A reversing entry makes it easier for accounting personnel to record the receipt of the interest, which could come many months later. The reversing entry establishes a debit balance in the Interest Income account. When the interest is received, the total interest received is credited to the Interest Income account. The new balance in the account reflects the amount of interest income earned in the current period.

An accrued expense must also be recorded as an adjusting entry at the end of a fiscal period. The adjusting entry increases a payable account and an expense account. The adjusting entry for accrued interest expense can be reversed by a reversing entry. The reversing entry establishes a credit balance in the Interest Expense account. When the interest is paid, the total interest paid is debited to the Interest Expense account. The new balance in the account reflects the amount of interest expense incurred in the current period.

Deferred revenue and deferred expenses occur when money is transferred before goods or services are provided. The company receiving the cash records a liability representing unearned income. The company paying the cash records an asset representing a prepaid expense. Both companies must record an adjusting entry at the end of the fiscal period. The company providing the goods or service will decrease the liability account and increase an income account. The company receiving the goods or service will decrease the asset account and increase an expense account.

DLEWIS33/ISTOCKPHOTO.COM

The Annual Report and the 10-K— Financial Information and More

Corporations publish annual reports to communicate the results of operations to interested parties, such as stockholders, creditors, and government agencies. Most companies post a copy of this report on their website. An annual report has two main sections:

1. *Management's Discussion and Analysis.* This section provides management with an opportunity to promote the corporation. Through the use of pictures, graphs, and narrative, management can highlight the achievements of the past fiscal year and present its plans for the future. Discussions of environmental and recycling programs, for example, could demonstrate how the corporation is socially responsible.

2. *Financial Statements.* The financial statements section contains several items in addition to basic financial statements. Most of the additional items are required by GAAP or the Securities and Exchange Commission. As a result, these items are similar among corporations.

   a. *Notes to the Financial Statements.* The notes contain additional, detailed information about items presented on the financial statements. For example, the note related to long-term debt would include the projected loan repayments for the next five years.

   b. *Auditor's Report.* The report of the independent auditor states that a public accounting firm has tested the financial statements for accuracy and fair presentation. The report gives the reader confidence to use the financial statements to make business decisions.

   c. *Financial Analysis.* Summary financial information, such as total assets, net income, and common financial ratios, are presented for several years. Company management is responsible for preparing and issuing the annual report.

Corporations are also required to file a yearly report to the Securities and Exchange Commission (SEC), called the 10-K. The SEC, in its role as regulator, sets forth specific requirements as to what is included in a 10-K filing. Besides the financial statements, the 10-K also includes detailed information about the business, its properties, executive compensation, fixed assets, organizational structure, and subsidiaries. Many companies are combining the annual report and the 10-K into one document which is given to all stockholders.

INSTRUCTIONS

Access an annual report using a library or the Internet and prepare a detailed outline of its contents. Summarize the major topics in *Management's Discussion and Analysis.* Did management do a good job of "putting its best foot forward?" Would you recommend that a friend purchase the corporation's stock? Support your answers.

Apply Your Understanding

INSTRUCTIONS: Download problem instructions for Excel, QuickBooks, and Peachtree from the textbook companion website at www.C21accounting.com.

21-1 Application Problem: Journalizing entries for accruals LO1, 2, 3, 4, 5, 6

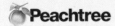**Peachtree**

1. Journalize and post adjusting and closing entries to the general journal.
2. Print the general journal and trial balance.
3. Journalize and post reversing entries.
4. Journalize and post notes payable and notes receivable transactions.

Quick Books

1. Journalize and post adjusting and closing entries to the journal.
2. Print the journal and trial balance.
3. Journalize and post reversing entries.
4. Journalize and post notes payable and notes receivable transactions.

1. Journalize and post adjusting, closing and reversing entries to the general journal.
2. Journalize and post notes payable and notes receivable transactions.
3. Print the worksheets.

Accounting forms and a partial unadjusted trial balance for Spano Corporation are given in the *Working Papers*. After each journal entry, update the T accounts given in the *Working Papers*. Your instructor will guide you through the following examples.

On December 31, 20X1, Spano Corporation has one note receivable outstanding, a 120-day, 6%, $16,000.00 note dated November 16, and one note payable outstanding, a 90-day, 6%, $18,000.00 note dated December 1.

Instructions:

1. Journalize the adjusting entries for accrued interest income and accrued interest expense on December 31. Use page 14 of a general journal.
2. Journalize the closing entries for interest income and interest expense using page 14 of a general journal.
3. Journalize the January 1, 20X2, reversing entries for accrued interest income and accrued interest expense on page 15 of a general journal.
4. Journalize the payment of cash for the maturity value of the note payable on March 1, 20X2. Check No. 321. Use page 25 of a cash payments journal.
5. Journalize the receipt of cash for the maturity value of the note receivable on March 16, 20X2. Receipt No. 587. Use page 16 of a cash receipts journal.
6. List the amount of interest income from this note receivable that will be shown on the income statements for 20X1 and 20X2.
7. List the amount of interest expense from this note payable that will be shown on the income statements for 20X1 and 20X2.

21-2 Application Problem: Journalizing entries for deferrals LO7, 8, 9, 10

The appropriate accounting forms are given in the *Working Papers*. After each journal entry, update the T accounts given in the *Working Papers*.

Instructions:

1. Journalize the following transactions for Deegs Company.
   - Oct. 1. Signed a contract to lease excess space to Sheldon Company for six months. Received cash in advance, $12,000.00. R164.
   - Dec. 31. Journalized the adjusting entry for rent earned.
2. Journalize the following transactions for Sheldon Company.
   - Oct. 1. Signed a contract to lease space from Deegs Company for six months. Paid cash in advance, $12,000.00. C377.
   - Dec. 31. Journalized the adjusting entry for rent expense.
3. What is the balance in the Prepaid Rent account? What does it represent?

Accounting forms and a partial unadjusted trial balance for Figlmiller Corporation are given in the *Working Papers.* Figlmiller Corporation collected $30,000 on November 1 for six months' rent. On December 31, 20X1, Figlmiller Corporation has one note receivable outstanding, a 90-day, 5%, $13,000.00 note dated December 1, and one note payable outstanding, a 120-day, 4%, $8,000.00 note dated November 16.

Instructions:

1. Journalize the adjusting entries for accrued interest income, accrued interest expense, and rent earned on December 31. Use page 14 of a general journal.

2. Journalize the closing entries for all income and expense accounts using page 14 of a general journal. Record the closing entry for both income accounts in one entry.

3. Journalize the January 1, 20X2, reversing entries for accrued interest income and accrued interest expense on page 15 of a general journal.

4. Journalize the receipt of cash for the maturity value of the note receivable on March 1, 20X2. Receipt No. 125. Use page 16 of a cash receipts journal.

5. Journalize the payment of cash for the maturity value of the note payable on March 16, 20X2. Check No. 185. Use page 25 of a cash payments journal.

6. List the amount of interest income from this note receivable that will be shown on the income statements for 20X1 and 20X2.

7. List the amount of interest expense from this note payable that will be shown on the income statements for 20X1 and 20X2.

8. What is the balance in the Prepaid Rent account on December 21, 20X1? What does it represent?

Peachtree

1. Journalize and post adjusting and closing entries to the general journal.
2. Print the general journal and trial balance.
3. Journalize and post reversing entries.
4. Journalize and post notes payable and notes receivable transactions.

Quick Books

1. Journalize and post adjusting and closing entries to the journal.
2. Print the journal and trial balance.
3. Journalize and post reversing entries.
4. Journalize and post notes payable and notes receivable transactions.

1. Journalize and post adjusting, closing, and reversing entries to the general journal.
2. Journalize and post notes payable and notes receivable transactions.
3. Print the worksheets.

The appropriate accounting forms are given in the *Working Papers*. After each journal entry, update the T accounts given in the *Working Papers*.

Marboe Fitness Center began operations on November 1, 20X1. It sells yearly memberships for $600, which allow the member full access to all exercise equipment in the center. By November 1, Marboe Fitness Center had sold 500 one-year memberships. Marboe Fitness Center also publishes a monthly magazine. By the end of November, Marboe had sold 1,000 one-year magazine subscriptions for $36.00 each. The first issue of the magazine was distributed on December 1, 20X1.

Instructions:

1. Journalize the adjusting entries for membership fees and magazine subscriptions earned.
2. What is the balance in the Unearned Membership Fees account? What does it represent?
3. What is the balance in the Unearned Magazine Subscriptions account? What does it represent?
4. GAAP requires that deferred revenue be recorded as it is earned. Revenue earned from a one-year magazine subscription is relatively easy to calculate. Each month, when a magazine is published, one-twelfth of the one-year subscription fee is earned for each subscription. Other forms of unearned revenue are not as easy to calculate and may not be earned evenly over time. A fitness center that sells one-year memberships can assume that the membership revenue is earned equally over time. However, if the fitness center feels that the membership is not earned equally over time, another method may be used to calculate the amount of revenue earned each month. Assume that Marboe Fitness Center does not believe membership revenue is earned equally over time. Develop a method for Marboe Fitness Center to calculate the amount of revenue earned each month.

21st Century Skills

FICO Scores—What's Your Number?

Theme: Financial, Economic, Business, and Entrepreneurial Literacy

Skills: Creativity and Innovation, Critical Thinking and Problem Solving, Communication and Collaboration, ICT Literacy

PARTNERSHIP FOR
21ST CENTURY SKILLS

Banks and other lenders provide consumer loans for cars, homes, home furnishings, etc. They also provide business loans. These lenders are well aware of the risks of not being repaid on time, and they take steps to minimize those risks. So, how do lenders determine if a business or individual is creditworthy (i.e., willing and able to repay a loan)?

Banks use credit scores to help predict the likelihood that individuals or businesses will repay their debt. The credit score is a numerical rating assigned to the borrower's credit information, which includes the way credit has been managed in the past.

For individuals, the most well-known type of credit score is FICO. FICO is named for the Fair Isaac Company, which developed the mathematical model in the 1950s. It calculates a score based on a person's credit report. It is important to remember that negative information remains on your credit report for seven to ten years. The three major credit bureaus that keep the credit history for scoring are Experian, Equifax, and TransUnion. Different scoring systems are used for rating businesses.

Many factors are taken into consideration to determine your FICO score. Among these are the amount you owe each month, your late-payment history, the length of your credit history, and the number of your recent credit applications. Income is not a factor because ability to pay is not necessarily an indicator of willingness to pay. The score, ranging from 300–850, often determines whether a person gets a loan and the interest rate they are charged. Many lenders consider someone with a FICO score over 720 to be a very good credit risk. A good score might also help someone get approved for an apartment, obtain employment, secure better insurance rates, or reduce deposits with utility companies. That is because a credit score is often seen as an indicator of character.

Your credit report should be reviewed regularly to uncover and correct any mistakes that might affect your FICO score. The Fair and Accurate Transactions Act of 2003 entitles everyone to a free report from each of the three agencies once a year. Students can begin a positive credit history by applying for a small amount of credit and paying on time and in full each month. Even your cell phone bill counts towards your credit history!

APPLICATION

1. Go to www.myfico.com. Determine the categories and percentages used to calculate your FICO score. Which category is the most important in determining the FICO score?

2. Create a table or spreadsheet with headings like the one below. Based on what you have learned, read the following scenarios and determine (a) if the impact is positive or negative on the FICO score, (b) the reason for the change, and (c) what needs to be done to improve the score if a negative impact was made. *Note*: If the impact was positive, only write "N/A".

Example:

Scenario	Impact	Reason for Change	Action to Remedy
Pays cell phone bill on time	+	*Timely Payments*	*N/A*
Overdue payment			
Obtains new car loan			
Pays off credit card			
Missed or late payment			

3. With a partner, create a one-minute public service announcement (poster, radio commercial, or video) informing other students of the FICO score and the impact it can have on their future.

Analyzing Nike's financial statements

Like most companies, Nike, Inc., records accrued liabilities at the end of a fiscal period in order for the financial statements to be accurate and up to date. Nike's accrued liabilities are often the largest single item in current liabilities. By looking at Nike's balance sheet, you cannot determine the makeup of its accrued liabilities. However, the notes to the financial statements usually give additional information about items such as accrued liabilities. Use the Consolidated Balance Sheets on page B-6 of Nike's 10-K report in Appendix B.

INSTRUCTIONS

1. What is the dollar amount of Nike's accrued liabilities as of May 31, 2011?

2. Find Note 5 on page B-14. Ignoring the Other category, list the names and amounts of the two largest accrued liabilities.

Chapter 22

End-of-Fiscal-Period Work for a Corporation

©DANIEL KOUREY, ISTOCK/©JIM PRUITT, ISTOCK

BLEND IMAGES/JUPITER IMAGES

Accounting In The Real World
Bank of America

Bank of America (BoA) is one of the largest financial services companies in the country. According to a recent annual report, BoA serves half of all U.S. households and operates in more than 40 countries. Chances are, you have a Bank of America branch office or ATM machine near you.

The recession that began in 2008 had a dramatic impact on financial institutions. One hard-hit area was the housing market. Housing prices plummeted, and many home mortgages were higher than the value of the mortgaged home. A mortgage that has a balance higher than the value of the property mortgaged is called an **underwater mortgage**. By the end of the first quarter of 2011, approximately 22.7% of all U.S. home mortgages were estimated to be underwater.

With a high percentage of mortgages underwater, mortgage lenders were faced with a greatly increased risk that homeowners would stop making their mortgage payments. Not making payments on a loan when they are due is called **defaulting** on the loan. When a mortgage is in default, the bank or finance company has the right to take possession of the property. When the bank or finance company takes possession of mortgaged property, it is called a **foreclosure**.

Foreclosures usually mean a loss for the mortgage holder, who must sell the property at a price less than the amount owed on the property. What is the impact of these foreclosures on the financial statements of the mortgage holder? Remember that GAAP requires a business to estimate the amount of receivables that will not be collected. Mortgages financed by BoA are listed as receivables on its balance sheet. Therefore, BoA must estimate the amount of these receivables that will not be paid in the future. This estimate is recorded in an account titled Allowance for Loans and Lease Losses.

BoA reported the following balances on its balance sheet:

2010: Loans and leases, $940,440,000,000; Allowance for loans and lease losses, $41,885,000,000

2009: Loans and leases, $900,128,000,000; Allowance for loans and lease losses, $37,200,000,000

CRITICAL THINKING

1. For 2010 and 2009, calculate what percent the allowance account is of the Loans and Leases account.

2. For which year was the percentage higher? What does this indicate about what Bank of America thinks about the rate of foreclosures?

Sources: www.credit.com/blog/2011/06 and CoreLogic.com.

Key Terms

- cash flow
- statement of cash flows
- operating activities
- investing activities
- financing activities

22-1 Preparing Adjusting Entries

LO1 Plan and record end-of-fiscal-period adjustments for a merchandising business organized as a corporation.

End-of-Fiscal-Period Work **LO1**

The end of a fiscal period is a busy time for a corporation. It begins with preparing an unadjusted trial balance to ensure that debits equal credits in the general ledger. The unadjusted trial balance and other financial data are used to plan and record adjusting entries. Once the adjusting entries are posted, an adjusted trial balance is prepared.

The adjusted trial balance is used to prepare the financial statements. The income statement is the first statement prepared. The amount of net income, selected balance sheet accounts, and other accounting information are used to prepare the statement of stockholders' equity. Summary amounts on this statement and the adjusted trial balance are used to prepare a balance sheet.

In preparation for recording transactions during the next period, closing and reversing entries are recorded and posted. The accounts are then ready to record transactions for the next fiscal period. Sun Treasures may prepare financial statements any time they are needed. However, Sun Treasures always prepares financial statements at the end of a fiscal year. [CONCEPT: Accounting Period Cycle]

ETHICS IN ACTION

Setting the Tone at the Top

A certain company's code of conduct prohibits employees from accepting gifts, favors, or entertainment that would influence their sound business decisions. Despite the rule, the company president is known to accept lavish gifts from suppliers. Do you think the employees will be motivated to adhere to the code of conduct?

The employees at the top of a company—managers, officers, and directors—must provide leadership in making ethical decisions. Among the many ways companies can "set the tone at the top" is to have a special code of conduct for members of the board of directors.

INSTRUCTIONS

Access the *Board of Directors Code of Conduct for Kellogg Company*. Determine whether directors can personally invest in the stock of companies that do business with Kellogg Company.

©LUCA DI FILIPPO, ISTOCK

Unadjusted Trial Balance

Sun Treasures' unadjusted trial balance prepared from the general ledger is shown below.

Sun Treasures, Inc.		
Unadjusted Trial Balance		
December 31, 20--		

ACCOUNT TITLE	DEBIT	CREDIT
Cash	43 8 4 8 68	
Petty Cash	4 5 0 00	
Accounts Receivable	52 4 8 1 37	
Allowance for Uncollectible Accounts		6 7 5 56
Notes Receivable	15 0 0 0 00	
Interest Receivable	—	
Merchandise Inventory	331 2 3 5 20	
Supplies—Office	89 6 4 0 00	
Supplies—Store	158 1 0 0 00	
Prepaid Insurance	54 8 7 2 35	
Office Equipment	325 6 4 8 16	
Accumulated Depreciation—Office Equipment		79 7 2 7 00
Store Equipment	1099 6 3 8 43	
Accumulated Depreciation—Store Equipment		337 9 0 2 00
Accounts Payable		15 4 6 2 50
Sales Tax Payable		6 4 7 31
Notes Payable		—
Interest Payable		—
Line of Credit		7 5 0 0 00
Unearned Rent Income		4 5 0 0 00
Employee Income Tax Payable		1 5 7 3 00
Social Security Tax Payable		3 0 0 0 80
Medicare Tax Payable		7 0 1 80
Medical Insurance Payable		3 2 1 24
Retirement Benefits Payable		4 7 5 00
Unemployment Tax Payable—State		3 5 00
Unemployment Tax Payable—Federal		2 3 6 25
Federal Income Tax Payable		—
Dividends Payable		—
Long-term Notes Payable		106 6 2 5 67
Bonds Payable		180 0 0 0 00
Capital Stock—Common ($10 par, 40,000)		400 0 0 0 00
Paid-in Capital in Excess of Par—Common		480 0 0 0 00
Capital Stock—Preferred ($50 par, 400)		20 0 0 0 00
Paid-in Capital in Excess of Par—Preferred		—
Retained Earnings		82 5 2 5 10
Dividends	21 2 0 0 00	
Income Summary	—	

(Continued on next page)

Unadjusted Trial Balance *(continued)*

ACCOUNT TITLE	DEBIT	CREDIT
	Sun Treasures, Inc.	
	Unadjusted Trial Balance	
	December 31, 20--	
Sales		2576 3 2 1 45
Sales Discount	15 4 5 7 93	
Sales Returns and Allowances	113 5 2 3 11	
Purchases	1307 1 6 0 50	
Purchases Discount		15 6 8 5 93
Purchases Returns and Allowances		1 1 5 0 40
Advertising Expense	58 0 0 0 00	
Cash Short and Over	2 4 1 7 25	
Credit Card Fee Expense	23 7 6 3 21	
Depreciation Expense—Office Equipment	—	
Depreciation Expense—Store Equipment	—	
Insurance Expense	—	
Miscellaneous Expense	38 0 1 0 66	
Payroll Taxes Expense	27 4 2 3 60	
Rent Expense	143 0 0 0 00	
Salary Expense	290 4 0 0 00	
Supplies Expense—Office	—	
Supplies Expense—Store	—	
Uncollectible Accounts Expense	—	
Utilities Expense	66 8 8 6 10	
Federal Income Tax Expense	23 0 0 0 00	
Interest Income		2 3 3 7 80
Rent Income		—
Gain on Plant Assets		18 2 3 1 00
Interest Expense	17 6 3 6 26	
Loss on Plant Assets	16 8 4 2 00	
Totals	4335 6 3 4 81	4335 6 3 4 81

Adjusting Entries for Uncollectible Accounts and Merchandise Inventory

ACCOUNT TITLE	DEBIT	CREDIT
Sun Treasures, Inc.		
Unadjusted Trial Balance		
December 31, 20--		
Accounts Receivable	52 4 8 1 37	
Allowance for Uncollectible Accounts		6 7 5 56
Merchandise Inventory	331 2 3 5 20	
Income Summary		
Uncollectible Accounts Expense		

Some general ledger accounts need to be brought up to date before financial statements are prepared. An unadjusted trial balance is used to plan and record the adjusting entries. Accounts are brought up to date by recording the adjustments in the general journal and then posting them to the general ledger.

Two methods are used to determine the amount of each adjustment. For some accounts, the calculated estimate of the account is also the amount used in the adjustment. These adjustments include interest income, depreciation expense, and interest expense.

Other accounts require estimating the end-of-period balance. The current balance is typically subtracted from the estimated end-of-period account balance to determine the amount of the adjustment. These adjustments include uncollectible accounts expense, merchandise inventory, supplies, prepaid insurance, and federal income tax expense.

Examples of both types of adjustments are shown on the following pages. Other adjustments were illustrated earlier in Part 3. Adjustments generally are made in the order that accounts are listed in the general ledger.

UNCOLLECTIBLE ACCOUNTS ADJUSTMENT

Sun Treasures estimates that $2,099.25 of its accounts receivable will not be collected. On December 31, the balance in the Allowance for Uncollectible Accounts account is $675.56. The amount of the adjusting entry is calculated as shown.

Desired Balance in Allowance Account	−	Current Balance in Allowance Account	=	Amount of Adjustment
$2,099.25	−	$675.56	=	$1,423.69

Uncollectible Accounts Expense is debited and Allowance for Uncollectible Accounts is credited for $1,423.69.

MERCHANDISE INVENTORY ADJUSTMENT

If the current balance in the Merchandise Inventory account is more than the actual inventory on hand at the end of the period, Income Summary is debited and Merchandise Inventory is credited. On December 31, the balance in the Merchandise Inventory account is $331,235.20. The actual inventory on hand on December 31 is $307,613.20. The amount of the adjusting entry is calculated as shown.

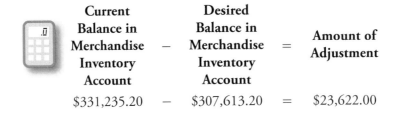

	Current Balance in Merchandise Inventory Account	−	Desired Balance in Merchandise Inventory Account	=	Amount of Adjustment
	$331,235.20	−	$307,613.20	=	$23,622.00

Income Summary is debited and Merchandise Inventory is credited for $23,622.00. If the current balance in Merchandise Inventory is less than the actual inventory on hand at the end of the period, Merchandise Inventory is debited and Income Summary is credited.

1 Debit Uncollectible Accounts Expense   **2** Credit Allowance for Uncollectible Accounts

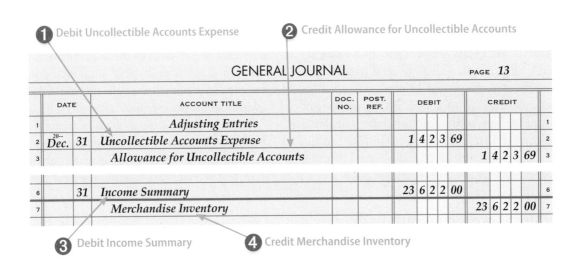

3 Debit Income Summary   **4** Credit Merchandise Inventory

Journalizing Adjustments for Uncollectible Accounts and Merchandise Inventory

1 Debit Uncollectible Accounts Expense for $1,423.69.

2 Credit Allowance for Uncollectible Accounts for $1,423.69.

3 Debit Income Summary for $23,622.00.

4 Credit Merchandise Inventory for $23,622.00.

Adjusting Entries for Supplies and Insurance

Sun Treasures, Inc. Unadjusted Trial Balance December 31, 20--		
ACCOUNT TITLE	**DEBIT**	**CREDIT**
Supplies—Store	158 1 0 0 00	
Prepaid Insurance	54 8 7 2 35	
Insurance Expense		
Supplies Expense—Store		

1 Debit Supplies Expense—Store

2 Credit Supplies—Store

	DATE	ACCOUNT TITLE	DOC. NO.	POST. REF.	DEBIT	CREDIT	
1		*Adjusting Entries*					1
10	31	Supplies Expense—Store			109 8 0 0 00		10
11		Supplies—Store				109 8 0 0 00	11
12	31	Insurance Expense			36 2 2 5 00		12
13		Prepaid Insurance				36 2 2 5 00	13

GENERAL JOURNAL PAGE 13

3 Debit Insurance Expense **4** Credit Prepaid Insurance

SUPPLIES—STORE ADJUSTMENT

The balance of Supplies—Store in the trial balance, $158,100.00, is the cost of supplies on hand at the beginning of the year plus the supplies purchased during the year. The supplies on hand on December 31 are counted and determined to be $48,300.00. To bring the account up to date, the balance of Supplies—Store needs to be decreased by $109,800.00 ($158,100.00 – $48,300.00), the cost of supplies used during the year. Supplies Expense—Store is debited and Supplies—Store is credited for the amount of the decrease.

PREPAID INSURANCE ADJUSTMENT

The balance of Prepaid Insurance in the trial balance, $54,872.35, is the cost of prepaid insurance remaining at the beginning of the year plus the cost of insurance purchased during the period. An analysis of the account determined that $18,647.35 of prepaid insurance premiums remain on December 31. To bring the account up to date, the balance of Prepaid Insurance needs to be decreased by $36,225.00 ($54,872.35 – $18,647.35), the cost of insurance that expired during the year. Insurance Expense is debited and Prepaid Insurance is credited for the amount of the decrease.

Journalizing Adjustments for Supplies and Insurance

1 Debit Supplies Expense—Store for $109,800.00.

2 Credit Supplies—Store for $109,800.00.

3 Debit Insurance Expense for $36,225.00.

4 Credit Prepaid Insurance for $36,225.00.

Federal Income Tax Adjustment

Sun Treasures, Inc.
Unadjusted Trial Balance
December 31, 20--

ACCOUNT TITLE	DEBIT	CREDIT
Federal Income Tax Payable		
Federal Income Tax Expense	23 0 0 0 00	

GENERAL JOURNAL

PAGE 13

	DATE	ACCOUNT TITLE	DOC. NO.	POST. REF.	DEBIT	CREDIT	
1		*Adjusting Entries*					1
22	31	Federal Income Tax Expense			2 9 9 2 22		22
23		Federal Income Tax Payable				2 9 9 2 22	23

1 Debit Federal Income Tax Expense   **2** Credit Federal Income Tax Payable

Detailed instructions for preparing the federal income tax adjustment were presented in Chapter 15. The first step is to calculate the corporation's net income before federal income tax. Sun Treasures' net income before federal income tax expense is $109,595.43.

The amount of federal income tax is calculated using tax rates provided by the Internal Revenue Service. The tax rate varies, depending on the amount of net income earned. The tax rates are given in the table below.

Tax Rate Schedule

If taxable income (line 30, Form 1120, or line 26, Form 1120-A) is:

Over—	But not over—	Tax is:	Of the amount over—
$0	50,000	15%	-0-
50,000	75,000	$7,500 + 25%	$50,000
75,000	100,000	13,750 + 34%	75,000
100,000	335,000	22,250 + 39%	100,000
335,000	10,000,000	113,900 + 34%	335,000
10,000,000	15,000,000	3,400,000 + 35%	10,000,000
15,000,000	18,333,333	5,150,000 + 38%	15,000,000
18,333,333	—	35%	-0-

CALCULATING FEDERAL INCOME TAX

The amount of taxable income is $109,595.43.
The amount over $100,000 is $9,595.43.
39% of $9,595.43 is $3,742.22
$22,250.00 + $3,742.22 = $25,992.22 Total Federal Income Tax

Sun Treasures has already paid $23,000.00. Therefore, the amount of federal income tax still due is $25,992.22 – $23,000.00 = $2,992.22. The estimated tax payments already made are subtracted from the total federal income tax expense to calculate the adjustment for federal income tax expense.

Total Federal Income Tax Expense	–	Estimated Federal Income Tax Already Paid	=	Accrued Federal Income Tax Expense
$25,992.22	–	$23,000.00	=	$2,992.22

Federal Income Tax Expense is debited and Federal Income Tax Payable is credited for the amount of the accrued taxes.

Journalizing Adjustment for Federal Income Tax Expense

1 Debit Federal Income Tax Expense for $2,992.22.

2 Credit Federal Income Tax Payable for $2,992.22.

Adjusting Entries

	DATE		ACCOUNT TITLE	DOC. NO.	POST. REF.	DEBIT	CREDIT	
1			*Adjusting Entries*					1
2	20-- Dec.	31	Uncollectible Accounts Expense			1 4 2 3 69		2
3			Allowance for Uncollectible Accounts				1 4 2 3 69	3
4		31	Interest Receivable			1 7 5 00		4
5			Interest Income				1 7 5 00	5
6		31	Income Summary			23 6 2 2 00		6
7			Merchandise Inventory				23 6 2 2 00	7
8		31	Supplies Expense—Office			76 4 4 0 00		8
9			Supplies—Office				76 4 4 0 00	9
10		31	Supplies Expense—Store			109 8 0 0 00		10
11			Supplies—Store				109 8 0 0 00	11
12		31	Insurance Expense			36 2 2 5 00		12
13			Prepaid Insurance				36 2 2 5 00	13
14		31	Depreciation Exp.—Office Equip.			25 1 4 6 00		14
15			Accum. Depr.—Office Equip.				25 1 4 6 00	15
16		31	Depreciation Exp.—Store Equip.			113 4 1 8 00		16
17			Accum. Depr.—Store Equip.				113 4 1 8 00	17
18		31	Interest Expense			7 1 0 84		18
19			Interest Payable				7 1 0 84	19
20		31	Unearned Rent Income			3 0 0 0 00		20
21			Rent Income				3 0 0 0 00	21
22		31	Federal Income Tax Expense			2 9 9 2 22		22
23			Federal Income Tax Payable				2 9 9 2 22	23

Sun Treasures' adjusting entries are shown above. The entries are posted to the general ledger to bring each account up to date. An adjusted trial balance is prepared. The adjusted trial balance is used to prepare financial statements.

Adjusted Trial Balance

After all adjusting entries are journalized and posted, another trial balance is prepared to prove the general ledger. The adjusted trial balance is shown below.

Sun Treasures, Inc. Adjusted Trial Balance December 31, 20--		
ACCOUNT TITLE	DEBIT	CREDIT
Cash	43 848 68	
Petty Cash	4 50 00	
Accounts Receivable	52 481 37	
Allowance for Uncollectible Accounts		2 099 25
Notes Receivable	15 000 00	
Interest Receivable	1 75 00	
Merchandise Inventory	307 613 20	
Supplies—Office	13 200 00	
Supplies—Store	48 300 00	
Prepaid Insurance	18 647 35	
Office Equipment	325 648 16	
Accumulated Depreciation—Office Equipment		104 873 00
Store Equipment	1099 638 43	
Accumulated Depreciation—Store Equipment		451 320 00
Accounts Payable		15 462 50
Sales Tax Payable		6 47 31
Notes Payable		—
Interest Payable		7 10 84
Line of Credit		7 500 00
Unearned Rent Income		1 500 00
Employee Income Tax Payable		1 573 00
Social Security Tax Payable		3 000 80
Medicare Tax Payable		7 01 80
Medical Insurance Payable		3 21 24
Retirement Benefits Payable		4 75 00
Unemployment Tax Payable—State		35 00
Unemployment Tax Payable—Federal		2 36 25
Federal Income Tax Payable		2 992 22
Dividends Payable		
Long-term Notes Payable		106 625 67
Bonds Payable		180 000 00

Sun Treasures, Inc.
Adjusted Trial Balance
December 31, 20--

ACCOUNT TITLE	DEBIT	CREDIT
Capital Stock—Common ($10 par, 40,000)		400 000 00
Paid-in Capital in Excess of Par—Common		480 000 00
Capital Stock—Preferred ($50 par, 400)		20 000 00
Paid-in Capital in Excess of Par—Preferred		————
Retained Earnings		82 525 10
Dividends	21 200 00	
Income Summary	23 622 00	
Sales		2576 321 45
Sales Discount	15 457 93	
Sales Returns and Allowances	113 523 11	
Purchases	1307 160 50	
Purchases Discount		15 685 93
Purchases Returns and Allowances		1 150 40
Advertising Expense	58 000 00	
Cash Short and Over	2 417 25	
Credit Card Fee Expense	23 763 21	
Depreciation Expense—Office Equipment	25 146 00	
Depreciation Expense—Store Equipment	113 418 00	
Insurance Expense	36 225 00	
Miscellaneous Expense	38 010 66	
Payroll Taxes Expense	27 423 60	
Rent Expense	143 000 00	
Salary Expense	290 400 00	
Supplies Expense—Office	76 440 00	
Supplies Expense—Store	109 800 00	
Uncollectible Accounts Expense	1 423 69	
Utilities Expense	66 886 10	
Federal Income Tax Expense	25 992 22	
Interest Income		2 512 80
Rent Income		3 000 00
Gain on Plant Assets		18 231 00
Interest Expense	18 347 10	
Loss on Plant Assets	16 842 00	
Totals	4479 500 56	4479 500 56

LO1 Plan and record end-of-fiscal-period adjustments for a merchandising business organized as a corporation.

Audit your understanding

1. Describe the two methods used to determine the amount of an adjustment.
2. Which accounts are used to adjust the Supplies account?

Work together 22-1

Recording adjusting entries and preparing an adjusted trial balance

Travel Lite Corporation's unadjusted trial balance and accounting forms are given in the *Working Papers*. Your instructor will guide you through the following example.

1. Using the following information, journalize the adjusting entries for the current year ended December 31.

Estimated uncollectible accounts based on aging accounts receivable	$ 3,697.32
Accrued interest income	137.50
Merchandise inventory	45,058.15
Supplies inventory	126.00
Value of prepaid insurance	1,535.80
Annual depreciation expense—equipment	2,250.00
Accrued interest expense	277.58
Prepaid rent income earned	1,000.00

2. Post the adjusting entries to the T accounts.
3. Using the tax table shown in this chapter, calculate federal income tax expense and journalize the income tax adjustment.
4. Post the federal income tax adjusting entry to the T accounts.
5. Using the unadjusted trial balance and the T accounts, complete the adjusted trial balance. Save your work to complete Work Together 22-2.

On your own 22-1

Recording adjusting entries and preparing an adjusted trial balance

Williams Corporation's unadjusted trial balance and accounting forms are given in the *Working Papers*. Work this problem independently.

1. Using the following information, journalize the adjusting entries for the current year ended December 31.

Estimated uncollectible accounts based on aging accounts receivable	$ 3,796.00
Accrued interest income	80.00
Merchandise inventory	98,996.13
Supplies inventory	401.25
Value of prepaid insurance	600.00
Annual depreciation expense—equipment	7,345.00
Accrued interest expense	150.00
Prepaid rent income earned	2,000.00

2. Post the adjusting entries to the T accounts.
3. Using the tax table shown in this chapter, calculate federal income tax expense and journalize the income tax adjustment.
4. Post the federal income tax adjusting entry to the T accounts.
5. Using the unadjusted trial balance and the T accounts, complete the adjusted trial balance. Save your work to complete On Your Own 22-2.

©CANDICE CUSACK, ISTOCK

LO2 Prepare an income statement for a merchandising business organized as a corporation.

LO3 Prepare a statement of stockholders' equity for a merchandising business organized as a corporation.

LO4 Prepare a balance sheet for a merchandising business organized as a corporation.

Income Statement LO2

Sun Treasures, Inc. Income Statement For Year Ended December 31, 20--					% OF SALES
Operating Revenue:					
Sales			2576 32 1 45		
Less: Sales Discount		15 45 7 93			
Sales Returns and Allowances		113 52 3 11	128 98 1 04		
Net Sales				2447 34 0 41	100.0
Cost of Merchandise Sold:					
Merchandise Inventory, Jan. 1, 20--			331 23 5 20		
Purchases		1307 16 0 50			
Less: Purchases Discount	15 68 5 93				
Purch. Returns and Allowances	1 15 0 40	16 83 6 33			
Net Purchases			1290 32 4 17		
Total Cost of Mdse. Avail. for Sale			1621 55 9 37		
Less Mdse. Inventory, Dec. 31. 20--			307 61 3 20		
Cost of Merchandise Sold				1313 94 6 17	53.7
Gross Profit				1133 39 4 24	46.3
Operating Expenses:					
Advertising Expense			58 00 0 00		
Cash Short and Over			2 41 7 25		
Credit Card Fee Expense			23 76 3 21		
Depr. Expense—Office Equipment			25 14 6 00		
Depr. Expense—Store Equipment			113 41 8 00		
Insurance Expense			36 22 5 00		
Miscellaneous Expense			38 01 0 66		
Payroll Taxes Expense			27 42 3 60		
Rent Expense			143 00 0 00		
Salary Expense			290 40 0 00		
Supplies Expense—Office			76 44 0 00		
Supplies Expense—Store			109 80 0 00		
Uncollectible Accounts Expense			1 42 3 69		
Utilities Expense			66 88 6 10		
Total Operating Expenses				1012 35 3 51	41.4

(Continued on next page)

Income Statement (*continued*)

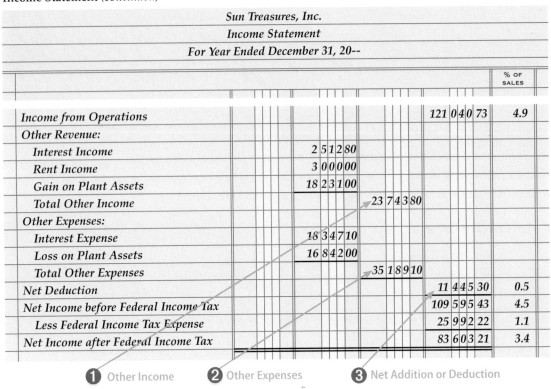

					% OF SALES
Income from Operations				121 04 0 73	4.9
Other Revenue:					
Interest Income		2 5 1 2 80			
Rent Income		3 0 0 0 00			
Gain on Plant Assets		18 2 3 1 00			
Total Other Income			23 7 4 3 80		
Other Expenses:					
Interest Expense		18 3 4 7 10			
Loss on Plant Assets		16 8 4 2 00			
Total Other Expenses			35 1 8 9 10		
Net Deduction				11 4 4 5 30	0.5
Net Income before Federal Income Tax				109 5 9 5 43	4.5
Less Federal Income Tax Expense				25 9 9 2 22	1.1
Net Income after Federal Income Tax				83 6 0 3 21	3.4

Sun Treasures, Inc.
Income Statement
For Year Ended December 31, 20--

❶ Other Income   ❷ Other Expenses   ❸ Net Addition or Deduction

Additional Items on an Income Statement

Sun Treasures' income statement is very similar to ThreeGreen's income statement, shown in Part 2. Both companies report net sales, net purchases, gross profit, income from operations, and other revenue (interest income). However, Sun Treasures lists the following additional items on its income statement:

(1) Rent income
(2) Gains and losses from the sale of plant assets
(3) Accruals for interest payable (interest expense)

These accounts are reported after income from operations. To help make decisions about current and future operations, Sun Treasures also analyzes relationships between revenue and expense items. Based on this analysis, Sun Treasures reports vertical analysis ratios for all major income statement items. Detailed procedures for preparing an income statement were presented in Chapter 16. The new items are highlighted in the illustration.

New Elements on the Income Statement for Sun Treasures

❶ Income from operations, $121,040.73, is the income earned only from normal business activities. Sun Treasures' normal business activities are selling souvenirs and tourist items. Interest earned on notes receivable, $2,512.80, rent income, $3,000.00, and gain from the sale of plant assets, $18,231.00, are not normal operating activities. Therefore, these accounts are reported after income from operations in a section labeled *Other Revenue*. The total of these Other Revenue accounts is $23,743.80.

❷ The interest expense on notes payable and lines of credit, $18,347.10, and the loss from the sale of plant assets, $16,842.00, are not normal operating activities. Therefore, these accounts are reported after income from operations in a section labeled *Other Expenses*. The total of these two Other Expenses accounts is $35,189.10.

❸ The difference between other revenue and other expenses, $11,445.30, is reported as a net addition or net deduction. The difference is added to or deducted from income from operations to determine the net income before federal income tax.

Statement of Stockholders' Equity LO3

Sun Treasures, Inc. Statement of Stockholders' Equity For Year Ended December 31, 20--			
Capital Stock—Common:			
$10.00 Par Value			
January 1, 20--, 39,400 Shares Issued		394 0 0 0 00	
Issued during Current Year, 600 Shares		6 0 0 0 00	
Bal., December 31, 20--, 40,000 Shares Issued			400 0 0 0 00
Paid-in Capital in Excess of Par—Common:			
Balance, January 1, 20--		462 0 0 0 00	
Issued during Current Year		18 0 0 0 00	
Balance, December 31, 20--			480 0 0 0 00
Capital Stock—Preferred:			
$50.00 Par Value, 6%			
January 1, 20--, 0 Shares Issued		—	
Issued during Current Year, 400 Shares		20 0 0 0 00	
Balance, December 31, 20--, 400 Shares Issued			20 0 0 0 00
Retained Earnings:			
Balance, January 1, 20--		82 5 2 5 10	
Net Income after Federal Income Tax for 20--	83 6 0 3 21		
Less Dividends Declared during 20--	21 2 0 0 00		
Net Increase during 20--		62 4 0 3 21	
Balance, December 31, 20--			144 9 2 8 31
Total Stockholders' Equity, December 31, 20--			1044 9 2 8 31

1 Paid-in Capital in Excess of Par—Common section

2 Preferred Stock section

The statement of stockholders' equity for Sun Treasures is similar to that for ThreeGreen in Part 2. Both companies report changes in the **Capital Stock** and **Retained Earnings** accounts. However, Sun Treasures has two additional equity accounts, so its statement of stockholders' equity has two additional sections: (1) Paid-in Capital in Excess of Par—Common and (2) Preferred Stock.

Detailed instructions for preparing the statement of stockholders' equity were presented in Chapter 16. The new sections are highlighted in the illustration.

> **New Elements on the Statement of Stockholders' Equity for Sun Treasures**
>
> **1** Changes in Paid-in Capital in Excess of Par—Common are listed in section 2. The ending balance, $480,000.00, is included in total stockholders' equity.
>
> **2** Changes in Preferred Stock are listed in section 3. The ending balance, $20,000.00, is included in total stockholders' equity.

Major corporations, especially those listed on the New York Stock Exchange (NYSE), publish lavish annual reports on their operations for the year. These annual reports are intended to summarize operations for their stockholders. They are also used to encourage investors to buy new issues of a company's stock. Most annual reports are available online as well.

Balance Sheet LO4

1 New current liability accounts

Sun Treasures, Inc.

Balance Sheet

December 31, 20--

Assets			
Current Assets:			
Cash		43 8 4 8 68	
Petty Cash		4 5 0 00	
Accounts Receivable	52 4 8 1 37		
Less Allowance for Uncollectible Accounts	2 0 9 9 25	50 3 8 2 12	
Notes Receivable		15 0 0 0 00	
Interest Receivable		1 7 5 00	
Merchandise Inventory		307 6 1 3 20	
Supplies—Office		13 2 0 0 00	
Supplies—Store		48 3 0 0 00	
Prepaid Insurance		18 6 4 7 35	
Total Current Assets			497 6 1 6 35
Plant Assets:			
Office Equipment	325 6 4 8 16		
Less Accumulated Depr.—Office Equipment	104 8 7 3 00	220 7 7 5 16	
Store Equipment	1099 6 3 8 43		
Less Accumulated Depr.—Store Equipment	451 3 2 0 00	648 3 1 8 43	
Total Plant Assets			869 0 9 3 59
Total Assets			1366 7 0 9 94
Liabilities			
Current Liabilities:			
Accounts Payable		15 4 6 2 50	
Sales Tax Payable		6 4 7 31	
Interest Payable		7 1 0 84	
Line of Credit		7 5 0 0 00	
Unearned Rent Income		1 5 0 0 00	
Employee Income Tax Payable		1 5 7 3 00	
Social Security Tax Payable		3 0 0 0 80	
Medicare Tax Payable		7 0 1 80	
Medical Insurance Payable		3 2 1 24	
Retirement Benefits Payable		4 7 5 00	
Unemployment Tax Payable—State		3 5 00	
Unemployment Tax Payable—Federal		2 3 6 25	
Federal Income Tax Payable		2 9 9 2 22	
Total Current Liabilities			35 1 5 5 96
Long-term Liabilities:			
Long-term Notes Payable		106 6 2 5 67	
Bonds Payable		180 0 0 0 00	
Total Long-term Liabilities			286 6 2 5 67
Total Liabilities			321 7 8 1 63
Stockholders' Equity			
Capital Stock—Common		400 0 0 0 00	
Paid-in Capital in Excess of Par—Common		480 0 0 0 00	
Capital Stock—Preferred		20 0 0 0 00	
Retained Earnings		144 9 2 8 31	
Total Stockholders' Equity			1044 9 2 8 31
Total Liabilities and Stockholders' Equity			1366 7 0 9 94

2 Long-term Liabilities section

3 Expanded Stockholders' Equity section

The balance sheet for Sun Treasures is similar to that for ThreeGreen in Part 2. Both balance sheets report assets, liabilities, and equity on a specific date. However, Sun Treasures has more current liability accounts, a new section, Long-term Liabilities, and more equity accounts. ThreeGreen only had current liabilities. Sun Treasures has both current and long-term liabilities. Each type of liability is listed separately and subtotaled. Total liabilities is also presented. Detailed procedures for preparing a balance sheet were presented in Chapter 16. The new items are highlighted in the illustration.

New Elements on the Balance Sheet for Sun Treasures

1 Several new current liabilities appear in the Current Liabilities section.

2 A new Long-term Liabilities section follows the Current Liabilities section. Each long-term liability account is listed, along with total long-term liabilities and total liabilities.

3 New stockholders' equity accounts are listed in the Stockholders' Equity section.

THINK LIKE AN ACCOUNTANT

Formatting Amounts in Financial Statements

The board of directors of Blanc Corporation is reviewing its financial statements. The president begins her presentation to the board by discussing sales trends. Which of these statements would the board members better understand?

1. Our sales for May were $542,349.31, an increase of $23,136.89 over April.
2. Our sales for May were $542 thousand, an increase of $23 thousand over April.

Does the board need to know the exact amount of sales? Will knowing about that extra $349.31 of sales cause the board to make any different decisions? Most people will better understand the second statement.

Amounts rounded to two, three, or four digits can provide an adequate level of information.

This level of accuracy is common in other areas of our daily living. Consider these examples. Speed limit signs have only two digits. Baseball batting averages are stated in three digits, such as .325. College grade point averages are also presented with three digits, such as 3.68.

Most corporations present their financial statements in thousands or millions. Notations such as *in thousands of dollars* or *$000s* are included in the statement headings. These notations inform the reader that the amounts are stated in thousands of dollars. A corporation can also replace digits with zeros. For example, the statement could round $12,345 to $12,000.

OPEN THE SPREADSHEET TLA_CH22
Follow the steps on the Instructions worksheet. Each worksheet contains a financial statement. Format each financial statement assuming it will be presented to a board of directors.

©DAN BACHMAN, ISTOCK

Audit your understanding

1. Why are other revenue and other expenses reported separately from sales, cost of merchandise sold, and operating expenses on the income statement?

2. What is an example of a long-term liability?

Work together 22-2

Preparing an income statement, statement of stockholders' equity, and balance sheet for a corporation

Use the adjusted trial balance from Work Together 22-1. Forms are given in the *Working Papers*. Your instructor will guide you through the following examples.

1. Complete the income statement for the current year. Calculate and record the following vertical analysis ratios: (a) cost of merchandise sold; (b) gross profit on operations; (c) total operating expenses; (d) income from operations; (e) net addition or deduction resulting from other revenue and expenses; and (f) net income before federal income tax. Round percentage calculations to the nearest 0.01%.

2. Complete the statement of stockholders' equity for the current year. As of January 1, Travel Lite Corporation had issued 4,500 shares of common stock with a par value of $1.00 per share. During the fiscal year, the corporation issued 500 additional shares of common stock. The balance in Paid-in Capital in Excess of Par—Common on January 1, 20--, was $8,000.00. As of January 1, Travel Lite had not issued any shares of preferred stock. During the fiscal year, it issued 500 shares of $10.00 par, 5% preferred stock at par value.

3. Complete the balance sheet for the current year. Save your work to complete Work Together 22-3.

On your own 22-2

Preparing an income statement, statement of stockholders' equity, and balance sheet for a corporation

Use the adjusted trial balance from On Your Own 22-1. Forms are given in the *Working Papers*. Your instructor will guide you through the following examples.

1. Complete the income statement for the current year. Calculate and record the following vertical analysis ratios: (a) cost of merchandise sold; (b) gross profit on operations; (c) total operating expenses; (d) income from operations; (e) net addition or deduction resulting from other revenue and expenses; and (f) net income before federal income tax. Round percentage calculations to the nearest 0.01%.

2. Complete the statement of stockholders' equity for the current year. As of January 1, Williams Corporation had issued 2,000 shares of common stock with a par value of $5.00 per share. During the fiscal year, the corporation issued 1,000 additional shares of common stock. The balance in Paid-in Capital in Excess of Par—Common on January 1, 20--, was $2,000. As of January 1, Williams Corporation had not issued any shares of preferred stock. During the fiscal year, it issued 1,000 shares of $10.00 par, 5% preferred stock at par value.

3. Complete the balance sheet for the current year. Save your work to complete On Your Own 22-3.

©CANDICE CUSACK, ISTOCK

LESSON

22-3 Preparing a Statement of Cash Flows

LO5 Prepare a statement of cash flows for a merchandising business organized as a corporation.

Statement of Cash Flows LO5

ThreeGreen, the company in Part 2, prepared three financial statements: income statement, statement of stockholders' equity, and balance sheet. Corporations are required to prepare one additional statement which addresses the changes in the business's cash for the period. The cash receipts and cash payments of a company are called **cash flow**. A financial statement that summarizes cash receipts and cash payments resulting from business activities during a fiscal period is called a **statement of cash flows**.

The statement of cash flows is different than the other financial statements in one major way—the basis it uses. The income statement, the statement of stockholders' equity, and the balance sheet are prepared using the accrual basis of accounting. This means that revenues are recorded when earned, not when cash is received and

expenses are included when incurred, not when cash is paid. The statement of cash flows is prepared using the cash basis of accounting. This means that the statement of cash flows only reports inflows and outflows of cash and excludes business transactions that do not affect cash. For example, interest accrued on a note receivable would not affect cash. Similarly, wages accrued but not paid during the period would not affect cash.

The purpose of the statement of cash flows is to provide important information to external parties such as stockholders and creditors. A business may have impressive profits, but may experience a cash shortage and have difficulty paying its bills. The statement of cash flows allows the reader to more fully understand how cash is acquired and how it is used by a company.

GLOBAL AWARENESS

Working in a Foreign Country

Does working in a foreign country appeal to you? Are you willing to pack your clothes and a few personal belongings and fly off for new adventures? Before you go, you will need to do some advance planning.

Many countries do not allow foreign workers. Those that do allow foreign workers may require a work permit. In some countries, you can only get a work permit if it can be proven that the position cannot be filled by a citizen of that country because of lack of skills or other reasons.

If you go to a country that does not require a work permit, you may be required to apply for and be granted a visa before you can enter the country. In addition, you may be required to provide proof of specific immunizations. Visas are often issued for

a limited time span, after which you must leave the country.

Perhaps the most important thing to consider is the culture and customs of the country, which may be very different than those to which you are accustomed. Understanding and tolerating these customs may be the ultimate test of your ability to live happily and successfully abroad.

CRITICAL THINKING

Choose a country in which you are interested. Search the Internet for suggestions on what is needed to work in that country, including work permits and visas. Also include what language is spoken in this country and what kind of climate you can tolerate. Summarize your findings in a one-paragraph written report.

©FONTMONSTER, ISTOCK

Cash Flows from Operating, Investing, and Financing Activities

The statement of cash flows is divided into three sections. The cash flows for each of these sections are calculated by analyzing the information presented in the ledger accounts and the other financial statements of the company.

CASH FLOWS FROM OPERATING ACTIVITIES

The cash receipts and payments necessary to operate a business on a day-to-day basis are called **operating activities**. Creditors, owners, and potential investors examine the operating activities to determine if the company generates sufficient cash to support future investments and long-term profitability.

CASH FLOWS FROM INVESTING ACTIVITIES

Cash receipts and cash payments involving the sale or purchase of assets used to earn revenue over a period of time are called **investing activities**. Financial analysts examine the investing activities to assess the future financial strength and profitability of a business. If a company is forced to sell buildings and equipment to raise cash for operations, there would soon be no more assets to use in operations.

CASH FLOWS FROM FINANCING ACTIVITIES

Cash receipts and payments involving debt or equity transactions are called **financing activities**. These activities usually involve borrowing money from creditors and repaying the principal or selling stock and paying dividends. Financing activities are often used to ensure that an adequate balance exists in the Cash account. If a business uses more cash than it receives, it must obtain additional financing. This often happens as a business expands operations, as Sun Treasures is doing. Extra cash is required to obtain inventory and assets for the new stores. If a business has excess cash, it can use it to repay loans, notes, and bonds.

A list of Sun Treasures' common inflows and outflows from operating, investing, and financing activities is presented.

Activity	Cash Inflows	Cash Outflows
Operating	Sale of merchandise Receipt of interest income Receipt of rent income	Payment for daily operations (advertising, insurance, interest, inventory, rent, salaries, taxes, utilities)
Investing	Sale of office equipment Sale of store equipment Sale of other investments	Purchase of office equipment Purchase of store equipment Purchase of other investments
Financing	Issuance of stock Issuance of long-term notes payable Issuance of bonds Borrowing cash against line of credit	Payment of dividends Payment of principal from long-term notes payable Payment of bond principal Making principal payments on line of credit

Companies often establish a line of credit with a bank. This credit can be used to pay invoices or make cash purchases, especially for urgent business needs that require an immediate cash payment. A line of credit is a short-term loan to the company, and interest must be paid on the loan. The advantage of having a line of credit is that the company will not need to take out a new loan every time cash is needed to operate the business.

Operating Activities Section of a Statement of Cash Flows

Sun Treasures' statement of cash flows is shown on the next page.

The operating activities section of the statement of cash flows can be prepared using one of two methods: the direct method or the indirect method. Sun Treasures uses the direct method to prepare the operating activities section of the statement of cash flows. The indirect method begins with net income and makes adjustments for noncash expenditures and other cash differences. Regardless of the method used, the net cash provided or used by operating activities is the same amount.

Sun Treasures has three sources of cash from operating activities: sales, interest, and rent. The amount of cash received for each of these items is not the same as the amount of sales, interest income, and rent income listed on Sun Treasures' income statement. Since the statement of cash flows is prepared on a cash basis, the amount listed is the total amount of cash received this period for each item. For example, Sun Treasures received

$4,500.00 for three months' rent on November 1. The amount listed on the statement of cash flows for rent received is $4,500.00. By December 31, Sun Treasures only earned $3,000.00 of rent income. Only the amount of rent income earned, $3,000.00, is reported on Sun Treasures' income statement. Likewise, other amounts on the statement of cash flows may not be the same as related amounts on the income statement or the statement of stockholders' equity.

The amount listed for sales and interest income is the actual amount of cash received for each item during this fiscal period. The amount is determined by examining the general ledger accounts and the financial statements.

The payments section is prepared in a similar manner. The actual amount of cash paid for each item must be determined. Sun Treasures lists the major operating items separately and adds smaller operating items together in a category called Other operating expenses.

DMITRIY SHIRONOSOV/SHUTTERSTOCK.COM

Completed Statement of Cash Flows

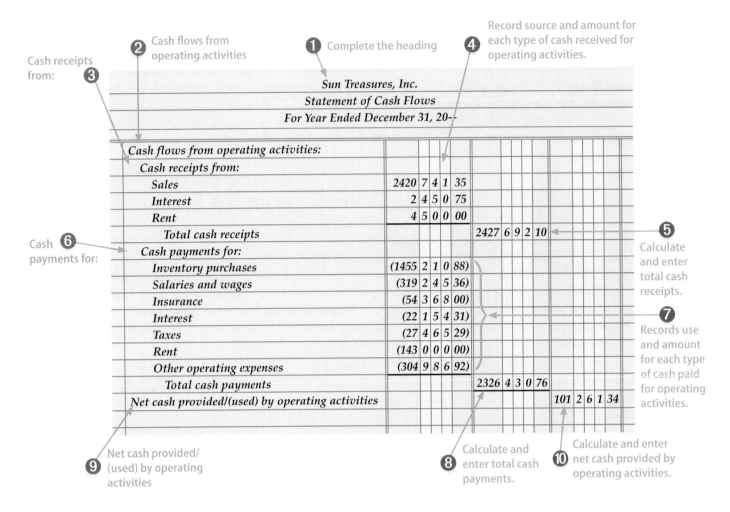

1 Complete the heading

2 Cash flows from operating activities

3 Cash receipts from:

4 Record source and amount for each type of cash received for operating activities.

6 Cash payments for:

9 Net cash provided/(used) by operating activities

5 Calculate and enter total cash receipts.

7 Records use and amount for each type of cash paid for operating activities.

8 Calculate and enter total cash payments.

10 Calculate and enter net cash provided by operating activities.

Sun Treasures, Inc.
Statement of Cash Flows
For Year Ended December 31, 20--

Cash flows from operating activities:			
Cash receipts from:			
Sales	2420 7 4 1 35		
Interest	2 4 5 0 75		
Rent	4 5 0 0 00		
Total cash receipts		2427 6 9 2 10	
Cash payments for:			
Inventory purchases	(1455 2 1 0 88)		
Salaries and wages	(319 2 4 5 36)		
Insurance	(54 3 6 8 00)		
Interest	(22 1 5 4 31)		
Taxes	(27 4 6 5 29)		
Rent	(143 0 0 0 00)		
Other operating expenses	(304 9 8 6 92)		
Total cash payments		2326 4 3 0 76	
Net cash provided/(used) by operating activities			101 2 6 1 34

Preparing the Operating Activities Section of a Statement of Cash Flows

1 Prepare the heading of the statement. The statement is prepared for the same period of time as the income statement.

2 Write the name of the first section, Cash flows from operating activities, on the first line.

3 Write the words Cash receipts from: on the next line.

4 Write the name and amount of each type of cash receipt for operating activities.

5 Calculate and enter total cash receipts.

6 Write the words Cash payments for: on the next line.

7 Write the name and amount of each type of cash payment for operating activities.

8 Calculate and enter total cash payments.

9 Write the words Net cash provided/(used) by operating activities on the next line.

10 Calculate and enter the net cash provided by operating activities, $101,261.34 ($2,427,692.10 − $2,326,430.76).

Investing Activities Section of a Statement of Cash Flows

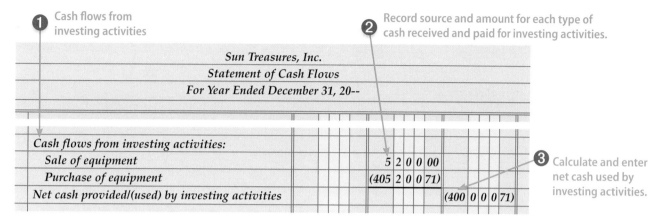

① Cash flows from investing activities

② Record source and amount for each type of cash received and paid for investing activities.

Sun Treasures, Inc.
Statement of Cash Flows
For Year Ended December 31, 20--

Cash flows from investing activities:		
Sale of equipment	5 2 0 0 00	
Purchase of equipment	(405 2 0 0 71)	
Net cash provided/(used) by investing activities		(400 0 0 0 71)

③ Calculate and enter net cash used by investing activities.

The remaining two sections of the statement of cash flows are prepared the same, regardless of the method used to prepare the operating activities section. The accountant for Sun Treasures examines the ledger accounts and other financial data to determine the actual cash received by investing activities and the actual cash paid for investing activities.

> **Preparing the Investing Activities Section of a Statement of Cash Flows**
>
> **①** Leaving one line blank, write the name of the second section, Cash flows from investing activities.
>
> **②** Write the name and amount of each type of cash receipt and cash payment for investing activities.
>
> **③** Calculate and enter the net cash used by investing activities, $(400,000.71) ($5,200.00 – $405,200.71).

Financing Activities Section of a Statement of Cash Flows

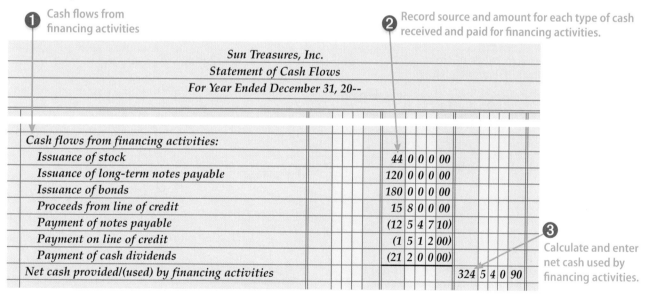

① Cash flows from financing activities

② Record source and amount for each type of cash received and paid for financing activities.

Sun Treasures, Inc.
Statement of Cash Flows
For Year Ended December 31, 20--

Cash flows from financing activities:		
Issuance of stock	44 0 0 0 00	
Issuance of long-term notes payable	120 0 0 0 00	
Issuance of bonds	180 0 0 0 00	
Proceeds from line of credit	15 8 0 0 00	
Payment of notes payable	(12 5 4 7 10)	
Payment on line of credit	(1 5 1 2 00)	
Payment of cash dividends	(21 2 0 0 00)	
Net cash provided/(used) by financing activities		324 5 4 0 90

③ Calculate and enter net cash used by financing activities.

The financing activities section is prepared in a manner similar to the investing activities section. Actual cash received by financing activities and actual cash paid for financing activities is determined and recorded on the statement of cash flows.

> **Preparing the Financing Activities Section of a Statement of Cash Flows**
>
> **①** Leaving one line blank, write the name of the third section, Cash flows from financing activities.
>
> **②** Write the name and amount of each type of cash receipt and cash payment for financing activities.
>
> **③** Calculate and enter the net cash provided by financing activities, $324,540.90 ($44,000.00 + $120,000.00 + $180,000.00 + $15,800.00 – $12,547.10 – $1,512.00 – $21,200.00).

Completing the Statement of Cash Flows

Sun Treasures, Inc.
Statement of Cash Flows
For Year Ended December 31, 20--

Cash flows from operating activities:			
Cash receipts from:			
Sales	2420 7 4 1 35		
Interest	2 4 5 0 75		
Rent	4 5 0 0 00		
Total cash receipts		2427 6 9 2 10	
Cash payments for:			
Inventory purchases	(1455 2 1 0 88)		
Salaries and wages	(319 2 4 5 36)		
Insurance	(54 3 6 8 00)		
Interest	(22 1 5 4 31)		
Taxes	(27 4 6 5 29)		
Rent	(143 0 0 0 00)		
Other operating expenses	(304 9 8 6 92)		
Total cash payments		(2326 4 3 0 76)	
Net cash provided/(used) by operating activities			101 2 6 1 34
Cash flows from investing activities:			
Sale of equipment		5 2 0 0 00	
Purchase of equipment		(405 2 0 0 71)	
Net cash provided/(used) by investing activities			(400 0 0 0 71)
Cash flows from financing activities:			
Issuance of stock		44 0 0 0 00	
Issuance of long-term notes payable		120 0 0 0 00	
Issuance of bonds		180 0 0 0 00	
Proceeds from line of credit		15 8 0 0 00	
Payment of notes payable		(12 5 4 7 10)	
Payment on line of credit		(1 5 1 2 00)	
Payment of cash dividends		(21 2 0 0 00)	
Net cash provided/(used) by financing activities			324 5 4 0 90
Net change in cash			25 8 0 1 53
Cash balance, January 1, 20--			18 0 4 7 15
Cash balance, December 31, 20--			43 8 4 8 68

Calculate net change in cash. **1**

Record cash balance on January 1. **2**

Record cash balance on December 31. Verify change in cash balance. **3**

The last three lines of the statement of cash flows show and verify the amount of increase or decrease in cash during the fiscal period. The net change in cash is calculated by netting out the totals of the three activities: Net cash provided by operating activities, $101,261.34, minus net cash used by investing activities, $400,000.71, plus net cash provided by financing activities, $324,540.90, equals net change in cash, $25,801.53.

The net change in cash is verified by adding it to the cash balance at the beginning of the period. The total should equal the ending balance in the Cash account.

Completing the Statement of Cash Flows

1 Calculate and record the net change in cash, $25,801.53.

2 Record the beginning cash balance, $18,047.15.

3 Record the ending cash balance, $43,848.68, and verify the net change in cash ($25,801.53 + $18,047.15 = $43,848.68).

The Enron Legacy

There was a time when Enron Corporation was an iconic symbol of American capitalism. The company was a leader in the production and trading of energy. Enron owned pipelines, power plants, natural gas distributors, and paper mills all over the world. Enron occupied a stunning office complex in Houston. For a short time, its famous crooked E logo adorned the home of Major League Baseball's Houston Astros.

Enron's growth and political power were headline news. Enron's revenue grew an astonishing 750% from 1996 to 2000. Its revenue of $101 billion in 2000 ranked it as one of the world's largest companies. *Fortune* magazine named Enron its "most innovative" company for six years. Enron was also well connected in national politics. Chief executive officer Ken Lay was a personal friend of President George W. Bush.

But underneath its pristine image was a corporate culture that motivated employees to take advantage of any situation to increase revenue and earnings. Enron's role in the 2000–2001 California energy crisis brought this culture to light. Legislation in California designed to control the energy prices charged to consumers had an unintended effect. California power companies had to pay market prices for extra energy while being limited to what they could charge the public. Enron schemed to inflate energy costs, causing wholesale electricity prices to skyrocket from $30 to $1,500 per megawatt hour. Enron was making huge profits while Californians were dealing with rolling blackouts. It certainly didn't help when president and chief operating officer Jeffrey Skilling was quoted as saying "What's the difference between California and the *Titanic*? At least when the *Titanic* went down … the lights were on."

A victim of accounting fraud and high debt, Enron filed for bankruptcy just over a year after its stock reached an all-time high of $90 per share. The accounting fraud included the abuse of revenue recognition rules, mark-to-market accounting, and special-purpose entities. These topics are well beyond the scope of this textbook. In fact, the complexity of these topics may have been beyond the ability or willingness of the financial community to understand.

Neither Enron nor its auditor, Arthur Andersen, survived the fraud. Numerous Enron officers were convicted of federal charges and sentenced to substantial jail terms. In a scene out of a Hollywood movie, Arthur Andersen staff shredded thousands of documents and e-mails related to its Enron audit. The accounting firm was convicted of obstruction of justice, an action that resulted in the firm's demise.

The Enron story has been told by numerous books and the documentary *The Smartest Guys in the Room*. The combined size and spectacular nature of the Enron and WorldCom frauds led to the passage of the Sarbanes-Oxley Act. The Act requires corporations to exert a higher level of internal control and executive responsibility over the fair presentation of financial information.

ACTIVITY

BelCorp Furniture has hired you to examine its purchases of materials. The company has reason to believe that its purchasing employees are favoring certain vendors.

INSTRUCTIONS

Open the spreadsheet FA_CH22 and complete the steps on the Instructions tab.

Sources: http://en.wikipedia.org; *Called to Account*, Paul M. Clikeman, Rutledge (New York and London), 2009; and *Business Fairy Tales*, Cecil W. Jackson, Thomson (Mason, Ohio), 2006.

End of Lesson Review

LO5 Prepare a statement of cash flows for a merchandising business organized as a corporation.

Terms Review

cash flow

statement of cash flows

operating activities

investing activities

financing activities

Audit your understanding

1. What basis is used to prepare the statement of cash flows?

2. List the three categories of activities used on the statement of cash flows.

Work together 22-3

Preparing a statement of cash flows for a corporation

Use the balance sheet from Work Together 22-2 and the information below. A form is given in the *Working Papers*. Your instructor will guide you through the following example.

Prepare a statement of cash flows for the current year.

Cash balance at the beginning of the period	$ 39,522.51

Cash receipts during the year:

Cash from sales	$598,236.31
Cash from interest	635.21
Cash from rent	4,000.00
Cash from sale of equipment	1,200.00
Cash from issuance of stock	17,500.00
Cash from issuance of bonds	10,000.00

Cash payments during the year:

Cash for inventory	$375,623.54
Cash for salaries and wages	85,807.14
Cash for insurance	4,254.35
Cash for interest	1,587.35
Cash for taxes	12,885.00
Cash for rent	16,248.65
Cash for other operating expenses	95,412.88
Cash for purchase of equipment	10,549.00
Cash for payment of notes payable	2,500.00
Cash for payment of dividends	21,200.00

On your own 22-3

Preparing a statement of cash flows for a corporation

Use the balance sheet from On Your Own 22-2 and the information below. A form is given in the *Working Papers*. Work the following problem independently.

Prepare a statement of cash flows for the current year.

Cash receipts during the year:

Cash from sales	$1,226,425.41
Cash from interest	377.00
Cash from rent	13,000.00
Cash from sale of equipment	13,200.00
Cash from issuance of stock	18,000.00
Cash from issuance of bonds	10,000.00

Cash payments during the year:

Cash for inventory	$ 805,412.20
Cash for salaries and wages	220,147.25
Cash for insurance	8,200.00
Cash for interest	915.00
Cash for taxes	28,000.00
Cash for rent	28,210.00
Cash for other operating expenses	95,214.20
Cash for purchase of equipment	75,000.00
Cash for payment of notes payable	7,500.00
Cash for payment of dividends	10,000.00
Cash balance at the beginning of the period	$ 6,023.29

22-4 Preparing Closing and Reversing Entries

LO6 Record closing entries for a merchandising business organized as a corporation.

LO7 Record reversing entries for a merchandising business organized as a corporation.

Closing Entry for Accounts with Credit Balances LO6

	DATE		ACCOUNT TITLE	DOC. NO.	POST. REF.	DEBIT	CREDIT	
1			*Closing Entries*					1
2	Dec.	31	Sales			2576 3 2 1 45		2
3			Purchases Discount			15 6 8 5 93		3
4			Purchases Returns and Allowances			1 1 5 0 40		4
5			Interest Income			2 5 1 2 80		5
6			Rent Income			3 0 0 0 00		6
7			Gain on Plant Assets			18 2 3 1 00		7
8			Income Summary				2616 9 0 1 58	8

GENERAL JOURNAL PAGE 14

① Debit the balance of every income statement account with a credit balance.

② Enter the total of the debit entries as a credit to Income Summary.

After financial statements are prepared, the adjusted trial balance is used to journalize the closing entries for a corporation. The income statement accounts with credit balances consist of the revenue accounts (Sales, Interest Income, Rent Income, and Gain on Plant Assets) and the contra cost accounts (Purchases Discount and Purchases Returns and Allowances). Closing entries are recorded on a new page of the general journal.

Journalizing a Closing Entry for Income Statement Accounts with Credit Balances

① Debit the balance of every income statement account with a credit balance.

② Enter the total of the debit entries, $2,616,901.58, as a credit to Income Summary.

In most commercial computerized accounting systems, year-end closing is performed by the software. The accountant selects a menu item to close the accounting records for the year, and the software automatically updates its database. In some systems, year-end closing cannot be undone.

Closing Entry for Accounts with Debit Balances

1 Enter Income Summary

Enter the total of the credit entries as a debit to Income Summary. **3**

GENERAL JOURNAL

PAGE 14

	DATE	ACCOUNT TITLE	DOC. NO.	POST. REF.	DEBIT	CREDIT	
1		*Closing Entries*					1
9	31	Income Summary			2509 6 7 6 37		9
10		Sales Discount				15 4 5 7 93	10
11		Sales Returns and Allowances				113 5 2 3 11	11
12		Purchases				1307 1 6 0 50	12
13		Advertising Expense				58 0 0 0 00	13
14		Cash Short and Over				2 4 1 7 25	14
15		Credit Card Fee Expense				23 7 6 3 21	15
16		Depreciation Expense—Office Equipment				25 1 4 6 00	16
17		Depreciation Expense—Store Equipment				113 4 1 8 00	17
18		Insurance Expense				36 2 2 5 00	18
19		Miscellaneous Expense				38 0 1 0 66	19
20		Payroll Taxes Expense				27 4 2 3 60	20
21		Rent Expense				143 0 0 0 00	21
22		Salary Expense				290 4 0 0 00	22
23		Supplies Expense—Office				76 4 4 0 00	23
24		Supplies Expense—Store				109 8 0 0 00	24
25		Uncollectible Accounts Expense				1 4 2 3 69	25
26		Utilities Expense				66 8 8 6 10	26
27		Federal Income Tax Expense				25 9 9 2 22	27
28		Interest Expense				18 3 4 7 10	28
29		Loss on Plant Assets				16 8 4 2 00	29

2 Credit the balance of every income statement account with a debit balance.

The income statement accounts with debit balances consist of the contra revenue accounts (Sales Discount and Sales Returns and Allowances), the cost (Purchases), and all expense accounts. Information needed for closing income statement debit balance accounts is obtained from the adjusted trial balance Debit column.

Because Cash Short and Over has a debit balance in this fiscal period, the account balance amount is closed to Income Summary with the debit balance accounts.

> **Journalizing a Closing Entry for Income Statement Accounts with Debit Balances**
>
> **1** Enter the account title Income Summary.
>
> **2** Credit the balance of every income statement account with a debit balance.
>
> **3** Enter the total of the credit entries, $2,509,676.37, as a debit to Income Summary.

Closing Entry to Record Net Income

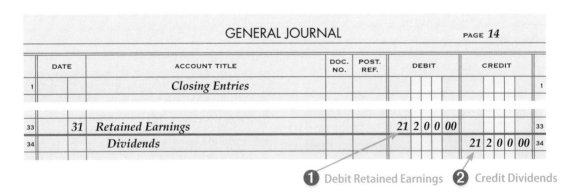

After closing entries for the income statement accounts are posted, Income Summary has a credit balance of $83,603.21. This credit balance equals the net income for the period.

As reported on the statement of stockholders' equity, the net income of a corporation increases Retained Earnings. Closing the balance of Income Summary actually increases the Retained Earnings account by the amount of net income. After the closing entry is posted, Income Summary has a zero balance.

A corporation having a net loss will have a debit balance in Income Summary. Retained Earnings would then be debited and Income Summary credited for the net loss amount. The entry would reduce the balance of Retained Earnings.

> **Journalizing a Closing Entry to Record Net Income in Retained Earnings**
>
> **1** Record a debit to Income Summary for the amount of net income, $83,603.21.
>
> **2** Record a credit to Retained Earnings for the same amount, $83,603.21.

Closing Entry for Dividends

Dividends reduce the earnings retained by a corporation, as reported on the statement of stockholders' equity. The closing entry reduces the balance in the Retained Earnings account by the amount of the dividends.

> **Journalizing a Closing Entry for Dividends**
>
> **1** Record a debit to Retained Earnings for the amount of dividends, $21,200.00.
>
> **2** Record a credit to Dividends for the same amount, $21,200.00.

Reversing Entries LO7

	DATE	ACCOUNT TITLE	DOC. NO.	POST. REF.	DEBIT	CREDIT	
1		*Adjusting Entries*					1
4	31	Interest Receivable			1 7 5 00		4
5		Interest Income				1 7 5 00	5
18	31	Interest Expense			7 1 0 84		18
19		Interest Payable				7 1 0 84	19
22	31	Federal Income Tax Expense			2 9 9 2 22		22
23		Federal Income Tax Payable				2 9 9 2 22	23

GENERAL JOURNAL PAGE 13

Reverse the entry that created a balance in Interest Receivable. ❶

GENERAL JOURNAL PAGE 1

	DATE	ACCOUNT TITLE	DOC. NO.	POST. REF.	DEBIT	CREDIT	
1		*Reversing Entries*					1
2	Jan. 20-- 1	Interest Income			1 7 5 00		2
3		Interest Receivable				1 7 5 00	3
4	1	Interest Payable			7 1 0 84		4
5		Interest Expense				7 1 0 84	5
6	1	Federal Income Tax Payable			2 9 9 2 22		6
7		Federal Income Tax Expense				2 9 9 2 22	7
8							8

Reverse the entry that created a balance in Interest Payable. ❷

Reverse the entry that created a balance in Federal Income Tax Payable. ❸

If an adjusting entry creates a balance in an asset or a liability account, the adjusting entry should be reversed. A review of Sun Treasures' adjusting entries shows that three adjusting entries created a balance in an asset or a liability account.

1. The adjusting entry for accrued interest income created a balance in the **Interest Receivable** account.
2. The adjusting entry for accrued interest expense created a balance in the **Interest Payable** account.
3. The adjusting entry for federal income tax expense created a balance in the **Federal Income Tax Payable** account.

> **Journalizing Reversing Entries**
>
> ❶ Reverse the entry that created a balance in Interest Receivable.
>
> ❷ Reverse the entry that created a balance in Interest Payable.
>
> ❸ Reverse the entry that created a balance in Federal Income Tax Payable.

Accounting Cycle for a Merchandising Business Organized as a Corporation

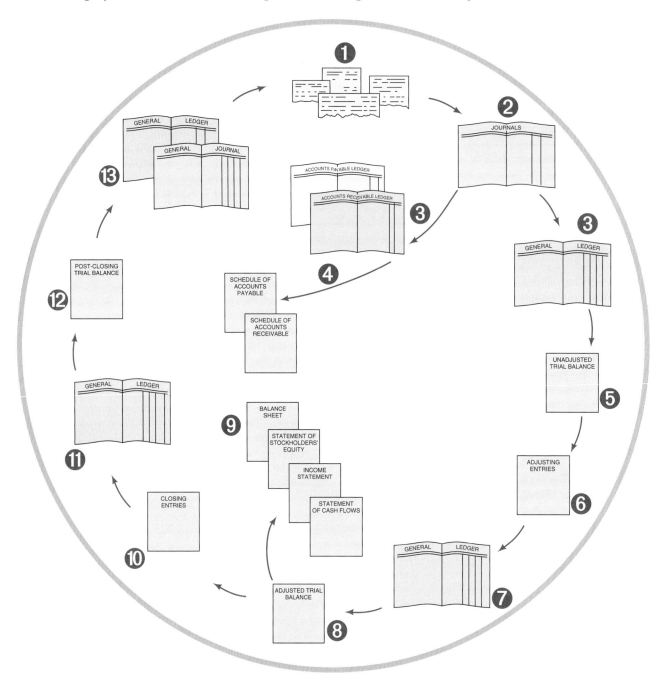

The accounting cycles are similar for merchandising businesses, regardless of how the businesses are organized. Variations occur in preparing financial statements. Variations also occur when reversing entries are recorded.

① Source documents are checked for accuracy, and transactions are analyzed into debit and credit parts.

② Transactions, from information on source documents, are recorded in journals.

③ Journal entries are posted to the accounts payable, accounts receivable, and general ledgers.

④ Schedules of accounts payable and accounts receivable are prepared from the subsidiary ledgers.

⑤ An unadjusted trial balance is prepared from the general ledger.

⑥ Adjusting entries are journalized.

⑦ Adjusting entries are posted to the general ledger.

⑧ An adjusted trial balance is prepared from the general ledger.

⑨ Financial statements are prepared from the adjusted trial balance.

⑩ Closing entries are journalized.

⑪ Closing entries are posted to the general ledger.

⑫ A post-closing trial balance is prepared from the general ledger.

⑬ Reversing entries are journalized and posted to the general ledger.

Information Technology Departments

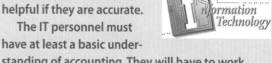

Most companies use some form of automated accounting software to record transactions, generate reports, and analyze financial results. For a small business, this software is usually a generic system that can easily be used by thousands of other businesses. These "one-size-fits-all" packages allow the user a few choices, but not great flexibility.

Larger companies, with information technology (IT) departments, may either develop their own accounting software programs internally or make major revisions in purchased programs to meet the company's needs. In addition to standard financial statements, company management may need unique reports for decision-making purposes. A standard accounting program assists in preparing the financial statements but is not programmed to gather data for the special reports. In this case, the IT department may attempt to revise the program.

These reports will only be helpful if they are accurate.

The IT personnel must have at least a basic understanding of accounting. They will have to work closely with accounting department personnel to ensure that the revised accounting software is measuring and reporting the data accurately. The more accounting knowledge the IT workers have, the easier it will be to communicate the needs of the accounting department and company management.

CRITICAL THINKING

1. As a class, identify a local business or government agency that has an information technology department. Choose a student to contact that organization to arrange an interview with a member of that department and two or three class representatives.

2. As a class, develop a list of questions that the class representatives should ask the IT representative.

3. After the interview, have the class representatives share their findings with the class.

End of Lesson Review

LO6 Record closing entries for a merchandising business organized as a corporation.

LO7 Record reversing entries for a merchandising business organized as a corporation.

Audit your understanding

1. What is used to prove the equality of debits and credits in the general ledger after closing entries are posted?

2. What are the four closing entries for a corporation?

3. Which accounts are closed to Retained Earnings?

Work together 22-4

Journalizing closing and reversing entries for a corporation

Use the accounting forms and financial statements from Work Together 22-1. General journal pages are given in the *Working Papers*. Your instructor will guide you through the following examples.

1. For the current year, journalize the closing entries using page 13 of a general journal.

2. For the following year, journalize the reversing entries using page 14 of a general journal.

On your own 22-4

Journalizing closing and reversing entries for a corporation

Use the accounting forms and financial statements from On Your Own 22-1. General journal pages are given in the *Working Papers*. Work this problem independently.

1. For the current year, journalize the closing entries using page 13 of a general journal.

2. For the following year, journalize the reversing entries using page 14 of a general journal.

©CANDICE CUSACK, ISTOCK

A Look at Accounting Software
Recurring Reversing Entries

A Look at Accounting Software in Chapter 15 showed the procedure for fully or partially automating transactions. This feature shows what happens when a recurring entry is set up for adjustments.

In this chapter, you learned about the need to accrue some types of revenue and expenses. You learned that accountants often prefer to reverse some adjusting entries. It was explained that reversing entries are not required, but doing so makes the accounting easier and less prone to error.

Reversing entries in a computerized accounting system are very easy to do. It is as simple as clicking a button on the Make Journal Entries window. The system does all the work.

When recurring entries and reversing entries work together, much of the work is reduced for the accounting staff and the chances for error are greatly reduced. It is important to remember, however, that accountants still need to determine which accounts to adjust and by what amounts.

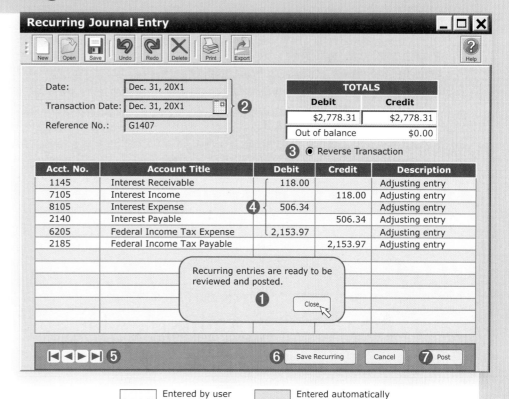

Recurring Journal Entry

Date: Dec. 31, 20X1
Transaction Date: Dec. 31, 20X1 ❷
Reference No.: G1407

TOTALS		
	Debit	Credit
	$2,778.31	$2,778.31
Out of balance		$0.00

❸ ● Reverse Transaction

Acct. No.	Account Title	Debit	Credit	Description
1145	Interest Receivable	118.00		Adjusting entry
7105	Interest Income		118.00	Adjusting entry
8105	Interest Expense	506.34		Adjusting entry
2140	Interest Payable		506.34	Adjusting entry
6205	Federal Income Tax Expense	2,153.97		Adjusting entry
2185	Federal Income Tax Payable		2,153.97	Adjusting entry

Recurring entries are ready to be reviewed and posted. ❶ [Close]

❺ ❻ [Save Recurring] [Cancel] ❼ [Post]

☐ Entered by user ☐ Entered automatically

❶ At the end of 20X0, Sun Treasures made the adjusting entries shown in the window and saved them as a recurring entry (Chapter 15). The posting option of "Edit before posting" was selected. Now, on December 31, 20X1, the system presents the recurring entries for review.

❷ The system automatically enters the system date, the transaction date, and the transaction reference number.

❸ When these adjustments were entered in 20X0, the accountant chose to reverse the entries and clicked the reverse transaction button. The system automatically posted a reversing entry on January 1, 20X1.

❹ These amounts were used for the adjustments on December 31, 20X0. The user will change them to the 20X1 amounts: Interest Receivable, $175.00; Interest Expense, $710.84; and Federal Income Tax Expense, $2,992.22.

❺ Other recurring transactions will have been presented by the system as well, including the adjusting entries that will not be reversed. The user can use the forward and back arrows to view those transactions.

❻ After the entries have been edited, the user can elect to save the edited recurring entry. That would be very helpful if adjusting entries were added or deleted with this year's adjustments.

❼ The user clicks Post to post the adjustments. The system will automatically post a reversing entry on January 1, 20X2.

Chapter Summary

Each adjusting entry affects an income statement account and a balance sheet account. Therefore, all adjusting entries must be accurately calculated and recorded. Any errors will affect the accuracy of both the income statement and the balance sheet.

Once the adjusting entries are journalized and posted, financial statements are prepared. The income statement is prepared first. The amount of net income is used in the statement of stockholders' equity, which is prepared second. The totals from the statement of stockholders' equity are used to prepare the balance sheet.

The statement of cash flows is also prepared. It contains three main sections: operating activities, investing activities, and financing activities. The statement of cash flows is prepared on a cash basis, meaning that it shows actual cash inflows and outflows.

Next, the closing entries are prepared and posted. The closing entries close all temporary accounts and transfer the balances through **Income Summary** to the **Retained Earnings** account. Only assets, liabilities, and equity accounts will have a balance going into the next fiscal period. A post-closing trial balance is completed to ensure that debits equal credits.

If a company chooses to use reversing entries, these entries are recorded as the first entries of the new fiscal period. Every adjusting entry that established a balance in a receivable or payable account is reversed.

EXPLORE ACCOUNTING

Audits Provide Stockholders with Positive Assurance

The financial statements are the responsibility of the company management. Stockholders want assurance that the financial statements of their corporation accurately present its financial condition and results of operations. To provide this assurance, corporations hire independent public accountants to audit the financial statements. Public accountants referred to as *auditors* provide the assurance of the accuracy of the financial statements. They also provide a written opinion that informs stockholders whether the financial statements can be relied upon for making informed business decisions.

Auditors examine accounting records to collect evidence that supports amounts in the financial statements. The auditors then form an opinion, which is the basis for a letter to the stockholders and directors. There are four types of audit opinions that the letter can communicate: unqualified, qualified, adverse, and disclaimer.

An unqualified opinion means the auditors feel that the financial statements fairly represent the financial position of the company without any exceptions (qualifications). This is the best opinion that an auditor can issue. It means that the auditor believes the company followed GAAP to prepare its financial statements—without exceptions.

A qualified opinion means the auditors feel that the financial statements fairly represent the financial position of the company, except for one or more minor issues (or qualifications).

An adverse opinion means the auditors feel the financial statements do not fairly represent the financial position of the company or that the financial statements do not follow GAAP.

A disclaimer means the auditors could not form an opinion as to whether the financial statements fairly represent the financial position of the company. This may happen because the company did not provide enough information to the auditors. It can also happen when the information needed to support the financial statements is not available because it has been destroyed by fire or natural disaster.

INSTRUCTIONS

Access an annual report using a library or the Internet. Read the opinion letter written by the company auditors. In a written report, list the name of the company, the date of the opinion, and which type of audit opinion the auditors gave the company. Include a copy of the auditors' letter with your report.

Apply Your Understanding

INSTRUCTIONS: Download problem instructions for Excel, QuickBooks, and Peachtree from the textbook companion website at www.C21accounting.com.

22-1 Application Problem: Recording adjusting entries and preparing an adjusted trial balance LO1

Handy Hardware Corporation's unadjusted trial balance and accounting forms are given in the *Working Papers*.

Instructions:

1. Using the following information, journalize the adjusting entries for the current year ended December 31.

Adjustment Information, December 31

Estimated uncollectible accounts based on aging accounts receivable	$ 13,832.96
Accrued interest income	630.00
Merchandise inventory	162,569.00
Supplies inventory	3,695.00
Value of prepaid insurance	8,360.00
Annual depreciation expense—equipment	13,034.00
Accrued interest expense	600.00
Prepaid rent income earned	4,000.00

2. Post the adjusting entries to the T accounts.

3. Using the tax table shown in this chapter, calculate federal income tax expense and journalize the income tax adjustment.

4. Post the federal income tax adjusting entry to the T accounts.

5. Using the unadjusted trial balance and the T accounts, complete the adjusted trial balance. Save your work to complete Problem 22-2.

22-2 Application Problem: Preparing an income statement, statement of stockholders' equity, and balance sheet for a corporation LO2, 3, 4

Use the adjusted trial balance from Problem 22-1. Forms are given in the *Working Papers*.

Instructions:

1. Complete the income statement for the current year. Calculate and record the following vertical analysis ratios: (a) cost of merchandise sold; (b) gross profit on operations; (c) total operating expenses; (d) income from operations; (e) net addition or deduction from other revenue and expenses; and (f) net income before federal income tax. Round percentage calculations to the nearest 0.01%.

2. Complete the statement of stockholders' equity for the current year. As of January 1, Handy Hardware Corporation had issued 15,000 shares of common stock with a par value of $1.00 per share. During the fiscal year, the corporation issued 5,000 additional shares of common stock. The balance in Paid-in Capital in Excess of Par—Common on January 1, 20--, was $20,000.00. As of January 1, Handy Hardware had not issued any shares of preferred stock. During the fiscal year, it issued 1,000 shares of $30.00 par, 5% preferred stock at par value.

3. Complete the balance sheet for Handy Hardware Corporation for the current year. Save your work to complete Problem 22-3.

22-3 Application Problem: Preparing a statement of cash flows for a corporation LO5

Use the balance sheet from Problem 22-2 and the information below. A form is given in the *Working Papers*.

Instructions:

Prepare a statement of cash flows for the current year.

Cash receipts during the year:

Cash from sales	$1,925,342.80
Cash from interest	754.14

Cash from rent	$ 12,000.00
Cash from sale of equipment	2,500.00
Cash from issuance of stock	65,000.00
Cash from issuance of bonds	8,000.00
Cash payments during the year:	
Cash for inventory	$1,371,254.10
Cash for salaries and wages	262,954.25
Cash for insurance	18,500.00
Cash for interest	7,050.50
Cash for taxes	25,650.00
Cash for rent	30,000.00
Cash for other operating expenses	171,501.54
Cash for purchase of equipment	40,000.00
Cash for payment of notes payable	20,000.00
Cash for payment of dividends	40,000.00
Cash balance at the beginning of the period	$ 11,010.61

22-4 Application Problem: Journalizing closing and reversing entries for a corporation LO6, 7

Use the accounting forms and financial statements from Problem 22-1 to complete this problem. General journal pages are given in the *Working Papers*.

Instructions:

1. For the current year, journalize the closing entries using page 13 of a general journal.

2. For the following year, journalize the reversing entries using page 14 of a general journal.

1. Journalize and post closing entries to the general journal.
2. Print the general journal and trial balance.
3. Journalize and post reversing entries to the general journal.

1. Journalize and post closing entries to the journal.
2. Print the journal and trial balance.
3. Journalize and post reversing entries to the journal.

1. Journalize and post closing and reversing entries to the general journal.
2. Print the worksheets.

22-M Mastery Problem: Journalizing adjustments, preparing financial statements, and journalizing end-of-fiscal-period entries for a corporation LO1, 2, 3, 4, 5, 6, 7

Ramel Corporation's unadjusted trial balance and accounting forms are given in the *Working Papers*.

Instructions:

1. Using the following information, journalize the adjusting entries for the current year ended December 31.

Adjustment Information, December 31

Estimated uncollectible accounts based on aging accounts receivable	$ 11,020.00
Accrued interest income	160.00
Merchandise inventory	581,489.16
Supplies inventory	620.01
Value of prepaid insurance	4,000.00
Annual depreciation expense—office equipment	10,960.00
Annual depreciation expense—store equipment	10,120.00
Accrued interest expense	625.00
Prepaid rent income earned	6,000.00

2. Post the adjusting entries to the T accounts.

3. Using the tax table presented in this chapter, calculate the federal income tax expense and journalize the income tax adjustment.

4. Post the federal income tax adjusting entry to the T accounts.

5. Using the unadjusted trial balance and the T accounts, complete the adjusted trial balance.

6. Complete the income statement for the current year. Calculate and record the following vertical analysis ratios: (a) cost of merchandise sold; (b) gross profit on operations; (c) total operating expenses; (d) income from operations; (e) net addition or deduction from other revenue and expenses; and (f) net income before federal income tax. Round percentage calculations to the nearest 0.01%.

7. Analyze the corporation's income statement by determining if vertical analysis ratios are within acceptable levels. If any vertical analysis ratio is not within an acceptable level, suggest steps that the company should take. The corporation considers the following ratios acceptable.

Cost of merchandise sold	Not more than 65.00%
Gross profit on operations	Not less than 35.00%
Total operating expenses	Not more than 30.00%
Income from operations	Not less than 5.00%
Net deduction from other revenue and expenses	Not more than 0.10%
Net income before federal income tax	Not less than 4.90%

8. Complete the statement of stockholders' equity for the current year. As of January 1, Ramel Corporation had issued 10,000 shares of common stock with a par value of $5.00 per share. During the fiscal year, the corporation issued 6,000 additional shares of common stock. The balance in Paid-in Capital in Excess of Par—Common on January 1, 20--, was $130,000.00. As of January 1, Ramel Corporation issued 1,500 shares of $20.00 par, 5% preferred stock. During the year, it issued 500 additional shares of preferred stock at par value.

9. Complete the balance sheet for Ramel Corporation for the current year.

10. Calculate the corporation's (a) working capital and (b) current ratio. Determine if these items are within acceptable levels. The corporation considers the following levels acceptable.

Working capital	Not less than $600,000.00
Current ratio	Between 5.0 to 1 and 6.0 to 1

11. Using the balance sheet and the following information, prepare a statement of cash flows for the current year.

Cash receipts during the year:	
Cash from sales	$4,211,326.34
Cash from interest	1,510.00
Cash from rent	9,000.00
Cash from sale of store equipment	3,500.00
Cash from issuance of stock	90,000.00
Cash payments during the year:	
Cash for inventory	$2,645,507.48
Cash for salaries and wages	844,521.30
Cash for insurance	30,000.00
Cash for interest	8,000.00
Cash for taxes	50,000.00
Cash for rent	90,000.00
Cash for other operating expenses	312,884.13
Cash for purchase of office equipment	48,651.87
Cash for purchase of store equipment	15,500.00
Cash for payment of notes payable	68,000.00
Cash for payment of bonds payable	150,000.00
Cash for payment of dividends	70,000.00
Cash balance at the beginning of the period	$ 72,764.94

12. Journalize the closing entries using page 16 of a general journal.

13. Journalize the reversing entries using page 17 of a general journal.

 Peachtree

1. Journalize and post adjusting and closing entries to the general journal.
2. Print the general journal and trial balance.
3. Journalize and post reversing entries to the general journal.

QB *Quick Books*

1. Journalize and post adjusting and closing entries to the journal.
2. Print the journal and trial balance.
3. Journalize and post reversing entries to the journal.

X

1. Journalize and post adjusting, closing, and reversing entries to the general journal.
2. Print the worksheets.

AAONLINE

1. Go to www.cengage.com/login
2. Click on **AA Online** to access.
3. Go to the online assignment and follow the instructions.

22-C Challenge Problem: Reversing entries L07

Elert Company's blank journals and T accounts are given in the *Working Papers*. On December 31, 20X1, Elert Company has one note receivable on its records. It is a $10,000.00, 90-day, 9% note. The accountant recorded the following adjusting entry related to this note:

GENERAL JOURNAL   PAGE 24

	DATE	ACCOUNT TITLE	DOC. NO.	POST. REF.	DEBIT	CREDIT	
1		*Adjusting Entries*					1
4	31	*Interest Receivable*			7 5 00		4
5		*Interest Income*				7 5 00	5

After closing entries were posted, the related accounts had the balances reflected in the following T accounts.

Notes Receivable	
Dec. 31 Bal. 10,000.00	

Interest Income	
Dec. 31 Closing 75.00	Dec. 31 Adj. 75.00

Interest Receivable	
Dec. 31 Adj. 75.00	

Instructions:

1. Assume that Elert Company uses reversing entries.
   a. Journalize the reversing entry and post the entry to the T accounts.
   b. Journalize the receipt of the note and interest on its due date, March 1, 20X2, using Check No. 441 as the source document. Post the entry to the T accounts.
   c. Complete the statements regarding how much interest income was recognized in 20X1 and 20X2.

2. Assume that Elert Company does not use reversing entries.
   a. Journalize the receipt of the note and interest on its due date, March 1, 20X2, using Check No. 441 as the source document. Post the entry to the T accounts.
   b. Complete the statements regarding how much interest income was recognized in 20X1 and 20X2.

3. Why would Elert choose to use reversing entries?

21st Century Skills

The Ins and Outs of Cash Flow

Theme: Financial, Economic, Business, and Entrepreneurial Literacy

Skills: Critical Thinking and Problem Solving, ICT Literacy

PARTNERSHIP FOR
21ST CENTURY SKILLS

One of the first things to do in managing personal finances is to understand the inflow and outflow of cash for a period of time. While a budget provides a plan for spending, a cash flow statement actually shows where the money came from and how it was spent. Learning to manage cash flow will prevent overspending and allow personal wealth-building.

A cash flow statement for personal use contains three parts: sources of income (inflows of cash), expenditures (outflows of cash), and the difference between the two amounts, the net cash flow.

Sources of income are more than just your salary. Income can be gifts, scholarships, and investment income. Basically, anything that brings in money is considered income.

Outflows of cash consist of all of your expenditures, both fixed and variable. Fixed expenditures are those costs that remain unchanged from one period to the next. These include rent, car payments, savings, and investments. Variable expenditures might include food, charitable contributions, gas, and clothing.

The last component of the cash flow statement is calculating the net cash flow. This is the cash inflow minus cash outflow. A positive number is good and means you have extra cash to invest toward financial goals and build personal wealth or even pay down debt. A negative balance is bad and means outflow is greater than inflow. A plan must be created to spend less or generate more income. One cannot become a millionaire if there is a deficit of cash.

Managing your cash flow allows you to direct the cash. Understanding money flow keeps you in control!

APPLICATION

1. Julia, a recent college graduate, just prepared a cash flow statement after her first month of employment at Hickman's Hometown Cuisine. Her cash flow statement showed the following for the month of August: cash inflow, $3,269.27 and cash outflow, $2,975.00. Julia also has student loan debt totaling $12,425.00. Julia would like to purchase a new computer. She does not have a savings plan or a retirement plan. Determine the amount of net cash at the end of August. What suggestions would you make for Julia to help her achieve her financial goals? Explain.

2. Elias works at Harmon's Historical Village, a living history museum. He received $4,971.65 during May for tips and wages earned by providing tours at the museum. His cash outflow for May was $5,325.19. Explain how Elias could have a negative cash flow, yet be able to make his payments.

3. Create an Excel spreadsheet with the following headings down the side (rows): Cash Inflow, Cash Outflow, and Net Cash Flow. The following headings should be placed at the top (columns): Recent College Graduate, Newly Married, Married with 3 Kids.

   a. Assume that you are a recent college graduate, newly married, and married with three children. Anticipate your sources of cash inflow and a list of expenditures (cash outflow) for the different stages in your life. Record your sources and estimations. Calculate your net cash flow.

   b. Explain how the various stages of your life might affect your cash flow statement.

Analyzing Nike's financial statements

As stated in this chapter, the Operating Activities section of the statement of cash flows can be prepared using the direct method or the indirect method. Sun Treasures used the direct method to prepare its statement of cash flows. Nike uses the indirect method. The only difference is in the operating activities section. Look at Nike's Consolidated Statements of Cash Flows on page B-7 in Appendix B. The "Cash provided by operations" section begins with net income and then makes adjustments not affecting cash and changes in certain other accounts. The Operating Activities section of Sun Treasures' statement of cash flows lists cash receipts and cash payments. Both companies arrive at an amount of cash flow from operating activities.

INSTRUCTIONS

1. List the cash provided by operations for Nike for the fiscal year 2011.
2. Did Nike's cash increase or decrease during the fiscal year ended 2011? By what amount?
3. What was the largest use of cash for financing activities for the fiscal year ended 2011?

Reinforcement Activity 3—Part B

An Accounting Cycle for a Corporation: End-of-Fiscal-Period Work

 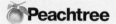 **AAONLiNE**

The plant asset records and ledgers used in Reinforcement Activity 3—Part A are needed to complete Reinforcement Activity 3—Part B.

Reinforcement Activity 3—Part B includes those accounting activities needed to complete the accounting cycle of Restaurant Warehouse, Inc.

INSTRUCTIONS

9. Record the 20X4 depreciation on the plant asset record of plant asset no. 422. (Plant assets 452 and 453 will not have depreciation in 20X4 because they were purchased at the end of the year.)

10. Prepare an unadjusted trial balance.

11. Use the information below, collected on December 31, to journalize the adjusting entries.

   a. Estimated uncollectible accounts based on aging accounts receivable, $1,261.20.

   b. Outstanding notes receivable consist of NR30, a 60-day, 11% note accepted from Northside Catering on December 7, 20X4, for an extension of time on its account, $7,200.00.

   c. Merchandise inventory, $150,983.90.

   d. Supplies inventory, $850.00.

   e. Value of prepaid insurance, $9,200.00.

   f. Estimate of office equipment depreciation, $15,040.00.

   g. Estimate of warehouse equipment depreciation, $28,420.00.

   h. Outstanding notes payable consist of (1) NP19, a 100-day, 9% note for $20,000.00 signed on October 31, 20X4, and (2) NP22, a 90-day, 10% note for $12,000.00 signed on December 28, 20X4.

   i. Rent earned, $3,000.00.

12. Post the adjusting entries in the general ledger.

13. Prepare an adjusted trial balance and total the columns.

14. Using the tax table shown in Chapter 22, calculate the federal income tax owed for the fiscal year.

15. Journalize and post the adjusting entry for federal income tax payable.

16. Complete the adjusted trial balance.

17. Prepare an income statement for the current year. Prepare a vertical analysis of each amount in the fourth column. Round calculations to the nearest 0.1%.

18. Prepare a statement of stockholders' equity. The company had 6,000 shares of $10.00 par value common stock and no shares of $50.00, 5% preferred stock outstanding on January 1. The company issued 500 shares of common stock and 300 shares of preferred stock during the year.

19. Prepare a balance sheet for the current year.

20. Use the Cash account and the information below to prepare a statement of cash flows for the current year.

Cash balance at the beginning of the period:	$ 15,250.25
Cash receipts during the year:	
Cash from sales	$1,534,072.65
Cash from interest	875.00
Cash from rent	10,000.00
Cash from sale of equipment	33,000.00
Cash from issuance of stock	40,000.00

Cash payments during the year:

Cash for inventory	$1,024,273.20
Cash for salaries and wages	210,573.25
Cash for insurance	15,000.00
Cash for interest	6,851.23
Cash for taxes	16,412.88
Cash for rent	48,000.00
Cash for other operating expenses	174,585.94
Cash for purchase of equipment	25,500.00
Cash for payment of bonds	40,000.00
Cash for payment of notes payable	17,000.00
Cash for payment of dividends	30,000.00

21. Journalize and post the closing entries.

22. Prepare a post-closing trial balance.

23. Journalize and post the reversing entries.

DIGITAL DIVERSIONS

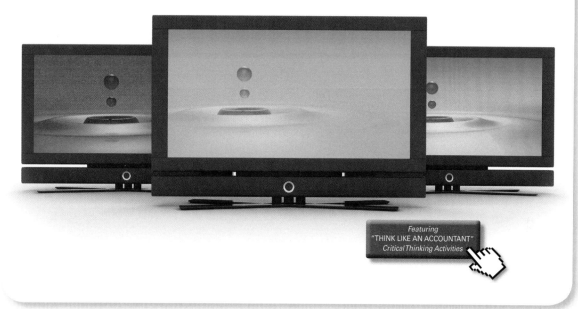

Featuring
"THINK LIKE AN ACCOUNTANT"
Critical Thinking Activities

This company covers an online merchandising business organized as a corporation with its company offices in Bradenton, Florida. Digital Diversions sells televisions, cell phones, MP3 players, computers, video games, and other electronics goods.

The business sells merchandise for cash and also subscribes to a national credit card service.

In addition, some sales are made on account to certain customers. In this simulation, you will do accounting work for Digital Diversions.

This real-life business simulation comes with source documents. It is available in manual and automated versions. The automated version is used with Automated Accounting Online software.

The following activities are included in this simulation:

1. Recording transactions in special journals from source documents.

2. Posting items to be posted individually to a general ledger and subsidiary ledger.

3. Posting column totals to a general ledger.

4. Preparing schedules of accounts receivable and accounts payable from subsidiary ledgers.

5. Preparing a trial balance on a work sheet.

6. Planning adjustments and completing a work sheet.

7. Preparing financial statements.

8. Journalizing and posting adjusting entries.

9. Journalizing and posting closing entries.

10. Preparing a post-closing trial balance.

11. Journalizing and posting reversing entries.

12. Completing the Think Like an Accountant Financial Analysis activities.

Part

4 Additional
Accounting Procedures

©OLGALIS, ISTOCK

MUST-HAVE GADGETS

Sarah Hatcher and Parker O'Reilly own a partnership called Must-Have Gadgets. The business sells accessories for electronic devices. The company accepts orders through its website and has customers in other countries.

Must-Have Gadgets rents the building that it uses for its operations. There are no employees; the partners do all the work in the company. Partners are not employees, and the money that partners receive from a partnership is not considered salaries. Therefore, Must-Have Gadgets does not need accounts for recording salaries and payroll taxes. Must-Have Gadgets will be used in Chapters 23 and 24 in Part 4 to illustrate the chapter concepts.

Chart of Accounts
MUST-HAVE GADGETS

GENERAL LEDGER

Balance Sheet Accounts

(1000) ASSETS
1100   Current Assets
1110   Cash
1120   Petty Cash
1130   Accounts Receivable
1135   Allowance for Uncollectible Accounts
1137   Time Drafts Receivable
1140   Merchandise Inventory
1150   Supplies
1160   Prepaid Insurance
1200   Plant Assets
1210   Office Equipment
1215   Accumulated Depreciation—Office Equipment

(2000) LIABILITIES
2100   Current Liabilities
2110   Accounts Payable

(3000) OWNERS' EQUITY
3110   Sarah Hatcher, Capital
3120   Sarah Hatcher, Drawing
3130   Parker O'Reilly, Capital
3140   Parker O'Reilly, Drawing
3150   Income Summary

Income Statement Accounts

(4000) OPERATING REVENUE
4110   Sales
4115   Sales Returns and Allowances
4120   Sales Discount

(5000) COST OF MERCHANDISE
5110   Purchases
5115   Purchases Returns and Allowances
5120   Purchases Discount

(6000) OPERATING EXPENSES
6110   Advertising Expense
6120   Credit Card Fee Expense
6130   Depreciation Expense—Office Equipment
6135   Insurance Expense
6140   Miscellaneous Expense
6150   Rent Expense
6160   Supplies Expense
6170   Uncollectible Accounts Expense

The chart of accounts for Must-Have Gadgets is illustrated above for ready reference as you study Part 4 of this textbook.

Chapter 23

Accounting for Partnerships

©DANIEL KOUREY, ISTOCK/©JIM PRUITT, ISTOCK

ROB MARMION/SHUTTERSTOCK.COM

Accounting In The Real World

Subway

More than 35,000 restaurants in 98 countries, easy-to-remember advertising slogans, and one of the fastest growing food chains in the world—that's Subway! But what else is there to know about Subway?

The first Subway shop was opened in 1965 by Fred DeLuca, a 17-year-old, recent high-school graduate. Fred had hopes of becoming a medical doctor but needed to earn money to pay for college. A family friend and doctor, Peter Buck, encouraged Fred to open a submarine sandwich shop. In addition, Dr. Buck handed Fred a $1,000 check and offered to become his partner. The first two shops were not successful, but the two partners continued to expand. In 1974, they decided to allow others to participate in the expansion of the company through franchising.

A franchise is a right granted to an individual or business to sell the products or services of another, larger business within a defined geographic area. The company granting the franchise is called the *franchisor*, and the holder of the franchise is called the *franchisee*. Franchisees typically receive support services from the franchisor, gain the advantage of national advertising, and receive rights to the use of the franchisor's trademarks.

Subway is a franchise company, which means that many local shops are owned by franchisees. To become a Subway franchisee, you must pay $15,000 up front, plus the cost of obtaining and preparing a shop. As a franchisee, you are able to take advantage of Subway's training programs and support, use its trademarks, and take advantage of nationwide purchase programs. Currently, a franchise pays 12.5% of weekly sales to Subway, which covers franchise royalties and advertising. The franchisee keeps any additional profit. A franchise is one way to own your own business while sharing in benefits that only large corporations can offer.

As with many franchise opportunities, Subway franchises are available to partners. Owning a franchise with a partner allows you to enter into business ownership with a smaller capital investment. It also allows you to benefit from the expertise of your partner(s).

CRITICAL THINKING

1. If you were going to start a business with someone else, how would you choose your partner?

2. Search the Internet for a franchise that is for sale. Write a report including the name of the franchise, the amount of investment required, the amount and kind of ongoing fees that must be paid, and what services are provided for these fees.

Key Terms

- partnership
- partner
- partnership agreement
- distribution of net income statement
- owners' equity statement
- liquidation of a partnership
- realization

23-1 Forming a Partnership

LO1 Journalize entries to record investments by partners.
LO2 Journalize entries to record withdrawals by partners.

Partnerships

Delgado Web Services, the business described in Part 1, is a proprietorship, a small business owned by one person. ThreeGreen Products, Inc., and Sun Treasures, Inc., the businesses described in Parts 2 and 3, are organized as corporations. Businesses that require the skills and capital of more than one person, but that do not wish to be organized as a corporation, may choose another form of business. A business in which two or more persons combine their assets and skills is called a **partnership**. Each member of a partnership is called a **partner**. As in other forms of ownership, reports and financial records of the business are kept separate from the personal records of the partners. [CONCEPT: Business Entity] Each form of ownership has its advantages and disadvantages. Some of these are listed below.

Form	Advantages	Disadvantages
Sole Proprietorship	1. Ease of formation 2. Retention of all profits 3. Total control 4. Simple tax structure	1. Unlimited liability 2. Less capital available 3. Limited vision and skills 4. Terminates with life of owner
Partnership	1. Ease of formation 2. More capital available 3. Share work; each partner can operate in their area of expertise 4. Simple tax structure	1. Unlimited liability 2. Liable for partner's actions 3. Must share profits 4. Hard to dissolve 5. Terminates with life of one partner
Corporation	1. Limited liability 2. Ease of transfer of ownership 3. Unlimited life of the organization; does not terminate with death of investor	1. Harder/more expensive to form 2. Less control 3. Double taxation 4. More government regulations

Partnership Agreements

A written agreement setting forth the conditions under which a partnership is to operate is called a **partnership agreement**. Legally, a partnership agreement may be either written or oral. However, a written agreement may limit misunderstandings in the future; therefore, a partnership agreement should be in writing. It should include the name of the business and the partners, the investments of each partner, the duties and responsibilities of each partner, how profits and losses are to be divided, what happens if a partner dies, how the partnership is to be dissolved, and the duration of the agreement.

PARTNERSHIP AGREEMENT

THIS CONTRACT is made and entered into this _____1st_____ day of __January, 20--__, by and between __Sarah Hatcher__ of ____Plano, TX____, and __Parker O'Reilly__ of ____Allen, TX____.

WITNESSETH: That the said parties have this date formed a partnership to engage in and conduct a business under the following stipulations which are part of this contract. The partnership will begin operation on __January, 1, 20--__.

FIRST: The business shall be conducted under the name __Must-Have Gadgets__, located initially at __2310 Premier Drive, Plano, TX 75075-2511__.

SECOND: The investment of each partner is: (first partner) ____Sarah Hatcher____: Cash of $____20,000.00____. (second partner) ____Parker O'Reilly____: Cash of $____20,000.00____ and total investment, $____40,000.00____.

THIRD: Both partners are to (a) participate in all general policy-making decisions, (b) devote full time and attention to the partnership business, and (c) engage in no other business enterprise without the written consent of the other partner. ____Sarah Hatcher____ to be general manager of the business's operations.

FOURTH: Neither partner is to become a surety bonding agent for anyone without the written consent of the other partner.

FIFTH: The partners will share equally in all profits and losses of the partnership.

SIXTH: No partner is to withdraw assets without the other partner's written consent.

SEVENTH: All partnership transactions are to be recorded in accordance with standard and generally accepted accounting procedures and concepts. The partners' records are to be open at all times for inspection by either partner.

EIGHTH: In case of either partner's death or legal disability, the equity of the partners is to be determined as of the time of the death or disability of the one partner. The continuing partner is to have first option to buy the deceased/disabled partner's equity at recorded book value.

NINTH: This partnership agreement is to continue indefinitely unless (a) terminated by death of one partner, (b) terminated by either partner giving the other partner written notice at least ninety (90) days prior to the termination date; or (c) terminated by written mutual agreement signed by both partners.

TENTH: At the termination of this partnership agreement, the partnership's assets, after all liabilities are paid, will be distributed according to the balance in partners' capital accounts.

IN WITNESS WHEREOF, the parties to this contract have set their hands and seals on the date and year written.

Signed: ___*Sarah Hatcher*___   (Seal) Date: ___January 1, 20--___

Signed: ___*Parker O'Reilly*___   (Seal) Date: ___January 1, 20--___

Initial Investments by Owners LO1

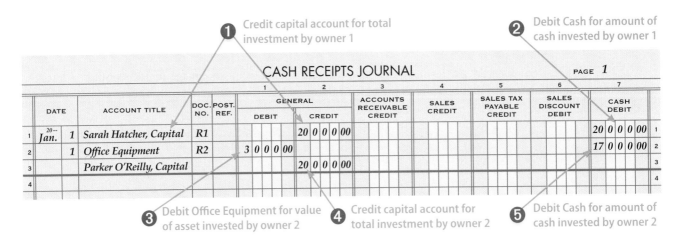

① Credit capital account for total investment by owner 1

② Debit Cash for amount of cash invested by owner 1

③ Debit Office Equipment for value of asset invested by owner 2

④ Credit capital account for total investment by owner 2

⑤ Debit Cash for amount of cash invested by owner 2

Must-Have Gadgets' partnership agreement calls for Sarah Hatcher to contribute cash and for Parker O'Reilly to contribute cash and office equipment to the new partnership. A separate journal entry is made for each partner's initial investment.

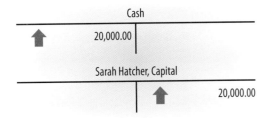

January 1. Received cash from partner, Sarah Hatcher, as an initial investment, $20,000.00. Receipt No. 1.

The asset account, Cash, increases by a debit, $20,000.00. The owner's capital account, Sarah Hatcher, Capital, increases by a credit, $20,000.00.

January 1. Received cash, $17,000.00, and office equipment valued at $3,000.00, from partner, Parker O'Reilly, as an initial investment. Receipt No. 2.

remember A partnership can consist of two or more partners. Partnerships are usually thought of as having only a few partners, but a partnership could have hundreds of partners.

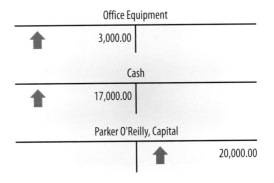

The asset account, Cash, increases by a debit, $17,000.00. The asset account, Office Equipment, increases by a debit, $3,000.00. The owner's capital account, Parker O'Reilly, Capital, increases by a credit, $20,000.00.

> **⚓ Journalizing Receipt of Partners' Initial Investment**
>
> **①** Credit Sarah Hatcher, Capital for the amount invested, $20,000.00.
>
> **②** Debit Cash for the same amount.
>
> **③** Debit Office Equipment for its value, $3,000.00.
>
> **④** Credit Parker O'Reilly, Capital for the total amount invested, $20,000.00.
>
> **⑤** Debit Cash for the amount invested, $17,000.00.

Withdrawal of Cash by Partner LO2

① Debit Parker O'Reilly, Drawing

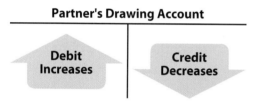

	DATE	ACCOUNT TITLE	CK. NO.	POST. REF.	GENERAL DEBIT	GENERAL CREDIT	ACCOUNTS PAYABLE DEBIT	PURCHASES DISCOUNT CREDIT	CASH CREDIT	
13	15	Parker O'Reilly, Drawing	12		7 5 0 00				7 5 0 00	13
14										14

CASH PAYMENTS JOURNAL   PAGE 1

② Credit Cash

During a fiscal period, partners may take assets out of the partnership in anticipation of the net income for the period. As in a proprietorship, assets taken out of a business for the personal use of an owner are known as *withdrawals*. The three types of assets generally taken out of a merchandising business are cash, supplies, and merchandise. The partnership agreement may limit the amount of assets that may be withdrawn.

Partner's Drawing Account

Debit Increases	Credit Decreases

While income increases the capital in the business, withdrawals reduce the amount of capital. The account titles of the partners' drawing accounts are Sarah Hatcher, Drawing and Parker O'Reilly, Drawing. Since capital accounts have credit balances, partners' drawing accounts have normal debit balances. Therefore, the drawing accounts increase by a debit and decrease by a credit, as shown in the T accounts.

January 15. Parker O'Reilly, partner, withdrew cash for personal use, $750.00. Check No. 12.

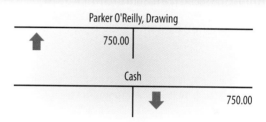

The owner's drawing account, Parker O'Reilly, Drawing, has a normal debit balance because withdrawals decrease owner's equity. Therefore, increases in withdrawals are recorded by a debit, $750.00. The asset account, Cash, decreases by a credit, $750.00.

✎ Journalizing Withdrawals of Cash by Partners

① **Debit** Parker O'Reilly, Drawing **for the amount withdrawn,** $750.00.

② **Credit Cash for the same amount.**

Can You Share Client Names?

After working six years with a national public accounting firm, Raymond Steele decided to venture out on his own. Raymond's new firm, Steele Consulting, specializes in helping companies that are facing severe financial difficulties. When delivering proposals to potential clients, Raymond proudly lists the names of his current clients.

The Code of Professional Conduct for the American Institute of Certified Public Accountants

"prohibits a member in public practice from disclosing confidential information without the client's consent." Raymond is aware of this rule but believes he is not violating it.

INSTRUCTIONS

Access the AICPA Code of Professional Conduct. Determine if Raymond's actions violate the confidentiality rule. (*Hint:* Remember that the Code includes rules, interpretations, and ethics rulings.)

Withdrawal of Supplies by Partner

1 Debit Sarah Hatcher, Drawing

	DATE		ACCOUNT TITLE	DOC. NO.	POST. REF.	DEBIT	CREDIT	
1	Jan. 20--	15	Sarah Hatcher, Drawing	M1		4 5 0 00		1
2			Supplies				4 5 0 00	2
3								3
4								4

GENERAL JOURNAL   PAGE 1

2 Credit Supplies

A partner usually withdraws cash for personal use. However, a partner may also withdraw supplies for personal use. This withdrawal increases the account balance of Sarah Hatcher, Drawing and decreases the Supplies account balance.

> **January 15. Sarah Hatcher, partner, withdrew supplies for personal use, $450.00. Memorandum No. 1.**

Sarah Hatcher's drawing account increases by a debit of $450.00. The asset account, Supplies, decreases by a credit of $450.00. This transaction is recorded in the general journal.

Sarah Hatcher, Drawing

450.00

Supplies

450.00

Journalizing Withdrawals of Merchandise by Partners

1 Debit Sarah Hatcher, Drawing for $450.00.

2 Credit Supplies for the same amount.

WHY ACCOUNTING?

Can Advertising Attract Tourists?

Advertising seems to be everywhere—on television, on your computer screen, enclosed with bills, on the inside and outside of public busses, and even in public bathrooms. Every year, we hear how much sponsors pay for a 30-second advertisement during the Super Bowl. There are even awards given for the best advertisements each year. But how do we know if the money spent on advertising is effective?

Many states have an office of tourism which, in the past, spent millions of dollars each year to attract tourists. Unfortunately, advertising is often the first cost to be cut from an unbalanced state budget. The *USA Today Travel* section reported that many states are decreasing the amount of money they budget for tourism. The state of Washington closed its tourism office completely, having to choose between public education and paying for glossy marketing campaigns.

With reduced budgets for tourism, many states are becoming more selective in where and how they advertise. Many are eliminating national television spots, focusing on target markets and lower-cost computer advertisements. Some tourism experts feel these cuts are shortsighted and will cost states more in lost tourism than was saved by the budget cuts.

CRITICAL THINKING

1. List two methods that a state tourism office could use to determine if advertising dollars were effective in bringing in tourists.

2. Use the Internet to research a state department of tourism. Find one fact published by that office relating to the amount budgeted for tourism, the amount of revenue generated from tourism dollars, or what means are used to attract tourism to the state.

Sources: "States Cut Back on Efforts to Draw Tourists," www.travel.usatoday.com, August 1, 2011; William Yardly, "A Tourism Office Falls Victim to Hard Times," *The New York Times*, July 11, 2011.

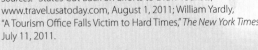

©ANEKCEN KOWEBHNKOB,/iSTOCK

LO1 Journalize entries to record investments by partners.

LO2 Journalize entries to record withdrawals by partners.

Terms Review

partnership

partner

partnership agreement

Audit your understanding

1. List at least three items that should be included in a partnership agreement.

2. Which accounts are debited and credited when a partner withdraws supplies from the partnership?

Work together 23-1

Journalizing partners' investments and withdrawals

Cash receipts, cash payments, and general journals are given in the *Working Papers*. Your instructor will guide you through the following examples.

Journalize the following transactions completed by Carpet World during April of the current year:

Transactions:

Apr. 1. Received cash of $15,000.00 and supplies valued at $4,000.00 from partner, Sofie Pavlov, as an initial investment. Receipt No. 1.

1. Received cash from partner, Noah Mancini, as an initial investment, $22,000.00. Receipt No. 2.

30. Sofie Pavlov, partner, withdrew cash for personal use, $1,000.00. Check No. 18.

30. Noah Mancini, partner, withdrew supplies for personal use, $1,200.00. Memorandum No. 6.

On your own 23-1

Journalizing partners' investments and withdrawals

Cash receipts, cash payments, and general journals are given in the *Working Papers*. Work this problem independently.

Journalize the following transactions completed by Ballo Brothers during October of the current year:

Transactions:

Oct. 1. Received cash of $30,000.00 and equipment valued at $10,000.00 from partner, Abdalla Ballo, as an initial investment. Receipt No. 1.

1. Received cash from partner, Rashad Ballo, as an initial investment, $36,000.00 Receipt No. 2.

30. Abdalla Ballo, partner, withdrew cash for personal use, $1,500.00. Check No. 47.

30. Rashad Ballo, partner, withdrew supplies for personal use, $1,900.00. Memorandum No. 8.

LESSON

23-2 Distribution of Net Income and Owners' Equity Statements

LO3 Prepare a distribution of net income statement for a partnership.

LO4 Prepare an owners' equity statement for a partnership.

Distribution of Net Income Statement LO3

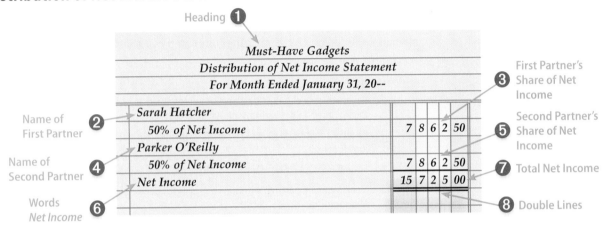

A partnership's net income or net loss may be divided in any way agreed upon by the partners in their partnership agreement. Sarah Hatcher and Parker O'Reilly, partners in Must-Have Gadgets, agreed to share net income or net loss equally.

A partnership's distribution of net income or net loss is usually shown on a separate financial statement. A partnership financial statement showing net income or loss distribution to partners is called a **distribution of net income statement**.

The income statement for a partnership is prepared in the same way as an income statement for a proprietorship, described in Chapter 7. Must-Have Gadgets' income statement shows a net income of $15,725.00 for the month ended January 31. This net income is used to prepare the distribution of net income statement.

↘ Preparing a Distribution of Net Income Statement

1 Write the heading of the distribution of net income statement on three lines.

2 Write one partner's name, Sarah Hatcher, on the first line at the extreme left.

3 Indent about one centimeter on the next line, and write Sarah Hatcher's share of net income as a percentage, 50.0% of Net Income. Write Ms. Hatcher's share of net income, $7,862.50 (50.0% × $15,725.00), in the amount column on the same line.

4 Write the other partner's name, Parker O'Reilly, on the next line.

5 Indent about one centimeter on the next line, and write Parker O'Reilly's share of net income as a percentage, 50.0% of Net Income. Write Mr. O'Reilly's share of net income, $7,862.50 (50.0% × $15,725.00), in the amount column on the same line.

6 Write Net Income on the next line at the extreme left of the wide column.

7 Add the distribution of net income and write the total amount, $15,725.00, in the amount column. Verify accuracy by comparing the total amount, $15,725.00, with the net income reported on the income statement, $15,725.00. The two amounts must be the same.

8 Rule double lines across the amount column to show that the distribution of net income statement has been verified as correct.

Distribution of Net Income Statement with Unequal Distribution

Computer Consulting						
Distribution of Net Income Statement						
For Year Ended December 31, 20--						
Ling Wang						
70% of Net Income	47	2	5	0	00	
Lucas Fornier						
30% of Net Income	20	2	5	0	00	
Net Income	67	5	0	0	00	

Regardless of how earnings are shared, the steps in preparing a distribution of net income statement are the same. The only difference is the description of how the earnings are to be shared by the partners.

Ling Wang and Lucas Fornier are partners in a business. Because Ms. Wang spends more time in the business than Mr. Fornier, the partners agree to share net income or loss unequally. Ms. Wang gets 70.0% of net income or loss. Mr. Fornier gets 30.0% of net income or loss. With a net income of $67,500.00, Ms. Wang receives 70.0%, or $47,250.00. Mr. Fornier receives 30.0%, or $20,250.00.

FINANCIAL LITERACY

Lease Agreements

Consumers should review their personal finances at least once a year to assess income and spending. It is a good time to review the cost of your living arrangements. Most financial experts recommend that no more than 30% of net pay be spent on housing.

While home ownership comes with tax advantages, privacy, and fewer restrictions, many find renting more appealing. The flexibility to relocate quickly and the benefit of maintenance-free living are two advantages to renting that many find attractive. Renters are sometimes tempted by luxuries, such as pools and clubhouses that come with the rental unit, to rush into a lease agreement without a full understanding of the costs or properly budgeting for them. A lease agreement is a binding legal contract for both the tenant and the landlord. It should not be rushed into.

In addition to listing the names of the lessor and the lessee and the address of the property, a lease agreement will also contain: the amount of the rent, when rent is due, additional fees for pets and/or parking, restrictions (including noise and visitors), lease start and end dates, amount of notice needed for termination, conditions upon which the landlord can enter the property, and signatures. A security deposit is almost always required. It is paid in advance to the landlord to cover possible damage to the property. It is reimbursed if the property is left as described in the lease agreement. The amount of the deposit is usually equivalent to one month's rent.

ACTIVITIES

Read and respond to the following items. Be sure to give reasons.

1. Brandon's lease just ended, and he moved to another apartment. Several months ago, Brandon allowed his friend Brady to stay with him temporarily. Now, Brandon's landlord will not return his $500 security deposit because of damage caused by his friend's dog. The landlord claims that the $500 will partially cover the cost of replacing carpeting in three rooms due to soiling and tears. Brandon disagrees because pets were allowed by the lease agreement, and he feels if anyone should incur the charges it should be Brady. Who is correct, Brandon or the landlord?

2. If you were the landlord, indicate at least five rules and/or restrictions that you would place in your lease agreement to protect yourself in the situations described in number 1.

3. Research the Federal Fair Housing Act and Fair Housing Amendments to determine what types of housing discrimination are legal.

Partners' Capital and Drawing Accounts

ACCOUNT *Sarah Hatcher, Capital*   **ACCOUNT NO.** *3110*

DATE	ITEM	POST. REF.	DEBIT	CREDIT	BALANCE DEBIT	BALANCE CREDIT
Jan. 1		CR1		20 000 00		20 000 00

ACCOUNT *Sarah Hatcher, Drawing*   **ACCOUNT NO.** *3120*

DATE	ITEM	POST. REF.	DEBIT	CREDIT	BALANCE DEBIT	BALANCE CREDIT
Jan. 15		G1	4 500 00		4 500 00	

ACCOUNT *Parker O'Reilly, Capital*   **ACCOUNT NO.** *3130*

DATE	ITEM	POST. REF.	DEBIT	CREDIT	BALANCE DEBIT	BALANCE CREDIT
Jan. 1		CR1		20 000 00		20 000 00

ACCOUNT *Parker O'Reilly, Drawing*   **ACCOUNT NO.** *3140*

DATE	ITEM	POST. REF.	DEBIT	CREDIT	BALANCE DEBIT	BALANCE CREDIT
Jan. 15		CP1	7 500 00		7 500 00	

The amount of net income earned is important to business owners. Owners are also interested in changes that occur in owners' equity during a fiscal period. A financial statement that summarizes the changes in owners' equity during a fiscal period is called an **owners' equity statement**. Business owners can review an owners' equity statement to determine if owners' equity is increasing or decreasing and what is causing the change. Three factors can change owners' equity:

1. Additional investments.
2. Withdrawals.
3. Net income or net loss.

An owners' equity statement shows information about changes in each partner's capital during a fiscal period. Information needed to prepare an owners' equity statement is obtained from the distribution of net income statement, shown on page 728, and the general ledger capital and drawing accounts shown above. The distribution of net income statement shows each partner's share of net income or net loss. Three kinds of information are obtained from each partner's capital and drawing account:

1. Beginning capital amount.
2. Any additional investments made during the fiscal period.
3. Each partner's withdrawal of assets during the fiscal period.

Owners' Equity Statement LO4

2 Name of First Partner   **1** Heading

Must-Have Gadgets Owners' Equity Statement For Month Ended January 31, 20--				
Sarah Hatcher				
Capital, January 1, 20--		20 0 0 0 00		
Share of Net Income	7 8 6 2 50			
Less Withdrawals	4 5 0 00			
Net Increase in Capital		7 4 1 2 50		
Capital, January 31, 20--			27 4 1 2 50	
Parker O'Reilly				
Capital, January 1, 20--		20 0 0 0 00		
Share of Net Income	7 8 6 2 50			
Less Withdrawals	7 5 0 00			
Net Increase in Capital		7 1 1 2 50		
Capital, January 31, 20--			27 1 1 2 50	
Total Owners' Equity, January 31, 20--			54 5 2 5 00	

First Partner's Ending Capital **3**

Name of Second Partner **4**

Second Partner's Ending Capital **5**

6 Total Owners' Equity   **7** Double Lines

Neither Sarah Hatcher nor Parker O'Reilly invested any additional capital during the month ended January 31 after the initial investments on January 1. Both partners withdrew either cash or supplies during the month.

Some businesses include the owners' equity statement information as part of the balance sheet. An example of this method of reporting changes in owner's equity is shown in Chapter 7.

Preparing an Owners' Equity Statement

1 Write the heading of the owners' equity statement on three lines.

2 Write the name Sarah Hatcher on the first line at the extreme left.

3 Calculate the net increase in capital and ending capital amount for Sarah Hatcher.

    a. Indent about one centimeter on the next line, and write Capital, January 1, 20--. Write the amount $20,000.00 in the second amount column. (This amount is obtained from the capital account.)

    b. Indent about one centimeter on the next line, and write Share of Net Income. Write the amount $7,862.50 in the first amount column. (This amount is obtained from the distribution of net income statement.)

    c. Indent about one centimeter on the next line, and write Less Withdrawals. Write the amount $450.00 in the first amount column. (This amount is obtained from the drawing account.)

    d. Indent about one centimeter on the next line, and write Net Increase in Capital. Write the amount $7,412.50 in the second amount column. ($7,862.50 – $450.00 = $7,412.50)

    e. Indent about one centimeter on the next line, and write Capital, January 31, 20--. Write the amount $27,412.50 in the third amount column. ($20,000.00 + $7,412.50 = $27,412.50)

4 Write the name Parker O'Reilly on the next line at the extreme left of the wide column.

5 Calculate the net increase in capital and ending capital amount for Parker O'Reilly. Follow Step 3.

6 Write Total Owners' Equity, January 31, 20-- on the next line at the extreme left of the wide column. Write the amount $54,525.00 in the third amount column.

7 Rule double lines across the three amount columns to show that the totals have been verified as correct.

Owners' Equity Statement with an Additional Investment and a Net Loss

J & J Tree Service																		
Owners' Equity Statement																		
For Year Ended December 31, 20--																		
Markus Jensen																		
Capital, January 1, 20--	100	1	6	0	00													
Plus Additional Investment	9	6	0	0	00													
Total						109	7	6	0	00								
Share of Net Loss	2	2	7	2	00													
Plus Withdrawals	14	2	0	8	00													
Net Decrease in Capital						16	4	8	0	00								
Capital, December 31, 20--											93	2	8	0	00			
Emma Johansen																		
Capital, January 1, 20--	98	7	2	0	00													
Plus Additional Investment	9	6	0	0	00													
Total						108	3	2	0	00								
Share of Net Loss	2	2	7	2	00													
Plus Withdrawals	14	4	9	6	00													
Net Decrease in Capital						16	7	6	8	00								
Capital, December 31, 20--											91	5	5	2	00			
Total Owners' Equity, December 31, 20--											184	8	3	2	00			

On December 31, the capital accounts of Markus Jensen and Emma Johansen showed additional investments of $9,600.00 each. Also, the income statement for their company, J & J Tree Service, showed a net loss of $4,544.00. The partners agreed to share net income or net loss equally. The owners' equity statement above shows the net loss as a deduction from the owners' capital.

Balance Sheet for a Partnership

Must-Have Gadgets													
Balance Sheet													
January 31, 20--													
Total Liabilities						32	8	4	1	00			
Owners' Equity													
Sarah Hatcher, Capital	27	4	1	2	50								
Parker O'Reilly, Capital	27	1	1	2	50								
Total Owners' Equity						54	5	2	5	00			
Total Liabilities and Owners' Equity						87	3	6	6	00			

The Asset and Liability sections of a balance sheet for a partnership are prepared in the same way as the Asset and Liability sections of a balance sheet for a proprietorship. The only section that is different is the Equity section. The Equity section lists the capital account for each partner. The balances of these two accounts are added together and listed as Total Owners' Equity. Total Liabilities and Total Owners' Equity are added together to determine Total Liabilities and Owners' Equity.

Careers In Accounting

Jenna Fitch
GOVERNMENTAL ACCOUNTANT

Jenna Fitch is an accountant for a midsized city in the state of Washington. A city government is not expected to make a profit. Therefore, the records kept by Ms. Fitch do not focus on revenues and expenses. Instead, the emphasis is on making sure that monies spent by the city are within specific limits. Each year, the city council presents and approves a budget for the coming year. Once approved, the budget must be followed. One of Ms. Fitch's major tasks is to make sure that the city does not spend more money in any budget category than was approved in the budget.

As a governmental accountant, Ms. Fitch follows different guidelines than would be followed by an accountant for a corporation. Instead of having one general ledger, Ms. Fitch keeps financial records for several separate funds, including a fire department fund, a water department fund, a fund for a street repaving project, and a general fund. She must keep separate records of revenues and expenditures for each fund.

Governmental accountants use a modified accrual basis of accounting as opposed to the accrual basis of accounting used by corporations. In the accrual basis, revenue is recognized when it is earned. In the modified accrual basis, revenue is recognized when it becomes both available and measurable.

Salary Range: Salaries vary depending on the type and size of government agency. The average salary for state and local agencies is $55,700. Federal agencies tend to be higher, with an average salary of $88,190.

Qualifications: A governmental accountant has to have many of the same qualifications as most other accountants. Minimum education for an entry-level position is a basic knowledge of accounting with some classes in not-for-profit accounting. Promotion to a manager-level position usually requires a bachelor's degree in accounting. Good communications skills are required, especially when working with donors or taxpayers.

Occupational Outlook: The growth for governmental accounting positions is projected to be in the average range (between 7% and 13%).

ACTIVITY
Research job openings for governmental accountants in your area. Record the educational requirements and the salary range for the position(s) listed. Summarize your findings in a written report.

Source: www.accountingedu.org.

End of Lesson Review

LO3 Prepare a distribution of net income statement for a partnership.

LO4 Prepare an owners' equity statement for a partnership.

Terms Review

distribution of net income statement

owners' equity statement

Audit your understanding

1. What information used to prepare an owners' equity statement is obtained from the distribution of net income statement?

2. What information used to prepare an owners' equity statement is obtained from the partners' capital and drawing accounts?

3. What is the procedure for calculating an owner's end-of-year capital when the partnership earned a net income for the year?

Work together 23-2

Preparing distribution of net income and owners' equity statements

Carpet World is a partnership owned by Sofie Pavlov and Noah Mancini. Information from Carpet World's general ledger and income statement is given below. Forms for completing this problem are given in the *Working Papers*. Your instructor will guide you through the following examples.

Net income for the month ended April 30	$32,600.00
Sofie Pavlov, Capital April 1 balance	19,000.00
Noah Mancini, Capital April 1 balance	22,000.00
Sofie Pavlov, Drawing April 30 balance	1,000.00
Noah Mancini, Drawing April 30 balance	1,200.00

1. Prepare a distribution of net income statement for Carpet World. Net income or loss is to be shared equally.

2. Using the balances of the general ledger capital and drawing accounts, prepare an owners' equity statement for Carpet World. No additional investments were made.

On your own 23-2

Preparing distribution of net income and owners' equity statements

Ballo Brothers is a partnership owned by Abdalla Ballo and Rashad Ballo. Information from Ballo Brothers' general ledger and income statement is given below. Forms for completing this problem are given in the *Working Papers*. Work this problem independently.

Net income for the month ended October 31	$62,500.00
Abdalla Ballo, Capital October 1 balance	40,000.00
Rashad Ballo, Capital October 1 balance	36,000.00
Abdalla Ballo, Drawing October 31 balance	1,500.00
Rashad Ballo, Drawing October 31 balance	1,900.00

1. Prepare a distribution of net income statement for Ballo Brothers. Net income or loss is to be distributed 60% to Abdalla Ballo and 40% to Rashad Ballo.

2. Using the balances of the general ledger capital and drawing accounts, prepare an owners' equity statement for Ballo Brothers. No additional investments were made.

©CANDICE CUSACK, ISTOCK

23-3 Dissolving a Partnership

LO5 Calculate and record a gain on realization.
LO6 Calculate and record a loss on realization.
LO7 Journalize entries to liquidate a partnership.

Account Balances Before Realization

	Cash			Accounts Payable	
Bal.	28,000.00			Bal.	8,500.00

	Supplies			Gerald Bakken, Capital	
Bal.	2,000.00			Bal.	22,000.00

	Machinery			Jon Bakken, Capital	
Bal.	25,000.00			Bal.	19,500.00

Accumulated Depreciation—Machinery		
	Bal.	5,000.00

If a partnership goes out of business, its assets are distributed to the creditors and partners. The process of paying a partnership's liabilities and distributing remaining assets to the partners is called **liquidation of a partnership**.

Cash received from the sale of assets during liquidation of a partnership is called **realization**. Typically, when a partnership is liquidated, the noncash assets are sold, and the available cash is used to pay the creditors.

Any remaining cash is distributed to the partners according to each partner's total equity.

On June 30, Gerald and Jon Bakken liquidated their partnership. At that time, adjusting entries were made and financial statements were prepared; then closing entries were journalized and posted. After the end-of-fiscal-period work was completed, the partnership had account balances as shown in the T accounts above.

A partnership usually tries to sell the business before it begins the process of liquidation.

Calculating Gain on Realization LO5

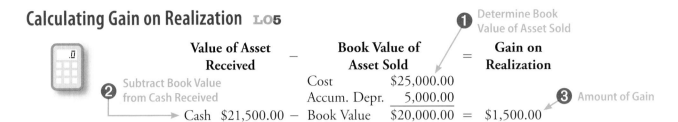

	Value of Asset Received	−	Book Value of Asset Sold	=	Gain on Realization

① Determine Book Value of Asset Sold

② Subtract Book Value from Cash Received

Cost $25,000.00
Accum. Depr. 5,000.00

Cash $21,500.00 − Book Value $20,000.00 = $1,500.00

③ Amount of Gain

Noncash assets might be sold for more than the recorded book value. When this happens, the amount received in excess of the book value is recorded as a gain on realization.

Gain on Realization	
	Gain recorded as a credit

A gain on realization is calculated as shown above. The account, Gain on Realization, is used to record the amount of the gain. Most companies will have to add this account to their charts of account. Gain on Realization is usually included in the Other Revenue section of the chart of accounts.

⬎ Calculating a Gain on Realization

① Determine the book value of the asset sold.

② Subtract the book value from the cash received.

③ Record the amount of gain on realization.

Recording a Gain on Realization

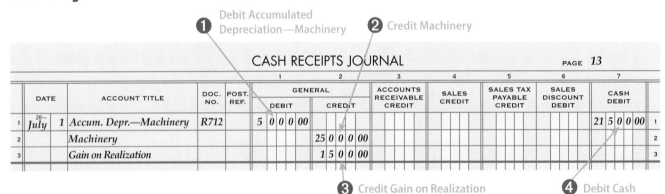

① Debit Accumulated Depreciation—Machinery

② Credit Machinery

CASH RECEIPTS JOURNAL PAGE 13

	DATE	ACCOUNT TITLE	DOC. NO.	POST. REF.	GENERAL DEBIT	GENERAL CREDIT	ACCOUNTS RECEIVABLE CREDIT	SALES CREDIT	SALES TAX PAYABLE CREDIT	SALES DISCOUNT DEBIT	CASH DEBIT	
1	July 1	Accum. Depr.—Machinery	R712		5 0 0 0 00						21 5 0 0 00	1
2		Machinery				25 0 0 0 00						2
3		Gain on Realization				1 5 0 0 00						3

③ Credit Gain on Realization

④ Debit Cash

July 1. Received cash from sale of machinery, $21,500.00: original cost, $25,000.00; total accumulated depreciation recorded to date, $5,000.00. Receipt No. 712.

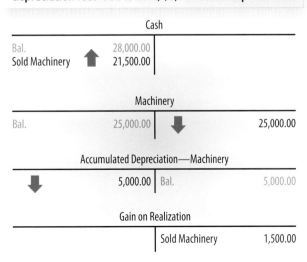

Cash

| Bal. | 28,000.00 | |
| Sold Machinery ⬆ | 21,500.00 | |

Machinery

| Bal. | 25,000.00 ⬇ | 25,000.00 |

Accumulated Depreciation—Machinery

| ⬇ | 5,000.00 | Bal. | 5,000.00 |

Gain on Realization

| | Sold Machinery | 1,500.00 |

The transaction is recorded in the cash receipts journal. After the transaction is posted, the Machinery and the Accumulated Depreciation—Machinery accounts will have a zero balance.

⬎ Recording a Gain on Realization

① **Debit** Accumulated Depreciation—Machinery **for** $5,000.00.

② **Credit** Machinery **for** $25,000.00, **the original cost of the machinery sold.**

③ **Credit** Gain on Realization **for** $1,500.00, **the amount of the gain.**

④ **Debit Cash for** $21,500.00, **the amount of cash received.**

Calculating Loss on Realization LO6

1 Determine Book Value of Asset Sold

2 Subtract Book Value from Cash Received

Value of Asset Received	−	Book Value of Asset Sold	=	Loss on Realization
Cash $1,700.00	−	Supplies $2,000.00	=	$(300)

3 Amount of Loss

Noncash assets might be sold for less than the recorded book value. When that happens, the amount by which the book value exceeds the amount received is recorded as a loss on realization.

```
              Loss on Realization
        ┌──────────────────┬──────────
   ⬆    │  Loss recorded   │
        │   as a debit     │
        └──────────────────┴──────────
```

A loss on realization is calculated as shown above. The account, Loss on Realization, is used to record the amount of the loss. Most companies will have to add this account to their charts of account. Loss on Realization is usually included in the Other Expenses section of the chart of accounts.

> **Calculating a Loss on Realization**
> **1** Determine the book value of the asset sold.
> **2** Subtract the book value from the cash received.
> **3** Record the amount of loss on realization.

Recording a Loss on Realization

1 Debit Loss on Realization

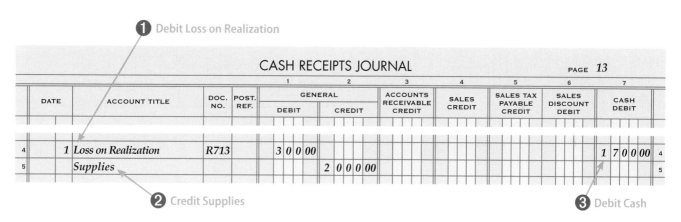

2 Credit Supplies

3 Debit Cash

July 1. Received cash from sale of supplies, $1,700.00; balance of Supplies account, $2,000.00. Receipt No. 713.

The transaction is recorded in the cash receipts journal. After the transaction is posted, the Supplies account will have a zero balance.

```
                    Cash
Bal.           28,000.00 │
Sold Machinery 21,500.00 │
Sold Supplies ⬆ 1,700.00 │

                  Supplies
Bal.            2,000.00 │ ⬇  2,000.00

              Loss on Realization
Sold Supplies    300.00  │
```

> **Recording a Loss on Realization**
> **1** Debit Loss on Realization for the amount of the loss, $300.00.
> **2** Credit Supplies for $2,000.00, the book value of the supplies sold.
> **3** Debit Cash for $1,700.00, the amount of cash received.

Liquidating Liabilities LO7

CASH PAYMENTS JOURNAL

PAGE **13**

| | | | | | GENERAL | | ACCOUNTS PAYABLE DEBIT | PURCHASES DISCOUNT CREDIT | CASH CREDIT |
DATE	ACCOUNT TITLE	CK. NO.	POST. REF.	DEBIT	CREDIT			
20-- July 1	✔	825				8 5 0 0 00		8 5 0 0 00

The partnership's available cash is used to pay creditors. The entry is recorded in the cash payments journal as shown.

> **July 1. Paid cash to all creditors for the amounts owed, $8,500.00. Check No. 825.**

After this entry is posted, the Accounts Payable account will have a zero balance.

Cash

Bal.	28,000.00	Paid Accts. Pay. ⬇ 8,500.00
Sold Machinery	21,500.00	
Sold Supplies	1,700.00	

Accounts Payable

⬇ 8,500.00	Bal.	8,500.00

ACCOUNT BALANCES AFTER LIQUIDATION OF NONCASH ASSETS AND PAYMENT OF LIABILITIES

When this transaction has been journalized and posted, the partnership has only five general ledger accounts with balances as shown.

Cash

Bal.	28,000.00	Paid Accts. Pay. 8,500.00
Sold Machinery	21,500.00	
Sold Supplies	1,700.00	
(New Bal.	42,700.00)	

Gerald Bakken, Capital

Bal.	22,000.00

Jon Bakken, Capital

Bal.	19,500.00

Gain on Realization

Sold Machinery	1,500.00
Bal.	1,500.00

Loss on Realization

Sold Supplies	300.00
Bal.	300.00

DISTRIBUTING LOSS OR GAIN ON REALIZATION

When all creditors have been paid, the balances of Gain on Realization and Loss on Realization are distributed to the partners based on the method of distributing net income or net loss as stated in the partnership agreement. The percentages for the Bakken partnership are Gerald Bakken, 60%, and Jon Bakken, 40%. The distribution of the balances of the two accounts is calculated as shown.

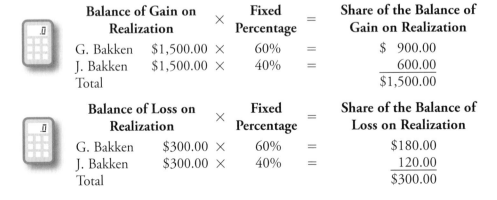

	Balance of Gain on Realization	×	Fixed Percentage	=	Share of the Balance of Gain on Realization
G. Bakken	$1,500.00	×	60%	=	$ 900.00
J. Bakken	$1,500.00	×	40%	=	600.00
Total					$1,500.00

	Balance of Loss on Realization	×	Fixed Percentage	=	Share of the Balance of Loss on Realization
G. Bakken	$300.00	×	60%	=	$180.00
J. Bakken	$300.00	×	40%	=	120.00
Total					$300.00

GENERAL JOURNAL

PAGE 7

	DATE		ACCOUNT TITLE	DOC. NO.	POST. REF.	DEBIT	CREDIT	
1			*Closing Entries*					1
2	July 6		*Gain on Realization*	M531		1 5 0 0 00		2
3			*Gerald Bakken, Capital*				9 0 0 00	3
4			*Jon Bakken, Capital*				6 0 0 00	4
5		6	*Gerald Bakken, Capital*	M532		1 8 0 00		5
6			*Jon Bakken, Capital*			1 2 0 00		6
7			*Loss on Realization*				3 0 0 00	7

Close Loss on Realization account.

Each partner's capital account is debited for the partner's share of the loss on realization.

> July 6. Recorded distribution of gain on realization: to Gerald Bakken, $900; to Jon Bakken, $600. Recorded distribution of loss on realization: to Gerald Bakken, $180.00; to Jon Bakken, $120.00. Memorandum Nos. 531 and 532.

After this entry is posted, the balances of Gain on Realization and Loss on Realization are zero. The total of the two capital accounts equals the balance of the Cash account.

Gerald Bakken, Capital

Share of loss	180.00	Bal.	22,000.00
		Share of gain	900.00
		(New Bal.	22,720.00)

Jon Bakken, Capital

Share of loss	120.00	Bal.	19,500.00
		Share of gain	600.00
		(New Bal.	19,980.00)

Gain on Realization

Distribution	1,500.00	Sold Machinery	1,500.00

Loss on Realization

Sold Supplies	300.00	Distribution	300.00

USING ONE REALIZATION ACCOUNT

The partnership in this lesson uses two separate realization accounts: one for loss on realization and one for gain on realization. A partnership could choose to use only one realization account. This account is usually titled Loss and Gain on Realization. When only one realization account is used, losses on realization are recorded on the debit side of the account and gains on realization are recorded on the credit side of the account. After all assets have been liquidated, the balance in this account will be equal to the net loss or net gain on realization and is closed into the partners' capital accounts.

Partnerships must file tax returns with the IRS to report how income was divided among the partners. However, partnerships do not pay income taxes. Net income passes through to the partners according to the terms of their partnership agreement. That income must be reported on each partner's individual tax return.

Distributing Remaining Cash to Partners

					GENERAL		ACCOUNTS PAYABLE DEBIT	PURCHASES DISCOUNT CREDIT	CASH CREDIT
	DATE	ACCOUNT TITLE	CK. NO.	POST. REF.	DEBIT	CREDIT			

CASH PAYMENTS JOURNAL — PAGE 13

					1	2	3	4	5
2	6	Gerald Bakken, Capital	826		22 7 2 0 00				22 7 2 0 00
3	6	Jon Bakken, Capital	827		19 9 8 0 00				19 9 8 0 00

Debit each partner's capital account for the amount of the account balance

Credit Cash for the amounts distributed

All remaining cash is distributed to the partners. The cash is distributed according to each partner's capital account balance, regardless of the method used to distribute net income or net loss.

July 6. Recorded final distribution of remaining cash to partners: to Gerald Bakken, $22,720.00; to Jon Bakken, $19,980.00. Check Nos. 826 and 827.

After these journal entries are journalized and posted as shown above, all of the partnership's general ledger accounts will have zero balances. The partnership is liquidated.

Cash

Bal.	42,700.00		22,720.00
(New Bal.	0.00)		19,980.00

Gerald Bakken, Capital

22,720.00	Bal.	22,720.00
	(New Bal.	0.00)

Jon Bakken, Capital

19,980.00	Bal.	19,980.00
	(New Bal.	0.00)

THINK LIKE AN ACCOUNTANT

Condensed Financial Statements

Large businesses have many levels of managers. Operational managers organize and monitor the daily activities of a business. Common tasks of an operational manager might include:

- Set employee work schedules.
- Purchase inventory and supplies.
- Plan advertising and promotions.

In contrast, strategic managers focus on the long-term operations of the business. Common tasks of a senior manager might include:

- Identify expansion opportunities.
- Make capital acquisition decisions.
- Determine dividends or partnership distributions.
- Hire and monitor operational managers.

The information needs of these managers differ. Operational managers need very detailed information. Senior managers prefer summarized information.

Even small businesses can have hundreds, even thousands, of general ledger accounts. This level of detail is necessary for operational managers to monitor daily activities. For example, a sales manager may use 30 or more accounts to classify the expenses of his department. In contrast, a strategic manager may only want to know the total of sales expenses.

A financial statement containing summarized amounts is referred to as a condensed financial statement. A condensed income statement might contain a single line for sales expenses. Strategic managers, investors, and government agencies require only condensed financial statements.

OPEN THE SPREADSHEET TLA_CH23

The worksheet contains the income statement of a partnership. Prepare the income statement so it can be used by any level of manager.

End of Lesson Review

LO5 Calculate and record a gain on realization.

LO6 Calculate and record a loss on realization.

LO7 Journalize entries to liquidate a partnership.

Terms Review

liquidation of a partnership

realization

Audit your understanding

1. How is a gain on realization recorded?
2. How is a loss on realization recorded?
3. Which accounts are debited when distributing remaining cash to partners during liquidation?

Work together 23-3

Liquidation of a partnership

Johanna and Stefan Salo agreed to liquidate their partnership on March 31 of the current year. On that date, after financial statements were prepared and closing entries were posted, the general ledger accounts had the balances shown in the *Working Papers*.

A cash receipts journal, a cash payments journal, and a general journal are provided in the *Working Papers*. Your instructor will guide you through the following examples.

Journalize the following transactions:

Transactions:

Apr. 1. Received cash from sale of office equipment, $12,000.00. R421.
    1. Received cash from sale of supplies, $1,900.00. R422.
    3. Received cash from sale of truck, $15,000.00. R423.
    5. Paid cash to all creditors for amounts owed. C547.
    6. Distributed balance of Gain on Realization to Johanna Salo, 60%; to Stefan Salo, 40%. M65.
    6. Distributed balance of Loss on Realization to Johanna Salo, 60%; to Stefan Salo, 40%. M66.
    6. Distributed remaining cash to partners. C548 and C549.

On your own 23-3

Liquidation of a partnership

Carlo Diaz and Olivia Thompson agreed to liquidate their partnership on June 30 of the current year. On that date, after financial statements were prepared and closing entries were posted, the general ledger accounts had the balances shown in the *Working Papers*.

A cash receipts journal, a cash payments journal, and a general journal are provided in the *Working Papers*. Work this problem independently.

Journalize the following transactions:

Transactions:

July 1. Received cash from sale of office equipment, $1,600.00. R348.
    1. Received cash from sale of supplies. $3,100.00. R349.
    3. Received cash from sale of truck, $10,800.00. R350.
    5. Paid cash to all creditors for amounts owed. C265.
    6. Distributed balance of Gain on Realization to Carlo Diaz, 60%; to Olivia Thompson, 40%. M33.
    6. Distributed balance of Loss on Realization to Carlo Diaz, 60%; to Olivia Thompson, 40%. M34.
    6. Distributed remaining cash to partners. C266 and C267.

A Look at Accounting Software

Setting Up a New Partnership

You were first introduced to the Company Setup window in Chapter 1, where a proprietorship was started. Setting up a partnership requires more information. In this chapter, you saw that Must-Have Gadgets was created on January 1, 20--, with two partners having equal shares in the business. The window at the right illustrates how that partnership might be set up in a computerized accounting system.

There are different types of partnership organization. Some of those types allow "limited" partners. That is, partners with limited liability. Must-Have Gadgets is a general partnership. Accounting software programs differ greatly in how partner information is entered, but the information illustrated here would be the minimum required.

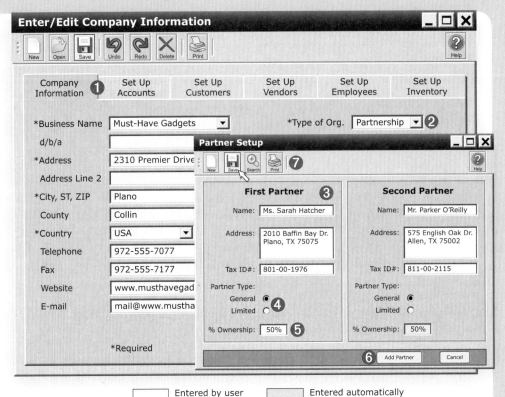

Entered by user   Entered automatically

1. The Company Setup window is opened from the System Manager window. The Company Information tab opens by default. When this tab is completed, the user would open other tabs to set up the general ledger accounts, customer and vendor accounts, etc. Must-Have Gadgets has no employees, so there would be no need to open that tab.

2. When the user selects Partnership from the drop-down list for the type of organization, the system knows that additional information is required, and a popup window opens to accept that information.

3. The minimum number of partners is two, so space is available to enter information for the two. The user would enter the names and addresses of both partners, along with their social security numbers (Tax ID#).

4. Must-Have Gadgets is a general partnership, so the user would click on the General button for both partners.

5. The percent ownership for each partner is entered. The system initially assumes that there are only two partners. As soon as the first percentage is entered, the system enters the balance of 100% for the other partner. The user can change the percentage if an entry error was made or if an additional partner is to be added. If these two percentages do not add up to 100%, the system will pop up a warning to the user to correct the entries or add another partner.

6. To add an additional partner, the user would click the Add Partner button. Clicking Cancel would close the window without saving, but the partnership cannot be set up in the system until this information is entered and saved.

7. The user clicks Save to exit the popup window. The popup will close and the user will continue entering information on the Company Information tab.

Chapter Summary

A partnership is one form of business ownership. It offers the advantage of sharing the work load, opportunity for more capital investment, and ease of formation. A written partnership agreement sets forth the conditions under which a partnership operates. Partners can invest cash or other assets in the partnership. A capital account is maintained for each partner. Investments by the partners are recorded in these capital accounts. Partners can also withdraw cash or merchandise from the partnership. Withdrawals by partners are recorded in temporary drawing accounts.

Partnership earnings are divided between the partners according to the terms of the partnership agreement. The ending capital balance for each partner reflects investments, share of earnings, and withdrawals. The balance sheet for a partnership is similar to that for a sole proprietorship except for the Equity section, which lists a capital account for each partner.

When a partnership is dissolved, several steps are required. First, noncash assets are sold, usually at either a gain or a loss. Then cash is used to pay any remaining liabilities. Finally, the remaining cash is distributed to the partners according to each partner's equity balance.

Is It Tax Avoidance or Tax Evasion?

EXPLORE ACCOUNTING

Once you start earning enough income, you will probably have to start paying some form of income tax to federal, state, and/or local governments. Some American taxpayers, both individuals and corporations, pay out a sizable percentage of their income for these taxes. However, we don't all pay out the same percent of our earnings in income tax. The United States has a graduated, or progressive, income tax system which increases the tax rate as income rises. However, due to provisions in the tax code, some individuals and corporations don't pay any income taxes at all.

Not paying taxes is not necessarily illegal. Using the provisions in the tax code to reduce one's taxes by legal means is known as *tax avoidance*, or more recently, *tax mitigation*. Not only can all tax-paying Americans apply tax laws to reduce the taxes they owe, but they are also encouraged to do so by the U.S. Legislature and courts of

law. A judge who became famous for his decisions on tax avoidance versus tax evasion once said "… for nobody owes any public duty to pay more than the law demands: taxes are enforced exactions, not voluntary contributions." Some tax avoidance methods include contributing income to charitable organizations, delaying the receipt of income through the use of approved retirement accounts, and decreasing taxable income by the payment of mortgage interest.

In contrast, using illegal methods to reduce one's taxes is known as *tax evasion* and is punishable by a fine and/or a prison sentence. The news media often report on prominent individuals or companies that have been found guilty of some form of tax evasion. Some tax evasion practices include failure to report all income earned, overstating expenses so as to lower taxable income, and overstatement of charitable contributions.

The Internal Revenue Service has a name for the difference between the amount of tax legally owed and the amount actually collected. It is called the *tax gap*. A recent study estimated the tax gap to be $450 billion.

INSTRUCTIONS

1. Use the Internet to search for a recent case of tax evasion. Write a summary of your findings including the name of the person, the method used to evade tax, and the punishment given.

2. Interview five people, asking them to give their views on tax avoidance versus tax evasion. Summarize your findings in a short written report.

Sources: Helvering v. Gregory, 69 F.2d 809, 810 (2d Cir.1934), aff'd, 293 U.S. 465, 55 S.Ct. 266, 79 L.Ed. 596 (1935); http://www.irs.gov/newsroom/article/0,,id=252038,00.html

©MAKHNACH_M_ISTOCK

Apply Your Understanding

INSTRUCTIONS: Download problem instructions for Excel, QuickBooks, and Peachtree from the textbook companion website at www.C21accounting.com.

23-1 Application Problem: Journalizing partners' investments and withdrawals LO1, 2

Cash receipts, cash payments, and general journals are given in the *Working Papers*.

Instructions:

Journalize the following transactions completed during May of the current year:

Transactions:

May 1. Received cash of $4,000.00 and equipment valued at $66,000.00 from partner, Alka Wozniak, as an investment. Receipt No. 1.

     1. Received cash from partner, Florian Kaminski, as an initial investment, $60,000.00. Receipt No. 2.

   30. Florian Kaminski, partner, withdrew cash for personal use, $7,200.00. Check No. 42.

   30. Alka Wozniak, partner, withdrew supplies for personal use, $9,600.00. Memorandum No. 8.

23-2.1 Application Problem: Preparing distribution of net income and owners' equity statements (net income) LO3, 4

Agnes Carlsson and Viktor Lindberg are partners in Sharp Appliances, a merchandising business. Forms for completing this problem are given in the *Working Papers*. The following information was taken from the records on December 31 of the current year.

Partner	Balance of Capital Account January 1	Balance of Drawing Account	Distribution of Net Income/Loss
Carlsson	$79,500.00	$8,775.00	60.0%
Lindberg	$71,300.00	$9,400.00	40.0%

Instructions:

1. On December 31, the partnership had a net income of $41,630.00. Prepare a distribution of net income statement for the partnership.

2. Prepare an owners' equity statement for Sharp Appliances. No additional investments were made.

23-2.2 Application Problem: Preparing an owners' equity statement (net decrease in capital) LO4

Heather Graham and Travis Owens are partners in Evergreen Gardens, a merchandising business. Forms for completing this problem are given in the *Working Papers*. The following information was taken from the records on December 31 of the current year.

Partner	Balance of Capital Account January 1	Balance of Drawing Account	Distribution of Net Income/Loss
Graham	$62,150.00	$6,975.00	$1,875.00
Owens	$59,000.00	$7,450.00	$1,875.00

Instructions:

Prepare an owners' equity statement for Evergreen Gardens. Additional investments made during the year: Heather Graham, $6,000.00; Travis Owens, $5,000.00.

23-3 Application Problem: Liquidating a partnership LO5, 6, 7

Rebecca and Doris Dixon agreed to liquidate their partnership on March 31 of the current year. On that date, after financial statements were prepared and closing entries were posted, the general ledger accounts had the following balances.

Cash	$10,000.00
Supplies	1,000.00
Office Equipment	20,000.00
Accumulated Depreciation—Office Equipment	11,000.00
Truck	34,000.00
Accumulated Depreciation—Truck	24,400.00
Accounts Payable	1,000.00
Rebecca Dixon, Capital	14,600.00
Doris Dixon, Capital	14,000.00

Instructions:

Journalize the following transactions which occurred during April of the current year:

Transactions:

Apr. 1. Received cash from sale of office equipment, $8,000.00. R364.
1. Received cash from sale of supplies, $400.00. R365.
3. Received cash from sale of truck, $10,000.00. R366.
5. Paid cash to all creditors for amounts owed. C534.
6. Distributed balance of Gain on Realization to Rebecca Dixon, 65%; to Doris Dixon, 35%. M141.
6. Distributed balance of Loss on Realization to Rebecca Dixon, 65%; to Doris Dixon, 35%. M142.
6. Distributed remaining cash to partners. C535 and C536.

Peachtree

1. Journalize and post transactions related to liquidating a partnership to the general journal.
2. Journalize and post the distribution of remaining cash in the Write Checks window.
3. Print the general journal and trial balance.

QuickBooks

1. Journalize and post transactions related to liquidating a partnership to the journal.
2. Journalize and post the distribution of remaining cash in the Write Checks window.
3. Print the journal and trial balance.

X (Excel)

1. Journalize transactions related to liquidating a partnership to the general journal.
2. Journalize and post the distribution of remaining cash to the cash payments journal.
3. Print the worksheets.

AAONLINE

1. Go to www.cengage.com/login
2. Click on **AA Online** to access.
3. Go to the online assignment and follow the instructions.

Sean and Shannon Fleming are partners in a business called CarpetClean. Journals and forms for completing this problem are given in the *Working Papers*. CarpetClean completed the following transactions during the current year.

Transactions:

Jan. 15. Received cash as an investment from partner, Sean Fleming, $12,000.00. Receipt No. 110.

     15. Received cash of $3,000.00 and equipment valued at $10,000.00 from partner, Shannon Fleming, as an investment. Receipt No. 111.

Mar. 31. Shannon Fleming, partner, withdrew supplies for personal use, $2,000.00. Memorandum No. 81.

     31. Sean Fleming, partner, withdrew cash for personal use, $1,600.00. Check No. 212.

Instructions:

1. Journalize the investments on January 15.

2. Journalize the withdrawals on March 31.

Additional information is given below.

Sean Fleming, Capital, January 1 balance	$35,620.00
Shannon Fleming, Capital, January 1 balance	31,760.00
Net income for the year ended December 31	29,200.00

3. Prepare a distribution of net income statement for CarpetClean for the year ended December 31. Net income or loss is to be distributed equally to the partners.

4. Using the balances of the general ledger capital accounts, prepare an owners' equity statement for CarpetClean for the year ended December 31. The investments made on January 15 are the only additional investments made by the partners this year. The withdrawals made on March 31 are the only withdrawals made by the partners this year.

The Flemings decided to liquidate CarpetClean and retire on December 31. On that date, after financial statements were prepared and closing entries were posted, the general ledger accounts had the following balances:

Cash	$108,980.00
Merchandise Inventory	4,000.00
Equipment	30,000.00
Accumulated Depreciation—Equipment	20,000.00
Accounts Payable	5,000.00
Sean Fleming, Capital	60,620.00
Shannon Fleming, Capital	57,360.00

The following transactions occurred on December 31 of the current year:

Transactions:

a. Received cash from the sale of merchandise inventory, $3,600.00. R345.

b. Received cash from the sale of equipment, $14,000.00. R346.

c. Paid cash to all creditors for amounts owed. C575.

d. Distributed balance of Gain on Realization to the partners on an equal basis. M288.

e. Distributed balance of Loss on Realization to the partners on an equal basis. M289.

f. Distributed remaining cash to partners. C576 and C577.

5. Journalize the transactions. Continue on the next available line of the journals used in instructions 1 and 2.

Peachtree

1. Journalize and post transactions related to liquidating a partnership to the general journal.

2. Journalize and post the distribution of remaining cash in the Write Checks window.

3. Print the general journal and trial balance.

QuickBooks

1. Journalize and post transactions related to liquidating a partnership to the journal.

2. Journalize and post the distribution of remaining cash in the Write Checks window.

3. Print the journal and trial balance.

1. Journalize transactions related to liquidating a partnership to the general journal.

2. Journalize and post the distribution of remaining cash to the cash payments journal.

3. Print the worksheets.

AAONLINE

1. Go to www.cengage.com/login

2. Click on **AA Online** to access.

3. Go to the online assignment and follow the instructions.

23-C Challenge Problem: Preparing a distribution of net income statement and an owners' equity statement with unequal distribution of net loss and additional investment LO3, 4

Kalima Verma and Amar Tambe are partners in a merchandising business, Travel Trinkets. Forms for completing this problem are given in the *Working Papers*. The following information was taken from the records on December 31 of the current year.

Partner	Balance of Capital Account January 1	Balance of Drawing Account	Distribution of Net Income/Loss
Verma	$62,647.00	$9,000.00	65.0%
Tambe	$50,980.50	$8,150.00	35.0%

Instructions:

1. On December 31, the partnership had a net loss of $16,170.00. Prepare a distribution of net income statement for the partnership.

2. Prepare an owners' equity statement for Travel Trinkets. Additional investments made during the year: Kalima Verma, $5,500.00; Amar Tambe, $4,750.00.

21st Century Skills

Time Value of Money—The Power of Compounding

Theme: Financial, Economic, Business, and Entrepreneurial Literacy

Skills: Flexibility and Adaptability, Initiative and Self-Direction

PARTNERSHIP FOR
21ST CENTURY SKILLS

The value of a dollar today is not the same as the value of that dollar at some point in the future. If you were asked whether you would prefer to receive $100 today or $100 a year from now, you'd take it today. If you don't actually need the money today, you might agree to wait a year if you are offered $105. Why? Because money has a time value. The time value of money is expressed as a rate of interest.

There are many terms used in the discussion and calculation of the time value of money. You may be familiar with some of them: simple interest, compound interest, present value, and future value. Simple interest is easy to understand. If you save $100 at 6% annual interest, you will get $6 more for every year the money is on deposit. After two years, you'd get back $112. Compound interest is harder to grasp because it depends on the number of times during each year that interest is added. Suppose interest is added every three months (quarterly). The interest rate is divided by four, so after three months your $100 earns 1.5% and is worth $101.50. After six months, another 1.5% is added, not just to the original $100, but to the $101.50. Now, the value is $103.02. After nine months, it's worth $104.57; after one year, its value is $106.14, and at the end of the second year, its value is $112.65. So quarterly compounding increased your return by $0.65 over the simple interest amount.

Using the above example, the present value of $100 has a future value of $112.65 in two years. The future value is what it will be worth at some time in the future given a specific rate of interest, the amount of time, and the number of compounding periods in each year. In the example, the interest rate is 6%, the time is two years, and the number of compounding periods is four.

Most people take home more money than they need to live on. If you begin saving that extra money when you are young, the time value of money will work for you. Save as early as you can. The sooner you begin, the more time your money has to grow. If you saved that $100 at 6% interest for 40 years, and the interest compounded every month, you could withdraw $1,095.75, nearly 11 times what you saved.

APPLICATION

1. Calculate the future value of an investment with a present value of $10,000 compounded monthly for one year at 6% interest. *Hint:* An interest rate of 6% compounded monthly means 6% divided by 12 months. Calculate the future value of the same investment at 6% simple interest. Explain the impact of time when calculating future value.

2. Calculate the future value of an investment presently worth $10,000 compounded annually for 20 years with interest rates of 2%, 4%, 6%, and 8%. Create a line graph to illustrate the different interest rates. Explain the importance of the interest rate in growing wealth.

Auditing for errors

Dorothy Wizen and Jonathan Yates are partners in New Market Foods. The following information was taken from the records on December 31 of the current year.

Partner	Balance of Capital Account January 1	Balance of Drawing Account	Distribution of Net Income/Loss
Wizen	$30,000.00	$4,600.00	40.0%
Yates	$24,000.00	$2,200.00	60.0%

On December 31, the partnership had a net income of $29,000.00. No additional investments were made.

REVIEW AND ANSWER

The following statements were prepared using the information above. Audit the statements. Prepare a list that describes any errors you discover and how they should be corrected.

New Market Foods		
Distribution of Net Income Statement		
December 31, 20--		
Dorothy Wizen		
40% of Net Income		14 5 0 0 00
Jonathan Yates		
60% of Net Income		14 5 0 0 00
Net Income		29 0 0 0 00

New Market Foods													
Owners' Equity Statement													
For Year Ended December 31, 20--													
Dorothy Wizen													
Capital, January 1, 20--						30	0	0	0	00			
Share of Net Income	14	5	0	0	00								
Less Withdrawals	4	6	0	0	00								
Net Increase in Capital						9	9	0	0	00			
Capital, December 31, 20--											39	9 0 0 00
Jonathan Yates													
Capital, January 1, 20--						42	0	0	0	00			
Share of Net Income	14	5	0	0	00								
Less Withdrawals	2	2	0	0	00								
Net Increase in Capital						16	7	0	0	00			
Capital, December 31, 20--											58	7 0 0 00
Total Owners' Equity, December 31, 20--											98	6 0 0 00

Analyzing Nike's financial statements

Look at the Liabilities and Shareholders' Equity section of Nike's Consolidated Balance Sheets in Appendix B on page B-6.

INSTRUCTIONS

How would this section be different if Nike were a partnership owned by two partners instead of a corporation?

Chapter 24

Recording International and Internet Sales

LEARNING OBJECTIVES

After studying Chapter 24, in addition to defining key terms, you will be able to:

LO1 Explain the purpose of entering the export and import markets.

LO2 Describe issues that must be considered before making international sales.

LO3 Explain the documentation that must be produced to process international sales.

LO4 Account for international sales.

LO5 Account for time drafts.

LO6 Account for an Internet sale.

Accounting In The Real World
Under Armour

It started with a problem and a former athlete's determination to find an alternative to his sweat-soaked cotton shirt. Kevin Plank's solution was a shirt that wicked the sweat from the body to increase speed and comfort. Kevin named the company Under Armour.

After only 14 short years, the company surpassed the $1 billion revenue mark! The manufacturing has grown from Plank's grandmother's row house to 26 manufacturing facilities in 22 countries outside of the United States.

In spite of its explosive revenue earnings, Under Armour still considers itself in the "early stages" of growth. Future growth plans include a move to develop an international presence. Currently, international sales account for only 4% of revenues. In an effort to expand globally, Under Armour has enhanced its website and mobile commerce.

Under Armour seeks to drive consumer demand by building brand awareness as a leading athletic performance brand. This strategy is executed partly by outfitting sports teams for such colleges as Auburn University and The University of Maryland, Plank's alma mater. Under Armour also has an emerging presence in the National Football League.

By focusing on athletic teams and having its products worn by leaders in the industry, Under Armour intends to appeal to athletes and consumers with active lifestyles around the globe.

CRITICAL THINKING

Doing business internationally involves risk that may interfere with payment and/or transportation. To reduce this risk and focus on its products, Under Armour has entered into an agreement with a third party called FiftyOne to help sell products and engage with online customers around the world. The services provided by FiftyOne include no-risk payments, tailored websites, and customer returns.

1. Evaluate the risks in doing business internationally.

2. List the factors that must be considered when creating a website that will be used in other countries.

3. Why would companies like Under Armour pay a third-party company to manage their website, payments, and returns? Is there a risk associated with a third party? Explain why or why not.

Key Terms

- exports
- imports
- contract of sale
- letter of credit
- bill of lading
- commercial invoice
- draft
- sight draft
- time draft
- trade acceptance

24-1 Recording International Sales

LO1 Explain the purpose of entering the export and import markets.
LO2 Describe issues that must be considered before making international sales.
LO3 Explain the documentation that must be produced to process international sales.
LO4 Account for international sales.
LO5 Account for time drafts.

International Sales LO1

Sales in the international market have become a major source of revenue for both small and large businesses. The growth of information technology tools and trading relationships in the twenty-first century has made it easier and less expensive to transact business internationally. It is no longer necessary to talk to your vendor or customer via telephone. E-mail, the Internet, and mobile devices have made it possible to do business in an interconnected world without much concern about time zones and business hours around the world.

Goods or services shipped out of a seller's home country to another country are called **exports**. Goods or services shipped into the buyer's home country from another country are called **imports**.

A company that conducts business across national borders is an international company. The number of international companies continues to grow as businesses are able to import materials or services that are less expensive or not available within their own country. Many companies have entered the export and import markets not only to expand their sales and profits, but also to maintain global competitiveness and provide products and services to meet customer demand.

Must-Have Gadgets imports merchandise such as digital cameras and cell phones from a variety of countries. Must-Have Gadgets also exports electronic gadgets such as earphones and tablet covers to customers around the world. Merchandise sold to individuals or other businesses within one's own country is referred to as *domestic sales*.

ETHICS IN ACTION

He's Guilty!

A company that believes one of its employees is stealing may obtain the services of a Certified Fraud Examiner (CFE). The CFE is trained to examine accounting records and obtain other evidence related to the alleged theft. CFEs often serve as expert witnesses in court. The *Code of Professional Standards* of the Association of Certified Fraud Examiners provides its members with guidance on how to serve as an expert witness. The Code states that the CFE should obtain evidence that provides a reasonable basis for his or her opinion. However, the CFE should never express an opinion on the guilt or innocence of any person.

INSTRUCTIONS

Access the *Code of Professional Standards* of the Association of Certified Fraud Examiners. Citing the section, what other advice does the Code provide a CFE when serving as an expert witness?

International Sales Compared with Domestic Sales LO2

Most domestic sales are for cash or on account after the customer's credit has been reviewed and approved. Because all transactions in the United States are covered by the same universal commercial laws and the same accounting standards, many transactions are based on trust. A customer with approved credit orders merchandise, the merchandise is shipped, and an invoice is sent by the vendor. After receiving the merchandise and invoice, the customer pays the vendor.

However, because of the increased complexities of international sales, several issues must be considered. The lack of uniform commercial laws between countries makes settlement of disputes more difficult.

Greater distances and sometimes more complex transportation methods increase the time to complete the transaction. Because it may be difficult to determine a customer's financial condition and to take legal action if a customer does not pay, the risk of uncollected amounts is increased. Unstable political conditions in some countries may affect the ability to receive payments from customers in those countries. Therefore, most businesses dealing in exports and/or imports follow a general process in international trade to ensure that the vendor receives payment for merchandise sold and the customer receives the merchandise ordered.

Processing an International Sale LO3

A document that details all the terms agreed to by seller and buyer for a sales transaction is called a **contract of sale**. The contract includes a description and quantity of merchandise, price, point of delivery, packing and marking instructions, shipping information, insurance provisions, and method of payment. A detailed contract of sale makes sales straightforward and eliminates confusion.

Must-Have Gadgets, located in Plano, Texas, contracts to sell merchandise to Serrano Company in Sao Paulo, Brazil. The contract price is $6,000.00 in U.S. dollars, and merchandise is to be delivered to Sao Paulo. Serrano Company is to pay transportation charges.

A letter issued by a bank guaranteeing that a named individual or business will be paid a specified amount provided stated conditions are met is called a **letter of credit**. The contract of sale between Must-Have Gadgets and Serrano specified a letter of credit as the method of payment. A letter of credit is known worldwide as a risk management tool for international transactions.

Serrano prepared an application with its bank, Banco do Rio, to issue a letter of credit. Banco do Rio

approved Serrano's application and issued the letter of credit. Banco do Rio forwarded the letter of credit to Must-Have Gadgets' bank, First Bank in Plano.

First Bank delivered the letter of credit to Must-Have Gadgets. Must-Have Gadgets reviewed the letter of credit to ensure that the provisions in the letter agreed with the contract of sale. Must-Have Gadgets then shipped the merchandise.

L.AARTIST/ISTOCKPHOTO.COM

The International Chamber of Commerce publishes "Incoterms" to attempt to coordinate international sales. This set of international rules interprets common sales terms used in foreign trade that are adopted by most international trade associations.

Collecting Payment for an International Sale

In order for Must-Have Gadgets to collect payment, three documents specified in the letter of credit must be submitted to First Bank: (1) a bill of lading, (2) a commercial invoice, and (3) a draft.

A receipt signed by the authorized agent of a transportation company for merchandise received that also serves as a contract for the delivery of the merchandise is called a **bill of lading**. The transportation company sends the bill of lading to Must-Have Gadgets when the merchandise is shipped. Must-Have Gadgets then prepares the other two documents. A statement prepared by the seller of merchandise addressed to the buyer showing a detailed listing and description of merchandise sold, including prices and terms, is called a **commercial invoice**. A written, signed, and dated order from one party ordering another party, usually a bank, to pay money to a third party is called a **draft**. A draft is sometimes referred to as a *bill of exchange*. A draft payable on sight when the holder presents it for payment is called a **sight draft**.

First Bank examines the documents submitted by Must-Have Gadgets to ensure that all terms of sale are in compliance with the letter of credit. First Bank then forwards the documents to Serrano's bank, Banco do Rio. Banco do Rio examines the documents to ensure they are in compliance with the terms and conditions of the letter of credit. When Banco do Rio determines that all documents are in compliance, it deducts the amount of the sight draft from Serrano's account and sends that amount, $6,000.00, to Must-Have-Gadgets' bank, First Bank in Plano.

Banco do Rio then forwards the documents to Serrano Company. By presenting the bill of lading and letter of credit to the transportation company, Serrano can receive the merchandise.

THINK LIKE AN ACCOUNTANT

Promoting Internet Sales

ArtCart is an Internet retail business that specializes in closeout art supplies. Similar to other Internet retail sites, selections are stored in an online shopping cart until the customer elects to check out.

To measure its success rate, ArtCart tracks the percentage of customers who complete their purchases. The company had been experiencing a success rate of approximately 82%. To encourage the remaining 18% of customers to complete their purchases, ArtCart introduced a discount program. Random customers are e-mailed a 10% discount offer one week after the items are entered in the shopping cart without being checked out. The 10% discount offer expires seven days later, thus encouraging immediate action by the customer.

Initial information seems to indicate that the discount program is working. Last December, over 70% of customers who received the discount offer checked out during the discount period. However, a new chief executive officer is questioning whether these sales would have been completed without the discount. She wonders whether the discount is simply changing when the customer checks out. If that is the case, the company is "giving away" 10% of its sales value on the discounted transactions.

OPEN THE SPREADSHEET TLA_CH24

The spreadsheet contains transaction information for January and February. Use the information to provide answers to the following questions:

1. After seven days, is there a significant difference between the success rates among customers who take the discount when checking out their shopping cart compared to those who aren't offered a discount?

2. What is the difference in the gross margin for discount sales versus nondiscount sales?

3. Apply the nondiscount success rate to the number of discount transactions. How many discount sales can be presumed to have been lost without the discount program?

4. Do you believe ArtCart's discount strategy is effective?

World Trade Organization

Decades ago, most U.S. businesses conducted their transactions within the boundaries of the United States. The majority of companies did not even consider going global for purchases or sales. U.S. laws governing patents, trade policies, and legal issues were in place to support a fair trade system. A company could expect its suppliers and customers to follow the laws.

Today, thousands of U.S. businesses either purchase or sell goods and services throughout the world. U.S. law does not apply to all international trade. There is a need for a set of international rules and guidelines to assist companies that wish to trade globally. The World Trade Organization (WTO) is attempting to negotiate these rules.

The WTO was formed in 1955 and is headquartered in Geneva, Switzerland. It is the only organization that focuses on rules for international trading. Currently, the WTO has 153 member countries and 30 "observer" governments, most of which are seeking membership. According to its website, the main function of the WTO "is to ensure that trade flows as smoothly, predictably and freely as possible."

The WTO has negotiated a variety of agreements with its member nations. It has a policy of one country, one vote. However, the consensus method is used and an actual vote has never taken place. Instead, member countries listen to opponents of an agreement and try to find ways to make the agreement acceptable to every member.

In addition to negotiating trade agreements, the WTO also implements and monitors agreements already in place. If a member country believes another country is not following the terms of an agreement, the WTO has a procedure for settling the dispute.

The WTO lists six principles that are fundamental to all WTO agreements: (1) non-discrimination, (2) more open trade, (3) predictable and transparent, (4) more competition, (5) benefits to less developed countries, and (6) protection of the environment.

The WTO publishes a variety of resources, many of which are available online. In addition to the legal texts of WTO agreements, the resources include economic research and analysis findings, the annual WTO report, international trade statistics, and the world trade report.

CRITICAL THINKING

1. Use the Internet to find three countries that fall into the following categories:
   a. Members of the WTO
   b. "Observers" of the WTO
   c. Neither members nor observers of the WTO
2. Find the top decision-making body on the WTO. In a few sentences, report the name of the body, when it meets, who attends, and what it does.

Journalizing an International Sale LO4

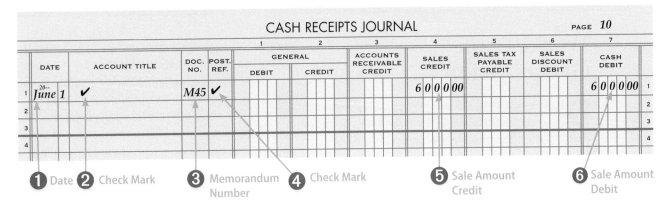

	DATE	ACCOUNT TITLE	DOC. NO.	POST. REF.	GENERAL DEBIT	GENERAL CREDIT	ACCOUNTS RECEIVABLE CREDIT	SALES CREDIT	SALES TAX PAYABLE CREDIT	SALES DISCOUNT DEBIT	CASH DEBIT	
1	20-- June 1	✔	M45	✔				6 0 0 0 00			6 0 0 0 00	1
2												2
3												3
4												4

❶ Date **❷** Check Mark **❸** Memorandum Number **❹** Check Mark **❺** Sale Amount Credit **❻** Sale Amount Debit

After receiving payment from Banco do Rio, First Bank deposits the payment for the sale in Must-Have Gadgets' account and sends Must-Have Gadgets a deposit slip for the amount deposited. After receiving the deposit slip from First Bank, Must-Have Gadgets prepares a memorandum as a source document for the cash received. The sale is then recorded as a cash sale.

Sales taxes are normally paid only on sales to the final consumer also referred to as the end user. Must-Have Gadgets' sale is to Serrano Company, a merchandising company. Therefore, sales tax is not collected.

The sales and collection process assured Must-Have Gadgets of receiving payment for its sale and Serrano Company of receiving the merchandise it ordered.

June 1. Recorded international cash sale, $6,000.00. Memorandum 45.

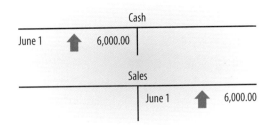

Recording an Entry for an International Sale

❶ Write the date, 20--, June 1, in the Date column.

❷ Place a check mark in the Account Title column to indicate that no account title needs to be entered.

❸ Write the source document number, M45, in the Doc. No. column.

❹ Place a check mark in the Post. Ref. column to indicate that the amounts on this line are not posted individually.

❺ Write the sale amount, $6,000.00, in the Sales Credit column.

❻ Write the sale amount, $6,000.00, in the Cash Debit column.

Visitors to foreign countries with a value added tax (VAT) typically are required to pay the VAT. However, if items purchased exceed a specified amount, a refund of a portion of the VAT can be requested.

Journalizing Time Drafts LO5

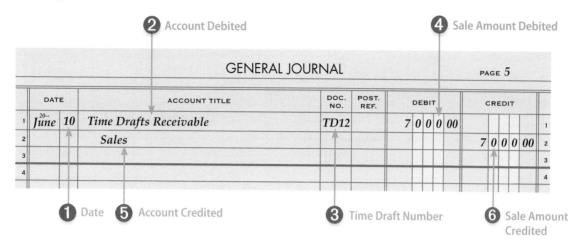

① Date **⑤** Account Credited   **③** Time Draft Number   **⑥** Sale Amount Credited

Must-Have Gadgets sold $7,000.00 of merchandise to Ramirez Co., located in Guadalajara, Mexico. The contract of sale with Ramirez was similar to the contract with Serrano Company, with one exception. Must-Have Gadgets agreed to delay receipt of payment 60 days. A draft that is payable at a fixed or determinable future time after it is accepted is called a **time draft**.

The sales process with Ramirez is the same as with Serrano, except Must-Have Gadgets submits with the documentation a time draft due 60 days from the date the draft is accepted. On June 10, all documentation for the Ramirez sale is verified to be correct by the seller's and buyer's banks, and Must-Have Gadgets' time draft is accepted.

After verifying the documentation, Ramirez's bank, Banco Mexico, returns the accepted time draft to Must-Have Gadgets and forwards the other documents to

Ramirez Co. Ramirez can receive the merchandise by presenting the bill of lading and letter of credit to the transportation company.

> **June 10.** Received a 60-day time draft from Ramirez Co. for an international sale, $7,000.00. Time Draft No. 12.

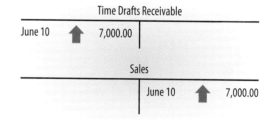

The minimum value added tax in the European Community is 15%; however, there is no additional local sales tax. The Philippines imposes a 12% VAT that applies to the sale, barter, or exchange of goods, properties, or services. Thailand applies a 7% VAT to selected beverages.

↻ Journalizing a Time Draft

① Write the date, 20--, June 10, in the Date column.

② Write Time Drafts Receivable in the Account Title column.

③ Write the time draft number, TD12, in the Doc. No. column.

④ Write the sale amount, $7,000.00, in the Debit column.

⑤ On the next line, indent and write Sales in the Account Title column.

⑥ Write the sale amount, $7,000.00, in the Credit column.

Journalizing Cash Receipts from Time Drafts

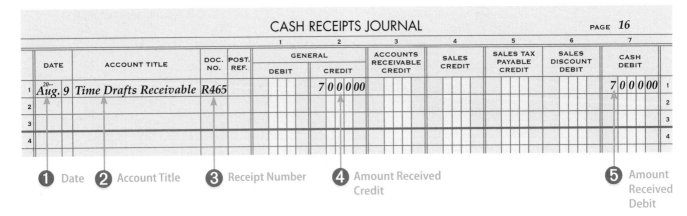

	DATE	ACCOUNT TITLE	DOC. NO.	POST. REF.	GENERAL DEBIT	GENERAL CREDIT	ACCOUNTS RECEIVABLE CREDIT	SALES CREDIT	SALES TAX PAYABLE CREDIT	SALES DISCOUNT DEBIT	CASH DEBIT	
1	Aug. 9 20--	Time Drafts Receivable	R465			7 0 0 0 00					7 0 0 0 00	1
2												2
3												3
4												4

CASH RECEIPTS JOURNAL   PAGE **16**

1. Date 2. Account Title 3. Receipt Number 4. Amount Received Credit 5. Amount Received Debit

When Ramirez's time draft is due and presented to its bank, Banco Mexico, the bank pays the draft. The payment process is the same as the payment of Serrano Company's sight draft.

> **August 9. Received cash for the value of Time Draft No. 12, $7,000.00. Receipt No. 465.**

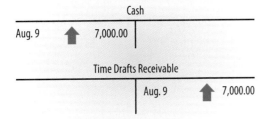

Cash

Aug. 9	7,000.00	

Time Drafts Receivable

	Aug. 9	7,000.00

The process used by Must-Have Gadgets for international sales relies upon letters of credit from banks to assure receipt of payment for those sales. Occasionally, Must-Have Gadgets grants an extension of time for payment to long-time international customers by submitting a time draft.

TRADE ACCEPTANCES

A form signed by a buyer at the time of a sale of merchandise in which the buyer promises to pay the seller a specified sum of money, usually at a stated time in the future, is called a **trade acceptance**.

A trade acceptance is similar to a draft except a draft is generally paid by a bank and a trade acceptance is paid by the buyer. A seller generally has much more assurance of receiving payment from a bank than from a buyer. Because of the many complexities, few businesses use trade acceptances in international sales. Some businesses, however, use trade acceptances for domestic sales to very reliable customers.

Journalizing Cash Received from a Time Draft

1. Write the date, 20--, Aug. 9, in the Date column.
2. Write Time Drafts Receivable in the Account Title column.
3. Write the source document number, R465, in the Doc. No. column.
4. Write the amount received, $7,000.00, in the General Credit column.
5. Write the same amount, $7,000.00, in the Cash Debit column.

remember — A sight draft and a time draft are similar. Both methods of international sales require the buyer's bank to guarantee the cash payment for the sale. The primary difference between a sight draft and a time draft is the timing of the payment. Cash payment of a time draft is delayed for a period of time after the delivery of the goods to the buyer.

Benford's Law

In 1925, Frank Benford, a scientist for General Electric, observed that the front pages of his logarithm book were worn from use more than the back pages. Prior to the age of computers, handheld calculators, and smartphones, scientists used a logarithm book to assist them in multiplying and dividing numbers. Being a good scientist, Benford questioned why he was using the front more than the back part of the book. The front part contained the logarithmic values for numbers beginning with 1 and continued through numbers beginning with 9 at the back of the book.

Benford began to test natural data sets and discovered a consistent number pattern. The frequency of the first digit of a number being a 1 was 30.1%, as shown in the following table. The size of the number is not important. Whether the number is 1.23, 123, or 123,000, each number begins with the number 1.

First Digit	Frequency of First Digit
1	30.1%
2	17.6%
3	12.5%
4	9.7%
5	7.9%
6	6.7%
7	5.8%
8	5.1%
9	4.6%

Named in honor of Frank Benford, Benford's Law only applies to natural data sets that have no artificial biases. For example, the ACT score that is between 1 and 36 is not a natural data set; nor are invoice numbers, weekly hours worked, or codes. Examples of natural data sets would include:

- Sales at a retail store
- Checking account balances at a bank
- Client investment accounts managed by a financial advisor
- Total assets of the S&P 500 companies

Auditors have discovered that they can apply Benford's Law to forensic accounting. Any significant difference between the expected frequency (Benford's Law) and the actual frequency of numbers indicates that some sort of bias exists. Whether the bias is a natural for the business or a result of a fraud requires additional investigation. For example, a grocery store may naturally have a higher proportion of transactions beginning with a 1 or 2; few customers purchase $300.00 or more of groceries at one time. In contrast, a dollar limit that requires management approval of a transaction may result in a fraudster entering a large number of transactions just under that limit.

ACTIVITY

Any time that BoardTown Stores is open, one employee is assigned the responsibility of maintaining the appearance of shelves. This employee returns misplaced merchandise to its proper location and neatly arranges items at the front of the shelves. Any damaged merchandise is removed from the shelves. After the items are scanned into a point-of-sale terminal located in a receiving area, they are packaged to be sold to a salvage business. The system removes the items from BoardTown's perpetual inventory.

Kelly Alford, the store manager, recently learned of Benford's Law and has asked you to analyze the transactions to remove damaged merchandise.

INSTRUCTIONS

Open the spreadsheet FA_CH24 and complete the steps on the Instructions tab.

Source: http://en.wikipedia.org.

End of Lesson Review

Terms Review

exports

imports

contract of sale

letter of credit

bill of lading

commercial invoice

draft

sight draft

time draft

trade acceptance

Audit your understanding

1. What are four of the issues that must be considered before making international sales?

2. What two purposes does a bill of lading serve?

3. How does a sight draft differ from a time draft?

4. Why do many companies dealing in international sales rely upon letters of credit from banks?

5. How does a trade acceptance differ from a draft?

Work together 24-1

Journalizing international sales transactions

The cash receipts and general journals for Nicola Maria Exports, Inc., are given in the *Working Papers*. Your instructor will guide you through the following examples.

1. Using the current year, journalize the following international sales on page 10 of a cash receipts journal and page 5 of a general journal. Sales tax is not charged on these sales. Source documents are abbreviated as follows: memorandum, M; time draft, TD; receipt, R.

Transactions:

July 11. Recorded an international cash sale, $12,000.00. M324.

16. Received a 30-day time draft from Sun Chan for an international sale, $16,000.00. TD31.

23. Received cash for the value of Time Draft No. 10, $22,000.00. R221.

2. Prove and rule the cash receipts journal.

On your own 24-1

Journalizing international sales transactions

The cash receipts and general journals for Courtney's Stone Collections are given in the *Working Papers*. Work this problem independently.

1. Using the current year, journalize the following international sales on page 17 of a cash receipts journal and page 8 of a general journal. Sales tax is not charged on these sales. Source documents are abbreviated as follows: memorandum, M; time draft, TD; receipt, R.

Transactions:

Oct. 8. Recorded an international cash sale, $8,400.00. M256.

17. Received a 45-day time draft from Ashley Patel for an international sale, $6,300.00. TD81.

30. Received cash for the value of Time Draft No. 73, $10,500.00. R205.

2. Prove and rule the cash receipts journal.

©CANDICE CUSACK, ISTOCK

LESSON
24-2 Recording Internet Sales

LO6 Account for an Internet sale.

Internet Sales

More companies are turning to the Internet, also referred to as *electronic commerce* or *e-commerce*, as an additional way of selling goods and services in order to compete globally. An explosive increase in Internet sales is likely due to a boost in global access to the Internet, buyer comfort and confidence in shopping online, and product availability and variety. Internet shopping provides customers the opportunity to browse the products offered by a company, compare competitors' products, and do so at a time and place convenient to the customer.

Selling goods over the Internet, however, also presents some challenges to the seller. The website developed must be easy to navigate and safe to use. Customers must feel that the website uses up-to-date security procedures to protect credit card information as it is being transmitted. The selling company must also be able to accept credit card sales, which means it must contract with a bank to offer this service or with a company that will offer this service to businesses for a fee.

Must-Have Gadgets has prepared a website that will accept credit card orders and transmit the sales information for immediate shipping and billing. An order confirmation is also immediately sent to the buyer, containing information about the order and expected shipping date.

Internet sales at Must-Have Gadgets must be completed with a credit card. At the end of each day, Must-Have Gadgets will be able to print out a terminal summary similar to the terminal summary discussed in Chapter 10. The terminal summary is used as the source document for recording online sales.

Wildlife Management

In many cities in the United States, the same thing happens each Friday afternoon. City dwellers pack up and vacate the city, choosing instead a quiet country experience. It might take place on a hiking trail, near a lake, or in the forest. If luck is with them, they may even spot some wildlife such as a deer.

Not everyone is excited about the increasing population of wildlife. Each year, deer alone cause millions of dollars of damage to U.S. agricultural crops. This causes a conflict between hunters, environmentalists, conservationists who want increased wildlife, and agricultural producers whose livelihood is threatened by wild animals.

Most states have a department or agency that is in charge of wildlife management. In order to help reach a balance, many states have a program through which producers receive payment for crop and animal losses due to wild animals. However, sometimes the cost of administrating such programs is higher than the amount actually paid out in losses. Administration costs are highest when losses are actually verified by wildlife officials. Without official verification, there is a risk that producers will claim more loss than actually occurred.

WHY ACCOUNTING?

Agriculture, Food & Natural Resources

CRITICAL THINKING

1. Assume you work in wildlife management. Develop a list of three things you could do to keep administration costs down, but at the same time, have some assurance that the loss claims you receive accurately reflect the loss that occurred.

2. Use the Internet to research crop and animal loss due to wild animals throughout the world. List three wild animals that cause this loss.

©ANEKCEN KOWEBHNKOB, ISTOCK

Journalizing an Internet Sale LO6

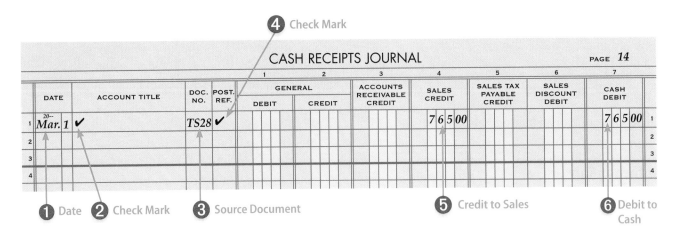

④ Check Mark

CASH RECEIPTS JOURNAL   PAGE 14

	DATE	ACCOUNT TITLE	DOC. NO.	POST. REF.	GENERAL DEBIT	GENERAL CREDIT	ACCOUNTS RECEIVABLE CREDIT	SALES CREDIT	SALES TAX PAYABLE CREDIT	SALES DISCOUNT DEBIT	CASH DEBIT	
1	20-- Mar. 1 ✔		TS28	✔				7 6 5 00			7 6 5 00	1
2												2
3												3
4												4

① Date   ② Check Mark   ③ Source Document   ⑤ Credit to Sales   ⑥ Debit to Cash

---

March 1. Recorded Internet credit card sales, $765.00. Terminal Summary 28.

Must-Have Gadgets processes its credit card sales at the end of each day. At the same time, the information is electronically transmitted to First Bank, with whom Must-Have Gadgets has contracted to process its credit card sales. This information is transferred to the Federal Reserve Bank and processed in a manner similar to checks. Therefore, Must-Have Gadgets considers these sales to be cash sales.

The asset account **Cash** has a normal debit balance and is debited for the amount of the credit card sales, $765.00. The **Sales** account has a normal credit balance. Therefore, **Sales** is credited for the amount of the sales, $765.00.

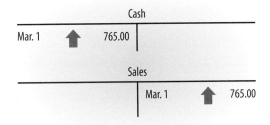

Recording an Entry for an Internet Sale

① Write the date, 20--, Mar. 1, in the Date column.

② Place a check mark in the Account Title column to indicate that no account title needs to be entered.

③ Write the source document number, TS28, in the Doc. No. column.

④ Place a check mark in the Post. Ref. column to indicate that the amounts on this line are not posted individually.

⑤ Write the sale amount, $765.00, in the Sales Credit column.

⑥ Write the sale amount, $765.00, in the Cash Debit column.

In order to process bank credit cards such as Visa and MasterCard, a business must set up a merchant account with a bank. The business pays a fee to the bank for processing credit card sales.

End of Lesson Review

LO6 Account for an Internet sale.

Audit your understanding

1. What are two reasons why a customer might prefer online shopping?
2. Why is a bank credit card sale treated the same as a cash sale?

Work together 24-2

Journalizing Internet sales transactions

The cash receipts journal for Julia's Organic Bakery is given in the *Working Papers*. Your instructor will guide you through the following examples.

Using the current year, journalize the following Internet sales on page 3 of a cash receipts journal.

Transactions:

Aug. 21. Recorded Internet credit card sales, $1,432.00. Terminal Summary 230.

27. Recorded Internet credit card sales, $2,010.00. Terminal Summary 231.

28. Recorded Internet credit card sales, $1,270.00. Terminal Summary 232.

On your own 24-2

Journalizing Internet sales transactions

The cash receipts journal for Rhonda's Gourmet Gifts is given in the *Working Papers*. Work this problem independently.

Using the current year, journalize the following Internet sales on page 11 of a cash receipts journal.

Transactions:

Feb. 7. Recorded Internet credit card sales, $125.00. Terminal Summary 44.

14. Recorded Internet credit card sales, $289.00. Terminal Summary 45.

28. Recorded Internet credit card sales, $338.00. Terminal Summary 46.

A Look at Accounting Software
Setting Up a New Customer

Merchandising businesses, whether wholesale or retail, have customers. Retail businesses don't typically keep subsidiary ledger accounts for all their customers because there are far too many of them and the sales volume to each customer is small. Merchandise businesses that sell wholesale typically do maintain accounts for each customer because those customers tend to make frequent purchases and their purchases are large enough to track. As with vendors, there are different types, or classes, of customers. Classes of customers might be based on sales contracts, government regulations, taxes, location, credit terms, product mix, etc. Accounting software systems allow businesses to set up different customer classes to enable recording and reporting accounting information accordingly.

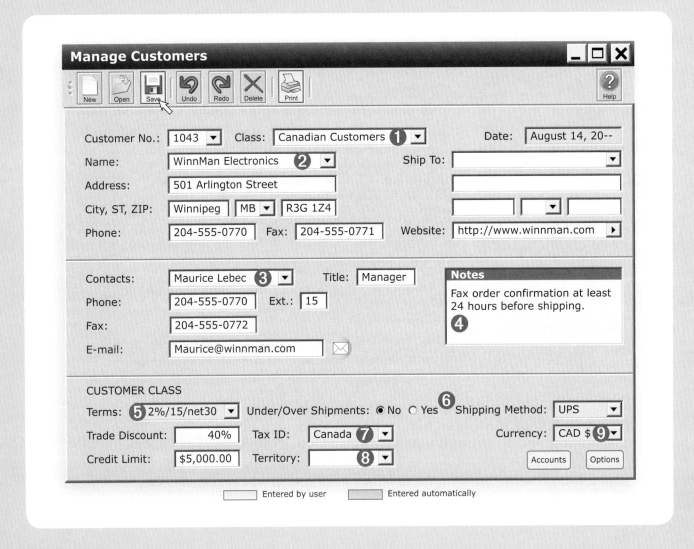

1. To set up a new customer, the user first assigns a customer number. If the business tracks customer sales by class, the user would click on the drop-down list and select the appropriate class for that customer.

2. Next, the user would enter the address, phone number, and web address of the customer. Some customers have multiple addresses—perhaps different branches or stores. The Ship To fields allow the business to track sales to each address while maintaining a total accounting of sales to the central account.

3. In business-to-business dealings, different types of contacts are involved. One person may be responsible for negotiating contracts, while another is responsible for placing orders. Another person may resolve problems with orders. Contact information, then, is very important to users of the accounting system.

4. The Notes field allows the user to record personal or business information about the contact and the business relationship.

5. When the different customer classes were set up, default settings for each class were entered. So, when the Canadian Customers class was selected, those fields with default settings were populated by the system. Alternate settings may be selected by the user as appropriate.

6. Sometimes the inventory of an item may not be sufficient to fill a customer's order. Or, prepackaged bundles of the item may contain quantities that don't match the order. For example, an item might be packaged with 24 items and the customer ordered 20. Many sales agreements allow the business to undership or overship quantities within certain limits. Some customers will not accept quantities other than what they ordered. When that is the case, the system will not allow an order to be filled with a lesser or greater quantity than the order.

7. There are many different tax codes to account for when selling to customers around the United States or around the world. Accounting systems allow businesses to set up different accounts to manage payment of those taxes. Setting a tax profile for each class simplifies this accounting. Canada, for example, has a general services tax which must be paid by the seller.

8. Large companies often manage their sales by geographic territories. Each territory generally has a sales manager and, perhaps, sales representatives. It is necessary in those situations to properly account for sales by territory.

9. For U.S. companies, international business can most often be conducted in U.S. dollars. However, it is sometimes necessary to conduct business in a foreign currency. Selling prices would then be quoted, and invoice payments would be received, in that currency. Currency conversions would generally be handled by the company's bank. However, accountants must enter currency exchange adjustments into the business's accounts.

Chapter Summary

Many companies have entered the export and import market to compete globally and to provide the products and services to meet customer demand.

International sales are more complex than domestic sales. The lack of universal commercial laws in other countries makes it challenging to settle disputes that could arise and affect payment. To process international sales, documentation such as a contract of sale, letter of credit, bill of lading, commercial invoice, and a sight or time draft must be produced for shipment and payment to occur.

Once business relationships have been established and trust is gained, a trade acceptance may be presented instead of a draft. A trade acceptance is an agreement from the buyer to pay directly in the future, unlike a draft for which payment is received from the buyer's bank.

Internet sales (or e-commerce) have exploded due to advances in technology and customers' growing comfort in buying online. Customers are enjoying the luxury of the shopping conveniences afforded by the Internet.

Internet sales are typically completed with a credit card. At the end of each day, the seller prints a terminal summary as a source document for recording online sales.

EXPLORE ACCOUNTING

A Sales Tax Dilemma

With Internet sales reaching over $165 billion and growing almost 15% annually, the issues of whether and how states should tax Internet sales are hot legislative topics.

Currently, sales tax is collected by the seller and paid to the state only on goods sold within the seller's state. Sellers do not collect sales tax on goods shipped outside the state, but buyers are technically required to pay a use tax to the state in which the good is used, consumed, or stored. Since the use tax is difficult to enforce, many states now want to make the sellers collect sales tax on goods purchased out of state on the Internet.

Many state lawmakers feel that online retailers who do not collect sales tax as "brick-and-mortar" retailers do are not doing their share. They argue that states are missing out on critical tax dollars.

Retailers are worried about competition from online sellers since Internet retailers can offer lower costs without collecting sales tax. Retailers say that imposing sales tax with e-commerce will remove the unfair advantage of Internet retailers and level the sales tax playing field.

Internet companies argue that they have to pay shipping. Additionally, they claim they do not use governmental services the way in-state retailers do, such as police/fire protection, and should not be required to charge and collect the sales tax.

A 1992 Supreme Court ruling says businesses must have a physical presence inside a state for the business to be required to collect sales tax. Many think since this decision originated with mail order sales that the definition of physical presence should be updated and broadened to include "a presence in the state" in an effort to address sales tax inequities.

State lawmakers are working hard to make an Internet sales tax a reality. Others are hopeful that Congress will finally step in and establish a federal law.

INSTRUCTIONS

1. Accountants must stay current on tax laws. Search the Internet to see what the current state law is pertaining to an Internet sales tax for your state.

2. Some think that having a "presence in the state" rather than a physical presence should be the requirement to collect sales tax. List three ways that one could have a "presence" and not necessarily a physical presence.

3. Compose a letter taking on the view of the consumer, brick-and-mortar retailer, state lawmaker, or Internet retailer stating your opinion about how Internet sales should or should not be taxed. Be sure to include at least three reasons why you support your decision.

Source: www.forbes.com.

Apply Your Understanding

INSTRUCTIONS: Download problem instructions for Excel, QuickBooks, and Peachtree from the textbook companion website at www.C21accounting.com.

24-1 Application Problem: Journalizing international sales transactions LO 4, 5

The cash receipts and general journals for Jan Hakeem Exports, Ltd. are given in the *Working Papers*.

Instructions:

1. Journalize the following international sales completed by Jan Hakeem Exports, Ltd. during June of the current year. Use page 12 of a cash receipts journal and page 5 of a general journal. Sales tax is not charged on these sales. Source documents are abbreviated as follows: memorandum, M; time draft, TD; receipt, R.

Transactions:

June   1.   Recorded an international cash sale, $14,000.00. M79.
     5.   Received a 30-day time draft from Bella Lamas for an international sale, $12,000.00. TD27.
     9.   Received cash for the value of Time Draft No. 24, $18,000.00. R115.
    12.   Received a 60-day time draft from Elias Harmon for an international sale, $7,000.00. TD33.
    19.   Received cash for the value of Time Draft No. 21, $22,000.00. R117.
    21.   Recorded an international cash sale, $13,500.00. M83.
    25.   Received a 30-day time draft from Juan Mendez for an international sale, $26,500.00. TD34.

2. Prove and rule the cash receipts journal.

 Peachtree

1. Journalize and post transactions related to international sales transactions to the general journal.
2. Journalize and post transactions related to cash receipts from international sales transactions.
3. Print the cash receipts journal, general journal, and trial balance.

 QuickBooks

1. Journalize and post transactions related to international sales transactions to the journal.
2. Journalize and post transactions related to cash receipts in the Receive Payments window.
3. Print the customer balance detail, journal, and trial balance.

Excel

1. Journalize and post transactions related to international sales transactions to the general journal.
2. Journalize and post transactions related to cash receipts from international sales transactions.
3. Print the cash receipts journal and general journal.

24-2 Application Problem: Journalizing Internet sales transactions LO 6

The cash receipts journal for Jeff's Sports Memorabilia is given in the *Working Papers*.

Instructions:

1. Journalize the following Internet sales completed by Jeff's Sports Memorabilia during August of the current year. Use page 15 of a cash receipts journal. Source documents are abbreviated as follows: terminal summary, TS.

Transactions:

Mar.   5.   Recorded Internet credit card sales, $799.00. TS113.
    13.   Recorded Internet credit card sales, $1,287.00. TS114.
    20.   Recorded Internet credit card sales, $1,109.00. TS115.
    27.   Recorded Internet credit card sales, $2,945.00. TS116.

2. Total and rule the cash receipts journal.

Dexter Corporation has both international and Internet sales.

Instructions:

1. Journalize the following transactions affecting sales and cash receipts completed during February of the current year. Use page 3 of both a general journal and a cash receipts journal. Source documents are abbreviated as follows: memorandum, M; receipt, R; time draft, TD; terminal summary, TS.

Transactions:

May 5. Received a 30-day time draft from Cooper Doi for an international sale, $3,000.00. TD10.
8. Recorded Internet credit card sales, $14,500.00. TS23.
12. Recorded an international cash sale, $8,800.00. M8.
14. Received cash for the value of Time Draft No. 4, $22,000.00. R35.
18. Recorded Internet credit card sales, $18,300.00. TS24.
21. Received cash for the value of Time Draft No. 7, $6,000.00. R37.
24. Recorded an international cash sale, $12,400.00. M12.
27. Recorded Internet credit card sales, $7,100.00. TS25.
28. Received a 30-day time draft from Strizi Percheki for international sale of merchandise, $5,000.00. TD11.

2. Prove and rule the cash receipts journal.

Peachtree	**QuickBooks**	**X**	**AA ONLINE**
1. Journalize and post transactions related to international sales transactions to the general journal.	1. Journalize and post transactions related to international sales transactions to the journal.	1. Journalize and post transactions related to international sales transactions to the general journal.	1. Go to www.cengage.com/login
2. Journalize and post transactions related to cash receipts from international sales transactions.	2. Journalize and post transactions related to cash receipts in the Receive Payments window.	2. Journalize and post transactions related to cash receipts from international sales transactions.	2. Click on **AA Online** to access.
3. Print the cash receipts journal, general journal, and trial balance.	3. Print the customer balance detail, journal, and trial balance.	3. Print the cash receipts journal and general journal.	3. Go to the online assignment and follow the instructions.

International sales can be stated in terms of U.S. dollars or in the foreign currency. The transaction statements below are stated in terms of the foreign currency of the customer.

Instructions:

1. Journalize the following transactions affecting sales. Use the foreign currency exchange rates given in the table below to translate the amount of the sales into U.S. dollars. Use page 11 of a cash receipts journal. Source documents are abbreviated as follows: memorandum, M. (*Hint:* Review the Global Awareness feature in Chapter 6.)

Transactions:

June 1. Recorded international cash sale, 6,207 Chinese yuan. M48.
8. Recorded international cash sale, 28,731 Mexican pesos. M53.
14. Recorded international cash sale, 4,631 New Zealand dollars. M59.
19. Recorded international cash sale, 453 European euros. M60.
28. Recorded international cash sale, 2,174,060 Indian rupees. M72.

Currency	1 U.S. Dollar Equals...
Chinese yuan	6.3883 yuan
European euro	0.73126 euro
Mexican peso	13.11144 pesos
New Zealand dollar	1.21711 New Zealand dollars
Indian rupee	47.79671 rupees

2. Prove and rule the cash receipts journal.

Crack Down on Identity Theft

Theme: Financial, Economic, Business, and Entrepreneurial Literacy

Skills: Critical Thinking and Problem Solving, Creativity and Innovation, ICT Literacy

PARTNERSHIP FOR
21ST CENTURY SKILLS

Millions have discovered the convenience of shopping on the Internet. Unfortunately, many have not considered the risk of releasing personal information to different websites. What would happen if someone stole personal or credit card information and charged thousands of dollars in someone else's name? This is a form of identity theft and is considered a crime.

Credit card fraud is the most common type of identity theft and is one of the fastest growing crimes in the United States. As many as 9 million Americans have their identities stolen each year. Unfortunately, the victims may be denied loans or job opportunities due to false information on their credit reports.

One way to protect against identity theft is to create strong passwords. A strong password consists of uncommon names and number combinations. Also, be cautious about e-mail scams and suspicious e-mails. Make sure the online business has a secure website and uses a security measure that scrambles your data as it passes through the Internet. This is called **encryption**; a closed padlock image will often appear on a website that uses encryption, or a pop-up window will indicate added security features. In addition, confirm the validity of the online business before conducting business and preferably look for a third-party endorsement such as the Better Business Bureau.

APPLICATION

1. List at least three other types of identity theft besides credit card fraud.
2. Compose a list of five ways in which consumers put themselves at risk for identity theft. For each of these risks, post reminders on a poster, produce a public service announcement, or create a "tweet of the day" on Twitter.

Analyzing Nike's financial statements

A majority of Nike's products are sold outside of the United States. As a result, transactions are conducted in multiple currencies. This exposes Nike to the effects of changes in foreign currency exchange rates, which could have a negative impact on its financial condition.

INSTRUCTIONS

Read the section of Note 1 entitled Foreign Currency Translation and Foreign Currency Transactions on page B-11 of Appendix B. In which financial statement do you find adjustments resulting from translating foreign functional currency financial statements into U.S. dollars?

Appendix A

Accounting Concepts

Since 1973, the Financial Accounting Standards Board (FASB) has assumed responsibility for setting financial accounting standards known as *Generally Accepted Accounting Principles* (GAAP). One of the first tasks of the FASB was to establish a framework that describes the concepts underlying GAAP. That framework continues to guide the FASB's development of new standards.

In the United States, GAAP serves as a guide for reporting and interpreting accounting information. The accounting principles described in this textbook are based on the application of the concepts underlying GAAP. These concepts are described below and referenced throughout the textbook.

In 1973, the international financial community formed an organization with the ambitious goal of creating a universal set of accounting standards. Similar to the FASB, the International Accounting Standards Board (IASB) uses a framework to develop its standards, known as *International Financial Reporting Standards* (IFRS, pronounced ī'-fers).

The FASB and IASB are committed to merging GAAP and IFRS to achieve one universal set of accounting standards. At the time this textbook was written, the FASB and IASB were working to establish a common framework. That framework will provide the foundation for development of accounting standards to be used around the world.

ACCOUNTING PERIOD CYCLE

Changes in financial information are reported for a specific period of time in the form of financial statements.

Financial statements summarize the financial information that a business records. The time period for which financial statements are prepared depends on the needs of the business. An accounting period may be one month, three months, six months, or one year. An accounting period of one year is a fiscal year. Publicly held corporations must prepare fiscal year financial statements. For tax purposes, every business prepares financial statements at the end of each year.

BUSINESS ENTITY

Financial information is recorded and reported separately from the owner's personal financial information.

A business exists separately from its owners. A business's records must not be mixed with an owner's personal records and reports. For example, a business owner may buy insurance to protect the business and insurance to protect the owner's home. Only the insurance obtained for the business is recorded in the business's financial records. Insurance purchased for the owner's personal home is recorded in the owner's personal financial records. One bank account is used for the business and another for the owner.

CONSISTENT REPORTING

The same accounting principles must be followed in the same way in each accounting period.

Business decisions are based on the financial information reported on financial statements. Some decisions require a comparison of current financial statements with previous financial statements. If accounting information is recorded and reported differently each accounting period, comparisons from one accounting period to another may not be possible. If a business were to include $100,000 of supply purchases as a cost of merchandise sold in one period and as an operating expense in the next period, a user of this information could not adequately compare the two accounting periods. Therefore, unless a change is necessary to make information more easily understood, accounting information is reported in a consistent way every accounting period.

FULL DISCLOSURE

Financial statements contain all information necessary to understand a business's financial condition.

Owners, managers, lenders, and investors rely on financial statements to make informed decisions. All relevant financial information must be adequately and completely disclosed on financial statements.

Assume a business only reports total liabilities of $200,000 on its balance sheet. If that total includes $75,000 in current liabilities, then the balance sheet does not adequately disclose the nature of the liabilities. The critical information not disclosed is that $75,000 is due within the current fiscal year. Full disclosure requires an income statement, a balance sheet, a statement of owners' equity, a statement of cash flows, and the notes to the financial statements.

GOING CONCERN

Financial statements are prepared with the expectation that a business will remain in operation indefinitely.

New businesses are started with the expectation that they will be successful. Accounting records and financial statements are designed as though businesses will continue indefinitely. For example, a business buys store equipment for $80,000. After yearly depreciation is recorded and reported based on the expected life of the equipment, the equipment's book value (cost less accumulated depreciation) is $44,000. If the business ended operations and the equipment had to be sold, the amount received might be less, or more, than the $44,000. However, accounting records are maintained with the expectation that the business will remain in operation indefinitely and that the cost will be allocated over the useful life of the equipment. The equipment value, therefore, is $44,000 on the records, regardless of what it may be worth when sold.

HISTORICAL COST

The actual amount paid for merchandise or other items bought is recorded.

The actual amount paid for an item in a business transaction may be different from its market value. For example, assume a business purchases a delivery truck that is advertised for sale at $28,500. The truck has a market value of $30,000. The business negotiated a purchase price of just $27,000. The amount recorded in the accounting records for the delivery truck is the "historical" cost, $27,000—the actual amount paid.

MATCHING EXPENSES WITH REVENUE

The revenue from business activities and the expenses associated with earning that revenue are recorded in the same accounting period.

Business activities for an accounting period are summarized in financial statements. To adequately report how a business performed during an accounting period, all revenue earned as a result of business operations must be reported. Likewise, all expenses incurred in producing the revenue during the same accounting period must be reported. Matching expenses with revenue gives a true picture of business operations for an accounting period. The timing of when cash is exchanged does not impact when a transaction is recorded as either revenue or expense.

For example, in February, assume a business performs $50,000 of services and uses $5,000 of supplies that were purchased in the prior fiscal year. Matching expenses with revenue results in net income of $4,500. Including all required expenses gives readers of the financial statements a more complete picture of the financial condition of the business.

MATERIALITY

Business activities creating dollar amounts large enough to affect business decisions should be recorded and reported as separate items in the accounting records and financial statements.

Business transactions are recorded in accounting records and reported in financial statements in dollar amounts. How the amounts are recorded and reported depends on the amount involved and the relative importance of the item in making business decisions. Dollar amounts that are large will generally be considered in making decisions about future operations. A separate accounting record is kept for items with dollar amounts large enough to be considered in making decisions about future operations. Dollar amounts that are small and not considered important in decision making may be combined with other amounts in the accounting records and financial statements.

NEUTRALITY

The process of making accounting estimates is free from bias.

Many accounting functions require a business to use estimates. These include the estimation of uncollectible accounts receivable and the assignment of a useful life and salvage value for a plant asset. A business must not set or alter these estimates to achieve some other goal, such as reducing net income to avoid income taxes. For example, a business could raise its estimate of uncollectible accounts receivable to reduce its operating income subject to income tax. However, in compliance with the neutrality principle, the book value of accounts receivable in the financial accounts must always be a reasonable and unbiased estimate of the money the business expects to collect in the future.

OBJECTIVE EVIDENCE

A source document is prepared for each transaction.

A source document is an original business paper indicating that a transaction did occur and that the amounts recorded in the accounting records are accurate and true.

For example, a check is the original business paper for cash payments. The original business paper for purchases on account is the purchase invoice. When accounting information reported on the financial statements needs to be verified, an accountant will first check the accounting record. If the details of an entry need further checking, an accountant will then check the business papers as objective evidence that the transaction did occur as recorded.

Many transactions in modern computerized accounting systems are entered directly into the system. Although no paper document is ever prepared, an electronic version of the document is available in the system. The electronic record provides the same objective evidence of the transaction as would a paper record.

REALIZATION OF REVENUE

Revenue is recorded at the time goods or services are sold.

A business may sell goods or services or both. Cash may be received at the time of sale, or the business may agree to receive payment at a later date. Regardless of when cash is actually received, the sale amount is recorded in the accounting records at the time of sale. For example, merchandise is sold for $3,500. The business agrees to an initial payment of $500 with the remaining balance to be divided in four monthly payments of $750 each. The full $3,500 of revenue is recorded at the time of the sale even though $3,000 will be collected later.

UNIT OF MEASUREMENT

Business transactions are reported in numbers that have common values—that is, using a common unit of measurement.

All transactions are recorded in accounting records in terms of money. Useful nonfinancial information may also be recorded to describe the nature of a business transaction. If part of the information in the accounting records is financial and part is nonfinancial, the financial statements will not be clear. For example, if a business states its sales in number of units sold (nonfinancial) and its expenses in dollars (financial), net profit cannot be calculated. Instead, total expenses (financial) are subtracted from the money taken in through sales (financial) to determine net profit.

NIKE INC

FORM 10-K
(Annual Report)

for the Period Ending 05/31/11

FORM 10-K

☑ ANNUAL REPORT PURSUANT TO SECTION 13 OR 15(D) OF THE SECURITIES EXCHANGE ACT OF 1934
FOR THE FISCAL YEAR ENDED MAY 31, 2011
OR

☐ TRANSITION REPORT PURSUANT TO SECTION 13 OR 15(D) OF THE SECURITIES EXCHANGE ACT OF 1934
FOR THE TRANSITION PERIOD FROM _____ TO _____

Commission File No. 1-10635

NIKE, INC.

(Exact name of Registrant as specified in its charter)

OREGON	**93-0584541**
(State or other jurisdiction of incorporation)	*(IRS Employer Identification No.)*
One Bowerman Drive Beaverton, Oregon	**97005-6453**
(Address of principal executive offices)	*(Zip Code)*

(503) 671-6453
(Registrant's Telephone Number, Including Area Code)

SECURITIES REGISTERED PURSUANT TO SECTION 12(B) OF THE ACT:	
Class B Common Stock	**New York Stock Exchange**
(Title of Each Class)	*(Name of Each Exchange on Which Registered)*

SECURITIES REGISTERED PURSUANT TO SECTION 12(G) OF THE ACT:
NONE

Indicate by check mark	YES	NO
• if the registrant is a well-known seasoned issuer, as defined in Rule 405 of the Securities Act.	☑	☐
• if the registrant is not required to file reports pursuant to Section 13 or Section 15(d) of the Act.	☐	☑
• whether the Registrant (1) has filed all reports required to be filed by Section 13 or 15(d) of the Securities Exchange Act of 1934 during the preceding 12 months (or for such shorter period that the Registrant was required to file such reports), and (2) has been subject to such filing requirements for the past 90 days.	☑	☐
• whether the registrant has submitted electronically and posted on its corporate Website, if any, every Interactive Data File required to be submitted and posted pursuant to Rule 405 of Regulation S-T (§229.405 of this chapter) during the preceding 12 months (or for such shorter period that the registrant was required to submit and post such files).	☑	☐
• if disclosure of delinquent filers pursuant to Item 405 of Regulation S-K (§229.405 of this chapter) is not contained herein, and will not be contained, to the best of Registrant's knowledge, in definitive proxy or information statements incorporated by reference in Part III of this Form 10-K or any amendment to this Form 10-K.	☐	☐
• whether the Registrant is a large accelerated filer, an accelerated filer, a non-accelerated filer, or a smaller reporting company. See the definitions of "large accelerated filer," "accelerated filer" and "smaller reporting company" in Rule 12b-2 of the Exchange Act.		

Large accelerated filer ☑	Accelerated filer ☐	Non-accelerated filer ☐	Smaller reporting company ☐

• whether the registrant is a shell company (as defined in Rule 12b-2 of the Act).	☐	☑

As of November 30, 2010, the aggregate market value of the Registrant's Class A Common Stock held by non-affiliates of the Registrant was $2,005,831,959 and the aggregate market value of the Registrant's Class B Common Stock held by non-affiliates of the Registrant was $33,459,424,185.

As of July 18, 2011, the number of shares of the Registrant's Class A Common Stock outstanding was 89,989,447 and the number of shares of the Registrant's Class B Common Stock outstanding was 384,840,843.

DOCUMENTS INCORPORATED BY REFERENCE:

Parts of Registrant's Proxy Statement for the Annual Meeting of Shareholders to be held on September 19, 2011 are incorporated by reference into Part III of this Report.

ITEM 6 Selected Financial Data

(In millions, except per share data and financial ratios)	Financial History				
	2011	2010	2009	2008	2007
Year Ended May 31,					
Revenues	$ 20,862	$ 19,014	$ 19,176	$ 18,627	$ 16,326
Gross margin	9,508	8,800	8,604	8,387	7,161
Gross margin %	45.6%	46.3%	44.9%	45.0%	43.9%
Restructuring charges	—	—	195	—	—
Goodwill impairment	—	—	199	—	—
Intangible and other asset impairment	—	—	202	—	—
Net income	2,133	1,907	1,487	1,883	1,492
Basic earnings per common share	4.48	3.93	3.07	3.80	2.96
Diluted earnings per common share	4.39	3.86	3.03	3.74	2.93
Weighted average common shares outstanding	475.5	485.5	484.9	495.6	503.8
Diluted weighted average common shares outstanding	485.7	493.9	490.7	504.1	509.9
Cash dividends declared per common share	1.20	1.06	0.98	0.875	0.71
Cash flow from operations	1,812	3,164	1,736	1,936	1,879
Price range of common stock					
High	92.30	78.55	70.28	70.60	57.12
Low	67.21	50.16	38.24	51.50	37.76
At May 31,					
Cash and equivalents	$ 1,955	$ 3,079	$ 2,291	$ 2,134	$ 1,857
Short-term investments	2,583	2,067	1,164	642	990
Inventories	2,715	2,041	2,357	2,438	2,122
Working capital	7,339	7,595	6,457	5,518	5,493
Total assets	14,998	14,419	13,250	12,443	10,688
Long-term debt	276	446	437	441	410
Redeemable Preferred Stock	0.3	0.3	0.3	0.3	0.3
Shareholders' equity	9,843	9,754	8,693	7,825	7,025
Year-end stock price	84.45	72.38	57.05	68.37	56.75
Market capitalization	39,523	35,032	27,698	33,577	28,472
Financial Ratios:					
Return on equity	21.8%	20.7%	18.0%	25.4%	22.4%
Return on assets	14.5%	13.8%	11.6%	16.3%	14.5%
Inventory turns	4.8	4.6	4.4	4.5	4.4
Current ratio at May 31	2.9	3.3	3.0	2.7	3.1
Price/Earnings ratio at May 31	19.2	18.8	18.8	18.3	19.4

Selected Quarterly Financial Data

(Unaudited)	1st Quarter		2nd Quarter		3rd Quarter		4th Quarter	
(In millions, except per share data)	2011	2010	2011	2010	2011	2010	2011	2010
Revenues	$ 5,175	$ 4,799	$ 4,842	$ 4,405	$ 5,079	$ 4,733	$ 5,766	$ 5,077
Gross margin	2,434	2,216	2,193	1,960	2,327	2,218	2,554	2,406
Gross margin %	47.0%	46.2%	45.3%	44.5%	45.8%	46.9%	44.3%	47.4%
Net income	559	513	457	375	523	496	594	522
Basic earnings per common share	1.17	1.06	0.96	0.77	1.10	1.02	1.27	1.08
Diluted earnings per common share	1.14	1.04	0.94	0.76	1.08	1.01	1.24	1.06
Weighted average common shares outstanding	479.6	485.8	477.9	487.2	475.3	484.4	469.3	484.4
Diluted weighted average common shares outstanding	488.6	491.6	487.6	494.5	485.5	492.3	478.7	493.9
Cash dividends declared per common share	0.27	0.25	0.31	0.27	0.31	0.27	0.31	0.27
Price range of common stock								
High	74.94	59.95	86.53	66.35	92.30	67.85	89.88	78.55
Low	67.21	50.16	72.13	53.22	81.46	60.89	75.45	66.99

Management's Annual Report on Internal Control Over Financial Reporting

Management is responsible for establishing and maintaining adequate internal control over financial reporting, as such term is defined in Rule 13a-15(f) and Rule 15d-15(f) of the Securities Exchange Act of 1934, as amended. Internal control over financial reporting is a process designed to provide reasonable assurance regarding the reliability of financial reporting and the preparation of the financial statements for external purposes in accordance with generally accepted accounting principles in the United States of America. Internal control over financial reporting includes those policies and procedures that: (i) pertain to the maintenance of records that, in reasonable detail, accurately and fairly reflect the transactions and dispositions of assets of the company; (ii) provide reasonable assurance that transactions are recorded as necessary to permit preparation of financial statements in accordance with generally accepted accounting principles, and that receipts and expenditures of the company are being made only in accordance with authorizations of our management and directors; and (iii) provide reasonable assurance regarding prevention or timely detection of unauthorized acquisition, use or disposition of assets of the company that could have a material effect on the financial statements.

While "reasonable assurance" is a high level of assurance, it does not mean absolute assurance. Because of its inherent limitations, internal control over financial reporting may not prevent or detect every misstatement and instance of fraud. Controls are susceptible to manipulation, especially in instances of fraud caused by the collusion of two or more people, including our senior management. Also, projections of any evaluation of effectiveness to future periods are subject to the risk that controls may become inadequate because of changes in conditions, or that the degree of compliance with the policies or procedures may deteriorate.

Under the supervision and with the participation of our Chief Executive Officer and Chief Financial Officer, our management conducted an evaluation of the effectiveness of our internal control over financial reporting based upon the framework in *Internal Control — Integrated Framework* issued by the Committee of Sponsoring Organizations of the Treadway Commission (COSO). Based on the results of our evaluation, our management concluded that our internal control over financial reporting was effective as of May 31, 2011.

PricewaterhouseCoopers LLP, an independent registered public accounting firm, has audited (1) the consolidated financial statements and (2) the effectiveness of our internal control over financial reporting as of May 31, 2011, as stated in their report herein.

Mark G. Parker
Chief Executive Officer and President

Donald W. Blair
Chief Financial Officer

Report of Independent Registered Public Accounting Firm

To the Board of Directors and Shareholders of NIKE, Inc.:

In our opinion, the consolidated financial statements listed in the index appearing under Item 15(a)(1) present fairly, in all material respects, the financial position of NIKE, Inc. and its subsidiaries at May 31, 2011 and 2010, and the results of their operations and their cash flows for each of the three years in the period ended May 31, 2011 in conformity with accounting principles generally accepted in the United States of America. In addition, in our opinion, the financial statement schedule listed in the appendix appearing under Item 15(a)(2) presents fairly, in all material respects, the information set forth therein when read in conjunction with the related consolidated financial statements. Also in our opinion, the Company maintained, in all material respects, effective internal control over financial reporting as of May 31, 2011, based on criteria established in *Internal Control — Integrated Framework* issued by the Committee of Sponsoring Organizations of the Treadway Commission (COSO). The Company's management is responsible for these financial statements and financial statement schedule, for maintaining effective internal control over financial reporting and for its assessment of the effectiveness of internal control over financial reporting, included in Management's Annual Report on Internal Control Over Financial Reporting appearing under Item 8. Our responsibility is to express opinions on these financial statements, on the financial statement schedule, and on the Company's internal control over financial reporting based on our integrated audits. We conducted our audits in accordance with the standards of the Public Company Accounting Oversight Board (United States). Those standards require that we plan and perform the audits to obtain reasonable assurance about whether the financial statements are free of material misstatement and whether effective internal control over financial reporting was maintained in all material respects. Our audits of the financial statements included examining, on a test basis, evidence supporting the amounts and disclosures in the financial statements, assessing the accounting principles used and significant estimates made by management, and evaluating the overall financial statement presentation. Our audit of internal control over financial reporting included obtaining an understanding of internal control over financial reporting, assessing the risk that a material weakness exists, and testing and evaluating the design and operating effectiveness of internal control based on the assessed risk. Our audits also included performing such other procedures as we considered necessary in the circumstances. We believe that our audits provide a reasonable basis for our opinions.

A company's internal control over financial reporting is a process designed to provide reasonable assurance regarding the reliability of financial reporting and the preparation of financial statements for external purposes in accordance with generally accepted accounting principles. A company's internal control over financial reporting includes those policies and procedures that (i) pertain to the maintenance of records that, in reasonable detail, accurately and fairly reflect the transactions and dispositions of the assets of the company; (ii) provide reasonable assurance that transactions are recorded as necessary to permit preparation of financial statements in accordance with generally accepted accounting principles, and that receipts and expenditures of the company are being made only in accordance with authorizations of management and directors of the company; and (iii) provide reasonable assurance regarding prevention or timely detection of unauthorized acquisition, use, or disposition of the company's assets that could have a material effect on the financial statements.

Because of its inherent limitations, internal control over financial reporting may not prevent or detect misstatements. Also, projections of any evaluation of effectiveness to future periods are subject to the risk that controls may become inadequate because of changes in conditions, or that the degree of compliance with the policies or procedures may deteriorate.

/s/ PRICEWATERHOUSECOOPERS LLP

Portland, Oregon
July 22, 2011

Consolidated Statements of Income

(In millions, except per share data)		Year Ended May 31,				
		2011		2010		2009
Revenues	$	20,862	$	19,014	$	19,176
Cost of sales		11,354		10,214		10,572
Gross margin		9,508		8,800		8,604
Demand creation expense		2,448		2,356		2,352
Operating overhead expense		4,245		3,970		3,798
Total selling and administrative expense		6,693		6,326		6,150
Restructuring charges (Note 16)		—		—		195
Goodwill impairment (Note 4)		—		—		199
Intangible and other asset impairment (Note 4)		—		—		202
Interest expense (income), net (Notes 6, 7 and 8)		4		6		(10)
Other (income), net (Note 17)		(33)		(49)		(89)
Income before income taxes		2,844		2,517		1,957
Income taxes (Note 9)		711		610		470
Net income	$	2,133	$	1,907	$	1,487
Basic earnings per common share (Notes 1 and 12)	$	4.48	$	3.93	$	3.07
Diluted earnings per common share (Notes 1 and 12)	$	4.39	$	3.86	$	3.03
Dividends declared per common share	$	1.20	$	1.06	$	0.98

The accompanying notes to consolidated financial statements are an integral part of this statement.

Consolidated Balance Sheets

	May 31,	
(In millions)	2011	2010
ASSETS		
Current assets:		
Cash and equivalents	$ 1,955 $	3,079
Short-term investments (Note 6)	2,583	2,067
Accounts receivable, net (Note 1)	3,138	2,650
Inventories (Notes 1 and 2)	2,715	2,041
Deferred income taxes (Note 9)	312	249
Prepaid expenses and other current assets	594	873
Total current assets	11,297	10,959
Property, plant and equipment, net (Note 3)	2,115	1,932
Identifiable intangible assets, net (Note 4)	487	467
Goodwill (Note 4)	205	188
Deferred income taxes and other assets (Notes 9 and 17)	894	873
TOTAL ASSETS	$ 14,998 $	14,419
LIABILITIES AND SHAREHOLDERS' EQUITY		
Current liabilities:		
Current portion of long-term debt (Note 8)	$ 200 $	7
Notes payable (Note 7)	187	139
Accounts payable (Note 7)	1,469	1,255
Accrued liabilities (Notes 5 and 17)	1,985	1,904
Income taxes payable (Note 9)	117	59
Total current liabilities	3,958	3,364
Long-term debt (Note 8)	276	446
Deferred income taxes and other liabilities (Notes 9 and 17)	921	855
Commitments and contingencies (Note 15)	—	—
Redeemable Preferred Stock (Note 10)	—	—
Shareholders' equity:		
Common stock at stated value (Note 11):		
Class A convertible — 90 and 90 shares outstanding	—	—
Class B — 378 and 394 shares outstanding	3	3
Capital in excess of stated value	3,944	3,441
Accumulated other comprehensive income (Note 14)	95	215
Retained earnings	5,801	6,095
Total shareholders' equity	9,843	9,754
TOTAL LIABILITIES AND SHAREHOLDERS' EQUITY	$ 14,998 $	14,419

The accompanying notes to consolidated financial statements are an integral part of this statement.

Consolidated Statements of Cash Flows

	Year Ended May 31,		
(In millions)	2011	2010	2009
Cash provided by operations:			
Net income	$ 2,133	$ 1,907	$ 1,487
Income charges (credits) not affecting cash:			
Depreciation	335	324	335
Deferred income taxes	(76)	8	(294)
Stock-based compensation (Note 11)	105	159	171
Impairment of goodwill, intangibles and other assets (Note 4)	—	—	401
Amortization and other	23	72	48
Changes in certain working capital components and other assets and liabilities excluding the impact of acquisition and divestitures:			
(Increase) decrease in accounts receivable	(273)	182	(238)
(Increase) decrease in inventories	(551)	285	32
(Increase) decrease in prepaid expenses and other current assets	(35)	(70)	14
Increase (decrease) in accounts payable, accrued liabilities and income taxes payable	151	297	(220)
Cash provided by operations	1,812	3,164	1,736
Cash used by investing activities:			
Purchases of short-term investments	(7,616)	(3,724)	(2,909)
Maturities of short-term investments	4,313	2,334	1,280
Sales of short-term investments	2,766	453	1,110
Additions to property, plant and equipment	(432)	(335)	(456)
Disposals of property, plant and equipment	1	10	33
Increase in other assets, net of other liabilities	(30)	(11)	(47)
Settlement of net investment hedges	(23)	5	191
Cash used by investing activities	(1,021)	(1,268)	(798)
Cash used by financing activities:			
Reductions in long-term debt, including current portion	(8)	(32)	(7)
Increase (decrease) in notes payable	41	(205)	177
Proceeds from exercise of stock options and other stock issuances	345	364	187
Excess tax benefits from share-based payment arrangements	64	58	25
Repurchase of common stock	(1,859)	(741)	(649)
Dividends — common and preferred	(555)	(505)	(467)
Cash used by financing activities	(1,972)	(1,061)	(734)
Effect of exchange rate changes	57	(47)	(47)
Net (decrease) increase in cash and equivalents	(1,124)	788	157
Cash and equivalents, beginning of year	3,079	2,291	2,134
CASH AND EQUIVALENTS, END OF YEAR	$ 1,955	$ 3,079	$ 2,291
Supplemental disclosure of cash flow information:			
Cash paid during the year for:			
Interest, net of capitalized interest	$ 32	$ 48	$ 47
Income taxes	736	537	765
Dividends declared and not paid	145	131	121

The accompanying notes to consolidated financial statements are an integral part of this statement.

Consolidated Statements of Shareholders' Equity

(In millions, except per share data)	Common Stock Class A Shares	Class A Amount	Class B Shares	Class B Amount	Capital in Excess of Stated Value	Accumulated Other Comprehensive Income	Retained Earnings	Total
BALANCE AT MAY 31, 2008	97	$ —	394	$ 3	$ 2,498	$ 251	$ 5,073	$ 7,825
Stock options exercised			4		167			167
Conversion to Class B Common Stock	(2)		2					—
Repurchase of Class B Common Stock			(11)		(6)		(633)	(639)
Dividends on Common stock ($0.98 per share)							(475)	(475)
Issuance of shares to employees			1		45			45
Stock-based compensation (Note 11):					171			171
Forfeiture of shares from employees			—		(4)		(1)	(5)
Comprehensive income:								
Net income							1,487	1,487
Other comprehensive income:								
Foreign currency translation and other (net of tax benefit of $178)						(335)		(335)
Net gain on cash flow hedges (net of tax expense of $168)						454		454
Net gain on net investment hedges (net of tax expense of $55)						106		106
Reclassification to net income of previously deferred net gains related to hedge derivatives (net of tax expense of $40)						(108)		(108)
Total comprehensive income						117	1,487	1,604
BALANCE AT MAY 31, 2009	95	$ —	390	$ 3	$ 2,871	$ 368	$ 5,451	$ 8,693
Stock options exercised			9		380			380
Conversion to Class B Common Stock	(5)		5					—
Repurchase of Class B Common Stock			(11)		(7)		(747)	(754)
Dividends on Common stock ($1.06 per share)							(515)	(515)
Issuance of shares to employees			1		40			40
Stock-based compensation (Note 11):					159			159
Forfeiture of shares from employees			—		(2)		(1)	(3)
Comprehensive income:								
Net income							1,907	1,907
Other comprehensive income (Notes 14 and 17):								
Foreign currency translation and other (net of tax benefit of $72)						(159)		(159)
Net gain on cash flow hedges (net of tax expense of $28)						87		87
Net gain on net investment hedges (net of tax expense of $21)						45		45
Reclassification to net income of previously deferred net gains related to hedge derivatives (net of tax expense of $42)						(122)		(122)
Reclassification of ineffective hedge gains to net income (net of tax expense of $1)						(4)		(4)
Total comprehensive income						(153)	1,907	1,754

| (In millions, except per share data) | Common Stock | | | | Capital in Excess of Stated Value | Accumulated Other Comprehensive Income | Retained Earnings | Total |
| | Class A | | Class B | | | | | |
	Shares	Amount	Shares	Amount				
BALANCE AT MAY 31, 2010	90	$ —	394	$ 3	$ 3,441	$ 215	$ 6,095	$ 9,754
Stock options exercised			7		368			368
Repurchase of Class B Common Stock			(24)		(14)		(1,857)	(1,871)
Dividends on Common stock ($1.20 per share)							(569)	(569)
Issuance of shares to employees			1		49			49
Stock-based compensation (Note 11):					105			105
Forfeiture of shares from employees			—		(5)		(1)	(6)
Comprehensive income:								
Net income							2,133	2,133
Other comprehensive income (Notes 14 and 17):								
Foreign currency translation and other (net of tax expense of $121)						263		263
Net loss on cash flow hedges (net of tax benefit of $66)						(242)		(242)
Net loss on net investment hedges (net of tax benefit of $28)						(57)		(57)
Reclassification to net income of previously deferred net gains related to hedge derivatives (net of tax expense of $24)						(84)		(84)
Total comprehensive income						(120)	2,133	2,013
BALANCE AT MAY 31, 2011	90	$ —	378	$ 3	$ 3,944	$ 95	$ 5,801	$ 9,843

The accompanying notes to consolidated financial statements are an integral part of this statement.

NOTE 1   Summary of Significant Accounting Policies

Description of Business

NIKE, Inc. is a worldwide leader in the design, marketing and distribution of athletic and sports-inspired footwear, apparel, equipment and accessories. Wholly-owned NIKE subsidiaries include Cole Haan, which designs, markets and distributes dress and casual shoes, handbags, accessories and coats; Converse Inc., which designs, markets and distributes athletic and casual footwear, apparel and accessories; Hurley International LLC, which designs, markets and distributes action sports and youth lifestyle footwear, apparel and accessories; and Umbro International Limited, which designs, distributes and licenses athletic and casual footwear, apparel and equipment, primarily for the sport of soccer.

Basis of Consolidation

The consolidated financial statements include the accounts of NIKE, Inc. and its subsidiaries (the "Company"). All significant intercompany transactions and balances have been eliminated.

Recognition of Revenues

Wholesale revenues are recognized when title passes and the risks and rewards of ownership have passed to the customer, based on the terms of sale. This occurs upon shipment or upon receipt by the customer depending on the country of the sale and the agreement with the customer. Retail store revenues are recorded at the time of sale. Provisions for sales discounts, returns and miscellaneous claims from customers are made at the time of sale. As of May 31, 2011 and 2010, the Company's reserve balances for sales discounts, returns and miscellaneous claims were $423 million and $371 million, respectively.

Shipping and Handling Costs

Shipping and handling costs are expensed as incurred and included in cost of sales.

Demand Creation Expense

Demand creation expense consists of advertising and promotion costs, including costs of endorsement contracts, television, digital and print advertising, brand events, and retail brand presentation. Advertising production costs are expensed the first time an advertisement is run. Advertising placement costs are expensed in the month the advertising appears, while costs related to brand events are expensed when the event occurs. Costs related to retail brand presentation are expensed when the presentation is completed and delivered. A significant amount of the Company's promotional expenses result from payments under endorsement contracts. Accounting for endorsement payments is based upon specific contract provisions. Generally, endorsement payments are expensed on a straight-line basis over the term of the contract after giving recognition to periodic performance compliance provisions of the contracts. Prepayments made under contracts are included in prepaid expenses or other assets depending on the period to which the prepayment applies.

Through cooperative advertising programs, the Company reimburses retail customers for certain costs of advertising the Company's products. The Company records these costs in selling and administrative expense at the point in time when it is obligated to its customers for the costs, which is when the related revenues are recognized. This obligation may arise prior to the related advertisement being run.

Total advertising and promotion expenses were $2,448 million, $2,356 million, and $2,352 million for the years ended May 31, 2011, 2010 and 2009, respectively. Prepaid advertising and promotion expenses recorded in prepaid expenses and other assets totaled $291 million and $261 million at May 31, 2011 and 2010, respectively.

Cash and Equivalents

Cash and equivalents represent cash and short-term, highly liquid investments with maturities of three months or less at date of purchase. The carrying amounts reflected in the consolidated balance sheet for cash and equivalents approximate fair value.

Short-Term Investments

Short-term investments consist of highly liquid investments, including commercial paper, U.S. treasury, U.S. agency, and corporate debt securities, with maturities over three months from the date of purchase. Debt securities that the Company has the ability and positive intent to hold to maturity are carried at amortized cost. At May 31, 2011 and 2010, the Company did not hold any short-term investments that were classified as trading or held-to-maturity.

At May 31, 2011 and 2010, short-term investments consisted of available-for-sale securities. Available-for-sale securities are recorded at fair value with unrealized gains and losses reported, net of tax, in other comprehensive income, unless unrealized losses are determined to be other than temporary. The Company considers all available-for-sale securities, including those with maturity dates beyond 12 months, as available to support current operational liquidity needs and therefore classifies all securities with maturity dates beyond three months at the date of purchase as current assets within short-term investments on the consolidated balance sheet.

See Note 6 — Fair Value Measurements for more information on the Company's short term investments.

Allowance for Uncollectible Accounts Receivable

Accounts receivable consists primarily of amounts receivable from customers. We make ongoing estimates relating to the collectability of our accounts receivable and maintain an allowance for estimated losses resulting from the inability of our customers to make required payments. In determining the amount of the allowance, we consider our historical level of credit losses and make judgments about the creditworthiness of significant customers based on ongoing credit evaluations. Accounts receivable with anticipated collection dates greater than 12 months from the balance sheet date and related allowances are considered non-current and recorded in other assets. The allowance for uncollectible accounts receivable was $124 million and $117 million at May 31, 2011 and 2010, respectively, of which $50 million and $43 million was classified as long-term and recorded in other assets.

Inventory Valuation

Inventories are stated at lower of cost or market and valued on a first-in, first-out ("FIFO") or moving average cost basis.

Property, Plant and Equipment and Depreciation

Property, plant and equipment are recorded at cost. Depreciation for financial reporting purposes is determined on a straight-line basis for buildings and leasehold improvements over 2 to 40 years and for machinery and equipment over 2 to 15 years. Computer software (including, in some cases, the cost of internal labor) is depreciated on a straight-line basis over 3 to 10 years.

Impairment of Long-Lived Assets

The Company reviews the carrying value of long-lived assets or asset groups to be used in operations whenever events or changes in circumstances indicate that the carrying amount of the assets might not be recoverable. Factors that would necessitate an impairment assessment include a significant adverse change in the extent or manner in which an asset is used, a significant adverse change in legal factors or the business climate that could affect the value of the asset, or a significant decline in the observable market value of an asset, among others. If such facts indicate a potential impairment, the Company would assess the recoverability of an asset group by determining if the carrying value of the asset group exceeds the sum of the projected undiscounted cash flows expected to result from the use and eventual disposition of the assets over the remaining economic life of the primary asset in the asset group. If the recoverability test indicates that the carrying value of the asset group is not recoverable, the Company will estimate the fair value of the asset group using appropriate valuation methodologies which would typically include an estimate of discounted cash flows. Any impairment would be measured as the difference between the asset groups carrying amount and its estimated fair value.

Identifiable Intangible Assets and Goodwill

The Company performs annual impairment tests on goodwill and intangible assets with indefinite lives in the fourth quarter of each fiscal year, or when events occur or circumstances change that would, more likely than not, reduce the fair value of a reporting unit or an intangible asset with an indefinite life below its carrying value. Events or changes in circumstances that may trigger interim impairment reviews include significant changes in business climate, operating results, planned investments in the reporting unit, or an expectation that the carrying amount may not be recoverable, among other factors. The impairment test requires the Company to estimate the fair value of its reporting units. If the carrying value of a reporting unit exceeds its fair value, the goodwill of that reporting unit is potentially impaired and the Company proceeds to step two of the impairment analysis. In step two of the analysis, the Company measures and records an impairment loss equal to the excess of the carrying value of the reporting unit's goodwill over its implied fair value should such a circumstance arise.

The Company generally bases its measurement of fair value of a reporting unit on a blended analysis of the present value of future discounted cash flows and the market valuation approach. The discounted cash flows model indicates the fair value of the reporting unit based on the present value of the cash flows that the Company expects the reporting unit to generate in the future. The Company's significant estimates in the discounted cash flows model include: its weighted average cost of capital; long-term rate of growth and profitability of the reporting unit's business; and working capital effects. The market valuation approach indicates the fair value of the business based on a comparison of the reporting unit to comparable publicly traded companies in similar lines of business. Significant estimates in the market valuation approach model include identifying similar companies with comparable business factors such as size, growth, profitability, risk and return on investment, and assessing comparable revenue and operating income multiples in estimating the fair value of the reporting unit.

The Company believes the weighted use of discounted cash flows and the market valuation approach is the best method for determining the fair value of its reporting units because these are the most common valuation methodologies used within its industry; and the blended use of both models compensates for the inherent risks associated with either model if used on a stand-alone basis.

Indefinite-lived intangible assets primarily consist of acquired trade names and trademarks. In measuring the fair value for these intangible assets, the Company utilizes the relief-from-royalty method. This method assumes that trade names and trademarks have value to the extent that their owner is relieved of the obligation to pay royalties for the benefits received from them. This method requires the Company to estimate the future revenue for the related brands, the appropriate royalty rate and the weighted average cost of capital.

Foreign Currency Translation and Foreign Currency Transactions

Adjustments resulting from translating foreign functional currency financial statements into U.S. dollars are included in the foreign currency translation adjustment, a component of accumulated other comprehensive income in shareholders' equity.

The Company's global subsidiaries have various assets and liabilities, primarily receivables and payables, that are denominated in currencies other than their functional currency. These balance sheet items are subject to remeasurement, the impact of which is recorded in other (income), net, within our consolidated statement of income.

Accounting for Derivatives and Hedging Activities

The Company uses derivative financial instruments to limit exposure to changes in foreign currency exchange rates and interest rates. All derivatives are recorded at fair value on the balance sheet and changes in the fair value of derivative financial instruments are either recognized in other comprehensive income (a component of shareholders' equity), debt or net income depending on the nature of the underlying exposure, whether the derivative is formally designated as a hedge, and, if designated, the extent to which the hedge is effective. The Company classifies the cash flows at settlement from derivatives in the same category as the cash flows from the related hedged items. For undesignated hedges and designated cash flow hedges, this is within the cash provided by operations component of the consolidated statements of cash flows. For designated net investment hedges, this is generally within the cash used by investing activities component of the cash flow statement. As our fair value hedges are receive-fixed, pay-variable interest rate swaps, the cash flows associated with these derivative instruments are periodic interest payments while the swaps are outstanding, which are reflected in net income within the cash provided by operations component of the cash flow statement.

See Note 17 — Risk Management and Derivatives for more information on the Company's risk management program and derivatives.

Stock-Based Compensation

The Company estimates the fair value of options and stock appreciation rights granted under the NIKE, Inc. 1990 Stock Incentive Plan (the "1990 Plan") and employees' purchase rights under the Employee Stock Purchase Plans ("ESPPs") using the Black-Scholes option pricing model. The Company recognizes this fair value, net of estimated forfeitures, as selling and administrative expense in the consolidated statements of income over the vesting period using the straight-line method.

See Note 11 — Common Stock and Stock-Based Compensation for more information on the Company's stock programs.

Income Taxes

The Company accounts for income taxes using the asset and liability method. This approach requires the recognition of deferred tax assets and liabilities for the expected future tax consequences of temporary differences between the carrying amounts and the tax basis of assets and liabilities. United States income taxes are provided currently on financial statement earnings of non-U.S. subsidiaries that are expected to be repatriated. The Company determines annually the amount of undistributed non-U.S. earnings to invest indefinitely in its non-U.S. operations. The Company recognizes interest and penalties related to income tax matters in income tax expense.

See Note 9 — Income Taxes for further discussion.

Earnings Per Share

Basic earnings per common share is calculated by dividing net income by the weighted average number of common shares outstanding during the year. Diluted earnings per common share is calculated by adjusting weighted average outstanding shares, assuming conversion of all potentially dilutive stock options and awards.

See Note 12 — Earnings Per Share for further discussion.

Management Estimates

The preparation of financial statements in conformity with generally accepted accounting principles requires management to make estimates, including estimates relating to assumptions that affect the reported amounts of assets and liabilities and disclosure of contingent assets and liabilities at the date of financial statements and the reported amounts of revenues and expenses during the reporting period. Actual results could differ from these estimates.

Recently Adopted Accounting Standards

In January 2010, the Financial Accounting Standards Board ("FASB") issued guidance to amend the disclosure requirements related to recurring and nonrecurring fair value measurements. The guidance requires additional disclosures about the different classes of assets and liabilities measured at fair value, the valuation techniques and inputs used, the activity in Level 3 fair value measurements, and the transfers between Levels 1, 2, and 3 of the fair value measurement hierarchy. This guidance became effective for the Company beginning March 1, 2010, except for disclosures relating to purchases, sales, issuances and settlements of Level 3 assets and liabilities, which will be effective for the Company beginning June 1, 2011. As this guidance only requires expanded disclosures, the adoption did not and will not impact the Company's consolidated financial position or results of operations.

In June 2009, the FASB issued a new accounting standard that revised the guidance for the consolidation of variable interest entities ("VIE"). This new guidance requires a qualitative approach to identifying a controlling financial interest in a VIE, and requires an ongoing assessment of whether an entity is a VIE and whether an interest in a VIE makes the holder the primary beneficiary of the VIE. This guidance became effective for the Company beginning June 1, 2010. The adoption of this guidance did not have an impact on the Company's consolidated financial position or results of operations.

Recently Issued Accounting Standards

In June 2011, the FASB issued new guidance on the presentation of comprehensive income. This new guidance requires the components of net income and other comprehensive income to be either presented in one continuous statement, referred to as the statement of comprehensive income, or in two separate, but consecutive statements. This new guidance eliminates the current option to report other comprehensive income and its components in the statement of shareholders' equity. While the new guidance changes the presentation of comprehensive income, there are no changes to the components that are recognized in net income or other comprehensive income under current accounting guidance. This new guidance is effective for the Company beginning June 1, 2012. As this guidance only amends the presentation of the components of comprehensive income, the adoption will not have an impact on the Company's consolidated financial position or results of operations.

In April 2011, the FASB issued new guidance to achieve common fair value measurement and disclosure requirements between U.S. GAAP and International Financial Reporting Standards. This new guidance, which is effective for the Company beginning June 1, 2012, amends current U.S. GAAP fair value measurement and disclosure guidance to include increased transparency around valuation inputs and investment categorization. The Company does not expect the adoption will have a material impact on its consolidated financial position or results of operations.

In October 2009, the FASB issued new standards that revised the guidance for revenue recognition with multiple deliverables. These new standards impact the determination of when the individual deliverables included in a multiple-element arrangement may be treated as separate units of accounting. Additionally, these new standards modify the manner in which the transaction consideration is allocated across the separately identified deliverables by no longer permitting the residual method of allocating arrangement consideration. These new standards are effective for the Company beginning June 1, 2011. The Company does not expect the adoption will have a material impact on its consolidated financial position or results of operations.

NOTE 2   Inventories

Inventory balances of $2,715 million and $2,041 million at May 31, 2011 and 2010, respectively, were substantially all finished goods.

NOTE 3   Property, Plant and Equipment

Property, plant and equipment included the following:

(In millions)	As of May 31, 2011	As of May 31, 2010
Land	$ 237	$ 223
Buildings	1,124	952
Machinery and equipment	2,487	2,217
Leasehold improvements	931	821
Construction in process	127	177
	4,906	4,390
Less accumulated depreciation	2,791	2,458
	$ 2,115	$ 1,932

Capitalized interest was not material for the years ended May 31, 2011, 2010, and 2009.

NOTE 4   Identifiable Intangible Assets, Goodwill and Umbro Impairment

Identified Intangible Assets and Goodwill

The following table summarizes the Company's identifiable intangible asset balances as of May 31, 2011 and 2010:

(In millions)	May 31, 2011			May 31, 2010		
	Gross Carrying Amount	Accumulated Amortization	Net Carrying Amount	Gross Carrying Amount	Accumulated Amortization	Net Carrying Amount
Amortized intangible assets:						
Patents	$ 80	$ (24)	$ 56	$ 69	$ (21)	$ 48
Trademarks	44	(25)	19	40	(18)	22
Other	47	(22)	25	32	(18)	14
TOTAL	$ 171	$ (71)	$ 100	$ 141	$ (57)	$ 84
Unamortized intangible assets — Trademarks			387			383
IDENTIFIABLE INTANGIBLE ASSETS, NET			$ 487			$ 467

The effect of foreign exchange fluctuations for the year ended May 31, 2011 increased unamortized intangible assets by approximately $4 million.

Amortization expense, which is included in selling and administrative expense, was $16 million, $14 million, and $12 million for the years ended May 31, 2011, 2010, and 2009, respectively. The estimated amortization expense for intangible assets subject to amortization for each of the years ending May 31, 2012 through May 31, 2016 are as follows: 2012: $16 million; 2013: $14 million; 2014: $12 million; 2015: $8 million; 2016: $7 million.

All goodwill balances are included in the Company's "Other" category for segment reporting purposes. The following table summarizes the Company's goodwill balance as of May 31, 2011 and 2010:

(In millions)	Goodwill	Accumulated Impairment	Goodwill, net
May 31, 2009	$ 393	$ (199)	$ 194
Other[1]	(6)	—	(6)
May 31, 2010	387	(199)	188
Umbro France[2]	10	—	10
Other[1]	7	—	7
MAY 31, 2011	$ 404	$ (199)	$ 205

(1)   Other consists of foreign currency translation adjustments on Umbro goodwill.

(2)   In March 2011, Umbro acquired the remaining 51% of the exclusive licensee and distributor of the Umbro brand in France for approximately $15 million.

Umbro Impairment in Fiscal 2009

The Company performs annual impairment tests on goodwill and intangible assets with indefinite lives in the fourth quarter of each fiscal year, or when events occur or circumstances change that would, more likely than not, reduce the fair value of a reporting unit or intangible assets with an indefinite life below its carrying value. As a result of a significant decline in global consumer demand and continued weakness in the macroeconomic environment, as well as decisions by Company management to adjust planned investment in the Umbro brand, the Company concluded sufficient indicators of impairment existed to require the performance of an interim assessment of Umbro's goodwill and indefinite lived intangible assets as of February 1, 2009. Accordingly, the Company performed the first step of the goodwill impairment assessment for Umbro by comparing the estimated fair value of Umbro to its carrying amount, and determined there was a potential impairment of goodwill as the carrying amount exceeded the estimated fair value. Therefore, the Company performed the second step of the assessment which compared the implied fair value of Umbro's goodwill to the book value of goodwill. The implied fair value of goodwill is determined by allocating the estimated fair value of Umbro to all of its assets and liabilities, including both recognized and unrecognized intangibles, in the same manner as goodwill was determined in the original business combination.

The Company measured the fair value of Umbro by using an equal weighting of the fair value implied by a discounted cash flow analysis and by comparisons with the market values of similar publicly traded companies. The Company believes the blended use of both models compensates for the inherent risk associated with either model if used on a stand-alone basis, and this combination is indicative of the factors a market participant would consider when performing a similar valuation. The fair value of Umbro's indefinite-lived trademark was estimated using the relief from royalty method, which assumes that the trademark has value to the extent that Umbro is relieved of the obligation to pay royalties for the benefits received from the trademark. The assessments of the Company resulted in the recognition of impairment charges of $199 million and $181 million related to Umbro's goodwill and trademark, respectively, for the year ended May 31, 2009. A tax benefit of $55 million was recognized as a result of the trademark impairment charge. In addition to the above impairment analysis, the Company determined an equity investment held by Umbro was impaired, and recognized a charge of $21 million related to the impairment of this investment. These charges are included in the Company's "Other" category for segment reporting purposes.

The discounted cash flow analysis calculated the fair value of Umbro using management's business plans and projections as the basis for expected cash flows for the next 12 years and a 3% residual growth rate thereafter. The Company used a weighted average discount rate of 14% in its analysis, which was derived primarily from published sources as well as our adjustment for increased market risk given current market conditions. Other significant estimates used in the discounted cash flow analysis include the rates of projected growth and profitability of Umbro's business and working capital effects. The market valuation approach indicates the fair value of Umbro based on a comparison of Umbro to publicly traded companies in similar lines of business. Significant estimates in the market valuation approach include identifying similar companies with comparable business factors such as size, growth, profitability, mix of revenue generated from licensed and direct distribution, and risk of return on investment.

Holding all other assumptions constant at the test date, a 100 basis point increase in the discount rate would reduce the adjusted carrying value of Umbro's net assets by an additional 12%.

NOTE 5 Accrued Liabilities

Accrued liabilities included the following:

(In millions)	May 31, 2011	May 31, 2010
Compensation and benefits, excluding taxes	$ 628	$ 599
Endorser compensation	284	267
Taxes other than income taxes	214	158
Fair value of derivatives	186	164
Dividends payable	145	131
Advertising and marketing	139	125
Import and logistics costs	98	80
Other[1]	291	380
	$ 1,985	$ 1,904

(1) Other consists of various accrued expenses and no individual item accounted for more than 5% of the balance at May 31, 2011 and 2010.

NOTE 6 Fair Value Measurements

The Company measures certain financial assets and liabilities at fair value on a recurring basis, including derivatives and available-for-sale securities. Fair value is a market-based measurement that should be determined based on the assumptions that market participants would use in pricing an asset or liability. As a basis for considering such assumptions, the Company uses a three-level hierarchy established by the FASB that prioritizes fair value measurements based on the types of inputs used for the various valuation techniques (market approach, income approach, and cost approach).

The levels of hierarchy are described below:

• Level 1: Observable inputs such as quoted prices in active markets for identical assets or liabilities.

• Level 2: Inputs other than quoted prices that are observable for the asset or liability, either directly or indirectly; these include quoted prices for similar assets or liabilities in active markets and quoted prices for identical or similar assets or liabilities in markets that are not active.

• Level 3: Unobservable inputs in which there is little or no market data available, which require the reporting entity to develop its own assumptions.

The Company's assessment of the significance of a particular input to the fair value measurement in its entirety requires judgment and considers factors specific to the asset or liability. Financial assets and liabilities are classified in their entirety based on the most stringent level of input that is significant to the fair value measurement.

The following table presents information about the Company's financial assets and liabilities measured at fair value on a recurring basis as of May 31, 2011 and 2010 and indicates the fair value hierarchy of the valuation techniques utilized by the Company to determine such fair value.

	May 31, 2011				
	Fair Value Measurements Using			Assets /Liabilities	
(In millions)	Level 1	Level 2	Level 3	at Fair Value	Balance Sheet Classification
ASSETS					
Derivatives:					
Foreign exchange forwards and options	$ —	$ 38	$ —	$ 38	Other current assets and other long-term assets
Interest rate swap contracts	—	15	—	15	Other current assets and other long-term assets
Total derivatives	—	53	—	53	
Available-for-sale securities:					
U.S. Treasury securities	125	—	—	125	Cash equivalents
Commercial paper and bonds	—	157	—	157	Cash equivalents
Money market funds	—	780	—	780	Cash equivalents
U.S. Treasury securities	1,473	—	—	1,473	Short-term investments
U.S. Agency securities	—	308	—	308	Short-term investments
Commercial paper and bonds	—	802	—	802	Short-term investments
Total available-for-sale securities	1,598	2,047	—	3,645	
TOTAL ASSETS	$ 1,598	$ 2,100	$ —	$ 3,698	
LIABILITIES					
Derivatives:					
Foreign exchange forwards and options	$ —	$ 197	$ —	$ 197	Accrued liabilities and other long-term liabilities
TOTAL LIABILITIES	$ —	$ 197	$ —	$ 197	

Using a Calculator and Computer Keypad

Kinds of Calculators

Many different models of calculators, both desktop and handheld, are available. All calculators have their own features and particular placement of operating keys. Therefore, it is necessary to refer to the operator's manual for specific instructions and locations of the operating keys for the calculator being used. A typical keyboard of a desktop calculator is shown in the illustration.

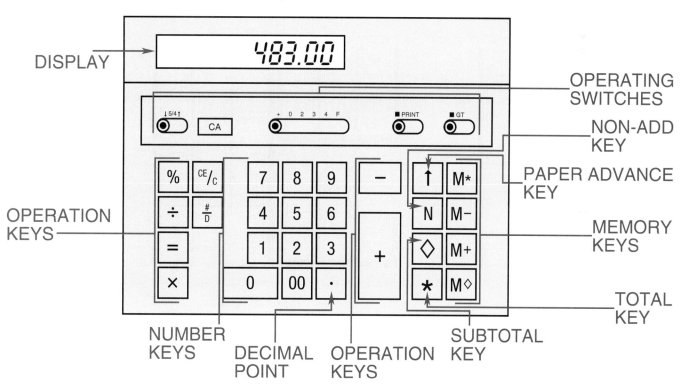

Desktop Calculator Settings

Several operating switches on a desktop calculator must be engaged before the calculator will produce the desired results.

The *decimal selector* sets the appropriate decimal places necessary for the numbers that will be entered. For example, if the decimal selector is set at 2, both the numbers entered and the answer will have two decimal places. If the decimal selector is set at F, the calculator automatically sets the decimal places. The F setting allows the answer to be unrounded and carried out to the maximum number of decimal places possible.

The *decimal rounding selector* rounds the answers. The down arrow position will drop any digits beyond the last digit desired. The up arrow position will drop any digits beyond the last digit desired and round the last digit up. In the 5/4 position, the calculator rounds the last desired digit up only when the following digit is 5 or greater. If the following digit is less than 5, the last desired digit remains unchanged.

The *GT* or *grand total switch* in the on position accumulates totals.

Kinds of Computer Keyboards

The computer has a keypad on the right side of the keyboard, called the *numeric keypad*. The two basic layouts for the numeric keypad, standard and enhanced, are shown in the illustration. On the standard keyboard, the directional arrow keys are found on the number keys. To use the numbers, press the key called *Num Lock*. (This key is found above the 7 key.) When the Num Lock is turned on, numbers are entered when the keys on the keypad are pressed. When the Num Lock is off, the arrow, Home, Page Up, Page Down, End, Insert, and Delete keys can be used.

The enhanced keyboards have the arrow keys and the other directional keys mentioned above to the left of the numeric keypad. When using the keypad on an enhanced keyboard, Num Lock can remain on.

The asterisk (*) performs a different function on the computer than the calculator. The asterisk on the calculator is used for the total while the computer uses it for multiplication.

Another difference is the division key. The computer key is the forward slash key (/). The calculator key uses the division key (÷).

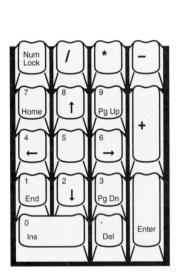

Standard
Keyboard Layout

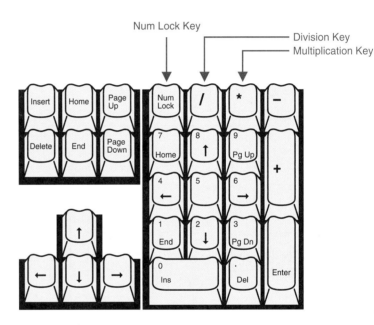

Enhanced
Keyboard Layout

Ten-Key Touch System

Striking the numbers 0 to 9 on a calculator or numeric keypad without looking at the keyboard is called the *touch system*. Using the touch system develops both speed and accuracy.

The 4, 5, and 6 keys are called the *home row*. If the right hand is used for the keyboard, the index finger is placed on the 4 key, the middle finger on the 5 key, and the ring finger on the 6 key. If the left hand is used, the ring finger is placed on the 4 key, the middle finger on the 5 key, and the index finger on the 6 key.

Place the fingers on the home row keys. Curve the fingers and keep the wrist straight. These keys may feel slightly concaved or the 5 key may have a raised dot. The differences in the home row allow the operator to recognize the home row by touch rather than by sight.

Maintain the position of the fingers on the home row. The finger used to strike the 4 key will also strike the 7 key and the 1 key. Stretch the finger up to reach the 7; then stretch the finger down to reach the 1 key. Visualize the position of these keys.

Again, place the fingers on the home row. Stretch the finger that strikes the 5 key up to reach the 8 key, then down to reach the 2 key. Likewise, stretch the finger that strikes the 6 key up to strike the 9 and down to strike the 3 key. This same finger will stretch down again to hit the decimal point.

If the right hand is used, the thumb will be used to strike the 0 and 00 keys and the little finger to strike the addition key. If the left hand is used, the little finger will be used to strike the 0 and 00 keys and the thumb to strike the addition key.

Handheld Calculators

Handheld calculators are slightly different from desktop calculators, not only in their size and features but also in their operation. Refer to the operator's manual for specific instructions for the calculator being used.

On a handheld calculator, the numeric keys are usually very close together. In addition, the keys do not respond to touch as easily as on a desktop calculator. Therefore, the touch system is usually not used on a handheld calculator.

Performing Mathematical Operations on Desktop Calculators

Mathematical operations can be performed on a calculator both quickly and efficiently. The basic operations of addition, subtraction, multiplication, and division are used frequently on a calculator.

ADDITION

Each number to be added is called an *addend*. The answer to an addition problem is called the *sum*.

Addition is performed by entering an addend and striking the addition key (+). All numbers are entered on a calculator in the exact order they are given. To enter the number 4,455.65, strike the 4, 4, 5, 5, decimal, 6, and 5 keys in that order, and then strike the addition key. Commas are not entered. Continue in this manner until all addends have been entered. To obtain the sum, strike the total key on the calculator.

SUBTRACTION

The top number or first number of a subtraction problem is called the *minuend*. The number to be subtracted from the minuend is called the *subtrahend*. The answer to a subtraction problem is called the *difference*.

Subtraction is performed by first entering the minuend and striking the addition key (+). The subtrahend is then entered, followed by the minus key (−), followed by the total key.

MULTIPLICATION

The number to be multiplied is called the *multiplicand*. The number of times the multiplicand will be multiplied

is called the *multiplier*. The answer to a multiplication problem is called the *product*.

Multiplication is performed by entering the multiplicand and striking the multiplication key (×). The multiplier is then entered, followed by the equals key (=). The calculator will automatically multiply and give the product.

DIVISION

The number to be divided is called the *dividend*. The number the dividend will be divided by is called the *divisor*. The answer to a division problem is called the *quotient*.

Division is performed by entering the dividend and striking the division key (÷). The divisor is then entered, followed by the equals key (=). The calculator will automatically divide and give the quotient.

CORRECTING ERRORS

If an error is made while using a calculator, several methods of correction may be used. If an incorrect number has been entered and the addition key or equals key has not yet been struck, strike the clear entry (CE) key one time. This key will clear only the last number that was entered. However, if the clear entry key is depressed more than one time, the entire problem will be cleared on some calculators. If an incorrect number has been entered and the addition key has been struck, strike the minus key one time only. This will automatically subtract the last number added, thus removing it from the total.

Performing Mathematical Operations on Computers and Handheld Calculators

On a computer keypad or a handheld calculator, addition is performed in much the same way as on a desktop calculator. However, after the + key is depressed, the

display usually shows the accumulated total. Therefore, the total key is not found. Some computer programs will not calculate the total until Enter is pressed.

Subtraction is performed differently on many computer keypads and handheld calculators. The minuend is usually entered, followed by the minus (–) key. Then the subtrahend is entered. Pressing either the + key or the = key will display the difference. Some computer programs will not calculate the difference until Enter is pressed.

Multiplication and division are performed the same way on a computer keypad and handheld calculator as on a desktop calculator. Keep in mind that computers use the * for multiplication and / for division.

Safety Concerns

Whenever electrical equipment such as a calculator or computer is being operated in a classroom or office, several safety rules apply. These rules protect the operator of the equipment, other persons in the environment, and the equipment itself.

1. Do not unplug equipment by pulling on the electrical cord. Instead, grasp the plug at the outlet and remove it.
2. Do not stretch electrical cords across an aisle where someone might trip over them.
3. Avoid food and beverages near the equipment where a spill might result in an electrical short.
4. Do not attempt to remove the cover of a calculator, computer, or keyboard for any reason while the power is turned on.
5. Do not attempt to repair equipment while it is plugged in.
6. Always turn the power off or unplug equipment when finished using it.

Calculation Drills

INSTRUCTIONS FOR DESKTOP CALCULATORS

Complete each drill using the touch method. Set the decimal selector at the setting indicated in each drill. Compare the answer on the calculator to the answer in the book. If the two are the same, progress to the next problem. It is not necessary to enter 00 in the cents column if the decimal selector is set at 0-F. However, digits other than zeros in the cents column must be entered, preceded by a decimal point.

INSTRUCTIONS FOR COMPUTER KEYPADS

Complete each drill using the touch method. There is no decimal selector on computer keypads. Set the number of decimal places as directed in the instructions for the computer program. In spreadsheets, for example, use the formatting options to set the number of decimal places. When the drill indicates "F" for floating, leave the computer application in its default format. Compare the answer on the computer monitor to the answer in the book. If the two are the same, progress to the next problem. It is not necessary to enter 00 in the cents column. However, digits other than zeros in the cents column must be entered, preceded by a decimal point.

DRILL C-1   Performing addition using the home row keys
Decimal Selector—2

4.00	44.00	444.00	4,444.00	44,444.00
5.00	55.00	555.00	5,555.00	55,555.00
6.00	66.00	666.00	6,666.00	66,666.00
5.00	45.00	455.00	4,455.00	44,556.00
4.00	46.00	466.00	4,466.00	44,565.00
5.00	54.00	544.00	5,544.00	55,446.00
6.00	56.00	566.00	5,566.00	55,664.00
5.00	65.00	655.00	6,655.00	66,554.00
4.00	64.00	644.00	6,644.00	66,555.00
5.00	66.00	654.00	6,545.00	65,465.00
49.00	561.00	5,649.00	56,540.00	565,470.00

DRILL C-2 Performing addition using the 0, 1, 4, and 7 keys
Decimal Selector—2

4.00	11.00	444.00	4,440.00	44,000.00
7.00	44.00	777.00	7,770.00	77,000.00
4.00	74.00	111.00	1,110.00	11,000.00
1.00	71.00	741.00	4,400.00	41,000.00
4.00	70.00	740.00	1,100.00	71,000.00
7.00	10.00	101.00	4,007.00	10,000.00
4.00	14.00	140.00	7,001.00	10,100.00
1.00	17.00	701.00	1,007.00	40,100.00
4.00	40.00	700.00	1,004.00	70,100.00
7.00	77.00	407.00	7,700.00	74,100.00
43.00	428.00	4,862.00	39,539.00	448,400.00

DRILL C-3 Performing addition using the 2, 5, and 8 keys
Decimal Selector—2

5.00	58.00	588.00	8,888.00	88,855.00
8.00	52.00	522.00	5,555.00	88,822.00
5.00	85.00	888.00	2,222.00	88,852.00
2.00	52.00	222.00	8,525.00	88,222.00
5.00	25.00	258.00	2,585.00	85,258.00
8.00	58.00	852.00	8,258.00	22,255.00
5.00	82.00	225.00	8,585.00	22,288.00
2.00	28.00	885.00	5,258.00	22,258.00
5.00	88.00	882.00	2,852.00	22,888.00
8.00	22.00	228.00	2,288.00	25,852.00
53.00	550.00	5,550.00	55,016.00	555,550.00

DRILL C-4 Performing addition using the 3, 6, 9, and decimal point keys
Decimal Selector—2

6.00	66.66	666.66	6,666.99	66,699.33
9.00	99.99	999.99	9,999.66	99,966.66
6.00	33.33	333.33	3,333.99	33,366.33
3.00	33.66	666.99	3,366.99	36,963.36
6.36	33.99	999.66	6,699.33	69,636.36
3.36	99.66	333.66	9,966.33	33,333.66
9.36	99.33	696.36	9,636.69	66,666.99
9.63	33.36	369.63	3,696.36	99,999.33
6.33	33.69	336.69	6,963.99	96,369.63
9.93	69.63	963.36	6,699.33	36,963.36
68.97	603.30	6,366.33	67,029.66	639,965.01

DRILL C-5 Performing subtraction using all number keys
Decimal Selector—F

456.73	789.01	741.00	852.55	987.98
−123.21	−456.00	−258.10	−369.88	−102.55
333.52	333.01	482.90	482.67	885.43

DRILL C-6 **Performing multiplication using all number keys**
Decimal Selector—F

654.05	975.01	487.10	123.56	803.75
× 12.66	× 27.19	× 30.21	× 50.09	× 1.45
8,280.273	26,510.5219	14,715.291	6,189.1204	1,165.4375

DRILL C-7 **Performing division using all number keys**
Decimal Selector—F

900.56	÷	450.28	=	2.
500.25	÷	100.05	=	5.
135.66	÷	6.65	=	20.4
269.155	÷	105.55	=	2.550023685*
985.66	÷	22.66	=	43.49779346*

Number of decimal places may vary, due to machine capacity.

Recycling Problems

1-R Recycling Problem: Determining how transactions change an accounting equation
LO4, 5, 6

Courtney McGraw operates a service business called Marry DJ's. Marry DJ's uses the accounts shown in the following accounting equation. Use the form in your *Recycling Problem Working Papers* to complete this problem.

Trans. No.	Assets						=	Liabilities	+	Owner's Equity
	Cash	+	Accts. Rec.—Big Day Planning	+	Supplies	+	Prepaid Insurance =	Accts. Pay.—Music Sources Co.	+	Courtney McGraw, Capital
Beg. Bal. 1.	2,500 +1,000		0		200		100	1,300		1,500 +1,000 (investment)
New Bal. 2.	3,500		0		200		100	1,300		2,500

Instructions:

For each transaction, complete the following. Transaction 1 is given as an example.

1. Analyze the transaction to determine which accounts in the accounting equation are affected.
2. Write the amount in the appropriate columns, using a plus (+) if the account increases or a minus (–) if the account decreases.
3. For transactions that change owner's equity, write in parentheses a description of the transaction to the right of the amount.
4. Calculate the new balance for each account in the accounting equation.
5. Before going on to the next transaction, determine that the accounting equation is still in balance.

Transactions:

1. Received cash from owner as an investment, $1,000.00.
2. Paid cash for rent, $700.00.
3. Paid cash for cell phone, $75.00.
4. Received cash from sales, $1,500.00.
5. Bought supplies on account from Music Sources Co., $350.00.
6. Sold services on account to Big Day Planning, $265.00.
7. Paid cash for advertising, $250.00.
8. Paid cash for supplies, $125.00.
9. Received cash on account from Big Day Planning, $150.00.
10. Paid cash on account to Music Sources Co., $200.00.
11. Paid cash for one month of insurance, $100.00.
12. Received cash from sales, $575.00.
13. Owner withdrew equity in the form of cash, $600.00.

2-R Recycling Problem: Analyzing transactions into debit and credit parts LO4, 5

Web World uses the following accounts.

Cash
Accounts Receivable—Janet East
Accounts Receivable—Adam Middleton
Supplies
Prepaid Insurance
Accounts Payable—Hilltop Supplies
Accounts Payable—Tech Supplies
Henry White, Capital

Henry White, Drawing
Sales
Advertising Expense
Miscellaneous Expense
Rent Expense
Repairs Expense
Utilities Expense

Instructions:

1. Prepare a T account for each account. Use the forms in your *Recycling Problem Working Papers*.

2. Analyze each transaction into its debit and credit parts. Write the debit and credit amounts in the proper T accounts to show how each transaction changes account balances.

Transactions:

Mar. 1. Received cash from owner as an investment, $3,500.00.
1. Paid cash for supplies, $800.00.
3. Paid cash for rent, $1,500.00.
4. Received cash from sales, $550.00.
7. Sold services on account to Janet East, $1,700.00.
8. Paid cash for insurance, $1,000.00.
10. Brought supplies on account from Tech Supplies, $200.00.
10. Paid cash for miscellaneous expense, $70.00.
14. Received cash from owner as an investment, $3,000.00.
16. Bought supplies on account from Hilltop Supplies, $280.00.
17. Received cash from sales, $750.00.
17. Received cash on account from Janet East, $800.00.
22. Paid cash for repairs, $215.00.
23. Paid cash on account to Tech Supplies, $100.00.
25. Paid cash for advertising, $1,100.00.
25. Sold services on account to Adam Middleton, $1,200.00.
29. Paid cash for electric bill (utilities expense), $250.00.
31. Paid cash to owner for personal use, $600.00.
31. Received cash on account from Adam Middleton, $700.00.

GreenThumb Landscaping uses the following accounts.

Cash
Accounts Receivable—Roseville Mall
Supplies
Prepaid Insurance
Accounts Payable—Central Supplies

Accounts Payable—Plant Warehouse
Noah Rasmussen, Capital
Noah Rasmussen, Drawing
Sales
Advertising Expense

Miscellaneous Expense
Rent Expense
Repairs Expense
Utilities Expense

Transactions:

Aug.
1. Received cash from owner as an investment, $16,000.00. R1.
2. Bought supplies on account from Central Supplies, $1,700.00. M1.
3. Paid cash for rent, $900.00. C1.
4. Paid cash for supplies, $300.00. C2.
5. Received cash from sales, $980.00. T5.
8. Paid cash on account to Central Supplies, $1,000.00. C3.
8. Paid cash for electric bill, $246.00. C4.
8. Sold services on account to Roseville Mall, $450.00. S1.
9. Paid cash for supplies, $90.00. C5.
10. Paid cash for repairs, $388.00. C6.
10. Received cash from sales, $476.00. T10.
11. Paid cash for miscellaneous expense, $40.00. C7.
11. Received cash from sales, $630.00. T11.
12. Received cash from sales, $900.00. T12.
15. Paid cash to owner as a withdrawal of equity for personal use, $4,000.00. C8.
15. Paid cash for supplies, $1,100.00. C9.
16. Received cash from sales, $850.00. T16.
17. Received cash on account from Roseville Mall, $230.00. R2.
17. Bought supplies on account from Plant Warehouse, $600.00. M2.
17. Received cash from sales, $500.00. T17.
19. Received cash from sales, $650.00. T19.
22. Received cash from sales, $610.00. T22.
23. Sold services on account to Roseville Mall, $582.00. S2.
24. Paid cash for advertising, $150.00. C10.
24. Received cash from sales, $300.00. T24.
25. Received cash from sales, $770.00. T25.
25. Bought supplies on account from Plant Warehouse, $60.00. M3.
26. Paid cash for insurance, $1,200.00. C11.
26. Received cash from sales, $300.00. T26.
29. Received cash on account from Roseville Mall, $350.00. R3.
31. Received cash from sales, $500.00. T31.
31. Paid cash to owner as a withdrawal of equity, $4,500.00. C12.

Instructions:

1. The journal for GreenThumb Landscaping is given in the *Recycling Problem Working Papers*. Use page 1 of the journal to journalize the transactions for August 1 through August 15. Source documents are abbreviated as follows: check, C; memorandum, M; receipt, R; sales invoice, S; calculator tape, T.

2. Use page 2 of the journal to journalize the transactions for the remainder of August.

4-R Recycling Problem: Journalizing transactions and posting to a general ledger LO3, 4, 5

Courtney Jerrold owns a service business called Repair It Now. Repair It Now's general ledger accounts are given in the *Recycling Problem Working Papers*.

Transactions:

Feb.   1. Received cash from owner as an investment, $5,500.00. R1.
       3. Received cash from sales, $900.00. T3.
       5. Paid cash for supplies, $400.00. C1.
       6. Sold services on account to Cindy West, $280.00. S1.
       9. Paid cash for miscellaneous expense, $50.00. C2.
    11. Paid cash for rent, $600.00. C3.
    13. Bought supplies on account from Chandler Supplies, $240.00. M1.
    13. Received cash from sales, $430.00. T13.
    16. Paid cash for advertising, $143.00. C4.
    18. Paid cash for electric bill, $230.00. C5.
    20. Paid cash on account to Chandler Supplies, $140.00. C6.
    20. Received cash on account from Cindy West, $150.00. R2.
    25. Paid cash for supplies, $150.00. C7.
    27. Received cash from sales, $2,100.00. T27.
    27. Paid cash for supplies, $80.00. C8.
    28. Received cash from sales, $110.00. T28.
    28. Paid cash to owner for a withdrawal of equity, $500.00. C9.

Instructions:

1. Open an account for Utilities Expense. Use the three-digit numbering system described in the chapter.

2. Journalize the transactions completed during February of the current year. Use page 1 of a journal. Source documents are abbreviated as follows: check, C; memorandum, M; receipt, R; sales invoice, S; calculator tape, T.

3. Post from the general journal to the general ledger.

5-R Recycling Problem: Reconciling a bank statement; journalizing a bank service charge, a dishonored check, and petty cash transactions LO4, 5, 6, 9, 10, 11

Alkar Kovac owns a business called Kovac Accounting. Selected general ledger accounts are given below.

110 Cash	140 Prepaid Insurance	530 Rent Expense
115 Petty Cash	320 Alkar Kovac, Drawing	535 Repairs Expense
120 Accounts Receivable—Latica Juric	510 Cash Short and Over	540 Supplies Expense
130 Supplies	520 Miscellaneous Expense	550 Utilities Expense

Instructions:

1. Journalize the following transactions completed during July of the current year. Use page 13 of the journal given in the *Recycling Problem Working Papers*. Source documents are abbreviated as follows: check, C; memorandum, M; calculator tape, T.

Transactions:

July 21. Paid cash to establish a petty cash fund, $200.00. C187.
    24. Paid cash for miscellaneous expense, $20.00. C188.
    26. Paid cash for supplies, $55.00. C189.
    27. Received notice from the bank of a dishonored check from Latica Juric, $110.00, plus $25.00 fee; total, $135.00. M36.
    28. Paid cash for repairs, $80.00. C190.
    31. Received cash from sales, $1,200.00. T31.
    31. Paid cash to owner for personal use, $750.00. C191.

2. Prepare a petty cash report for July 31 of the current year using the following information: Petty cash slips supported payment of $108.00 for Supplies and $80.00 for Miscellaneous Expense. Actual amount of cash in the petty cash box is $10.00.

3. Continue using the journal and journalize the following transaction:

Transaction:

July 31. Paid cash to replenish the petty cash fund, $190.00. C192.

4. On July 31 of the current year, Kovac Accounting received a bank statement dated July 30. Prepare a bank statement reconciliation. Use July 31 of the current year as the date. The following information is obtained from the July 30 bank statement and from the records of the business.

Bank statement balance	$2,552.00
Bank service charge	20.00
Outstanding deposit, July 31	1,200.00
Outstanding checks, Nos. 191 and 192	
Checkbook balance on Check Stub No. 193	2,832.00

5. Continue using the journal and journalize the following transaction:

Transaction:

July 31. Received bank statement showing July bank service charge, $20.00. M37.

On June 30 of the current year, Destin Heating Repair has the following general ledger accounts and balances. The business uses a monthly fiscal period. A work sheet is given in the *Recycling Problem Working Papers*.

	Account Balances	
Account Titles	**Debit**	**Credit**
Cash	$11,316.00	
Petty Cash	600.00	
Accounts Receivable—Jennifer Ford	6,044.00	
Supplies	3,420.00	
Prepaid Insurance	4,400.00	
Accounts Payable—Coastal Supplies		$ 2,000.00
Isabel Ybarra, Capital		18,008.00
Isabel Ybarra, Drawing	1,760.00	
Income Summary		
Sales		13,600.00
Advertising Expense	1,800.00	
Cash Short and Over	8.00	
Insurance Expense		
Miscellaneous Expense	760.00	
Rent Expense	1,500.00	
Supplies Expense		
Utilities Expense	2,000.00	

Instructions:

1. Prepare the heading and trial balance on a work sheet. Total and rule the Trial Balance columns.
2. Analyze the following adjustment information into debit and credit parts. Record the adjustments on the work sheet.

Adjustment Information, June 30

Supplies inventory	$ 880.00
Value of prepaid insurance	3,600.00

3. Total and rule the Adjustments columns.
4. Extend the up-to-date balances to the Balance Sheet or Income Statement columns.
5. Rule a single line across the Income Statement and Balance Sheet columns. Total each column. Calculate and record the net income or net loss. Label the amount in the Account Title column.
6. Total and rule the Income Statement and Balance Sheet columns.
7. A journal and general ledger accounts are given in the *Recycling Problem Working Papers*. The general ledger accounts do not show all details for the fiscal period. The balance shown in each account is the account's balance before adjusting entries are posted. Use page 11 of a journal. Journalize and post the adjusting entries.

Forms are given in the *Recycling Problem Working Papers*. The following information is obtained from the work sheet of Destin Heating Repair for the month ended April 30 of the current year.

| | ACCOUNT TITLE | INCOME STATEMENT | | BALANCE SHEET | | |
		DEBIT	CREDIT	DEBIT	CREDIT	
1	Cash			6 9 6 0 00		1
2	Petty Cash			1 5 0 00		2
3	Accounts Receivable—Jennifer Ford			1 9 6 00		3
4	Supplies			7 8 0 00		4
5	Prepaid Insurance			8 0 0 00		5
6	Accounts Payable—Coastal Supplies				1 1 1 2 00	6
7	Isabel Ybarra, Capital				9 3 3 6 00	7
8	Isabel Ybarra, Drawing			6 0 0 00		8
9	Income Summary					9
10	Sales		3 2 7 0 00			10
11	Advertising Expense	4 5 0 00				11
12	Cash Short and Over	2 00				12
13	Insurance Expense	1 5 6 00				13
14	Miscellaneous Expense	8 4 00				14
15	Rent Expense	5 0 0 00				15
16	Supplies Expense	1 4 0 0 00				16
17	Utilities Expense	1 6 4 0 00				17
18		4 2 3 2 00	3 2 7 0 00	9 4 8 6 00	10 4 4 8 00	18
19	Net Loss		9 6 2 00	9 6 2 00		19
20		4 2 3 2 00	4 2 3 2 00	10 4 4 8 00	10 4 4 8 00	20
21						21

Instructions:

1. Prepare an income statement for the month ended April 30 of the current year.

2. Calculate and record the ratios for total expenses and net loss. Place the percentage for net loss in parentheses to show that it is for a net loss. Round percentage calculations to the nearest 0.1%.

3. Prepare a balance sheet for April 30 of the current year.

Destin Heating Repair's partial work sheet for the month ended April 30 of the current year is given below. The general ledger accounts are given in the *Recycling Problem Working Papers*. The general ledger accounts do not show all details for the fiscal period. The balance shown in each account is the account's balance before closing entries are posted.

		5	6	7	8	
		INCOME STATEMENT		BALANCE SHEET		
	ACCOUNT TITLE	DEBIT	CREDIT	DEBIT	CREDIT	
1	Cash			6 9 6 0 00		1
2	Petty Cash			1 5 0 00		2
3	Accounts Receivable—Jennifer Ford			1 9 6 00		3
4	Supplies			7 8 0 00		4
5	Prepaid Insurance			8 0 0 00		5
6	Accounts Payable—Coastal Supplies				1 1 1 2 00	6
7	Isabel Ybarra, Capital				9 3 3 6 00	7
8	Isabel Ybarra, Drawing			6 0 0 00		8
9	Income Summary					9
10	Sales		3 2 7 0 00			10
11	Advertising Expense	4 5 0 00				11
12	Cash Short and Over	2 00				12
13	Insurance Expense	1 5 6 00				13
14	Miscellaneous Expense	8 4 00				14
15	Rent Expense	5 0 0 00				15
16	Supplies Expense	1 4 0 0 00				16
17	Utilities Expense	1 6 4 0 00				17
18		4 2 3 2 00	3 2 7 0 00	9 4 8 6 00	10 4 4 8 00	18
19	Net Loss		9 6 2 00	9 6 2 00		19
20		4 2 3 2 00	4 2 3 2 00	10 4 4 8 00	10 4 4 8 00	20
21						21

Instructions:

1. Continue on page 7 of the journal. Journalize and post the closing entries.
2. Prepare a post-closing trial balance.

9-R Recycling Problem: Journalizing purchases, cash payments, and other transactions
LO6, 7, 8, 10

G&S Enterprises sells electrical supplies.

Instructions:

1. Using the journals given in the *Recycling Problem Working Papers*, journalize the following transactions completed during August of the current year. Use page 8 of a purchases journal and page 12 of a cash payments journal. Post the following transactions when journalized: (1) transactions impacting Accounts Payable to the accounts payable subsidiary ledger, and (2) cash payments, entered in a general amount column of the cash payments journal, to the general ledger. Source documents are abbreviated as follows: check, C; purchase invoice, P.

Transactions:

Aug. 3. Purchased merchandise on account from Brown Company, $3,460.00. P288.
    4. Paid cash on account to Curtis Supply, $2,615.00, covering P285, less 2% discount. C621.
    7. Purchased merchandise on account from Nolen & Shaw, $4,660.00. P289.
    8. Paid cash to Spring Communications for telephone bill, $189.00. C622.
    9. Paid cash on account to Nolen & Shaw, $4,190.00, covering P287, less 2% discount. C623.
    10. Paid cash to West End Supply for store supplies, $129.00. C624.
    12. Purchased merchandise for cash from Washburn Industries, $518.00. C625.
    13. Purchased merchandise on account from Curtis Supply, $2,450.00. P290.
    14. Paid cash on account to Brown Company, $3,215.00, covering P281. No cash discount was offered. C626.
    17. Purchased merchandise on account from Holliman Industries, $3,570.00. P291.
    18. Paid cash to Roadway Signs for advertising, $900.00. C627.
    20. Paid cash on account to Holliman Industries, $3,210.00, covering P284. No cash discount was offered. C628.
    22. Purchased merchandise on account from Brown Company, $1,590.00. P292.
    23. Paid cash to Krestor Electronics for merchandise, $821.00. C629.
    25. Paid cash to River Electric for the electric bill, $292.00. C630.
    31. Replenished the $200.00 petty cash fund. Receipts were submitted for the following: office supplies, $62.36, and miscellaneous, $34.95. A cash count shows $100.69 in the petty cash box. C631.

2. Total and rule the purchases journal.

3. Post the purchases journal to the general ledger.

4. Total, prove, and rule the cash payments journal.

5. Post the special columns of the cash payments journal to the general ledger.

6. Prepare a schedule of accounts payable as of August 31.

10-R Recycling Problem: Journalizing sales and cash receipts transactions

LO2, 3, 4, 5, 6, 7

Forshee Supply sells stationery and business forms.

The sales journal, cash receipts journal, account receivable ledger forms, and selected general ledger accounts are given in the *Recycling Problem Working Papers*.

Instructions:

1. Journalize the following transactions completed during the remainder of May in the appropriate journal. Use page 5 of a sales journal and page 6 of a cash receipts journal. Post any transaction impacting Accounts Receivable to the accounts receivable subsidiary ledger when the transaction is journalized. The sales tax rate is 6%. Source documents are abbreviated as follows: receipt, R; sales invoice, S; terminal summary, TS.

Transactions:

May 3. Received cash on account from Mooreville City Schools, covering S402 for $1,625.00. R512.
      5. Sold merchandise on account to Joseph Architects, $1,158.00, plus sales tax. S422.
      6. Recorded cash and credit card sales, $2,148.32, plus sales tax, $128.90; total, $2,277.22. TS12.
      8. Received cash on account from JRD Hotel Group, $3,145.62, covering S421, less a 2% discount. R513.
    12. Sold merchandise on account to Mooreville City Schools, $2,640.00. Mooreville City Schools is exempt from sales tax. S423.
    14. Received cash on account from Joseph Architects, $1,227.48, covering S422, less a 2% discount. R514.
    22. Recorded cash and credit card sales, $3,118.31, plus sales tax, $187.10; total, $3,305.41. TS13.
    23. Sold merchandise on account to Best Dean & Atkins, $985.00, plus sales tax. S424.
    30. Sold merchandise on account to Joseph Architects, $813.00, plus sales tax. S425.

2. Total, prove, and rule the sales journal.

3. Post the sales journal to the general ledger.

4. Total and prove the cash receipts journal.

5. Prove cash. On May 31, the balance on the next unused check stub was $12,448.22.

6. Rule the cash receipts journal.

7. Post the cash receipts journal to the general ledger.

8. Prepare a schedule of accounts receivable.

11-R Recycling Problem: Journalizing and posting transactions using a general journal and a cash payments journal LO2, 3, 4, 5, 6, 8

Journals and selected accounts payable, accounts receivable, and general ledger accounts for Backley Farms are given in the *Recycling Problem Working Papers*.

Instructions:

1. Journalize the following transactions during December of the current year. Use page 13 of a general journal. Journalize the January transaction on page 17 of a cash payments journal. Source documents are abbreviated as follows: memorandum, M; debit memorandum, DM; credit memorandum, CM; sales invoice, S; check, C.

Transactions:

Dec. 4. Bought office supplies on account from Nickels Company, $112.00. M124.
     6. Granted credit to Down Under for spoiled merchandise, $62.50, plus sales tax, $3.13, from S522; total, $65.63. CM34.
     9. Returned merchandise to Koppens Distributing, $623.00. DM22.
   15. The board of directors declared a dividend of $0.25 per share; capital stock issued is 10,000 shares. M125.
   18. Granted credit to Carol's Café for merchandise returned, $41.00, plus sales tax, $2.05, from S528; total, $43.05. CM35.
   21. Learned that a sale on account to Ribs-N-More was incorrectly charged to the account of Ribbin's Place, $512.50. M126.
   26. Returned merchandise to Deaton Stores, $169.52. DM23.
Jan. 15. Paid cash for dividend declared December 15. C904.

2. Post each general journal entry to the appropriate subsidiary ledger and the general ledger.

3. Post the January 15 transaction in the General Debit column of the cash payments journal.

12-R Recycling Problem: Preparing a semimonthly payroll LO3, 4, 6, 9

Prior pay period paycheck stubs and selected payroll data for Crusoe Company are provided in a payroll register in the *Recycling Problem Working Papers*.

Instructions:

1. Complete the payroll register. Use the tax withholding tables in Chapter 12 to find the federal income tax withholding for each employee. Calculate withholdings for social security and Medicare taxes using 6.2% and 1.45% tax rates, respectively. None of the employees has accumulated earnings greater than the social security tax base. The voluntary deductions are not eligible to be deducted from total earnings to calculate payroll taxes.

2. Prepare a check for the total amount of the net pay. Make the check payable to Second National Bank, Payroll Account 945-12-1648, and sign your name as the manager of Crusoe Company.

3. Prepare payroll checks for Angie C. Barnes, Check No. 611, and Bert M. Clayton, Check No. 612. Sign your name as the manager of Crusoe Company. Record the two payroll check numbers in the payroll register.

13-R Recycling Problem: Journalizing payroll transactions LO2, 3, 5

Novus Company completed payroll transactions during the period January 1 to February 15 of the current year. Payroll tax rates are as follows: social security, 6.2%; Medicare, 1.45%; FUTA, 0.8%; SUTA, 5.4%. No total earnings have exceeded the tax base for calculating unemployment taxes. Novus Company is a monthly schedule depositor for payroll taxes.

Instructions:

1. Journalize the following transactions on page 16 of the cash payments journal and page 14 of the general journal given in the *Recycling Problem Working Papers*. Source documents are abbreviated as follows: check, C; memorandum, M.

Transactions:

Jan. 15. Paid cash for December's payroll tax liability. Withheld taxes from December payrolls: employee income tax, $772.00; social security tax, $763.84; and Medicare tax, $178.64. C743.

15. Paid cash for semimonthly payroll. Total earnings, $6,580.00; withholdings: employee income tax, $463.00; health insurance premiums, $410.00 (calculate the social security and Medicare deductions). C744.

15. Recorded employer payroll taxes expense for the January 15 payroll. M92.

15. Paid cash for employees' health insurance premiums, $820.00. C745.

31. Paid cash for semimonthly payroll. Total earnings, $6,130.00; withholdings: employee income tax, $426.00; health insurance premiums, $410.00 (calculate the social security and Medicare deductions). C762.

31. Recorded employer payroll taxes expense for the January 31 payroll. M96.

31. Paid cash for FUTA tax liability for quarter ended December 31, $40.53. C763.

31. Paid cash for SUTA tax liability for quarter ended December 31, $273.60. C764.

Feb. 15. Paid cash for the January liability for employee income tax, social security tax, and Medicare tax. C790.

15. Paid cash for semimonthly payroll. Total earnings, $5,998.00; withholdings: employee income tax, $412.00; health insurance premiums, $430.00 (calculate the social security and Medicare deductions). C791.

15. Recorded employer payroll taxes expense. M102.

2. Prove and rule the cash payments journal.

14-R Recycling Problem: Recording entries for uncollectible accounts LO2, 3, 4, 5, 6, 7, 8

A general journal, a cash receipts journal, and selected accounts receivable and general ledger accounts for RPW Industries are given in the *Recycling Problem Working Papers*. The following transactions relating to uncollectible accounts receivable occurred during December of the current year.

Instructions:

1. Journalize the following transactions. Use page 16 of a general journal and page 22 of a cash receipts journal. Post transactions in the general journal to the general ledger and the accounts receivable ledger when the transaction is journalized. Post any transaction in the cash receipts journal impacting Accounts Receivable to the accounts receivable ledger when the transaction is journalized.

Transactions:

Dec. 2. Wrote off Trinity Corporation's past-due account as uncollectible, $841.32. M121.
   6. Received cash from Classic Interiors for the maturity value of NR12, a 60-day, 9% note for $3,800.00. R647.
   9. Specialty Supply dishonored NR6, a 90-day, 8% note, for $5,600.00. M124.
   13. Received cash in full payment of Lowndes Company's account, previously written off as uncollectible, $948.15. M126 and R650.
   17. Wrote off Denton Company's past-due account as uncollectible, $2,315.00. M129.
   20. Received cash from Doughty & Bolden for the maturity value of NR10, a 120-day, 8% note for $6,000.00. R655.
   28. Accepted a 120-day, 8% note from Adcock Corporation for an extension of time on its account, $3,520.00. NR14.

2. Prove the cash receipts journal. Post the total of the Accounts Receivable Credit column to the general ledger account.

3. Journalize the December 31 adjusting entry for estimated uncollectible accounts expense for the year. Use page 17 of the general journal. Use the aging of accounts receivable schedule given in the *Recycling Problem Working Papers* to calculate the adjustment. Post the adjusting entry to the general ledger accounts.

15-R Recycling Problem: Journalizing adjusting entries and preparing an adjusted trial balance LO2, 3, 4, 6, 7, 8, 9

Page 18 of a general journal, a partially completed adjusted trial balance, and selected general ledger accounts for Northern Outlets are given in the *Recycling Problem Working Papers*.

Instructions:

1. Use the following information collected on December 31 to prepare the adjusting entries.

a.	Estimate of uncollectible accounts receivable	$ 840.00
b.	Office supplies inventory	1,260.00
c.	Store supplies inventory	994.00
d.	Value of prepaid insurance	2,400.00
e.	Merchandise inventory	64,184.00
f.	Note receivable, 120-day, 8% note, dated November 15	
g.	Estimate of office equipment depreciation	3,450.00
h.	Estimate of store equipment depreciation	9,420.00

2. Post the adjusting entries to the general ledger.

3. Record all account balances, except for Federal Income Tax Expense, on an adjusted trial balance.

4. Using the tax table shown in Chapter 15, calculate the federal income tax owed for the fiscal year.

5. Journalize and post the adjusting entry for federal income tax payable.

6. Complete the adjusted trial balance.

7. Total, prove, and rule the adjusted trial balance.

16-R Recycling Problem: Preparing financial statements and closing entries LO1, 2, 3, 4

The adjusted trial balance for Pacific Corporation for the year ended December 31 of the current year and forms for completing this problem are given in the *Recycling Problem Working Papers*.

Instructions:

1. Prepare an income statement. The beginning balance of Merchandise Inventory is $96,673.67.

2. Prepare a vertical analysis of each amount in the fourth amount column. Round percentage calculations to the nearest 0.1%.

3. Prepare a statement of stockholders' equity. The company had 60,000 shares of $1.00 par value stock outstanding on January 1. The company issued an additional 5,000 shares during the year.

4. Prepare a balance sheet for the current year.

5. Journalize the closing entries on page 20 of the general journal.

17-R Recycling Problem: Analyzing financial statements LO1, 2, 3, 4, 5, 6, 7, 8

The income statement and balance sheet for International Spices and forms for completing this problem are given in the *Recycling Problem Working Papers*.

Instructions:

1. Prepare a vertical analysis of the income statement and balance sheet. Round percentage calculations to the nearest 0.1%.

2. Prepare a horizontal analysis of the comparative income statement and balance sheet. Round percentage calculations to the nearest 0.1%.

3. Compare the actual vertical analysis ratios to management's benchmark ratios. Identify whether each ratio is within management's target range.

4. Using the following information, calculate the following ratios for the current year: (a) earnings per share, (b) dividend yield, and (c) price-earnings ratio. Round the dividend yield to the nearest 0.01%. Round the price-earnings ratio to the nearest 0.1. Evaluate each ratio relative to prior year ratios.

Number of shares outstanding	10,000
Dividends per share	$0.50
Market price	$96.50

5. Calculate the (a) working capital and (b) current ratio. Round the current ratio to the nearest 0.01. Determine if these ratios are within management's target range.

18-R Recycling Problem: Journalizing transactions related to debt and equity financing

LO2, 4, 5

The journals and loan payment schedule for Best Appliances are given in the *Recycling Problem Working Papers*.

Instructions:

Using the current year, journalize the following transactions on page 9 of a cash receipts journal, page 8 of a cash payments journal, and page 7 of a general journal. Refer to the loan payment schedule when journalizing the December 1 transaction. Source documents are abbreviated as follows: check, C; receipt, R; memorandum, M.

Transactions:

July   1.   Issued twenty 20-year, 8%, $5,000.00 bonds. R465.
       4.   Drew $32,700.00 on its line of credit. R469.
       6.   Sold 200 shares of 6.0%, $50.00 par value preferred stock at par value. R472.
       8.   Issued 3,000 shares of $10.00 par value common stock at par value. R476.
      12.   Signed a 150-day, 10% note to Gaston Company for an extension of time on its account payable, $8,600.00. M49.
      29.   Issued 2,000 shares of $10.00 par value common stock at $10.80 per share. R487.
Aug.   1.   Signed a five-year, 8% note, $50,000.00. R489.
Dec.   1.   Paid cash for the December payment on the August 1 note payable, $1,013.82. C822.
       2.   Paid cash for the monthly payment on its line of credit: principal, $2,000.00, plus interest, $106.68. C823.
       9.   Paid cash for the maturity value of the July 12 note payable to Gaston Company, $8,600.00, plus interest. C834.
      31.   Paid cash for the semiannual interest on bonds. C849.

19-R Recycling Problem: Recording transactions for plant assets

LO1, 2, 3, 4, 5, 6, 7, 8, 9, 10, 11

Innsbruck Accounting records plant assets in two accounts: Equipment, Account No. 1205, and Furniture, Account No. 1215. Equipment is depreciated using the straight-line method. Furniture is depreciated using the double declining-balance method. Forms are given in the *Recycling Problem Working Papers*.

Instructions:

1.   Record the following transactions completed during 20X1 on page 1 of a cash payments journal.

Transactions:

Jan.   5.   Bought a computer (equipment) and a work station (furniture): cost, $51,000.00. C310. Computer: estimated value, $17,000.00; estimated salvage value, $1,000.00; estimated useful life, 8 years; plant asset No. 333; serial number, 1455WZM-8. Work station: estimated value, $34,000.00; estimated salvage value, $2,000.00; estimated useful life, 4 years; plant asset No. 334; serial number, 44-5K26YT.
Feb. 26.   Paid property taxes on plant assets assessed at $400,000.00. The tax rate is 0.9%. C335.
Apr.   5.   Bought a copier: cost, $8,600.00; estimated salvage value, $600.00; estimated useful life, 5 years; plant asset No. 335; serial number, LK8GJY. C361.

2.   Complete Section 1 of a plant asset record for each new plant asset.

3.   Use the form provided in the *Recycling Problem Working Papers* to calculate beginning book value, annual depreciation, accumulated depreciation, and ending book value for each new plant asset.

4.   Complete Section 3 of the plant asset records for 20X1–20X4.

5.   Record the following transactions completed during 20X5. Use page 2 of a cash receipts journal and page 1 of a general journal.

Transactions:

Jan.   6.   Received cash for sale of a work station, plant asset No. 334, $2,200.00. R278.
July   2.   Received cash for sale of a computer, plant asset No. 333, $7,500.00. M65 and R310.
Dec. 31.   Recorded the adjusting entry for depreciation. Total 20X5 depreciation expense of furniture was $29,500.00. Total 20X5 depreciation expense of equipment was $65,750.00.

6.   Complete the plant asset records for each plant asset sold during 20X5.

7.   Complete Section 3 of the plant asset record for the copier for 20X5.

20-R Recycling Problem: Determining the cost of inventory using the FIFO, LIFO, and weighted-average inventory costing methods LO2, 3, 4

Dan's Fans began the year with 30 units of its model K45-3SPD ceiling fan in beginning inventory. Each unit sells for $99.95. The following transactions involving model K45-3SPD occurred during the year. Forms are given in the *Recycling Problem Working Papers*. Source documents are abbreviated as follows: purchase invoice, P; sales invoice, S.

Transactions:

Jan.	6.	Purchased 25 units from Westingplace Company for $45.00 per unit, 2/10, n/30. P232.
Apr.	5.	Sold 40 units to Heights Builders, n/30. S315.
	14.	Purchased 25 units from Westingplace Company for $45.60 per unit, 2/10, n/30. P246.
July	5.	Sold 30 units to Cherry Hill Resort, n/30. S346.
Aug.	3.	Purchased 25 units from Westingplace Company for $46.25 per unit, 2/10, n/30. P259.
Dec.	2.	Sold 10 units to Blaine Builders, n/30. S402.
	12.	Purchased 25 units from Westingplace Company for $46.60 per unit, 2/10, n/30. P278.

Instructions:

1. Enter the transactions on the stock record and determine the number of units in ending inventory.

2. Calculate the cost of ending inventory using the FIFO, LIFO, and weighted-average methods.

3. Which of the inventory costing methods resulted in the lowest cost of merchandise sold? Merchandise available for sale is the total cost of beginning inventory plus all purchases during the year.

21-R Recycling Problem: Journalizing entries for accruals and deferrals LO1, 2, 3, 4, 5, 6, 7, 8

Accounting forms and a partial unadjusted trial balance for Fuenfigger Corporation are given in the *Recycling Problem Working Papers*. Fuenfigger Corporation collected $36,000 on November 1 for six months' rent. On December 31, 20X1, Fuenfigger Corporation has one note receivable outstanding, a 120-day, 6%, $20,000.00 note dated December 1, and one note payable outstanding, a 60-day, 8%, $25,000.00 note dated November 16. After each journal entry, update the T accounts given in the *Recycling Problem Working Papers*.

Instructions:

1. Journalize the adjusting entries for accrued interest income, accrued interest expense, and rent earned on December 31. Use page 14 of a general journal.

2. Journalize the closing entries for all income and expense accounts using page 14 of a general journal. Record the closing entry for both income accounts in one entry.

3. Journalize the January 1, 20X2, reversing entries for accrued interest income and accrued interest expense on page 15 of a general journal.

4. Journalize the payment of cash for the maturity value of the note on January 15, 20X2. Check No. 190. Use page 25 of a cash payments journal.

5. Journalize the receipt of cash for the maturity value of the note on March 31, 20X2. Receipt No. 205. Use page 16 of a cash receipts journal.

6. List the amount of interest income from the note receivable that will be shown on the income statements for 20X1 and 20X2.

7. List the amount of interest expense from the note payable that will be shown on the income statements for 20X1 and 20X2.

8. What is the balance in the Prepaid Rent account on December 31, 20X1? What does it represent?

Stowe Corporation's unadjusted trial balance and accounting forms are given in the *Recycling Problem Working Papers*.

Instructions:

1. Using the following information, journalize the adjusting entries for the current year ended December 31.

Adjustment Information, December 31

Estimated uncollectible accounts based on aging accounts receivable	$ 3,632.00
Accrued interest income	52.80
Merchandise inventory	191,891.42
Supplies inventory	200.00
Value of prepaid insurance	1,240.00
Annual depreciation expense—office equipment	3,616.00
Annual depreciation expense—store equipment	3,340.00
Accrued interest expense	206.25
Rent income earned	1,980.00

2. Post the adjusting entries to the T accounts.

3. Using the tax table presented in this chapter, calculate the federal income tax expense and journalize the income tax adjustment.

4. Post the federal income tax adjusting entry to the T accounts.

5. Using the unadjusted trial balance and the T accounts, complete the adjusted trial balance.

6. Complete the income statement for the current year. Calculate and record the following component percentages: (a) cost of merchandise sold; (b) gross profit on operations; (c) total operating expenses; (d) income from operations; (e) net addition or deduction from other revenue and expenses; and (f) net income before federal income tax. Round percentage calculations to the nearest 0.1%. Round net addition or deduction from other revenue and expenses *up* to the nearest 0.1%.

7. Analyze the corporation's income statement by determining if component percentages are within acceptable levels. If any component percentage is not within an acceptable level, suggest steps that the company should take. The corporation considers the following component percentages acceptable.

Cost of merchandise sold	Not more than 67.0%
Gross profit on operations	Not less than 33.0%
Total operating expenses	Not more than 27.0%
Income from operations	Not less than 8.0%
Net deduction from other revenue and expenses	Not more than 0.10%
Net income before federal income tax	Not less than 7.90%

8. Complete the statement of stockholders' equity for the current year. As of January 1, Stowe Corporation had issued 16,000 shares of common stock with a par value of $1.00 per share. During the fiscal year, the corporation issued 10,000 additional shares of common stock. The balance in Paid-in Capital in Excess of Par—Common on January 1, 20--, was $40,000.00. As of January 1, Stowe Corporation had issued 2,700 shares of $5.00 par, 5% preferred stock. No additional shares of preferred stock were issued during the year.

9. Complete the balance sheet for Stowe Corporation for the current year.

10. Calculate the corporation's (a) working capital and (b) current ratio. Determine if these items are within acceptable levels. The corporation considers the following levels acceptable.

Working capital	Not less than $200,000.00
Current ratio	Between 4.5 to 1 and 5.0 to 1

11. Using the balance sheet and the following information, prepare a statement of cash flows for the current year.

Cash receipts during the year:

Cash from sales	$1,439,078.18
Cash from interest	447.68
Cash from rent	1,980.00
Cash from sale of store equipment	4,200.00
Cash from issuance of stock	30,000.00

Cash payments during the year:

Cash for inventory	$ 966,504.49
Cash for salaries and wages	283,775.68
Cash for insurance	8,000.00
Cash for interest	2,450.45
Cash for taxes	16,000.00
Cash for rent	29,700.00
Cash for other operating expenses	140,258.66
Cash for purchase of office equipment	5,000.00
Cash for purchase of store equipment	1,500.00
Cash for payment of notes payable	3,500.00
Cash for payment of bonds payable	2,000.00
Cash for payment of dividends	21,120.00
Cash balance at the beginning of the period	$ 22,731.58

12. Journalize the closing entries using page 16 of a general journal.

13. Journalize the reversing entries using page 17 of a general journal.

23-R Recycling Problem: Recording partners' investments and withdrawals, preparing financial statements, and liquidating a partnership LO1, 2, 3, 4, 5, 6, 7

Johannes Kilmeta and Joseph Schwantz are partners in a business called J & J Painters. Journals and forms for completing this problem are given in the *Recycling Problem Working Papers*. J & J Painters completed the following transactions during the current year.

Transactions:

Jan. 15. Received cash of $1,000.00 and equipment valued at $4,000.00 from partner, Johannes Kilmeta, as an investment. Receipt No. 521.

15. Received cash from partner, Joseph Schwantz, as an investment, $5,000.00. Receipt No. 522.

July 31. Joseph Schwantz, partner, withdrew merchandise for personal use, $4,000.00. Memorandum No. 291.

31. Johannes Kilmeta, partner, withdrew cash for personal use, $4,000.00. Check No. 625.

Instructions:

1. Journalize the investments on January 15.

2. Journalize the withdrawals on July 31.

Additional information is given below.

Johannes Kilmeta, Capital, January 1 balance	$11,200.00
Joseph Schwantz, Capital, January 1 balance	11,200.00
Net income for the year ended December 31	14,800.00

3. Prepare a distribution of net income statement for J & J Painters. Net income or loss is to be distributed equally to the partners.

4. Using the balances of the general ledger capital accounts, prepare an owners' equity statement for J & J Painters. The investments made on January 15 are the only additional investments made by the partners this year. The withdrawals made on July 31 are the only withdrawals made by the partners this year.

The partners decided to liquidate J & J Painters on December 31. On that date, after financial statements were prepared and closing entries were posted, the general ledger accounts had the following balances.

Cash	$41,200.00
Merchandise Inventory	3,000.00
Equipment	28,000.00
Accumulated Depreciation—Equipment	25,000.00
Accounts Payable	8,000.00
Johannes Kilmeta, Capital	19,600.00
Joseph Schwantz, Capital	19,600.00

The following transactions occurred on December 31 of the current year.

Transactions:

 a. Received cash from the sale of merchandise inventory, $3,300.00. R773.

 b. Received cash from the sale of equipment, $2,000.00. R774.

 c. Paid cash to all creditors for amounts owed. C718.

 d. Distributed gain on realization and loss on realization to the partners on an equal basis. M337 and M338.

 e. Distributed remaining cash to partners. C719 and C720.

5. Journalize the transactions. Continue on the next available line of the journals used in instructions 1 and 2.

24-R Recycling Problem: Recording international and Internet sales LO4, 5, 6

Connections Trade, Inc., sells costume jewelry domestically and internationally. The company has Internet sales as well. Journals and forms for completing this problem are given in the *Recycling Problem Working Papers*.

Instructions:

1. Journalize the following transactions affecting sales and cash receipts completed during October of the current year. Use page 24 of a general journal and a cash receipts journal. Source documents are abbreviated as follows: memorandum, M; receipt, R; time draft, TD; and terminal summary, TS.

Transactions:

Oct. 3. Received a 30-day time draft from Taiwan Importers for an international sale, $5,200.00. TD61.
     6. Recorded Internet credit card sales, $6,450.00. TS350.
   10. Recorded international cash sale, $12,600.00. M61.
   13. Recorded Internet credit card sales, $6,750.00. TS320.
   14. Received cash for the value of Time Draft No. 68, $2,000.00. R102.
   18. Received cash for the value of Time Draft No. 71, $6,800.00. R110.
   20. Recorded Internet cash sale, $18,200. TS321.
   24. Recorded international cash sale, $9,500.00. M75.
   27. Recorded Internet cash sale, $3,100.00. TS322.
   30. Received a 30-day time draft from Swedish Gems for international sale of merchandise, $18,025.00. TD62.

2. Prove and rule the cash receipts journal.

Appendix E

Answers to Audit Your Understanding

Chapter 1, Lesson 1-1, page 9
1. Accounting is the process of planning, recording, analyzing, and interpreting financial information.
2. Accounting provides financial information to everyone who needs it to make good business decisions.
3. Answers will vary but may include creating a personal budget or providing information for a loan or credit card application.

Chapter 1, Lesson 1-2, page 17
1. Answers will vary but should include businesses that perform activities for a fee, such as dry cleaners, car washes, or landscapers.
2. The right side must also be increased.
3. If one account is increased, another account on the same side of the equation must be decreased by the same amount.
4. Purchasing on account means buying items or services and paying for them at a future date.

Chapter 1, Lesson 1-3, page 22
1. Owner's equity is increased.
2. Owner's equity is increased.
3. Owner's equity is decreased.

Chapter 2, Lesson 2-1, page 35
1.

Assets	=	Liabilities	+	Owner's Equity
Left side		Right side		

2. (1) Assets are on the left side of the accounting equation. Therefore, assets increase on the left, or debit, side of the account. (2) Liabilities and the owner's capital account are on the right side of the accounting equation. Therefore, liabilities and the owner's capital account increase on the right, or credit, side of the account.

Chapter 2, Lesson 2-2, page 42
1. The questions used to analyze a transaction are: (1) Which accounts are affected? (2) How is each account classified? (3) How is each classification changed? (4) How is each amount entered in the accounts?
2. The affected accounts are Supplies and Accounts Payable.

Chapter 2, Lesson 2-3, page 49
1. Communications Expense and Cash
2. Accounts Receivable and Sales
3. Cash and Accounts Receivable
4. Debit because withdrawals decrease owner's equity
5. Credit because revenue increases owner's equity

Chapter 3, Lesson 3-1, page 64
1. By date.
2. Source documents are one way to verify the accuracy of a specific journal entry.
3. Date, debit, credit, and source document.

Chapter 3, Lesson 3-2, page 69
1. Prepaid Insurance
2. Supplies
3. Accounts Payable
4. Cash

Chapter 3, Lesson 3-3, page 75
1. Cash
2. Sales
3. Sales
4. C (for check)
5. R (for receipt)

Chapter 3, Lesson 3-4, page 80

1. When there is insufficient space to record any more entries.
2. Draw neat lines through all parts of the incorrect entry. Journalize the entry correctly on the next blank line.
3. Draw neat lines through all incorrect parts. Record the correct items on the same lines as the incorrect items, directly above the canceled parts.

Chapter 4, Lesson 4-1, page 97

1. The first digit indicates in which general ledger division the account is located. The second and third digits indicate the location of the account within that division.
2. (1) Write the account title after the word *Account* in the heading. (2) Write the account number after the words *Account No.* in the heading.

Chapter 4, Lesson 4-2, page 108

1. (1) Write the date in the Date column of the account. (2) Write the journal page number in the Post. Ref. column of the account. (3) Write the amount in the Debit or Credit column. (4) Calculate and write the new account balance in the Balance Debit or Balance Credit column. (5) Return to the journal and write the account number in the Post. Ref. column of the journal.
2. Whenever the debits in an account exceed the credits, the balance is a debit. Whenever the credits in an account exceed the debits, the balance is a credit.
3. The cash balance as shown in the checkbook and the cash balance in the Cash account.

Chapter 4, Lesson 4-3, page 113

1. A journal entry made to correct an error in the ledger.
2. When a transaction has been improperly journalized and posted to the ledger.
3. (1) Draw a line through the incorrect amount. (2) Write the correct amount just above the correction in the same space. (3) Recalculate the account balance.
4. (1) Draw a line through the incorrect item in the account. (2) Record the posting in the correct amount column. (3) Recalculate the account balance.

Chapter 5, Lesson 5-1, page 128

1. Blank endorsement, special endorsement, and restrictive endorsement.

2. (1) Write the amount of the check after the dollar sign at the top of the stub. (2) Write the date of the check on the Date line. (3) Write to whom the check is to be paid on the *To* line. (4) Record the purpose of the check on the *For* line. (5) Write the amount of the check after the words *Amt. This Check.* (6) Calculate the new checking account balance and record it in the amount column on the last line of the stub.
3. (1) Write the date. (2) Write to whom the check is to be paid following the words *Pay to the order of.* (3) Write the amount in figures following the dollar sign. (4) Write the amount in words and draw a line through the unused space up to the word *Dollars.* (5) Write the purpose of the check on the line labeled *For.* (6) Sign the check.

Chapter 5, Lesson 5-2, page 134

1. (1) A service charge may not have been recorded in the depositor's business records. (2) Outstanding deposits may be recorded in the depositor's records but not on a bank statement. (3) Outstanding checks may be recorded in the depositor's records but not on a bank statement. (4) A depositor may have made a math or recording error.
2. An outstanding check.

Chapter 5, Lesson 5-3, page 139

1. (1) The check appears to be altered. (2) The signature on the check does not match the signature on the signature card. (3) The amounts written in figures and in words do not agree. (4) The check is postdated. (5) The person who wrote the check has stopped payment on it. (6) The account of the person who wrote the check has insufficient funds to pay the check.
2. Cash.
3. Cash.

Chapter 5, Lesson 5-4, page 146

1. For making small cash payments for which writing a check is not time- or cost-effective.
2. The check issued to replenish petty cash is a credit to Cash and does not affect Petty Cash.

Chapter 6, Lesson 6-1, page 162

1. Name of the business, name of report, and date of report.
2. All general ledger accounts are listed in the Trial Balance columns of a work sheet, even if some accounts do not have balances.

Chapter 6, Lesson 6-2, page 168

1. An expense should be reported in the same fiscal period that it is used to produce revenue.

2. (1) What is the balance of the account to be adjusted? (2) What should the balance be for this account? (3) What must be done to correct the account balance? (4) What adjustment is made?

Chapter 6, Lesson 6-3, page 175

1. Balance Sheet Credit column.
2. Balance Sheet Debit column.
3. Subtract the smaller total from the larger total to find the difference.
4. The difference between two column totals can be divided evenly by 9.
5. A slide.

Chapter 6, Lesson 6-4, page 179

1. To update general ledger accounts at the end of a fiscal period.
2. Adjustments column of the work sheet.
3. Supplies Expense and Insurance Expense.

Chapter 7, Lesson 7-1, page 198

1. Heading, revenue, expenses, and net income or net loss.
2. Total Expenses *divided by* Total Sales *equals* Total Expenses Ratio.
3. Net Income *divided by* Total Sales *equals* Net Income Ratio.

Chapter 7, Lesson 7-2, page 205

1. Heading, assets, liabilities, and owner's equity.
2. Capital Account Balance *plus* Net Income (or *less* Net Loss) *less* Drawing Account Balance *equals* Current Capital.

Chapter 8, Lesson 8-1, page 222

1. Beginning balances.
2. Changes in the owner's capital account for a single fiscal period.
3. (1) An entry to close income statement accounts with credit balances. (2) An entry to close income statement accounts with debit balances. (3) An entry to record net income or net loss and close the Income Summary account. (4) An entry to close the owner's drawing account.

Chapter 8, Lesson 8-2, page 230

1. To assure a reader that a balance has not been omitted.
2. Only those with balances (permanent accounts).
3. Because they are closed and have zero balances.
4. (1) Analyze transactions. (2) Journalize. (3) Post. (4) Prepare work sheet. (5) Journalize and post adjusting entries. (6) Prepare financial statements. (7) Journalize and post closing entries. (8) Prepare post-closing trial balance.

Chapter 9, Lesson 9-1, page 248

1. A retail merchandising business sells to those who use or consume the goods. A wholesale merchandising business buys and resells merchandise primarily to other merchandising businesses.
2. A corporation, through the rights granted in its charter, has the legal rights of a person.
3. Proprietorships have a single capital and drawing account for the owner. A corporation has separate capital accounts for the stock issued and for the earnings kept in the business.
4. The sum of the subsidiary ledger accounts is equal to the balance in the general ledger controlling account.
5. Debit Balance.

Chapter 9, Lesson 9-2, page 254

1. With a periodic inventory system, the value of the inventory is determined by a physical count. With a perpetual inventory system, the value of the inventory on hand is determined by a continuous record of increases and decreases.
2. In a perpetual inventory system, purchases are recorded in the Merchandise Inventory account. In a periodic inventory system, purchases are recorded in the Purchases account.
3. Purchases journal, cash payments journal, sales journal, cash receipts journal.
4. Special amount columns are used for frequently occurring transactions.
5. All transactions for purchasing merchandise on account involve a debit to Purchases and a credit to Accounts Payable.
6. Using special amount columns eliminates writing general ledger account titles in the Account Title column, which saves time and helps to reduce mistakes.
7. A purchase invoice lists the vendor name and address; the date; the quantity, description, and price of each item; and the total amount of the purchase.

Chapter 9, Lesson 9-3, page 259

1. Posting frequently to the accounts payable ledger helps ensure that vendor accounts are paid on time and that the business can continue purchasing goods and services on account.
2. It provides an audit trail that allows an employee to trace the transaction back to the journal and page number.
3. To provide an audit trail to the account where the transaction was posted.

Chapter 9, Lesson 9-4, page 266

1. $480.00.
2. To encourage early payment.
3. Cash payment transactions that do not occur often.
4. Two ten means 2% of the invoice amount may be deducted if the invoice is paid within 10 days of the invoice date. Net thirty means that the total invoice amount must be paid within 30 days.
5. The titles of the accounts for which the petty cash funds were used.
6. As a debit.

Chapter 9, Lesson 9-5, page 273

1. Accounts Payable Debit.
2. (1) Rule a single line across all amount columns. (2) Write the date in the Date column. (3) Write *Totals* in the Account Title column. (4) Write each column total below the single line. (5) Rule a double line across all amount columns.
3. A controlling account balance in a general ledger must equal the sum of all account balances in a subsidiary ledger.

Chapter 10, Lesson 10-1, page 289

1. Markup is the amount added to the cost of merchandise to set the selling price.
2. The total of the accounts in the accounts receivable subsidiary ledger equals the balance in the controlling account, Accounts Receivable.
3. Credit Balance.
4. Accounts Receivable.
5. As a percent of sales.
6. The amount of sales tax collected is a business liability until paid to the government.

Chapter 10, Lesson 10-2, page 293

1. (1) Accounts Receivable is debited. (2) Sales is credited. (3) Sales Tax Payable is credited.
2. (1) Write the date. (2) Write the sales journal page number in the Post. Ref. column of the ledger account. (3) Enter the debit and credit amounts. (4) Calculate and record the new account balance. (5) Write the customer account number in the Post. Ref. column of the sales journal.

Chapter 10, Lesson 10-3, page 301

1. Before any sale is entered, the number, description, price, and quantity on hand of each item of merchandise are stored in the POS terminal.
2. A batch report can be detailed, showing each credit card sale, or a summary of the number and total of sales by credit card type.

3. If a customer pays the amount owed within 10 days, the sales invoice amount is reduced 2%. Otherwise, the net amount is due in 30 days.

Chapter 10, Lesson 10-4, page 309

1. Accounts Receivable Credit column.
2. Accounts receivable trial balance.

Chapter 11, Lesson 11-1, page 326

1. When the transaction cannot be recorded in a special journal.
2. After each general journal entry is recorded.
3. A purchases return is credit allowed for the purchase price of returned merchandise. A purchases allowance is credit allowed for part of the purchase price of merchandise that is not returned, such as for units that are damaged but still usable or of a different quality than that ordered.
4. Better information is provided if purchases returns and allowances are credited to a separate account. A business can then track the amount of purchases returns and allowances in a fiscal period to evaluate the efficiency of its purchasing activities.

Chapter 11, Lesson 11-2, page 331

1. A sales return is credit allowed to a customer for the sales price of returned merchandise. A sales allowance is credit allowed to a customer for part of the sales price of merchandise that is not returned, such as for a shortage in a shipment.
2. Credit memorandum.
3. To provide better information, enabling management to quickly learn if the percent of sales returns and allowances to sales is greater than expected.
4. Sales Returns and Allowances and Sales Tax Payable are debited; Accounts Receivable is credited.

Chapter 11, Lesson 11-3, page 336

1. Stockholders' Equity.
2. Most corporations have many stockholders. It is not practical to have a separate owner's equity account for each stockholder.
3. Retained Earnings.
4. At the end of the fiscal period, temporary accounts are closed to Retained Earnings. Net income increases Retained Earnings; dividends reduce Retained Earnings.
5. The board of directors must declare a dividend.

Chapter 12, Lesson 12-1, page 350

1. The total amount earned by all employees for a pay period.

2. Employees can swipe their name badges, key in personal identification numbers, or press a finger on a biometric pad to record their arrival or departure.

3. This act requires most businesses involved in interstate commerce to pay employees at least 1½ times the normal hourly rate for hours worked in excess of 40 hours per week.

4. 1½ times the normal hourly rate for hours worked more than 8 hours per day or 40 hours per week.

Chapter 12, Lesson 12-2, page 357

1. Form W-4, Employee's Withholding Allowance Certificate.

2. Employee marital status and number of withholding allowances.

3. Both the employee and employer.

4. Only the contributions to a 401(k) and an IRA are deducted from earnings before payroll taxes are calculated.

5. The withdrawals from the 401(k) and an IRA are subject to income taxes; withdrawals from a Roth IRA are tax free.

Chapter 12, Lesson 12-3, page 363

1. The payroll register summarizes the payroll for one pay period and shows total earnings, payroll withholdings, and net pay for all employees.

2. By subtracting total deductions from total earnings.

3. Because a business must send quarterly and annual reports to federal and state governments showing employee taxable earnings and taxes withheld from employee earnings.

Chapter 12, Lesson 12-4, page 368

1. (1) To help protect and control payroll payments. (2) Payroll checks require space to record earnings and deduction information.

2. The payroll register, employee earnings record, and prior pay period paycheck stub.

3. Each employee's net pay is deposited to his or her bank account. Individual checks are not written and do not have to be distributed. However, each direct deposit employee will receive a printed or electronic statement of earnings and deductions that supports the amount deposited.

Chapter 13, Lesson 13-1, page 381

1. Salary Expense.

2. Employee Income Tax Payable.

3. Social Security Tax Payable.

4. Medicare Tax Payable.

Chapter 13, Lesson 13-2, page 386

1. Social security: 6.2% of employee earnings up to a maximum of $106,800.00 in each calendar year; Medicare: 1.45% of total employee earnings; FUTA: 0.8% on the first $7,000.00 earned by each employee; SUTA: 5.4% on the first $7,000.00 earned by each employee.

2. The first $7,000.00.

Chapter 13, Lesson 13-3, page 391

1. By January 31 of the following year.

2. Federal income tax, social security tax, and Medicare tax.

Chapter 13, Lesson 13-4, page 397

1. By the 15th day of the following month.

2. Using the Electronic Federal Tax Payment System.

Chapter 14, Lesson 14-1, page 417

1. The contra asset account Allowance for Uncollectible Accounts and the expense account Uncollectible Accounts Expense.

2. The allowance method of recording losses from uncollectible accounts attempts to match the expense of uncollectible accounts in the same fiscal year that the related sales are recorded.

3. (1) Percent of sales method. (2) Percent of accounts receivable method.

4. The account is not affected.

Chapter 14, Lesson 14-2, page 424

1. The balance of the customer account is an actual uncollectible amount and no longer an estimate of an uncollectible amount.

2. The book value is the same because the same amount is deducted from the Accounts Receivable and the allowance accounts.

3. To show an accurate credit history.

Chapter 14, Lesson 14-3, page 430

1. The receipt of cash from sales does not occur at the same time and in amounts sufficient to pay for needed purchases and expenses.

2. A note can be useful in a court of law as written evidence of a debt.

3. Ten cents will be paid for the use of each dollar borrowed for a full year.

4. The words (1) *Accepted note* and (2) *Dishonored note* are written in the Item column of the customer's account.

Chapter 15, Lesson 15-1, page 445

1. Federal income tax expense.

2. (1) What is the balance of the account being adjusted?

(2) What should the balance be for this account?

(3) What must be done to correct the account balance?

(4) What adjustment is made?

3. Supplies Expense—Office and Supplies—Office.

4. Insurance Expense and Prepaid Insurance.

Chapter 15, Lesson 15-2, page 449

1. A physical inventory is conducted.

2. Debit Merchandise Inventory and credit Income Summary.

3. Daily.

4. The adjusting entry for accrued revenue increases a revenue account (a credit) and increases a receivable account (a debit).

Chapter 15, Lesson 15-3, page 454

1. Current assets and plant assets.

2. Original cost, salvage value, and useful life.

3. Land.

4. No change.

Chapter 15, Lesson 15-4, page 462

1. A business can examine each account to determine if the account needs adjustment.

2. By the order the accounts appear in the trial balance, beginning with assets or revenue.

3. All income statement debit accounts, excluding Federal Income Tax Expense, and all income statement credit accounts.

4. Bracket minimum tax, $7,500.00; marginal tax rate, 25%.

Chapter 16, Lesson 16-1, page 481

1. The Cost of Merchandise Sold section.

2. Beginning Merchandise Inventory, *plus* Purchases, *equals* Total Cost of Merchandise Available for Sale, *less* Ending Merchandise Inventory, *equals* Cost of Merchandise Sold.

3. The interest earned on notes receivable is not a normal operating activity.

Chapter 16, Lesson 16-2, page 485

1. The changes in a corporation's ownership for a fiscal period.

2. Capital Stock and Retained Earnings.

3. In the Capital Stock general ledger account.

4. The Retained Earnings amount on the unadjusted trial balance.

5. A corporation can assign any par value allowed by laws in the state in which it incorporates.

6. The income statement.

Chapter 16, Lesson 16-3, page 493

1. Current assets and plant assets.

2. (1) The balance of the asset account, (2) the balance of the contra asset account, and (3) the book value.

3. Mortgage payable.

4. From the statement of stockholders' equity.

5. Schedule of accounts payable and schedule of accounts receivable.

Chapter 16, Lesson 16-4, page 501

1. From the adjusted trial balance.

2. Income Summary.

Chapter 16, Lesson 16-5, page 505

1. General ledger accounts that have balances. Accounts are listed in the same order as they appear in the general ledger.

2. To prove the equality of debits and credits in the general ledger.

3. (a) An adjusted trial balance is prepared from the general ledger. (b) Financial statements are prepared from the adjusted trial balance.

Chapter 17, Lesson 17-1, page 521

1. (1) Actual ratios from prior fiscal periods, (2) industry standards published by industry organizations, (3) business plans, and (4) unexpected events.

2. If the increase in markup is too large, a decrease in sales revenue could occur for two reasons: (1) the sales price may exceed what customers are willing to pay or (2) customers may elect to purchase from competing businesses having lower prices.

3. Purchase merchandise in larger quantities or from other vendors offering a lower cost.

4. Operating expense ratio.

5. (1) Reduce operating expenses, (2) modify the benchmark, or (3) increase net sales.

Chapter 17, Lesson 17-2, page 527

1. (a) These are typically two of its largest asset accounts for a retail merchandising business. (b) Second, industry standards are available for these accounts.

2. A ratio below the target range may indicate that a company is restricting customers' ability to purchase on account. This action may have a negative effect on sales.

3. The business may not be stocking an adequate supply or variety of merchandise.

4. The company should prepare a list of the inventory items having the largest cost. The company should assess whether the proper quantity of each item is available for sale. Future inventory purchases

should ensure that the optimal quantity on hand is maintained.

5. The business must be able to pay its liabilities on a timely basis. If sales decline during difficult financial times, a business may be unable to make its monthly payments.

Chapter 17, Lesson 17-3, page 532

1. If management took actions that should have decreased supplies expense by significantly more than 2.0%, then only a 2.0% decrease would be unfavorable.
2. The document filed with the Securities and Exchange Commission contains a section titled *Management's Discussion and Analysis of Financial Condition and Results of Operations*. Management often uses these ratios to explain the current year's results of operations compared to previous years.

Chapter 17, Lesson 17-4, page 537

1. Each corporation's EPS is a unique number because corporations can issue any number of shares. As a result, the earnings of each corporation are divided by a different number of shares.
2. Investors.
3. High.
4. High.
5. Balance sheet.
6. Working capital is a measure of the financial resources available for the daily operations of the business.
7. The current ratio permits a business to compare itself to its industry or to provide a convenient relative measurement from year to year regarding the company's ability to pay current liabilities when due.

Chapter 18, Lesson 18-1, page 557

1. The loan agreement specifies the maximum amount that can be borrowed, the interest rate, term of the agreement, and repayment terms.
2. Prime plus 3%.
3. A non-operating expense.
4. In a section titled Other Expenses.

Chapter 18, Lesson 18-2, page 564

1. To convince the bank that it can repay the loan.
2. The bank can take the collateral and sell it to pay off the debt.
3. Use of funds, business experience, market demand, financial projections, collateral, and capital profile.
4. Investor B.

5. Bonds generally have extended terms such as 5, 10, or 20 years. Also, bonds payable tend to be issued for larger amounts than notes payable.

Chapter 18, Lesson 18-3, page 568

1. No. Dividends do not have to be paid to stockholders unless the earnings are sufficient to warrant such payments.
2. By the dividend rate and par value.
3. Preferred, then common.
4. To earn dividends.

Chapter 18, Lesson 18-4, page 573

1. Lines of credit, notes payable, bonds, common stock, and preferred stock.
2. Interest rates, impact on earnings, repayment terms, ownership control, and debt ratio.
3. The borrowed funds must be invested in the business to earn income higher than the interest charged on the borrowed funds.
4. Highly leveraged or over-leveraged.
5. The debt ratio of the corporation exceeds its debt ratio benchmark.

Chapter 19, Lesson 19-1, page 588

1. Office Equipment is debited; Cash is credited.
2. So that each plant asset can be depreciated individually.
3. Land and anything attached to the land.

Chapter 19, Lesson 19-2, page 593

1. Matching Expenses with Revenue.
2. Original cost, estimated salvage value, and estimated useful life.

Chapter 19, Lesson 19-3, page 597

1. Depreciation is credited to the contra account, Accumulated Depreciation, rather than crediting the asset account.
2. The balance of the asset account is not changed.

Chapter 19, Lesson 19-4, page 602

1. Disposal date, disposal method, and disposal amount.
2. Partial year's depreciation.
3. Cash received less the book value of the asset sold.
4. Other Expenses.

Chapter 19, Lesson 19-5, page 606

1. Depreciation rate.
2. Double declining-balance method.
3. Depreciation expense declines each year.
4. Its estimated salvage value.

Chapter 19, Lesson 19-6, page 609

1. Amortization Expense.
2. Patent.

Chapter 20, Lesson 20-1, page 625

1. (1) Excess inventory requires that a business spend money for expensive store and warehouse space. (2) Excess inventory uses capital that could be invested in other assets to earn a profit for the business. (3) Excess inventory requires that a business spend money for expenses, such as taxes and insurance premiums, which increase with the cost of the merchandise inventory. (4) Excess inventory may become obsolete and unsalable.
2. At the end of a fiscal year.
3. A business frequently establishes its fiscal year to end when inventory normally is at a minimum because it takes less time to count a smaller inventory.
4. A customary practice is to take a physical inventory at the end of the fiscal year. The physical inventory results are then compared with the perpetual inventory records and the perpetual records are corrected to reflect the actual quantity on hand as determined by the physical inventory.

Chapter 20, Lesson 20-2, page 632

1. The price of merchandise purchased first should be charged against current revenue.
2. Each item in ending inventory is recorded at the earliest prices paid for the merchandise.
3. FIFO.
4. Using the same inventory costing method for all fiscal periods provides financial statements that can be compared with other fiscal period statements. If a business changes inventory cost methods, part of the difference in gross profit and net income may be caused by the change in methods.

Chapter 20, Lesson 20-3, page 635

1. By using the gross profit method of estimating inventory.
2. Actual net sales and net purchases amounts, the beginning inventory amount, and the gross profit percentage.
3. The beginning inventory for the month is the same as the ending inventory from the previous month.

Chapter 21, Lesson 21-1, page 656

1. Realization of Revenue.
2. To avoid the inconvenience of determining how much, if any, of each cash payment is for interest income incurred and accrued during the previous year and how much is incurred in the current year.

Companies that choose to use reversing entries do not want to force their accountants to go back and check prior entries when notes are paid in the next period.

Chapter 21, Lesson 21-2, page 663

1. A liability account.
2. An expense account.

Chapter 22, Lesson 22-1, page 684

1. (1) For some accounts, the calculated estimate of the account is also the amount used in the adjusting entry. (2) Other accounts have a current balance when the adjustment is planned. The current balance is typically subtracted from the estimated account balance to determine the amount of the adjustment.
2. Supplies Expense is debited; Supplies is credited.

Chapter 22, Lesson 22-2, page 690

1. Sales, cost of merchandise sold, and operating expenses are used to determine income from operations. Other revenue and other expenses, such as interest income, rent income, interest expense, and gains or losses on plant assets, are not normal business activities. Therefore, they are not included in calculating income from operations and are reported separately.
2. Student answers will vary but could include: bonds payable, long-term notes payable, or mortgage payable.

Chapter 22, Lesson 22-3, page 698

1. Cash basis.
2. (1) Operating activities, (2) investing activities, and (3) financing activities.

Chapter 22, Lesson 22-4, page 706

1. A post-closing trial balance.
2. (1) Closing entry for income statement accounts with credit balances (revenue and cost accounts). (2) Closing entry for income statement accounts with debit balances (cost, contra revenue, and expense accounts). (3) Closing entry to record net income or net loss in the Retained Earnings account and to close the Income Summary account. (4) Closing entry for the Dividends account.
3. Income Summary and Dividends.

Chapter 23, Lesson 23-1, page 727

1. Student answers should include three of the following: the name of the business and the partners, the

investments of each partner, the duties and responsibilities of each partner, how profits and losses are to be divided, what happens if a partner dies, how the partnership is to be dissolved, and the duration of the agreement.

2. The partner's drawing account increases by a debit; Supplies decreases by a credit.

Chapter 23, Lesson 23-2, page 734

1. Each partner's share of net income or net loss.
2. Beginning capital amount, any additional investments made during the fiscal period, and each partner's withdrawal of assets during the fiscal period.
3. Compute ending capital as follows: Share of Net Income or Loss *less* Withdrawals *equals* Net Increase/Decrease in Capital. Beginning Capital *plus* Net Increase/Decrease in Capital *equals* Ending Capital.

Chapter 23, Lesson 23-3, page 741

1. As a credit to the Gain on Realization account.
2. As a debit to the Loss on Realization account.
3. Each partner's capital account.

Chapter 24, Lesson 24-1, page 760

1. (1) The lack of uniform commercial laws among countries makes settlement of disputes more difficult.

(2) Greater distances and sometimes more complex transportation methods increase the time to complete the transaction. (3) Because it may be difficult to determine a customer's financial condition and to take legal action if a customer does not pay, the risk of uncollected amounts is increased. (4) Unstable political conditions in some countries may affect the ability to receive payments from those countries.

2. The bill of lading serves as a receipt for merchandise received and as a contract for the delivery of the merchandise.
3. A sight draft is payable when the holder presents it for payment. A time draft is payable at a fixed or determinable future time after it is accepted.
4. To assure receipt of payment for those sales.
5. A draft is generally paid by a bank, and a trade acceptance is paid by the buyer. A seller generally has much more assurance of receiving payment from a bank than from a buyer.

Chapter 24, Lesson 24-2, page 763

1. To browse and compare the products offered by companies, and to do so at a convenient time and place for the customer.
2. Credit card sales information is processed in a manner similar to checks. Therefore, these sales are considered cash sales.

Glossary

401(k) A qualified retirement plan sponsored by an employer. (p. 356)

Accelerated depreciation Any method of depreciation which records greater depreciation expense in the early years and less depreciation expense in the later years. (p. 603)

Account A record that summarizes all the transactions pertaining to a single item in the accounting equation. (p. 14)

Account balance The difference between the increases and decreases in an account. (p. 14)

Account number The number assigned to an account. (p. 94)

Account title The name given to an account. (p. 14)

Accounting The process of planning, recording, analyzing, and interpreting financial information. (p. 6)

Accounting clerk An accounting worker who processes routine details about accounting transactions. (p. 142)

Accounting cycle The series of accounting activities included in recording financial information for a fiscal period. (p. 229)

Accounting equation An equation showing the relationship among assets, liabilities, and owner's equity. (p. 13)

Accounting period *See* fiscal period. (p. 159)

Accounting system A planned process designed to compile financial data and summarize the results in accounting records and reports. (p. 6)

Accounts payable Amounts to be paid in the future for goods or services already acquired. (p. 39)

Accounts payable ledger The subsidiary ledger containing vendor accounts. (p. 246)

Accounts payable trial balance *See* schedule of accounts payable. (p. 272)

Accounts receivable Amounts to be received in the future due to the sale of goods or services. (p. 44)

Accounts receivable ledger A subsidiary ledger containing all accounts for charge customers. (p. 284)

Accounts receivable trial balance *See* schedule of accounts receivable. (p. 308)

Accrual An entry recording revenue before the cash is received, or an expense before the cash is paid. (p. 648)

Accrual basis of accounting Reporting income when earned and expenses when incurred. (p. 163)

Accrued expenses Expenses incurred in one fiscal period, but not paid until a later fiscal period. (p. 652)

Accrued interest expense Interest incurred but not yet paid. (p. 652)

Accrued interest income Interest earned but not yet received. (p. 448)

Accrued revenue Revenue earned in one fiscal period but not received until a later fiscal period. (p. 447)

Accumulated depreciation The total amount of depreciation expense that has been recorded since the purchase of a plant asset. (p. 451)

Accumulated earnings The total gross earnings year to date for an employee. (p. 355)

Activity-based costing (ABC) Allocating factory overhead based on the level of major activities. (p. 638)

Adjusted gross income The amount of total income minus adjustments, reported on Form 1040. (p. 367)

Adjusted trial balance A trial balance prepared after adjusting entries are posted. (pp. 180, 457)

Adjusting entries Journal entries recorded to update general ledger accounts at the end of a fiscal period. (p. 176)

Adjustments Changes recorded on a work sheet to update general ledger accounts at the end of a fiscal period. (p. 163)

Aging of accounts receivable Analyzing accounts receivable according to when they are due. (p. 414)

Allowance method Crediting the estimated value of uncollectible accounts to a contra account. (p. 412)

Amortization The spreading of the cost of an intangible asset over its useful life. (p. 608)

Articles of incorporation A legal document that identifies basic characteristics of a corporation, which is a part of the application submitted to a state to become a corporation. (p. 244)

Assessed value The value of an asset determined by tax authorities for the purpose of calculating taxes. (p. 587)

Asset Anything of value that is owned. (p. 7)

Audit An examination of financial records, accounts, and supporting documents to check their accuracy. (p. 233)

Audit trail A paper or electronic path that provides a documented history of a transaction. (p. 233)

Auditor The accountant who conducts the audit. (p. 233)

B

Bad debt *See* uncollectible accounts. (p. 412)

Balance sheet A financial statement that reports assets, liabilities, and owner's equity on a specific date. (p. 169)

Bank statement A report of deposits, withdrawals, and bank balances sent to a depositor by a bank. (p. 129)

Batch report A report of credit card sales produced by a point-of-sale terminal. (p. 295)

Batching out The process of preparing a batch report from a point-of-sale terminal. (p. 295)

Beginning inventory The amount of inventory on hand at the beginning of a fiscal period. (p. 446)

Benchmark A standard used to compare financial performance. (p. 516)

Bill of exchange *See* draft. (p. 754)

Bill of lading A receipt signed by the authorized agent of a transportation company for merchandise received that also serves as a contract for the delivery of the merchandise. (p. 754)

Blank endorsement An endorsement consisting only of the endorser's signature. (p. 124)

Board of directors A group of persons elected by the stockholders to govern a corporation. (p. 333)

Bond A long-term promise to pay a specified amount on a specified date and to pay interest at stated intervals. (p. 562)

Bond issue All bonds representing the total amount of a loan. (p. 562)

Book value The difference between an asset's account balance and its related contra account balance. (p. 412)

Book value of a plant asset The original cost of a plant asset minus accumulated depreciation. (p. 451)

Book value of accounts receivable The difference between the balance of Accounts Receivable and its contra account, Allowance for Uncollectible Accounts. (p. 412)

Budget A financial road map used by individuals and companies as a guide for spending and saving. (p. 193)

Business ethics The use of ethics in making business decisions. (p. 8)

Business plan A formal written document that describes the nature of a business and how it will operate. (p. 10)

Canceled check A check which has been paid by the bank. (p. 129)

Capital The assets or other financial resources available to a business. (p. 244)

Capital account An account used to summarize the owner's equity in a business. (p. 14)

Capital expenditures Purchases of plant assets used in the operation of a business. (p. 558)

Capital stock The total shares of ownership in a corporation. (p. 244)

Cash basis of accounting Reporting income when the cash is received and expenses when the cash is paid. (p. 163)

Cash discount A deduction that a vendor allows on an invoice amount to encourage prompt payment. (p. 260)

Cash flow The cash receipts and cash payments of a company. (p. 691)

Cash over A petty cash on hand amount that is more than the recorded amount. (p. 143)

Cash payments journal A special journal used to record only cash payment transactions. (p. 260)

Cash receipts journal A special journal used to record only cash receipt transactions. (p. 296)

Cash sale A sale in which the customer pays for the total amount of the sale at the time of the transaction. (p. 294)

Cash short A petty cash on hand amount that is less than the recorded amount. (p. 143)

Certified public accountant (CPA) An accountant who has passed the uniform certified public accounting exam and met the licensing requirement for a state. (p. 157)

Chart of accounts A list of accounts used by a business. (p. 36)

Charter A state approves the formation of a corporation by issuing a charter, the legal right for a business to conduct operations as a corporation. (p. 244)

Check A business form ordering a bank to pay cash from a bank account. (p. 60)

Checking account A bank account from which payments can be ordered by a depositor. (p. 123)

Closing entries Journal entries used to prepare temporary accounts for a new fiscal period. (p. 215)

Code of conduct A statement that guides the ethical behavior of a company and its employees. (p. 122)

Collateral Assets pledged to a creditor to guarantee repayment of a loan. (p. 559)

Commercial invoice A statement prepared by the seller of merchandise addressed to the buyer showing a detailed listing and description of merchandise sold, including prices and terms. (p. 754)

Commission A method of paying an employee based on the amount of sales the employee generates. Commissions are normally calculated as a percent of an employee's sales. (p. 346)

Comparative financial statements Financial statements that provide information for multiple fiscal periods. (pp. 207, 517)

Compound interest Interest paid on an original amount deposited in a bank plus any interest that has been paid. (p. 11)

Comptroller *See* controller. (p. 385)

Contra account An account that reduces a related account on a financial statement. (p. 263)

Contract of sale A document that details all the terms agreed to by seller and buyer for a sales transaction. (p. 753)

Controller The chief accountant in an organization, having responsibility for both financial and managerial accounting activities. Sometimes called *comptroller*. (p. 385)

Controlling account An account in a general ledger that summarizes all accounts in a subsidiary ledger. (p. 246)

Corporation An organization with the legal rights of a person which many persons or other corporations may own. (p. 244)

Correcting entry If a transaction has been improperly journalized and posted to the ledger, the incorrect journal entry should be corrected with an additional journal entry, called a correcting entry. (p. 109)

Cost accounting The field of accounting that identifies and measures costs. (p. 563)

Cost of capital The ratio of interest and dividend payments to the proceeds from debt and capital financing. (p. 569)

Cost of goods sold *See* cost of merchandise sold. (p. 476)

Cost of merchandise The amount a business pays for goods it purchases to sell. (p. 250)

Cost of merchandise sold The original price of all merchandise sold during a fiscal period. (p. 476)

Cost of sales *See* cost of merchandise sold. (p. 476)

Credit An amount recorded on the right side of an account. (p. 33)

Credit limit The maximum outstanding balance allowed to a customer by a vendor. (p. 267)

Credit line *See* line of credit. (p. 552)

Credit memorandum A form prepared by the vendor showing the amount deducted for returns and allowances. (p. 327)

Creditor A person or business to whom a liability is owed. (p. 16)

Current assets Cash and other assets expected to be exchanged for cash or consumed within a year. (p. 450)

Current liabilities Liabilities due within a short time, usually within a year. (p. 489)

Current ratio A ratio that measures the relationship of current assets to current liabilities. (p. 535)

Debit An amount recorded on the left side of an account. (p. 33)

Debit card A bank card that automatically deducts the amount of a purchase from the checking account of the cardholder. (p. 138)

Debit memorandum A form prepared by the customer showing the price deduction taken by the customer for a return or an allowance. (p. 322)

Debt financing Obtaining capital by borrowing money for a period of time. (p. 552)

Debt ratio Total liabilities divided by total assets. (p. 526)

Declaring a dividend Action by a board of directors to distribute corporate earnings to stockholders. (p. 333)

Declining-balance method of depreciation A type of accelerated depreciation that multiplies the book value of an asset by a constant depreciation rate to determine annual depreciation. (p. 603)

Defaulting Not making payments on a loan when they are due. (p. 673)

Deferral An entry recording the receipt of cash before the related revenue is earned, or payment of cash before the related expense is incurred. (p. 648)

Deferred expenses Payments for goods or services which have not yet been received. *See also* prepaid expense. (p. 660)

Deferred revenue Cash received for goods or services which have not yet been provided. (p. 658)

Deficit A negative balance that remains after total expenses are subtracted from total income. (p. 193)

Deposit The payment of payroll taxes to the government. (p. 392)

Deposit slip A bank form which lists the checks, currency, and coins an account holder is adding to a bank account. (p. 123)

Depreciation A loss in the usefulness of a plant asset as a result of wear or obsolescence. (p. 450)

Depreciation expense The portion of a plant asset's cost that is transferred to an expense account in each fiscal period during that asset's useful life. (p. 450)

Direct deposit The payment of an employee's net pay using electronic funds transfer. (p. 366)

Direct write-off method Recording uncollectible accounts expense only when an amount is actually known to be uncollectible. (p. 419)

Discount period The period of time during which a customer may take a cash discount. (p. 263)

Dishonored check A check that a bank refuses to pay. (p. 135)

Dishonored note A note that is not paid when due. (p. 429)

Distribution of net income statement A partnership financial statement showing net income or loss distribution to partners. (p. 728)

Dividend yield The relationship between dividends per share and market price per share. (p. 534)

Dividends Earnings distributed to stockholders. (p. 332)

Double declining-balance method of depreciation A declining-balance rate that is two times the straight-line rate. (p. 603)

Double-entry accounting The recording of debit and credit parts of a transaction. (p. 59)

Draft A written, signed, and dated order from one party ordering another party, usually a bank, to pay money to a third party. (p. 754)

Due date The date by which an invoice must be paid. (p. 252)

Earnings per share Net income after federal income tax divided by the number of outstanding shares of stock. (p. 533)

EFT *See* electronic funds transfer. (p. 137)

Electronic funds transfer A computerized cash payments system that transfers funds without the use of checks, currency, or other paper documents. (p. 137)

Employee earnings record A business form used to record details of an employee's earnings and deductions. (p. 360)

Ending inventory The actual count of merchandise at the end of a fiscal period. (p. 446)

Endorsement A signature or stamp on the back of a check transferring ownership. (p. 124)

Endorsement in full *See* special endorsement. (p. 124)

Entrepreneur Someone who owns, operates, and takes the risk of a business venture. (p. 5)

Entry Information for each transaction recorded in a journal. (p. 59)

Equities Financial rights to the assets of a business. (p. 13)

Equity The difference between assets and liabilities. (p. 7)

Equity financing Obtaining capital by issuing stock in a corporation. (p. 565)

Ethics The principles of right and wrong that guide an individual in making decisions. (p. 8)

Exhibit *See* supporting schedule. (p. 492)

Expense The cost of goods or services used to operate a business. (p. 19)

Exports Goods or services shipped out of a seller's home country to another country. (p. 752)

Face amount *See* principal. (p. 425)

Factory overhead All expenses other than direct materials and direct labor that apply to making products. (p. 638)

Federal unemployment tax A federal tax paid by employers to administer the unemployment program. (p. 382)

FIFO *See* first-in, first-out inventory costing method. (p. 626)

File maintenance The procedure for arranging accounts in a general ledger, assigning account numbers, and keeping records current. (p. 95)

Financial accounting The area of accounting which focuses on reporting information to external users. (p. 190)

Financial leverage The ability of a business to use borrowed funds to increase its earnings. (p. 571)

Financial ratio A comparison between two components of financial information. (p. 195)

Financial statements Financial reports that summarize the financial condition and operations of a business. (p. 6)

Financing activities Cash receipts and payments involving debt or equity transactions. (p. 692)

First-in, first-out inventory costing method Using the price of merchandise purchased first to calculate the cost of merchandise sold first. (p. 626)

Fiscal period The length of time for which a business summarizes its financial information and reports its financial performance. (p. 159)

Fiscal year A fiscal period consisting of 12 consecutive months. (p. 159)

Foreclosure When the bank or finance company takes possession of mortgaged property. (p. 673)

Forensic accountant An accountant who combines accounting and investigating skills to uncover suspected fraudulent business activity, or to prevent such activity. (p. 48)

Franchise A right granted to an individual or business to sell the products or services of another, larger business within a defined geographical area. (p. 55)

FUTA *See* federal unemployment tax. (p. 382)

GAAP Generally accepted accounting principles. The standards and rules that accountants follow while recording and reporting financial activities. (p. 11)

Gain An increase in equity resulting from activity other than selling goods or services. (p. 600)

Gain on plant assets An increase in equity that results when a plant asset is sold for more than book value. (p. 600)

General amount column A journal amount column that is not headed with an account title. (p. 260)

General journal A journal with two amount columns in which all kinds of entries can be recorded. (p. 320)

General ledger A ledger that contains all accounts needed to prepare financial statements. (p. 94)

Generally accepted accounting principles *See* GAAP. (p. 11)

Gross earnings *See* total earnings. (p. 346)

Gross margin Gross profit as a percent of net sales. (p. 518)

Gross pay *See* total earnings. (p. 346)

Gross profit The operating revenue remaining after cost of merchandise sold has been deducted. (p. 476)

Gross profit margin *See* gross margin. (p. 518)

Gross profit method of estimating inventory Estimating inventory by using the previous year's percentage of gross profit on operations. (p. 633)

Gross profit on sales *See* gross profit. (p. 476)

Gross wages *See* total earnings. (p. 346)

Horizontal analysis A comparison of one item on a financial statement with the same item on a previous period's financial statement. (p. 528)

Imports Goods or services shipped into the buyer's home country from another country. (p. 752)

Income from operations The operating revenue remaining after the cost of merchandise sold and operating expenses have been deducted. (p. 478)

Income statement A financial statement showing the revenue and expenses for a fiscal period. (p. 170)

Individual retirement account (IRA) A qualified retirement plan that provides most individuals with a deferred federal income tax benefit. (p. 356)

Intangible asset An asset that does not have physical substance. (p. 607)

Intellectual property Anything, or any process, that is protected by patent, trademark, or copyright. *See also* intangible asset. (p. 648)

Interest An amount paid for the use of money for a period of time. (p. 11)

Interest expense Interest accrued on borrowed funds. (p. 555)

Interest income The interest earned on money loaned. (p. 428)

Interest rate The percentage of the principal that is due for the use of the funds secured by a note. (p. 425)

Interim financial statements Financial statements providing information for a time period shorter than the fiscal year. (p. 207)

Internal controls Processes and procedures employed within a business to ensure that its operations are conducted ethically, accurately, and reliably. (p. 338)

Inventory A list of assets, usually containing the value of individual items. (p. 249)

Inventory record A form used during a physical inventory to record information about each item of merchandise on hand. (p. 622)

Investing activities Cash receipts and cash payments involving the sale or purchase of assets used to earn revenue over a period of time. (p. 692)

Invoice A form describing the goods or services sold, the quantity, the price, and the terms of sale. (p. 60)

IRA *See* individual retirement account. (p. 356)

Issue date The date on which a business issues a note, bond, or stock. (p. 565)

Journal A form for recording transactions in chronological order. (p. 58)

Journalizing Recording transactions in a journal. (p. 58)

Language of business *See* accounting. (p. 6)

Last-in, first-out inventory costing method Using the price of merchandise purchased last to calculate the cost of merchandise sold first. (p. 627)

Ledger A group of accounts. (p. 94)

Letter of credit A letter issued by a bank guaranteeing that a named individual or business will be paid a specified amount provided stated conditions are met. (p. 753)

Liability An amount owed. (p. 7)

LIFO *See* last-in, first-out inventory costing method. (p. 627)

Line of credit A bank loan agreement that provides immediate short-term access to cash. (p. 552)

Liquid assets *See* quick assets. (p. 535)

Liquidation of a partnership The process of paying a partnership's liabilities and distributing remaining assets to the partners. (p. 735)

Liquidity ratio A ratio that measures the ability of a business to pay its current financial obligations. (p. 535)

List price The retail price listed in a catalog or on an Internet site. (p. 260)

Long-term liabilities Liabilities owed for more than a year. (p. 489)

Lookback period The 12-month period that ends on June 30th of the prior year that is used to determine how frequently a business must deposit payroll taxes. (p. 392)

Loss A decrease in equity resulting from activity other than selling goods or services. (p. 601)

Loss on plant assets The decrease in equity that results when a plant asset is sold for less than book value. (p. 601)

Lower of cost or market inventory costing method (LCM) Using the lower of cost or market price to calculate the cost of ending merchandise inventory. (p. 631)

Maker of a note The person or business that signs a note and thus promises to make payment. (p. 425)

Managerial accounting The area of accounting that focuses on reporting information to internal users. (p. 190)

Marginal tax rate The tax rate associated with a tax bracket. (p. 458)

Market ratio A ratio that measures a corporation's financial performance in relation to the market value of its stock. (p. 534)

Market value The price that must be paid to replace an asset. (p. 631)

Markup The amount a business adds to the cost of merchandise to establish the selling price. (p. 284)

Maturity date The date on which the principal of a note is due to be repaid. (p. 425)

Maturity value The amount that is due on the maturity date of a note. (p. 427)

Medicare tax A federal tax paid for hospital insurance. (p. 355)

Memorandum A form on which a brief message is written to describe a transaction. (p. 61)

Merchandise Goods that a business purchases to sell. (p. 244)

Merchandise inventory The goods a business has on hand for sale to customers. (p. 249)

Merchandising business A business that purchases and resells goods. (p. 244)

Net income The difference between total revenue and total expenses when total revenue is greater. (p. 171)

Net loss The difference between total revenue and total expenses when total expenses are greater. (p. 172)

Net pay Earnings paid to an employee after payroll taxes and other deductions. (p. 359)

Net price The price after the trade discount has been deducted from the list price. (p. 260)

Net realizable value The amount of accounts receivable a business expects to collect. (p. 412)

Net sales The amount of sales, less sales discounts and sales returns and allowances. (p. 475)

Net worth statement A formal report that shows what an individual owns, what an individual owes, and the difference between the two. (p. 7)

Nominal accounts *See* temporary accounts. (p. 215)

Non-operating expense Expenses that are not related to a business's normal operations. (p. 555)

Non-sufficient funds check A check dishonored by the bank because of insufficient funds in the account of the maker of the check. (p. 135)

Normal balance The side of an account that is increased is called the normal balance of the account. (p. 33)

Note *See* promissory note. (p. 425)

Note payable A promissory note signed by a business and given to a creditor. (p. 425)

Note receivable A promissory note that a business accepts from a person or business. (p. 425)

NSF check *See* non-sufficient funds check. (p. 135)

Number of days' sales in inventory A financial ratio determined by dividing 365 days by the inventory turnover ratio. (p. 642)

Opening an account Writing an account title and number on the heading of an account. (p. 96)

Operating activities The cash receipts and payments necessary to operate a business on a day-to-day basis. (p. 692)

Operating expense ratio Total operating expenses as a percent of net sales. (p. 519)

Operating expenses The expenses incurred by a business in its normal operations. (p. 478)

Operating income *See* income from operations. (p. 478)

Operating margin Income from operations as a percent of net sales. (p. 519)

Operating revenue The revenue earned by a business from its normal business operations. (p. 475)

Owner's equity The amount remaining after the value of all liabilities is subtracted from the value of all assets. (p. 13)

Owners' equity statement A financial statement that summarizes the changes in owners' equity during a fiscal period. (p. 730)

Par value A value assigned to a share of stock and printed on the stock certificate. (pp. 483, 565)

Partner Each member of a partnership. (p. 722)

Partnership A business in which two or more persons combine their assets and skills. (p. 722)

Partnership agreement A written agreement setting forth the conditions under which a partnership is to operate. (p. 722)

Pay period The number of days or weeks of work covered by an employee's paycheck. (p. 346)

Pay yourself first A budgeting strategy of setting aside at least 10% of after-tax income for saving and investing. (p. 193)

Payee The person or business to whom the amount of a note is payable. (p. 425)

Payroll The total amount earned by all employees for a pay period. (p. 346)

Payroll clerk The accounting staff position that compiles and computes payroll data, then prepares, journalizes, and posts payroll transactions. (p. 346)

Payroll deduction Any amount withheld from an employee's gross earnings. (p. 352)

Payroll register An accounting form that summarizes the earnings, deductions, and net pay of all employees for one pay period. (p. 358)

Payroll taxes Taxes based on the payroll of a business. (p. 351)

Percent of accounts receivable method A method that uses an analysis of accounts receivable to estimate the amount that will be uncollectible. (p. 413)

Percent of sales method A method used to estimate uncollectible accounts receivable which assumes that a percentage of each sales dollar will eventually become uncollectible. (p. 413)

Periodic inventory A merchandise inventory evaluated at the end of a fiscal period. (p. 249)

Permanent accounts Accounts used to accumulate information from one fiscal period to the next. (p. 215)

Perpetual inventory An inventory determined by keeping a continuous record of increases, decreases, and the balance on hand of each item of merchandise. (p. 249)

Personal net worth The difference between personal assets and personal liabilities. (p. 7)

Personal property All property not classified as real property. (p. 587)

Petty cash An amount of cash kept on hand and used for making small payments. (p. 140)

Petty cash slip A form showing proof of a petty cash payment. (p. 141)

Physical inventory A periodic inventory conducted by counting, weighing, or measuring items of merchandise on hand. (p. 249)

Plant asset record An accounting form on which a business records information about each plant asset. (p. 594)

Plant assets Physical assets that will be used for a number of years in the operation of a business. (p. 450)

Point-of-sale (POS) terminal A specialized computer used to collect, store, and report all the information about a sales transaction. (p. 294)

Post-closing trial balance A trial balance prepared after the closing entries are posted. (p. 228)

Postdated check A check with a future date on it. (p. 126)

Posting Transferring information from a journal entry to a ledger account. (p. 98)

Preferred stock A class of stock that gives preferred shareholders preference over common shareholders in dividends along with other rights. (p. 567)

Prepaid expense Cash paid for an expense in one fiscal period that is not used until a later period. *See also* deferred expenses. (p. 163)

Price-earnings ratio The relationship between the market value per share and earnings per share of a stock. (p. 534)

Prime interest rate The interest rate charged to a bank's most creditworthy customers. (p. 552)

Principal The original amount of a note, sometimes referred to as the *face amount*. (p. 425)

Profit margin Net income after federal income tax as a percent of net sales. (p. 517)

Profitability ratio A ratio that measures the ability of a business to generate income. (p. 516)

Promissory note A written and signed promise to pay a sum of money at a specified time. (p. 425)

Proprietorship A business owned by one person. (p. 10)

Proving cash Determining that the amount of cash agrees with the balance of the cash account in the accounting records. (p. 107)

Public accounting firm An accounting business that helps other businesses with accounting issues. (p. 233)

Purchase invoice An invoice used as a source document for recording a purchase on account transaction. (p. 252)

Purchase on account A transaction in which the items purchased are to be paid for later. (p. 252)

Purchase order A form requesting that a vendor sell merchandise to a business. (p. 251)

Purchases allowance Credit allowed for part of the purchase price of merchandise that is not returned, resulting in a decrease in the customer's account payable to the vendor. (p. 322)

Purchases discount When a company that has purchased merchandise on account takes a cash discount. (p. 263)

Purchases journal A special journal used to record only purchases of merchandise on account. (p. 252)

Purchases return Credit allowed for the purchase price of returned merchandise, resulting in a decrease in the customer's account payable to the vendor. (p. 322)

Qualified retirement plan A retirement savings plan approved by the Internal Revenue Service that provides individuals with a tax benefit. *See also* 401(k), individual retirement account, Roth IRA. (p. 356)

Quick assets Cash and other current assets that can be quickly converted into cash. (p. 535)

Quick ratio A ratio that measures the relationship of quick assets to current liabilities. (p. 535)

Rate of return on sales *See* operating margin. (p. 519)

Ratio analysis The calculation and interpretation of a financial ratio. (p. 195)

Real accounts *See* permanent accounts. (p. 215)

Real estate *See* real property. (p. 587)

Real property Land and anything attached to the land. (p. 587)

Realization Cash received from the sale of assets during liquidation of a partnership. (p. 735)

Receipt A business form giving written acknowledgement for cash received. (p. 61)

Recurring entries Transactions that are set up for automated entry in computerized accounting systems. (p. 463)

Recurring transactions *See* recurring entries. (p. 463)

Requisition A form requesting the purchase of merchandise. (p. 251)

Residual value *See* salvage value. (p. 450)

Restrictive endorsement An endorsement restricting further transfer of a check's ownership. (p. 125)

Retail merchandising business A merchandising business that sells to those who use or consume the goods. (p. 244)

Retained earnings An amount earned by a corporation and not yet distributed to stockholders. (p. 332)

Return on investment The ratio of the money earned on an investment relative to the amount of the investment. (p. 584)

Return on sales (ROS) The ratio of net income to total sales. (p. 196)

Revenue An increase in equity resulting from the sale of goods or services. (p. 18)

Revenue expenditure The payment of an operating expense necessary to earn revenue. (p. 552)

Reversing entry An entry made at the beginning of one fiscal period to reverse an adjusting entry made in the previous fiscal period. (p. 649)

ROI *See* return on investment. (p. 584)

Rollover The movement of funds from one qualified retirement plan to another. (p. 520)

Roth individual retirement account (Roth IRA) A qualified retirement plan that allows tax-free withdrawals from the account. (p. 356)

Salary A fixed annual sum of money divided among equal pay periods. (p. 346)

Salary expense The total of gross earnings for all employees earning hourly wages, salaries, and commissions. (p. 378)

Sale on account A sale for which payment will be received at a later date. (p. 18)

Sales allowance Credit allowed to a customer for part of the sales price of merchandise that is not returned, resulting in a decrease in the accounts receivable of the merchandising business. (p. 327)

Sales discount A cash discount on a sale taken by the customer. (p. 296)

Sales invoice An invoice used as a source document for recording a sale on account. A sales invoice is also referred to as a *sales ticket* or a *sales slip*. (p. 60)

Sales journal A special journal used to record only sales of merchandise on account. (p. 287)

Sales return Credit allowed to a customer for the sales price of returned merchandise, resulting in a decrease in the accounts receivable of the merchandising business. (p. 327)

Sales slip *See* sales invoice. (p. 60)

Sales tax A tax on a sale of merchandise or services. (p. 286)

Sales ticket *See* sales invoice. (p. 60)

Salvage value The amount that will be received for an asset at the time of its disposal. (p. 450)

Schedule of accounts payable A listing of vendor accounts, account balances, and the total amount due to all vendors. Some businesses call this listing an *accounts payable trial balance*. (p. 272)

Schedule of accounts receivable A listing of customer accounts, account balances, and total amount due from all customers. (p. 308)

Scrap value *See* salvage value. (p. 450)

Selling price The amount a business receives from the sale of an item of merchandise. (p. 284)

Service business A business that performs an activity for a fee. (p. 10)

Share of stock A unit of ownership in a corporation. (p. 244)

Sight draft A draft payable on sight when the holder presents it for payment. (p. 754)

Social security tax A federal tax paid for old-age, survivors, and disability insurance. (p. 355)

Sole proprietorship *See* proprietorship. (p. 10)

Solvency ratio A ratio that measures the ability of a business to pay its long-term liabilities. (p. 526)

Source document A business paper from which information is obtained for a journal entry. (p. 59)

Special amount column A journal amount column headed with an account title. (p. 252)

Special endorsement An endorsement indicating a new owner of a check. (p. 124)

Special journal A journal used to record only one kind of transaction. (p. 251)

Stakeholders Any persons or groups who will be affected by an action. (p. 191)

State unemployment tax A state tax paid by employers that is used to pay benefits to unemployed workers. (p. 382)

Stated interest rate The interest rate used to calculate periodic interest payments on a bond. (p. 562)

Statement of cash flows A financial statement that summarizes cash receipts and cash payments resulting from business activities during a fiscal period. (p. 691)

Statement of stockholders' equity A financial statement that shows changes in a corporation's ownership for a fiscal period. (p. 482)

Stock ledger A file of stock records for all merchandise on hand. (p. 623)

Stock record A form used to show the kind of merchandise, quantity received, quantity sold, and balance on hand. (p. 623)

Stockholder The owner of one or more shares of stock. (p. 244)

Straight-line method of depreciation Recording an equal amount of depreciation expense for a plant asset in each year of its useful life. (p. 451)

Subledger *See* subsidiary ledger. (p. 246)

Subsidiary ledger A ledger that is summarized in a single general ledger account. Accountants often refer to a subsidiary ledger as a *subledger*. (p. 246)

Supplementary report *See* supporting schedule. (p. 492)

Supporting schedule A report prepared to give details about an item on a principal financial statement. (p. 492)

Surplus A positive balance that remains after total expenses are subtracted from total income. (p. 193)

SUTA *See* state unemployment tax. (p. 382)

T account An accounting device used to analyze transactions. (p. 33)

Tax base The maximum amount of earnings on which a tax is calculated. (p. 355)

Tax bracket Each tax rate and taxable income amount on one line of a tax table. (p. 458)

Taxable income The amount of total income minus adjustments, deductions, and exemptions that is used to calculate income tax. (p. 367)

Temporary accounts Accounts used to accumulate information until it is transferred to the owner's capital account. (p. 215)

Term *See* time of a note. (p. 425)

Terminal summary The report that summarizes the cash and credit card sales of a point-of-sale terminal. A terminal summary is also known as a *Z tape*. (p. 294)

Terms of sale An agreement between a buyer and a seller about payment for merchandise. (p. 252)

Time clock A device used to record the dates and times of every employee's arrivals and departures. (p. 347)

Time draft A draft that is payable at a fixed or determinable future time after it is accepted. (p. 757)

Time of a note The length of time from the signing date to the maturity date, usually expressed as the number of days. (p. 425)

Total earnings The total amount paid by a business for an employee's work, earned by a wage, salary, or commission. (p. 346)

Total income The sum of all sources of income reported on Form 1040. (p. 367)

Trade acceptance A form signed by a buyer at the time of a sale of merchandise in which the buyer promises to pay the seller a specified sum of money, usually at a stated time in the future. (p. 758)

Trade discount A reduction in the list price granted to a merchandising business. (p. 260)

Transaction Any business activity that changes assets, liabilities, or owner's equity. (p. 14)

Trend analysis An analysis of changes over time. (p. 517)

Trial balance A proof of the equality of debits and credits in a general ledger. (p. 160)

Unadjusted trial balance A trial balance prepared before adjusting entries are posted. (p. 441)

Uncollectible accounts Accounts receivable that cannot be collected. (p. 412)

Underwater mortgage A mortgage that has a balance higher than the value of the mortgaged property. (p. 673)

Unearned revenue *See* deferred revenue. (p. 658)

Useful life The period of time over which an asset contributes to the earnings of a business. (p. 450)

Vendor A business from which merchandise, supplies, or other assets are purchased. (p. 246)

Vertical analysis Reporting an amount on a financial statement as a percentage of another item on the same financial statement. (p. 195)

Voided check A check that cannot be processed because the maker has made it invalid. (p. 127)

Voucher check A check which has a detachable check stub, or *voucher*, that contains detailed information about the cash payment. (p. 364)

Wage The amount paid to an employee for every hour worked. (p. 346)

Wage garnishment A process that requires an employer to withhold a portion of an employee's paycheck to pay a court-ordered debt settlement. (p. 393)

Weighted-average inventory costing method Using the average cost of beginning inventory plus merchandise purchased during a fiscal period to calculate the cost of merchandise sold. (p. 628)

Wholesale merchandising business A business that buys and resells merchandise primarily to other merchandising businesses. (p. 244)

Withdrawals Assets taken from the business for the owner's personal use. (p. 20)

Withholding allowance A deduction from total earnings for each person legally supported by a taxpayer, including the employee. (p. 352)

Work sheet A columnar accounting form used to summarize the general ledger information needed to prepare financial statements. (p. 159)

Working capital The amount of total current assets less total current liabilities. (p. 535)

Writing off an account Canceling the balance of a customer account because the customer does not pay. (p. 418)

Z tape *See* terminal summary. (p. 294)

401(k) *401(k)* Un plan de jubilación calificado que es patrocinado por un empleador. (p. 356)

Accelerated depreciation *Depreciación acelerada* Cualquier método de depreciación que registra mayores gastos de depreciación en los primeros años y menos gastos de depreciación en los últimos años. (p. 603)

Account *Cuenta* Un archivo que resume todas las transacciones en relación a un solo artículo en la ecuación de contabilidad. (p. 14)

Account balance *Saldo de la cuenta* La diferencia entre los aumentos y reducciones en una cuenta. (p. 14)

Account number *Número de cuenta* El número asignado a una cuenta. (p. 94)

Account title *Título de cuenta* El nombre dado a una cuenta. (p. 14)

Accounting *Contabilidad* El proceso de planificar, registrar, analizar, e interpretar información financiera. (p. 6)

Accounting clerk *Auxiliar de contabilidad* Un trabajador de contabilidad quien procesa detalles rutinarios sobre las transacciones de contabilidad. (p. 142)

Accounting cycle *Ciclo contable* La serie de actividades de contabilidad incluidas en el registro de la información financiera en un período fiscal. (p. 229)

Accounting equation *Ecuación de contabilidad* Una ecuación que muestra la relación entre activos, responsabilidades, y capital del dueño. (p. 13)

Accounting period *Período de contabilidad* (Véase fiscal period *período fiscal*.) (p. 159)

Accounting system *Sistema de contabilidad* Un proceso planificado diseñado de acumular datos financieros y hacer un resumen de los resultados en registros y reportes de contabilidad. (p. 6)

Accounts payable *Cuentas por pagar* Cantidades a ser pagadas en el futuro por los bienes y servicios ya adquiridos. (p. 39)

Accounts payable ledger *Libro mayor de cuentas por pagar* El libro mayor auxiliar que contiene las cuentas de los proveedores. (p. 246)

Accounts payable trial balance *Balance de comprobación de cuentas por pagar* (Véase schedule of accounts payable *calendario de cuentas por pagar*.) (p. 272)

Accounts receivable *Cuentas por cobrar* Cantidades a ser recibidas en el futuro debido a la venta de bienes o servicios. (p. 44)

Accounts receivable ledger *Libro mayor de cuentas por cobrar* Un libro mayor auxiliar que contiene sólo cuentas para clientes a crédito. (p. 284)

Accounts receivable trial balance *Balance de comprobación de cuentas por cobrar* (Véase schedule of accounts receivable *calendario de cuentas por cobrar*.) (p. 308)

Accrual *Acumulación* Una entrada registrando ganancia antes de que el efectivo sea recibido, o un gasto antes de que el efectivo sea pagado. (p. 648)

Accrual basis of accounting *Base de acumulación de contabilidad* Reportar los ingresos cuando se ganen y los gastos cuando sean incurridos. (p. 163)

Accrued expenses *Gastos acumulados* Gastos incurridos durante un período fiscal, pero pagados en otro período fiscal posterior. (p. 652)

Accrued interest expense *Gasto del interés acumulado* Interés incurrido, pero aún no pagado. (p. 652)

Accrued interest income *Ganancia del interés acumulado* Interés ganado, pero aún no recibido. (p. 448)

Accrued revenue *Ingreso acumulado* Ingreso ganado en un período fiscal, pero no recibido hasta un período fiscal posterior. (p. 447)

Accumulated depreciation *Depreciación acumulada* La cantidad total de gastos de depreciación que se ha registrado desde la compra de un activo fijo. (p. 451)

Accumulated earnings *Ingresos acumulados* El total de los ingresos brutos de un empleado del año. (p. 355)

Activity-based costing (ABC) *Determinación de costo por actividad (costeo ABC)* Asignar los gastos generales de la fábrica basados en el nivel de actividades mayores. (p. 638)

Adjusted gross income *Ingreso bruto ajustado* La cantidad de ingreso total menos los ajustes reportados en el formulario 1040. (p. 367)

Adjusted trial balance *Balance de comprobación ajustado* Un balance de comprobación después de registrarse los asientos de ajuste. (p. 457)

Adjusting entries *Asientos de ajuste* Asientos registrados en el diario para poner al corriente las cuentas del libro mayor al final de un período fiscal. (p. 176)

Adjustments *Ajustes* Cambios registrados en una hoja de trabajo para poner al corriente las cuentas del libro mayor al final de un período fiscal. (p. 163)

Aging of accounts receivable *Antigüedad de cuentas por cobrar* Analizar las cuentas por cobrar de acuerdo a cuando se deben de pagar. (p. 414)

Allowance method *Método de concesión* Acreditar el valor estimado de cuentas incobrables a una contra cuenta. (p. 412)

Amortization *Amortización* Distribuir el costo de un activo intangible a lo largo de su utilidad de vida. (p. 608)

Articles of incorporation *Acta constitutiva de una sociedad* Un documento legal que identifica las características básicas de una corporación, lo cual es parte de la solicitud sometida al estado para volverse una corporación. (p. 244)

Assessed value *Valor asesorado* El valor de un bien determinado por autoridades de impuestos para calcular los impuestos. (p. 587)

Asset *Activo* Cualquier cosa de valor que se posee. (p. 7)

Audit *Auditoría* Un análisis de los archivos financieros, cuentas, y documentos que los apoyen para verificar su precisión. (p. 233)

Audit trail *Pista de auditoría* Un papel o trayectoria electrónica que provee una historia documentada de una transacción. (p. 233)

Auditor *Auditor* El contador quien lleva a cabo la auditoría. (p. 233)

Bad debt *Deuda irrecuperable* (Véase uncollectible accounts *cuentas incobrables*.) (p. 412)

Balance sheet *Balance general* Un estado financiero que informa sobre los activos, las obligaciones y el capital propio en una fecha específica. (p. 169)

Bank statement *Estado de cuenta bancaria* Un informe de depósitos, retiros y saldo bancario, enviado por un banco a un depositante. (p. 129)

Batch report *Reporte colectivo* Un reporte de las ventas de tarjetas de crédito producido por una terminal de punto de venta. (p. 295)

Batching out *Procesamiento colectivo* El proceso de preparar un reporte de ventas de tarjetas de crédito producidas por una terminal de punto de venta. (p. 295)

Beginning inventory *Inventario inicial* La cantidad de inventario a la mano al comienzo de un período fiscal. (p. 446)

Benchmark *Estándar de comprobación* Un estándar utilizado para comparar el desempeño financiero. (p. 516)

Bill of exchange *Letra de cambio* (Véase draft *letra de cambio*.) (p. 754)

Bill of lading *Conocimiento de embarque* Un recibo firmado por el agente autorizado de una compañía de transportación para la mercancía recibida, que también sirve como un contrato para la entrega de la misma. (p. 754)

Blank endorsement *Endoso en blanco* Un endoso que consiste únicamente de la firma del endosante. (p. 124)

Board of directors *Consejo directivo* Un grupo de personas elegidas por los accionistas para dirigir una corporación. (p. 333)

Bond *Bono* Una promesa de largo plazo de pagar una cantidad específica en una fecha específica y de pagar interés a intervalos estipulados. (p. 562)

Bond issue *Emisión de bonos* Todos los bonos que representan la cantidad total de un préstamo. (p. 562)

Book value *Valor contable* La diferencia entre el saldo de cuenta de un activo y el saldo de su contra cuenta relacionada. (p. 412)

Book value of a plant asset *Valor contable de un activo fijo* El costo original de un activo fijo menos la depreciación acumulada. (p. 451)

Book value of accounts receivable *Valor contable de cuentas por cobrar* La diferencia entre el saldo de cuentas por cobrar y su contra cuenta, la asignación de cuentas incobrables. (p. 412)

Budget *Presupuesto* Una guía financiera utilizada por los individuos y compañías como una guía de gastos y ahorros. (p. 193)

Business ethics *Ética de negocios* El uso de ética en tomar decisiones de negocios. (p. 8)

Business plan *Plan de negocios* Un documento formal por escrito que describe la naturaleza de un negocio y como va a funcionar. (p. 10)

Canceled check *Cheque cancelado* Un cheque que ha sido pagado por el banco. (p. 129)

Capital *Capital* Los activos u otros recursos financieros disponibles para un negocio. (p. 244)

Capital account *Cuenta de capital* Una cuenta utilizada para resumir el capital propio en un negocio. (p. 14)

Capital expenditures *Gastos de capital* Compras de activos fijos utilizados en la operación de un negocio. (p. 558)

Capital stock *Capital social* El número total de acciones en propiedad en una corporación. (p. 244)

Cash basis of accounting *Principio contable de caja* Reportar los ingresos cuando sean recibidos y los gastos cuando el dinero sea pagado. (p. 163)

Cash discount *Descuento en efectivo* Una deducción que un vendedor permite en una factura para motivar un pago rápido. (p. 260)

Cash flow *Flujo de caja* Los recibos y pagos de efectivo de una compañía. (p. 691)

Cash over *Exceso de caja* Una cantidad de efectivo disponible que es mas de la cantidad registrada. (p. 143)

Cash payments journal *Diario de pagos en efectivo* Un diario especial que se usa para registrar únicamente transacciones de pago en efectivo. (p. 260)

Cash receipts journal *Diario de recibos en efectivo* Un diario especial que se usa para registrar únicamente transacciones de recibo en efectivo. (p. 296)

Cash sale *Venta al contado* Una venta en la el cliente paga la cantidad total de la venta en el momento de la transacción. (p. 294)

Cash short *Dinero en efectivo de menos* Una cantidad de efectivo disponible que es menos de la cantidad registrada. (p. 143)

Certified public accountant (CPA) *Contador público* Un contador quien ha pasado el examen uniforme de certificación para contadores y ha llenado los requerimientos estatales para su licencia. (p. 157)

Chart of accounts *Plan de cuentas* Una lista de cuentas que se usa en un negocio. (p. 36)

Charter *Acta constitutiva* Un estado autoriza la formación de una corporación al otorgar una acta constitutiva, el derecho legal de que un negocio opere como una corporación. (p. 244)

Check *Cheque* Un documento de negocios ordenándole a un banco que pague en efectivo de una cuenta bancaria. (p. 60)

Checking acccount *Cuenta de cheques* Una cuenta bancaria de la cual los pagos son ordenados por un depositante. (p. 123)

Closing entries *Asiento de cierre* Los asientos en el diario que se usan para preparar cuentas temporales para un período fiscal nuevo. (p. 215)

Code of conduct *Código de conducta* Una declaración que guía el comportamiento de ética de una compañía y sus empleados. (p. 122)

Collateral *Colateral o garantía* Los activos prometidos a un acreedor para garantizar el pago de un préstamo. (p. 559)

Commercial invoice *Factura comercial* Un informe preparado por el vendedor de la mercancía y dirigido al comprador, que muestra un listado detallado y la descripción de la mercancía vendida, incluyendo precios y términos. (p. 754)

Commission *Comisión* Un método de pagarle a un empleado basado en la cantidad de generada en ventas por el empleado. Las comisiones normalmente son calculadas como un porcentaje de las ventas de empleado. (p. 346)

Comparative financial statements *Estados financieros comparativos* Informes financieros que proveen información de múltiples períodos fiscales. (pp. 207, 517)

Compound interest *Interés compuesto* El interés pagado sobre una cantidad original depositada en un banco más cualquier interés que se haya pagado. (p. 11)

Comptroller *Contralor* (Véase controller *controlador.*) (p. 385)

Contra account *Contra cuenta* Cuenta que reduce una cuenta relacionada en un estado financiero. (p. 263)

Contract of sale *Contrato de venta* Un documento que detalla todos los términos acordados por el vendedor y el comprador para una transacción de venta. (p. 753)

Controller *Controlador* El contador principal en una organización, teniendo la responsabilidad de las actividades de financieras y las administrativas. A veces llamado *contralor.* (p. 385)

Controlling account *Cuenta de control* Una cuenta en el libro mayor general que resume todas las cuentas de un libro mayor auxiliar. (p. 246)

Corporation *Corporación* Una organización con los derechos legales de una persona y de la cual varias personas u otras corporaciones son dueñas. (p. 244)

Correcting entry *Asiento de corrección* Si una transacción ha sido asentada inapropiadamente y contabilizado en el diario, el asiento incorrecto debería de ser corregido con un asiento adicional, llamado un asiento de corrección. (p. 109)

Cost accounting *Contabilidad de costos* La división de contabilidad que identifica las medidas de los costos. (p. 563)

Cost of capital *Costo de capital* El índice de interés y pagos de dividendos a los fondos de deudas y financiamiento de capital. (p. 569)

Cost of goods sold *Costo de bienes vendidos* (Véase cost of merchandise sold *costo de mercancía vendida.*) (p. 476)

Cost of merchandise *Costo de la mercancía* El precio que un negocio paga por la mercancía que compra para vender. (p. 250)

Cost of merchandise sold *Costo de mercancía vendida* El precio original de toda la mercancía vendida durante un período fiscal. (p. 476)

Cost of sales *Costo de ventas* (Véase cost of merchandise sold *costo de mercancía vendida.*) (p. 476)

Credit *Crédito* La cantidad registrada en el lado derecho de una cuenta. (p. 33)

Credit limit *Límite de crédito* La cantidad máxima pendiente que se le permite a un cliente por parte del vendedor. (p. 267)

Credit line *Línea de crédito* (Véase line of credit *línea de crédito.*) (p. 552)

Credit memorandum *Memorándum de crédito* Un documento preparado por el vendedor que muestra la cantidad deducida por las devoluciones y concesiones. (p. 327)

Creditor *Acreedor* Una persona u organización a quien se le debe una obligación. (p. 16)

Current assets *Activos actuales* El efectivo y otros activos que se espera que se intercambien por efectivo o que se consuman dentro de un año. (p. 450)

Current liabilities *Obligaciones actuales* Las obligaciones que se deben dentro den un corto plazo, generalmente dentro de año. (p. 489)

Current ratio *Índice actual* Un índice que mide la relación actual de los activos actuales con las obligaciones actuales. (p. 535)

Debit *Débito* Una cantidad registrada en el lado izquierdo de una cuenta. (p. 33)

Debit card *Tarjeta de débito* Una tarjeta bancaria que automáticamente deduce la cantidad de una compra de la cuenta de cheques del tarjeta habiente. (p. 138)

Debit memorandum *Memorándum de débito* Un documento preparado por el cliente que muestra la deducción de precio tomada por el cliente por una devolución o concesión. (p. 322)

Debt financing *Financiamiento de deuda* Obteniendo capital al pedir prestado por un período de tiempo. (p. 552)

Debt ratio *Índice de deuda* El total de las obligaciones dividido por el total de los activos. (p. 526)

Declaring a dividend *Declaración de dividendos* La acción tomada por el consejo directivo para distribuir las ganancias de la corporación a los accionistas. (p. 333)

Declining-balance method of depreciation *Método de depreciación de saldo decreciente* Un tipo de depreciación acelerada que multiplica el valor contable de un activo por un índice de depreciación constante para determinar su depreciación. (p. 603)

Defaulting *Incumplimiento* No hacer los pagos de un préstamo cuando se vencen. (p. 673)

Deferral *Aplazamiento* Un asiento registrando el recibo de efectivo antes de que los ingresos relacionados son ganados, o pagos de efectivo antes de que los gastos relacionados sean incurridos. (p. 648)

Deferred expenses *Gastos diferidos* Pagos por bienes o servicios que aun no se han recibido. (Véase también prepaid expense *gastos pre pagados*.) (p. 660)

Deferred revenue *Ingresos diferidos* Efectivo recibido por bienes y servicios que aun no han sido proveídos. (p. 658)

Deficit *Déficit* Un saldo negativo que permanece después de que el total de gastos es restado del ingreso total. (p. 193)

Deposit *Depósito* El pago de impuestos de nomina al gobierno. (p. 392)

Deposit slip *Comprobante de depósito* Un formulario del banco que muestra los cheques, billetes, y monedas que un cuenta habiente está añadiendo a una cuenta bancaria. (p. 123)

Depreciation *Depreciación* Una pérdida en la utilidad de un activo fijo como el resultado del desgasto u obsolescencia. (p. 450)

Depreciation expense *Gasto de depreciación* La porción del costo de un activo fijo que es transferida a una cuenta de gastos cada período fiscal durante la vida de utilidad de ese activo. (p. 450)

Direct deposit *Depósito directo* El pago neto de nomina de un empleado utilizando la transferencia electrónica de fondos. (p. 366)

Direct write-off method *Método de pérdida directa* Registrar los gastos de cuentas incobrables solamente cuando en verdad se sabe que una cantidad es incobrable. (p. 419)

Discount period *Período de descuento* El período de tiempo durante el cual el cliente puede tomar un descuento de efectivo. (p. 263)

Dishonored check *Cheque rechazado* Un cheque que el banco rehúsa pagar. (p. 135)

Dishonored note *Letra rechazada* Una letra que no se paga cuando se vence. (p. 429)

Distribution of net income statement *Declaración de distribución de ingreso neto* Un estado financiero de sociedad que muestra la distribución de las ganancias o pérdidas netas a los socios. (p. 728)

Dividend yield *Rendimiento de dividendo* La relación entre los dividendos por acción y el precio del mercado de cada acción. (p. 534)

Dividends *Dividendos* Las ganancias que se distribuyen a los accionistas. (p. 332)

Double declining-balance method of depreciation *Método de depreciación de saldo doblemente decreciente* Un índice de depreciación de saldo que es dos veces la del índice sencilla. (p. 603)

Double-entry accounting *Contabilidad de partida doble* El registro de las partes de débito y crédito de una transacción. (p. 59)

Draft *Letra de cambio* Una orden escrita, firmada y fechada por un partido, ordenando a otro partido, generalmente un banco, que pague dinero a un tercer partido. (p. 754)

Due date *Fecha de vencimiento* La fecha en la cual una factura debe ser pagada. (p. 252)

Earnings per share *Ganancia por acción* Ganancias netas después del impuesto fiscal dividido por la cantidad pendiente de acciones. (p. 533)

EFT *EFT* (Véase electronic funds transfer *transferencia electrónica de fondos*.) (p. 137)

Electronic funds transfer *Transferencia electrónica de fondos* Un sistema computarizado de pagos de dinero, el cual transfiere fondos sin el uso de cheques, moneda, u otro documento de papel. (p. 137)

Employee earnings record *Registro de ganancias de los empleados* Un documento de negocios que registra todos los detalles de las ganancias y deducciones de un empleado. (p. 360)

Ending inventory *Inventario final* La cuenta actual de mercancía al final de un período fiscal. (p. 446)

Endorsement *Endoso* Una firma o sello en la parte trasera de un cheque para transferir la titularidad. (p. 124)

Endorsement in full *Endoso completo* Un endoso que indica un nuevo propietario del cheque (Véase special endorsement *endoso especial*.) (p. 124)

Entrepreneur *Empresario* Alguien quien es dueño, administra, y toma el riesgo de iniciar un negocio. (p. 5)

Entry *Asiento* Información de cada transacción registrada en un diario. (p. 59)

Equities *Derechos de propiedad* Los derechos financieros a los activos de un negocio. (p. 13)

Equity *Patrimonio neto* La diferencia entre los activos y las obligaciones. (p. 7)

Equity financing *Financiación de patrimonio* Obtener capital al emitir acciones de una corporación. (p. 565)

Ethics *Ética* Los principios del bien y el mal que guían a un individuo al tomar decisiones. (p. 8)

Exhibit *Anexo* Informe preparado que da detalles sobre un artículo en un estado financiero principal (Véase supporting schedule *plan de apoyo*.) (p. 492)

Expense *Gasto* El costo de los bienes y servicios utilizados para operar un negocio. (p. 19)

Exports *Exportaciones* Bienes o servicios enviados del país de origen del vendedor a otro país. (p. 752)

Face amount *Valor nominal* (Véase principal *principal*.) (p. 425)

Factory overhead *Gastos fijos de fábrica* Todos los gastos aparte de los materiales y mano de obra directa que aplican para fabricar productos. (p. 638)

Federal unemployment tax *Contribución federal para el desempleo* Un impuesto federal pagado por los empleados para administrar el programa de desempleo. (p. 382)

FIFO *PEPS* (Véase first-in, first-out inventory costing method *método de costos de inventario de primero en entrar, primero en salir*.) (p. 626)

File maintenance *Mantenimiento de archivos* El procedimiento de ordenar cuentas en un libro mayor general, asignando números de cuenta y manteniendo los registros al corriente. (p. 95)

Financial accounting *Contabilidad financiera* La división de contabilidad que se enfoca en reportar información a los usuarios externos. (p. 190)

Financial leverage *Apalancamiento financiero* La habilidad de un negocio de utilizar fondos prestados para aumentar sus ganancias. (p. 571)

Financial ratio *Proporción financiera* Una comparación entre dos componentes de información financiera. (p. 195)

Financial statements *Estados de cuenta financieros* Reportes financieros que resumen las condiciones y operaciones financieras de un negocio. (p. 6)

Financing activities *Actividades financieras* Recibos y pagos de dinero que involucran transacciones de deuda o patrimonio neto. (p. 692)

First-in, first-out inventory costing method *Método de costos de inventario de primero en entrar, primero en salir* Utilizando el precio de la mercancía comprada primero para calcular el costo de la mercancía que se vende primero. (p. 626)

Fiscal period *Período fiscal* El plazo de tiempo en el cual un negocio resume su información financiera y reporta su desempeño financiero. (p. 159)

Fiscal year *Año fiscal* Un período fiscal que consiste de doce meses consecutivos. (p. 159)

Foreclosure *Embargo hipotecario* Cuando el banco o compañía financiera toma posesión de una propiedad hipotecada. (p. 673)

Forensic accountant *Contador forense* Un contador quien combina la contabilidad con las habilidades de investigación para descubrir la sospecha de actividad fraudulenta, o de prevenir tal actividad. (p. 48)

Franchise *Franquicia* Un derecho otorgado a un individuo o negocio para vender productos o servicios de otro negocio más grande dentro de un área geográfica definida. (p. 55)

FUTA *FUTA* (Véase federal unemployment tax *contribución federal para el desempleo*.) (p. 382)

GAAP *GAAP* Principios de Contabilidad Generalmente Aceptados. Los estándares y normas que los contadores siguen mientras que registran y reportan actividades financieras. (p. 11)

Gain *Beneficio* Un incremento en el patrimonio neto que resulta de actividades aparte de vender bienes y servicios. (p. 600)

Gain on plant assets *Ganancia sobre activos fijos* Un aumento en el patrimonio cuando un activo fijo es vendido por más de su valor contable. (p. 600)

General amount column *Columna de cantidad general* Una columna de cantidad de un diario que no tiene el título de cuenta. (p. 260)

General journal *Libro diario general* Un libro con dos columnas para cantidades en la cual todo tipo de asientos pueden ser registrados. (p. 320)

General ledger *Libro mayor general* Un libro mayor que contiene todas las cuentas necesarias para preparar estados financieros. (p. 94)

Generally accepted accounting principles *Principios de Contabilidad Generalmente Aceptados* (Véase GAAP.) (p. 11)

Gross earnings *Ganancia bruta* (Véase total earnings *ganancia total*.) (p. 346)

Gross margin *Margen bruto* Ganancia bruta como un porcentaje de ventas netas. (p. 518)

Gross pay *Sueldo bruto* (Véase total earnings *ganancia total*.) (p. 346)

Gross profit *Ganancia bruta* (Véase gross profit on sales *ganancia bruta de ventas*.) (p. 476)

Gross profit margin *Margen de ganancia bruta* (Véase gross margin *margen bruto*.) (p. 518)

Gross profit method of estimating an inventory *Método de ganancia bruta para estimar un inventario* Un estimado del inventario mediante el uso de los porcentajes de ganancia bruta de años anteriores en operaciones. (p. 633)

Gross profit on sales *Ganancia bruta de ventas* El ingreso operativo restante después de que se deduzca el costo de la mercancía vendida. (p. 476)

Gross wages *Salario bruto* (Véase total earnings *ganancia total*.) (p. 346)

Horizontal analysis *Análisis horizontal* Una comparación de un artículo en un estado financiero con el mismo artículo en un estado financiero del período anterior. (p. 528)

Imports *Importaciones* Bienes o servicios enviados al país del comprador desde otro país. (p. 752)

Income from operations *Ingresos por operaciones* El ingreso operativo que queda después de que se deduzcan los costos de la mercancía vendida y los gastos operativos. (p. 478)

Income statement *Estado de ingresos* Un estado financiero que muestra los gastos e ingresos durante un período fiscal. (p. 170)

Individual retirement account (IRA) *Cuenta Individual de Jubilación (IRA)* Una cuenta de jubilación calificada que provee a la mayoría de los individuos con el beneficio de impuestos diferidos. (p. 356)

Intangible asset *Activo intangible* Un activo que no tiene forma física. (p. 607)

Intellectual property *Propiedad intelectual* Cualquier cosa o proceso que está protegido por patente, marca registrada, o derechos de autor. (Véase también intangible asset *activo intangible*.) (p. 648)

Interest *Interés* Una cantidad que se paga por el uso de dinero durante un período de tiempo. (p. 11)

Interest expense *Gastos de interés* El interés que se acumula en dinero que se ha tomado prestado. (p. 555)

Interest income *Ingresos de interés* El interés que se gana por dinero prestado. (p. 428)

Interest rate *Tasa de interés* El porcentaje del capital que se debe por el uso de los fondos garantizados por una letra. (p. 425)

Interim financial statements *Estados financieros provisionales* Estados financieros que proveen información por un período menor que el año fiscal. (p. 207)

Internal controls *Controles internos* Procesos y procedimientos empleados dentro de un negocio para asegurar que sus operaciones son manejadas con ética, con precisión, y confiabilidad. (p. 338)

Inventory *Inventario* Un listado de activos, que generalmente contiene el valor de artículos individuales. (p. 249)

Inventory record *Registro de inventario* Un formulario que se usa durante un inventario físico para registrar información acerca de cada artículo de mercancía a la mano. (p. 622)

Investing activities *Actividades de inversión* Recibos y pagos de dinero que involucran la venta o compra de activos utilizados para generar ingresos sobre un período de tiempo. (p. 692)

Invoice *Factura* Un formulario que describe los bienes o servicios vendidos, la cantidad, el precio, y los términos de venta. (p. 60)

IRA *IRA* (Véase individual retirement account *cuenta individual de jubilación*.) (p. 356)

Issue date *Fecha de emisión* La fecha en la cual un negocio emite una letra, bono, o acción. (p. 565)

Journal *Diario* Un formulario para registrar transacciones en orden cronológico. (p. 58)

Journalizing *Asentar en el diario* Registrar las transacciones en un diario. (p. 58)

Language of business *Lenguaje de negocios* (Véase accounting *contabilidad*.) (p. 6)

Last-in, first-out inventory costing method *Método de inventario de costos del último en entrar, primero en salir* Se usa el precio de la mercancía que se compra al último para calcular el costo de la mercancía que se vende primero. (p. 627)

Ledger *Libro mayor* Un grupo de cuentas. (p. 94)

Letter of credit *Carta de crédito* Una carta emitida por un banco garantizando que cierto individuo o negocio se le pagará una cantidad específica siempre y cuando las condiciones establecidas se cumpla. (p. 753)

Liability *Obligación* Una cantidad que debe. (p. 7)

LIFO *LIFO* (Véase last-in, first-out inventory costing method *método de inventario de costos del último en entrar, primero en salir*.) (p. 627)

Line of credit *Línea de crédito* Un acuerdo de préstamo bancario que provee acceso inmediato de corto plazo a efectivo. (p. 552)

Liquid assets *Activos líquidos* (Véase quick assets *activos realizables*.) (p. 535)

Liquidation of a partnership *Disolución de una sociedad* El proceso de pagar las obligaciones de la sociedad y distribuir los activos restantes entre los socios. (p. 735)

Liquidity ratio *Coeficiente de liquidez* Un índice que mide la habilidad de un negocio de pagar sus obligaciones financieras actuales. (p. 535)

List price *Precio de lista* El precio minorista impreso en un catálogo o un sitio de Internet. (p. 260)

Long-term liabilities *Obligaciones de largo plazo* Las obligaciones que se deben por más de un año. (p. 489)

Lookback period *Período retroactivo* El período de 12 meses que termina el 30 de Junio del año anterior que se usa para determinar que tan frecuentemente un negocio debe depositar los impuestos de nomina. (p. 392)

Loss *Pérdida* Una reducción en el patrimonio que resulta de actividades aparte de vender bienes y servicios. (p. 601)

Loss on plant assets *Pérdidas en activos fijos* La reducción en el patrimonio que resulta cuando un activo fijo se vende por menos del valor contable. (p. 601)

Lower of cost or market inventory costing method (LCM) *Método de inventario de costo de mercado del menor costo (LCM)* Utilizando el más bajo del costo o del valor de mercado para csalcular el costo del inventario final de mercancías. (p. 631)

Maker of a note *Girador de una letra* La persona o negocio que firma una letra y así promete hacer el pago de la misma. (p. 425)

Managerial accounting *Contabilidad administrativa* El área de contabilidad que se enfoca en reportar la información a los usuarios internos. (p. 190)

Marginal tax rate *Índice de impuestos marginal* El índice de impuestos asociado con una tabla de impuestos. (p. 458)

Market ratio *Índice de mercado* Un índice que mide el desempeño económico de una corporación en relación al valor de mercado de sus acciones. (p. 534)

Market value *Valor de mercado* El precio que se debe pagar para reemplazar un activo. (p. 631)

Markup *Aumentar en precio* La cantidad que un negocio le añade al costo de la mercancía para establecer el precio de venta. (p. 284)

Maturity date *Fecha de vencimiento* La fecha en la cual el principal de una letra se debe pagar. (p. 425)

Maturity value *Valor de vencimiento* La cantidad que se debe en la fecha de vencimiento de una letra. (p. 427)

Medicare tax *Impuestos de Medicare* Impuesto federal que se paga para seguro de hospital. (p. 355)

Memorandum *Memorándum* Un documento en el cual se escribe un mensaje breve para describir una transacción. (p. 61)

Merchandise *Mercancía* Bienes que un negocio compra para vender. (p. 244)

Merchandise inventory *Inventario de mercancía* Los bienes que un negocio tiene a la mano para la venta a clientes. (p. 249)

Merchandising business *Negocio mercantil* Un negocio que compra y revende bienes. (p. 244)

Net income *Ingreso neto* La diferencia entre el ingreso total y los gastos totales cuando el ingreso total es mayor. (p. 171)

Net loss *Pérdida neta* La diferencia entre el ingreso total y los gastos totales cuando los gastos son mayores. (p. 172)

Net pay *Pago neto* La ganancia total que se le paga a un empleado después que los impuestos de nómina y otras deducciones. (p. 359)

Net price *Precio neto* El precio después de que se ha deducido el descuento comercial del precio de lista. (p. 260)

Net realizable value *Valor neto realizable* La cantidad de cuentas por cobrar que un negocio anticipa cobrar. (p. 412)

Net sales *Ventas netas* El total de las ventas menos los descuentos, devoluciones y concesiones. (p. 475)

Net worth statement *Declaración de valor neto* Un informe formal que muestra lo que un individuo tiene, lo que debe, y la diferencia entre las dos. (p. 7)

Nominal accounts *Cuenta nominal* (Véase temporary accounts *cuentas temporales*.) (p. 215)

Non-operating expense *Gastos no operativos* Los gastos que no están relacionados con las operaciones diarias del negocio. (p. 555)

Non-sufficient funds check *Cheque sin fondos* Un cheque que no es honrado por el banco porque no hay suficientes fondos en la cuenta del girador del cheque. (p. 135)

Normal balance *Balance normal* El lado de una cuenta que se aumenta, se le llama el balance normal de la cuenta. (p. 33)

Note *Letra* (Véase promissory note *pagare*.) (p. 425)

Note payable *Letra por pagar* Un pagare firmada por un negocio y otorgada a un acreedor. (p. 425)

Note receivable *Letra por cobrar* Un pagare que un negocio acepta de una persona o negocio. (p. 425)

NSF check *Cheque NSF* (Véase non-sufficient funds check *cheque sin fondos*.) (p. 135)

Number of days' sales in inventory *Número de días de inventario para la venta* Un índice financiero que se determina al dividir 365 días por el índice de rotación de inventario. (p. 642)

Opening an account *Apertura de cuenta* Escribir un título y número de cuenta en el encabezado de la misma. (p. 96)

Operating activities *Actividades operativas* Los recibos de dinero y pagos necesarios para operar un negocio día a día. (p. 692)

Operating expense ratio *Índice de gastos operativos* El total de los gastos operativos como un porcentaje de las ventas netas. (p. 519)

Operating expenses *Gastos operativos* Los gastos incurridos por un negocio durante su operación normal. (p. 478)

Operating income *Ingreso operativo* (Véase income from operations *ingresos por operaciones*.) (p. 478)

Operating margin *Margen operativo* Los ingresos operativos como un porcentaje de las ventas netas. (p. 519)

Operating revenue *Ingreso operativo* Los ingresos generados por un negocio de sus operaciones normales. (p. 475)

Owner's equity *Capital propio* La cantidad que queda después que el valor las obligaciones es restada del valor de los activos. (p. 13)

Owner's equity statement *Estado de cuenta de capital propio* Un estado financiero que resume los cambios en el capital propio durante un período fiscal. (p. 730)

Par value *Valor nominal* Un valor asignado a una acción e impreso en el certificado de acciones. (pp. 483, 565)

Partner *Socio* Cada miembro de una sociedad. (p. 722)

Partnership *Sociedad* Un negocio en el cual dos o más personas combinan sus activos y sus habilidades. (p. 722)

Partnership agreement *Convenio de sociedad* Un acuerdo escrito que establece las condiciones bajo las cuales opera una sociedad. (p. 722)

Pay period *Período de pago* El número de días o semanas laborales que cubre un cheque de nomina del empleado. (p. 346)

Pay yourself first *Cóbrese usted primero* Una estrategia de presupuestar al apartar al menos el 10% de ingresos después de impuestos para ahorrar e invertir. (p. 193)

Payee *Beneficiario* La persona o negocio a quien se le paga la cantidad de la letra. (p. 425)

Payroll *Nómina* La cantidad total que ganan todos los empleados durante un período de pago. (p. 346)

Payroll clerk *Empleado de nomina* El puesto de contabilidad que recopila y calcula los datos de nomina, luego prepara, asienta, y reporta las transacciones de nomina. (p. 346)

Payroll deduction *Deducción de nomina* Cualquier cantidad deducida de las ganancias brutas de un empleado. (p. 352)

Payroll register *Registro de nomina* Un formulario de contabilidad que resume las ganancias, deducciones, y pago neto de todos los empleados por un período de pago. (p. 358)

Payroll taxes *Impuestos de nómina* Impuestos basados en la nómina de un negocio. (p. 351)

Percent of accounts receivable method *Método de porcentaje de cuentas por cobrar* Un método que usa el análisis de cuentas por cobrar para calcular la cantidad que será incobrable. (p. 413)

Percent of sales method *Método de porcentaje de ventas* Un método usado para calcular las cuentas por cobrar incobrables, el cual asume que un porcentaje de cada dólar de venta eventualmente se volverá incobrable. (p. 413)

Periodic inventory *Inventario periódico* Un inventario de mercancía evaluado al final de un período fiscal. (p. 249)

Permanent accounts *Cuentas permanentes* Las cuentas que se usan para acumular información de un período fiscal a otro. (p. 215)

Perpetual inventory *Inventario perpetuo* Un inventario determinado mediante el constante registro de aumentos, reducciones, y saldos a la mano de cada artículo de mercancía. (p. 249)

Personal net worth *Valor neto personal* La diferencia entre los activos y las obligaciones personales. (p. 7)

Personal property *Propiedad personal* Toda la propiedad no clasificada como propiedad inmueble. (p. 587)

Petty cash *Caja chica* Una cantidad de dinero en efectivo que se tiene a la mano y se usa para hacer pagos menores. (p. 140)

Petty cash slip *Recibo de caja chica* Un documento que comprueba un pago de la caja chica. (p. 141)

Physical inventory *Inventario físico* Un inventario periódico al contar, pesar, o midiendo artículos de mercancía a la mano. (p. 249)

Plant asset record *Registro de activo fijo* Un formulario de contabilidad en el cual se registra la información de cada activo fijo de un negocio. (p. 594)

Plant assets *Activos fijos* Activos físicos que se usarán durante un número de años en la operación de un negocio. (p. 450)

Point-of-sale (POS) terminal *Terminal de punto de venta* Un computadora especializada que se usa para recolectar, guardar, y reportar toda la información de una transacción de venta. (p. 294)

Post-closing trial balance *Balance de comprobación posterior al cierre* Un balance de comprobación preparado después de pasar los asientos de cierre. (p. 228)

Postdated check *Cheque posfechado* Un cheque con una fecha futura. (p. 126)

Posting *Pasar asientos* Transferir información de un asiento diario a una cuenta del libro mayor. (p. 98)

Preferred stock *Acción preferente* Un tipo de acción que le da preferencia a los accionistas privilegiados sobre los accionistas comunes en cuanto a los dividendos y otros derechos. (p. 567)

Prepaid expense *Gasto pre pagado* Dinero pagado por un gasto en un período fiscal el cual no es utilizado hasta un período después. (Véase también *deferred expenses* *gastos diferidos*.) (p. 163)

Price-earnings ratio *Índice de ganancias sobre precio* La relación entre el valor de mercado por acción y las ganancias por acción de una inversión. (p. 534)

Prime interest rate *Tase de interés preferencial* La tasa de interés que se le cobra a los clientes más dignos de crédito de un banco. (p. 552)

Principal *Principal* La cantidad original de una letra, a veces se le refiere como el *valor nominal*. (p. 425)

Profit margin *Margen de ganancia* Ingreso neto como un porcentaje de ventas netas después de los impuestos fiscales. (p. 517)

Profitability ratio *Índice de rentabilidad* Un índice que mide la habilidad de un negocio de generar ingresos. (p. 516)

Promissory note *Pagaré* Una promesa por escrito y firmada para pagar una suma de dinero a una fecha específica. (p. 425)

Proprietorship *Empresa de propietario único* Un negocio cuyo dueño es una sola persona. (p. 10)

Proving cash *Verificación de efectivo* Determinando que la cantidad de efectivo concuerde con el balance de cuenta de efectivo en los registros de contabilidad. (p. 107)

Public accounting firm *Despacho de contabilidad* Un negocio de contabilidad que le ayuda a otros negocios en cuestiones de contabilidad. (p. 233)

Purchase invoice *Factura de compra* Una factura que se usa como documento original para registrar una compra en una transacción de cuenta. (p. 252)

Purchase on account *Comprar a cuenta* Una transacción en la cual los artículos comprados serán pagados después. (p. 252)

Purchase order *Orden de compra* Un documento que solicita que un proveedor le venda mercancía a un negocio. (p. 251)

Purchases allowance *Concesión de compras* Crédito que se asigna a una parte del precio de compra de la mercancía que no se devuelve y que resulta en una reducción en la cuenta del cliente pagadero al vendedor. (p. 322)

Purchases discount *Descuento de compras* Cuando una compañía que compra mercancía a cuenta toma un descuento de efectivo. (p. 263)

Purchases journal *Diario de compras* Un diario especial que se usa solamente para registrar las transacciones de compras a cuenta. (p. 252)

Purchases return *Devolución de compras* Crédito permitido por el precio de compra de la mercancía devuelta, lo que resulta en una reducción en la cuenta del cliente pagadero al vendedor. (p. 322)

Qualified retirement plan *Plan de jubilación calificado* Una cuenta de ahorros para la jubilación que es aprobada por el Servicio de Impuestos Internos que les provee a los individuos con un beneficio de impuestos. (Véase también *401(k), Cuenta Individual de Jubilación, Roth IRA*.) (p. 356)

Quick assets *Activos realizables* Efectivo y otros activos actuales que se pueden convertir rápidamente en efectivo. (p. 535)

Quick ratio *Índice de realización* Un índice que mide la relación de los activos realizables a las responsabilidades actuales. (p. 535)

Rate of return on sales *Índice de beneficio en ventas* (Véase *operating margin* *margen operativo*.) (p. 519)

Ratio analysis *Análisis del índice* El cálculo e interpretación del índice financiero. (p. 195)

Real accounts *Cuentas reales* (Véase *permanent accounts* *cuentas permanentes*.) (p. 215)

Real estate *Bienes raíces* (Véase *real property* *propiedad de inmuebles*.) (p. 587)

Real property *Propiedad de inmuebles* Terreno y cualquier cosa unida al terreno. (p. 587)

Realization *Ganancia* Efectivo recibido de la venta de activos durante la disolución de una sociedad. (p. 735)

Receipt *Recibo* Un documento de negocios que muestra por escrito la aceptación del dinero recibido. (p. 61)

Recurring entries *Asientos recurrentes* Las transacciones que se preparan para asientos automáticos en sistemas de contabilidad computarizadas. (p. 463)

Recurring transactions *Transacciones recurrentes* (Véase recurring entries *asientos recurrentes*.) (p. 463)

Requisition *Requisición* Un documento solicitando la compra de mercancía. (p. 251)

Residual value *Valor residual* (Véase salvage value *valor de recuperación*.) (p. 450)

Restrictive endorsement *Endoso restrictivo* Un endoso que restringe transferencias futuras de la propiedad de un cheque. (p. 125)

Retail merchandising business *Negocio de comercio minorista* Un negocio que le vende a aquellos quienes usen o consuman los bienes. (p. 244)

Retained earnings *Ganancias retenidas* Una cantidad que gana una corporación y aún no distribuida a los accionistas. (p. 332)

Return on investment *Rendimiento de la inversión* La porción de dinero ganado sobre una inversión relativo a la cantidad de la inversión. (p. 584)

Return on sales (ROS) *Rendimiento de ventas (RDV)* La porción de ingresos netos de las ventas totales. (p. 196)

Revenue *Ganancia* Un aumento en capital que resulta de la venta de bienes y servicios. (p. 18)

Revenue expenditure *Inversión de ingresos* El pago de un gasto operativo para generar ganancias. (p. 552)

Reversing entry *Asiento revertido* Un asiento hecho al principio de un período fiscal para revertir un asiento de ajuste hecho en el período fiscal anterior. (p. 649)

ROI *ROI* (Véase return on investment *rendimiento de la inversión*.) (p. 584)

Rollover *Reinversión* El traslado de fondos de un plan de jubilación calificado a otro. (p. 520)

Roth individual retirement account (Roth IRA) *Cuenta individual de jubilación tipo Roth (Roth IRA)* Un plan de jubilación calificado que permite retiros que son libres de impuestos de la cuenta. (p. 356)

Salary *Sueldo* Una suma fija de dinero dividida igualmente entre los períodos de pago. (p. 346)

Salary expense *Gasto salarial* La suma de todas las ganancias de todos los empleados ganando por hora, por sueldo, y comisiones. (p. 378)

Sale on account *Venta a cuenta* Una venta por la cual el pago será recibido en una fecha posterior. (p. 18)

Sales allowance *Concesión de ventas* Crédito permitido a los clientes por parte del precio de venta que es devuelta, lo cual resulta en una reducción en las cuentas por cobrar del negocio mercantil. (p. 327)

Sales discount *Descuento de venta* Un descuento en el precio de una venta por el cliente. (p. 296)

Sales invoice *Factura de venta* Una factura que se usa como un documento original para registrar una venta a cuenta. Una factura de venta también es referida como un *recibo de venta*. (p. 60)

Sales journal *Diario de ventas* Un diario especial que se usa para registrar únicamente las ventas de mercancía a cuenta. (p. 287)

Sales return *Devolución de venta* Crédito permitido a un cliente por el precio de compra de la mercancía devuelta, lo cual resulta en una reducción en las cuentas por cobrar del negocio mercantil. (p. 327)

Sales slip *Recibo de venta* (Véase sales invoice *factura de venta*.) (p. 60)

Sales tax *IVA* Un impuesto sobre la venta de mercancías o servicios. (p. 286)

Sales ticket *Recibo de venta* (Véase sales invoice *facture de venta*.) (p. 60)

Salvage value *Valor de recuperación* La cantidad que será recibida por un activo al tiempo de su eliminación. (p. 450)

Schedule of accounts payable *Plan de cuentas por pagar* Una lista de cuentas de proveedores, saldos de las cuentas, y la cantidad total que se debe a todos los proveedores. A esto algunos negocios les llaman *balance de comprobación de cuentas por pagar*. (p. 272)

Schedule of accounts receivable *Plan de cuentas por cobrar* Un listado de cuentas de clientes, saldos de las cuentas y la cantidad total que deben todos los clientes. (p. 308)

Scrap value *Valor residual* (Véase salvage value *valor de recuperación*.) (p. 450)

Selling price *Precio de menudeo* La cantidad que un negocio recibe de la venta de un artículo de mercancía. (p. 284)

Service business *Negocio que provee servicio* Un negocio que desempeña una actividad a cambio de una cuota. (p. 10)

Share of stock *Unidad de acción* Una unidad de titularidad en una corporación. (p. 244)

Sight draft *Letra a la vista* Una letra pagable a la vista cuando el portador la presenta para su pago. (p. 754)

Social security tax *Impuesto del seguro social* Un impuesto federal que se paga para los de la tercera edad, sobrevivientes, y seguro de incapacidad. (p. 355)

Sole proprietorship *Propietario único* (Véase proprietorship *empresa de propietario único*.) (p. 10)

Solvency ratio *Proporción de solvencia* Una proporción que mide la habilidad de un negocio de pagar sus obligaciones a largo plazo. (p. 526)

Source document *Documento original* Un documento de negocios del cual se obtiene información para asentar en un diario. (p. 59)

Special amount column *Columna de cantidad especial* Una columna de cantidad en un diario con un título de cuenta. (p. 252)

Special endorsement *Endoso especial* Un endoso que indica un nuevo dueño de un cheque. (p. 124)

Special journal *Diario especial* Un diario que se usa para registrar solamente un tipo de transacción. (p. 251)

Stakeholders *Interesados* Cualquier persona o grupo que será afectada por una acción. (p. 191)

State unemployment tax *Impuesto estatal para el desempleo* Un impuesto estatal pagado por los empleados y que se usa para pagar beneficios a los trabajadores desempleados. (p. 382)

Stated interest rate *Tasa de interés especificada* La tasa de interés que se usa para calcular los pagos de interés periódicos de un bono. (p. 562)

Statement of cash flows *Declaración de flujo de efectivo* Una estado financiero que resume los recibos y pagos de dinero que resultan de las actividades de negocios durante un período fiscal. (p. 691)

Statement of stockholders' equity *Estado financiero del capital de accionistas* Un estado financiero que muestra cambios en la titularidad de una corporación durante un período fiscal. (p. 482)

Stock ledger *Libro mayor de existencias* Un archivo para el registro de existencias de la mercancía a la mano. (p. 623)

Stock record *Registro de existencias* Un documento que se usa para mostrar la clase de mercancía, la cantidad recibida, la cantidad vendida y el saldo a la mano. (p. 623)

Stockholder *Accionista* Dueño de una o más acciones en una corporación. (p. 244)

Straight-line method of depreciation *Método de depreciación de línea directa* El registro de una cantidad igual de gasto de depreciación para un activo fijo en cada año de su vida útil. (p. 451)

Subledger *Libro auxiliar* (Véase subsidiary ledger *libro mayor auxiliar*.) (p. 246)

Subsidiary ledger *Libro mayor auxiliar* Un libro mayor que resume en una sola cuenta del libro mayor general. Los contadores a menudo se refieren a un libro mayor auxiliar como un *libro auxiliar*. (p. 246)

Supplementary report *Informe suplementario* (Véase supporting schedule *plan de apoyo*.) (p. 492)

Supporting schedule *Plan de apoyo* Un informe preparado para dar detalles de un artículo en un estado financiero principal. (p. 492)

Surplus *Excedente* Un balance positivo que queda después de que los gastos totales son restados del ingreso total. (p. 193)

SUTA *SUTA* (Véase state unemployment tax *impuesto estatal para el desempleo*.) (p. 382)

T account *Cuenta T* Un aparato de contabilidad que se usa para analizar transacciones. (p. 33)

Tax base *Base de impuestos* La cantidad máxima de ganancias sobre la cual se calculan los impuestos. (p. 355)

Tax bracket *Escala contributiva* Cada índice de impuestos e ingresos sujetos a impuestos en una sola línea de una tabla de impuestos. (p. 458)

Taxable income *Ingresos sujetos a impuestos* La cantidad de ingreso total menos los ajustes, deducciones y exenciones que se usa para calcular el impuesto fiscal. (p. 367)

Temporary accounts *Cuentas temporales* Cuentas que se usan para acumular información hasta que sean transferidas a la cuenta de principal del titular. (p. 215)

Term *Termino* (Véase time of a note *plazo de una nota*.) (p. 425)

Terminal summary *Resumen de terminal* El reporte que resume las ventas en efectivo y de crédito de un terminal de punto de venta. Un resumen de sistema también es conocido como una *cinta Z*. (p. 294)

Terms of sale *Condiciones de venta* Un acuerdo entre el comprador y el vendedor sobre el pago de la mercancía. (p. 252)

Time clock *Reloj de control de asistencia* Un aparato que registra las fechas y horas de llegadas y partidas de cada empleado. (p. 347)

Time draft *Letra de cambio a término* Una letra que será pagada a un plazo o futuro determinado después de que sea aceptada. (p. 757)

Time of a note *Termino de una letra* El plazo de tiempo de la fecha de firma a la fecha de vencimiento, generalmente expresado como número de días. (p. 425)

Total earnings *Ganancia total* La cantidad total pagado por un negocio por el trabajo de un empleado, ya sea por hora, salarial, o de comisión. (p. 346)

Total income *Ingreso total* La suma de todas las fuentes de ingresos reportados en el formulario 1040. (p. 367)

Trade acceptance *Acuerdo comercial* Un documento firmado por un comprador en el momento de la venta de mercancía, en la cual el comprador se compromete a pagar al vendedor una suma específica de dinero, generalmente, en un tiempo establecido en el futuro. (p. 758)

Trade discount *Descuento comercial* Una rebaja en el precio de lista garantizado a un negocio mercantil. (p. 260)

Transaction *Transacción* Cualquier actividad de negocio que cambie activos, obligaciones, o capital. (p. 14)

Trend analysis *Análisis de tendencias* Un análisis de cambios al paso del tiempo. (p. 517)

Trial balance *Balance de comprobación* Una prueba de la igualdad de débitos y créditos en el libro mayor general. (p. 160)

Unadjusted trial balance *Balance de comprobación no ajustado* Un balance de comprobación antes de que los asientos de ajuste sean registrados. (p. 441)

Uncollectible accounts *Cuentas incobrables* Cuentas por cobrar que no pueden ser cobradas. (p. 412)

Underwater mortgage *Hipoteca sobrevalorada* Una hipoteca que tiene un balance mayor que el valor de la propiedad hipotecada. (p. 673)

Unearned revenue *Ingreso no ganados* (Véase deferred revenue *ingresos diferidos*.) (p. 658)

Useful life *Vida útil* El período de tiempo sobre el cual un activo contribuye a las ganancias de un negocio. (p. 450)

Vendor *Proveedor* Un negocio del cual se compran mercancías, provisiones, y otros activos. (p. 246)

Vertical analysis *Análisis vertical* Reportar una cantidad en un estado financiero como un porcentaje de otro artículo en el mismo estado financiero. (p. 195)

Voided check *Cheque cancelado* Un cheque que no puede ser procesado porque el mercado lo ha hecho invalido. (p. 127)

Voucher check *Comprobante de cheque* Un cheque que tiene un talón desprendible, o *comprobante*, que contiene información detallada sobre el pago de dinero. (p. 364)

Wage *Salario* La cantidad que se le paga a un empleado por cada hora laboral. (p. 346)

Wage garnishment *Retención de salario* Un proceso que requiere que un empleador retenga una porción del cheque de pago del empleado para pagar una liquidación de cuenta por orden del tribunal. (p. 393)

Weighted-average inventory costing method *Método de inventario de costo promedio* Utilizando el costo promedio del inventario inicial más las mercancías compradas durante un período fiscal para calcular el costo de la mercancía vendida. (p. 628)

Wholesale merchandising business *Negocio de ventas al mayoreo* Un negocio que compra y revende mercancías principalmente a otros negocios mercantiles. (p. 244)

Withdrawals *Retiros* Los activos retirados de un negocio para el uso personal del dueño. (p. 20)

Withholding allowance *Deducción en la retención* Una deducción del ingreso total por cada persona legalmente mantenida por el contribuyente, incluyendo al empleado. (p. 352)

Work sheet *Hoja de trabajo* Un formulario de contabilidad que contiene columnas que se usa para resumir la información del libro general mayor que es necesario para preparar estados financieros. (p. 159)

Working capital *Capital de trabajo* La cantidad del total de los activos actuales menos el total de las obligaciones actuales. (p. 353)

Writing off an account *Cancelación de una cuenta* Cancelar el saldo de la cuenta de un cliente por incumplimiento de pago. (p. 418)

Z tape *Cinta Z* (Véase terminal summary *resumen de terminal*.) (p. 294)

Index

Features Index

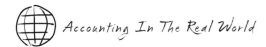

Accounting In The Real World

Careers In Accounting

ETHICS IN ACTION

EXPLORE ACCOUNTING

FINANCIAL LITERACY

FORENSIC ACCOUNTING

GLOBAL AWARENESS

THINK LIKE AN ACCOUNTANT

WHY ACCOUNTING?